Human Intestinal Flukes

Jong-Yil Chai

Human Intestinal Flukes

From Discovery to Treatment and Control

Springer

Jong-Yil Chai
Department of Tropical Medicine and Parasitology
Seoul National University College of Medicine
Seoul, South Korea

Institute of Parasitic Diseases, Korea Association
of Health Promotion
Seoul, South Korea

ISBN 978-94-024-1702-9 ISBN 978-94-024-1704-3 (eBook)
https://doi.org/10.1007/978-94-024-1704-3

This Springer imprint is published by the registered company Springer Nature B.V.
The registered company address is: Van Godewijckstraat 30, 3311 GX Dordrecht, The Netherlands

Preface

Digenetic trematodes are an important group of parasites infecting humans and animals. They are morphologically characterized by dorsoventrally flat body and the presence of at least two suckers, oral and ventral suckers, and, in some cases, another sucker, i.e., the genital sucker. They are exclusively parasitic and, in most cases, hermaphroditic, with the exception of schistosomes, which have separate sex. Trematodes can be classified into two large categories, namely, contact (water)-borne and foodborne species. The former is a highly important group, i.e., schistosomes (family Schistosomatidae), which can cause infections in mesenteric and vesical blood vessels of animals and humans. The latter is another important group causing infections in the alimentary tract, including the bile duct, intestine, esophageal wall, pancreatic duct, or the lung parenchyma and extrapulmonary locations.

More than one billion people are estimated to be at risk of infection with foodborne trematodes, and about 56 million were infected as of 2005 (Fürst et al. 2012). These foodborne trematodes are largely classified into liver, lung, and intestinal flukes. Among them, intestinal flukes are the largest group in which at least 74 species are involved in causing zoonotic infections in humans (Yu and Mott 1994; Chai 2007). The number of people infected with these flukes is estimated to be about seven million people worldwide (Toledo et al. 2014). However, this may be a far underestimate of the actual number.

The zoonotic intestinal flukes are morphologically diverse and comprise of a total of 38 genera belonging to 16 families: the Heterophyidae (*Metagonimus*, *Heterophyes*, *Haplorchis*, *Acanthotrema*, *Apophallus*, *Ascocotyle*, *Centrocestus*, *Cryptocotyle*, *Heterophyopsis*, *Procerovum*, *Pygidiopsis*, *Stellantchasmus*, and *Stictodora*), Echinostomatidae (*Echinostoma*, *Isthmiophora*, *Echinochasmus*, *Acanthoparyphium*, *Artyfechinostomum*, *Echinoparyphium*, *Himasthla*, and *Hypoderaeum*), amphistomes (*Fischoederius*, *Gastrodiscoides*, and *Watsonius*), Diplostomidae (*Neodiplostomum* and *Fibricola*), Fasciolidae (*Fasciolopsis*), Gymnophallidae (*Gymnophalloides*), Lecithodendriid-like flukes (*Caprimolgorchis* and *Phaneropsolus*), Plagiorchiidae (*Plagiorchis*), Brachylaimidae (*Brachylaima*), Strigeidae (*Cotylurus*), Microphallidae (*Gynaecotyla* and *Microphallus*), Isoparorchiidae (*Isoparorchis*), Troglotrematidae (*Nanophyetus*), and

Cyathocotylidae (*Prohemistomum*) (Yu and Mott 1994; Chai and Lee 2002; Fried et al. 2004; Chai 2007; Chai et al. 2009). Life cycles and geographical distributions are diverse and characteristic for each species.

Intestinal fluke infections are commonly considered as tropical endemic diseases in Asian countries where six million people are infected (Fürst et al. 2012). However, the geographical limits and the population at risk are currently expanding and changing in relation to factors such as growing international markets, improved transportation systems, changes in eating habits in western countries, and demographic changes (Toledo et al. 2014). Global warming and environmental changes may be another important factor for the endemicity changes. The pathogenicity of intestinal flukes is generally mild, but investigation is needed to see how it is in immunocompromised individuals. There are problems to be solved for specific diagnosis of intestinal fluke infections (Chai et al. 2005). In this book, characteristics of each species of intestinal fluke, in terms of biology, epidemiology, host-parasite relationships, pathogenicity, clinical aspects, diagnosis, and treatment, are reviewed in detail.

Seoul, South Korea Jong-Yil Chai

References

Chai JY (2007) 2. Intestinal flukes. In Food-borne parasitic zoonoses: fish and plant-borne parasites. In Murrell KD, Fried B (eds) World class parasites. Springer, New York. pp 53–115

Chai JY, Lee SH (2002) Food-borne intestinal trematode infections in the Republic of Korea. Parasitol Int 51:129–154

Chai JY, Murrell KD, Lymbery AJ (2005) Fish-borne parasitic zoonoses: status and issues. Int J Parasitol 35:1233–1254

Chai JY, Shin EH, Lee SH et al (2009) Foodborne intestinal flukes in Southeast Asia. Korean J Parasitol 47(suppl):S69–S102

Fried B, Graczyk TK, Tamang L (2004) Food-borne intestinal trematodiases in humans. Parasitol Res 93:159–170

Fürst T, Keiser J, Utzinger J (2012) Global burden of human food-borne trematodiasis: a systematic review and meta-analysis. Lancet Infect Dis 12:210–221

Toledo R, Munoz-Antoli C, Esteban JG (2014) Chapter 7. Intestinal trematode infections. In Toledo R, Fried B (eds) Digenetic trematodes. Springer, New York. Adv Exp Med Biol 766:201–240

Yu SH, Mott KE (1994) Epidemiology and morbidity of food-borne intestinal trematode infections. Trop Dis Bull 91:R125–R152

Acknowledgments

I am greatly indebted to late Prof. Byong-Seol Seo, Seoul National University College of Medicine, Seoul, South Korea, who encouraged and guided me to begin studies on human intestinal flukes from 1976 until 1991 when he passed away. My sincere thanks are also delivered to Prof. Emeritus Soon-Hyung Lee, Seoul National University, who greatly encouraged and helped me to continue my studies on intestinal flukes until the present. I am also grateful to Prof. Emeritus Han-Jong Rim, Korea University School of Medicine, Seoul, South Korea, who guided me to begin international collaborations with China, Lao PDR, Tanzania, Cambodia, and Myanmar. Many research papers were published on intestinal flukes particularly resulting from Korea-Lao PDR project and Korea-Cambodia project.

I would like to extend my special thanks to my lifelong colleagues and coworkers in intestinal fluke studies: Prof. Sung-Tae Hong (Seoul National University, Seoul, South Korea), Prof. Sung-Jong Hong (Chung-Ang University, Seoul, South Korea), Prof. Woon-Mok Sohn (Gyeongsang National University, Jinju, South Korea), Prof. Sun Huh (Hallym University, Chuncheon, South Korea), Prof. Jae-Ran Yu (Konkuk University, Seoul, South Korea), Prof. Weon-Gyu Kho (Inje University, Busan, South Korea), Prof. Min-Ho Choi (Seoul National University), Prof. Min Seo (Dankook University, Cheonan, South Korea), Prof. Yun-Kyu Park (Inha University, Incheon, South Korea), Prof. Eun-Hee Shin (Seoul National University), Prof. Eun-Taek Han (Kangwon National University, Chuncheon, South Korea), and Prof. Min-Jae Kim (Asan Medical Center, Seoul, South Korea). I cannot forget the excellent research works of my colleagues, late Dr. Sang-Mee Guk (Seoul National University) and late Dr. Jae-Hwan Park (Seoul National University). My special thanks are extended to Prof. Emeritus Duk-Young Min (Eulji University, Daejeon, South Korea), Prof. Keeseon S. Eom (Chungbuk National University, Cheongju, South Korea), and Prof. Tai-Soon Yong (Yonsei University, Seoul, South Korea) who collaborated with me in international collaboration projects. I also thank all the staff and members of Korea Association of Health Promotion, for their kindness in helping and encouraging me to write this book. Particular thanks are delivered to my former and current laboratory members at the Department of Tropical Medicine and Parasitology, Seoul National University College of Medicine and Institute of Parasitic Diseases, Korea Association of Health Promotion, Seoul, South Korea: Mr. Keon Hoon Lee, Mr. Jeong-Gyu Lee, Dr. Bong-Kwang Jung, Ms. Jaeeun Cho (currently in the United States), Ms. Hyemi Song, Ms. Hyemi Lim, Ms. Sooji Hong, Mr. Taehee Chang, Ms. Jaein Ryu, and Ms. Hyejoo Shin (helped me with line drawings). Lastly, my sincere appreciation should go to Mr. Jae-Lip Kim (helped me with line drawings and laboratory works), Mr. Deok-Gyu Kim (helped me with line drawings), and Mr. Sung-Yil Choi (helped me with ultrastructural studies of intestinal flukes).

Contents

About the Author

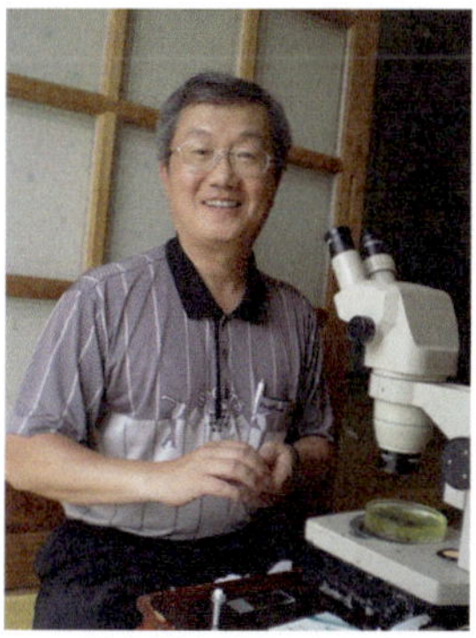

Prof. Dr. **Jong-Yil Chai** Emeritus Professor at the Department of Tropical Medicine and Parasitology, Seoul, South Korea, has been investigating diseases caused by intestinal parasites, including flukes, roundworms, and protozoans for over 40 years in the South Korea. He also worked in other Asian countries, including China, Thailand, Lao PDR, Cambodia, Vietnam, Myanmar, and Indonesia, and in Africa (especially Tanzania). He has published 10 books and more than 600 original research papers on parasitology and tropical medicine. He has been serving as the Editor of *The Korean Journal of Parasitology* since 2006. He is also serving as the President of *World Federation of Parasitologists* since 2018 and the Treasurer of *International Federation for Tropical Medicine* since 2012. He is the President of *Korea Association of Health Promotion* since January 2016.

Chapter 1
Heterophyids

1.1 Family Heterophyidae

Morozov (1952) enlisted 6 subfamilies in the family Heterophyidae Leiper, 1909, namely, Apophallinae Ciurea, 1924, Centrocestinae Looss, 1899, Cryptocotylinae Lühe, 1909, Euryhelminae Morozov, 1951, Heterophyinae Ciurea, 1924, and Metagoniminae Ciurea, 1924. Yamaguti (1958), removing Euryhelminae, added 9 more subfamilies which included Ascocotylinae Yamaguti, 1958, Galactosominae Ciurea, 1933, Haplorchinae Looss, 1899, Novemtestinae Yamaguti, 1958, Opisthometrinae Yamaguti, 1958, Pygidiopsinae Yamaguti, 1958, Scaphanocephalinae Yamaguti, 1958, Stictodorinae Yamaguti, 1958, and Tetracladinae Yamaguti, 1958, totaling 14 subfamilies. However, Pearson (2008) deferred the use of subfamilies of the Heterophyidae because their usefulness must await revision to be redefined by molecular studies, particularly in reference to the systematic value of the ventrogenital complex. He enlisted 36 recognized genera (*Acanthotrema* Travassos, 1928, *Acetodextra* Pearse, 1924, *Adleriela* Witenberg, 1930, *Alloheterophyes* Pearson, 1999, *Apophallus* Lühe, 1909, *Ascocotyle* Looss, 1899, *Centrocestus* Looss, 1899, *Cercarioides* Witenberg, 1929, *Condylocotyla* Pearson and Prévot, 1985, *Cryptocotyle* Lühe, 1899, *Euhaplorchis* Martin, 1950, *Euryhelmis* Poche, 1926, *Galactosomum* Looss, 1899, *Haplorchis* Looss, 1899, *Haplorchoides* Chen, 1949, *Heterophyes* Cobbold, 1886, *Heterophyopsis* Tubangui and Africa, 1938, *Heterotetrophyes* Leonov, 1957, *Irinaia* Caballero y C. and Bravo Hollis, 1966, *Metagonimus* Katsurada, 1912, *Neostictodora* Sogandares-Bernal, 1959, *Opisthometra* Poche, 1926, *Pandiontrema* Oshimarin, 1963, *Phocitrema* Goto and Ozaki, 1930, *Phocitremoides* Martin, 1950, *Pholeter* Odhner, 1914, *Procerovum* Onji and Nishio, 1916, *Protoheterophyes* Pearson, 2002, *Pseudexorchis* Yamaguti, 1938, *Pseudopygidiopsis* Yamaguti, 1971, *Pygidiopsis* Looss, 1907, *Pygidiopsoides* Martin, 1951, *Scaphanocephalus* Jägerskiöld, 1903, *Stellantchasmus* Onji and Nishio, 1916, *Stictodora* Looss, 1899, and *Tetracladium* Kulachkova,

J.-Y. Chai, *Human Intestinal Flukes*,
https://doi.org/10.1007/978-94-024-1704-3_1

1954) and 3 additional genera as *incertae sedis*. Among them, 13 genera (30 species) are known to infect humans (Chai 2007).

Phylogenetic studies were performed on 3 related families (Opisthorchiidae, Heterophyidae, and Cryptogonimidae) of the superfamily Opisthorchioidea Looss, 1899 analyzing the 18S rDNA and ITS sequences, and it was revealed that the family Opisthorchiidae and Heterophyidae are inseparable from each other, with the former nested within the latter (Thaenkham et al. 2012). It is accepted that the morphology and life cycles of these 2 families are highly similar, and they are phylogenetically close to each other. Within the family Heterophyidae, a few studies have been available in molecular aspects. Phylogenetic trees using the 18S rDNA sequences showed close relationships of *Metagonimus* spp. with those of *Haplorchis, Procerovum, Galactosomum,* and *Haplorchoides*, and those using ITS2 sequences revealed close relationships between *Metagonimus* spp. with *Euryhelmis, Haplorchis,* and *Procerovum* spp. (Thaenkham et al. 2012). Phylogenetic groups could also be formed based on the sequence of the mitochondrial cytochrome *c* oxidase 1 (*CO1*) gene; they were *Haplorchis taichui* group, *Haplorchis pumilio* group, and other heterophyids group (Chontananarth et al. 2014).

Among the 13 genera known to infect humans, 7 major genera with more than 2 species involved include *Metagonimus, Heterophyes, Haplorchis, Centrocestus, Procerovum, Pygidiopsis,* and *Stictodora.* Total 28 species of heterophyid flukes are known to cause human infections around the world (Table 1.1). They are contracted to humans by ingesting raw or improperly cooked freshwater or brackish water fish (Chai 2007). In view of the wide geographical distribution and the number of infected people around the world, *Metagonimus, Heterophyes,* and *Haplorchis* are the 3 major genera which are highlighted in this review. Only the species reported from humans (either natural or experimental) are described in detail, and the other species without human infections are briefly given only by their names with literature background as potentially zoonotic species.

1.2 *Metagonimus*

Flukes of the genus *Metagonimus* Katsurada, 1912 differ from those of *Heterophyes* and *Heterophyopsis* in that the former has a smaller, submedian-located ventral sucker and no genital sucker, whereas the latter 2 have a bigger and almost median-located ventral sucker and a prominent genital sucker (Chai 2007; Yu and Chai 2010, 2013). Whereas *Metagonimus* has 2 testes, *Haplorchis* and *Procerovum* have only one testis (Chai and Jung 2017). In addition, *Haplorchis, Procerovum,* and *Stictodora* have prominent gonotyl(s) armed with several to numerous rodlets, superimposed on the submedially located ventral sucker but *Metagonimus* has less apparent gonotyls (Chai 2015). *Pygidiopsis* is characterized by having a small median-located ventral sucker and the presence of a ventrogenital apparatus armed with total 12–15 min spines on the right and left sides of the ventrogenital sac (Chai et al. 1986). *Centrocestus* has minute circumoral spines on the oral sucker, and its

Table 1.1 Dimensions of adults, eggs, cercariae, and metacercariae of zoonotic heterophyid species

Species	Adults (mm)	Eggs (μm)	Cercariae (μm) Body (tail length)	Metacercariae (μm)
Metagonimus yokogawai	0.80–1.32 × 0.42–0.54	26–30 × 15–18	175–238 × 56–77 (340–420)	143–190 × 129–163
Metagonimus takahashii	0.86–1.19 × 0.44–0.57	30–36 × 17–20	235–300 × 100–138 (415–535)	150–163 × 143–153
Metagonimus miyatai	1.00–1.30 × 0.46–0.63	29–32 × 17–20	196–230 × 56–66 (343–390)	144–180 × 126–154
Metagonimus minutus	0.43–0.50 × 0.25–0.40	21–24 × 12–15	Not found	144–162 × 125–160
Metagonimus katsuradai	0.32–0.45 × 0.20–0.25	27–29 × 15–17	266–336 × 112–133 (420–490)	168–200 × 152–190
Heterophyes heterophyes	0.60–2.70 × 0.20–0.90	23–29 × 13–15	60–105 × 92 (499–619)	130–260
Heterophyes nocens	0.82–1.02 × 0.52–0.63	23–29 × 13–15	175–238 × 56–77 (340–420)	130–220 × 80–170
Heterophyes dispar	0.40–1.40 × 0.20–0.40	19–25 × 13–15	176–224 × 68–81 (493)	130–260
Haplorchis taichui	0.43–1.18 × 0.17–0.26	22–32 × 11–17	89–124 × 31–43 (250–350)	190–220 × 160–190
Haplorchis pumilio	0.29–0.43 × 0.20–0.26	28–33 × 15–19	189–215 × 69–96 (440)	140–150
Haplorchis yokogawai	0.50–0.72 × 0.18–0.32	26–31 × 14–17	68–96 × 37–50	170–240 × 150–230
Haplorchis vanissimus	0.47–0.57 × 0.12–0.18	23–26 × 11–13	Not found	Not found
Acanthotrema felis	0.43–0.57 × 0.24–0.31	25–28 × 13–17	Not found	216–254 × 152–185
Apophallus donicus	1.12–1.30 × 0.58–0.72	25–35 × 15–20	190 × 80 (258)	93–108
Ascocotyle (Phagicola) longa	0.85–1.00 × 0.27–0.35	16–18 × 9–11	110–125 × 60–95 (179)	225–240 × 215–235
Centrocestus armatus	0.36–0.63 × 0.18–0.28	31–33 × 15–20	97–125 × 49–69 (74–122)	200–250 × 100–120
Centrocestus cuspidatus	0.50 × 0.35	30 × 15	Not described	Not described
Centrocestus formosanus	0.41–0.52 × 0.16–0.20	32–35 × 17–20	47–122 × 26–71 (62–98)	190 × 140
Centrocestus kurokawai	0.36 × 0.18	33–40 × 17–21	Not found	Not found
Cryptocotyle lingua	1.2–2.0 × 0.40–0.90	42–48 × 20–22	140–180 × 52–65 (not given)	110–120 × 80–90
Heterophyopsis continua	2.0–2.8 × 0.42–0.53	24–28 × 14–19	Not found	440–475 × 435–470

(continued)

Table 1.1 (continued)

Species	Adults (mm)	Eggs (μm)	Cercariae (μm) Body (tail length)	Metacercariae (μm)
Procerovum calderoni	0.36–0.47×0.15–0.24	27–30 × 11–13	84–168 × 56–70 (280–336)	150–180 × 105–135
Procerovum varium	0.26–0.28 × 0.09–0.12	24–28 × 12–16	140–160 × 60–72 (316–340)	200–220 × 160–200
Pygidiopsis genata	0.35–0.70 × 0.16–0.40	17–22 × 9–13	108–140 × 40–70 (385–420)	120–210
Pygidiopsis summa	0.58–0.85 × 0.29–0.41	19–24 × 11–13	180–210 × 75–93 (350–420)	190–290 × 160–290
Stellantchasmus falcatus	0.39–0.78 × 0.31–0.40	24–30 × 10–13	55–116 × 34–64 (240–370)	150–200 × 130–190
Stictodora fuscata	0.90–0.98 × 0.38	34–38 × 20–23	Not found	190–300 × 170–270
Stictodora lari	0.70–0.86 × 0.27–0.36	28–33 × 17–20	219 × 87 (429)	390–430 × 320–350

ventral sucker is located median (Yu and Chai 2010, 2013; Chai 2015). *Metagonimus* is morphologically close to *Stellantchasmus* in having a small, laterally deviated ventral sucker, but differs from the latter in the absence of an elongated sac-like seminal vesicle with a muscular expulsor at the opposite side of the ventral sucker (Yu and Chai 2010, 2013; Chai 2015).

After the genus *Metagonimus* was erected with *M. yokogawai* as the type species (Katsurada 1912a, b; Yokogawa 1913a; Ito 1964a), 9 more species have been described. They include *M. ovatus* (Yokogawa 1913b); *M. takahashii* (Suzuki 1930), *M. minutus* (Katsuta 1932), *M. katsuradai* (Izumi 1935), *M. otsurui* (Saito and Shimizu 1968), *M. miyatai* (Saito et al. 1997), *M. hakubaensis* (Shimazu 1999), *M. pusillus* (Tatonova et al. 2017), and *M. suifunensis* (Shumenko et al. 2017) (Table 1.2). Ransom (1920) synonymized *M. ovatus* with *M. yokogawai,* and Morozov (1952) and Yamaguti (1958, 1971, 1975) did not list *M. ovatus* as a distinct species. However, Shimazu and Kino (2015) acknowledged the validity of *M. ovatus* because the shorter termination of intestinal ceca of *M. ovatus* (ending at the anterior half of the testicular zone) compared with that of *M. yokogawai* (entering into the post-testicular zone) is a significant and specific character.

Among the 10 species of *Metagonimus*, *M. yokogawai, M. takahashii*, and *M. miyatai* are the 3 major human-infecting species in Japan and South Korea (Chai et al. 2005, 2009, 2015). With regard to *M. katsuradai*, an experimental human infection was reported to be successful (Izumi 1935) but no natural human infections have been discovered. *M. minutus* is listed as a human-infecting species (Yu and Mott 1994) but no literature background is available to verify this. *M. otsurui* was first reported from experimental hamsters fed the metacercariae from freshwater fish (Saito and Shimizu 1968), and later the Japanese water shrew was found to

Table 1.2 Species of *Metagonimus* reported in the literature

Species with nominators	Human infection	Area (Country)
Metagonimus yokogawai (Katsurada, 1912) Katsurada, 1912	Yes	China, Europe[a], India, Japan, South Korea, Taiwan, Russia
Metagonimus takahashii (Takahashi, 1929) Suzuki, 1930	Yes	Japan, South Korea
Metagonimus miyatai Saito, Chai, Kim, Lee and Rim, 1997	Yes	Japan, South Korea
Metagonimus minutus Katsuta, 1932	Yes[b]	Taiwan
Metagonimus katsuradai Izumi, 1935	Yes[c]	Japan, Russia
Metagonimus hakubaensis Shimazu, 1999	No	Japan
Metagonimus otsurui Saito and Shimizu, 1968	No	Japan
Metagonimus ovatus Yokogawa, 1913	No	Japan
Metagonimus pusillus Tatonova, Shumenko and Besprozvannykh, 2017	No	Russia
Metagonimus suifunensis Shumenko, Tatonova and Besprozvannykh, 2017	No	Russia

Information updated from Chai and Jung (2017)
[a]Countries include Bulgaria, Czech Rep., Romania, Serbia, Spain, and Ukraine. The specific diagnosis of the parasite needs to be further studied in these countries
[b]Experimental human infection was reported
[c]Listed as a human-infecting species (Yu and Mott 1994) without proper literature background

be naturally infected (Shimazu and Urabe 2002). However, it was never discovered from humans. *M. hakubaensis* was originally found from experimental rats fed the metacercariae in lampreys (Shimazu 1999) but human infection is yet unknown.

The geographical distribution of human metagonimiasis is mainly in the Far East, including the South Korea (= South Korea), China, Japan, and the Far Eastern Russia (Chai et al. 2005, Chai 2015). The diagnosis of metagonimiasis using fecal smears is often problematic because mixed infections with liver flukes, such as *Clonorchis sinensis*, or other heterophyid flukes, in particular *Heterophyes nocens*, *Heterophyopsis continua, Pygidiopsis summa,* and *Stellantchasmus falcatus,* are not uncommon (Lee et al. 1984a, 2012; Chai and Lee 2002). Immunological, molecular, and genetic techniques are at times needed for discriminating infections with different genera and even different species of *Metagonimus* (Chai et al. 1989; Yang et al. 2000; Yu and Chai 2010, 2013).

Among the 8 *Metagonimus* spp. reported to date, 5 species, namely, *M. yokogawai, M. takahashii*, *M. miyatai, M. minutus* (human infection with this species has no proper literature background) and *M. katsuradai* (only experimentally proven to be able to infect humans) have been listed as human-infecting species (Yu and Mott 1994; Chai 2007, Chai et al. 2009; Yu and Chai 2013; Chai 2015). However, in true sense, only the former 3 species have public health significance. Here, the epidemiological characteristics of these 3 species are discussed. It is worthy of mentioning that some of old literature on *M. yokogawai* is actually referring to *M. takahashii* or *M. miyatai*, and caution is required when reviewing *M. yokogawai sensu stricto* (Chai et al. 2009; Chai 2015).

A brief history of the discovery, taxonomic debates if any, and morphological and biological characteristics of each *Metagonimus* species are given as follows:

1.2.1 Metagonimus yokogawai

1.2.1.1 *Metagonimus yokogawai* (Katsurada, 1912) Katsurada, 1912

[syn. *Heterophyes yokogawai* Katsurada, 1912; *Heterophyes yokogawai* Yokogawa, 1912; *Loxotrema ovatum* Kobayashi, 1912; *Yokogawa yokogawai* Leiper, 1913; *Loossia romanica* Ciurea, 1915; *Loossia parva* Ciurea, 1915; *Loossia dobrogensis* Ciurea, 1915; *Loxotrema yokogawai* (Kobayashi) Kobayashi, 1925]

Taxonomy and Morphology

This species (Figs. 1.1 and 1.2) was originally described from an experimental dog fed the metacercariae in the sweetfish (*Plecoglossus altivelis*) from Taiwan and

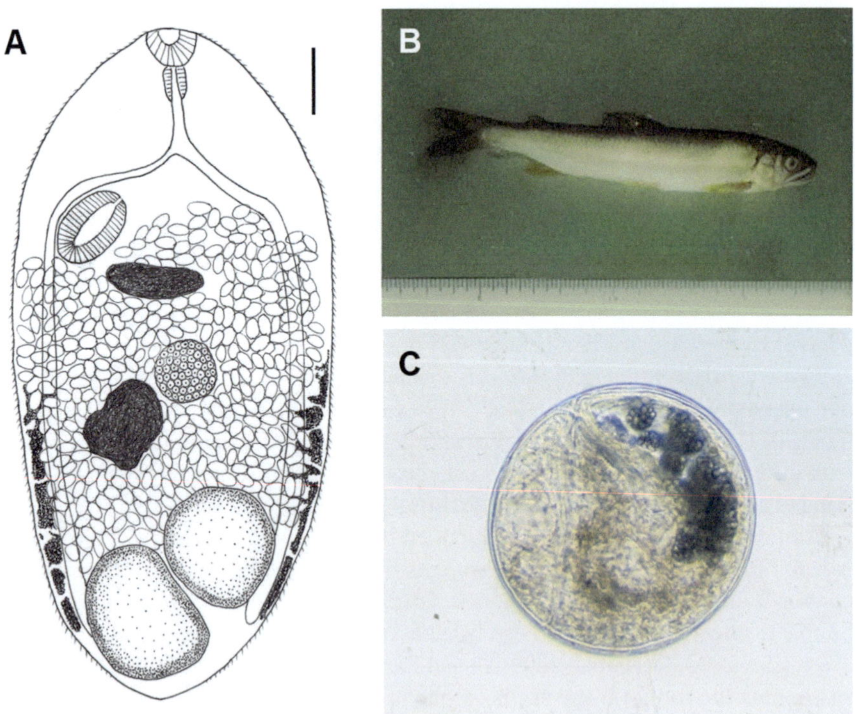

Fig. 1.1 *Metagonimus yokogawai*. (**a**) Line drawing of an adult worm (original figure). Scale bar = 0.1 mm (**b**) The fish intermediate host, sweetfish (*Plecoglossus altivelis*) (**c**) A metacercaria isolated from the sweetfish. ×100

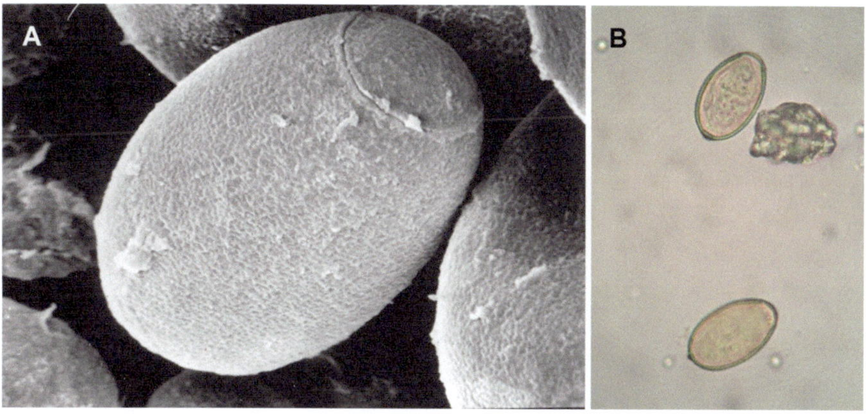

Fig. 1.2 Eggs of *Metagonimus yokogawai*. (**a**) Scanning electron microscopic view. The egg size is 28 μm in length and 17 μm in width (**b**) Two eggs from the distal part of the uterus of an adult worm. The same size of the eggs as (**a**)

named as *Heterophyes yokogawai* on 31 May 1912 (Katsurada 1912a). However, the adult worm morphology was significantly different from that of *Heterophyes* (whereas *Heterophyes* has a large and median-located ventral sucker, the flukes obtained had a small and submedian-located ventral sucker), and subsequently it was renamed as *Metagonimus yokogawai* in the same year, on 31 October 1912 (Katsurada 1912b). A detailed description of the worm morphology was subsequently described by Yokogawa (1913a). On the other hand, the identical species was also discovered in Japan and reported as *Loxotrema ovatum* on 10 October 1912 (Kobayashi 1912). As the Kobayashi's proposal of *L. ovatum* preceded the Katsurada's proposal of *M. yokogawai*, Kobayashi (1925) insisted to call this trematode as *Loxotrema yokogawai* admitting the priority of the species name '*yokogawai*'. However, Faust and Nishigori (1926) found that the genus name "*Loxotrema*" was preoccupied by a molluscan species by Gabb in 1868 and gave an opinion that it should be called as *Metagonimus yokogawai*.

The characteristic morphological features of *Metagonimus* spp. (Fig. 1.3a–c) include a minute body (0.5–1.5 mm in length), a small laterally deviated ventral sucker with no ventrogenital apparatus and no genital sucker, a medially-located ovary, and 2 testes located almost side-by-side or a little oblique near the posterior extremity (Ito 1964a; Chai et al. 2009; Yu and Chai 2013). The adult flukes of *M. yokogawai* (Fig. 1.3a) are 0.80–1.32 mm long and 0.42–0.54 mm wide, slightly smaller than those of *M. takahashii* (Fig. 1.3c), 0.86–1.19 mm long and 0.44–0.57 mm wide, and *M. miyatai* (Fig. 1.3b), 1.00–1.30 mm long and 0.46–0.63 mm wide (Saito et al. 1997; Chai 2015). The eggs of *M. yokogawai* (Fig. 1.2a, b) are 26–30 μm long and 15–18 μm wide, also smaller than those of *M. takahashii*, 30–36 μm long and 17–20 μm wide, and *M. miyatai,* 29–32 μm long and 17–20 μm wide, although there are some overlaps in the range (Chai et al. 1993a). *M. minutus* differs from *M. yokogawai, M. takahashii*, and *M. miyatai* in having a smaller body

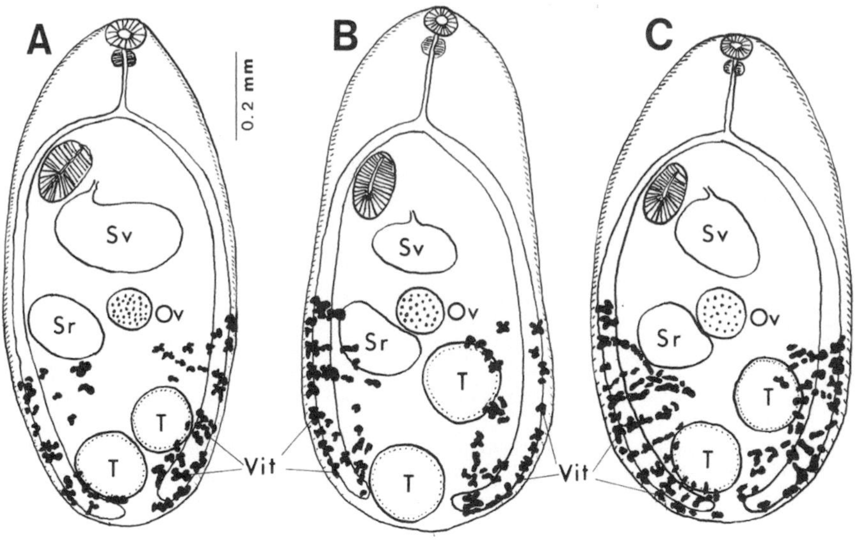

Fig. 1.3 Comparative morphology of *Metagonimus yokogawai* (**a**), *M. miyatai* (**b**), and *M. takahashii* (**c**) adult flukes. Abbreviations: *ov* ovary, *T* testis, *Sr* seminal receptacle, *Sv* seminal vesicle, *Vit* vitelline follicles. Reproduced from Chai et al. (1993a) Korean J Parasitol 31:99–108 with permission

(0.46 × 0.28 mm) and egg size (23 × 13 μm) (Katsuta 1932; Chai et al. 1993a). The adult flukes of *M. katsuradai, M. otsurui,* and *M. hakubaensis* differ from those of *M. yokogawai, M. takahashii, M. miyatai*, and *M. minutus* in that the formers have a larger ventral sucker than the oral sucker (Izumi 1935; Chai et al. 1993a; Shimazu 1999).

M. yokogawai has a unique position and arrangement of 2 testes which are closely adjacent to each other near the posterior extremity (Chai et al. 2009; Yu and Chai 2013; Shimazu and Kino 2015). By contrast, in *M. miyatai* and *M. takahashii*, the 2 testes are more or less separated from each other (Chai et al. 1991; Saito et al. 1997; Chai 2015). In addition, the vitelline follicles of *M. yokogawai* extend in lateral fields from the level of the ovary down to the posterior end of the posterior testis, but not beyond the posterior testis (Saito et al. 1997; Chai 2015). In *M. miyatai,* vitelline follicles distribute from the level of the ovary down to the anterior level of the posterior testis; there is no vitellaria distribution beyond the posterior testis (Chai et al. 1993a; Saito et al. 1997). However, in *M. takahashii*, vitelline follicles are abundant from the level of the ovary down to the posterior testis and usually extend beyond the posterior testis level (Chai et al. 1993a; Saito et al. 1997). Moreover, *M. yokogawai* has the uterine tubule which never overlaps or crosses over the middle portion of the anterior testis, whereas *M. takahashii* and *M. miyatai* have the uterine tubules which overlap the whole anterior testis (Chai et al. 1993a; Saito et al. 1997). *M. suifunensis* was reported to be morphologically close to *M.*

yokogawai, M. takahashii, and *M. miyatai*; however, it differed from the 3 species in molecular characteristics (Shumenko et al. 2017).

The adult flukes of *M. yokogawai* differ from those of *M. takahashii* and *M. miyatai* in their tegumental ultrastructures (Lee et al. 1984b; Fujino et al. 1989; Chai et al. 1998, 2000a). Scanning electron microscopy showed that, on the lip of the oral sucker, type II sensory papillae (swollen tegumental surface without a cilium), 7–9 in numbers, are present in all of the 3 *Metagonimus* spp. Type I papillae are also present in all 3 *Metagonimus* spp. However, type III sensory papillae (round swelling of tegumental ridge) are observed only in *M. yokogawai* (Lee et al. 1984b) but not in *M. takahashii* (Chai et al. 2000a) and *M. miyatai* (Chai et al. 1998). In the inner side of the oral sucker, 2 large and 4 small type I papillae (ciliated knob-like tegumental swelling) are recognized in *M. takahashii* (Chai et al. 2000a) and *M. miyatai* (Chai et al. 1998) but this is unknown in *M. yokogawai* (Lee et al. 1984b). Several other minor differences among the 3 *Metagonimus* spp. were described (Fujino et al. 1989; Chai et al. 2000a). The body wall ultrastructure of *M. takahashii* (under the name *M. yokogawai takahashii*) was also studied using transmission electron microscopy (Inatomi et al. 1968). It is covered with non-nucleated integument of a syncytial structure, which is limited by the plasma membrane at the outer surface and the basement of the integument at the inner side, which is a common and basic structure for the trematode tegument (Inatomi et al. 1968).

Life Cycle

M. yokogawai has several developmental stages during its life cycle. These include the eggs, miracidia, sporocysts, rediae, daughter rediae, cercariae, metacercariae, and adults (Beaver et al. 1984). When the eggs are liberated from the intestinal tract of the definitive host, they already contain mature miracidia and enter the surrounding water and then small streams and rivers. The first intermediate host, *Semisulcospira* snails, ingests the fully embryonated, unhatched eggs (Beaver et al. 1984). A first sporocyst generation and 2 redial generations are then developed, and finally the characteristic lophocercus cercariae, with pigmented eyespots (= ophthalmo-pleuro-lophocercus cercariae), abundant penetration glands, and a distinctive anterior end having an anteroventral mouth (= oral sucker) and a pair of clustered penetration gland openings, are liberated from the snail host and begin to swim (Beaver et al. 1984). Swimming cercariae find freshwater fish, the second intermediate host, attach to their scales, in the skin, or in the flesh, and become encysted which we call metacercariae (Beaver et al. 1984). The metacercariae can persist in the fish muscle for at least 2.5 years and can live throughout the life span of the fish host (Yu and Chai 2013; Chai 2015). Ingestion of raw or improperly cooked fish flesh causes human infections.

Semisulcospira libertina and *Semisulcospira coreana* have been reported to be the molluscan intermediate host of *M. yokogawai* (Ito 1964b; Cho et al. 1984). The cercarial body is 175–238 μm long and 56–77 μm wide and the tail is 340–420 μm long and 31–35 μm wide (Ito 1964b). Many cercariae recognizable by their prominent eye spots are contained in the daughter redia (Ito 1964b). Oral spines are nearly 30 in total number, with the posterior row being 4 spines (Ito 1964b; Saito 1972).

The most important fish host for *M. yokogawai* is the sweetfish *Plecoglossus altivelis* (Fig. 1.1b) in South Korea and Japan (Ito 1964a; Chai and Lee 2002; Sohn 2009; Chai 2007, 2015). The dace *Tribolodon hokonensis* and *Tribolodon taczanowskii,* and the perch *Lateolabrax japonicus* have also been reported as the fish host for *M. yokogawai* (Ahn 1983; Chai 2007; Chai et al. 2009; Yu and Chai 2013; Chai 2015). The metacercarial cyst (Fig. 1.1c) is round or elliptical, 143–190 μm in length and 129–163 μm in width, with the cyst wall thickness of 2.6–3.9 μm (Hong and Seo 1969). The excysted metacercariae are 252–320 μm long and 163–190 μm wide (Hong and Seo 1969). The metacercariae of *M. yokogawai* resemble the metacercariae of *Clonorchis sinensis* but can be differentiated from it by a smaller ventral sucker compared with the oral sucker, whereas in *C. sinensis* the ventral sucker is markedly larger than the oral sucker. The metacercarial distribution within the sweetfish body is as follows: 62.8% in the muscle, 29.3% in the subcutaneous tissues, and 7.7% on the scales (Hong and Seo 1969).

The natural definitive hosts are humans and animals, including fish-eating mammals and birds (Chai et al. 2009). Dogs (Muto 1917; Komiya 1965; Cho et al. 1981), rats (Seo et al. 1981a, b), cats (Huh et al. 1993), foxes (Miyamoto 1985), boars (Komiya 1965) and kites (bird) (Miyamoto 1985) have been known to be the natural definitive hosts. However, the significance of each animal host as the source of human infections has not been properly evaluated (Chai 2007; Chai et al. 2009; Yu and Chai 2013). Mice, rats, cats, dogs, gerbils, hamsters, and ducks are experimental definitive hosts for *M. yokogawai* (Kagei and Kihata 1970; Guk et al. 2005; Chai et al. 2009; Li et al. 2010, 2013, Chai 2017). The development of *M. yokogawai* has been studied most frequently in small experimental animals, including mice and rats, and rarely hamsters, guinea pigs, chicks, ducks, and rabbits (Takahashi 1929; Koga 1938; Gushima 1939; Komiya et al. 1958; Yokogawa and Sano 1968; Hong and Seo 1969; Li et al. 2010, 2013, Chai 2017). Guk et al. (2005) studied on the growth and development of *M. yokogawai* in different strains of mice (BALB/c, ddY, C57BL/6J, C3H/HeN, and A/J) and found that ddY mice were the most suitable host for *M. yokogawai* with the highest worm recovery rate. In vitro culture of the metacercariae of *M. yokogawai* to egg-laying adults was tried by Yasuraoka and Kojima (1970). It was possible to cultivate *M. yokogawai* metacercariae into adults in NCTC medium supplemented with chick embryo extract and human serum, with appearance of 70–90 eggs in the uterus at day 17 post-culture (Yasuraoka and Kojima 1970).

Epidemiology and Geographical Distribution

Among the 3 *Metagonimus* species of public health importance, *M. yokogawai* is the most widely spread and most highly prevalent species. The principal mode of human infection is consumption of raw or improperly cooked flesh of freshwater fish, notably the sweetfish (*Plecoglossus altivelis*) and the dace (*Tribolodon taczanowskii*) in Far Eastern countries (Yu and Chai 2013; Chai 2015). Pickled, salted, or fermented fish, as well as cooking knife and chopping board contaminated with the metacercariae may also cause human infections; however, such possibilities are relatively low. Large or small endemic foci with low, medium, or high prevalence

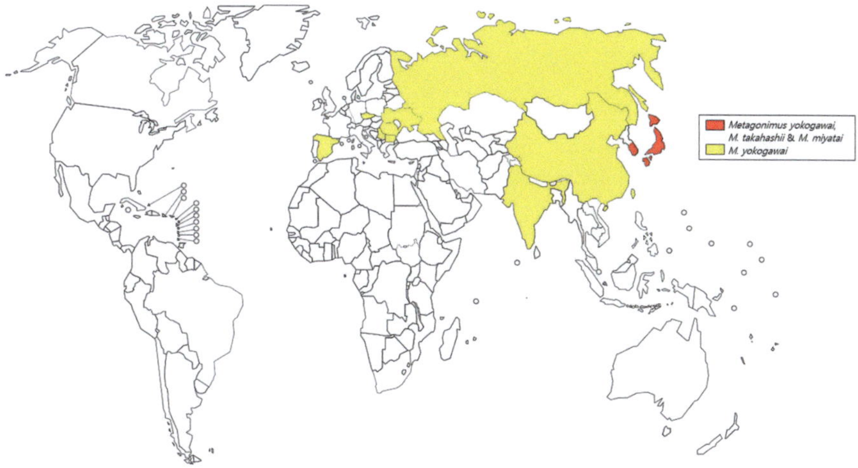

Fig. 1.4 Global distribution of *Metagonimus* spp. (*M. yokogawai, M. takahashii,* and *M. miyatai*) based on the presence of their life cycles

among human population are scattered along riverside areas of these countries, where local people traditionally eat raw fish (Yu and Chai 2013; Chai 2015). The major endemic areas are South Korea, Japan, China, Taiwan, India, and far eastern parts of Russia (Fig. 1.4) (Yu and Chai 2013; Chai 2015). Indonesia and the Philippines have sometimes been included among the countries where *M. yokogawai* is distributed (Harinasuta et al. 1987; Yu and Mott 1994; Fried et al. 2004). However, the related original literature is difficult to find. Reports on *M. yokoagwai* have also been available from several European countries, including Bulgaria, Czech Republic, Romania, Serbia, Spain, and Ukraine (see below), although the specific diagnosis of the parasite should be further studied.

China Little information has been available regarding *M. yokogawai* infection in humans and animals in mainland China. It was briefly mentioned that human infections exist in Guangdong, Anhui, Hubei, and Zhejiang Province (Yu and Mott 1994). In Heilongjiang Province, 6.2% of 178 farm dogs were reported to be infected with 2–7850 specimens of *M. yokogawai* per dog (Wang et al. 2006). In Yunnan Province, the cercariae of *M. yokogawai* were detected from *Semisulcospira libertina* snails (Chen et al. 2009). In Guangxi Province, 18 of 31 fish species, including *Zacco platypus* and *Hemibarbus maculatus*, were infected with *M. yokogawai* metacercariae (Sohn et al. 2009). It is interesting to note that in Guangxi Province 8 human infections were confirmed by genetic analysis of fecal eggs (Jeon et al. 2012).

Europe The existence of *M. yokogawai* (in some references described as *Metagonimus* sp.) have been reported in fish hosts and wild animals of several European countries, including Romania (Ciurea 1924), Bulgaria (Nachev and Sures 2009; Ondračkova et al. 2012), Czech Republic (Francová et al. 2011), Serbia (Cakić et al. 2007; Djikanovic et al. 2012), Spain (Toledo et al. 2014), and Ukraine

(Davydov et al. 2011; Korol et al. 2016). No human infections have been reported in these countries.

India Two cases of heterophyid egg positives (designated as *M. yokogawai* infection) were detected in India (Mahanta et al. 1995; Uppal and Wadhwa 2005). However, adult flukes were not confirmed.

Japan Since the first discovery of *M. yokogawai*, numerous epidemiological studies have been performed in Japan (Ito 1964a). It was originally thought that *M. yokogawai* infection is distributed nationwide with the exception of Hokkaido (Ito 1964a). Later, however, the presence of its life cycle in Hokkaido was recognized (Miyamoto 1985). Until the 1960s, the reported prevalence in humans ranged 0.5–35.1% depending on the locality (Ito 1964a). In 1953, the prevalence of *M. yokogawai* in Shikoku Island divided into 4 prefectural areas (Kagawa, Tokushima, Kochi, and Ehime Prefectures) was 7.2% on average (1.6–12.6% by prefecture) (Hunter et al. 1953). A small riverside village in Shizuoka prefecture revealed an egg positive rate of 15.0% (38/253) among the people (Yokogawa et al. 1962). Thus, the prevalence in humans was generally lower than that in South Korea. However, in some areas, for example, those along the Takatsu River, Shimane Prefecture, the prevalence among riparian residents was high up to 71.9% among 798 examined (Kagei 1965). Two areas surveyed in Akita Prefecture revealed 8.5% and 45.9% egg prevalence among the residents (Yoshimura et al. 1972). Kagei and Kihata (1973) surveyed 26 areas of Japan and reported *M. yokogawai* egg positive rates of 0–73.9%. Three areas of Shimane Prefecture showed the highest prevalence (73.9%, 71.9%, and 57.1%, respectively) followed by areas of Hiroshima (38.9%), Kochi (33.2%), Kagoshima (28.0%), and Saga Prefecture (27.0%). The prevalence in humans was positively correlated with the metacercarial density in the sweetfish caught in each area (Kagei and Kihata 1973). An epidemiological survey performed in 1982–1988 around the Hamamatsu Lake, Shizuoka Prefecture revealed 13.2% egg positive rate among 4524 lakeside people examined (Ito et al. 1991). Thereafter, no information is available on the prevalence of human infection in Japan. However, it is presumed that the prevalence has been decreasing until now.

With regard to metacercarial infection in fish host, 121 (93.1%) out of 130 sweetfish collected from the Takatsu River, Shimane Prefecture were found infected, with the average number of metacercariae per fish of 297–13,452, which varied by month or season (Kagei et al. 1966). Subsequently, 10 Prefectures, including Gifu, Kyoto, Hyogo, Okayama, Shimane, Yamaguti, Ehime, Kochi, Miyazaki, Kumamoto, and Kagoshima, were verified to be high endemic areas with heavy metacercarial burdens, >1000 per sweetfish (Kagei and Oshima. 1968). It is interesting to note that in a small village of Akita Prefecture, the infection rate and the metacercarial density were markedly higher in the dace (*Tribolodon hakonensis*), 100% (30/30) and 270 metacercariae per fish, respectively, compared to the sweetfish, 96% (24/25) and 17 metacercariae per fish (Yoshimura et al. 1972). However, Kagei and Kihata (1973) reported the metacercarial density in the sweetfish from 26 areas of Japan; an area of Kochi Prefecture showed the highest metacercarial burden (38,250/fish) followed by areas of Shimane (10,804–19,900/fish), Yamaguti (14,850/fish), Hiroshima (2000/fish), and Saga Prefecture (1400/fish). Kagei et al. (1975) also reported that another fish species, *Salangichthys microdon*, is infected with *M. yokogawai* metacercariae, although the infection rate and the metacercarial density are relatively low. In Hokkaido, daces are an important fish host, with 5.6–100% prevalence and 2–102.5 metacercariae/fish (Miyamoto and Kutsumi 1978). Around the Lake Hamamatsu in Shizuoka Prefecture, 26.6–100% of the sweetfish were infected with *M. yokogawai* metacercariae depending on different streams, with the metacercarial density of 0.7–23,305 per fish (Ito et al. 1991). Later, in 18 small rivers in Shizuoka Prefecture, the prevalence of *M. yokogawai* metacercariae was examined in the sweetfish; it ranged 0–100%, with variable metacercarial density per fish (Kino et al. 2006).

Various mammalian and avian species have been known to be natural definitive host for *M. yokogawai* in Japan, including the dog, cat, pig, rodents, foxes, and a few species of birds (Ito 1964a). In Hokkaido, red foxes and black kites (bird) were found to be natural definitive hosts (Miyamoto 1985).

South Korea Since the first discovery of an endemic focus in a southern area located along the Miryang River (Chun 1960a), many epidemiological studies have been performed. The results have revealed that almost all small streams to large rivers in eastern and southern coastal areas were found to be endemic areas of *M. yokogawai* (Seo et al. 1981a; Chai and Lee 2002; Chai 2007; Chai et al. 1977, 2009). The Sumjin, Tamjin, and Boseong Rivers, Geoje Island, and Osip Stream in Samcheok-shi (Gangwon-do) have been the highest endemic areas with 20–70% egg positive rates of the riparian residents (Yeo and Seo 1971; Chai et al. 1977; Soh and Ahn 1978; Ahn 1984; Chai et al. 2000b, 2009, 2015). Although the intensity of infection has slightly decreased in some areas (Lee et al. 2008), high endemicity is still persisting in others (Chai et al. 2015). However, the national prevalence of heterophyid eggs (mostly *M. yokogawai*) among the Korean people was 0.50% and 0.26% in 2004 and 2012, respectively, showing a decreasing pattern (Kim et al. 2009; Korean CDC 2013). The number of infected people currently in South Korea is estimated to be about 130,000 (Korean CDC 2013).

Regarding the infection status of fish host with *M. yokogawai* metacercariae, an earlier study performed in Jeju-do (formerly Cheju-do) Island reported av. 90.3% (56/62) positive rate of the sweetfish collected from 3 different localities (Kang et al. 1964). Subsequently, at a lower reach of the Hyungsan River, Kyeongsangbuk-do Province, 75 (40.5%) of 185 daces (*Tribolodon taczanowskii*) were reported to be positive for *M. yokogawai* metacercariae; the metacercarial density was low (Choi et al. 1966). Later, the Seomjin River showed that the infection rate of the sweetfish was 100% with the average metacercarial density per fish of 3851 (Hong and Seo 1969). In the Tamjin River, 100% infection rate of the sweetfish was reported with an average metacercarial density of 15,688 per fish (Chai et al. 1977). Along the Boseong River, a tributary of the Seomjin River, 100% metacercarial prevalence with an average metacercarial density per fish of 22,650 was also documented (Soh and Ahn 1978). In comparison, the sweetfish caught from small streams running into the eastern coast (Gangwon-do) were found to harbor lower numbers of metacercariae ranging from 0 (Namdaecheon, Yangyang-gun) to 1643 metacercariae per fish (Oshipcheon, Samcheok-gun) (Seo et al. 1982). The Namdaecheon, Yangyang-gun is located in the northernmost part of the eastern coast of South Korea, and thus the absence of metacercarial infection in the sweetfish caught from this area drew a considerable attention. However, contradictory results were reported from 3 different surveys performed in this area (Song et al. 1985; Sohn et al. 1990; Cho et al. 2014). Whereas Song et al. (1985) and Cho et al. (2014) detected a small number of metacercariae from the sweetfish in this area (av. 11.6 and 49.0 metacercariae per fish, respectively), Sohn et al. (1990) could not detect any metacercariae from this stream.

Song et al. (1985) surveyed on the status of metacercarial infection in the sweetfish from 70 small streams along eastern and southern coastal areas and found that 432 (64.7%) of 668 sweetfish examined were infected with *M. yokogawai* metacercariae, with the average metacercarial density per fish of 640. Thereafter, no active surveys were performed on the infection status of sweetfish until 2011 when 88 (60.7%) of 145 sweetfish caught from 10 streams of eastern and southern coastal areas were found to be infected with *M. yokogawai* metacercariae; at this time, the average number of metacercariae per sweetfish was 61 (Cho et al. 2011). These two figures (Song et al. 1985; Cho et al. 2011) showed that the prevalence of metacercariae in sweetfish is sustained but the metacercarial density per fish is decreasing. However, Sohn et al. (2018) recently found surprisingly heavy metacercarial burdens (under the name *Metagonimus* spp.) in sweetfish caught from the upper, middle, and lower reaches of the Seomjin River (av. 3146, 2875, and 8727 metacercariae/fish, respectively) and those caught from the middle and lower reaches of the Tamjin River (av. 1339 and 841, respectively). This discrepancy particularly in the Seomjin River may be either due to a seasonal tendency of metacercarial burdens or because of a small number of fish (2–3 sweetfish each) examined in the Seomjin River (Sohn et al. 2018). On the other hand, the metacercarial infection status examined in the dace (*Tribolodon taczanowskii*) caught from the Seomjin River revealed a total of 8767 metacercariae of *Metagonimus* spp. (the majority being *M. yokogawai* with a few *M. miyatai* and *M. takahashii*) from 15 fish, with an average number per fish of 584 (Chai et al. 1991). Little information is available on the infection status in the dace in South Korea.

Natural definitive hosts for *M. yokogawai* are cats, dogs, and rodents. Four (9.8%) of 41 cats purchased from a market in Seoul had *M. yokogawai* infection (Huh et al. 1993), and 78 (17.8%) of 438 feral cats purchased from a market in Busan were infected with *M. yokogawai* adult flukes (described under the name *Metagonimus* sp.) (Table 1.3) (Sohn and Chai 2005). Recently, 61 (30.0%) of 203 stray cats captured around the Seomjin River was infected with an average of 105.7 adult flukes of *Metagonimus* spp. (presumed to be *M. yokogawai*) (Shin et al. 2015). As for dogs, few studies have been performed on their infection status with *M. yokogawai*. One (1.0%) of 102 stray dogs caught in Gyeonggi-do (formerly Kyonggi-do) was found to have 57 *M. yokogawai* worms (Cho et al. 1981). Four (2.4%) of 170

Table 1.3 Heterophyid flukes recovered from 438 feral cats purchased in a market in Pusan, South Korea

Heterophyid species	No. (%) of cats infected	No. worms recovered	
		Total (average no./cat)	Range of worm load
Acanthotrema felis	5 (1.1)	370 (74.0)	1–238
Centrocestus armatus	5 (1.1)	135 (27.0)	2–105
Cryptocotyle concava	13 (3.0)	286 (22.0)	1–267
Heterophyes nocens	106 (24.2)	4052 (38.2)	1–389
Heterophyopsis continua	58 (13.2)	696 (12.0)	1–135
Metagonimus spp.[a]	78 (17.8)	11,598 (148.7)	1–3984
Pygidiopsis summa	92 (21.0)	6478 (70.4)	1–1486
Procerovum varium	1 (0.002)	3 (3.0)	–
Stellantchasmus falcatus	9 (2.1)	377 (41.9)	1–270
Stictodora fuscata	15 (3.4)	91 (6.1)	1–21
Stictodora lari	2 (0.46)	18 (9.0)	1–17

Data from Sohn and Chai (2005)
[a]Including *M. yokogawai, M. takahashii,* and *M. miyatai*

wild rats captured from various localities were found infected with *M. yokogawai*, 1–38 worms per rat (Seo et al. 1981b).

Of considerable interest is that the eggs of *M. yokogawai* were detected from Korean mummies of the 17th century, Joseon Dynasty (Seo et al. 2008; Shin et al. 2009). It is thus apparent that the life cycle of *M. yokogawai* was actively maintained around 400 years ago in South Korea (Seo et al. 2008). The area where the mummy was found (Seo et al. 2008) is now a well-known high endemic area of *M. yokogawai* infection (Yeo and Seo 1971; Chai and Lee 2002; Chai et al. 2009).

Taiwan The metacercariae of *M. yokogawai* were originally described from the sweetfish *Plecoglossus altivelis* in Taiwan by S. Yokogawa in 1912 (Ito 1964a). After then, human infections with *M. yokogawai* were occasionally found (Chen 1991). However, little investigation has been available regarding the prevalence and geographical distribution of *M. yokogawai* infection in humans and animals (Li et al. 2013). Also there were few reports on fish intermediate hosts. A recent survey added several fish species as the second intermediate host for *M. yokogawai* in Taiwan; *Opsariichthys pachycephalus* (syn. *Zacco pachycephalus*), *Zacco platypus, Varicorhinus barbatulus, Acrosscheilus formosanus, Distoechodon turmirostris, Himibarbus labeo,* and *Sinibrama macrops* (Li et al. 2010, 2013).

Russia The Amur and Ussuri valleys of the Khabarovsk territory have been known to be endemic areas of *M. yokogawai* (Yu and Mott 1994). In this territory, the prevalence was 1–2% among the total population but it was 20–70% among the ethnic minority (Yu and Mott 1994). In the north of Sakhalin Island, the infection rate was 10% among ethnic minorities and 1.5% among Russians, and sporadic cases were also reported in the Amur district and the Primorye territory (Yu and

Mott 1994; Chai 2015). In the Khabarovsk territory, the population at risk was once estimated to be 859,000, which is 14.7% of the total population in this territory (Yu and Mott 1994).

Other Countries In USA, at least 4 articles reported *M. yokogawai* infection among Southeast Asian refugees (Tittle et al. 1982; Sutherland et al. 1983; Nutman et al. 1987) or in a Caucasian American female who traveled to the Orient (Goldsmith 1978). In one study, adult flukes were recovered after anthelmintic treatment; the infection was presumed to have acquired during her travel to the Orient (Goldsmith 1978). However, in the other 3 studies, only eggs were detected in feces, and adult flukes were not identified (Tittle et al. 1982; Sutherland et al. 1983; Nutman et al. 1987). Considering that the refugees were from Cambodia, Lao PDR, or Vietnam (Tittle et al. 1982; Sutherland et al. 1983; Nutman et al. 1987), the eggs they found may have been those of *Haplorchis* spp. or *Opisthorchis viverrini*, rather than those of *M. yokogawai* which is not distributed in these countries.

1.2.2 Metagonimus takahashii

1.2.2.1 *Metagonimus takahashii* (Takahashi, 1929) Suzuki, 1930

[syn. *Metagonimus yokogawai ovatus* Asada, 1934; *Metagonimus yokogawai* var. *takahashii* Morishita, 1951; *Metagonimus yokogawai* Koga type by Koga, 1938 and Saito, 1984]

Taxonomy and Morphology

This species (Fig. 1.5a, b) was originally reported by S. Takahashi from the small intestine of mice and dogs fed the metacercariae encysted in various freshwater fish species in Japan (Takahashi 1929). When this species was first reported, it was just called as a larger egg-type *M. yokogawai* because its eggs were larger than those of *M. yokogawai* and the worm was morphologically so similar to *M. yokogawai* (Takahashi 1929). A year later, it was reported as a new species, *M. takahashii*, admitting that the larger egg size is enough to be a specific character (Suzuki 1930). Yamaguti (1934) recovered numerous adult flukes from the small intestine of foxes in Siga Prefecture, Japan and assigned them as *M. takahashii*. However, the validity of this new species was put to a question because its morphological difference from *M. yokogawai* was minor, and the name was compromised as *M. yokogawai ovatus* by Asada (1934). Kogame (1939) agreed to use the name *M. yokogawai ovatus* for the large egg-type *Metagonimus* reported by Takahashi. After then, Miyata (1944) treated *M. takahashii* as a separate species from *M. yokogawai* admitting that in addition to the different egg size the former has the right testis more posterior than the left testis and the uterus extends to the posterior margin of the right testis and the latter has 2 testes lying almost horizontally and the uterus ended in front of the anterior margin of the 2 testes. However, the taxonomic debates on *M. takahashii*

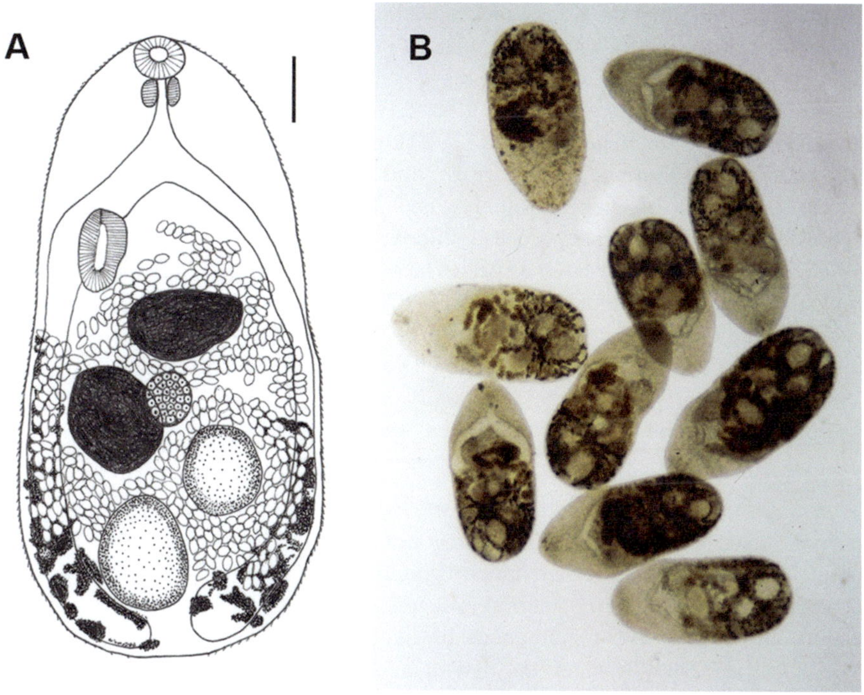

Fig. 1.5 *Metagonimus takahashii*. (**a**) Line drawing of an adult worm (original figure). Scale bar = 0.1 mm (**b**) Several adult flukes recovered from a human case. ×40

continued and a new name, *M. yokogawai* var. *takahashii,* was proposed by Morishita in 1951 (Ito 1964a; Takahashi 1967). Subsequently, Ochi (1957), Takahashi (1967) and Ito (1964a) used this name. However, Komiya (1965) called it as either *M. yokogawai takahashii* or simply *M. yokogawai* (synonymizing *M. takahashii* Suzuki 1930 with *M. yokogawai*) in his review book, "Metacercariae in Japan and Adjacent Territories".

Even after then, the taxonomic validity of *M. takahashii* continued to be the subject of study by Japanese parasitologists. Saito (1972, 1973) was one of them who strongly supported the validity of *M. takahashii* based not only on its remarkably larger egg size than *M. yokogawai* but also on differential morphologies of larval and adult stages and also by the different host specificities of the 2 species at experimental infection with the cercariae. It seems that, thereafter, the name *M. takahashii* has been settled, although *M. yokogawai takahashii* continued to be used for a while (Kamiya et al. 1975; Miyamoto and Kutsumi 1978). Later, Saito (1984) grouped *Metagonimus* spp. flukes into 2; one is the large ventral sucker group (in comparison to the oral sucker) which included *M. yokogawai* and *M. takahashii*, and the other is the small ventral sucker group which included *M. katsuradai* and *M. otsurui*. He described 2 more types in the former group; Miyata type and Koga type (Saito 1984). The Miyata type was later described as a new species, *M. miyatai*

(Saito et al. 1997) and the Koga type, encysting in the scale of the dace *Tribolodon hakonensis* (Koga 1938), was synonymized with *M. takahashii* by the present author (Chai et al. 1991).

Adult flukes of *M. takahashii* are 0.86–1.19 mm long and 0.44–0.57 mm wide, and their eggs are 30–36 μm long and 17–20 μm wide (Saito et al. 1997; Chai 2015). They differ from those of *M. yokogawai* and *M. miyatai* in the position of the 2 testes, distribution of vitelline follicles, and size of their eggs (Saito 1984; Chai et al. 1993a; Chai 2015). They are also different from *M. katsuradai, M. otsurui*, and *M. hakubaensis* in that the latter 3 species have a smaller ventral sucker than the oral sucker (Saito 1984; Shimazu 1999; Chai 2015). *M. minutus* has a larger ventral sucker than the oral sucker but differs from *M. takahashii* and *M. yokogawai* in having a smaller body and eggs, larger seminal vesicle, and different fish host (Katsuta 1932; Chai et al. 1993a).

For comparative surface ultrastructures, see *M. yokogawai*.

Life Cycle

Semisulcospira spp., including *Semisulcospira libertina* and *Semisulcospira coreana,* have been recognized as the snail hosts for *M. takahashii* (Saito 1972; Cho et al. 1984). They produce cercariae of the ophthalmo-pleurolo-phocercous type, characterized by possessing a pair of eyespots and a long slender tail without bifurcation but covered with membranous fin-like structure (Saito 1972; Chai 2015). When they are shed in water, they swim freely and infect freshwater fish (Saito 1972; Chai 2015). They attach to the skin or scale of the fish host and penetrate into the dermis and then the muscles leaving their tail outside the body of the fish (Chai 2015). The fish hosts for *M. takahashii* were reported to be the crussian carp *Carassius auratus* (Fig. 1.6), carp *Cyprinus carpio*, dace *Tribolodon taczanowskii*, and perch *Lateolabrax japonicus* (Takahashi 1929; Saito 1984; Sohn 2009; Chai 2015). Saito (1972) compared the morphology of cercariae and metacercariae of *M. takahashii* in comparison to that of *M. yokogawai*. The size of *M. takahashii* cercariae is 235–300 μm long and 100–138 μm wide for the body and 415–535 μm long and 30–55 μm wide for the tail (Saito 1972). The cercariae have 5 posterior oral spines on the oral sucker (*M. yokogawai* has 4 posterior spines) and different size and arrangement of the 7 pairs of penetration gland cells (2 longitudinal rows in *M. takahashii*, but longitudinal and transverse rows in *M. yokogawai*) (Saito 1972). The metacercariae of *M. takahashii* are brownish, whereas those of *M. yokogawai* are yellowish, and their excretory bladder is dark blue in the former and black in the latter (Saito 1972). The metacercarial cyst of *M. taklahashii* is 150–163 μm long and 143–153 μm wide (Saito 1972). *M. takahashii* metacercariae are found mostly from the scale of the fish, whereas those of *M. yokogawai* are found from the muscle, skin, and scales (Saito 1984).

The natural definitive hosts for *M. takahashii* are mice, rats, dogs, cats, and other mammals and fish-eating birds including pelicans, kites, and other avian species (Takahashi 1929; Yamaguti 1958; Kamiya et al. 1975; Ahn 1993). Adult specimens of *Metagonimus* sp. were recovered from migrating large egrets (*Egretta alba modesta*) in South Korea (Ryang et al. 1991); this is considered to be *M. takahashii*

Fig. 1.6 A carp, *Carassius auratus*, a fish intermediate host of *Metagonimus takahashii*

infection according to the figures shown by the authors. The experimental definitive hosts include mice (Takahashi 1929; Guk et al. 2005, Chai 2017), rats and dogs (Takahashi 1929, Chai 2017), cats (Kim et al. 2006, Chai 2017), hamsters (Saito 1972; Chai et al. 1991; Rim et al. 1996, Chai 2017), and rabbit (as Koga type) (Kogame 1939). Guk et al. (2005) studied on the growth and development of *M. takahashii* in different strains of mice (BALB/c, ddY, C57BL/6J, C3H/HeN, and A/J) and reported that mice were a generally not so good experimental host, although BALB/c, ddY, and C3H/HeN mice were slightly better than C57BL/6J and A/J mice.

Epidemiology and Geographical Distribution

M. takahashii is widely spread around small streams, rivers, ponds, or lakes. The principal mode of human infection is consumption of raw or improperly cooked freshwater fish, particularly the carp (*Carassius auratus* or *Cyprinus carpio*) in South Korea and Japan (Fig. 1.4) (Chai 2015). Pickled, salted, or fermented fish, as well as cooking knife and chopping board contaminated with the metacercariae may also cause human infections, although such possibility is quite low.

Japan After *M. takahashii* was first found and described as a new species in Japan (Suzuki 1930), articles regarding its existence have been published (Ito 1964a; Saito 1972, 1973). However, because of taxonomic debates and confusion between *M. takahashii* and *M. yokogawai*, its precise epidemiological characteristics, including the prevalence and geographical distribution of human infections, have not been clearly defined (Chai 2015). It is of note that in Okayama City 43 (0.64%) of 6680 residents were infected with *M. takahashii*, whereas 54 (0.81%) were infected with *M. yokogawai* (Takahashi 1929). In Fuchu City, Hiroshima Prefecture, 11 (4.8%) of 231 residents examined were infected with *M. takahashii*, whereas 81 (35.1) were infected with *M. yokogawai* (Asada et al. 1957). Around the Lake Biwa, *Semisulcospira* snails collected from the water drainage system were found to be infected with the cercariae of *M. takahashii*, together with those of *M. yokogawai, M. hakubaensis, M. otsurui,* and *M. katsuradai* (Urabe 2003).

South Korea The existence of *M. takahashii* was first documented by recovery of adult flukes from experimental rabbits fed the metacercariae from carps (Chun 1960b). The presence of human infections (mixed with *Metagonimus* sp., which was presumed to be *M. miyatai*) was first demonstrated through recovery of adult flukes in riparian people along the Hongcheon River, Gangwon-do (Ahn and Ryang 1988). Subsequently, an endemic area of *M. takahashii* was discovered in Umsong-gun, Chunchungnam-do Province, along the upper reaches of the Namhan River (Chai et al. 1993a). The inhabitants in this area were mixed-infected with *M. miyatai*, with an egg positive rate of 9.7% for both species (Chai et al. 1993a). Presumably, *M. takahashii* is distributed along many small rivers and streams in inland areas of South Korea (Yu and Chai 2010, 2013). The major source of human infection is crucian carp *Carassius carassius* (Chai 2015). However, perch, *Lateolabrax japonicus*, has been identified as another source of human infection, particularly in Gyeongsangnam-do (formerly Kyongsangnam-do) Province (Kim et al. 2006). A recent survey performed along the Boseong River, Jeollanam-do (formerly Chollanam-do) (*M. yokogawai* endemic area) detected 3293 specimens of *M. takahashii* from 11 riparian residents out of a total of 70,223 intestinal fluke specimens (mostly *M. yokogawai*) (Chai et al. 2015).

1.2.3 Metagonimus miyatai

1.2.3.1 *Metagonimus miyatai* Saito, Chai, Kim, Lee and Rim, 1997

[syn. *Metagonimus yokogawai* Miyata type by Saito, 1984]

Taxonomy and Morphology
This species (Fig. 1.7a, b) was proposed as a specific level by Saito et al. (1997) based on adult flukes collected from dogs and hamsters experimentally fed the metacercariae from the sweetfish, dace, common fat-minnow *Morocco steindachneri*, pale chub *Zacco platypus*, and dark chub *Zacco temmincki* in South Korea and Japan. This fluke was actually first found (shown only by a figure drawing) by Katsurada (1912c) together with *M. yokogawai* in Taiwan but at that time Katsurada regarded it as a paratype specimen of *M. yokogawai* (Saito et al. 1997). Later, flukes of the same species were found in Japan (Miyata 1941). However, its specific status was not acknowledged for a long time, and no special name was given until 1984 when S. Saito began to call it as the '*Metagonimus* Miyata type' (Saito 1984). In the meantime, in South Korea, Kim (1980) reported a peculiar finding that where the sweetfish is unavailable *Metagonimus* eggs and worms not identifiable as *M. yokogawai* or *M. takahashii* were recovered from the people residing along the Gum River basin, Chungcheongnam-do and described the worms as *Metagonimus* sp. After Miyata type was reported by Saito (1984), Kim et al. (1987) further studied on *Metagonimus* flukes prevalent along the Gum River and the Daecheong Reservoir and reported them as the *Metagonimus* Miyata type of Saito (1984). Subsequently, the specific level of this fluke became acknowledged and described as a new species, *M. miyatai* (Saito et al. 1997). Human infections have been reported from South Korea and Japan (Saito et al. 1997; Chai et al. 1993a, 2015).

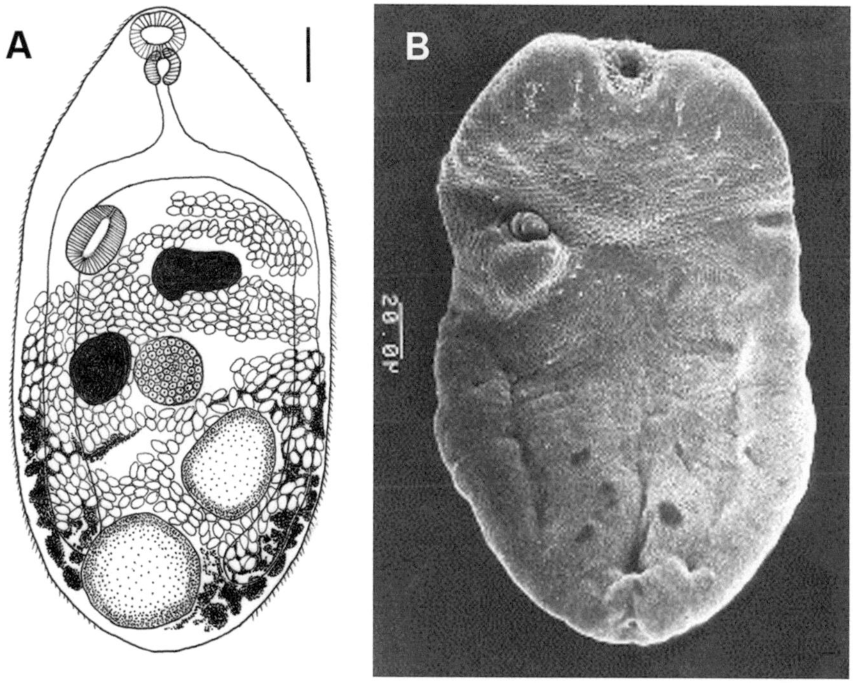

Fig. 1.7 *Metagonimus miyatai*. (**a**) Line drawing of an adult worm (original figure). Scale bar = 0.1 mm (**b**) Scanning electron microscopic view of a 2-week-old adult fluke. Reproduced from Chai et al. (1998) Korean J Parasitol 36:217–225 with permission

Adult flukes of *M. miyatai* (Figs. 1.7a, b and 1.8a) are 1.00–1.30 mm long and 0.46–0.63 mm wide, and the eggs are 29–32 µm long and 17–20 µm wide (Saito et al. 1997; Chai 2015). Its specific morphology includes 2 markedly separated testes from each other, with the posterior one located very close to the posterior wall of the worm, vitelline follicles never distributing beyond the posterior testis, and the egg size which is intermediate (Fig. 1.8b) between those of *M. yokogawai* and *M. takahashii* (Chai et al. 1993a; Saito et al. 1997; Yu and Chai 2013; Chai 2015). *M. miyatai* is also genetically distinct from *M. yokogawai* and *M. takahashii* (Yu et al. 1997a, b; Lee et al. 1999; Yang et al. 2000). *M. miyatai* differs morphologically from *M. minutus* in its larger body and egg size (Katsuta 1932; Chai et al. 1993a). It also differs from *M. katsuradai, M. otsurui,* and *M. hakubaensis* in that the latter 3 species have a smaller ventral sucker compared with the oral sucker, whereas in *M. miyatai*, the ventral sucker is larger than its oral sucker (Shimazu 1999; Chai et al. 1993a; Saito et al. 1997).

For comparative surface ultrastructures, see *M. yokogawai*.

Life Cycle

The snail host for *M. miyatai* includes *Semisulcospira libertina, Semisulcospira dolorosa, Semisulcospira globus,* and *Koreanomelania nodifila* (Kim 1980; Kim

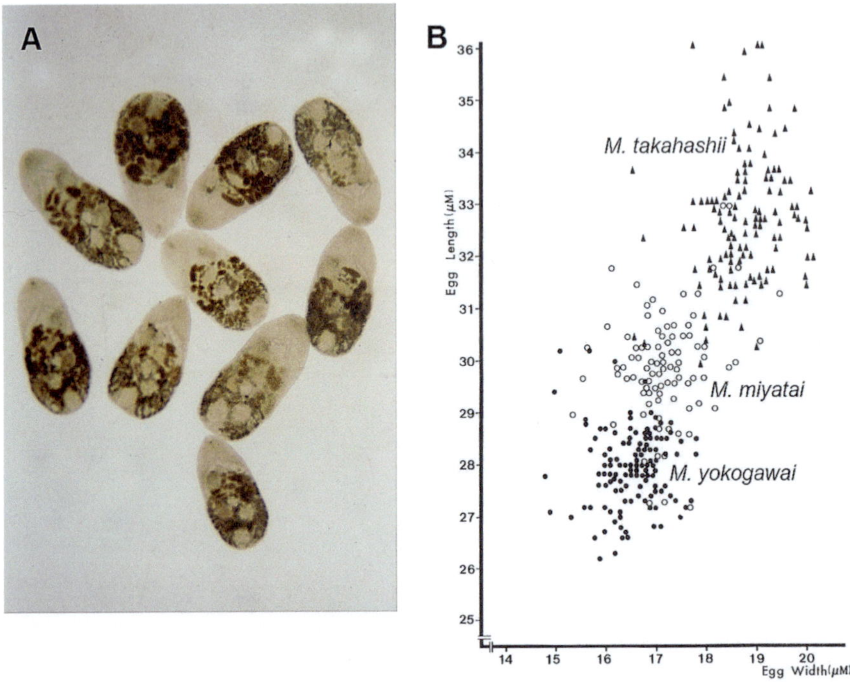

Fig. 1.8 *Metagonimus miyatai.* (**a**) Several adult flukes recovered from a human case. ×40 (**b**) Comparative measurements of eggs of *M. miyatai* with those of *M. yokogawai* and *M. takahashii.* Reproduced from Chai et al. (1993a) Korean J Parasitol 31:99–108 with permission

et al. 1987; Shimazu 2002). Daughter rediae contain ophthalmo-pleuro-lophocercus cercariae, and the cercariae are 196–230 μm long and 56–66 μm wide and the tail is 343–390 μm long (Shimazu 2002). The number of oral spines is 4 in the first or posteriormost row on the oral sucker of the cercariae, the same number as that of *M. yokogawai*, and the penetration gland cells are 7 pairs and arranged almost in 2 longitudinal rows (Shimazu 2002). The metacercariae of *M. miyatai* have been detected in *Zacco platypus* (Fig. 1.9a), *Zacco temminckii, Plecoglossus altivelis, Tribolodon hakonensis, Tribolodon taczanowskii*, *Opsariichthys bidens*, *Morocco steindachneri*, and *Phoxinus lagowskii steindachneri* (Saito et al. 1997; Shimazu 2002; Sohn 2009). The metacercarial cyst (Fig. 1.9b) is 144–180 μm long and 126–154 μm wide, and the size of excysted metacercariae is 256–340 μm by 110–150 μm (Shimazu 2002). Most of the metacercariae of *M. miyatai* occur under the scale of the sweetfish, dace, pale, chub, dark chub, and common fat-minnow (Saito et al. 1997).

Natural definitive hosts of *M. miyatai* include the dog, red fox, raccoon dog, and black-eared kite (Saito et al. 1997; Chai 2015). Mice, rats, hamsters, and dogs are experimental definitive hosts for *M. miyatai* (Kim 1980; Kim et al. 1987; Chai et al. 1991; Ahn and Ryang 1995; Saito et al. 1997; Shimazu 2002). Guk et al. (2005) studied on the growth and development of *M. miyatai* in different strains of mice

Fig. 1.9 *Metagonimus miyatai.* (**a**) The pale chub, *Zacco platypus*, a fish intermediate host of *Metagonimus miyatai*. About 10 cm in length (**b**) A group of metacercariae encysted on a scale of a pale chub. ×40

(BALB/c, ddY, C57BL/6J, C3H/HeN, and A/J) and reported that mice were generally not a susceptible animal host, although ddY and C57BL/6J mice were slightly better than the other 4 strains of mice.

Epidemiology and Geographical Distribution

Among the 3 *Metagonimus* species of public health importance, *M. miyatai* seems to be the second widely spread and prevalent species. The principal mode of human infection is consumption of raw or improperly cooked freshwater fish, particularly the minnows (*Zacco platypus*) in South Korea and Japan (Fig. 1.4) (Chai 2015). Numerous endemic areas are scattered along riparian villages of these countries, where local people traditionally eat raw fish (Yu and Chai 2013; Chai 2015). Pickled, salted, or fermented fish, as well as cooking knife and chopping board contaminated with the metacercariae may also cause human infections; however, such possibility is relatively low.

Japan The Miyata type of *Metagonimus* (now *M. miyatai*) was originally found in Japan (Miyata 1941, 1944). However, epidemiological studies, particularly on human infections, are scarce. With regard to animal definitive hosts, Saito et al. (1997) listed dogs, foxes, raccoon dogs, and black-eared kites in Shimane, Kochi, and Yamagata Prefectures. Cercariae and rediae were found in *Semisulcospira* snails (Shimazu 2002). Metacercariae were detected in *Phoxinus lagowski steindachneri* fish in Hiroi River basin, Nagano Prefecture (Shimazu 2002). Later, many small rivers of Shizuoka Prefecture were found to have fish infected with *M. miyatai* metacercariae (Kino et al. 2006).

South Korea The presence of human infections with this species (under the name *Metagonimus* sp.) was first reported by Kim (1980) in Geum River by detecting eggs in the feces which were slightly larger in size than those of *M. yokogawai* and recovery of adult flukes from several human cases. Eighteen of 22 species of freshwater fish, including *Zacco platypus* and *Pseudogobio esocinus*, collected from this river were positive for metacercariae of this species (Kim 1980). Later, Kim et al. (1987) performed another survey on this species around the Lake Daecheong and upper reaches and designated the worms as *Metagonimus* Miyata type of Saito (1984). In this survey, *Zacco platypus* and *Opsariichthys bidens* were the most heavily infected fish species (Kim et al. 1987). In Hongcheon River basin, Gangwon-do Province, 7.4% egg prevalence of *Metagonimus* spp. was detected among the riparian people, and the adult flukes recovered from the people were *Metagonimus* Miyata type (written as *Metagonimus* sp.) and *M. takahashii* (Ahn and Ryang 1988). The metacercariae of Miyata type were detected also in the dace *Tribolodon taczanowskii* caught from the Seomjin River (Chai et al. 1991). Adult flukes were recovered from 32 riverside people living along the Namhan river in Umsong-gun (these people were concurrently infected with *M. takahashii* with the egg prevalence of 9.7%) and Yongwol-gun (infected only with *Metagonimus* Miyata type and the prevalence was 48.1%) (Chai et al. 1993a). Another survey performed in several rivers of Gangwon-do Province reported the presence of *Metagonimus* Miyata type metacercariae in freshwater fish species, including *Zacco platypus* and *Opsariichthys bidens* (Ahn 1993). Adult flukes of *Metagonimus* Miyata type were also recovered from residents along the Hantaan River, Chorwon-gun (Park et al. 1993) and Talchongang (River), Chungwon-gun (Yu et al. 1994). *Metagonimus* adult flukes, erroneously written as *M. takahashii*, recovered from 6 people in Keochang-gun, Gyeongsangnam-do Province are now regarded as adult flukes of *M. miyatai* (Son et al. 1994). The cercariae and metacercariae of this species were detected in a stream near Cheonan City, Chungcheongnam-do Province (Nam 1997). Subsequently, *Metagonimus* Miyata type was designated as a new species, *M. miyatai*, based on specimens collected from South Korea and Japan (Saito et al. 1997). According to a recent survey, 343 specimens out of a total of 70,223 intestinal fluke specimens recovered from 11 riparian people residing along the Boseong River, Jeollanam-do Province were confirmed to be *M. miyatai*, although the majority was *M. yokogawai* (Chai et al. 2015).

1.2.4 Metagonimus minutus

1.2.4.1 *Metagonimus minutus* Katsuta, 1932

Taxonomy and Morphology

This species (Fig. 1.10a) was originally described based on adult flukes recovered from cats and mice experimentally fed the metacercariae in the brackish water mullet in Taiwan (Katsuta 1932). Its body and egg sizes are smaller than those of *M. yokogawai, M. takahashii*, and *M. miyatai* (Katsuta 1932; Ito 1964a; Saito et al. 1997). The body size of *M. minutus* (0.432–0.504 by 0.252–0.396 mm) is slightly larger than that of *M. katsuradai* (0.315–0.450 by 0.200–0.250 mm) but its egg size is smaller (21–24 by 12–15 μm) than that of *M. katsuradai* (27–29 by 15–17 μm) (Katsuta 1932; Izumi 1935). The size ratio of the oral and ventral suckers is also a characteristic feature; in *M. minutus*, the oral sucker is smaller than the ventral sucker, whereas, in *M. katsuradai,* the oral sucker is bigger than the ventral sucker (Katsuta 1932; Izumi 1935; Chai 2015). *M. minutus* has been listed as a human-infecting intestinal fluke species, but without proper literature background (Yu and Mott 1994).

Life Cycle
The molluscan host of *M. minutus* has not been reported. The fish host is the brackish water fish, *Mugil cephalus*, and the metacercariae are found in the scales, gills, and fins (Katsuta 1932). The metacercarial cysts are 144–162 by 125–160 μm in size, and the excysted metacercariae are 252–315 μm long and 75–108 μm wide (Katsuta 1932). Natural definitive hosts are yet unknown, and cats and mice were used as experimental definitive hosts (Katsuta 1932).

Epidemiology and Geographical Distribution
This species was originally reported in Taiwan (Katsuta 1932). Eating the raw or improperly cooked flesh of mullets in endemic areas is a risk factor. No reports are available regarding the distribution of this species in other countries.

1.2.5 Metagonimus katsuradai

1.2.5.1 *Metagonimus katsuradai* Izumi, 1935

Taxonomy and Morphology
This species (Fig. 1.10b) was originally described in Japan based on adult flukes from rats, mice, rabbits, dogs, and cats experimentally infected with the metacercariae obtained from freshwater fish which included *Pseudorasbora parva, Zacco platypus*, and *Tanakia lanceolata* (Izumi 1935). The possibility of human infection was experimentally proven by infection to author himself and family (Izumi 1935). The body size of *M. katsuradai* (0.315–0.450 by 0.200–0.250 mm) is slightly smaller than that of *M. minutus* (0.432–0.504 by 0.252–0.396 mm) but its egg size (27–29 by 15–17 μm) is larger than that of *M. minutus* (21–24 by 12–15 μm) (Katsuta 1932; Izumi 1935). *M. katsuradai* differs from *M. yokogawai*, *M. takahashii, M. miyatai*, and *M. minutus* in having a smaller ventral sucker than the oral sucker (Izumi 1935; Yu and Chai 2013; Chai 2015). It also differs from *M. otsurui* in the position of the seminal receptacle; in the left side of the ovary in *M. katsuradai* and in the right side of the ovary in *M. otsurui* (Saito and Shimizu 1968). It differs from *M. hakubaensis* in its long ceca that enter the post-testicular region compared with the short ceca ending at the mid-level of the posterior testis (Shimazu 1999).

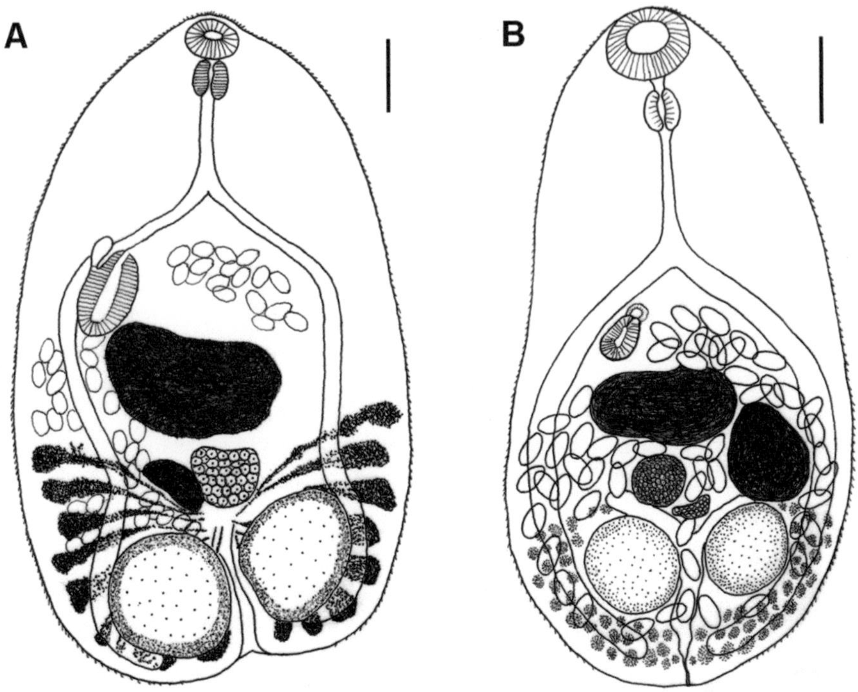

Fig. 1.10 Line drawings of *Metagonimus minutus* (**a**) and *Metagonimus katsuradai* (**b**) adult flukes. Scale bar = 0.05 mm (**a**) Redrawn from the figure in Katsuta (1932) Taiwan Iggakai Zasshi31:26–39 (**b**) Redrawn from the figure in Izumi (1935) Tokyo Iji Shinshi no. 2929:1224–1236

Life Cycle

The molluscan host of *M. katsuradai* is *Semisulcospira libertina* in Japan (Kurokawa 1939) and *Juga tegulata* in Russia (Besprozvannykh et al. 1987). The cercariae are pleurolophocercous type, and 266–336 μm long and 112–133 μm wide, and the tail is 420–490 μm long and 34–42 μm wide (Ito 1964b). The fish host is freshwater fish, including *Tanakia* (formerly *Acheilognathus*) *lanceolata, Tanakia oryzae, Tanakia limbata, Tanakia rhombea, Tanakia moriokae, Pseudorasbora parva, Zacco platypus*, and *Gnathopogon elongatus* (Izumi 1935; Ito 1964a; Shimazu 2003). The metacercariae are found in the scale, gill, fin, and subcutaneous tissues of these fish (Komiya 1965). The metacercarial cysts are 168–200 by 152–190 μm in size, and the excysted metacercariae are 214–294 μm long and 130–160 μm wide (Shimazu 2003). Dogs are the only natural definitive host ever reported (Yoshikawa et al. 1940), and the experimental definitive hosts include humans, mice, white mice, rats, rabbits, puppies, kittens, ducks and golden hamsters (Izumi 1935; Kurokawa 1939; Shimazu 2003).

Epidemiology and Geographical Distribution
Consumption of raw or improperly cooked freshwater fish, notably the carp (*Zacco platypus* and others), is a risk factor (Ito 1964a). Pickled, salted, or fermented fish, as well as cooking knife and chopping board contaminated with the metacercariae may also cause human infections. This fluke is distributed in Japan and Russia (Izumi 1935; Besprozvannykh et al. 1987).

Japan The distribution of *M. katsuradai* is mostly confined to Japan (Ito 1964a). In Hyogo Prefecture, the cercarial infection rate of *Semisulcospira* snails was 2.0% for *M. yokogawai*, 8.6% for *M. takahashii,* and 1.9% for *M. katsuradai* (Kurokawa 1939). In Kobe City, *M. katsuradai* was found to be infected in dogs (Ito 1964a). Around the Lake Biwa, cercariae of *M. katsuradai* (having 6 oral spines) were discovered (Urabe 2003). The possibility of human infection was proven by experimental infection of humans (Izumi 1935); however, natural human cases have never been documented.

Russia The existence of *M. katsuradai* life cycle in Russia was first documented by Besprozvannykh et al. (1987) in the southern Primorye region through discovery of cercariae in *Juga tegulata* snails and metacercariae in 6 species of freshwater fish. Later, infection of *Juga* snails was also found in rivers of the Maritime Territory (Besprozvannykh 1994). Without firm evidence such as recovery of worms, *M. katsuradai* is listed among the human-infecting trematodes in the Primorye Territory (Emolenko et al. 2015).

1.2.6 Potentially Zoonotic Metagonimus *spp.*

Potentially zoonotic *Metagonimus* spp. include *M. ovatus* Yokogawa, 1913 (reviewed by Shimazu and Kino 2015), *M. otsurui* Saito and Shimizu, 1968, *M. hakubaensis* Shimazu, 1999, *M. pusillus* Tatonova et al., 2017, and *M. suifunensis* Shumenko et al., 2017.

1.2.7 Genomics and Proteomics

Molecular genetic studies have shown that *M. yokogawai, M. takahashii,* and *M. miyatai* are distinct to each other (Yu and Chai 2010, 2013). The polymerase chain reaction-based restriction fragment length polymorphism (PCR-RFLP) patterns of *M. yokogawai, M. takahashii,* and *M. miyatai* were analyzed using the internal transcribed spacer 1 (ITS1) of ribosomal RNA and mitochondrial cytochrome *c* oxidase 1 (CO1) (Yu et al. 1997a). The restriction fragment patterns of ITS1 products treated with *Rsa*I, *Alu*I, and *Msp*I enzymes showed multiple bands of different size between the 3 species of *Metagonimus* (Yu et al. 1997a). With regard to CO1 gene, the restriction of PCR products with *Rsa*I and *Alu*I also produced differentially fragmented banding patterns (Yu et al. 1997a). In addition, PCR analysis based on random amplification of polymorphic DNA (RAPD) technique using random 10-mer oligonucleotide primers also showed clearly distinguishable patterns between *M. yokogawai* and *M. miyatai* (Yu et al. 1997b). Subsequently, simple sequence repeat anchored PCR using primers of 3' or 5' termini of (CA)n repeats showed distinguishable banding patterns among the 3 species of *Metagonimus* (Yang et al. 2000).

Chromosomes and karyotypes were also used to differentiate *M. yokogawai, M. takahashii,* and *M. miyatai* (Lee et al. 1999). The number of bivalents in the first meiotic division of *M. takahashii* was 9 (n = 9), whereas the diploid numbers of *M. miyatai* and *M. yokogawai* were 18 (2n = 18) and 32 (2n = 32), respectively (Lee et al. 1999). The chromosomes of *M. miyatai* consisted of 1 pair of metacentric, 7 pairs of submetacentric, and 1 pair of telocentric chromosomes, whereas those of *M. yokogawai* had 2 pairs of metacentric, 11 pairs of submetacentric, and 3 pairs of subtelocentric chromosomes (Lee et al. 1999).

Gene sequence studies were also performed on 28S ribosomal DNA (rDNA) and CO1 of 3 *Metagonimus* species (Lee et al. 2004). The length of the D1 region of 28S rDNA sequence of the 3 *Metagonimus* species was 248 bp and its G+C content is 52% (Lee et al. 2004). The length of the mitochondrial CO1 sequence averaged 400 bp with a G+C content ranging from 44% (*M. miyatai*) to 46% (*M. takahashii*) and 47% (*M. yokogawai*) (Lee et al. 2004). Nucleotide sequence differences were 23.0% (92/400 bp) between *M. miyatai* and *M. takahashii*, 16.2% (65/400 bp) between *M. miyatai* and *M. yokogawai*, and 13.2% (53/400 bp) between *M. takahashii* and *M. yokogawai* (Lee et al. 2004). In addition, the aligned sequences of 28S D1 rDNA and CO1 gene of *M. yokogawai, M. takahashii,* and *M. miyatai* showed high similarities with those of other intestinal trematodes, including *Pygidiopsis summa* and *Stellantchasmus falcatus* (Lee et al. 2004). By the neighbor-joining and parsimony methods, *M. takahashii* and *M. yokogawai* were placed in the same clade, whereas *M. miyatai* was placed in a different clade (Lee et al. 2004), which was agreed by another study group (Thaenkham et al. 2012). Meanwhile, a numerical taxonomy study revealed that *M. miyatai* was classified as a subspecies level of *M. takahashii*, whereas *M. yokogawai* and *M. takahashii* were distinct taxa (Kim et al. 1991).

Another phylogenetic study on the genus *Metagonimus* was performed using 6 species available in Japan; *M. yokogawai, M. takahashii, M. miyatai, M. hakubaensis, M. katsuradai,* and *M. otsurui* (Pornruseetairatn et al. 2016). The results revealed that the former 4 species (*M. yokogawai, M. takahashii, M. miyatai,* and *M. hakubaensis*) were grouped into one big clade, and the latter 2 species (*M. katsuradai* and *M. otsurui*) formed another clade, based on a combined 28S rDNA, ITS2, and *cox*1 sequence dataset (Pornruseetairatn et al. 2016). *M. suifunensis* was recently reported as a new species based on molecular analysis of ITS1-5.8S-ITS2 region and 28S nuclear rDNA of adult worms; *M. suifunensis* formed a separate group from *M. yokogawai, M. takahashii, M. miyatai, M. hakubaensis, M. katsuradai*, and *M. otsurui* (Shumenko et al. 2017). On the other hand, another new species reported from Russia, *M. pusillus* was genetically close to *M. katsuradai* and *M. otsurui*; all these 3 species have smaller sized ventral sucker compared to their oral suckers (Tatonova et al. 2017).

Whole genome sequencing of *Metagonimus* spp. has not yet been tried. No information is available regarding proteomics of *Metagonimus* spp.

1.2.8 Pathology and Immunology

When a definitive host, including mammals and birds, ingest the metacercariae of *Metagonimus* spp., they pass through the stomach and go down to the duodenum or jejunum. They enter into the space between intestinal villi and then invade into the crypt of Lieberkühn for 2–3 days. After then, they come out of the crypt and stay between the villi (intervillous space) or migrate to the lumen side of the small intestine. However, unless the host is immunocompromised, the habitat of adult flukes is confined to the mucosa (villi and crypt) and the worms never invade deeper layers of the submucosa, muscularis mucosa, or serosa. They become adult flukes within 5 days after infection and lay eggs which pass through the intestine and go to the environment.

Living in the mucosa of the small intestine, the adult worms give mechanical, chemical, and immunological stimuli to the host. These stimuli together elicit local and systemic inflammatory responses of the host. Thus, mild to severe mucosal inflammations, i.e., duodenitis, jejunitis, or ileitis occurs according to locations in the small intestine. These pathological changes in the mucosa lead to difficulty in nutrient absorption from the intestine. Increase in permeability in the intestinal mucosa was reported in mice experimentally infected with *M. yokogawai* (Ohnishi and Taufen 1984). The resulting watery diarrhea seems to be due to poor absorption of intestinal secretions from secretory crypt cells (Cho et al. 1985). Decreased enzyme activities were suggested to be associated with malabsorption and diarrhea in acute *M. yokogawai* infection (Hong et al. 1991).

An earlier study on the intestinal pathology of *M. yokogawai*-infected experimental animals was reported in Japan (Koga 1938; Gushima 1939). However, gross and microscopic findings based on modern pathological terms and concepts were reported by Chai (1979), Lee et al. (1981), and Kang et al. (1983) using rats, cats, and dogs as experimental hosts. The major histopathological findings were villous atrophy and crypt hyperplasia, with variable degrees of inflammatory reactions (Fig. 1.11). The infected mucosa showed blunting and fusion of the villi, edema of the villus tips, congestion, goblet cell hyperplasia, mastocytosis, and inflammatory cell infiltrations in the villous stroma, with decreased villus/crypt height ratios (Chai 1979; Chai et al. 1993b; Chai and Lee 2002). These histopathological findings observed in experimental animals seem to occur almost similarly in human metagonimiasis patients. For example, a histopathological study of the small intestine was possible in a patient naturally infected with *M. yokogawai*, and almost similar intestinal histopathology was observed (Chi et al. 1988). In immunocompetent ani-

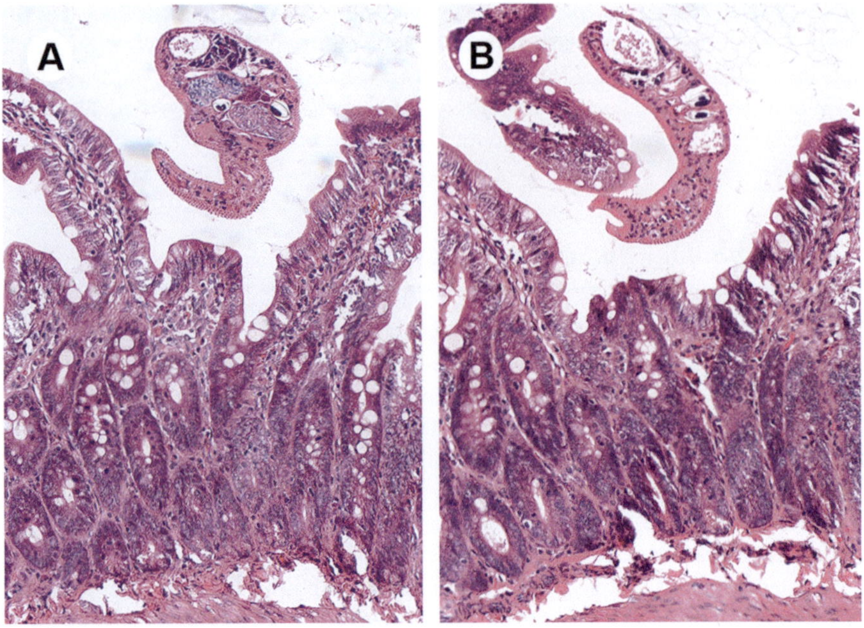

Fig. 1.11 Intestinal sections of rats (**a**, **b**) experimentally infected with the metacercariae of *Metagonimus yokogawai*. Day 5 after infection. Intestinal mucosa shows atrophy, and crypts are hyperplastic. Goblet cell hyperplasia is also seen. ×200

mals, the location of worms was confined to the intestinal mucosa (Chai 1979; Kang et al. 1983; Rho et al. 1984; Jang et al. 1985). However, immunosuppression of mice by prednisolone injection allowed a deeper invasion of the worms into the submucosa (Chai et al. 1995a). Moreover, immunosuppression enhanced survival of worms and prolonged their life spans (Fig. 1.12) (Chai et al. 1984, 1995a). Intestinal histopathology due to *M. yokogawai* infection was normalized at 3–4 weeks after the infection (Chai et al. 1995a).

Similar intestinal histopathology was observed in *M. miyatai*-infected mice; however, the degree of mucosal damage was less severe than in *M. yokogawai*-infected mice (Yu et al. 1997c). This was suggested by stronger expression patterns of the proliferating cell nuclear antigen (PCNA) in the intestinal mucosa of *M. miyatai*-infected mice than in *M. yokogawai*-infected mice (Yu et al. 1997c). In other *Metagonimus* spp., no information is available on the pathogenesis and pathology of infected definitive hosts.

It is of interest to note that several heterophyid species, namely *Stellantchasmus falcatus*, *Haplorchis* spp., and *Procerovum* spp., caused erratic extraintestinal parasitism in man, which is often fatal (Africa et al. 1940). The most frequently affected site was the heart valve, brain, and spinal cord, where eggs and adult flukes originating from the small intestinal mucosa embolised in the blood vessels of these remote tissues (Africa et al. 1940). It was suggested that such erratic parasitism may have

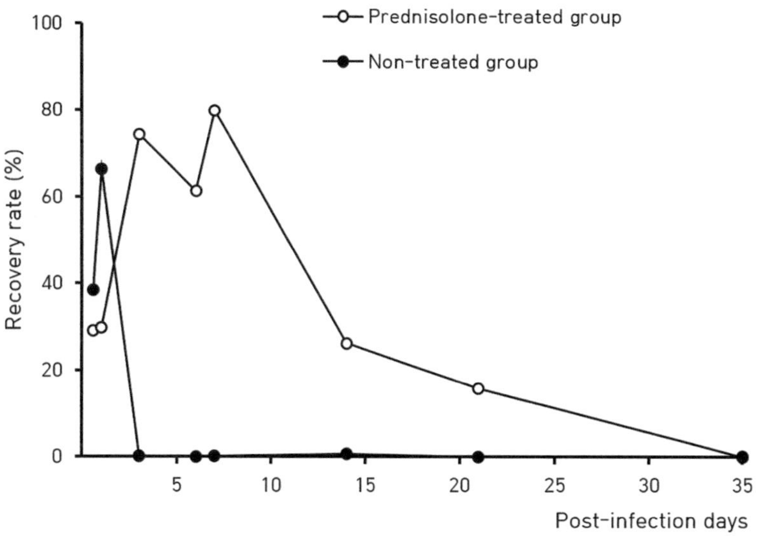

Fig. 1.12 Chronological worm recovery of *Metagonimus yokogawai* from prednisolone-treated (immunosuppressed) ICR mice in comparison with non-treated (immunocompetent) ICR mice. Redrawn from Chai et al. (1984) Korean J Parasitol 22:153–160

occurred in immunocompromised patients (Yokogawa 1940). *M. yokogawai* worms were found to have invaded the submucosa of the small intestine in immunosuppressed mice (Chai et al. 1995a). Therefore, *Metagonimus* spp. are highly suggested to be able to cause such erratic parasitism in immunocompromised patients. Actually, in a patient infected with *Metagonimus,* intracerebral hemorrhage and diabetes mellitus occurred, and it was suggested that both manifestations seem to be due to an acute complication, and diabetes mellitus may also be a chronic sign (Yamada et al. 2008). Further studies are required to elucidate the pathogenicity of *Metagonimus* flukes.

There may be strong host protective mechanisms against *M. yokogawai* and other heterophyid fluke infections. However, immunophysiology and immunopathogenesis due to these fluke infections have seldom been studied in contrast to other intestinal helminth infections, including nematode infections (Castro 1989). Host protective mechanisms against *Metagonimus* worms seem to be significant viewing from the fact that the intestinal histopathology caused by *M. yokogawai* was normalized around 3–4 weeks after the infection (Chai 1979; Chai et al. 1995a). One of the possible immune effectors for the spontaneous recovery of the histopathology includes intestinal intraepithelial lymphocytes (IELs) that increase remarkably along the villous epithelial layer of infected rats (Chai et al. 1994). IELs are known to consist mainly of $CD8^+$ cytotoxic T-cells (Chai et al. 1994). Another effector cell is lamina propria lymphocytes (LPLs) that are chiefly composed of IgA producing B-cells (Chai et al. 1994). Mucosal mast cells were suggested as a third effector responsible for the worm expulsion from infected rats (Chai et al. 1993b). In addition, goblet cells are the fourth effector for expulsion of worms (Chai et al.

2009). Eosinophils were also increased in the peripheral blood of *M. yokogawai*-infected mice at day 7 post-infection in a primary infection and at an earlier time (at day 5) in a secondary infection (Ohnishi 1987). However, intensive studies are required to understand the precise roles of mucosal mast cells, goblet cells, and eosinophils in the host defense against *Metagonimus* spp. infections.

It is interesting to refer to the results of Hong et al. (1993) who infected *Neodiplostomum seoulense* (under the name *Fibricola seoulensis*) first and thereafter challenged *M. yokogawai* infection to rats and observed the worm recovery and intestinal histopathology. The results revealed that the pre-established *N. seoulense* infection in the duodenum of the rats affected adversely the settlement of *M. yokogawai* flukes in the jejunum or ileum. This less settlement of *M. yokogawai* may be due to local non-specific immune responses in the intestinal mucosa of the rats. It has been reported recently that *M. yokogawai*-infected mice displayed altered gut microbiome in the cecum; several *Lactobacillus* species with known immunomodulatory role in immune-mediated diseases were increased significantly in infected mice compared to uninfected controls (Kim et al. 2018).

Immunogold studies have revealed that the antigenicity of *M. yokogawai* is originating from the syncytial tegument, tegumental cell cytoplasms, vitelline cells, and epithelial lamellae of the cecum (Ahn et al. 1991; Rim et al. 1992). To investigate the specific antigens of *M. yokogawai*, a SDS-PAGE/immunoblot analysis was undertaken on crude extracts of metacercariae, which showed that out of 14 protein bands found, 11 reacted with infected human sera, and among them 66 kDa and 22 kDa proteins were the specific antigens (Lee et al. 1993). Han et al. (2014) detected an interesting somatic antigen, 100 kDa in size (Fig. 1.13), from the tegumental layer of *M. yokogawai* adults, which commonly reacts against various kinds of trematodes including *Gymnophalloides seoi* (intestinal fluke), *Paragonimus westermani* (lung fluke), and *Clonorchis sinensis* and *Fasciola hepatica* (liver flukes).

1.2.9 Clinical Manifestations, Diagnosis and Treatment

Clinical symptoms due to *Metagonimus* spp. infections are generally mild and transient, unless the patients are heavily infected, complicated with other diseases, or immunocompromised (Chai and Lee 2002; Chai et al. 2009; Yu and Chai 2013). In *M. yokogawai* infection, the most frequent clinical symptoms are abdominal pain, diarrhea, lethargy, anorexia, malabsorption, and weight loss (Cho et al. 1984; Seo et al. 1985). In association with diarrhea and malabsorption, decreased enzyme activities were observed in the small intestine of *M. yokogawai*-infected animals (Hong et al. 1991).

The severity of clinical symptoms is closely related to individual worm burdens; heavier infections tend to suffer from severer clinical course and illness. The degree of clinical symptoms may also be related to host susceptibility as well as acquired immunity of individual patients (Chai 2007). Some individuals may undergo a latent or subclinical course even when they have considerable degrees of worm

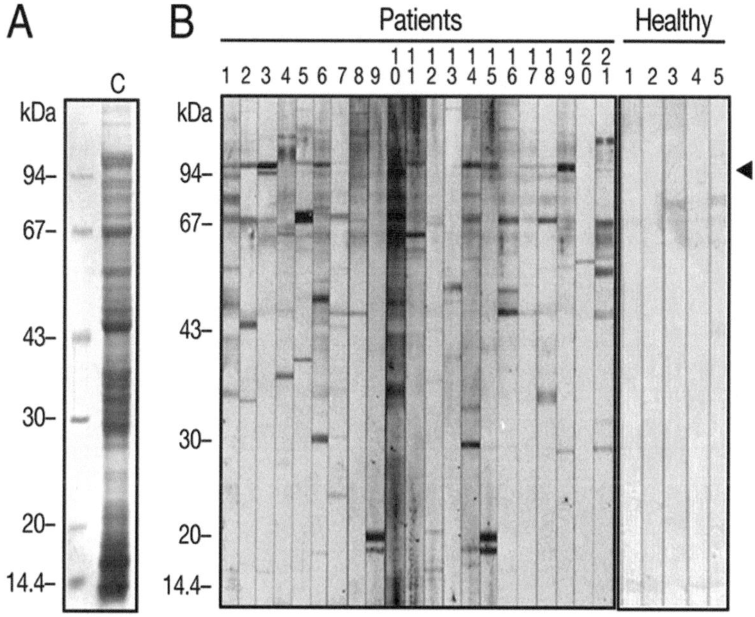

Fig. 1.13 A 100 kDa antigen of *Metagonimus yokogawai* reacting with infected patients' sera in immunoblot analysis. This antigen appeared to commonly react with other trematode species, including *Clonorchis sinensis, Paragonimus westermani*, and *Gymnophalloides seoi*. Reproduced from Han et al. (2014) Korean J Parasitol 52:201–204 with permission

burden. Reversely, some others who have relatively low worm burdens may suffer from a significant degree of clinical symptoms. This difference may be due to different susceptibility of hosts to the pathogenicity of *Metagonimus* spp. worms. Acquired immunity is also a significant factor for clinical manifestations of the patients. For example, new visitors to endemic areas who had a first time infection suffer from a severe illness (Chai et al. 2009). On the other hand, long-time residing residents in endemic areas generally complain of milder symptoms than what may be expected (Seo et al. 1985). Probably they are infected repeatedly and may be protected from severe pathology and symptoms caused by *M. yokogawai* worms. An example for this includes a most heavily infected case of *M. yokogawai* infection among the Korean literature, who resided in a highly endemic area harboring as many as 63,587 worms and complained of only minor gastrointestinal troubles, i.e., indigestion and epigastric pain (Seo et al. 1985).

The immunocompetency of the host is also important in clinical manifestations of metagonimiasis (Chai 2007). Immunocompetent patients can easily overcome the disease, the course of which is generally mild and transient. However, in immunocompromised individuals, *M. yokogawai* infection may cause severe clinical manifestations, possibly including erratic parasitism in vital organs as reported in other heterophyid fluke infections (Africa et al. 1940; Chai 2007; Yu and Chai 2013). For example, a severe clinical case of *M. yokogawai* infection was complicated with multiple intracerebral hemorrhages and diabetes mellitus; patients like this may have been immunosuppressed though it was not confirmed in this case (Yamada et al. 2008).

The diagnosis of *Metagonimus* spp. infection is usually based on recovery of eggs in fecal examinations (Chai 2007). In field conditions, direct smear, cellophane thick smear, or Kato-Katz thick smear techniques can be applied, whereas, in laboratories equipped with centrifuges, concentration techniques, including formalin-ether sedimentation technique and brine (or zinc sulfate) floatation techniques, can be used (Yu and Chai 2013). A confirmatory diagnosis can be made when adult flukes were detected during gastroduodenoscopy, surgical procedures in the intestine, or at autopsy. However, a practical way in the field or laboratory is recovery of adult flukes from diarrheic stools following anthelmintic treatment and purging (Chai 2007).

An important diagnostic limitation of fecal examinations is that *Metagonimus* spp. eggs closely resemble those of other heterophyid fluke species (*Heterophyes nocens, Heterophyopsis continua, Stellantchasmus falcatus, Pygidiopsis summa, Haplorchis* spp., and *Stictodora* spp.) (Chai 2015). Moreover, *Metagonimus* spp. eggs are also morphologically similar to the eggs of small liver flukes (*Clonorchis sinensis, Opisthorchis viverrini,* and *Opisthorchis felineus*) and lecithodendriid flukes (*Prosthodendrium molenkampi* and *Phaneropsolus bonnei*) (Lee et al. 2012). Therefore, in areas with mixed infections, specific diagnosis is almost impossible unless the adult flukes are recovered. Therefore, when the diagnosis is based only on fecal eggs, it should be expressed as a broad term, i.e., small trematode eggs (STE), minute intestinal fluke eggs (MIF eggs), or at least heterophyid fluke eggs (Lee et al. 1984a, 2012).

It is true that specific diagnosis of heterophyid eggs is usually difficult. However, close observations and measurements of *Metagonimus* spp. eggs may help differential diagnosis (Lee et al. 1984a, 2012). For example, the eggs of *M. yokogawai* can be differed from other heterophyid eggs by their elliptical shape with length/width ratio of 1.5–2.1, clean shell surface, less prominent operculum, no shoulder rims, and dark yellow or brown color (Lee et al. 1984a, 2012). The eggs of *M. takahashii* (30.5–35.5 μm in length) and *M. miyatai* (28.5–31.5 μm in length) are slightly bigger than those of *M. yokogawai* (26.5–29.0 μm) and otherwise morphologically very similar to each other (Chai et al. 1993a; Lee et al. 2012).

The eggs of *Heterophyes nocens* are similar to those of *M. yokogawai*, but the former is a little smaller in size and has slight attenuations at one or both ends (Lee et al. 1984a, 2012). The eggs of *Heterophyopsis continua* are broadly oval in shape, slightly smaller in size, but practically difficult to differentiate from those of *M. yokogawai* (Lee et al. 1984a, 2012). The eggs of *Pygidiopsis summa* are characteristically small and pyriform in shape and thus quite easy to differentiate from those of *M. yokogawai* eggs (Lee et al. 1984a, 2012). Nevertheless, the specific diagnosis only based on fecal eggs is difficult in areas of no previously known endemicity, as well as in areas with mixed heterophyid fluke infections (Chai 2007). In these cases, recovery of adult flukes from definitive hosts, including humans and animals, is essential to provide a specific diagnosis.

There could be false egg negative cases among light infection cases with *M. yokogawai*, for example, with less than 100 worms in an infected person (Chai and Lee 2002). In the human host, the number of eggs produced per day per worm (EPDPW) for *M. yokogawai* was reported to be only 14–64 eggs (Seo et al. 1985). In experimental dogs, the EPDPW of *M. yokogawai* was 35–45, similar to that in humans (Ahn et al. 1981). Therefore, the detectability of eggs in the feces from such low worm burden cases is negligible (Chai and Lee 2002). In these cases, serological tests, in particular ELISA, are helpful (Chai et al. 1989; Cho et al. 1987).

Molecular techniques, including PCR or PCR-RFLP, can be used to detect *Metagonimus* spp. infections in the feces (Jeon et al. 2012) or food materials (Pyo et al. 2013). For example, PCR technique could differentiate *M. yokogawai* infection from *C. sinensis* or *Haplorchis taichui* infection with detection of mixed-infection cases also (Jeon et al. 2012). Using PCR-RFLP technique, targeting 18S rRNA, trematode infections in aquatic food samples could be detected, for example, *M. yokogawai* infection in fish and *Gymnophalloides seoi* infection in oysters (Pyo et al. 2013). Whereas digestion with the restriction enzyme *Msp1* could not differentiate *M. yokogawai* and *Heterophyopsis continua*, digestion with Hinf1 could differentiate *M. yokogawai* from *H. continua* (Pyo et al. 2013).

Praziquantel is the drug of choice for all heterophyid fluke infections, including *Metagonimus* spp. infections (Chai 2007). A single oral dose of 10–20 mg/kg praziquantel is satisfactory, with 95–100% cure rate for *M. yokogawai* infection (Rim et al. 1978; Lee et al. 1984c). Praziquantel is highly safe without particular adverse reactions at this dose even in children and pregnant women (Chai 2013).

Hamajima et al. (1979) studied on in vitro effects of bithionol and menichlopholan on *M. takahashii* worms and reported that the effects of these drugs were better to *M. takahashii* than to *C. sinensis* or *Paragonimus miyazakii*. Mehlhorn et al. (1983) studied the effects of praziquantel on the tegumental ultrastructure of *M. yokogawai* and several other trematode species and reported that all the species of worms displayed severe tegumental vacuolization within 5 min after exposure to the drug followed by rupture of the vacuoles and marked destruction of the whole tegumental surface.

1.2.10 Prevention and Control

Health education not to consume raw or undercooked fish responsible for *Metagonimus* spp. infection will help prevention of the disease (Chai 2015; Chai and Jung 2017). However, it is practically difficult to achieve it because of the old tradition of enjoying raw fish dish which is hardly possible to change.

The control measures for metagonimiasis include control of the snail host, *Semisulcospira* spp., control of the fish hosts, for example, the sweetfish and dace in the case of *M. yokogawai*, and mass chemotherapy of residents in endemic areas (Chai 2015; Chai and Jung 2017). However, snail control and fish control are practically difficult to perform successfully (Chai 2015). In addition, mass chemotherapy can temporarily reduce the prevalence and infection intensity (worm load) but reinfection continues to occur in endemic areas unless the consumption of raw or improperly cooked fish is completely stopped (Chai 2015).

The infectivity of *M. yokogawai* metacercariae in fish can be controlled by gamma-irradiation at 200 Gy (Chai et al. 1995b). However, this method is not feasible in the field due to various reasons such as the necessity of an irradiator, high cost, and low preference of irradiated fish by the consumers (Chai et al. 1995b). Brining and pickling may also reduce the parasite hazard in a fish; however, some zoonotic trematode metacercariae require up to 8 days in 30% brine to be killed (WHO 1995).

1.3 *Heterophyes*

The adult flukes of *Heterophyes*, together with those of the genus *Heterophyopsis*, have a peculiar genital organ which is called 'genital sucker' (Chai 2007, 2014). The genital sucker is not a true sucker but a well-developed sucker-like structure containing the terminal genitalia with an opening and equipped with a protrusible gonotyl armed with minute spines called rodlets. This is a character distinct from other genera of the Heterophyidae (Yamaguti 1958; Chai 2014). *Heterophyes* flukes are characterized by their minute body (0.4–2.7 mm long), a large and median ventral sucker, presence of a prominent genital sucker, and 2 adjacent testes near the posterior end of the body (Chai and Jung 2017).

In addition to the presence of a genital sucker, *Heterophyes* has a large median ventral sucker, whereas *Metagonimus* has a small submedian ventral sucker (Chai 2007, 2014, 2015). *Stellantchasmus* lacks a genital sucker and has a small, dextrally deviated ventral sucker and an elongated sac-like seminal vesicle connected to a muscular expulsor at the opposite side of the ventral sucker (Chai 2007, 2014). *Procerovum* and *Haplorchis* have only a single testis but *Heterophyes* has 2 testes (Chai 2007, 2014). *Heterophyopsis* has an elongated body and 2 obliquely tandem testes, whereas the body of *Heterophyes* is elongate, pyriform to elliptical, and its 2 testes are located side by side (Chai 2007). The ventral suckers of *Pygidiopsis* and *Heterophyes* are both median; however, that of the former is small and equipped anterosinistrally with a small genital apparatus, whereas that of the latter is large and equipped posterosinistrally with a large genital sucker (Chai 2007). *Centrocestus* differs from *Heterophyes* in having minute circumoral spines around the oral sucker (Chai 2007).

Flukes of the genus *Heterophyes* were first discovered by Bilharz in 1851 at an autopsy of an Egyptian and named as *Distomum heterophyes* by von Siebold in 1852 (Chai 2007, 2014). Subsequently, Cobbold (1866) created the genus *Heterophyes* and described *Heterophyes aegyptiaca* (later synonymized with *H. heterophyes* by Witenberg 1929). *D. heterophyes* was redescribed by Looss (1894), and a new species *Distomum fraternum* (= *Heterophyes fraternus*) was described (Looss 1894), which was also synonymized with *H. heterophyes* by Witenberg

(1929). Stiles and Hassal (1900) assigned *D. heterophyes* to genus *Heterophyes* and renamed it as *H. heterophyes*. Another species, *Heterophyes persicus*, was reported under the name *Cotylogonimus persicus* from a Persian wolf (Braun 1901); however, this species was later synonymized with *H. heterophyes* (Witenberg 1929). Looss (1902) added 6 new *Heterophyes* species, including *Heterophyes aequalis, Heterophyes dispar, Heterophyes dispar limatus, Heterophyes heterophyes sentus, Heterophyes inops,* and *Heterophyes palidus.* However, 2 of them (*H. heterophyes sentus* and *H. palidus*) were synonymized with *H. heterophyes, H. inops* was regarded as a synonym of *H. aequalis,* and *H. dispar limatus* was treated as a synonym of *H. dispar* (Witenberg 1929).

Thereafter, *Heterophyes elliptica* (Yokogawa 1913) and *Heterophyes nocens* (Onji and Nishio 1916) were discovered in Taiwan and Japan, respectively. In addition, in Japan, *Heterophyes katsuradai* was added as a new species (Ozaki and Asada 1926). However, the validity of *H. elliptica* is questionable (Waikagul and Pearson 1989), and *H. katsuradai* has been considered a synonym of *H. nocens* (Witenberg 1929; Waikagul and Pearson 1989).

Another species, named as *Heterophyes indica,* was reported from dogs in India (Rao and Ayyar 1932), and *Heterophyes superspinata* was described in Kazachstan (Laonov and Belogurov 1965). *Heterophyes pleomorphis* was recorded in Uganda (Bwangamoi and Ojok 1977), and *Heterophyes bitorquatus* and *Heterophyes chini* were reported in Malaysia (Borneo) (Pearson and Pearson 1981). However, *H. chini* and *H. superspinata* (synonymizing *H. bitorquatus*) were moved to a new genus *Alloheterophyes* Pearson 1999, which differs from *Heterophyes* in having a seminal vesicle consisted with 2 tandem chambers, a uterine seminal receptacle, and several other characters (Pearson 1999).

Therefore, a total of 18 species or subspecies (Table 1.4) have so far been documented in the genus *Heterophyes*, among which 3 species (including one synonym) were moved to *Alloheterophyes*. Out of the remaining 15 *Heterophyes* species, *H. aequalis, H. dispar, H. heterophyes, H. nocens, H. indica*, and *H. pleomorphis* are now recognized as valid species, and 3 of them, *H. nocens, H. heterophyes* and *H. dispar,* are known to infect humans (Chai 2014). Human infections with these *Heterophyes* spp. are prevalent in the Far East, the Middle East, Egypt, Sudan, and southeastern Europe (Chai 2014).

Only 3 species, i.e., *H. heterophyes, H. nocens,* and *H. dispar*, have so far been known to infect humans; however, a few others, particularly *H. aequalis*, are potential species that may cause human infections. Caution is needed to refer to some literature which deals with *H. nocens* as a synonym of *H. heterophyes*. Now it is well acknowledged that *H. nocens* is an oriental species that occur in the Far East (including South Korea and Japan), and *H. heterophyes*, together with *H. dispar*, are the species occurring in the Mediterranean (including Egypt and Sudan) and Middle East (including Saudi Arabia and Yemen) regions. Infected people can immigrate to other countries; for example, Egypt to France (Rousset and Pasticier 1972), Japan to France (Lamy et al. 1976), Egypt to Japan (Kagei et al. 1980), Sudan to South Korea (Eom et al. 1985a), Saudi Arabia to South Korea (Chai et al. 1986).

Table 1.4 Species of *Heterophyes* reported in the literature

Species with nominator	Human infection	Area (Country)
Heterophyes heterophyes (von Siebold, 1852) Stiles and Hassal, 1900	Yes	Egypt, Greece, India, Iran, Israel, Italy, Japan[a], South Korea[a], Kuwait, Sri Lanka, Saudi Arabia, Spain, Sudan, Thailand, Tunisia, Turkey, United Arab Emirate, Yemen
Heterophyes nocens Onji and Nishio, 1916	Yes	China, Japan, South Korea, Thailand (?)
Heterophyes dispar Looss, 1902	Yes	Egypt, South Korea[b], Middle East
Heterophyes aequalis Looss, 1902	No	Egypt, Middle East
Heterophyes indica Rao and Ayyar, 1931	No	India
Heterophyes pleomorphis Bwangamoi and Ojok, 1977	No	Uganda
Other species[c]		

Information updated from Chai and Jung (2017)

[a]Imported human cases were reported in Japan (Kagei et al. 1980) and South Korea (Eom et al. 1985; Chai et al. 1986)

[b]Imported human cases were reported in South Korea (Eom et al. 1985; Chai et al. 1986)

[c]Other species include *H. aegyptiaca* Cobbold 1866 (synonymized with *H. heterophyes* by Witenberg 1929), *H. fraternus* (Looss 1894) (synonymized with *H. heterophyes* by Witenberg 1929), *H. persicus* (Braun 1901) (synonymized with *H. heterophyes* by Witenberg 1929), *H. heterophyes sentus* Looss 1902 (synonymized with *H. heterophyes* by Witenberg 1929), *H. inops* Looss 1902 (synonymized with *H. heterophyes* by Witenberg 1929), *H. palidus* Looss 1902 (synonymized with *H. heterophyes* by Witenberg 1929), *H. dispar limatus* Looss 1902 (synonymized with *H. dispar* by Witenberg 1929), *H. elliptica* Yokogawa 1913 (questionable species, Waikagul and Pearson 1989), *H. katsuradai* Ozaki and Asada 1926 (synonymized with *H. nocens* by Witenberg 1929), *H. superspinata* Laonov and Belogurov 1965 (transferred to *Alloheterophyes* by Pearson 1999), *H. bitorquatus* Pearson and Pearson 1981 (synonymized with *H. superspinata* and transferred to *Alloheterophyes* by Pearson 1999), and *H. chini* Pearson and Pearson 1981 (transferred to *Alloheterophyes* by Pearson 1999)

A brief history of the discovery, taxonomic debates, and morphological and biological characteristics of each *Heterophyes* species are given in the following section. However, regarding the phylogenetic relationships of *Heterophyes* spp. and other heterophyid species, further studies are required to draw firm conclusions.

1.3.1 Heterophyes heterophyes

1.3.1.1 *Heterophyes heterophyes* (v. Siebold, 1852) Stiles and Hassal, 1900

[syn. *Heterophyes aegyptiaca* Cobbold, 1866; *Distomum heterophyes* Looss, 1894; *Distomum fraternus* Looss, 1894; *Cotylogonimus persicus* Braun, 1901; *Heterophyes heterophyes sentus* Looss, 1902; *Heterophyes pallidus* Looss, 1902; *Heterophyes persicus* Looss, 1902]

Taxonomy and Morphology

This species (Fig. 1.14a, b) was first discovered by Bilharz in 1851 at autopsy of an Egyptian in Cairo, and is now known to cause human infections along the Nile Delta of Egypt and Sudan, the Middle East, India, Sri Lanka, and southeastern Europe (Macy 1953; Himonas 1964; Yu and Mott 1994; Mahanta et al. 1995; Pica et al. 2003; Fried et al. 2004; Chai et al. 2005). It was originally described as *Distomum heterophyes* (von Siebold 1852; Looss 1894) but the same fluke was found by many other authors and reported as *Distoma heterophyes hominis, Dicrocoelium heterophyes, Fasciola heterophyes, Mesogonimus heterophyes,* or *Cenogonimus heterophyes* (Ransom 1920; Witenberg 1929). After creation of the genus *Heterophyes* by Cobbold (1866), the name of this fluke was settled as *H. heterophyes* (Stiles and Hassal 1900). Several endemic foci have also been reported in Asia (Yu and Mott 1994); however, the worm may have been confused with *H. nocens*. Imported human infections were reported from people who returned from Egypt to Japan (Kagei et al. 1980) and from Sudan and Saudi Arabia to South Korea (Eom et al. 1985a; Chai et al. 1986).

Adult flukes of *H. heterophyes* are minute, ovoid to elliptical, elongate, or pyriform in shape (Witenberg 1929; Chai 2014). Their unique morphologies include the

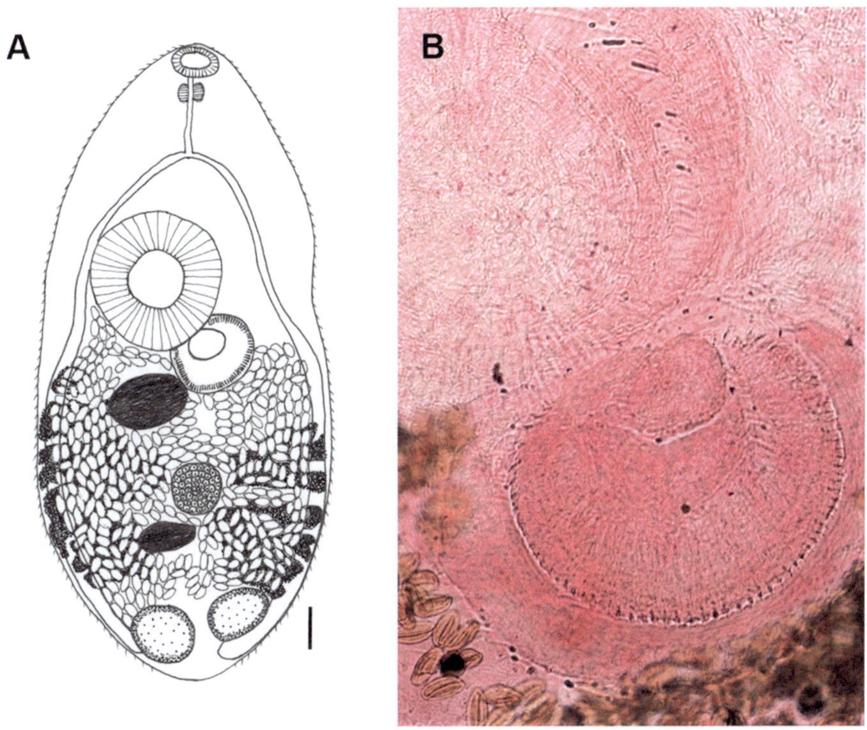

Fig. 1.14 *Heterophyes heterophyes*. (**a**) Line drawing of an adult worm (original figure). Scale bar = 0.1 mm (**b**) Enlarged view of the ventral and genital suckers and rodlets on the gonotyl. ×400

presence of 2 side-by-side testes near the posterior extremity of the body, a large ventral sucker (about 0.15 mm in diameter) which is located median, and a large submedian (posterosinistral) genital sucker (Figs. 1.14b and 1.15a) armed with 70–85 chitinous rodlets on the gonotyl (Chai 2007, 2014). *H. heterophyes* adults (0.6–2.7 mm long and 0.2–0.9 mm wide) differ from *H. nocens* adults (0.82–1.02 mm long and 0.52–0.63 mm wide) mainly in the number of rodlets on the gonotyl; 50–62 in *H. nocens* (Fig. 1.15b) and 70–85 in *H. heterophyes* (Witenberg 1929; Chai et al. 1994, 2009). The adults of *H. dispar* (0.4–1.4 mm long and 0.2–0.4 mm wide) are slightly smaller in body size (Fig. 1.15c) and have smaller sizes of the genital sucker and smaller numbers of rodlets on the gonotyl (22–35) compared with those of *H. heterophyes* and *H. nocens* (Witenberg 1929; Chai et al. 1986, 2009). The eggs of *H. heterophyes* (23–29 μm long and 13–15 μm wide) are similar to those of *H. nocens* (23–29 μm long and 13–15 μm wide) but slightly larger than those of *H. dispar* (21–25 μm long and 13–15 μm wide) (Witenberg 1929; Chai et al. 1986; Lee et al. 2012). The cercariae are pleurolophocercous type, with pigmented eye-spots (= ophthalmo-pleuro-lophocercus cercariae), and the cercarial body is 60–105 μm long and 92 μm wide, with 2 anterior rows of 7–10 small preoral spines and one posterior row of 4–6 larger spines, and a long tail of 499–619 μm long and 23–35 μm wide, which closely resembles those of other heterophyid species (Martin 1959). Metacercarial cysts are globular or slightly oval, 130–260 μm in diameter, and usually found in fish muscles (Chai 2014).

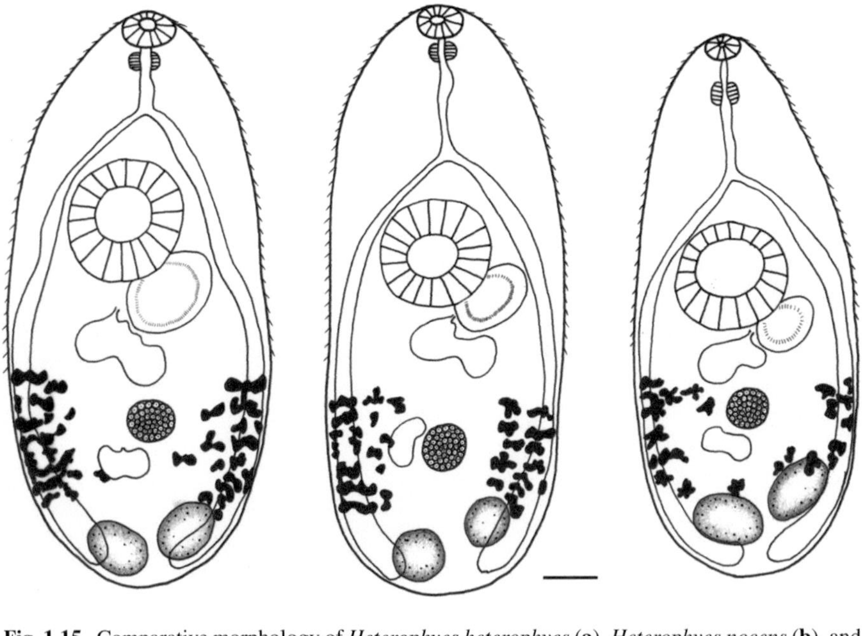

Fig. 1.15 Comparative morphology of *Heterophyes heterophyes* (**a**), *Heterophyes nocens* (**b**), and *Heterophyes dispar* (**c**) adult flukes. Scale bar = 0.1 mm

Life Cycle

H. heterophyes has several developmental stages. The eggs are minute, operculate, ovoid, and light brown (Beaver et al. 1984). They contain a fully developed miracidium and hatch after ingestion by an appropriate freshwater snail (Bearup 1958), for example, *Pirenella conica* in Egypt and the Middle East (Beaver et al. 1984; Taraschewski 1984). A sporocyst and one to 2 redial generations are developed and from which the cercariae with eyespots resembling those of *Metagonimus yokogawai* finally emerge (Beaver et al. 1984). They enter between the scales of freshwater or brackish water fish, including mullets (*Mugil cephalus, Mugil capito, Mugil auratus, Mugil saliens,* and *Mugil chelo*), *Tilapia* fish (*Oreochromis niloticus* and *Tilapia zilli*), and gobies/other fish (*Aphanius fasciatus, Barbus canis*, *Sciaena aquilla*, *Solea vulgaris,* and *Acanthogobius* sp.), and encyst chiefly in the muscle of these fish host (Paperna and Overstreet 1981; Velasquez 1982). Among them, the mullet (*Mugil cephalus*) is the representative species responsible for the transmission of *Heterophyes* (Khalil 1923). The longevity of metacercariae in the fish is unknown, but they may be able to survive for several years or throughout the life span of the fish hosts. In salted fish, they can survive only up to 7 days (Yu and Mott 1994). The larva inside the cyst is usually folded on itself showing the oral sucker, ventral sucker, genital sucker with gonotyl spines, and excretory vesicle filled with refractile globules (Chai 2014).

A variety of mammals and birds, including dogs, cats, wolves, bats, rats, foxes, sea gulls, and pelicans, are natural definitive hosts and take the role of reservoir hosts (Macy 1953; Yamaguti 1958; Dissanaike 1961; Ito 1964a; Chai 2014). Rats, dogs, cats, foxes, badgers, pigs, macaques, and gulls can be used as experimental definitive hosts (Chai 2014). The life span in the canine or feline host is 1–4 months but may be longer in humans (Chai 2014).

Epidemiology and Geographical Distribution

The principal mode of human infections with *H. heterophyes* is consuming raw or improperly cooked flesh of fish intermediate hosts, notably mullets and gobies (Chai 2014). Human and/or animal infections have been reported in Northern Africa (Egypt, Sudan, and Tunisia), Europe (Spain, Italy, Greece, Turkey, Israel, and Palestine), the Middle East (Saudi Arabia, Iran, United Arab Emirates, Kuwait, and Yemen), India, Sri Lanka, and Thailand (Fig. 1.16) (Yu and Mott 1994; Chai 2014; Tandon et al. 2015). East Asian countries, including China, Taiwan, Russia (far eastern parts), the Philippines, and Indonesia, were also recorded as endemic areas of *H. heterophyes* (Velasquez 1982; Yu and Mott 1994; Hung et al. 2013); however, the parasite may be *H. nocens*, a closely related species (Chai 2014). About 30 million people are estimated to be infected with *H. heterophyes* (Mehlhorn 2015).

Egypt Heterophyiasis due to *H. heterophyes* is highly endemic in Egypt (Youssef and Uga 2014). Human infections are prevalent in the northern part of the Nile Delta, particularly around Lakes Manzala, Burullus, and Edku, where fishermen and domestic animals frequently consume fish (Yu and Mott 1994). Khalil (1933) reported an extremely high prevalence (88%) of this fluke among schoolchildren at Mataria on Lake Manzala, and Wells and Blagg (1956) also reported a high

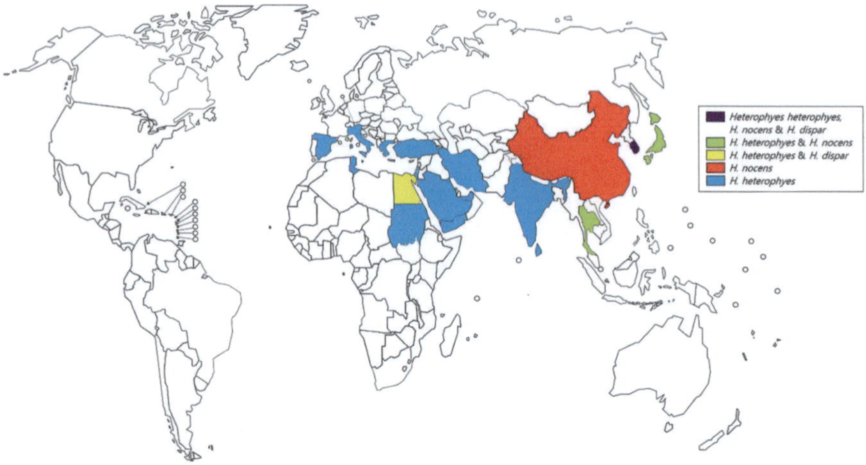

Fig. 1.16 Global distribution of *Heterophyes* spp. (*H. heterophyes, H. nocens,* and *H. dispar*) based on the presence of their life cycles

prevalence (36%) among children living near the Lake Burullus. During the 1930s–1950s, 36–90% of schoolchildren and 22% of adults were found to be infected with this fluke in the northern parts of Nile Delta (Chai 2014). In Dakahlia Governorate, 229 human cases were reported, and the disease was common in both urban and rural localities owing to the habit of consuming salted or insufficiently baked fish (Sheir and Aboul-Enein 1970). However, the prevalence began to decline in the 1960s–1980s to 2.5–10.0% in these areas (Rifaat et al. 1980; Youssef et al. 1987; Chai 2014). Near Lake Manzala, Nagathy and Khalil (1964) reported about 10% prevalence among the lakeside people, and Rifaat et al. (1980) found average 2.5% prevalence in the same area. Yet, near Lake Edku, the prevalence of *H. heterophyes* among 2219 individuals was 33.8% demonstrating still considerably high endemicity of this fluke in northern parts of Nile Delta (Abou-Basha et al. 2000). In Qalyobia Governorate, 13.3% prevalence of *H. heterophyes* infection was found among the local residents (Lobna et al. 2010). In the same area, metacercariae of *H. heterophyes* were detected in 22% of brackish water fish and 32% of freshwater fish (Lobna et al. 2010). Similarly, in Dakahlia Governorate, 57.9% of freshwater and brackish water fish were positive for metacercariae of *H. heterophyes* (Hegazi et al. 2014). Among 295 field rats from Dakahlia Governorate, 23 (7.8%) were infected with *H. heterophyes* (Abo-Shady et al. 1983). In a northern region of Nile Delta, the prevalence of *H. heterophyes* in cats was 3% (Khalafalla 2011). According to a study in Alexandria Governorate, 27.2% of stray dogs and 11.4% of stray cats were found infected with *H. heterophyes* adult flukes (Karema 2012). In Beni Suef Province, the prevalence of *H. heterophyes* in cats was 3.2% (El-Dakhly et al. 2017). In Kafrelsheikh Province, 24 (24.0%) of 100 tilapia fish (*Oreochromis niloticus*) examined were positive for heterophyid metacercariae (inclusive of *H. heterophyes* and *H. aequalis*) (Kirrella et al. 2018).

It is interesting to note that some Japanese immigrants living in Egypt were found positive for heterophyid eggs (including *H. heterophyes*); the prevalence was 11% in 2005, 11% in 2006, 15% in 2007, and 14% in 2008 (Okuzawa et al. 2010). There was a positive association between heterophyid infection and the length of stay of Japanese people in Egypt (Okuzawa et al. 2010).

Greece Two human patients were detected by recovery of fecal eggs in Greece by Sphangos in 1953; subsequently, 5 (17.9%) of 28 stray dogs necropsied were found harbouring *H. heterophyes* in their intestines (Himonas 1964).

India Maplestone and Bhaduri (1940) reported the presence of this fluke among dogs in India.

Iran The prevalence of heterophyid flukes (including *H. heterophyes*) in humans and animals in Iran was first documented by Massoud et al. (1981). In 13 villages of Khuzestan, the prevalence ranged 2–24% (av. 8%) among residents (Massoud et al. 1981). The postmortem examination of carnivores in the same area, 14.2% of jackals, 33.3% of foxes, and 2.5% of dogs were infected with heterophyid flukes, which included *H. heterophyes, Metagonimus yokogawai,* and *H. nocens* (under the name *H. katsuradai*) (Massoud et al. 1981). Another study reported 1.9% egg positive rate for heterophyids among 984 persons in rural areas of Khuzestan province; however, adult worms were not identified from these persons (Farahnak and Massoud 1996).

Israel (Palestine) Witenberg (1929) found *H. heterophyes* adults in dogs, cats, foxes, short-toed eagle, and also in experimentally infected rabbits fed infected fish.

Italy One case of a dog from Sardinia was found to be infected with *H. heterophyes* (Deiana 1961).

Kuwait A survey during 1979–1980 in Kuwait reported 3.4% (7/208) of stray dogs examined were infected with *H. heterophyes* (Abdul-Salam 1986). Subsequently, 2 of 103 stray cats (1.9%) were found infected with *H. heterophyes* (Abdul-Salam and Baker 1990). Later, El-Azazy et al. (2015) reported that 15.8% among 240 stray cats were infected with 141 ± 17 adult flukes of *H. heterophyes*. Interestingly, they also reported 2.9% prevalence of *H. nocens* infection among the same group of cats; this needs further clarification.

Saudi Arabia Metacercariae of *H. heterophyes* were detected in mullets *Mugil cephalus* from Najran region, Saudi Arabia; the positive rate was 5% among 20 fish examined and the metacercarial density per infected fish was 1.3 (Khalil et al. 2014).

Spain A case of anaphylactic reaction (fish allergy) concurrent with *H. heterophyes* infection was reported in a 29-year-old woman (Martinez-Alonso et al. 1999).

Sri Lanka Seven (24.1%) of 29 dogs from Colombo were found heavily infected with *H. heterophyes* (Dissanaike 1961).

Sudan Few epidemiological surveys have been undertaken regarding the prevalence of *H. heterophyes* in the first, second, and definitive hosts, although some humans (Koreans) who lived in Sudan were found to have been infected with *H. heterophyes* and *H. dispar* (Eom et al. 1985a). It was only recently that the metacercariae of *Heterophyes* (presumed to be *H. heterophyes*) were detected in mullets (12% of examined fish) caught from Sudanese Red Sea waters (Gumaa et al. 2015).

Thailand In Bangkok, 3 (3.3%) of 90 stray dogs harboured a total of 133 adult specimens of *H. heterophyes* (Ito 1962).

Tunisia Taraschewski and Nicolaidou (1987) mentioned that *H. heterophyes* adults were reported from natural definitive hosts in Tunisia.

Turkey Metacercariae were detected in mullets (*Mugil cephalus*) caught from Aegean Sea in 1981 (Öktener et al. 2010).

United Arab Emirates In Dubai, a survey of stray cats revealed 2.5% prevalence (6 of 240 cats examined) of *H. heterophyes* (Schuster et al. 2009).

Yemen A bat from Yemen was found infected with *H. heterophyes* (Macy 1953).

Other Countries Imported human infections were reported in France (Rousset and Pasticier 1972), South Korea (Eom et al. 1985a; Chai et al. 1986), and Japan (Kagei et al. 1980), among people who returned from Egypt, Saudi Arabia, or Sudan. In USA, a 36-year-old Chinese male immigrant for 5 years suffered from increasing abdominal distention, epigastric and right upper quadrant pain, followed by severe diarrhea were coinfected with *H. heterophyes* and *Clonorchis sinensis* (Coleman et al. 1958). Ching (1961) performed a stool survey in Hawaii and detected eggs of heterophyids (written as *Heterophyes* sp.) from 41 (3.0%) of 1380 samples; however, adult flukes were not identified. In USA, a 48-year-old American female was also found to be infected with *H. heterophyes* (the species is uncertain because only eggs were detected in her stool) after eating 'sushi' in a local Japanese restaurant (Adams et al. 1986). Nutman et al. (1987) detected heterophyid eggs (diagnosed as *H. heterophyes*) in stool specimens of 4 (3.0%) of 128 Southeast Asian refugees (from Vietnam, Lao PDR, and Cambodia) in USA; however, the eggs may have been those of other species, including *Haplorchis* spp or *Opisthorchis viverrini*. In Brazil, eggs of *Heterophyes* sp. or *Metagonimus* sp. were detected in 3 villagers from Sâo Lourenço; however, adult flukes were not recovered, and specific diagnosis of these cases remain to be determined (Gonçalves et al. 1990).

1.3.2 Heterophyes nocens

1.3.2.1 *Heterophyes nocens* Onji and Nishio, 1916

[syn. *Heterophyes katsuradai* Ozaki and Asada, 1926]

Taxonomy and Morphology

This species (Fig. 1.17a, b) was first reported in Japan by Onji and Nishio (1916) based on adult flukes recovered from experimental dogs and cats fed the metacercariae encysted in mullets, *Mugil cephalus*. It is now known to occur as human infections in Japan, China, and South Korea (Yokogawa et al. 1965; Xu and Li 1979; Seo et al. 1981a; Chai et al. 1984, 1985). However, in case of China, the species was described under the name *H. heterophyes* (Xu and Li 1979), which is now considered to be *H. nocens* (Chai 2007).

There were taxonomic debates on this species. Soon after this species was described, Cort and Yokogawa (1921) supported the validity of this species enlisting differential points from Egyptian *H. heterophyes*. However, Lane (1922), Leiper (1922), and Faust and Nishigori (1926) denied its validity and synonymized it with *H. heterophyes*. Meanwhile, Ciurea (1924) admitted *H. nocens* and included it in

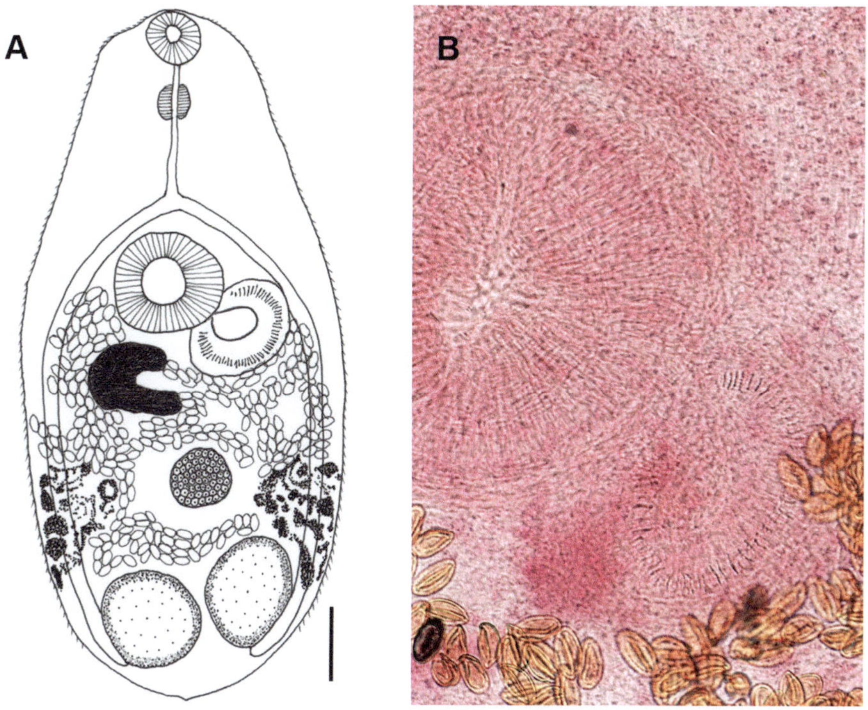

Fig. 1.17 *Heterophyes nocens*. (**a**) Line drawing of an adult worm (original figure). Scale bar = 0.1 mm (**b**) Enlarged view of the ventral and genital suckers and rodlets on the gonotyl. ×400

the list of valid *Heterophyes* species. Witenberg (1929) raised a question about the validity of *H. nocens* but provisionally retained *H. nocens* as a distinct species. Hasegawa (1931) also enlisted *H. nocens* as a distinct species. Nevertheless, Asada (1934) proposed to call it as a subspecies, *H. heterophyes nocens,* in order to compromise the taxonomic situation of *H. nocens*. In 1953, K Morishita agreed to the compromise but suggested to call it as a variant, *H. heterophyes* var. *nocens* (Ito 1964a). Even thereafter, the status of *H. nocens* was not settled. Some Japanese authors used *H. heterophyes* var. *nocens* (Ito 1964a; Yokogawa et al. 1965) or *H. heterophyes nocens* (Ito et al. 1967; Suzuki et al. 1982), and others used *H. nocens* (Komiya 1965). In South Korea, Seo et al. (1980, 1981a, b) and Chai et al. (1984, 1985) used the subspecies name, *H. heterophyes nocens*, but Chai et al. (1986) began to use *H. nocens*. Thereafter, in both countries, the name *H. nocens* has been consistently used until now (Sohn et al. 1989; Chai et al. 1992, 1994; Ryang et al. 1999; Kino et al. 2002; Chai et al. 2004, 2005, 2009).

H. nocens adult flukes are elongate, elliptical, or pyriform (Fig. 1.18a), 0.82–1.02 mm long and 0.52–0.63 mm wide, and morphologically close to *H. heterophyes* (Chai et al. 1986, 1994). The only recognizable difference is the smaller number (50–62) of rodlets on the gonotyl of the genital sucker (Fig. 1.17b) in com-

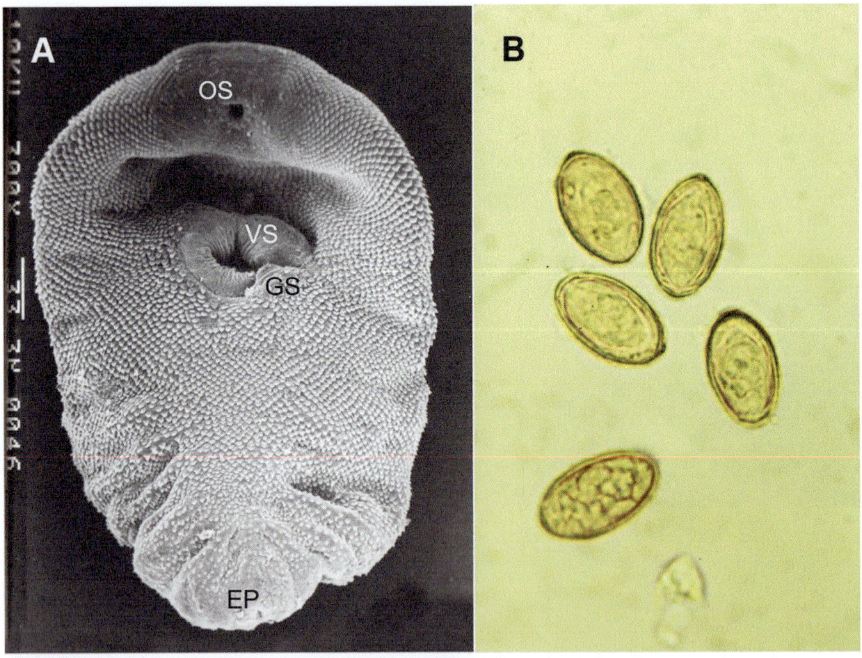

Fig. 1.18 *Heterophyes nocens.* (**a**) Scanning electron microscopic view of an adult fluke recovered from an experimental cat at week 3 post-infection. Abbreviations: OS, oral sucker; VS, ventral sucker; GS, genital sucker; EP, excretory pore. Reproduced from Chai et al. (1992) Korean J Parasitol 30:75–82 with permission (**b**) Eggs from the distal part of the uterus of an adult worm, 26.5 μm in average length and 16 μm in average width

parison to that in *H. heterophyes* (70–85) (Taraschewski 1984; Chai et al. 1986, 1994; Chai and Lee 2002). *H. dispar* has a slightly smaller body (0.4–1.4 mm long and 0.2–0.4 mm wide) and also has a smaller-sized genital sucker and smaller numbers (22–35) of rodlets on the gonotyl compared to *H. nocens* and *H. heterophyes* (Witenberg 1929; Chai et al. 1986, 2009). *H. aequalis* is also smaller than *H. nocens* in body size, has relatively short ceca, and has a smaller number (14–25) of rodlets on the gonotyl than *H. nocens* and *H. dispar* (Witenberg 1929; Chai et al. 1986). The eggs of *H. nocens* (23–29 μm long and 13–15 μm wide) are similar to those of *H. heterophyes* but slightly larger than those of *H. dispar* (21–25 μm long and 13–15 μm wide) (Witenberg 1929; Chai et al. 1986; Lee et al. 2012). *H. nocens* eggs are minute, operculate, ovoid, and light brown, and contain a fully developed miracidium (Fig. 1.18b). The cercariae are ophthalmo-pleuro-lophocercous type, and 175–238 μm long and 56–77 μm wide, and the tail is 340–420 μm long and 31–35 μm wide (Ito 1964b). The metacercarial cysts are globular or elliptical, 130–220 μm long and 80–170 μm wide (Komiya 1965).

The surface ultrastructure was studied in *H. nocens* adult flukes recovered from experimentally cats (Fig. 1.18a) and a naturally infected human patient (Chai et al. 1992). The tegumental ultrastructure is generally similar to that of other heterophyids; however, the genital sucker morphology, including the number of gonotyl spines and the distribution patterns of tegumental spines and sensory papillae are characteristic features of *H. nocens* (Chai et al. 1992).

Life Cycle

Eggs of *H. nocens* hatch after ingestion by an appropriate brackish water snail, for example, *Cerithidea cingulata* (= *Tympanotonus microptera*) or *Cerithidea fluviatilis* (Asada 1928; Ito 1964b; Chai et al. 2009). A sporocyst and a few redial generations are developed and from which ophthalmo-pleuro-lophocercus cercariae finally emerge (Beaver et al. 1984). The cercariae can survive as long as 42–54 h in sea water (Chai 2014). They enter between the scales of brackish water fish, including mullets (Fig. 1.19a) and gobies (Fig. 1.19b) (*Mugil cephalus, Liza menada, Tridentiger obscurus, Glossogobius brunnaeus, Therapon oxyrhynchus,* and *Acanthogobius flavimanus*) (Ito 1964a; Komiya 1965; Sohn 2009). A species of freshwater carp, *Pseudorasbora parva* (Sohn and Choi 1997) and 2 species of brackish water gobies, *Boleophthalmus pectinirostris* and *Scartelaos* sp. (Sohn et al. 2005), can also be fish hosts for *H. nocens*. The metacercariae encyst chiefly in the muscle of fish, particularly in the hypochondrial region (Komiya 1965). The larva inside the cyst (Fig. 1.19c, d) characteristically reveals its oral sucker, ventral sucker, genital sucker with gonotyl spines, and excretory vesicle filled with refractile granules (Chai 2014). The longevity of metacercariae in the fish is unknown, but they may be able to survive for several years or throughout the life span of the fish hosts (Chai 2014). In salted fish, they may survive only up to 7 days (Yu and Mott 1994).

Domestic or feral cats, dogs, and rats are natural definitive hosts (Yoshikawa et al. 1940; Ito 1964a; Eom et al. 1985b; Sohn and Chai 2005; Shin et al. 2015). Mice and rats can be experimental definitive hosts (Chai et al. 2009; Chai 2014).

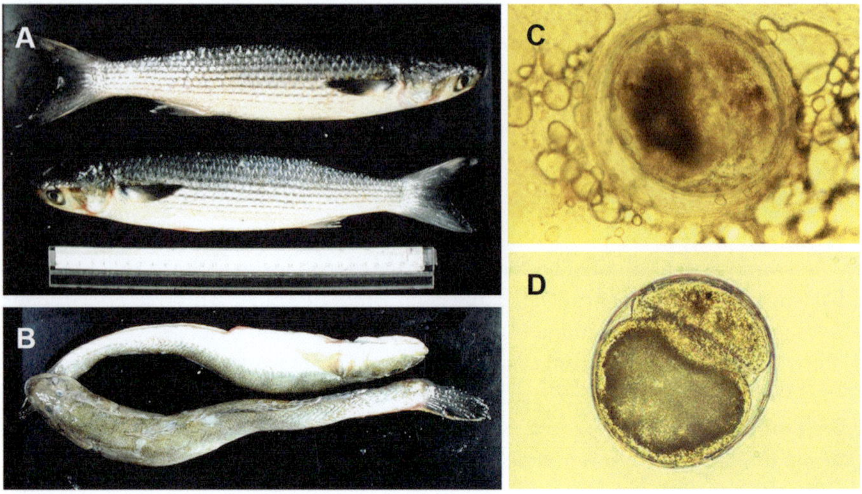

Fig. 1.19 *Heterophyes nocens*. (**a**) The mullet, *Mugil cephalus*, a fish intermediate host (**b**) The goby, *Acanthogobius flavimanus*, another fish host (**c**) Metacercaria encysted in the soft tissue of a mullet. ×200 (D) Metacercaria isolated from the flesh of a goby. ×200

The life span in animal host is 1–4 months but may be longer in humans (Chai 2014).

Epidemiology and Geographical Distribution
The mode of human infection with *H. nocens* is the same as that of *H. heterophyes*. Raw or improperly cooked mullets and gobies are the major source of infection (Chai 2014; Chai and Jung 2017). Endemic areas are scattered along riverside areas of South Korea, Japan, and probably China and Taiwan (Fig. 1.16). In South Korea, about 50,000 people are estimated to be infected with this fluke (Chai and Lee 2002).

China Human infections were reported in provinces of mainland China (Guangdong, Hubei, and Beijing) and Taiwan under the name *H. heterophyes* (Yu and Mott 1994), but the parasite may have been actually *H. nocens* (Chai 2014).

Japan In an earlier report from Fukuoka and Kumamoto Prefecture, *H. nocens* (under the name *H. heterophyes*) infection was identified in 3 human cases (Nagata 1914). Thereafter, Onji (1915) reported 18.5% prevalence of *H. nocens* among inhabitants in Yamaguchi Prefecture. Later, an epidemiological survey performed in Chiba Prefecture revealed that the heterophyid egg positive rate among residents was 8.0% in Goi-Machi village and 9.0% in Misaki-Machi village (Yokogawa et al. 1965). Based on worm recovery results from some patients, the former village was verified to have mixed infections with *H. nocens* and *M. yokogawai*, whereas the latter village had mostly *Pygidiopsis summa* infections (Yokogawa et al. 1965). Ito et al. (1967) reported that the prevalence of *H. nocens* in Harai village of Izu peninsula, Shizuoka Prefecture was 20.7% in 1959 but 6 years after mass treatment, inhibition of raw fish eating, and health education, it was decreased to 3.4%. In Kochi

Prefecture, 13 heterophyid egg positive people were treated with kamala (anthelmintic drug) and from 7 of them specimens of *Metagonimus* spp. (596 worms) and *H. nocens* (2 worms) were recovered (Suzuki et al. 1982). Human *H. nocens* infection was also reported from Chugoku and Hiroshima Prefectures (Suzuki et al. 1982). More recently, 2 lakeside villages of Mikkabi-cho, north end of Hamana Lake, Shizuoka Prefecture were found to have 7.5% and 10.5% prevalence of *H. nocens* eggs (Kino et al. 2002).

South Korea The metacercariae of *H. nocens* were first detected in the mullet *M. cephalus* captured in 3 southern coastal areas (Seo et al. 1980). They were fed to mice and rats and adult flukes were confirmed (Seo et al. 1980). A human case was first identified in a man residing in a seashore village along the Western Sea (= Yellow Sea) by Seo et al. (1981a). Thereafter, succeeding cases human were reported from various coastal areas (Chai et al. 1984, 1985). Subsequently, among human populations, over 40% prevalences were detected in various southwestern coastal areas, i.e., Jeollanam-do and Gyeongsangnam-do Province (Chai et al. 1994, 1997, 1998; Park et al. 2007). For example, in a coastal village of Shinan-gun, Jeollanam-do Province, 43% of the residents were found infected with *H. nocens* (Chai et al. 1994). Moreover, another coastal village in Muan-gun, Jeollanam-do revealed 75% prevalence of heterophyid eggs among the inhabitants; they were verified to be mixed-infected with *H. nocens* (all of 20 worm-recovered cases) and *Pygidiopsis summa* (18 of 20 worm-recovered cases) (Table 1.5) (Chai et al. 1997). In these areas, individual worm burdens of *H. nocens* ranged 3–1338 (average 237 worms per person) (Chai et al. 1994, 1997, 1998). Later, numerous endemic foci were found in coastal islands located in the western and southern sea and have been added to the list of endemic areas (Chai et al. 2004; Guk et al. 2007). It is interesting to note that, in an inland area of Boseong-gun (Boseong River) where *M. yokogawai* is prevalent with a low grade mixed-infection with *M. takahashii* and *M. miyatai*, a few adult specimens of *H. nocens* were recovered from some riparian residents (Chai et al. 2015). *H. nocens* adult flukes have been recovered from stray cats in Gyeongbuk Province (Lee 1979) and Busan (Sohn and Chai 2005), domestic cats in Seoul and other areas (Eom et al. 1985b), feral cats caught on Aphaedo Island (Shin et al. 2009), and stray cats from areas near Seomjin-gang (River) (Shin et al. 2015).

The status of metacercarial infection in brackish water fish, including mullets *Mugil cepahlus* and gobies *Acanthogobius flavimanus,* was first surveyed in coastal areas of South Korea by Seo et al. (1981c). The mullets were collected from total 14 localities and the gobies were from 5 localities, and mullets from 5 areas (5/14 areas) and gobies from 2 areas (2/5 areas) were positive for *H. nocens* metacercariae (Seo et al. 1981c). The metacercarial density was not so high per infected fish, 2–67 in mullets and 1–16 in gobies (Seo et al. 1981c). Later, mullets *Mugil cephalus* and redlip mullets *Chelon haematocheilus*, were caught in Jinju-man (Bay), Gyeongsangnam-do Province and examined for *H. nocens* metacercariae (Kim et al. 2006). The infection rate of the mullet with *H. nocens* metacercariae was 40%, with an average metacercarial burden of 8.5 per infected fish, and in the redlip mul-

Table 1.5 Recovery of heterophyid fluke specimens from villagers of a seashore village in Muan-gun, Jeollanam-do, South Korea[a]

Villager code	Age & sex	No. of specimens recovered *Heterophyes nocens*	*Pygidiopsis summa*	*Heterophyopsis continua*	*Stictodora fuscata*	*Gymnophalloides seoi*
1	43 F	1338	21	0	76	1
2	33 F	1049	143	1	0	0
3	56 F	325	30	0	0	0
4	40 M	295	25	0	5	0
5	61 M	209	44	1	0	0
6	70 M	137	111	0	49	2
7	60 F	121	13	0	0	0
8	35 F	100	21	0	0	0
9	50 M	80	70	0	34	0
10	61 M	44	2	0	0	0
11	60 M	34	2	0	0	0
12	46 F	25	0	0	0	0
13	40 F	23	1	0	0	0
14	51 M	22	13	0	0	0
15	49 M	20	13	0	0	0
16	62 M	17	3	0	0	1
17	33 F	9	1	0	0	0
18	46 F	8	170	0	0	0
19	71 F	5	0	0	0	0
20	58 M	3	20	0	0	0
Total		3864	703	2	164	4

[a]Data from Chai et al. (1997)

let, the prevalence of *H. nocens* metacercariae was 16.7%, with the metacercarial burden per infected fish of 2.0 (Kim et al. 2006). In gobies, a recent report showed that the infection rate of those caught from Muan-gun and Shinan-gun with *H. nocens* metacercariae was 55.0% (22/40) in total (Sohn et al. 2018). The metacercarial burden per fish was 2.5 in Muan-gun (Sohn et al. 2018).

Other Countries The life cycle of *H. nocens* may be present in Thailand, since cercariae of *Heterophyes* sp. were recovered from brackish water snails in coastal areas (Namchote et al. 2015). A case of *H. nocens* infection (under the name *H. heterophyes*) was reported in France; the case was a French professor visiting Japan and consumed raw fish and aquatic plants there (Lamy et al. 1976).

1.3.3 Heterophyes dispar

1.3.3.1 *Heterophyes dispar* Looss, 1902

[syn. *Heterophyes dispar limatus* Looss, 1902]

Taxonomy and Morphology

H. dispar (Fig. 1.20a, b) was first discovered in the intestines of dogs and cats in Egypt (Looss 1902), and then from mammals, including foxes and wolves, in the northern Africa and eastern Mediterranean, including Greece and Israel (Palestine) (Witenberg 1929; Taraschewski and Nicolaidou 1987; Yu and Mott 1994; Chai 2014). Human infections were reported from 2 Korean men who returned from Saudi Arabia (Chai et al. 1986) and from Thailand (Kaewkes et al. 1992; Yu and Mott 1994).

There were taxonomic debates on *H. dispar* and *H. aequalis*, both of which were first described by Looss (1902) in Egypt. Whereas Witenberg (1929) and Wells and Randall (1956) acknowledged the validity of these 2 species, Kuntz and Chandler

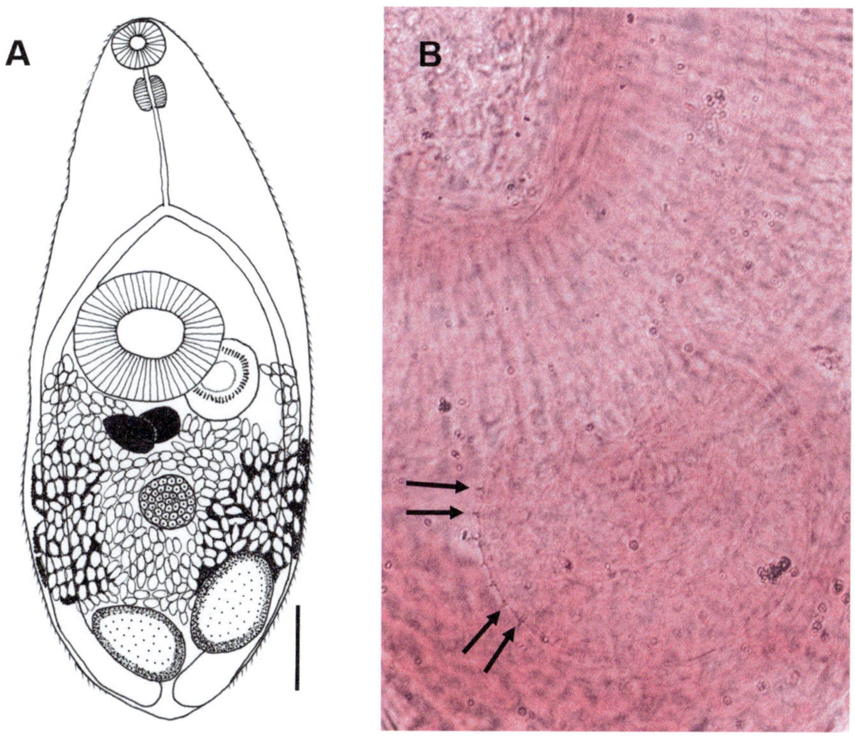

Fig. 1.20 *Heterophyes dispar*. (**a**) Line drawing of an adult worm (original figure). Scale bar = 0.1 mm (**b**) Enlarged view of the ventral and genital suckers and rodlets (arrows) on the gonotyl. ×400

(1956a, b) synonymized *H. dispar* with *H. aequalis*. However, *H. dispar* is distinct from *H. aequalis* in the larger number of rodlets (22–35) on the gonotyl compared with *H. aequalis* (14–25) and long ceca extending down to the posterior margin of 2 testes in *H. dispar*, whereas they are ending before the anterior margin of 2 testes in *H. aequalis* (Looss 1902; Witenberg 1929). In addition, the habitat selection of *H. dispar* and *H. aequalis* was different in various experimental animals, including dogs, cats, and rats; the former showed a preference for the anterior small intestine (duodenum and proximal jejunum), whereas the latter preferred the lower small intestine (posterior jejunum and ileum) (Taraschewski 1987). Based on this difference and also with others, Taraschewski (1985a, b, 1987) acknowledged the validity of both species.

H. dispar adults are elliptical or pyriform, and slightly smaller (0.4–1.4 mm long and 0.2–0.4 mm wide) than those of *H. heterophyes* and *H. nocens* (Chai et al. 1986, 2009; Chai 2014). However, the morphology of internal organs is similar to one another. The only recognizable difference is the smaller number (22–35) of rodlets on the gonotyl of the genital sucker in *H. dispar* compared to that in *H. heterophyes* (70–85) and *H. nocens* (50–62) (Chai et al. 1986, 1994; Chai 2014). *H. aequalis* is similar in body size with *H. dispar*, but has relatively short ceca, and has a smaller number (14–25) of rodlets on the gonotyl than *H. dispar* (Witenberg 1929; Chai et al. 1986). The eggs of *H. dispar* (19–25 μm long and 13–15 μm wide) are slightly smaller than those of *H. heterophyes* or *H. nocens* (Chai et al. 1986; Chai 2014). Descriptions of the cercariae of *H. dispar* are not available to the author's hand; however, Kuntz and Chandler (1956b) described the cercariae of *H. aequalis* (they considered *H. dispar* as a synonym of *H. aequalis*). The cercariae (under the name *H. aequalis*) are biocellate and pleurolophocercous type, and the cercarial body is 176–224 (av. 205) μm long and 68–81 (av. 76) μm wide, and the tail is 471–513 (av. 493) μm long and 26–29 (av. 27) μm wide (Kuntz and Chandler 1956b). The metacercariae of the 3 species of *Heterophyes* occurring in the Middle East, i.e., *H. heterophyes, H. dispar,* and *H. aequalis*, are so similar morphologically, that it was impossible to differentiate them (Witenberg 1929). They are almost round, and 130–260 μm in diameter (Witenberg 1929).

Life Cycle

The life cycle is similar to that of *H. heterophyes* (Chai 2014). Freshwater or brackish water snails, *Pirenella conica*, serve as the first intermediate hosts, and freshwater or brackish water fish, including *Mugil cephalus, Mugil capito, Mugil auratus, Epinephelus enaeus, Tilapia simonis, Tilapia nilotica, Tilapia zilli, Lichia amia, Lichia glauca, Barbus canus, Solea vulgaris*, and *Sciaena aquilla* are the important second intermediate hosts (Witenberg 1929; Wells and Randall 1956; Paperna and Overstreet 1981; Taraschewski 1984). They usually encyst in the striped muscle of the fish host, but also in heart muscles, connective tissues, and fatty tissues (Witenberg 1929; Chai 2014). The longevity of metacercariae in fish is unknown, but they may be able to survive for several years or throughout the life span of the fish hosts (Chai 2014). Natural definitive hosts include dogs, cats, wolves, jackals, foxes, and kites (Witenberg 1929; Wells and Randall 1956; Chai 2014). Pups, rabbits, rats, cats, and red foxes were used as experimental definitive hosts (Taraschewski 1985b; Chai 2014).

Epidemiology and Geographical Distribution

Human infections can occur when fish intermediate hosts, including *Mugil* spp., are eaten raw or under inadequately cooked conditions (Chai 2014). However, human infections were unknown before 1986 when 2 Korean men who returned from Saudi Arabia were found infected with this fluke together with *H. heterophyes* (Eom et al. 1985a; Chai et al. 1986). This fluke is known to be distributed in Egypt, North Africa, the Eastern Mediterranean, and India (Fig. 1.16) (Gupta et al. 2008; Hung et al. 2013). Human infection was found in Thailand (Kaewkes et al. 1992; Yu and Mott 1994), but no detailed description of the case has been available and whether the case was imported or not is uncertain. In Egypt, 2 of 14 stray dogs in Ismailia City were found infected with *H. dispar* adult flukes (El-Gayar 2007). Later, El-Azazy et al. (2015) reported in Egypt that 10.8% among 240 stray cats were infected with 83 ± 12 adult flukes of *H. dispar*. In Madras, India, a high infection rate (96%) of domestic cats with *H. dispar* was reported (Gupta et al. 2008).

1.3.4 Potentially Zoonotic Heterophyes *spp.*

Potentially zoonotic *Heterophyes* spp. include *H. aequalis* Looss, 1902, *H. indica* Rao and Ayyar, 1931, and *H. pleomorphis* Bwangamoi and Ojok, 1977.

1.3.5 Genomics and Proteomics

Genomics and proteomics of *Heterophyes* spp. flukes have seldom been studied. In GenBank, only the sequences of mitochondrial cytochrome *c* oxidase subunit 1 (CO1) and a nuclear ribosomal gene (28S rDNA) of *H. nocens* are available (AF188119 and AF181890, respectively) (Masala et al. 2016). According to Masala et al. (2016), metacercariae of *H. heterophyes* (together with a few *H. nocens*?) and seemingly *H. dispar* were detected in gray mullets caught from Sardinia (western Mediterranean Sea); ITS2 was sequenced and compared between *H. heterophyes, H. nocens* (?), and *H. dispar* from Sardinia, and *H. nocens* from South Korea. The results revealed that *H. heterophyes* and *H. nocens* (?) from Sardinia formed one clade, whereas *H. nocens* from South Korea was grouped into another distinct cluster (Masala et al. 2016). A numerical taxonomy study also revealed that *H. heterophyes, H. nocens, H. dispar* are all distinct taxa (Kim et al. 1991).

1.3.6 Pathology and Immunology

The virulence of *Heterophyes* flukes might be different by different parasite species (Chai 2014); however, there have been no studies supporting this hypothesis. Two principal factors related to virulence include mechanical and chemical irritations by the flukes (Chai 2014). Mechanical irritation is chiefly caused by movement of worms which can give harmful effects to the intestinal mucosa, in particular, villous and crypt layers of the small intestine (Chai 2014). Chemical substances produced by the flukes, which include secretory-excretory proteins (ESP), can play a role for not only antigens but also toxins to the host (Chai 2014).

The intestinal histopathology in *Heterophyes* spp. infection (Fig. 1.21) is essentially the same as that seen in *M. yokogawai* infection. The adult flukes of *H. heterophyes* or *H. nocens* (Ryang et al. 1999) parasitize the middle part of the small intestines; within the crypts of Lieberkühn in early stages of the infection (by day 2–3 post-infection), and between villi in later stages (Hamdy and Nocola 1980; Chai 2014). They can elicit mild inflammatory reactions, together with ulcers, irritation, and superficial necrosis of the site of their attachment to the host intestinal mucosa (Yu and Mott 1994; Fried et al. 2004; Toledo et al. 2014). Villous atrophy and crypt hyperplasia are the major histopathologic features, accompanied by

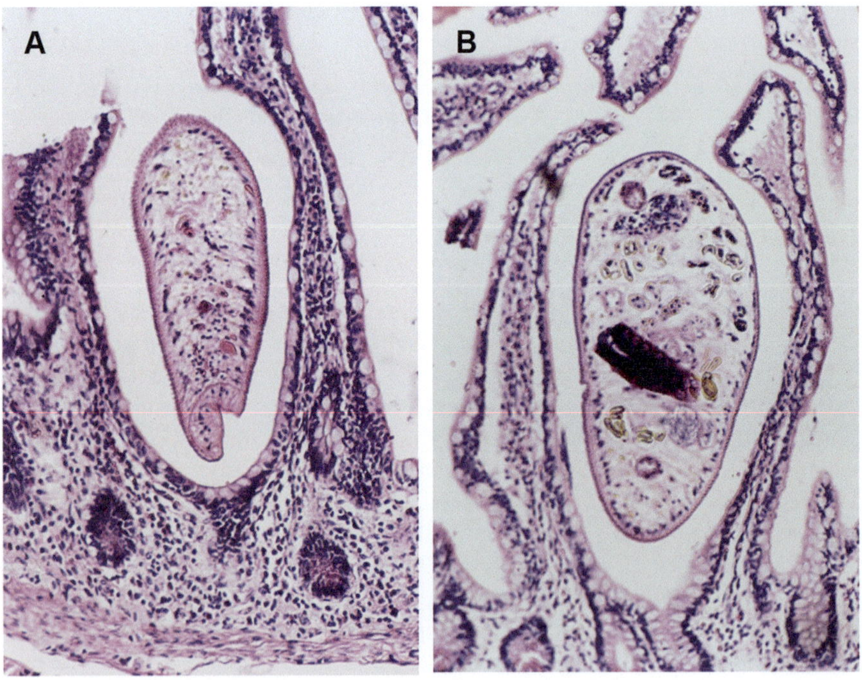

Fig. 1.21 Intestinal sections of a human patient (**a**, **b**) naturally infected with *Heterophyes nocens*. Intestinal mucosa shows atrophy. Goblet cell hyperplasia is also seen. ×100

inflammatory cell infiltrations (Hamdy and Nicola 1980; Ashour et al. 2014; Chai 2014). However, involvement of Peyer's patches and mesenteric lymph nodes by adult flukes were frequently seen in experimental dogs and cats (Hamdy and Nicola 1980). In avian hosts, like sea gulls, the flukes frequently invade extraintestinal or somatic tissues and organs, in particular, the liver, pancreas, and bile duct (Chai 2014). However, in mammalian hosts, this possibility has not been confirmed. Immune responses of the host against the flukes or their ESP may be too strong (hypersensitive) that the host immunity can damage reversely the host itself (Chai 2014). The affected mucosa may undergo hypersensitive and allergic reactions, including severe catarrhal inflammation and loss of villi (Chai 2014). Pathogenicity is also related to other host-parasite relationships, including the intensity of infection; heavier infections generally undergo severer illnesses (Chai 2014).

Several heterophyid species, namely *Haplorchis* spp., *Stellantchasmus falcatus*, and *Procerovum* spp., can cause erratic extraintestinal parasitism in man, which is often fatal (Africa et al. 1940). The most frequently affected site was the heart valve, brain, and spinal cord, where eggs and adult flukes originating from the small intestinal mucosa embolised the blood vessels of these tissues (Africa et al. 1940). It was suggested that such erratic parasitism should occur in immunocompromised patients (Yokogawa 1940). In this respect, it is of note that eggs of *H. heterophyes* (Gallais et al. 1955; Collomb and Bert 1959; Collomb et al. 1960) and *H. nocens* (under the name *H. heterophyes*) (Zhang et al. 1990) were found encapsulated in the brain of patients with neurological symptoms. *H. nocens* eggs were also detected within an intestinal tumor near the appendix in a 10-year old girl in Japan (Nakano and Inuoe 1955).

The risk of ectopic *Heterophyes* infection, particularly due to *H. heterophyes*, was studied in experimental rats in Egypt (Elsheikha 2007). In 4 of 20 rats, *H. heterophyes* eggs and/or immature worms were found in the intestinal wall, lymph nodes, liver, and spleen which evidently demonstrated the potential to cause extraintestinal spreading of the infection (Elsheikha 2007). In addition, the mechanisms of extraintestinal spreading were suggested to include underlying diseases which can lead to the patient more susceptible to *Heterophyes* infection, as well as immunosuppression as a predisposing factor, and malnutrition and/or malabsorption secondary to villus ischemia and enterocyte destruction induced by *Heterophyes* infection (Elsheikha 2007). Another histopathological study demonstrated deposition of antigens or immune complexes in the kidneys and brain of experimental mice; these deposits were thought to play important roles in histopathological changes in the kidneys and brain (Daoud 2012). Proteolytic activity was demonstrated in *H. heterophyes* adult flukes which seemed to play an important role for invasion of the parasite inside the intestinal wall of the hosts (Danasory and Hamdy 1980).

Host immune responses and immunity have been seldom studied in *Heterophyes* spp. infections. There may be strong host protective mechanisms against *Hetrophyes* spp. infections. However, immunophysiology and immunopathogenesis due to these fluke infections have seldom been studied in contrast to other intestinal helminth infections, including nematodes or other intestinal trematodes such as *M.*

yokogawai or echinostomes. The fact that intestinal histopathology induced by heterophyids is spontaneously restored indicates the development of host protective immunity (Toledo et al. 2014). Elevated levels of IgG, IgM, and IgE have been detected in the serum of humans infected with *H. heterophyes* (El-Ganayni et al. 1989; Martínez-Alonso et al. 1999; Toledo et al. 2014). IgG, IgM, and IgA were also increased in the intestine of infected human patients (El-Ganayni et al. 1989).

1.3.7 Clinical Manifestations, Diagnosis and Treatment

The most frequent clinical manifestations in heterophyiasis patients are mild to moderate degrees of abdominal pain, diarrhea, lethargy, anorexia, and weight loss (Chai 2014; Chai and Jung 2017). However, the severity of symptoms may vary and depend on host-side factors such as the intensity of infection (the number of infected worms) in each patient, immune status of the patient, and previous history of infection with these flukes. Heavier infection cases tend to suffer from more severe illnesses, whereas lightly infected cases may undergo a subclinical course. Immunocompetent patients can endure the infection only with mild clinical symptoms but immunocompromised patients may undergo severe clinical course, including erratic parasitism (= extraintestinal heterophyiasis) in the heart, brain, and spinal cord, as reported by Africa et al. (1940). Both *H. heterophyes* and *H. nocens* (presumably) are suspected as the causes of cerebral manifestations, including epilepsy, brain abscess, or brain cyst (Gallais et al. 1955; Collomb and Bert 1959; Collomb et al. 1960; Zhang et al. 1990). In an interesting case of acute appendicitis in a 10-year old girl in Japan, *H. nocens* eggs were demonstrated within the tumor formed near the appendix (Nakano ad Inuoe 1955). Village people who are repeatedly infected with *Heterophyes* spp. seem to get acquired immunity and may easily endure the infection; however, a new visitor to an endemic area may suffer from severer illnesses. Clinico-pathological significance of *Heterophyes* flukes should be further investigated in detail.

The detection of *Heterophyes* spp. infection is usually done by recovery of eggs in the feces. Smear techniques, such as the direct smear, cellophane thick smear, and Kato-Katz thick smear, can be applied in the laboratory and in the field (Chai 2014). Concentration techniques, including formalin-ether sedimentation and brine floatation, are performed in laboratories equipped with centrifuges (Chai 2014). However, in areas of mixed infections with other heterophyid species, specific diagnosis is problematic (Chai 2014). In addition, detecting eggs in the feces is often failed in light infection cases and it is necessary to use immunological or molecular detection techniques (Chai 2014).

Heterophyes eggs can be differentiated from those of *Clonorchis, Opisthorchis*, or other heterophyid species (Chai 2014). However, it is only with difficulty and needs experience. The eggs of *H. heterophyes* and *H. nocens* are similar and characterized by their length of 0.023–0.027 mm and 0.024–0.029 mm, respectively, ellipsoid to ovoid in shape with a length/width ratio of 1.5–2.1, clean shell surface, less prominent operculum, no shoulder rims, and yellowish brown in color (Lee et al. 1984, 2012). The eggs of *H. dispar* are similar to those of *H. heterophyes* or *H. nocens*, with the exception of their smaller size (Chai 2014). There could be false egg negative cases among the light infection cases, for example, with less than 100 worms in an infected person; in such cases the probability to detect eggs in the feces is almost negligible (Chai and Lee 2002).

In such cases, serological tests, including ELISA, and genetic techniques, including polymerase chain reaction (PCR), may be helpful (Chai 2014). Little study has been available on these techniques. In dogs, 3 immunodiagnostic methods, including counter current immunoelectrophoresis, intradermal test, and indirect fluorescent immunoassay, were tried to detect serum antibodies against *H. heterophyes* (Elshazly et al. 2008). The intradermal test revealed 100% sensitivity and 90% specificity (Elshazly et al. 2008). Molecular diagnostic studies are not yet available. The diagnosis of erratic parasitism in the heart, brain, or spinal cord is impossible unless biopsy or necropsy is done on the affected lesion (Chai 2014).

The drug of choice for individual treatment of *Heterophyes* spp. infection is praziquantel, at a single oral dose of 10–20 mg/kg praziquantel (Chai 2013). The effect is highly satisfactory, with over 95% cure rate (Ata et al. 1988; El-Hawy et al. 1988). Niclosamide can also be used (El-Hawy et al. 1988).

1.3.8 Prevention and Control

Proper disposal of human or animal feces can reduce the infection source (*Heterophyes* eggs) to the snail intermediate host (Chai 2014). However, control of the snail host is hardly feasible. Also, fish control, including the mullets, and reservoir host control are impractical. One of the most efficient preventive measures is to persuade people to cook fish before eating (Chai 2014). However, public health workers have experienced how difficult it is to persuade people in endemic areas to change their long-tradition of eating raw or undercooked fish (Chai 2014). Because of this strong food tradition, prevention of heterophyiasis at the consumer level is highly difficult (Chai 2014).

Heating fish for 10–15 min at 70 °C could inactivate metacercariae; however, data are insufficient to determine the exact time-temperature treatment baseline. A review of available data on processing conditions identified some parameters for heating, pickling, salting, freezing, and irradiating fish for inactivation of parasites (WHO 1995). Freezing and storing at −20 °C or below for 7 days, or freezing at −35 °C or below until solid and storing at −35 °C or below for 15 h, or freezing at −35 °C or below until solid, and storing at −20 °C or below for 24 h is sufficient to kill parasites (WHO 1995).

Brining and pickling may also reduce the parasite hazard in a fish; however, some zoonotic trematode metacercariae require up to 8 days in 30% brine to be killed (WHO 1995). The effectiveness of smoking to a temperature of 65 °C is considered to be effective for parasitic nematodes in fish, but there is little research on this process for intestinal trematodes, including *Heterophyes* (Chai 2014).

1.4 *Haplorchis*

The adult flukes of the genus *Haplorchis* Looss 1899, *Procerovum* Onji and Nishio 1916, *Haplorchoides* Chen 1949, *Euhaplorchis* Martin 1950, and *Pygidiopsoides* Martin 1951 are differentiated from those of the other genera of the Heterophyidae in that they have a single testis (Yamaguti 1958; Chai 2007; Thaenkham et al. 2012). Flukes of *Haplorchis* are characterized by the presence of only one testis and a small armed ventral sucker lacking a gonotyl and they lack the expulsor-style distal part of the seminal vesicle which is present in genera *Procerovum* and *Stellantchasmus* (Pearson and Ow-Yang 1982).

The ventral sucker of *Metagonimus* is markedly submedian (dextral) but that of *Haplorchis* is only slightly submedian or almost median (Chai 2007). *Heterophyes* has 2 testes whereas *Haplorchis* has a single testis (Ito 1964a; Chai 2007, 2014). *Heterophyopsis* has an elongated body and 2 obliquely tandem testes, whereas the body of *Haplorchis* is ovoid to elliptical and it has a single testis (Chai 2007). *Pygidiopsis* has a ventrogenital apparatus consisting of a small median ventral sucker and antero-sinistrally a genital apparatus armed with a small number of rodlets (Chai 2007). *Centrocestus* differs from *Haplorchis* in having minute circumoral spines around the oral sucker (Chai 2007).

Flukes of the genus *Haplorchis* were first discovered in Egypt and described under the name *Distomum cahirinus* and *Monostomum pumilio* (Looss 1896). The genus *Haplorchis* was created later by Looss (1899) including *Haplorchis cahirinus* (Looss 1896) and *Haplorchis pumilio* (Looss 1896). However, Witenberg (1929) proposed to transfer *H. cahirinus* to another family because it is an intestinal parasite of fish in its adult stage, whereas *H. pumilio* is an intestinal parasite of birds and mammals. In Taiwan, Nishigori (1924) created a new genus *Monorchotrema* and assigned 2 species; *Monorchotrema taihokui* and *Monorchotrema taichui* which were recovered from experimentally infected dogs, cats, and rats fed the metacercariae in fish. Subsequently, Faust and Nishigori (1926) worked out their whole life cycles. Witenberg (1929) discovered specimens of *M. taichui* and *M. taihokui* (using the genus name as *Monorchitrema*) from Israel (Palestine) dogs, cats, and birds, and suggested strongly that *Monorchitrema* should be a synonym of *Haplorchis.* Witenberg (1929) further suggested that *M. taihokui* should be a synonym of *Haplorchis pumilio.* Soon after this, Katsuta (1932a, 1932b) in Taiwan successively found metacercariae and adults of *Monorchotrema microrchia* and *Monorchotrema yokogawai,* respectively. Later, *M. microrchia* was synonymized with *Haplorchis taichui* and *M. yokogawai* was renamed as *Haplorchis yokogawai* (Chen 1936). Tubangui (1933) added another species named *Haplorchis anguillarum* but this species has 2 testes; so, Chen (1936) did not acknowledge the validity of this species. Later, Tubangui and Africa (1938) transferred this species to the genus

Gallactosomum. Gohar (1934) described another species, *Haplorchis milvi*, from Egyptian kites. Reviewing all these historical events, Chen (1936) listed tentatively 4 species in the genus *Haplorchis*; *H. pumilio* (type species), *H. taichui, H. yokogawai,* and *H. milvi*. However, Chen (1936) suggested that *H. milvi* may fall into synonymy with *H. yokogawai* if the type specimen is re-studied. Later, Chen (1949) did not mention on *H. milvi*, and Kuntz and Chandler (1956) proposed to regard *H. milvi* as a synonym of *H. yokogawai*.

In Egypt, Khalil (1932) described the life cycle of *Haplorchis pleurolophocerca* (under the name *Kasr aini*) originating from *Cercaria pleurolophocerca* named by Sonsino in 1892. The name *H. pleurolophocerca* was used by Price (1940). Toledo et al. (2014) listed this species among the human-infecting *Haplorchis* species. However, Pearson (1964) suggested this species to be a synonym of *H. pumilio*. In India, Dayal (1935) reported *Monorchotrema taakree* adults from the intestinal of a freshwater fish but this species was later transferred to the genus *Haplorchoides* (Yamaguti 1958). Africa and Garcia (1935) described *Haplorchis calderoni* from the small intestine of dogs, cats, and humans in the Philippines but this species was transferred to the genus *Procerovum* after Price (1940). Africa (1938) added 2 more *Haplorchis* species. One was *H. vanissimus* (as *H. vanissima*) recovered from the small intestine of humans, and the other was *H. sisoni* collected from the small intestine of cats and dogs experimentally infected with metacercariae from fish. Later, *H. sisoni* was synonymized with *Procerovum varium* (Pearson 1964). In the meantime, in Hainan Island, China, Kobayasi (1942) described 6 additional species of *Haplorchis; H. yokogawai* var. *elliptica, H. minutus, H. cordatus, H. hoihowensis, H. macrovesica,* and *H. microvesica*. However, all these species were synonymized with other pre-existing taxa; *H. yokogawai* var. *elliptica* was synonymized with *H. yokogawai* (Pearson 1964), *H. macrovesica* was with *P. calderoni* (Chen 1949), and *H. minutus, H. cordatus, H. hoihowensis,* and *H. microvesica* were with *P. varium* (Pearson 1964). Later, Kobayasi (1954) proposed a new species, *H. nhatrangensis*, from experimentally infected puppies and cats with metacercariae in fish from French Indo-China. Pearson (1964) thoroughly reviewed the reported species of *Haplorchis* but did not mention about *H. nhatrangensis.* Now it appears that *H. nhatrangensis* is morphologically not significantly different from *H. yokogawai*; therefore, it can be treated as a synonym of *H. yokogawai*. Three new species were described by Pearson (1964), i.e., *H. sprenti, H. parataichui*, and *H. wellsi*, and 3 questional species, *H. pearsoni* Fernando 1933, *H. butei* Chatterji 1948, and *H. tagorai* Chatterji 1949 were mentioned. Later, Pearson and Ow-Yang (1982) described 2 more new species (*H. parapumilio* and *H. paravanissimus*) and finally enlisted 9 species in this genus, *H. taichui, H. parataichui, H. pumilio, H. parapumilio, H. vanissimus, H. paravanissimus, H. wellsi, H. yokogawai,* and *H. sprenti*.

Therefore, at present 9 species (Table 1.6) can be recognized as valid species in the genus *Haplorchis*. Among them, *H. taichui, H. pumilio, H. yokogawai,* and *H. vanissimus* are human-infecting species. Human infections with *Haplorchis* spp. are prevalent in Southeast Asia, including countries located in Indo-China Peninsula, Taiwan, and the Philippines, and also probably in Egypt (Chai 2007; Chai and Jung 2017).

Table 1.6 Species of *Haplorchis* reported in the literature

Species with nominator	Human infection	Area (Country)
Haplorchis taichui (Nishigori, 1924) Chen, 1936	Yes	Bangladesh, China, Egypt, India, Iraq, Israel, Kuwait, Lao PDR, Malaysia, Myanmar, The Philippines, Sri Lanka, Taiwan, Thailand, USA (Hawaii), Vietnam
Haplorchis pumilio (Looss, 1896) Looss, 1899	Yes[a]	Australia, Cambodia, China, Egypt, India, Iraq, Israel, Kenya, Lao PDR, Malaysia, Mexico, Myanmar, Peru, The Philippines, Sri Lanka, Taiwan, Thailand, USA, Venezuela, Vietnam
Haplorchis yokogawai (Katsuta, 1932) Chen, 1936	Yes	Australia, Cambodia, China, Egypt, India, Indonesia, Kuwait, Lao PDR, Malaysia, Myanmar, The Philippines, Sri Lanka, Taiwan, Thailand, USA (Hawaii), Vietnam
Haplorchis vanissimus (Africa, 1938) Yamaguti, 1958	Yes	Australia, The Philippines
Haplorchis parapumilio Pearson and Ow-Yang, 1982	No	Indonesia
Haplorchis parataichui Pearson, 1964	No	Australia
Haplorchis paravanissimus Pearson and Ow-Yang, 1982	No	Australia
Haplorchis sprenti Pearson, 1964	No	Australia
Haplorchis wellsi Pearson, 1964	No	Taiwan

Information updated from Chai and Jung (2017)
[a]A natural human case co-infected with *H. pumilio*, *Gymnophalloides seoi,* and *Gynaecotyla squatarolae* has been reported in South Korea (Chung et al. 2011). However, South Korea is tentatively not listed as an endemic area of *Haplorchis* spp.

Only 4 of the 9 *Haplorchis* species, including *H. taichui, H. pumilio, H. yokogawai,* and *H. vanissimus*, have so far been reported from human infections. Three species, namely, *H. taichui, H. pumilio,* and *H. yokogawai* are distributed widely in Southeast Asia, including China and Taiwan, Indochina Peninsula, and the Middle East and North Africa, including Israel (Palestine) and Egypt (Velasquez 1982; Yu and Mott 1994). *H. vanissimus* was reported only in the Philippines (Africa 1938) and Australia (Pearson 1964).

A brief history of the discovery, taxonomic debates, and morphological and biological characteristics of each *Haplorchis* species are given in the following section.

1.4.1 Haplorchis taichui

1.4.1.1 *Haplorchis taichui* (Nishigori, 1924) Chen, 1936

[syn. *Monorchotrema taichui* Nishigori, 1924; *Monorchotrema microrchia* Katsuta, 1932; *Haplorchis microrchis* (Katsuta) Yamaguti, 1958]

Taxonomy and Morphology

This species (Fig. 1.22a, b) was originally described from birds and mammals caught in the middle part of Taiwan (Nishigori 1924). Subsequently, its complete life cycle has been elucidated by Faust and Nishigori (1926). Later, *Monorchotrema microrchia* was reported as a new species in Taiwan (Katsuta 1932a); however, this species was synonymized with *H. taichui* (Chen 1936). Now *H. taichui* is known to be distributed in Asian-Pacific Region and the Middle east (Egypt, Israel, and Palestine) (Pearson 1964; Velasquez 1982; Yu and Mott 1994; Chai et al. 2005a, 2009a). Human infections are not infrequently found in Thailand, Lao PDR, Vietnam, the Philippines, and South China (Velasquez 1982; Yu and Mott 1994; Belizario et al. 2004; Chai et al. 2009a).

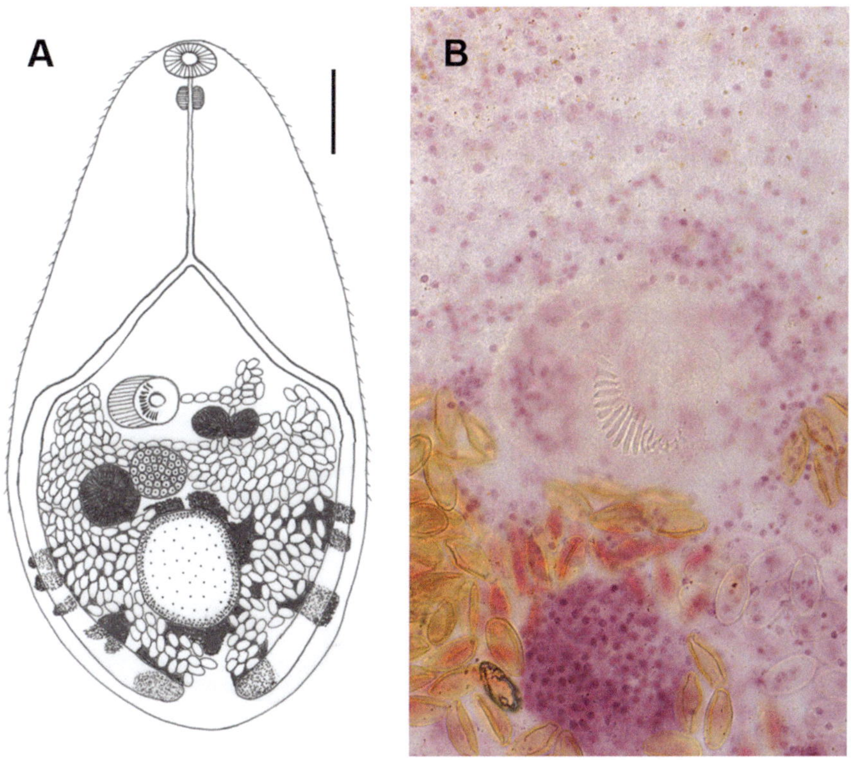

Fig. 1.22 *Haplorchis taichui*. (**a**) Line drawing of an adult worm (original figure). Scale bar = 0.1 mm (**b**) Enlarged view of the ventral sucker and rodlets on the gonotyl. ×400

The body is oval in shape, with flattened dorsal and ventral sides; the size of adult flukes is 0.43–1.18 mm long and 0.17–0.26 mm (Faust and Nishigori 1926). In adults, the most specific morphological feature for differentiation from other *Haplorchis* species is the size, shape, and number of spines (Fig. 1.22b) on the ventral sucker (Ujiie 1936; Chen 1936; Pearson and Ow-Yang 1982). *H. taichui* has a semi-lunar group of 12–16 long, crescentic, and hollow spines (Fig. 1.22b) up to 19–30 μm long and a sinistral patch of very minute solid spines up to 4 μm long (Pearson and Ow-Yang 1982). *H. parataichui* is morphologically most similar to *H. taichui*, and it has 15–21 long and hollow spines up to 17 μm long and characteristically a large single sclerite on the dorsal lip at the opposite side of the spines (Pearson and Ow-Yang 1982). In addition, the testis of *H. taichui* exceeds ceca but that of *H. parataichui* does not exceed ceca (Pearson and Ow-Yang 1982). Other species can be differentiated by the presence of minute sclerites on the ventral sucker (*H. pumilio, H. parapumilio, H. vanissimus,* and *H. paravanissimus*), remarkably large ventral sucker (*H. wellsi*), or a ventral sucker smaller than the oral sucker (*H. yokogawai* and *H. sprenti*) (Pearson and Ow-Yang 1982). The eggs of *H. taichui* are 22–32 (av 27.0) × 11–17 (av. 14.1) μm, operculate, ovoid, and light yellow, containing a mature miracidium (Ditrich et al. 1992a). They are slightly smaller in size than the eggs of *H. pumilio* or *H. yokogawai* (Faust and Nishigori 1926; Tesana et al. 1991; Ditrich et al. 1992a).

The cercariae are ophthalmo-pleuro-lophocercus type, with the cercarial body of 89–124 μm long and 31–43 μm wide, with 3 rows of small preoral spines (4 in the first and 5–8 in the second and third), and a long tail of 250–350 μm × 16–22 μm in size, and closely resemble those of other heterophyid species (Ito 1964b; Ditrich et al. 1992b). The metacercarial cysts are elliptical, 190–220 × 160–190 μm, showing the oral sucker, ventral sucker, a baseball glove-shaped ventrogenital sac with 12–16 spines on the ventral sucker, and O-shaped excretory vesicle filled with refractile globules (Rim et al. 2008).

The tegumental ultrastructure of *H. taichui* was studied by Fujino et al. (1989) using adult flukes recovered from experimentally infected hamsters. Almost all surface of the adult worm was covered with scale-like spines, and sensory papillae were present on the anterior two-thirds of the body (Fujino et al. 1989). The opening of the ventrogenital complex was devoid of spines and appeared as a round or slit-like depression of the tegument (Fujino et al. 1989). Sclerites of the ventrogenital complex were not visible in normal, undamaged specimens (Scholz et al. 1991a). *H. taichui* had 10–12 digited, somewhat robust teeth-like tegumental spines, whereas *H. yokogawai* revealed finer and more numerous (14–16) spine teeth (Scholz et al. 1991a). The eggs of *H. taichui* had slender coiled structures on the shell surface with no apparent shoulders, whereas those of *H. pumilio* had surface granular tubercles with minute shoulders on the operculum (Fujino et al. 1989). Ditrich et al. (1992a) observed filamentous structures on the shell surface of *H. taichui, H. yokogawai,* and *Stellatchasmus falcatus*.

Life Cycle

The eggs of *H. taichui* contain a fully matured miracidium and hatch in water (Faust and Nishigori 1926). The miracidium penetrates the tissues of the snail to which it is adapted and metamorphoses into a sporocyst; rediae are produced parthenogenetically within these sporocysts, and after 5–6 weeks mature cercariae develop within the rediae (Faust and Nishigori 1926). The snail intermediate hosts are freshwater snails (thiarid snails), which inluded *Melania obliquegranosa* in Taiwan (experimental) (Faust and Nishigori 1926), *Melanoides tuberculata* and *Melania juncea* in the Philippines (Velasquez 1973a), and *Tarebia granifera* in Hawaii (Martin 1958). Rediae are elongated and recovered from the digestive gland of the snails (Martin 1958; Ito 1964b; Velasquez 1973a). Cercariae are ophthalmo-pleurolophocercus type, with 3 rows of small preoral spines (4 in the first and 5–8 in the second and third), and closely resemble those of other heterophyid species (Ito 1964b; Ditrich et al. 1992b).

They enter between the scales of freshwater fish (Fig. 1.23a), including *Hampala macrolepidota, Hampala dispar, Mystacoleucus marginatus,* and *Barbodes gonionotus* (Scholz et al. 1990) and *Cyclocheilichthys repasson, Cyclocheilichthys armatus, Onychostoma elongatum, H. dispar, Labiobarbus leptocheila,* and *Cirrhinus molitorella* in Lao PDR (Rim et al. 2008), *Cyprinus carpio, Cyprinus auratus, Zacco platypus, Pseudorasbora parva, Rhodeus ocellatus, Gambusia affinis, Puntius orphoides, Puntius leiacanthus, Puntius gonionotus, Puntius binotatus, Puntius palata,* and *Opicephalus striatus* in the Philippines (Velasquez 1973b, 1982). The fish hosts reported in Thailand include *H. dispar, Puntius gonionotus, Puntius leiacanthus, Cyclocheilichthyes armatus, Mystacoleucus atridorsalis,* and *Cirrhinus julleine* (Srisawangwong et al. 1997), *Raiamas guttatus, Mystacoleucus marginatus*, and *Henichorhynchus siamensis* (Kumchoo et al. 2005), and *Barbodes gonionotus, Hampala macrolepidota, Henicorhynchus siamensis, Labiobarbus siamemsis, Morulius chrysophykkadian, Mystacoleucus marginatus, Puntioplites*

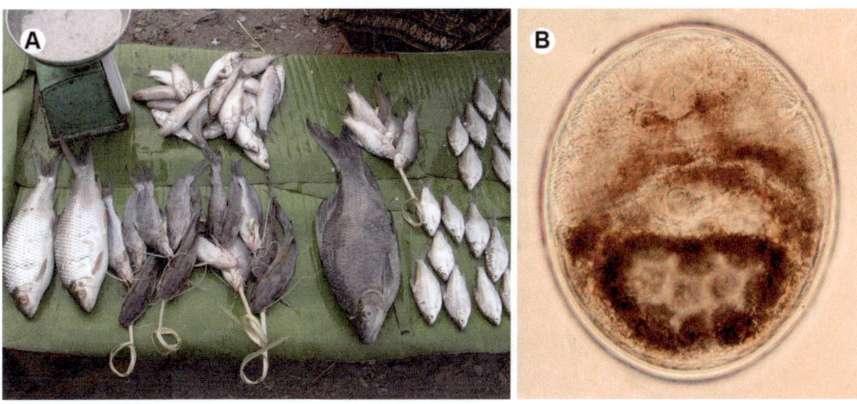

Fig. 1.23 *Haplorchis taichui*. (**a**) Freshwater fish sold in a local market in Vientiane, Lao PDR. Some of these fish are the second intermediate hosts (**b**) Metacercaria isolated from the flesh of a freshwater fish. ×200

proctozysron, and *Systomus orphoides* (Nithikathkul and Wongsawad 2008). In Taiwan, *Hemiculter leucisculus* (Ooi et al. 1997) and *Ctenopharyngodon idellus* (Wang et al. 2002) are also fish hosts for *H. taichui* (Ooi et al. 1997). In mainland China (Nanning, Guangxi Province), *Hypophthalmichthys molitrix, Carassius carassius, Hemibarbus maculatus, Toxabramis houdemeri, Squalidus argentatus, Cyprinus carpio, Abbotina rivularis, Hemiculter leucisculus, Culter Recurviceps, Saurogobio dabryi,* and *Chanodichthys dabryi* have been proved to be the fish hosts for *H. taichui* (Sohn et al. 2009).

The metacercariae (Fig. 1.23b) encyst in the cartilage of the dorsal fin, head, buccal cavity, and gill (Komiya 1965) or muscles and flesh (Ditrich et al. 1990) of these fish hosts. The metacercariae can also be located in muscles of the fish. The longevity of metacercariae in the fish is unknown, but they may be able to survive for several years or throughout the life span of the fish hosts. In 'pla-som' Thai traditional dish which is usually consumed after 3 days of preparation, the metacercariae can survive only 1 day, so eating 'pla-som' may be safe from infection; however, in 'lab-pla' dish which is usually consumed immediately after preparation, the metacercariae can survive longer than 3 h after preparation and may be the major source of infection (Sukontason et al. 1998).

Birds and mammals, including dogs, cats, and humans, have been reported as the natural definitive hosts (Yamaguti, 1958). Experimental definitive hosts include mice, rats, hamsters, guinea pigs, rabbits, cats, and dogs (Faust and Nishigori 1926; Sukontason et al. 2001). A human was also successfully infected with this fluke after swallowing the fish flesh (Faust and Nishigori 1926). The metacercariae develop into adults within 7–9 days in these experimental animals (Faust and Nishigori 1926). The worms initially invade the upper part of the small intestine, but as they mature, they parasitize more and more commonly the middle and lower parts of the small intestine (Faust and Nishigori 1926). Their longevity in humans and animals may be shorter than a few months. The egg laying capacity of *H. taichui* was studied in 25 human patients in Thailand; the number of eggs per day per worm was 82 (Sato et al. 2009a).

Epidemiology and Geographical Distribution

The principal mode of human infection with *H. taichui* is consumption of raw or improperly cooked flesh of freshwater fish. In Thailand and Lao PDR, fermentation is a traditional preservation procedure for freshwater fish, and consumption of semi-fermented fish shortly after preparation increases the risk of human infections with liver (*Opisthorchis viverrini*) and intestinal flukes (*H. taichui, H. pumilio,* and *H. yokogawai*) (Sukontason et al. 1998). Thereby, local fish dishes, notably 'koi-pla', 'pla-som', 'pla-la', and 'lab-pla' are the source of human infections; although, their relative importance is different by each type of dish preparation (Sukontason et al. 1998). Among them, 'lab-pla' and 'pla-som' are more important sources of infection (Radomyos et al. 1998; Sukontason et al. 1998; Onsurathum et al. 2016). Whereas in 'pla-som' which is usually consumed after 3 days of preparation, the metacercariae can survive only 1 day, so eating 'pla-som' may be safe from infection, in 'lab-pla' which is usually consumed immediately after preparation, the metacercariae can survive longer than 3 h after preparation and thus may be the major source of infection (Sukontason et al. 1998). In the Philippines, a local fish dish called 'kinilaw' (freshwater fish seasoned only with salt and vinegar) is popularly consumed (Belizario et al. 2004). Other types of local fish dish in the Philippines include 'sabaw' (boiling fish for several minutes) and 'sugba' (grilling over charcoal) (Belizario et al. 2004). In Vietnam, raw or pickled fish, for example, slices of silver carp, sold in Vietnamese restaurants are popularly consumed (Dung et al. 2007). The geographical distribution (Fig. 1.24) of *H. taichui* is now extended to Thailand, Lao PDR, Cambodia, Vietnam, South China, Taiwan, the Philippines, USA (Hawaii), Egypt, Israel (Palestine), Iraq, Bangladesh, India, Sri Lanka, Malaysia, and Myanmar (Pearson and Ow-Yang 1982; Velasquez 1982; Yu and Mott 1994; Chai et al. 2005a, 2009a, 2014, 2017).

Bangladesh Yu and Mott (1994) and Hung et al. (2013) listed Bangladesh among the countries where *H. taichui* is distributed.

China The metacercariae of *H. taichui* were detected from various kinds of fish in Hainan Island (Kobayasi 1968). However, the presence of human *H. taichui* infection was first documented from Guangxi Province in 2004 (Li et al. 2010). Later, in several different areas of Guangxi Province, 28.0–70.6% (av. 59.6%) prevalence was obtained by fecal examination for small trematode eggs; PCR analysis of the feces revealed that 29 of 46 egg positive cases were due to *H. taichui* (Jeon et al. 2012). The metacercariae of *H. taichui* were detected in 22 of 27 freshwater fish examined in Mashan-xian (total number of metacercariae; 540), and 60 of 68 freshwater fish in Nanning City (total number of metacercariae; 4975), Guangxi Province (Sohn et al. 2009).

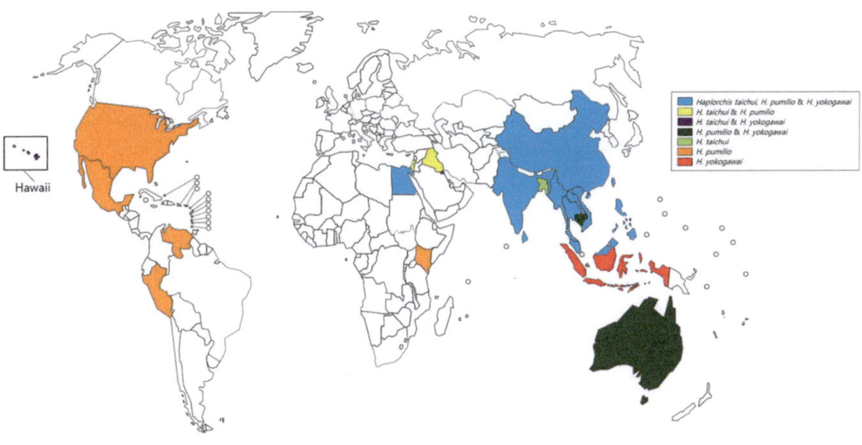

Fig. 1.24 Global distribution of *Haplorchis* spp. (*H. taichui, H. pumilio,* and *H. yokogawai*) based on the presence of their life cycles

Egypt The presence of *H. taichui* in Egypt was first documented by Gohar (1934) from Egyptian kites *Milvus migrans*. Subsequently, Abdel-Azim (1938) found a few specimens of *H. taichui* adults from dogs in Cairo and Upper Egypt. Kuntz and Chandler (1956) also detected this parasite in a cat from Giza Province and a dog in Cairo. The cercariae of *Haplorchis* sp. (*H. taichui* or *H. yokogawai*) were found in brackish water snails, *Pirenella conica*, in several lakes of Upper Egypt (Martin 1959). Later, in 3 localities of Egypt, the metacercariae of *H. taichui,* together with those of *H. pumilio,* were detected in *Tilapia galilae, Tilapia ouria, Tilapia zilii,* and *Tilapia nilotica* fish (Mahdy and Shaheed 2001). It seems that the prevalence of *H. taichui* is much lower than that of *H. pumilio* or *H. yokogawai* in Egypt.

India Odening (1962) reported the occurrence of *Haplorchis* spp. adults in birds and mammals. The metacercariae were recovered from 4 species of freshwater fish, including *Cirrhina reba, Amblypharyngodon mola, Labeo bata,* and *Puntius* sp. (Nath and Pande 1970). In 1964, Simha and Deshpande collected *H. taichui* specimens from foxes *Vulpes bengalensis* in Hyderabad; many other reports on intermediate and definitive hosts are also available from India (Pearson and Ow-Yang 1982).

Iraq *H. taichui* was recovered from domestic dogs in Baghdad by Shaheen et al in 1962 (Pearson and Ow-Yang 1982).

Israel (Palestine) Witenberg (1929) reported *Monorchotrema taichui* (synonym of *H. taichui*) from naturally infected dogs, cats, and a bird (*Larus* sp.) near the Lake Tiberias. Witenberg (1929) also obtained experimentally this fluke after feeding dogs with various species of fish having the metacercariae.

Kuwait In a survey of stray cats, 9 (3.8%) of 240 examined were found to be infected with adult flukes of *H. taichui* (El-Azazy et al. 2015).

Lao PDR The first report of *H. taichui* infection in 5 Laotians was published by Giboda et al. (1991). Thereafter, Rim et al. (2003) reported that the overall positive rate of small trematode eggs (*O. viverrini, H. taichui,* or other minute intestinal flukes) in fecal examinations of Loatian people in 17 provinces and Vientiane Municipality was 10.9% (3263/29,846). According to locality, Vientiane Municipality and Phongsali, Khammouane, Savannakhet, Saravane, Champasak, and Attapeu Provinces revealed higher prevalences (over 10%) than the other provinces (Rim et al. 2003). Chai et al. (2005b) performed worm recovery of *O. viverrini, H. taichui,* or other minute intestinal flukes from small trematode egg positive cases in 2 areas of Lao PDR; the intensity of infection and relative proportion of each fluke species varied by locality along the Mekong River. For example, Vientiane Municipality was highly prevalent with *O. viverrini* worms with a small number of intestinal flukes, including *H. taichui*, but Saravane Province was severely infected with *H. taichui* worms with a small number of *O. viverrini* specimens (Chai et al. 2005b). Hyperendemicity, with high prevalence and heavy worm burden, of *H. taichui* in

Saravane Province was again documented (Chai et al. 2013). In Savannakhet Province, the prevalence of small trematode eggs among the riparian people was 67.1% (658/981), and the worms recovered after chemotherapy and purging of 29 egg-positive people consisted of similar numbers of *O. viverrini* (3347 worms) and *H. taichui* (2977 worms) and smaller numbers of other intestinal fluke species (Chai et al. 2007). In Khammouane Province, the prevalence of small trematode eggs among the riparian people was higher than in Savannakhet Province, 81.1% (1007/1242), and the worms recovered after chemotherapy and purging of 33 egg-positive people consisted of remarkably higher numbers of *H. taichui* (10,691 worms) and *Caprimolgorchis molenkampi* (7510 worms) (under the name *Prosthodendrium molenkampi*) than *O. viverrini* (1377 worms) and *Phaneropsolus bonnei* (910 worms) (Chai et al. 2009b). Similar trends were reported in Vientiane, Savannakhet, and Saravane Province (Sayasone et al. 2009). An interesting finding was that the high prevalence (18.4%) of small trematode eggs notified in Phongsali Province (Rim et al. 2003) was later confirmed to be exclusively due to *H. taichui* and *H. yokogawai* infections but not to *O. viverrini* infection based on worm recovery results of 10 volunteers (Chai et al. 2010). Also in Champasak Province, the infection was mostly due to intestinal flukes, in particular, *H. taichui* followed by *H. pumilio* but only a few specimens of *O. viverrini* were recovered in a few cases (Chai et al. 2013). Exclusive infections only with *H. taichui*, followed by *H. yokogawai* and *H. pumilio,* with no *O. viverrini,* were also confirmed in 10 small trematode egg positive cases in Luang Prabang Province (Sohn et al. 2014). One of 12 helminth egg positive people in Xieng Khouang Province revealed 93 specimens of *H. taichui*, where *H. pumilio* infection was confirmed in 8 of 12 people (total 2268 specimens) (Chai et al. 2015). With regard to animal reservoir hosts, 40.7% of domestic cats (11/27) from Nam Ngum water reservoir area, north of Vientiane, were found to be infected with *H. taichui* (total number of worms; 473) (Ditrich et al. 1990).

The metacercariae of *H. taichui* were detected in a high proportion of freshwater fish caught from different localities of Lao PDR (Rim et al. 2008, 2013). In Vientiane Municipality, 10.0–72.7% of freshwater fish examined were infected with an average of 1.0–17.5 metacercariae of *H. taichui* per fish (Rim et al. 2008). In Savannakhet Province, 8.0–40.0% of freshwater fish examined were infected with an average of 1.0–4.5 metacercariae of *H. taichui* per fish (Rim et al. 2008). However, the prevalence and metacercarial burden was much greater in Luang Prabang Province; 86.4% of freshwater fish examined were infected with an average of 260 metacercariae of *H. taichui* per fish (Rim et al. 2013). Similar high prevalence and intensity of *H. taichui* metacercariae were seen in freshwater fish caught in Khammouane and Saravane Province (Rim et al. 2013).

Malaysia In Ranau and Inanam, North Borneo, *H. taichui* specimens were recovered in the small intestine of Brahminy kites (Pearson and Ow-Yang 1982).

Myanmar The metacercariae of *H. taichui* were detected in 58 (42.3%) of 137 freshwater fish (metacercarial density; av. 42.9/fish) purchased in a local market in Yangon (Chai et al. 2017).

The Philippines In an examination of 27 cattle egrets caught near Manila City, Africa et al. (1936) recovered adult specimens of *H. taichui* or *H. pumilio* in their small intestines. Later, the Lake Lanao, Marawi City, Mindanao Island and U.P. rice paddies, Diliman, Quezon City, and Luzon Island have been listed as endemic areas of *H. taichui* based on fish infections with metacercariae (Velasquez 1973b). Regarding human infections, less than 1% of population is estimated to be infected with heterophyid flukes (Eduardo 1991). However, in southern Mindanao, 36.0% (87/242) egg positive rate was reported; *H. taichui* adult flukes were recovered from some of these patients (Belizario et al. 2004).

Sri Lanka Adults of *H. taichui* were recovered from cats in Gomarankadawelo (Pearson and Ow-Yang 1982).

Taiwan *H. taichui* was originally discovered from Taiwan (Nishigori 1924; Faust and Nishigori 1926). However, there have been few succeeding studies on this fluke in Taiwan. Between 1984 and 1987, metacercariae of *Haplorchis* spp. (may have included *H. taichui*) were detected from freshwater fish in Sun Moon Lake (Cheng 1988). Thereafter, another study in Sun Moon Lake detected the metacercariae of *H. taichui* (4064 of 4223 metacercariae examined under light microscopy) from *Hemiculter leucisculus* (Ooi et al. 1997). In Meinung Township, 451 *Ctenopharyngodon idellus* were examined and 3.3% were found to be positive for *H. taichui* metacercariae (Wang et al. 2002).

Thailand *H. taichui* specimens were collected from stray dogs, 12 (13.3%) of 90 examined, in Bangkok; 1–76 specimens were collected from each dog (Ito et al. 1962). Kliks and Tantachamrun (1974) found this fluke in domestic cats from Chiang Mai; they also detected the metacercariae in freshwater fish (*Puntius leiachanthus, Puntius goniotonus,* and *Puntius orphoides*) and the cercariae from the freshwater snail *Melanoides tuberculata*. Human infection with *Haplorchis* spp. was first recorded in Thailand by Manning and Lertpraesert (1971) and Manning et al. (1971), and then by Kliks and Tantachamrun (1974) and Radomyos et al. (1984). Subsequently, northern parts of Thailand (Nan, Phrae, Uttaradit, Phitsanulok, Phetchabun, Phichit, Sukhothai, Kamphaeng Phet, Nakhon Sawan, Tak, Lampang, Phayao, Chiang Rai, Chiang Mai, Mae Hong Son, and Lamphun Provinces) were found to be endemic areas of *H. taichui*, together with *H. pumilio, H. yokogawai*, and *Opisthorchis viverrini* (Radomyos et al. 1998). The prevalence of *H. taichui* among 431 people from these areas who were subjected to worm recovery after anthelmintic treatment and purging was 63.1%, whereas *O. viverrini* worms were recovered only from 11.6% of them (Radomyos et al. 1998). In another study performed in Phrae Province, 613 km north of Bangkok, the prevalence of *H. taichui* worms among 87 worm-recovery cases was 64.4%, whereas that of *O. viverrini* was 4.6% (Pungpak et al. 1998). In Nan Province, 37 of 50 praziquantel-treated patients were positive for *H. taichui* worms in their diarrheic stools, with average 62 worms per case (5–1520 by individual person), whereas in Lampang Province, 69 of 100 patients revealed *H. taichui* worms, with av. 326 worms per case (1–4277 by individual) (Wijit et al. 2013). In northeastern parts, such as Khon Kaen Province, heterophyid trematodes are common among villagers who enjoy eating insufficiently cooked or raw freshwater fish (Srisawangwong et al. 1997). In 6 species of freshwater fish commonly eaten by the people, the metacercariae of *H. taichui* were the most highly prevalent of all metacercariae which included *H. pumilio, Centrocestus formosanus,* or *O. viverrini* (Srisawangwong et al. 1997). However, little information is available regarding human infections with *H. taichui* in Khon Kaen areas. In Chiang Mai Province, studies have also revealed that the metacercariae of *H. taichui* were up to 384 times more prevalent than those of *O. viverrini* (Sukontason et al. 1999a). Another study in Chiang Mai Province reported that 91.7% of freshwater fish examined (266/290) were positive for *H. taichui* metacercariae; their intensity of infection averaged 242.9 metacercariae per fish (Kumchoo et al. 2005).

USA (Hawaii) Martin (1958) studied on the infection status of *Tarebia granifera* snails with the cercariae of *H. taichui* in Kaneoha, Oahu; the infection rate of the snails was 7%. No further studies have been published in Hawaii.

Vietnam Until 2003, only liver flukes, especially *C. sinensis* and *O. viverrini*, were recognized as foodborne zoonotic trematodes in Vietnam (De et al. 2003). Shortly after then, however, the presence of minute intestinal trematodes, including *H. taichui, H. pumilio,* and *H. yokogawai*, has been confirmed in human infections in 2 communes of Nam Dinh Province, a northern part of Vietnam (Dung et al. 2007). The prevalence of small trematode eggs among riparian people in this area was 64.9% (399/615), and 1–307 specimens of *H. taichui* were recovered in 23 of 33 volunteers who received praziquantel treatment and purging (Dung et al. 2007). However, the positive rate, as well as the worm numbers recovered, was much higher for *H. pumilio* than *H. taichui, H. yokogawai,* or others (Dung et al. 2007). Later, in another commune in Nam Dinh Province, 22.7% (92/405) of household members were positive for small trematode eggs and total 124 specimens of *H. taichui* were recovered from 10 volunteers (De and Le 2011). In 2 different communes of Nam Dinh Province, the metacercariae of *H. taichui* were detected in 0–50% of freshwater fish examined, whereas those of *H. pumilio* were found in 50–100% of them (Skov et al. 2009). Similarly, in freshwater fish purchased from Nam Dinh Province, the metacercariae of *H. taichui* were detected in 60% (3/5 fish; average 2 metacercariae per fish) of *Rasbora aurotaenia* (Chai et al. 2012). In Ninh Binh Province, 20.5% (381/1857) of commune people were positive for small trematode eggs; examination of freshwater fish from this area revealed 56.1% (271/483 fish) positive rate for foodborne zoonotic trematode metacercariae which consisted of *Haplorchis spp., Procerovum varium, Centrocestus formosanus*, and others (Hung et al. 2015). In another northern area, Nghe An Province, dogs (30.0–38.8%), cats (48.6–51.4%), and pigs (7.9–14.0%) were positive for small trematode eggs by different fecal examination techniques, such as Kato-Katz technique, formalin-ether sedimentation technique, and combined technique (Anh et al. 2008). Also in Nghe An Province, a small proportion (1.0–1.9%) of fish from nursery and grow-out systems were infected with metacercariae of *H. taichui*, whereas a large proportion

(41.1–45.2%) harboured metacercariae of *H. pumilio* (Chi et al. 2008). In southern parts of the country, Tien Giang Province and Can Tho City, a small proportion of cultured fish was infected with the metacercariae of *H. taichui*; a higher proportion of the fish was positive for *H. pumilio* (Thien et al. 2007).

1.4.2 Haplorchis pumilio

1.4.2.1 *Haplorchis pumilio* (Looss, 1896) Looss, 1899

[syn. *Monostomum pumilio* Looss, 1896; *Monorchotrema taihokui* Nishigori, 1924; *Kasr aini* Khalil, 1932; *Haplorchis pleurolophocerca* (Sonsino, 1892) Price, 1940; *Haplorchis taihokui* (Nishigori) Yamaguti, 1958]

Taxonomy and Morphology
This species (Fig. 1.25a, b) was originally described in Egypt under the name *Monostomum pumilio* based on adult flukes recovered from the small intestine of birds and mammals (Looss 1896). Subsequently, the genus *Haplorchis* was erected by Looss (1899) and this species was named as *Haplorchis pumilio*. In 1892, in Egypt, Sonsino reported *Cercaria pleurolophocerca* from brackish water snails. Later, Khalil (1932) described its life cycle and named its adults as *Kasr aini*. Price (1940) renamed it as *Haplorchis pleurolophocerca*. However, Pearson (1964)

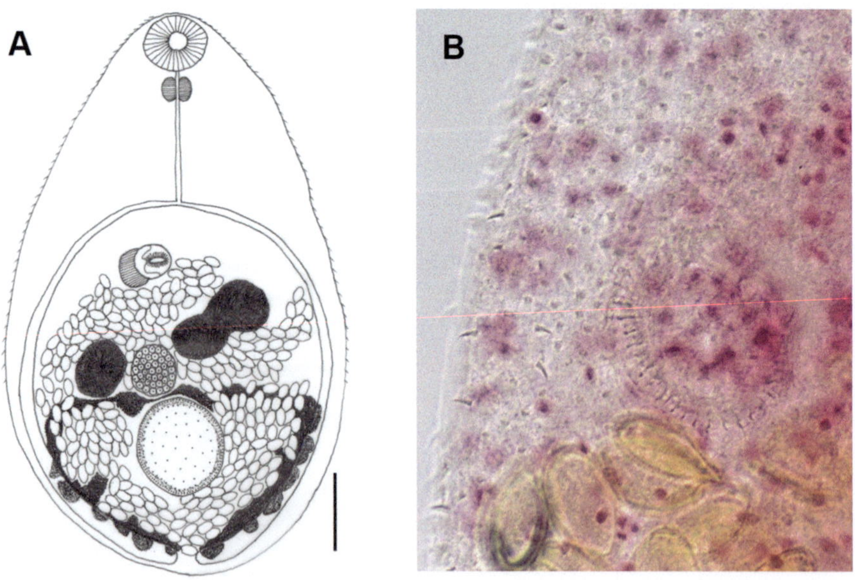

Fig. 1.25 *Haplorchis pumilio*. (**a**) Line drawing of an adult worm (original figure). Scale bar = 0.1 mm (**b**) Enlarged view of the ventral sucker and rodlets on the gonotyl. ×400

suggested this species to be a synonym of *H. pumilio*. In Taiwan, flukes of the same species were discovered and described under the name *Monorchotrema taihokui* (Nishigori 1924). However, Witenberg (1929) suggested that *M. taihokui* should be a synonym of *H. pumilio,* and Chen (1936) regarded *M. taihokui* as a synonym of *H. pumilio.* This species is now known to be distributed widely in Asia, Africa, the Middle East (Witenberg 1929; Pearson 1964; Pearson and Ow-Yang 1982; Velasquez 1982; Yu and Mott 1994; Chai et al. 2014), and even in North and South Americas (Diaz et al. 2008; Huston et al. 2014). Human infections were reported in most of the above countries except Americas (Yu and Mott 1994; Chai et al. 2009a).

The most specific morphological feature for differentiation from other *Haplorchis* species is the size, shape, and number of spines on the ventral sucker (Ujiie 1936; Chen 1936; Pearson and Ow-Yang 1982). The body of *H. pumilio* is oval, and dorsal and ventral sides are flattened; the size of adult flukes is 0.29–0.43 mm long and 0.20–0.26 mm (Faust and Nishigori 1926). *H. pumilio* has a circle of 32–40 I- or Λ-shaped sclerites, 2.5–5.9 μm long, interrupted dorsally between latero-dorsal lobes of the ventral sucker, and a few to 9 small simple spines of various lengths on latero-dorsal and mid-dorsal lobes, respectively (Pearson 1964; Pearson and Ow-Yang 1982). *H. parapumilio* is morphologically most similar to *H. pumilio*, and it has 23–32 I- or Λ-shaped sclerites with the last dorsal ones twice as long as others (Pearson and Ow-Yang 1982). Other species can be differentiated by the presence of a semi-lunar group of 12–16 long, crescentic, and hollow spines up to 19–30 μm long and a sinistral patch of very minute solid spines up to 4 μm long (*H. taichui*), 15–21 hollow spines up to 17 μm long (*H. parataichui*), ventral sucker with 4 lobes and armed with spines (*H. vanissimus*), ventral sucker without lobes and spines interrupted mid-ventrally (*H. paravanissimus*), remarkably large ventral sucker (*H. wellsi*), or a ventral sucker smaller than the oral sucker (*H. yokogawai* and *H. sprenti*) (Pearson and Ow-Yang 1982). The eggs of *H. pumilio* are small, operculate, ovoid, light brown, and 28–33 (av. 30.8) μm long and 15–19 (av. 17.3) μm (Ditrich et al. 1992a), slightly larger than those of *H. taichui* or *H. yokogawai* (Fujino et al. 1989; Ditrich et al. 1992a).

The cercariae are ophthalmo-pleuro-lophocercus type, with the cercarial body of 189–215 μm long and 69–96 μm wide and a tail of 440 × 29 μm in size, with 3 rows of small preoral spines (4 in the first, 5 in the second, and 6 in the third) and closely resemble those of other heterophyid species (Ito 1964b). The metacercarial cysts are round (Fig. 1.26a), 140–150 μm in diameter, showing the oral sucker, ventral sucker armed with hyaline, deer horn-like minute spines, 36–42 in number, and O-shaped excretory vesicle filled with refractile globules (Komiya 1965).

The tegumental ultrastructure of *H. pumilio* was studied by Srisawangwong et al. (1989) and Fujino et al. (1989) using adult specimens and/or eggs recovered from experimentally infected hamsters. Almost all surface of the adult worm was covered with scale-like spines, and many sensory papillae were present on the anterior two-thirds of the body the distribution of which was bilaterally symmetrical, in groups, or singly between spines (Srisawangwong et al. 1989). The eggs of *H. pumilio* had surface granular tubercles with minute shoulders on the operculum, whereas those of *H. taichui* had slender coiled structures on the surface with no apparent shoulders

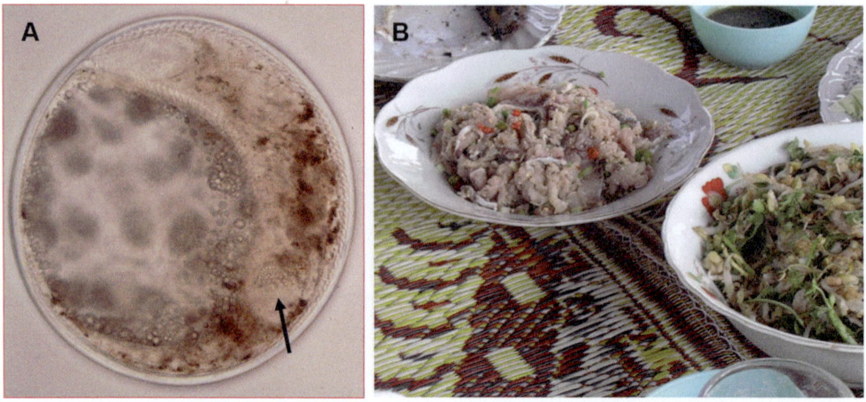

Fig. 1.26 *Haplorchis pumilio*. (**a**) Metacercaria isolated from the flesh of a freshwater fish showing the rodlets (arrow) on the gonotyl. ×200 (**b**) Fish dishes, a potential source of human infections. Vientiane, Lao PDR

(Fujino et al. 1989). Similar findings were reported by other workers (Tesana et al. 1991; Ditrich et al. 1992a).

Life Cycle

The eggs of *H. pumilio* contain a fully matured miracidium and hatch in water (Faust and Nishigori 1926). The mature miracidium has a small anterior cone devoid of cilia; they penetrate the tissues of the snail and metamorphose into a sporocyst; finally, rediae are produced parthenogenetically within these sporocysts, and after 30–40 days cercarial progeny develops within the rediae (Faust and Nishigori 1926). The snail host is *Melania reiniana* var. *hitachiens* (experimental) in Taiwan (Faust and Nishigori 1926; Velasquez 1982) or *Melanoides* (= *Thiara*) *tuberculata* (natural) in Taiwan (Lo and Lee 1996; Wang et al. 2002), India (Umadevi and Madhavi 2006), Egypt (Khalifa et al. 1977; Sommerville 1982; Saad and Abed 1995), and Peru (Pulido-Murillo et al. 2018). Rediae are yellowish brown in color and recovered from the digestive gland of the snails (Ito 1964b; Velasquez 1973a).

The second intermediate host is freshwater or brackish water fish belonging to the Cyprinidae, Siluridae, and Cobitidae, similar to *H. tachui* (Faust and Nishigori 1926; Velasquez 1982). They include *Mugil capito, Ophicephalus striatus, Glossogobius giurus, Therapon plumbeus, Gerris filamentosus, Teuthis javus, Ambassis buruensis, Astatotilapia desfontainesi, Acanthogobius* spp., *Anabas* spp., *Carrssius* spp., *Cyprinus* spp., *Tilapia simonis, Tilapia galilea, Tilapia nilotica, Barbus canis, Barbus longiceps,* and *Puntius binotatus* in the Philippines and other countries (Velasquez 1982). In Lao PDR, *Hampala macrolepidota* and *Esomus longimana* have been reported as the fish hosts (Scholz et al. 1990; Scholz 1991). In Southern China, *H. pumilio* metacercariae were detected in *Microphysogobio fukiensis, Pseudohemiculter dispar, Opsariichthys bidens, Hemibarbus maculatus, Puntius semifascioliatus, Carassius auratus, Melzia lineata, Hypophthalmichthys molitrix, Pseudorasbora parva, Acheilognathus tonkinensis, Toxabramis houdemeri,*

Squalidus argentatus, Cyprinus carpio, Hemiculter leucisculus, Saurogobio dabryi, Culter recurviceps, and *Chanodichthys dabryi* (Sohn et al. 2009). In Taiwan, *Carassius auratus, Clarias fuscus, Channa formosana, Pseudorasbora parva, Phodens ocellatus, Gambusia affinis, Polyacanthus operculatus, Clenophalus tadianus, Misgurnus anguillicaudatus, Parasilurus asotus, Zacco platypus, Cyprinus carpio, Hemiculter leucisculus* and *Ctenopharyngodon idellus* were reported as the fish hosts (Faust and Nishigori 1926; Ooi et al. 1997; Wang et al. 2002). In Vietnam, *Pangasianodon hypophthalmus, Clarias sp., Trichogaster trichopterus,* and *Anabas testudineus* were identified as the fish host for *H. pumilio* (Thien et al. 2007). In Thailand, *Hampala dispar, Puntius gonionotus, Puntius leiacanthus, Cyclocheilichthyes armatus, Mystacoleucus atridorsalis,* and *Cirrhinus julleine* were reported (Srisawangwong et al. 1997). In Vietnam, *Ctenopharyngodon idellus, Hypophthalmichthys molitrix, Labeo rohita, Cirrhnus mrigalo,* and Pacu (scientific name not described) were found to be infected with *H. pumilio* metacercariae (Phan et al. 2010). In Egypt, *Gambusia affinis, Tilapia nilotica, Tilapia zilli, Sarotherodon mossambicus, Sarotherodon spilurus,* and *Sarotherodon galilaea* were reported as the experimental fish hosts (Khalifa et al. 1977; Sommerville 1982). *Tilapia* sp. and *Bagrus bayad* were confirmed to be fish host in Egypt (Tawfik et al. 2000). In India, *Channa punctatus, Channa orientalis, Puntius sophore, Gambusia affinis, and fingerlings of Cyprinus carpio,* and *Therapon jarbua* were found naturally infected and *Therapon jarbua, Esomus danricus,* and *Oreochromis mossambicus* were suitable experimental hosts (Umadevi and Madhavi 2006).

The metacercariae encyst in the head, thorax, gill, buccal cavity, and cartilage in tail (Komiya 1965); however, they also encyst in the muscle of these fish hosts (Ditrich et al. 1990). The longevity of metacercariae in the fish is unknown, but they may be able to survive for years or throughout the life span of the fish hosts.

Fish-eating birds and mammals, including dogs, cats, and humans, have been reported as the natural definitive hosts (Yamaguti 1958; Yu and Mott 1994). Experimental definitive hosts include mice, rats, hamsters, guinea pigs, rabbits, cats, and dogs (Faust and Nishigori 1926; Chai et al. 2012; Nissen et al. 2013; Songsri et al. 2018). The metacercariae develop into adults within 7–9 days in these experimental animals (Faust and Nishigori 1926; Chai et al. 2012). The worms invade the upper part of the small intestine, penetrating deeply between the villi, where they gradually develop to adulthood (Faust and Nishigori 1926). Ten to 13 days after infection, all the worms fully mature, and each organ becomes perfectly developed (Faust and Nishigori 1926). The longevity of adult flukes in humans and animals may be shorter than a few months.

Epidemiology and Geographical Distribution

The principal mode of human infection with *H. pumilio* is consumption of raw or improperly cooked flesh of freshwater fish. In Vietnam, where this parasite is highly endemic, raw or pickled fish, for example, slices of silver carp, sold in Vietnamese restaurants is a major source of infection (Dung et al. 2007). In Thailand and Lao PDR, where fermentation is a traditional preservation method for freshwater fish, semi-fermented fish shortly after preparation is the major source of human infections with liver (*Opisthorchis viverrini*) and intestinal flukes (*H. pumilio, H. taichui,* and *H. yokogawai*) (Sukontason et al. 1998). Practically, local fish dishes (Fig. 1.26b), namely 'Koi-pla', 'lab-pla', and 'pla-som' are important sources of infection (Radomyos et al. 1998; Sukontason et al. 1998; Onsurathum et al. 2016). The 'pla-som' is usually consumed after 3 days of preparation, and the metacercariae can survive only 1 day; therefore, eating 'pla-som' may be relatively safe from infection (Sukontason et al. 1998). However, in 'lab-pla' which is usually consumed immediately after preparation, the metacercariae can survive longer than 3 h after preparation and thus may be the major source of infection (Sukontason et al. 1998). *H. pumilio* is distributed in Vietnam, Thailand, Lao PDR, Cambodia, Myanmar, South China, Taiwan, the Philippines, Australia, Egypt, Kenya, Israel (Palestine), Iraq, India, Sri Lanka, Malaysia, Mexico, Venezuela, and USA (Fig. 1.24) (Witenberg 1929; Pearson 1964; Pearson and Ow-Yang 1982; Velasquez 1982; Yu and Mott 1994; Scholz et al. 2001; Diaz et al. 2008; Chai et al. 2005a, 2009a, 2014, 2017; Huston et al. 2014).

Australia Adult flukes were recovered in the lower third of the small intestine of water rats (*Hydromys chrysogaster*) caught from Brisbane, Queensland (Pearson 1964).

Cambodia Before 2014, no reports were available regarding the existence of *Haplorchis* spp. in Cambodia. Recently, however, a fish survey in Pursat Province, near the Lake Tonlesap, revealed the infection of freshwater fish *Henicorhynchus lineatus* and *Pristolepis fasciata* with the metacercariae of *H. pumilio* (Chai et al. 2014). No human cases have been detected until present.

China The metacercariae of *H. pumilio* were detected from various kinds of fish in Hainan Island (Kobayasi 1968). The presence of human *H. pumilio* infection was first documented in Guangdong Province in 1964 (Li et al. 2010). Later, however, little information is available regarding the distribution of this parasite in China. The cercariae of this parasite were detected in *Melanoides tuberculata* snails collected in Fujian Province (Cheng et al. 1998). The metacercariae of *H. pumilio* were detected from freshwater fish including *Pseudorasbora parva* in Pinyuan County, Guangdong Province (Cheng et al. 2000). The metacercariae were also detected in 34 of 42 freshwater fish examined in Mashan-xian (total number of metacercariae; 7057), 67 of 74 fish in Nanning City (3554), and 34 of 34 fish in Binyang-xian (2046), Guangxi Province (Sohn et al. 2009).

Egypt *H. pumilio* was originally described in Egypt (Looss 1896). Later, Gohar (1934) found *H. pumilio*, together with *H. taichui* and *H. milvi* (synonym of *H. yokogawai*) from Egyptian kites *Milvus migrans*. Kuntz and Chandler (1956) also detected this parasite in 40 cats from Mediterranean Coast, Cairo, Giza Province or Faiyum Province, 2 dogs in Cairo, 1 fox and 2 shrews from Giza Province, and 1 kite from Faiyum Province. Human *H. pumilio* infection in Egypt was first documented by Khalifa et al. (1977) in a 9-year-old child passing diarrheic stools.

Otherwise, human infections have seldom been reported in Egypt. Later, in 3 localities of Egypt, the metacercariae of *H. pumilio,* together with those of *H. taichui,* were detected in *Tilapia galilae, Tilapia ouria, Tilapia zilii,* and *Tilapia nilotica* fish (Mahdy and Shaheed 2001). The life cycle and larval morphology was studied by Saad and Abed (1995) using *Melanoides tuberculata* as the snail host and *Gambusia affinis, Ctenopharyngodon idellus,* and *Tilapia nilotica* as fish hosts. Adult flukes were recovered from experimental dogs fed the metacercariae from fish hosts (Tawfik et al. 2000). The prevalence of *H. pumilio* is much higher than that of *H. taichui* or *H. yokogawai* in Egypt.

India The occurrence of *Haplorchis* spp. or *H. pumilio* metacercariae in freshwater fish was reported by several workers and adult flukes were recovered in birds and mammals (Odening 1962; Pearson and Ow-Yang 1982; Umadevi and Madhavi 2006).

Iraq *H. pumilio* was recovered from domestic dogs in Baghdad by Shaheen et al in 1962 (Pearson and Ow-Yang 1982).

Israel (Palestine) Witenberg (1929) reported *Monorchotrema taihokui* (synonym of *H. pumilio*) from naturally infected dogs and cats around Lake Tiberias and also dogs and cats experimentally infected with the metacercariae in *Tilapia* fish.

Kenya Cultured *Tilapia* fish from a fish farm were commonly infected with the metacercariae of *H. pumilio* (Sommerville 1982).

South Korea A 5-year old child was found to be naturally infected with one specimen of *H. pumilio*, together with 841 *Gymnophalloides seoi* and *3 Gynaecotyla squatarolae* specimens (Chung et al. 2011). However, South Korea is tentatively not listed as an endemic area of *Haplorchis* spp.

Lao PDR The existence of *H. pumilio* in Lao PDR was first documented by Ditrich et al. (1990) in domestic cats and freshwater fish (*Hampala macrolepidota*). Scholz et al. (1990) and Scholz (1991) also detected *H. pumilio* metacercariae in 2 species of freshwater fish, *Hampala macrolepidota* and *Esomus longimana*. The presence of human *H. pumilio* infection was first documented by Chai et al. (2005b) based on recovery of adult flukes after praziquantel treatment and purging. Total 1125 specimens of *H. pumilio* were recovered in 15 patients from Saravane Province and 1 specimen in one patient from Vientiane province (Chai et al. (2005b). Later, in Saravane and Champasak Province, 796 and 247 adult specimens of *H. pumilio* were recovered in 5 and 5 patients, respectively (Chai et al. 2013). In the meantime, Rim et al. (2003) reported that the overall positive rate of small trematode eggs, including *O. viverrini, H. taichui,* and *H. pumilio*, in fecal examinations of Laotian people in 17 provinces and Vientiane Municipality was 10.9% (3263/29,846). Vientiane Municipality and Phongsali, Khammouane, Savannakhet, Saravane, Champasak, and Attapeu Provinces revealed higher prevalences (over 10%) than the other provinces (Rim et al. 2003). In Savannakhet Province, the prevalence of small trematode eggs among the riparian people was 67.1% (658/981), and a small proportion of recovered worms (80 among 7693 fluke specimens) were *H. pumilio* from 3 patients (Chai et al. 2007). In Savannakhet, and Saravane Province, 2–41 *H. pumilio* specimens were recovered from a few patients (Sayasone et al. 2009). In Luang Prabang Province, total 41 specimens of *H. pumilio* were recovered in 4 of 10 patients (Sohn et al. 2014). In Xieng Khouang Province, 2268 specimens of *H. pumilio* were harvested from 8 of 12 helminth egg positive people; *H. taichui* was recovered only in one person (93 specimens) (Chai et al. 2015). With regard to animal reservoir hosts, 18.5% of domestic cats (5/27) from Nam Ngum water reservoir area was found to be infected with *H. taichui* (total number of worms; 473) (Ditrich et al. 1990).

Malaysia In Ranau, North Borneo, *H. pumilio* specimens were recovered in the small intestine of reptiles (*Cerberus rhynchops* and *Varanus salvator*) and a leopard cat (*Prionailurus bengalensis borneoensis*) (Fischthal and Kuntz 1965a, b). Domestic cats and dogs from Kuala Lumpur were found infected with *H. pumilio*, and 13 specimens of *H. pumilio* were recovered from a Brahminy kite in East Malaysia (Pearson and Ow-Yang 1982).

Mexico Scholz et al. (2001) reported the presence of *H. pumilio* metacercariae in freshwater fishes, including *Dormitator latifrons* and *Gobiomorus maculatus*, from Jalisco and Tabasco.

Myanmar The metacercariae of *H. pumilio* were detected in 96 (49.0%) of 196 freshwater fish (metacercarial density; av. 23.6/fish) purchased in a local market in Yangon (Chai et al. 2017).

Peru *Melanoides tuberculata* snails were found to play the role of the first intermediate host of *H. pumilio* and *Centrocestus formosanus* (Pulido-Murillo et al. 2018).

The Philippines Africa et al. (1936) recovered adult specimens of *H. pumilio* or *H. taichui* in the small intestines of 27 cattle egrets caught near Manila City. Later, the Lake Lanao, Marawi City, and Mindanao Island are endemic areas of *H. pumilio* based on recovery of metacercariae in fish (Velasquez 1973b). Human infections with *H. pumilio* have not been documented.

Sri Lanka Adults of *H. pumilio* were recovered from dogs in Colombo (Pearson and Ow-Yang 1982).

Taiwan *H. pumilio* was originally discovered in Egypt (Looss 1896) but subsequently discovered also in Taiwan under the name *Monorchotrema taihokui* (Nishigori 1924; Faust and Nidhigori 1926). Human experimental infection was found to be successful (Faust and Nishigori 1926). However, there have been few succeeding studies on human infections with this fluke in Taiwan. In domestic cats from Hsin-chu Prefecture, adult flukes of *H. pumilio* were recovered in 1959 (Fischthal and Kuntz 1975). Between 1984 and 1987, metacercariae of *Haplorchis* spp. (may have included *H. pumilio* and *H. taichui*) were detected from freshwater fish in Sun Moon Lake (Cheng 1988). The cercariae of *H. pumilio* were detected in *Melanoides tuberculata* snails (under the name *Thiara tuberculata*) in Kinmen Islands (Chao et al. 1993). Another study in Sun Moon Lake detected the metacercariae of *H. taichui* (90 of 4223 metacercariae examined under light microscopy) from *Hemiculter leucisculus* (Ooi et al. 1997). Later, in Meinung Township, 451 *Ctenopharyngodon idellus* were examined and 16.2% (73 fish) were found to be positive for *H. pumilio* metacercariae (Wang et al. 2002).

Thailand Twelve human cases infected with *H. pumilio* were reported by Radomyos et al. (1983, 1984); these were the first report of human *H. pumilio* infection in Thailand. Subsequently, based on adult worm recovery, northern parts of Thailand (Nan, Phrae, Tak, Lampang, Phayao, Chiang Rai, and Chiang Mai Provinces) were found to be endemic areas of *H. pumilio*, together with *H. taichui, H. yokogawai*, and *Opisthorchis viverrini* (Radomyos et al. 1998). The prevalence of *H. pumilio* among 431 volunteer people who were subjected to worm recovery after anthelmintic treatment and purging was 3.0%, whereas *H. taichui* and *O. viverrini* worms were recovered from 63.1% and 11.6%, respectively (Radomyos et al. 1998). In Khon Kaen Province, a northeastern part, the metacercariae of *H. pumilio* were detected in several species of freshwater fish, although the metacercarial numbers were lower than those of *H. taichui* (Srisawangwong et al. 1997). Little information is available regarding human infections with *H. pumilio* in Khon Kaen areas. In Chiang Mai Province, *H. pumilio* metacercariae were detected only in 2 fish species (av. 1.81 metacercariae /fish), whereas *H. taichui* metacercariae were found in 8 fish species (av. 48.9 metacercariae/fish) (Sukontason et al. 1999a).

USA Cercariae of *H. pumilio* were detected from the freshwater snails *Melanoides tuberculata,* and it is likely that the life cycle of *H. pumilio* has become established in many of the aquatic systems, including the San Marcos River (Hays County, Texas) and San Felipe Springs (Val Verde County, Texas) (Huston et al. 2014). However, as of yet, there have been no published reports of *H. pumilio* metacercariae in second intermediate hosts, and neither there have been any reports of definitive hosts infected with *H. pumilio* (Huston et al. 2014).

Venezuela The presence of *H. pumilio* life cycle has been recently identified in Venezuela (Diaz et al. 2008). The snail host was *Melanoides tuberculata*, and the fish host was *Rivulus harti*; experimental infection of ducks fed the fish revealed the adult flukes in their small intestine (Diaz et al. 2008).

Vietnam Until 2003, in Vietnam, only liver flukes, especially *C. sinensis* and *O. viverrini*, were recognized as foodborne zoonotic trematodes (De et al. 2003). However, soon after then, the presence of minute intestinal trematodes, including *H. pumilio, H. taichui,* and *H. yokogawai*, has been confirmed in human infections in 2 communes of Nam Dinh Province, a northern part of Vietnam (Dung et al. 2007). The prevalence of small trematode eggs among riparian people in this area was 64.9% (399/615), and 1–4525 specimens of *H. pumilio* were recovered in all of 33 volunteers who received praziquantel treatment and purging (Dung et al. 2007). The positive rate, as well as the intensity of infection, of *H. pumilio* was much higher than those of *H. taichui* and *H. yokogawai* (Dung et al. 2007). Later, in another commune in Nam Dinh Province, 22.7% (92/405) of household members were positive for small trematode eggs and total 200 specimens of *H. taichui* were recovered from 10 volunteers (De and Le 2011). In 2 different communes of Nam Dinh Province, the metacercariae of *H. pumilio* were detected in 50–100% of freshwater fish examined, whereas those of *H. taichui* were found in 0–50% of them (Skov et al. 2009). Later, in freshwater fish purchased from Hanoi City and Nam Dinh Province, the metacercariae of *H. pumilio* were detected in 73.8% (45/61 fish) with an average metacercarial burden per fish of 129 in Hanoi and 85.5% (59/69 fish) with an average metacercarial burden per fish of 15 in Nam Dinh Province (Chai et al. 2012). In Ninh Binh Province, 20.5% (381/1857) of commune people were positive for small trematode eggs; examination of freshwater fish from this area revealed 56.1% (271/483 fish) positive rate for foodborne zoonotic trematode metacercariae which consisted of *Haplorchis* spp. and other minute intestinal trematodes (Hung et al. 2015). In another northern area, Nghe An Province, dogs (30.0–38.8%), cats (48.6–51.4%), and pigs (7.9–14.0%) were positive for small trematode eggs by different fecal examination techniques, such as Kato-Katz technique, formalin-ether sedimentation technique, and combined technique (Anh et al. 2008). Also in Nghe An Province, a large proportion (41.1–45.2%) of fish from nursery and grow-out systems were infected with metacercariae of *H. pumilio*, whereas a small proportion (1.0–1.9%) harboured metacercariae of *H. taichui* (Chi et al. 2008). Similarly, in southern parts of Vietnam, i.e., Tien Giang Province and Can Tho City, a high proportion of cultured fish was positive for *H. pumilio* metacercariae, whereas only a small proportion of them was infected with *H. taichui* metacercariae (Thien et al. 2007).

1.4.3 Haplorchis yokogawai

1.4.3.1 *Haplorchis yokogawai* (Katsuta, 1932) Chen, 1936

[syn. *Monorchotrema yokogawai* Katsuta, 1932; *Haplorchis milvi* Gohar, 1934; *Haplorchis yokogawai* var. *elliptica* Kobayashi, 1942; *Haplorchis nhatrangensis* Kobayasi, 1954]

Taxonomy and Morphology

This species (Fig. 1.27a, b) was originally described in Taiwan under the name *Monorchotrema yokogawai* from adult flukes obtained in the small intestine of dogs and cats experimentally fed the metacercariae encysted in the mullet *Mugil*

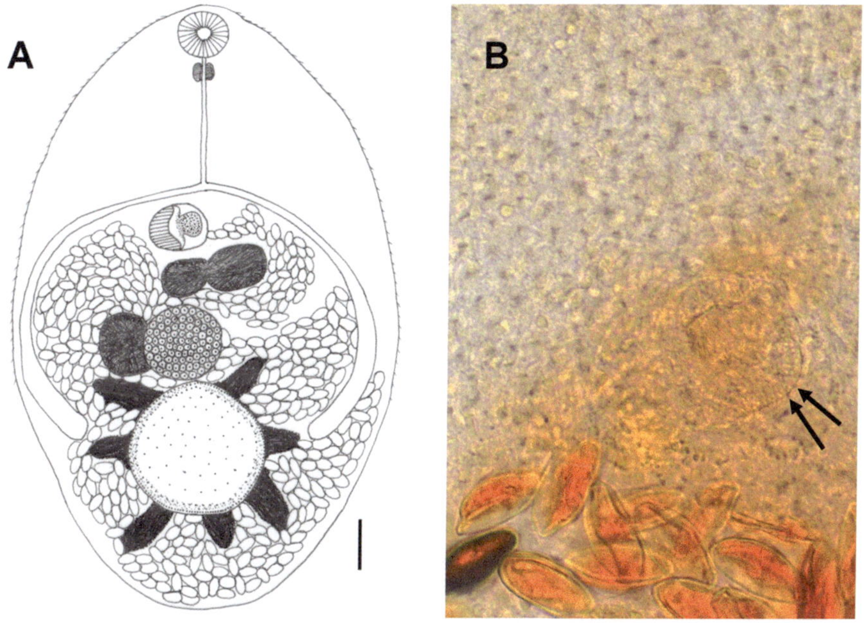

Fig. 1.27 *Haplorchis yokogawai.* (**a**) Line drawing of an adult worm (original figure). Scale bar = 0.05 mm (**b**) Enlarged view of the ventral sucker and rodlets (arrows) on the gonotyl. ×400

cephalus (Katsuta 1932b). Chen (1936) renamed this species as *Haplorchis yokogawai*. Prior to this, Gohar (1934) described a species, *Haplorchis milvi*, from the Egyptian kites. However, Chen (1936) mentioned on this species but suggested that *H. milvi* may fall into synonymy with *H. yokogawai* if the type specimen is restudied. Later, Kuntz and Chandler (1956) proposed to regard *H. milvi* as a synonym of *H. yokogawai*. In Southern China (Hainan Island), Kobayasi (1942) reported *Haplorchis yokogawai* var. *elliptica* from experimental dogs fed the metacercariae in mullets. However, Pearson (1964) synonymized this species with *H. yokogawai*. Later, Kobayasi (1954) described another new species, *H. nhatrangensis*, from puppies and cats fed the metacercariae in fish from French Indo-China. However, *H. nhatrangensis* is not significantly different from *H. yokogawai*, and it should be treated as a synonym of *H. yokogawai*. This species has been reported mostly in Asian-Pacific countries, the Middle East, North Africa, and Oceania (Pearson 1964; Velasquez 1982; Yu and Mott 1994; Chai et al. 2014, 2017). Human infections were reported mainly in Asian countries (Yu and Mott 1994; Chai et al. 2009a).

The most specific morphological feature for differentiation from other *Haplorchis* species is the size, shape, and number of spines on the ventral sucker (Ujiie 1936; Chen 1936; Pearson and Ow-Yang 1982). The body is ovoid to oval and flat on dorsal and ventral sides; the adult flukes are 0.50–0.72 mm long and 0.18–0.32 mm (Katsuta 1932b). *H. yokogawai* has a small ventral sucker with its apex comprising a large ventral lobe armed with numerous tiny spines (<1 μm long) and a pair of large variable-sized sclerites ventro-dextrally, and 3 small lobes (one sinistral, one dorsal, and one dextral) armed with tiny spines (Chen 1936; Pearson and Ow-Yang 1982). The total number of tiny spines (Fig. 1.27b) on the ventral sucker was reported to be 70–74 (Katsuta 1932b) but difficult to count by other authors (Chen 1936; Pearson 1964; Pearson and Ow-Yang 1982). Ceca of *H. yokogawai* exceed the middle level of the testis (Pearson and Ow-Yang 1982). *H. sprenti* is most similar to *H. yokogawai* in the armature of the ventral sucker but the former differs from the latter in lacking the 2 large variable-sized sclerites on the ventral lobe and having ceca not exceeding the middle of the testis (Pearson and Ow-Yang 1982). *H. pumilio* is morphologically similar to *H. yokogawai* but the latter has 23–32 I- or Λ-shaped sclerites on the ventral sucker (Pearson and Ow-Yang 1982). Other species can be differentiated by the presence of 15–21 large spines up to 17 μm long (*H. parataichui*), ventral sucker with 4 lobes and armed dorsal pocket (*H. vanissimus*), ventral sucker without lobes but with armed dorsal pocket with tiny spines interrupted mid-ventrally (*H. paravanissimus*), or remarkably large ventral sucker (*H. wellsi*) (Pearson and Ow-Yang 1982). The eggs of *H. yokogawai* are small, operculate, ovoid, light brown, and 26–31 (av. 28.6) μm long and 14–17 (av. 15.4) μm (Ditrich et al. 1992a), and slightly smaller than those of *H. taichui* or *H. pumilio* (Fujino et al. 1989; Ditrich et al. 1992a).

The cercariae are ophthalmo-pleuro-lophocercus type, smaller than those of *H. taichui* and *H. pumilio*, with the cercarial body of 68–96 μm × 37–50 μm and the tail of 310–353 μm × 15–21 μm in size, with 3 rows of small preoral spines (6 in the first row), and closely resemble those of other heterophyid species (Ito 1964b). The metacercarial cysts are elliptical, 170–240 × 150–230 μm, showing the oral sucker, U-shaped ventral sucker armed with minute barely visible spines, 70–74 in number, and O-shaped excretory vesicle occupying the great part of the posterior body (Rim et al. 2008).

The tegumental ultrastructure of *H. yokogawai* was studied by Scholz et al. (1991a) using adult flukes recovered from naturally infected domestic cats. The tegumental surface of the adult worm was covered with scale-like spines, and sensory papillae were present on the anterior two-thirds of the body (Scholz et al. 1991a). The opening of the ventrogenital complex was devoid of spines, and sclerites of the ventrogenital complex were not visible in normal, undamaged specimens (Scholz et al. 1991a). *H. yokogawai* had fine 14–16 digitated tegumental spines, whereas *H. taichui* revealed somewhat robust, less digitated (12–14) spines (Scholz et al. 1991a). The eggs of *H. yokogawai* had some filamentous structure on the surface and no apparent shoulders were recognizable (Ditrich et al. 1992a).

Life Cycle

The eggs of *H. yokogawai* contain a fully matured miracidium and hatch in water. The mature miracidium penetrate the tissues of the snail and metamorphose into a sporocyst; finally, rediae are produced within these sporocysts, and after 30–40 days cercarial progeny develops within the rediae (see for *H. pumilio* and *H. taichui* in Faust and Nishigori 1926). The snail host is *Melanoides* (= *Thiara*) *tuberculata* or *Stenomelania newcombi* (Ito 1964b; Velasquez 1982). Rediae are slender and elongated to saccular and recovered from the digestive gland of the snails (Martin 1958; Ito 1964b). Cercariae are ophthalmo-pleuro-lophocercus type, smaller than those of *H. taichui* and *H. pumilio*, and invade the skin of freshwater or brackish water fish (Ito 1964b; Ditrich et al. 1992b).

The fish hosts reported include *Gerris kapas, Amphacanthus javus, Ophicephalus stratus, Ambassis burunensis, Hemiramphus georgii, Mugil affinis, Puntius orphoides, Puntius leicanthus, Puntius gonionotus, Clarias fuscus, Boleophthalmus* spp., *Pectinirostris* spp., *Mullus* spp., and *Misgurnus* spp. in Taiwan, the Philippines, South China, Malaysia, northern Thailand, India, Australia, and Egypt (Velasquez 1982). In addition, in Vietnam, *Cirrhinus molitorella, Hypophthalmichthys molitrix, Carassius auratus, Albulichthys albuloides, Parabramis pekinensis, Ctenopharyngodon idella, barbodes balleroides, Anabas testudineus, Puntius semifasciolatus, Rasbora aurotaenia, Colia lindmani, Trichogaster trichopterus,* and *Acheilgnathus barbatulus* have been found to harbor the metacercariae (Chai et al. 2012). In Lao PDR, *Onychostoma elongatum, Onychostoma fusiforme, Cyclocheilichthys apogon, Cyclocheilichthys armatus, Cyclocheilichthys enoplos, Cyclocheilichthys furcatus, Cyclocheilichthys repasson, Hampala dispar, Labiobarbus leptocheila, Osteochilus hasseltii, Cirrhinus molitorella, Hypsibarbus wetmorei, Hypsibarbus lagleri, Hypsibarbus pierri, Scaphognathops bandanensis, Sinibrama melrosei, Mystacoleucus ectypus, Mystacoleucus greenwayi, Lobocheilos rhabdoura, Crossocheilus oblongus, Puntioplites proctozysron, Poropuntius dearatus, Paralaubuca barroni,* and *Puntius brevis* (Rim et al. 2008, 2013) were reported as the fish hosts from different localities. In Cambodia, *Puntioplites proctozysron, Cirrhinus jullieni, Labeo chrysphekadion, Lobocheilos rhabdoura,* and *Barbonymus altus* were reported as the fish hosts (Chai et al. 2014). In India, *Mugil cepahlus, Liza macrolepis,* and *Valamugil cunnesius* were shown to be fish hosts for *H. yokogawai* (Rekharani and Madhavi 1985). In Egypt, *Tilapia nilotica* and *Gambusia affinis* were experimental fish hosts for *H. yokogawai* (Fahmy et al. 1986) and *Tilapia nilotica* and *Tilapia zilli* were also natural fish hosts (Lobna et al. 2010). The metacercariae encyst predominantly in fins and scales (Ditrich et al. 1990). The longevity of metacercariae may be relatively short.

Fish-eating birds and mammals, including dogs, cats, cattle, and humans, have been reported as the natural definitive hosts (Yamaguti 1958; Yu and Mott 1994). Experimental definitive hosts include mice, cats, dogs, and humans (Katsuta 1932b). The metacercariae develop into adults within 7–9 days in these experimental animals (Katsuta 1932b). It seems that the worms invade the mucosa of the small intestine and penetrate deeply between the villi, where they gradually develop to adult flukes (see Faust and Nishigori 1926 for *H. taichui* and *H. pumilio*). The longevity of adult flukes in humans and animals may be shorter than a few months.

Epidemiology and Geographical Distribution

Humans are contracted with *H. yokogawai* through consumption of raw or improperly cooked flesh of freshwater fish. In Thailand and Lao PDR, consumption of semi-fermented fish shortly after preparation is the major risk for human infections with liver (*Opisthorchis viverrini*) and intestinal flukes (*H. yokogawai* and other minute intestinal flukes) (Sukontason et al. 1998). Practically, local fish dishes, notably 'lab-pla' and 'pla-som' are important sources of infection (Radomyos et al. 1998; Sukontason et al. 1998; Onsurathum et al. 2016). In 'lab-pla', the metacercariae can survive longer than 3 h after preparation, but 'lab-pla' is usually consumed immediately after preparation (Sukontason et al. 1998); therefore, 'lab-pla' may be the major source of infection among Thai and Laotians. In the Philippines, local fish dishes called 'kinilaw' (freshwater fish seasoned only with salt and vinegar), 'sabaw' (boiling fish for several minutes), and 'sugba' (grilling over charcoal) are popularly consumed and seem to be the source of infection with *Haplorchis* spp. (Belizario et al. 2004;). In Vietnam, raw or pickled fish, for example, slices of silver carp, is an example of the infection source (Dung et al. 2007). The presence of this fluke has been reported in the Philippines, South China, Taiwan, Malaysia, Indonesia, Thailand, Lao PDR, Cambodia, Myanmar, Vietnam, India, Sri Lanka, Kuwait, Australia, USA (Hawaii), and Egypt (Pearson 1964; Velasquez 1982; Yu and Mott 1994; Chai et al. 2005a, 2009a, 2014, 2017).

Australia Adult flukes were recovered in the lower portion of the small intestine of domestic cats, water rats (*Hydromys chrysogaster*), and whistling eagle (*Haliastur sphenurus*) caught from Brisbane, Queensland (Pearson 1964).

Cambodia Before 2014, no reports were available regarding the existence of *Haplorchis* spp. in Cambodia. Recently, however, a fish survey in Pursat Province, near the Lake Tonlesap, revealed the infection of freshwater fish *Puntioplites falcifer* with the metacercariae of *H. yokogawai* (Chai et al. 2014). No human infections have been detected until present.

China Chen (1936) detected infection of dogs and cats from Canton (Guangdong) with *H. yokogawai*. The metacercariae of *H. yokogawai* and *H. yokogawai elliptica* Kobayasi, 1942 (synonymized with *H. yokogawai* by Pearson 1964) were detected from various kinds of fish in Hainan Island (Kobayasi 1942, 1968). The presence of human *H. pumilio* infection was first documented in Guangdong Province in 1979 (Li et al. 2010). Later, however, little information is available regarding the distribution of this parasite in China.

Egypt The presence of *H. yokogawai* in Egypt (erroneously described as *H. pumilio*; Kuntz and Chandler 1956) was first documented by Gohar (1934) from Egyptian kites *Milvus migrans*. Kuntz and Chandler (1956) also detected this parasite in 16 cats from Mediterranean Coast, Cairo, and Giza Province, 2 dogs in Cairo, and one kite in Faiyum Province. The cercariae of *Haplorchis* sp. (*H. yokogawai* or *H. taichui*) were found in brackish water snails, *Pirenella conica*, in several lakes of Upper Egypt (Martin 1959). The metacercariae of *H. yokogawai* were collected from fish in Assiut Province and successfully infected to dogs and cats (Fahmy et al. 1976). Later, in the same province, natural infection of freshwater snails, *Melanoides tuberculata*, with cercariae were detected which were experimentally infected to *Tilapia nilotica* and *Gambusia affinis* fish, and finally adult flukes were obtained from experimental rats (Fahmy et al. 1986). In Dakhalia Governorate, *H. yokogawai* metacercariae were detected from 2 species of freshwater fish, i.e., *Tilapia nilotica* and *Tilapia zilli* (Elshazly et al. 2007). Later, in Ismailia area, 165 of 173 *Tilapia zilli* were infected with heterophyid metacercariae, and 162 (93.6%) of 173 fish were infected with *H. yokogawai*, with metacercarial density of 4–370 per fish (Ibrahim and Soliman 2010). Lobna et al. (2010) detected metacercariae of various species of heterophyids which includes *H. yokogawai* from *Tilapia nilotica* and *Tilapia zilli* caught at Qalyobia and Dakahlia Governorates and obtained adult flukes after feeding them to puppies.

India Gupta and Pande (1965) detected *H. yokogawai* adults in domestic dogs and cats from Mathura. The metacercariae were recovered from 4 species of freshwater fish, including *Cirrhina reba, Amblypharyngodon mola, Labeo bata,* and *Puntius* sp. (Nath and Pande 1970) and 3 species of mullets, including *Mugil cepahlus, Liza macrolepis,* and *Valamugil cunnesius* (Rekharani and Hadhavi 1985). In 1971, Srivastava detected adult flukes from pheasant crows (*Centropus sinensis*) from Mathura (Pearson and Ow-Yang 1982).

Indonesia Lie Kian Joe (1951) reported adult fluke infections in humans and cats in Java, and found metacercariae in *Clarias batrachus* fish.

Kuwait One (0.4%) of 240 stray cats examined was found to be infected with adult flukes of *H. yokogawai* (El-Azazy et al. 2015).

Lao PDR The existence of *H. yokogawai* in Lao PDR was first documented by Ditrich et al. (1990) in 11 domestic cats. The presence of human *H. yokogawai* infection was first documented by Chai et al. (2005b) based on recovery of adult flukes after praziquantel treatment and purging. Total 65 specimens of *H. yokogawai* were recovered in 2 patients from Vientiane Province and 22 specimens in one patient from Saravane province (Chai et al. 2005b). Low grade infections were detected in Savannakhet Province; 2 of 29 people treated with praziquantel and purging expelled 3 specimens of *H. yokogawai* (Chai et al. 2007). In another study in Savannakhet and Saravane Province, 154 specimens of *H. yokogawai* were recovered from a small number of patients (Sayasone et al. 2009). Phongsali Province was subsequently confirmed to be an endemic area of *Haplorchis* spp., predominantly with *H. taichui* (861 specimens from 8 of 10 volunteers) and with a smaller number of *H. yokogawai* (59 specimens from 6 of 10 volunteers) but not *O. viverrini* infection based on worm recovery (Chai et al. 2010). Similarly, in Luang Prabang Province, total 83 specimens of *H. yokogawai* were recovered in 5 of 10 patients (Sohn et al. 2014). With regard to animal reservoir hosts, 40.7% of domestic cats (11/27) from Nam Ngum water reservoir area was found to be infected with *H. yokogawai* (total number of worms; 322) (Ditrich et al. 1990).

The metacercariae of *H. yokogawai* were detected in a high proportion of freshwater fish caught from different localities of Lao PDR (Rim et al. 2008, 2013). In

Vientiane Municipality, 10.0–100% of freshwater fish examined were infected with an average of 5.0–335.0 metacercariae of *H. yokogawai* per fish in Vientiane Municipality; *H. yokogawai* metacercariae were not detected in Savannakhet Province (Rim et al. 2008). In Luang Prabang Province; 70.8% of freshwater fish examined were infected with an average of 362 metacercariae of *H. yokogawai* per fish (Rim et al. 2013). Similar high prevalence and intensity of *H. yokogawai* metacercariae were seen in freshwater fish caught in Khammouane and Saravane Province (Rim et al. 2013).

Malaysia In East Malaysia, 13 specimens of *H. yokogawai* were recovered from a Brahminy kite (Pearson and Ow-Yang 1982). It is also stated that the life cycle of *H. yokogawai* is distributed in Malaysia (Hung et al. 2013).

Myanmar The metacercariae of *H. yokogawai* were detected in 40 (50.0%) of 80 freshwater fish (metacercarial density; av. 30.6/fish) purchased in a local market in Yangon (Chai et al. 2017).

The Philippines Human infections with *H. yokogawai* were described by Africa et al. (1940) from 16 of 33 human autopsies in the Philippines. Later, however, the presence of this parasite has seldom been traced. Vasquez-Colet and Africa (1940) detected the metacercariae of *H. yokogawai* in several species of fishes. The metacercariae were also found in milkfish obtained from fishponds in Malabon, Rizal (Velasquez 1983).

Sri Lanka In 1971, Kannangara detected *H. yokogawai* adults in domestic dogs and fishing cats (*Felis viverrina*) from Gomarankadawela (Pearson and Ow-Yang 1982).

Taiwan *H. yokogawai* was originally discovered from dogs and cats fed infected mullets Taiwan, and the possibility of human infection was proved by a human experimental infection (Katsuta 1932b). However, there have been few succeeding studies on this fluke in Taiwan.

Thailand *H. yokogawai* specimens were collected from stray dogs, 2 (2.2%) of 90 examined, in Bangkok; 14–57 specimens were collected from each dog (Ito et al. 1962). Kliks and Tantachamrun (1974) found this fluke in domestic cats from Chiang Mai; they also detected the metacercariae in freshwater fish (*Puntius leiachanthus, Puntius goniotonus,* and *Puntius orphoides*) and the cercariae from the freshwater snail *Melanoides tuberculata*. Human infection with *Haplorchis yokogawai* was first recorded by Manning and Lertpraesert (1971) and Manning et al. (1971), and then by Kliks and Tantachamrun (1974) and Radomyos et al. (1984). Subsequently, northern parts of Thailand (Nan, Phrae, Uttaradit, Phitsanulok, Phetchabun, Nakhon Sawan, Tak, Lampang, Phayao, Chiang Rai, and Chiang Mai Provinces) were found to have human cases infected with *H. yokogawai*, in co-infection with *H. taichui, H. pumilio,* and *Opisthorchis viverrini* (Radomyos et al.

1998). In these areas, the prevalence of *H. yokogawai* among 431 people who were subjected to worm recovery after anthelmintic treatment and purging was 10.4% (Radomyos et al. 1998). In another study performed in Phrae Province, the prevalence of *H. yokogawai* among 87 worm-recovery cases was 2.3%, much lower than 64.4% of *H. taichui* (Pungpak et al. 1998).

USA (Hawaii) Martin (1958) reported that *Stenomelania newcombi* snails from Oahu were the first intermediate host of *H. yokogawai*, and the metacercariae were experimentally established in Chinese catfish *Clarias fuscus*; cats were a successful experimental definitive host, and night herons were found a natural definitive host.

Vietnam Until 2003, only liver flukes (*Clonorchis sinensis* and *Opisthorchis viverrini*) were recognized as foodborne zoonotic trematodes in Vietnam (De et al. 2003). Shortly after then, the presence of minute intestinal trematodes, including *H. yokogawai,* together with *H. pumilio* and *H. taichui* has been confirmed in human infections in 2 communes of Nam Dinh Province, a northern part of Vietnam (Dung et al. 2007). However, the prevalence and worm burden of *H. yokogawai* were markedly lower than those of *H. pumilio* and *H. taichui* (Dung et al. 2007). In Ninh Binh Province, 20.5% (381/1857) of commune people were positive for small trematode eggs; examination of freshwater fish from this area revealed 56.1% (271/483 fish) positive rate for foodborne zoonotic trematode metacercariae (Hung et al. 2015); however, the prevalence of *H. yokogawai* seems to be very low. In another northern area, Nghe An Province, dogs (30.0–38.8%), cats (48.6–51.4%), and pigs (7.9–14.0%) were positive for small trematode eggs but infections due to *H. yokogawai* may be low (Anh et al. 2008). Also in Nghe An Province, a very low proportion (0.2%) of fish from grow-out systems were infected with metacercariae of *H. yokogawai*, whereas a large proportion (41.1%) harboured metacercariae of *H. pumilio* (Chi et al. 2008).

1.4.4 Haplorchis vanissimus

1.4.4.1 *Haplorchis vanissimus* (Africa, 1938) Yamaguti, 1958

[syn. *Haplorchis vanissima* Africa, 1938]

Taxonomy and Morphology

This species was originally described from adult flukes recovered at an autopsy of a Filipino in the Philippines and described under the name *Haplorchis vanissima* (Africa 1938). Abdel-Azim (1938) found specimens with similar morphology from Egyptian dogs and argued that *H. vanissimus* is a synonym of *H. milvi* which was originally described from Egyptian kites (Gohar 1934). However, Kuntz and Chandler (1956) pointed out that Abdel-Azim probably had found *H. yokogawai*, not *vanissimus*. Later, this species was found in pelicans and wild mammals in Australia (Pearson and Ow-Yang 1982).

The specific morphological characters of *H. vanissimus* include the presence of 4 armed lobes and an armed dorsal pocket on the ventral sucker with spines continuous across the width of ventral face (Pearson and Ow-Yang 1982). It is readily distinguished from the other species of *Haplorchis* (*H. pumilio, H. parapumilio, H. taichui, H. parataichui, H. yokogawai, H. wellsi,* and *H. sprenti*) by the form and spination of the ventral sucker and especially by the occurrence of spines in the dorsal pocket of the ventrogenital sac (Pearson 1964; Pearson and Ow-Yang 1982). The most closely resembled species is *H. paravanissimus* which has a simple ventral sucker without obvious lobes and the presence of minute spines interrupted mid-ventrally (Pearson and Ow-Yang 1982).

Adult flukes of *H. vanissimus* are small, pyriform, divided by constriction into fore- and hindbody, and 0.47–0.57 (av. 0.51) mm in toal length and 0.12–0.18 (av. 0.14) mm in width of the forebody (Pearson 1964). The eggs (ueterine) are small, ovoid, and 23–26 (av. 25) μm long and 11–13 (av. 12) μm wide (Pearson 1964). Larval stages, including the cercariae and metacercariae have not been found.

Life Cycle

The life cycle of this species is poorly known. The snail host is unknown. Probably freshwater fish play the role of the second intermediate hosts (Yu and Mott 1994). Humans are a natural definitive host (Africa 1938). In Australia, fish-eating birds, such as *Phalacrocorax ater* (little black cormorant), *Haliastur sphenurus* (whistling eagle), and *Nycticorax caledonicus* (nankeen night heron), were found to be natural definitive hosts (Pearson 1964). Dogs and cats are also included among the definitive hosts of *H. vanissimus* (Hung et al. 2013). The habitat of adult flukes in the avian hosts is the lower third of the small intestine (Pearson 1964).

Epidemiology and Geographical Distribution

After this species was first reported at an autopsy of a Filipino in the Philippines (Africa 1938) and morphologically redescribed by Pearson (1964) based on specimens recovered from naturally infected birds in Brisbane, Australia, few studies have been performed regarding the life cycle and epidemiology of this parasite. No further human infections have been documented. Freshwater fish species may play the role of the source of human infection; however, the practical mode of human infection or the type of fish dish involved is unknown. The geographical distribution of this fluke is confined to the Philippines and Australia.

1.4.5 Potentially Zoonotic **Haplorchis** *spp.*

Potentially zoonotic *Haplorchis* spp. include *H. parataichui* Pearson, 1964; *H. sprenti* Pearson, 1964; *H. wellsi* Pearson, 1964; *H. parapumilio* Pearson and Ow-Yang, 1982; *H. paravanissimus* Pearson and Ow-Yang, 1982.

1.4.6 Genomics and Proteomics

A rapid and sensitive tool for detecting *H. taichui* with low DNA concentrations and for distinguishing *H. taichui* from *Opisthorchis viverrini, H. pumilio,* and *H. yokogawai* has been developed by Thaenkham et al. (2007). They used mitochondrial cytochrome *c* oxidase subunit I (COI) gene, and by polymerase chain reaction (PCR) at 56°C, only *H. taichui* could be amplified, whereas by PCR at 50°C-56°C, *H. pumilio* and *H. yokogawai* were amplified with low sensitivity (Thaenkham et al. 2007). In addition, PCR-restriction fragment length polymorphism (RFLP) profiles were suggested to be useful for diagnosing mixed *H. taichui* and *O. viverrini* infection (Thaenkham et al. 2007). Subsequently, PCR diagnosis was applied to field surveys and it was shown to be valuable and sensitive diagnostic tool for low-intensity *H. taichui* and *O. viverrini* infection (Lovis et al. 2009). Moreover, the high annealing temperature-based random amplified polymorphic DNA (HAT-RAPD) technique was developed using specific primers to discriminate *H. taichui* infection from various other infections, including *O. viverrini* and *Stellantchasmus falcatus* which generated a 256 bp amplicon and showed a positive result only for *H. taichui* (Wongsawad et al. 2009). A multiplex PCR assay was also developed using specific primers for *H. taichui* derived from HAT-RAPD (Wongsawad and Wongsawad 2012). PCR targeting ITS1 and ITS2 regions of ribosomal DNA revealed useful results; particularly in ITS2 region, the amplicon size for *H. taichui* was significantly different from that of *O. viverrini, C. sinensis,* and *H. pumilio* (Sato et al. 2009b). Molecular techniques were also applied to determine the prevalence of *H. taichui* cercariae in the snail host in Chiang Mai Province, Thailand; the positive rate of *H. taichui* from specific PCR was 9.7% (Chontananarth and Wongsawad 2010). Molecular techniques were also used in Vietnam (De and Le 2011; Le et al. 2017), China (Jeon et al. 2012), and Thailand (Wongsawad et al. 2012; Sato et al. 2015) to detect human infections with *H. pumilio* and *H. taichui* (Vietnam) and *H. taichui* (China and Thailand). The complete mitochondrial genome of *H. taichui* was obtained and comparatively analyzed with other trematodes (Lee et al. 2013). However, Lao, Thai, and Vietnamese populations of *H. taichui* are genetically distant from one another (Thaenkham et al. 2016). Dung et al. (2013) studied on genetic variation of 3 Vietnamese isolates and attributed the low gene flow among them to topographic features that isolated them geographically, including mountainous and wetland areas. However, based on the results of mitochondrial *COX1* gene analysis, another hypothesis was made in Thailand, Lao PDR, and Vietnam that the population structure of *H. taichui* is affected by the national border rather than environmental factors such as common river basins and distribution of intermediate hosts (Thaenkham et al. 2016). Further studies are required to elucidate this point.

1.4.7 Pathology and Immunology

In the Philippines, Africa et al. (1940) reported extraintestinal heterophyidiasis (cardiac, cerebral, and spinal) in humans based on autopsy findings. Six species of heterophyid flukes, including 3 *Haplorchis* spp. (*H. taichui, H. yokogawai,* and *H. vanissimus*), *Stellantchasmus falcatus, Procerovum calderoni,* and *Microphallus brevicaeca* (syn. *Heterophyes brevicaeca* Africa and Garcia 1935; *Spelotrema brevicaeca* Tubangui and Africa 1938; *Carneophallus brevicaeca* Velasquez, 1975), were reported to be involved in causing intestinal, other visceral, or both infections. Many of the patients died due to these complications. Yokogawa (1940) suggested that these patients may have been immunocompromised to become unable to resist otherwise mild heterophyid or microphallid infections. However, the pathogenicity, as well as the pathology of each *Haplorchis* species infection, has not been well established. In Thailand, a human autopsy case infected with *H. taichui* and 2 infected with *H. yokogawai* were reported from Udonthani Province (Manning and Lertpraesert 1971; Manning et al. 1971). Another human case was subsequently reported in Chiang Mai, Thailand; worm sections were found deep in the crypt of the ileum (Kliks and Tantachamrun 1974). Later, 3 more human cases infected with *H. taichui* were reported with evidence of this infection as a pathogenic parasite (Sukontason et al. 2005). Surgical resection of the small intestines revealed the pathological features of mucosal ulceration, mucosal and submucosal hemorrhages, fusion and shortening of villi, chronic inflammation, and fibrosis of the submucosa; *H. taichui* worms were found with their mouth-parts attached to the mucosal epithelium and distorting the epithelial lining (Sukontason et al. 2005). Moreover, *H. taichui* was suggested to be an etiological agent of irritable bowel syndrome-like symptoms in humans (Watthanakulpanich et al. 2010).

Host immune responses against *Haplorchis* spp. infection have seldom been studied, despite the suggestion that the visceral spreading of *Haplorchis* and other minute intestinal flukes may occur in immunocompromised patients (Yokogawa 1940). Sukontason et al. (2001), Kumchoo et al. (2003), and Saenphet et al. (2008) demonstrated spontaneous expulsion of worms from the intestine of mice, chicks, and rats experimentally infected with *H. taichui* within 9, 48, and 28 days post infection, respectively, which demonstrate the development of innate and/or acquired immunity of the host. Mucosal mast cells (MMCs) were significantly increased in number in infected rats peaking at day 21 post infection (Saenphet et al. 2008). Eosinophil counts and serum IgE levels were elevated after infection which peaked at day 14 post infection (Saenphet et al. 2008). In humans infected with *H. taichui*, serum antibodies (probably IgG) against *H. taichui* were increased as measured by ELISA; enzyme-linked immunoelectron transfer (EITB) assay was useful to discriminate *H. taichui* infection (10 kDa band) from *O. viverrini* infection (70 kDa band) (Ditrich et al. 1991).

1.4.8 Clinical Manifestations, Diagnosis and Treatment

Few reports have been available regarding the clinical symptoms and signs of human *Haplorchis* spp. infection. This was partly due that humans in endemic areas are usually mixed-infected with other foodborne trematodes infecting the liver or intestine, namely, *O. viverrini,* or other *Haplorchis* spp., other heterophyid or lecithodendriid flukes (see *Caprimolgorchis molenkampi* and *Phaneropsolus bonnei*). Africa et al. (1940) presumed that the symptoms due to *Haplorchis* spp. infection may be intestinal disturbances such as colicky pain and mucous diarrhea, and the degree of such symptoms would depend upon the number of worms that had invaded the glands of Lieberkühn, the extent of penetration, or of the destruction or necrosis of the epithelium occasioned by the presence of worms. Recently, it was reported that *H. taichui* infection may cause irritable bowel syndrome-like symptoms, and the patients may complain of dyspepsia, nausea, vomiting, lassitude, abdominal pain, flatulence, loose fecal excretion, fever, pallor, abdominal distension, and jaundice with enlarged liver (Watthanakulpanich et al. 2010).

The detection of *Haplorchis* spp. infection is usually done by recovery of eggs in the feces. Smear (direct smear, cellophane thick smear, and Kato-Katz thick smear) or concentration techniques (formalin-ether sedimentation and brine floatation) can be applied in the field or laboratory where appropriate. However, in areas of mixed infections with other heterophyid or opisthorchiid species, specific diagnosis is problematic (Chai and Lee 2002). In addition, detecting eggs of *Haplorchis* spp. in the feces frequently fails in light infections and it is necessary to use immunological or molecular detection techniques.

Eggs of *Haplorchis* spp. can be differentiated with difficulty from those of *Clonorchis, Opisthorchis*, or other heterophyid flukes (Fujino et al. 1989; Tesana et al. 1991; Ditrich et al. 1992a). The eggs of *H. taichui* are 27.0–27.8 μm × 13.7–14.1 μm in size and slightly smaller than those of *H. pumilio* which are 30.8 ± 0.8 μm × 17.3 ± 0.7 μm in size (Ditrich et al. 1992a). The length and weight of *H. yokogawai* eggs are between the 2 species of eggs (Ditrich et al. 1992a). All these eggs of 3 species are ellipsoid to ovoid in shape with an average length/width ratio of 1.8 (*H. pumilio*), 1.9 (*H. yokogawai*), or 1.9–2.0 (*H. taichui*) (Ditrich et al. 1992a). They have relatively clean shell surface, distinct (*H. pumilio*), indistinct (*H. taichui* and *H. yokogawai*) shoulders, and yellowish brown in color (Fujino et al. 1989; Tesana et al. 1991; Ditrich et al. 1992a). Potassium permanganate staining was introduced by Sukontason et al. 1999b) in order to distinguish the eggs of *H. taichui* and *P. bonnei* from those of *O. viverrini*; the staining made the muskmelon patterns on the egg shell surface of *O. viverrini* more clearly visible (Sukontason et al. 1999b).

There could be false egg negative cases among light infection cases, for example, with less than 100 worms in an infected person; in such cases the probability to detect eggs in the feces is almost negligible (Chai and Lee 2002). In such cases, serological tests, including ELISA, and genetic techniques, including PCR, may be helpful. Thaenkham et al. (2007) developed a rapid and sensitive tool for detecting

H. taichui with low DNA concentrations and for distinguishing *H. taichui* from *Opisthorchis viverrini, H. pumilio,* and *H. yokogawai*. They further suggested that PCR-RFLP profiles would be useful for diagnosing mixed *H. taichui* and *O. viverrini* infection. PCR diagnosis was also applied to detect low-intensity *H. taichui* and *O. viverrini* infections in field surveys (Lovis et al. 2009). HAT-RAPD technique was developed to discriminate *H. taichui* infection from various other infections, including *O. viverrini* and *S. falcatus* which generated a 256 bp amplicon and showed a positive result only for *H. taichui* (Wongsawad et al. 2009). A multiplex PCR assay based on HAT-RAPD results was also developed for detecting *H. taichui* (Wongsawad and Wongsawad 2012). PCR targeting ITS1 and ITS2 regions of ribosomal DNA revealed useful results; particularly in ITS2 region, the amplicon size for *H. taichui* was significantly different from that of *O. viverrini, C. sinensis,* and *H. pumilio* (Sato et al. 2009b). However, Sato et al. (2010) reported that PCR for copro-DNA targeting ITS1 and ITS2 regions could detect lower number of *H. taichui* cases than those with *H. taichui* worms expelled after treatment, whereas the same DNA technique was excellent for copro-detection of *O. viverrini* infection. Molecular techniques were also used in Vietnam (De and Le 2011), China (Jeon et al. 2012), and Thailand (Wongsawad et al. 2012; Sato et al. 2015) to detect human infections with *H. pumilio* and *H. taichui* (Vietnam) and *H. taichui* (China and Thailand).

However, the diagnosis of erratic parasitism in the heart, brain, or spinal cord is impossible unless biopsy or necropsy is done on the affected lesion (Chai 2014; Chai and Jung 2017). Detection of serum antibodies or parasite genetic markers cannot discriminate intestinal versus visceral infections. Cardiac ultrasonography combined with serum antibody and molecular tests would help the diagnosis of possible cardiac infections with heterophyid fluke infections.

The drug of choice for individual treatment of *Haplorchis* spp. infection is praziquantel, at a single oral dose of 40 mg/kg praziquantel (Pungpak et al. 1998; Radomyos et al. 1998; Sayasone et al. 2009; Chai et al. 2010, 2013; Sohn et al. 2014). However, reduced doses, for example, 20–30 mg/kg, were also useful to treat individual patients in endemic areas (Chai et al. 2005a, 2007, 2009b). Experimental use of niclosamide also showed an excellent efficacy against adult worms of *H. taichui* (Kumchoo et al. 2007).

1.4.9 Prevention and Control

Proper disposal of human or animal feces can reduce the infection source (*Haplorchis* spp. eggs) to the environment. However, control of the snail host is hardly feasible. Also, fish control, including the fish, and reservoir host control are hardly practicable. One of the most efficient preventive measures is to persuade people to cook fish before eating as in other heterophyid infections (Chai 2014). However, it is extremely difficult to persuade people in endemic areas to change their long-tradition of eating raw or undercooked fish (Chai 2014).

Heating fish for 10–15 min at 70 °C could inactivate metacercariae; however, data are insufficient to determine the exact time-temperature treatment baseline. A review of available data on processing conditions identified some parameters for heating, pickling, salting, freezing, and irradiating fish for inactivation of parasites (WHO 1995). Freezing and storing at −20 °C or below for 7 days, or freezing at −35 °C or below until solid and storing at −35 °C or below for 15 h, or freezing at −35 °C or below until solid, and storing at −20 °C or below for 24 h is sufficient to kill parasites (WHO 1995).

Pickling may reduce the parasite hazard in a fish dish. The metacercariae of heterophyids can survive only 1 day in pickled fish dish; therefore, consuming 'pla-som' after 3 days of preparation would be safe from infection (Sukontason et al. 1998). However, the metacercariae of heterophyids can survive longer than 3 h in 'lab-pla' which is usually consumed immediately after preparation; therefore, this type of fish dish may be dangerous for parasite infection (Sukontason et al. 1998). Smoking to a temperature of 65°C can be considered for parasitic nematodes in fish, but little is known on this process for intestinal trematodes, including *Haplorchis* and *Heterophyes* (Chai 2014).

1.5 *Acanthotrema*

1.5.1 Acanthotrema felis

1.5.1.1 *Acanthotrema felis* Sohn, Han and Chai, 2003

This species (Fig. 1.28) was first described from the small intestine of stray cats in South Korea (Sohn et al. 2003a). Subsequently, a single adult specimen was found from a 70-year-old Korean woman residing in a coastal area of South Korea (Cho et al. 2010). Thereafter, 4 more human infections with low worm burdens (total 10 worms) were detected in South Korea (Chai et al. 2014). There have been no reports on this fluke in other countries (Table 1.7). *Acanthotrema armata* was reported from an avian species *Larus audouinii* in Spain (Lafuente et al. 2000). They (Lafuente et al. 2000) included 2 more species in this genus; *A. hancocki* (Martin 1950) which was originally reported as *Parastictodora hancocki*, and *A. martini* (Sogandares-Bernal 1959) which was originally reported as *Neostictodora martini*. Sohn et al. (2003a) added 3 more new combinations in this genus; *A. tridactyla* (originally *Stictodora tridactyla* by Martin and Kuntz 1955), *A. tanayensis* (originally *Stictodora tanayensis* by Velasquez 1973), and *A. cursitans* (formerly *Stictodora cursitans*; Kinsella and Heard 1974). Therefore, total 7 species are now known in *Acanthotrema* (Sohn et al. 2003a).

The adult fluke of *A. felis* is 0.43–0.57 mm long and 0.22–0.31 mm wide, and the eggs are 25–28 × 13–17 μm in size (Sohn et al. 2003a). They characteristically have a ventrogenital sac armed with 3 sclerites (2 long and pointed and 1 short and thumb-like) (Sohn et al. 2003a). The life cycle is only partially known. The cercar-

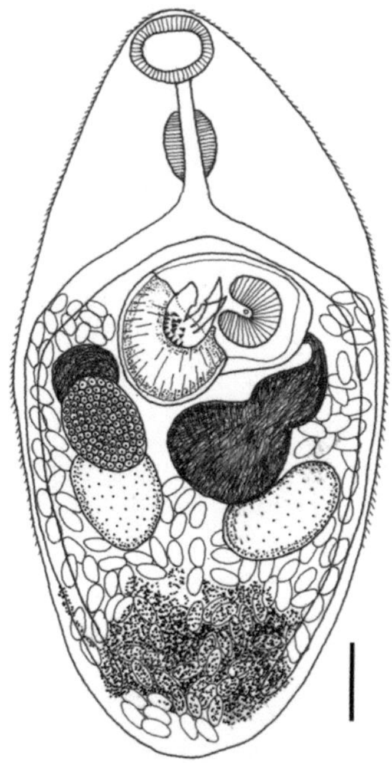

Fig. 1.28 Line drawing of an adult fluke of *Acanthotrema felis*. Redrawn from the figure in Sohn et al. (2003a) J Parasitol 89:154–158. Scale bar = 0.05 mm

iae and other moluscan larval stages have not yet been found. The metacercariae were discovered from the goby, *Acanthogobius flavimanus*, a brackish water fish species; they were experimentally fed to kittens, and adult flukes were harvested 7 days later (Sohn et al. 2003b). Later, Cho et al. (2012) detected *A. felis* metacercariae in 31 (91.2%) of 34 gobies, *A. flavimanus*, examined. The metacercariae are elliptical, yellowish brown, and 216–254 μm long and 152–185 μm wide; they also show a ventrogenital sac armed with 3 sclerites (Sohn et al. 2003b). Only cats were reported to be the natural definitive host (Sohn and Chai 2005; Shin et al. 2009, 2015), for example, 5 (1.1%) of 438 stray cats collected from Pusan were infected with a total of 370 specimens of *A. felis* (Sohn and Chai 2005). The surface ultrastructure was studied by Sohn et al. (2003c). The structure is similar to that of other heterophyid trematodes; however, the tegumental surface of the ventrogenital sac which showed protuberances with minute spines but without sensory papillae was suggested to be characteristic for *A. felis* (Sohn et al. 2003c).

Other Potentially Zoonotic *Acanthotrema* **spp.** *A. acanthotrema* Travassos, 1928; *A. hancocki* (Martin, 1950) Lafuente et al., 2000; *A. tridactyla* (Martin and Kuntz, 1955) Sohn et al., 2003; *A. martini* (Sogandares-Bernal, 1959) Lafuente et al., 2000; *A. tayanensis* (Velasquez, 1973) Sohn et al., 2003; *A. cursitans* (Kinsella and Heard, 1974) Sohn et al., 2003; *A. armata* Lafuente et al., 2000 (reported by Sohn et al. 2003a).

Table 1.7 Geographical distribution of zoonotic heterophyids other than *Metagonimus*, *Heterophyes*, and *Haplorchis*

Species & Nominator	Country/Region
Acanthotrema felis Sohn, Han, and Chai, 2003	South Korea
Apophallus donicus (Skrjabin and Lindtrop, 1919) Price, 1931	Canada, Europe, Ukraine, USA
Ascocotyle (*Phagicola*) *longa* Ransom, 1920	Brazil, Colombia, Czech Republic, Egypt, Georgia, Germany, Greece, Israel, Mexico, Panama, Peru, Romania, Turkey, USA
Centrocestus armatus Tanabe, 1922	Japan, South Korea
Centrocestus cuspidatus (Looss, 1896) Looss, 1899	China, Egypt, Kuwait, Taiwan, Tunisia
Centrocestus formosanus Nishigori, 1924	Brazil, China, Colombia, Costa Rica, Croatia, Egypt, India, Japan, Lao PDR, Mexico, The Philippines, Taiwan, Thailand, Tunisia, Turkey, USA, Vietnam
Centrocestus kurokawai Kurokawa, 1935	Japan
Cryptocotyle lingua (Creplin, 1825) Fischoeder, 1903	Denmark, England, Greenland, Iceland, Japan, North America, Norway, Russia, Ukraine
Heterophyopsis continua (Onji and Nishio, 1916) Price, 1940	China, Japan, South Korea, Saudi Arabia, Thailand, United Arab Emirates, Vietnam
Procerovum calderoni (Africa and Garcia, 1935) Price, 1940	China, Egypt, The Philippines
Procerovum varium Onji and Nishio, 1916	Australia, Cambodia, China, Egypt, India, Japan, South Korea, Lao PDR, The Philippines, Vietnam
Pygidiopsis genata Looss, 1907	Egypt, Iran, Israel, Kuwait, Romania, The Philippines, Tunisia, Ukraine
Pygidiopsis summa Onji and Nishio, 1916	Japan, South Korea, Vietnam
Stellantchasmus falcatus Onji and Nishio, 1916	Australia, China, India, Iran, Israel, Japan, South Korea, Lao PDR, The Philippines, Taiwan, Thailand,USA (Hawaii), Vietnam
Stictodora fuscata (Onji and Nishio, 1916) Yamaguti, 1958	Japan, South Korea, Kuwait
Stictodora lari Yamaguti, 1939	Australia, Japan, South Korea, Russia, Vietnam

Information updated from Chai and Jung (2017) Food Waterb Parasitol 8–9:33–63

1.6 *Apophallus*

1.6.1 Apophallus donicus

1.6.1.1 *Apophallus donicus* (Skrjabin and Lindtrop, 1919) Price, 1931

This species (Fig. 1.29) was first described from the small intestine of dogs, cats, rats, foxes, and rabbits (experimental) in Europe and North America (Table 1.7) (Yamaguti 1958, 1971). The adult fluke is 1.12–1.30 mm long and 0.58–0.72 mm wide, and the eggs are 25–35 × 15–20 μm in size (Yamaguti 1971). Its

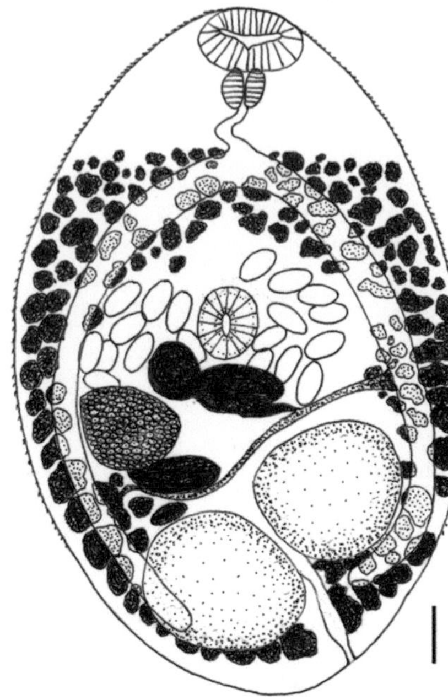

Fig. 1.29 Line drawing of an adult fluke of *Apophallus donicus*. Redrawn from the figure in Niemy and Macy (1974) Proc Helminthol Soc Wash 41:223–229. Scale bar = 0.1 mm

morphological details were described by Niemi and Macy (1974). Experimental infection of a human with this species was successful in the United States (USA) (Niemi and Macy 1974). Other reports of human infections are available in USA (Schell 1985). The cercariae are shed by the stream snail, *Flumenicola virens* and *Lithoglyphus naticoides* (Niemi and Macy 1974; Hung et al. 2013). The cercaria is pleuro-lophocercous type; its body is 190 μm long and 80 μm wide, and the tail is 332–370 (av. 258) μm long (Niemi and Macy 1974). The cercariae were found to encyst in hatchery-reared coho salmon, *Oncorhynchus kisutch* (Niemi and Macy 1974). Many kinds of fish, including blackside dace, suckers, squawfish, redside shiners, and rainbow trout were found naturally infected with the metacercariae (Niemi and Macy 1974). The metacercariae are spherical, with outer fibrous wall, and 93–108 (av. 103) μm in diameter (Niemi and Macy 1974). Reservoir hosts include dogs, cats, rats, foxes, rabbits, and various species of birds (Yamaguti 1958; Yu and Mott 1994; Hung et al. 2013). Its distribution among wild mammals (redfox, raccoon dog, and American mink) in Ukraine was recently reported (Korol et al. 2016).

Other Potentially Zoonotic *Apophallus* **spp.** *A. bacalloti* Morozov, 1952; *A. brevis* Ransom, 1929; *A. crami* Price, 1931; *A. eccentricus* Africa and Garcia, 1935; *A. imperator* Lyster, 1940; *A. lari* (Leonov, 1957); *A. lerouxi* Rayski and Fahmy, 1962; *A. majori* Szidat, 1924; *A. microtestis* (Leonov, 1957); *A. mühlingi* (Jägerskiöld, 1899); *A. similis* (Ransom, 1920) Price, 1931; *A. venustus* (Ransom, 1920); *A. microsoma* Ferguson et al., 2012 (reviewed by Ferguson et al. 2012).

1.7 *Ascocotyle*

1.7.1 Ascocotyle longa

1.7.1.1 *Ascocotyle (Phagicola) longa* Ransom, 1920

Species of *Ascocotyle* Looss 1899 (subgenus *Phagicola* Faust 1920) are intestinal parasites of fish-eating birds and mammals in Europe, Asia, Africa, and the Americas (Yu and Mott 1994). *Ascocotyle longa* was originally described based on specimens from Alaskan fox (*Vulpes lagopus*) from National Zoological Park in Washington DC, USA (Ransom 1920). The distribution of this species is now known to be almost worldwide (Table 1.7); North (Mexico and USA) and South America (Brazil, Colombia, Panama, and Peru), Europe (Czech Republic, Germany, Greece, and Romania), Africa (Egypt), and the Middle East (Georgia, Israel, Palestine, and Turkey) (Scholz 1999). The taxonomic status of this species in relation to other related species has been extensively studied (Scholz 1999).

The size of the adult fluke (Fig. 1.30) is 0.85–1.0 mm by 0.27–0.35 mm, and the size of eggs is 16–18 μm long and 9–11 μm wide (Ransom 1920). The morphological details of this species in relation to other species were given by Scholz (1999). Ten cases of human infections presumably due to this species (described as *Phagicola* sp.) were first reported in Brazil in 2 papers (Chieffi et al. 1990, 1992). Subsequently, Antunes and Almeida-Dias (1994) added 10 more human patients who consumed raw mullets in previous 4 months in Brazil. The natural and experi-

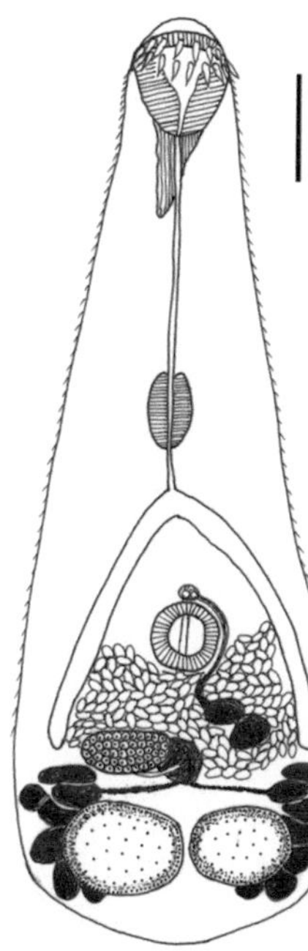

Fig. 1.30 Line drawing of an adult fluke of *Ascocotyle longa*. Redrawn from the figure in Scholz (1999) Syst Parasitol 43:147–158. Scale bar = 0.1 mm

mental first intermediate host is the cochliopid snail *Heleobia australis* in Brazil (Simões et al. 2010). The cercariae are pleuro-lophocercous type, and its body is 110–125 μm long and 60–95 μm wide, and the tail is 170–185 (av. 179) μm in length (Simões et al. 2010). Fish, in particular, various species of mullets (*Mugil* spp., including *Mugil liza*, and *Liza haematocheilus*) serve as the second intermediate host (Chieffi et al. 1992; Oliveira et al. 2007; Simões et al. 2010; Borges et al. 2018; Sarabeev et al. 2019). The metacercariae are encysted in body musculature, heart, stomach, liver, kidneys, spleen, gonads, and mesentery of the fish host; they are oval, thin-walled, and translucent, and 225–240 (av. 232) μm long and 215–235 (av. 229) μm wide (Simões et al. 2010). Various kinds of birds, including the pelican and eagle, and mammals, particularly dogs, are the reservoir hosts of this fluke (Chieffi et al. 1990, 1992; Simões et al. 2010). Hamsters were an experimental definitive host (Simões et al. 2010).

Other Potentially Zoonotic *Ascocotyle* **(***Phagicola***) spp.** *A.* (*P.*) *arnaldoi* Travassos, 1929; *A.* (*P.*) *ascolonga* Witenberg, 1929; *A.* (*P.*) *byrdi* (Robinson, 1956); *A.* (*P.*) *longicollis* (Kuntz and Chandler, 1956); *A.* (*P.*) *inglei* (Hutton and Sogandares-Bernal, 1959) (reviewed by Scholz 1999); *A.* (*P.*) *angrense* Travassos, 1916; *A.* (*P.*) *diminuta* (Stunkard and Havilland, 1924) (Núñez 1993).

1.8 *Centrocestus*

1.8.1 Centrocestus armatus

1.8.1.1 *Centrocestus armatus* (Tanabe, 1922) Price, 1932

[syn. *Stamnosoma nycticoracis* Izumi, 1935]

This species (Fig. 1.31) was originally reported from dogs, cats, rabbits, rats, and mice experimentally fed cyprinoid fish harboring the metacercariae in Japan (Tanabe 1922). Yamaguti (1958) synonymized *Stamnosoma nycticoracis* Izumi, 1935 obtained from herons and several other species of birds, cats, and foxes with *C. armatus*. One of the morphological characteristics of *C. armatus* is the presence of 42–48 circumoral spines on the oral sucker (Hong et al. 1988). Only a small number of intrauterine eggs, the median location of the ovary, and the side-by-side location of 2 testes are other characteristics (Chai 2007). Regarding human infections, a successful experimental infection was reported in Japan when this fluke was first reported as a new species (Tanabe 1922). Later, a naturally infected human case was reported in South Korea (Hong et al. 1988). To date, the geographical distribution of this species is limited to South Korea and Japan (Fig. 1.32; Table 1.7).

The adult flukes are 0.35–0.63 mm long and 0.18–0.28 mm wide (Tanabe 1922). The egg size is 31–33 μm long and 15–20 μm wide (Hong et al. 1988). The first intermediate host is the fresh water snail, *Semisulcospira libertina* (Takahashi 1929; Komatsu et al. 2014). The cercariae are oval in shape and transparent; its body is

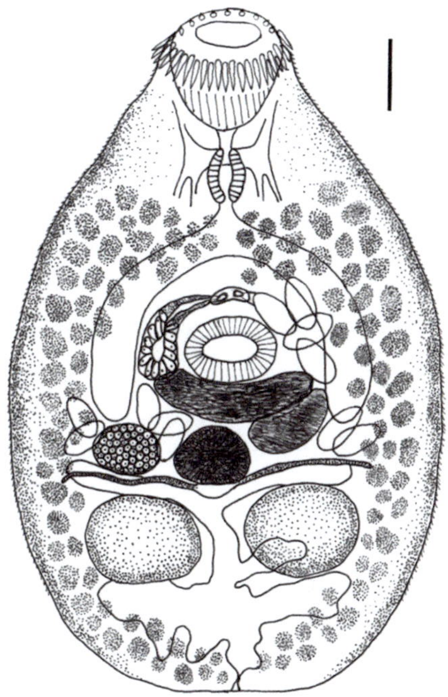

Fig. 1.31 Line drawing of an adult fluke of *Centrocestus armatus*. Redrawn from the figure in Tanabe (1922) Kyoto Igaku Zasshi 19:239–252. Scale bar = 0.05 mm

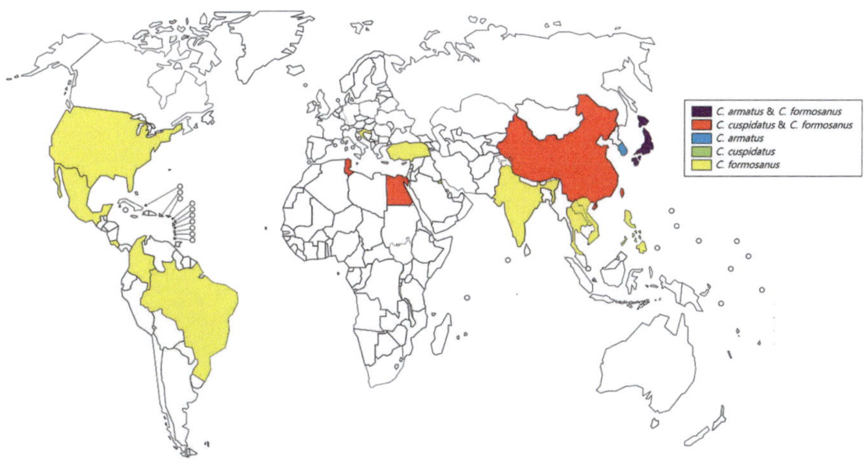

Fig. 1.32 Global distribution of *Centrocestus* spp. (*C. armatus, C. formosanus,* and *C. cuspidatus*) based on the presence of their life cycles

97–125 μm long and 49–69 μm wide, and the tail is 74–122 μm long and 12–19 μm wide (Takahashi 1929). The second intermediate hosts are various species of freshwater fish, such as, *Zacco platypus*, *Nipponocypris temminckii* (= *Zacco temminckii*), *Rhodeus ocellatus*, *Gobius similis*, *Pseudorasbora parva*, *Pelteobagrus fulvidraco,* and *Acanthogobius flavimanus* (Lee et al. 1984; Hong et al. 1989a; Komatsu et al. 2014; Sohn et al. 2018). The metacercariae are elongated elliptical in shape, tapering on both ends, and 200–250 μm long and 100–120 μm wide (Komiya 1965). The large egrets *Egretta alba modesta* (Ryang et al. 1991), kites, herons, and 3 unidentified avian species (Komatsu et al. 2014), dogs, rabbits, rats, cats, and humans (Sohn and Chai 2005; Hung et al. 2013; Shin et al. 2015) have been reported to be the natural definitive hosts. Rats were a useful experimental definitive host that allowed full development of worms within day 3 post-infection (Hong et al. 1989b). However, hamsters were the better experimental definitive host compared with rats, mice, and chicks (Kimura et al. 2007).

1.8.2 Centrocestus cuspidatus

1.8.2.1 *Centrocestus cuspidatus* (Looss, 1896) Looss, 1899

This species (Fig. 1.33) was originally reported from a naturally infected dog in Egypt (Ransom 1920). Later, human infections were found in Egypt and Taiwan (Yu and Mott 1994) and also in Fujian Province, China (Li et al. 2010); however, the precise literature background is unavailable. The distribution of this fluke (Fig. 1.32; Table 1.7) extends from Egypt (Ransom 1920; Martin 1959) to Kuwait (El-Azazy

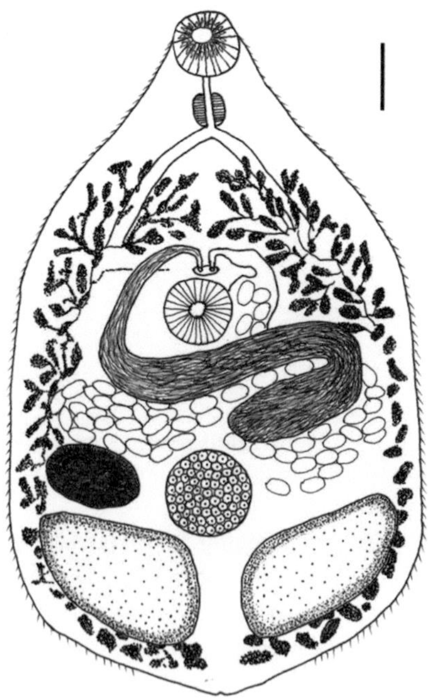

Fig. 1.33 Line drawing of an adult worm of *Centrocestus cuspidatus*. Redrawn from the figure in Ransom (1920) Proc US Nat Mus 57(2322):527–573. Scale bar = 0.05 mm

et al. 2015), Tunisia (Yamaguti 1958), Taiwan (Yu and Mott 1994), and China (Li et al. 2010).

The adult worm is 0.50 mm long and 0.35 mm wide, and has 36 circumoral spines (Ransom 1920). The egg size is 30 μm by 15 μm (Ransom 1920). However, its life history is poor known. The snail intermediate host is known to be *Oncomelania formosana* (Hung et al. 2013); however, the description of the cercariae is not available. The second intermediate host was confirmed to be freshwater fish, including *Gambusia* sp. (Martin 1958; Yamaguti 1975). The metacercariae are equipped with 2 rows of 18 spines each on the oral sucker (Martic 1958); however, the dimension of the metacercariae is unavailable. The reservoir hosts include dogs, cats, foxes, rats, yellow-billed kites (*Milvus parasiticus*), and chickens (Yu and Mott 1994; Hung et al. 2013; El-Azazy et al. 2015). Adult flukes were obtained experimentally from rats fed the fish *Astatotilapia desfontainesi* (Yamaguti 1958) and chicks fed the metacercariae from *Gambusia* (Yamaguti 1975).

1.8.3 Centrocestus formosanus

1.8.3.1 *Centrocestus formosanus* (Nishigori, 1924) Price, 1932

[syn. *Centrocestus cuspidatus caninus* Leiper 1913; *Stephanopirumus longus* Onji and Nishio 1916; *Centrocestus caninus* Travassos 1922]

This species (Fig. 1.34a, b) was originally described from experimental dogs, cats, mice, rats, and ducks fed freshwater fish containing the metacercariae and found also in a naturally infected night herons (*Nycticorax nycticorax*) in Taiwan (Nishigori 1924). Prior to this, *Centrocestus cuspidatus caninus* was described by Leiper in 1913 based on a single poorly preserved specimen (Ransom 1920). This was later called as *C. caninus* by Travassos in 1922 (Yamaguti 1971). However, Faust and Nishigori (1926) synonymized *C. caninus* with *Stamnosoma formosanum* (now *C. formosanus*). Morozov (1952) acknowledged *C. armatus, C. cuspidatus,* and *C. formosanus* but not *C. caninus* within the genus *Centrocestus.* However, Yamaguti (1958) accepted *C. caninus* synonymizing *C. formosanus, C. yokogawai* Kobayasi 1942, and *Stephanopirumus longus* Onji and Nishio 1916 with *C. caninus*. Waikagul et al. (1997) followed the acceptance of *C. caninus* by Yamaguti (1958). However, synonymizing *C. formosanus* with *C. caninus* is problematic not only because the latter is based only on a single specimen whereas the former is based on a sufficient number of specimens but because many workers have used the name *C. formosanus* rather than *C. caninus* (Chai et al. 2013a). Finally, Chai et al. (2013a) proposed to accept *C. armatus, C. cuspidatus, C. formosanus, C. kurokawai* (Kurokawa 1935), *C. polyspinosus* (Kobayasi 1942), and *C. asadai* (Mishima 1959) in the genus *Centrocestus.*

Regarding the human infection with *C. formosanus*, an experimental infection was performed successfully when this species was first reported as a new species (Nishigori 1924). After then, possible occurrence of natural human infections was

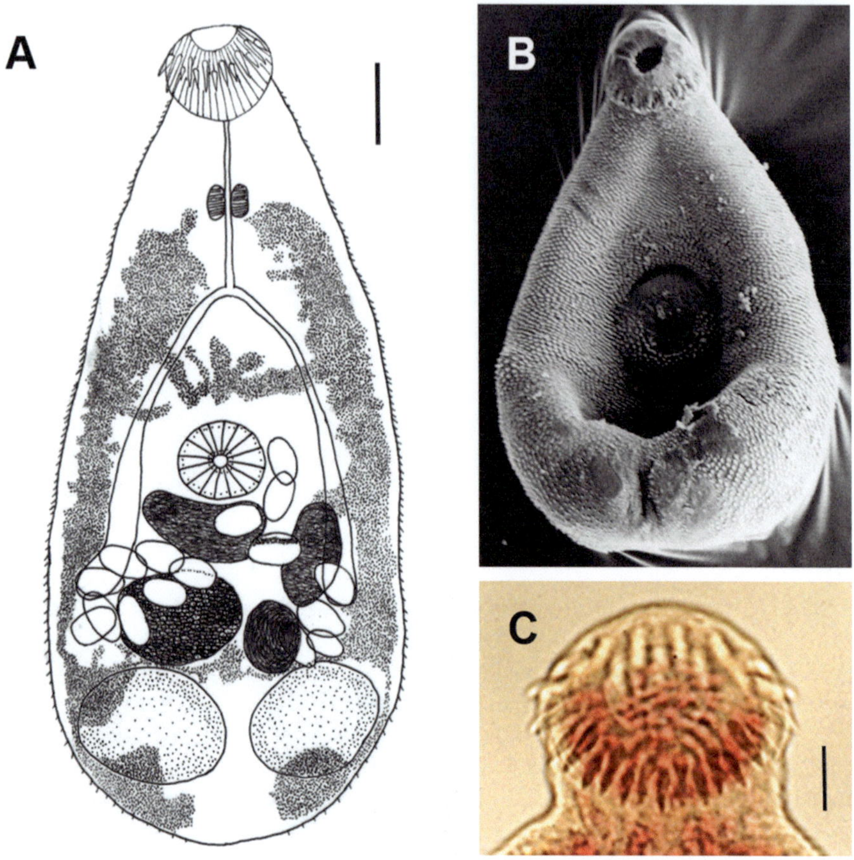

Fig. 1.34 *Centrocestus formosanus*. (**a**) Line drawing of an adult fluke recovered from a village resident in Vientiane Municipality, Lao PDR. Redrawn from the figure in Chai et al. (2013a) J Parasitol 99:531-536. Scale bar = 0.05 mm (**b**) Scanning electron microscopic view of an adult fluke (body length; 280 μm) recovered from an experimentally infected ICR mouse at day 7 post-infection. (**c**) Oral sucker of an adult fluke showing circumoral spines. Scale bar = 100 μm (**b**, **c**) Reproduced from the figure in Han et al. (2008) Korean J Parasitol 46:49–53 with permission

suggested by several authors (Ito 1964; Premvati and Pande 1974). In Hiroshima, Japan, a young farmer was found to be naturally infected with *C. formosanus var. kurokawai* (Kurokawa 1935). However, *C. formosanus* var. *kurokawai* is now treated as a separate species, *C. kurokawai* (Yamaguti 1958, 1971). Harinasuta et al. (1987) listed *C. formosanus* among the human-infecting trematode species in China and Taiwan but there were no literature backgrounds. Li et al. (2010) listed *C. formosanus* as one of the human infecting helminths found in 1979 in Guangdong Province, China but there was no related literature. The first documentation of human *C. formosanus* infection was done in Fujian Province, China by Chen et al. (1991). Yu and Mott (1994) described the presence of human *C. formosanus* infections in Taiwan and the Philippines; however, it is unclear whether these reports were truly based on identification of adult worms. Waikagul et al. (1997) reported 2 human cases infected with *C. formosanus* (under the name *C. caninus*) in Thailand based on recovery of adult flukes. The next report on natural human *C. formosanus* infections (3 cases) was published from Vietnam (De and Le 2011). Although there are no detailed worm descriptions, the figures of the whole worm and of the 32 circumoral spines on the oral sucker apparently indicate that the worms are *C. formosanus* (De and Le 2011). Thereafter, ten additional human cases were reported from Lao PDR by recovery of adult flukes after chemotherapy and purging (Chai et al. 2013a, b, 2015).

This species is now known to be distributed in Taiwan, China, Japan, the Philippines, India, Vietnam, Lao PDR, Thailand, Turkey, Croatia, USA (Hawaii, Florida, Texas, and Utah), Mexico, Colombia, Peru, Brazil, Costa Rica, Egypt, and Tunisia (Fig. 1.32; Table 1.7) (Chen 1942; Martin 1958; Yamaguti 1975; Madhavi 1986; Yu and Mott 1994; Waikagul et al. 1997; Scholz and Salgado-Maldonado 1999; Mitchell et al. 2000; Velásquez et al. 2006; Gjurčevic et al. 2007; Thien et al. 2007; Chi et al. 2008; De and Le 2011; Pinto et al. 2013; Chai et al. 2013a, b; Najet et al. 2014; Yousif et al. 2016; Pulido-Murillo et al. 2018). It is interesting to note that *C. formosanus* is an exotic trematode species in the Americas (USA, Mexico, Costa Rica, and Brazil) that originated from Southeast Asia from the late 1950s (Scholz and Salgado-Maldonado 1999; Mitchell et al. 2000; Cortés et al. 2010; Pinto and de Melo 2010). In Mexico, this trematode was most likely introduced with the importation of the snail intermediate host *Melanoides tuberculata* from Asia in 1979 (Scholz and Salgado-Maldonado 1999). Human infections are yet unknown in USA, Mexico, and Brazil (Chai et al. 2013a). However, the metacercariae of this trematode infect the gill of various species of fish and cause serious losses among fish raised by tropical fish producers; they are also believed to be harmful to wild fish populations (Mitchell et al. 2000). The life cycle of *C. formosanus* was successfully completed in the laboratory in Egypt using infected snail host (*Melanoides tuberculata*) from Giza Governorate, Egypt, aquarium-reared *Gambusia affinis* fish as the second host, and rats (*Rattus norvegicus*) as the final host (Yousif et al. 2016).

The adult fluke is morphologically characterized by having 30–36 circumoral spines (Fig. 1.34c) (Chen 1942). They are 0.41–0.52 mm in length and 0.16–0.20 mm in width, and the size of their eggs is 32–35 μm by 17–20 μm (Chai et al. 2013a). The cercariae are found in the snail, *Semisulcospira libertina* in Taiwan (Nishigori 1924; Ito 1964), *Stenomelania newcombi* in Hawaii (Martin 1958), and *Melanoides tuberculata* in Taiwan (Chao et al. 1993; Lo and Lee 1996), USA, Mexico, Peru, and Brazil (Scholz and Salgado-Maldonado 1999; Mitchell et al. 2000; Pulido-Murillo et al. 2018; Pinto et al. 2018). The cercarial body is 47–122 μm long and 26–71 μm wide, and its tail is 62–98 μm long and 11–15 μm wide (Nishigori 1924). Various species of fish, including *Pseudorasbora parva, Ophicephalus striatus, Misgurnus anguillicaudatus, Zacco platypus, Anabas testudineus, Gambusia affinis, Astyanax fasciatus, Oreochromis aureus, Cyprinus carpio, Carassius auratus, Hampala dispar, Puntius brevis, Puntius gonionotus, Puntius leiacanthus, Etheostoma fonticola, Cyclocheilichthys armatus, Cyclocheilichthys repasson,*

Mystacoeleucus atridorsalis, Mystacoeleucus greenwayi, Physoschistura meridionalis, Puntioplites proctozysron, Hypsibarbus pierrei, Osteochilus hasselti, Cirrhinus molitorella, Tilapia nilotica, and *Tilapia zillii*, serve as the second intermediate host (Chen 1942; Martin 1958; Waikagul et al. 1997; Srisawangwong et al. 1997; Mitchell et al. 2000; Han et al. 2008; Rim et al. 2008, 2013). The metacercariae are elliptical, and 190 μm long and 140 μm wide (Nishigori 1924). Natural definitive hosts other than humans are fish-eating birds and mammals, such as the green heron (*Butorides vitrescens*), heron (*Butorides striatus*), pond heron (*Ardeola grayii*), night heron (*Nycticorax nycticorax*), great egret (*Ardea alba*), and dog (Chen 1942; Premvati and Pande 1974; Scholz and Salgado-Maldonado 1999; Mitchell et al. 2000). Experimental definitive hosts include mice, rats, dogs, cats, rabbits, and ducks (Nishigori 1924; Chen 1942; Waikagul et al. 1997; Saenphet et al. 2006a; Han et al. 2008; Pinto et al. 2015).

Saenphet et al. (2006b) studied on mucosal mast cell responses in rats experimentally infected with *C. formosanus* (under the name *C. caninus*); their possible role in worm expulsion was suggested. Pinto et al. (2015) studied on the worm burden, morphology, and fecundity of *C. formosanus* in immunosuppressed mice. They reported that the worm burden in dexamethasone-treated mice was significantly greater than that in the control (immunocompetent) mice, and the parasites recovered from immunosuppressed mice were larger, with more developed reproductive structures and greater number of intrauterine eggs than in control mice.

1.8.4 Centrocestus kurokawai

1.8.4.1 *Centrocestus kurokawai* (Kurokawa, 1935) Yamaguti, 1958

This species (Fig. 1.35) was originally reported from a naturally infected human in Hiroshima Prefecture, Japan under the name *C. formosanus* var. *kurokawai* (Kurokawa 1935). The adult worm has 38 or 40 circumoral spines (Kurokawa 1935). Subsequently, it was treated as a distinct species by Yamaguti (1958). Later, however, Yamaguti (1971) suggested that *C. kurokawai* could be identical with *C. armatus*. Ito (1964) and Yu and Mott (1994) continued to use *C. formosanus* var. *kurokawai* or *C. kurokawai* for this species. On the other hand, Waikagul et al. (1997) synonymized them and used the name *C. armatus* for *C. kurokawai*. However, Chai et al. (2013a) retained the name *C. kurokawai* in consideration that the number of circumoral spines (38 or 40) might be a specific feature. This species has never been reported from other countries.

The average length of adult flukes is 0.36 mm, the average width is 0.18 mm, and their egg size is 33–40 μm by 17–21 μm (Kurokawa 1935). No information is available on the intermediate hosts and reservoir hosts. The second intermediate host may be species of freshwater fish (Yu and Mott 1994).

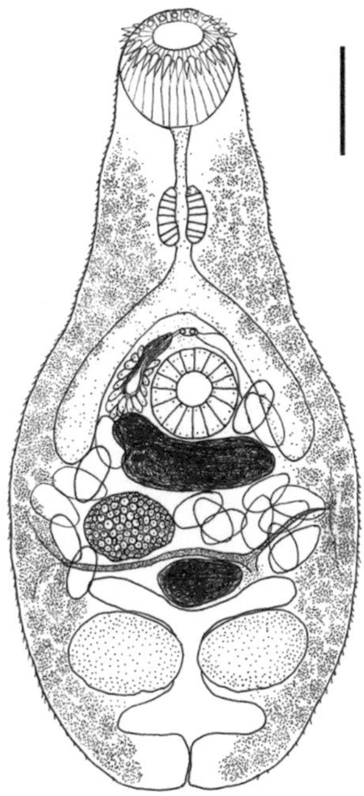

Fig. 1.35 Line drawing of an adult fluke of *Centrocestus kurokawai*. Redrawn from the figure in Kurokawa (1935) Tokyo Iji Shinshi no. 2915:293–298. Scale bar = 0.05 mm

Potentially Zoonotic *Centrocestus* **spp.** Other potentially zoonotic *Centrocestus* spp. include *C. asadai* Mishima, 1959 and *C. polyspinosus* Kobayasi, 1942a (reviewed by Chai et al. 2013a).

1.9 *Cryptocotyle*

1.9.1 Cryptocotyle lingua

1.9.1.1 *Cryptocotyle lingua* (Creplin, 1825) Fischoeder, 1903

This species was (Fig. 1.36) originally described as *Distoma lingua* by Creplin in 1825 from the intestine of an avian species *Larus marinus* (Stunkard 1930) and was renamed in 1903 as *Cryptocotyle lingua* by Fischoeder (Ransom 1920). It has since been described from various fish-eating birds and mammals including cats, dogs, rats, foxes, *Larus*, gulls, terns, and herons in Europe (including England, Denmark, Iceland, Greenland, and Norway), Ukraine, Russia, North America, and Japan (Stunkard 1930; Yamaguti 1958; Kristoffersen 1991; Huxham et al. 1993; Saeed et al. 2006; Christensen et al. 2015; Korol et al. 2016) (Table 1.7).

The adult flukes are 1.2–2.0 mm long and 0.4–0.9 mm wide, and their eggs are 42–48 μm long and 20–22 μm wide (Yamaguti 1971). Human infection with this fluke was reported only one time in Greenland (Babbott et al. 1961). Although adult

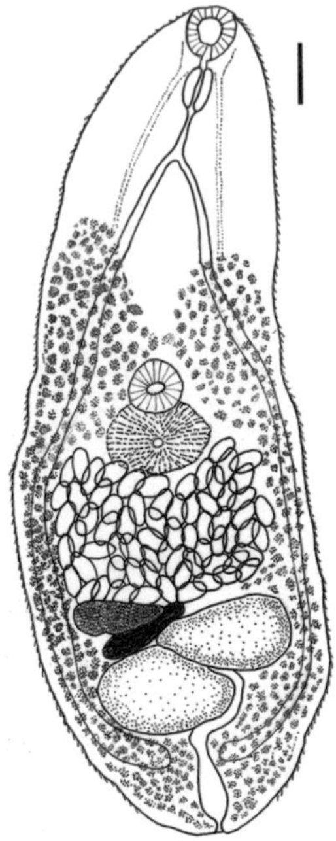

Fig. 1.36 Line drawing of an adult fluke of *Cryptocotyle lingua*. Redrawn from the figure in Stunkard (1930) J Morphol Physiol 50:143–191. Scale bar = 0.1 mm

flukes were not identified in this study, it seems that the egg size of 40–50 by 24–28 μm (significantly larger than the other members of heterophyids) strongly suggested them to be *C. lingua* (Babbott et al. 1961). Cercariae develop in littorina snails, *Littorina littorea* (Yamaguti 1958, 1975); the cercarial body is 140–180 μm long and 52–65 μm wide (the length of the tail not given) (Yamaguti 1975). The metacercariae encyst in several species of fish *Gobius ruthensparri, Labrus bergylta,* and mullet *Chelon labrosus* (Yamaguti 1958; Matthews and Matthews 1993). They are oval in shape, and 110–120 μm long and 80–90 μm wide (Yamaguti 1975). Adults can be grown in gulls by feeding metacercarial cysts (Yamaguti 1958).

Other Potentially Zoonotic *Cryptocotyle* **spp.** *C. badamshini* (Kurochkin, 1959) Yamaguti, 1971; *C. concava* (Creplin, 1925) Fischoeder, 1903; *C. jejuna* (Nicoll, 1907) Ransom, 1920; *C. macrorhinis* (MacCallum, 1916) Yamaguti, 1971; *C. quinqueangularis* (Skrjabin, 1923) Witenberg, 1929; *C. ransomi* (Isaichkov, 1924) Delianova, 1957; *C. thapari* McIntosh, 1953 (reviewed by Yamaguti 1971).

1.10 *Heterophyopsis*

1.10.1 Heterophyopsis continua

1.10.1.1 *Heterophyopsis continua* (Onji and Nishio, 1916) Price, 1940

[syn. *Heterophyes continuus* Onji and Nishio, 1916; *Pseudoheterophyes continua* Yamaguti, 1939]

This parasite (Fig. 1.37a) was first discovered in Japan from experimental cats fed the mullet *Mugil cephalus* that harbored the metacercariae and described under the name *Heterophyes continuus* (Onji and Nishio 1916). However, this parasite was morphologically unique from *Heterophyes* having an elongated body and the

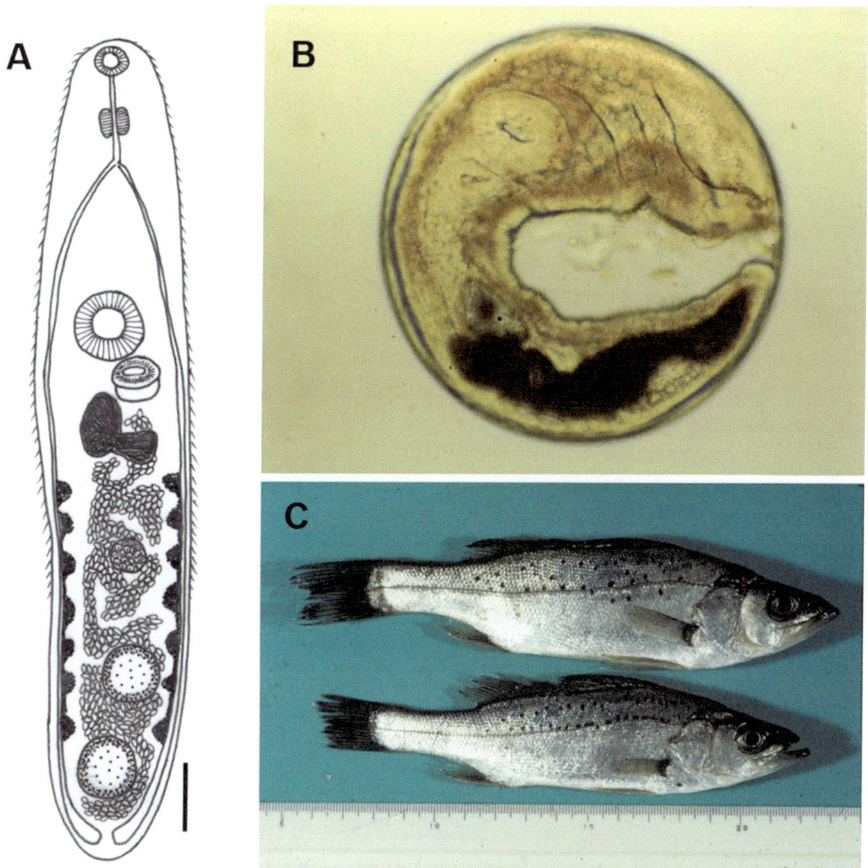

Fig. 1.37 *Heterophyopsis continua*. (**a**) Line drawing of an adult fluke (original figure). Scale bar = 0.2 mm (**b**) The perch, *Lateolabrax japonicus*, the fish intermediate host (**c**) A metacercaria isolated from the muscle of a perch. ×200

genital sucker separated from the ventral sucker. Later, Africa and Garcia (1935) described a closely similar parasite recovered from dogs, cats, and birds and named it as *Heterophyes expectans*. After then, Tubangui and Africa (1938) created a new genus *Heterophyopsis* for this and named it as *Heterophyopsis expectans*. Yamaguti (1939) also created a new genus *Pseudoheterophyes* and assigned *H. continuus* to this genus by naming it as *Pseudoheterophyes continua*. Yamaguti (1939) also described a new subspecies in this genus, *P. continua major*, which was recovered from an avian host. However, Africa et al. (1940) and Price (1940) synonymized *Pseudoheterophyes* with *Heterophyopsis* and thereafter, the status of the genus *Heterophyopsis* has been settled. Later, *Heterophyopsis yehi* was described as a new species from dogs in Ceylon, Sri Lanka (Dissanaike 1961), but Pearson (1973) transferred this species to *Galactosomum*, so the name became *Galactosomum yehi*. *Heterophyopsis neimongolis* was recorded from birds in Nei Mongol Autonomous Region, China (Qiu et al. 1984). Also, *Heterophyopsis guangxiensis* was described as a new species from a bird in China (Ho and He 1986), and *Heterophyopsis hawaiiensis* was reported as a new species from a Hawaiian monk seal in Hawaii, USA (Dailey et al. 2004).

The size of *H. continua* adults is 2.0–2.8 mm long and 0.42–0.53 mm wide, and morphologically differs from other heterophyids in the elongate body, genital sucker located separately at a slightly postero-sinistral position from the ventral sucker, and 2 obliquely tandem testes (Seo et al. 1984; Chai and Lee 2002; Chai et al. 2009). The eggs are 24–28 × 14–19 μm in size (Seo et al. 1984; Lee et al. 1984, 2012). The cercariae have not been found. The metacercariae are almost round (Fig. 1.37b) and 440–475 × 435–470 μm in size, with a relatively thick cyst wall and Y-shaped excretory bladder (Sohn 2009; Chai et al. 2012). The surface ultrastructure of several developmental stages of *H. continua* was studied, and it was reported that the tegumental processes were band-like in metacercariae but changed into cobblestone-like in 2-day juvenile flukes and velvety in 3-day old worms (Hong et al. 1991).

The first intermediate host is yet unknown. Metacercariae encyst most commonly in the perch *Lateolabrax japonicus* (Fig. 1.37c) or goby *Acanthogobius flavimanus* (Chun 1960; Seo et al. 1984; Chai et al. 2005; Kim et al. 2006; Sohn et al. 2009; Cho et al. 2012). Other fish hosts include shad *Konosirus* (= *Clupanodon*) *punctatus* (Chun 1960; Sohn et al. 1994; Kim et al. 2006; Cho et al. 2012), conger eel *Conger myriaster* (Kim et al. 1996), sweetfish *Plecoglossus altivelis* (Cho and Kim 1985), gobies *Boleophthalmus pectinirostris* and *Scartelaos* sp. (Sohn et al. 2005), *Mugil cephalus* (Kim et al. 2006), *Harengula zunasi* (Yamaguti 1942), and groupers *Epinephelus bleekeri* and *Epinephelus coioides* (Vo et al. 2008, 2011; Thanh et al. 2009). Seasonal features of metacercarial occurrence were studied in the perch; *H. continua* metacercariae occur as a small to mid-sized form in July, grow to a larger form by August, and attain infectivity to experimental chicks after 2 months in the perch (Hong 2012). A recent study in South Korea reported that the infection rate of gobies caught from 6 localities of western and southern coastal areas with *H. continua* metacercariae was 38.2% on average (Sohn et al. 2018). The metacercarial burden per fish ranged 1–21 (Sohn et al. 2018).

Humans (Chai et al. 2005, 2009), domestic or feral cats (Eom et al. 1985; Sohn and Chai 2005; Schuster et al. 2009; Chai et al. 2013), dogs (Yamaguti 1958), ducks (Onji and Nishio 1916), and sea-gulls (Yamaguti 1939) were reported to be natural definitive hosts. Experimental definitive hosts include cats (Onji and Nishio 1916), dogs (Chun 1960; Ito et al. 1962; Seo et al. 1984) and domestic chicks (Hong et al. 1990, 1991; Shin et al. 2015).

The presence of human infections was mentioned in Japan (Yamaguti 1958; Komiya and Suzuki 1966); however, no proper literature background is available for this. Subsequently, in South Korea, 2 natural human infections were first discovered (Seo et al. 1984). The patients were residents of seashore villages in southern parts of South Korea and enjoyed eating raw flesh of brackish water fish, including the perch (Seo et al. 1984). Total 17 human cases, including the first 2 cases, have been confirmed by recovery of adult flukes in South Korea (Hong et al. 1996; Guk et al. 2006; Park et al. 2007; Chai et al. 1997, 1998, 2004, 2014, 2015). Now the geographical distribution of *H. continua* (Table 1.7) includes South Korea (Seo et al. 1984; Chai et al. 2005, 2009), China (Chen 1948), Japan (Yamaguti 1958; Komiya and Suzuki 1966), Thailand (Ito et al. 1962), Vietnam (Vo et al. 2008; Chai et al. 2012), Saudi Arabia (under the name *Heterophyopsis* sp.; Kalantan et al. 2000), and United Arab Emirates (Schuster et al. 2009).

The pathogenicity and pathology in *H. continua* infection remain unknown. One of the reasons is mixed-infection in almost all reported cases with other heterophyid or opisthorchiid flukes (Hong et al. 1996; Guk et al. 2006; Park et al. 2007; Chai et al. 1997, 1998, 2004, 2014, 2015). Another reason is low worm burdens in most of the reported patients not enough to cause significant clinical problems. The diagnosis of human *H. continua* infection is problematic because it is difficult to discriminate the eggs from those of other heterophyids in fecal examinations (Lee et al. 1984, 2012). For differential diagnosis of metacercariae in food samples, including fish, PCR-RFLP assay was tried targeting their 18S rRNA; using *MSP1* it was possible to discriminate *H. continua* and *Heterophyes nocens* from other trematodes like *Clonorchis sinensis* and *Pygidiopsis summa* (Pyo et al. 2013). *Hinf1* digested *H. nocens* but not *H. continua*, thus this technique could discriminate the 2 fluke species (Pyo et al. 2013). A numerical taxonomy study on heterophyid flukes reported that *H. continua* were more closely related to *Stictodora* spp. rather than to *Heterophyes* or *Metagonimus* (Kim et al. 1991). Human infections can be treated successfully using praziquantel (Hong et al. 1996; Guk et al. 2006; Park et al. 2007; Chai et al. 1997, 1998, 2004, 2014, 2015). In vitro effects of praziquantel on *H. continua* were reported (Woo et al. 1990).

Other Potentially Zoonotic *Heterophyopsis* spp. *H. expectans* (Africa and Garcia, 1935) Tubangui and Africa, 1938; *H. continua major* (Yamaguti, 1939) Yamaguti, 1958; *H. neimongolis* Qiu, Zhang and Li, 1984; *H. guangxiensis* Ho and He, 1986; *H. hawaiiensis* Dailey, Kliks and Demaree, 2004.

1.11 *Procerovum*

1.11.1 Procerovum calderoni

1.11.1.1 *Procerovum calderoni* (Africa and Garcia, 1935) Price, 1940

[syn. *Monorchotrema calderoni* Africa and Garcia, 1935; *Haplorchis calderoni* Africa, 1938; *Haplorchis macrovesica* Kobayasi, 1942]

This species was originally described from dogs, cats, and 2 humans in the Philippines under the name *Monorchotrema calderoni* (Africa and Garcia 1935). It was later renamed as *Haplorchis calderoni* (Africa 1938); however, it was subsequently assigned to *Procerovum* Onji and Nishio 1916 by Price (1940). It can be discriminated from *Procerovum varium* in that the former has an extensively long expulsor, whereas the latter has a comparatively shorter expulsor (Pearson 1964). This fluke has been reported from the Philippines (Africa and Garcia 1935; Velasquez 1973a, b), China (Kobayasi 1968; Yu and Mott 1994), and Egypt (Shalaby et al. 1993; Tawfik et al. 2000) (Fig. 1.38; Table 1.7).

The adult flukes are 0.360–0.465 mm long and 0.150–0.235 mm wide, and the eggs are 27–30 × 11–13 μm in size (Velasquez 1973a). The rediae are elongate and develop in the digestive gland of the snail host (Velasquez 1973b). The cercariae are parapleurolophocercus type, with rectangular eyespots, and the cercarial body is 84–168 μm long and 56–70 μm wide; the tail is 280–336 μm long; the metacercariae are 150–180 by 105–135 μm in size (Velasquez 1973b). The first intermediate host is the brackish water snail, *Sermyla riquetti* (= *Thiara riquetti*) (Velasquez 1973b). The second intermediate hosts are freshwater or brackish water fish, including *Ophiocephalus striatus, Glossogobius giurus, Mollienesia latipinna, Mugil* sp., *Creisson validus, Butis amboinensis, Chanos chanos, Platycephalus indicus, Mugil*

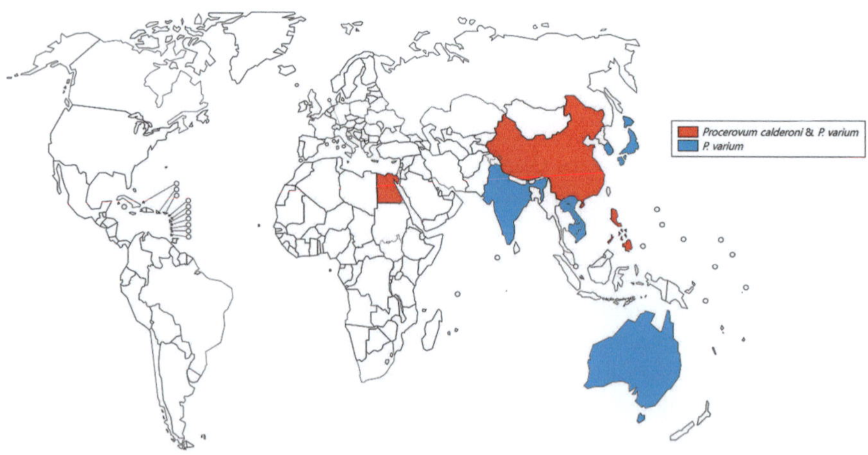

Fig. 1.38 Global distribution of *Procerovum* spp. (*P. calderoni* and *P. varium*) based on the presence of their life cycles

dussumieri, Pelates quadrilineatus, Hemirhamphus georgi, Scatophagus argus, Oxyurichthys microlepis, Anabas testudineus, and *Tilapia nilotica* (Velasquez 1973a, b; Shalaby et al. 1993; Yu and Mott 1994). Natural reservoir hosts as we all as experimental hosts are dogs and cats (Velasquez 1973b).

1.11.2 Procerovum varium

1.11.2.1 *Procerovum varium* Onji and Nishio, 1916

[syn. *Procerovum sisoni* Africa, 1938; *Haplorchis minutus* Kobayasi, 1942; *Haplorchis hoihowensis* Kobayasi, 1942; *Haplorchis cordatus* Kobayasi, 1942; *Haplorchis microvesica* Kobayasi, 1942]

This parasite (Fig. 1.39a) was originally described from experimental dogs infected with the metacercariae encysted in the mullet *Mugil cephalus* in Japan (Onji and Nishio 1916). Later, Kobayasi (1942) described *Haplorchis minutus, H. hoihowensis, H. cordatus,* and *H microvesica* from Hainan Island, China; however, these were all synonymized with *P. varium* by Pearson (1964). *Procerovum sisoni*

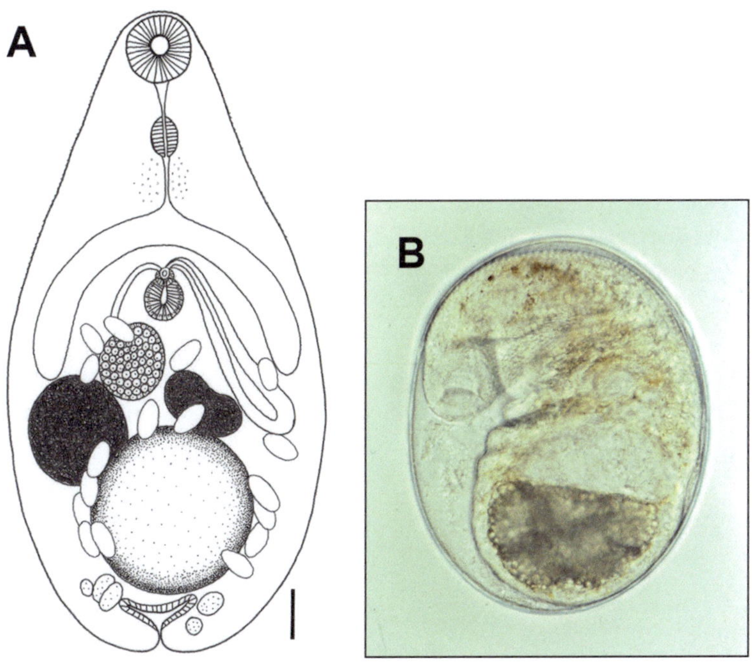

Fig. 1.39 *Procerovum varium*. (**a**) Line drawing of an adult fluke. Redrawn from the figure in Pearson (1964) Parasitology 54:601–676. Scale bar = 0.05 mm (**b**) Metacercaria isolated from a fish intermediate host, *Anabas testudineus*, in Hanoi, Vietnam. Reproduced from the figure in Chai et al. (2012) Korean J Parasitol 50:317–325 with permission

was raised as a new species by Africa (1938), and it was redescribed by Chen (1949); however, this species was later synonymized with *P. varium* (Pearson 1964; Umadevi and Madhavi 2000). Experimental human infections were reported in Japan (Aokage 1956; Komiya and Suzuki 1966). There have been no reports on natural human intestinal infections with adult flukes. However, it is of particular interest that cercariae of *P. varium* shed from *Melanoides tuberculata* snails caused ocular inflammation in children bathed in water in India, the parasite species of which was confirmed by molecular studies (Arya et al. 2016). In Taiwan, aquacultured Japanese eels were found to be infected with the metacercariae of *Procerovum cheni*, related species to *P. varium*, in the eyes (Ooi et al. 1999). It is now known to be distributed in Japan, China, the Philippines, Cambodia, Lao PDR, Vietnam, Australia, India, South Korea, and Egypt (Umadevi and Madhavi 2000; Sohn and Chai 2005; Vo et al. 2008; Thanh et al. 2009; Chai et al. 2014; Eom et al. 2015; Hung et al. 2015; El-Dakhly et al. 2017) (Table 1.7).

The adult flukes are 0.26–0.28 mm long and 0.94–1.20 mm wide, and the eggs are 24–28 × 12–16 μm in size (Umadevi and Madhavi 2000). The cercariae are para-pleuro-lophocercus type, with rectangular eyespots, and the cercarial body is 140–160 μm long and 60–72 μm wide; the tail is 316–340 μm long; the metacercariae (Fig. 1.39b) are 200–220 by 160–200 μm in size (Umadevi and Madhavi 2000). The first intermediate host is the brackish water snail, *Melanoides* (= *Thiara*) *tuberculata* (Umadevi and Madhavi 2000). The second intermediate hosts are freshwater or brackish water fish, including *Mugil affinis, Mugil cephalus, Oryzias melastigma, Platycephalus indicus, Mollienesia latipinna, Scatophagus argus, Chanos chanos, Oxyurichthys microlepis, Hemirhamphus georgi,* groupers *Epinephelus bleekeri* and *Epinephelus coioides*, and climbing perch *Anabas testudineus* (Velasquez 1973a; Yu and Mott 1994; Umadevi and Madhavi 2000; Vo et al. 2008; Thanh et al. 2009; Skov et al. 2009; Chai et al. 2012, 2014). Natural infection of cats was discovered in South Korea (Sohn and Chai 2005; Chai et al. 2013; Shin et al. 2015), and that of birds (pond herons) was found in India (Umadevi and Madhavi 2000). Adult flukes were successfully reared in dogs (Onji and Nishio 1916), chicks, ducklings, and mice (Umadevi and Madhavi 2000).

Potentially Zoonotic *Procerovum* spp. Potentially zoonotic *Procerovum* spp. include *P. cheni* Hsu, 1950 and *P. bartillans* Pearson, 1964 (see Pearson 1964).

1.12 *Pygidiopsis*

1.12.1 Pygidiopsis genata

1.12.1.1 *Pygidiopsis genata* Looss, 1907

This species (Fig. 1.40) was first discovered in the small intestine of a pelican in Cairo, Egypt (Looss 1907; Ransom 1920). Subsequently, it was also found in pelicans in Romania (Ciurea 1924), dogs in China (it should be verified whether the species was actually *P. genata* or a related species *P. summa*) (Faust and Nishigori 1926), and dogs and cats (both hosts were experimentally infected) in the Philippines (Africa and Garcia 1935; Africa et al. 1940). *P. genata* was also detected among the trematode parasites from a Persian wolf and from the intestine of dogs and cats in Israel (Palestine) (Witenberg 1929). In Egypt, this parasite has been found from cats, dogs, foxes, shrews, rats, kites, and ducks (Abdel Azim 1938; Kuntz and Chandler 1956) and subsequently in humans by recovery of eggs in fecal examinations (Youssef et al. 1987a). The metacercariae were detected in goby fish in Ukraine (Kvach 2002) and *Astatotilapia desfontiansei* in Tunisia (Balozet and Callot 1939). Recently, this parasite was recovered from birds in Israel (Dzikowski et al. 2004) and stray cats in Kuwait (El-Azazy et al. 2015). Kuntz and Chandler (1956) treated *P. summa* and *Pygidiopsis plana* as synonyms of *P. genata*, without proper explanations. However, both of these 2 species should be treated as distinct species because of various significant points (Diaz et al. 2014; Sohn et al. 2016). Molecular analysis

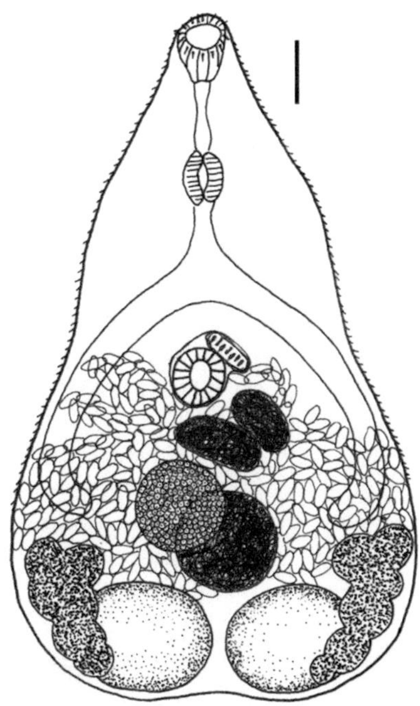

Fig. 1.40 Line drawing of an adult fluke of *Pygidiopsis genata*. Redrawn from the figure in Witenberg (1929) Ann Trop Med Parasitol 23:131–268. Scale bar = 0.05 mm

using rDNA ITS1 and ITS2 revealed that *P. genata* is genetically more close to *Phagicola longa* and *Ascocotyle pindoramensis* than *Metagonimus yokogawai* and *Haplorchis pumilio* (Al-Kandari et al. 2015).

The adult flukes are 0.35–0.70 mm long and 0.16–0.40 mm wide, and the eggs are 17–22 × 9–13 μm in size (Witenberg 1929; Youssef et al. 1987b). The oral sucker has 16 small spines around the oral aperture which are seen only in fresh preparations (Witenberg 1929). The snail hosts are *Melanoides tuberculata* (Youssef et al. 1987b) and *Melanopsis costata* (Dzikowski et al. 2004). The rediae occur in spaces within the digestive gland of the snail host, and the cercariae are biocellate, phototropic, and pleuro-lophocercous, and emerge from the snail at noon (Youssef et al. 1987b). The cercariae are ovoid; their body is 108–140 (av. 130) μm long and 40–70 (av. 60) μm wide, and the tail is 385–420 μm long and 13–17 μm wide (Youssef et al. 1987b). The second intermediate hosts are brackish water fish, including *Tilapia galilea, Tilapia nilotica, Tilapia simonis,* and *Barbus canis* (Witenberg 1929), *Mugil capito* (Fahmy and Selim 1959), *Tilapia zilli* and *Tilapia nilotica* (Mahdy and Shaheed 2001; Ibrahim and Soliman 2010; Lobna et al. 2010), and experimentally *Gambusia affinis* and *Tilapia nilotica* (Youssef et al. 1987b). The metacercariae are spherical or subspherical, 120–210 μm in diameter, and usually encyst in the head, tail, and muscles of the fish hosts (Youssef et al. 1987b; Hegazi et al. 2014). Natural definitive hosts include pelicans, wolves, cats, dogs, foxes, shrews, rats, kites, and ducks (Looss 1907; Witenberg 1929; Kuntz and Chandler 1956; El-Dakhly et al. 2017). Experimental hosts include mice, rats, and hamsters (Mansour et al. 1981).

Molecular analysis of 18S rDNA and ITS1 and ITS2 regions revealed specific links between the pleurolophocercous cercariae that emerged from *M. costata* snails, the metacercariae from the fish *Tilapia zilli*, and the adult flukes found in the cormorant (a bird), and thus was helpful for elucidation of the life cycle (Dzikowski et al. 2004).

Human infections were unknown before 1987 when eggs were detected in human fecal examinations from Maryut area on Manzala Lake, Egypt; the egg positive rate was 2.7% (2/73) (Youssef et al. 1987a). Although the adult flukes were not identified, the eggs of *P. genata* were morphologically well discriminated from those of *Heterophyes heterophyes* (Youssef et al. 1987a). However, trials to obtain adult flukes are required to definitely confirm the zoonotic potential of this parasite in Egypt. The existence of human infections in other countries, including the Philippines, Romania, Iran, Israel (Palestine), Ukraine, Tunisia, and Kuwait, should be determined (Fig. 1.41; Table 1.7). The pathogenicity and pathology, symptoms and signs, and other characteristics of this fluke infection are unknown. Diagnosis can be done by detecting eggs in the feces or recovery of adult flukes following chemotherapy and purging. Treatment can be successfully done using praziquantel. Avoidance of raw or undercooked brackish water fish, including mullets and gobies, can prevent human infections.

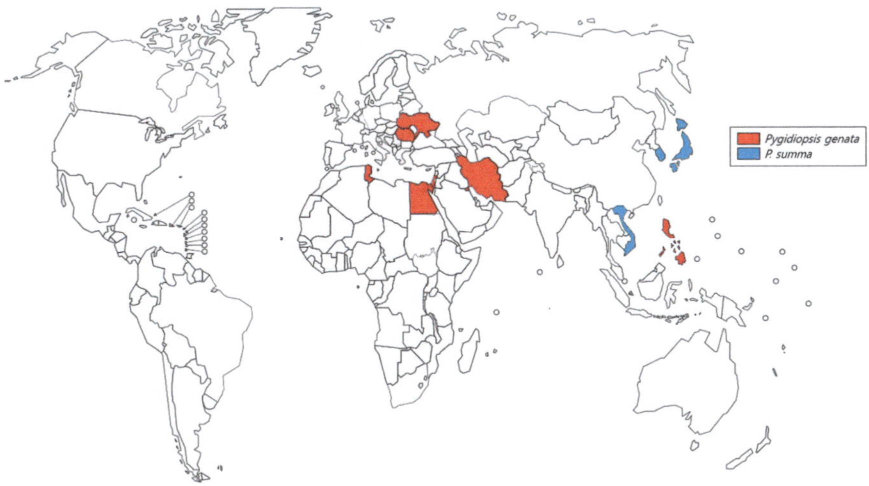

Fig. 1.41 Global distribution of *Pygidiopsis* spp. (*P. genata* and *P. summa*) based on the presence of their life cycles

1.12.2 Pygidiopsis summa

1.12.2.1 *Pygidiopsis summa* Onji and Nishio, 1916

This species (Fig. 1.42a, b) was originally described from dogs fed brackish water fish infected with the metacercariae in Japan (Nishio 1915; Onji and Nishio 1916). It is now known to be present in Japan, South Korea, and Vietnam (Yokogawa et al. 1965; Seo et al. 1981a, b; Vo et al. 2008; Sohn et al. 2016). Human infections with *P. summa* were first reported by detection of eggs in human feces in Japan (Takahashi 1929). Subsequently, adult flukes were identified from humans in Japan (Yokogawa et al. 1965) and South Korea (Seo et al. 1981a). In South Korea, 8 people residing in a salt-farm village of Okku-gun, Jeollabuk-do (formerly Chollabuk-do) who habitually ate the raw flesh of the mullet were proved to be infected with *P. summa* through recovery of adult flukes after bithionol treatment and purging (Seo et al. 1981a). In another coastal area of South Korea, 18 heterophyid egg-positive people were found to be mixed-infected with *P. summa* and *Heterophyes nocens* (Chai et al. 1994). Eighteen more cases were detected in another coastal area, Muan-gun, Jeollanam-do, from whom total 703 adult specimens of *P. summa* were recovered (Chai et al. 1997). Five more cases were detected in Buan-gun, Jeollabuk-do, and total 1732 adult specimens were collected (Chai et al. 1998). Subsequently, more wide distribution of this parasite has been found along the western and southern coastal islands of South Korea, although the egg positive rate was remarkably higher for *Heterophyes nocens* (11.0%) than that for *P. summa* (1.2%) (Chai et al. 2004).

The taxonomic relationships of *P. summa* with other trematode parasites were studied by Lee et al. (2007). Using 28S rDNA D1 gene analysis, *P. summa* was shown to be located in the same clade as *Paragonimus westermani* and the next

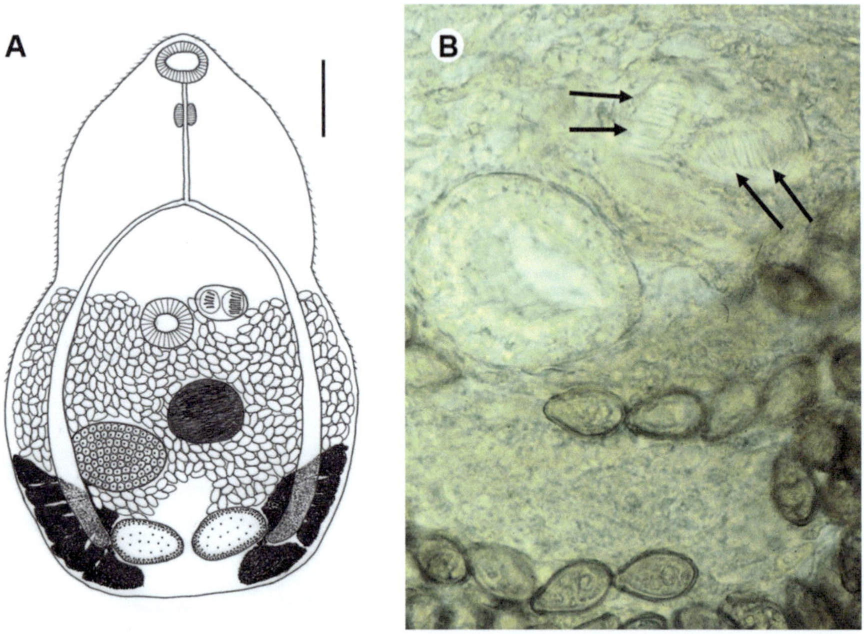

Fig. 1.42 *Pygidiopsis summa*. (**a**) Line drawing of an adult fluke (original figure). Scale bar = 0.1 mm (**b**) Enlarged view of the ventrogenital apparatus containing the ventral sucker and rodlets (arrows; 5–6 on the left and 7–9 on the right side) on the gonotyl. ×400

clade to *Metagonimus yokogawai* and *M. takahashii,* whereas *Clonorchis sinensis* and *Plagiorchis muris* were put in the same clade (Lee et al. 2007). However, analysis of mitochondrial cytochrome *c* oxidase subunit 1 (mCO1) showed more proximity of *P. summa* to *C. sinensis* than to *P. westermani, M. yokogawai,* and *M. takahashii* (Lee et al. 2007). A numerical taxonomy study on various heterophyid flukes reported that *P. summa* were more closely related to *Stellantchasmus falcatus* rather than to *Heterophyes* or *Metagonimus* (Kim et al. 1991).

The worms are characterized by a small concave body, median location of the ventral sucker, unique morphology of the ventrogenital apparatus (Fig. 1.42b), side-by-side location of the 2 testes (Chai et al. 1986), and small pyriform eggs with no distinct muskmelon patterns on the shell (Lee et al. 1984). The adult flukes are 0.58–0.85 mm long and 0.29–0.41 mm wide, and the eggs are 19–24 × 11–13 μm in size (Chai et al. 1986). The life cycle of *P. summa* has been elucidated by Ochi (1931) in Yamaguti, Hiroshima, and Okayama Prefectures, Japan. Rediae are light yellowish and cylindrical measuring 700–800 × 175 μm, and found in a brackish water snail *Tympanotonus microptera* (= *Cerithidea fluviatilis*) (Fig. 1.43a) in South Korea (personal observation) and in Japan (Ochi 1931). A few cercariae and many germ balls are contained in a redia (Ochi 1931). The cercariae are para-pleurolophocercus type (Fig. 1.43b), with rectangular or star-shaped eyespots, with the cercarial body of 180–210 μm long and 75–93 μm wide and a tail of 350–420 μm

Fig. 1.43 *Pygidiopsis summa*. (**a**) The snail intermediate host, *Cerithidea fluviatilis*, collected from a tidal flat in Okku-gun, Jeollabuk-do, South Korea (**b**) Cercaria emerged from the snail host, having the cercarial body of 200 µm in length and the tail of 380 µm long

long and 52–55 µm wide (Ochi 1931). Its oral sucker is armed with 2 rows of 8 oral spines and 12 circularly arranged smaller-sized spines (Ochi 1931). The metacercariae are detected in the gill and muscle of the mullets *Mugil cephalus, Liza menada,* redlip mullets *Chelon haematocheilus*, and goby *Acanthogobius flavimanus* (Onji and Nishio 1916; Takabayashi 1953; Chun 1963; Seo et al. 1981b; Sohn et al. 1994; Kim et al. 2006; Sohn 2009; Cho et al. 2012). The metacercariae are 190–290 by 160–290 µm in size and morphologically distinct by an X-shaped excretory bladder (Fig. 1.44a) (Seo et al. 1981b). The natural infection of domestic or feral cats (Eom et al. 1985; Sohn and Chai 2005; Shin et al. 2009, 2015) and raccoon dogs (Shin et al. 2009) have been reported. Experimental hosts include rats, cats, and dogs (Ochi 1931; Chun 1963).

The surface ultrastructure of *P. summa* was studied on adult flukes (Chai et al. 2002). The worm is calabash-form with its posterior part broader than the anterior part; tegumental spines with 14–20 tips are densely distributed and type I (uniciliated knob-like swellings) and type II sensory papillae (aciliated round swellings) are distributed around the oral and ventral suckers (Chai et al. 2002). The severe digitation of the tegumental spines resembled that of *H. nocens* (Chai et al. 2002).

This fluke is distributed mainly in the brackish water zone in Japan, South Korea, and Vietnam (Table 1.7) where brackish water fish, the source of infection, are available. In South Korea, a salt farm village near an estuary (Fig. 1.45) located in Okku-gun, Jeollanam-do was found to be an endemic focus of this fluke infection (Seo et al. 1981a).

The pathogenicity and pathology (Seo et al. 1986) as well as mucosal immune responses of the host against *P. summa* infection (Chai et al. 2014b) were studied in

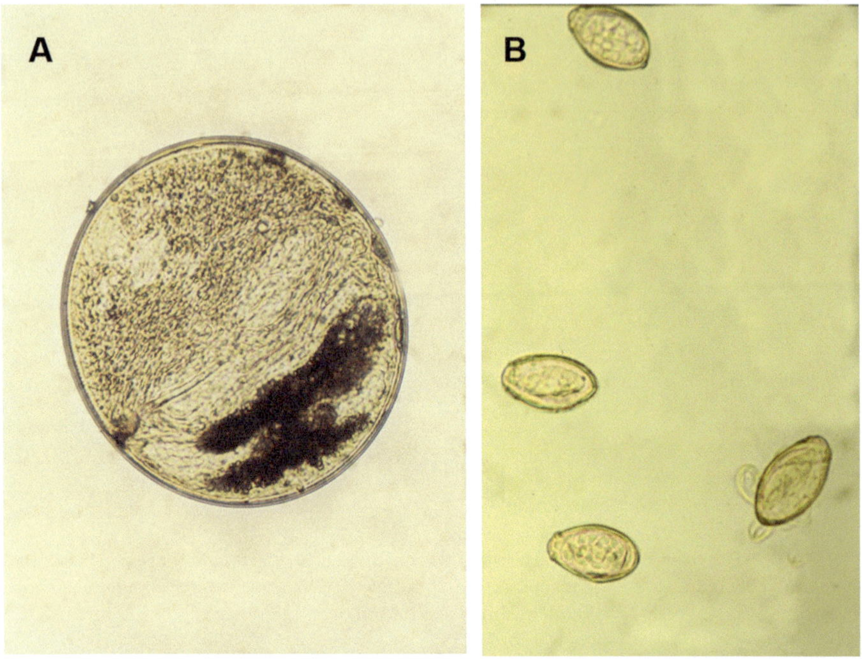

Fig. 1.44 *Pygidiopsis summa*. (**a**) Metacercaria isolated from the muscle of a mullet, *Mugil cephalus*, in South Korea showing X-shaped excretory bladder. ×200 (**b**) Eggs from the distal part of the uterus of an adult worm, 21.6 μm in average length and 12.1 μm in average width

Fig. 1.45 Irrigation channel in a salt farm in Okku-gun, Jeollabuk-do, an endemic area of *Pygidiopsis summa* in South Korea. The mullet fish are frequently available in this channel

experimental animals, including rats and mice. The mucosal pathology (Fig. 1.46a, b) was severe in rodent intestines and characterized by villous atrophy accompanied by crypt hyperplasia and severe stromal inflammation (Seo et al. 1986). However, no deep invasion of worms beyond the submucosal level was found, and the intestinal lesion was restored from 3 weeks after the infection (Seo et al. 1986). Immune effectors in the intestinal mucosa against *P. summa* infection included intraepithelial lymphocytes, goblet cells, mast cells, and IgA (Chai et al. 2014b).

Nevertheless, the symptoms and signs due to *P. summa* infection are known to be generally mild and transient (Chai and Lee 2002; Chai et al. 2005, 2009). One of the reasons is mixed-infection of the majority of human cases with other heterophyid flukes such as *Heterophyes nocens* (Chai et al. 1994, 1997, 1998, 2004). The most heavily infected person ever documented was a 52-year-old Korean man; from him 4045 adult specimens of *P. summa* were recovered after chemotherapy and purging (Seo et al. 1981a). In this patient, no significant symptoms or signs were complained, and the only abnormal laboratory finding was slight eosinophilia of 7% (Seo et al. 1981a).

The specific diagnosis of human *P. summa* infection is problematic because it is difficult to discriminate the eggs from those of other heterophyids or opisthorchiids in fecal examinations (Lee et al. 1984, 2012). However, a favorable point is that the

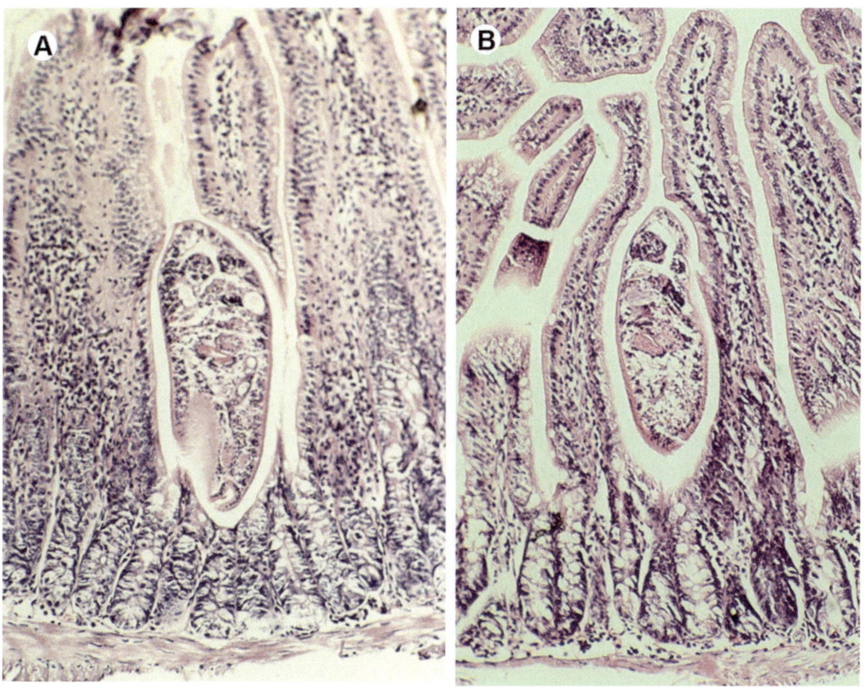

Fig. 1.46 Intestinal sections of mice (**a**, **b**) experimentally infected with *Pygidiopsis summa*. Intestinal mucosa shows atrophy, and crypts are hyperplastic. ×100 (**a**) Reproduced from the figure in Seo et al. (1986) Seoul J Med 27:125-134 with permission

size of eggs is very small (Fig. 1.44b), therefore, is helpful for their differential diagnosis in fecal examinations (Lee et al. 1984, 2012; Chai et al. 2004). This (smaller size of eggs compared with those of *Heterophyes* or *Haplorchis*) is also applicable to *P. genata* infection in Egypt (Youssef et al. 1987a). For differential diagnosis of metacercariae in food samples, including fish, PCR-RFLP assay was tried targeting their 18S rRNA; using *Hinf1* it was possible to discriminate *H. continua* and *P. summa* (Pyo et al. 2013). Human infections can be treated successfully using praziquantel (Chai et al. 1994, 1997, 1998, 2004, 2014a) or bithionol (Seo et al. 1981a).

Potentially Zoonotic *Pygidiopsis* spp. Potentially zoonotic *Pygidiopsis* spp. include *P. plana* (Linton, 1928), *P. macrostomum* Travassos, 1928, *P. pindoramensis* Travassos, 1929, *P. marivillai* Refuerzo and Garcia, 1937, *P. phalacrocoracis* Yamaguti, 1939, *P. piclaumoreli* Dollfus and Capron, 1958, *P. anterouteria* (Nasir and Diaz, 1971), *P. pelecani* Wang, 1982, *P. ardeae* Køie, 1990, *P. crassus* Ostrowski de Núñez, 1995, *P. australis* Ostrowski de Núñez, 1995 and *P. himantopae* (Dronen et al., 2005) (see Sohn et al. 2016).

1.13 *Stellantchasmus*

1.13.1 Stellantchasmus falcatus

1.13.1.1 *Stellantchasmus falcatus* Onji and Nishio, 1916

[syn. *Diorchitrema pseudocirrata* Witenberg, 1929; *Stellantchasmus formosanus* Katsuta, 1931; *Stellantchasmus amplicaecalis* Katsuta, 1932]

This species (Fig. 1.47a, b) was originally reported from cats, dogs, and a bird experimentally fed the mullet harboring the metacercariae in Japan (Onji and Nishio 1916, 1924). Witenberg (1929) created a new genus *Diorchitrema* for the flukes obtained from the intestine of dogs and cats from Israel (Palestine) and reported them as *D. pseudocirrata*. However, Ciurea (1933) and Price (1940) synonymized *Diorchitrema* with *Stellantchasmus*, and Alicata and Schattenburg (1938) placed *D. pseudocirrata* as a synonym of *S. falcatus*. In the meantime, *Stellantchasmus formosanus* was described from experimental cats, dogs, mice, and a human infected with the metacercariae encysted in the mullet *Mugil cephalus* in Taiwan (Katsuta 1931), and *Stellantchamus amplicaecalis* from dogs, cats, and mice fed the metacercariae from mullets in Taiwan (Katsuta 1932). However, both of these species were synonymized with *S. falcatus* (Pearson 1964).

Human infections with *S. falcatus* were first reported by recovery of eggs in human feces (105 of 6680 inhabitants) in Japan, but the adult flukes were not identified (Takahashi 1929). Katsuta (1931, 1932) succeeded in infecting himself with *S. formosanus* but failed to infect with *S. amplicaecalis*, respectively (both species are synonyms of *S. falcatus*). Africa and Garcia (1935) was the first to detect people

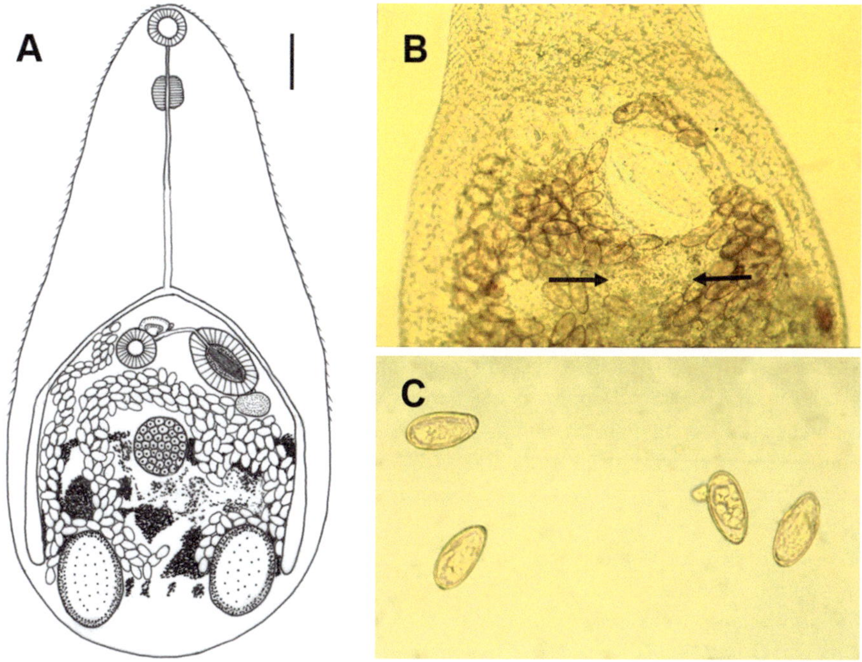

Fig. 1.47 *Stellantchasmus falcatus*. (**a**) Line drawing of an adult fluke (original figure). Scale bar = 0.05 mm (**b**) Close-up view of the ventrogenital apparatus (the ventral sucker and the distal part of the seminal vesicle) and the proximal part of the seminal vesicle (arrows). ×200. Reproduced from the figure in Seo et al. (1984) Korean J Parasitol 22:43–50 with permission (**c**) Eggs from the distal part of the uterus of an adult worm, 27.2 μm in average length and 12.5 μm in average width

infected with *S. falcatus* (under the name *D. pseudocirrata*) by adult worm recovery in the Philippines. Later, they corrected the name of the parasite as *S. falcatus* (Africa et al. 1940). Thereafter, a few human cases were found by recovery of adult flukes in Hawaii (Alicata and Schattenburg 1938; Glover and Alicata 1957), Japan (Kagei et al. 1964; Ito 1964a), Thailand (Kliks and Tantachamrun 1974; Tantachamrun and Kliks 1978; Radomyos et al. 1990), South Korea (Seo et al. 1984; Hong et al. 1986; Sohn et al. 1989; Chai et al. 1998), and Vietnam (Dung et al. 2007). Three additional species of *Stellantchamus* have been described by Pearson (1964) and Pearson and Ow-Yang (1982); *S. aspinosus* Pearson 1964, *S. gallinae* (Oshmarin 1970) Pearson and Ow-Yang 1982, and *S. batillans* (Pearson 1964) Pearson and Ow-Yang 1982. Later, *S. aspinosus* and *S. batillans* were reported again in Australia from water rats (Smales and Cribb 1997).

There has been debate on the taxonomy of *S. falcatus* (freshwater type) found in the northern part of Thailand which is transmitted by freshwater fish, namely, half-beaked fish *Dermogenys pusillus* and climbing perch *Anabas testudineus* (Wongsawad and Wongsawad 2010), in comparison to the original *S. falcatus* (brackish water type) which is mediated by brackish water fish, in particular, mullets *Mugil* spp. or *Liza* spp. (Chai and Lee 2002; Chai et al. 2005, 2009). In Thailand, both types are found, and morphologically, there are only minor differences in body size, organ arrangement, and the prepharynx length between the adults of the 2 types (Wongsawad and Wongsawad 2010). The genomic DNAs of *S. falcatus* freshwater type (Wongsawad et al. 2006; Wongsawad and Wongsawad 2010) and brackish water type (Wongsawad and Wongsawad 2010) were successfully isolated and analyzed for molecular differentiation of these 2 types using the HAT-RAPD method. Several primers, namely, OPA-09, OPN-03, and OPAD-01, successfully differentiated the genomic DNA of *S. falcatus* brackish water type from that of *S. falcatus* freshwater type, generating type-specific HAT-RAPD fragments (Wongsawad and Wongsawad 2010). From this observation, they strongly suggested that the 2 types of *S. falcatus* may be different species (Wongsawad and Wongsawad 2010). This point needs further verification with further researches. Sequences of the nuclear ribosomal DNA genes, including 18S rDNA, 28S rDNA, and ITS2 region, were used for analysis of the phylogenetic relationships of *S. falcatus* with other heterophyid and opisthorchiid trematodes (Thaenkham et al. 2010; Sripalwit et al. 2015). *S. falcatus* was phylogenetically far from *Haplorchis* spp, and *Procerovum* spp., and it was indicated that *S. falcatus* might have diverged first from a common ancestor of Haplorchiinae species (Thaenkham et al. 2010). Similarly, *S. falcatus* was far from *Haplorchoides* sp., *Centrocestus* spp., *Metagonimus yokogawai*, and *Opisthorchis viverrini* (Sripalwit et al. 2015). A numerical taxonomy study reported that *S. falcatus* was more closely related to *Pygidiopsis summa* rather than to *Heterophyes* or *Metagonimus* (Kim et al. 1991).

The adult flukes of *S. falcatus* are 0.39–0.78 mm long and 0.31–0.40 mm wide and morphologically characterized by its pyriform shape with the presence of a small submedian ventral sucker and an expulsor type elongated sac-like seminal vesicle (Fig. 1.47b) (Seo et al. 1984; Chai and Lee 2002). Their eggs are elongated oval in shape (Fig. 1.47c), yellowish, and 24–30 × 10–13 μm in size; they lack the muskmelon pattern on the shell surface (Seo et al. 1984). The life cycle studies were actively performed in Hawaii (Martin 1958; Noda 1959) and some studies on the fish host were performed in Japan (Onji and Nishio 1916), Taiwan (Katsuta 1931, 1932), and South Korea (Chai and Sohn 1988). The snail host was confirmed to be the brackish water snail *Stenomelania newcombi, Thiara granifera*, and *Thiara granifera mauiensis* in Hawaii (Martin 1958; Noda 1959) and *Melanoides tuberculata* in Egypt (Boulos and Samra 1985). Two generations of rediae, each measuring 112–420 × 56–112 μm, were found to develop in the digestive gland of the snails (Martin 1958). The cercariae are ocellate and pleuro-lophocercous with a double left eyespot and a single right eyespot, with their body 55–116 (av. 91) × 34–64 (av. 47) μm in size and tail 240–370 (av. 320) μm long and 11–20 (av. 17) μm wide; they have 5 oral spines in the first row and 7–10 oral spines in the second and third rows, respectively (Martin 1958). The second intermediate host was shown to be brackish water fish, in particular, the mullet *Mugil cephalus* (Fig. 1.48a), other *Mugil* sp., *Liza menada,* and *Liza haematocheila* (Alicata and Schattenburg 1938; Otagaki and Kanemitsu 1953; Martin 1958; Kobayasi 1968; Rekharani and Madhavi 1985; Chai and Sohn 1988), goby *Acanthogobius flavimanus* (Kanemitsu 1953), *Xenentodon*

Fig. 1.48 *Stellantchasmus falcatus*. (**a**) A mullet, *Mugil cephalus*, the fish intermediate host (**b**) A metacercaria isolated from the muscle of a mullet. ×200 Reproduced from the figure in Chai and Sohn (1988) Korean J Parasitol 26:65–68 with permission

cacila, Xenentodon canciloides (Scholz et al. 1990; Ditrich et al. 1990), and giant gouramy *Osphronemus gourami* (Thien et al. 2007). However, freshwater fish, in particular, the half-beaked fish *Dermogenus pusillus* and climbing perch *Anabas testudineus* also serve as the second intermediate host in the northern part of Thailand (Wongsawad et al. 2004; Wongsawad and Wongsawad 2010). The identity of these 2 types of *S. falcatus* remains to be further verified. The metacercarial cysts (Fig. 1.48b) are elliptical, 150–200 × 130–190 μm in size, and found mainly in the muscle of the fish (Ito 1964b; Chai and Sohn 1988). Natural definitive hosts are stray cats, dogs, pigs, rats, humans, and birds (Takahashi 1929; Ash 1962; Seo et al. 1984; Smales and Cribb 1997; Sohn and Chai 2005; Farahnak et al. 2004; Anh et al. 2009; Shin et al. 2015). Experimental hosts include chicks, mice, rats, cats, dogs, and humans (Katsuta 1931; Alicata and Schattenburg 1938; Wongsawad et al. 1998; Saenphet et al. 2003; Ramsuk et al. 2004). Rats were shown to be a better experimental host than mice (Saenphet et al. 2003).

The surface ultrastructure of *S. falcatus* was studied on metacercariae and adult flukes (Wongsawad et al. 1997). The metacercarial cysts were found in groups from the body cavity of the fish host *D. pusillus*; they have wide and shallow groove on the surface of the cyst (Wongsawad et al. 1997). The adult worms are pyriform with its posterior part broader than the anterior part; tegumental spines with 7–9 tips are densely distributed, and club-like sensory papillae, unique for *S. falcatus*, are observed (Wongsawad et al. 1997). The fine structure of the secretory vesicle in *S. falcatus* cercariae was studied by Singh et al. (1977).

Now the existence of this fluke is known in Japan, the Philippines, Hawaii, South Korea, China, Taiwan, Lao PDR, Vietnam, Thailand, Australia, India, Iran, and Israel (Palestine) (Fig. 1.49; Table 1.7) (Witenberg 1929; Katsuta 1931, 1932; Africa et al. 1940; Chen 1951; Martin 1958; Ito 1964a; Pearson 1964; Kobayasi 1968; Rekharani and Madhavi 1985; Ditrich et al. 1990; Radomyos et al. 1990; Smales and Cribb 1997; Wongsawad et al. 1997, 1998; Chai and Lee 2002; Farahnak et al. 2004; Dung et al. 2007; Chi et al. 2008).

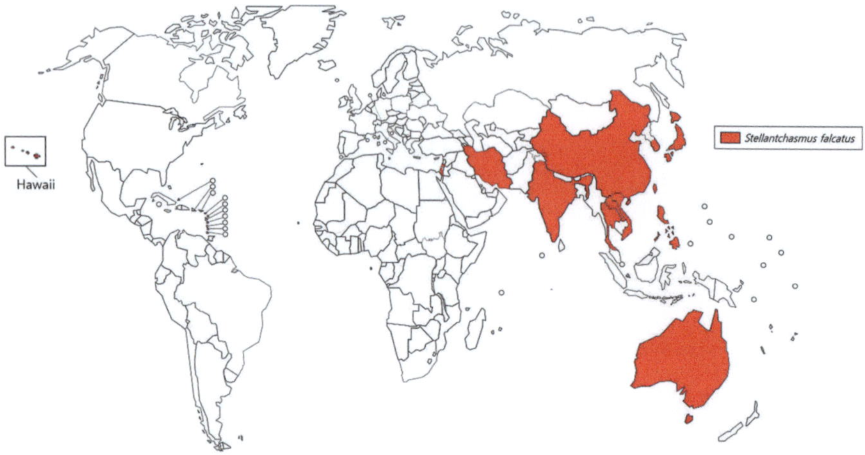

Fig. 1.49 Global distribution of *Stellantchasmus falcatus* based on the presence of their life cycles

Despite that *S. falcatus* was involved in causing erratic parasitisms in the heart, brain, and spinal cord of humans (Africa et al. 1940), the pathogenicity and pathology as well as mucosal immune responses of the host against *S. falcatus* infection has been seldom studied. However, innate immunity against *S. falcatus* infection was demonstrated in mice and rats; in the former, the worms spontaneously expelled within a week after infection, and in the latter, the worms expelled after 28 days (Saenphet et al. 2003). The number of blood eosinophils was increased from the first week of infection and remained relatively high until the worms are expelled from these rodent hosts (Saenphet et al. 2003).

The symptoms and signs due to *S. falcatus* infection are known to be generally mild and transient (Chai and Lee 2002; Chai et al. 2009). One of the reasons is mixed-infections in the majority of human cases with other heterophyid flukes such as *Heterophyes nocens* and *Pygidiopsis summa* (Chai et al. 1998, 2004). However, *S. falcatus* worms were discovered among the trematodes involved in erratic parasitisms in humans in the Philippines (Africa et al. 1940). It was suggested that such patients may have been immunocompromised (Yokogawa 1940); in such conditions, the worms could penetrate deep into the submucosa and mesenteric vessels, and liberate eggs in the blood streams. It is of considerable interest that a neorickettsia-like organism (SF strain) was isolated from the metacercariae of *S. falcatus*, although the pathogenicity of SF strain neorickettsia to humans have not been clarified (Fukuda and Yamamoto 1981).

The specific diagnosis of human *S. falcatus* infection is problematic because it is difficult to discriminate the eggs from those of other heterophyids or opisthorchiids in fecal examinations (Lee et al. 1984, 2012 Ditrich et al. 1992). However, a favorable point is that the egg shape is typically elongated; thus, is helpful for their differential diagnosis in fecal examinations (Lee et al. 1984, 2012). Human infections can be treated successfully using praziquantel (Seo et al. 1984; Chai et al. 1998, 2004) or niclosamide (Ramsuk et al. 2004).

Potentially Zoonotic *Stellantchasmus* spp. Potentially zoonotic *Stellantchasmus* spp. include *S. aspinosus* Pearson, 1964, *S. gallinae* (Oshmarin, 1970) Pearson and Ow-Yang, 1982, and *S. batillans* (Pearson, 1964) Pearson and Ow-Yang, 1982 (reviewed by Pearson and Ow-Yang 1982).

1.14 *Stictodora*

1.14.1 Stictodora fuscata

1.14.1.1 *Stictodora fuscata* (Onji and Nishio, 1916) Yamaguti, 1958

[syn. *Cornatrium fuscatum* Onji and Nishio, 1916]

The genus *Stictodora* was first established by Looss (1899) in Egypt using *Stictodora sawakinensis* as the type. After then, in Japan, Onji and Nishio (1916, 1924) created a genus *Cornatrium* and included 4 species; *C. adulescentium, C. fuscatum, C. perpendiculum,* and *C. pusyllum.* However, *Cornatrium* has been synonymized with *Stictodora*, and the names were changed into *S. adulescentia, S. fuscata, S. perpendiculum,* and *S. pusylla* (Yamaguti 1958). Thereafter, including *S. manilensis* (Africa and Garcia 1935), *S. guerreroi* (Garcia and Refuerzo 1938), *S. diplachantha* (Johnston 1943), and *S. hainanensis* (Kobayasi 1942), a total of about 20 additional had been reported (Yamaguti 1971; Kharoo and Dhar 1984; Qiu and Zhang 1986; Dronen et al. 2007; Das et al. 2014). However, *S. hainanensis* was synonymized with *S. manilensis* (Chen 1951), and several other species were transferred to different genera, such as *Galactosomum* (Pearson 1973) or *Acanthotrema* (Sohn et al. 2003). The species retaining taxonomic validity are listed below.

S. fuscata (Fig. 1.50a) was originally described from cats experimentally fed infected mullets in Japan (Onji and Nishio 1916). The adult fluke is morphologically characterized by the presence of a gonotyl superimposed on the ventral sucker and armed with 12 chitinous spines, a metraterm (Fig. 1.50b), and 2 testes located obliquely in the middle field of the body (Chai et al. 1988). The presence of human infection with this fluke was briefly mentioned by Yamaguti (1958, 1971) but the literature background is unavailable. The first human infection with *S. fuscata* was discovered from a Korean young man (reported under the name *Stictodora* sp.), who favoured eating raw mullets and gobies (Chai et al. 1988). Thereafter, about 35 human infection cases have been detected by recovery of adult flukes in seashore villages in South Korea (Chai et al. 1994, 1997, 1998, 2004; Guk et al. 2006; Park et al. 2007; Chai et al. 2014, 2015). The existence of *S. fuscata* life cycle has been reported in South Korea (Chai et al. 2009), Japan (Komiya 1965), and Kuwait (Abdul-Salam et al. 2000) (Table 1.7).

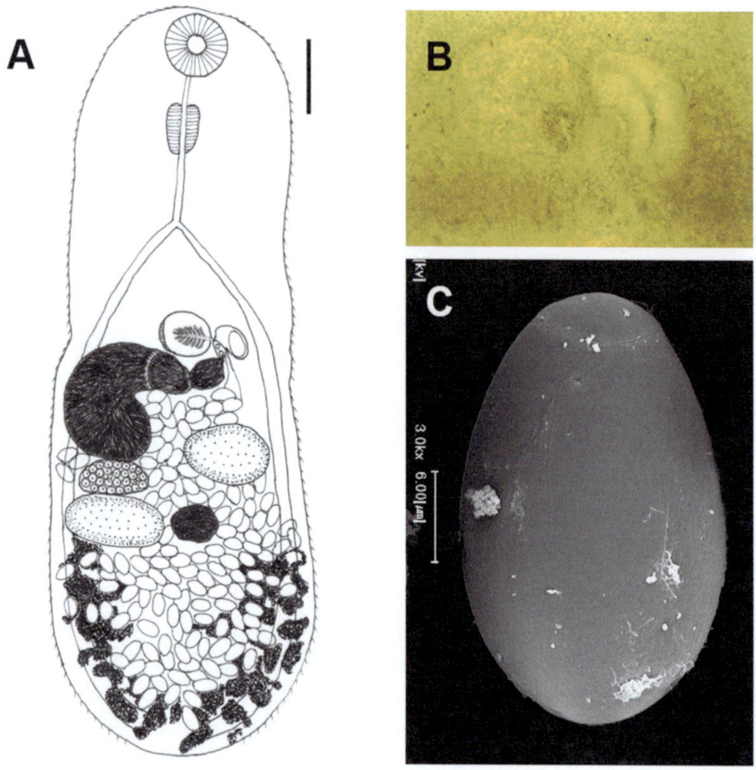

Fig. 1.50 *Stictodora fuscata*. (**a**) Line drawing of an adult fluke (original figure). Scale bar = 0.1 mm (**b**) Close-up view of the ventrogenital sac (the ventral sucker, gonotyl with minute spines, and the metraterm). ×200. Reproduced from the figure in Chai et al. (1988) Korean J Parasitol 26:127–132 with permission (**c**) Scanning electron microscopic view of an egg (33.6 μm in length) recovered from a naturally infected human in South Korea

Adult flukes of *S. fuscata* are 0.90–0.98 mm long and 0.38 mm wide, and their eggs (Fig. 1.50c) are 34–38 × 20–23 μm in size (Chai et al. 1988). The cercariae have not been discovered. The metacercariae are elliptical, and 190–300 μm by 170–270 μm long (Sohn et al. 1994b).

The surface ultrastructure of *S. fuscata* has been studied by Sohn (2000) and Abdul-Salam et al. (2000). The body was pyriform or leaf-like and ventrally concave, and the body surface is covered with cobblestone-like cytoplasmic processes (Abdul-Salam et al. 2000). The tegumental spines are digitated into 9–12 points at the tip at the anterior portion, 5–6 and 7–8 in the middle, and 2–3 and peg-like at the posterior part (Abdul-Salam et al. 2000; Sohn 2000). The type I sensory papillae were distributed in single or grouped form symmetrically around the oral sucker (Sohn 2000). The ventrogenital opening is armed with protruding gonotyl spines and also sperms discharged from the genital pore (Sohn 2000).

The life cycle of *S. fuscata* is poorly known. The snail intermediate host is not yet discovered (Komiya 1965; Chai et al. 2009). The second intermediate host is brackish water fish, including mullets *Mugil cephalus* in Japan and South Korea (Onji and Nishio 1916; Sohn et al. 1994a) and *Liza macrolepis* in Kuwait (Abdul-Salam et al. 2000), and redlip mullets *Chelon haematocheilus* and gobies *Acanthogobius flavimanus* in South Korea (Sohn et al. 1994a, b; Cho et al. 2012). However, a freshwater fish *Pseudorasbora parva* could also be a fish host in Japan (Hasegawa 1934). The metacercariae are detected in the mesenterium and adjacent fat tissues (Komiya 1965), or muscle, head tissue, and viscera of the fish (Sohn et al. 1994b). A recent study in South Korea reported that the infection rate of gobies caught from 4 localities of western and southern coastal areas with *S. fuscata* metacercariae was 61.3% on average (Sohn et al. 2018). The metacercarial burden per fish ranged from 3 to 1081 (Sohn et al. 2018).

The natural definitive hosts include cats, dogs, and humans (Onji and Nishio 1916; Yamaguti 1958; Sohn and Chai 2005; Shin et al. 2009; Chai et al. 2009, 2013). Avian species can also play the role of natural definitive hosts of this fluke (Komiya 1965; Yamaguti 1971). Cats are an experimental definitive host (Onji and Nishio 1916; Sohn et al. 1994b; Sohn 2000; Abdul-Salam et al. 2000).

The pathogenicity and pathology as well as host immune responses are unknown. Clinical manifestations in heavily infected cases (more than 100 worms) remain to be determined. However, most of the human cases were mixed-infected with other intestinal flukes (Chai et al. 1994, 1997, 1998, 2004). Therefore, symptoms elicited solely by *S. fuscata* infection are difficult to know. The diagnosis of eggs in fecal examinations is difficult, but the eggs of *S. fuscata* is larger (33.6 μm in average length) than the eggs of other heterophyid species (smaller than 30 μm with the exception of *Metagonimus takahashii* and *M. miyatai* eggs) (Lee et al. 2012). Treatment is successful with praziquantel 10 mg/kg in a single dose (Chai et al. 2014, 2015).

1.14.2 Stictodora lari

1.14.2.1 *Stictodora lari* Yamaguti, 1939

This fluke (Fig. 1.51a, b) was first discovered in the small intestine of the sea gull *Larus crassirostris* in Japan (Yamaguti 1939). Later *S. lari* was found in Australia (Bearup 1961; Howell 1973), Russia (Belogurov et al. 1968), South Korea (Chai et al. 1989), and Vietnam (Anh et al. 2009) (Table 1.7). Its morphological characters include a gonotyl armed with 70–80 min spines arranged in 2 groups; one densely crowded group of 30–40 spines and the other linearly-arranged group containing 30–40 spines, which make a C-form (Fig. 1.51b) or a comma- or reversed comma-shape (Chai et al. 1989). Human infections were first documented by Chai et al. (2002) in South Korea; 6 human patients were found infected with 1–10 specimens of *S. lari* recovered after anthelmintic treatment and purging of coastal

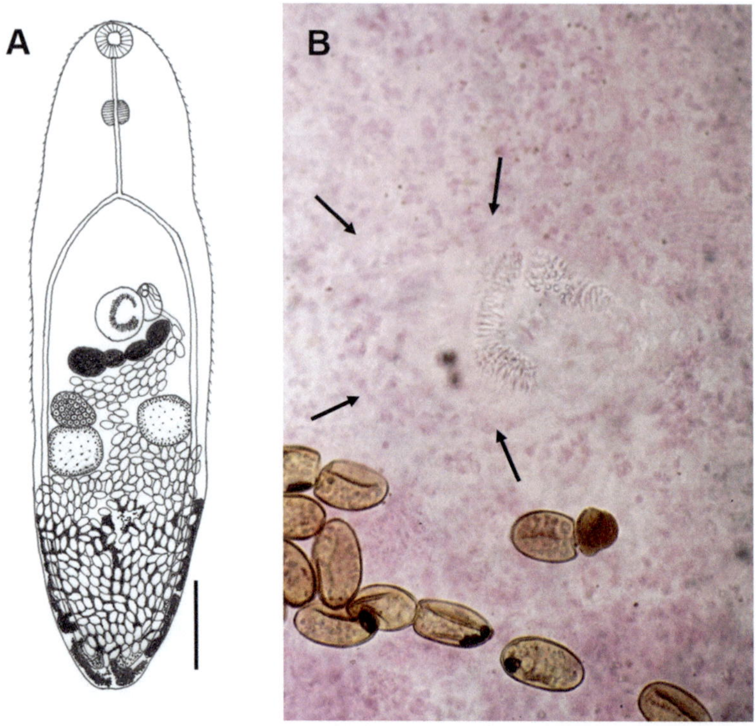

Fig. 1.51 *Stictodora lari*. (**a**) Line drawing of an adult fluke (original figure). Scale bar = 0.1 mm (**b**) Close-up view of the ventrogenital sac (the ventral sucker and the gonotyl with minute spines arranged in "C-shape". ×400

village residents in a southern part of South Korea. Subsequently, 4 additional cases were detected from a southern island, South Korea (Chai et al. 2004). In Muan-gun, South Korea, another human case was found (Cho et al. 2010). A numerical taxonomy study reported that *S. lari* is more close to *H. continua* than to *P. summa, H. nocens,* or *S. falcatus* (Kim et al. 1991).

Adult flukes of *S. lari* are elongate (Fig. 1.51a), and 0.70–0.86 mm long and 0.27–0.36 mm wide in specimens from human infections (Chai et al. 2002) and 0.95–1.18 mm long and 0.26–0.32 mm wide in those obtained experimentally from a puppy and kittens (Chai et al. 1989). The eggs are oval, dark brown, thick-shelled without musk-melon appearance, and 28–33 µm long (av. 30) and 17–20 (av. 19) µm wide (Chai et al. 1989). The life cycle and larval stages of *S. lari* were studied in Australia (Bearup 1961) and South Korea (Chai et al. 1989). The first intermediate host is the brackish water gastropod *Velacumantus australis* in Australia (Bearup 1961; Appleton 1983) but unknown in South Korea. Rediae, 0.148 by 0.022 mm, were found in the mantle and digestive gland of the snail; cercariae were pleuro-lophocercous type with eyespots, body being 219 μm long ad 87 μm wide and tail being 429 μm long and 31 μm wide (Bearup 1961). A group of oral spines are seen (difficult to see in cercariae but can be visible in metacercariae) in small pit anterior to the mouth opening; 16 spines are arranged in a circle projecting from the pit (Bearup 1961). Cercariae were experimentally exposed to freshwater fish *Gambusia* and *Lebistes*, and metacercariae were obtained; the metacercarial cyst was 180 μm in diameter at 2 h after infection, but it grew to become 400 μm at 26 days (Bearup 1961). In gobies *A. flavimanus*, a natural fish host in South Korea (Chai et al. 1989; Cho et al. 2012), the metacercarial cyst is elliptical and 390–430 μm long and 320–350 μm wide (Chai et al. 1989). In Australia, a number of estuarine fish species, including *Flavingobius lateralis obliquus, Atherinosoma microstoma, Urocampus carinorostris, Waiteopsis paludis, Mugil* sp., and *Gambusia affinis* have been identified to be the fish hosts (Bearup 1961). In gobies, metacercariae are mainly found in the head tissue of the fish (Chai et al. 1989), whereas in *Gambusia affinis*, an experimental host, they are scattered throughout the body muscles and rarely in the liver (Bearup 1961). A recent study in South Korea reported that the infection rate of gobies caught from 7 western and southern coastal areas with *S. lari* metacercariae was 45.3% on average (Sohn et al. 2018). The metacercarial burden per fish ranged from 2 to 1090 (Sohn et al. 2018).

Natural definitive hosts include feral cats (Sohn and Chai 2005; Chai et al. 2013; Shin et al. 2015), humans (Chai et al. 2002), and dogs (Anh et al. 2009). Cats, dogs, and seagulls were used as experimental definitive hosts (Belogurov et al. 1968; Bearup 1961; Chai et al. 1989).

The pathogenicity and pathology as well as host immune responses against *S. lari* infection are unknown. However, as most of the human cases detected were infected only with a small number of worms (Chai et al. 2002, 2004; Cho et al. 2010), clinical manifestations seem to be negligible. The diagnosis of human *S. lari* infection by fecal examinations is difficult. Treatment is successful with praziquantel 10 mg/kg in a single dose (Chai et al. 2002, 2004).

Potentially Zoonotic *Stictodora* spp. Potentially zoonotic *Stictodora* spp. include *S. adulescentia* (Onji and Nishio, 1916) Yamaguti, 1958, *S. alykhani* Das et al., 2014, *S. allicoli* Kharoo and Dhar, 1984, *S. caballeroi* Martin, 1955, *S. cablei* Dronen et al., 2007, *S. diplacantha* Johnston, 1943, *S. guerreroi* Garcia and Refuerzo, 1936, *S. japonica* Yamaguti, 1939, *S. lariformicola* Sogandares-Bernal and Walton, 1965, *S. macrotestis* Belopol'skaia, 1963, *S. manilensis* Africa and Garcia, 1935, *S. mergi* Yamaguti, 1939, *S. morosovi* Laonov, 1957, *S. palmifera* Vasquez-Colet, 1944, *S. perpendiculum* (Onji and Nishio, 1916) Yamaguti, 1958, *S. petrowi* Oshmarin, 1963, *S. pusilla* (Onji and Nishio, 1916) Yamaguti, 1958, *S. sawakinensis* Looss, 1899, *S. sclerogonocotyla* Paperna, 1964, *S. thapari* Witenberg, 1953, and *S. yantainensis* Qiu and Zhang, 1986 (see Yamaguti 1971; Kharoo and Dhar 1984; Qiu and Zhang 1986; Dronen et al. 2007; Das et al. 2014).

References

References for Section 1.1

Chai JY (2007) Intestinal flukes. In: Murrell KD, Fried B (eds) Food-borne parasitic zoonoses. Fish and plant-borne parasites. Springer, New York, pp 53–115

Chontananarth T, Wongsawad C, Chomdej S et al (2014) Molecular phylogeny of trematodes in family Heterophyidae based on mitochondrial cytochrome *c* oxidase subunit I (COI). Asian Pac J Trop Med 7:446–450

Morozov FN (1952) Superfamily Heterophyoidea Faust, 1929. In: Skrjabin KI (ed) Trematodes of animals and man, vol 6. Academy of Sciences of the Union of Soviet Socialist Republics, Moscow, pp 153–412 (in Russian)

Pearson J (2008) Family Heterophyidae Leiper, 1909. In: Bray RA, Gibson DI, Jones A (eds) Keys to the Trematoda, vol 3. CAB International, Wallingford, pp 113–124

Thaenkham U, Blair D, Nawa Y et al (2012) Families Opisthorchiidae and Heterophyidae: are they distinct? Parasitol Int 61:90–93

Yamaguti S (1958) Systema Helminthum. Vol. I. The digenetic trematodes of vertebrates (Part I). Interscience Publishers Inc, New York, pp 1–979

References for Section 1.2

Africa CM, de Leon W, Garcia EY (1940) Visceral complications in intestinal heterophyidiasis of man. Acta Med Philippina, Monogr Ser 1:1–132

Ahn YK (1983) *Lateolabrax japonicus*, a role of the second intermediate host of *Metagonimus yokogawai*. New Med J 26:135–139 (in Korean)

Ahn YK (1984) Epidemiological studies on *Metagonimus yokogawai* infection in Samcheok-gun, Kangwon-do, Korea. Korean J Parasitol 22:161–170 (in Korean)

Ahn YK (1993) Intestinal flukes of genus *Metagonimus* and their second intermediate hosts in Kangwon-do. Korean J Parasitol 31:331–340 (in Korean)

Ahn YK, Ryang YS (1988) Epidemiological studies on *Metagonimus* infection along the Hongcheon river, Kangwon Province. Korean J Parasitol 26:207–213 (in Korean)

Ahn YK, Ryang YS (1995) Growth, egg-laying and life span of Miyata type of genus *Metagonimus* (Trematoda: Heterophyidae) in the final hosts. J Wonju Med Coll 8:1–12 (in Korean)

Ahn YK, Soh CT, Lee SK (1981) Egg laying capacity of *Metagonimus yokogawai*. Yonsei Reports Trop Med 12:11–16

Ahn H, Rim HJ, Kim SJ (1991) Antigenic localities in the tissues of *Metagonimus yokogawai* observed by immunogold labeling method. Korean J Parasitol 29:245–257 (in Korean)

Asada J (1934) On *Metagonimus yokogawai* and its related species. *Rinsho Igaku* (Clinical Medicine) 22:43–56 (in Japanese)

Asada J, Kaji F, Ochi G et al (1957) On the prevalent occurrence of metagonimiasis caused by *Plecoglossus altivelis* of the Ashida River, Hiroshima Prefecture. Tokyo Iji Shinshi 74:325–330 (in Japanese)

Beaver PC, Jung RC, Cupp EW (1984) Clinical parasitology, 9th edn. Lea and Febiger, Philadelphia

Besprozvannykh VV (1994) The epizootiological problems of trematodiases in the Maritime Territory. Med Parazitol (Mosk) 3:28–31 (in Russian)

Besprozvannykh VV, Ermolenko AV, Dvoryadkin VA (1987) Occurrence of *Metagonimus katsuradai* Izumi, 1935 (Trematoda: Heterophyidae) in the southern Primor'e region. In Mamaev YL (ed) Gel'minty I vyzyvaemye imi zabollevaniya. Vladivostock, Russia, pp 47–52

Cakic P, Paunovic M, Bojana S et al (2007) *Metagonimus yokogawai*, a new parasitic trematoda species in ichthyoparasitofauna of the Serbia. Acta Veterinaria (Beograd) 57:537–543

Castro GA (1989) Immunophysiology of enteric parasitism. Parasitol Today 5:11–19

Chai JY (1979) Study on *Metagonimus yokogawai* (Katsurada, 1912) in Korea V. Intestinal pathology in experimentally infected albino rats. Seoul J Med 20:104–117

Chai JY (2007) Intestinal flukes. In: Murrell KD, Fried B (eds) Food-borne parasitic zoonoses. Fish and plant-borne parasites. Springer, New York, pp 53–115

Chai JY (2013) Praziquantel in treatment of trematode and cestode infections. Infect Chemother 45:32–43

Chai JY (2015) *Metagonimus*. In Xiao L, Ryan U, Feng Y (eds) Biology of foodborne parasites. CRC Press/Taylor & Francis Group, Boca Raton, pp 427–443

Chai JY (2017) *Metagonimus*. In Liu (ed) Laboratory models for foodborne infections, Food microbiology series. CRC Press/Taylor & Francis Group, Boca Raton, pp 743–763

Chai JY, Lee SH (2002) Food-borne intestinal trematode infections in the Republic of Korea. Parasitol Int 51:129–154

Chai JY, Jung BK (2017) Fishborne zoonotic heterophyid infections: an update. Food Waterborne Parasitol 8-9:33–63

Chai JY, Cho SY, Seo BS (1977) Study on *Metagonimus yokogawai* (Katsurada, 1912) in Korea. IV. An epidemiological investigation along Tamjin River basin, South Cholla Do. Korean J Parasitol 15:115–120

Chai JY, Seo BS, Lee SH (1984) Study on *Metagonimus yokogawai* (Katsurada, 1912) in Korea VII. Susceptibility of various strains of mice to *Metagonimus* infection and effect of prednisolone. Korean J Parasitol 22:153–160

Chai JY, Seo BS, Lee SH et al (1986) Growth and development of *Pygidiopsis summa* in rats and mice with a supplementary note on its morphological characters. Korean J Parasitol 24:55–62

Chai JY, Yu JR, Lee SH et al (1989) An egg-negative patient of acute metagonimiasis diagnosed serologically by ELISA. Seoul J Med 30:139–142

Chai JY, Sohn WM, Kim MH et al (1991) Three morphological types of the genus *Metagonimus* encysted in the dace, *Tribolodon taczanowskii*, caught from the Sumjin River. Korean J Parasitol 29:217–225

Chai JY, Huh S, Yu JR et al (1993a) An epidemiological study of metagonimiasis along the upper reaches of the Namhan River. Korean J Parasitol 31:99–108

Chai JY, Kim TH, Kho WG et al (1993b) Mucosal mast cell responses to experimental *Metagonimus yokogawai* infection in rats. Korean J Parasitol 31:129–134

Chai JY, Yun TY, Kim J et al (1994) Chronological observation on intestinal histopathology and intraepithelial lymphocytes in the intestine of rats infected with *Metagonimus yokogawai*. Korean J Parasitol 32:215–221 (in Korean)

Chai JY, Kim J, Lee SH (1995a) Invasion of *Metagonimus yokogawai* into the submucosal layer of the small intestine of immunosuppressed mice. Korean J Parasitol 33:313–321

Chai JY, Kim SJ, Kook J et al (1995b) Effects of gamma-irradiation on the survival and development of *Metagonimus yokogawai* metacercariae in rats. Korean J Parasitol 33:297–303

Chai JY, Kang YJ, Choi SY et al (1998) Surface ultrastructure of *Metagonimus miyatai* metacercariae and adults. Korean J Parasitol 36:217–225

Chai JY, Guk SM, al HET (2000a) Surface ultrastructure of *Metagonimus takahashii* metacercariae and adults. Korean J Parasitol 38:9–15

Chai JY, Han ET, Park YK et al (2000b) High endemicity of *Metagonimus yokogawai* infection along residents of Samcheok-shi, Kangwon-do. Korean J Parasitol 38:33–36

Chai JY, Murrell KD, Lymbery AJ (2005) Fish-borne parasitic zoonoses: status and issues. Int J Parasitol 35:1233–1254

Chai JY, Shin EH, Lee SH et al (2009) Foodborne intestinal flukes in Southeast Asia. Korean J Parasitol 47(Suppl):S69–S102

Chai JY, Jung BK, Kim DG et al (2015) Heterophyid trematodes recovered from people residing along the Boseong River, South Korea. Acta Trop 148:142–146

Chen ER (1991) Current status of food-borne parasitic zoonoses in Taiwan. Southeast Asian J Trop Med Public Health 22(Suppl):62–64
Chen Y, Zhang W, Tian M et al (2009) Investigation of snails transmitting parasitic diseases in Yunnan Province. J Pathogen Biol (China) 4:211–214 (in Chinese)
Chi JG, Kim CW, Kim JR et al (1988) Intestinal histopathology in human metagonimiasis with ultrastructural observations of parasites. J Korean Med Sci 3:171–177
Cho SY, Kang SY, Ryang YS (1981) Helminthes infections in the small intestine of stray dogs in Ejungbu City, Kyunggi Do, Korea. Korean J Parasitol 19:55–59
Cho SY, Kang SY, Lee JB (1984) Metagonimiasis in Korea. Arzneimittelforschung 34(9B):1211–1213
Cho SY, Kim SI, Earm YE et al (1985) A preliminary observation on water content of small intestine in *Metagonimus yokogawai* infected dog. Korean J Parasitol 23:175–177
Cho SY, Kim SY, Kang SY (1987) Specific IgG antibody response in experimental cat metagonimiasis. Korean J Parasitol 25:149–153
Cho SH, Kim TS, Na BK et al (2011) Prevalence of *Metagonimus* metacercariae in sweetfish, *Plecoglossus altivelis*, from eastern and southern coastal areas in Korea. Korean J Parasitol 49:161–165
Cho SH, Lee WJ, Kim TS et al (2014) Prevalence of zoonotic trematode metacercariae in freshwater fish from Gangwon-do, Korea. Korean J Parasitol 52:399–412
Choi DW, Lee JT, Hwang HK et al (1966) Studies on the larval trematodes from brackish water fishes. 2. Observation on *Metagonimus yokogawai* Katsurada, 1912. Korean J Parasitol 4:33–37 (in Korean)
Chun SK (1960a) A study on *Metagonimus yokogawai* from *Plecoglossus altivelis* in the Miryang River. Bull Pusan Fish Coll 3:24–33 (in Korean)
Chun SK (1960b) A study on the metacercaria of *Metagonimus takahashii* and *Exorchis oviformis* from *Carassius carassius*. Bull Pusan Fish Coll 3:31–39 (in Korean)
Ciurea J (1924) Heterophyidés de la Faune Parasitaire de Roumanie. Parasitology 16:1–25 (in French)
Davydov ON, Lysenko VN, Kurovskaya LY et al (2011) Species diversity of carp, *Cyprinus carpio* (Cypriniformes, Cyprinidae), parasites in some cultivation regions. Vestnik Zoologii 45:e9
Djikanovic V, Paunovic M, Nikolic V et al (2012) Parasitofauna of freshwater fishes in the Serbian open waters: a checklist of parasites of freshwater fishes in Serbian open waters. Rev Fish Biol Fish 22:297–324
Emolenko AV, Bespozvannykh VV, Rumyantseva EE et al (2015) Pathogens of human trematodiases in the Primorye Terrotory. Med Parazitol (Mosk) (2):6–10 (in Russian)
Faust EC, Nishigori M (1926) The life cycles of two new species of Heterophyidae parasitic in mammals and birds. J Parasitol 13:91–131
Francová K, Ondračkova M, Polačik M et al (2011) Parasite fauna of native and non-native populations of *Neogobius melanostomus* (Pallas, 1814) (Gobiidae) in the longitudinal profile of the Danube River. J Appl Ichthyol 27:879–886
Fujino T, Higo H, Ishii Y et al (1989) Comparative studies on two similar species of *Haplorchis* and *Metagonimus* (Trematoda: Heterophyidae) – surface ultrastructure of adults and eggs. Proc Helminthol Soc Wash 56:35–41
Goldsmith RS (1978) Chronic diarrhea in returning travelers: intestinal parasitic infection with the fluke *Metagonimus yokogawai*. South Med J 71:1513–1515
Guk SM, Park JY, Seo M et al (2005) Susceptibility of inbred mouse strains to infection with three species of *Metagonimus* prevalent in the Republic of Korea. J Parasitol 91:12–16
Gushima M (1939) Studies on the immunity of *Metagonimus yokogawai*. Igaku Kenkyu 13:1713–1796 (in Japanese)
Hamajima F, Fujino T, Yamagami K et al (1979) Studies on the *in vitro* effects of bithionol and menichlopholan on flukes of *Clonorchis sinensis, Metagonimus takahashii* and *Paragonimus miyazakii*. Int J Parasitol 9:241–249

Han ET, Yang HJ, Park YJ et al (2014) *Metagonimus yokogawai*: a 100-kDa somatic antigen commonly reacting with other trematodes. Korean J Parasitol 52:201–204

Harinasuta T, Bunnag D, Radomyos P (1987) Intestinal fluke infections. In Bailliere's clinical tropical medicine and communicable. Diseases 2(3):695–721

Hong NT, Seo BS (1969) Study on *Metagonimus yokogawai* (Katsurada, 1912) in Korea. Korean J Parasitol 7:129–142

Hong SJ, Woo HC, Lee SY et al (1993) Worm recovery and small intestinal lesions of albino rats coinfected with *Fibricola seoulensis* and *Metagonimus yokogawai*. Korean J Parasitol 31:109–116

Hong ST, Yu JR, Myong NH et al (1991) Activities of brush border membrane bound enzymes of the small intestine in *Metagonimus yokogawai* infection in mice. Korean J Parasitol 29:9–20

Huh S, Sohn WM, Chai JY (1993) Intestinal parasites of cats purchased in Seoul. Korean J Parasitol 31:371–373

Hunter GW III, Ritchie LS, Pan C et al (1953) Parasitological studies in the far east IX. An epidemiologic survey of Shikoku Island, Japan. Jpn J Med Sci Biol 6:45–55

Inatomi S, Tongu Y, Sakumoto D et al (1968) The ultrastructure of helminth 2. The body wall of *Metagonimus takahashii* Suzuki, 1930. Jpn J Parasitol 17:455–460 (in Japanese)

Ito J (1964a) *Metagonimus* and other human heterophyid trematodes. Progr Med Parasitol Japan 1:314–393

Ito J (1964b) A monograph of cercariae in Japan and adjacent territories. Progr Med Parasitol Japan 1:395–550

Ito J, Mochizuki H, Ohno Y et al (1991) On the prevalence of *Metagonimus* sp. among the inhabitants at Hamamatsu basin in Shizuoka prefecture, Japan. Jpn J Parasitol 40:274–278

Izumi M (1935) Studies on a new species of *Metagonimus* and its life cycle. Tokyo Iji Shinshi 2929:1224–1236 (in Japanese)

Jang YK, Kang SY, Kim SI et al (1985) In situ posture of anterior body of *Metagonimus yokogawai* in experimentally infected dog. Korean J Parasitol 23:203–213

Jeon HK, Lee D, Park H et al (2012) Human infections with liver and minute intestinal flukes in Guangxi, China: analysis by DNA sequencing, ultrasonography, and immunoaffinity chromatography. Korean J Parasitol 50:391–394

Kagei N (1965) Epidemiological studies of metagonimiasis in Japan. I. Epidemological survey of metagonimiasis among the Takatsu River, Shimane Prefecture. Bull Inst Public Health Japan 14:213–227 (in Japanese)

Kagei N, Oshima T (1968) Nationwide epiemiological surveys on the metacercariae of *Metagonimus yokogawai* in "ayu", *Plecoglossus altivelis*, in Japan. Jpn J Parasitol 17:461–470 (in Japanese)

Kagei N, Kihata M (1970) On the development of *Metagonimus yokogawai* (Katsurada, 1912) (Heterophyidae, Trematoda) in laboratory animals. Rep Nat Inst Pub Hyg (Japan) 19:48–63 (in Japanese)

Kagei N, Kihata M (1973) Epidemiological studies on metagonimiasis – correlation between the metacercaria-incidence in "ayu" *Plecoglossus altivelis*, and egg-positive rates in the residents. Jpn J Parasitol 22:218–221 (in Japanese)

Kagei N, Sasa M, Mitsui G et al (1966) Metagonimiasis in Amami Islands, South Japan. Bull Inst Public Health Japan 15:142–146 (in Japanese)

Kagei N, Kihata M, Hirayama T et al (1975) Epidemiological study on *Metagonimus yokogawai* infection of *Salangichthys microdon* Bleeker from Japan. Bull Inst Public Health Japan 24:7–17 (in Japanese)

Kamiya H, Seki N, Tada Y et al (1975) Helminths of stray dogs in Sapporo. II. Jpn J Parasitol 24:41–47 (in Japanese)

Kang SY, Loh IK, Park YH et al (1964) Studies on *Metagonimus yokogawai* infected in *Plecoglossus altivelis* collected in Cheju Province. J Korea Med Ass 7:470–476 (in Korean)

Kang SY, Cho SY, Chai JY et al (1983) A study on intestinal lesions of experimentally reinfected dogs with *Metagonimus yokogawai*. Korean J Parasitol 21:58–73

Katsurada F (1912a) On the genus *Heterophyes* in Japan. Okayama Igakkai Zasshi 268:373–380 (in Japanese)

Katsurada F (1912b) On a new trematode, *Metagonimus yokogawai*. Tokyo Iji Shinshi 1796:3483–3489 (in Japanese)

Katsurada F (1912c) *Heterophyes* in Japan. II. Creation of a new genus *Metagonimus*. Okayama Igakkai Zasshi 273:768–778 (in Japanese)

Katsuta I (1932) Studies on the metacercariae of Formosan brackish water fishes (2) On a new species, *Metagonimus minutus* n. sp. parasitic in *Mugil cephalus*. Taiwan Iggakai Zasshi 31:26–39 (in Japanese)

Kim CH (1980) Study on the *Metagonimus* sp. in Gum River basin, Chungchung-nam Do, Korea. Korean J Parasitol 18:215–228 (in Korean)

Kim CH, Kim NM, Lee CH et al (1987) Studies on the *Metagonimus* fluke in the Daecheong reservoir and the upper stream of Geum River, Korea. Korean J Parasitol 25:69–82 (in Korean)

Kim KH, Yoon YM, Lee JS et al (1991) A numerical taxonomic study on heterophyid trematodes. Korean J Parasitol 29:55–65 (in Korean)

Kim DG, Kim TS, Cho SH et al (2006) Heterophyid metacercarial infections in brackish water fishes from Jinju-man (Bay), Kyongsangnam-do, Korea. Korean J Parasitol 44:7–13

Kim TS, Cho SH, Huh S et al (2009) A nationwide survey on the prevalence of intestinal parasitic infections in the Republic of Korea, 2004. Korean J Parasitol 47:37–47

Kim JY, Kim EM, Yi MH et al (2018) Intestinal fluke *Metagonimus yokogawai* infection increases probiotic Lactobacillus in mouse cecum. Exp Parasitol 193:45–50

Kino H, Suzuki T, Oishi H et al (2006) Geographical distribution of *Metagonimus yokogawai* and *M. miyatai* in Shizuoka Prefecture, Japan, and their site preferences in the sweetfish, *Plecoglossus altivelis*, and hamsters. Parasitol Int 55:201–206

Kobayashi H (1912) On a new genus of trematode (a preliminary report). Dobutsugaku Zasshi 24(289):603–608 (in Japanese)

Kobayashi H (1925) On the scientific name of *Metagonimus yokogawai*. Chosen Igakkai Zasshi (55):404 (in Japanese)

Koga G (1938) Studies on the genus *Metagonimus*. Igaku Kenkyu 12:3471–3528 (in Japanese)

Kogame Y (1939) On *Metagonimus yokogawai ovatus* (Kobayashi, 1913) found from *Tribolodon hakonensis* in Daiseiji River, Ishikawa Prefecture, Japan. Tokyo Iji Shinshi 3127:793–796 (in Japanese)

Komiya Y (1965) Metacercariae in Japan and adjacent territories. Progree Med Parasitol Japan 2:1–328

Komiya Y, Ito J, Yamamoto S (1958) Studies on *Metagonimus yokogawai* infected in a brackish water fish *Salangichthys microdon* from the lake Kasumigaura. Jpn J Parasitol 7:7–11 (in Japanese)

Korean Centers for Disease Control and Prevention (2013) National statistics of intestinal parasitic infections (the 9th Report). Osong, Korea, pp 1–210. ISBN: 978-89-6838-009-9

Korol EN, Varodi EI, Kornyushin VV et al (2016) Helminths of wild predatory mammals (Mammalia, Carnivora) of Ukraine. Trematodes. Vestnik Zoologii 50:301–308

Kurokawa T (1939) Studies on the genus *Metagonimus*, especially on the life history of *M. katsuradai* Izumi, 1935 and determination of its first intermediate host. Tokyo Iji Shinshi 3161:2877–2885 (in Japanese)

Lee JB, Chi JG, Lee SK et al (1981) Study on pathology of metagonimiasis in experimentally infected cat intestine. Korean J Parasitol 19:109–129

Lee SH, Hwang SW, Chai JY et al (1984a) Comparative morphology of eggs of heterophyids and *Clonorchis sinensis* causing human infections in Korea. Korean J Parasitol 22:171–180

Lee SH, Seo BS, Chai JY et al (1984b) Study on *Metagonimus yokogawai* (Katsurada, 1912) in Korea. VII. Electron microscopic observation of the tegumental structure. Korean J Parasitol 22:1–10 (in Korean)

Lee SH, Chai JY, Hong SJ et al (1984c) Anthelmintic effect of praziquantel (Distocide®) against *Metagonimus yokogawai* infection. J Korean Soc Chemother 2:167–171 (in Korean)

Lee SC, Chung YB, Kong Y et al (1993) Antigenic protein fractions of *Metagonimus yokogawai* reacting with patient sera. Korean J Parasitol 31:43–48

Lee SU, Huh S, Park GM et al (1999) A cytogenetic study on human intestinal trematodes of the genus *Metagonimus* (Digenea: Heterophyidae) in Korea. Korean J Parasitol 37:237–241

Lee SU, Huh S, Sohn WM et al (2004) Sequence comparisons of 28S ribosomal DNA and mitochondrial cytochrome *c* oxidase subunit I of *Metagonimus yokogawai, M. takahashii* and *M. miyatai*. Korean J Parasitol 42:129–134

Lee JJ, Kim HJ, Kim MJ et al (2008) Decrease of *Metagonimus yokogawai* endemicity along the Tamjin River basin. Korean J Parasitol 46:289–291

Lee JJ, Jung BK, Lim H et al (2012) Comparative morphology of minute intestinal fluke eggs that can occur in human stools in the Republic of Korea. Korean J Parasitol 50:207–213

Li MH, Liao CW, Lee YL et al (2010) Infectivity and development of *Metagonimus yokogawai* in experimentally infected domestic ducks (*Cairina muschata*). Vet Parasitol 168:45–50

Li MH, Juang HI, Chen PL et al (2013) *Metagonimus yokogawai*: metacercariae survey in fishes and its development to adult worms in various rodents. Parasitol Res 112:1647–1653

Mahanta J, Narain K, Srivastava VK et al (1995) Heterophyid eggs in human stool samples in Assam: first report for India. Indian J Commun Dis 27:142–145

Mehlhorn H, Kojima S, Rim HJ et al (1983) Ultrastructural investigations on the effects of praziquantel on human trematodes from Asia: *Clonorchis sinensis, metagonimus yokogawai, Opisthorchis viverrini, Paragonimus westermani* and *Schistosoma japonicum*. Arzneimit-Forsch/Drug Res 33:91–98

Miyamoto K (1985) Studies on zoonoses in Hokkaido 7. Survey of natural definitive hosts of *Metagonimus yokogawai*. Jpn J Parasitol 34:371–376 (in Japanese)

Miyamoto K, Kutsumi H (1978) Studies on zoonoses in Hokkaido, Japan 2. On the second intermediate hosts of *Metagonimus yokogawai* in Asahikawa City, Kamikawa District. Jpn J Parasitol 27:445–452 (in Japanese)

Miyata I (1941) I. Supplements to the taxonomic knowledge of trematodes of the genus *Metagonimus*. Shokubutsu Oyobi Dobutsu 9:533-534 (in Japanese).

Miyata I (1944) Comments on the classification of trematodes of the genus *Metagonimus*. Dobutsugaku Zasshi 56:16–19 (in Japanese)

Morozov FN (1952) Superfamily Heterophyoidea Faust, 1929. In Skrjabin KI (ed) Trematodes of animals and man, vol 6. Academy of Sciences of the Union of Soviet Socialist Republics, Moscow, pp 153–412 (in Russian)

Muto S (1917) Studies on human trematodes caused by their intermediate host, freshwater fish in Biwa-Lake, especially on *Metagonimus yokogawai* from Cyprinidae. Nippon Shokakibyo Gakkai Zasshi 16:135–166 (in Japanese)

Nachev N, Sures B (2009) The endohelminth fauna of barbel (*Barbus barbus*) correlates with water quality of the Danube River in Bugaria. Parasitology 136:545–000

Nam HS (1997) The *Metagonimus* sp. in a stream of Yeonchun Ri, Buk Myeon, Chunan City, Korea. J Soonchunhyang Med Coll 3:485–490

Nutman TB, Ottesen EA, Ieng S et al (1987) Eosinophilia in Southeast Asian refugees: evaluation at a referral center. J Infect Dis 155:309–313

Ochi G (1957) Studies on the genus *Metagonimus* in Japan. Tokyo Iji Shinshi 74:591–599

Ohnishi Y (1987) Eosinophil responses in the mice infected with *Metagonimus yokogawai*. Jpn J Parasitol 36:271–275

Ohnishi Y, Taufen M (1984) Increase of permeability in the intestinal mucosa of mice infected with *Metagonimus yokogawai*. Jpn J Vet Sci 46:885–887

Ondračkova M, Slovačkova I, Trichkova T et al (2012) Shoreline distribution and parasitic infection of black-striped pipefish *Syngnathus abaster* Risso, 1827 in the low River Danube. J Appl Ichthyol 28:590–596

Park MS, Kim SW, Yang YS et al (1993) Intestinal parasite infections in the inhabitants along the Hantan River, Chorwon-gun. Korean J Parasitol 31:375–378

Pornruseetairatn S, Kino H, Shimazu T et al (2016) A molecular phylogeny of Asian species of the genus *Metagonimus* (Digenea)-small intestinal flukes-based on representative Japanese population. Parasitol Res 115:1123–1130

Pyo KH, Kang EY, Hwang YS et al (2013) Species identification of medically important trematodes in aquatic food samples using PCR-RFLP targeting 18S rRNA. Foodborne Pathog Dis 10(3):1–3

Ransom BH (1920) Synopsis of the trematode family Heterophyidae with descriptions of a new genus and five new species. Proc US Nat Mus 57(2322):527–573

Rho IH, Kim SI, Kang SY et al (1984) Observation on the pathogenesis of villous changes in early phase of experimental metagonimiasis. Chung-Ang J Med 9:67–77 (in Korean)

Rim HJ, Chu DS, Lee JS et al (1978) Anthelmintic effects of various drugs against metagonimiasis. Korean J Parasitol 16:117–122 (in Korean)

Rim HJ, Kim SJ, Yang MG (1992) Antigenic localities in the tissues of *Metagonimus yokogawai* in the period of growth. Korean J Parasitol 30:309–321 (in Korean)

Rim HJ, Kim KH, Joo KH (1996) Classification of host specificity of *Metagonimus* spp. from Korean freshwater fish. Korean J Parasitol 34:7–14

Ryang YS, Ahn YK, Yoon MB (1991) Trematode infections in the small intestine of *Egretta alba medesta* in Kanhwon-do. Korean J Parasitol 29:227–233 (in Korean)

Saito S (1972) On the differences between *Metagonimus yokogawai and Metagonimus takahashii* I. The morphological comparisons. Jpn J Parasitol 21:449–458 (in Japanese)

Saito S (1973) On the differences between *Metagonimus yokogawai and Metagonimus takahashii* II. The experimental infections to the second intermediate hosts. Jpn J Parasitol 22:39–44 (in Japanese)

Saito S (1984) On the synonymy of the trematodes of the genus *Metagonimus*. Report Parasite Classif Morphol Seminar (Japan) 2:1–5 (in Japanese)

Saito S, Shimizu T (1968) A new trematode, *Metagonimus otsurui* sp. nov. from the fresh-water fishes (Trematoda: Heterophyidae). Jpn J Parasitol 17:167–174

Saito S, Chai JY, Kim KH et al (1997) *Metagonimus miyatai* sp. nov. (Digenea: Heterophyidae), a new intestinal trematode transmitted by freshwater fishes in Japan and Korea. Korean J Parasitol 35:223–232

Seo BS, Lee SH, Cho SY et al (1981a) An epidemiological study on clonorchiasis and metagonimiasis in riverside areas in Korea. Korean J Parasitol 19:137–150

Seo BS, Cho SY, Hong ST et al (1981b) Studies on parasitic helminths of Korea V. Survey on intestinal trematodes of house rats. Korean J Parasitol 19:131–136

Seo BS, Hong ST, Chai JY et al (1982) Study on *Metagonimus yokogawai* (Katsurada, 1912) in Korea. IV. Geographical distribution of metacercarial infection in sweetfish along the east and south coast. Korean J Parasitol 29:28–32 (in Korean)

Seo BS, Lee SH, Chai JY et al (1985) Intensity of *Metagonimus yokogawai* infection among inhabitants in Tamjin River basin with reference to its egg laying capacity in human host. Seoul J Med 26:207–212

Seo M, Shin DH, Guk SM et al (2008) *Gymnophalloides seoi* eggs from the stool of a 17th century female mummy found in Hadong, Republic of Korea. J Parasitol 94:467–472

Shimazu T (1999) *Metagonimus hakubaensis* sp. n. (Digenea, heterophyidae) from Nagano, Japan: morphology and life cycle. Bull Nat Sci Mus Tokyo Ser A 25:87–99

Shimazu T (2002) Life cycle and morphology of *Metagonimus miyatai* (Digenea: Heterophyidae) from Nagano, Japan. Parasitol Int 51:271–280

Shimazu T (2003) Morphology of metacercariae and adults of *Metagonimus katsuradai* Izumi (Digenea, Heterophyidae) from Shiga, Japan. Bull Nat Sci Mus Tokyo (Ser A) 29:47–51

Shimazu T, Urabe M (2002) Morphology and life cycle of *Metagonimus otsurui* (Digenea: Heterophyidae) from Nara, Japan. Bull Nat Sci Mus Tokyo Ser A 28:21–28

Shimazu T, Kino H (2015) *Metagonimus yokogawai* (Trematoda: Heterophyidae): from discovery to designation of a neotype. Korean J Parasitol 53:627–639

Shin DH, Lim DS, Choi KJ et al (2009) Scanning electron microscope study of ancient parasite eggs recovered from Korean mummies of the Joseon Dynastry. J Parasitol 95:137–145

Shin SS, Oh DS, Ahn KS et al (2015) Zoonotic intestinal trematodes in stray cats (*Felis catus*) from riverside areas of the Republic of Korea. Korean J Parasitol 53:209–213

Shumenko PG, Tatonova YV, Besprozvannkh VV (2017) *Metagonimus suifunensis* sp. n. (Trematoda: Heterophyidae) from the Russian Southern Far East: morphology, life cycle, and molecular data. Parasitol Int 66:982–991

Soh CT, Ahn YK (1978) Epidemiological study on *Metagonimus yokogawai* infection along Boseong River in Jeonra Nam Do, Korea. Korean J Parasitol 16:1–13 (in Korean)

Sohn WM (2009) Fish-borne zoonotic trematode metacercariae in the Republic of Korea. Korean J Parasitol 47(Suppl):S103–S113

Sohn WM, Chai JY (2005) Infection status with helminthes in feral cats purchased from a market in Busan, Republic of Korea. Korean J Parasitol 43:93–100

Sohn WM, Hong ST, Chai JY et al (1990) Infection status of sweetfish from Kwangjung-stream and Namdae-stream in Yangyang-gun, Kangwon-do with the metacercariae of *Metagonimus yokogawai*. Korean J Parasitol 28:253–255 (in Korean)

Sohn WM, Eom KS, Min DY et al (2009) Fishborne trematode metacercariae in freshwater fish from Guangxi Zhuang Autonomous Region, China. Korean J Parasitol 47:249–257

Sohn WM, Na BK, Cho SH et al (2018) Infection status with *Metagonimus* spp. metacercariae in fishes from Seomjin-gang and Tamjin-gang in Republic of Korea. Korean J Parasitol 56:351–358

Son WY, Huh S, Lee SU et al (1994) Intestinal trematode infections in the villagers in Koje-myon, Kochang-gun, Kyongsangnam-do, Korea. Korean J Parasitol 32:149–155

Song CY, Lee SH, Jeon SR (1985) Studies on the intestinal fluke, *Metagonimus yokogawai* Katsurada, 1912 in Korea. IV. Geographical distribution of sweetfish and infection status with *Metagonimus* metacercariae in South-Eastern area of Korea. Korean J Parasitol 23:123–138

Sutherland JE, Avant RF, Franz WB et al (1983) Indochinese refugee health assessment and treatment. J Fam Pract 16:61–67

Suzuki S (1930) Yokogawa's *Metagonimus*. List of publications on special animals in Okayama prefecture. Okayama Prefectural Report:146

Takahashi S (1929) On the life-history of *Metagonimus yokogawai*, a new species of *Metagonimus* and *Exorchis major*. Okayama Igakkai Zasshi (479):2687–2755 (in Japanese)

Takahashi S (1967) Studies on the genus *Metagonimus*. Okayama Igakkai Zasshi 79:43–49 (in Japanese)

Thaenkham U, Blair D, Nawa Y et al (2012) Families Opisthorchiidae and Heterophyidae: are they distinct? Parasitol Int 61:90–93

Tittle BS, Harris JA, Chase PA et al (1982) Health screening of Indochinese refugee children. Am J Dis Child 136:697–700

Toledo R, Muñoz-Antoli C, Esteban JG (2014) Intestinal trematode infections. In: Digenetic Trematodes, Toledo R, Fried B (eds). Springer, New York, USA. Adv Exp Med Biol 766:201–240

Tatonova YV, Shumenko PG, Besprozvannykh VV (2017) Description of *Metagonimus pusillus* sp. nov. (Trematoda: Heterophyidae): phylogenetic relationships within the genus. J Helminthol. https://doi.org/10.1017/S0022149X17001146

Uppal B, Wadhwa V (2005) Rare case of *Metagonimus yokogawai*. Indian J Med Microbiol 23:61–62

Urabe M (2003) Trematode fauna of prosobranch snails of the genus *Semisulcospira* in Lake Biwa and the connected drainage system. Parasitol Int 52:21–34

Wang CR, Qiu JH, Zhao JP et al (2006) Prevalence of helminthes in adult dogs in Heilongjiang Province, the People's Republic of China. Parasitol Res 99:627–630

WHO (1995) Control of Foodborne Trematode Infections. Report of a WHO Study Group. Geneva: WHO. WHO Tech Report Ser 849:1–157

Yamada SM, Yamada S, Takada H et al (2008) A case of metagonimiasis complicated with multiple intracerebral hemorrhages and diabetes mellitus. J Nippon Med Sch 75:32–35

Yamaguti S (1934) Studies on the helminth fauna of Japan. Part 3. Avian trematodes, II. Jpn J Zool V:543–583

Yamaguti S (1958) Systema Helminthum. Vol. I. The digenetic trematodes of vertebrates (Part I). Interscience Publishers Inc, New York, pp 1–979

Yamaguti S (1971) Synopsis of digenetic trematodes of vertebrates, vol I. Keigaku Publishing Co, Tokyo, pp 1–1074

Yamaguti S (1975) Synoptical review of life histories of digenetic trematodes of vertebrates. Keigaku Publishing Co, Tokyo. pp 1–590 with 219 figure plates

Yang HJ, Guk SM, Han ET et al (2000) Molecular differentiation of three species of *Metagonimus* by simple sequence repeat anchored polymerase chain reaction (SSR-PCR) amplification. J Parasitol 86:1170–1172

Yasuraoka K, Kojima K (1970) In vitro cultivation of the heterophyid trematode, *Metagonimus yokogawai*, from the metacercaria to adult. Jpn J Parasitol 23:199–210

Yeo TO, Seo BS (1971) Studies on *Metagonimus yokogawai* (Katsurada, 1912) in Korea III. Epidemiological observation of human *Metagonimus* infection in Hadong area, South Kyongsang Do. Seoul J Med 12:259–268

Yokogawa M, Sano M (1968) Studies on the intestinal flukes IV. On the development of the worm in the experimentally infected animals with metacercariae of *Metagonimus yokogawai*. Jpn J Parasitol 17:540–545 (in Japanese)

Yokogawa M, Sano M, Takahashi T et al (1962) Studies on *Metagonimus yokogawai* Katsurada, 1913 in Ohama-machi, Shizuoka Prefecture. Jpn J Parasitol 11:157–164 (in Japanese)

Yokogawa S (1913a) On a new trematode which takes *Plecoglossus altivelis* as second intermediate host-*Metagonimus*. Tokyo Igakkai Zashii 27:685–709 (in Japanese)

Yokogawa S (1913b) On a new species of the genus *Metagonimus, Metagonimus ovatus* n. sp. Tokyo Igakkai Zasshi 27:1705–1709 (in Japanese)

Yokogawa S (1940) On the visceral heterophyidiasis, especially on the etiology of heart, brain and spinal cord heterophyidiasis. Taiwan Igakkai Zasshi 39:1729–1730 (in Japanese)

Yoshikawa M, Miyata I, Uesugi S (1940) Contributions to the knowledge of dog parasites in Kobe City. Nippon Juigakkai Zasshi 2:450–464 (in Japanese)

Yoshimura H, Ohmori Y, Tani S et al (1972) Epidemological studies of metagonmiasis in Chokai village, Akita Prefecture. Jpn J Parasitol 21:400–407 (in Japanese)

Yu JR, Chai JY (2010) Chapter 59. *Metagonimus*. In Liu D (ed) Molecular detection of foodborne pathogens. CRC Press (Taylor & Francis Group), Boca Raton, pp 805–811

Yu JR, Chai JY (2013) *Metagonimus*. In Liu D (ed) Molecular detection of human parasitic pathogens. CRC Press (Taylor & Francis Group), Boca Raton, pp 389–398

Yu SH, Mott KE (1994) Epidemiology and morbidity of food-borne intestinal trematode infections. Trop Dis Bull 91:R125–R152

Yu JR, Kwon SO, Lee SH (1994) Clonorchiasis and metagonimiasis in the inhabitants along Talchongang (River), Chungwon-gun. Korean J Parasitol 32:267–269

Yu JR, Chung JS, Huh S et al (1997a) PCR-RFLP pattern of three kinds of *Metagonimus* in Korea. Korean J Parasitol 35:271–276

Yu JR, Chung JS, Chai JY (1997b) Different RAPD patterns between *Metagonimus yokogawai* and *Metagonimus* Miyata type. Korean J Parasitol 35:295–298

Yu JR, Myong N, Chai JY (1997c) Expression patterns of proliferating cell nuclear antigen in the small intestine of mice infected with *Metagonimus yokogawai* and *Metagonimus* Miyata type. Korean J Parasitol 35:239–244

References for Section 1.3

Abdul-Salam JM (1986) Intestinal helminth parasites of stray dogs in Kuwait. Arab Gulf. J Sci Res (B: Agricult Biol Sci) 4:659–663

Abdul-Salam JM, Baker K (1990) Prevalence of intestinal helminths in stray cats in Kuwait. Pakistan Vet J 10:17–21

Abo-Shady AF, Ali MM, Hegazi MM et al (1983) Helminth fauna of rats from Dakahlia Governorate, Egypt. J Egypt Soc Parasitol 13:391–396

Abou-Basha LM, Abdel-Fattah OP et al (2000) Epidemiological study of heterophyiasis among humans in an area of Egypt. East Mediterranean Health J 6:932–938 (in Arabic)

Adams KO, Jungkind DL, Bergquist EJ et al (1986) Intestinal fluke infection as a result of eating sushi. Am J Cli Pathol 86:688–689

Africa CM, de Leon W, Garcia EY (1940) Visceral complications in intestinal heterophyidiasis of man. Acta Med Philippina, Monogr Series 1:1–132

Asada J (1928) Studies on *Heterophyes* prevalent in humans in Japan. An experimental study on life cycle of *Heterophyes heterophyes* and decision of its first intermediate host. Tokyo Iji Shinshi 2564:6–12 (in Japanese)

Asada J (1934) On *Metagonimus yokogawai* and its related species. *Rinsho Igaku* (Clin Med) 22:43–56 (in Japanese)

Ashour DS, Othman AA, Radi DA (2014) Insights into regulatory molecules of intestinal epithelial cell turnover during experimental infection by *Heterophyes heterophyes*. Exp Parasitol 143:48–54

Ata AA, Attia M, Soliman HM et al (1988) Effect of praziquantel on *Heterophyes heterophyes*. J Egypt Soc Parasitol 18:515–518

Beaver PC, Jung RC, Cupp EW (1984) Clinical parasitology, 9th edn. Lea and Febiger, Philadelphia

Bearup AJ (1958) Trematode parasites in esturine fish. Australian J Sci 20:219

Braun M (1901) Zur Kentniss der Trematoden der Säugethiere. Zool Jahrb 14:311–348

Bwangamoi O, Ojok L (1977) Helminthiasis in dogs in Uganda. IV. *Heterophyes pleomorphis* sp. n. (Trematoda: Heterophyidae) from the small intestine of dogs in Kampala. Bull Anim Health Product Africa, pp 427–430

Chai JY (2007) Intestinal flukes. In: Murrell KD, Fried B (eds) Food-borne parasitic zoonoses. Fish and plant-borne parasites. Springer, New York, pp 53–115

Chai JY (2013) Praziquantel in treatment of trematode and cestode infections. Infect Chemother 45:32–43

Chai JY (2014) Helminth-Trematode. *Heterophyes heterophyes*. In Encyclopedia of food safety, vol. 2. Elsevier, Amsterdam, pp 158–163

Chai JY (2015) *Metagonimus*. In Xiao L, Ryan U, Feng Y (eds) Biology of foodborne parasites. CRC Press/Taylor & Francis Group, Boca Raton, pp 427–443

Chai JY, Lee SH (2002) Food-borne intestinal trematode infections in the Republic of Korea. Parasitol Int 51:129–154

Chai JY, Jung BK (2017) Fishborne zoonotic heterophyid infections: an update. Food Waterborne Parasitol 8-9:33–63

Chai JY, Seo BS, Lee SH (1984) Studies on intestinal trematodes in Korea XI. Two cases of human infection by *Heterophyes heterophyes nocens*. Korean J Parasitol 22:37–42

Chai JY, Hong SJ, Sohn WM et al (1985) Further cases of human *Heterophyes heterophyes nocens* infection in Korea. Seoul J Med 26:197–200

Chai JY, Seo BS, Lee SH et al (1986) Human infections by *Heterophyes heterophyes* and *H. dispar* imported from Saudi Arabia. Korean J Parasitol 24:82–88

Chai JY, Chung HL, Choi MH et al (1992) Surface ultrastructure of *Heterophyes nocens* (Trematoda: Heterophyidae). Korean J Parasitol 30:75–82

Chai JY, Nam HK, Kook J et al (1994) The first discovery of an endemic focus of *Heterophyes nocens* (Heterophyidae) infection in Korea. Korean J Parasitol 32:157–161

Chai JY, Kim IM, Seo M et al (1997) A new focus of *Heterophyes nocens*, *Pygidiopsis summa*, and other intestinal flukes in a coastal area of Muan-gun, Chollanam-do. Korean J Parasitol 35:233–238

Chai JY, Song TE, Han ET et al (1998) Two endemic foci of heterophyids and other intestinal fluke infections in southern and western coastal areas in Korea. Korean J Parasitol 36:155–161

Chai JY, Park JH, Han ET et al (2004) Prevalence of *Heterophyes nocens* and *Pygidiopsis summa* infections among residents of the western and southern coastal islands of the Republic of Korea. Am J Tro Med Hyg 71:617–622

Chai JY, Murrell KD, Lymbery AJ (2005) Fish-borne parasitic zoonoses: status and issues. Int J Parasitol 35:1233–1254

Chai JY, Shin EH, Lee SH et al (2009) Foodborne intestinal flukes in Southeast Asia. Korean J Parasitol 47(Suppl):S69–S102

Chai JY, Jung BK, Kim DG et al (2015) Heterophyid trematodes recovered from people residing along the Boseong River, South Korea. Acta Trop 148:142–146

Ching HL (1961) Internal parasites of man in Hawaii with special reference to heterophyid flukes. Hawaii Med J 20:442–445

Cho SH, Lee WJ, Kim TS et al (2014) Prevalence of zoonotic trematode metacercariae in freshwater fish from Gangwon-do, Korea. Korean J Parasitol 52:399–412

Ciurea PJ (1924) Heterophyidae de la faune Parasitaire de Roumanie. Parasitology 16:1–25 (in French)

Cobbold S (1866) Tapeworms (human entozoa), their Sources, Nature and Treatment. London, pp 1–83

Coleman JM, Halpin RW, Kuterman G (1958) Clonorchiasis infection caused by *Clonorchis sinensis*: report of a case. Am J Gastroenterol 30:509–517

Collomb H, Bert J (1959) Parasite epilepsy of unusual origin: distomiasis (due to *Heterophyes heterophyes*). Neurochirugie 5:330–333

Collomb H, Deschiens R, Demarchi J (1960) On 2 cases of cerebral distomiasis caused by *Heterophyes heterophyes*. Bull Soc Pathol Exot Filiales 53:144–147

Cort WW, Yokogawa S (1921) A new human trematode from Japan. J Parasitol 8:66–69

Danasory ME, Hamdy EI (1980) Proteolytic action of extracts of adult *Heterophyes heterophyes*. J Egypt Med Assoc 63:185–188

Daoud A (2012) Experimental heterophyiasis: histopathological and immunological study. Int Symp Front Immunol Inflam 254. World Allergy J (abstracts):S100

Deiana S (1961) *Phagicola italica* (Alessandrini, 1906) ed. *Heterophyes heterophyes* Siebold (1852), parassitti del cane in Sardegna. Rev Parassitol 22:185–192 (in Italian)

Dissanaike AS (1961) On some helminths of dogs in Colombo and their bearing on human infections, with a description of a new trematode *Heterophyopsis yehi* sp. nov. (Heterophyidae). Ceylon J Med Sci 10:1–14

Elshazly AM, Elsheikha HM, Rahbar MH et al (2008) Comparison of three immunodiagnostic tests for experimental *Heterophyes heterophyes* infection in dogs. Vet Parasitol 151:196–202

El-Azazy OME, Ibrahim Abdou NEM, Khalil AI et al (2015) Potential zoonotic trematodes recovered in stray cats from Kuwait Municipality, Kuwait. Korean J Parasitol 53:279–287

El-Dakhly MM, Aboshinaf ASM, El-Nahass E et al (2017) A preliminary study on the helminth fauna in necropsied stray cats (*Felis catus*) in Beni-Suef, Egypt. J Adv Vet Res 7:87–92

El-Ganayni GA, Youssef ME, Handousa AE et al (1989) Serum and intestinal immunoglobulin levels in heterophyidiasis. J Egypt Soc Parasitol 19:219–223

El-Gayar AK (2007) Studies on some trematode parasites of stray dogs in Egypt with a key to the identification of intestinal trematodes of dogs. Vet Parasitol 144:360–365

El-Hawy AM, El-Nasr MSS, Abdel Rahman MM (1988) The cure rates of patients infected with heterophyiasis and treated with praziquantel versus niclosamide. J Egypt Soc Parasitol 18:437–442

Elsheikha HM (2007) Heterophyosis: risk of ectopic infection. Vet Parasitol 147:341–342

Eom KS, Yoo HW, Chung MS et al (1985a) Heterophyid trematodes (*Heterophyes heterophyes* and *H. dispar*) human infections imported from Sudan to Korea. Korean J Parasitol 23:360–361. (abstract in Korean)

Eom KS, Son SY, Lee JS et al (1985b) Heterophyid trematodes (*Heterophyopsis continua*, *Pygidiopsis summa* and *Heterophyes heterophyes nocens*) from domestic cats in Korea. Korean J Parasitol 23:197–202

Farahnak A, Massoud J (1996) The prevalence of Heterophyidae family in humans and animals in Khuzestan Province. J Kerman Univ Med Sci 3:181–184 (in Arabic)

Faust EC, Nishigori M (1926) The life cycles of two new species of Heterophyidae parasitic in mammals and birds. J Parasitol 13:91–131

Fried B, Graczyk TK, Tamang L (2004) Food-borne intestinal trematodiases in humans. Parasitol Res 93:159–170

Gallais P, Paillas P, Collomb H et al (1955) Anatomo-pathological study of a parasitic cerebral cyst in man. Bull Soc Pathol Exot Filiales 48:830–832 (in French)

Gonçalves JF, Tanabe M, Medeiros FPM et al (1990) Parasitological and serological studies on amoebiasis and other intestinal parasitic infections in the rural sector around recife, Northeast Brazil. Rev Inst Med Trop 32:428–435

Guk SM, Shin EH, Kim JL et al (2007) A survey of *Heterophyes nocens* and *Pygidiopsis summa* metacercariae in mullets and gobies along the coastal areas of the Republic of Korea. Korean J Parasitol 45:205–211

Gumaa N, AbdulRaheem EM, Nur-Eldaiem Z et al (2015) New record of trematode metacercaria as zoonotic parasite in mullet fish of the Sudanese Red Sea waters. J Biomed Pharmaceut Res 4:66–69

Gupta N, Gupta DK, Shalaby S (2008) Parasitic zoonotic infections in Egypt and India: an overview. J Parasit Dis 32:1–9

Hamdy EI, Nicola E (1980) On the histopathology of the small intestine in animals experimentally infected with *H. heterophyes*. J Egypt Med Assoc 63:179–184

Hasegawa A (1931) Taxonomic study on the genus *Heterophyes* in Japan. Okayama Igakkai Zasshi 43:502–503 (in Japanese)

Hegazi MA, Hassan AT, Al-Nashar TM et al (2014) Encysted metacercariae of family Heterophyidae in infected fish in Dakahlia Governorate, an endemic focus in Egypt. J Egypt Soc Parasitol 44:547–558

Himonas CA (1964) *Heterophyes heterophyes* from dogs in Greece. J Parasitol 50:79

Hung NM, Madsen H, Fried B (2013) Global status of fish-borne zoonotic trematodiasis in humans. Acta Prasitol 58:231–258

Ito J (1964a) *Metagonimus* and other human heterophyid trematodes. Progr Med Parasitol Japan 1:314–393

Ito J (1964b) A monograph of cercariae in Japan and adjacent territories. Progr Med Parasitol Japan 1:395–550

Ito J, Papasarathorn T, Tongkoom B (1962) An investigation of parasitic helminths of stray dogs in Bangkok. Jpn J Med Sci Biol 15:53–60

Ito J, Mochizuki H, Noguchi M (1967) An epidemiological study of human helminths in rural areas of Shizuoka Prefecture. IV. Three human trematodes. Jpn J Parasitol 16:134–138 (in Japanese)

Kaewkes S, Elkins DB, Pearson JC et al (1992) The taxonomy and epidemiology of minute intestinal flukes in northeast Thailand. The XIII International Congress for tropical medicine and malaria, Pattaya, Thailand. Abstract 2:207

Kagei N, Hayashi S, Kato K (1980) On the heterophyid trematode (*Heterophyes heterophyes*) infection cases imported from Egypt to Japan. Jpn J Trop Med 8:1–7 (in Japanese)

Karema ME (2012) Investigation on some internal parasites affecting stray dogs and cats. Alexandria J Vet Sci 35:211–219

Khalafalla RE (2011) A survey study on gastrointestinal parasites of stray cats in northern region of Nile Delta, Egypt. PLoS One 6:e20282

Khalil M (1923) A preliminary note on the second intermediate host of *Heterophyes* in Egypt. J Helminthol 1:141–142

Khalil M (1933) The life history of the human trematode parasite *Heterophyes heterophyes* in Egypt. Lancet 222:537

Khalil MI, El-Shahawy IS, Abdelkader HS (2014) Studies on some fish parasites of public health importance in the southern area of Saudi Arabia. Braz J Vet Parasitol 23:435–442

Kim KH, Yoon YM, Lee JS et al (1991) A numerical taxonomic study on heterophyid trematodes. Korean J Parasitol 29:55–65 (in Korean)

Kim DG, Kim TS, Cho SH et al (2006) Heterophyid metacercarial infections in brackish water fishes from Jinju-man (Bay), Kyongsangnam-do, Korea. Korean J Parasitol 44:7–13

Kino H, Oishi H, Ohno Y et al (2002) An endemic human infection with *Heterophyes nocens* Onji et Nishio, 1916 at Mikkabi-cho, Shizuoka, Japan. Jpn J Trop Med Hyg 30:301–304

Kirrella GAK, Elhawary NM, Bazh EK et al (2018) *Oreochromis niloticus* and *Clarias gariepinus* fish infected with digenean metacercariae: experimental infection of puppies and some chemical alterations in fish. Asian J Anim Vet Adv 13:352–359

Komiya Y (1965) Metacercariae in Japan and adjacent territories. Progress Med Parasitol Japan 2:1–328

Kuntz RE, Chandler AC (1956a) Studies on Egyptian trematodes with special reference to the heterophyid of mammals. I. Adult flukes, with descriptions of *Phagicola longicollis* n. sp., *Cynodiplostomum namrui* n. sp., and a *Stephanoprora* from cats. J Parasitol 42:445–459

Kuntz RE, Chandler AC (1956b) Studies on Egyptian trematodes with special reference to the heterophyid of mammals. II. Embryonic development of *Heterophyes aequalis* Looss. J Parasitol 42:613–625

Lamy C, Duhamel C, Morel C et al (1976) A case of intestinal fluke infection. Nouv Presse Med 5:1005–1006 (in French)

Lane C (1922) A note on *Heterophyes nocens* as a distinct species of trematode parasite. Lancet 2:505

Laonov VA, Belogurov O (1965) New species of trematode from the common tern in Kamchatka –*Heterophyes superspinatus* sp. nov. Raboty po Gel'minthologii k 40-letiya Nauchnoii Pedaogogicheskoi Deyatel'nosti Prof. A.A. Soboleva. Vladivostok, Russia. Academia Nauk. pp 119–120

Lee HS (1979) A survey on helminth parasites of cats in Gyeongbug area. Korean J Vet Res 19:57–61 (in Korean)

Lee SH, Hwang SW, Chai JY et al (1984) Comparative morphology of eggs of heterophyids and *Clonorchis sinensis* causing human infections in Korea. Korean J Parasitol 22:171–180

Lee JJ, Jung BK, Lim H et al (2012) Comparative morphology of minute intestinal fluke eggs that can occur in human stools in the Republic of Korea. Korean J Parasitol 50:207–213

Leiper T (1922) A helminthological review. Trop Dis Bull 20:364–365

Lobna SMA, Metawea YF, Elsheikha HM (2010) Prevalence of heterophyiosis in Tilapia fish and humans in northern Egypt. Parasitol Res 107:1029–1034

Looss A (1894) Ueber den Bau *Distomum heterophyes* v. Sieb. und *Distomum fraternum* n. sp. Kassel, pp 1–59

Looss A (1902) Notizen zur Helminthologie Aegyptens. V. Eine Revision der Fasciolidengattung *Heterophyes* Cobb. Centralbl Bakteriol 32:886–891

Macy RW (1953) First report of the human intestinal fluke *Heterophyes heterophyes* from a Yamen bat, *Rhinolophus clivosus acrotis*. J Parasitol 39:571

Mahanta J, Narain K, Srivastava VK (1995) Heterophyid eggs in human stool specimens in Assam: first report for India. J Commun Dis 27:142–145

Maplestone PA, Bhaduri NV (1940) The helminth parasites of dogs in Calcutta and their bearing on human parasitology. Ind J Med Res 28:595–604

Martin WE (1959) Egyptian heterophyid trematodes. Trans Am Microscop Soc 78:172–181

Martínez-Alonso JC, Armentia A, Vega JM et al (1999) Anaphylactic reaction concurrent with *Heterophyes heterophyes* infestation. Rev Esp Alergol Immunol Clin 14:37–39 (in Spanish)

Masala S, Piras MC, Sanna D et al (2016) Epidemiological and molecular data of zoonotic trematode metacercariae found in the muscle of grey mullets (Osteichthys: Mugilidae) from Sardinia (western Mediterranean Sea). Parasitol Res 115:3409–3417

Massoud J, Jalali H, Reza M (1981) Studies on trematodes of the family Heterophyidae (Odhner, 1914) in Iran. 1. Preliminary epidemiological surveys in man and carnivores in Khuzestan. J Helminthol 55:255–260

Mehlhorn H (2015) *Heterophyes heterophyes*. Encyclop Parasitol. https://doi.org/10.1007/978-3-642-27769-6_1452-2

Nagata H (1914) On the small intestinal fluke belonging to *Heterophyes* among the Japanese people. Igaku Chuo Zasshi 11:1009–1017 (in Japanese)

Nagaty HF, Khalil HM (1964) Incidence of helminth infections among the outpatients in the clinic of Mataria collective unit, Dakahlia Governorate, UAR. J Egypt Med Assoc 47:341–346

Nakano T, Inoue M (1955) A human case of intestinal tumor caused by deposited eggs of *Heterophyes heterophyes nocens*. Gekkano Ryoiki 3:272–274 (in Japanese)

Namchote S, Sritongtae S, Butnin S et al (2015) Larval stage of trematodes obtained from brackish water snails in the central and east coast of the gulf of Thailand. Sci Res Essays 10:386–401

Nutman TB, Ottesen EA, Ieng S et al (1987) Eosinophilia in Southeast Asian refugees: evaluation at a referral center. J Infect Dis 155:309–313

Okuzawa E, Hamada A, Fukushima S et al (2010) Prevalence of heterophyid infection among Japanese residents of Egypt (2005-2008) and its association with length of stay. Trop Med Health 38:143–146

Öktener A, Yurdakul N, Alas A et al (2010) Fish-borne parasitic zoonoses in Turkish waters. Gazi Univ J Sci 23:255–260

Onji Y (1915) Studies on the heterophyid metacercaria in *Mugil cephalus* (I). Tokyo Iji Shinshi (1918):875–883 (in Japanese)

Onji Y, Nishio T (1916) On the trematodes whose intermediate host is brackish water fishes. Chiba Igaku Semmon Gakko Zasshi 81&82:229–249

Ozaki Y, Asada J (1926) A new human trematode, *Heterophyes katsuradai* n. sp. J Parasitol 12:215–218

Paperna I, Overstreet RM (1981) Parasites and diseases of mullets (Mugilidae). In: Oren OH (ed) Aquaculture of grey mullets. Cambridge University Press, Cambridge, pp 411–493

Park JH, Kim JL, Shin EH et al (2007) Guk SM, Park YK, Chai JY. A new endemic focus of *Heterophyes nocens* and other heterophyid infections in a coastal area of Gangjin-gun, Jeollanam-do. Korean J Parasitol 45:33–38

Pearson JC (1999) Proposed division of the genus *Heterophyes* Cobbold, 1865 (Trematoda: Heterophyidae). Syst parasitol 43:11–15

Pearson JC, Pearson OC (1981) Two new species of the trematode genus *Heterophyes* from Sarawak. Sarawak Museum J 29:171–189

Pica R, Castellano C, Cilia C et al (2003) Intestinal fluke infections: the heterophyids. Clin Ter 154:61–63

Rao MAN, Ayyar LSP (1932) *Heterophyes* species from dogs in Madras. Indian Vet J 8:251–253

Ransom BH (1920) Synopsis of the trematode family Heterophyidae with descriptions of a new genus and five new species. Proc US Nat Mus 57(2322):527–573

Rifaat MM, Salem SAM, El Kholy SI et al (1980) Studies on the incidence of *Heterophyes heterophyes* in Dakahlia Governorate. J Egypt Soc Parasitol 10:369–373

Rousset JJ, Pasticier A (1972) Two cases of heterophyid infection. Epidemiological and clinical aspects and importance of opsopathology. Ann Parasitol Hum Comp 47:465–474 (in French)

Ryang YS, Lee CY, Lee KJ et al (1999) An incidental case of human *Heterophyes nocens* infection diagnosed by sectional morphology in a biopsy specimen of the small intestine. Korean J Parasitol 37:189–194

Schuster RK, Thomas K, Sivakumar S et al (2009) The parasite fauna of stray cats (*Felis catus*) in Dubai, United Arab Emirates. Parasitol Res 105:125–134

Seo BS, Cho SY, Chai JY et al (1980) Studies on intestinal trematodes in Korea. II. Identification of the metacercariae of *Heterophyes heterophyes nocens* in mullets of three southern coastal areas. Seoul J Med 21:116–124

Seo BS, Hong ST, Chai JY (1981a) Studies on intestinal trematodes in Korea III. Natural human infections of *Pygidiopsis summa* and *Heterophyes heterophyes nocens*. Seoul J Med 22:228–235

Seo BS, Cho SY, Hong ST et al (1981b) Studies on parasitic helminths of Korea V. Survey on intestinal trematodes of house rats. Korean J Parasitol 19:131–136

Seo BS, Hong ST, Chai JY et al (1981c) Studies on intestinal trematodes in Korea IV. Geographical distribution of *Pygidiopsis* and *Heterophyes* metacercariae. Seoul J Med 22:236–242

Sheir ZM, Aboul-Enein ME (1970) Demographic, clinical and therapeutic appraisal of heterophyiasis. J Trop Med Hyg 73:148–152

Shin EH, Park JH, Guk SM et al (2009) Intestinal helminth infections in feral cats and a raccoon dog on Aphaedo Island, Shinan-gun, with a special note on *Gymnophalloides seoi* infection in cats. Korean J Parasitol 47:189–191

Shin SS, Oh DS, Ahn KS et al (2015) Zoonotic intestinal trematodes in stray cats (*Felis catus*) from riverside areas of the Republic of Korea. Korean J Parasitol 53:209–213

Sohn WM (2009) Fish-borne zoonotic trematode metacercariae in the Republic of Korea. Korean J Parasitol 47(suppl):S103–S113

Sohn WM, Choi YS (1997) Infection status with trematode metacercariae in the fresh-water fish from Chunamchosuchi (pond), Uichang-gun, Kyongsangnam-do, Korea. Korean J Parasitol 35:165–170

Sohn WM, Chai JY (2005) Infection status with helminthes in feral cats purchased from a market in Busan, Republic of Korea. Korean J Parasitol 43:93–100

Sohn WM, Chai JY, Lee SH (1989) Two cases of natural human infection by *Heterophyes nocens* and the infection status of heterophyid metacercariae in mullets from Samcheonpo, Kyongnam Province. Inje Med J 10:443–450 (in Korean)

Sohn WM, Kim JA, Chai JY (2005) Two species of goby, *Boleophthalmus pectinirostris* and *Scartelaos* sp., as the new second intermediate hosts of heterophyid fluke in Korea. Korean J Parasitol 43:161–164

Sohn WM, Na BK, Cho SH et al (2018) Infections with zoonotic trematode metacercariae in yellow goby, *Acanthogobius flavimanus*, from coastal areas of Republic of Korea. Korean J Parasitol 56:259–265

Stiles CW, Hassal A (1900) Notes on Parasites. 16th Annual Report on Bureau of Animal Industry. Washington, DC, pp 559–611

Suzuki N, Kumazawa H, Araki T et al (1982) Occurrence of *Heterophyes heterophyes nocens* Onji et Nishio, 1916 in man in Kochi Prefecture. Jpn J Parasitol 31:271–274

Tandon V, Shylla JA, Ghatani S et al (2015) Neglected tropical diseases: trematodiases-The Indian scenario. Proc Nat Acad Sci India (Sect B Biol Sci) 85:901–907

Taraschewski H (1984) Die Trematoden der gattung *Heterophyes* Taxonomie, Biologie, Epidemiologie. PhD dissertation to Universität Hohenheim, Germany. 1984, pp 1–169

Taraschewski H (1985a) Investigations on the prevalence of *Heterophyes* species in twelve populations of the first intermediate host in Egypt and Sudan. J Trop Med Hyg 88:265–271

Taraschewski H (1985b) Transmission experiments on the host specificity of *Heterophyes* species in 16 potential definitive hosts. Z Parasitenkd 71:505–518

Taraschewski H (1987) Experiments on habitat selection of *Heterophyes* species in different definitive hosts. J Helminthol 61:33–42

Taraschewski H, Nicolaidou A (1987) *Heterophyes* in Greece: record of *H. heterophyes, H. aequalis* and *H. dispar* from the first intermediate host, *Pirenella conica*. J Helminthol 61:28–32

Toledo R, Munoz-Antoli C, Esteban JG (2014) Intestinal trematode infections. In: Toledo R, Fried B (eds) Digenetic Trematodes, Springer, New York, USA. Adv Exp Med Biol 766:201–240

Velasquez CC (1982) Heterophyidiasis, In: Steele JH (ed) CRC Handbook series in zoonoses, section C: parasitic zoonoses, vol III (Trematode Zoonoses). CRC Press, Boca Raton, pp 99–107

von Siebold T (1852) Beitrage zur Helminthographia, humana. Zeitschr Wiss Zool IV:53–76

Waikagul J, Pearson JC (1989) *Heterophyes nocnes* Onji and Nishio, 1916 (Digenea: Heterophyidae) from the water rat, *Hydromys chrysogaster* Geoffroy, 1804 in Australia. Syst Parasitol 13:53–61
Wells WH, Blagg W (1956) A survey of human intestinal parasites in a fishing village of northern Egypt. Am J Trop Med Hyg 5:266–268
Wells WH, Randall BH (1956) New hosts for trematodes of the genus *Heterophyes* in Egypt. J Parasitol 42:287–292
WHO (1995) Control of foodborne Trematode infections. Report of a WHO Study Group. Geneva: WHO. WHO Tech Report Ser 849:1–157
Witenberg G (1929) Studies on the trematode – family Heterophyidae. Ann Trop Med Parasitol 23:131–268
Xu BK, Li DN (1979) Rare human parasites in China. Natl Med J China 59:286–290
Yamaguti S (1958) Systema Helminthum. Vol. I. The digenetic trematodes of vertebrates (Part I). Interscience Publishers Inc, New York, pp 1–979
Yamaguti S (1975) Synoptical review of life histories of digenetic trematodes of vertebrates. Keigaku Publishing Co, Tokyo, pp 1–590 with 219 figure plates
Yokogawa S (1913) A new species of the genus *Heterophyes*, i.e., *Heterophyes elliptica*. J Bacteriol (217):789–802 (in Japanese)
Yokogawa S (1940) On the visceral heterophyidiasis, especially on the etiology of heart, brain and spinal cord heterophyidiasis. Taiwan Igakkai Zasshi 39:1729–1730 (in Japanese)
Yokogawa M, Sano M, Itabashi T et al (1965) Studies on the intestinal flukes II. Epidemiological studies on heterophyid trematodes of man in Chiba Prefecture. Jpn J Parasitol 14:577–585
Yoshikawa M, Miyata I, Uesugi S (1940) Contributions to the knowledge of dog parasites in Kobe City. Nippon Juigakkai Zasshi 2:450–464 (in Japanese)
Youssef AI, Uga S (2014) Review of parasitic zoonoses in Egypt. Trop Med health 42:3–14
Youssef MM, Mansour NS, Awadalla HN et al (1987) Heterophyid parasites of man from Idki, Maryut and Manzala Lakes areas in Egypt. J Egyp Soc Parasitol 17:475–479
Yu SH, Mott KE (1994) Epidemiology and morbidity of food-borne intestinal trematode infections. Trop Dis Bull 91:R125–R152
Zhang SL, Yuan EE, Zhang SS et al (1990) Case report: brain abscess caused by heterophyid eggs. Chinese J Parasitol Parasit Dis 8:173 (in Chinese)

References for Section 1.4

Abdel-Azim M (1938) On the intestinal helminths of dogs in Egypt. J Egypt Med Assoc 21:118–122
Africa CM (1938) Description of three trematodes of the genus *Haplorchis* (Heterophyidae) with notes on two other Philippine members of this genus. Phil J Sci 66:299–307
Africa CM, Garcia EY (1935) Two more new heterophyid trematodes from the Philippines. Phil J Sci 57:443–450
Africa CM, de Leon W, Garcia EY (1936) Somatic heterophyidiasis in fish-eating birds, II. Presence of adults and eggs in the bile ducts of the cattle egret. Phil J Sci 61:227–234
Africa CM, de Leon W, Garcia EY (1940) Visceral complications in intestinal heterophyidiasis of man. Acta Med Philippina Monogr Ser 1:1–132
Anh NTL, Phuong NT, Ha GH et al (2008) Evaluation of techniques for detection of small trematode eggs in faeces of domestic animals. Vet Parasitol 156:346–349
Belizario VY Jr, de Laon WU, Bersabe MJJ et al (2004) A focus of human infection by *Haplorchis taichui* (Trematoda: Heterophyidae) in the Southern Philippines. J Parasitol 90:1165–1169
Chai JY (2007) Intestinal flukes. In: Murrell KD, Fried B (eds) Food-borne parasitic zoonoses, fish and plant-borne parasites. Springer, New York, pp 53–115
Chai JY (2014) Helminth-Trematode. *Heterophyes heterophyes*. In: Encyclopedia of food safety, vol 2. Elsevier, Amsterdam, pp 158–163

Chai JY, Lee SH (2002) Food-borne intestinal trematode infections in the Republic of Korea. Parasitol Int 51:129–154
Chai JY, Jung BK (2017) Fishborne zoonotic heterophyid infections: an update. Food Waterborne Parasitol 8-9:33–63
Chai JY, Murrell KD, Lymbery AJ (2005a) Fish-borne parasitic zoonoses: status and issues. Int J Parasitol 35:1233–1254
Chai JY, Park JH, Han ET et al (2005b) Mixed infections with *Opisthorchis viverrini* and intestinal flukes in residents of Vientiane Municipality and Saravane Province in Laos. J Helminthol 79:283–289
Chai JY, Han ET, Guk SM et al (2007) High prevalence of liver and intestinal fluke infections among residents of Savannakhet Province, Laos. Korean J Parasitol 45:213–218
Chai JY, Shin EH, Lee SH et al (2009a) Foodborne intestinal flukes in Southeast Asia. Korean J Parasitol 47(Suppl):S69–S102
Chai JY, Han ET, Shin EH et al (2009b) High prevalence of *Haplorchis taichui, Prosthodendrium molenkampi*, and other helminth infections among people in Khammouane province, Lao PDR. Korean J Parasitol 47:243–247
Chai JY, Yong TS, Eom KS et al (2010) Prevalence of the intestinal flukes *Haplorchis taichui* and *H. yokogawai* in a mountainous area of Phongsaly Province, Lao PDR. Korean J Parasitol 48:339–342
Chai JY, De NV, Sohn WM (2012) Foodborne trematode metacercariae in fish from northern Vietnam and their adults recovered from experimental hamsters. Korean J Parasitol 50:317–325
Chai JY, Yong TS, Eom KS et al (2013) Hyperendemicity of *Haplorchis taichui* infection among riparian people in Saravane and Champasak Province, Lao PDR. Korean J Parasitol 51:305–311
Chai JY, Sohn WM, Na BK et al (2014) Zoonotic trematode metacercariae in fish from Phnom Penh and Pursat, Cambodia. Korean J Parasitol 52:35–40
Chai JY, Sohn WM, Jung BK et al (2015) Intestinal helminths recovered from humans in Xieng Khouang Province, Lao PDR with a particular note on *Haplorchis pumilio* infection. Korean J Parasitol 53:439–445
Chai JY, Sohn WM, Na BK et al (2017) Zonotic trematode metacercariae in fish from Yangon, Myanmar and their adults recovered from experimental animals. Korean J Parasitol 55:631–641
Chao D, Wang LC, Huang TC (1993) Prevalence of larval helminths in freshwater snails of the Kinmen Islands. J Helminthol 67:259–264
Chen HT (1936) A study of the Haplorchinae (Looss 1899) Poche 1926 (Trematoda: Heterophyidae). Parasitology 28:40–55
Chen HT (1949) Systematic consideration of some heterophyid trematodes in the subfamilies Haplorchinae and Stellantchasminae. Ann Trop Med Parasitol 43:304–312
Cheng CW (1988) Studies on genus *Haplorchis* trematode in Taiwan. Hirosaki Med J 40:130–154 (in Japanese)
Cheng Y, Xu G, Guo Z et al (1998) Survey on natural infection of cercariae in snail host and experimental infection of *Haplorchis pumilio*. Chinese J Schistosomiasis Cont 10
Cheng Y, Li Y, Lin J et al (2000) Survey of mixed infections with fish-borne trematodes in Piyuan county and DNA (RAPD) analysis. Chinese J Zoon 16:52–55
Chi TTK, Dalsgaard A, Turnbull JF et al (2008) Prevalence of zoonotic trematodes in fish from a Vietnamese fish-farming community. J Parasitol 94:423–428
Chontananarth T, Wongsawad C (2010) Prevalence of *Haplorchis taichui* in field-collected snails: a molecular approach. Korean J Parasitol 48:343–346
Chung OS, Lee HJ, Kim YM et al (2011) First report of human infection with *Gynaecotyla squatarolae* and first Korean record of *Haplorchis pumilio* in a patient. Parasitol Int 60:227–229
Dayal J (1935) Studies on the trematode parasites of Indian fishes. 1. A new trematode *Monorchotrema taakree* n. sp. from a freshwater fish, *Pseudeutropius taakree,* from Lucknow. Proc Indian Acad Sci 2:403–409

De NV, Le TH (2011) Human infections of fish-borne trematodes in Vietnam: prevalence and molecular specific identification at an endemic commune in Nam Dinh province. Exp Parasitol 129:355–361

De NV, Murrell KD, Cong LD et al (2003) The food-borne trematode zoonoses of Vietnam. The current status of parasitic diseases in Vietnam. Southeast Asian J Trop Med Pub Health 34(suppl 1):1–34

Diaz MT, Hernandez LE, Bashirullah AK (2008) Studies on the life cycle of *Haplorchis pumilio* (Looss, 1896) (Trematoda: Heterophyidae) in Venezuela. Rev Cientif, FCV-LUZ 18:35–42

Ditrich O, Scholz T, Giboda M (1990) Occurrence of some mediacally important flukes (Trematoda: Opisthorchiidae and Heterophyidae) in Nam Ngum Water Reservoir, Laos. Southeast Asian J Trop Med Public Health 21:482–488

Ditrich O, Kopacek P, Giboda M et al (1991) Serological differentiation of human small fluke infeccyions using *Opisthorchis viverrini* and *Haplorchis taichui* antigens. Southeast Asian J Trop Med Public Health 22(Suppl):174–178

Ditrich O, Giboda M, Scholz T (1992a) Comparative morphology of eggs of the haplorchiinae (Trematoda: Heterophyidae) and some other medically important heterophyid and opisthorchiid flukes. Folia Parasitol 39:123–132

Ditrich O, Našincová V, Scholz T et al (1992b) Larval stages of medically important flukes (Trematoda) from Vientiane Province, Laos. Part II. Cercariae. Ann Parasitol Hum Comp 67:75–81

Dung DT, De NV, Waikagul J et al (2007) Fishborne zoonotic intestinal trematodes, Vietnam. Emerg Infec Dis 13:1828–1833

Dung DT, Hop NT, Thaenkham U et al (2013) Genetic differences among Vietnamese *Haplorchis taichui* populations using the COI genetic marker. J Helminthol 87:66–70

Eduardo SL (1991) Food-borne parasitic zoonoses in the Philippines. Southeast Asian J Trop Med Pub Health 22:16–22

El-Azazy OME, Ibrahim Abdou NEM, Khalil AI et al (2015) Potential zoonotic trematodes recovered in stray cats from Kuwait Municipality, Kuwait. Korean J Parasitol 53:279–287

Elshazly AM, Soltan DM, Shahat SA et al (2007) Natural infection of fresh and brackish water fish with heterophyid encysted metacercariae in Dakhalia Governorate, Egypt. J Egypt Soc Parasitol 37:999–1010

Fahmy MA, Mandour AM, El-Naffar MK (1976) Successful infection of dogs and cats by *Prohemistomum vivax* Sonsino, 1893 and *Haplorchis yokogawai* Katsuta, 1932. J Egypt Soc Parasitol 6:77–82

Fahmy MA, Kahlifa R, Makhlouf LM (1986) Studies on heterophyid cercariae from Assiut Province. II. The life cycle of *Haplorchis yokogawai* (Katsuta, 1936) (Trematoda: Heterophyidae). Assiut Vet Med J 16:119–133

Faust EC, Nishigori M (1926) The life cycles of two new species of Heterophyidae parasitic in mammals and birds. J Parasitol 13:91–131

Fischthal JH, Kuntz RE (1965a) Digenetic trematodes of amphibians and reptiles from North Borneo (Malaysia). Proc Helminthol Soc Washington 32:63–71

Fischthal JH, Kuntz RE (1965b) Six digenetic trematodes of mammals from North Borneo (Malaysia). Proc Helminthol Soc Washington 32:154–159

Fischthal JH, Kuntz RE (1975) Some digenetic trematodes of mammals from Taiwan. Proc Helminthol Soc Washington 42:149–157

Fujino T, Higo H, Ishii Y et al (1989) Comparative studies on two similar species of *Haplorchis* and *Metagonimus* (Trematoda: Heterophyidae) – surface ultrastructure of adults and eggs. Proc Helminthol Soc Wash 56:35–41

Giboda M, Ditrich O, Scholz T et al (1991) Human *Opisthorchis* and *Haplorchis* infection in Laos. Trans Roy Soc Trop Med Hyg 85:538–540

Gohar N (1934) Les trématodes parasites du milan egyptien *Milvus mgrans* avec description d'une nouvelle espéce et remarques sur les genres *Haplorchis* Looss 1899 et *Monorchotrema* Nishigori 1924. Ann Parasitol Hum Comp 12:218–227 (in French)

Gupta VP, Pande BP (1965) On the heterophyid genus *Haplorchis* Looss, 1899 in Indian dog with a brief note on the species reported from other hosts. Agra Univ J Res 13:161

Hung NM, Madsen H, Fried B (2013) Global status of fish-borne zoonotic trematodiasis in humans. Acta Prasitol 58:231–258

Hung NM, Dung DT, Anh NTL et al (2015) Current status of fish-borne zoonotic trematode infections in Gia Vien district, Ninh Bin province, Vietnam. Parasit Vectors 8:21

Huston DC, Worsham MD, Huffman DG et al (2014) Infection of fishes, including threatened and endangered species by the trematode parasite *Haplorchis pumilio* (Looss, 1896) (Trematoda: Heterophyidae). Bioinv Rec 3:189–194

Ibrahim MM, Soliman MFM (2010) Prevalence and site preferences of heterophyid metacercariae in *Tilapia zilli* from Ismalia Fresh Water Canal, Egypt. Parasite 17:233–239

Ito J (1964a) A monograph of cercariae in Japan and adjacent territories. Progr Med Parasitol Japan 1:395–550

Ito J (1964b) *Metagonimus* and other human heterophyid trematodes. Progr Med Parasitol Japan 1:314–393

Ito J, Papasarathorn T, Tongkoom B (1962) An investigation of parasitic helminths of stray dogs in Bangkok. Jpn J Med Sci Biol 15:53–60

Jeon HK, Lee D, Park H et al (2012) Human infections with liver and minute intestinal flukes in Guangxi, China: analysis by DNA sequencing, ultrasonography, and immunoaffinity chromatography. Korean J Parasitol 50:391–394

Katsuta I (1932a) Studies on trematodes that take brackish water fish as the second intermediate host in Taiwan (3rd Report). *Monorchotrema microrchia* which takes *Mugil cephalus* as its intermediate host. Taiwan Igakkai Zasshi 31:160–175 (in Japanese)

Katsuta I (1932b) Studies on trematodes that take brackish water fish as the second intermediate host in Taiwan (4th Report). *Monorchotrema yokogawai* which takes *Mugil cephalus* as its intermediate host. Taiwan Igakkai Zasshi 31:253–265 (in Japanese)

Khalifa R, El-Naffar MK, Arafa MS (1977) Studies on heterophyid cercariae from Assiut Province, Egypt. I. Notes on the life cycle of *Haplorchis pumilio* (Looss, 1896) with a discussion on previously described species. Acta Parasitol Pol 25:25–38

Khalil M (1932) The life history of a heterophyid parasite in Egypt. C R Congr Int Med Trop Hyg 4:137–146

Kliks M, Tantachamrun T (1974) Heterophyid (Trematoda) parasites of cats in north Thailand, with note on a human case found at necropsy. Southeast Asian. J Trop Med Public Health 5:547–555

Kobayasi H (1942) Studies on trematodes in Hainan Island. II. Trematoda found in the intestinal tract of dogs by experimental feeding with certain fresh and brackish water fish. Jpn J Med Sci Pathol 6:187–227

Kobayasi H (1954) Studies on flukes in French Indochina. On a new species of fluke including in the genus *Haplorchis, Haplorchis nhatrangensis* n. sp. Jpn J Rural Med 11:20–24

Kobayasi H (1968) Reports on scientifical works. Studies on trematode in Hainan island, South China and Viet-Nam (French Indo-China). A monograph

Komiya Y (1965) Metacercariae in Japan and adjacent territories. Progr Med Parasitol Japan 2:1–328

Kumchoo K, Wongsawad C, Chai JY et al (2003) Recovery and growth of *Haplorchis taichui* (Trematoda: Heterophyidae) in chicks. Southeast Asian J Trop Med Public Health 34:718–722

Kumchoo K, Wongsawad C, Chai JY et al (2005) High prevalence of *Haplorchis taichui* metacercariae in cyprinoid fish from Chiang Mai Province. Thailand. Southeast Asian J Trop Med Public Health 36:451–455

Kumchoo K, Wongsawad C, Vanittanakom P et al (2007) Effect of niclosamide on the tegumental surface of *Haplorchis taichui* using scanning electron microscopy. J Helminthol 81:329–337

Kuntz RE, Chandler AC (1956) Studies on Egyptian trematodes with special reference to the heterophyid of mammals. I. Adult flukes, with descriptions of *Phagicola longicollis* n. sp., *Cynodiplostomum namrui* n. sp., and a *Stephanoprora* from cats. J Parasitol 42:445–459

Le TH, Nguyen KT, Nguyen NT et al (2017) The ribosomal transcription units of *Haplorchis pumilio* and *H. taichui* and the use of 28S rDNA sequences for phylogenetic identification of common heterophyids in Vietnam. Parasit Vectors 10:17

Lee D, Choe S, Park H et al (2013) Complete mitochondrial genome of *Haplorchis taichui* and comparative analysis with other trematodes. Korean J Parasitol 51:719–726

Li T, He S, Zhao H et al (2010) Major trends in human parasitic diseases in China. Trends Parasitol 26:264–270

Lie Kian J (1951) Some human flukes from Indonesia. Docum Neerl Indones Morb Trop 3:105–116

Lo CT, Lee KM (1996) Pattern of emergence and the effects of temperature and light on the emergence and survival of heterophyid cercariae (*Centrocestus formosanus* and *Haplorchis pumilio*). J Parasitol 82:347–350

Lobna SMA, Metawea YF, Elsheikha HM (2010) Prevalence of heterophyiosis in Tilapia fish and humans in Northern Egypt. Parasitol Res 107:1029–1034

Looss A (1896) Researches sur la faune parasitaire de l'Egypte. Première partie. Mém Inst égypt (Egypte) 3:1–252

Looss A (1899) Weitere Beitrage zur Kentniss der Trematoden-Fauna Aegyptens, zugleich Versuch einer naturalischen Gliedrung des Genus *Distomum* Retzius. Zool Yb 12:521–784

Lovis L, Mak TK, Phongluxa K et al (2009) PCR diagnosis of *Opisthorchis viverrini* and *Haplorchis taichui* infections in a Lao community in an area of endemicity and comparison of diagnostic methods for parasitological field surveys. J Clin Microbiol 47:1517–1523

Mahdy OA, Shaheed IB (2001) Studies on metacercarial infection among *Tilapia* species in Egypt. Helminthologia 38:35–42

Manning GS, Lertprasert P (1971) Four new trematodes of man from Thailand. Trans Roy Soc Trop Med Hyg 65:101–102

Manning GS, Lertprasert P, Watanasirmkit K et al (1971) A description of newly discovered intestinal parasites endemic to northern Thailand. J Med Ass Thailand 54:466–474

Martin WE (1958) The life histories of some Hawaiian heterophyid trematodes. J Parasitol 44:305–318

Martin WE (1959) Egyptian heterophyid trematodes. Trans Am Microscop Soc 78:172–181

Nath D, Pande BP (1970) Identity of the three heterophyid metacercariae infesting some of the freshwater fishes. Curr Sci 39:325–326

Nishigori M (1924) Two new trematodes of the family Heterophyidae found in Formosa. Taiwan Igakkai Zasshi 237:569–570 (in Japanese)

Nissen S, Nguyen LAT, Dalsgaard A et al (2013) Experimental infection with the small intestinal trematode, *Haplorchis pumilio*, in young dogs. Vet Parasitol 191:138–142

Nithikathkul C, Wongsawad C (2008) Prevalence of *Haplorchis taichui* and *Haplorchoides* sp. metacercariae in freshwater fish from water reservoirs, Chiang Mai, Thailand. Korean J Parasitol 46:109–112

Odening K (1962) Trematoden aus indischen Vögeln des Berliner Tierparks. Z Parasitenkd 21:381–425

Onsurathum S, Pinlaor P, Charoensuk L et al (2016) Contamination of *Opisthorchis viverrini* and *Haplorchis taichui* metacercariae in fermented fish products in northeastern Thailand markets. Food Cont 59:493–498

Ooi HK, Chen CI, Lin SC et al (1997) Metacercariae in fishes of Sun Moon Lake which is an endemic area for *Clonorchis sinensis* in Taiwan. Southeast Asian J Trop Med Pub Health 28:222–223

Pearson JC (1964) A revision of the subfamily Haplorchinae Looss, 1899 (Trematoda: Heterophyidae). Parasitology 54:601–676

Pearson JC, Ow-Yang CK (1982) New species of *Haplorchis* from Southeast Asia, together with keys to the *Haplorchis*-group of heterophyid trematodes of the region. Southeast Asian J Trop Med Pub Health 13:35–60

Phan VT, Ersbøll AK, Nguyen TT et al (2010) Freshwater aquaculture nurseries and infection of fish with zoonotic trematodes, Vietnam. Emerg Infect Dis 16:1905–1909

Price EW (1940) A review of the trematode superfamily Opisthorchioidea. Proc Helminthol Soc Wash 7:1–13

Pulido-Murillo EA, Furtado LFV, Melo A et al (2018) Fishborne zoonotic trematodes transmitted by *Melanoides tuberculata* snails, Peru. Emerg Infect Dis 24:606–608

Pungpak S, Radomyos P, Radomyos B et al (1998) Treatment of *Opisthorchis viverrini* and intestinal fluke infections with praziquantel. Southeast Asian J Trop Med Public Health 29:246–249

Radomyos P, Bunnag D, Harinasuta T (1983) *Haplorchis pumilio* (Looss) infection in man in northeastern Thailand. Southeast Asian J Trop Med Publ Health 14:223–227

Radomyos P, Bunnag D, Harinasuta T (1984) Worms recovered in stool following praziquantel treatment. Arzneim/Forch (Drug Res) 34:1186–1188

Radomyos P, Wongsaroj T, Wilairatana P et al (1998) Opisthorchiasis and intestinal fluke infections in northern Thailand. Southeast Asian J Trop Med Public Health 29:123–127

Rekharani Z, Madhavi R (1985) Digenetic trematodes from mullets of Visakhapatnam (India). J Nat Hist 19:929–951

Rim HJ, Chai JY, Min DY et al (2003) Prevalence of intestinal parasite infections on a national scale among primary schoolchildren in Laos. Parasitol Res 91:267–272

Rim HJ, Sohn WM, Yong TS et al (2008) Fishborne trematode metacercariae detected in freshwater fish from Vientiane Municipality and Savannakhet Province, Lao PDR. Korean J Parasitol 46:253–260

Rim HJ, Sohn WM, Yong TS et al (2013) Fishborne trematode metacercariae in Luang Prabang, Khammouane, and Saravane Province, Lao PDR. Korean J Parasitol 51:107–114

Saad AIA, Abed GH (1995) Studies on the life cycle of *Haplorchis pumilio* (Looss, 1896) Looss, 1899 with morphological redescription of larval and adult stages. J Egypt Soc Parasitol 25:795–806

Sato M, Sanguankiat S, Pubampen S et al (2009a) Egg paying capacity of *Haplorchis taichui* (Digenea: Heterophyidae) in humans. Korean J Parasitol 47:315–318

Sato M, Thaengkham U, Dekumyoy P et al (2009b) Discrimination of *O. viverrini, C. sinensis, H. pumilio* and *H. taichui* using nuclear DNA-based PCR targeting ribosomal DNA ITS regions. Acta Trop 109:81–83

Sato M, Pongvongsa T, Sanguankiat S et al (2010) Copro-DNA diagnosis of *Opisthorchis viverrini* and *Haplorchis taichui* infection in an endemic area of Lao PDR. Southeast Asian J Trop Med Public Health 41:28–35

Sato M, Pongvongsa T, Sanguankiat S et al (2015) Patterns of trematode infections of *Opisthorchis viverrini* (Opisthorchiidae) and *Haplorchis taichui* (Heterophyidae) in human populations from two villages in Savannakhet Province, Lao PDR. J Helminthol 89:439–445

Saenphet S, Wongsawad C, Saenphet K et al (2008) *Haplorchis taichui*: worm recovery rate and immune responses in infected rats (*Ratus norvegicus*). Exp Parasitol 120:175–179

Sayasone S, Vonghajack Y, Vanmany M et al (2009) Diversity of human intestinal helminthiasis in Lao PDR. Trans Roy Soc Trop Med Hyg 103:247–254

Scholz T (1991) Metacercariae of trematodes from fish in Vientina Province. Laos. Acta Soc Zool Bohemoslov 55:130–145

Scholz T, Ditrich O, Giboda M (1990) Larval stages of medically important flukes (Trematoda) from Vientiane Province, Laos. Part I. Metacercariae. Ann Parasitol Hum Comp 65:238–243

Scholz T, Ditrich O, Tuna M et al (1991a) Study on the body surface of *Haplorchis yokogawai* (Katsuta, 1932) and *H. taichui* (Nishigori, 1924) (Trematoda: Heterophyidae). Southeast Asian J Trop Med Public Health 22:443–448

Scholz T, Ditrich O, Tuna M et al (1991b) Differential diagnosis of opisthorchiid and heterophyid metacercariae (Trematoda) infecting flesh of cyprinid fish from Nam Ngum Dam in Laos. Southeast Asian J Trop Med Public Health 22(Suppl):171–173

Scholz T, Aguirre-Macedo ML, Salgado-Maldonado G (2001) Trematodes of the family Heterophyidae (Digenea) in Mexico: a review and new host and geographical records. J Nat Hist 35:1733–1772

Skov J, Kania PW, Dalsgaard A et al (2009) Life cycle stages of heterophyid trematodes in Vietnamese freshwater fishes traced by molecular and morphometric methods. Vet Parasitol 160:66–75

Sohn WM, Eom KS, Min DY et al (2009) Fishborne trematode metacercariae in freshwater fish from Guangxi Zhuang Autonomous Region, China. Korean J Parasitol 47:249–257

Sohn WM, Yong TS, Eom KS et al (2014) Prevalence of *Haplorchis taichui* among humans and fish in Luang Prabang Province, Lao PDR. Acta Trop 136:74–80

Sommerville C (1982) The life history of *Haplorchis pumilio* (Looss, 1896) from cultured tilapias. J Fish Dis 5:233–241

Songsri J, Boonmars T, Boonjaraspinyo S et al (2018) Syrian hamster (*Mesocricetus auratus*) as an animal model for *Haplorchis taichui* infection: biology, morphology, and pathology. Thai J Vet Med 48:479–486

Srisawangwong T, Kanla P, Tesana S et al (1989) Scanning electron microscopy of the tegumental surface of adult *Haplorchis pumilio* (Looss). J Helminthol 63:141–147

Srisawangwong T, Sithithaworn P, Tesana S (1997) Metacercariae isolated from cyprinoid fishes in Khon Kaen district by digestion technic. Southeast Asian J Trop Med Pub Health 28:224–226

Sukontason K, Methanitikorn R, Sukontason K et al (1998) Viability of metacercariae in northern Thai traditional foods. Southeast Asian J Trop Med Pub Health 29:714–716

Sukontason K, Piangjai S, Muangyimpong Y et al (1999a) Prevalence of trematode metacercariae in cyprinoid fish of Ban Pao District, Chiang Mai province, Northern Thailand. Southeast Asian J Trop Med Pub Health 30:365–370

Sukontason K, Piangjai S, Sukontason K et al (1999b) Potassium permanganate staining for differentiation of the surface morphology of *Opisthorchis viverrini, Haplorchis taichui,* and *Phaneropsolus bonnei* eggs. Southeast Asian J Trop Med Pub Health 30:371–374

Sukontason K, Sukontason KL, Boonsriwong N et al (2001) Development of *Haplorchis taichui* (Trematoda: heterophyidae) in *Mus musculus* mice. Southeast Asian J Trop Med Pub Health 32(Suppl 2):43–47

Sukontason K, Unpunyo P, Sukontason KL et al (2005) Evidence of *Haplorchis taichui* infection as a pathogenic parasite: three case reports. Scand J Infect Dis 37:388–390

Tawfik MAA, Elnawawi FA, Shaapan RM (2000) Studies on some fish-borne trematodes in Egypt. Egyptian J Vet Sci 34:39–48

Tesana S, Srisawangwonk T, Kaewkes S et al (1991) Eggshell morphology of the small eggs of human trematodes in Thailand. Southeast Asian J Trop Med Public Health 22:631–636

Thaenkham U, Visetsuk K, Dung DT et al (2007) Discrimination of *Opisthorchis viverrini* and *Haplorchis taichui* using COI sequence marker. Acta Trop 103:26–32

Thaenkham U, Blair D, Nawa Y, Waikagul J (2012) Families Opisthorchiidae and Heterophyidae: are they distinct? Parasitol Int 61:90–93

Thaenkham U, Phuphisut O, Nuamtanong S et al (2016) Population structure of *Haplorchis taichui* in Indochina revealed by mitochondrial *COX1* sequence. J Helminthol (submitted)

Thien PC, Dalsgaard A, Thanh BN et al (2007) Prevalence of fishborne zoonotic parasites in important cultured fish species in the Mekong Delta, Vietnam. Parasitol Res 107:1277–1284

Toledo R, Munoz-Antoli C, Esteban JG (2014) Intestinal trematode infections. In Digenetic Trematodes, Toledo R, Fried B (eds.). Springer, New York, USA. Adv Exp Med Biol 766:201–240

Tubangui MA (1933) Trematode parasites of Philippine vertebrates. IV. Description of new species and classification. Philip J Sci 52:167–197

Tubangui MA, Africa CM (1938) The systematic position of some trematodes-reported from the Philippines. Phil J Sci 67:117–125

Ujiie N (1936) Differentiation of the species of Monorchotrema from Formosa. Taiwan Igakkai Zasshi 35:938–946 (in Japanese)

Umadevi K, Madhavi R (2006) The life cycle of *Haplorchis pumilio* (Trematoda: Heterophyidae) from the Indian region. J Helminthol 80:327–332

Vasquez-Colet A, Africa CM (1940) Morphological studies on various Philippine heterophyid metacercariae with notes on the incidence, site, and degree of metacercarial infection in three species of marine fish. Phil J Sci 72:395–419

Velasquez CC (1973a) Molluscan stages of *Haplorchis taichui* (Nishigori) in *Melania juncea* Lea in the Philippines. J Parasitol 59:281

Velasquez CC (1973b) Observations on some Heterophyidae (Trematoda: Digenea) encysted in Philippine fishes. J Parasitol 59:77–84

Velasquez CC (1982) Heterophyidiasis. In: Steele JH (ed) CRC handbook series in zoonoses, section C: parasitic zoonoses, vol III (Trematode Zoonoses). CRC Press, Boca Raton, pp 99–107

Velasquez CC (1983) Pests/parasites and diseases of milkfish in the Philippines. In: Juario JV et al (eds) Advances in milkfish biology and culture. Proceedings of the 2nd International milkfish aquaculture conference, 4–8 October, 1983. Iloilo City, Philippines, pp 155–159

Wang JJ, Chung LY, Lee JD et al (2002) *Haplorchis* infections in intermediate hosts from a clonorchiasis endemic area in Meinung, Taiwan, Republic of China. J Helminthol 76:185–188

Watthanakulpanich D, Waikagul J, Maipanich W et al (2010) *Haplorchis taichui* as a possible etiologic agent of irritable bowel syndrome-like symptoms. Korean J Parasitol 48:225–229

WHO (1995) Control of Foodborne Trematode Infections. Report of a WHO Study Group. Geneva, WHO. WHO Tech Report Ser 849:1–157

Wijit A, Morakote N, Klinchid J (2013) High prevalence of haplorchiasis in Nan and Lampang Provinces, Thailand, proven by adult worm recovery from suspected opisthorchiasis cases. Korean J Parasitol 51:767–769

Witenberg G (1929) Studies on the trematode – family Heterophyidae. Ann Trop Med Parasitol 23:131–268

Wongsawad C, Wonsawad P (2012) *Opisthorchis viverrini* and *Haplorchis taichui*: development of a multiplex PCR assay for their detection and differentiation using specific primers derived from HAT-RAPD. Exp Parasitol 132:237–242

Wongsawad C, Wonsawad P, Chai JY et al (2009) *Haplorchis taichui*, Witenberg, 1930: development of a HAT-RAPD marker for the detection of minute intestinal fluke infection. Exp Parasitol 123:158–161

Wongsawad C, Phalee A, Noikong W et al (2012) Co-infection with *Opisthorchis viverrini* and *Haplorchis taichui* detected by human fecal examination in Chomtong district, Chiang Mai Province, Thailand. Parasitol Int 61:56–59

Yamaguti S (1958) Systema Helminthum. Vol. I. The digenetic trematodes of vertebrates (Part I). Interscience Publishers Inc, New York, pp 1–979

Yokogawa S (1940) On the visceral heterophyidiasis, especially on the etiology of heart, brain and spinal cord heterophyidiasis. Taiwan Igakkai Zasshi 39:1729–1730 (in Japanese)

Yu SH, Mott KE (1994) Epidemiology and morbidity of food-borne intestinal trematode infections. Trop Dis Bull 91:R125–R152

References for Section 1.5

Chai JY, Kim JL, Seo M (2014) Four human cases of *Acanthotrema felis* (Digenea: Heterophyidae) infection in Korea. Korean J Parasitol 52:291–294

Cho SH, Cho PY, Lee DM et al (2010) Epidemiological survey on the infection of intestinal flukes in residents of Muan-gun, Jeollanam-do, the Republic of Korea. Korean J Parasitol 48:133–138

Cho SH, Kim IS, Hwang EJ et al (2012) Infection status of esturine fish and oysters with intestinal fluke metacercariae in Muan-gun, Jeollanam-do, Korea. Korean J Parasitol 50:215–220

Kinsella JM, Heard RW III (1974) Morphology and life cycle of *Stictodora cursitans* n. comb. (Trematoda: Heterophyidae) from mammals in Florida salt marshes. Trans Am Microscop Soc 93:408–412

Lafuente M, Roca V, Carbonell E (2000) Description of *Acanthotrema armata* n. sp. (Trematoda: Heterophyidae) from *Larus audouinii* (Aves: Laridae), with an amended diagnosis of the genus *Acanthotrema* Travassos, 1928. Syst Parasitol 45:131–134

Martin WE (1950) *Parastictodora hancocki* n. gen., n. sp. (Trematoda: Heterophyidae), with observation on its life cycle. J Parasitol 36:360–370

Martin WE, Kuntz RE (1955) Some Egyptian heterophyid trematodes. J Parasitol 41:374–382

Shin EH, Park JH, Guk SM et al (2009) Intestinal helminth infections in feral cats and a raccoon dog on Aphaedo Island, Shinan-gun, with a special note on *Gymnophalloides seoi* infection in cats. Korean J Parasitol 47:189–191

Shin SS, Oh DS, Ahn KS et al (2015) Zoonotic intestinal trematodes in stray cats (*Felis catus*) from riverside areas of the Republic of Korea. Korean J Parasitol 53:209–213

Sohn WM, Chai JY (2005) Infection status with helminthes in feral cats purchased from a market in Busan, Republic of Korea. Korean J Parasitol 43:93–100

Sohn WM, Han ET, Chai JY (2003a) *Acanthotrema felis* n. sp. (Digenea: Heterophyidae) from the small intestine of stray cats in the Republic of Korea. J Parasitol 89:154–158

Sohn WM, Han ET, Seo M et al (2003b) Identification of *Acanthotrema felis* (Digenea: Heterophyidae) metacercariae encysted in the brackish water fish *Acanthogobius flavimanus*. Korean J Parasitol 41:101–105

Sohn WM, Seo M, Chai JY (2003c) Surface ultrastructure of the adult stage of *Acanthotrema felis* (Trematoda: Heterophyidae). Korean J Parasitol 41:107–111

Velasquez CC (1973) Observations on some Heterophyidae (Trematoda: Digenea) encysted in Philippine fishes. J Parasitol 59:77–84

References for Section 1.6

Ferguson JA, Locke SA, Font WF et al (2012) *Apophallus microsoma* n. sp. from chicks infected with metacercariae from coho salmon (Oncorhynchus kisutch) and review of the taxonomy and pathology of the genus *Apophallus* (Heterophyidae). J Parasitol 98:1122–1132

Niemi DR, Macy RW (1974) The life cycle and infectivity to man of *Apophallus donicus* (Skrjabin and Lindtrop, 1919) (Trematoda: Heterophyidae) in Oregon. Proc Helminthol Soc Washington 41:223–229

Schell SC (1985) Handbook of Trematodes of North America North of Mexico. University Press of Idaho, Moscow, Idaho, USA, pp 1–263

Yamaguti S (1958) Systema Helminthum. Vol. I. The digenetic trematodes of vertebrates (Part I). Interscience Publishers Inc, New York, pp 1–979

Yamaguti S (1971) Synopsis of digenetic trematodes of vertebrates, vol I. Keigaku Publishing Co, Tokyo, pp 1–1074

Yu SH, Mott KE (1994) Epidemiology and morbidity of food-borne intestinal trematode infections. Trop Dis Bull 91:R125–R152

References for Section 1.7

Antunes SA, Almeida-Dias ER (1994) *Phagicola longa* (Trematoda: Heterophyidae) em mugilídeos estocados resfriados e seu consume cru em São Paulo, SP. Hig Alim 8:41–42

Borges JN, Lopes KC, Santos CP (2018) Viability of *Ascocotyle* (*Phagicola*) *longa* (Trematoda: Heterophyidae) metacercariae from mullets (*Mugil liza*) from Rio de Janeiro, Brazil after exposure to freezing and heating in the temperature range from −30 °C to 180 °C. Food Contr 89:117–122

Chieffi PP, Leite OH, Dias RMD, Torres DMA, Mangini ACS (1990) Human parasitism by *Phagicola* sp. (Trematoda, Heterophyidae) in Cananéia, São Paulo State, Brazil. Rev Inst Med Trop São Paulo 32:285–288

Chieffi PP, Gorla MCO, Torres DM et al (1992) Human infection by *Phagicola* sp. (Trematoda, Heterophyidae) in the municipality of Registro, São Paulo State, Brazil. J Trop Med Hyg 95:346–348

Núñez MO (1993) Life-history studies of heterophyid trematodes in the Neotropical Region: *Ascocotyle* (*Phagicola*) *diminuta* (Stunkard & Haviland, 1924) and *A.* (*P.*) *angrense* Tranvassos, 1916. Syst Parasitol 24:191

Oliveira SA, Blazquez FJH, Antunes SA, Maria AAM (2007) *Ascocotyle* (*Phagicola*) *longa* Ransom, 1920 (Digenea: Heterophyidae) metacercariae, in *Mugil platanus* in estuarine of Cananéia, SP, Brazil. Ciencia Rural, Santa Maria 37:1056–1059 (in Portuguese)

Ransom BH (1920) Synopsis of the trematode family Heterophyidae with descriptions of a new genus and five new species. Proc US Nat Mus 57(2322):527–573

Sarabeev V, Balbuena JA, Morand S (2019) Aggregation patterns of helminth populations in the introduced fish, *Liza haematocheilus* (Teleosti: Mugillidae): disentangling host-parasite relationships. Int J Parasitol 49:83–91

Scholz T (1999) Taxonomic study of *Ascocotyle* (*Phagicola*) *longa* Ransom, 1920 (Digenea: Heterophyidae) and related taxa. Syst Parasitol 43:147–158

Simões SBE, Barbosa HS, Santos CP (2010) The life cycle of *Ascocotyle* (*Phagicola*) *longa* (Digenea: Heterophyidae), a causative agent of fish-borne trematodes. Acta Trop 113:226–233

Yu SH, Mott KE (1994) Epidemiology and morbidity of food-borne intestinal trematode infections. Trop Dis Bull 91:R125–R152

References for Section 1.8

Chai JY (2007) Intestinal flukes. In: Murrell KD, Fried B (eds) Food-borne parasitic zoonoses. Fish and plant-borne parasites. Springer, New York, pp 53–115

Chai JY, Sohn WM, Yong TS et al (2013a) *Centrocestus formosanus* (Heterophyidae): human infections and the infection source in Lao PDR. J Parasitol 99:531–536

Chai JY, Yong TS, Eom KS et al (2013b) Hyperendemicity of *Haplorchis taichui* infection among riparian people in Saravane and Champasak Province, Lao PDR. Korean J Parasitol 51:305–311

Chai JY, Sohn WM, Jung BK et al (2015) Intestinal helminths recovered from humans in Xieng Khouang Province, Lao PDR with a particular note on *Haplorchis pumilio* infection. Korean J Parasitol 53:439–445

Chao D, Wang LC, Huang TC (1993) Prevalence of larval helminths in freshwater snails of the Kinmen Islands. J Helminthol 67:259–264

Chen HT (1942) The metacercaria and adult of *Centrocestus formosanus* (Nishigori, 1924), with notes on the natural infection of rats and cats with *C. armatus* (Tanabe, 1922). J Parasitol 28:285–298

Chen YZ, Xu XL, Chen BJ et al (1991) First report on human infection of *Centrocestus formosanus* (in Fujian). Chin J Parasitol Parasit Dis 9:273

Chi TTK, Dalsgaard A, Turnbull JF, Tuan PA, Murrell KD (2008) Prevalence of zoonotic trematodes in fish from a Vietnamese fish-farming community. J Parasitol 94:423–428

Cortés DA, Dolz G, Zúñiga JJR, Rocha AEJ, Aláan DL (2010) *Centrocestus formosanus* (Opisthorchiida: Heterophyidae) como causa de muerte de alevines de tilapia gris *Oreochromis niloticus* (Perciforme: Cichlidae) en el Pacifico seco de Costa Rica. Rev Biol Trop 58:1453–1465

De NV, Le TH (2011) Human infections of fish-borne trematodes in Vietnam: prevalence and molecular specific identification at an endemic commune in Nam Dinh province. Exp Parasitol 129:355–361

El-Azazy OMS, Abdou NEM, Khalil AI et al (2015) Potential zoonotic trematodes recovered in stray dogs from Kuwait Municipality, Kuwait. Korean J Parasitol 53:279–287

Faust EC, Nishigori M (1926) The life cycles of two new species of Heterophyidae parasitic in mammals and birds. J Parasitol 13:91–131

Gjurčevic E, Petrinec Z, Kozaric Z et al (2007) Metacercariae of *Centrocestus formosanus* in goldfish (*Carassius auratus* L.) imported into Croatia. Helminthologia 44:214–216

Han ET, Shin EH, Phommakorn S et al (2008) *Centrocestus formosanus* (Digenea: Heterophyidae) encysted in the freshwater fish, *Puntius brevis*, from Lao PDR. Korean J Parasitol 46:49–53

Harinasuta T, Bunnag D, Radomyos P (1987) Intestinal fluke infections. In Bailliere's clinical tropical medicine and communicable diseases. 2(3):695–721

Hong SJ, Seo BS, Lee SH, Chai JY (1988) A human case of *Centrocestus armatus* infection in Korea. Korean J Parasitol 26:55–60

Hong SJ, Woo HC, Kim IT (1989a) Study on *Centrocestus armatus* in Korea I. Infection status of *Zacco platypus* and *Z. temminckii* with the metacercariae of *C. armatus*. Korean J Parasitol 27:41–46 (in Korean)

Hong SJ, Woo HC, Kim IT (1989b) Study on *Centrocestus armatus* in Korea II. Recovery rate, growth and development of worms in albino rats. Korean J Parasitol 27:47–56

Hung NM, Madsen H, Fried B (2013) Global status of fish-borne zoonotic trematodiasis in humans. Acta Prasitol 58:231–258

Ito J (1964) *Metagonimus* and other human heterophyid trematodes. Progr Med Parasitol Japan 1:314–393

Kimura D, Paller VG, Uga S (2007) Development of *Centrocestus armatus* in different final hosts. Vet Parasitol 146:367–371

Kobayasi H (1942) Studies on trematoda in Hainan Island. Determination of the second intermediate hosts of trematodes and trematodes found in the intestinal tracts of dogs by experimental feeding with fish in Hainan Island. Jpn J Med Sci 6:181–185

Komatsu S, Kimura D, Paller VGV, Uga S (2014) Dynamics of *Centrocestus armatus* transmission in endemic river in Hyogo Prefecture, Japan. Trop Med Health 42:35–42

Komiya Y (1965) Metacercariae in Japan and adjacent territories. Progr Med Parasitol Japan 2:1–328

Kurokawa T (1935) On a new species of *Stamnosoma* found from a man. Tokyo Iji Shinshi 2915:293–298 (in Japanese)

Lee JK, Lee HI, Baek BK et al (1984) Survey on encysted cercariae of trematodes from freshwater fishes in Tongjin riverside areas in Korea. Korean J Parasitol 22:190–202 (in Korean)

Li T, He S, Zhao H, Zhao G, Zhu XQ (2010) Major trends in human parasitic diseases in China. Trends Parasitol 26:264–270

Lo CT, Lee KM (1996) Pattern of emergence and the effects of temperature and light on the emergence and survival of heterophyid cercariae (*Centrocestus formosanus* and *Haplorchis pumilio*). J Parasitol 82:347–350

Madhavi R (1986) Distribution of metacercariae of *Centrocestus formosanus* (Trematoda: Heterophyidae) on the gills of *Aplocheilus panchax*. J Fish Biol 29:685–690

Martin WE (1958) The life cycle of some Hawaiian heterophyid trematodes. J Parasitol 44:305–321

Martin WE (1959) Egyptian heterophyid trematodes. Trans Am Microscop Soc 78:172–181

Mishima T (1959) On a new species of the genus *Centrocestus* with its life history. Tokyo Iji Shinshi 76:292–299

Mitchell AJ, Salmon MJ, Huffman DG, Goodwin AE, Brandt TM (2000) Prevalence and pathogenicity of a heterophyid trematode infecting the gills of an endangered fish, the fountain darter, in two central Texas spring-fed rivers. J Aquat Anim Health 12:283–289

Morozov FN (1952) Superfamily Heterophyoidea Faust, 1929. In Skrjabin KI (ed) Trematodes of animals and man, vol 6, Academy of Sciences of the Union of Soviet Socialist Republics, Moscow, pp 153–412 (in Russian)

Najet G, Sabah D, Hayet H et al (2014) *Melanoides tuberculata* as intermediate host of *Centrocestus formosanus* (Nishigori, 1924) in Tunisia. African J Biotechnol 13:2774–2777

Nishigori M (1924) On a new trematode, *Stamnosoma formosanum* n. sp., and its life history. Taiwan Igakkai Zasshi 234:181–228 (in Japanese)

Oliveira SA, Blazquez FJH, Antunes SA, Maria AAM (2007) *Ascocotyle* (*Phagicola*) *longa* Ransom, 1920 (Digenea: Heterophyidae) metacercariae, in *Mugil platanus* in estuarine of Cananéia, SP, Brazil. Ciencia Rural, Santa Maria 37:1056–1059 (in Portuguese)

Pinto HA, de Melo AL (2010) *Melanoides tuberculata* (Mollusca: Thiaridae) as an intermediate host of *Centrocestus formosanus* (Trematoda: Heterophyidae) in Brazil. Rev Instit Med Trop São Paulo 52:207–210

Pinto HA, Mati ALT, de Melo AL (2013) New records and a checklist of trematodes from Butorides striata (AvesL Ardeidae). Rev Mexicana Biodiversidad 84:1100–1110

Pinto HA, Mati VLT, de Melo AL (2015) Experimental centrocestiasis: worm burden, morphology and fecundity of *Centrocestus formosanus* (Trematoda: Heterophyidae) in dexamethasone immunosuppressed mice. Parasitol Int 64:236–239

Pinto HA, Conçalves NQ, López-Hernandez D et al (2018) The life cycle of a zoonotic parasite reassessed: experimental infection of *Melanoides tuberculata* (Mollusca: Thiaridae) with *Centrocestus formosanus* (Trematoda: Heterophyidae). PLoS One 13:e0194161

Premvati G, Pande V (1974) On *Centrocestus formosanus* (Nishigori, 1924) Price, 1932 and its experimental infections in white leghorn chicks. Jpn J Parasitol 23:79–84

Pulido-Murillo EA, Furtado LFV, Melo A et al (2018) Fishborne zoonotic trematodes transmitted by *Melanoides tuberculata* snails, Peru. Emerg Infect Dis 24:606–608

Ransom BH (1920) Synopsis of the trematode family Heterophyidae with descriptions of a new genus and five new species. Proc US Nat Mus 57(2322):527–573

Rim HJ, Sohn WM, Yong TS et al (2008) Fishborne trematode metacercariae detected in freshwater fish from Vientiane Municipality and Savannakhet Province, Lao PDR. Korean J Parasitol 46:253–260

Rim HJ, Sohn WM, Yong TS et al (2013) Fishborne trematode metacercariae in Luang Prabang, Khammouane, and Saravane Province, Lao PDR. Korean J Parasitol 51:107–114

Ryang YS, Ahn YK, Yoon MB (1991) Trematode infections in the small intestine of *Egretta alba medesta* in Kanhwon-do. Korean J Parasitol 29:227–233 (in Korean)

Saenphet S, Wongsawad C, Saenphet K et al (2006a) Chronological observations of intestinal histopathology in rats (*Rattus novegicus*) infected with *Centrocestus caninus*. Southeast Asian J Trop Med Pub Health 37(Suppl 3):69–73

Saenphet S, Wongsawad C, Saenphet K et al (2006b) Mucosal mast cell responses in rats (*Rattus novegicus*) experimentally infected with *Centrocestus caninus*. Southeast Asian J Trop Med Pub Health 37:446–451

Scholz T (1999) Taxonomic study of *Ascocotyle* (*Phagicola*) *longa* Ransom, 1920 (Digenea: Heterophyidae) and related taxa. Syst Parasitol 43:147–158

Scholz T, Salgado-Maldonado G (1999) The introduction and dispersal of *Centrocestus formosanus* (Nishigori, 1924) (Digenea: Heterophyidae) in Mexico: a review. Am Midland Naturalist 143:185–200

Shin SS, Oh DS, Ahn KS et al (2015) Zoonotic intestinal trematodes in stray cats (*Felis catus*) from riverside areas of the Republic of Korea. Korean J Parasitol 53:209–213

Sohn WM, Chai JY (2005) Infection status with helminthes in feral cats purchased from a market in Busan, Republic of Korea. Korean J Parasitol 43:93–100

Sohn WM, Na BK, Cho SH et al (2018) Infections with zoonotic trematode metacercariae in yellow goby, *Acanthogobius flavimanus*, from coastal areas of Republic of Korea. Korean J Parasitol 56:259–265

Srisawangwong T, Sithithaworn P, Tesana S (1997) Metacercariae isolated from cyprinoid fishes in Khon Kaen district by digestion technic. Southeast Asian J Trop Med Pub Health 28:224–226

Takahashi S (1929) A contribution to the life-history of *Stamnosoma armatum* Tanabe. Okayama Igakkai Zasshi 41:1759–1771 (in Japanese)

Tanabe H (1922) Studien uber die Trematoden mit Susswasser-fischen als Zwischenwirt. I. *Stamnosoma armatum* n. g., n. sp. Kyoto Igaku Zasshi 19:239–252 (in Japanese)

Thien PC, Dalsgaard A, Thanh BN et al (2007) Prevalence of fishborne zoonotic parasites in important cultured fish species in the Mekong Delta, Vietnam. Parasitol Res 107:1277–1284

Velásquez LE, Bedoya JC, Areiza A, Vález I (2006) First record of *Centrocestus formosanus* (Digenea: Heterophyidae) in Colombia. Rev Mexicana Biodiversidad 77:119–121

Waikagul J, Wongsaroj T, Radomyos P et al (1997) Human infection of *Centrocestus caninus* in Thailand. Southeast Asian J Trop Med Pub Health 28:831–835

Yamaguti S (1958) Systema Helminthum. Vol. I. The digenetic trematodes of vertebrates (Part I). Interscience Publishers Inc, New York, pp 1–979

Yamaguti S (1971) Synopsis of digenetic trematodes of vertebrates, vol I. Keigaku Publishing Co., Tokyo, pp 1–1074

Yamaguti S (1975) Synoptical review of life histories of digenetic trematodes of vertebrates. Keigaku Publishing Co, Tokyo, pp 1–590 with 219 figure plates

Yousif F, Ayoub M, Tadros M et al (2016) The first record of *Centrocestus formosanus* (Nishigori, 1924) (Digenea: Heterophyidae) in Egypt. Exp Parasitol 168:56–61

Yu SH, Mott KE (1994) Epidemiology and morbidity of food-borne intestinal trematode infections. Trop Dis Bull 91:R125–R152

References for Section 1.9

Babbott FL, Frye WW, Gordon JE (1961) Intestinal parasites of man in Arctic Greenland. Am J Trop Med Hyg 10:185–190

Christensen ND, Skirnisson K, Nielsen OK (2015) The parasite fauna of the gyrfalcon (*Falco rusticolus*) in Iceland. J Wildl Dis 51:929–933

Huxham M, Raffaelli D, Pike A (1993) The influence of *Cryptocotyle lingua* (Digenea: Platyhelminthes) infections on the survival and fecundity of *Littorina littorea* (Gastropoda: Prosobranchia); an ecological approach. J Exp Mar Biol Ecol 168:223–238

Korol EN, Varodi EI, Kornyushin VV et al (2016) Helminths of wild predatory mammals (Mammalia, Carnivora) of Ukraine. Trematodes. Vestnik Zoologii 50:301–308

Kristoffersen R (1991) Occurrence of the digenean *Cryptocotyle lingua* in farmed Arctic charr *Salvelinus alpinus* and periwinkles *Littorina littorea* sampled close to charr farms in northern Norway. Dis Aquat Org 12:59–65

Matthews RA, Matthews BF (1993) *Cryptocotyle lingua* in mullet, *Chelon labrosus*; significance of metacercarial excretory proteins in the stimulation of the immune response. J Helminthol 67:1–9

Ransom BH (1920) Synopsis of the trematode family Heterophyidae with descriptions of a new genus and five new species. Proc US Nat Mus 57(2322):527–573

Saeed I, Maddox-Hyttel C, Monrad J et al (2006) Helminths of red foxes (*Vulpes vulpes*) in Denmark. Vet Parasitol 139:168–179

Stunkard HW (1930) The life history of *Cryptocotyle lingua* (Creplin), with notes on the physiology of the metacercariae. J Morphol Physiol 50:143–191

Yamaguti S (1958) Systema Helminthum. Vol. I. The digenetic trematodes of vertebrates (Part I). Interscience Publishers Inc, New York, pp 1–979

Yamaguti S (1971) Synopsis of digenetic trematodes of vertebrates, vol I. Keigaku Publishing Co, Tokyo, pp 1–1074

Yamaguti S (1975) Synoptical review of life histories of digenetic trematodes of vertebrates. Keigaku Publishing Co, Tokyo, pp 1–590 with 219 figure plates

References for Section 1.10

Africa CM, Garcia EY (1935) Two more new heterophyid trematodes from the Philippines. Phil J Sci 57:443–450

Africa CM, de Leon W, Garcia EY (1940) Visceral complications in intestinal heterophyidiasis of man. Acta Med Philippina Monogr Ser (1):1–132

Chai JY, Lee SH (2002) Food-borne intestinal trematode infections in the Republic of Korea. Parasitol Int 51:129–154

Chai JY, Kim IM, Seo M et al (1997) A new focus of *Heterophyes nocens*, *Pygidiopsis summa*, and other intestinal flukes in a coastal area of Muan-gun, Chollanam-do. Korean J Parasitol 35:233–238

Chai JY, Song TE, Han ET et al (1998) Two endemic foci of heterophyids and other intestinal fluke infections in southern and western coastal areas in Korea. Korean J Parasitol 36:155–161

Chai JY, Park JH, Han ET et al (2004) Prevalence of *Heterophyes nocens* and *Pygidiopsis summa* infections among residents of the western and southern coastal islands of the Republic of Korea. Am J Tro Med Hyg 71:617–622

Chai JY, Murrell KD, Lymbery AJ (2005) Fish-borne parasitic zoonoses: status and issues. Int J Parasitol 35:1233–1254

Chai JY, Shin EH, Lee SH et al (2009) Foodborne intestinal flukes in Southeast Asia. Korean J Parasitol 47(Suppl):S69–S102

Chai JY, De NV, Sohn WM (2012) Foodborne trematode metacercariae in fish from northern Vietnam and their adults recovered from experimental hamsters. Korean J Parasitol 50:317–325

Chai JY, Bahk YY, Sohn WM (2013) Trematodes recovered in the small intestine of stray cats in the Republic of Korea. Korean J Parasitol 51:99–106

Chai JY, Kim JL, Seo M (2014) Four human cases of *Acanthotrema felis* (Digenea: Heterophyidae) infection in Korea. Korean J Parasitol 52:291–294

Chai JY, Jung BK, Kim DG et al (2015) Heterophyid trematodes recovered from people residing along the Boseong River, South Korea. Acta Trop 148:142–146

Chen HT (1948) A preliminary note on heterophyid trematodes from China. Science (Shanghai) 30:17

Cho SY, Kim SI (1985) *Plecoglossus altivelis* as a new fish intermediate host of *Heterophyopsis continua*. Korean J Parasitol 23:173–174

Cho SH, Kim IS, Hwang EJ et al (2012) Infection status of esturine fish and oysters with intestinal fluke metacercariae in Muan-gun, Jeollanam-do, Korea. Korean J Parasitol 50:215–220

Chun SK (1960) A study on some trematodes whose intermediate hosts are brackish water fish (I) The life history of *Heterophyes continus,* the intermediate host of which is *Lateolabrax japonicus*. Bull Pusan Fish Coll 3:40–44

Dailey MD, Kliks MM, Demares RS (2004) *Heterophyopsis hawaiiensis* n. sp. (Trematoda: Heterophyidae) from the Hawaiian Monk Seal, *Monachus schauinslandi* Matschie, 1905 (Carnivora: Phocidae). Comp Parasitol 71:9–12

Dissanaike AS (1961) On some helminths of dogs in Colombo and their bearing on human infections, with a description of a new trematode *Heterophyopsis yehi* sp. nov. (Heterophyidae). Ceylon J Med Sci 10:1–14

Eom KS, Son SY, Lee JS et al (1985) Heterophyid trematodes (*Heterophyopsis continua*, *Pygidiopsis summa* and *Heterophyes heterophyes nocens*) from domestic cats in Korea. Korean J Parasitol 23:197–202

Guk SM, Park JH, Shin EH et al (2006) Prevalence of *Gymnophalloides seoi* infection in coastal villages of Haenam-gun and Yeongam-gun, Republic of Korea. Korean J Parasitol 44:1–5

Ho KT, He JZ (1986) A new species of the genus *Heterophyopsis* from bird in Guangxi, China (Trematoda: Heterophyidae). Acta Zootaxon Sin:1986–1904

Hong SJ (2012) Seasonal features of *Heterophyopsis continua* metacercariae in perches, *Lateolabrax japonicus*, and infectivity to the final host. Parasitol Res 110:1209–1212

Hong SJ, Lee SH, Chai JY et al (1990) Recovery rate, growth and development of *Heterophyopsis continua* in experimental chicks. Korean J Parasitol 28:53–62

Hong SJ, Chai JY, Lee SH (1991) Surface ultrastructure of the developmental stages of *Heterophyopsis continua* (Trematoda: Heterophyidae). J Parasitol 77:613–620

Hong SJ, Chang CK, Lee DH et al (1996) One human case of natural infection by *Heterophyopsis continua* and three other species of intestinal trematodes. Korean J Parasitol 34:87–90

Ito J, Papasarathorn T, Tongkoom B (1962) An investigation on parasitic helminths of stray dogs in Bangkok. Jpn J Med Sci Biol 15:53–60

Kalantan AMN, Arfin M, Mosjen AAA (2000) Digenetic trematodes of Larus genei (Lariformes: Laridae) caught from Al-Rames Coast of Al-Qateef in Eastern Province of Saudi Arabia. Pakistan J Biol Sci 3:1708–1711

Kim KH, Yoon YM, Lee JS et al (1991) A numerical taxonomic study on heterophyid trematodes. Korean J Parasitol 29:55–65 (in Korean)

Kim KH, Choi ES, Rim HJ (1996) *Conger myriaster*, a new second intermediate host of *Heterophyopsis continua* (Digenea: Heterophyidae). Korean J Parasitol 34:283–285

Kim DG, Kim TS, Cho SH et al (2006) Heterophyid metacercarial infections in brackish water fishes from Jinju-man (Bay), Kyongsangnam-do, Korea. Korean J Parasitol 44:7–13

Komiya Y, Suzuki N (1966) The metacercariae of trematodes belonging to the family Heterophyidae from Japan and adjacent territories. Jpn J Parasitol 15:208–214 (in Japanese)

Lee SH, Hwang SW, Chai JY et al (1984) Comparative morphology of eggs of heterophyids and *Clonorchis sinensis* causing human infections in Korea. Korean J Parasitol 22:171–180

Lee JJ, Jung BK, Lim H et al (2012) Comparative morphology of minute intestinal fluke eggs that can occur in human stools in the Republic of Korea. Korean J Parasitol 50:207–213

Onji Y, Nishio T (1916) On the trematodes whose intermediate host is brackish water fishes. Chiba Igaku Semmon Gakko Zasshi 81 & 82:229–249 (in Japanese)

Park JH, Guk SM, Shin EH et al (2007) A new focus of *Gymnophalloides seoi* infection on Aphae Island, Shinan-gun, Jeollanam-do. Korean J Parasitol 45:39–44

Pearson JC (1973) A revision of the subfamily Haplorchinae Looss, 1899 (Trematoda: Heterophyidae). II. Genus *Galactosomum*. Phil Trans Roy Soc Lond (B Biol Sci) 266:341–447

Price EW (1940) A review of the trematode superfamily Opisthorchioidea. Proc Helminthol Soc Wash 7:1–13

Pyo KH, Kang EY, Hwang YS et al (2013) Species identification of medically important trematodes in aquatic food samples using PCR-RFLP targeting 18S rRNA. Foodborne Pathog Dis 10:1–3

Qiu ZZ, Zhang RS, Li QK (1984) On some trematodes of the family Heterophyidae from birds in Lake Wuliangsuhai, Nei Mongol Autonomous Region. Acta Zootax Sin:1984–1902

Schuster RK, Thomas K, Sivakumar S et al (2009) The parasite fauna of stray cats (*Felis catus*) in Dubai, United Arab Emirates. Parasitol Res 105:125–134

Seo BS, Lee SH, Chai JY et al (1984) Studies on intestinal trematodes in Korea. XIII. Two cases of natural human infection by *Heterophyopsis continua* and the status of metacercarial infection in brackish water fishes. Korean J Parasitol 22:51–60

Shin SS, Oh DS, Ahn KS et al (2015) Zoonotic intestinal trematodes in stray cats (*Felis catus*) from riverside areas of the Republic of Korea. Korean J Parasitol 53:209–213

Sohn WM (2009) Fish-borne zoonotic trematode metacercariae in the Republic of Korea. Korean J Parasitol 47(Suppl):S103–S113

Sohn WM, Chai JY (2005) Infection status with helminthes in feral cats purchased from a market in Busan, Republic of Korea. Korean J Parasitol 43:93–100

Sohn WM, Han GG, Kho WG et al (1994) Infection status with the metacercariae of heterophyid flukes in the brackish water fish from Haenam-gun, Chollanam-do. Korean J Parasitol 32:163–169 (in Korean)

Sohn WM, Kim JA, Chai JY (2005) Two species of goby, *Boleophthalmus pectinirostris* and *Scartelaos* sp., as the new second intermediate hosts of heterophyid fluke in Korea. Korean J Parasitol 43:161–164

Sohn WM, Na BK, Cho SH (2009) *Echinostoma hortense* and heterophyid metacercariae encysted in yellowfin goby, *Acanthogobius flavimanus*, from Shinan-gun and Muan-gun (Jellanam-do), Korea. Korean J Parasitol 47:307–310

Sohn WM, Na BK, Cho SH et al (2018) Infections with zoonotic trematode metacercariae in yellow goby, *Acanthogobius flavimanus*, from coastal areas of Republic of Korea. Korean J Parasitol 56:259–265

Thanh BN, Dalsgaard A, Evenson Ǿ et al (2009) Survey for fishborne zoonotic metacercariae in farmed grouper in Vietnam. Foodborne Pathog Dis 6:1037–1039

Tubangui MA, Africa CM (1938) The systematic position of some trematodes-reported from the Philippines. Phil J Sci 67:117–125

Vo DT, Murrell D, Dalsgaard A et al (2008) Prevalence of zoonotic metacercariae in two species of groupers, *Epinephelus coioides* and *Epinephelus bleekeri*, and flathead mullet, *Mugil cephalus*, in Vietnam. Korean J Parasitol 46:77–82

Vo DT, Bristow GA, Vo DT et al (2011) Digenean trematodes of cultured grouper (*Epinephelus coioides* and *E. bleekeri*) in Khanh Hoa Province. Vietnam. Dis Asian Aquacult 7:39–52 *In* Bondad-Reantaso MG et al eds, Diseases of Asian Aquaculture. VII. Fish Health Section, Asian Fisheries Society, Selangor, Malaysia

Woo HC, Suh MD, Hong SJ (1990) In vitro effect of praziquantel on *Heterophyopsis continua* by scanning electron microscopic observation. Korean J Vet Res 30:487–497 (in Korean)

Yamaguti S (1939) Studies on the helminth fauna of Japan. Part 25. Trematodes of birds, IV. Jpn J Zool 8:129–210

Yamaguti S (1942) Studies on the helminth fauna of Japan. Part 38. Larval trematodes of fishes. Jpn J Med Sci (Bacteriol Parasitol) 2:131–160

Yamaguti S (1958) Systema Helminthum. Vol. I. The digenetic trematodes of vertebrates (Part I). Interscience Publishers Inc, New York, pp 1–979

References for Section 1.11

Africa CM (1938) Description of three trematodes of the genus *Haplorchis* (Heterophyidae) with notes on two other Philippine members of this genus. Phil J Sci 66:299–307

Africa CM, Garcia EY (1935) Two more new heterophyid trematodes from the Philippines. Phil J Sci 57:443–450

Aokage K (1956) Studies on trematode parasites of brackish water fishes in Chugoku coast of Setonaikai. Tokyo Iji Shinshi 73:217–224 (in Japanese)

Arya LK, Rathinam SR, Lalitha P et al (2016) Trematode fluke *Procerovum varium* as cause of ocular inflammation in children, South India. Emerg Infect Dis 22:192–200

Chai JY, De NV, Sohn WM (2012) Foodborne trematode metacercariae in fish from northern Vietnam and their adults recovered from experimental hamsters. Korean J Parasitol 50:317–325

Chai JY, Bahk YY, Sohn WM (2013) Trematodes recovered in the small intestine of stray cats in the Republic of Korea. Korean J Parasitol 51:99–106

Chai JY, Sohn WM, Na BK et al (2014) Zoonotic trematode metacercariae in fish from Phnom Penh and Pursat, Cambodia. Korean J Parasitol 52:35–40

Chen HT (1949) Systematic consideration of some heterophyid trematodes in the subfamilies Haplorchinae and Stellantchasminae. Ann Trop Med Parasitol 43:304–312

Eom KS, Park HS, Lee D et al (2015) Infection status of zoonotic trematode metacercariae in fishes from Vientiane Municipality and Champasak Province in Lao PDR. Korean J Parasitol 53:447–453

El-Dakhly MM, Aboshinaf ASM, El-Nahass E et al (2017) A preliminary study on the helminth fauna in necropsied stray cats (*Felis catus*) in Beni-Suef, Egypt. J Adv Vet Res 7:87–92

Hung NM, Dung DT, Anh NTL et al (2015) Current status of fish-borne zoonotic trematode infection in Gia Vien district, Ninh Binh Province, Vietnam. Parasit Vectors 8:21

Kobayasi H (1942) Studies on trematodes in Hainan Island. II. Trematoda found in the intestinal tract of dogs by experimental feeding with certain fresh and brackish water fish. Jpn J Med Sci Pathol 6:187–227

Kobayasi H (1968) Reports on scientifical works. Studies on trematode in Hainan island, South China and Viet-Nam (French Indo-China). A monograph

Komiya Y, Suzuki N (1966) The metacercariae of trematodes belonging to the family Heterophyidae from Japan and adjacent territories. Jpn J Parasitol 15:208–214 (in Japanese)

Onji Y, Nishio T (1916) On the trematodes whose intermediate host is brackish water fishes. Chiba Igaku Semmon Gakko Zasshi 81 & 82:229–249 (in Japanese)

Ooi HK, Wang WS, Tu CY et al (1999) Natural mass infection by heterophyid metacercariae in aquacultured Japanese ell in Taiwan. Dis Aquat Org 35:31–36

Pearson JC (1964) A revision of the subfamily Haplorchinae Looss, 1899 (Trematoda: Heterophyidae). I. The *Haplorchis* group. Parasitology 54:601–676

Price EW (1940) A review of the trematode superfamily Opisthorchioidea. Proc Helminthol Soc Wash 7:1–13

Shalaby SI, Riegler G, Esposito P et al (1993) Trematode parasites transmitted to man and fish-eating mammals through *Tilapia nilotica*. I. Experimental infection. Acta Mediter Pathol Infect Trop 12:107–110

Shin SS, Oh DS, Ahn KS et al (2015) Zoonotic intestinal trematodes in stray cats (*Felis catus*) from riverside areas of the Republic of Korea. Korean J Parasitol 53:209–213

Skov J, Kania PW, Dalsgaard A et al (2009) Life cycle stages of heterophyid trematodes in Vietnamese freshwater fishes traced by molecular and morphometric methods. Vet Parasitol 160:66–75

Sohn WM, Chai JY (2005) Infection status with helminthes in feral cats purchased from a market in Busan, Republic of Korea. Korean J Parasitol 43:93–100

Tawfik MAA, Elnawawi FA, Shaapan RM (2000) Studies on some fish-borne trematodes in Egypt. Egyptian J Vet Sci 34:39–48

Thanh BN, Dalsgaard A, Evenson Ǿ et al (2009) Survey for fishborne zoonotic metacercariae in farmed grouper in Vietnam. Foodborne Pathog Dis 6:1037–1039

Umadevi K, Madhavi R (2000) Observations on the morphology and life-cycle of *Procerovum varium* (Onji & Nishio, 1916) (Trematoda: Heterophyidae). Syst Parasitol 46:215–225

Velasquez CC (1973a) Observations on some Heterophyidae (Trematoda: Digenea) encysted in Philippine fishes. J Parasitol 59:77–84

Velasquez CC (1973b) Life cycle of *Procerovum calderoni* (Africa and garcia, 1935), Price, 1940 (Trematoda: Digenea: Heterophyidae). J Parasitol 59:813–816

Vo DT, Murrell D, Dalsgaard A et al (2008) Prevalence of zoonotic metacercariae in two species of grouper, *Epinephelus coioides* and *Epinephelus bleekeri*, and flathead mullet, *Mugil cephalus*, in Vietnam. Korean J Parasitol 46:77–82

Yu SH, Mott KE (1994) Epidemiology and morbidity of food-borne intestinal trematode infections. Trop Dis Bull 91:R125–R152

References for Section 1.12

Abdel Azim M (1938) On the intestinal helminths of dogs in Egypt. J Egypt Med Assoc 21:118–122

Africa CM, Garcia EY (1935) Two more new heterophyid trematodes from the Philippines. Phil J Sci 57:443–450

Africa CM, de Leon W, Garcia EY (1940) Visceral complications in intestinal heterophyidiasis of man. Acta Med Philippina Monogr Ser 1:1–132

Al-Kandari WY, Alnaqeeb MA, Isaac AM et al (2015) Molecular characterization of *Stictodora tridactyla* (Trematode: Heterophyidae) from Kuwait Bay using rDNA ITS and mtCO1. Parasitol Res 114:4259–4266

Balozet L, Callot J (1939) Trematodes de Tunisie. 3. Superfamilie Heterophyoidea. Arch Institut Pasteur Tunis 28:34–63

Chai JY, Lee SH (2002) Food-borne intestinal trematode infections in the Republic of Korea. Parasitol Int 51:129–154

Chai JY, Seo BS, Lee SH et al (1986) Growth and development of *Pygidiopsis summa* in rats and mice with a supplementary note on its morphological characters. Korean J Parasitol 24:55–62

Chai JY, Nam HK, Kook J et al (1994) The first discovery of an endemic focus of *Heterophyes nocens* (Heterophyidae) infection in Korea. Korean J Parasitol 32:157–161

Chai JY, Kim IM, Seo M et al (1997) A new focus of *Heterophyes nocens*, *Pygidiopsis summa*, and other intestinal flukes in a coastal area of Muan-gun, Chollanam-do. Korean J Parasitol 35:233–238

Chai JY, Song TE, Han ET et al (1998) Two endemic foci of heterophyids and other intestinal fluke infections in southern and western coastal areas in Korea. Korean J Parasitol 36:155–161

Chai JY, Sohn WM, Choi SY et al (2002) Surface ultrastructure of *Pygidiopsis summa* (Digenea: Heterophyidae) adult flukes. Korean J Parasitol 40:107–112

Chai JY, Park JH, Han ET et al (2004) Prevalence of *Heterophyes nocens* and *Pygidiopsis summa* infections among residents of the western and southern coastal islands of the Republic of Korea. Am J Tro Med Hyg 71:617–622

Chai JY, Murrell KD, Lymbery AJ (2005) Fish-borne parasitic zoonoses: status and issues. Int J Parasitol 35:1233–1254

Chai JY, Shin EH, Lee SH et al (2009) Foodborne intestinal flukes in Southeast Asia. Korean J Parasitol 47(Suppl):S69–S102

Chai JY, Kim LJ, Seo M (2014a) Four human cases of *Acanthotrema felis* (Digenea: Heterophyidae) infection in Korea. Korean J Parasitol 52:291–294

Chai JY, Park YJ, Park JH et al (2014b) Mucosal immune responses of mice experimentally infected with *Pygidiopsis summa* (Trematoda: Heterophyidae). Korean J Parasitol 52:27–33

Cho SH, Kim IS, Hwang EJ et al (2012) Infection status of esturine fish and oysters with intestinal fluke metacercariae in Muan-gun, Jeollanam-do, Korea. Korean J Parasitol 50:215–220

Chun SK (1963) On some trrematodes whose intermediate hosts are brackish water fish (II). The life history of *Pygidiopsis summus* the intermediate host of which is *Mugil cephalus*. Bull Fish Coll Pusan Nat Univ 5:1–6

Ciurea PJ (1924) Heterophyidae de la faune Parasitaire de Roumanie. Parasitology 16:1–25 (in French)

Diaz MT, Gómez Z, Bashirullah AK et al (2014) Partial life cycle of *Pygidiopsis australis* Ostrowski de Nuñez, 1996 (Digenea: Heterophyidae) in Venezuela. Revista Cientifica (FCV-LUZ) 24:83–87

Dzikowski R, Levy MG, Poore MF et al (2004) Use of rDNA polymorphism for identification of Heterophyidae infecting freshwater fishes. Dis Aquat Organ 59:35–41

Eom KS, Son SY, Lee JS et al (1985) Heterophyid trematodes (*Heterophyopsis continua*, *Pygidiopsis summa* and *Heterophyes heterophyes nocens*) from domestic cats in Korea. Korean J Parasitol 23:197–202

El-Azazy OMS, Abdou NEM, Khalil AI et al (2015) Potential zoonotic trematodes recovered in stray dogs from Kuwait Municipality, Kuwait. Korean J Parasitol 53:279–287

El-Dakhly MM, Aboshinaf ASM, El-Nahass E et al (2017) A preliminary study on the helminth fauna in necropsied stray cats (*Felis catus*) in Beni-Suef, Egypt. J Adv Vet Res 7:87–92

Fahmy MAM, Selim MK (1959) Studies on some trematode parasites of dogs in Egypt with special reference to the role played by fish in their transmission. Z Parasitenkd 19:3–13

Faust EC, Nishigori M (1926) The life cycles of two new species of Heterophyidae parasitic in mammals and birds. J Parasitol 13:91–131

Hegazi MA, Hassan AT, Al-Nashar TM et al (2014) Encysted metacercariae of family Heterophyidae in infected fish in Dakahlia Governorate, an endemic focus in Egypt. J Egypt Soc Parasitol 44:547–558

Ibrahim MM, Soliman MFM (2010) Prevalence and site preferences of heterophyid metacercariae in *Tilapia zilli* from Ismalia Fresh Water Canal, Egypt. Parasite 17:233–239

Kim KH, Yoon YM, Lee JS et al (1991) A numerical taxonomic study on heterophyid trematodes. Korean J Parasitol 29:55–65 (in Korean)

Kim DG, Kim TS, Cho SH et al (2006) Heterophyid metacercarial infections in brackish water fishes from Jinju-man (Bay), Kyongsangnam-do, Korea. Korean J Parasitol 44:7–13

Kuntz RE, Chandler AC (1956) Studies on Egyptian trematodes with special reference to the heterophyid of mammals. I. Adult flukes, with descriptions of *Phagicola longicollis* n. sp., *Cynodiplostomum namrui* n. sp., and a *Stephanoprora* from cats. J Parasitol 42:445–459

Kvach Y (2002) Helminthes of goby fish of the Hryhoryivsky estuary (Black Sea, Ukraine). Vesnik Zool 36:71–76

Lee SH, Hwang SW, Chai JY et al (1984) Comparative morphology of eggs of heterophyids and *Clonorchis sinensis* causing human infections in Korea. Korean J Parasitol 22:171–180

Lee SU, Chun HC, Huh S (2007) Molecular phylogeny of parasitic Platyhelminthes based on sequences of partical 28S rDNA D1 and mitochondrial cytochrome *c* oxidase subunit 1. Korean J Parasitol 45:181–189

Lee JJ, Jung BK, Lim H et al (2012) Comparative morphology of minute intestinal fluke eggs that can occur in human stools in the Republic of Korea. Korean J Parasitol 50:207–213

Lobna SMA, Metawea YF, Elsheikha HM (2010) Prevalence of heterophyiosis in *Tilapia* fish and humans in Northern Egypt. Parasitol Res 107:1029–1034

Looss A (1907) Notizen zur Helminthologie Aegyptens. VII. Ueber einige neue Trematoden der äegyptischen Fauna. Centralbl Bakteriol 43:478–490

Mahdy OA, Shaheed IB (2001) Studies on metacercarial infection among *Tilapia* species in Egypt. Helminthologia 38:35–42

Mansour NS, Youssef M, Awadalla HN et al (1981) Susceptibility of small laboratory animals to *Pygidiopsis genata* (Trematoda: Heterophyidae). J Egypt Soc Parasitol 11:225–234

Nishio T (1915) On a new trematode of genus *Pygidiopsis*. Tokyo Iji Shinshi (1923):1139–1142 (in Japanese)

Ochi S (1931) Studies on the trematodes whose intermediate hosts are brackish water fishes-On the life cycle of Pygidiopsis summus. Tokyo Iji Shinshi 2712:346–353 (in Japanese)

Onji Y, Nishio T (1916) On the trematodes whose intermediate host is brackish water fishes. Chiba Igaku Semmon Gakko Zasshi 81&82:229–249 (in Japanese)

Pyo KH, Kang EY, Hwang YS et al (2013) Species identification of medically important trematodes in aquatic food samples using PCR-RFLP targeting 18S rRNA. Foodborne Pathog Dis 10:1–3

Ransom BH (1920) Synopsis of the trematode family Heterophyidae with descriptions of a new genus and five new species. Proc US Nat Mus 57(2322):527–573

Seo BS, Hong ST, Chai JY (1981a) Studies on intestinal trematodes in Korea. III. Natural human infections of *Pygidiopsis summa* and *Heterophyes heterophyes nocens*. Seoul J Med 22:228–235

Seo BS, Hong ST, Chai JY et al (1981b) Studies on intestinal trematodes in Korea IV. Geographical distribution of *Pygidiopsis* and *Heterophyes* metacercariae. Seoul J Med 22:236–242

Seo BS, Cheong SK, Chai JY et al (1986) Histopathology of small intestine of rats and mice experimentally infected with *Pygidiopsis summa*. Seoul J Med 27:125–134

Shin EH, Park JH, Guk SM et al (2009) Intestinal helminth infections in feral cats and a raccoon dog on Aphaedo Island, Shinan-gun, with a special note on *Gymnophalloides seoi* infection in cats. Korean J Parasitol 47:189–191

Shin SS, Oh DS, Ahn KS et al (2015) Zoonotic intestinal trematodes in stray cats (*Felis catus*) from riverside areas of the Republic of Korea. Korean J Parasitol 53:209–213

Sohn WM (2009) Fish-borne zoonotic trematode metacercariae in the Republic of Korea. Korean J Parasitol 47(Suppl):S103–S113

Sohn WM, Chai JY (2005) Infection status with helminthes in feral cats purchased from a market in Busan, Republic of Korea. Korean J Parasitol 43:93–100

Sohn WM, Han GG, Kho WG et al (1994) Infection status with the metacercariae of heterophyid flukes in the brackish water fish from Haenam-gun, Chollanam-do. Korean J Parasitol 32:163–169 (in Korean)

Sohn WM, Kim DG, Jung BK et al (2016) *Pygidiopsis cambodiensis* n. sp. (Digenea: Heterophyidae) from experimental hamsters infected with metacercariae in mullets from Cambodia. Parasitol Res 115:123–130

Takabayashi Y (1953) Studies on trematode cysts in the fish in Yamaguchi Prefecture. Gifu Ika Daigaku Kiyo (3):219–226 (in Japanese)

Takahashi S (1929) On the eggs of *Stellantchasmus falcatus* and *Pygidiopsis summus* found in human stools which are similar to those of the liver fluke. Okayama Igakkai Zasshi 41:1502–1513 (in Japanese)

Vo DT, Murrell D, Dalsgaard A et al (2008) Prevalence of zoonotic metacercariae in two species of groupers, *Epinephelus coioides* and *Epinephelus bleekeri*, and flathead mullet, *Mugil cephalus*, in Vietnam. Korean J Parasitol 46:77–82

Witenberg G (1929) Studies on the trematode – family Heterophyidae. Ann Trop Med Parasitol 23:131–268

Yokogawa M, Sano M, Itabashi T et al (1965) Studies on the intestinal flukes II. Epidemiological studies on heterophyid trematodes of man in Chiba Prefecture. Jpn J Parasitol 14:577–585

Youssef MM, Mansour NS, Awadalla HN et al (1987a) Heterophyid parasites of man from Idku, Maryut and Manzala Lakes areas in Egypt. J Egypt Soc Parasitol 17:475–479

Youssef MM, Mansour NS, Hammouda NA et al (1987b) Studies on some developmental stages in the life cycle of *Pygidiopsis genata* Looss, 1907 (Trematoda: Heterophyidae) from Egypt. J Egypt Soc Parasitol 17:463–474

References for Section 1.13

Africa CM, Garcia EY (1935) Two more new heterophyid trematodes from the Philippines. Phil J Sci 57:443–450

Africa CM, de Leon W, Garcia EY (1940) Visceral complications in intestinal heterophyidiasis of man. Acta Med Philippina Monogr Ser 1:1–132

Alicata JE, Schattenburg OL (1938) A case of intestinal heterophyidiasis of man in Hawaii. J Am Med Assoc 110:1100–1101

Anh NTL, Phuong NT, Johansen MV et al (2009) Prevalence and risks for fishborne zoonotic trematode infections in domestic animals in a highly endemic area of North Vietnam. Acta Trop 112:198–203

Ash LR (1962) Helminth parasites of dog and cats in Hawaii. J Parasitol 48:63–65

Boulos LM, Samra LMA (1985) Studies on some of the developmental stages in the life cycle of *Stellantchasmus falcatus* (Trematoda: heterophyidae) in Egypt. J Egypt Soc Parasitol 15:397–402

Chai JY, Sohn WM (1988) Identification of *Stellantchasmus falcatus* metacercariae encysted in mullets in Korea. Korean J Parasitol 26:65–68

Chai JY, Lee SH (2002) Food-borne intestinal trematode infections in the Republic of Korea. Parasitol Int 51:129–154

Chai JY, Song TE, Han ET et al (1998) Two endemic foci of heterophyids and other intestinal fluke infections in southern and western coastal areas in Korea. Korean J Parasitol 36:155–161

Chai JY, Park JH, Han ET et al (2004) Prevalence of *Heterophyes nocens* and *Pygidiopsis summa* infections among residents of the western and southern coastal islands of the Republic of Korea. Am J Tro Med Hyg 71:617–622

Chai JY, Murrell KD, Lymbery AJ (2005) Fish-borne parasitic zoonoses: status and issues. Int J Parasitol 35:1233–1254

Chai JY, Shin EH, Lee SH et al (2009) Foodborne intestinal flukes in Southeast Asia. Korean J Parasitol 47(Suppl):S69–S102

Chen HT (1951) *Stictodora manilensis* and *Stellantchamus falcatus* from Hong Kong, with a note on the validity of other species of the two genera (Trematoda: Heterophyidae). Lingnan Sci J 23:165–175

Chi TTK, Dalsgaard A, Turnbull JF, Tuan PA, Murrell KD (2008) Prevalence of zoonotic trematodes in fish from a Vietnamese fish-farming community. J Parasitol 94:423–428

Ciurea I (1933) Les vers parasites de l'homme, des mammiferes et des oiseaux provenant des poisons du Danube et de la Mer Noir. Premier Memoire. Trematodes, famille Heterophyidae

Odhner, aver un essai de classification des Trematodes de la superfamille Heterophyoidea Faust. Arch Rom Pathol Exp Microbiol 6:4–134 in Germany

Ditrich O, Scholz T, Giboda M (1990) Occurrence of some mediacally important flukes (Trematoda: Opisthorchiidae and Heterophyidae) in Nam Ngum Water Reservoir, Laos. Southeast Asian J Trop Med Public Health 21:482–488

Ditrich O, Giboda M, Scholz T (1992) Comparative morphology of eggs of the haplorchiinae (Trematoda: Heterophyidae) and some other medically important heterophyid and opisthorchiid flukes. Folia Parasitol 39:123–132

Dung DT, De NV, Waikagul J et al (2007) Fishborne zoonotic intestinal trematodes, Vietnam. Emerg Infec Dis 13:1828–1833

Farahnak A, Shiekhian R, Mobedi I (2004) A faunistic survey on the bird helminth parasites and their medical importance. Iran J Public Health 33:40–46

Fukuda T, Yamamoto S (1981) Neorickettsia-like organism isolated from metacercaria of a fluke, *Stellantchasmus falcatus*. Jpn J Med Sci Biol 34:103–107

Glover MA, Alicata JE (1957) Intestinal heterophyidiasis. Hawaii Med J 16:636 & 688

Hong ST, Chai JY, Lee SH (1986) Ten human cases of *Fibricola seoulensis* infection and mixed one with *Stellantchasmus* and *Metagonimus*. Korean J Parasitol 24:94–96

Ito J (1964a) *Metagonimus* and other human heterophyid trematodes. Progr Med Parasitol Japan 1:314–393

Ito J (1964b) A monograph of cercariae in Japan and adjacent territories. Progr Med Parasitol Japan 1:395–550

Kagei N, Oshima T, Ishikawa K et al (1964) Two cases of human infection with *Stellantchasmus falcatus* Onji et Nishio 1915 (Heterophyidae) in Kochi Prefecture. Jpn J Parasitol 13:472–478 (in Japanese)

Kanemitsu T (1953) Studies on trematodes which take brackish water fish as the intermediate host, especially those belonging to *Heterophyes*. Kyoto Igaku 6:270–283 (in Japanese)

Katsuta I (1931) Studies on trematodes that take brackish water fish as the second intermediate host in Taiwan. I. On a new trematode *Stellantchasmus formosanus* which takes *Mugil cephalus* as its intermediate host. Taiwan Igakkai Zasshi 30:1404–1417 (in Japanese)

Katsuta I (1932) Studies on trematodes that take brackish water fish as the second intermediate host in Taiwan. 5. On a new trematode *Stellantchasmus amplicaecalis* which takes *Mugil cephalus* as its intermediate host. Taiwan Igakkai Zasshi 31:457–471 (in Japanese)

Kim KH, Yoon YM, Lee JS et al (1991) A numerical taxonomic study on heterophyid trematodes. Korean J Parasitol 29:55–65 (in Korean)

Kliks M, Tantachamrun T (1974) Heterophyid (Trematoda) parasites of cats in north Thailand, with note on a human case found at necropsy. Southeast Asian J Trop Med Pub Health 5:547–555

Kobayasi H (1968) Reports on scientifical works. Studies on trematode in Hainan island, South China and Viet-Nam (French Indo-China). A monograph

Lee SH, Hwang SW, Chai JY et al (1984) Comparative morphology of eggs of heterophyids and *Clonorchis sinensis* causing human infections in Korea. Korean J Parasitol 22:171–180

Lee JJ, Jung BK, Lim H et al (2012) Comparative morphology of minute intestinal fluke eggs that can occur in human stools in the Republic of Korea. Korean J Parasitol 50:207–213

Martin WE (1958) The life cycle of some Hawaiian heterophyid trematodes. J Parasitol 44:305–321

Noda K (1959) The larval development of *Stellantchasmus falcatus* (Trematoda: Heterophyidae) in the first intermediate host. J Parasitol 45:635–642

Onji Y, Nishio T (1916) On the trematodes whose intermediate host is brackish water fishes. Chiba Igaku Semmon Gakko Zasshi 81&82:229–249 (in Japanese)

Onji Y, Nishio T (1924) A monograph of intestinal trematodes. Chiba Igakkai Zasshi 2:113–161 (in Japanese)

Otagaki H, Kanemitsu T (1953) On the trematode cysts of brackish water fishes from the market in Binan district, Hiroshima Prefecture. Tokyo Iji Shinshi 70:575–578 (in Japanese)

Pearson JC (1964) A revision of the subfamily Haplorchinae Looss, 1899 (Trematoda: Heterophyidae). I. The *Haplorchis* group. Parasitology 54:601–676

Pearson JC, Ow-Yang CK (1982) New species of *Haplorchis* from Southeast Asia, together with keys to the *Haplorchis*-group of heterophyid trematodes of the region. Southeast Asian J Trop Med Public Health 13:35–60

Price EW (1940) A review of the trematode superfamily Opisthorchioidea. Proc Helminthol Soc Wash 7:1–13

Radomyos P, Charoenlarp P, Radomyos B et al (1990) Two human cases of *Stellantchasmus falcatus* (Trematoda: Heterophyidae) infection in northeastern Thailand. Jpn J Parasitol 39:7–11

Ramsuk A, Wongsawad C, Wongsawad P et al (2004) Treatment of *Stellantchasmus falcatus* in *Gallus gallus domesticus* by niclosamide and some anthelminthic plants. Southeast Asian J Trop Med Pub Health 35(Suppl 1):296–298

Rekharani Z, Madhavi R (1985) Digenetic trematodes from mullets of Visakhapatnam (India). J Nat Hist 19:929–951

Saenphet S, Wongsawad C, Saenphet K et al (2003) Susceptibility of rodents to *Stellantchasmus falcatus* infection. Southeast Asian J Trop Med Pub Health 34(Suppl 2):123–127

Scholz T, Ditrich O, Giboda M (1990) Larval stages of medically important flukes (Trematoda) from Vientiane Province, Laos. Part I. Metacercariae. Ann Parasitol Hum Comp 65:238–243

Seo BE, Lee SH, Chai JY et al (1984) Studies on intestinal trematodes in Korea, XII. Two cases of human infection by *Stellantchasmus falcatus*. Korean J Parasitol 22:43–50

Shin SS, Oh DS, Ahn KS et al (2015) Zoonotic intestinal trematodes in stray cats (*Felis catus*) from riverside areas of the Republic of Korea. Korean J Parasitol 53:209–213

Singh AP, Noda K, Lim D (1977) Fine structure of the secretory vesicle in cercariae of *Stellantchasmus falcatus*. J Arizona Acad Sci 12:23–28

Smales LR, Cribb TH (1997) Helminth parasite communities of the water-rat, *Hydromys chrysogaster*, from Queensland. Wildl Res 24:445–457

Sohn WM, Chai JY (2005) Infection status with helminthes in feral cats purchased from a market in Busan, Republic of Korea. Korean J Parasitol 43:93–100

Sohn WM, Chai JY, Lee SH (1989) A human case of *Stellantchasmus falcatus* infection. Korean J Parasitol 27:277–279

Sripalwit P, Wongsawad C, Chontananarth T et al (2015) Development and phylogenetic characteristics of *Stellantchasmus falcatus* (Trematoda: Heterophyidae) from Thailand. Korean J Parasitol 53:201–207

Takahashi S (1929) On the eggs of *Stellantchasmus falcatus* and *Pygidiopsis summus* found in human stools which are similar to those of the liver fluke. Okayama Igakkai Zasshi 41:1502–1513 (in Japanese)

Tanabe H (1922) Studien uber die Trematoden mit Susswasser-fischen als Zwischenwirt. I. *Stamnosoma armatum* n. g., n. sp. Kyoto Igaku Zasshi 19:239–252 (in Japanese)

Tantachamrun T, Kliks M (1978) Heterophyid infection in human ileum: report of three cases. Southeast Asian J Trop Med Pub Health 9:228–231

Thaenkham U, Dekumyoy P, Komalamisra C et al (2010) Systematics of the subfamily Haplorchiinae (Trematoda: Heterophyidae), based on nuclear ribosomal DNA genes and ITS2 region. Parasitol Int 59:460–465

Thien PC, Dalsgaard A, Thanh BN et al (2007) Prevalence of fishborne zoonotic parasites in important cultured fish species in the Mekong Delta, Vietnam. Parasitol Res 107:1277–1284

Witenberg G (1929) Studies on the trematode – family Heterophyidae. Ann Trop Med Parasitol 23:131–268

Wongsawad C, Wongsawad P (2010) Molecular markers for identification of *Stellantchasmus falcatus* and a phylogenetic study using the HAT-RAPD method. Korean J Parasitol 48:303–307

Wongsawad C, Rojanapaibul A, Vanittanakom P (1997) Surface ultrastructure of encysted metacercariae and of adult *Stellantchasmus* sp. (Trematoda: Heterophyidae). J E M S T (Thailand) 11:19–26

Wongsawad C, Chariyahpongpun P, Namue C (1998) Experimental host of *Stellantchasmus falcatus*. Southeast Asian J Trop Med Pub Health 29:406–409

Wongsawad C, Rojtinnakorn J, Wongsawad P et al (2004) Helminths of vertebrates from Mae Sa stream, Chiang Mai, Thailand. Southeast Asian J Trop Med Pub Health 35(Suppl 1):140–146
Wongsawad C, Wongsawad P, Chai JY et al (2006) DNA quatities and qualities from various stages of some trematodes using optical and HAT-RAPD methods. Southeast Asian J Trop Med Pub Health 37(Suppl 3):62–68
Yokogawa S (1940) On the visceral heterophyidiasis, especially on the etiology of heart, brain and spinal cord heterophyidiasis. Taiwan Igakkai Zasshi 39:1729–1730 (in Japanese)

References for Section 1.14

Abdul-Salam A, Nair SB, Ashkanani H (2000) Surface ultrastructure of *Stictodora fuscatum* (Trematoda: Heterophyidae) from Kuwait Bay. Parasitol al día 24:1–2
Africa CM, Garcia EY (1935) Two more new heterophyid trematodes from the Philippines. Phil J Sci 57:443–450
Anh NTL, Phuong NT, Johansen MV et al (2009) Prevalence and risks for fishborne zoonotic trematode infections in domestic animals in a highly endemic area of North Vietnam. Acta Trop 112:198–203
Appleton CC (1983) Studies on *Austrobilharzia terrigalensis* (Trematoda: Schistosomatidae) in the Swan estuary, Western Australia: frequency of infection in the intermediate host population. Int J Parasitol 13:51–60
Bearup AJ (1961) Observations on the life cycle of *Stictodora lari* (Trematoda: Heterophyidae). Proc Linnean Soc New South Wales 86:251–257
Belogurov OI, Leonov VA, Zueva LS (1968) Helminth fauna of fish eating birds (gulls and guillemots) from the coast of the Sea of Okhotsk. In Skryabin LI, Mamaev YL (eds) Helminth of animals of the Pacific Ocean, pp 105–124
Chai JY, Hong SJ, Lee SH et al (1988) *Stictodora* sp. (Trematoda: Heterophyidae) recovered from a man in Korea. Korean J Parasitol 26:127–132
Chai JY, Park SK, Hong SJ et al (1989) Identification of *Stictodora lari* (Heterophyidae) metacercariae encysted in the brackish water fish, *Acanthogobius flavimanus*. Korean J Parasitol 27:253–259
Chai JY, Nam HK, Kook J et al (1994) The first discovery of an endemic focus of *Heterophyes nocens* (Heterophyidae) infection in Korea. Korean J Parasitol 32:157–161
Chai JY, Kim IM, Seo M et al (1997) A new focus of *Heterophyes nocens*, *Pygidiopsis summa*, and other intestinal flukes in a coastal area of Muan-gun, Chollanam-do. Korean J Parasitol 35:233–238
Chai JY, Song TE, Han ET et al (1998) Two endemic foci of heterophyids and other intestinal fluke infections in southern and western coastal areas in Korea. Korean J Parasitol 36:155–161
Chai JY, Han ET, Park YK et al (2002) *Stictodora lari* (Digenea: Heterophyidae): the discovery of the first human infections. J Parasitol 88:627–629
Chai JY, Park JH, Han ET et al (2004) Prevalence of *Heterophyes nocens* and *Pygidiopsis summa* infections among residents of the western and southern coastal islands of the Republic of Korea. Am J Tro Med Hyg 71:617–622
Chai JY, Shin EH, Lee SH et al (2009) Foodborne intestinal flukes in Southeast Asia. Korean J Parasitol 47(Suppl):S69–S102
Chai JY, Bahk YY, Sohn WM (2013) Trematodes recovered in the small intestine of stray cats in the Republic of Korea. Korean J Parasitol 51:99–106
Chai JY, Kim LJ, Seo M (2014) Four human cases of *Acanthotrema felis* (Digenea: Heterophyidae) infection in Korea. Korean J Parasitol 52:291–294
Chai JY, Jung BK, Kim DG et al (2015) Heterophyid trematodes recovered from people residing along the Boseong River, South Korea. Acta Trop 148:142–146

Chen HT (1951) *Stictodora manilensis* and *Stellantchamus falcatus* from Hong Kong, with a note on the validity of other species of the two genera (Trematoda: Heterophyidae). Lingnan Sci J 23:165–175

Cho SH, Cho PY, Lee DM et al (2010) Epidemiological survey on the infection of intestinal flukes in residents of Muan-gun, Jeollanam-do, the Republic of Korea. Korean J Parasitol 48:133–138

Cho SH, Kim IS, Hwang EJ et al (2012) Infection status of esturine fish and oysters with intestinal fluke metacercariae in Muan-gun, Jeollanam-do, Korea. Korean J Parasitol 50:215–220

Das SN, Ghazi RR, Bushra G (2014) *Stictodora* (*Stictodora*) *alykhani* sp. nov. (Trematoda: Heterophyidae) from the bird *Ardes grayii* in Jamshoro Sindh, Pakistan. Int Res J (Flora and Fauna) 20:151–155

De NV, Le TH (2011) Human infections of fish-borne trematodes in Vietnam: prevalence and molecular specific identification at an endemic commune in Nam Dinh province. Exp Parasitol 129:355–361

Diaz MT, Gómez Z, Bashirullah AK et al (2014) Partial life cycle of *Pygidiopsis australis* Ostrowski de Nuñez, 1996 (Digenea: Heterophyidae) in Venezuela. Revista Cientifica (FCV-LUZ) 24:83–87

Dronen NO, Blend CK, Gardner SL et al (2007) *Stictodora cablei* n. sp. (Digenea: Heterophyidae) from the royal tern, *Sterna maxima* (Laridae: Sterninae) from Puerto Rico and the Brazos County area of the Texas Gulf coast, U.S.A. with a list of other endohelminths recovered in Texas. Zootaxa 1432:35–56

Garcia EY, Refuerzo PG (1936) Two more species of the genus *Stictodora* Looss, 1899, in the Philippines with description of a new species. Phil J Sci 60:137–141

Guk SM, Park JH, Shin EH et al (2006) Prevalence of *Gymnophalloides seoi* infection in coastal villages of Haenam-gun and Yeongam-gun, Republic of Korea. Korean J Parasitol 44:1–5

Hasegawa T (1934) On the trematode metacercariae encysted in *Pseudorasbora parva*. Okayama Igakkai Zasshi 46:1397–1434 (in Japanese)

Howell MJ (1973) The resistance of cysts of *Stictodora lari* (Trematoda: Heterophyidae) to encapsulation by cells of the fish host. Int J Parasitol 3:653–659

Johnston TH (1943) Trematodes from Australian birds. I. Cormorants and darters. Trans Roy Soc South Australia 66:226–242

Kim KH, Yoon YM, Lee JS et al (1991) A numerical taxonomic study on heterophyid trematodes. Korean J Parasitol 29:55–65 (in Korean)

Kobayasi H (1942) Studies on trematodes in Hainan Island. II. Trematoda found in the intestinal tract of dogs by experimental feeding with certain fresh and brackish water fish. Jpn J Med Sci Pathol 6:187–227

Komiya Y (1965) Metacercariae in Japan and adjacent territories. Progr Med Parasitol Japan 2:1–328

Lee JJ, Jung BK, Lim H et al (2012) Comparative morphology of minute intestinal fluke eggs that can occur in human stools in the Republic of Korea. Korean J Parasitol 50:207–213

Looss A (1899) Weitere Beitrage zur Kentniss der Trematoden-Fauna Aegyptens, zugleich Versuch einer naturalischen Gliedrung des Genus *Distomum* Retzius. Zool Yb 12:521–784

Onji Y, Nishio T (1916) On the trematodes whose intermediate host is brackish water fishes. Chiba Igaku Semmon Gakko Zasshi 81&82:229–249 (in Japanese)

Onji Y, Nishio T (1924) A monograph of intestinal trematodes. Chiba Igakkai Zasshi 2:113–161 (in Japanese)

Park JH, Guk SM, Shin EH et al (2007) A new focus of *Gymnophalloides seoi* infection on Aphae Island, Shinan-gun, Jeollanam-do. Korean J Parasitol 45:39–44

Pearson JC (1973) A revision of the subfamily Haplorchinae Looss, 1899 (Trematoda: Heterophyidae). II. Genus *Galactosomum*. Phil Trans Roy Soc Lond (B Biol Sci) 266:341–447

Qiu ZZ, Zhang RS (1986) The preliminary report of digenetic trematodes of terrestrial vertebrates from Kun Yu Mountain, Tantai, Province Shandong, China. Acta Sci Nat Univ Nankaiensis 2:137–146 (in Chinese)

Shin EH, Park JH, Guk SM et al (2009) Intestinal helminth infections in feral cats and a raccoon dog on Aphaedo Island, Shinan-gun, with a special note on *Gymnophalloides seoi* infection in cats. Korean J Parasitol 47:189–191

Shin SS, Oh DS, Ahn KS et al (2015) Zoonotic intestinal trematodes in stray cats (*Felis catus*) from riverside areas of the Republic of Korea. Korean J Parasitol 53:209–213

Sohn WM (2000) Surface ultrastructure of *Stictodora fuscatum* (Trematoda: Heterophyidae). Korean J Elect Microsc 30:205–212 (in Korean)

Sohn WM, Chai JY (2005) Infection status with helminthes in feral cats purchased from a market in Busan, Republic of Korea. Korean J Parasitol 43:93–100

Sohn WM, Han GG, Kho WG et al (1994a) Infection status with the metacercariae of heterophyid flukes in the brackish water fish from Haenam-gun, Chollanam-do. Korean J Parasitol 32:163–169 (in Korean)

Sohn WM, Chai JY, Lee SH (1994b) *Stictodora fuscatum* (Heterophyidae) metacercariae encysted in gobies, Acanthogobius flavimanus. Korean J Parasitol 32:143–148

Sohn WM, Han ET, Chai JY (2003) *Acanthotrema felis* n. sp. (Digenea: Heterophyidae) from the small intestine of stray cats in the Republic of Korea. J Parasitol 89:154–158

Sohn WM, Na BK, Cho SH et al (2018) Infections with zoonotic trematode metacercariae in yellow goby, *Acanthogobius flavimanus*, from coastal areas of Republic of Korea. Korean J Parasitol 56:259–265

Yamaguti S (1958) Systema Helminthum. Vol. I. The digenetic trematodes of vertebrates (Part I). Interscience Publishers Inc, New York, pp 1–979

Yamaguti S (1971) Synopsis of digenetic trematodes of vertebrates, vol I. Keigaku Publishing Co., Tokyo, pp 1–1074

Chapter 2
Echinostomes

2.1 Family Echinostomatidae

The family Echinostomatidae Looss, 1899 (= echinostomes) was created with the type genus *Echinostoma* Rudolphi, 1809 (Looss 1899). They are predominantly parasites of birds, but also of mammals, including humans, and rarely fish and reptiles (Yamaguti 1958). Echinostome flukes are morphologically characterized by the presence of a head collar with collar spines around the oral sucker. The number and arrangement of collar spines is an important key for taxonomic purposes (Toledo et al. 2006).

Bashikirova (1947) enlisted 8 subfamilies in the family Echinostomatidae, including Echinostomatinae Looss, 1899, Echinochasminae Odhner, 1910, Himasthlinae Odhner, 1910, Pegosomatinae Skrjabin and Schulz, 1938, Cotylotretinae Skrjabin and Schulz, 1938, Stephanoproraoidinae Skrjabin and Schulz, 1938, Chaunocephalinae Travassos, 1922, and Sodalinae Skrjabin and Schulz, 1938. Yamaguti (1958) retained 6 among them, including Echinostomatinae, Echinochasminae, Himasthlinae, Pegosomatinae (as Pegosominae Odhner, 1910), Chaunocephalinae, and Sodalinae, and added 3 new subfamilies Balfourinae, Ignaviinae, and Pelmatostominae. Later, Kostadinova (2005) added Nephrostominae Mandheim, 1943 and a new subfamily Ruffetrematinae Kostadinova, 2005, but excluded Balfourinae Yamaguti, 1958; thus, 10 subfamilies were enlisted in Echinostomatidae (46 genera, including 2 subgenera). However, recently, Tkach et al. (2016) studied on the phylogenetic relationships of the superfamily Echinostomatoidea using partial sequences of the nuclear 28S rDNA, and elevated the systematic rank of Echinochasminae and Himasthlinae to full family status to become Echinochasmidae and Himasthlidae, respectively. However, in this book, using these new family names is deferred until consent is gathered and further back-up data are published.

Species of medical importance are almost exclusively included in the subfamilies Echinostomatinae, Echinochasminae, and Himasthlinae. In the subfamily

J.-Y. Chai, *Human Intestinal Flukes*,
https://doi.org/10.1007/978-94-024-1704-3_2

Echinostomatinae, total 19 genera were enlisted (Kostadinova 2005). Among them, 4 genera are medically important; *Echinostoma* Rudolphi, 1809, *Echinoparyphium* Dietz, 1909, *Hypoderaeum* Dietz, 1909, and *Isthmiophora* Lühe, 1909 (Chai 2009, 2015). In the Echinochasminae, 8 genera and 2 subgenera were enlisted; among them, only *Echinochasmus* Dietz, 1909 (syn. *Episthmium* Lühe 1909) is zoonotic (Kostadinova 2005; Chai 2009, 2015). In the Himasthlinae, 7 genera were included, and 3 among them, *Artyfechinostomum* Lane, 1915, *Himasthla* Dietz, 1909, and *Acanthoparyphium* Dietz, 1909, have been reported to infect humans (Kostadinova 2005; Chai 2009, 2015). Thus, 8 genera (20 species) are currently regarded as medically important ones, reducing 1 genus *Episthmium* (synonymized with *Echinochasmus* by Kostadinova 2005) listed in Chai (2009, 2015). In this chapter, these 8 genera (*Echinostoma, Isthmiophora, Echinochasmus, Acanthoparyphium, Artyfechinostomum, Echinoparyphium, Himasthla,* and *Hypoderaeum*) and their diseases are briefly reviewed.

For generic and specific differentiation of echinostome flukes, various morphological features of adult flukes have been used (Kostadinova and Gibson 2000; Maldonado et al. 2003). These included the number, shape, arrangement, and relative size of collar spines, the position of the cirrus sac and structure of the seminal vesicle, the development of the pars prostatica, the size and armament of the cirrus, the position of the ovary and testes, the location and structure of vitellaria, the nature of the tegumental armament, the presence of a uroproct, and the body shape in terms of length/width ratios (Kostadinova and Gibson 2000; Maldonado et al. 2003). In addition, cercarial morphology (Kanev et al. 1995), cercarial chetotaxy (Kostadinova 1999; Toledo et al. 2000), and genetic characteristics, including gene sequences (Morgan and Blair 1995; Fujino et al. 1995; Sorensen et al. 1998; Kostadinova et al. 2003), are also used for specific identification.

Echinostomes of medical significance can be morphologically classified into 3 groups (Beaver et al. 1984). The biggest group is those with collar spines arranged in 2 rows, interrupted ventrally but not dorsally (*Echinostoma, Isthmiophora, Echinoparyphium*, and *Hypoderaeum*). The second group is those with collar spines arranged in a single or alternative rows, interrupted both ventrally and dorsally (*Echinochasmus*). The third group is those with collar spines arranged usually in a single row, interrupted ventrally but not dorsally (*Acanthoparyphium, Artyfechinostomum,* and *Himasthla*). At present, a total of 23 echinostome species are classified as human-infecting species (Table 2.1); *Echinostoma revolutum, Echinostoma cinetorchis, Echinostoma lindoense, Echinostoma paraensei, Echinostoma ilocanum, Echinostoma macrorchis, Echinostoma angustitestis, Echinostoma aegyptiacum, Isthmiophora hortensis, Isthmiophora melis, Echinochasmus japonicus, Echinochasmus perfoliatus, Echinochasmus liliputanus, Echinochasmus fujianensis, Echinochasmus jiufoensis, Echinochasmus caninus, Acanthoparyphium tyosenense, Artyfechinostomum malayanum, Artyfechinostomum sufrartyfex, Artyfechinostomum oraoni, Echinoparyphium recurvatum, Himasthla muehlensi,* and *Hypoderaeum conoideum* (revised from Chai 2009, 2015). The presence of human infection with *E. aegyptiacum* is based on a report from Fujian

Table 2.1 Dimensions of adults, eggs, cercariae, and metacercariae of zoonotic echinostome species

Species (no. of collar spines)	Adults (mm)	Eggs (μm)	Cercariae (μm) body (tail length)	Metacercariae (μm)
Echinostoma revolutum (37)	9.50–11.85 × 1.45–2.09	108–125 × 57–75	265–375 × 128–154 (414–430)	132–152
Echinostoma cinetorchis (37)	10.8–12.6 × 2.6–3.2	99–116 × 65–76	150–174 × 102–121 (225–255)	134–139
Echinostoma lindoense (37)	13.0–15.0 × 2.5–3.0	92–124 × 65–76	332–474 × 130–185 (427–490)	120–130
Echinostoma paraensei (37)	7.5–16.0 × 0.79–1.95	104–122 × 74–86	228–275 × 117–136	132–148
Echinostoma ilocanum (51)	5.46–9.20 × 0.62–1.56	89–118 × 52–66	224–275 × 71–86 (377–387)	93–110
Echinostoma macrorchis (45)	4.6–7.8 × 1.3	81–100 × 54–65	340–350 × 140–165 (350–365)	139–159 × 99–120
Echinostoma angustitestis (41)	5.6 × 0.43	77–80 × 52–55	Not found	Not found
Echinostoma aegyptiacum (45)	5.60–7.25 × 0.65–1.05	96–123 × 57–69	Not found	Not found
Isthmiophora hortensis (27)	5.38–6.46 × 1.36–1.83	127–139 × 71–81	253–347 × 119–173 (436–485)	140–174 × 123–166
Isthmiophora melis (27)	4.56–7.35 × 1.01–1.35	121–139 × 78–88	384 × 80 (545)	152–170 × 145–170
Echinochasmus japonicus (24)	0.45–1.38	77–90	110–170 × 70–100 (84–140)	77–80 × 54–60
Echinochasmus perfoliatus (24)	0.5–1.2	96–102	130 × 75 (110)	92–108 × 71–97
Echinochasmus liliputanus (24)	1.68–1.76 × 0.23–0.40	95–116	130–140 × 98–120 (110–140)	78–86 × 56–70
Echinochasmus fujianensis (24)	1.25–1.79 × 0.38–0.52	98–113 × 64–72	127–132 × 78–86 (125–130)	98–114 × 76–88
Echinochasmus jiufoensis (24)	0.55–0.79 × 0.24–0.30	100–115 × 72–79	Not found	Not found
Echinochasmus caninus (24)	0.88–1.21 × 0.36–0.46	84 × 50–60	Not found	Not known

(continued)

Table 2.1 (continued)

Species (no. of collar spines)	Adults (mm)	Eggs (μm)	Cercariae (μm) body (tail length)	Metacercariae (μm)
Acanthoparyphium tyosenense (23)	1.76–2.00 × 0.40–0.54	78–93 × 63–73	330–510 × 160–200 (310–370)	420–460
Artyfechinostomum malayanum (43)	6.0–8.1 × 1.6–2.0	120–135 × 68–75	205–315 × 100–180 (285–480)	145–165
Artyfechinostomum sufrartyfex (43)	12.0–18.0 × 5.4–6.0	90–120 × 60–70	327 × 186 (352)	143 × 104
Artyfechinostomum oraoni (41)	4.0–5.1 × 0.70–0.75	131–140 × 73–80	Not found	Not found
Echinoparyphium recurvatum (45)	3.5–4.7 × 0.50–0.65	82–97 × 54–59	235–291 × 112–138 (496–556)	140–150 × 135–146
Himasthla muehlensi (31)	11.0–17.7 × 0.40–0.48	114–149 × 62–85	Not found	Not found
Hypoderaeum conoideum (49)	7.3–11.4 × 1.1–1.6	95–108 × 61–68	242–422 × 83–197	134–154

Province, China (Cheng et al. 2005). The zoonotic echinostomes are distributed mainly in Southeast Asia and the Far East (Rim 1982; Chai 2009, 2015).

For phylogenetic studies of echinostome flukes, internal transcribed spacers (ITS1 and ITS2), 28S, 18S, and 5.8S ribosomal DNA, nicotinamide adenine dinucleotide dehydrogenase (NADH) subunit 1 (ND1), and mitochondrial cytochrome *c* oxidase 1 (CO1) genes have been analyzed. Among them, ND1, in comparison with ITS1, ITS2, and CO1, was identified as the most suitable marker for identifying echinostome species and strains, in particular, the 37 collar-spined group (Morgan and Blair 1998a, b; Kostadinova and Gibson 2000). In addition, the use of ITS2 and ND1, along with partial 28S sequences, could add some more insight into the taxonomic status of the Echinostomatidae (Marcilla 2009). For example, the utility of ITS2 sequences was found to be useful for understanding the taxonomic status of *Isthmiophora hortensis*, which was amended from the original name *Echinostoma hortense* (Kostadinova and Gibson 2002; Kostadinova et al. 2003). The 28S rDNA sequences were useful to analyze the phylogenetic relationships of the echinostome superfamilies (Tkach et al. 2016). Detailed discussions will be given in each section dealing with each particular echinostome species.

Echinostomes have a 3-host life cycle which involves the first intermediate host (aquatic snail), the second intermediate host (snail, clam, fish, amphibia, and reptile), and the definitive host (fish, reptile, bird, and mammal) (Toledo et al. 2006; Chai 2009, 2015). The eggs are immature when laid, but mature to become miracidia after leaving the host, and hatch in about 3 weeks in the environment (Rim 1982). The miracidia enter the snail host, where they develop into mother rediae and then, daughter rediae, and cercariae (Beaver et al. 1984). The cercariae have well-developed tails and usually bear collar spines around the oral sucker similar to that of the adults (Rim 1982). The mature cercariae may directly encyst within the body of their snail host, or escape from the snail and encyst in other snails of the same or different species; they may also encyst in bivalves, insects, tadpoles and frogs, fish, or on vegetation (Rim 1982). The encysted metacercariae are round to oval, and show 2 branches of the excretory bladder filled with coarse granules and a head collar with collar spines (Rim 1982).

The principal mode of infection in the definitive host is consumption of the second intermediate hosts harboring the metacercariae. However, it has been postulated that humans can also be infected through drinking untreated water containing echinostome cercariae, which could become encysted when exposed to the human gastric juice (Xiao et al. 2005). In the definitive host, including humans, the main habitat is the small intestine, and probably less frequently the pyloric area of the stomach (Chai 2007, 2009). The clinical symptoms in humans are mostly gastrointestinal, including abdominal pain, diarrhea, weakness, and weight loss (Chai et al. 2009; Chai 2015).

The history of discovery, taxonomic debates, life cycles, kinds of intermediate and definitive hosts, epidemiology and geographical distribution, pathogenesis, pathology, and immunology, symptoms and signs, diagnosis and treatment, and prevention and control of each human-infecting echinostome are described in this chapter.

2.2 *Echinostoma*

Human-infecting echinostomes are largely divided into 3 groups (families) as already mentioned. The biggest group is the Echinostomatidae which includes 4 genera of medical significance, i.e., *Echinostoma, Isthmiophora, Echinoparyphium,* and *Hypoderaeum*. Among them, *Echinostoma* spp. are the most important group, and most extensive studies have been performed on this genus. *Isthmiophora* is another important genus, since one of the major human-infecting echinostomes in the Far East, formerly *Echinostoma hortense,* has been transferred to this genus under a new name *I. hortensis* (Kostadinova and Gibson 2002).

Echinostoma differs morphologically from *Echinoparyphium* in several points. The collar spines of *Echinostoma* are not sharply pointed but those of *Echinoparyphium* are sharply pointed (Kostadinova 2005). In addition, the body of *Echinostoma* is medium to large and its forebody is very short to short, whereas the body of *Echinoparyphium* is small to medium and its forebody is long to very long (Kostadinova 2005). *Hypoderaeum* has a weakly developed head collar, small-sized collar spines, and short uterine loop, whereas *Echinostoma* has a well-developed collar, large-sized collar spines, and long and numerous-looped uterus (Kostadinova 2005). *Isthmiophora* has short uterine field, pre-equatorial or equatorial testes, very long post-testicular field, and armed cirrus, whereas *Echinostoma* has long uterine field, postequatorial testes, not very long post-testicular field, and unarmed cirrus (Kostadinova 2005).

In the genus *Echinostoma*, the type species being *E. revolutum* (Froelich, 1802) Looss, 1899, numerous species have been described from birds and mammals worldwide. Yamaguti (1971) listed 101 species reported from birds and 22 species from mammals. The host specificity of *Echinostoma* spp. is quite strong, and only 3 species among them, *E. revolutum, E. rodriguesi* Hsu et al., 1968, and *E. katsuradai* Kurisu, 1930, were those that infect both mammals and birds (Yamaguti 1971). Thus, total 120 nominal species of *Echinostoma* have been enlisted by Yamaguti (1971). Later, however, many of them were synonymized with the others, and some new taxons were also described.

Echinostoma spp. can have a wide range of collar spine numbers, from 31 to 55 (Kostadinova 2005); for example, *E. anseries* (31-collar spined) (Yamaguti 1939a), *E. revolutum* (37-collar spined), *E. aegyptiacum* (43–45 collar spined) (Khalil and Abaza 1924), and *E. ilocanum* (49–55 collar spined) (Lie and Nasemary 1973). Among them, those having 37 collar spines are most common and are called either as 37-collar spined group or *E. revolutum* group, or simply '*revolutum*' group (Huffman and Fried 1990; Fried and Graczyk 2004; Toledo et al. 2009). There have long been debates on the taxonomy and classification of these '*revolutum*' group echinostomes.

Kanev (1994) and Kanev et al. (1995a, b) listed 5 species in the 37-collar spined group, namely, *E. revolutum* (sensu stricto), *E. trivolvis* (Cort, 1914) Kanev, 1985, *E. caproni* Richard, 1964, *E. jurini* (Skvortsov, 1924), and *E. echinatum* (Zeder, 1803). Kanev (1994) synonymized *E. audyi* Lie and Umathevy, 1965, *E. ivaniosi* Mahandas, 1973, and *E. paraulum* Dietz, 1909 with *E. revolutum*. Also, *E. sisjakowi* (Skvortsov, 1924) Yamaguti, 1958, *E. orlovi* Romashov, 1966, and *E. bolschewense* (Kotova, 1939) Nasincova, 1991 were synonymized with *E. jurini* (Kanev et al. 1995a). Further, Kanev et al. (1995b) synonymized some descriptions of *E. echinatum* (Zeder, 1803), *E. revolutum* (Froelich, 1802), *E. paraulum* Dietz, 1909, *E. armigerum* Barker and Irvine, 1915, *E. coalitum* Barker and Beaver, 1915, *E. collawayensis* Barker and Noll, 1915, *Echinoparyphium contiguum* Barker and Bastron, 1915, and *E. multispinosum* Vigueras, 1944 with *E. trivolvis*. In addition, Kanev (1985), Huffman and Fried (1990), Kanev (1994), and Kanev et al. (1987, 1995a, b) synonymized *E. lindoense* Sandground and Bonne, 1940, *E. barbosai* Lie and Basch, 1966, *E. miyagawai* of Kosupko, and *E. revolutum* of Nasincova with *E. echinatum*. Huffman and Fried (1990) synonymized *E. liei* Jeyarasasingam et al., 1972, *E. togoensis* Jourdan and Kulo, 1981, and *E. paraensei* Lie and Basch, 1967 with *E. caproni*.

Later, however, *E. paraensei* was acknowledged as a distinct species because of its unique isoenzymatic patterns (Sloss et al. 1995) and unique DNA sequences (Morgan and Blair 1995). Fried and Huffman (1996) and Kostadinova and Gibson (2000) accepted *E. paraensei* as a distinct species. In addition, Kostadinova and Gibson (2000) and Kostadinova et al. (2000a, b) reconsidered *E. miyagawai* Ishii, 1932 as a distinct species. They rather questioned about the taxonomic status of *E. echinatum*.

In the meantime, *E. parvocirrus* was reported as a new 37-collar spined group in Guadeloupe, French West Indies (Nassi and Dupouy 1988), and *E. friedi* was described as a new 37-collar spined species in Spain (Toledo et al. 2000). Thus, Kostadinova and Gibson (2000) listed 8 species in the '*revolutum*' group, which included *E. revolutum* (sensu stricto), *E. jurini, E. trivolvis, E. paraensei, E. caproni, E. miyagawai, E. parvocirrus,* and *E. friedi*. Kostadinova et al. (2003) assigned *E. revolutum* of Morgan and Blair (1995, 1998a, b) from Australia as *E. robustum* Yamaguti, 1935, although they did not favor the validity of *E. robustum* until further studies are performed on its larval and adult stages. *E. robustum* has been reported continuously in Europe, North and South Americas, and Oceania (Kotelnikof 1961; Rayski and Fahmy 1962; Fagasinski 1962; Alekseev 1968; Detwiler et al. 2010).

In the meantime, *E. deserticum* was reported as a new 37-collar spined species from Africa (Kechemir et al. 2002), and *E. luisreyi* was described as a new 37-collar spined species from Brazil (Maldonado et al. 2003). Thus, Fried and Graczyk (2004) listed 10 species of 37-collar spined *Echinostoma* group, including the 5 species (*E. revolutum, E. trivolvis, E. caproni, E. jurini*, and *E. echinatum*) acknowledged by Kanev and coworkers (Kanev et al. 1987; Kanev 1994; Kanev et al. 1995a, b), 3 new species (*E. parvocirrus, E. friedi,* and *E. luisreyi*), and 2 species not recognized by Kanev and coworkers (*E. paraensei* and *E. miyagawai*). However, Fried and Graczyk (2004) did not mention *E. robustum* and *E. deserticum*. Subsequently, Toledo et al. (2009) listed 10 species, including *E. deserticum,* but excluding *E. echinatum* and *E. robustum*.

However, based on molecular, morphological, and ecological data, the classification of 37-collar spined *Echinostoma* species and geographical distribution of each species became more problematic and have been continuously changing (Georgieva et al. 2013, 2014; Faltýnková et al. 2015). It is noteworthy that, using molecular techniques, a lot of new cryptic 37-collar spined *Echinostoma* species have been discovered in different parts of the world (Georgieva et al. 2013, 2014; Faltýnková et al. 2015). Synonymies ever reported based only on morphological characters are being reconsidered until the results are firmly supported by molecular evidences.

In Europe, for instance, 2 new 37-collar spined species were recently described, i.e., *E. nasincovae* (Faltýnková et al. 2015) and *Echinostoma* sp. IG (Georgieva et al. 2013). In addition, *E. bolschewense* which was synonymized with *E. jurini* by Kanev (1994) and *E. paraulum* synonymized with *E. revolutum* by Kanev et al. (1995a) were reconsidered as distinct species (Georgieva et al. 2014; Faltýnková et al. 2015). The synonymy of *E. bolschewense* with *E. jurini* proposed by Kanev et al. (1995a) was denied because of morphologcal differences in their cercariae; rather, *E. jurini* was not recognized as a distinct species (Faltýnková et al. 2015). In addition, *E. friedi* was suggested to be a synonym of *E. miyagawai* by Georgieva et al. (2013, 2014). *E. robustum* Yamaguti, 1935 was once synonymized with *E. revolutum* by Dubinina and Bezubik, but later acknowledged as a distinct species based on specimens harvested from a duck in UK (Rayski and Fahmy 1962). Thereafter, *E. robustum* was recorded from birds in Poland (Fagasinski 1962) and

Table 2.2 Continental distribution of 37-collar-spined *Echinostoma* spp.

Continent	Species distributed
Africa	*E. caproni, E. deserticum*
Asia	*E. revolutum* (*s.s.*), *E. cinetorchis, E. lindoense, E. miyagawai, E. robustum*
Europe	*E. revolutum* (*s.s.*), *E. bolschewense, E. miyagawai, E. nasincovae, E. paraulum, E. robustum, Echinostoma* sp. IG
North/Central America	*E. revolutum* (*s.s.*), *E. robustum, E. parvocirrus, E. trivolvis*
Oceania	*E. revolutum* (*s.s.*), *E. robustum, E. paraensei*
South America	*E. revolutum* (*s.s.*), *E. barbosai, E. luisryi, E. paraensei, E. robustum, E. rodriguesi*

Russia (Kotelnikof 1961; Alekseev 1968). Put together, in Europe, 7 species of 37-collar spined echinostomes can be currently acknowledged; *E. revolutum* (sensu stricto), *E. bolschewense, E. miyagawai, E. nasincovae, E. paraulum, E. robustum,* and *Echinostoma* sp. IG (Rayski and Fahmy 1962; Faltýnková et al. 2015) (Table 2.2).

In Africa, more than 5 species of 37-collar spined echinostomes were described, including *E. caproni* (Richard 1964; Richard and Brygoo 1978), *E. deserticum* (Kechemir et al. 2002), *E. revolutum* (Bisseru 1967), *E. liei* (Jeyarasasingam et al. 1972), and *E. togoensis* (Jourdane and Kulo 1981). However, Kanev (1994) suggested that *E. revolutum* described by Bisseru (1967) was actually identical to *E. caproni*. Also, Fried and Huffman (1996) reported that the studies performed under the names *E. revolutum, E. liei,* and *E. togoensis* using materials from Africa actually dealt with *E. caproni*. Therefore, only 2 species, *E. caproni* and *E. deserticum* are currently recognizable as the 37-collar spined group present in Africa (Table 2.2).

Regarding the North and Central American group of 37-collar spined echinostomes, the taxonomy has not yet been properly revised or settled (Georgieva et al. 2014). In North America, 5 species were reported at an earlier time, which included *E. trivolvis, E. armigerum, E. coalitum, E. collawayensis,* and *Echinoparyphium contiguum* (Kanev et al. 1995a; Georgieva et al. 2014). Beaver (1937) treated 4 of the above (*E. armigerum, E. coalitum, E. collawayensis,* and *E. contiguum*) as synonyms of *E. revolutum*. Later, however, Kanev (1985) pointed out that the *E. revolutum* of Beaver (1937) was identical with *E. trivolvis*. Thus, many of the articles published from North America under the name *E. revolutum* were reconsidered to have actually dealt with *E. trivolvis*. Sorensen et al. (1997, 1998) was the first who confirmed the true existence of *E. revolutum* in North America. Later, based on *nd1* gene sequences, the American *E. revolutum* was shown to be genetically different from European populations, and further studies were needed on the taxonomy of North American 37-collar spined echinostomes (Detwiler et al. 2010; Georgieva et al. 2014). In addition, Detwiler et al. (2010) detected the presence of *E. robustum* from Indiana and Minnesota, USA, and Brazil. From Guadeloupe (French West Indies), *E. parvocirrus* was reported (Nassi and Dupouy 1988). Thus, in North and Central America, 4 species can be listed as the '*revolutum*' group; *E. revolutum, E. robustum, E. parvocirrus,* and *E. trivolvis* (Nassi and Dupouy 1988; Detwiler et al. 2012) (Table 2.2).

In South America, 9 species, namely, *E. revolutum, E. barbosai, E. erraticum* Lutz, 1924, *E. microrchis* Lutz, 1924, *E. neglectum* Lutz, 1924, *E. nephrocystis* Lutz, 1924, *E. paraensei, E. rodriguesi*, and *E. luisreyi* Maldonado et al., 2003 have been described (Lutz 1924; Beaver 1937; Maldonado et al. 2001a, 2003). The presence of *E. revolutum* in Brazil has been reported by various workers, including Brasil and Amato (1992), as reviewed by Maldonado and Lanfredi (2009). *E. barbosai* was synonymized with *E. echinatum* by Kanev et al. (1987); however, the status of *E. echinatum* is now not recognized by other workers (Georgieva et al. 2014; Faltýnková et al. 2015). Thus, the name *E. barbosai* should be retained until further confirmatory studies are performed. Beaver (1937) treated the 4 species reported from Brazil by Lutz (1924), i.e., *E. erraticum, E. microrchis, E. neglectum,* and *E. nephrocystis,* as a synonym of *E. revolutum*. However, Kanev et al. (1995b) was of opinion that the *E. revolutum* assigned by Beaver (1937) was actually *E. trivolvis*. Nevertheless, Kanev et al. (1995b) did not recognize the presence of *E. trivolvis* in South America. Then, how could the 4 species reported by Lutz (1924) be truly equal to *E. trivolvis*? Or is each species valid? Anyhow, the presence of *E. trivolvis* in South America remains to be confirmed, and the synonymy of the 4 South American species proposed by Beaver (1937) needs re-verification. The presence of *E. robustum* in South America was first suggested by molecular analysis of materials obtained from Brazil (Detwiler et al. 2010). Therefore, the existence of 6 species of 37-collar spined echinostomes, including *E. revolutum, E. barbosi, E. luisreyi, E. paraensei, E. robustum,* and *E. rodriguesi,* is at present recognized in South America (Table 2.2). It is of considerable interest that in a mummified human body in Brazil, eggs presumed to be of *E. paraensei* (or *E. luisreyi*) were detected by a molecular technique (Leles et al. 2014).

In Asia, at least 5 species, including *E. revolutum* (Lee et al. 1990a; Sohn et al. 2011a; Saijuntha et al. 2011a, b, c; Chai et al. 2011, 2012; Chantima et al. 2013), *E. cinetorchis* Ando and Ozaki, 1923 (Seo et al. 1980; Lee et al. 1990b), *E. miyagawai* (Chu et al. 1973; Eom et al. 1984), *E. lindoense* (Sandground and Bonne 1940), and *E. robustum* (Islam et al. 1988) were reported as the 37-collar spined echinostomes (Table 2.2). However, recent molecular studies have revealed that the Asian *E. revolutum* is genetically different from that of the other continent; it was closest to an Australian isolate deposited in GenBank (Saijuntha et al. 2011a). In addition, there has been found a cryptic species infecting humans in Cambodia and Lao PDR genetically different from but morphologically close to *E. revolutum* (Cho 2016); this species is expected to be assigned as a new species in the near future. With regard to *E. cinetorchis*, Beaver (1937) synonymized this species with *E. trivolvis* (erroneously with *E. revolutum*; emended by Kanev 1985). However, *E. cinetorchis* is characteristic in having 2 testes which are mobile to other locations of the body; one or both testes even disappear from the body after they grow to be adults (Rim 1982; Chai 2007, 2009, 2015). Molecular, morphological, and ecological studies are needed to determine the validity of this species.

Also, *E. miyagawai* in Asia has seldom been the subject of molecular and ecological studies. Kanev et al. (1987) synonymized *E. lindoense* with *E. echinatum*; however, the status of *E. echinatum* is now questioned by many workers (Kostadinova and Gibson 2000; Georgieva et al. 2014; Faltýnková et al. 2015), and the name *E. lindoense* should be retained.

In Oceania, 3 echinostome species have been recognized to be existing (Table 2.2). In Australia, *E. revolutum* (suspected as *E. robustum* by Kostadinova et al. 2003) and *E. paraensei* were discovered by molecular analysis (Morgan and Blair 1998b). In New Zealand, a species closely allied to *E. revolutum* was found from molecular analysis (Morgan and Blair 1998b).

Therefore, as the 37-collar spined echinostomes around the world, at least 17 species should be considered; *E. revolutum* (sensu stricto), *E. barbosi, E. bolschewense, E. caproni, E. cinetorchis, E. deserticum, E. lindoense E. luisreyi, E. miyagawai, E. nasincovae, E. paraensei, E. paraulum, E. parvocirrus, E. robustum, E. rodriguesi, E. trivolvis,* and *Echinostoma* sp. IG. Among them, zoonotic echinostomes are at least 4 species, namely, *E. revolutum, E. cinetorchis, E. lindoense*, and *E. paraensei* (Chai 2009, 2015; Leles et al. 2014).

Non-37-collar spined *Echinostoma* spp. listed in this section as zoonotic species include *E. ilocanum* (Garrison, 1908) Odhner, 1911 (49–51 collar spined) (Cheng et al. 2005; Chai 2009), *E. aegyptiacum* Khalil and Abaza, 1924 (43–45 collar spined), *E. angustitestis* Wang, 1977 (41-collar spined), and *E. macrorchis* Ando and Ozaki, 1923 (43–47 collar spined). *E. ilocanum* has been reported from the Philippines (Garison 1908), Thailand (Radomyos et al. 1982), Cambodia (Sohn et al. 2011b), and Lao PDR (Chai et al. 2018). *E. aegyptiacum* has been originally reported in Egypt (Khalil and Abaza 1924), and then in Japan (Yamaguti 1939b), Taiwan (Fischthal and Kuntz 1975), China (Cheng et al. 2005), and Vietnam (Toan et al. 2008). *E. angustitestis* was originally reported from dogs in China (Wang 1977) and then found in humans in China (Cheng et al. 1992); it has been reported only in China (Yu and Mott 1994). *E. macrorchis* was first discovered in Japan (Ando and Ozaki 1923), and later found in Taiwan (Fischthal and Kuntz 1975, 1981; Lo 1995), Lao PDR (Sohn et al. 2013), and South Korea (Sohn and Na 2017).

Therefore, in the present section, 8 species of *Echinostoma* infecting humans, including 4 37-collar spined group and 4 non-37-collar spined *Echinostoma* spp., together with several potentially zoonotic *Echinostoma* spp. are described. Experimental human infection with *E. miyagawai* was reported to be successful in China (Wu 2013); however, this species was included among the potentially zoonotic *Echinostoma* species because of lack of detailed information. Natural human infection with *E. paraulum* was also reported in Yunnan Province in China (Li et al. 2010; Wu 2013) but the taxonomic status of this species has been unstable (debates on its synonymy with *E. revolutum* have not been completely resolved), so that this species is not included among the zoonotic *Echinostoma* species in this review book.

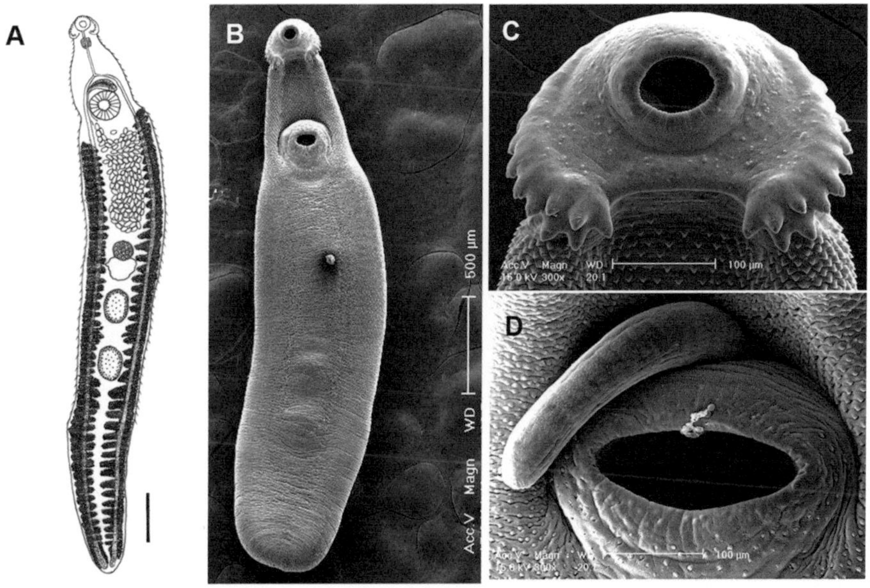

Fig. 2.1 *Echinostoma revolutum*. (**a**) Line drawing of an adult worm (original figure). Scale bar = 1 mm (**b**–**d**) Scanning electron microscopic views of a 2-week-old adult fluke recovered from an experimental hamster. Reproduced from Chai et al. (1998) Korean J Parasitol 49:449–455 with permission (**b**) Whole worm (**c**) Oral sucker and collar spines (**d**) Ventral sucker and an unarmed cirrus that come out from the genital pore

2.2.1 Echinostoma revolutum

2.2.1.1 *Echinostoma revolutum* (Froelich, 1802) Dietz, 1909

[syn: *Echinostoma revolutum* var. *japonicum* Kurisu, 1932; *Echinostoma audyi* Lie and Umathevy, 1965; *Echinostoma ivaniosi* Mahandas, 1973]

Taxonomy and Morphology

This (Fig. 2.1a, b) is the oldest echinostome species (subfamily Echinostominae) ever recorded and the representative species of the so-called 37-collar spined echinostomes or '*revolutum*' group echinostomes (Huffman and Fried 1990; Kanev 1994; Fried and Graczyk 2004). It was originally described as *Fasciola revoluta* by Froelich in 1802 in Germany with adult specimens recovered from the large intestine of naturally infected wild ducks *Anas boschas fereae* dissected in 1798 (Kanev 1994). Rudolphi in 1809 established a new group, *Echinis* (*Echinostoma*) for this fluke, in the genus *Distoma* Retzius, 1786. Independently from this, Zeder in 1803 established a new name for a morphologically similar echinostome from Germany, *Distoma echinatum* (Toledo et al. 2014a). *D. echinatum* was renamed as *E. echinatum* by de Blainville in 1828 (Dietz 1910). After Rudolphi established *Echinostoma* in 1809, for 100 years, until the study of Dietz (1909, 1910), practically almost all collar-spined worms found in Europe were diagnosed either as *D. echinatum* or as *E. echinatum* (Kanev 1994). However, Dietz (1909, 1910) restored the validity of *F. revoluta*, renaming it as *E. revolutum*, and synonymized *E. echinatum* with *E. revolutum*. This was a big milestone for the taxonomy of '*revolutum*' group echinostomes. Nevertheless, the taxonomic validity of *E. echinatum* has long been debated even until the present (Kostadinova and Gibson 2000; Kostadinova et al. 2000b; Georgieva et al. 2014; Faltýnková et al. 2015). In addition, more than 120–200 nominal species have been described and included in the genus *Echinostoma* (Yamaguti 1958; Kostadinova et al. 2003), and at least 17 species are now considered to be valid in the '*revolutum*' group (see above). Human infection with *E. revolutum* was first documented in Taiwan (Anazawa 1929), and the prevalence in Taiwan among human population was reported to be 0.11–0.65% (Lu 1982). Further human infections were detected in mainland China, Indonesia, Thailand, Cambodia, Lao PDR, and Russia (Chai 2015). Now, *E. revolutum* is regarded as an intestinal fluke of the duck, goose, muskrat, as well as humans in Asia, Europe, Africa, New Zealand, and North and South Americas (Kanev 1994; Yu and Mott 1994; Fried and Graczyk 2004; Chai 2009, 2015).

The characteristic morphology of *E. revolutum* includes the presence of 37 collar spines (Fig. 2.1c), which are arranged conspicuously as 5-6-15-6-5, including 5 corner spines and 6 lateral ones on each side in single rows, and 15 dorsal spines in a double row (Kostadinova et al. 2000b). The adult flukes are 9.50–11.85 × 1.45–2.09 mm, and eggs are 108–125 × 57–75 μm in size (Faltýnková et al. 2015). The cercarial body and tail (length) of *E. revolutum* was reported to be 265–315 μm long and 128–154 μm wide and 414–430 μm long and 39–50 μm wide, respectively (Kanev 1994). The metacercariae are spherical or subspherical, 132–152 μm in diameter (Kanev 1994).

Kanev (1994) stated that the '*revolutum*' group cannot be identified each other only by the morphology of adult flukes, but they can be more clearly discriminated by the morphology of larval stages (in particular, cercariae) and host-parasite relationships, including the kinds and species of intermediate hosts. However, some other workers reported discriminating features in their adult morphologies. For example, the ventral sucker of *E. revolutum* is bigger (and wider) than that of *E. miyagawai* in comparison with the width of the body at the level of the ventral sucker in each species (Kostadinova et al. 2000b). In addition, the vitellaria distributing along both lateral sides of the body become confluent in the posterior part of the body in *E. miyagawai* adults; however, they do not become confluent in *E. revolutum* adults (Kostadinova et al. 2000b). The adult flukes of *E. revolutum* are significantly larger (about a double) in size than those of *E. nacincovae*, and the angle and lateral spines of *E. revolutum* are distinctly longer than those of *E. nacincovae* (Faltýnková et al. 2015). The 2 testes of *E. revolutum* are usually intact, located tandom in the posterior part of the body but those (one or both testes) of *E. cinetorchis* frequently disappear from the body after they grow up to be adults (Chai 2009, 2015). For differential points between *E. revolutum* and other 'revolutum' group in Europe, including *E. bolschewense, E. miyagawai, Echinostoma* sp. IG, and *E. paraulum*, see Faltýnková et al. (2015).

The tegumental ultrastructure of *E. revolutum* (probably *E. trivolvis*) was studied during their development from metacercariae to adults in the chick embryo and chicks (Fried and Fujino 1984). The development was essentially the same in the 2 different conditions; on the chorioallantois and in vivo of chick (Fried and Fujino 1984). During the development of metacercariae into juveniles and adolescents, the tegument changed from smooth to granular, and sensory papillae on the suckers became well-defined. The collar spines became thicker and more curved, and the tegumental spines showed marked changes in size, shape, and distribution on both ventral and dorsal aspects of the body (Fried and Fujino 1984). The oral sucker and the collar lacked tegumental spines (Fig. 2.1c) (Kanev et al. 1999). Three types of sensory papillae were observed; ciliated knob-like papillae (type I), non-ciliated papillae with a step-like elevation of the tegument (type II), and round, swollen, or sometimes spherical papillae (type III). The type I papillae were common in juvenile flukes, whereas the type II and type III papillae were found mainly on the lip of the oral and ventral suckers of adolescent worms (Fried and Fujino 1984). An unarmed cirrus is seen protruded out of the genital pore (Fig. 2.1d).

Life Cycle

E. revolutum has several developmental stages, including the egg, miracidium, sporocyst, redia, daughter redia, cercaria, metacercaria, and adult (Kanev 1994). The first eggs appear in the feces 10 days after infection in birds; they are unembryonated, yellowish-brown, and equipped with a small operculum and abopercular thickening (Kanev 1994). At a constant temperature of 28 °C, eggs kept in distilled water yielded fully-developed miracidia within 9–12 days; exposure to light stimulates hatching of miracidia (Kanev 1994). Miracidia penetrate into the snail host at mantle edge or along edges of foot, and after 48 h, sporocysts develop in the ventricular cavity of the snail heart; they are contractile, elongate sacs attached by their broader end to heart muscle and with narrow end free in the heart cavity, containing germ balls and 1–2 rediae (Kanev 1994). The first generation rediae (mother rediae) are motile, colorless, with collar conspicuous and gut reaching almost to the locomotor organs, and produce daughter rediae (Kanev 1994). Daughter rediae (second and third generation rediae) may contain up to 30 cercariae, in addition to a number of germ balls (Kanev 1994). Cercariae are echinostome-type with an oral sucker surrounded by a spiny collar (Schell 1970). Penetration gland cells are present along the esophagus of the cercariae with 4 inconspicuous gland duct openings on the dorsal lip of the oral sucker; paraesophageal gland cell outlets are also present, 16–20 in number (Kanev 1994). The snail host so far reported is *Lymnaea stagnalis* (Kanev 1994; Fáltynková et al. 2015), *Lymnaea swinhoei, Austropeplea ollula* (syn. *Lymnaea ollula*) (Ito 1964), *Lymnaea elodes* (Sorensen et al. 1997; Sorensen and Minchella 1998; Fried et al. 1997), *Lymnaea tomentosa* (Davis 2005), *Lymnaea glabra* (Rondelaud et al. 2015), *Radix auricularia, Radix peregra,* and *Stagnicola palustris* (Fáltynková et al. 2015).

The cercariae escape from the snail and swim in water. They then infect the same or different snail species, invade into the pericardial sac or posterior kidney region of the snail, and are encysted to become metacercariae (Kanev 1994). However, in

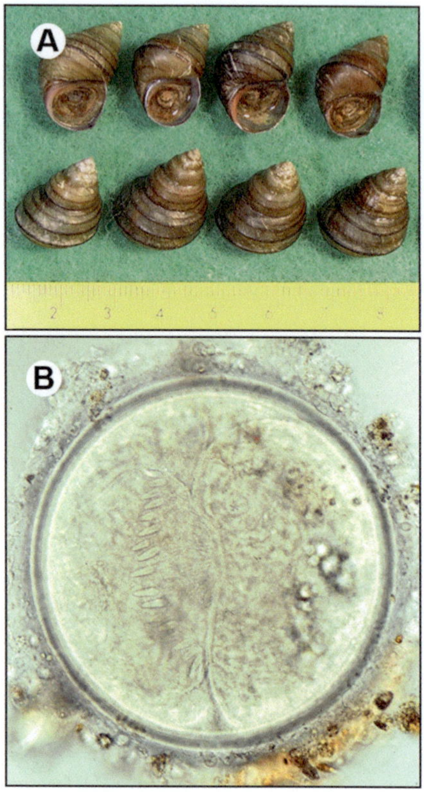

Fig. 2.2 *Echinostoma revolutum*. (**a**) *Filopaludina* sp. snails, a second intermediate host, purchased in a local market of Nam Dinh Province, Vietnam (**b**) Metacercaria isolated from the snail host showing the collar spines on the head collar.×200

Lymnaea tomentosa snails, in most cases the cercariae encysted without emerging from the snails (Davis 2005). Sometimes, metacercariae are found in the mantle and soft tissues of snails already harbouring rediae and cercariae of the same species; in some cases, metacercariae are also found within their rediae (Kanev 1994). The metacercariae become infective to the definitive host within 1–2 days; they may survive 18 months in the snail (Kanev 1994).

The snail species playing the role of a second intermediate host include *Lymnaea stagnalis, Fossaria truncatula* (syn. *Lymnaea truncatula*), *Austropeplea ollula* (syn. *Lymnaea ollula*), *Lymnaea swinhoei, Lymnaea elodes, Lymnaea tomentosa, Corbicula fluminea, Physa acuta, Planorbis corneus, Radix auricularia, Radix lagotis, Radix peregra, Semisulcospira cancellata, Semisulcospira palustris, Stagnicola palustris*, and *Filopaludina* sp. (Fig. 2.2a) (Komiya 1965; Alekseev 1968; Kanev 1994; Sorensen et al. 1997; Davis 2005; Chai et al. 2011; Georgieva et al. 2013; Fáltynková et al. 2015). Frogs (*Rana temporaria* and *Rana ridibunda*) and turtles (*Emys orbicularis*) also can serve as the second intermediate host; in these hosts, the metacercariae (Fig. 2.2b) are found in the kidney and eye cavity (Kanev 1994).

The natural and experimental definitive hosts include various species of birds, including pigeons, ducks, chickens, and geese (Kanev 1994; Sorensen et al. 1997; Davis 2005; Saijuntha et al. 2010a; Fáltynková et al. 2015). Kanev (1985, 1994) and Kanev et al. (1995a) argued that only birds can play the role of the definitive host for *E. revolutum*. Fried and Graczyk (2004) and Toledo et al. (2009) accepted this concept. However, there have been reports on *E. revolutum* infections in mammalian animals (Yamaguti 1958; Chai et al. 2009b; Toledo and Esteban 2016). This issue needs to be clarified though molecular and ecological studies on larval and adult flukes in different localities and different hosts. The first report of mammalian infection with *E. revolutum* was a human infection in a 31-year-old Taiwanese woman (Anazawa 1929). Thereafter, a lot of papers have reported human infections in Taiwan (based on recovery of echinostome eggs), with the prevalence ranging from 0.11% to 0.65% during 1929–1979 (Lu 1982). Small endemic foci or a few cases of human infection have been discovered in Peoples' Republic of China, Indonesia, Thailand, Cambodia, and Lao PDR (Rim 1982; Radomyos et al. 1994, 1998; Yu and Mott 1994; Ashford and Crewe 2003; Sohn et al. 2011a; Chai et al. 2012). Adult flukes were also recovered in vertebrate animals (mammals) other than humans, i.e., musk rats (Rankin 1946; Detwiler et al. 2012), house rats (Lee et al. 1990a; Maldonado and Lanfredi 2009), field rats (Bonne et al. 1953), cats (Sohn and Chai 2005), and wild boars (Maldonado and Lanfredi 2009). It is of note that Detwiler et al. (2012) performed molecular analysis of echinostome flukes recovered from musk rats in Virginia, USA, and the presence of *E. revolutum* haplotypes was confirmed in one musk rat. Therefore, it can be said safely that *E. revolutum* is a parasite of birds and also mammals.

In the definitive hosts, adult worms live in the posterior part of the small intestine, cecum, and rectum; egg production begins about 10–14 days after infection, for example, in young pigeons; 18-day worms were all fully gravid (Kanev 1994; Fáltynková et al. 2015). Under laboratory conditions, worms live between 4 and 8 weeks (Kanev 1994). Experimental definitive hosts included pigeons (Kanev 1994; Fáltynková et al. 2015), chickens (Humphries et al. 1997; Sorensen et al. 1997, 1998; Detwiler et al. 2010), ducks, fowls, white rats, dogs (Tsuchimochi 1924; Anazawa 1929), and hamsters (Chai et al. 2011; Chantima et al. 2013).

Epidemiology and Geographical Distribution

Kanev (1994) suggested that adults of *E. revolutum* cannot be identified using only morphological criteria. In addition, Kanev (1994) strongly suggested that *E. revolutum* is exclusively an avian parasite but not a mammalian parasite. If these suggestions are accepted, all the literature dealing with human *E. revolutum* infection may be problematic. However, as already mentioned, Detwiler et al. (2012) confirmed the presence of *E. revolutum* in a musk rat in Virginia, USA by molecular methods and concluded that *E. revolutum* is a parasite of birds but also of mammals. Yamaguti (1971) and Rim (1982) also regarded *E. revolutum* as a parasite of both birds and mammals. The present author agrees to regard *E. revolutum* as a parasite of both birds and mammals, although more data are needed to clearly elucidate this point.

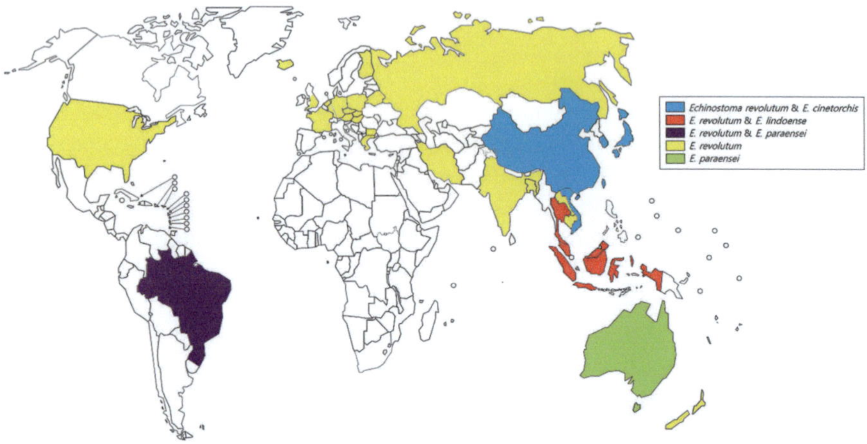

Fig. 2.3 Global distribution of 37-collar spined *Echinostoma* spp. (*E. revolutum, E. cinetorchis, E. lindoense,* and *E. paraensei*) based on the presence of their life cycles

The principal mode of infection in birds or mammals, including humans, is consumption of raw or undercooked snails, which include *Lymnaea, Fossaria, Austropeplea, Corbicula, Physa, Planorbis, Radix, Semisulcospira,* and *Filopaludina* spp. (Komiya 1965; Alekseev 1968; Kanev 1994; Sorensen et al. 1997; Davis 2005; Chai et al. 2011; Fáltynková et al. 2015). Frogs and turtles can also be the infection source to humans (Kanev 1994). The geographical distribution of *E. revolutum* is now acknowledged to be almost cosmopolitan, with the exception of the African Continent. The presence of its larvae or adults has been reported from 33 countries in Europe, Asia, North and South Americas, and Oceania (32 if Australia is excluded) (Fig. 2.3; Table 2.3). In these countries, avian species, in particular, ducks, fowls, and pigeons, in Europe, Asia, North and South Americas, and Oceania are not uncommonly infected with this echinostome species. However, human infections (if the diagnosis is correct) have been reported from 6 Asian countries but never from Europe, Americas, and Oceania.

Australia The presence or not of *E. revolutum* life cycle in Australia is to be determined firmly. Three strains, collected as metacercariae having 37 collar spines, were molecularly identified as *E. revolutum* (Morgan and Blair 1998b). However, Kostadinova et al. (2003) reviewed this and had an opinion that the Australian isolates were close to *E. robustum*, although they did not readily recognize the validity of *E. robustum*.

Austria Austria is included among the countries of distribution of *E. revolutum* (Kanev 1994).

Bangladesh Out of 100 domestic ducks examined in Mymensingh District, 9 (9.0%) harboured *E. revolutum* worms, with the worm density of 1–6 specimens (mean 2) per duck (Islam et al. 1988). In another study, 63 (30.6%) of 206 ducks

Table 2.3 Global distribution of 37-collar-spined *Echinostoma* spp.

Species & Nominator	Continent (Country/Region)
Echinostoma revolutum (Froelich, 1802) Dietz, 1909*	*Asia* (Bangladesh, Cambodia, China, India, Indonesia, Japan, South Korea, Lao PDR, Malaysia, Taiwan, Thailand, Vietnam), *Europe* (Austria, Belarus, Bulgaria, Czech Rep., England, Finland, France, Germany, Greece, Hungary, Iceland, The Netherlands, Poland, Russia, Slovak Rep., Yugoslavia), *The Middle East* (Iran), *Oceania* (New Zealand), *North America* (USA; Indiana, Minnesota), *South America* (Brazil)
Echinostoma cinetorchis Ando and Ozaki, 1924*	China, Japan, South Korea, Taiwan, Vietnam
Echinostoma lindoense Sandground and Bonne, 1940*	Indonesia, Malaysia, Thailand
Echinostoma paraensei Lie and Basch, 1967*	Australia, Brazil
Echinostoma barbosai Lie and Basch, 1966	Brazil
Echinostoma bolschewense (Kotova, 1939) Nasincova, 1991	Czech Rep., Russia, Slovak Rep.
Echinostoma caproni Richard, 1964	Cameroon, Congo, Egypt, Madagascar
Echinostoma deserticum Kechemir et al., 2002	Algeria, Niger
Echinostoma luisreyi Maldonado et al., 2003	Brazil
Echinostoma miyagawai Ishii, 1932	*Asia* (Japan, South Korea, Lao PDR, Thailand), *Europe* (Bulgaria, Czech Rep., Poland, Spain, Ukraine)
Echinostoma nasincovae Faltýnková et al. (2015)	Czech Rep., Slovak Rep.
Echinostoma paraulum Dietz, 1909	Czech Rep., Germany
Echinostoma parvocirrus Nassi and Dupouy, 1988	French West Indies (Guadeloupe)

(continued)

Table 2.3 (continued)

Species & Nominator	Continent (Country/Region)
Echinostoma robustum Yamaguti, 1935	*Asia* (Bangladesh), *Europe* (England, Germany, Poland, Russia), *Oceania* (Australia), *North America* (USA; Indiana, Minnesota), *South America* (Brazil)
Echinostoma rodriguesi Hsu et al., 1968	Brazil
Echinostoma trivolvis (Cort, 1914) Kanev, 1985	Canada, USA (Indiana, Minnesota, Wisconsin)
Echinostoma sp. IG Georgieva et al., 2013	England, Germany, Iceland

*Human infections have been reported

from the same district were infected with *E. revolutum* (Yousuf et al. 2009). A recent study in Mymensingh District collected a total of 31 flukes from 11 ducks in 2015, and nuclear ribosomal ITS2 and mitochondrial *nad1* sequences of the flukes were analyzed (Mohanta et al. 2019). No human infection has been discovered.

Belarus Domestic and wild mammals in Belorussian Polesie have been found to have 3 species of echinostomes, including *E. revolutum, Isthmiophora melis,* and *Echinochasmus perfoliatus* (Shimalov and Shimalov 2002).

Brazil Various avian (*Cairina moschata, Gallus gallus,* and *Passe domesticus*) and mammalian (*Rattus norvegicus* and *Sus scrofa*) animals were reported to be the natural definitive hosts (Maldonado and Lanfredi 2009).

Bulgaria Studies were carried out on experimental conditions of the complete life history, morphological structure, and ecology of echinostome species (Kanev and Odening 1983). At least 2 echinostome species, presumably *E. lindoense* and *E. audyi*, were present (Kanev and Odening 1983). However, *E. audyi* was synonymized with *E. revolutum* by Kanev (1994). Rediae of *E. revolutum* were obtained from naturally and experimentally infected *Lymnaea stagnalis* snails (Mustafa 1994).

Cambodia Human infections were identified by recovery of adult worms in 4 schoolchildren in Pursat Province (Sohn et al. 2011a). In 4 different schools located along the Tonle Sap Lake, Pursat Province, the prevalence of echinostome eggs (most were presumed to be *E. revolutum*) among schoolchildren ranged 7.5–22.4% (Sohn et al. 2011a). In another area, Bat Dambang Province, the echinostome egg positive rate (species undetermined) was 4.8% among kindergarten children (Park et al. 2004). In Takeo Province, the echinostome eggs (species undetermined) were found in 3.6% among general people surveyed (Yong et al. 2012). Similarly, in

Kratie Province, 71 (3.4%) of 2101 riparian people were positive for echinostome eggs (species undetermined) (Sohn et al. 2012). Cercariae and metacercariae have never been detected. Natural definitive hosts are unknown.

China Human cases were recorded in Yunnan and Guangdong Province (Yu and Mott 1994). However, the prevalence of human infections is unknown. *Gyraulus convexusculus, Hippeutis cantori*, *Lymnaea plicatula*, and *Segmentina* (*Polypylis*) *hemisphaerula* snails were reported to be the second intermediate hosts in Fujian Province (Chen et al. 1985). Chickens, ducks, and other avian species were found to be the natural definitive hosts (Chen et al. 1985).

Czech Republic An avian host (*Buteo buteo*) was reported to be a natural definitive host (Maldonado and Lanfredi 2009).

England Kanev (1994) included England among the countries where *E. revolutum* is distributed.

Findland The first intermediate host was reported to be *Lymnaea stagnalis* and *Lymnaea peregra* (Maldonado and Lanfredi 2009).

France The first intermediate host was reported to be *Lymnaea glabra* and *Galba trunctatula* in Brenne Regional Natural Park (Rondelau et al. 2015, 2016).

Germany Cercariae of *E. revolutum* were obtained from *Lymnaea stagnalis* snails collected in fish ponds near Höchstadt/Aisch (Haas et al. 1995). Later, white storks (*Ciconia ciconia*) were found to be natural definitive host for *E. revolutum* (Schuster et al. 2002).

Greece One mute swan (*Cygnus olor*) from a northern area was found to be infected with *E. revolutum* (Papazahariadou et al. 2008).

Hungary Hamsters (*Cricetus cricetus*) from Tiszavasvári were found infected with *E. revolutum* (Matskási 1971).

Iceland The cercariae of *E. revolutum* were detected in *Radix peregra* snails from the Lake Myvatn (Georgieva et al. 2013).

India The presence of the life cycle of *E. revolutum* has been reported in India. *Lymnaea auricularia* var. *rufescens* was found to be the common first and second intermediate host; pigeons and fowls were successfully infected with the metacercariae (Patnaik and Ray 1966). Natural infection of domestic ducks with adult worms was also reported (Kishore and Sinha 1982). *Echinostoma ivaniosi* was reported as a new species (Mohandas 1973); however, because of no difference in the morphology and biology of larval and adult worms it was synonymized with *E. revolutum* (Kanev 1994). The first intermediate host was *Lymnaea luteola* and

Lymnaea acuminata, and the second intermediate host was *Lymnaea luteola, Lymnaea acuminata, Indoplanorbis exustus,* and *Idiopoma dissimilis* (Mohandas 1973). Human infection with *E. revolutum* has never been reported.

Indonesia Three human infections were reported in 1953 (Bonne et al. 1953); 2 were postmortem cases infected each with a single worm, and another was infected with more than 85 specimens in an 8-year-old boy. Lie (1964) considered these human cases to be *E. lindoense*; however, this needs verification. The infection rates are usually low (around 1%). There was a high endemic focus in the Lindu Valley of Central Sulawesi with 24–96% prevalence for echinostome infections (species undetermined) (Carney 1991). However, foodborne trematodiases in this area were almost eliminated (Graczyk and Fried 1998). It is of note that parasitic zoonoses, including echinostomiasis, were a reemerging disease as the popularity of exotic foods being served in Korean and Japanese restaurants spread throughout Indonesian cities (Kusharyono and Sukartinah 1991). Human infections are attributed to eating freshwater snails and clams.

Iran Various species of birds captured from Khuzestan Province harboured 24 species of intestinal helminths including *E. revolutum* (Farahnak et al. 2004).

Japan This echinostome was discovered in birds near Osaka, Tokyo, and Sapporo (Yamashita 1964). The tufted duck, *Aythya fuligula*, was a natural definitive host (Yamaguti 1933). The velvet scoters, *Melanitta fusca stejnegeri*, around Lake Biwa were also confirmed to be a natural definitive host (Yamaguti 1934). Life history studies have seldom been performed in Japan.

South Korea The first report of *E. revolutum* was the discovery of an infection in a wild duck (*Anas platyrhynchus platyrhynchus*) in Busan area (Isshiki 1934). Thereafter, 5 species of domestic or wild birds, including fowls and ducks (*Gallus domesticus, Anas poecilorhyncha zanorhyncha, Anas fulcata, Anas platyrhynchus platyrhynchus,* and *Aythya fuligula*) have been found as the natural definitive host in different areas of South Korea (Jang 1958; Chu et al. 1973). Later, a house rat (*Rattus norvegicus*) was found to be infected with a total of 28 specimens (Lee et al. 1990a). Thereafter, 2 of 438 feral cats were found to be infected with a total of 7 specimens of *E. revolutum* (Sohn and Chai 2005).

Lao PDR Human infections were reported in 3 patients from Khammouane Province based on recovery of adult worms (Chai et al. 2012). The prevalence of echinostome eggs (species undetermined) in fecal examinations ranged 0.2–1.3% in Vientiane, Saravane, Savannakhet, and Khammouane Province (Chai et al. 2005, 2007, 2009c). Cercariae and metacercariae have never been detected. As to the natural definitive host, 46 adult specimens of *E. revolutum* were collected from a duck farm (number of ducks examined is unknown) in Vientiane Province (Saijuntha et al. 2011b).

Malaysia With the exception of *Artyfechinostomum malayanum,* no other human-infecting echinostome species were described until 1965 (Rim 1982; Graczyk and Fried 1998). However, *Echinostoma audyi* was described as a new echinostome species infecting avian hosts (experimental), including ducklings, pigeons, and little cuckoo doves, in Kuala Lumpur and Kuala Pilah (Lie and Umathevy 1965). *Lymnaea rubiginosa* served as the first intermediate host, and the same and other snail species, including *Gyraulus convexiusculus, Indoplanorbis exustus, Pila scutata,* and *Bellamya ingallsiana* served as the second intermediate hosts (Lie and Umathevy 1965). Later, however, Kanev (1994) synonymized *E. audyi* with *E. revolutum* for various reasons. Thus, the presence of *E. revolutum* life cycle is now recognized in Malaysia.

The Netherlands Nine avian species were reported to harbor the adult flukes of *E. revolutum* (Borgsteede et al. 2000).

New Zealand Adult echinostomes having 37 collar spines removed from a wild goose (*Branta canadensis*) were diagnosed as *E. revolutum* through molecular analysis (Morgan and Blair 1998b). Later, one of 9 black-backed gull (*Larus dominicanus*) was found to harbor 1 adult specimen of *E. revolutum* (Latham and Poulin 2002). *E. revolutum* adult flukes were recovered from the intestine of wild Canada geese (*Branta canadensis*), and eggs were obtained from the individual worm dissections to culture in vitro and infect the snails *Lymnaea tomentosa* where the parasite developed to cercariae and then metacercariae (Davis 2005).

Poland *E. revolutum* adults were recovered from the domestic poultry in Poland between 1955 and 1959 (Fagasinski 1962). Native cercariae of *E. revolutum* emerged from *Lymnaea stagnalis* and *Planorbarius corneus* were experimentally infected to immigrant snails (*Potamopyrgus antipodarum*) successfully (Żbikowski and Żbikowska 2009).

Russia The first intermediate host (experimental) was reported to be *Radix auricularia, Radix lagotis, Planorbis* sp., and *Semisulcospira cancellata* (Alekseev 1968). The second intermediate host was, in addition to these 4 snail species, *Vivipara ussuriensis, Cristaria plicata,* corixids, *Acheilognathus chankaensis,* and *Rana temporaria* (Alekseev 1968). Racoon dogs and American minks introduced the Volga Delta harboured specimens of *E. revolutum* and *Echinochamus perfoliatus* (Ivanov and Semenova 2000). There has been no record on human infections.

Slovak Republic Three species of birds (*Anser albitrans, Anser tabalis,* and *Branta canadensis*) were reported to be the natural definitive hosts (Maldonado and Lanfredi 2009).

Taiwan The first human infection with *E. revolutum* was discovered by Anazawa (1929) from a 31-year-old Taiwanese woman by recovery of 18 adult worms after treatment with oleoresin of aspidium. Anazawa (1929) also discovered 47 (0.39%)

fecal echinostome egg-positive cases (species undetermined) among 12,055 people examined. The second case of *E. revolutum* infection was a 9-year-old girl, and the third case was a school child, from both of whom the adult flukes were recovered and morphologically identified (Lu 1982). The prevalence of human infections with echinostomes (species undetermined), from 1929 to 1979, in different areas of Taiwan was reported to be between 0.11% and 0.65% (Lu 1982). After then, however, no proper data have been available to estimate the status of human infection with *E. revolutum* in Taiwan.

Regarding the infection status of larval stages in snail hosts, not many studies are available. Anazawa (1929) reported that the cercarial infection rate of *Lymnaea swinhoei* was 2.6% on average. Tsuchimochi (1924) found cercariae in 548 (9.6%) of 5722 *Lymnaea ollula* snails. Anazawa (1929) also reported *Corbicula producta* and *Unio spinfoei* snails as the second intermediate host, which are popularly consumed after salting overnight; the metacercarial positive rate of the former snail species was up to 96% in highly prevalent areas. With regard to the definitive host, Tsuchimochi (1924) found *E. revolutum* adult worms from domestic ducks in Taiwan. Adult flukes were also recorded from civet cats in Taipei and Lo-tung areas (Fischthal and Kunz 1975).

Thailand Bhaibulaya et al. (1966) first found a human infection with *E. revolutum*, and only a few reports have been available on recovery of adult flukes from humans in Thailand. For example, some specimens recovered in 4 (0.6%) out of 681 helminth egg positive (*O. viverrini* or *Taenia* sp.) residents from 16 provinces in northeast Thailand after chemotherapy were *E. revolutum* adult flukes (Radomyos et al. 1994, 1998). However, it is of note that in one region of northeast Thailand, greater than 50% of the stool samples contained echinostome eggs (species undetermined) (Graczyk and Fried 1998). Also of note is that echinostomiasis is particularly prevalent in rural Thai women of child-bearing age (Sanchaisuriya et al. 1993). The first intermediate host is *Indoplanorbis exustus* and *Lymnaea rubiginosa* in Thailand (Harinasuta et al. 1987). The second intermediate hosts include *Physa occidentalis, Lymnaea* sp., *Clea helena, Eiriesia eyriesi, Bithynia funiculata, Bithynia siamensis siamensis, Filopaludina dollaris, Filopaludina sumatrensis polygramma, Filopaludina martensi martensi,* and *Idiopoma umbilicata* snails and tadpoles (Yu and Mott 1994; Chantima et al. 2013; Tesana et al. 2014). With regard to the definitive host, as many as 76.7% of domestic ducks from a market in Bangkok were found infected with echinostome flukes, in particular, *E. revolutum* (828 among 976 specimens) and *Hypoderaeum conoideum* (148 of 976 specimens) (Pethleart et al. 2005). Free-grazing ducks from slaughterhouses in central, north, and northeastern Thailand revealed high prevalences of *E. revolutum* adult flukes (Saijuntha et al. 2013).

USA Regarding *Echinostoma* spp. in North America, Beaver (1937) treated the previously reported 4 species (*Echinostoma armigerum, Echinostoma coalitum, Echinostoma collawayensis,* and *Echinostoma contiguum*) as the synonyms of *E. revolutum.* Later, however, Kanev (1985) indicated that *E. revolutum* of Beaver

(1937) was considered to be actually dealing with *E. trivolvis*. Sorensen et al. (1997, 1998) was the first who confirmed the true existence of *E. revolutum* in North America. The first intermediate host was confirmed to be *Lymnaea elodes* in seral sites of northern Indiana (Sorensen et al. 1997, 1998; Sorensen and Minchella 1998). *Planorbella trivolvis* (= *Helisoma trivolvis*) snails could also serve as the first intermediate host of *E. revolutum* in Connecticut (Holland et al. 2007) and Indiana (Detwiler et al. 2010). The second intermediate hosts can be various snail species, including *Lymnaea* spp. and *Physa* spp., and various fish and amphibian species (Johnson and McKenzie 2009). The natural definitive hosts included domestic ducks, domestic pigeons, domestic chickens, black-headed munia, spoted munia, little cuckoo dove, and Java sparrows (Johnson and McKenzie 2009). The reason for overall distribution of *E. revolutum* is not well understood in North America is probably due, in part, to misclassification as *E. trivolvis* in some regions (Johnson and McKenzie 2009). It is of note that *Echinostoma* spp. eggs were detected in 4 (0.3%) of 1478 Southeast Asian refugees living in Massachusetts; however, they are not considered to be due to infections in USA because they newly arrived there (DeGirolami and Kimber 1983).

Vietnam Kanev (1994) mentioned that *E. revolutum* is distributed in Vietnam based on cercariae and experimentally grown adults. Quite recently, Chai et al. (2011) discovered the metacercariae of *E. revolutum* from *Filopaludina* snails purchased from a local market in Nam Dinh Province; the identification was based on adult flukes recovered from experimentally infected hamsters. A total of 30 helminth species have been reported from dogs in Vietnam, including *E. revolutum* (Bang and Cuong 2015).

Yugoslavia Ducks (*Anas platyrhynchus*) were found to be the natural definitive host (Kanev 1994).

2.2.2 Echinostoma cinetorchis

2.2.2.1 *Echinostoma cinetorchis* Ando and Ozaki, 1923

Taxonomy and Morphology

E. cinetorchis (Fig. 2.4a, b) was originally described in Japanese based on specimens recovered from the small intestine of wild rats in Japan (Ando and Ozaki 1923). This species was redescribed by Dollfus (1925a) in French. It was subsequently found in dogs in Taiwan (Sugimoto 1933; Fischthal and Kuntz 1975), mice, rats, and dogs in South Korea (Seo et al. 1964, 1981; Cho et al. 1981; Chai et al. 2009a), and field rats (Fujian Province), house rats (Jilin Province), and dogs (Sichuan Province) in China (Chen et al. 1985). Recently, *E. cinetorchis* was also found from chickens and ducks in Vietnam (Anh et al. 2010). Its characteristic morphology includes abnormal location and disappearance of one or both testes after

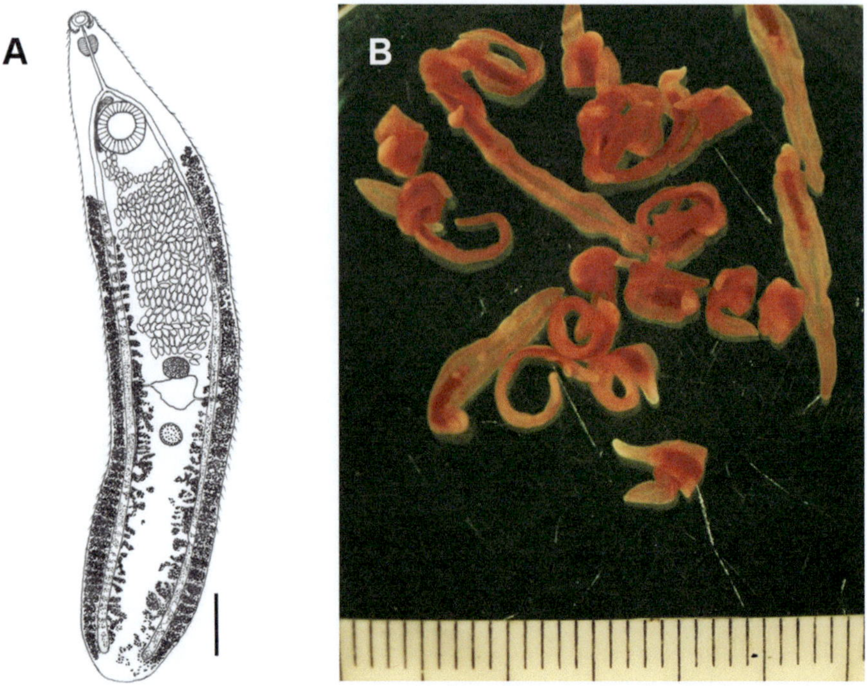

Fig. 2.4 *Echinostoma cinetorchis*. (**a**) Line drawing of an adult worm (original figure). Scale bar = 1 mm (**b**) Adult flukes recovered from experimentally infected rats. Red color in worms indicate the uterus filled with eggs

they grow to be adults, and the presence of 37 collar spines around the oral sucker (Chai and Lee 2002; Chai et al. 2009b). Beaver (1937) obtained adult echinostomes reared from *Cercaria trivolvis* in the laboratory and assigned them as *E. revolutum*. He synonymized *E. cinetorchis* with *E. revolutum* because of their morphologic similarities, including the number of collar spines (n = 37) and dimensions of internal organs and eggs. In addition, he further synonymized 13 species, including *E. sudanense* Odhner, 1911, *E. miyagawai* Ishii, 1932, and *E. paraulum* Dietz, 1909, with *E. revolutum*.

However, the synonymy between *E. cinetorchis* and *E. revolutum* by Beaver (1937) is not justified due to various reasons, in particular, the unique feature of *E. cinetorchis* having testes that move to abnormal locations and even disappear from the body after the worms grow up to be adults. In addition, Kanev (1985) recognized *E. revolutum* of Beaver (1937) as *E. trivolvis* based on various differential points between the 2 species. Human infection with *E. cinetorchis* was first reported in Japan (Takahashi et al. 1930a, b; Kawahara and Yamamoto 1933), and then in South Korea (Seo et al. 1980; Ryang et al. 1986; Lee et al. 1988b; Son et al. 1994; Jung et al. 2014). Now, it is well known as a zoonotic echinostome species infecting humans, rodents, and poultries in Asian countries (Chai et al. 2009a, b; Maldonado and Lanfredi 2009; Anh et al. 2010; Toledo and Esteban 2016).

Adult flukes of *E. cinetorchis* are morphologically characterized by having 37 collar spines, which are arranged as 6-6-13-6-6, including 6 corner spines and 6 lateral ones on each side in single rows, and 13 dorsal spines in a double row (Seo et al. 1980). The adult flukes are 10.8–12.6 × 2.6–3.2 mm, and eggs (Fig. 2.5a) are 99–116 × 65–76 μm in size (Seo et al. 1980). *E. cinetorchis* is morphologically close to *E. revolutum*, but differs in the arrangement of collar spines (6 corner spines in *E. cinetorchis* vs 5 corner spines in *E. revolutum*) and the location of the testes (2 testes at normal tandem position in *E. revolutum* vs. abnormal locations and even disappearance of one or both testes in *E. cinetorchis*). The size (length) of cercarial body and tail of *E. cinetorchis* has been reported variable, either as small as 150–174 (av. 164) μm long and 102–121 (av. 109) μm wide and 225–255 (av. 237) μm long and 35–46 (av. 39) μm wide, respectively (Lee et al. 1990b) or as big as 300 μm and 550 μm, respectively (Takahashi 1927). The cercarial body and tail (length) of *E. revolutum* was reported to be 265–315 μm long and 128–154 μm wide and 414–430 μm long and 39–50 μm wide, respectively (Kanev 1994). The detailed morphology of *E. cinetorchis* cercariae, such as the number of penetration gland cells and the number of paraesophageal gland pores, remains to be determined. The metacercariae of *E. cinetorchis* (Fig. 2.5b) and *E. revolutum* are similar to each other in size

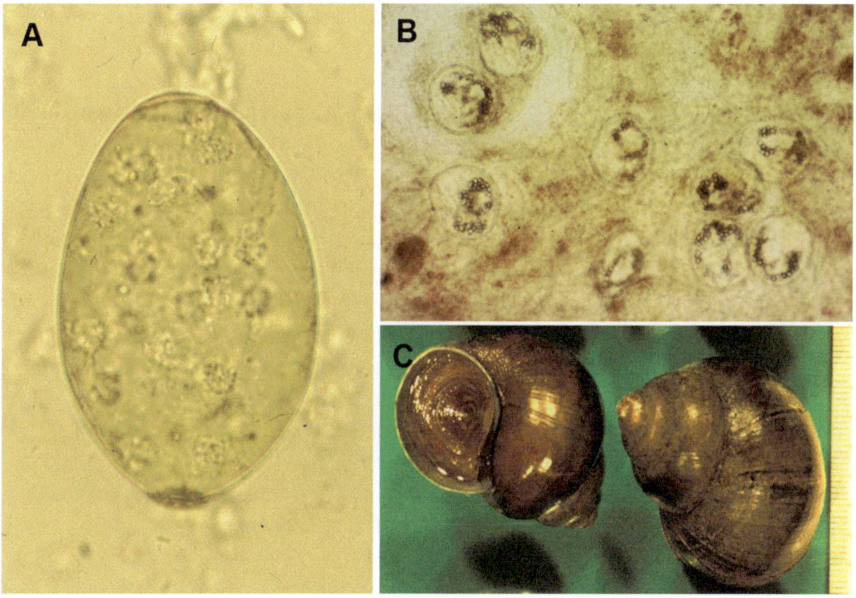

Fig. 2.5 *Echinostoma cinetorchis*. (**a**) Egg recovered in the feces of a naturally infected patient in South Korea. This egg is 99 × 63 μm in size and shows a prominent operculum, thin and transparent shell, and abopercular wrinkle or knob. Reproduced from the figure in Chai (2009) The Biology of Echinostomes (Fried B, Toledo R, eds). Springer, New York, USA with permission (**b**) A group of metacercariae encysted in the posterior abdominal wall of a loach, *Misgurnus anguillicaudatus*, a second intermediate host. ×100 (**c**) Large snails, *Cipangopaludina* sp., another second intermediate host

and shape, i.e., globular and 134–139 μm in diameter for the former (Lee et al. 1990b), and spherical and 132–152 μm in diameter for the latter (Kanev 1994).

The tegumental ultrastructures of juvenile and adult *E. cinetorchis* were studied using worms recovered from experimentally infected rats fed the metacercariae from the laboratory-infected snail host, *Hippeutis cantori* (Lee et al. 1992). The 3-day-old juvenile flukes were elongated and ventrally curved, with their ventral sucker located near the anterior 2/5 of the body (Lee et al. 1992). The lip of the oral and ventral suckers had 8 and 5 type II sensory papillae (aciliated·round swellings), respectively, and between the tegumental spines, a few type III papillae (pit-type sensory papillae) were observed (Lee et al. 1992). Tongue or spade-shaped spines were distributed anteriorly to the ventral sucker, whereas peg-like spines were distributed posteriorly (Lee et al. 1992). The 16-day-old adult flukes were leaf-like, and their oral and ventral suckers became closer; type I (ciliated knob-like swellings) sensory papillae were distributed on the tegument anterior to the ventral sucker, and type II and type III papillae were seen on the head crown and the lip of the oral and ventral suckers (Lee et al. 1992).

Life Cycle

E. cinetorchis has the life cycle stages of the egg, miracidium, sporocyst, redia, daughter redia, cercaria, metacercaria, and adult. The first eggs appear in the feces 11–12 days after infection in experimental dogs, rats, and mice (Yamashita 1964). The eggs are unembryonated, yellowish-brown, and equipped with a small operculum and abopercular wrinkles or thickening (Seo et al. 1980; Chai and Lee 2002). At a constant temperature of 28 °C, eggs kept in water yielded fully-matured miracidia at 24 days; the hatched miracidia were equipped with numerous cilia and actively moved in water (Lee et al. 1990b). When they were in contact with the snail, *Hippeutis cantori*, they penetrated into the mantle or tentacle of the snail and developed into sporocysts, rediae, daughter rediae, and finally cercariae (Lee et al. 1990b). At day 66 following exposure to the snail, larval stages, including rediae (mother rediae), daughter rediae (containing cercariae), cercariae, and metacercariae were detected from the infected snails (Lee et al. 1990b). The daughter rediae are elongated and sac-shaped, and have a muscular pharynx, intestinal caecum (filled with brownish material), and 7–14 cercariae; the cercariae are echinostome-type and have a snake head-shaped body and a rod-like tail; the body is equipped with a head collar (collar spines are hard to identify), 2 suckers, a pharynx, 2 caeca, excretory granules, and a germ cell primordium (Lee et al. 1990b). The numbers of penetration gland cells and paraesophageal gland cell outlets remain to be determined.

The snail host (first intermediate host) so far confirmed is *Hippeutis cantori* (Lee et al. 1990b), *Segmentina hemisphaerula* (syn. *S. mica*) (Takahashi 1927; Chung et al. 2001a), *Austropeplea ollula* (syn. *Lymnaea ollula*), and possibly *Fossaria truncatula* (syn. *Lymnaea truncatula*) (Chung et al. 2001b). The second host includes a variety of animal species ranging from snails to fish, and amphibia (Yamashita 1964; Rim 1982; Chai et al. 2009b). The snail species, *Hippeutis cantori, Semisulcospira hemisphaerula, Austropeplea ollula* (syn. *Lymnaea ollula*), and

Fossaria truncatula (syn. *Lymnaea truncatula*) were experimentally proven to be the first as well as the second intermediate hosts (Lee et al. 1990b; Chung et al. 2001a, b). Other freshwater snails, including *Radix auricularia coreana, Physa acuta, Cipangopaludina chinensis malleata*, *Cipangopaludina* sp. (Fig. 2.5c), *Corbicula fluminea*, *Pisidium coreanum,* and potentially *Biomphalaria glabrata* have also been proved to be or suggested to be the second intermediate hosts (Ahn et al. 1989; Chung and Jung 1999; Chung et al. 2001c, d; Park et al. 2006a). In addition, tadpoles of *Rana nigromaculata, Rana rugosa, Rana japonica, Rana catesbiana* (Ando and Tsuyuki 1923; Hirazawa 1929), and freshwater fish, especially the loach *Misgurnus anguillicaudatus* (Saito and Tani 1982; Seo et al. 1984), have proven to be second intermediate hosts. Encystment of cercariae in vitro and development into metacercariae were possible using RPMI 1640 medium plus 10% fetal bovince serum (Park et al. 2006b).

The natural definitive hosts include humans (Chai et al. 2009b), rats (Ando and Ozaki 1923; Seo et al. 1964, 1981), mice (Chai et al. 2009b; Sohn et al. 2014), dogs (Sugimoto 1933; Cho et al. 1981), chickens, and ducks (Kurisu 1932; Anh et al. 2010). Experimental infection has been successful in rats and mice (Makino et al. 1982; Lee et al. 1988a, 1990b; Chung and Jung 1999). Adult worms live in the posterior part of the small intestine of definitive hosts; egg production begins about 10 days after infection in experimental rats; 16-day worms were all fully gravid (Seo et al. 1984). Adult worms live longer than 4 weeks in experimental mice, and some of the worms can live longer than 12 weeks in experimental rats (Seo et al. 1984; Lee et al. 1988a).

Epidemiology and Geographical Distribution

The principal mode of infection in mammals, including humans, and birds is consumption of raw or undercooked molluscan species, amphibia, or fish (Yamashita 1964; Chai 2009). The geographical distribution is confined to Asian countries, including Japan, Taiwan, China, South Korea, Indonesia, and Vietnam (Table 2.3) (Yu and Mott 1994; Chai 2009; Anh et al. 2010; Hung et al. 2013). Beaver et al. (1984) mentioned that human infections with *E. cinetorchis* were incidentally found at necropsies in Indonesia; however, no proper literature background is available now.

China Infections in field rats (Fujian Province), house rats (Jilin Province), and dogs (Sichuan Province) were reported (Chen et al. 1985).

Indonesia It has been mentioned that *E. cinetorchis* is distributed in Indonesia (Hung et al. 2013).

Japan Several human infections were discovered in Kumamoto and Aichi Prefectures and Kobe City (Takahashi et al. 1930a, b; Kawahara and Yamamoto 1933; Moriyama 1952; Hyodo and Matsuyama 1958, under the name *E. revolutum*). Natural infections in house rats were reported in Hiroshima, Gifu, Shiga, Kagoshima, and Saga Prefectures, and Nagoya and Kobe City (Ando and Ozaki 1923; Ando and Tsuyuki 1923; Yamashita 1964). The prevalence ranged from 0.67% to 1.2% among house rats in these areas (Yamashita 1964). Infection in domestic fowls were reported in Osaka City and Hiroshima and Okayama Prefectures (Kurisu 1932). In raccoon dogs, 3 (15%) of 20 examined in Aomori and Akita Prefecture were found to be infected with 1–28 specimens of *E. cinetorchis* (Sato et al. 1999). *Segmentina nitidella* was identified to be the first intermediate host (Takahashi 1927). The same snail species (*S egmentina nitidella*) and *Gyraulus hiemantium, Viviparus malleatus, Lymnaea japonica, Cipangopaludina japonica* snails, fish (loach, *Misgurnus* sp.), giant salamanders, frogs, and tadpoles were reported to be the second intermediate hosts harbouring the metacercariae (Ito 1964; Yamashita 1964; Komiya 1965; Okahashi 1966; Makino et al. 1982; Saito and Tani 1982).

South Korea A human case of *E. cinetorchis* infection was found in a 60-year-old woman in Gyeonggi-do (Province) from whom 8 adult flukes were recovered (Seo et al. 1980). It was not able to determine the source of infection in this case. Thereafter, total 5 human cases have been described (Ryang et al. 1986; Lee et al. 1988b; Son et al. 1994; Jung et al. 2014). The source of infection in the second case was presumed to be the large snail (*Cipangopaludina* sp.) (Ryang et al. 1986) and that of the last human case was raw frogs (Jung et al. 2014). A single adult specimen was recovered from a house rat in Gyeonggi-do (Seo et al. 1964), and subsequently total 45 specimens were obtained from 13 infected rats from Gyeonggi-do and Chungcheongbuk-do (Seo et al. 1981). Later, 5 (0.4%) out of 1366 and 1 (0.8%) out of 133 field mice (*Apodemus agrarius*) caught from Gyeonggi-do and Gyeongsangnam-do were found infected with *E. cinetorchis*, respectively (Chai et al. 2009a; Sohn et al. 2014). In Ejungbu City, Gyeonggi-do, infection in 2 (2.8%) of 72 stray dogs was reported (Cho et al. 1981). Cercariae were shed from *Hippeutis* sp. snails experimentally infected with miracidia cultivated in the laboratory (Ahn et al. 1989). Metacercariae were first detected in loaches (*M. anguillicaudatus*) caught from Jeollanam-do and Gyeongsangnam-do (Seo et al. 1984). Thereafter, the metacercariae of *E. cinetorchis* have been found in *Hippeutis cantori* snails (Lee et al. 1988a), *Cipangopaludina chinensis malleata* (Chung and Jung 1999), *Segmentina hemisphaerula* (Chung et al. 2001a), and *Austropeplea ollula* (Chung et al. 2001b). *Corbicula fluminea* (Chung et al. 2001c), *Biomphalaria glabrata* (Chung et al. 2001d), and *Pisidium coreanum* (Park et al. 2006a) were confirmed experimentally to be potential second intermediate hosts.

Taiwan After a naturally infected dog was reported in Taipei (Sugimoto 1933), house rats (Fischthal and Kuntz 1975) and house mice (Fischthal and Kuntz 1981) were found to be natural definitive hosts.

Vietnam Chickens and ducks in Nghia Lac (2.0% and 4.0%, respectively) and Nghia Phu communes (6.0% and 20.0%, respectively) were found to be infected with *E. cinetorchis* (Anh et al. 2010).

2.2.3 Echinostoma lindoense

2.2.3.1 *Echinostoma lindoense* Sandground and Bonne, 1940

Taxonomy and Morphology

E. lindoense (Fig. 2.6a) was first described from human population in the Lake Lindoe region of Central Celebes, Indonesia (Sandground and Bonne 1940). The prevalence was about 50% (24–96%) among 176 inhabitants of 3 villages (Sandground and Bonne 1940). Later, however, the introduction of the fish *Tilapia* into this lake led to almost extinction of *Corbicula* mussels, the major source of human infection, and then human infections vanished (Cross 1984; Yu and Mott 1994). This echinostome was also discovered in humans in Jakarta, Indonesia and then animals, including rats in Malaysia, Thailand, and the Philippines (Lie 1964; Lie et al. 1973; Eduardo and Lee 2006). Echinostomes similar in their structure and biology to *E. lindoense* were also found in Brazil (Lie 1968) and European countries, including Bulgaria, Poland, Czecho Republic,

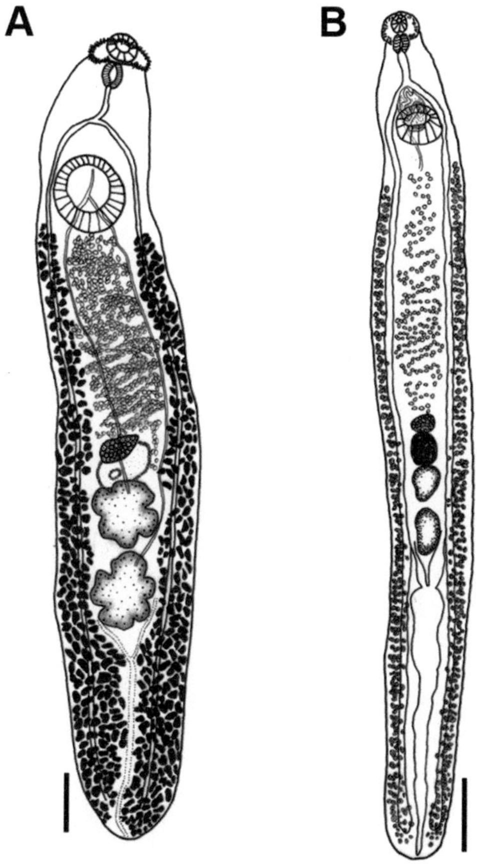

Fig. 2.6 Line drawings of *Echinostoma lindoense* (**a**) and *Echinostoma paraensei* (**b**) adult flukes. Scale bar = 1 mm (**a**) Redrawn from the figure in Sandground and Bonne (1940) Am J Trop Med 20:511–536 (**b**) Redrawn from the figure in Lie and Basch (1967) J Parasitol 53:1192–1199

Slovak Republic, Germany, Austria, England, and Russia (Vasilev et al. 1982; Lie and Kanev 1983). In the meantime, *Echinostoma barbosi,* a 37-collar spined echinostome morphologically similar to *E. lindoense*, was described as a new species in Brazil (Lie and Basch 1966).

The major differential points of *E. lindoense* from the pre-existing type species, *E. revolutum,* were in the morphology of the larval stages (particularly in cercariae); *E. lindoense* has 2 dorsal, 2 ventral, and 2 small ventrolateral tail fin folds, whereas *E. revolutum* has only one small dorsal fin fold near the tip of the cercarial tail (Lie and Kanev 1983). It is also of note that the testes of *E. lindoense* are deeply indented (Asian strain) or superficially lobed (Brazilian strain; the name of this echinostome needs further studies), but those of *E. revolutum* are smooth or only slightly lobated (Lie 1968; Kanev 1994). *E. lindoense* has shorter and wider collar spines compared to *E. revolutum* which has longer and slender collar spines (Bonne et al. 1953).

As the larval and adult stages of *E. lindoense* from Asia were morphologically and biologically almost similar to those of *E. echinatum* originating from Germany, *E. lindoense* was once synonymized with *E. echinatum* by Kanev and coworkers (Kanev 1985, 1994; Kanev et al. 1987, 1995a, b). Also, *E. barbosai, E. miyagawai*, and *E. revolutum* of Nasincova were synonymized with *E. echinatum* (Kanev 1994). The synonymy of *E. lindoense* with *E. echinatum* was accepted by Huffman and Fried (1990), Haseeb and Eveland (2000), Chai et al. (2009b), Toledo et al. (2014a, b), and Toledo and Esteban (2016). However, Kostadinova and Gibson (2000) and Kostadinova et al. (2000a, b) questioned about the taxonomic validity of *E. echinatum*, because of its many uncertain points, for example, a wide range (more than 20) of the number of paraesophageal gland-cell outlets in cercariae. It was also pointed out that *E. echinatum* has not been justified in a taxonomic publication. The questionable status of *E. echinatum* (i.e., *species inquirenda*) was agreed in subsequent publications, including Georgieva et al. (2013, 2014) and Fáltynková et al. (2015). Therefore, in this review book, *E. lindoense* is treated as a valid species.

Adult flukes of *E. lindoense* are morphologically characterized by having 37 collar spines, which are arranged as 5-7-13-7-5, including 5 corner spines and 7 lateral ones on each side in single rows, and 13 dorsal spines in alternative rows (Sandground and Bonne 1940). The adult flukes are 13.0–15.0 × 2.5–3.0 mm, and eggs are 92–124 × 65–76 μm in size (Sandground and Bonne 1940). The cercarial body and tail of *E. lindoense* measured 332–474 μm by 130–185 μm and 427–490 μm by 40–60 μm, respectively (Lie 1968). The penetration gland cells are 4–5 pairs, and the exact number of paraesophageal gland pores is unknown. The metacercariae of *E. lindoense* are globular and 120–130 μm in diameter (Sandground and Bonne 1940). The tegumental papillae on 6 species of echinostome cercariae were studied, and the distribution and numerical patterns of papillae were similar in 2 closely related species, for example, those having the same collar spine numbers, *E. lindoense* and *E. revolutum* (under the name *E. audyi*) (Lie 1966).

Life Cycle

E. lindoense has the life cycle stages of eggs, miracidia, sporocysts, rediae, cercariae, metacercariae, and adults (Lie 1964). The eggs are unembryonated, yellowish-brown, and equipped with a small operculum and abopercular wrinkles or thickening. Miracidia develop into sporocysts, rediae (at least 3 generations), and then cercariae in freshwater snails *Anisus sarasinorum* (= *Gyraulus sarasinorum*) or *Anisus convexiusculus* (= *Gyraulus convexiusculus*) (Bonne et al. 1953; Lie 1964, 1968). Miracidia penetrate the snail only after accidental touching of the snail, and cercariae are usually shed in small numbers and not every day (Lie 1964). The second intermediate hosts are several species of snails or mussels, including *Gyraulus convexiusculus, Lymnaea rubiginosa, Indoplanorbis exustus, Viviparus rudipelis, Corbicula lindoensis, Corbicula subplanta, Idiophoma javanica, Biomphalaria glabrata,* and tadpoles of *Rhacophorus leucomystax* (Bonne et al. 1953; Lie 1964; Lie and Heyneman 1975; Carney et al. 1980). The natural definitive hosts include domestic ducks and geese (Lie 1964). Mice, rats, pigeons, ducklings, and goslings were susceptible experimental hosts (Sandground and Bonne 1940; Bonne et al. 1953; Lie 1964). Natural human infections were discovered in the Lake Lindoe region of Central Celebes and Jakarta, Indonesia (Sandground and Bonne 1940; Lie 1964). Humans were also experimentally infected with this fluke with these worms which were capable of persisting in the intestine for at least 10 months (Sandground and Bonne 1940).

Epidemiology and Geographical Distribution

Corbicula lindoensis is an important source of human infection with *E. lindoense* in Lake Lindoe villages, Indonesia (Bonne et al. 1953). Steaming or boiling of these mussels before eating in these areas is incompletely done in a very primitive way (Bonne et al. 1953). Malaysia, the Philippines, and Thailand were also reported to have *E. lindoense* life cycle (Lie 1964; Lie et al. 1973; Eduardo and Lee 2006) (Table 2.3). Although Lie (1968) and Lie and Kanev (1983) reported that echinostomes similar in structure and biology to *E. lindoense* were also found in Brazil and European countries, including Bulgaria, Poland, Czecho Republic, Slovak Republic, Germany, Austria, England, and Russia, in this chapter, these countries were not included among the list of countries where *E. lindoense* is distributed.

Indonesia In the Lake Lindu Valley of central Sulawesi, surveys of stool specimens from 1937 to 1956 demonstrated a consistently high prevalence of *E. lindoense* infection (Carney et al. 1980). The prevalence ranged 84–96% in Anca village, 29–62% in Tomado village, and 24–45% in Langko village around the lake; the average prevalence was 42.6% (Carney et al. 1980; Graczyk and Fried 1998). However, the prevalence in these villages became 0% in 2 successive surveys (1971 and 1972); thus, human *E. lindoense* infection in these areas were considered eliminated (Carney et al. 1980). This elimination of human *E. lindoense* infection was considered to be greatly due to introduction of *Tilapia* fish to the lake which led to almost extinction of *Corbicula* mussels, the major source of human infection (Graczyk and Fried 1998). Thereafter, around 1% prevalence of human echinostome (species undetermined) infections was reported in Indonesia (Carney 1991). In West Kalimantan, Borneo, echinostome eggs (species undetermined) were observed in fecal examinations (Cross et al. 1976). The transmission foci in Lindu Valley remained at moors and marshes around the lake where a variety of freshwater mollusks thrive and support the larval stages of this echinostome; naturally infected mollusks and mammals were found in accessible areas along the north, west, and south coastal plains of the Lindu Valley (Carney et al. 1980). However, it is of note that echinostomiasis was regarded a reemerging disease as the popularity of exotic foods served in Korean and Japanese restaurants spread throughout Indonesian cities (Kusharyono and Sukartinah 1991).

Malaysia This echinostome was found in the Malaysian snails *Gyraulus convexiusculus* and domestic ducks and possibly geese in Kuala Lumpur area (Lie 1964). In addition, *Gyraulus convexiusculus* snails harbouring the larval stages were air-shipped from Kuala Lumpur to San Francisco and used for a comparative study with a similar strain from Brazil (Lie 1968).

The Philippines The presence of *E. lindoense* was reported from field rats (*Rattus mindanensis mindanensis*) caught from Bay, Laguna in Luzon (Eduardo and Lee 2006).

Thailand It was reported that *E. lindoense* is a common parasite in Thailand (Lie et al. 1973).

2.2.4 Echinostoma paraensei

2.2.4.1 *Echinostoma paraensei* Lie and Basch, 1967

Taxonomy and Morphology

This species (Fig. 2.6b) was first described from experimental hamsters, mice, and rats fed the metacercariae from naturally infected *Biomphalaria* snails in Belo Horizonte (BH), Minas Gerais State, Brazil (Lie and Basch 1967). This BH strain of *E. paraensei* has been kept in the laboratory using hamsters and *Biomphalaria* snails in Loker laboratory, University of New Mexico, USA (Maldonado et al. 2001a). Later, this fluke was detected from naturally infected water rats, *Nectomys squamipes*, and experimental mice, *Mus musculus*, in Brazil (Maldonado et al. 2001a, b, c). *E. paraensei* was also discovered in Australia analyzing mitochondrial ND1 gene sequences (Morgan and Blair 1998b). So far, only mammals have been proved to be the definitive host of this fluke (Kostadinova and Gibson 2000; Maldonado et al. 2001a, b, c). It is of note that recently eggs of *E. paraensei* (or less probably *E. luisreyi*) were detected in the coprolite of a mummified human body in Brazil using molecular techniques, suggesting that echinostomiasis due to *E. paraensei* (or *E. luisreyi*) may be a zoonotic disease in Brazil (Leles et al. 2014). However, there is no contemporary evidence of human infections in enzootic areas of this fluke.

Kanev (1985) considered *E. paraensei* a synonym of *E. caproni* based on the fact that this echinostome also uses species of *Biomphalaria* as the first intermediate host. Christensen et al. (1990) also synonymized *E. paraensei* with *E. caproni*. Huffman and Fried (1990) followed this synonymy. However, Sloss et al. (1995) showed distinct isoenzyme systems between *E. paraensei* and *E. caproni* and denied this synonymy. In addition, Morgan and Blair (1995) analyzed rDNA ITS sequences of *Echinostoma* spp. flukes and concluded that *E. paraensei* and *E. trivolvis* are very close relatives and both are distant from *E. caproni*. Petrie et al. (1996) observed significantly different banding patterns of *E. paraensei* and *E. caproni* in random amplification of polymorphic DNA (RAPD) analysis. Host-parasite relationships, including susceptibility of mice and hamsters to infection with *E. paraensei* and *E. caproni*, and behavior of their miracidia in water were also remarkably different by species of echinostomes (Meece and Nollen 1996). The metacercariae of *E. paraensei* and *E. caproni* showed specific differences in terms of excystation rate in media and also morphological features (Fried and Reddy 1997). Consequently, Fried and Huffman (1996) and Toledo et al. (2009) accepted *E. paraensei* as a distinct species.

Adult flukes of *E. paraensei* are morphologically close to *E. revolutum, E. lindoense,* and *E. barbosai* (Lie and Basch 1967). *E. paraensei* has 37 collar spines, which are arranged as 5-7-13-7-5 or 5-6-15-6-5, including 5 corner spines and 6 or 7 lateral ones on each side in single rows, and 13 or 15 dorsal spines in 2 alternating rows (Lie and Basch 1967). The most specific character of this fluke is 5–11 smaller-sized dorsalmost collar spines compared to other collar spines (Lie and Basch 1967). The adult flukes are 7.5–16.0 × 0.79–1.95 mm, and eggs are 104–122 × 74–86 μm in size (Lie and Basch 1967). The cercarial body and tail measured 228–275 μm by 117–136 μm and 412–490 μm by 41–47 μm, respectively (Lie and Basch 1967). The penetration gland cells have 6–8 duct openings, but paraesophageal gland cells are absent (Lie and Basch 1967). The metacercariae of *E. paraensei* are spherical and 132–148 μm in diameter (Lie and Basch 1967).

The surface ultrastructures of larval and adult flukes of *E. paraensei* were reported by various workers using scanning electron microscopy (Maldonado et al. 2001a; Pinheiro et al. 2004a, b). The adult flukes were characterized by having smaller-sized dorsal collar spines compared to lateral and corner spines, which was a differential feature from other echinostome species (Maldonado et al. 2001a). The tegumental spines were scale-like but the region between the genital pore and the acetabulum lacks the tegumental spines (Maldonado et al. 2001a). A folded protuberance with a pore was seen just posterior to the genital pore, and numerous randomly distributed small, domed, ciliated type I sensory papillae were seen on the tegument of the acetabulum (Maldonado et al. 2001a). The miracidial body was covered by cilia except at the terebratorium region (anteriormost introverted region), and the terebratorium was retractable, presenting folds and a corrugated surface with profiles of cytoplasmic expansions, forming network of anastomosing folds (Pinheiro et al. 2004a). Rediae typically had an oral aperture, pharynx, digestive cecum, collar region, and birth papilla; uniciliated papillae were observed in the mouth region, and numerous tegumental folds but not microvilli were seen on the surface of the rediae (Pinheiro et al. 2004b). Cercariae have an elongated body with muscular striations all over the surface; the tail is long with a thicker tip that narrows at the end, with 2 dorsal, 2 ventral, and 2 lateral fin-folds (Matos et al. 2018).

Life Cycle

The freshwater snails *Biomphalaria glabrata, Physa rivalis* (Brazil), and *Glyptophysa* sp. (Australia), serve as the natural first intermediate host (Lie and Basch 1967; Morgan and Blair 1998b). *Biomphalaria glabrata, Physa marmorata,* and *Lymnaea columella* were also experimentally infected with the miracidia (Maldonado et al. 2001b). Eggs appear in stools of hamsters, rats, and mice 11–16 days after infection; they experimentally hatch 11 days after incubation in distilled water and hatching is stimulated with light (Lie and Basch 1967). Miracidia swim in water for several hours being positively phototactic, and then enter the snail through its exposed parts while shedding the epidermal plates; complete penetration takes about half an hour (Lie and Basch 1967). Miracidia develop into sporocysts (elongated sac-like) within the ventricle cavity of the snail, sometimes also in the aorta or tissue surrounding the pulmonary cavity (Lie and Basch 1967). Mother rediae, with large or small pharynx, are produced 6 or more days after exposure with miracidia; they migrate to various organs of the snail, i.e., in the blood sinus along the intestine where they pass through the liver and to ovotestis or in the venous sinuses around the pulmonary cavity; they produce daughter rediae (Lie and Basch 1967; Sapp et al. 1998). A characteristic precocious mother redia (PMR) is produced in a sporocyst attached to the inner surface of the host's ventricle and develops before other mother rediae; PMR is released as early as 6 days post-exposure (Sapp et al. 1998). After the PMR is released, the remaining redial embryos begin to develop into mother rediae; daughter rediae develop within the body of PMR (Sapp et al. 1998). Cercariae are released 25 days after exposure; they are negatively phototactic, swim in water with body curled ventrally, and live for 6 h in the absence of a second intermediate host (Lie and Basch 1967). The same snail host *Biomphalaria glabrata, Biomphalaria straminea*, and other species of freshwater snails can serve as the second intermediate host; the metacercarial cysts are formed in the pericardial sac of these snails or the posterior part of the kidney (Lie and Basch 1967). In vitro metacercarial cyst formation was observed (Stein and Basch 1977).

The natural definitive host is water rats *Nectomys squamipes* (Maldonado et al. 2001a, b, c). Experimental hosts included mice, rats, and hamsters; in these animals worms survived more than 5 months but heavy infection killed these animals (Lie and Basch 1967).

Epidemiology and Geographical Distribution

There has been no evidence of contemporary human infection with this echinostome; thus, no epidemiological studies have been performed on human infections. Only the eggs of *E. paraensei* (or less probably *E. luisreyi*) were detected in the coprolite of a mummified human body in Brazil (Leles et al. 2014); thus, a zoonotic nature of this echinostome is suggested. The source of infection in the mummy is uncertain. The geographical distribution of *E. paraensei* has been reported only in Brazil and Australia (Table 2.3) (Lie and Basch 1967; Morgan and Blair 1998b).

Australia An echinostome isolate molecularly compatible to *E. paraensei* was obtained from a permanent pond in Townsville in North Queensland (Morgan and Blair 1998b). The host was *Glyptophysa* sp. snails from which echinostome cercariae (PCerc-1, closely allied to *E. paraensei* from Brazil) were recovered (Morgan and Blair 1998b).

Brazil Cercariae of *E. paraensei* were first found in *Biomphalaria glabrata* snails from Belo Horizonte (BH isolate), Caratinga, and Bambuli (all in the State of Minas Gerais) (Lie and Basch 1967). Later, a new geographical isolate (RJ isolate) was obtained from naturally infected semi-aquatic rats *Nectomys squamipes* in Sumidouro, Rio de Janeiro State (Maldonado et al. 2001a). It is interesting to note that coprolites from a mummified human body dated 560 ± 40 before present found in Peruaçu Valley, Minas Gerais revealed echinostome eggs which were molecularly close to *E. paraensei* (Leles et al. 2014). Echinostome eggs suggestive of *E. paraensei* (by molecular analysis) were also found from the felid coprolites from Pernambuco State, Brazil (Sianto et al. 2016).

2.2.5 Echinostoma ilocanum

2.2.5.1 *Echinostoma ilocanum* (Garrison, 1908) Odhner, 1911

[syn. *Euparyphium ilocanum* Tubangui, 1931]

Taxonomy and Morphology
The eggs of *E. ilocanum* were first discovered in the feces of 5 prisoners in Manila, the Philippines in 1907 (Garrison 1908). One of the 5 infected cases was treated with male-fern, and 21 adult worms were recovered in the feces; the adult worm (Fig. 2.7) was described as *Fascioletta ilocana* (Garrison 1908; Cross and Basaca-Sevilla 1986). Garrison sent 4 worms to Odhner who noted several morphologic features indicating that the worms belong to the genus *Echinostoma* (Odhner 1911). Tubangui (1931) redescribed the species based on worms recovered from rats and placed it in the genus *Euparyphium*. Bashkirova (1947), Bonne et al. (1953), and Skrjabin and Bashikirova (1956) followed this placement. However, Yamaguti (1958) did not agree to this and assigned it in *Echinostoma*, which has thereafter been agreed by many succeeding workers (Lie and Nasemary 1973; Radomyos et al. 1982; Cross and Basaca-Sevilla 1986; Kostadinova and Gibson 2002; Sohn et al. 2011b). Consequently, the name *Echinostoma ilocanum* has been settled. The presence of this echinostome species has been reported from Asian countries.

The characteristic morphology of *E. ilocanum* includes the presence of 51 (49–60) collar spines, including 5 angle spines (3 oral and 2 aboral) and 12–14 lateral spines on each side and 13–15 dorsal spines, and globular or oblong and rarely deeply lobed testes (Bonne et al. 1953; Lie and Nasemary 1973; Rim 1982; Radomyos et al. 1982; Chai et al. 2018). The adult flukes are 5.46–9.20 × 0.62–

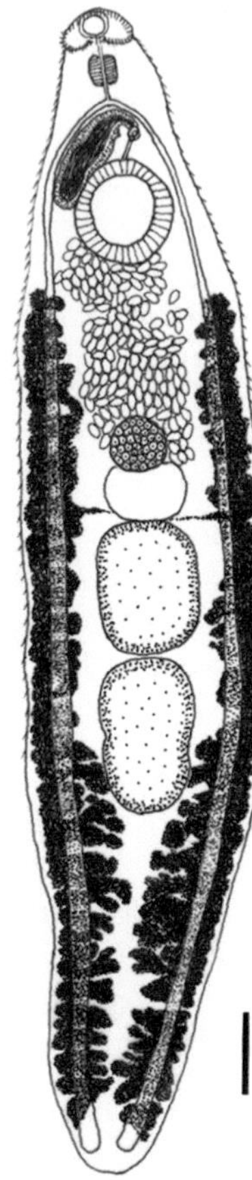

Fig. 2.7 Line drawing of an adult fluke of *Echinostoma ilocanum* (original figure). Scale bar = 0.5 mm

1.56 mm in size and elongate with maximum width at uterine region (Lie and Nasemary 1973). The uterine and fecal eggs are 89–118 μm long and 52–66 μm wide (Lie and Nasemary 1973; Radomyos et al. 1982; Sohn et al. 2011b). The cercariae are long-tailed, and 224–275 μm long and 71–86 μm wide, with a long tail of 377–387 μm long and 40–51 μm wide (Lie and Nasemary 1973). The metacercarial cysts are spherical, and 93–110 μm in diameter and occurs in the pericardial sac and posterior part of kidney of the snails and in the kidneys of tadpoles (Lie and Nasemary 1973).

Adult flukes tend to be tapering at both ends, and in particular, somewhat pointed toward the posterior end. Their anterior two-thirds dorsally and anterior three-fourth ventrally and laterally are covered with scale-like spines (Lie and Nasemary 1973). The location of the ovary is mostly median near the equatorial level of the body and rarely slightly submedian. Vitellaria extend from the level of the middle portion of the uterine tubule down to the posterior end of the body. A characteristic feature of *E. ilocanum* is the variability of the number of collar spines on the oral sucker, 49–55 (Lie and Nasemary 1973) or even 50–60 (Bonne et al. 1953). However, the most common number has been 49–51 (Rim 1982; Radomyos et al. 1982; Cross and Basaca-Sevilla 1986; Sohn et al. 2011b; Chai et al. 2018). Another characteristic morphological feature of *E. ilocanum* is the shape of 2 testes, most frequently globular or oblong, but sometimes one or both testes show shallow or moderate indentations near their equator portion (Bonne et al. 1953; Lie and Nasemary 1973). In rare instances, deep indentations are observed on one or both testes (Radomyos et al. 1982; Grover et al. 1998). The tegumental ultrastructure of *E. ilocanum* has never been studied using a scanning electron microscope.

Life Cycle

The life history of *E. ilocanum* was experimentally completed in Kuala Lumpur, Malaysia (Lie and Nasemary 1973). The eggs were obtained from experimental rats infected with metacercariae encysted in various freshwater snails, including *Lymnaea rubiginosa* (Lie and Nasemary 1973). The first intermediate hosts are *Gyraulus convexiusculus, Gyraulus prashadi,* or *Hippeutis* snails (Lie and Nasemary 1973; Eduardo 1991; Yu and Mott, 1994). Eggs appear in the feces of experimental rats 14 days after the infection, and eggs hatch in 9 days after keeping in distilled water (Lie and Nasemary 1973). The body of miracidia is covered with 4 rows of ciliated epidermal plates; they penetrate into the snail host in the mantle edge and along the edges of the foot, shedding the epidermal cells during penetration; they rarely also penetrate other exposed parts, such as the antennae and head region (Lie and Nasemary 1973). Sporocysts develop in the ventricular cavity of the heart of the snail; they develop into contractile, elongated sacs, containing 1–2 gray rediae (Lie and Nasemary 1973). Rediae are released from sporocysts 8–9 days after exposure, migrate to hemolymph space surrounding the viscera, and mature 18–22 days after exposure, producing daughter rediae (Lie and Nasemary 1973). From day 25–29 post-exposure all or almost all rediae produce cercariae; each redia contains 13 cercariae, and the total number of rediae in each snail ranges 30–60 (Lie and Nasemary 1973). Cercariae are covered with scale-like spines and sensory papillae, having genital primordia (2 masses of cells, one at anterior margin of acetabulum, and the other between acetabulum and base of tail); tail without fins (Lie and Nasemary 1973). Metacercarial cysts are spherical and encyst in the pericardial sac and posterior part of the kidney of *Gyraulus convexiusculus* and *Lymnaea rubiginosa,* and in the kidney of tadpoles (Lie and Nasemary 1973). The sources of human infections are rather large snails *Pila conica, Pila luzonica* (the Philippines), and *Viviparus javanicus* (Java) (Beaver et al. 1984; Cross and Basaca-Sevilla 1986). Rats (*Rattus norvegicus* and *Rattus argentiventer*), dogs, and probably cats also are reservoir hosts (Lie and Nasemary 1973; Cross and Basaca-Sevilla 1986). Experimental hosts included white rats, mice, and hamsters (Lie and Nasemary 1973; Cross and Basaca-Sevilla 1986).

Epidemiology and Geographical Distribution

Pila luzonica snails are an important source of human infection with *E. ilocanum* in the Philippines; there are groups such as the Ilocanos who eat *Pila luzonica* uncooked (Cross and Basaca-Sevilla 1986). In Ilocos areas, the snail meat is seasoned with vinegars, chili, lemon, or calamansi; some people cut the snails and salt or season them with a fermented shrimp sauce called "bagoong" (Cross and Basaca-Sevilla 1986). Infections in males often occur while fishing or farming, and snails from the fields and streams are eaten straightly from the shell (Cross and Basaca-Sevilla 1986). The presence of this echinostome species has been reported from the Philippines (Eduardo 1991), Indonesia (Celebes and Java) (Bonne et al. 1953), Malaysia (Lie and Nasemary 1973), China (Yu and Mott 1994), Thailand (Radomyos et al. 1982), India (Grover et al. 1998), Cambodia (Sohn et al. 2011b), and Lao PDR (Chai et al. 2018) (Table 2.4). Human infections were identified in the Philippines, Indonesia, Thailand, China, Cambodia, and Lao PDR (Garrison 1908; Bonne et al. 1953; Radomyos et al. 1982; Eduardo 1991; Yu and Mott 1994; Sohn et al. 2011b; Chai et al. 2018).

Cambodia Nine (0.7%) of 1287 residents in 7 villages of Oddar Meanchey Province were positive for echinostome eggs; 2 of the 9 cases were treated with praziquantel and purged, and total 14 adult flukes of *E. ilocanum* were recovered (Sohn et al. 2011b).

China Dogs mostly from Canton were found infected with various trematode species, including *E. ilocanum* (Chen 1934). Later, the prevalence among dogs in Canton (Guangdong Province) was reported to be 13.5% (Yu and Mott 1994). Human infections were found in Yunnan Province in 1964 (Yu and Mott 1994; Li et al. 2010). Studies on the life cycle of this echinostome have not been published.

India An 8-year-old girl (a migrant from a village in Bihar) complaining of vomiting, diarrhea, and swelling of the feet for 7 days was confirmed to be infected with *E. ilocanum*; the adult worm was found among the vomitus, and eggs were found in stool specimens (Grover et al. 1998). She recalled having eaten roasted snails and fish (Grover et al. 1998).

Indonesia Occurrence of human infections with *E. ilocanum* was first mentioned by Sandground (1938) who discovered 22 egg-positive patients among lunatics at the Lengteng Agoeng Rural Colony for the insane (outside Batavia); adult flukes were recovered from 11 of the 22 patients after treatment with tetrachlorethylene (Sandground 1938). Soon after this, another human case was detected in a native of Batam in West Java (Sandground 1939). Later, human infections were also found at autopsies of patients from a lunatic asylum living together in a colony near Batavia; more than 250 specimens were collected in a single patient (Bonne et al. 1953). The first intermediate host was confirmed to be *Gyraulus convexisculus*, and the second hosts (natural and experimental) were *Lymnaea rubiginosa brevis, Viviparus javanicus,* and *Pila conica* (Sandground 1938). The common field rat (*Rattus ratus brevicaudatus*) was an important reservoir host (Sandground 1938).

Lao PDR Adult specimens, 658 in total number, were recovered from 2 riparian people residing along the Mekong River in Savannakhet Province, Lao PDR after treatment with praziquantel and purging (Chai et al. 2018). The source of human infections is unknown.

Table 2.4 Geographical distribution of zoonotic echinostomes other than 37-collar spined *Echinostoma* spp.

Species & Nominator	Country/Region
Acanthoparyphium tyosenense Yamaguti, 1939	Japan, South Korea
Artyfechinostomum malayanum (Leiper, 1911) Mendheim, 1943	China, India, Indonesia, Lao PDR, Malaysia, The Philippines, Singapore, Thailand
Artyfechinostomum oraoni Bandyopadhyay, Manna and Nandy, 1989	India
Artyfechinostomum sufrartyfex Lane, 1915	India, Vietnam (?)
Echinoparyphium recurvatum (von Linstow, 1873) Lühe, 1909	Bangladesh, Bulgaria, Canada, China, Croatia, Czech Rep., Egypt, England, India, Indonesia, Japan, South Korea, Mexico, The Philippines, New Zealand, Poland, Russia, Spain, Taiwan, Thailand, USA
Echinostoma angustitestis Wang, 1977	China
Echinostoma aegyptiacum Khalil and Abaza, 1924	China, Egypt, Japan, Taiwan, Turkey, Vietnam
Echinostoma ilocanum (Garrison, 1908) Odhner, 1911	Cambodia, China, India, Indonesia, Lao PDR, Malaysia, The Philippines, Thailand
Echinostoma macrorchis Ando and Ozaki, 1923	Japan, South Korea, Lao PDR, Taiwan
Echinochasmus caninus (Verma, 1935) n. comb.	China, India, Thailand, Vietnam
Echinochasmus fujianensis Cheng et al., 1992	China
Echinochasmus japonicus Tanabe, 1926	China, Japan, South Korea, Kuwait, Lao PDR, Russia, Taiwan, Thailand, Vietnam
Echinochasmus jiufoensis Yu and Mott, 1994	China
Echinochasmus liliputanus (Looss, 1896) Odhner, 1910	China, Egypt, Israel, Sri Lanka, Syria
Echinochasmus perfoliatus (Ratz, 1908) Gedoelst, 1911	Bulgaria, China, Croatia, Denmark, Egypt, England, Hungary, India, Italy, Japan, South Korea, Poland, Romania, Russia, Serbia, Taiwan, Thailand, Ukraine, Vietnam
Himasthla muehlensi Vogel, 1933	North America
Hypoderaeum conoideum (Bloch, 1872) Dietz, 1909	Bangladesh, China, Indonesia, Japan, Mexico, North America, Russia, Spain, Taiwan, Thailand
Isthmiophora hortensis (Asada, 1926) Kostadinova and Gibson, 2002	China, Japan, South Korea
Isthmiophora melis (Schrank, 1788) Lühe, 1909	Belarus, Bulgaria, Canada, Czech Republic, England, France, Germany, Hungary, Lithuania, Poland, Romania, Russia, Taiwan, Ukraine, USA

Malaysia Larval stages of *E. ilocanum* were found in West Malaysia during a survey of echinostome infections in freshwater snails; adult worms were maintained in laboratory rats (Lie and Nasemary 1973). The first intermediate host was confirmed to be *Gyraulus convexiusculus,* and the second hosts included *Gyraulus convexiusculus, Lymnaea rubiginosa*, and tadpoles (Lie and Nasemary 1973). Experimental infection was successful in white rats, and natural adult worm infections were found in rats (*Rattus argentiventer*) (Lie and Nasemary 1973). Human infections are yet unknown.

The Philippines Five of over 5000 prisoners examined in Manila were positive for echinostome eggs, and from one of the 5 positive prisoners 21 adult worms were recovered (Garrison 1908). Five more human cases were detected in Zambales, Luzon (Hilario and Wharton 1917). Later, during 17 years, 3% of over 30,000 Philippino people examined were found to be passing echinostome eggs (species undetermined), and it was assumed that most of the eggs were *E. ilocanum* (Cross and Basaca-Sevilla 1986). In northern Luzon, adult flukes were recovered from treated people, and the egg prevalence averaged 11% (7–17% by different age group) among 7417 Ilocanos examined (Cross and Basaca-Sevilla 1986). However, *E. ilocanum* prevalence became low, 2–14% during 1978–1984 in Ilocos Sur area, where repeated mebendazole treatments were performed to control intestinal capillariasis among these people (Cross and Basaca-Sevilla 1986). A planorbid snail, *Gyraulus phrasadi*, was confirmed to be the first intermediate host, and the source of human infection was *Pila luzonica* snails (Eduardo 1991).

Thailand Human infections were first discovered in 10 patients (from northeastern parts of Thailand) who were echinostome egg-positive and treated with praziquantel; a total of 375 adult specimens (37.5 per patient) were recovered (Radomyos et al. 1982). Later, total 51 patients were reported also from northeast Thailand from whom adult flukes were confirmed (Radomyos et al. 1994). Studies on intermediate hosts and reservoir hosts are not available.

2.2.6 Echinostoma macrorchis

2.2.6.1 *Echinostoma macrorchis* Ando and Ozaki, 1923

Taxonomy and Morphology

E. macrorchis (Fig. 2.8a) was first described from naturally infected rats, *Rattus rattus* and *Rattus norvegicus,* in Japan (Ando and Ozaki 1923). Subsequently, the first human infection case was reported in Japan (Majima 1927), and another human case was added in Japan (Okabe and Okabe 1972). Experimental infection of albino rats with the metacercariae were reported to be successful (Ochi 1931). Ishii (1935) found naturally infected rats in Tokyo area, Japan, and Ito and Itagaki (2003) recovered adult flukes from *Apodemus speciosus* mice in Japan. This fluke was also found

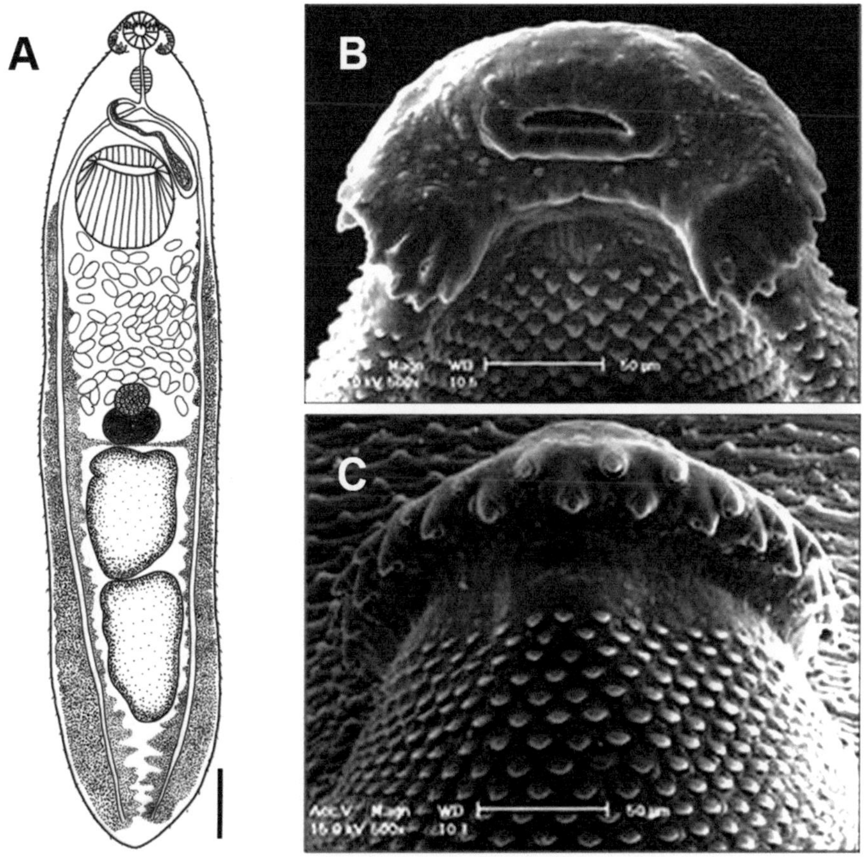

Fig. 2.8 *Echinostoma macrorchis*. (**a**) Line drawing of an adult worm (original figure). Scale bar = 0.5 mm (**b**, **c**) Scanning electron microscopic views of a 2-week-old adult fluke recovered from an experimental rat. Reproduced from Sohn et al. (2013) Korean J Parasitol 51:191–196 with permission (**b**) Oral sucker and collar spines, ventral view (**c**) Oral sucker and collar spines arranged alternatively, dorsal view

in Japanese moles (Yokohata et al. 1989). In Taiwan, naturally infected rats were reported (Fischthal and Kuntz 1975, 1981), and its life cycle was completed in the laboratory using mice and rats as the definitive hosts (Lo 1995). The presence of its life cycle was recently confirmed in Lao PDR (Sohn et al. 2013) and South Korea (Sohn and Na 2017).

The adult flukes are leaf-like, 4.6–7.8 mm long, and up to 1.3 mm wide (Ochi 1931; Rim 1982). It has a total of 43–47 collar spines (usually 45) in 2 alternating rows (Fig. 2.8b, c) (Rim 1982). The corner spines are usually 6 in number on each side (Ando and Ozaki 1923; Ochi 1931; Lo 1995) but it can be 5 in rare instances (Sohn et al. 2013; Sohn and Na 2017). The eggs are relatively small, 81–89 μm long, and 54–58 μm wide (Ando and Ozaki 1923); however, they can be as big as

95–100 μm long and 55–65 μm wide in fresh adult specimens (Ochi 1931). Two characteristic morphological features of this species are the number of corner spines (6 in most cases) and the size and shape of 2 testes (large size and somewhat quadriangular shape with more or less irregular surface) (Ando and Ozaki 1923). This fluke closely resembles *E. aegyptiacum* which has 43–45 collar spines and moderately big testes (Khalil and Abaza 1924). To assess the taxonomic validity of these 2 species, molecular studies will be useful. This species also closely resembles *Euparyphium murinum*, but the latter genus (*Euparyphium*) has a very short uterine tubule and only a small number of uterine eggs (Kostadinova and Gibson 2002). The cercarial body is spindle-shaped, and 340–350 μm long and 140–165 μm wide, and the tail is 350–365 μm long and 50–60 μm wide (Ito 1964). The metacercariae are round (Fig. 2.9a) or spleen-shaped, and 139–159 μm long and 99–120 μm wide with double thin layers (Komiya 1965).

Life Cycle

The life cycle of *E. macrorchis* was elucidated in Japan by Takahashi (1927) and Ochi (1931). The eggs develop and hatch in water, and miracidia swim in water waiting for infection to the first intermediate host, *Segmentina hemisphaerula* (= *Segmentina mica*) and *Gyraulus hiemantium* or *Gyraulus chinensis* (= *Planorbis compressus japonicus*) (Takahashi 1927; Rim, 1982). Miracidia develop into sporocysts, and then rediae and daughter rediae are produced; cercariae are found mainly

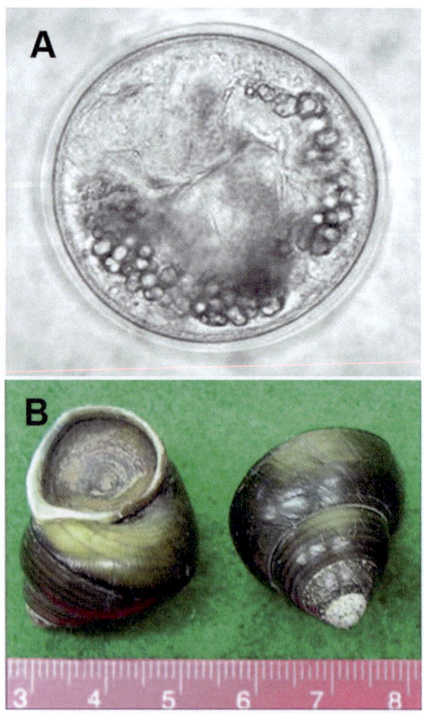

Fig. 2.9 *Echinostoma macrorchis*. (**a**) Metacercaria isolated from the snail host. x 200 (**b**) The snails, *Cipangopaludina* sp., purchased in a local market in Vientiane, Lao PDR, a second intermediate host. (**a**, **b**). (Reproduced from Sohn et al. (2013) Korean J Parasitol 51:191–196 with permission)

in the liver of these snail hosts (Ochi 1931). Metacercarial cysts are formed under the mantle and in the wall of the head and liver of freshwater snails, *Segmentina hemisphaerula, Gyraulus chinensis* (or *Gyraulus hiemantium*), *Cipangopaludina* spp., including *Cipangopaludina chinensis malleata* (= *Viviparus malleatus*) (Fig. 2.9b) and *Cipangopaludina japonica, Parafossarulus striatulus, Bulimus striatus*, and *Lymnaea japonica* (Yamashita 1964; Komiya 1965; Yu and Mott, 1994; Sohn et al. 2013; Sohn and Na 2017). Metacercariae are also found in the kidneys of tadpoles of frogs (*Rana nigromaculata, Rana catesbiana, Rana rugosa,* and *Rana latouchi*) and larvae of salamanders (*Hynobius nigrescens*) (Yamashita 1964; Lo 1995). Mice and rats are natural definitive hosts (Ishii 1935; Yamashita 1964). An avian species, *Capella gallinago gallinago,* has also been added to the natural definitive hosts in Japan (Yamashita 1964). Human infections were reported only in Japan (Majima 1927).

Epidemiology and Geographical Distribution

There have been only 2 reports of natural human infections with this echinostome (Majima 1927; Okabe and Okabe 1972). The infection source of the first patient (12-year-old boy infected with 34 specimens of *E. macrorchis*) was uncertain, but it was presumed to be salamanders, since he ate 10 small raw salamanders with his friends. The second case was a 48-year-old man residing in Saga City who expelled 31 specimens of *E. macrorchis* together with 2 other species of trematodes; the infection source of this patient was uncertain (Okabe and Okabe 1972). This fluke is geographically distributed in Japan, South Korea, Lao PDR, and Taiwan (Table 2.4) (Okabe and Okabe 1972; Fischthal and Kuntz 1975, 1981; Sohn et al. 2013; Sohn and Na 2017).

Japan *E. macrorchis* was first discovered in house rats from Gifu, Shiga, and Hiroshima Prefectures (Ando and Ozaki 1923). Subsequently, a human infection case was discovered in Saga Prefecture (Majima 1927). Later, the infection rate of rats in Kagoshima and Saga Prefectures was reported to be 0.5% and 0.4–3.2%, respectively (Yamashita 1964). Infection was also recognized in a bird from Kyushu Prefecture (Yamashita 1964). Takahashi (1927) and Ochi (1931) discovered larval stages of this fluke in Fukuoka Prefecture and Tokyo Prefecture, respectively. Ishii (1935) found white rats infected with *E. macrorchis* in Tokyo Prefecture. A second human case was found in Saga City (Okabe and Okabe 1972). In Miyagi, Fukushima, and Niigata Prefectures, *E. macrorchis* infection was found in Japanese moles (Mogera wogura and Mogera tokudae) (Yokohata et al. 1989). More recently, 1.7% of 58 wild rodents (field mice *Apodemus speciosus*) were found infected with *E. macrorchis* (Ito and Itagaki 2003).

South Korea Its existence was first confirmed by discovery of metacercariae in *Cipangopaludina chinensis malleata* snails collected from various localities, including Imsil-gun, Hwasun-gun, Shinan-gun, and Jinju City; adult flukes were recovered from experimentally infected rats (Sohn and Na 2017). Human infections are yet unknown.

Lao PDR Metacercariae of *E. macrorchis* were discovered in *Cipangopaludina* snails purchased from a market in Vientiane Municipality, and adult flukes were recovered in experimentally infected rats and a cat (Sohn et al. 2013). No other studies have been performed.

Taiwan The first report of *E. macrorchis* was the discovery of this species in rodents (*Rattus rattus* and *Rattus norvegicus*) from Chang-hua and Taipei Prefectures (Fischthal and Kuntz 1975). It was also recovered in Formosan brown country rats (*Rattus losea*) and common rats (*Rattus norvegicus*) from Taipei, Ping-tung, and Chang-hua Prefectures (Fischthal and Kuntz 1981). Tadpoles of *R. latouchi* collected from a ditch in Taipei City harboured echinostome metacercariae in their kidneys; they were fed to mice which grew to be adults of *E. macrorchis* (Lo 1995). *Gyraulus chinensis* snails present in the same ditch was later found shedding the cercariae of *E. macrorchis*; infected snails were also collected from caltrop ponds in Kaohsiung City (Lo 1995). Human infections are yet unknown.

2.2.7 Echinostoma angustitestis

2.2.7.1 *Echinostoma angustitestis* Wang, 1977

Taxonomy and Morphology

E. angustitestis (Fig. 2.10a) was first described from dogs experimentally infected with metacercariae isolated from freshwater fish (Yu and Mott 1994). Human infections were reported from 2 cases in Fujian Province, China (Cheng et al. 1992). Later, livestock and/or poultries were found to be infected with this fluke in China, although no detailed results were given (Zhan et al. 2017).

The morphology of the adult fluke is not well known, and the original report of Wang PQ is not available on-line or in the library. The only one referable we found was Fauna Sinica edited by Chen et al. (1985). The adult fluke is 5.6 mm in length and 0.43 in width. The head collar is equipped with a total of 41 collar spines arranged in 2 alternating rows. The corner spines are 4 on each side (in the figure they look like 5 on each side). The egg is 77–80 × 52–55 μm in size (Chen et al. 1985). The most characteristic feature of this species is the size and shape of the 2 testes; narrow and elongated. No studies have been reported regarding its surface ultrastructures. The cercariae and metacercariae have not been found.

Life Cycle

The complete life cycle of *E. angustitestis* has not yet been determined. However, the first intermediate host is supposed to be *Parafossarulus* spp. and *Oncomelania* spp., the second intermediate host is freshwater fish, and the natural definitive host is livestock, including dogs (Yu and Mott 1994; Hung et al. 2013; Zhan et al. 2017).

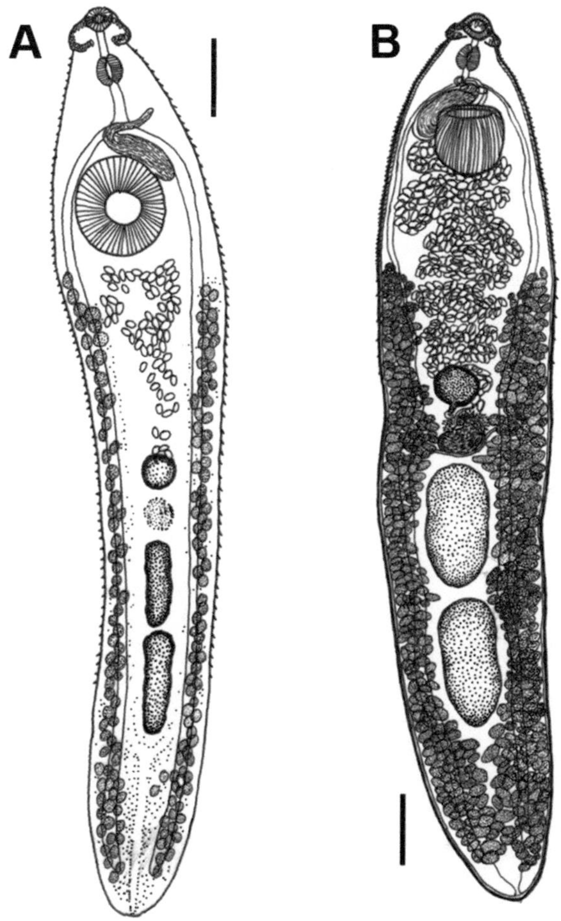

Fig. 2.10 Line drawings of *Echinostoma angustitestis* (**a**) and *Echinostoma aegyptiacum* (**b**) adult flukes. (**a**) Redrawn from the figure in Chen et al. (1985) Fauna Sinica, Science Press, Beijing, China. Scale bar = 0.5 mm (**b**) Redrawn from the figure in Yamaguti (1939b) Jpn J Med Sci (VI. Bacteriol Parasitol) 1:131–153. Scale bar = 0.5 mm

Epidemiology and Geographical Distribution
The source of human infections is presumed to be freshwater fish (Yu and Mott 1994). This fluke is known to be distributed only in 2 provinces (Fujian and Anhui) of China (Cheng et al. 1992; Chen et al. 2013; Zhan et al. 2017) (Table 2.4).

China This species was originally recovered from the intestine of dogs experimentally infected with the metacercariae from freshwater fish in Fujian Province in 1977 (Yu and Mott 1994). Two human infections were reported in Fujian Province (Cheng et al. 1992; Yu and Mott 1994). Chen et al. (2013) compared morphological characteristics of 5 echinostome species occurring in Fujian Province, including *E. angustitestis, E. aegyptiacum, Echinochasmus japonicus, Echinochasmus perfoliatus,* and *Echinochasmus fujianensis*. Infection in domestic animals with *E. angustitestis* has been reported from Anhui Province (Zhan et al. 2017).

2.2.8 Echinostoma aegyptiacum

2.2.8.1 *Echinostoma aegyptiacum* Khalil and Abaza, 1924

Taxonomy and Morphology

E. aegyptiacum (Fig. 2.10b) was first discovered in the small intestine of a naturally infected rat in Cairo, Egypt in 1924 and described under the name *Echinostoma aegyptiaca* (Khalil and Abaza 1924; Dollfus 1925b). Yamaguti (1939b) redescribed this species based on specimens from experimentally infected rats in Japan under the name *Echinostoma aegyptiacum.* Azim synonymized this species with *Echinoparyphium recurvatum* in 1930, but Yamaguti (1971) did not agree to this synonymy. This fluke was later detected in the stomach and small intestine of the brown country rat and the Norway rat in Taiwan (Fischthal and Kuntz 1975), house rats in Vietnam (Toan et al. 2008), and wild rats in Turkey (Gürler and Bakan 2017). Human infection was reported in Fujian Province, China (Cheng et al. 2005), but there are no details of the human infections with no description of adult worms.

Adult flukes of *E. aegyptiacum* are elongate, with parallel sides and more or less pointed extremities, 5.60–7.25 mm long and 0.65–1.05 mm wide, and beset with 43–45 collar spines in 2 alternating rows (Yamaguti 1939b). The corner spines are 4–5 in number (usually 5) (Yamaguti 1939b). The eggs are 100 μm long and 57 μm wide (Khalil and Abaza 1924) or 96–123 μm long and 57–69 μm wide (Yamaguti 1939b). Morphologically this species most closely resembles *E. macrorchis,* and no clear differential keys have been described, except on the size of the testes, bigger in *E. macrorchis* than in *E. aegyptiacum*. In *E. macrorchis*, the testis size increases markedly in older worms and can be smaller in younger flukes (Sohn and Na 2017). Thus, the 2 species may be a synonym of the other. To elucidate this point, molecular studies are necessary. Surface ultrastructure of this fluke has never been reported. The cercariae and metacercariae have not been found.

Life Cycle

The complete life cycle of *E. aegyptiacum* has not been elucidated. The natural definitive host includes Formosan brown country rats (*Rattus losea*), Norway rats (*Rattus norvegicus*), and house rats (*Rattus rattus*) (Fischthal and Kuntz 1975; Toan et al. 2008; Gürler and Bakan 2017). Humans are also a natural definitive host (Cheng et al. 2005).

Epidemiology and Geographical Distribution

The source of human or animal infections is unknown. This fluke is known to be distributed in Egypt (Khalil and Abaza 1924), Japan (Yamaguti 1939b), Taiwan (Fischthal and Kuntz 1975), Vietnam (Toan et al. 2008), Turkey (Gürler and Bakan 2017), and China (Cheng et al. 2005; Chen et al. 2013) (Table 2.4). Human infections were reported only in China (Cheng et al. 2005).

China Human infections were reported for the first time in Fujian Province (Cheng et al. 2005). Chen et al. (2013) compared morphological characteristics of 5 echinostome species occurring in Fujian Province, including *E. aegyptiacum, E. angustit-*

estis, Echinochasmus japonicus, Echinochasmus perfoliatus, and *Echinochasmus fujianensis.* Further details of human infections with *E. aegyptiacum*, including the infection source, have not been elucidated. Infection in domestic animals has been reported from Anhui Province (Zhan et al. 2017).

Egypt This fluke was first discovered from a house rat in Cairo and reported as a new species; 7 adult flukes were recovered in the small intestine of the rat (Khalil and Abaza 1924). Thereafter, few study has been reported on this species in Egypt.

Japan Yamaguti (1939b) found this species from a laboratory rat. The morphology of this species was redescribed. No further studies have been available.

Taiwan Some of echinostome flukes recovered from rats in Taipei, Chang-hua, and Ping-tung Prefectures were assigned as *E. aegyptiacum* (Fischthal and Kuntz 1975). Further reports were not followed.

Turkey *E. aegyptiacum* was recovered from house rats (*Rattus norvegicus*) (Gürler and Bakan 2017).

Vietnam House rats (*Rattus flavipectus*) from Ha Tinh and Nghe An Provinces were infected with various helminth species including *E. aegyptiacum* (Toan et al. 2008).

2.2.9 Potentially Zoonotic **Echinostoma** *spp.*

Potentially zoonotic *Echinostoma* spp. include *E. barbosi* Lie and Basch, 1966, *E. bolschewense* (Kotova, 1939) Nasincova, 1991, *E. caproni* Richard, 1964, *E. deserticum* Kechemir et al., 2002, *E. luisreyi* Maldonado et al., 2003, *E. miyagawai* Ishii, 1932, *E. nasincovae* Faltýnková et al., 2015, *E. paraulum* Dietz, 1909, *E. parvocirrus* Nassi and Dupouy, 1988, *E. robustum* Yamaguti, 1935, *E. rodriguesi* Hsu et al., 1968, and *E. trivolvis* (Cort, 1914) Kanev, 1985 (see Fried and Graczyk 2004; Toledo et al. 2009; Detwiler et al. 2012; Georgieva et al. 2013; Faltýnková et al. 2015).

2.2.10 Genomics and Proteomics

For better understanding of the study trends of genomics and proteomics of echinostome flukes belonging to the genus *Echinostoma*, data published on zoonotic as well as non-zoonotic species of *Echinostoma* were both subjected to a review here. However, genetic information on echinostomes is scarce, and there were no full genome sequencing projects for echinostomes (Marcilla 2009; Toledo et al. 2011). The number of gene sequence data is not many, and most of the data obtained were used for phylogenetic and taxonomic studies (Marcilla 2009; Toledo and Fried 2013). Inevitably, this low number of gene sequences in the database made it fail to identify the proteins from peptides obtained from echinostomes (Marcilla 2009). Among the zoonotic species, *E. paraensei* was the most frequently studied species, and *E. revolutum* was the next one. Among the non-zoonotic species, *E. caproni* was the most frequently studied species. Adult flukes and larval stages (sporocysts, cercariae, and metacercariae) were both the subjects used for molecular analysis. In *E. paraensei*, the expressed sequence tags (EST) that have 358 sequence entries (obtained from sporocysts) generated from the suppression subtractive hybridization (SSH) library constituted the only EST data available for echinostomes (Nowak and Loker 2005). For *E. revolutum, E. caproni*, and other echinostomes, 1–17 DNA molecules were analyzed in GenBank until 2008 (Marcilla 2009). New cDNA and genomic libraries are required for further echinostome genetic studies. There have been few studies on microarrays or reverse genetics of echinostomes (Chai et al. 2009b).

The major molecules used for molecular studies of echinostomes were ribosomal DNA (rDNA) and mitochondrial DNA (mtDNA), with a few exceptions that included enolase gene (Marcilla 2009). Internal transcribed spacers (ITS-1 and ITS-2) and 28S, 18S, and 5.8S rDNA were the most popularly analyzed DNA molecules, and nicotinamide adenine dinucleotide dehydrogenase (NADH) subunit 1 (ND1) and cytochrome *c* oxidase 1 (CO1) have been the most commonly used mitochondrial markers (Marcilla 2009). ITS-1, ITS-2, and 5.8S ribosomal DNA were used to study 8 echinostome species; it was found that 5 ('*revolutum*' group) of the 8 species revealed distinguishable ITS data from the others, but within the '*revolutum*' group, there found only low sequence divergence (Morgan and Blair 1995). Sorensen et al. (1998) detected high levels of intraspecific variation among ITS sequences of *E. revolutum* and *E. caproni*. Morgan and Blair (1998a, b) used ND1 as a marker for species and strain detection of echinostomes within the group.

To identify the species and strains of 37-collar spined echinostomes, ND1 was confirmed to be the most suitable marker, in comparison with CO1, ITS-1, and ITS-2 (Morgan and Blair 1998a, b; Kostadinova et al. 2003). Based on morphological as well as molecular analysis of ND1, a new cryptic species of 37-collar spined group, designated as *Echinostoma* sp. IG, was described in Germany and Iceland (Georgieva et al. 2013). Analysis of ND1 together with ITS-1/5.8S/ITS-2 gene clusters also helped differential diagnosis of *Echinoparyphium ellisi* from *E. revolutum* and supported the distinct status of 3 isolates of *E. revolutum* from Europe, North America, and Australia (Kostadinova et al. 2003). A combined analysis of ND1 and CO1, and comparison of the data with those reported on ITS loci, was also used to examine the phylogenetic relationships of 9 cryptic lineages of echinostomes in North and South America, including 5 species of *Echinostoma,* 1 species of *Hypoderaeum*, and 3 species of *Echinoparyphium* (Detwiler et al. 2010). In addition, ND1 phylogeny of echinostomes from muskrats in Virginia, USA demonstrated that they were infected with 5 echinostome lineages, including 3 *E. trivolvis* lineages, 1 *E. revolutum*, and 1 *Echinoparyphium* lineage 1 (Detwiler et al. 2012). A combination of ND1 and ITS-2 analyses of echinostome metacercariae collected from snails in 8 sites of Lamphun Province, Thailand revelaed genetic heterogeneity and possible cryptic speciation (Noikong et al. 2014). ND1 and CO1 were also used to analyze the taxonomic properties of echinostomes from ducks in Thailand and Lao PDR, and it was concluded that they belonged to *E. revolutum* and *E. miyagawai*, but *E. revolutum* from these areas (Asia) was genetically different from those reported from America, Europe, and Australia (Nagatani et al. 2015). Analysis of partial fragments of ND1 and 28S rRNA genes of echinostomes from birds in New Zealand revealed that they consisted of *E. miyagawai, Echinoparyphium ellisi*, and 2 new species, *Echinostoma novaezealandense* and *Echinoparyphium poulini* (Georgieva et al. 2017).

Meanwhile, ITS-1 sequence alone was also used to compare the genetic characteristics of *E. revolutum* and *E. recurvatum* in Thailand (Saijuntha et al. 2011a). Tantrawatpan et al. (2013) used ITS-1 and ITS-2 sequences for differentiation of *A. malayanum* and *A. sufrartyfex*, although the latter was synonymized with the former due to morphological similarity (Chai 2009). Analysis of ITS-2 sequences was also helpful to understand the taxonomic status of *Echinostoma hortense*, which was proposed to be transferred to *Isthmiophora* and rename as *I. hortensis* (Kostadinova et al. 2003). Partial sequences of 28S rDNA, in combination with ITS-2 and ND1, were used for taxonomic studies at a supraspecific level within the Echinostomatidae family (Marcilla 2009). Using partial sequences of 28S rDNA, in combination with isoenzyme analysis of mannose phosphate isomerase and malic enzyme, the taxonomic validity of *Echinostoma caproni* and *Echinostoma friedi* were strengthened (Marcilla 2009); however, *E. friedi* was later suggested to be a synonym of *E. miyagawai* based on combined sequence analysis of ND1 and 28S rDNA (Georgieva et al. 2013, 2014). Partial sequences of 28S rDNA were also useful to analyze the phylogenetic relationships of the superfamily Echinostomatoidea, and it was proposed to elevate the systematic level of subfamilies Echinochasminae and Himasthlinae into families Echinochasmidae and Himasthlidae (Tkach et al. 2016). Among the zoonotic *Echinostoma* spp., molecular data have been available in *E. revolutum* (ITS-1/5.8S rDNA/ITS-2, 18S rDNA, 28S rDNA, CO1, and ND1), *E. paraensei* (ITS-1/5.8S rDNA/ITS-2, 18S rDNA, 28S rDNA, CO1, and ND1), and *E. cinetorchis* (28S rDNA and ND1).

Polymerase chain reaction-based restriction fragment length polymorphism (PCR-RFLP) analysis and random amplification of polymorphic DNA (RAPD) analysis were also used for molecular taxonomic studies of echinostomes (Toledo and Fried 2013). Sorensen et al. (1998) noted intraspecific variation in ITS sequences of different *E. trivolvis* isolates from North America, which was further supported by PCR-RFLP assay of the same locus. Fujino et al. (1995, 1997) used RAPD assay to differentiate *E. trivolvis* and *E. caproni* using genomic DNA from adults and metacercariae with satisfactory results. RAPD technique was also applied for molecular characterization of *E. paraensei* and *E. caproni* (Petrie et al. 1996).

Proteomics of parasites collectively refers to a way to link any protein in or from the parasite to its encoding DNA (Marcilla 2009). However, the application of proteomics to echinostome proteins is only very recent, and there have been very few publications (Toledo et al. 2011). The major limitation in proteomic studies is the lack of sufficient genomic data, although some data have been accumulated on the proteins secreted from echinostomes. The difficulty of proteomics research is also due to the difficulty of in vitro culture of echinostomes and thus in obtaining sufficient amount of materials for biochemical studies (Marcilla 2009). Identification of echinostome proteins was possible in some parts because they are homologous to other trematode proteins, i.e., schistosomes (Marcilla 2009). However, more than 75% of echinostome proteins may not present sufficient homology with schistosomes to allow for proper identification (Toledo et al. 2011). Moreover, not all the available data for other trematode species likes schistosomes are useful in searches using routine bioinformatics tools (Toledo et al. 2011). Moreover, half of the proteins identified in schistosomes from their transcriptomes do not have a known function, or are even species-specific, thus increasing the difficulties when working with other trematodes like echinostomes (Toledo et al. 2011).

The study of echinostome proteins has been initiated by Taft and Fried (1968), who first showed an evidence of the presence of cytochrome oxidase in *E. revolutum* (actually *E. trivolvis*). Subsequently, larval proteins of *E. lindoense* were obtained from the snail host, *Biomphalaria glabrata* (Heyneman et al. 1971). Haque and Siddiqi (1982) obtained electrophoretic profiles of acid and alkaline phosphatases of *Artyfechinostomum malayanum* (under the name *Echinostoma malayanum*). This was the first isoenzyme study on echinostomes, and then isoenzymes were popularly used to differentiate the species of echinostomes. For example, isoenzyme patterns of *E. caproni* and *E. liei* were compared, and it was strongly suggested that *E. togoensis* is a subspecies of *E. caproni* (Voltz et al. 1987). Also the taxonomic validity of *E. caproni* and *E. freidi* was examined by isoenzyme analysis of 2 diagnostic loci, i.e., mannose phosphate isomerase and malic enzyme (Marcilla 2009). Multilocus enzyme electrophoresis was used to differentiate *E. revolutum* and *H. conoideum* (Saijuntha et al. 2010a) and *E. revolutum* and *A. malayanum* (Saijuntha et al. 2010b). Intraspecific diversity of *E. revolutum* was also reported using multilocus enzyme electrophoresis among geographically (Thailand and Lao PDR) and temporally isolated populations (Saijuntha et al. 2011b).

In studies of echinostome proteins, the material most frequently used was excretory-secretory products (ESP), because these materials constitute the initial contact parasites with the host and environment (Toledo et al. 2011). In rediae of *E. trivolvis*, the presence of heme was demonstrated using laser desorption mass spectrometry (Pisciotta et al. 2005). In *E. friedi* adults (a synonym of *E. miyagawai*; Georvieva et al. 2014), various kinds of proteins (actin, tropomyosin, and paramyosin), enzymes (enolase, glyceraldehyde-3-phosphate dehydrogenase, aldolase, and glutathion-S-transferase), and a stress-related protein (heat shock protein-70) have been identified from ESP using 2-dimensional electrophoresis (2DE) (Bernal et al. 2006). Also in *E. caproni* sporocysts and adults, superoxide dismutase, glutathion-S-transferase, aldo-keto-reductase, triose phosphate isomerase, glyceraldehyde-3-phosphate dehydrogenase, aldolase, enolase, and calreticulin (Guillou et al. 2007), enolase (Marcilla et al. 2007), heat shock protein-70 (Higón et al. 2008), and 39 parasite proteins largely including glycolytic enzymes (Sotillo et al. 2010) were identified from their ESP. Cortés et al. (2016) found that definitive hosts (rats and mice) influence the proteomic profile of ESP of *E. caproni*; 19 differential protein spots were discovered on 2-dimensional gel electrophoresis images; 14 were overexpressed in mice and 5 were overexpressed in rats. The over expressed proteins in mice were mainly antioxidant and detoxifying enzymes such as glutathion-S-transferase, hydroxyacylglutathion hydrolase, and thiopurine S-transferase, and metabolic enzymes like enolase, leucine aminopeptidase or malate dehydrogenase; these proteins were suggested to protect the parasites and be involved in establishment of chronic infections in mice (Cortés et al. 2016).

2.2.11 Pathology and Immunology

The pathogenicity of echinostome flukes to the definitive host is not well known and remains to be further studied (Toledo et al. 2006a; Chai 2007; Chai et al. 2009b). In addition, the target species were in most cases non-zoonotic *Echinostoma* spp., namely, *E. caproni* (Bindseil and Christensen 1984, under the name of *E. revolutum*; Christensen et al. 1988; Kim and Fried 1989; Isaacson et al. 1989; Fried et al. 1990; Toledo et al. 2006a) and *E. trivolvis* (Huffman et al. 1986, 1988; Fried et al. 1988; Christensen et al. 1988; Fujino et al. 1993). Histopathological studies have seldom been performed in zoonotic *Echinostoma* spp., in particular, *E. revolutum* (in true sense), *E. cinetorchis* (except a report by So 1955), *E. paraensei, E. lindoense,* and *E. ilocanum*. Some studies were performed in *I. hortensis* (under the name *Echinostoma hortense*), an important zoonotic echinostome species in the Far East (Chai 2009), which will be introduced and discussed in the next section (*Isthmiophora*).

So far we know, the pathogenicity of *Echinostoma* spp. is complex and diverse depending on a wide variety of host and parasite factors (Toledo et al. 2006a; Chai et al. 2009b). Simonsen et al. (1989) suggested that the mucosal changes in *E. caproni* infection in mice could be induced by parasite-side factors including the worm feeding activity, mechanical irritation, and the release of toxic substances, and host-side factors such as immune responses of the host to the parasite. However, little is known about the detailed mechanisms inducing pathological alterations in affected intestinal tissues (Toledo et al. 2006a). With regard to parasite-related factors, mechanical worm movement and toxic and immunogenic effects induced by their excretory-secretory products (ESP) seem to be 2 major factors. Host-side factors may include natural resistance (anatomical, biological, and ecological barriers) and immune responses of the host (local/systemic, innate/acquired, humoral/cellular, T-helper 1/T-helper 2, and so on).

An important parasite-side factor is the intensity of infection (= worm load), which appears to be highly important not only in the pathogenicity but also in the severity of the clinical diseases (Yamashita 1964; Rim 1982). So (1955) infected white rats with 300–500 metacercariae of *E. cinetorchis* and observed heavy lesions in the small intestine. He (So 1955) also reported that over 30 worms could be fatal to young rats, and worms intruded into the liver (bile duct) in a case of heavy infection. Fried et al. (1988, 1990) infected hamsters with 1, 2, or 5 (low doses) metacercariae of *E. trivolvis* (under the name *E. revolutum*) and *E. caproni* and observed host intestinal histopathology; the results showed no significant differences in the intestinal histopathogy. However, when 20 metacercariae of *E. caproni* (under the name *E. revolutum*) were given to mice, significant changes occurred in the small intestine of infected mice (Bindseil and Christensen 1984).

Toxic metabolites are another parasite-derived factor responsible for eliciting the pathogenicity. Echinostomes secrete/excrete various antigenic proteins which are contained in somatic organs, tissues, or in ESP (Toledo et al. 2009). For example, 4 parasite surface antigens were isolated using Western blot analysis of juvenile and adult *E. caproni*-derived ESP (2 fractions) and detergent solubilized products (2 fractions); these antigens were thought to cause significant stimuli to the host (Andressen et al. 1989). Bernal et al. (2006) identified 10 kinds of proteins (skeletal proteins, glycolytic enzymes, detoxifying enzymes, and heat shock proteins) from ESP of *E. miyagawai* (under the name *E. friedi*). Carpena et al. (2007) also observed the existence of somatic polypeptides that were specifically expressed depending on the host species (hamsters and rats) infected with *E. miyagawai* (under the name *E. friedi*).

In intestinal histopathological sections of rodents infected with *Echinostoma* spp., the worms were located in the lumen of the upper small intestine, and the pathological changes were chiefly observed at the attachment sites of the echinostomes (Toledo et al., 2006a). The flukes were seen to tightly pinch and suck the mucosa with their oral suckers, and it seemed that the mucosal layer was eventually eaten by the flukes (Chai 2015). In mice infected with *E. caproni*, villous atrophy, crypt hyperplasia, and subepithelial fibrosis were conspicuous features observed in the small intestine, and these changes were thymus-independent (Bindseil and Christensen 1984). In Wistar rats (less compatible host) and hamsters (highly compatible host) infected with *E. caproni*, the intestinal histopathology was compared; villous atrophy, including fused villi, and eroded and destroyed villi was a common feature in both rats and hamsters (Toledo et al. 2006b). However, in rats local inflammatory responses were weak and goblet cell hyperplasia was remarkable, whereas in hamsters local inflammatory responses were strong but goblet cell hyperplasia was weak (Toledo et al. 2006b). This difference was related to the early expulsion of worms from rats and chronic retention of worms in hamsters (Toledo et al. 2006b). In chicks infected with *E. caproni*, atrophic villi, hypertrophied circular musculature with collagen-like fibers, and hemorrhagic zones were observed; cephalic spines of worms were seen to abrade the host mucosa, and the brush borders of epithelial cells and goblet cells were frequently lost in the mucosa of the infected ileum (Kim and Fried 1989). Hemorrhagic areas were also observed in the small intestine of hamsters infected with *E. caproni* (Isaacson et al. 1989).

Similar intestinal histopathology was reported in *E. trivolvis* infection; villous atrophy, crypt hyperplasia, inflammation of the stroma, decreased villus/crypt ratios, and focal loss of the mucosal tissue were common findings in the small intestine of experimentally infected hamsters (Huffman et al. 1986). The damages at the mucosa were so severe that in focal areas massive destruction and detachment of villi, at times complete loss of the mucosal integrity and ulcerations, were observed (Huffman et al. 1986). Goblet cell hyperplasia and mucosal mast cell hyperplasia were observed in the small intestine of *E. trivolvis*-infected BALB/c mice, whereas in athymic nude mice goblet cell hyperplasia similarly occurred but mast cell hyperplasia did not occur (Fujino et al. 1993). However, hemorrhagic areas which were frequently observed in *E. caproni* infection in hamsters (Isaacson et al. 1989) and chicks (Kim and Fried 1989) were not observed in *E. trivolvis* infection in hamsters (Huffman et al. 1986). Also *E. caproni* tends to penetrate to the crypt layer of the intestinal mucosa, whereas *E. trivolvis* remains at the tip of the villi (Isaacson et al. 1989). The attachment site of *E. caproni* at the host intestinal mucosa revealed no changes in cellular composition and no specific cellular responses, gradually reduced in size, and disappeared after mechanical removal of the parasites from unfixed tissue in saline (in vitro) (Simonsen et al. 1989). Further studies are required to confirm this in other species of *Echinostoma*.

It is of considerable interest to note that some echinostome species, *E. cinetorchis* (So 1955) and *E. trivolvis* (Huffman et al. 1986, 1988, under the name of *E. revolutum*) can cause extraintestinal lesions, whereas *E. caproni* may not cause such infections (Isaacson et al. 1989). In *E. cinetorchis* infection in rats, So (1955) observed that some worms intruded into the liver in a case of heavy infection. Similarly, *E. trivolvis* was also found to have penetrated the liver causing necrosis and hemorrhage of the surrounding area and laid eggs there (Huffman et al. 1986). A further study by Huffman et al. (1988) reported that *E. trivolvis* can cause extraintestinal infections in the liver, gall bladder, pancreas, and stomach and elicit damages of the organs and introduction of bacteria into the liver parenchyma, resulting in suppurative hepatitis, perbiliary necrosis, hemorrhage, egg granuloma, and fibrosis in the liver. In contrast, no parasites or eggs were found in the liver of *E. caproni*-infected hamsters or chicks (Isaacson et al. 1989; Kim and Fried 1989). Isaacson et al. (1989) explained that only 3% of the total number of *E. caproni* parasitized the duodenum, and all others were located in the lower portion of the intestine; thus they may not easily migrate up the bile duct to the liver of hamsters. Liver damages seen in *E. caproni*-infected hamsters (Isaacson et al. 1989) were suggested to have been due to bacterial infections; damages in the area of the sphincter Oddi by *E. caproni* nay result in backflow of intestinal bacteria and account for the suppurative liver lesions. These differences in the pathogenicity and pathology of echinostomes seem to vary on the species of parasite (Isaacson et al. 1989).

Studies on host resistance and immunity against echinostomes have been performed by various workers; however, there are still much to be further clarified. The immunological studies are regarding local or systemic immunity, innate or acquired immunity, humoral or cellular immunity, and T-helper-1 (Th1) or T-helper-2 (Th2) immunity, and have been studied in infections with *E. caproni, E. trivolvis, E. paraensei, E. friedi*, *E. revolutum*, and *I. hortensis* (Fried and Graczyk 2004; Toledo et al. 2006a; Chai 2009, 2015). The studies using *I. hortensis* will be described in the following section (see *Isthmiophora*).

It has been learned from previous studies that the rodent hosts exhibit various types of host-parasite relationships. One of the interesting immunological phenomena is the so-called 'spontaneous expulsion' of parasites from their hosts (Toledo et al. 2006a), which has been reported more popularly in nematode-rodent models (Anthony et al. 2007). In trematodes, including echinostomes, this kind of adult worm expulsion from the rodent host has been reported since the end of the 1980s. Toledo et al. (2006a) stated that the worm expulsion occurs with different dynamics depending on the models used in different parasite as well as host species. In *Echinostoma* spp., this interesting phenomenon has been studied popularly in *E. trivolvis, E. caproni,* and *E. friedi* (Fujino et al. 1993; Brunet et al. 2000; Toledo et al. 2003, 2006a, b). This spontaneous worm expulsion is less likely to occur in the human host; for example, in humans experimentally infected with *E. lindoense*, adult flukes persisted at least 10 months (Sandground and Bonne 1940).

The susceptibility of mice, rats, and hamsters to *E. trivolvis* and *E. caproni* has been shown to be dependent upon the parasite as well as host species. Whereas *E. trivolvis* (under the name *E. revolutum*) survived for long periods of time in golden hamsters, it was eliminated quickly from the small intestine of ICR mice within 3–4 weeks post-infection (Hosier and Fried 1986; Mabus et al. 1988; Weinstein and Fried 1991), BALB/c mice within 2 weeks (Fujino et al. 1993), and C3H mice by day 12 post-infection (Fujino and Fried 1993a). *E. caproni* produces chronic infections in hamsters and mice but the worms are expelled in 6–7 weeks in rats (Odaibo et al. 1988; Toledo et al. 2004a). In NMRI mice, *E. caproni* was retained for more than 16 weeks (Odaibo et al. 1988), and in ICR mice *E. caproni* induced a chronic infection (Weinstein and Fried 1991). It is also interesting to note that *E. miyagawai* (under the name *E. friedi*) survived for at least 12 weeks in hamsters but the infection was terminated at 3–4 weeks in rats (Toledo et al. 2003). The survival of echinostomes can be prolonged by immunosuppressive treatment (Fujino et al. 1996a) or concurrent infection with other parasite such as *Schistosoma mansoni* (Christensen et al. 1985). McMaster et al. (1995) observed increased worm recovery, decreased total white blood cell counts, and decreased relative spleen weight in hamsters infected with *E. trivolvis* and *E. caproni* on day 14 post-infection. Fujino et al. (1996a) observed delayed worm expulsion of *E. trivolvis* in dexamethasone-treated C3H/HeN mice.

Several types of possible immune effectors, namely, goblet cells (Fujino and Fried 1993b; Fujino et al. 1993, 1996a, 1998a, b, 2000), mast cells (Fujino et al. 1993), eosinophils (Bindseil and Christensen 1984), neutrophils and mononuclear inflammatory cells (Muñoz-Antoli et al. 2007), antibodies (Agger et al. 1993), and cytokines (Brunet et al. 2000) have been suggested to be associated with the worm expulsion of echinostomes. However, the role of mast cells is controversial (Toledo et al. 2006a). Mastocytosis was pronounced in the intestinal mucosa of BALB/c mice at day 17 post-infection with *E. trivolvis* which coincided with worm expulsion, in contrast to the athymic nude mice in which there was no increase of mucosal mast cell numbers (Fujino et al. 1993). Nevertheless, worm expulsion occurred in athymic nude mice, and the worm expulsion kinetics was similar to that of conventional BALB/c mice, which suggested that mast cell hyperplasia in BALB/c mice may not be related to worm expulsion but may be a secondary response due to the presence of the worms (Fujino et al. 1993). On the other hand, importance of goblet cells has been generally acknowledged. In *E. trivolvis* (under the name *E. revolutum*) infection, proliferation of intestinal goblet cells was notified in golden hamsters (Huffman et al. 1986). However, in *E. caproni*-infected mice, chronic infection was accompanied by reduced goblet cell numbers (Bindseil and Christensen 1984; Weinstein and Fried 1991; Fujino and Fried 1993b). In *E. trivolvis*-infected mice, the goblet cell numbers increased coinciding with worm expulsion, and worm expulsion was delayed when mice were treated with dexamethasone (Fujino et al. 1993, 1996a). Also, dexamethasone administration to immunodeficient SCID mice delayed the expulsion of *E. trivolvis* (Fujino et al. 1998a). Similar effects of immunosuppression by dexamethasone were also observed in golden hamsters infected with *E. caproni* and *E. trivolvis* (McMaster et al. 1995). Mucins increased by a primary *Nippostrongylus brasiliensis* infection in the intestine of mice were suggested to be responsible for a rapid expulsion of a subsequent challenge infection with *E. caproni* or *E. trivolvis* (Fujino et al. 1996b). However, a contradicting result was also observed in RAG-2-deficient mice infected with *E. caproni*, a mouse strain of genetically lacking B- and T-lymphocytes; goblet cell hyperplasia was marked in RAG-2-deficient mice but worms survived as they did in normal ICR mice (Frazer et al. 1999). This result suggested that other immune mechanisms are also involved in worm expulsion of echinostomes (Toledo et al. 2006a).

In addition to goblet cells and mast cells, eosinophils were listed as a potential immune effector for expulsion of echinostome worms (Toledo et al. 2006a). In *E. caproni* (Bindseil and Christensen 1984) and *E. trivolvis* (Fujino et al. 1996b) infections in mice, eosinophil infiltration was a characteristic histopathological feature in the intestinal mucosa. Also, Hansen et al. (1991) demonstrated increased levels of peripheral eosinophilia in rats infected with *E. caproni* in close relationship with the worm burden and suggested a potential role of eosinophils in the regulatory response against *E. caproni* in rats. As another candidate of immune effectors, in addition to goblet cells, mucosal neutrophils and mononuclear inflammatory cells in the mesentery were suggested to be essential in determining the course of *E. caproni* infection in mice (Muñoz-Antoli et al. 2007).

Antibodies and cytokines were also suggested to be important components of systemic as well as local defense mechanisms against echinostomes (Agger et al. 1993; Sotillo et al. 2007; Brunet et al. 2000). It has been noted that antibodies are simultaneously and constantly trapped by secretion from worms at the infection sites which seems to be a novel mechanism of parasite immune evasion from the host (Cortés et al. 2017). However, elevated levels of IgG, IgM, and IgA have been detected in serum as well as the small intestine of mice infected with *E. caproni* (Agger et al. 1993; Sotillo et al. 2007). It was also shown that antibodies in mouse serum covered the surface of *E. caproni* (under the name *E. revolutum*) in vitro, and worms obtained from immune mice were found to be covered by antibodies (Simonsen and Andersen 1986). In *E. caproni* infection, the kinetics of IgM, IgA, and IgG subclasses were observed in the serum and intestine of experimentally infected rats and mice (Sotillo et al. 2007). In mice (worms expel late), the level of IgG2a in serum remained constant during the course of *E. caproni* infection, whereas in rats (worms quickly expel), the IgG2a responses were increased in the intestine; this result suggests strongly that IgG2a is significantly related with worm expulsion (Sorillo et al. 2007). Since IgG2a is an important element mediating T-helper-2 (Th2) immune responses of mice (Sotillo et al. 2007; Shin et al. 2007), the expulsion of echinostomes from the host intestine is suggested to be mediated by a Th2 type immune response.

Th1 and Th2 cytokine profiles were studied in rodent hosts experimentally infected with *E. caproni* (Brunet et al. 2000). Upon antigen stimulation, mesenteric lymphnode cells from *E. caproni*-infected mice produced significantly higher levels of a Th1 cytokine IFN-γ in vitro for 3 weeks; during this period they were unable to expel *E. caproni* worms (Brunet et al. 2000). However, injection of these mice with anti-IFN-γ monoclonal antibodies was found to be effective in reducing the worm load of *E. caproni* (Brunet et al. 2000). Thus, echinostome chronic infection in mice is biased toward a Th1 phenotype characterized by production of IFN-γ, IL-12, and TNF-α, and worm rejection by the host is closely related to Th2 responses which are mediated by IL-4 and IL-5 (Brunet et al. 2000; Toledo and Fried 2005). It is interesting to note that some factors in mouse serum, suggested to be a kind of cytokine, were shown to induce retraction of collar spines of *E. trivolvis* adult flukes probably enhancing worm expulsion (Fujino et al. 1994).

2.2.12 Clinical Manifestations, Diagnosis and Treatment

Morbidity and mortality due to echinostomiasis are difficult to assess in endemic areas because of a prolonged latent phase, a short acute phase, asymptomatic presentations, and also because of a similarity of clinical symptoms caused by other intestinal helminthiases (Graczyk and Fried 1998). The major clinical symptoms in echinostome infections include abdominal pain, diarrhea, easy fatigue, and loss of body weight (Rim 1982; Chai and Lee 2002; Fried and Graczyk 2004). The clinical manifestations of human echinostomiasis may be more severe than those produced by other intestinal trematodes, though the clinical features greatly depend on the parasite load (Chai 2009; Toledo et al. 2014b). One of the reasons for this includes the size and volume of the parasite; whereas heterophyid flukes are small and generally 0.5–2 mm in length, echinostomes, in particular, *Echinostoma* spp. and *Isthmiophora* spp. are large and generally 5.0–20.0 mm in length (Chai 2007, 2009). Thus, it can be accepted that mechanical irritation must be greater by echinostome adults than heterophyid fluke adults. However, reports on clinical symptoms and signs in human *Echinostoma* spp. infection are scarce.

A patient infected with *E. cinetorchis* suffered from diarrhea which was cured after treatment with anthelmintics (Yamashita 1964). Another patient having *E. cinetorchis* infection experienced intermittent abdominal pain, nausea, vomiting, indigestion, diarrhea, and constipation (Seo et al. 1980). Upper abdominal discomfort accompanied with duodenal ulcer was reported in a patient infected with *E. cinetorchis* (Makino et al. 1982). Two additional *E. cinetorchis* patients reported suffered from polyuria, weight loss, and loose stool in one patient, and general weakness in another patient (Ryang et al. 1986). A colonoscopy case was proved to be infected with 2 live worms of *E. cinetorchis* in the ascending colon; the patient suffered from right lower quadrant abdominal pain for 5 days (Jung et al. 2014). Patients infected with *E. ilocanum* experienced epigastric pain, abdominal pain, intestinal colic, diarrhea, constipation, flatulence, anorexia, and headache (Radomyos et al. 1982; Beaver et al. 1984). A young girl infected with *E. ilocanum* suffered from vomiting, diarrhea, and swelling of the feet for 7 days (Grover et al. 1998). In 2 patients infected with *E. ilocanum*, occasional gastrointestinal discomfort, indigestion, and diarrhea occurred; however, the clinical symptoms were mild (Sohn et al. 2011b). Some reports mentioned headache, dizziness, abdominal discomfort, and anemia as the symptoms of *E. ilocanum* infection (Cross and Basaca-Sevilla 1986). It is of note that among 18 American tourists to Kenya and Tanzania who were echinostome egg positive in fecal examinations (adult flukes were not recovered), 10 had moderately severe abdominal cramps and loose or watery stools (Poland et al. 1985). The clinical signs, including laboratory findings, in *Echinostoma* spp. infection are poorly known (Chai 2009). Peripheral blood eosinophilia is commonly observed in *E. cinetorchis* infected patients (Lee et al. 1988b). In experimental rats infected with *E. paraensei*, liver enzymes such as aspartate aminotransferase (AST), alanine aminotransferase (ALT), gamma-glutamyl transferase, and bilirubin, and glucose were elevated at weeks 1 and 2 after infection while total proteins were decreased at week 1 (Garcia et al. 2011). In the same experimental setting using rats, red blood cells, hematocrit, and hemoglobin were significantly decreased at week 1 suggesting normocystic normochromic anemia (Garcia et al. 2012). However, in human patients, these should be determined.

The diagnosis of human echinostomiasis is usually based on recovery of eggs in fecal examinations (Chai and Lee 2002) or can be done using immunological methods such as enzyme-linked immunosorbent assay (ELISA) (Toledo et al. 2006a). In fecal examinations, the eggs of different echinostome species exhibit similar size, shape, and morphology, so that specific diagnosis is usually difficult or frequently not possible. Only in rare instances, careful microscopic observations with measurements of the eggs may suggest specific diagnosis in known endemic areas with a single or mixed echinostome species infection (Chai 2009). For example, *E. lindoense* eggs are apparently bigger than *E. angustitestis* eggs; thus, a specific diagnosis can be done in endemic areas (Chai 2009). Therefore, if specific diagnosis of echinostome infections are preferred, recovery and identification of adult worms is strongly recommended (Chai and Lee 2002; Chai 2007, 2009).

The echinostome eggs are oval in most cases with a germ cell and yolk inside, yellowish, with a thin and refractory shell, and with a small, inconspicuous operculum located at the anterior end, and abopercular wrinkles or thickening at the terminal end (Chai 2009). In thick smears like Kato-Katz slides, the operculum, germ cell, and abopercular wrinkles may be difficult to see (Chai 2009). The sizes of human-infecting echinostome eggs are in the range, 0.066–0.149 mm in length and 0.043–0.090 mm in width, and those of *Echinostoma* spp. eggs are 0.077–0.124 mm in length and 0.052–0.076 mm in width (Chai 2009).

The detectability of echinostome eggs in the feces is remarkably different depending on the species (and genera) of echinostomes and worm load (Chai and Lee 2002). In *Echinostoma* spp. infections, the egg detectability is relatively high because the adult worms have a long uterine tubule and contain a plenty of eggs (more than 200) in their uteri. For example, *E. cinetorchis* sometimes contain more than 300 uterine eggs, so the infection is easily detected in fecal examination even if the patient was infected with only a single worm (Lee et al. 1988b). The detectability of eggs in the feces also depends on the egg laying capacity of each echinostome species (Chai and Lee 2002). Although its uterine tubule is short and contains not so many eggs, *Isthmiophora hortensis* (under the name *Echinostoma hortense*) infection is easily detected probably due to a high egg laying capacity and active deposition of eggs (Seo et al. 1985). In contrast, *Echinochasmus japonicus* and *Acanthoparyphium tyosenense* have a short uterine tubule and contain only a small number of eggs, 1–5 and 20–50, respectively; therefore, the detectability of eggs in the feces is comparatively low (Chai and Lee 2002).

ELISA has been developed to detect antibodies against *E. caproni, E. revolutum* or *E. friedi* (Toledo et al. 2006a). Using crude adult worm antigen, anti-*E. caproni* IgM was detected in serum of mice from week 2 post-infection, and IgG and IgA from week 4 post-infection (Agger et al. 1993). Using surface glycocalyx membrane crude antigen of adult *E. caproni,* IgG was detected in serum of mice from day 8 post-infection, which peaked at days 14–18 post-infection (Graczyk and Fried 1994). When excretory-secretory antigen of *E. caproni* was used, anti-*E. caproni* IgG was detected in serum of mice from week 2 post-infection (Toledo et al. 2005). Similar results were reported for *E. trivolvis* infection in mice; anti-*E. trivolvis* IgG was detected from day 10 post-infection (Graczyk and Fried 1995). However, a major limitation of these methods is that antibody response indicates previous exposures to echinostome infections rather than active infections (Toledo et al. 2006a). To overcome this limitation, a coproantigen capture ELISA was developed in *E. caproni* infection in hamsters and rats which appeared to be a rapid and sensitive method detecting antigens in the feces from as early as day 1–2 post-infection, allowing to distinguish between past and active infections (Toledo et al. 2004b).

In human echinostomiasis due to *Echinostoma* spp. infection, praziquantel in a single oral dose of 10–20 mg/kg can cure the disease (Lee et al. 1988b; Chai 2009). In experimental mice infected with *E. paraensei*, higher doses of praziquantel (50–100 mg/kg) was necessary to obtain a cure (Ferraz et al. 2012). Ultrastructural observations on the effects of praziquantel demonstrated an intense vacuolization of the tegument of *E. paraensei*, appearance of autophagic vacuoles, and swelling of the basal infolds of the tegumental syncytium (Gonçalves et al. 2013). Albendazole may also be effective for treatment of *Echinostoma* spp. infection (Chai 2007, 2009). In experimental NMRI mice, artemisinin derivatives, including artesunate (700 mg/kg) and artemether (1100 mg/kg), were shown to kill all *E. caproni* worms infected (Keiser et al. 2006).

2.2.13 Prevention and Control

Eating raw or improperly cooked freshwater fish, fresh or brackish water snails, or amphibians like frogs should be avoided to prevent *Echinostoma* spp. infections (Chai 2007). An herbicide named "Roundup" in Brazil was shown to have suppressive effects on hatching and survival of *E. paraensei* eggs in vitro and thus dynamics of transmission of this echinostome could be affected by this herbicide in the natural environments (Monte et al. 2016).

2.3 *Isthmiophora*

The genus *Isthmiophora* (subfamily Echinostominae) was established by Lühe in 1909 using *I. melis* reported from rodents by Schrank in 1788 as the type species (Yamaguti 1958; Kostadinova 2005a). Thereafter, taxonomic debates have continued until recently (Kostadinova and Gibson 2002; Kostadinova 2005a). Odhner in 1910 did not agree to the validity of *Isthmiophora*, and Bashikirova (1947) and Skrjabin and Bashikirova (1956) assigned *I. melis* in *Eupharyphium* Dietz, 1909 as *Euparyphium melis*. However, Yamaguti (1958) retained the genus *Isthmiophora*, and Dönges (1970) accepted *Isthmiophora* as a valid genus. Kostadinova and Gibson (2002) re-defined *Isthmiophora* genus comparing with *Euparyphium* Dietz, 1909, and included 6 species in *Isthmiophora*, namely, *I. melis* (Schrank, 1788) Lühe, 1909, *I. inermis* (Fuhrmann, 1904) Kostadinova and Gibson, 2002, *I. beaveri* (Yamaguti, 1958) Kostadinova and Gibson, 2002, *I. lukjanovi* (Cherkova, 1971) Kostadinova and Gibson, 2002, *I. citellicola* (Kadenatsii in Skrjabin and Bashikirova 1956) Kostadinova and Gibson, 2002, and *I. hortensis* (Asada, 1926) Kostadinova and Gibson, 2002. Among them, 2 species, namely, *I. hortensis* and *I. melis* are classified as zoonotic echinostomes.

I. hortensis was previously assigned to *Echinostoma* as *E. hortense* (Asada 1926) but transferred to *Isthmiophora* after morphological (Kostadinova and Gibson 2002) and molecular studies (Kostadinova et al. 2003). In addition, Kostadinova et al. (2003) suggested that 5 Australian (Townsville) isolates of *Echinostoma* sp. designated by Morgan and Blair (1998a) should be affiliated to *Isthmiophora*. This needs further verification. *I. melis* which was placed in *Isthmiophora* (Lühe 1909) was later transferred to either *Euparyphium* (Beaver et al. 1984) or *Echinostoma* (Harinasuta et al. 1987) but has been returned to a species belonging to *Isthmiophora* (Fried 2001; Kostadinova and Gibson 2002). Two macerated specimens recovered from a man in Japan were assigned as a new species of *Psilorchis* (*Psilorchis hominis*) (Psilostomidae) (Kifune and Takao 1973); however, they were considered unquestionably belong to *Isthmiophora* (Kostadinova 2005b).

The adults of the genus *Isthmiophora* Lühe, 1909 are characterized by the presence of 27 collar spines, and their testes are irregular in shape or lobed and located in the middle of the posterior half of the body (Fried 2001). Kostadinova and Gibson

(2002) listed further important characters of *Isthmiophora* as the considerably more anterior position of the testes (pre-equatorial or equatorial), the presence of an armed cirrus, the small head collar with a faint ventral ridge, the differing size of the dorsal collar spines (oral longer than aboral), the short forebody and uterus, and large eggs. The genus *Euparyphium* is morphologically close to *Isthmiophora.* Kostadinova and Gibson (2002) listed 4 species in *Euparyphium*; *E. capitaneum* Dietz, 1909, *E. murinum* Tubangui, 1931, *E. guerreroi* Tubangui, 1931, and *E. albuferensis* Esteban et al., 1997. *Euparyphium* differs from *Isthmiophora* by having an elongate filiform body, strongly elongate testes, unspined tegument, unspined cirrus, and smaller sized eggs; *Isthmiophora* has a plump body, large irregularly rounded testes, spined tegument, armed cirrus, and large eggs (Dietz 1909; Lühe 1909; Mendheim 1943; Kostadinova and Gibson 2002). The genus *Echinostoma* also has some morphological features similar to *Isthmiophora. Echinostoma* has a long uterine field, postequatorial testes with not very long post-testicular field, and an unarmed cirrus, whereas *Isthmiophora* has a short uterine field, pre-equatorial or equatorial testes and very long post-testicular field, and an armed cirrus (Kostadinova 2005a). *Echinoparyphium* is another genus morphologically close to *Isthmiophora* and *Euparyphium* (Toledo et al. 1998; Kostadinova and Gibson 2002). The generic characters of *Echinoparyphium* include small to medium body, presence of 29–45 sharply pointed collar spines in double row, dorsal aboral spines longer than dorsal oral spines, angle spines (4–5 on each side) longer than marginal spines, post-testicular field not very long, and small sized eggs, not numerous (Kostadinova 2005a). In comparison, *Isthmiophora* has medium to large body, presence of not sharply pointed 27–29 collar spines with dorsal spines in double row, dorsal aboral spines shorter than oral spines, angle spines (4 on each side) slightly longer than marginal spines, very long post-testicular field, and large sized eggs, not numerous (Kostadinova 2005a). *Hypoderaeum* is also similar to *Isthmiophora* in that they both have an elongate, medium to large body size, small head collar, short uterus, and long post-testicular length; however, *Hypoderaeum* has a bluntly ended anterior end with a very short forebody, a very weakly developed collar, and an unarmed cirrus, whereas *Isthmiophora* has a moderately short forebody, a small but distinct collar, and an armed cirrus (Kostadinova 2005a).

In this section, 2 species of *Isthmiophora* infecting humans, having 27 collar spines and distributed in Asia (*I. hortensis*) or Europe and North America (*I. melis*), together with a few potentially zoonotic *Isthmiophora* spp. are described.

2.3.1 Isthmiophora hortensis

2.3.1.1 *Isthmiophora hortensis* (Asada, 1926) Kostadinova and Gibson, 2002

[syn. *Echinostoma hortense* Asada, 1926; *Echinostoma campi* Ono, 1930; *Euparyphium amurensis* Besprozvannykh, 2001]

Taxonomy and Morphology

I. hortensis (Fig. 2.11a) was originally described as *Echinostoma hortense* based on specimens obtained from experimental rats and dogs infected with metacercariae in tadpoles of *Rana* and *Bufo* spp. (Asada 1926, 1939). It was found again in naturally infected rodents in Japan (Yamaguti 1933, 1939), South Korea (Park 1938, Seo et al. 1964, 1981), and China (Fan and Sun, 1989). In the meantime, *Echinostoma campi* was reported as a new species from dogs (natural and experimental) and rats (experimental) in Manchuria, China (Ono 1930). Its metacercariae were found from both amphibia (tadpoles) and fish (loach; *Misgurnus* sp.); for this reason, this echinostome was considered distinct from *E. hortense* (reported only from amphibians by that time) and assigned as a new species *E. campi* (Ono 1930). Yamaguti (1958)

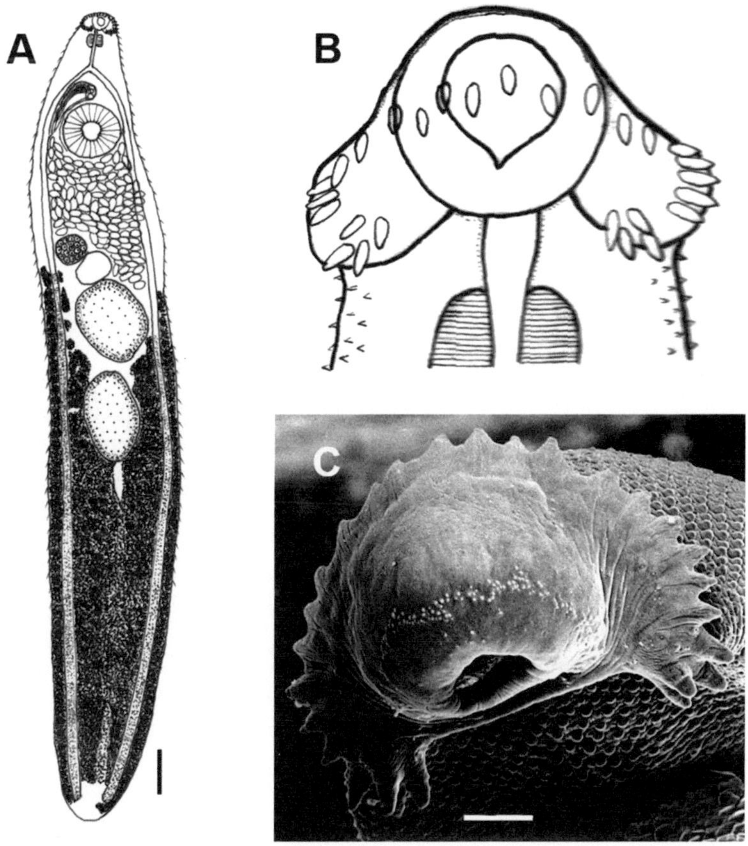

Fig. 2.11 *Isthmiophora hortensis*. (**a**) Line drawing of an adult worm (original figure). Scale bar = 1 mm (**b**) Collar spines (n = 27) around the oral sucker of a 28-day-old adult fluke recovered from an experimental rat. (Reproduced from Seo et al. (1980) Seoul J Med 21:21–29 with permission). (**c**) Scanning electron microscopic view of the head collar, with collar spines (n = 27) of a 4-week-old adult fluke recovered from an experimental rat. (Reproduced from Lee et al. (1986) Korean J Parasitol 24:63–70 with permission)

was of opinion that *E. campi* is a synonym of *E. hortense*, but Okamoto (1954) objected to this synonymy. However, Arizono et al. (1976), Tani (1976a), and Chai et al. (1985a) followed the synonymy proposed by Yamaguti (1958) accepting that both amphibians and fish can be the second intermediate host of *E. hortense*. Thereafter, the name *E. hortense* had been used until recently.

However, Kostadinova and Gibson (2002) notified that the morphologic characters given by Asada (1926, 1939), Park (1938), Yamaguti (1933, 1939, 1941), and Saito (1984) for *E. hortense* suggested that this species agrees better with the diagnostic features of the genus *Isthmiophora*. They subsequently confirmed the affiliation of the specimens of *E. hortense* (from South Korea) with *Isthmiophora* (*I. hortensis* n. comb.) based on morphologic characters such as short uterine field (5.7–8.0% of the total body length), pre-equatorial or equatorial testes, very long post-testicular field (37.6–42.2% of body length), 27 collar spines (Fig. 2.11b, c) of which angle spines (4 on each side) are slightly longer than marginal ones, dorsal spines in oral and aboral rows of different sizes, anterior limit of vitellaria at ovarian or mid-uterine level, and armed cirrus (Kostadinova and Gibson 2002). Kostadinova et al. (2003) performed molecular analyses of the internal transcribed spacer (ITS) locus of genomic DNA and nicotinamide adenine dinucleotide dehydrogenase (NADH) subunit 1 (ND1) locus of mitochondrial genes from a lot of echinostome species. As a result, based on ND1 data, they justified the taxonomic transfer of *E. hortense* to *Isthmiophora*. This new combination is followed by Sato and Suzuki (2006), Sato et al. (2006), Qiu et al. (2017), and Sohn et al. (2017). The author agrees to the new combination for this important zoonotic echinostomes.

Euparyphium amurensis was described as a new species from Russian-Far East on the basis of 5 experimentally raised adults from rats fed the metacercariae (Besprozvannykh 2001). However, the descriptions of *E. amurensis* were closely corresponded to *I. hortensis* in terms of most morphological and metrical features (Kostadinova and Gibson 2002). Therefore, the author treated *E. amurensis* as a synonym of *I. hortensis*.

Human infections with *I. hortensis* were first documented in Japan by Tani et al. (1974), Arizono et al. (1976), and Tani (1976a). Subsequently, human *I. hortensis* infection was discovered in South Korea (Seo et al. 1983; Ryang et al. 1985; Lee et al. 1986b) and China (Chen et al. 1993). An endemic focus with 15 human infections were reported from Akita Prefecture, Japan (Tani 1976a), and a larger endemic focus with 59 human infections (22.4% of 263 inhabitants) were discovered in Cheongsong-gun (County), Gyeongsangbuk-do (Province), South Korea (Lee et al. 1988). In China, 6 out of 10 hospitalized patients with hepatitis in Liaoning Province were found infected with *I. hortensis* (Chen et al. 1993).

The morphological characters of *I. hortensis* include the presence of dorsally uninterrupted 27 collar spines (Fig. 2.11b, c) with a poorly developed ventral ridge and a submedially located ovary (Chai and Lee 2002; Kostadinova and Gibson 2002). The collar spines are blunt-ended, with dorsal spines arranged in 2 alter native rows and lateral spines arranged in a single row; angle spines are 4 on each side and longer than marginal ones, and oral spines are slightly longer than aboral ones (Kostadinova and Gibson 2002). The adult flukes are leaf-like,

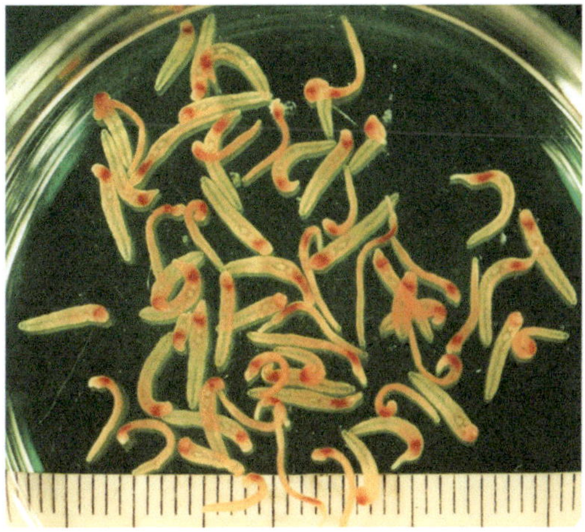

Fig. 2.12 Adult flukes of *Isthmiophora hortensis* recovered from experimentally infected rats. Red color in worms indicate the uterus filled with eggs

with a red-colored spot near the anterior end when life (Fig. 2.12), and 5.38–6.46 × 1.36–1.83 mm in size, and the eggs are 127–139 × 71–81 μm in size (Seo et al. 1983; Kostadinova and Gibson 2002). The most important key to differentiate *I. hortense* from *I. melis* is the location of the cirrus sac; it is located between intestinal bifurcation and ventral sucker in *I. hortensis* but it is located antero-dorsal to the ventral sucker in *I. melis* (Kostadinova and Gibson 2002). *I. hortensis* has usually 27 collar spines but *I. lukjanovi* and *I. citellicola* have 29 collar spines (Kostadinova and Gibson 2002). Whereas *I. hortensis* has a more anterior distribution of vitellaria (at level of the ovary) and anterior testis broadly oval and posterior testis elongate-oval, *I. inermis* has a less anterior distribution of vitellaria, at level of anterior testis, and elongate testes (Kostadinova and Gibson 2002). *I. beaveri* is differed from *I. hortensis, I. melis,* and *I. inermis* in that *I. beaveri* has an equatorial anterior testis and relatively short post-testicular field, but the 3 latters have a pre-equatorial anterior testis and longer post-testicular field (Kostadinova and Gibson 2002).

The tegumental ultrastructure of *I. hortensis* adult flukes (4-week-old in rats) (Lee et al. 1986a) was generally similar to that of other echinostomes, including *E. trivolvis* (Fried and Fujino 1984). It was characterized by a leaf-like body, with ventrally curved anterior end, looking like "e" or "c" shape (Lee et al. 1986a). The tegument of the whole body was wrinkled transversely and covered with cobblestone-like cytoplasmic processes (Lee et al. 1986a). The lip of the oral sucker had aciliated round swollen (type II) sensory papillae on its ventral half and had uniciliated knob-like (type I) sensory papillae on the dorsal outer surface (Lee et al. 1986a). The ventral sucker was aspinous and had many type I sensory papillae arranged in a circular band on its outer surface, and the tegument around the genital opening was devoid of sensory papillae but of similar feature to the ventral sucker (Lee et al. 1986a). Scale-like spines with broad base and round tip were distributed densely on the tegument anterior to the ventral sucker but they became sparse in the posterior half of the ventral surface, finally to disappear at posterior extremity; a few type I sensory papillae were observed to the ventral surface (Lee et al. 1986a). However, type III sensory papillae which was observed in *E. trivolvis* (Fried and Fujino 1984) were not found in *I. hortensis* (Lee et al. 1986a).

Life Cycle

I. hortensis has the life cycle stages of the egg, miracidium, sporocyst, redia, daughter redia, cercaria, metacercaria, and adult (Lee et al. 1991). The snail intermediate hosts were confirmed to be *Lymnaea pervia* (Fig. 2.13a), *Lymnaea ollula, Lymnaea japonica*, and *Radix auricularia coreana* (Ono 1930; Asada 1939; Ahn and Ryang 1986; Ahn and Kang 1988; Lee et al. 1991). Cercariae (Fig. 2.13b) shed from these snails enter various kinds of second intermediate hosts, including the amphibians such as the tadpoles of *Rana* spp. and *Bufo* spp., and the larva of *Hynobius* spp. (Asada 1939; Komiya 1965) and freshwater fish including the loaches (*Misgurnus anguillicaudatus* and *Misgurnus mizolepis*) and *Acanthogobius flavimanus, Acheilognathus moriokae*, *Odontobutis obscura interrupta* (Fig. 2.14a), *Moroco oxycephalus, Coreoperca kawamebari*, *Squalidus coreanus,* and *Carassius carassius* (experimental) in Japan and South Korea (Ono 1930; Tani 1976a, b; Seo et al. 1980; Chai et al. 1985a; Ahn et al. 1985; Ryang et al. 1985; Lee et al. 1988; Ryang 1990; Sohn et al. 2018). In loaches, the metacercariae were predominantly found in head tissues and soft tissues, in particular, around the mesentery (Okahashi 1966) or perianal area (Tani 1976b; Saito and Tani 1982; Chai et al. 1985a). A species of brackish water fish, *Acanthogobius flavimanus* (= yellowfin goby), has been added among the second intermediate hosts of *I. hortensis* in Shian-gun and Muan-gun,

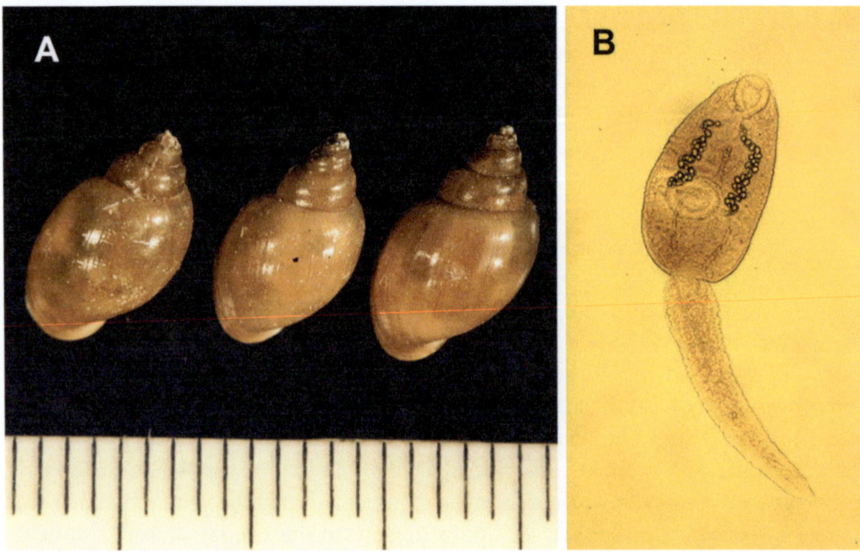

Fig. 2.13 *Isthmiophora hortensis*. (**a**) Freshwater snails, *Lymnaea pervia*, the first intermediate host (**b**) Cercaria shed from the snail host. The cercarial body is 300 μm long, and the tail is 450 μm long

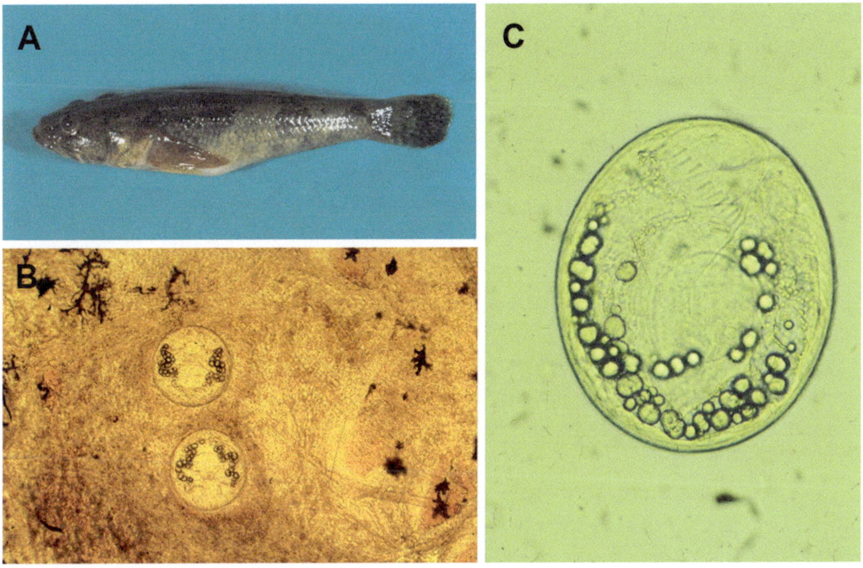

Fig. 2.14 *Isthmiophora hortensis*. (**a**) Freshwater fish, *Odontobutis obscura interrupta*, a second intermediate host in an endemic area of Cheongsong-gun, Gyeongsangbuk-do, South Korea. (**b**) Two metacercariae in the gill of an experimentally infected tadpole of *Rana* sp. in the laboratory. ×100 (**c**) Metacercaria isolated from the gill of an infected tadpole in the laboratory. ×400. (**a**–**c**). (Reproduced from the figure in Chai (2009) The Biology of Echinostomes (Fried B, Toledo R, eds). Springer, New York, USA with permission)

South Korea (Sohn et al. 2009). Tadpoles of *Rana nigromaculata* were also experimentally proven to be a second intermediate host having metacercariae in the gill (Fig. 2.14b, c) (Lee et al. 1991). In South Korea, 41.6% (64 of 154 loaches *Misgurnus anguillicaudatus* examined in 4 areas were found infected with *I. hortensis* metacercariae (Chai et al. 1985a). In Liaoning Province of China, 69.7% of the loach *Misgurnus anguillicaudatus* purchased from a local market was infected with *I. hortensis* metacercariae (Chen et al. 1993). In addition, the loaches from Nenjiang River, Heilongjiang Province, China, were also found infected with the metacercariae of *I. hortensis* (Qiu et al. 2017). Natural definitive hosts include mice (Sohn et al. 2014, 2017), rats (Park 1938; Seo et al. 1964, 1981), dogs (Ono 1930; Tani 1976b; Cho et al. 1981; Okanishi et al. 2013), cats (Sohn and Chai 2005; Shin et al. 2015; Sohn et al. 2017), raccoon dogs (Sato and Suzuki 2006; Sato et al. 2006), martens (Sato et al. 1999), weasels (Sato et al. 1999), and wild boars (Sohn et al. 2017). Mice, rats, and humans have also been shown to be experimentally susceptible to *I. hortensis* infection (Ono 1930; Seo et al. 1980, 1985; Lee et al. 2004).

The complete life cycle was successfully maintained in the laboratory using *Lymnaea* snails and tadpoles of *Rana nigromaculata* as the first and second intermediate hosts, respectively, and ICR mice as the experimental definitive host (Lee et al. 1991). Eggs were obtained by in vitro maintenance of adult flukes (in Tyrode solution) recovered from experimental rats fed the metacercariae in loaches, *Misgurnus anguillicaudatus*, at week 3 post-infection (Lee et al. 1991). The eggs were incubated in distilled water at 28–29 °C in an incubator and 13 days later hatched under sun light with emergence of miracidia (Lee et al. 1991). Miracidia were made contact with *Lymnaea pervia* snails cultivated and maintained in the laboratory, and the infected snails were kept for 30 days until cercariae emerge from the snails (Lee et al. 1991). Sporocysts were detected at day 7 post-infection, and full developed mother rediae containing daughter rediae were recovered from day 14 post-infection; daughter rediae were containing mature cercariae at day 30 post-infection (Lee et al. 1991). It took 30–31 days from miracidial infection to cercarial shedding in snails (Lee et al. 1991). The cercarial body was 253–347 μm long and 119–173 μm wide on average, and the tail was 436–485 μm long and 40–64 μm wide; the cercariae had a weakly developed head collar, and it was unable to recognize the presence of collar spines (Lee et al. 1991). The cercariae were infected to laboratory-reared tadpoles of *Rana nicromaculata*, and from day 1 post-infection mature metacercariae infective to mice were harvested from the posterior abdominal wall and gill of tadpoles (Lee et al. 1991). More than 30% of metacercariae aged from day 1 (one metacercaria among 30 given were already infective to mice at 6 h) to day 50 post-infection to tadpoles were successfully infected to ICR mice (Lee et al. 1991). The metacercarial cyst was 140–174 μm long and 123–166 μm wide, and the average size of excysted metacercariae were 426 μm in length and 203 μm in width (Lee et al. 1991). The head collar and collar spines were clearly visible in metacercariae (Lee et al. 1991).

The development of metacercariae to adults in the definitive host was studied by various workers (Saito 1984; Seo et al. 1985; Lee et al. 1991). Up to 90% of the metacercariae of 9 days old in tadpoles were infective to mice (Seo et al. 1980; Lee et al. 1991). The growth of genital organs such as the testes, ovary, and cirrus pouch in experimental rats was morphologically accomplished in 6–7 days (Saito 1984). The growth curve of the sexual organs showed S-shaped lines, while that of the other parenchymal organs (such as suckers, pharynx, and head collar) was straight lines until day 10–14 post-infection (Saito 1984; Seo et al. 1985). The entry of sperms into the female reproductive system may take place ventrally via the genital pore and uterus but not dorsally via the Laurer's canal (Saito 1984). The prepatent period was 10–12 days in rats and 16–17 days in humans (experimental infection); the egg production reaches a peak at day 32–33 post-infection and decreased thereafter (Seo et al. 1985). The number of eggs per gram of feces was 390 at day 32–33 post-infection in humans and 417 at day 34–36 post-infection in rats (Seo et al. 1985).

In human volunteers infected with *I. hortensis*, fecal eggs began to be detected around day 16–17 post-infection and continued to be detected until day 70–90 post-infection (Tani 1979). The number of eggs per gram of feces (EPG) peaked to be 22–30 on day 20–30 post-infection, and then decreased thereafter quickly (Tani 1979).

Epidemiology and Geographical Distribution

Human infections with *I. hortensis* have been found in Japan, South Korea, and China (Fig. 2.15; Table 2.4) (Tani et al. 1974; Arizono et al. 1976; Tani 1976a; Seo et al. 1983; Chen et al. 1993; Chai and Lee 2002). The principal mode of human infection is consumption of raw freshwater fish, in particular, loaches in Japan (Tani 1976a, b) and China (Chen et al. 1993), and presumably carps, *Odontobutis obscura interrupta* and *Moroco oxycephalus,* in South Korea (Lee et al. 1988).

China In 1930, *Echinostoma campi* was reported as a new echinostome species in Mukden, Manchuria which takes both tadpoles and loaches as the second intermediate host, and dogs (natural and experimental) and rats (experimental) as the definitive hosts (Ono 1930). It looked different from *I. hortensis* (= *E. hortense*) in that *E. campi* takes fish as the second intermediate host, whereas *I. hortensis* takes amphibians as the second intermediate host in its original description (Asada 1926). However, *E. campi* was later synonymized with *I. hortensis* (under the name *E. hortense*) (Yamaguti 1958), although Okamoto (1954) supported the validity of *E. campi*. According to Ono (1930), 2 (0.65%) of 308 stray dogs harboured one specimen each of *I. hortensis* adults, and about 20% of *Lymnaea* sp. snails shed the cercariae. The cercariae were infective not only to tadpoles but also to freshwater fish, including the loach, silver carp, and gold fish (Ono 1930). Based on infections in intermediate and definitive hosts, the areas of *I. hortensis* distribution included Fujian, Shanghai, Liaoning, and Jilin Provinces (Chen et al. 1985). Heilongjiang, Guangxi, and Anhui Provinces were added among the localities where *I. hortensis* is distributed (Fan and Sun 1989; Liu and Shi 2011; Zhan et al. 2017; Qiu et al. 2017).

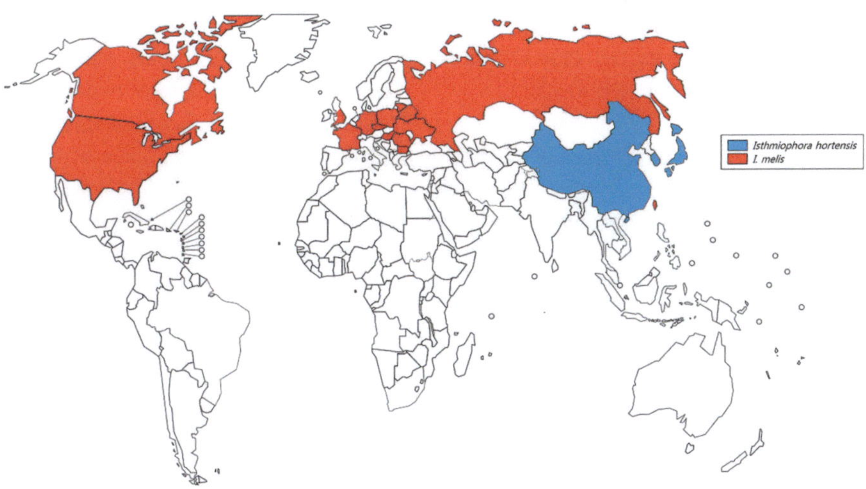

Fig. 2.15 Global distribution of *Isthmiophora* spp. (*I. hortensis* and *I. melis*) based on the presence of their life cycles

The first case of human *I. hortens is* infection was reported from Harbin, Heilongjiang Province; the patient had the history of eating raw loaches and complained of dizziness, adynamia, and upper abdominal pain, and expelled 70 adult specimens after anthelmintic treatment (Fan and Sun 1989). Subsequently, in Liaoning Province, 6 out of 10 hospitalized hepatitis patients who had eaten raw loach were found infected with *I. hortensis*, and out of 33 loaches purchased from the region, metacercariae of *I. hortensis* were detected in 23 (69.7%), with particular location in perianal soft tissues (Chen et al. 1993). Two human cases were later detected in Guangxi Province; 4 and 3 adult specimens each of *I. hortensis* were recovered after anthelmintic medication (Liu and Shi 2011). The presence of *I. hortensis* in domestic animals (kinds of animal not specified) was also confirmed in Huainan areas of north Anhui Province (Zhan et al. 2017). In Nanjiang River, Heilongjiang Province, 19 (4.0%) of 476 loaches, *Misgurnus anguillicaudatus*, was found infected with the metacercariae of *I. hortensis* (Qiu et al. 2017).

Japan *I. hortensis* was originally reported from experimental rats near Tokyo, Japan (Asada 1926) and then natural infections were found in field rats (*Rattus norvegicus*; locality unknown) and weasels (*Mustela sibirica itasi*) near Kyoto (Yamaguti 1933, 1939). Later, in Hokkaido, Kamiya and Ishigaki (1972) also found this echinostome in weasels. The first human infection case was discovered in Akita Prefecture and reported under the name *Echinostoma* sp. (Tani et al. 1974). Subsequently, 15 (0.2%) of 6356 persons examined in several villages of Akita Prefecture revealed echinostome eggs in their feces, and after treatment with an anthelmintic drug (Kamala) 12 adult specimens were recovered from 2 patients which were morphologically identified as *I. hortensis* (under the name *Echinostoma hortense*) (Tani 1976a). The source of infection was suggested to be raw freshwater fish, particularly the loach (*Misgurnus anguillicaudatus*) (Tani 1976a). Separately from this, Arizono et al. (1976) discovered 4 human cases of *I. hortensis* (under the name *Echinostoma hortense*) in Osaka or Kobe Prefecture. The source of infection was also the loach, and the metacercariae recovered from the loach were experimentally fed to 2 human volunteers and 3 experimental dogs; adult flukes were recovered from dogs at day 33 post-infection and eggs of *I. hortensis* were detected in the feces of humans at day 16 post-infection (Arizono et al. 1976). A human case was added from Shimane Prefecture who consumed raw loaches, and it was estimated that about 20 human *I. hortensis* infections were reported by this time in Japan (Makino et al. 1982). Thereafter, human *I. hortensis* infection has been found sporadically, including 6 more cases diagnosed by gastrointestinal endoscopy in different parts of Japan (Kyoto, Hokkaido, Tottori, Ehime, and Okayama Prefectures) (Hamamoto et al. 1997; Tanaka et al. 2008).

In addition to loaches, Tani (1976b) added another freshwater fish species, *Acheilognathus moriokae* (Japanese bittering), as the second intermediate host, and *Rattus norvegicus* (brown rat), *Mustela sibirica* (weasel), *Maltes melampus* (marten), and *Canis familiaris* (dog) as the natural definitive host in Akita Prefecture. Tani (1976c) further studied on the susceptibility of humans and various kinds of animals to *I. hortensis* infection and reported that rats were the most highly susceptible host, whereas humans were a less susceptible host. In Asahikawa City of Hokkaido, Miyamoto et al. (1983) reported that 14 (93.3%) of 15 feral minks (*Mustela vison*) were infected with adult flukes of *I. hortensis*, and the metacercariae of *I. hortensis* were detected in the soft tissue around the anus of the Asian pound loaches (*Misgurnus anguillicaudatus*) and Siberian stone loaches (*Barbatula toni*); *Lymnaea japonica* snails were found to be the first intermediate host of *I. hortensis* in this area. Harada et al. (1983) was the first who detected 2 human cases diagnosed by gastrointestinal endoscopy in Kyoto; one case was mixed-infected with *Echinochasmus japonicus* which was recovered after anthelmintic treatment and purging. In Wakayama Prefecture, 26 (4.9%) of 531 feral raccoons (*Procyon lotor*) examined were identified as *I. hortensis* based on morphological and molecular studies (Sato and Suzuki 2006). Okanishi et al. (2013) extracted 2 adult specimens of *I. hortensis* from a dog suffering from severe enteritis with vomiting and diarrhea using gastrointestinal endoscopy.

South Korea Park (1938) first reported the presence of this species in South Korea; 15 adult specimens of *I. hortensis* were recovered from 5 rats captured around Seoul. After then, various species of rodents (*Rattus norvegicus, Rattus rattus alexandrius, Apodemus agrarius, Mus musculus yamashinai,* and *Microtus fortis pellcius*) captured from Chulwon, Geumhwa, Cheongpyong, Paju, Pocheon, and Seoul were found infected with *I. hortensis* (Seo et al. 1964). Subsequently, a dog from Iksan area, Jeollabuk-do (Province) was infected with this species (misdiagnosed as *Euparyphium melis*) (Rhee and Rim 1970). Later, this fluke was recovered from 4 (5.6%) of 72 stray dogs caught from Ejungbu City, Gyeonggi-do (Province) (Cho et al. 1981). Another survey of house rats revealed *I. hortensis* infection in 16 (9.4%) out of 170 rats caught from different localities; infected rats were detected from Gapyong, Namyangju, Yongin, Youngweol, Jungwon, Hadong, and Naju areas (Seo et al. 1981). Around this time, the metacercariae of *I. hortensis* were first found in loaches *Misgurnus anguillicaudatus* in an area of Hwaseong-gun, Gyeonggi-do (Seo et al. 1980).

The first report of human *I. hortensis* infection was published in 1983 (Seo et al. 1983). The patient was a 21-year-old man, and several echinostome eggs were found in routine fecal examination; after treatment with praziquantel 20 mg/kg in a single dose, an adult specimen was recovered together with 4 specimens of the liver fluke *Clonorchis sinensis* (Seo et al. 1983). His infection source with *I. hortensis* was unclear, although he recalled to have consumed various kinds of freshwater fish under raw conditions; but he denied having eaten raw loaches (Seo et al. 1983). The second and third human infections were discovered in Gangwon-do (Province); both cases revealed eggs of 0.108–0.142 mm by 0.066–0.078 mm in the feces, and from one patient 6 adult specimens were recovered after treatment with praziquantel 10 mg/kg in a single dose (Ryang et al. 1985). The 2 patients ate raw freshwater fish, including carps and minnows (*Zacco platypus, Carrasius auratus,* and *Moroco oxycephalus*), and 3 (3.6%) out of 84 *Morocco oxycephalus* fish caught around the village and examined were positive for *I. hortensis* metacercariae (Ryang et al. 1985). Later, an epidemiological survey was undertaken along the Namhan River, and 2 (0.3%) of 745 people were positive for *I. hortensis* eggs in their feces; one (2.9%) of 29 house rats caught around the village was positive for *I. hortensis* eggs in the feces (Ahn and Ryang 1986). Four species of 14 freshwater fish species examined were confirmed to be the second intermediate host; *Misgurnus anguillicaudatus, Misgurnus mizolepis, Morocco oxycephalus,* and *Odontobutis obscura interrupta*; one snail species, *Radix auricularia coreana*, was confirmed to be the first intermediate host in this area (Ahn and Ryang 1986). Two more patients were confirmed as *I. hortensis* infection in a university hospital in Seoul; one was egg positive but recovery of adult worms was unsuccessful; the other was egg positive and 21 adult flukes were recovered after treatment with praziquantel 12 mg/kg in a single dose, together with 8 specimens of *Metagonimus takahashii* (Lee SK et al. 1986).

Subsequently, an endemic focus of *I. hortensis* infection was discovered in a village of Cheongsong-gun (County), Gyangsangnam-do (Province), where the eggs of *I. hortensis* was positive in 59 (22.4%) of 263 residents examined; 35 of 59 egg positive cases were treated with praziquantel 10 mg/kg in a single dose, and 1–649 (mean 51) adult specimens of *I. hortensis* were recovered from each case (Lee SK et al. 1988). Three of the 35 worm-positive cases expelled more than 100 worms; 134, 475, and 649, respectively (Lee SK et al. 1988). In this study, a freshwater fish species, *Squalidus coreanus*, has been added as a new second intermediate host of *I. hortensis* (Lee et al. 1988). Around the Choongju Lake and upper streams of Namhan River, 3 echinostome egg positive cases were detected; one patient was considered an *E. cinetorchis* infection, and the other 2 were considered *I. hortensis* infection; adult flukes were recovered from one of these 2 patients (Ryang 1990). Two fish species, *Coreoperca kawamebari* and *Acanthogobius flavimanus*, was newly added as a second intermediate host of *I. hortensis* (Ryang 1990; Sohn et al. 2018). Further, 11 (9.5%) of 116 villagers in a rural village of Geochang-gun (County), Gyeongsangnam-do (Province) were positive for *I. hortensis* eggs in the feces and 7 of them expelled a total of 452 (6–227 by individual) adult flukes after praziquantel (10 mg/kg in a single dose) treatment and purgation (Son et al. 1994). During one-year period of 1996, 5 cases of *I. hortensis* infection were detected in a university hospital in Seoul by recovery of adult flukes after medication with praziquantel (Kim and Cho 1996).

Clinical cases of *I. hortensis* infection were occasionally diagnosed by gastrointestinal endoscopy (Chai et al. 1994; Lee and Hong 2002; Cho et al. 2003; Chang et al. 2005; Park and Kim 2006). The first case was a 55-year-old man living in Hamyang-gun (County), Gyeongsangnam-do (Province) who had the clinical symptoms of epigastric pain and hematemesis; endoscopy revealed lesions of early gastric cancer and duodenal ulcerations (Chai et al. 1994). A penetrating parasite into the duodenal mucosa was picked out under endoscopy and the worm was morphologically identified as *I. hortensis*, and after treatment with praziquantel 10 mg/kg in a single dose 3 more specimens of *I. hortensis* adults, together with 7 specimens of *Metagonimus* sp., were recovered (Chai et al. 1994). The second clinical case was a 40-year-old Korean woman who complained of acidic belching, epigastric discomfort, dizziness, and weight loss of 2 kg; upper endoscopy revealed 2 worms in the stomach; one was penetrating into the mucosa on the lesser curvature of the antrum, the other was attached to the mucosal surface of the great curvature of the antrum; she often consumed raw freshwater fish (Lee and Hong 2002). The third case was a 81-year-old Korean man who complained of epigastric discomfort of several days duration; upper endoscopy revealed 2 worms in the duodenal bulb area and were removed using an endoscopic forcep; he often consumed raw freshwater fish, including the loach (Cho et al. 2003). The fourth clinical case was a 55-year-old woman who complained of upper abdominal pain and discomfort which persisted for 2 weeks; upper gastroduodenoscopy, 2 motile flukes were found attached to the duodenal bulb, and retrieved with endoscopic forceps; she had the history of eating raw frog meat which was suggested as the infection source (Chang et al. 2005). Another clinical case was a 75-year-old female who complained of nausea, vomiting, and epigastric pain that had persisted for 1 month; 2 live worms were removed from the mucosal surface of the duodenal bulb area under endoscopy; her infection source was presumed to be the loaches purchased from a local market which were consumed raw (Park and Kim 2006).

Russia *Euparyphium amurensis* described as a new species from Russian-Far East on the basis of 5 specimens recovered from experimentally infected rats fed the metacercariae (Besprozvannykh 2001). However, *E. amurensis* was close to *I. hortensis* in terms of most morphological and metrical features (Kostadinova and Gibson 2002); thus, in this book it is considered that *I. hortensis* is existing in Russia.

2.3.2 Isthmiophora melis

2.3.2.1 *Isthmiophora melis* (Schrank, 1788) Lühe, 1909

[syn. *Echinostoma trigonocephalum* (Rudolphi, 1802) Cobbold, 1860; *Echinostoma spiculator* (Dujardin, 1845) Cobbold, 1860; *Echinostoma melis* (Schrank, 1788) Dietz, 1909; *Euparyphium melis* (Schrank, 1788) Railliet, 1919; *Euparyphium suinum* Ciurea, 1921; *Euparyphium jassyense* Leon and Ciurea, 1922; *Echinocirrus melis* (Schrank, 1788) Mendheim, 1943]

Taxonomy and Morphology
I. melis (Fig. 2.16) was originally reported as *Fasciola melis* by Schrank F. von B. in 1788 from rodents and carnivores in Europe and North America (Yamaguti 1958). In 1802, Rudophi C. A. named this echinostome as *Fasciola trigonocephala* (Yamaguti 1958). Later, Lühe (1909) proposed the genus *Isthmiophora* taking *I. melis* as the type species (Kostadinova and Gibson 2002). At the same time, Dietz (1909) placed *I. melis* in *Echinostoma* as *Echinostoma melis* and created the genus *Euparyphium* using *E. capitaneum* as the type species. In 1919, Railliet A. assigned *I. melis* in the genus *Euparyphium*, and named it as *Euparyphium melis* (Kostadinova and Gibson 2002). Thereafter, taxonomic confusion continued on this species, and

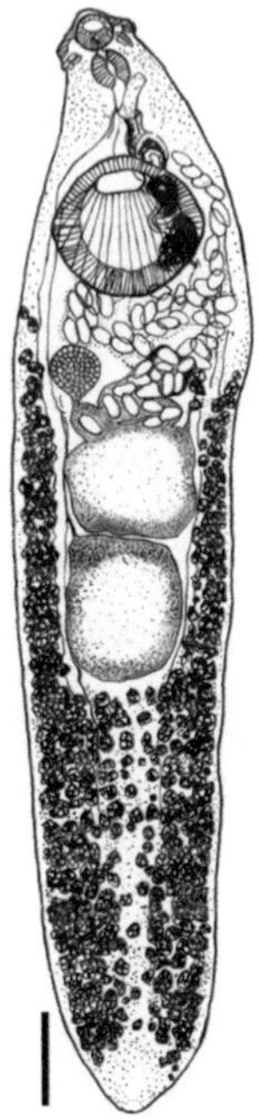

Fig. 2.16 Line drawing of an adult fluke of *Isthmiophora melis*. Scale bar = 1 mm. (Redrawn from the figure in Dönges (1967) Z Parasitenkd 29:1–14)

it had been either placed in *Echinostoma* (as *E. jassyense*, Harinasuta et al. 1987) or in *Euparyphium* (Nicoll 1923; Beaver 1941; Skrjabin and Bashikirova 1956; Gupta 1962; Beaver et al. 1984) or *Isthmiophora* (Yamaguti 1958; Smales and Blankespoor 1984; Fried 2001; Kostadinova and Gibson 2002). Yamaguti (1958) and Kostadinova (2005a) acknowledged both *Isthmiophora* and *Euparyphium* genera and assigned *I. melis* as the type species of *Isthmiophora* and *E. capitaneum* as the type of *Euparyphium*. Beaver (1941) reported the life cycle of *Euparyphium melis* in USA (Douglas Lake, Michigan and Minnesota) and Canada (Ontario); however, Yamaguti (1958) named this species as an American form of *Euparyphium,* and named *E. beaveri*. Later, however, Kostadinova and Gibson (2002) transferred this species to *Isthmiophora* under the name *I. beaveri*.

Human infection with *I. melis* was first confirmed by Leon in 1916 in a diarrheic patient in Romania (Beaver et al. 1984) and then in another case at autopsy of a Chinese patient (Hsü 1940). Later, human infections were reported in Taiwan, and Liaoning Province, China (Yu and Mott 1994). The source of human infections in China was presumed to be the tadpoles (Hsü 1940) and the loach, *Misgurnus anguillicaudatus* (Yu and Mott 1994). The snail *Lymnaea stagnalis* was found to be the first intermediate host (Dönges and Götzelmann 1977), and amphibians and fish were the second intermediate host (Motzel and Haas 1985; Radev et al. 2009). In Belarus, domestic and wild vertebrate animals were found to be infected with this fluke (Shimalov and Shimalov 2002a).

The morphological characters of *I. melis* include the presence of dorsally uninterrupted 27 collar spines, including 8 (4 + 4) corner spines on each side (Rim 1982;

Kostadinova and Gibson 2002). The collar spines are blunt-pointed; corner spines (2 dorsal and 2 ventral) are longer than marginal ones; lateral spines are in single row; dorsal spines are in double row; and oral spines are slightly longer than aboral ones (Kostadinova and Gibson 2002). The adult flukes are 4.56–7.35 × 1.01–1.35 mm, and eggs are 121–139 × 78–88 µm in size (Kostadinova and Gibson 2002). The cercariae are elongate but with stout proportions, relatively transparent, and 384 µm long and 80 µm wide, and the tail is 545 µm long and 52 µm wide (Beaver 1941). The metacercariae are almost spherical, extremely thin-walled, and 152–170 µm long and 145–170 µm wide (Beaver 1941).

The most important key to differentiate *I. melis* adults from those of *I. hortensis* is the location of the cirrus sac; it is located antero-dorsal to the ventral sucker in *I. melis* whereas it is located between intestinal bifurcation and ventral sucker in *I. hortensis* (Kostadinova and Gibson 2002). *I. melis* has 27 collar spines but *I. lukjanovi* and *I. citellicola* have 29 collar spines (Kostadinova and Gibson 2002). Whereas *I. melis* has a more anterior distribution of vitellaria (at level of the ovary) and anterior testis broadly oval and posterior testis elongate-oval, *I. inermis* has a less anterior distribution of vitellaria, at level of anterior testis, and elongate testes (Kostadinova and Gibson 2002). *I. beaveri* is differed from *I. melis* in that *I. beaveri* has an equatorial anterior testis and relatively short post-testicular field, but *I. melis* has a pre-equatorial anterior testis and longer post-testicular field (Koatadinova and Gibson 2002).

The tegumental ultrastructure of *I. melis* adult flukes (dissected from wild mink) suited by Smales and Blankespoor (1984) was generally similar to that of other echinostomes, including *E. trivolvis* (Fried and Fujino 1984). The tegument of the whole body was covered with cobblestone-like cytoplasmic processes (Smales and Blankespoor 1984). The anterior end containing the oral sucker and head collar was aspinous but had 2 concentric rings of sensory papillae on the lip of the oral sucker and many papillae between the oral sucker and spiny collar and between and around collar spines (Smales and Blankespoor 1984). The collar spines were completely retractable into pockets in the tegument (Smales and Blankespoor 1984). On the anterior 3 quarters of the ventral body surface and the anterior dorsum, blunt and rounded tegumental spines were scattered (Smales and Blankespoor 1984). However, the tegument surrounding the ventral sucker and the genital pore was aspinous; the rim of the ventral sucker was encircled by numerous large domed papillae, and the genital pore was surrounded by 3–4 papillae (Smales and Blankespoor 1984). The cirrus was not armed with spines, more or less cylindrical, and had the same tegumental pattern as the body surface, with papillae scattered over the visible portion (Smales and Blankespoor 1984). The body surface was covered with secretory material, bead-like droplets (Smales and Blankespoor 1984).

Life Cycle

I. melis has the life cycle stages of the egg, miracidium, sporocyst, more than 4 generations of rediae (mother rediae I and II, daughter rediae I and II, and intermediate rediae), cercaria, metacercaria, and adult (Dönges 1971; Dönges and Götzelmann 1977; Grabda-Kazubska and Laskowski 1996). The snail intermediate host was reported to be *Lymnaea stagnalis* (Dönges and Götzelmann 1977; Radev et al. 2009) and *Planorbis* sp. (in Wales, UK) (Kostadinova et al. 2003), and the second intermediate hosts are amphibians including tadpoles and fish including the loach (in China) (Yu and Mott 1994). The definitive hosts are more than 30 species of wild vertebrates, including rodents such as *Apodemus agrarius, Apodemus sylvaticus, Rattus norvegicus,* and *Mus musculus*, foxes, martens, badgers, hedghogs, and minks distributed in Europe, Asia, and North America (Radev et al. 2009; Hildebrand et al. 2015; Nugaraitė et al. 2017).

Dönges and Götzelmann (1975) studied the life cycle of *I. melis* and found that *L. stagnalis* snails were infected with the miracidia, and they began to shed cercariae 49–53 days later. These cercariae were experimentally infected to tadpoles of *Xenopus laevis*, and the metacercariae recovered from these tadpoles were orally given to experimental ferrets (*Putorius furo*) and jirds (*Meriones unguiculatus*), the feces of which became positive for eggs after 12 days and 10 days, respectively (Dönges and Götzelmann 1975). Dönges (1971) reported that miracidium-sporocyst generation of *I. melis* is followed by at least 4 generations of rediae in snails; 2 mother rediae generations having a large pharynx and 2 daughter rediae generations having a small pharynx; after a period (somewhat shorter in small hosts and longer in large hosts) most embryos within daughter rediae begin to develop into cercariae. It was thus considered that the number of redial generations is potentially unlimited (Dönges 1971). Thus, transplantation of rediae from infected snails to uninfected snails was tried which resulted in a success, and a redial transplantation strain of *I. melis* has been established in the laboratory; it was stated that a total of 45 transplantation steps have been continued for 8 years, which corresponded to a minimum of 93 redial generations (2 generations of macropharyngeate rediae and 91 generations of micropharyngeate rediae) (Dönges and Götzelmann 1975).

Epidemiology and Geographical Distribution

I. melis is a very common and widely distributed species in various localities of Europe, Asia, and North America (Table 2.4) (Yamaguti 1971; Radev et al. 2009). Human infections were reported from Romania and China (Hsü 1940; Beaver et al. 1984; Yu and Mott 1994). The source of infection in the Romanian patient was unclear; however, the Chinese second case may have swallowed infected tadpoles on his journey (Hsü 1940). Raw loaches were also suggested to be a source of human infection in China (Yu and Mott 1994).

Belarus Ten (20.0%) of 50 American mink collected from Belorussian Polesie were infected with *I. melis* together with various other intestinal helminths (Shimalov and Shimalov 2001). In addition, domestic and wild animals (including European polecat) in Belorussian Polesie have been found to have 3 species of human-infecting echinostomes, including *I. melis, E. revolutum*, and *Echinochasmus perfoliatus* (Shimalov and Shimalov 2002a). Out of 40 European polecats examined in Belorussian Polesie, 19 (47.5%) were infected with *I. melis* (Shimalov and Shimalov 2002b).

Bulgaria Adult specimens of *I. melis* were collected from European polecats (*Mustela putorius*) caught at Lake Srebarna (Kostadinova and Gibson 2002).

Canada American minks were found to harbor the adult flukes of *I. melis* (Law and Kennedy 1932; Gupta 1962).

China A human case was reported at autopsy of a Chinese male who died of chronic myelogenous leukemia; 2 specimens were recovered from the small intestine, and it was suggested that the patient may have swallowed tadpoles on his journey (Hsü 1940). Another human infection was discovered from Liaoning Province in 1963 presumably due to eating raw loaches (Yu and Mott 1994). This species had been found from various wild animals near Beijing (Chen et al. 1985).

Czech Republic Adult specimens obtained from hedgehogs and badgers in Zahlinice were used for morphological and molecular studies (Hildebrand et al. 2015).

England This echinostome was reported from dogs and cats (Nicoll 1923). Molecular analysis was performed using rediae and cercariae from *Planorbis* sp. collected from Wales (Kostadinova et al. 2003).

France Some of American minks and European minks were found to be positive for *I. melis* in their intestines (Torres et al. 2008).

Germany The snails *Lymnaea stagnalis* infected with *I. melis* rediae and cercariae are ubiquitous (Dönges 1967, 1970, 1971; Dönges and Götzelmann 1975). Also, uninfected *Lymnaea stagnalis* were collected from the Federsee, a South German lake, made as an inbred laboratory strain in University of Würzberg, and used to infect with *I. melis* miracidia or rediae and for various other experimental studies (Dönges 1971). Naturally infected *Lymnaea stagnalis* shedding *I. melis* cercariae were collected near the town of Erlangen and transferred to Sofia (Bulgaria) for experiments (Mustafova et al. 1991). In addition, *Lymnaea stagnalis* snails collected in fish ponds near Hochstadt/Aisch were shedding the cercariae of *I. melis* (Loy et al. 2001). Feral American minks (*Mustela vision*) were found to be infected with *I. melis* (Zschille et al. 2004).

Hungary In 6 localities, *I. melis* adult flukes were recovered from foxes and polecats (Sugár and Matskási 1962). Rats (*Rattus norvegicus*) from Agárd, Pákozd were also found infected with *I. melis* (Matskási 1971).

Lithuania American minks (*Neovison vison*) and European polecats (*Mustela putorius*) collected from different parts of Lithuania were commonly infected with *I. melis* (Nugaraitė et al. 2017).

Poland Soltys (1962) recorded adult *I. melis* from various wild animals, including *Putorius putorius, Mustela erminea, Mustela nivalis, Meles meles,* and *Manes manes*. Naturally infected *Lymnaea stagnalis* originating from a large clay pit situated near a town Grodzisk Mazowiecki, about 30 km to the west from Warzawa; adult worms were confirmed after experimental infection to tadpoles and then to white mice (Grabda-Kazubska and Laskowski 1996). Rodents (*Apodemus agrarius*) captured in Lower Silesia and American mink (*Neovison vison*) obtained from the Polish Academy of Sciences (the capture locality unknown) were infected with adult *I. melis* (Hildebrand et al. 2015).

Romania A human case was found in 1916 by Leon having diarrhea (Beaver et al. 1984). No further reports have been available.

Russia Muskrats imported from North America and settled in the Volga Delta were found be infected with *I. melis* (Ivanov and Semenova 2000). Racoon dogs imported from Voronezh oblast and acclimated in the Volga Delta were also found to be infected with *I. melis* (Ivanov and Semenova 2000). Later, American minks in Russia were reported to be infected with *I. melis* (Nugaraitė et al. 2017).

Taiwan Human infections were found in Taiwan (Cross 1974). The geographical distribution and life cycle of this echinostome is to be determined.

Ukraine Specimens of *I. melis* collected from Kherson region were used for the analysis of large subunit ribosomal DNA (lsrDNA) in comparison with other digenean trematodes (Tkach et al. 2000). Five adult specimens were collected from *Meles meles* (Kostadinova and Gibson 2002). Adult specimens were collected also from the redfox (*Vulpes vulpes*) (positive rate 1.2%), raccoon dog (*Nyctereutes procyonis*) (14.3%), American mink (*Neovison vison*) (61.5%), stone marten (*Martes foina*) (1.0%), and polecat (*Mustela eversmanni*) (50.0%) from Cherkasy and Kyiv regions (Korol et al. 2016).

USA Adult flukes were dissected from wild mink (*Mustela vison*) (Smales and Blankespoor 1984).

2.3.3 Potentially Zoonotic **Isthmiophora** *spp.*

Potentially zoonotic *Isthmiophora* spp. include *I. beaveri* (Yamaguti, 1941) Kostadinova and Gibson, 2002, *I. inermis* (Fuhrmann, 1904) Kostadinova and Gibson, 2002, *I. lukjanovi* (Cherkova, 1971) Kostadinova and Gibson, 2002, and *I. citellicola* (Kadenatsii in Skrjabin and Bashikirova, 1956) Kostadinova and Gibson, 2002 (see Kostadinova and Gibson 2002).

2.3.4 Genomics and Proteomics

The karyotype of *I. hortensis* (under the name *E. hortense*) was widely different from that of *E. cinetorchis*, and the chromosome number of *I. hortensis* was n = 10, 2n = 20, whereas that of *E. cinetorchis* was n = 11, 2n = 22 (Terasaki et al. 1982). It was suggested that the basic chromosome number of *Echinostoma* spp. flukes is n = 11, 2n = 22, and *I. hortensis* is the heteroploid with one pair of chromosomes attached to another pair (Terasaki et al. 1982). This difference appears to be very big, so it was used for supporting and justifying the transference of *E. hortense* to another genus *Isthmiophora* (Kostadinova and Gibson 2002). The karyotype of *I. melis* (Mustafova et al. 1991) was similar to that of *I. hortensis* (Terasaki et al. 1982). The number of chromosomes was n = 10, 2n = 20 for *I. melis* (Mustafova et al. 1991). However, it was suggested that the fundamental number of arms in the karyotype of *I. melis* should be 22 (Mustafova et al. 1991). Although this suggestion needs verification, the same number of chromosomes in *I. hortensis* and *I. melis*, both n = 10, 2n = 20, are acceptable, and unique from *Echinostoma* spp., for example, *E. revolutum* (or *E. trivolvis*), *E. cinetorchis,* and *E. miyagawai*, which have n = 11, 2n = 22 chromosomes (Churchill 1950; Terasaki et al. 1982; Barsiene and Kiseliene 1991).

Mitochondrial cytochrome *c* oxidase subunit I (COI) and nicotinamide adenine dinucleotide dehydrogenase subunit 1 (ND1) of different echinostome species revealed that *I. hortensis* and a number of Australian isolates exhibited a distinct clustering pattern from other echinostomes, indicating a different generic affiliation (Morgan and Blair 1998a, b). Subsequently, Kostadinova et al. (2003) analyzed ND1 sequences of 37 different echinostome species and internal transcribed spacer (ITS) sequences of 15 different species, and the phylogenetic trees inferred from the results confirmed its affiliation to *Isthmiophora* rather than *Echinostoma*. Later, Sato and Suzuki (2006) analyzed the nucleotide sequences of ITS-1, ITS-2, CO1, and ND1 of their *I. hortensis* specimens recovered from feral raccoons in Japan; ITS-1 (444 bp) and ITS-2 (440 bp) showed 99% homology with *I. hortensis* and 92–94% homology with *I. melis* and the data of CO1 and ND1 also supported that their specimens should be classified as *I. hortensis* (Sato and Suzuki 2006). Complete mitochondrial genome of *I. hortensis* was recently analyzed by Liu et al. (2016) in China, and the results revealed that the mitochondrial genome size was 14,994 bp, smaller than that of *Eurytrema pancreaticum* (15,031 bp), *Haplorchis taichui* (15,130 bp), *Metagonimus yokogawai* (15,258 bp), and *Schistosoma haematobium* (15,003 bp). The mitochondrial genome of *I. hortensis* lacked *atp8* gene, which is similar to other digenean trematodes (Lee et al. 2013; Liu et al. 2016). Though *I. hortensis* and *Hypoderaeum conoideum* beong to the same family, the length of their CO3 genes were very different; that of *I. hortensis* was shorter than *H. conoideum* by 312 bp (Liu et al. 2016).

Large subunit ribosomal DNA (lsrDNA) of *I. melis* was analyzed by Tkach et al. (2000) using specimens obtained from *Nytereutes procyonoides* in Ukraine and used as the outgroup to determine the phylogenetic relationships of 13 families of order Plagiorchiata; it was shown that *I. melis* was well clustered with *Psilochasmus oxyurus* (Psilostomatidae), a closely neighboured family. Kostadinova et al. (2003) was the first who analyzed ND1 and ITS sequences of *I. melis* from rediae and cercariae from sail hosts and compared with those of *I. hortensis*; it was evident that *E. hortense* of Asada (1926) belongs to *Isthmiophora*. Kudlai et al. (2015) reviewed the genetic information of various echinostomes and other trematodes and confirmed the systematic conclusions of Kostadinova and Gibson (2002) and Kostadinova et al. (2003) regarding the taxonomic relationships of *Isthmiophora* and *Euparyphium*. Hildebrand et al. (2015) studied on the molecular characteristics of *I. melis* specimens isolated from different host species and came to a conclusion that the specimens from field mice (*Apodemus agrarius*) were definitely confirmed to be a species of *Isthmiophora* based on SSU and LSU of rDNA sequences and to specifically as *I. melis* based on characteristics of less conservative markers, such as ITS1/ITS2 of rDNA and CO1 of mtDNA. Specimens from European badger (*Meles meles*), American mink (*Neovison vison*), and European hedgehog (*Erinaceus europaeus*) shared this molecular identity, with only minimal (1.4%) variation within the CO1 gene (Hildebrand et al. 2015). There is no available information regarding the proteomics of *Isthmiophora* spp.

2.3.5 Pathology and Immunology

The intestinal histopathology and cellular reactions in *I. hortensis* infection was studied in laboratory rodents (Lee et al. 1990; Chai and Lee 2002; Park et al. 2005). The pathological features were essentially the same as observed in other echinostome infections, for example, *E. trivolvis* and *E. caproni* (Huffman et al. 1986; Isaacson et al. 1989; Toledo et al. 2006a, b). The worms of *I. hortensis* were located in the lumen of the upper small intestine, and the pathological changes were chiefly observed at the attachment sites of the worms (Lee et al. 1990; Chai and Lee 2002). The flukes were seen to tightly pinch and suck the mucosa with their oral suckers (Fig. 2.17a, b), and it seemed that the mucosal tissue was eventually eaten by the flukes (Chai 2009; Chai et al. 2009). The major histopathological findings included villous atrophy, crypt hyperplasia, stromal inflammation, decreased villus/crypt ratios, mastocytosis, goblet cell hyperplasia, and focal loss of the mucosal tissues (Lee et al. 1990; Kim et al. 2000; Park et al. 2005). The mucosal damages were so severe that in focal areas massive destruction and detachment of villi, at times complete loss of the mucosal integrity and ulcerations, were observed (Lee et al. 1990; Chai et al. 2009). These pathological features were similar to those observed in patients with severe catarrhal enteritis (Chai and Lee 2002).

In *I. hortensis* infection, pathological lesions in the gastrointestinal tract of human patients were reported based on endoscopic findings (Harada et al. 1983; Chai et al. 1994; Hamamoto et al. 1997; Lee and Hong 2002; Cho et al. 2003; Chang et al. 2005; Park and Kim 2006; Tanaka et al. 2008). Gastroduodenal endoscopy of a 55-year-old Korean man revealed 3 ulceration spots at the posterior wall of the

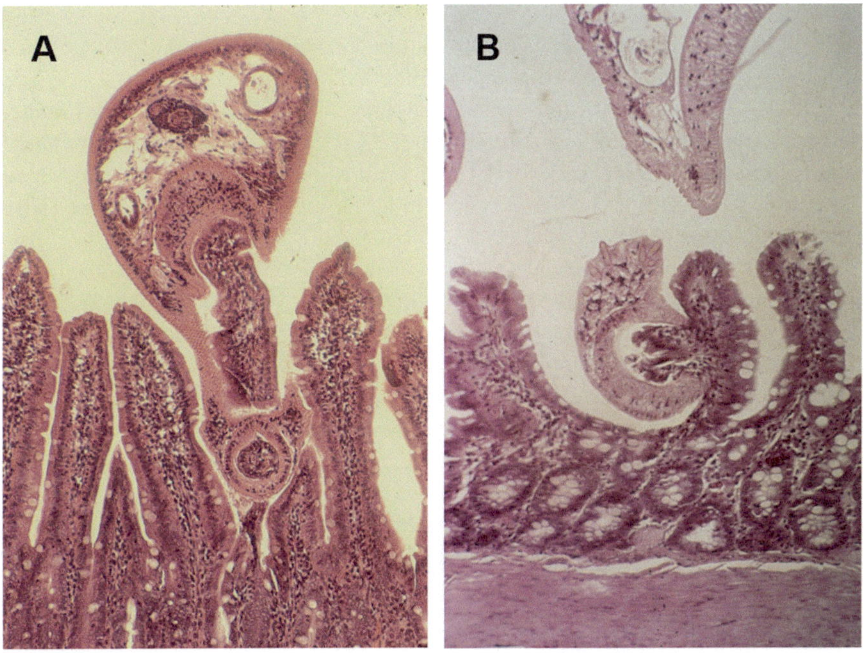

Fig. 2.17 Intestinal sections of rats (**a**, **b**) experimentally infected with the metacercariae of *Isthmiophora hortensis*. Day 7 (**a**) and day 22 (**b**) after infection. Intestinal mucosa shows atrophy and stromal inflammations, and crypts reveal hyperplasia. Goblet cells also show hyperplasia, particularly in (**b**). ×200 (**a**, **b**). (Reproduced from the figure in Lee et al. (1990) Korean J Parasitol 28:45–52 with permission)

stomach near the pylorus; one of the ulcers was attached by a large trematode parasite, and bleeding was seen from the ulcer (Chai et al. 1994). The relationship between *I. hortensis* infection and mucosal bleeding remained to be elucidated (Chai et al. 1994). However, in some human cases, *I. hortensis* infection was incidentally found with no special symptoms (Hamamoto et al. 1997). Symptoms and signs in human patients infected with *I. hortensis* are described in the next section. There is no available information regarding the pathology and pathogenesis of *I. melis* infection.

Immunology of echinostomiasis has been studied extensively in animal-infecting species, for example, *E. caproni, E. trivolvis,* and *E. friedi* (Toledo et al. 2006a). Among the zoonotic echinostomes, *I. hortensis* has been mostly frequently subjected to immunological studies (Chai 2009; Cho et al. 2007; Ryang et al. 2007; Chai 2015). A type of natural immunity of the host against intestinal helminth infections is the spontaneous expulsion of primary infections (Toledo et al. 2006a). This interesting phenomenon has been observed in various echinostome-rodent host models, including *I. hortensis, E. trivolvis, E. caproni,* and *E. friedi* in mice and rats (Tani and Yoshimura 1988; Fujino et al. 1993; Kim et al. 2000; Brunet et al. 2000; Lee et al. 2004; Toledo et al. 2006a, b). However, the dynamics are different depending on different parasite and host species, and even host strain (Fujino and Fried 1993; Toledo et al. 2006b; Cho et al. 2007). In *I. hortensis* infection, C57BL/6 mice began to expel worms from week 3 post-infection (Tani and Yoshimura 1988; Lee et al. 2004). It is also interesting to note that whereas BALB/c mice rejected *I. hortensis* worms within week 3 post-infection, C3H/HeN mice and ICR mice retained worms until week 5 and week 7 post-infection, respectively (Lee et al. 2004). In Sprague-Dawley rats, *I. hortensis* stayed longer than in any strain of mice (Kim et al. 2000; Lee et al. 2004).

Mucosal mast cells and goblet cells were suggested to be associated with the worm expulsion of *I. hortensis* from rodent hosts (Kim et al. 2000; Park et al. 2005). In experimental rats, mast cells began to increase in number from day 3 post-infection and peaked on day 35, and then decreased slowly until day 56 post-infection; the worm expulsion occurred most actively from day 42 to day 56 (Kim et al. 2000). Therefore, it was suggested that intestinal mastocytosis may play an important role in expulsion of *I. hortensis* (Kim et al. 2000). Later, however, it was suggested that goblet cells, rather than mast cells, may play more critical role in expulsion of *I. hortensis* (Park et al. 2005). In other echinostome species, for example, *E. trivolvis*, it was suggested that intestinal mastocytosis may not be related with worm expulsion but may be a secondary response to the presence of worms in the intestine (Fujino et al. 1993). In *I. hortensis* infection, further researches are necessary to elucidate this point.

It is agreed that Th1 and Th2 cytokines are closely related with worm expulsion of echinostomes, including *I. hortensis*, from mice (Cho et al. 2007; Ryang et al. 2007). Whereas Th1 cytokines (IL-12, TNF-α, and IFN-γ) are associated with retention of worms for a long time, Th2 cytokines (IL-4 and IL-5) are associated with expulsion of worms from the host (Brunet et al. 2000; Toledo and Fried 2005). *I. hortensis* infection in BALB/c mice, a resistant mouse strain, exhibited higher protein expression of IL-4 and IL-5 as well as stronger mRNA expressions of IL-4 and IL-5 in their splenocytes, than C3H/HeN mice, a susceptible strain which undergoes a chronic infection (Cho et al. 2007; Ryang et al. 2007). Treatment of BALB/c mice with kitotifen, an anti-allergic drug, suppressed the mRNA levels of IL-4 and IL-5 and elevated the worm recoveries from this mouse strain (Ryang et al. 2007).

The immunological effects of electrolyzed reduced water on *I. hortensis* infection was investigated in C57BL/6 mice; feeding electrolyzed reduced water to these mice revealed influences on local immune responses (elevating Th1 cytokines such as IL-1β and TNF-α) in the small intestines but not on systemic immune responses (Lee et al. 2009).

2.3.6 Clinical Manifestations, Diagnosis and Treatment

The major clinical symptoms due to echinostome infections are mostly gastrointestinal, including abdominal pain, diarrhea, easy fatigue, and loss of body weight (Tani 1979; Rim 1982; Chai and Lee 2002; Fried et al. 2004). However, considering the severe mucosal damages, including ulcerations of the mucosa in naturally infected patients (Chai et al. 1994) and experimental rats infected with *I. hortensis* (Lee et al. 1990), the symptoms seem to be severer than those seen in other intestinal fluke infections, for example, heterophyid fluke infections. A patient infected with *I. hortensis* complained of lower abdominal pain, diarrhea, tenesmus, easy fatigue, and urinary incontinence (Lee et al. 1986b). It is notifiable that human patients infected with *I. hortensis* infection suffered from severe epigastric discomfort and ulcerative lesions in the stomach or duodenum who were diagnosed by identification of worms through gastrointestinal endoscopy (Fig. 2.18a, b) (Chai et al. 1994; Lee and Hong 2002; Cho et al. 2003; Chang et al. 2005; Park and Kim 2006; Tanaka et al. 2008). In South Korea, more than 5 patients have been diagnosed via gastrointestinal endoscopy (Chai et al. 1994; Lee and Hong 2002; Cho et al. 2003; Chang et al. 2005; Park and Kim 2006), and in Japan, more than 6 patients have been diagnosed via gastrointestinal endoscopy (5 patients) (including magnifying endoscopy) or colonoscopy (one patient) (Tanaka et al. 2008).

The first endoscopy-diagnosed patient in South Korea (Chai et al. 1994) was admitted to a hospital because of epigastric pain and hematemesis, and in gastroduodenoscopy an adult fluke was seen attached at the lesion, which was removed by an endoscopic clipper. After praziquantel treatment 3 more adult flukes were recovered from the feces; the patient had eaten different kinds of raw freshwater fish (Chai et al. 1994). Another endoscopy-diagnosed patient experienced acute epigastric pain and diarrhea of 1-month duration accompanied by acidic belching, dizziness, and 2 kg weight loss, and vague epigastric discomfort for a year duration (Lee and Hong 2002). The third patient complained of epigastric discomfort for several days (Cho et al. 2003), and the fourth patient suffered from upper abdominal pain and discomfort which persisted for 2 weeks (Chang et al. 2005). The fifth patient had epigastric discomfort for 1 month, and indigestion, anorexia, dizziness, head-

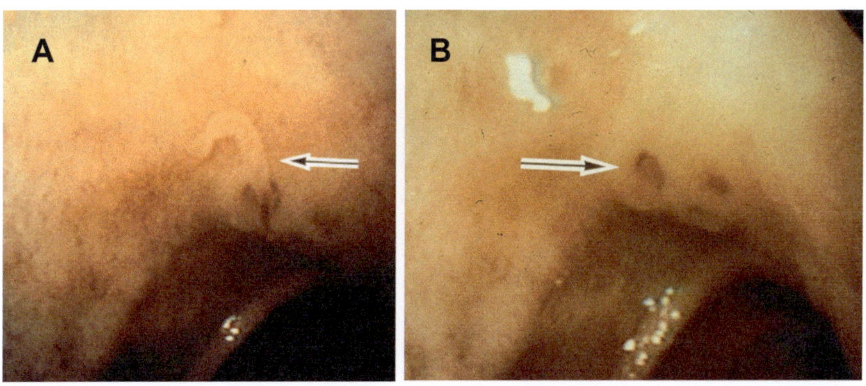

Fig. 2.18 *Isthmiophora hortensis*. (**a**) Gastroduodenal endoscopy of a patient showing an adult worm attached to an ulcerated lesion in the distal part of the stomach and bleeding (arrow), before removing the worm (**b**) Same after removal of the worm. Note mucosal ulcers (arrow) at the place where the worm attached (**a**, **b**). (Reproduced from the figure in Chai et al. (1994) Korean J Parasitol 32:201–204 with permission)

ache, nausea and vomiting occurred at times; the patient was hospitalized because nausea and vomiting became severer (Park and Kim 2006). The first endoscopy-diagnosed *I. hortensis* patient was reported in 1983; the chief complaints were diarrhea and epigastric pain (Tanaka et al. 2008). The second and third patients had the similar symptoms of diarrhea and epigastric pain; the fourth patient had no noticeable clinical symptoms (Tanaka et al. 2008). The fifth patient complained of abdominal pain and fever, and *I. hortensis* was found at the terminal ileum through colonoscopy; the sixth patient had abdominal discomfort, and the lesion was the duodenum (Tanaka et al. 2008).

The clinical signs, including laboratory findings, in echinostomiasis are poorly known (Chai 2009). Peripheral blood eosinophilia has been commonly observed in naturally infected patients (Lee et al. 1988; Tanaka et al. 2008). Also in 5 human volunteers infected with *I. hortensis*, eosinophilia was observed in all patients from day 30 until day 80–100 post- infection (in one patient eosinophilia continued until day 200) (Tani 1979). The level of eosinophilia in *I. hortensis* infection was dependent upon individual worm burdens; 11–24% (av. 17%) among the patients with more than 100 worms (Fig. 2.19), 4–21% (av. 10%) among those with 51–100 worms, and 2–14% (av. 5%) among those with less than 50 worms (Lee et al. 1988). Other clinical laboratory findings in *I. hortensis* infection included elevation of C-reactive protein, IgE, IgG, IgM, IgA, white blood cells, and carcinoembryonic antigen levels (Tani 1979; Tanaka et al. 2008).

The diagnosis of human *I. hortensis* or *I. melis* infection is based on recovery of eggs in fecal examinations (Chai 2009, 2015). The eggs of *I. hortensis* and *I. melis* are large, yellowish, and oval with a thin and refractory shell, a germ cell and yolk inside, a small inconspicuous operculum at the anterior end, and abopercular wrinkles or thickening at the terminal end (Chai 2007, 2009). In Kato-Katz fecal smears, the operculum, germ cell, and abopercular wrinkles may be difficult to see (Chai

Fig. 2.19 Total 649 adult specimens of *Isthmiophora hortensis* recovered from a single patient in Cheongsong-gun, Gyeongsangnam-do, South Korea. The worms are coiled as "C-shaped" objects. (Reproduced from the figure in Chai (2009) The Biology of Echinostomes (Fried B, Toledo R, eds). Springer, New York, USA with permission)

2009, 2015). The size of *I. hortensis* eggs is in the range 0.127–0.139 × 0.071–0.081 mm (Seo et al. 1983), and that of *I. melis* eggs is 0.121–0.139 × 0.078–0.088 mm (Kostadinova and Gibson 2002). In endemic areas with mixed infections of *I. hortensis* and *E. cinetorchis*, careful microscopic observations with measurements of the eggs can provide a specific diagnosis because of the apparently larger size of *I. hortensis* eggs than *E. cinetorchis* eggs (Ryang 1990; Chai 2007, 2009, 2015). However, recovery and identification of the adult fluke is strongly recommended, if a definite diagnosis is preferred (Chai 2007, 2009). In fecal examinations, the egg detectability is considerably high in infections with *I. hortensis* (Seo et al. 1985) and *E. cinetorchis* (Seo et al. 1984), whereas it is very low in infections with *Echnochasmus japonicus* (Chai et al. 1985b) and *Acanthoparyphium tyosenense* (Chai et al. 2001). This difference is due to remarkably different numbers of intrauterine eggs and the different egg laying capacity (Chai 2007, 2009).

Human *I. hortensis* infection can be treated successfully using 10–20 mg/kg praziquantel in a single oral dose (Lee et al. 1988; Chai et al. 1994; Chai 2007, 2009). Albendazole may also be effective (Chai 2009, 2015).

2.3.7 *Prevention and Control*

Avoidance of eating raw or improperly cooked amphibians (tadpoles or frogs) and freshwater fish (especially the loach) is the most important and feasible method to prevent *I. hortensis* or *I. melis* infections.

2.4 *Echinochasmus*

The genus *Echinochasmus* (subfamily Echinochaminae) was established by Dietz in 1909 using *Echinochasmus coaxatus* Dietz, 1909 as the type, and *Echinochasmus euryporus* (Looss) and *Echinochasmus boleocephalus* (v. Linstow) as the other 2 members (Price 1931). Meanwhile, the genus *Episthmium* was established by Lühe in 1909 using *Episthmium africanum* (Stiles) as the type, and *Episthmium bursicola* (Creplin) as another member (Price 1931). Odhner (1910) did not agree to *Episthmium* as a new genus, synonymized *Episthmium* with *Echinochasmus*, and renamed *Episthmium africanum* and *Episthmium bursicola* as *Echinochasmus africanus* and *Echinochasmus bursicola*, respectively. Later, Verma (1935) created a new genus *Episthochasmus* for worms obtained from dogs in Calcutta, India and named it as *Episthochasmus caninum*. In 1941, Bashikirova E. I. treated *Echinochasmus*, *Episthmium*, *Episthochasmus*, and *Monilifer* (a genus created by Dietz in 1909) as 4 subgenera of *Echinochasmus* Dietz, 1909 (Bashikirova 1947). Later, Yamaguti (1958) acknowledged *Echinochasmus, Episthmium,* and *Monilifer* as distinct genera and treated only *Episthochasmus* as a synonym of *Episthmium*. However, Kostadinova and Gibson (2001) suggested that *Episthmium* may be synonymous with *Echinochasmus,* and subsequently Kostadinova (2005) synonymized *Episthmium* Lühe, 1909 and *Episthochasmus* Verma, 1935 with *Echinochasmus* Dietz, 1909 and transferred *Monilifer* to a subgenus of *Stephanoprora.* In addition, Kostadinova (2005) synonymized the genera *Allechinostomum* Odhner, 1910, *Heterechinostomum* Odhner, 1910, and *Velamenophorus* Mendheim, 1940 with *Echinochasmus* Dietz, 1909. Thus, the taxonomic status of *Echinochasmus caninus* (syns. *Episthmium caninum, Episthochasmus caninum*) has been settled.

Echinochasmus liliputanus (Looss, 1896) is the oldest zoonotic *Echinochasmus* species among the literature. It was originally found from dogs and cats in Egypt in 1896 and described as *Echinostomum liliputanum* Looss, 1896 (Bashikirova 1947; Yamaguti 1958). Odhner (1910) assigned this species as *Echinochasmus liliputanus*. The next old zoonotic *Echinochasmus* is *Echinochasmus perfoliatus* (v. Rátz, 1908) Gedoelst, 1911. It was originally found from the intestine of dogs and cats in Hungary in 1908 and described as *Echinostomum perfoliatum* (Skrjabin and Bashikirova 1956; Yamaguti 1958, 1971; Rim 1982). Dietz (1909, 1910) considered this echinostome better fit to *Echinochasmus* but retained the old name. Meanwhile, Railliet and Henry (1909) found the same parasite and named it as *Echinostoma gregale* (later synonymized with *Echinochasmus perfoliatus* by Sprehn in 1932). In 1911, Gedoelst assigned this echinostome in *Echinochasmus* with the name of *Echinochasmus perfoliatus* (Yamaguti 1971). Tubangui (1922) found this species from dogs in China and described it as a subspecies *Echinochasmus perfoliatus shieldsi*; however, Yamashita (1937) synonymized this with *E. perfoliatus*. In 1915, Tanabe H. discovered a similar-shaped echinostome from an experimental cat fed *Acheilognathus intermedia* fish in Japan and provisionally named it as *Echinochasmus perfoliatus* var. *japonicus*. However, later, Tanabe (1922) synonymized this with *E. perfoliatus*. Several years later, Tanabe (1926) discovered a new species, *Echinochasmus japonicus*.

Thereafter, 2 more zoonotic *Echinochasmus* species were discovered in China. In Guangzhou, a new species named as *Echinochasmus jiufoensis* was discovered at autopsy of a 6-month-old girl who died from pneumonia and dehydration (Liang and Ke 1988). In Fujian Province, *Echinochasmus fujianensis* was described as a new species based on specimens obtained from humans, dogs, cats, pigs, and rats (Cheng et al. 1992).

Flukes of the genus *Echinochasmus* had been assigned to belong to the subfamily Echinochasminae under the family Echinostomatidae (Yamaguti 1958). However, Tkach et al. (2016) recently studied on phylogenetic relationships of the superfamily Echinostomatoidea using partial sequences of the nuclear 28S rDNA, and elevated the status of the subfamily Echinochasminae to a family level Echinochasmidae. This was supported by Le et al. (2016) based on the complete mitochondrial genome analysis of *Echinochasmus japonicus*. Also, the subfamilies Echinostomatinae and Himasthlinae were elevated to family levels Echinostomatidae and Himasthlidae, respectively (Tkach et al. 2016). The present author would like to accept this new taxonomic movement; however, in this review book the old classification (Yamaguti 1958, 1971) is used for convenience.

The generic characteristics of *Echinochasmus* include distinct head collar, collar spines all in a single row, dorsal interruption of collar spines narrow, 2 angle spines, internal seminal vesicle saccular and bipartite, tegumental spines small in size and dense in forebody only, and ceca blind (Kostadinova 2005). *Echinochasmus* is different from *Echinostoma* and *Isthmiophora* in its smaller body size, collar spines dorsally interrupted, no ventral ridge on head collar, and very short uterus with fewer number of uterine eggs (Yamaguti 1958; Fried 2001; Kostadinova 2005). *Echinochasmus* is similar to *Echinoparyphium* in its small body size and elongate-oval shape, long forebody, and short uterus (Fried 2001). However, *Echinochasmus* has dorsally interrupted collar spines (arranged in a single row) whereas *Echinoparyphium* has dorsally uninterrupted collar spines (arranged in a double row), and the former does not have a ventral ridge on the head collar whereas the latter has a ventral ridge on the head collar (Fried 2001).

Within the genus *Echinochasmus*, more than 70 species have been described in the literature including those listed under the genus *Episthmium* and other genera (Yamaguti 1958, 1971). Among them, 6 species, namely, *Echinochasmus japonicus* Tanabe, 1926, *Echinochasmus perfoliatus* (Ratz, 1908) Gedoelst, 1911, *Echinochasmus lilliputanus* (Looss, 1896) Odhner, 1910, *Echinochasmus fujianensis* Cheng et al., 1992, *Echinochasmus jiufoensis* Liang and Ke, 1988, and *Echinochasmus caninus* (Verma, 1935) Kostadinova, 2005 have been reported from human infections. In this section, these 6 zoonotic species and several potentially zoonotic *Echinochasmus* species are described.

2.4.1 Echinochasmus japonicus

2.4.1.1 *Echinochasmus japonicus* Tanabe, 1926

Taxonomy and Morphology

E. japonicus (Fig. 2.20a, b) was first described by Tanabe (1926) based on specimens obtained from experimental animals such as dogs, cats, rats, mice, and birds fed the metacercariae encysted in freshwater fish in Japan. Now *E. japonicus* is known to distribute in the Far East (Yamashita 1964; Chai and Lee 2002; Chai 2007, 2009, 2015), Indochina Peninsula (Ito 1962; Ito et al. 1962; Radomyos et al. 1998; Chai et al. 2012; Besprozvannykh et al. 2013), and Kuwait (El-Azazy et al. 2015). An experimental human infection was first reported in Taiwan (Ujiie 1936a) but natural human infections were not confirmed for a long time. Natural human infections were first reported in Fujian Province, China; the prevalence among people was 8.5% (egg-positive in 43 of 504 people examined) (Lin et al. 1982). Another human case was found in Guangxi Province in the same year (Liu et al. 1982). A year later, a human infection case was reported from Japan (Harada et al. 1983). Subsequently, 4 human cases were detected through recovery of adult flukes (1–43 in number of specimens) in South Korea (Seo et al. 1985). Later, natural human infections have been discovered in various provinces of China (Lin et al. 1985; Zhu et al. 1986; Yu

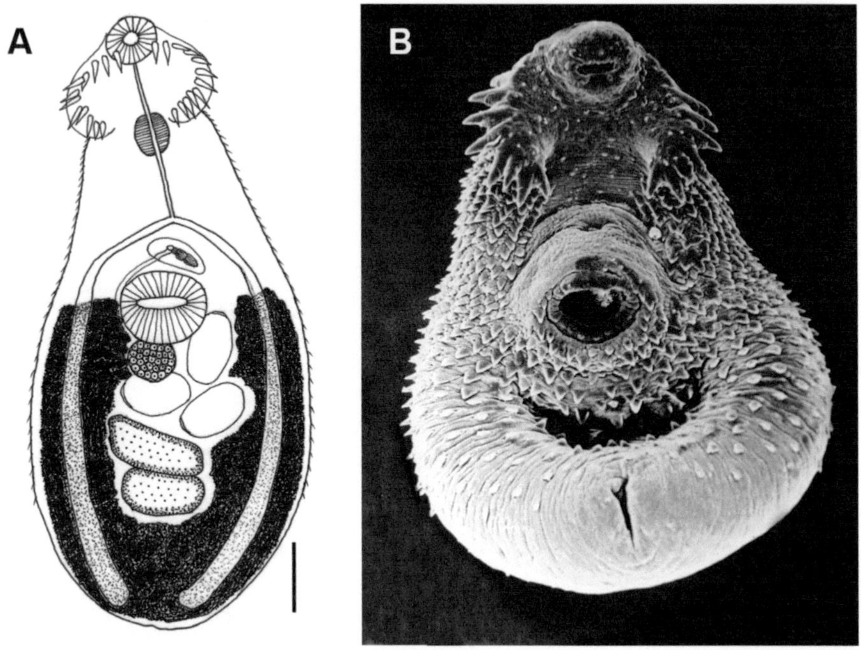

Fig. 2.20 *Echinochasmus japonicus*. (**a**) Line drawing of an adult worm (original figure). Scale bar = 0.05 mm (**b**) Scanning electron microscopic views of a 2-week-old adult fluke recovered from an experimental rat. (Reproduced from Lee et al. (1987) Korean J Parasitol 25:51–58 with permission)

and Mott 1994), Thailand (Radomyos et al. 1998), Lao PDR (Sayasone et al. 2009a; Chai et al. 2012), and Vietnam (Le et al. 2016). Infection in domestic animals (dogs, cats, and pigs) was reported in Vietnam (Anh et al. 2009a, b), and the presence of its life cycle has been confirmed in Primorye region, Russia (Besprozvannykh 2009).

The characteristic morphology of *E. japonicus* includes a small plump body (Fig. 2.20b), 24 dorsally interrupted collar spines, 2 large and tandem testes, and a very small number (usually less than 5) of uterine eggs (Chai and Lee 2002; Chai et al. 2009a). One of the most closely resembled species to *E. japonicus* is *E. perfoliatus*; however, they can be differed from each other in various points (Rim 1982; Seo et al. 1985; Chai et al. 1985). *E. japonicus* has a smaller (0.45–1.38 mm long) and oval or plump body, 2 closely adjacent tandem testes located in the posterior one-third of the body, vitellaria from acetabular level to the posterior end of the body, a very small number of uterine eggs (less than 3), and smaller egg size (77–90 μm long) (Yamashita 1964; Rim 1982; Seo et al. 1985; Chai et al. 1985). *E. perfoliatus* has a larger (0.5–12 mm) and slender to elongated body, 2 tandem testes located in posterior one-fourth of the body, vitellaria from genital pore level to the posterior end of the body, a larger number of uterine eggs (more than 4–5), and larger egg size (90–135 μm long) (Yamashita 1964; Rim 1982; Seo et al. 1985; Chai et al. 1985). In addition, the collar spines of *E. perfoliatus* are arranged in a single row, whereas their dorsal spines of *E. japonicus* are arranged in a double row (Chen et al. 1985). *E. liliputanus* is also very close to *E. japonicus*; however, *E. liliputanus* (1.68–1.76 mm long) is larger than *E. japonicus* (0.45–1.38 mm long), and has a head collar (0.126–0.184 mm long) bearing 24 collar spines arranged in a single row and round cirrus sac, where *E. japonicus* has a head collar (0.144–0.160 mm long) bearing 24 collar spines arranged in a double row and elongated cirrus sac; the collar spines of *E. japonicus* (35–45 μm long) are sharply pointed and longer than those of *E. liliputanus* (21–28 μm long) (Chen et al. 1985). The eggs are bigger in *E. liliputanus* (95–116 μm long) than in *E. japonicus* (77–90 μm long) (Chen et al. 1985; Seo et al. 1985). The vitellaria of *E. japonicus* extends from the posterior margin of the ventral sucker to the posterior end of the body, whereas those of *E. liliputanus* extends from the middle level of the uterus to the posterior end of the body (Chen et al. 1985). *E. japonicus* is differed from *E. fujianensis* in its smaller body, smaller number of uterine eggs (less than 3 in *E. japonicus* and 4–20 in *E. fujianensis*), smaller size of the head collar bearing 24 spines arranged in a double row (single row in *E. fujianensis*) and longer and more sharply pointed collar spines (shorter and less sharply pointed collar spines in *E. fujianensis*) (Cheng et al. 1992). Another zoonotic *Echinochasmus* species, *E. jiufoensis*, is differed from *E. japonicus* in its peculiar arrangement of the 2 testes, which are diagonal or somewhat transversal instead of tandem (Liang and Ke 1988). *E. caninus* (syn. *Episthmium caninum*) is differed from all other species of *Echinochasmus* in that the former has a profusely developed and extending vitellaria into the forebody (Yamaguti 1958, 1971).

The cercarial body of *E. japonicus* is 110–170 × 70–100 μm, and the tail is 84–140 × 16–22 μm in size (Yamaguti 1951; Ito 1964). It has 7 pairs of penetrating gland cells in front of the ventral sucker (Yamaguti 1951; Ito 1964). The metacercarial cysts are elliptical and 77–80 × 54–60 μm in size, equipped with total 24 collar spines which are interrupted dorsally (Komiya 1965). Its head glands are 6 in number lying dorsal to the oral sucker (Komiya 1965). The metacercariae of *E. japonicus* are morphologically very similar to those of *E. perfoliatus* (Komiya 1965) and it is practically very difficult if the metacercariae of the 2 species are mixed-infected in a single fish. The only apparent difference is the smaller size (77–80 × 54–60 μm) of the metacercariae of *E. japonicus* than those (92–108 × 71–97 μm) of *E. perfoliatus* (Komiya 1965).

The tegumental ultrastructure was studied by Lee et al. (1987) on adult flukes obtained from albino rats experimentally fed the metacercariae from a carp, *Pseudorasbora parva*. The worms were minute and plumpy gourd-shaped with attenuated anterior end and round posterior end (Lee et al. 1987). The tegument of the whole body was wrinkled transversely and covered with cobblestone-like cytoplasmic processes (Lee et al. 1987). The head collar was armed with total 24 collar spines which were dorsally interrupted (Lee et al. 1987). The oral and ventral suckers were muscular and equipped with numerous type II sensory papillae, and the genital opening was seen between the 2 suckers (Lee et al. 1987). The tegumental spines were spade-shaped with broad base and pointed tip; they were compact on the anterolateral tegument or dorsal surface of the anterior body (Lee et al. 1987).

Two types papillae, uni-ciliated (type I) and round swollen papillae without a cilium (type II) were observed; type I papillae were chiefly distributed on ventral surfaces, and type II papillae were seen on the lip of 2 suckers (Lee et al. 1987).

Life Cycle

E. japonicus has several developmental stages, including the egg, miracidium, sporocyst, mother redia, daughter redia, cercaria, metacercaria, and adult (Ujiie 1936a, b; Yamashita 1964; Lin et al. 1990). The first eggs appear in the feces 5–6 days after infection in experimental mice (Chai et al. 1985). The eggs are immature, oval, yellowish-brown, and equipped with a small operculum with abopercular wrinkle or knob (Ujiie 1936b; Choi et al. 2006). The eggs incubated in water at 23–30 °C produced miracidia in 4 days (Ujiie 1936a); miracidia begin to hatch on day 8 after incubation (Lin et al. 1990). The miracidia penetrate into the snail host *Parafossarulus* (*Bulimus*) *striatulus japonicus, Parafossarulus manchouricus, Digoniostoma funiculata, Oncomelania* spp, *Pila* spp., *Gyraulus* spp., *Alocinma longicornis*, or *Melanoides tuberculata*, and sporocysts, rediae, and cercariae develop in the snails (Yamaguti 1951; Ito 1962; Cheng and Fan 1989; Choi et al. 2006; Hung et al. 2013). The rediae are 0.6–1.4 mm long and 0.14–0.20 mm wide; the pharynx of the rediae is 34–40 μm in diameter (Yamaguti 1951). In *Parafossarulus striatulus*, cercariae mature and emerge from the snails 60 days after infection with the miracidia (Lin et al. 1990). The cercariae have an ovoid body and a short tail, but at this stage no head collar or collar spines are recognizable around the oral sucker (Choi et al. 2006). The oral sucker, when contracted, shows a slit-like opening, where 4 non-ciliated round swollen sensory papillae (type II papillae) are located (Choi et al. 2006). Seven pairs of penetrating gland cells are seen in front of the ventral sucker (Yamaguti 1951; Ito 1964). Sensory papillae with cilia (type I) are observed on the ventral surface just posterior to the oral sucker; the ventral sucker is muscular without tegumental spines or sensory papillae (Choi et al. 2006).

The development in as well as emergence of *E. japonicus* cercariae from *P. striatulus* snails is closely related to temperature and light (Cheng et al. 1990). When the infected snails were kept at water temperature of 27–32 °C, the germinal cells and germ balls in the daughter rediae multiplied continually into cercariae, and their majority emerged (Cheng et al. 1990). However, at water temperature below 24 °C, multiplication was hindered and emergence of cercariae obviously decreased, and cercarial shedding stopped at water temperature of 14 °C (Cheng et al. 1990). The rate and degree of infection with the metacercariae were generally higher in small-sized fish than large-sized ones; this was probably because the cercariae are tactic to light and active in shallow water where they are constantly in contact with small fishes (Cheng et al. 1990).

Various kinds of freshwater or brackish water fish, including *Pseudorasbora parva* (Fig. 2.21a), *Hypomesus olidus, Plecoglossus altivelis, Acheilognathus intermedius, Gnathopogon elongatus, Gnathopogon strigatus, Hemibarbus barbus, Macropodus opercularis, Zacco platypus, Carassius auratus, Salangichthys microdon, Misgurnus anguillicaudatus,* and *Acanthogobius flavimanus,* have

Fig. 2.21 *Echinochasmus japonicus*. (**a**) Freshwater fish, *Pseudorasbora parva*, a second intermediate host (**b**) Metacercaria isolated from the flesh of the fish. ×200

been reported to be the second intermediate host of *E. japonicus* (Tanabe 1926; Mori 1935; Kogame 1941; Yamashita 1964; Hung et al. 2013). Yamaguti (1951) added tadpoles of *Rana rugosa* as another second intermediate host of *E. japonicus* in which the successful development of the cercariae into metacercariae was experimentally proved. The metacercariae (Fig. 2.21b) are found exclusively in the gill of the fish or tadpoles (Yamashita 1964; Komiya 1965). Hasegawa (1926) gave infected sweetfish (*Plecoglossus altivelis*) to dogs and confirmed the occurrence of their eggs on the 9th day. In addition, Hasegawa (1926) also gave the metacercariae from *Pseudorasbora parva* to mice, and after 4 h freed larvae were found in the intestine. In rats, the parasites became adult flukes in 7 days (Hasegawa 1926). However, in dogs and cats, the worms grew quickly within 4 days having a few eggs in the uterus, and full maturation was recognized in 18 days (Ujiie 1936a). In experimental chicks, the metacercariae from *Pseudorasbora parva* and tadpoles of *Rana rugosa* became adult flukes in 14 days (Yamaguti 1951). Natural infections in ducks (Eom et al. 1984), egrets (Ryang et al. 1991), and cats (Sohn and Chai 2005) have been confirmed by the recovery of adult flukes. Dogs were added to the natural definitive host of this echinostome in China (Zhou and Wang 1987).

Epidemiology and Geographical Distribution

The geographical distribution of *E. japonicus* has been extended from Asian countries, including Japan, Taiwan, China, South Korea, Thailand, Lao PDR, Vietnam, and Russia (Fig. 2.22; Table 2.4) (Ujiie 1936a; Harada et al. 1983; Lin et al. 1985; Seo et al. 1985; Zhu et al. 1986; Radomyos et al. 1998; Chi et al. 2008; Besprozvannykh 2009; Sayasone et al. 2009a, b; Chai et al. 2012) to the Middle East (Kuwait) (El-Azazy et al. 2015). Natural and experimental human infections have been reported only from Asian countries, including Taiwan (experimental), China (hereafter; natural), Japan, South Korea, Thailand, Lao PDR, and Vietnam (Ujiie 1936a; Lin et al. 1982; Harada et al. 1983; Seo et al. 1985; Zhu et al. 1986; Radomyos et al. 1998; Sayasone et al. 2009a; Chai et al.

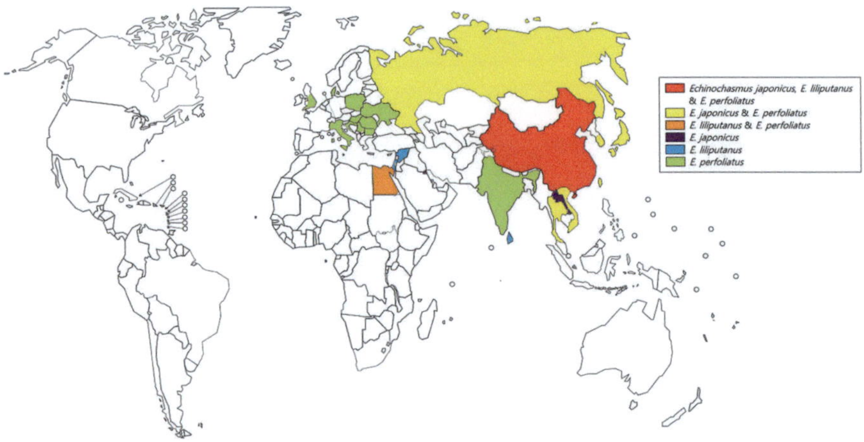

Fig. 2.22 Global distribution of *Echinochasmus* spp. (*E. japonicus, E. perfoliatus,* and *E. liliputanus*) based on the presence of their life cycles

2012; Le et al. 2016). The main mode of infection is consumption of raw freshwater fish; however, accidental infection may also occur if infected tadpoles (or frogs) are eaten raw or in undercooked conditions.

China The metacercariae of *E. japonicus* were detected from the gill of 2 freshwater fish species (*Pseudorasbora parva* and *Sarcocheilichthys sinensis*) obtained from a market in Shanghai (Komiya and Murase 1952). Thereafter, natural human infections with this fluke (8.5%; 43/504) were reported for the first time in the world literature from residents of Fujian Province; the prevalence among dogs was 43.3% (54/119), and that in cats was 15.7% (8/58) (Lin et al. 1982). A case of human infection was also detected in Guangxi Province (Liu et al. 1982). Subsequently, in Fujian (8 counties) and Guangdong Province (one county), 178 (4.9%) of 3639 residents were found positive for eggs in their feces (Lin et al. 1985). In addition, 412 (39.7%) of 1039 dogs and 34 (9.5%) of 357 cats from these areas were also positive for eggs, and various kinds of fish, including *Pseudorasbora parva*, harboured the metacercariae (Lin et al. 1985). Total 24 species of freshwater fish from South Fujian Province were examined and 22 species were found infected with *E. japonicus* metacercariae (Cheng et al. 1986). To evaluate the therapeutic effect of praziquantel against this echinostome infection, a total of 49 human patients infected with *E. japonicus* in Fujian Province were subjected to a treatment with Pyquiton (praziquantel) 5–20 mg/kg in a single dose; they were well tolerated the treatment and the therapeutic efficacy was satisfactory (Zhu et al. 1986). In Jiangxi (Zhou and Wang 1987) and Heilongjiang Province (Zhou et al. 1987), natural infection of dogs was confirmed. In Fujian Province, *Melanoides tuberculata* (Cheng and Fang 1989) and *Parafossarulus striatulus* (Cheng et al. 1990; Lin et al. 1990) were found as the snail intermediate host of *E. japonicus*. In 6 counties of Fujian and Guangdong Provinces, the prevalence was reported to be 4.9% in humans, 39.7% among dogs, and 9.5% among cats (Yu and Mott 1994). In Anhui Province, the prevalence of *E.*

japonicus among some residents was reported to be 1.4% in 1993 (Wu 2013). Molecular diagnosis using random amplified polymorphic DNA (RAPD) analysis was tried to differentiate 4 zoonotic *Echinochasmus* species occurring in China, namely, *E. japonicus, E. perfoliatus, E. liliputanus,* and *E. fujianensis* (Cheng et al. 1999). In Pinyuan County of Guangdong Province, RAPD analysis in combination with morphological studies were performed to diagnose trematode metacercariae encysted in 11 species of freshwater fish, including *Pseudorasbora parva*; 6 trematode species were confirmed including *E. japonicus, E. perfoliatus,* and *E. fujianensis* (Cheng et al. 2000a). In Heilongjiang Province, 2 (1.1%) of 178 adult dogs killed and examined for their intestinal helminths revealed 5–380 specimens of *E. japonicus* (Wang et al. 2006). Chen et al. (2013) compared morphological characteristics of 5 echinostome species occurring in Fujian Province, including *E. japonicus, E. perfoliatus, E. fujianensis, Echinostoma angustitestis,* and *Echinostoma aegyptiacum.*

Japan Tanabe (1926) first described *E. japonicus* as a new species based on adult flukes collected from experimental dogs, cats, rats, mice, and fowls fed the metacercariae encysted in various species of freshwater fish. Hasegawa (1926) gave sweetfish (*P. altivelis*) to dogs and confirmed the occurrence of eggs on day 9 post-infection. Kurisu (1932) observed infection of domestic fowls (5/316; 1.6%) in Osaka, Okayama, and Hiroshima Prefectures. Mori (1935) demonstrated the successful development of *E. japonicus* metacercariae from *Salangichthys microdon* fish in experimental rats, puppies, kittens, and fowls. Yamaguti (1939) detected natural infection of *Egretta intermedia* (Lake Ogura), *Nycticorax nycticorax* (Lake Biwa), *Milvus migrans* (near Kyoto), and *Bucephala clangula* (Kanazawa) with this echinostome. Kogame (1941) detected the metacercariae from the loach (*Misgurnus anguillicaudatus*) in Hiroshima Prefecture. Yamaguti (1951) confirmed that *Parafossarulus striatulus japonicus* snails are the first intermediate host of *E. japonicus*, and also demonstrated that, in addition to freshwater fish, tadpoles of *Rana rugosa* can play the role of a second intermediate host. In Tokushima Prefecture, the cercarial infection rate of *E. japonicus* in *Parafossarulus manchouricus* snails revealed almost no change from 1955 (1.21%) through 1963 (1.22%); however, the metacercarial infection rate of freshwater fish (*Pseudorasbora parva*) was reduced from 66.9% in 1954–1956 to 10.0% in 1963–1964 in Naruto City and from 63.5% in 1954–1956 to 16.7% in 1961–1962 in Anan City (Yamaguchi 1967). Infection in a red fox (*Vulpes vulpes schlencki*) was reported from Hokkaido based on adult specimens (7 in number) recovered (Kamiya and Ohbayashi 1975). The first human natural infection in Japan was reported from a 48-year-old male who complained of upper abdominal pain and watery diarrhea and had a clinical history of gastric ulcer for 3 years; 41 specimens of *E. japonicus* were recovered after treatment with kamala followed by bithionol together with 8 specimens of *Isthmiophora hortensis* (under the name *Echinostoma hortense*) (Harada et al. 1983).

South Korea The existence of the life cycle was first verified by Chun (1962); he detected the metacercariae of *E. japonicus* from the gill of freshwater fish, including *Pseudorasbora parva* and *Carassius auratus* (*Carassius carassius*) caught in Nakdong River. Thereafter, many large and small rivers were confirmed to have freshwater fish infected with *E. japonicus* metacercariae. For example, *Carassius auratus* caught from Kimhae (Nakdong River), Ulsan (Taewha River), Pohang (streams), and Gunsan (Mangyeong River) were found infected with *E. japonicus* metacercariae (Chun 1964). The metacercariae (under the name *Echinochasmus* sp. 2; smaller metacercariae) were also detected in various species of freshwater fish, including *Pseudorasbora parva, Puntungia herzi, Gnathopogon coreanus, Carassius auratus,* and *Acheilognathus* sp., caught from Kumho River, Gyeongsangbuk-do (Province) (Lee 1968). A similar study was performed in Osip stream (Yeongdeok, Gyeongsangbuk-do) in which *Carassius carassius* and *Gnathopogon atromaculatus* fish were positive for *Echinochasmus* species metacercariae (Lee et al. 1979). Another study in Kumho River revealed infection of *Achelognathus taenianalis, Gnathopogon atromaculatus, Hemibarbus labeo, Pseudogobio esocinus, Pseudorasbora parva,* and *Zacco platypus* with *Echinochasmus* sp. metacercariae (Hwang and Choi 1980). The cercariae of *E. japonicus* were detected in *Parafossarulus manchouricus* snails collected from the middle and lower reaches of Mangyeong River, Jeollabuk-do (Province); the cercarial positive rate was 8.0% (137/1713) (Rhee et al. 1983a). The metacercariae were found in *Hypomesus olidus* and *Pseudorasbora parva* fish caught from Mangyeong River (Rhee et al. 1983b). Subsequently, in Tongjin River, Jeollabuk-do, 17 species of freshwater fish, including *Abbotina springeri, Carassius auratus, Cultriculus eigenmanni, Gnathopogon majimae, Gnathopogon coreanus, Hemibarbus longirostris, Pseudogobio eosinus, Pseudorasbora parva, Puntungia herzi,* and *Zacco platypus*, were verified as the second intermediate host (Rhee et al. 1984). In Hyungsan River, Gyeongsangbuk-do (Province), 5 species of freshwater fish, including *Carassius auratus, Gnathopogon atromaculatus, Pseudorasbora parva, Zacco platypus, Zacco teminchkii,* and *Plecoglossus altivelis*, were found to harbour the metacercariae (under the name *Echinochasmus* sp.) (Joo 1984). Infection of the definitive host was first confirmed in 2 of 105 domestic ducks from different parts of South Korea (Eom et al. 1984). The first report of human *E. japonicus* infection among Koreans was published by Seo et al. (1985) who recovered 1–43 adult specimens from 4 patients who habitually consumed freshwater fish; the patients were co-infected with other intestinal flukes, including *Metagonimus yokogawai, Heterophyes nocens, Pygidiopsis summa, Isthmiophora hortensis,* and *Taenia saginata* (probably *Taenia asiatica*). Chai et al. (1985) detected the metacercariae of *E. japonicus* from *Pseudorasbora parva* and observed the worm development in experimentally infected mice; the worms sexually matured within 5 days and attained maximum body growth within 7 days. Lee et al. (1987) studied on the tegumental ultrastructure of adult flukes. Choi et al. (1990a) detected the metacercariae of *Echinochasmus* sp. in freshwater fish (*Carassius auratus, Gnathopogon atromaculatus, Paracheilognathus rhombea,* and *Pseudorasbora parva*) from Chongdo stream (Choi et al. 1990a) and Yang River (Choi et al. 1990b), Gyeongsangbuk-do (Province). On the other hand, Ryang et al. (1991) detected adult specimens of *E. japonicus* from the small intestine of egrets (*Egretta alba modesta*) in Hoengseong-gun, Gangwon-do (Province); the infection rate of the egrets was 50.0% and the average intensity of infection was 16.5 (9–24) worms per bird. One specimen of *E. japonicus* was recovered from one (1.2%) of 85 field mice (*Apodemus agrarius*) examined (Yong et al. 1991). Later, Rim et al. (1996) detected the metacercariae of *E. japonicus* from various species of freshwater fish, including *Pseudorasbora parva, Squalidus chankaensis tsuchigae* (syn. *Gnathopogon atromaculatus*), and *Zacco platypus*, from Taewha, Hyeongsan, and Nakdong River. Sohn and Choi (1997) detected the metacercariae in 2 fish species (*Pseudorasbora parva* and *Acanthorhodeus asmussi*) from Choonam Reservoir, Uichang-gun, Gyeongsangnam-do (Province). Natural infection in feral cats was reported by Sohn and Chai (2005) in which 18 (4.1%) of 438 cats were infected with 1–146 (total 411) specimens of *E. japonicus*; the worm morphology from these cats was described later by Chai et al. (2013). Choi et al. (2006) successfully maintained its partial life cycle from cercariae to adults in the laboratory using *Pseudorasbora parva* as the second intermediate host and rats, chicks, and ducks as the definitive host, respectively. Adult specimens were recovered from one (1.9%) of 54 shrews (*Crocidura lasiura*) captured in Gyeonggi-do (Province) (Chai et al. 2009b).

Kuwait Adult flukes of *E. japonicus* were reported from stray cats from Kuwait Municipality, Kuwait; the prevalence was 1.67% (4/240) and the mean intensity was 5 specimens per cat (El-Azazy et al. 2015).

Lao PDR The first report of human infection with *E. japonicus* was documented from Savannakhet Province in 2009; 3 patients were confirmed by recovery of adult flukes, 2, 4, and 4 in number of recovered specimens (Sayasone et al. 2009a, b). Subsequently, 7 human cases were also found in Khammouane Province; total 33 specimens were recovered after anthelmintic (praziquantel) treatment and purging (Chai et al. 2012). However, some of the specimens were later confirmed to be *Episthmium caninum* which is to be published later.

Taiwan Ujiie (1936a) himself and another volunteer swallowed each 50 metacercariae of *E. japonicus*, and after 7–8 days a few eggs were detected in their feces. On day 20 after the infection, 2–3 adult specimens were recovered from their feces, and it was proved that humans can be infected with this echinostome (Ujiie 1936a). Severe infections in ducks raised in the paddy-fields and parasitized by 1000–4000 specimens, which were in most cases fatal with symptoms including a swollen caecum, were reported in southern Taiwan (Lee et al. 1976). Later, adult specimens were also collected from the small intestine of small mammals (*Suncus murinus*) in Chang-hua Prefecture (Fischthal and Kuntz 1981).

Thailand The presence of *E. japonicus* life cycle in Thailand was first notifed by Ito et al. (1962) who investigated on the parasitic helminths of stray dogs found in Bangkok; 5 (5.5%) of 90 dogs were infected with 4, 7, 14, 41, and 260 specimens, respectively. Subsequently, its cercariae were detected in 2 of 800 *Digoniostoma* *funiculata* snails collected from Mahasarakhan Province (Ito 1962). Human *E. japonicus* infection was first reported by Radomyos et al. (1994, 1998) in a male patient from a northeastern part of Thailand.

Russia Filimonova (1973–1974, 1979) first confirmed the presence of the life cycle of *E. japonicus* in West Siberia, including Novosibirsk Region. Thereafter, the cercariae, metacercariae, and adults were studied in Primorye Region; the snail host was *Parafossarulus spiridonovi*, and the fish hosts were *Rhodeus sericeus sericeus, Pseudorasbora parva* and *Percottus glehni* (Besprozvannykh 2009). Chickens (*Gallus gallus domesticus*) were experimentally proved to be definitive host (Besprozvannykh 2009).

Vietnam Adult worms were first discovered by Le (2000). Thereafter, the metacercariae of *E. japonicus* was detected for the first time in Vietnam (Nghe An Province) in a freshwater fish species (*Labeo rohita*), although the prevalence and intensity were very low (Chi et al. 2008). The adult flukes were also found in domestic dogs and pigs from Nghe An Province; the prevalence was 29.6% (8/27) in dogs and 60.0% (3/5) in pigs with the infection intensity of 38 ± 79 and 3 ± 3 specimens, respectively (Anh et al. 2009a). In another Province (Nam Dinh Province), the adult flukes were found in domestic cats; the prevalence was 30% (6/20) and the infection intensity was 15 ± 17 specimens per cat (Anh et al. 2009b). The snail intermediate host was confirmed to be *Parafossarulus striatulus* in Nam Dinh Province, the metacercariae were found in the gill of freshwater fish species *Rhodeus sericeus sericeus* and *Pseudorasbora parva* (experimentally proved), and chickens (*Gallus gallus domesticus*) were experimentally determined as the definitive host (Besprozvannykh et al. 2013). It seems that human case reports have never been published in Vietnam. However, Le et al. (2016) used adult flukes (morphologically confirmed as *E. japonicus*) recovered from human patients in Phu Tho, Ha Noi, and Hoa Binh Provinces, Vietnam for analysis of the mitochondrial genome.

2.4.2 Echinochasmus perfoliatus

2.4.2.1 *Echinochasmus perfoliatus* (Ratz, 1908) Gedoelst, 1911

[syn. *Echinostomum perfoliatum* v. Ratz, 1908; *Echinostoma gregale* Railliet and Henry, 1909; *Echinochasmus perfoliatus* var. *japonicus* Tanabe, 1915; *Echinochasmus perfoliatus shieldsi*, Tubangui, 1922]

Taxonomy and Morphology

This echinostome (Fig. 2.23) was first found from the intestine of 2 dogs in Bucharest, Romania by Motas and Straulescus in 1902 and reported it under the name *Distoma echinatum* (Tanabe 1922; Tubangui 1922). It was renamed as *Echinostomum perfoliatum* by v. Ratz in 1908 based on specimens obtained from

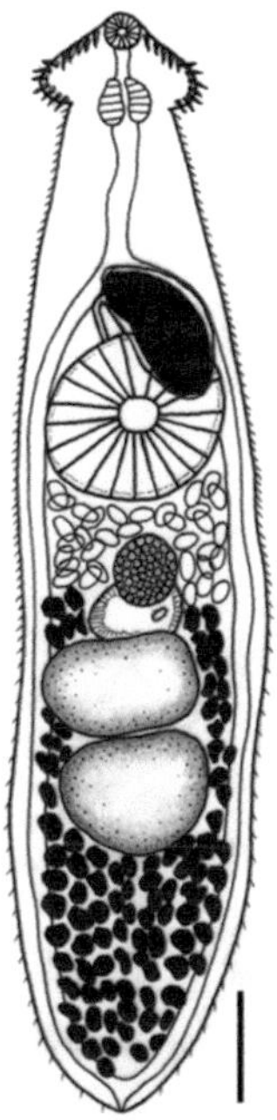

Fig. 2.23 Line drawing of an adult fluke of *Echinochasmus perfoliatus*. Scale bar = 0.05 mm. (Modified from the figure in Hirazawa (1928) Tokyo Iji Shinshi no. 2577:1328–1334)

dogs and cats in Hungary (Tanabe 1922; Tubangui 1922). Dietz (1909, 1910) considered this echinostome better fit to *Echinochasmus*; however, the old name was retained. Meanwhile, Railliet and Henry (1909) found the same parasite in Romania and named it as *Echinostoma gregale*; however, this species was later synonymized with *Echinochasmus perfoliatus* (Skrjabin and Bashikirova 1956). Gedoelst (1911) was the first who assigned this echinostome in *Echinochasmus* using the name *E. perfoliatus*. Tubangui (1922) found the same species from dogs in China and described it as a subspecies *Echinochasmus perfoliatus shieldsi*; however, Yamashita (1937) synonymized it with *E. perfoliatus*. In Japan, Tanabe H. discovered in 1915 a similar-shaped echinostome from an experimental cat fed *Acheilognathus intermedia* fish and provisionally named it as *Echinochasmus perfoliatus* var. *japonicus* (Yamashita 1964). However, later, Tanabe (1922) himself reported this again as *E. perfoliatus*.

This echinostome is now a common parasite in the small intestines of dogs, cats, pigs, and foxes in Hungary, Italy, Romania, Poland, Denmark, Bulgaria, England, Croatia, Russia, Ukraine, Egypt, India, Japan, China, Taiwan, South Korea, Thailand, and Vietnam (Nicoll 1923; Rim 1982; Yu and Mott 1994; Shimalov and Shimalov 2002; Saeed et al. 2006; Chai et al. 2009a; Otranto et al. 2017). However, human infections have been reported only from Japan, China, and India. An experimental human infection was first reported in Japan (Tanabe 1922), and subsequently a natural human infection was discovered in Japan (Hirazawa 1928). Later, in 1979, in Wuhan Province, China, about 14,000 worms were found in the small intestine at an autopsy of a child who died of the infection, and the prevalence in the residence area of this case was 1.84% (34/1846) (Wuhan Medical College 1979; Yu and Mott 1994). Subsequently, another human case, 40-year-old male, was reported in Fujian Province, China from whom 128 adult specimens of *E. perfoliatus* were recovered after anthelmintic treatment (Lin and Cheng 1981). In Anhui Province, China, 11 (1.1%) of 997 residents were found positive for *E. perfoliatus* eggs and total 171 adult flukes were recovered after treatment and purging (Jiang et al. 1988). Thereafter, many human infections were added in various parts of China (Guangdong, Fujian, Anhui and Hubei Provinces) (Yu and Mott 1994). Bhalerao (1935) listed *E. perfoliatus* as a parasite of the cat, dog, and human in India, although no details of human infections are available among the literature.

The characteristic morphology of *E. perfoliatus* includes a slender and elongated body, larger than the closely related species, *E. japonicus*, equipped with 24 dorsally and ventrally interrupted collar spines, 2 tandem testes, and a small number (usually less than 10) of uterine eggs (Chai and Lee 2002; Chai 2007; Chai et al. 2009a). *E. perfoliatus* can be differentiated from *E. japonicus* in various points (Rim 1982; Seo et al. 1985; Chai et al. 1985). *E. perfoliatus* has a larger (0.5–12.0 mm) and slender body, 2 tandem testes located in posterior one-fourth of the body, vitellaria from genital pore level to the posterior end of the body, a larger number of uterine eggs (more than 4–5, up to 10), and larger egg size (90–135 μm long) (Yamashita 1964; Rim 1982). On the other hand, *E. japonicus* has a smaller (0.45–1.38 mm long) body size, oval or plump in shape, 2 closely adjacent tandem testes located in the posterior one-third of the body, vitellaria from acetabular level to the posterior end of the body, a very small number of uterine eggs (less than 3), and smaller egg size (77–90 μm long) (Yamashita 1964; Rim 1982; Seo et al. 1985; Chai et al. 1985). *E. liliputanus* is also close to *E. perfoliatus*. However, *E. liliputanus* (1.68–1.76 mm long) is smaller than *E. perfoliatus*, and has a small head collar (126–184 μm long) bearing 24 collar spines arranged in a single row and slightly elongated cirrus sac, where *E. perfoliatus* has a larger head collar (270–400 μm long) bearing 24 collar spines arranged in a single row and markedly elongated cirrus sac; the collar spines of *E. perfoliatus* (68–70 μm long) are more sharply pointed and longer than those of *E. liliputanus* (21–28 μm long) (Chen et al. 1985). The eggs are bigger in *E. perfoliatus* (96–102 μm long) than in *E. liliputanus* (80–88 μm long) (Chen et al. 1985). The vitellaria of *E. perfoliatus* extends from the genital pore level to the posterior end of the body, whereas those of *E. liliputanus* extends from the middle level of the uterus to the posterior end of the body (Chen et al. 1985). *E. perfoliatus* is differed from *E. fujianensis* in its larger body, smaller number of uterine eggs (less than 10 in *E. perfoliatus* and 4–20 in *E. fujianensis*), larger size of the head collar and longer and a little sharply pointed collar spines (shorter and less sharply pointed collar spines in *E. fujianensis*) (Cheng et al. 1992). *E. jiufoensis* is differed from *E. perfoliatus* in its peculiar arrangement of the 2 testes, which are diagonal or somewhat transversal instead of tandem (Liang and Ke 1988). *E. caninus* (syn. *Episthmium caninum*) is differed from all other species of *Echinochasmus* in that the former has a profusely developed and extensive vitellaria reaching into the forebody (Yamaguti 1958, 1971).

The cercarial body of *E. perfoliatus* is inverted oval and flat, and 130 μm long and 75 μm wide in living specimens; the tail is shorter than the body length, 110 μm long and 22 μm wide (Komiya 1951). The metacercarial cysts are elliptical and 92–108 × 71–97 μm in size, equipped with total 24 collar spines arranged in a single row which are interrupted dorsally and ventrally (Komiya 1965). Its head glands are lying dorsally anterior to posterior margin of the oral sucker, their opening being on dorsal upper margin of the oral sucker (Komiya 1965). The metacercariae of *E. perfoliatus* are morphologically very similar to those of *E. japonicus* (Komiya 1965) and it is practically very difficult if the metacercariae of the 2 species are mixed-infected in a single fish. The only apparent difference is the larger size (92–108 × 71–97 μm) of the metacercariae of *E. perfoliatus* than those of *E. japonicus* (77–80 × 54–60 μm) (Komiya 1965).

The tegumental ultrastructure of *E. perfoliatus* larvae or adults has never been documented.

Life Cycle

Developmental stages of *E. perfoliatus* have been described, including the egg, miracidium, sporocyst, mother redia, daughter redia, cercaria, metacercaria, and adult (Tanabe 1922; Komiya 1951; Yamashita 1964). Mature flukes were obtained in 8–20 days in experimental cats and pigs (producing eggs) and worms survived 132–168 days in these hosts (Sosipatrov 1964). Tanabe (1922) obtained eggs at 36 days after experimental infection of himself with the metacercariae isolated from *Opsariichthys uncirostris* fish. The eggs are immature, oval, yellowish-brown, and equipped with a small operculum with abopercular wrinkle or knob (Tanabe 1922). The eggs incubated in water at 37 °C produced miracidia in 7 days (Tanabe 1922) and miracidia begin to hatch when they became matured (Tanabe 1922). In another experiment, the optimum temperature for the development of eggs was 30 °C and miracidia hatched in 8 days in both dark and light; no development of miracidia occurred below 6 °C (Sosipatrov 1964). Sahai and Srivastava (1970) also observed hatching of miracidia in 8 days at 37.5 °C and in 10 days at 30 °C after culture. The miracidia exhibited a rudimentary eye spot on days 2–3 after culture in water at 30 °C and the eye spot was distinctly pigmented on day 5; on day 8–9 they were fully developed with cilia and a clearly duplicated eye spot (Sahai and Srivastava 1970).

The first intermediate host includes *Parafossarulus* (*Bulimus*) *striatulus, Parafossarulus manchouricus, Bithynia leachi, Lymnaea stagnalis,* and *Radix ovata* (experimental), and sporocysts, rediae, and cercariae develop in these snails (Komiya 1949, 1951; Ito 1964; Sosipatrov 1964). The mother rediae are 1.8–2.1 mm long and 0.7–0.8 mm wide and the daughter rediae are 1.5–1.8 mm long and 0.3–0.7 mm wide; both are echinostome type (Komiya 1951). The pharynx (0.1 × 0.05 mm) of mother rediae is larger than that of daughter rediae; daughter rediae contain 10–13 germ balls and more than 10 cercariae (Komiya 1951). The cercarial shedding occurred on days 43–63 after miracidial infection in *Bithynia leachi* and *Lymnaea stagnalis* snails (Sosipatrov 1962). The cercarial movement was alike that of the usual cercariae of xiphidious type; the cercarial body surface was smooth and had no spines or scales (Komiya 1951). Several short sensory hairs were seen on both lateral margins of the body; rod-like cystogenous gland materials were compacted within the body (Komiya 1951). The collar spines were not developed to be recognizable; the genital primordia were undifferentiated and recognized as 2 masses of cells located along the anterior and posterior margins of the acetabulum, respectively (Komiya 1951).

Various kinds of freshwater or brackish water fish, including *Pseudorasbora parva, Plecoglossus altivelis, Acheilognathus rhombea, Acheilognathus lanceolata, Acanthogobius flavimanus, Gnathopogon elongatus, Zacco platypus, Zacco temminckii, Opsariichthys uncirostris, Odontobutis obscura, Pseudogobio esocinus, Carassius auratus, Puntungia herzi, Misgurnus anguillicaudatus, Mugil cephalus; Lateolabrax japonicus, Sarcocheilichthys variegatus, Salangichthys microdon,* and *Tridentiger obscurus* have been reported to be the second intermediate host of *E. perfoliatus* (Fahmy and Selim 1959; Yamashita 1964; Komiya 1965; Rim 1982). The metacercariae are found exclusively in the gill of the fish (Yamashita 1964; Komiya 1965). The cercariae were, when exposed to small *Pseudorasbora parva* fish, sucked into the mouth of the fish and their majority seemed to have been caught in the gills; 3 h later many cercarial bodies were found in the gill and several of them were already encysted (Komiya 1951). Three days after this infection, all cercariae were encysted to become metacercariae; 7 days after the infection the collar spines began to be observed with great effort (Komiya 1951).

The natural definitive hosts include humans, rats, cats, dogs, foxes, badgers, fowls, pigs, and wild boars (Yamashita 1964; Komiya 1965; Rim 1982; Hung et al. 2013). Experimental definitive hosts included dogs, cats, ducks, chickens, and pigs (Tanabe 1922; Fahmy and Selim 1959; Sosipatrov 1961a, 1964). In cats and pigs experimentally infected with the metacercariae, adult flukes were recovered at day 8–20 post-infection, and the adult flukes survived 132–168 days in pigs (Sosipatrov 1964).

Epidemiology and Geographical Distribution

The geographical distribution of *E. perfoliatus* is wide, from Far Asian countries, including Japan, China, South Korea, and Russia to many European countries (Fig. 2.22; Table 2.4) (Rim 1982; Yu and Mott 1994; Chai et al. 2009a; Otranto et al. 2017). However, natural and experimental human infections have been reported only from Japan, China, and India (Bhalerao 1935; Hirazawa 1928; Yu and Mott 1994). The main mode of infection is consumption of raw freshwater fish. Dogs, cats, pigs, and foxes are important reservoir hosts (Chai et al. 2009a).

Bulgaria The metacercariae of *E. perfoliatus* were detected in black-stripped pipefish (*Syngnathus abaster*) caught from the lower River Danube; the prevalence was 4% and the intensity 0.8 ± 4.1 (Ondračková et al. 2012).

China Tubangui (1922) obtained adult specimens of this fluke and described it as a subspecies, *E. perfoliatus shieldsi*; however, Yamashita (1937) synonymized this subspecies with *E. perfoliatus*. Thereafter, Chen (1934), Wu (1937), Kuo and Kiang (1943), Zhou and Wang (1987), and Zhao et al. (2001) obtained *E. perfo-*

liatus specimens from dogs in Canton (Guangdong), Shanghai, Chengtu, Nanchang and Ruichang (Anhui Province), and Nanhai, respectively. The first human infection case was reported by Lin and Cheng (1981) from Fujian Province. Thereafter, human infections were also detected in Anhui Province; 11 (1.1%) of 997 examinees for their stool specimens were positive for echinostome eggs and total 171 adult specimens were recovered from the 11 cases after anthelmintic treatment and purging (Jiang et al. 1988). The presence of human infections was also confirmed in Hubei Province (Chen and Yang 1988). Praziquantel treatment was tried for the treatment of *E. perfoliatus* and *Metagonimus yokogawai* infections (Xu et al. 1988). Molecular diagnosis using random amplified polymorphic DNA (RAPD) analysis was tried to differentiate zoonotic *Echinochasmus* species occurring in China, namely, *E. perfoliatus, E. japonicus, E. liliputanus,* and *E. fujianensis* (Cheng et al. 1999). In Guangdong Province (Pinyuan County), RAPD analysis in combination with morphological studies were performed to diagnose trematode metacercariae encysted in 11 species of freshwater fish, including *P. parva*; 6 trematode species, including *E. perfoliatus, E. japonicus,* and *E. fujianensis* were confirmed (Cheng et al. 2000a). The metacercariae of *E. perfoliatus* were detected in the gill of *Zacco platypus* caught from Yangshuo, Guangxi Zhuang Autonomous Region (Sohn et al. 2009). In Fujian Province, morphological characteristics of 5 echinostome species occurring in this region, including *E. perfoliatus, E. japonicus, E. fujianensis, Echinostoma angustitestis,* and *Echinostoma aegyptiacum* were analyzed (Chen et al. 2013). In Guangxi Province, feral dogs (10.0%; 4/40) and cats (25.6%; 10/39) were found to be infected with *E. perfoliatus* (Fang et al. 2015).

Croatia Six (12.8%) of 47 wild boars (*Sus scrofa*) from eastern Croatia were found infected with *E. perfoliatus*; total 141 specimens were collected from 6 wild boars (Rajković-Janje et al. 2002).

Denmark Fourteen (1.3%) of 1040 Danish red foxes examined during 1997–2002 were infected with *E. perfoliatus* and the mean intensity of infection in these animals was 4.6 worms per animal (Saeed et al. 2006). Red foxes from Copenhagen were infected with *E. perfoliatus*, whereas those from Southern Jutland were not infected with this echinostome (Al-Sabi et al. 2014).

Egypt Abdel Azim (1938) reported that *E. perfoliatus* is a common intestinal parasite in dogs in Lower and Upper Egypt. One adult specimen was found in a dog fed on *Mugil* fish (Fahmy and Selim 1959). Adult specimens were also recovered in dogs fed *Tilapia* sp. and *Bagrus bayad* fish from the Nile River (Tawfik et al. 2000).

England This echinostome was listed as an intestinal fluke of the cat, dog, and pig (Nicoll 1923).

Hungary Six years after the first discovery of this echinostome in 1902 in Romania (reported as *Distoma equinatum*), it was renamed as *Echinostomum perfoliatum* by

v. Ratz in 1908 based on specimens obtained from dogs and cats in Hungary (Tanabe 1922; Tubangui 1922).

India Chandler (1925) mentioned the common occurrence of *E. perfoliatus* in dogs in Calcutta, and Bhalerao (1935) listed *E. perfoliatus* as a parasite of cat, dog, and man. Adult specimens of *E. perfoliatus* were also obtained from cats in Calcutta and Mukteswar (Bhalerao 1936) and dogs in Orissa (Patnaik 1959), Bihar (Kumar and Sahai 1972), and Bareilly (Sahai and Srivastava 1970). In wild carnivores, such as rusty spotted cats, *E. perfoliatus* is listed as an important small intestinal trematode (Acharjyo 2004).

Italy Beaver et al. (1984) and Hung et al. (2013) listed Italy among the countries where *E. perfoliatus* was reported.

Japan Adult specimens of *E. perfoliatus* were obtained from the small intestine of cats and dogs fed various kinds (11 species) of freshwater fish from Kyoto, Okayama, Shiga, and Tokyo (Tanabe 1915, 1922). The species of freshwater fish included *Acheilognathus intermedia, Brevigobio kawabatae, Chanogobius macrognathus, Fluvidraco nudiceps, Gnathopogon elongatus, Mogurnda obscura, Opsariichthys uncirostris, Pseudoperilampus typus, Pseudorasbora parva, Zacco platypus,* and *Zacco temminckii.* Tanabe (1922) succeeded in infecting himself with *E. perfoliatus* by swallowing 6 metacercariae separated from the gill of *Opsariichthys uncirostris*; the eggs were detected in his feces at day 36 after the infection. Meanwhile, Muto (1918) gave *Pseudogobio esocinus* and *Acheilognathus intermedia* fish to puppies and obtained adult flukes; he obtained eggs in the feces of the puppies after 21–23 days. The eggs believed to have been *E. perfoliatus* were discovered from human feces several times until 1928 (Yamashita 1964). However, Hirazawa (1928) was the first who confirmed 5 adult flukes from a 14-year-old patient living in Osaka City. Kurisu (1932) obtained adult specimens from fowls of Osaka, Hiroshima, and Okayama. Okabe (1940) listed various species of freshwater fish transmitting *E. perfoliatus*, including *Plecoglossus altivelis, Phoxis lagowskii, Tridentiger obscurus, Carassius auratus, Puntungia herzi,* and *Acheilognathus rhombea.* Abe (1941) reported that *Rhodeus lanceolata* fish can transmit the metacercariae of *E. perfoliatus*. Several reports were made regarding the snail intermediate host in Japan (Yamashita 1964); however, the definite decision of the snail host as *Parafossarulus* (*Bithynia*) *striatulus* was done by Komiya (1949, 1951). Otagaki and Kanemitsu (1953) added *Salangichthys microdon, Acanthogobius flavimanus,* and *Glossogobius giuris* among the list of fish intermediate host. Okahashi (1966) added loaches (*Misgurnus anguillicaudatus*) in the list of fish intermediate hosts. Yamaguchi (1967) found the cercariae of *E. perfoliatus* in *Parafossarulus manchouricus* snails in 3 (0.03%) of 10,400 snails examined in Tokushima Prefecture; he also detected its metacercariae in *Pseudorasbora parva* fish, 52 (6.9%) of 756 fish examined in 1954–1956, 2 (2.7%) of 450 fish in 1962–1963, and 4 (4.0%) of 100 fish in 1963–

1964 in Naruto City. Ritchie et al. (1952, 1953) reported infection of people with *E. perfoliatus* (only by recovery of eggs in the feces) in 4 of 1239 people from Saga-Fukuoka and Kumamoto Prefectures in 1952 and one of 2525 individuals from the Tone River area (Chiba, Ibaraki, and Saitama Prefectures) in 1953, respectively. Thereafter, almost no literature is available regarding recovery of *E. perfoliatus* from people or intermediate hosts. In 2012, a checklist of parasites of freshwater and brackish water fish in Hiroshima Prefecture included *E. perfoliatus* that occurs in this region (Nagasawa and Nitta 2012).

South Korea The first report of this echinostome species was published by Chun (1962); he discovered the metacercariae of *E. perfoliatus* in freshwater fish species, including *Carassius auratus, Pseudorasbora parva, Culter brevicauda, Gnathopogon coreanus, Zacco platypus,* and *Zacco temminckii* from Myungji, Kimhae, and Milyang areas. Chun (1964) also reported *Carassius auratus* fish as the fish host for *E. perfoliatus*. The adult specimens were detected in naturally infected cats from Gyeongsangbuk-do (Province) (Lee 1979). The metacercariae (under the name *Echinochasmus* sp. 1; bigger metacercariae) were detected in various species of freshwater fish, including *Pseudorasbora parva, Puntungia herzi, Gnathopogon coreanus, Carassius auratus,* and *Acheilognathus* sp., caught from Kumho River, Gyeongsangbuk-do (Province) (Lee 1968). A similar study was performed in Osip stream (Yeongdeok, Gyeongsangbuk-do) in which *Carassius auratus* and *Gnathopogon atromaculatus* fish were positive for *Echinochasmus* species metacercariae (Lee et al. 1979). Another study in Kumho River revealed infection of *Achelognathus taenianalis, Gnathopogon atromaculatus, Hemibarbus labeo, Pseudogobio esocinus, Pseudorasbora parva,* and *Zacco platypus* with *Echinochasmus* sp. metacercariae (Hwang and Choi 1980). In Hyungsan River, Gyeongsangbuk-do (Province), 5 species of freshwater fish, including *Carassius auratus, Gnathopogon atromaculatus, Pseudorasbora parva, Zacco platypus, Zacco teminchkii,* and *Plecoglossus altivelis*, were found to harbor the metacercariae (under the name *Echinochasmus* sp.) (Joo 1984). Thereafter, no reports on *E. perfoliatus* have been available. Human *E. perfoliatus* infection has never been documented.

Poland Adult flukes of *E. perfoliatus* were recovered in one (4.0%) of 25 racoon dogs necropsied in Poland (Machnicka et al. 2003).

Romania In 1902, *E. perfoliatus* was first found from the intestine of 2 dogs in Bucharest, Romania by Motas and Straulescus and reported under the name *Distoma echinatum* (Tanabe 1922; Tubangui 1922). Later, Railliet and Henry (1909) found the same parasite in dogs and named it as *Echinostoma gregale*; this was later synonymized with *E. perfoliatus* (Skrjabin and Bashikirova 1956). Ciurea (1915, 1920) found this echinostome in the intestine of dogs (adults) and freshwater fish (metacercariae) from Romania.

Russia *E. perfoliatus* infection was repeatedly reported in pigs and was considered an important pathogen to pigs; 127 pigs died in the Astrakhan region in the course of an epidemic of *E. perfoliatus* infection (Chebotarev et al. 1960). The main symptoms in infected pigs (intensity of 5000–15,000 worms per pig) in this area included diarrhea, accelerated pulse and breathing, periodical rise in the body temperature, pericardial spasms, and enlargement of the lymph nodes; pathological changes were observed in the small intestine and other organs and tissue, such as the heart, brain, lungs, and skeletal muscles (Sosipatrov 1961a, b). Sosipatrov (1962) found 9.96% and 6.7% of snails *Bulinus leachi* and *Lymnaea stagnalis* infected with the cercariae of *E. perfoliatus*, respectively, and 22 species of fish acting as the second intermediate host. Hexachloroethane was used for treatment of pig infection, whereas kamala, filixan, and carbon tetrachloride were ineffective (Proshin 1962). Sosipatrov (1964) studied on the life cycle of *E. perfoliatus* and found that 22 of 27 local fish species were capable of transmitting this echinostome; however, infection to the frog (*Rana temporaria*) and molluscs was not successful. Argentophilic structures of the miracidium were studied by Dimitrov et al. (1998) using the material obtained from Vladivostok. Far East Russia. Adult specimens were recovered from raccoon dogs and American minks (Ivanov and Semenova 2000). Domestic and wild animals were found to be infected with echinostome species, including *E. perfoliatus* (Shimalov and Shimalov 2002).

Serbia During 1993–2000, a total of 108 adult red foxes were examined for their intestinal parasites, and *E. perfoliatus* was detected in 14.8% of the foxes (Pavlović et al. 2011).

Taiwan Yu and Mott (1994) and Hung et al. (2013) listed Taiwan among the countries where *E. perfoliatus* is existing.

Thailand Four of 54 leopards, 2 of 3 leopard cats, and 2 of 16 cats from Huai Kha Wildlife Sanctuary were positive for echinostomatid eggs (presumed to be those of *Echinostoma ilocanum* or *E. perfoliatus*) (Patton and Robinowitz 1994).

Ukraine Wild animal species, including the redfox (*Vulpes vulpes*), raccoon dog (*Nyctereutes procyonis*), and American mink (*Neovison vison*), were recorded to have infections with *E. perfoliatus* (Korol et al. 2016).

Vietnam An available literature reported that 4 (16.0%) of 25 dogs from Nam Dinh Province harboured 5 ± 3 specimens of *E. perfoliatus* (Anh et al. 2009b). The infection of dogs with *E. perfoliatus* has been commonly documented in Vietnam (Bang and Cuong 2015). Human infection was reported in Hanoi but the prevalence was not reported (Hung et al. 2013).

2.4.3 Echinochasmus liliputanus

2.4.3.1 *Echinochasmus liliputanus* (Looss, 1896) Odhner, 1910

[syn. *Echinostomum liliputanum* Looss, 1896]

Taxonomy and Morphology

This echinostome (Fig. 2.24) was originally described by Looss (1896) based on adult specimens obtained from birds (*Milvus migrans, Pernis apivorus,* and *Ardea cinerea*), cats, and dogs in Egypt, Syria, and Israel (Palestine) (Witenberg 1932; Kuntz and Chandler 1956). Subsequently, Witenberg (1932) discovered its metacercariae from freshwater fish (*Tilapia* and *Nemachilus*) from Israel (Palestine), which were fed to experimental cats and dogs, and eggs were obtained in the stool of these animals in a fortnight. Later, in Egypt, *E. liliputanus* was found again in dogs, cats, and a fox (Kuntz and Chandler 1956). This species was also reported from vertebrate animals in Sri Lanka (Kannangara 1971) and raccoon dogs (*Nyctereutes procyonoides*) in China (Cheng and Ye 1988). Human infection are known only in China (Xiao et al. 1992; Yu and Mott 1994).

The adult flukes are variable in size, from 0.5 to 0.8 mm long and 0.2 mm wide (Witenberg 1932) to 1.68–1.76 mm long and 0.23–0.40 mm wide (Chen et al. 1985) or 1.52–2.06 mm long and 0.47–0.56 mm wide (Xiao et al. 1992). They have a slightly elongated ovoid body, a reniform head collar with 24 collar spines arranged in a single row, interrupted dorsally and ventrally, 2 tandem testes, a small number

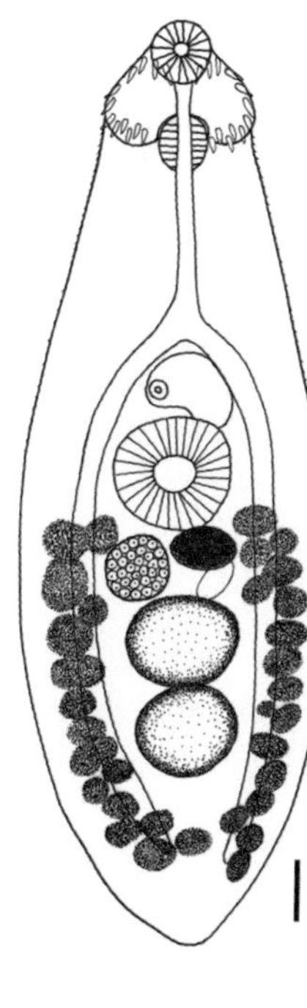

Fig. 2.24 Line drawing of an adult fluke of *Echinochasmus liliputanus*. Scale bar = 0.05 mm. (Modified from the figure in Fahmy and Selim (1959) Z Parasitenkd 19:3–13)

(usually 1–2, rarely up to 6–7) of uterine eggs, and vitellaria which do not extend anteriorly up to the level of the ventral sucker (Witenberg 1932; Chen et al. 1985; Xiao et al. 1992). *E. liliputanus* is morphologically close to *E. japonicus*. The former has a slightly elongated body but the latter has an oval or plump body (Chen et al. 1985). The vitellaria of *E. japonicus* are more extensively distributed, from the acetabular level to the posterior end of the body, but those of *E. japonicus* are less extensive, from the middle level of the uterus to the posterior end of the body (Chen et al. 1985). The egg size is smaller for *E. japonicus* (62–64 μm long) than *E. liliputanus* (80–88 μm long or 95–116 μm long) (Chen et al. 1985; Xiao et al. 1992). The collar spines of *E. japonicus* are characteristically longer and more sharply pointed than those of *E. liliputanus* (Chen et al. 1985). *E. liliputanus* is also close to *E. perfoliatus*. However, *E. liliputanus* (0.5–2.1 mm long) is smaller in body size than *E. perfoliatus* (0.5–12.0 mm), and has a small head collar (0.126–0.184 mm long) and slightly elongated (kidney-shaped) cirrus sac, where *E. perfoliatus* has a larger head collar (0.27–0.40 mm long) and markedly elongated cirrus sac; the collar spines of *E. liliputanus* (21–28 μm long) are shorter than those of *E. perfoliatus* (68–70 μm long) and less sharply pointed (Chen et al. 1985). The eggs of *E. liliputanus* are variable in size, 80–88 μm long and 54–66 μm wide (Chen et al. 1985) or 95–116 μm long and 54–73 μm (Xiao et al. 1992), smaller than or as large as those of *E. perfoliatus* (96–102 μm long and 56–60 μm wide) (Chen et al. 1985). The vitellaria of *E. liliputanus* extend from the middle level of the uterus to the posterior end of the body, whereas those of *E. perfoliatus* extend from the genital pore level to the posterior end of the body (Chen et al. 1985). *E. liliputanus* is differed from *E. fujianensis* (oval in shape) in its elongated body, smaller number of uterine eggs (less than 6–7 in *E. liliputanus* and 4–20 in *E. fujianensis*), and less extensive distribution of vitellaria, i.e., from the middle level of the uterus to the posterior end of the body in *E. liliputanus*, but from the cirrus sac level to the posterior end of the body in *E. fujianensis* (Chen et al. 1985; Cheng et al. 1992). *E. jiufoensis* is differed from *E. liliputanus* in its peculiar arrangement of the 2 testes, which are diagonal or somewhat transversal instead of tandem (Liang and Ke 1988). *E. caninus* (syn. *Episthmium caninum*) is differed from all other species of *Echinochasmus* in that the former has a profusely developed and extensive vitellaria reaching into the forebody (Yamaguti 1958, 1971).

The cercarial body of *E. liliputanus* is oval and flat, and 130–140 μm long and 98–120 μm wide; the tail length is similar to its body length, 110–140 μm long and 28–30 μm wide (Chen et al. 1985). The metacercarial cysts are small and elliptical, 78–86 × 56–70 μm in size, equipped with total 24 collar spines arranged in a single row which are interrupted dorsally and ventrally (Chen et al. 1985). The metacercariae of *E. liliputanus* are morphologically similar to those of *E. japonicus* and *E. perfoliatus* (Chen et al. 1985). The only apparent difference is the larger size (92–108 × 71–97 μm) of the metacercariae of *E. perfoliatus* than those of *E. liliputanus* (78–86 × 56–70 μm) (Chen et al. 1985).

The tegumental ultrastructure of *E. liliputanus* was studied by Wu et al. (1997) on adult flukes recovered from experimentally infected dogs using a scanning electron microscope. Most of the body surface was covered with tegumental spines except for the collar, acetabulum, and the posterior aspect of the body; there were 3 types of papillae on the tegument (2 ciliated and one aciliated types) (Wu et al. 1997). On the acetabulum total 32 protruded aciliate papillae were seen (Wu et al. 1997).

Life Cycle

The life cycle of *E. liliputanus* has not yet been extensively studied. However, it has been known that freshwater snails *Parafossarulus striatulus* (Chen et al. 1985; Yu and Mott 1994) and *Bellamya aeruginosa* (Xiao et al. 2000) are the first intermediate host, and freshwater fish species (more than 20 species of 9 families, including *Pseudorasbora parva,* goldfish, *Mugil capito*, and *Tilapia nilotica*) play the role of the second intermediate host (Fahmy and Selim 1959; Yu and Mott 1994; Wu 2013). In fish hosts, the metacercariae are encysted in the gill in most cases (Wu 2013). It is of special interest to note that both cercariae and metacercariae of *E. liliputanus* can infect the human host; therefore, *E. liliputanus* is regarded as both a water-borne and a fish-borne echinostome (Xiao et al. 1995a, b, c, 2005; Wu 2013). The natural definitive hosts include humans, dogs, cats, badgers (*Meles meles leptorhynchus*), foxes (*Vulpes vulpes hoole*), raccoon dogs (*Nyctereutes procyonoides procyonoides*), and birds (*Pernis apivorus, Milvus aegypticus, Milvus parasiticus,* and *Ardes cinerea*) (Chen et al. 1985; Yu and Mott 1994; El-Gayar 2007). Dogs, rabbits, cats, and mice were confirmed to be useful experimental definitive hosts (Xiao et al. 2000).

In a laboratory setting in Anhui Province, China, the cercariae were detected from the snail host (*Bellamya aeruginosa*) at days 103–140 days after experimental exposure of the snails to eggs in April-May; however, longer days (more than 300 days) were needed in September-October (Xiao et al. 2000). In the field, cercarial shedding occurred from late July and peaked in September-November, and disappeared by early December (Xiao et al. 1995a). In October (mean temperature, 23.2 °C), the largest number of cercariae, up to 209,200 daily/snail, were reproduced from the daughter rediae within a snail (Xiao et al. 2000). The cercariae were phototactic and emerged from the epitaenial fold of the positive snails mainly during the daytime (08:00–16:00); the newly shed cercariae tended to distribute with the surface water, maximum 6 cm deep from the surface, and the time of 50% mortality of the newly emerged cercariae at 6 °C, 20 °C, and 30 °C was 259 h, 106 h, and 69 h, respectively (Xiao et al. 2000). The infectivity of the cercariae to fish hosts was cercarial age-dependent; it peaked at 9 h after the emergence (over 64% were infective); it decreased rapidly to below 1% by 72 h after the emergence (Xiao et al. 2000). The cercariae were also infective directly to the definitive hosts, including dogs and human volunteers (Xiao et al. 1995b). Nine dogs and 2 human volunteers were orally (by drinking water) exposed to the cercariae (1500–88,000 cercariae individually) of *E. liliputanus*; in human volunteers, eggs appeared in their stools on days 15–16 post-infection, and in dogs, the eggs first appeared in the feces at day 14 post infection and the worm recovery rate was 4.0% (Xiao et al. 1995b). Xiao et al. (2005) examined in vitro and in vivo encystment of *E. liliputanus* cercariae; the in vitro encystment occurred in the gill of goldfish, a second intermediate host for this echinostome. The cercariae also encysted in various dilutions of Locke's solution, NaCl solution, artificial gastric juice, and human gastric juice; when treated with a bile salt medium the in vitro formed cysts were capable of excysting (Xiao et al. 2005). In addition, cysts formed in vitro (especially in human gastric juice) and in vivo were both capable of infecting experimental rabbits, so that it was concluded that these results might be helpful in elucidating the mechanisms of the infection of humans through swallowing the cercariae in water (Xiao et al. 2005).

Epidemiology and Geographical Distribution

The geographical distribution of *E. liliputanus* is relatively limited; Egypt, Syria, Israel (Palestine), Sri Lanka, and China are the so far known areas of distribution (Fig. 2.22; Table 2.4) (Witenberg 1932; Kuntz and Chandler 1956; Kannangara 1971; Cheng and Ye 1988; Hung et al. 2013). Human infections were first discovered in Anhui Province, China, with the prevalence of 13.4% among 2426 people examined (Xiao et al. 1992). In the same place, dogs (60%) and cats (45%) were also found to be infected (Xiao et al. 1992). Since then, more than 2500 human infection cases were reported in Anhui Province, China (Xiao et al. 2005). In countries other than China, no human infections have been discovered.

It was postulated in Auhui Province, China that humans can be infected with this echinostome through drinking untreated water containing the cercariae, since the infection rate was only 1.5% in the inhabitants who did not drink raw water, whereas it was 20.1% among those who used to drink raw water (Xiao et al. 1995c). An experimental study was undertaken to explain the mechanism of the human oral infection with cercariae, and the phenomenon of cercarial encystment in the presence of human gastric juice was proposed as a possible mechanism (Xiao et al. 2005). The main risk factors for *E. liliputanus* infection included drinking unboiled water, eating the snails (Viviparidae), using the ditch as the source of drinking water, and brushing the teeth or rinsing the mouth with the water from the ditch (Wang et al. 1999).

China The presence of the life cycle in China was first documented in 1964–1965 in Fujian Province; *Parafossarulus striatulus* was found to be the snail intermediate host (Chen et al. 1985). After then, Cheng and Ye (1988) found adults of *E. liliputanus* in raccoon dogs from Hunan Province. Human infections with *E. liliputanus* were first discovered in Anhui Province with the prevalence rate of 13.4% among 2426 people examined (Xiao et al. 1992). Higher infection rates were observed in males (14.2%) than in females (12.6%) and in age groups 3–15 years (22.7%) and 16–30 years (16.4%) than in others. In the same place, the infection rates of dogs and cats were 60% (21/35) and 45% (5/11), respectively (Xiao et al. 1992). Subsequently, Xiao et al. (1994) conducted another epidemiological survey and reported an overall prevalence among people was 13.7% with no significant difference in the infection rates between males and females. The infection rate was closely related to age with higher rates occurring in relatively younger persons; the age group 3–30 years had 78.3% of the total infections (Xiao et al. 1994). Since then, more than 2500 human infection cases have been reported in Anhui Province, China (Xiao et al. 2005). Wang et al. (1993) determined the therapeutic efficacy of praziquantel (referred to as pyquiton in China) for the treatment of human *E. liliputanus* infection; 200 human cases were divided into 2,5, 5.0, and 10.0 mg/kg dose groups, and 1 month after the treatment the cure rates were 96.5%, 98.7%, and 100%, respectively. The clinical symptoms in these patients included abdominal pain, abdominal distention, diarrhea, and anorexia (Wang et al. 1993). Human infections by drinking unboiled water containing the cercariae and also by eating raw fish containing the metacercariae were reported by Xiao et al. (1995b, c). People in an endemic area claimed that they did not eat raw fish (Xiao et al. 1995c). In a longitudinal survey in a primary school in Anhui Province, China, *E. liliputanus* infection in children reached a peak in September and October when drinking untreated water occurs most often; the annual infection rate in children was 31.9% (Wang et al. 1998). In addition to drinking unboiled water, eating the snails (Viviparidae), using the ditch as the source of drinking water, and brushing the teeth or rinsing the mouth with the water from the ditch were main risk factors for *E. liliputanus* infection (Wang et al. 1999). A molecular study using random amplified polymorphic DNA (RAPD) analysis to differentiate 4 zoonotic *Echinochasmus* species occurring in China, including *E. liliputanus*, *E. japonicus, E. perfoliatus,* and *E. fujianensis* resulted to be successful; however, it was suggested that *E. liliputanus* Anhui strain and *E. fujianensis* may be the same species (Cheng et al. 1999). Xiao et al. (2005) examined in vitro and in vivo encystment of *E. liliputanus* cercariae, and it was found that the in vitro encystment occurred in the gill of goldfish and also in various dilutions of Locke's solution, NaCl solution, artificial gastric juice, and human gastric juice. In addition, the cysts formed in human gastric juice were capable of infecting experimental rabbits, and thus it was strongly suggested that humans can be infected with this echinostome by swallowing the cercariae in drinking water from the ditches (Xiao et al. 2005). In Guangxi Province, feral dogs (4 of 40 examined) were found to be infected with a variety of intestinal helminths, including *E. liliputanus* (Fang et al. 2015).

Egypt In 1896, Looss A. discovered adult specimens of *E. liliputanus* from birds (*Milvus migrans, Pernis apivorus,* and *Ardea cinerea*), cats, and dogs in Egypt, Syria, and Israel (Palestine) and reported as a new species, *Echinostomum liliputanum* (Witenberg 1932; Kuntz and Chandler 1956). Later, this echinostome was found again in dogs, cats, and a fox (Abdel Azim 1939; Kuntz and Chandler 1956; Fahmy and Selim 1959; El-Gayar 2007). White rats and chickens experimentally infected with trematode metacercariae in freshwater fish from Ismalia Province, Egypt harboured adult specimens of various helminths, including *E. liliputanus* (Abou-Eisha et al. 2008; Saleh et al. 2009). Natural infection of stray cats with *E. liliputanus* was recently reported from Beni-Suef Province (El-Dakhly et al. 2017).

Israel (Palestine) Four of 27 cats and one of 27 dogs were found infected with this echinostome species (Witenberg 1932). Subsequently, its metacercariae were detected in freshwater fish (*Tilapia* and *Nemachilus*), which were fed to experimental cats and dogs, and eggs were obtained in the stool of these animals (Witenberg 1932).

Sri Lanka This echinostome was recorded from the intestine of a few species of vertebrates in Ceylon (Kannangara 1971).

Syria This echinostome was discovered in an avian species (*Ardea cinerea*) from Syria (Witenberg 1932; Yamaguti 1971).

2.4.4 Echinochasmus fujianensis

2.4.4.1 *Echinochasmus fujianensis* Cheng et al., 1992

Taxonomy and Morphology

Echinochasms fujianensis was first discovered from humans, dogs, cats, pigs, and rats in Longhai County, Fujian Province, China (Cheng et al. 1992). Thereafter, this species was also found in Guangdong Province, China (Cheng et al. 2000a). It has been found only in China. It is recognized that *E. fujianensis* is the most dominant species among the 3 common *Echinochasmus* species existing in China (Fujian, Hubei, Anhui, and Guangdong Provinces), i.e., *E. fujianensis, E. japonicus*, and *E. perfoliatus* (Cheng et al. 1999, 2000a). Human infections were so far confirmed in Fujian Province.

The adult worms are 1.25–1.79 mm long and 0.375–0.518 mm wide, and their eggs are 98–113 µm long and 64–72 µm wide (Cheng et al. 1992). It has a prominent head collar with 24 collar spines arranged in a single row, interrupted dorsally, with 4 corner spines on each side; its vitellaria distribution is more extensive (from the anterior end of the ventral sucker to the posterior end of the body) than 2 other *Echinochasmus* species, *E. japonicus* and *E. liliputanus* (from the posterior end of the ventral sucker to the posterior end of the body) (Cheng et al. 1992). *E. perfoliatus* is larger in body and head collar size than *E. fujianensis*, and the former has more than 20 uterine eggs, whereas the latter has 4–20 uterine eggs (Cheng et al. 1992). *E. fujianensis* also differs genetically from *Echinochasmus japonicus* as revealed by random amplified polymorphic DNA analysis (RAPD) patterns (Cheng et al. 1999). *E. jiufoensis* is differed from *E. fujianensis* in its peculiar arrangement of the 2 testes, which are diagonal or somewhat transversal instead of tandem (Liang and Ke 1988). *E. caninus* (syn. *Episthmium caninum*) is differed from *E. fujianensis* in its more extensive distribution of vitellaria into the anterior part of the body (Yamaguti 1958, 1971).

The cercarial body of *E. fujianensis* were heart-shaped and 127–132 µm long and 78–86 µm wide, and its tail was 125–130 µm long and 20–23 µm wide (Cheng et al. 1992, 1994). The cercarial body of *E. fujianensis* was similar in size to those of *E. perfoliatus* and *E. liliputanus* but apparently larger than those of *E. japonicus* (Cheng et al. 1992). The metacercariae are elliptical and 98–114 µm long and 76–88 µm wide; they are larger than those of *E. liliputanus* (78–86 µm long and 56–70 µm wide) and *E. japonicus* (69–80 µm long and 52–67 µm wide) but as large as those of *E. perfoliatus* (95–120 µm long and 70–91 µm wide) (Cheng et al. 1992).

Surface ultrastructural studies of *E. fujianensis* have not yet been performed.

Life Cycle

Its first intermediate host has been experimentally proven to be a species of freshwater snail, *Bellamya aeruginosa* (Cheng et al. 1992) and *Oncomelania* spp. (Hung et al. 2013). Natural infection of *Bellamya aeruginosa* snails were also confirmed; 4.7% of 147 field collected snails were cercaria-positive (Cheng et al. 1992). The daughter rediae were 0.61–1.4 mm long and 0.14–0.25 mm wide (Cheng et al. 1992, 1994). Encysted metacercariae were found in the gills of freshwater fish, including *Pseudorasbora parva* and *Cyprinus carpio* (Cheng et al. 1992; Yu and Mott 1994). The natural definitive hosts included humans, dogs, cats, pigs, and rats (Cheng et al. 1992, 1994).

Epidemiology and Geographical Distribution

The geographical distribution of *E. fujianensis* has been confined to Fujian, Hubei, Anhui, and Guangdong Provinces of China (Table 2.4) (Cheng et al. 1992; Yu and Mott 1994; Cheng et al. 2000a). However, the distribution in China may be wider than reported. The main mode of infection in humans is considered to be consumption of raw freshwater fish (Cheng et al. 1992).

China This echinostome was first described based on adult specimens obtained from humans, dogs, cats, pigs, and rats in Fujian Province (Cheng et al. 1992). In Fujian Province, the egg positive rate of residents was 2.5% (13 persons) among 528 examined; 1–13 adult specimens were recovered individually from 9 egg-positive cases after anthelmintic treatment (Cheng et al. 1992). In 5 localities of southern Fujian Province, the prevalence among residents was 3.2% (1.6–7.8%); two-thirds of the infected people were 3–15 years of age. The therapeutic efficacy of praziquantel and mebendazole-medicated salt in treatment of human *E. fujianensis* infection was evaluated, and it has been confirmed that praziquantel is the drug of choice for this infection and mebedazole-medicated salt can also be used, although the efficacy is lower than that of praziquantel, when there are co-infections with nematodes (Cheng et al. 1997). In Hubei, Anhui, and Fujian Provinces, China, molecular studies using random amplified polymorphic DNA (RAPD) analysis of 4 zoonotic *Echinochasmus* species, including *E. fujianensis, E. liliputanus*, *E. japonicus,* and *E. perfoliatus* suggested that *E. liliputanus* Anhui strain and *E. fujianensis* may be the same species (Cheng et al. 1999). The metacercariae of *E. fujianensis* were also found in the gills of in freshwater fish from Pinyuan County, Guangdong Province; they were experimentally fed to dogs and cats, and adult flukes were obtained (Cheng et al. 2000a, b). Molecular studies using RAPD and isoelectric focusing electrophoresis, and isoenzyme analyses of lactic dehydrogenase revealed that *E. fujianensis* Fujian and Guangdong strains are identical and the same species (Cheng et al. 2000a, b; Xu et al. 2002). Morphological characteristics (adults and eggs) of 5 echinostome species, including 3 *Echinochasmus* spp. (*E. fujianensis, E. japonicus,* and *E. perfoliatus*), *Echinostoma angustitestis*, and *E. aegyptiacum* were compared (Chen et al. 2013).

2.4.5 Echinochasmus jiufoensis

2.4.5.1 *Echinochasmus jiufoensis* Yu and Mott, 1994

Taxonomy and Morphology

A new species of *Echinochasmus, E. jiufoensis,* was discovered at autopsy of a 6-month-old girl who died from pneumonia and dehydration in Guangzhou, China (Liang and Ke 1988). This echinostome has 24 collar spines arranged in a single row, interrupted dorsally and ventrally, and is closely allied to *Echinochasmus beleocephalus* Dietz, 1909; however, it is distinguished from the latter in several points (Liang and Ke 1988; Yu and Mott 1994). The 2 testes of *E. jiufoensis* are arranged somewhat diagonally or even transversely, whereas those of *E. beleocephalus* and 4 other zoonotic *Echinochasmus* spp. (*E. japonicus, E. perfoliatus, E. liliputanus,* and *E. fujianensis*) are at tandem position (Liang and Ke 1988). The eggs of *E. jiufoensis* are larger than those of *E. beleocephalus* (Liang and Ke 1988).

The adult flukes are rather plump than elongated, and 0.55–0.79 mm long and 0.24–0.30 mm wide; their eggs are 100–115 μm long and 72–79 μm wide (Liang and Ke 1988). The uterus is short, and there are only 1–3 uterine eggs. The cercariae and metacercariae have never been detected.

Life Cycle

The life cycle and route of infection in the infected child are not completely known (Liang and Ke 1988). Freshwater snails, including *Oncomelania* spp., and molluscan and fish species, were suggested to be the first and second intermediate hosts, respectively (Hung et al. 013). The natural definitive hosts include humans, dogs, cats, and pigs (Hung et al. 2013).

Epidemiology and Geographical Distribution

No information is available on the epidemiological characteristics of this echinostome. It was found only once in a child from a suburb of Guangzhou, China (Table 2.4) (Liang and Ke 1988).

China A 6-month old child (girl) who died from pneumonia and dehydration in Guangzhou was found to have a new species of *Echinochasmus*; at autopsy 4 adult specimens were recovered from the intestinal tract (Liang and Ke 1988).

2.4.6 Echinochasmus caninus

2.4.6.1 *Echinochasmus caninus* (Verma, 1935) n. comb.

[syn. *Episthochasmus caninum* Verma, 1935; *Episthmium caninum* (Verma, 1935) Yamaguti, 1958]

Taxonomy and Morphology

This species (Fig. 2.25) was originally reported by Verma (1935) in India based on worms obtained from dogs in Calcutta, India as a new genus and a new species, *Episthochasmus caninum*. In 1941, Bashikirova E. I. treated *Episthochasmus, Echinochasmus*, *Episthmium,* and *Monilifer* as 4 subgenera of *Echinochasmus* Dietz, 1909 (Bashikirova 1947). Kobayasi (1942) found the metacercariae of this echinostome in fish *Macropodus opercularis* and adult flukes in dogs from Hainan Island, China. Yamaguti (1958) treated *Episthochasmus* as a synonym of *Episthmium* and acknowledged *Echinochasmus, Episthmium,* and *Monilifer* as 3 distinct genera. Gupta and Pande (1963) treated *Episthmium caninum* as a synonym of *Echinochasmus corvus* Bhalerao, 1926, which was reported from the intestine of a Burmese house-crow (*Corvus insolens*). However, Yamaguti (1971) did not accept this synonymy. Later, Kostadinova and Gibson (2001) suggested that *Episthmium* may be a synonym of *Echinochasmus,* and Kostadinova (2005) synonymized *Episthmium* Lühe, 1909 with *Echinochasmus* Dietz, 1909. Thus, the taxonomic status of *Echinochasmus caninus* has been settled. Three human infections were reported from northeast Thailand (Radomyos et al. 1985, 1991), and the source of infection was presumed to be a freshwater fish, *Macropodus opercularis* (Harinasuta et al. 1987; Tungtrongchitr and Radomyos 1989; Radomyos et al. 1998).

The adult flukes of *E. caninus* are delicate, thin, and semi-transparent except in the region of testes where they look whitish opaque (Verma 1935). They are elongated oval or plump in shape and 0.88–1.21 mm long and 0.36–0.46 mm wide (Verma 1935). The collar spines are prominent, 24 in number, and arranged in a

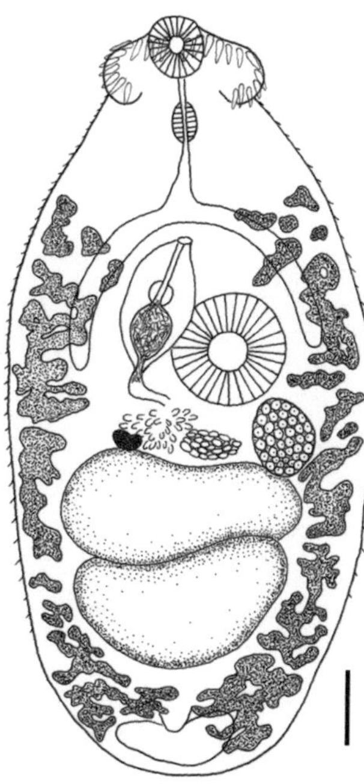

Fig. 2.25 Line drawing of an adult fluke of *Echinochasmus caninus*. Scale bar = 0.1 mm. (Modified from the figure in Verma (1935) Proc Ind Acad Sci 1:837–856)

single (dorsal spines) or double row (ventral and lateral spines), interrupted dorsally and ventrally; 2 of the dorsal spines of each side overlap the oral sucker in most specimens (Verma 1935; Radomyos et al. 1985). The number of uterine eggs are few (0–3 eggs per worm), and the egg size is 84 μm long and 50–60 μm wide (Verma 1935). The vitellaria are distributed profusely from the intestinal bifurcation level to the posterior end of the body (Verma 1935). *E. caninus* is differed from all other zoonotic *Echinochasmus* spp. mainly in the extent of the vitellaria in the anterior body (Verma 1935). The cercariae have not been discovered. The metacercariae were detected by Kobayasi (1942) in Hainan Island, China but the dimension of the metacercariae was not given.

Life Cycle
The first intermediate host has not yet been documented. The fish host *Macropodus opercularis* has been found in Hainan Island, China (Kobayasi 1942). The natural definitive host is dogs (Verma 1935; Kobayasi 1942) and humans (Radomyos et al. 1985, 1991, 1994, 1998).

Epidemiology and Geographical Distribution
The geographical distribution of this echinostome is confined to India, Thailand, China, and Vietnam (Table 2.4) (Verma 1935; Kobayasi 1942; Radomyos et al. 1985, 1991; Hung et al. 2013). The source of human infection is probably freshwater fish, *Macropodus opercularis* (Radomyos et al. 1985; Tungtrongchitr and Radomyos 1989).

China Kobayasi (1942) first detected the metacercariae of this echinostome in the freshwater fish *Macropodus opercularis* and also adult flukes in the intestine of dogs from Hainan Island, China. The presence of this echinostome is now also known in Guangdong Province (Chen et al. 1985).

India This echinostome species was first described based on specimens deposited in Indian Museum, Calcutta, which were collected from the intestine of dogs (Verma 1935). Rao B.V. in 1958 found this echinostome in Madras (Gupta and Pande 1963). Gupta and Pande (1963) found this fluke in dogs, cats, and jackals from Gorakhpur and Mathura; but they assigned their flukes as *Echinochasmus corvus*, synonymizing *Episthmium caninum* with *E. corvus*.

Thailand Radomyos et al. (1985) first detected a human case infected with this species; 18 specimens were recovered after anthelmintic treatment of a 44-year-old Thai farmer from Roi-Et Province. The source of infection was presumed to be raw freshwater fish (Radomoys et al. 1985; Tungtrongchitr and Radomyos 1989), as Kobayasi (1942) found the metacercariae of this species in *Macropodus opercularis* fish from Hainan Island, China. Two more human cases were found among the residents of Yasothorn and Kalasin Provinces, northeast Thailand (Radomyos et al. 1991, 1994, 1998).

Vietnam It has been stated that *E. caninus* is distributed in Vietnam (Hung et al. 2013).

2.4.7 *Potentially Zoonotic* Echinochasmus *spp.*

Potentially zoonotic *Echinostoma* spp. include *E. beleocephalus* (von Linstow, 1873) Dietz, 1909, *E. elongatus* Miki, 1923, *E. grandis* Kurisu, 1931, *E. magnovatus* (Stunkard and Haviland, 1923) Yamaguti, 1958, *E. milvi* Yamaguti, 1939, *E. modax* (Looss, 1932) Yamaguti, 1958, and *E. tobi* Yamaguti, 1939 (see Yamaguti 1939, 1971).

2.4.8 *Genomics and Proteomics*

Karyological studies have been seldom performed on *Echinochasmus* spp.; information is available only in 2 non-zoonotic species, *E. beleocephalus* (2n = 14) and *E. bursicola* (2n = 18) (Barsiene and Kiseliene 1990). A molecular study using random amplified polymorphic DNA (RAPD) technique was performed to differentiate 4 zoonotic *Echinochasmus* species occurring in China, namely, *E. japonicus, E. perfoliatus, E. liliputanus,* and *E. fujianensis* (Cheng et al. 1999). RAPD analysis in combination with morphological studies were used to diagnose trematode metacercariae encysted in 11 species of freshwater fish (including *P. parva*) in Pinyuan County of Guangdong Province; the results confirmed the presence of 6 trematode species, including *E. japonicus, E. perfoliatus,* and *E. fujianensis* (Cheng et al. 2000a). Lactic dehydrogenase isoenzymes and their proteins were analyzed on Guangdong and Fujian strains of *E. fujianensis*; minor differences were noted between the 2 geographical strains (Cheng et al. 2000b). Proteins and genomic DNAs of Guangdong and Fujian strains of *E. fujianensis* were analyzed using RAPD technique and isoelectric focusing electrophoresis; the results confirmed that the 2 geographical strains are one species (Xu et al. 2002). In phylogenetic trees based on ITS2 and 28S rDNA, a close phylogenetic relationship was suggested between *Echinochasmus* Dietz, 1909 and *Stephanoprora* Odhner, 1902 (Stanevičiūte et al. 2015).

Tkach et al. (2016) analyzed partial 28S rDNA of 80 echinostome species (superfamily Echinostomatoidea), including *E. japonicus* and several non-zoonotic *Echinochasmus* spp., and elevated the systematic rank of Echinochasminae and Himasthlinae to full family status to become Echinochasmidae and Himasthlidae, respectively. The complete mitochondrial genome of *E. japonicus* was reported by Le et al. (2016) from Vietnam. The circular mitochondrial molecule of this species was 15,865 bp in length, containing 12 protein-coding regions, 2 ribosomal RNA genes, and 22 transfer RNA genes (Le et al. 2016). Phylogenetic analysis of concatenated mitochondrial protein sequences of 40 trematode species (including *E. japonicus*) and strains supported the elevation of the subfamily Echinochasminae to a family level Echinochasmidae (Le et al. 2016) which was proposed by Tkach et al. (2016).

2.4.9 Pathology and Immunology

The pathogenicity of zoonotic *Echinochasmus* spp. to the human host remains to be determined. A human patient infected with *E. japonicus* (41 adult worms were recovered after anthelmintic treatment) had the clinical complaints of abdominal pain and watery diarrhea (Harada et al. 1983). However, this patient was co-infected with eight worms of *Isthmiophora hortensis* (Harada et al. 1983); therefore, the symptoms may have been due to *I. hortensis* infection rather than *E. japonicus* infection because the worm size of *I. hortensis* is much bigger than that of *E. japonicus* and thus the pathogenicity seems much greater for *I. hortensis*. However, severe *E. japonicus* infections in ducks raised in the paddy-fields, parasitized by 1000–4000 adult specimens, were in most cases fatal with symptoms including a swollen cecum in southern Taiwan (Lee et al. 1976). Therefore, a critically important factor for high pathogenicity seems to be the intensity of infection.

In addition, *E. perfoliatus* is known to be highly pathogenic to pigs (Chebotarev et al. 1960; Sosipatrov 1961a, b). A high fatality of pigs was reported; 127 pigs were dead in Astrakhan region of Russia probably due to a co-infection of *E. perfoliatus* with *Physocephalus sexalatus* (a nematode parasite of pigs and boars) (Chebotarev et al. 1960). Pathological changes were observed not only in the small intestines of pigs but also in extraintestinal organs, including the heart, brain, lungs, and skeletal muscles (Sosipatrov 1961a, b). This extraintestinal involvement of *E. perfoliatus* infection should be highlighted in the pathogenicity of *Echinochasmus* flukes in pigs and other definitive hosts. The number of *E. perfoliatus* worms in dead pigs varied from 15,000 to 18,000 per pig (Sosipatrov 1962). The pathogenicity of *E. liliputanus, E. fujianensis, E. jiufoensis,* and *E. caninus* has seldom been the subject of studies.

2.4.10 Clinical Manifestations, Diagnosis and Treatment

The clinical manifestations of *E. japonicus* infection in China included abdominal pain, diarrhea, abdominal tenderness, anorexia, and anemia (Lin et al. 1982). In South Korea, human cases mixed infected with *E. japonicus* and *Metagonimus yokogawai* complained of abdominal pain and diarrhea (Seo et al. 1985). With regard to *E. perfoliatus* infection, a patient reported from China had the clinical complaints of abdominal pain, diarrhea, constipation, and eosinophilia (Lin and Cheng 1981). In *E. liliputanus* infection, abdominal pain, distention of the abdomen, diarrhea, and anorexia were the major symptoms complained by the patients (Wang et al. 1993). In pigs heavily infected with *E. perfoliatus*, the principal clinical symptoms included diarrhea, accelerated pulse and breathing, periodical rise in the body temperature, periodical spasms, and enlargement of the lymph nodes (Sosipatrov 1961a, b).

The diagnosis of *Echinochasmus* spp. infection relies on recovery of suspected eggs from the feces of patients. However, specific diagnosis or even generic diagnosis is usually difficult and hardly possible because their eggs are highly similar to one another both in size and shape. Recovery of adult flukes after anthelmintic treatment and purging is necessary if the specific diagnosis is ultimately required. However, in already known endemic areas, recovery of characteristic echinostome eggs is enough to provide the diagnosis. In Astrakhan region of Russia where pig *E. perfoliatus* infection prevailed, stool sedimentation techniques as well as direct stool smears were helpful for detection of the eggs in pig stools (Sosipatrov 1961a, b). In Fujian Province, China, the comparative egg morphologies of 5 species of zoonotic echinostome species, including *E. japonicus, E. perfoliatus,* and *E. fujianensis*, were analyzed (Chen et al. 2013). It was stated that the eggs of *E. japonicus* are yellowish brown in color, whereas those of *E. perfoliatus* and *E. fujianensis* are golden yellow; the opercula of *E. japonicus* and *E. fujianensis* eggs are prominent but that of *E. perfoliatus* eggs is less apparent; the egg shell is relatively thick in *E. perfoliatus* but relatively thin in *E. japonicus* and *E. fujianensis* (Chen et al. 2013).

Molecular diagnosis of larval or adult *Echinochasmus* spp. has been tried. In Fujian Province, Cheng et al. (1999) used random amplified polymorphic DNA (RAPD) analysis of adult flukes to differentiate zoonotic *Echinochasmus* species occurring in China, namely, *E. perfoliatus, E. japonicus, E. liliputanus,* and *E. fujianensis.* In Guangdong Province (Pinyuan County), RAPD analysis in combination with morphological studies were performed to diagnose trematode metacercariae encysted in 11 species of freshwater fish, including *P. parva*; the results confirmed the presence of 6 trematode species, including *E. perfoliatus, E. japonicus,* and *E. fujianensis* (Cheng et al. 2000a). In addition, isoelectric focusing electrophoresis and isoenzyme analyses of lactic dehydrogenase were tried to differentiate *Echinochasmus* spp. (Cheng et al. 2000b; Xu et al. 2002).

In pigs, hexachloroethan at a weekly dose of 0.4 g/kg for several weeks gave good results for treatment of *E. perfoliatus* infection but kamala, fillxan, and carbon tetrachloride were ineffective (Proshin 1962). For human *E. japonicus* infection, praziquantel (Pyquiton) was tried and showed excellent results; 5 mg/kg or 10 mg/kg in a single dose revealed 100% or 94.1% cure rate, respectively, when estimated at 1 month later (Zhu et al. 1986). The drug was well tolerated by the patients (Zhu et al. 1986). Similar therapeutic trial was successfully performed on patients infected with *E. perfoliatus* (Xu et al. 1988) and *E. liliputanus* using praziquantel (Wang et al. 1993). The cure rate was 96.5%, 98.7%, and 100% by 2.5, 5.0, and 10.0 mg/kg praziquantel, respectively, used in a single dose (Wang et al. 1993). For *E. fujianensis* infection, praziquantel (2.5 mg/kg or 5.0 mg/kg) and mebendazole-medicated salt (400 mg or 800 mg) were used, and the results revealed 92.3% and 100% cure rates with praziquantel and 71.4% and 85.2% cure rates with mebendazole, respectively (Cheng et al. 1997).

2.4.11 Prevention and Control

Eating raw or improperly cooked freshwater fish (all *Echinochasmus* spp. infections), or amphibians like tadpoles or frogs (*E. japonicus* infection), should be avoided to prevent zoonotic *Echinochasmus* spp. infections.

2.5 *Acanthoparyphium*

2.5.1 Acanthoparyphium tyosenense

2.5.1.1 *Acanthoparyphium tyosenense* Yamaguti, 1939

The genus *Acanthoparyphium* (subfamily Himasthlinae) was erected by Dietz in 1909 using *A. phoenicopteri* (Lühe, 1909) from a bird *Phenicopterus roseus* in Tunisia as the type species (Yamaguti 1958). Now at least 15 species are included in this genus (Chai et al. 2001). *A. tyosenense* was originally described based on worms obtained from the small intestines of the duck *Melanitta fusca stejnegeri* and *Melanitta nigra americana* caught in South Korea (Yamaguti 1939). Skrjabin and Bashikirova (1956) and Chen et al. (1985) treated *A. tyosenense* as a synonym of a related species, *Acanthoparyphium kurogamo*, which caused some taxonomic confusion. However, Chai et al. (2001), after review of the original specimens of *A. tyosenense* and *A. kurogamo* stored in Meguro Parasitological Museum, Tokyo, Japan, came to a conclusion that the 2 species are clearly distinct from each other. Natural human infections were discovered in 10 patients who resided in 2 coastal villages in Jeollabuk-do (Province), South Korea (Chai et al. 2001, 2009). The patients recalled that they had eaten improperly cooked marine bivalves and gastropods. The geographical distribution of this echinostome has been limited to South Korea and Japan (Kim et al. 2004).

The adult flukes (Fig. 2.26a) are 1.76–2.00 mm long and 0.40–0.54 mm wide (from humans) or 2.48–3.13 mm long and 0.52–0.73 mm wide (from experimental chicks) (Chai et al. 2001). It is equipped with a characteristic head collar with total 23 collar spines arranged in a single row, without ventral corner spines, a long cirrus sac reaching beyond the posterior margin of the acetabulum, and vitellaria extending to the level of the cirrus sac or the Mehlis' gland (Chai et al. 2001). Its eggs are 78–93 μm long and 63–73 μm wide (in humans) or 105–111 μm long and 55–63 μm wide (in humans) (Chai et al. 2001). The cercarial body is 330–510 μm long and 160–200 μm wide and their tails are 310–370 μm long and 40–50 μm wide (Ito 1957). The metacercariae are 420–460 μm in diameter (Chai et al. 2001). *A. tyosenense* adults are differed from *Acanthoparyphium kurogamo* adults mainly in the body shape and position of the acetabulum and testes (Chai et al. 2001). The former has its maximum breadth near the rounded posterior end, whereas the latter has the maximum breadth near its equatorial line; the acetabulum of the former is located at

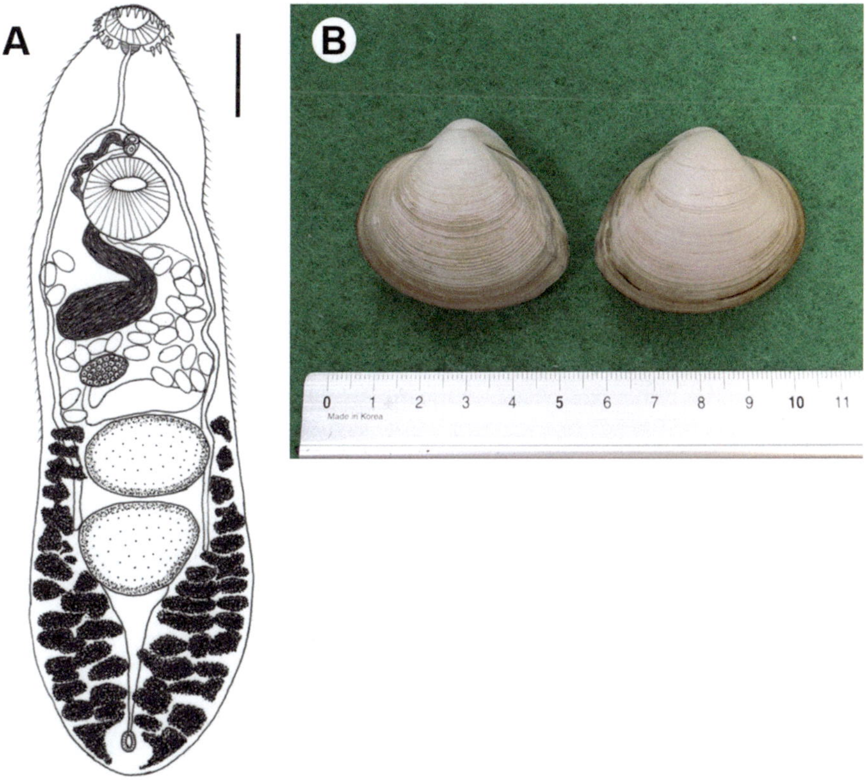

Fig. 2.26 *Acanthoparyphium tyosenense*. (**a**) Line drawing of an adult worm (original figure). Scale bar = 0.2 mm (**b**) A brackish water bivalve, *Mactra veneriformis*, collected from an estuary in a southwestern part of South Korea, a second intermediate host

the posterior part of the anterior third of the body but that of the latter is at the junction between the anterior and middle third of the body (Chai et al. 2001). The anterior testis of *A. tyosenense* is located just postequatorial and its posterior testis is at the junction between the middle and posterior third of the body, but in *A. kurogamo* the anterior testis is located at the junction between the middle and posterior thirds of the body (Chai et al. 2001). *A. tyosenense* also resembles *Acanthoparyphium melanittae* and *Acanthoparyphium charadrii*; but *A. melanittae* has an extremely anterior extension of the vitellaria to the level of the acetabulum, and *A. charadrii* has a more laterally deviated ovary and a slightly less anterior extension of the vitellaria (Yamaguti 1939a). *Acanthoparyphium marilae* is another species to be differed from *A. tyosenense*; the former species has a much restricted distribution of the vitellaria only from the middle level of the posterior testis to the posterior end of the body (Han and Chai 2008), whereas in the latter the vitellaria are distributed from the anterior end level of the anterior testis to the posterior end of the body (Chai et al. 2001).

The surface ultrastructure of *A. tyosenense* has been studied using juvenile (1- to 3-day-old worms) and adult flukes recovered in chicks experimentally infected with the metacercariae from the brackish water bivalve, *Mactra veneriformis* (Fig. 2.26b) (Han et al. 2011). The juvenile worms were minute in size and curved ventrally showing 23 collar spines arranged in a single row; in adults, the lip of the oral sucker had 7 single aciliated sensory papillae and 4 grouped uniciliated sensory papillae (Han et al. 2011). The ventral sucker had 25 aciliated round swellings on its lip, and the anterolateral surface between the 2 suckers was densely packed with tongue-shaped tegumental spaines, and the ventral surface just posterior to the ventral sucker was covered with peg-like spines (Han et al. 2011). Refractile, peg-like spines were seen on the anterolateral surface, whereas scale-like spines with round tips and broad base were sparsely distributed posterior to the ventral sucker (Han et al. 2011). The cirrus was characteristically protruding and armed with minute spines (Han et al. 2011).

Ito (1957) discovered a new echinostome cercaria named as *Cercaria yamagutii* in brackish water snails (*Tympanotonus microptera, Cerithidea largillierti,* and *Cerithidea cingulata*) from Tokyo Bay, Japan which is now considered to be identical with the cercaria of *A. tyosenense* released from the marine megagastropods (*Lunatia fortuni* and *Glossaulax didyma*) in South Korea (Kim and Yu 2001). The metacercariae were detected in brackish water bivalves and gastropods, including *Mactra veneriformis, Mactra sulcataria, Mactra chinensis, Solen strictus, Solen grandis, Ruditapes philippinarum, Cyclina sinensis, Meretrix petechialis,* and *Neverita bicolor* (Kim 1988; Chai et al. 2001; Kim and Yu 2001; Kim et al. 2004; Chung et al. 2007). In addition to the ducks, *Melanitta fusca stejnegeri* and *Melanitta nigra americana,* Chung et al. (2007) added the great knot (*Calidris tenuirostris*) and the turnstone (*Arenaria interpres*) to the natural definitive hosts of *A. tyosenense*. Kim and Chun (1969) and Kim (1988) infected the metacercariae to the sea gull (*Larus crassiostris*) and successfully obtained the adult flukes. Adult flukes were also experimentally obtained from domestic chicks (Chai et al. 2001; Han et al. 2003). In chicks, the worms grew quickly to become ovigerous adults in 5 days and survived at least up to 38 days, chiefly parasitizing in the jejunum; the number of uterine eggs reached a peak during day 10 and day 15 after infection (Han et al. 2003).

The source of human infections is brackish water bivalves and other mollusks, including *Mactra* spp., *Solen* spp., *Ruditapes philippinarum, Cyclina sinensis, Meretrix petechialis,* and *Neverita bicolor*, which are popularly eaten raw by the local people (Kim 1988; Chai et al. 2001; Kim and Yu 2001; Kim et al. 2004; Chung et al. 2007; Chai 2009). The metacercariae were detected in western coastal areas of Jeollabuk-do and Chungcheongnam-do (Province), South Korea, including Naecho-do, Gimje City (Simpo), Gunsan City, Buan-gun, Taean-gun, and Gochang-gun (Kim 1988; Chai et al. 2001; Kim and Yu 2001; Kim et al. 2004; Chung et al. 2007; Sohn et al. 2017). The distribution of this species is known in South Korea (Chai et al. 2001) and Japan (Ito 1957) (Table 2.4).

Other *Acanthoparyphium* **spp.** *A. charadrii* Yamaguti, 1939; *A. haematopi* Ku and Chiu 1979; *A. kurogamo* Yamaguti, 1939; *A. loborchis* Wang, 1977; *A. macrachan-*

thum (Rybakov and Lukomskaya, 1988; *A. marilae* Yamaguti, 1934; *A. melanittae* Yamaguti, 1939; *A. ochthodromi* Tubangui, 1933; *A. pagollae* Cable et al., 1960; *A. paracharadrii* (Velasquez, 1964); *A. phoenicopteri* Johnston, 1917; *A. spinulosum* Johnston, 1917; *A. spinulosum suzugamo* Yamaguti, 1939; *A. squatarolae* Yamaguti, 1934 (see Chai et al. 2001).

2.6 *Artyfechinostomum*

2.6.1 Artyfechinostomum malayanum

2.6.1.1 *Artyfechinostomum malayanum* (Leiper, 1911) Mendheim, 1943

[syn. *Echinostomum malayanum* Leiper, 1911; *Euparyphium malayanum* (Leiper, 1911) Leiper, 1915; *Isthmiophora malayana* (Leiper, 1911) Yamaguti, 1958]

This echinostome (Fig. 2.27a) (subfamily Himasthlinae) was first described by Leiper in 1911 under the name *Echinostomum malayanum* based on adult specimens obtained from the intestine of 2 Tamil people from Singapore and Kuala Lumpur, Malaysia (Bonne et al. 1953; Beaver et al. 1984; Chai 2009, 2015). Odhner (1913) redescribed the morphology of this echinostome under the name *Echinostomum malayanum*. Leiper (1915) renamed this parasite as *Euparyphium malayanum*, and Skrjabin and Bashikirova (1956) followed this name. However, Mendheim (1943) and Bisseru (1957) transferred this echinostome to *Artyfechinostomum*, and Yamaguti (1958) transferred this to *Isthmiophora*. Jain (1960a) agreed to use *Artyfechinostomum* for this echinostome but synonymized *A. malayanum* with *A. sufrartyfex*, another species (type species of *Artyfechinostomum*) reported from an Assamese girl in India (Lane 1915). However, Lie (1963a) was skeptical on the validity of *Artyfechinostomum* and used *Echinostoma* for this echinostome. Thereafter, taxonomic confusion has been continued for a long time even until present. Four kinds of generic names have been used for this echinostome; *Echinostoma* (Mukherjee and Ghosh 1968; Jaw and Lo 1974; Mohandas and Nadakal 1978; Beaver et al. 1984; Monzon and Kitikoon 1989; Maji et al. 1993; Yu and Mott 1994; Radomyos et al. 1998; Maleewong et al. 2003; Belizario et al. 2007; Saijuntha et al. 2010; Srisawangwong et al. 2011; Wu 2013; Noikong and Wongsawad 2014; Khanna et al. 2016; Songsri et al. 2016), *Euparyphium* (Acharjyo 2004), *Isthmiophora* (Yamaguti 1971; Chen et al. 1985), or *Artyfechinostomum* (Premvati and Pande 1974; Eduardo 1989, 1991; Brier 1992; Roy and Tandon 1992; Divina and Pulmano 1996; Kostadinova and Gibson 2002; Kostadinova et al. 2002; Chai et al. 2009, 2012; Veciana et al. 2012; Tantrawatpan et al. 2013; Sohn et al. 2017). The author thinks that the generic name of this echinostome should be *Artyfechinostomum* based on its morphological features and the species name *Artyfechinostomum malayanum* is the correct one.

Taxonomic debates have been continued regarding the synonymy of *A. malayanum* and *A. sufrartyfex*. When Lane (1915) reported *A. sufrartyfex* from an Indian girl, Leiper (1915) suggested *A. sufrartyfex* to be identical with *A. malayanum* (under the name *Euparyphium malayanum*). On the other hand, Mendheim (1943) and Bisseru (1957) listed *A. malayanum* (Leiper, 1911) and *A. sufrartyfex* Lane, 1915 as separate species. Jain (1960a) listed 3 species in *Artyfechinostomum*, including *A. sufrartyfex* Lane, 1915 (treating *A. malayanum* as a synonym of *A. sufrartyfex*), *A. indicum* (Bhalerao 1931), and *A. mehrai* (Faruqui 1930) Jain, 1957. However, Mukherjee and Ghosh (1968), Mohandas (1971), and Premvati and Pande (1974) compared *A. malayanum* and *A. sufrartyfex* and synonymized the latter with the former. Kostadinova et al. (2002) also suggested that *A. malayanum* and *A. sufrartyfex* may be conspecific. However, Kostadinova (2005) used *A. sufrartyfex* as the type species of the genus *Artyfechinostomum* and Kostadinova and Gibson (2002) listed *A. malayanum* as a distinct species. Thus, Kostadinova and coworkers tentatively acknowledged both species. In addition, Tantrawatpan et al. (2013) performed a molecular study on *A. malayanum* and *A. sufrartyfex* using ITS1 and ITS2 sequences, and argued that the 2 species are distinct from each other. Toledo and Esteban (2016) treated them as 2 geographically distinct species. In this context, the taxonomic debates on *A. malayanum* and *A. sufrartyfex* are still continuing and remain to be further studied. In this review book, the author treated *A. malayanum* and *A. sufrartyfex* as separate species.

The adult flukes of *A. malayanum* (Fig. 2.27a) are plump or elongated oval, ventrally curved, and 6.0–8.1 mm long and 1.6–2.0 mm wide (Sohn et al. 2017). Their morphological characters include the unique arrangement and number of the collar spines, distribution of body spines, 2 deeply lobed testes, a feature which is also found in young worms, large cirrus, usually extending somewhat beyond the acetabulum, distribution of vitellaria with the anterior margin at the level of the acetabulum, and the relatively broad size of the body, the broadest of the human echinostomes (Lie 1963a). Their head collar is small but distinct bearing total 43 (39–45) collar spines, with dorsal spines arranged in 2 alternating rows and lateral spines are in a single row, with 5 end group spines on each side (Lie 1963a; Premvati and Pande 1974; Sohn et al. 2017). The eggs are operculate, ovoid to ellipsoid (Fig. 2.27b), and 120–135 μm long and 68–75 μm wide (Sohn et al. 2017). The cercarial body is 205–315 μm long and 100–180 μm wide and the tail is 285–480 μm long and 40–50 μm wide (Lie 1963b). The metacercariae are round (Fig. 2.27c), 145–165 μm in diameter (Sohn et al. 2017), or slightly elliptical, 129–153 μm long and 96–123 μm wide (Lie and Virik 1963). The cyst wall is about 2.5 μm thick (Lie 1963b). Although *A. sufrartyfex* is morphologically similar to *A. malayanum*, it differed from the latter in the morphology of collar spines, shape of the body and ventral sucker, and size of the eggs (Lie 1963a). *A. sufrartyfex* has 43–45 collar spines arranged in double rows (both lateral and dorsal spines), but *A. malayanum* has the same number of collar spines with dorsal spines arranged in 2 alternating rows but lateral spines in a single row (Lie 1963a). The body of the adult worms of *A. sufrartyfex* has an enlargement towards the posterior extremity with a constriction in the acetabular region (Lane 1915; Lie 1963a); however, this shape is seen in *A. malayanum* particularly in somewhat macerated worms which have died before fixation (Lie 1963a). The eggs of *A. sufrartyfex* are 90–113 μm long and 58–75 μm wide, whereas those of *A. malaya-*

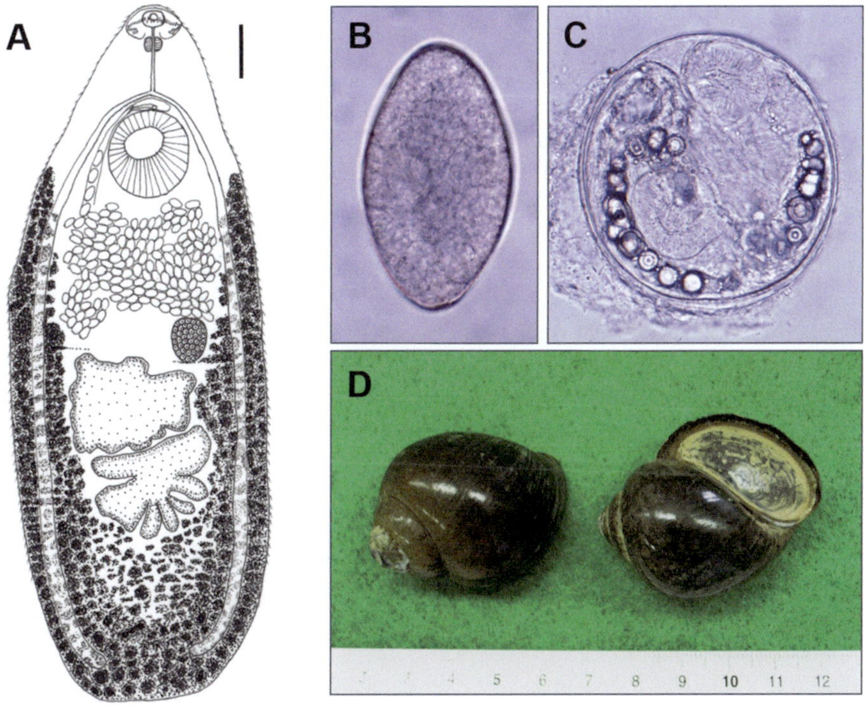

Fig. 2.27 *Artyfechinostomum malayanum.* (**a**) Line drawing of an adult fluke (original figure). Scale bar = 0.5 mm (**b**) Egg in the feces of an experimentally infected hamster. This egg measures 125 × 70 μm (**c**) Metacercaria isolated from the gastropod host. ×200 (**d**) A freshwater gastropod, *Pila* sp., a second intermediate host (**b–d**). (Reproduced from Sohn et al. (2017) Korean J Parasitol 55:341–345 with permission)

num measure 90–159 (or 120–135) μm long and 60–93 (68–75) μm wide; they considerably overlap each other (Lie 1963a; Sohn et al. 2017). The differential points of *A. oraoni* from *A. malayanum* include 41 collar spines arranged in a single row, smaller body size (4.0–5.1 mm), bigger size of the acetabulum, almost no lobed 2 testes, and difference in the egg size range (102–150 μm long and 60–90 μm wide) (Bandyopadhyay et al. 1989).

The first intermediate host is freshwater snails, *Indoplanorbis exustus,* and *Gyraulus convexiusculus,* and the cercariae encyst in various species of snails, i.e., *Indoplanorbis exustus, Pila* sp. (Fig. 2.27d) (including *P. scutata*), *Lymnaea* (*Bullastra*) *cumingiana, Lymnaea rubiginosa, Gyraulus convexiusculus, Radix quadrasi, Physastra hungerfordiana, Viviparus javanicus,* and *Digoniostoma pulchella* (Lie and Virik 1963; Monzon and Kitikoon 1989; Yu and Mott 1994; Namue and Wongsawad 1997; Belizario et al. 2007). Certain species of fish and tadpoles may also serve as the second intermediate host (Monzon et al. 1993; Namue and Wongsawad 1997). Natural definitive hosts other than humans include rats, cats, dogs, pigs, mice, hamsters, monkeys, and house-shrews (Bisseru 1957; Lie 1963b;

Premvati and Pande 1974; Eduardo 1989; Yu and Mott 1994; Divina and Pulmano 1996; Belizario et al. 2007; Veciana et al. 2012). Experimental hosts included rats, hamsters, and mice (Lie and Virik 1963; Songsri et al. 2016).

The eggs of *A. malayanum*, when kept in tap water in a petri-dish at room temperature, they started to hatch on the 9th day (Lie and Virik 1963). When miracidia were exposed to *Indoplanorbis exustus* snails, they penetrated the snails mainly in the head region, and on the 15th and 23rd day, rediae and daughter rediae were observed, and from the 44th to 46th day cercariae were released (Lie and Virik 1963). The cercariae were armed with 43 collar spines but no tegumental spines were seen on the body surface (Lie and Virik 1963). When 3 cercariae-positive *Indoplanorbis exustus* snails were transferred to an aquarium containing 10 *Lymnaea rubiginosa* snails, and then a new batch of 10 *Lymnaea rubiginosa* snails were added; all *Lymnaea* snails were subsequently positive for the metacercariae (Lie and Virik 1963). The metacercariae were found mainly in the kidney of the naturally and experimentally infected snails (Lie and Virik 1963; Mohandas and Nadakal 1978). Adult flukes were harvested from experimental animals at days 14–18 post-infection (Lie and Virik 1963). In mice, adult worms survived at least more than 12 weeks (Srisawangwong et al. 2004). However, worm recovery, eggs per worm, and eggs per gram of feces were higher in hamsters than in rats and mice; gerbils were found refractory to infection with *A. malayanum* (Songsri et al. 2016).

Surface ultrastructure of *A. malayanum* (under the name *Echinostoma malayanum*) was studied by Tesana et al. (1987) in Thailand. The adult flukes were obtained from experimental infection of metacercariae to rats; the total number of collar spines was 41 (2–4 spines may have been missing), including a pair of 5 corner spines on each side, a pair of 10 lateral spines, and 11 dorsal spines (5 oral and 6 aboral) (Tesana et al. 1987). Sensory papillae were found more densely on the head collar and on the ventral body surface; dome-shaped sensory papillae were seen only on the head collar (Tesana et al. 1987).

The geographical distribution of *A. malayanum* extends from India, Indonesia, Lao PDR, Malaysia, the Philippines, and Thailand to China and Singapore (Fig. 2.28; Table 2.4) (Lane 1915; Bonne et al. 1953; Lie and Virik 1963; Maji et al. 1993; Radomyos et al. 1998; Belizario et al. 2007; Chai et al. 2012).

Molecular studies on *A. malayanum* have been studied by a few researchers. Multilocus enzyme electrophoresis was performed on 22 enzymes encoding a presumptive 30 loci to explore the genetic variation and differentiation of *A. malayanum* and *Echinostoma revolutum* isolated from Khon Kaen, Thailand; the results revealed that the 2 echinostome species had fixed genetic differences at 70% of the loci (Saijuntha et al. 2010). Genetic differentiation between *A. malayanum* and *A. sufrartyfex* was studied using an analysis of ITS1 and ITS2 loci of rDNA; the results revealed that out of 699 bp of combined ITS1 and ITS2 sequences 18 variable nucleotide positions (2.58%) were observed, and 17 could be used as diagnostic position between the 2 species, which may sufficiently suggest that the synonymy of these species is not valid (Tantrawatpan et al. 2013).

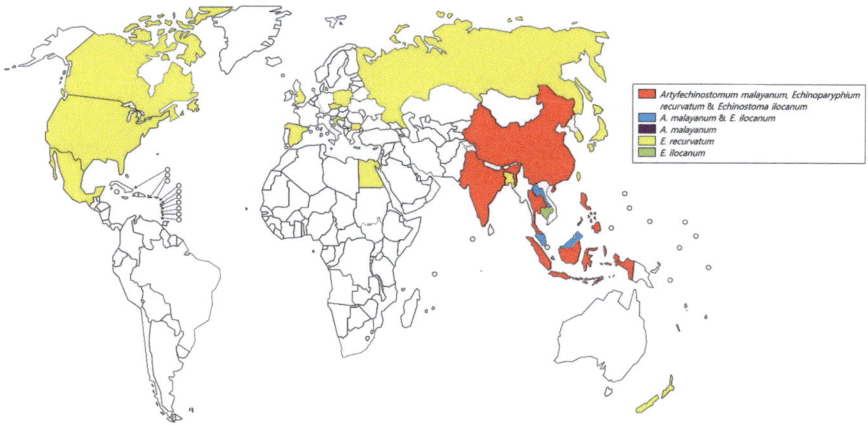

Fig. 2.28 Global distribution of *Artyfechinostomum malayanum, Echinoparyphium recurvatum,* and *Echinostoma ilocanum* based on the presence of their life cycles

Infection with *A. malayanum* causes lysis and destruction of intestinal mucosa and moderates hyperplasia of the epithelial cells; light infection caused little injury, however, in acute infection hemorrhagic inflammation, severe enteritis, and the presence of lymphocytes were observed (Mohandas and Nadakal 1978). Short villi and goblet cell proliferation were apparent in infected animals compared with uninfected controls (Songsri et al. 2016). The potentiality of this echinostome to elicit diarrhea has been well established in experimental animals (Lie and Viril 1963) and found also in natural human infections (Maji et al. 1993). The severity of the symptoms may be dependent upon the intensity of infection; it is notable that a 12-year girl form North Sumatra, Indonesia harbored as many as 750 worms (Bonne et al. 1953). Immunity to this echinostome species has seldom been the study subject. However, Mohandas and Nadakal (1978) reported crowding effect in the length of *A. malayanum* in rats. Development of concomitant and protective immunity has been found in experimental mice repeatedly infected with *A. malayanum* (Srisawangwong et al. 2011).

In Malaysia, *Pila* snails are sold in markets and often eaten by certain groups of people; they are usually well-cooked before being eaten but accidental human infection can occur when cooking of the snail is inadequate (Lie and Virik 1963). In India, human cases consumed naturally infected *Pila scutata* snails (Singh 1991). In the Philippines, ingestion of raw or half-cooked *Lymnaea* (*Bullastra*) *cumingiana* snails after treatment with salt or 'bagoong' (salted fish paste) is related to infection with *A. malayanum* (Tangtrongchitr and Monzon 1991). In addition, Belizario et al. (2007) reported that all echinostome (*A. malayanum*)-infected patients in the Philippines had a history of having eaten the snail dishes, 'kulol' and 'kiambu-ay', prepared raw with coconut milk and lime juice ('kinilaw'), especially when found in greater abundance during the rainy season. In Chiang Mai, Thailand, 10.5% of 38 rats were found infected with *A. malayanum* (Namue and Wongsawad 1997).

2.6.2 Artyfechinostomum sufrartyfex

2.6.2.1 *Artyfechinostomum sufrartyfex* Lane, 1915

[syn. *Paryphostomum sufrartyfex* (Lane, 1915) Bhalerao, 1931; *Artyfechinostomum mehrai* (Faruqui, 1930) Jain, 1960]

Lane (1915) found an echinostome fluke (subfamily Himasthlinae) from an Assamese girl in India and named it as *Artyfechinostomum sufrartyfex*. Later, this echinostome (Fig. 2.29) was also found in pigs (Ahluwalia 1962), a cat and a dog (Dubey et al. 1969), and a human (Reddy and Varmah 1950) in India. Leiper (1915) suggested *A. sufrartyfex* to be identical with *A. malayanum* (under the name *Euparyphium malayanum*), and Bhalerao (1931) treated *A. sufrartyfex* as a member of *Paryphostomum* and named it as *P. sufrartyfex*. However, Mendheim (1943), Bisseru (1957), and Jain (1960a) transferred this echinostome to *Artyfechinostomum*. Mendheim (1943) and Bisseru (1957) treated *A. sufrartyfex* Lane, 1915 and *A. malayanum* (Leiper, 1911) as separate species, and Yadav (1959) included *A. sufrartyfex* Lane, 1915, *A. malayanum* (Leiper, 1911), *A. indicum* (Bhalerao, 1931), and *A. mehrai* (Faruqui, 1930) Jain, 1957 in the genus *Artyfechinostomum*. Jain (1960a) listed only 3 species in this genus, *A. sufrartyfex, A. indicum*, and *A. mehrai,* synonymizing *A. malayanum* with *A. sufrartyfex*. Mukherjee and Ghosh (1968), Mohandas (1971), and Premvati and Pande (1974) also compared *A. sufrartyfex* and *A. malayanum* but synonymized the former with the latter (*A. malayanum*). However, Kostadinova et al. (2002) retained *A. sufrartyfex* as the type species of

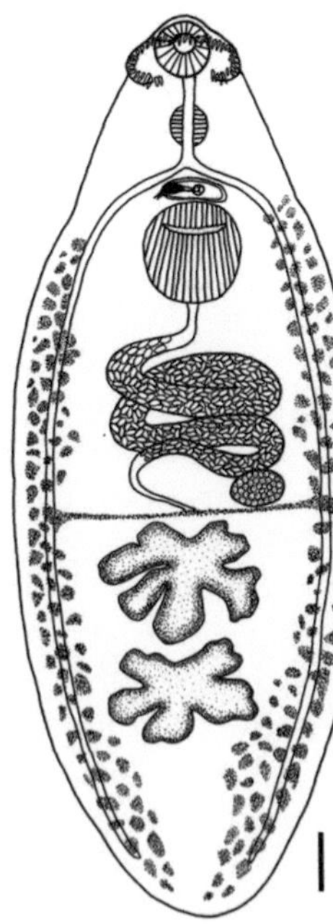

Fig. 2.29 Line drawing of an adult fluke of *Artyfechinostomum sufrartyfex*. Scale bar = 1 mm. (Modified from the figure in Reddy and Varmah (1950) Ind Med Gazatte 85:837–856)

Artyfechinostomum, although they suggested possible synonymy of *A. malayanum* and the type species. Recently, Tantrawatpan et al. (2013) performed a molecular study on *A. sufrartyfex* and *A. malayanum* using ITS1 and ITS2 sequences, and concluded that the 2 species may be distinct from each other. Toledo and Esteban (2016) treated them as 2 geographically distinct species; *A. malayanum* is distributed in China, India, Indonesia, Lao PDR, Thailand, Malaysia, the Philippines, and Singapore, whereas the distribution of *A. sufrartyfex* is largely confined to India (Table 2.4). *A. sufrartyfex* was also reported from the domestic pig, black rat, and Asian palm civet (Ngo et al. 2011) and the lizard (*Varanus nebulosus*) in southern Vietnam (Tran et al. 2016). However, it will be needed to reconfirm the specific diagnosis of these worms. Collectively, the synonymy of *A. sufrartyfex* and *A. malayanum* is still continuing and remains to be determined.

On the other hand, *Cercaria mehrai* Faruqui, 1930 was described based on echinostome cercariae found in *Indoplanorbis exustus* snails collected from the Allahabad district, India (Faruqui 1930). Jain (1958, 1960b) studied on the life cycle of this echinostome and described its larval (rediae, cercariae, and metacercariae) and adult stages and named it as *Artyfechinostomum mehrai* (Faruqui, 1930) Jain, 1960. However, Ahluwalia (1962) and Premvati and Pande (1974) was of opinion that *A. mehrai* is synonymous with *A. sufrartyfex*. The author follows this synonymy. The first human infection with *A. mehrai* was reported from a 14-year-old Hindu girl, India with a history of diarrhea, vomiting, anorexia, and loss of weight, and worms were recovered from the vomitus and gastric contents (Raghunathan and Srinivasan 1962). Subsequently, a fatal case (30-year-old Hindu woman) infected with *A. mehrai* was reported by Reddy et al. (1964) in India, and a third case (9-year-old boy) with bowel perforation was also reported from India (Kaul et al. 1974). Kostadinova et al. (2002) was of opinion that *A. mehrai* is a synonym of *A. sufrartyfex*. Thus, in this review book, *A. mehrai* is treated as a synonym of *A. sufrartyfex*.

The adult flukes of *A. sufrartyfex* are 12.0–18.0 mm long and 5.4–6.0 mm wide and have a thick, fleshy, oblong body with a pinkish color in the living state; in some cases, a constriction on the sides, near the level of the acetabulum, is observed (Ahluwalia 1962). Their head collar is small but distinct bearing total 43 collar spines, arranged in 2 alternating rows (both dorsal and lateral spines), with 5 end group spines on each side (Ahluwalia 1962; Lie 1963a). They have a very long, muscular, and closely coiled cirrus extending beyond the posterior margin of the ventral sucker, submedian ovary, and 2 deeply lobated testes, and are same as *A. malayanum* in these characters (Ahluwalia 1962; Sohn et al. 2017). The eggs are operculate, ovoid to ellipsoid, and 90–120 μm long and 60–70 μm wide (Ahluwalia 1962). The cercarial body (under the name *A. mehrai*) is 327 μm long and 186 μm wide and the tail is 352 μm long (Jain 1958). The metacercariae (under the name *A. mehrai*) are round, 143 μm long and 104 μm wide (Jain 1958).

A. sufrartyfex is morphologically very similar to *A. malayanum* (Lie 1963a). It has 43 collar spines arranged in double rows (both lateral and dorsal spines); however, *A. malayanum* has the same number of collar spines with dorsal spines arranged in 2 alternating rows but lateral spines in a single row (Lie 1963a). The body of the adult worms of *A. sufrartyfex* has an enlargement towards the posterior extremity with a constriction in the acetabular region (Lane 1915; Lie 1963a); however, *A. malayanum* has an elongated oval body with the maximum breadth near the uterine tubule or ovarian level (Lie 1963a). The eggs of *A. sufrartyfex* are 90–120 μm long and 60–70 μm wide, whereas those of *A. malayanum* measure 90–159 (or 120–135) μm long and 60–93 (68–75) μm wide; they considerably overlap each other (Lie 1963a; Sohn et al. 2017). The differential points of *A. oraoni* from *A. sufrartyfex* include 41 collar spines arranged in a single row, smaller body size (4.0–5.1 mm), bigger size of the acetabulum, almost no lobed 2 testes, and difference in the egg size range (102–150 μm long and 60–90 μm wide) (Bandyopadhyay et al. 1989).

The first intermediate host is freshwater snails, *Indoplanorbis exustus* and *Lymnaea luteola* (Ramanujachari and Alwar 1954; Raghunathan and Srinivasan 1962). The miracidia of *A. sufrartyfex* which hatch in 11 days in water may infect small *Lymnaea luteola* (Ramanujachari and Alwar 1954). Metacercarial stages may occur either in freshwater fish (like *Bourbus stigma*), freshwater snails (*Digoniostoma pulchella, Indoplanorbis exustus,* and *Lymnaea luteola*), or pond-frogs (*Rana cyanophlyctis*) (Jain 1958; Raghunathan and Srinivasan 1962; Nath 1969). The metacercariae are encysted in the kidneys in pond-frogs (Nath 1974). The definitive hosts of this fluke include humans, pigs (natural and experimental), dogs, cats, and rats (experimental) in India (Ramanujachari and Alwar 1954; Ahluwalia 1962; Lie 1963b; Dubey et al. 1969; Nath 1969). Humans may be infected by ingesting imperfectly cooked fish or snails (Raghunathan and Srinivasan 1962). The presence of *A. sufrartyfex* in areas other than India was documented from the domestic pig, black rat, and Asian palm civet (Ngo et al. 2011) and the lizard (*Varanus nebulosus*) in southern Vietnam (Tran et al. 2016), although the specific diagnosis of these worms needs re-evaluation.

ITS1 and ITS2 regions of rDNA were studied on *A. sufrartyfex* from India; ITS1 was most closely similar to that of *Echinostoma caproni* (under the name *E. liei*) and ITS2 was most similar to *Echinostoma trivolvis* (Tandon et al. 2008). However, they did not analyze intraspecific variations. Genetic differentiation of *A. sufrartyfex* from *A. malayanum* was studied by Tantrawatpan et al. (2013) using an analysis of ITS1 and ITS2 loci of rDNA. The results revealed that, out of 699 bp of combined ITS1 and ITS2 sequences, 18 variable nucleotide positions (2.58%) were observed, and 17 could be used as diagnostic position between the 2 species, which may sufficiently suggest that the synonymy of these species is not valid (Tantrawatpan et al. 2013).

In the intestinal section of a cat naturally infected with *A. sufrartyfex*, the flukes were found at different depths of the jejunum, some had reached the muscular is mucosa, and some had invaded the submucosa and muscular coats of the nodulated portion (Dubey et al. 1969). Several specimens were found completely occupying the intestinal glands, with suckers closely applied to the host's tissue; the tracts left over by the migrating flukes were often consisting of macrophages, lymphocytes, and neutrophils (Dubey et al. 1969). In dogs, the duodenum was congested, and the flukes lay embedded deep in the duodenal mucosa causing minute ulcerations at places from where the flukes were retracted; the places left after the retraction of the worm showed desquamation of the epithelium, hypertrophy of the goblet cells, congestion, edema, and marked infiltration with lymphocytes, macrophages, and plasma cells (Dubey et al. 1969). In experimentally infected pups, mild hemorrhagic enteritis was seen at day 14 post-infection with slight thickening of the duodenal wall (Nath 1974).

In endemic areas of the states of Bihar and Jharkhand, India, the giant freshwater snail, *Pila globosa*, is consumed raw by the local people, who believe it to be a source of strength to weak or ailing children; *Pila* sp., also known as the apple snail, is the carrier of the infective stage and thus a potent source of infection to humans with *A. sufrartyfex* (Tandon et al. 2015). Root-tuber extract of *Fleningia vestita*, a leguminous plant from India, was highly effective in killing *A. sufrartyfex* adult fluke in vitro (Roy and Tandon 1996).

2.6.3 Artyfechinostomum oraoni

2.6.3.1 *Artyfechinostomum oraoni* Bandyopadhyay, Manna and Nandy, 1989

This echinostome (subfamily Himasthlinae) was reported from a group of 20 human infections in a tribal community near Calcutta, India (Bandyopadhyay and Nandy 1986; Bandyopadhyay et al. 1989). In a life cycle study, the freshwater snail, *Lymnaea* sp., was experimentally proven to be a first intermediate host, producing rediae on 32nd day post-infection; however, the cercariae were not observed (Maji et al. 1995). The source of human infections has not yet been discovered. It has been proven that *A. oraoni* provoked fatal diarrhea in naturally infected pigs (Bandyopadhyay et al. 1995).

Adult flukes of *A. oraoni* are leaf-like with narrowed anterior and posterior ends, with the middle portion considerably broad, 4.0–5.1 mm long and 0.70–0.75 mm wide (acetabular level) or 1.81–1.90 mm wide (posterior testis level) (Bandyopadhyay et al. 1989). The eggs are operculate, oval, and light creamy in color; uterine eggs are 102–150 μm long and 60–90 μm wide and fecal eggs are 131–140 μm long and 73–80 μm wide (Bandyopadhyay et al. 1989). The differential points of *A. oraoni* from *A. sufrartyfex* include 41 collar spines arranged in a single row (*A. sufrartyfex* has 43 collar spines arranged in double row) (Lie 1963a), smaller body size (12.0–18.0 mm long in *A. sufrartyfex*), bigger size of the acetabulum, almost no lobed 2 testes, and difference in the egg size range (120–135 μm long and 68–75 μm wide in *A. sufrartyfex*) (Bandyopadhyay et al. 1989). The cercariae and metacercariae have not been detected. The distribution of this species is so far confined to India (Table 2.4).

Potentially Zoonotic *Artyfechinostomum* **spp.** Potentially zoonotic *Artyfechinostomum* spp. include *A. africanum* Albaret et al., 1990, *A. indicum* (Bhalerao, 1931), *A. neotoma* (Jain, 1953) Kostadinova et al., 2002, *A. palustris*

(Chatterji, 1932), *A. palustris rattus* (Jain, 1953), *A. paradoxuri* Baugh, 1962, and *A. shubhrai* (Agrawal, 1963) Yamaguti, 1971 (see Yamaguti 1971; Kostadinova et al. 2002; Sohn et al. 2017).

2.7 *Echinoparyphium*

2.7.1 Echinoparyphium recurvatum

2.7.1.1 *Echinoparyphium recurvatum* (von Linstow, 1873) Lühe, 1909

[syn. *Echinoparyphium koidzumii* Tsuchimochi, 1924]

This echinostome (Fig. 2.30a) (subfamily Echinostomatinae) was first reported by von Linstow in 1873 based on adult specimens recovered in a species of duck (scaup), *Anas marila* (= *Aythya marila*) in Germany under the name *Distomum recurvatum* (Lühe 1909; Dietz, 1910). In 1892, the name was changed into *Echinostomum recurvatum* by Stossich (Dietz, 1910). The genus *Echinoparyphium* was erected by Dietz (1909) using *E. elegans* (Looss, 1899) Dietz, 1909 as the type. Subsequently, this echinostome was named as *Echinoparyphium recurvatum* by Lühe (1909). *Echinoparyphium koidzumii* was described as a new species recovered in domestic fowls from Taiwan (Tsuchimochi 1924); however, Yamaguti (1933) synonymized this species with *E. recurvatum*. Thereafter, until the 1970s, at least 151 species names have been reported in this genus (Yamaguti 1971; Buscher 1978; Kanev 1990). However, the taxonomic positions of many species are unstable and problematic (Huffman and Fried 2012). McCarthy (1990) reported 2 sympatric sibling species in the so-called *E. recurvatum* complex. Furthermore, Kiseliene and Grabda-Kazubska (1993) and Fried (2001) suggested that the *E. recurvatum* complex consist of at least 3 species, including 2 other similar species, i.e., *Echinoparyphium pseudorecurvatum* reported from Poland (Kiseliene and Grabda-Kazubska 1990) and *Echinoparyphium mordwilkoi* reported from Russia (Skrjabin 1915). *E. recurvatum* is now a cosmopolitan species infecting various species of birds and mammals (Beaver et al. 1984; Yu and Mott 1994; Chai 2009; Chai et al. 2009).

A human infection was first found from a Japanese living in Taiwan who suffered from nephritis; one echinostome specimen was recovered in the feces after anthelmintic treatment (Akagi 1916) which was sent to Dr. Morishita K. and diagnosed as *E. recurvatum* (under the name *E. koidzumii* which is now a synonym of *E. recurvatum*) (Anazawa 1929; Yamashita 1964; Beaver et al. 1984). The second report was made by Lie (1951) in Jakarta, Indonesia based on 2 human autopsies. The third was made by Bonne et al. (1953) in several autopsies of patients from a lunatic asylum living together in a rural colony near Batavia, Indonesia; the patients were mixed infections with *Echinostoma ilocanum*. The fourth report was made by Fain and Galal (1977) in Egypt who recovered 5 specimens of *E. recurvatum* in a man from Upper Egypt. Another human case was reported from Egypt in an autopsy (Beaver et al. 1984).

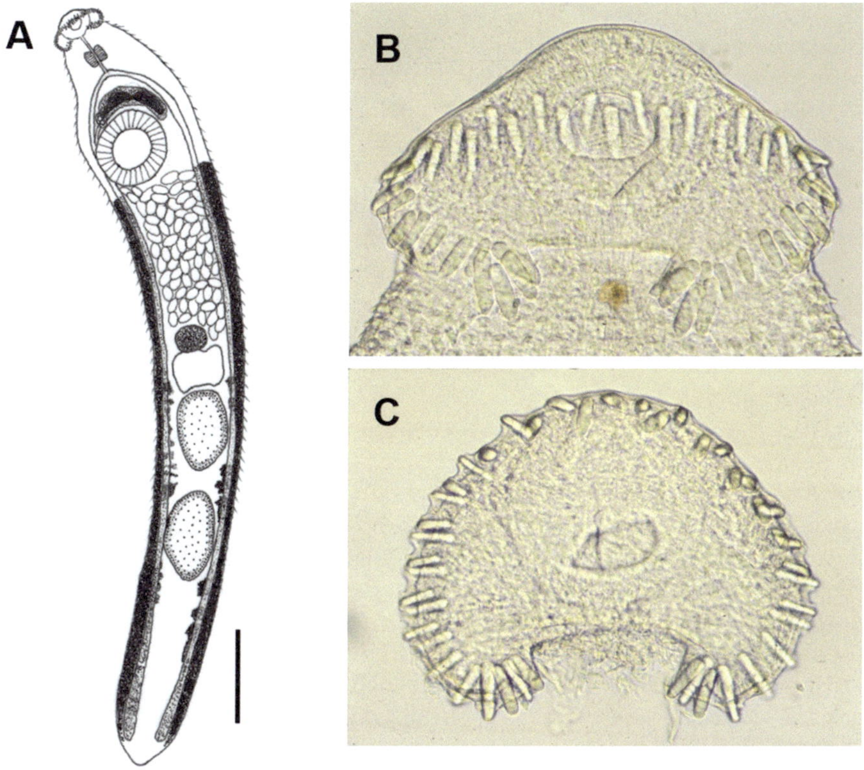

Fig. 2.30 *Echinoparyphium recurvatum* based on specimens recovered from a naturally infected rat in Yangyang-gun, Gangwon-do, South Korea (**a**) Line drawing of an adult fluke (original figure). Scale bar = 0.5 mm. Drawn from the figure in Chai (2009) The Biology of Echinostomes. Springer (**b**, **c**) Head collars of adult flukes showing 45 collar spines. Ventral view (**b**); En face view (**c**). Reproduced from the figure in Chai (2009) The Biology of Echinostomes. Springer, New York, USA

The adult flukes have a relatively small and narrow body, 3.5–4.7 mm long and 0.5–0.65 mm wide, having a head collar with 45 collar spines arranged in 2 alternating rows and 4–5 end group spines on each side (Fig. 2.30b, c), a large ventral sucker, a short uterus with only a few eggs, but no seminal receptacle (Buscher 1978; Rim 1982; Lee et al. 1990). The uterine eggs are 82–97 μm long and 54–59 μm wide (Lee et al. 1990). The cercariae are spindle-shaped in life, with a markedly developed head collar armed with 45 collar spines; the cercarial body is 235–291 μm long and 112–138 μm wide, and the tail is 469–556 μm long and 49–61 μm wide (Sohn 1998). The metacercariae have 2 walls, a thick hyaline and a thin elastic walls, with the characteristic head collar equipped with 45-collar spines and numerous excretory granules; they are almost spherical and 140–150 μm long and 135–146 μm wide (Sohn 1998).

The differential points of *E. recurvatum* from *E. elegans* in the adult morphology include the presence of 45 collar spines (*E. elegans* has 43 spines) and the absence of a seminal receptacle (*E. elegans* has one) (Buscher 1978). Among those having 45 collar spines, *E. ralphaudyi* Lie, 1975 differs from *E. recurvatum* in having the pars prostatica, *E. baculoides* Dollfus, 1951 and *E. ellisi* Johnston and Simpson, 1944 differs in having vitellaria confluent posterior to testes (*E. recurvatum* has vitellaria not confluent posterior to testes), *E. mordwilkoi* Skrjabin, 1915 has vitellaria extending anteriorly to posterior edge of the ventral sucker (in *E. recurvatum*, vitellaria are not extending anteriorly to the posterior edge of the ventral sucker), and *E. hydromyos* Angel, 1966 has a seminal receptacle (Buscher 1978). *E. flexum* (Linton, 1892) also has vitellaria extending anteriorly to posterior edge of the ventral sucker, unlike *E. recurvatum*; however, it was synonymized with *E. recurvatum* by Senger (1954).

The surface ultrastructure of *E. recurvatum* juvenile and adult flukes was studied by Sohn et al. (2002) with specimens obtained from experimental chicks (*Gallus domesticus*) in South Korea and McCarthy (2011) on the worms recovered from experimentally infected mallards (*Anas platyrhynchos*) in southern UK. One to 5-day old worms recovered in experimentally infected chicks were elongated and ventrally concave, and covered with peg-like tegumental spines with a sharp-pointed tip except in areas adjacent to the head collar and excretory pore; type I sensory papillae (uniciliated round swellings) were distributed on the lip of the oral sucker, and grouped uniciliated papillae were around the oral sucker (Sohn et al. 2002). The areas on the ventral sucker were aspinous and with no sensory papillae; tegumental spines on the ventral surface posterior to the ventral sucker became gradually sparse and disappeared on the tegument of the posterior body (Sohn et al. 2002). The 15-day old worms were stout, and their tegumental surface was generally similar to that of juvenile worms; however, the tegumental spines were tongue-shaped without a pointed tip (Sohn et al. 2002). McCarthy (2011) reported that the tegumental features of *E. recurvatum* adults (15-day old) obtained from UK were very similar to those reported from South Korea by Sohn et al. (2002), and the rounded and scale-like (McCarthy 2011) or spade- or tongue-shaped (Sohn et al. 2002) tegumental spines of *E. recurvatum* were unique from those of *E. mordwilkoi* which had thorn-shaped tegumental spines.

The first intermediate host is planorbid or lymnaeid snails, including *Physa alexandrina, Physa fontinalis, Planorbis planorbis, Lymnaea pervia, Lymnaea peregra, Valvata piscinalis*, and *Radix auricularia coreana* (Evans and Gordon 1983; McCarthy 1990; Sohn 1998). The metacercariae encyst in tadpoles and frogs of *Rana temporaria,* and also in snails, *Pisidium subtruncatum, Valvata piscinalis* (Evans et al. 1981), *Physa fontinalis* (Evans and Gordon 1983), *Planorbis planorbis* and *Lymnaea* sp. (Yamashita 1964; Yu and Mott 1994), *Lymnaea swinhoei, Lymnaea ollula* (Tsuchimochi 1924), *Lymaea peregra* (McCarthy 2011), *Radix auricularia coreana* (Sohn 1998), *Lymnaea stagnalis* (Yurlova et al. 2006), and *Physella cubensis* (Sereno-Uribe et al. 2015). The definitive hosts include house rats (Lee et al. 1990), wild rats (*Arvicanthis niloticus*) (Beaver et al. 1984), dogs (Abdel Azim 1939), and various species of birds (Yamaguti 1958).

In *Radix auricularia coreana* snails, 3 larval stages, namely, rediae, cercariae, and metacercariae, are simultaneously found; in a southern area of South Korea, 52 (49.0%) out of 106 examined were positive for these larval stages (Sohn 1998). The rediae are elongate sac-like, 2.4 mm long and 0.3 mm wide, with a muscular pharynx and brownish ceca reaching from the posterior to the anterior half of the body; the cercariae are equipped with 45 collar spines on the head collar, and when they were exposed to the *Radix auricularia* snails and a fish species, the loach (*Misgurnus anguillicaudatus*), the infection was successful; however, mud-snails (*Cypangopaludina* sp.) were not infected (Sohn 1998). The rediae are very active and located in the digestive gland of infected snails; they are packed with numerous elongate rediae of various sizes (Huffman and Fried 2012). Histochemical studies were performed on rediae and cercariae of *E. recurvatum* regarding enzyme activities of acid and alkaline phosphatases and non-specific esterases; it was revealed that these enzyme activities were strong in the cuticle and suckers of developing cercariae probably in association with cellular differentiation in these areas (Probert 1966). The cercariae emerge throughout a day in a moderate number, but the greatest number are shed between 9:00 and 12:00 in the morning; they swim actively, exhibit a creeping motion and remain alive for about 24 h in water (Huffman and Fried 2012). At 18 °C the maximum life span of the cercariae was 48 h, and 50% survival occurred at 30.5 h; infectivity of the cercariae to the second intermediate host (*Lymnaea peregra*) was maximal approximately 2 h after emission from the first intermediate host (Evans and Gordon 1983). The metacercariae are detected in the mantle cavity, pericardial cavity, kidney lumen, or liver of these snails (Tsuchimochi 1924; Adam and Lewis 1992). Chicks and ducks were used to infect with the metacercariae; the worm recovery rate from chicks was 7.0–22.6% from day 5 to day 17 post-infection (Sohn 1998). The egg producing maturity was attained in 7–10 days in experimentally infected ducks but eggs appeared in their feces at 15 days (Tsuchimochi 1924). The maximum survival time was approximately 28 days in ducklings, and the time to 50% parasite survival was 12.5 days (Evans 1983).

In Taiwan, this echinostome (under the name *E. koidzumii*) was discovered in domestic ducks and fowls (Tsuchimochi 1924). In Japan, this echinostome (under the name *E. koidzumii*) was reported from domestic and wild ducks (Ishii 1932). Yamaguti (1933, 1934, 1939) also found *E. recurvatum* in various species of birds, including wild ducks, in Japan. In the Philippines, *E. recurvatum* was found from birds together with *E. revolutum* (Tubangui 1932). A variant, named *E. recurvatum* var. *indiana,* was recorded by Verma (1936) in India. Abdel Azim (1939) obtained *E. recurvatum* worms from experimentally infected dogs in Egypt. This echinostome was also recovered from California and Florida turkeys (Annereaux 1940; Hon et al. 1975) and muskrats in Minnesota (Penner 1940), Maine (Meyer and Reilly 1950), and Ohio, USA (Beckett and Gallicchio 1967). The cercariae were found in *Helisoma trivolvis* snails in Lafayette, Indiana, USA (Senger 1954). Various species of birds are infected with this echinostome in Russia (Bashikirova 1947). Soulsby (1955) reported heavy infections of mute swans with *E. recurvatum* in Somerset, UK, and Keymer et al. (1962) recorded infection of wild and domestic birds, including tufted ducks (*Aythya fuligula*), pintail mallard (*Anas acuta*), scaup (*Aythya marila*), goosander (*Mergus merganser*), and mute swan (*Cygnus olor*), with this fluke in UK. In addition to China, Egypt, UK, India, Japan, the Philippines, Russia, Indonesia, Taiwan, and USA, the geographical distribution of this echinostome extends to New Zealand (Weeks 1982; Fredensborg et al. 2004), Canada (Bush and Holmes 1986), Bulgaria (Dimitrov 1990), South Korea (Lee et al. 1990), Spain (Toledo et al. 1998), Poland (Fagasinski 1962; Grabda-Kazubska et al. 1998), Czech Republic (Faltýnková 2005), Bangladesh (Yousuf et al. 2009), Thailand (Saijuntha et al. 2011a, b, 2013), Croatia (Lajtner 2012), and Mexico (Sereno-Uribe et al. 2015) (Table 2.4).

In the human host, the pathogenicity and clinical manifestations of *E. recurvatum* infection are unknown. However, in avian hosts, *E. recurvatum* seems highly pathogenic if a large number of worms are infected, and also possibly in mammals. Annereaux (1940) reported debilitation and death in domestic turkeys resulting from heavy infections with *E. recurvatum* in USA. Also, Soulsby (1955) reported that heavy infections in mute swans with this echinostome, including many immature worms, caused emaciation, catarrhal enteritis, and heavy mortality on the river Axe in Somerset, UK (Soulsby 1955).

A phylogenetic study was performed on *E. recurvatum* and related species and genera of Echinostomatidae occurring in Europe using internal transcribed spacer (ITS) region of rDNA; *E. recurvatum, E. elegans,* and *E. pseudorecurvatum* were closely correlated one another, whereas other genera *Pseudoechinoparyphium* (*P. echinatum*) and *Hypoderaeum* (*H. conoideum*) were more distant from *E. recurvatum* (Grabda-Kazubska et al. 1998). However, Kostadinova et al. (2003) analyzed ITS and nicotinamide adenine dinucleotide dehydrogenase subunit 1 (ND1) loci of various echinostome species and found that *Echinostoma* is represented as a paraphyletic taxon with *E. recurvatum* (both ITS and ND1 trees), and *Isthmiophora, Echinoparyphium aconiatum,* and *Hypoderaeum conoideum* were nested within it. Saijuntha et al. (2011a) also reported that *E. recurvatum* and *Echinostoma revolutum* in Thailand are clustered as sister taxa but not with other members of *Echinoparyphium*, which agreed to a previous report (Saijunthat et al. 2011b) based on alloenzyme electrophoresis and mitochondrial DNA sequencing that *E. recurvatum* and *E. revolutum* in Southeast Asia are sister species. In Mexico, sequences of ITS1, 5.8S and ITS2 rDNA were obtained from adult flukes (recovered in naturally infected shoveler duck *Anas clypeata*) and cercariae and metacercariae (isolated from *Physella cubensis* snails) and confirmed the presence of *E. recurvatum* in central Mexico (Sereno-Uribe et al. 2015).

Potentially zoonotic *Echinoparyphium* spp. Potentially zoonotic *Echinoparyphium* spp. include *E. aconiatum* Dietz, 1909; *E. bioccalerouxi* Dollfus, 1953; *E. combesi* Kechimer, 1980; *E. contiguum* Barker 1915; *E. dunni* Lie and Umathevy, 1965; *E. elegans* (Looss, 1899) Dietz, 1909; *E. ellisi* Johnston and Simpson, 1944; *E. flexum* (Linton, 1892) Dietz, 1910; *E. hydromyos* Angel, 1966; *E. japonicum* Ando and Ozaki, 1923; *E. mordwilkoi* Skrjabin, 1915; *E. pseudorecurvatum* Kiseliene and Grabda-Kazubska, 1990; *E. ralphaudyi* Lie et al., 1975; *E. rubrum* Kanev et al.,

1998; *E. schulzi* Matevossian, 1951; *E. sisjakowi* Skvortsov, 1934; *E. speotyto* Buscher, 1978; *E. spinosus* Singh et al., 2002; *E. taipeiensis* Fischthal and Kuntz, 1976 (see Buscher 1978; Chen et al. 1985; Huffman and Fried 2012).

2.8 *Himasthla*

2.8.1 Himasthla muehlensi

2.8.1.1 *Himasthla muehlensi* Vogel, 1933

This echinostome (Fig. 2.31) (subfamily Himasthlinae) was obtained by Prof. Mühlens after a purgative treatment of a German patient who lived in Colombia and traveled to New York, USA where he had eaten raw clams *Venus mercenaria* and developed a gastrointestinal disease when he came back to Hamburg, Germany (Vogel 1933; Beaver et al. 1984). The genus *Himasthla* was erected by Dietz in 1909 with *Himasthla rhigedana* as the type species (Dietz 1910). After then, more than 25 species have been described in this genus; the majority (22 species) are parasites of birds, and 2 and 1 species are parasites of fish and a human, respectively (Diaz and Cremonte 2004). *H. muehlensi* (5 specimens) was initially described to have 32 collar spines (Vogel 1933); however, Stunkard (1939) re-examined the specimens of Dr. Vogel and came to a conclusion that the number of

Fig. 2.31 Line drawing of an adult fluke of *Himasthla muehlensi*. Scale bar = 1 mm. (Modified from the figure in Vogel (1933) Zentralbl Bakteriol Parasitenkd Infekt 127:387–391)

collar spines of *H. muehlensi* is 31. In 1940, Mendheim suggested a possible identity of *H. muehlensi* with *Himasthla elongata* (Mehlis, 1831) Dietz, 1909; however, the number of collar spines in *H. elongata* is 29, so *H. muehlensi* having 31 collar spines is certainly distinct from *H. elongata* (Stunkard 1960). On the other hand, Stunkard (1938, 1960) suggested a possible synonymy between *H. muehlensi* Vogel, 1933 and *Himasthla quissetensis* (Miller and Northup, 1926) Stunkard, 1934 and also between *H. quissetensis* and *Himasthla alincia* Dietz, 1909; thus, a synonymy of 3 species, *H. muehlensi, H. quissetensis,* and *H. alincia*, was raised. However, the anterior distribution of vitellaria is different among the 3 species; in *H. muehlensi*, the vitellaria reach almost up to the posterior margin of the cirrus sac, but in *H. alincia*, the vitellaria distribution is limited some distance beyond the posterior margin of the cirrus sac, and in *H. quissetensis*, the vitellaria distribute more anteriorly up to the level of the cirrus sac (Vogel 1933; Stunkard 1938; Han et al. 2009). Nevertheless, this possible synonymy needs further verification, although a brawback is that after the original description of *H. muehlensi*, no succeeding reports have been published on this species (it is considered a parasite of North America) (Table 2.4).

Adult flukes of *H. muehlensi* have a remarkably elongated (11.0–17.7 mm in length) and narrow body (0.40–0.48 mm) (Vogel 1933; Diaz and Cremonte 2004). They have a total of 31 collar spines (originally reported to have 32 spines), including 27 spines in an uninterrupted horseshoe pattern on the dorsum and around the sides, and 2 on each side of the ventral corner (Beaver et al. 1984). The size of irregularly ovoid eggs inside of the uterus was 114–149 μm long and 62–85 μm wide (Vogel 1933). The life cycle of *H. muehlensi* has not been elucidated, except a speculation that the source of the human infection may have been a kind of mollusk the patient consumed, *Venus mercenaria*. Stunkard (1938) examined a large number of this mollusk purchased from the New York market but failed to detect the metacercariae. As in other *Himasthla* spp., the first intermediate host of *H. muehlensi* may be a marine prosobranch gastropod species, and the second intermediate host may include the marine prosobranch gastropods, marine bivalves, and marine annelids (Fried 2001). It is likely that birds and mammals (accidentally) are the definitive hosts (Fried 2001).

Other *Himasthla* spp. of taxonomic importance Potentially zoonotic *Himasthla* spp. include *H. alincia* Dietz, 1909; *H. catoptrophori* Dronen et al., 1998; *H. californiensis* (Adams and Martin, 1963) Deblock, 1966; *H. compacta* Stunkard, 1960; *H. elongata* (Mehlis, 1831) Dietz, 1909; *H. escamosa* Diaz and Cremonte, 2004; *H. kusasigi* Yamaguti, 1939; *H. larina* Ishikulov and Kuklin, 1998; *H. leptosoma* (Creplin, 1829) Dietz, 1909; *H. limnodromi* Didyk and Burt, 1997; *H. littorinae* Stunkard, 1966; *H. mcintosh* Stunkard, 1960; *H. piscicola* Stunkard, 1960; *H. quissetensis* (Miller and Northup, 1926) Stunkard, 1934; *H. rhigedana* Dietz, 1909 (see Yamaguti 1971; Stunkard 1960; Diaz and Cremonte 2004).

2.9 *Hypoderaeum*

2.9.1 Hypoderaeum conoideum

2.9.1.1 *Hypoderaeum conoideum* (Bloch, 1872) Dietz, 1909

[syn. *Psilochasmus lecithosus* Otte, 1926; *Hypoderaeum sinensis* Hsü, 1932; *Hypoderaeum magnocirrus* Verma, 1936]

This species (Fig. 2.32) (subfamily Echinostominae) was originally described from birds in Germany by Bloch in 1872 under the name *Cucullanus conoideus* (Skrjabin and Bashikirova 1956). The name was changed several times into *Festucaria anatis* and *Festucaria boschadis* by Schrank in 1788 and 1790, respectively, *Distoma anatis* by Zeder in 1800, *Fasciola appendiculata* by Froelich in 1802, and *Distomum oxycephalum* by Rudolphi in 1819, *Echinostoma oxycephalum* by Cobbold in 1861, *Distomum echinatum* by von Linstow in 1873, *Echinostomum echinatum* by Stossich in 1892, and *Distoma froelichii* by Kowalewski in 1894 (Dietz 1910; Skrjabin and Bashikirova 1956; Yamaguti 1971). The name was further changed into *Echinostomum conoideum* by Kowalewski in 1897, *Opistorchis pianae* by Galli-Valerio in 1898, and then finally into *Hypoderaeum conoideum* by Dietz in 1909 (Dietz 1909, 1910). Later, *Psilochasmus lecithosus* was reported by Otte in 1926 but synonymized with *H. conoideum* (Yamaguti 1971), and *Hypoderaeum sinensis* was described by Hsü in 1932, and *Hypoderaeum magnocirrus* was reported by Verma in 1936; however, they were also synonymized with *H.*

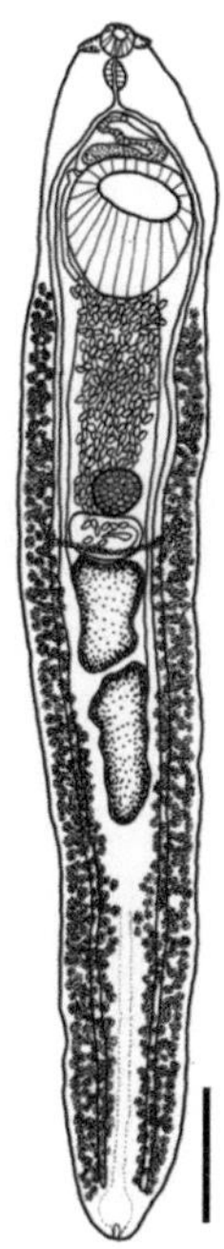

Fig. 2.32 Line drawing of an adult fluke of *Hypoderaeum conoideum*. Scale bar = 1 mm. (Modified from the figure in Morishita and Tsuchimochi (1925) Taiwan Igakkai Zasshi no. 243:544–562)

conoideum (Skrjabin and Bashikirova 1956). This echinostome is now known to be a common intestinal fluke of birds, including the duck, goose, fowl, swan, aquatic birds, and pigeon in Europe, Russia (Siberia), Mexico, North America, and Asia, including Bangladesh, Japan, China, Taiwan, Indonesia, and Thailand (Table 2.4) (Yamaguti 1958, 1971; Rim 1982; Toledo et al. 1996; Yousuf et al. 2009). Human infection was found in an area of northeast Thailand, where 55% of 254 persons examined were found to be infected with this echinostome (Yokogawa et al. 1965).

Adult flukes are slightly elongated attaining a maximum width at the junction between the first and second thirds of the body and 7.3–11.4 mm long and 1.1–1.6 mm wide; they have a poorly developed head collar with 47–54 (usually 49, mean 52) collar spines; 4 corner spines on each side and 39–45 lateral and dorsal spines arranged in 2 alternating rows (Rim 1982; Toledo et al. 1996). Their anteriormost portion of the body is markedly reduced in length, and the distance between the oral and ventral suckers are short (Rim 1982; Toledo et al. 1996). The eggs are 95–108 μm long and 61–68 μm wide (Rim 1982). The cercarial body is 242–422 μm long and 83–197 μm wide, and the tail is 231–575 μm long and 31–82 μm wide (Muňoz-Antolí et al. 2000). The metacercarial cyst is round and 134–154 μm in diameter, covered with outer cyst wall of 6–11 μm thickness and inner wall of 1.3–1.6 μm thickness (Muňoz-Antolí et al. 2000).

The first intermediate hosts are freshwater snails, *Lymnaea peregra*, *Lymnaea stagnalis, Lymnaea limosa, Lymnaea ovata, Lymnaea palustris, Lymnaea rubiginosa, Lymnaea tumida, Planorbis corneus, Indoplanorbis exustus,* and the same snail species and tadpoles are the second intermediate hosts (Yamaguti 1958; Yurlova 1987; Haas et al. 1995; Toledo et al. 1999). *Lymnaea peregra* and *Lymnaea corvus* were experimentally proved to be susceptible first intermediate host in Spain (Toledo et al. 1999). Chicks and ducks were used as the experimental definitive hosts (Muňoz-Antolí et al. 2000).

In Thailand, *H. conoideum* was reported from humans and birds (Yokogawa et al. 1965; Harinasuta et al. 1987). In Taiwan, fowls and ducks were found infected with *H. conoideum* (Morishita and Tsuchimochi 1925). In Spain, the life cycle of *H. conoideum* has been discovered near Albufera Natural Park (Toledo et al. 1996, 1998, 1999; Muňoz-Antolí et al. 2000). In Russia, waterfowls of Karelia were found to be infected with various species of trematodes, including *H. conoideum* (Jakovleva et al. 2012).

Potentially zoonotic *Hypoderaeum* spp. Potentially zoonotic *Hypoderaeum* spp. include *H. batanguensis* (Tubangui, 1932) Bashikirova, 1941; *H. charadrii* Tubangui and Masiluňgan, 1935; *H. cubanicum* (Artjuch, 1958) Jatschenko, 1987; *H. dingeri* Lie, 1964; *H. essexense* (Khan, 1960) Khan, 1962; *H. gnedini* Bashikirova, 1941; *H. magnicirrusa* Verma, 1936; *H. mainpuria* Verma, 1936; *H. microspina* (Singh, 1954) Skrjabin and Bashikirova, 1956; *H. skrjabini* Oschmarin, 1946; *H. sobolevi* Alekseev, 1965; *H. vigi* Bashikirova, 1941 (see Skrjabin and Bashikirova 1956; Yamaguti 1971).

References

References for Section 2.1

Bashikirova EI (1947) Family Echinostomatidae Dietz, 1909. In: Skrjabin KI (ed) Trematodes and animals and man, vol 1. Akademiya Nauk Publishers, Moscow, pp 310–391

Beaver PC, Jung RC, Cupp EW (1984) Clinical parasitology, 9th edn. Lea and Febiger, Philadelphia

Chai JY (2007) Intestinal flukes. In: Murrell KD, Fried B (eds) Food-borne parasitic zoonoses. Fish and plant-borne parasites. Springer, New York, pp 53–115

Chai JY (2009) Echinostomes in humans. In: Fried B, Toledo R (eds) The biology of echinostomes. Springer, New York, pp 147–183

Chai JY (2015) Chapter 19. Echinostomes. In: Xiao L, Ryan U, Feng Y (eds) Biology of foodborne parasites. CRC Press, Taylor & Francis Group, Boca Raton, pp 427–443

Chai JY, Shin EH, Lee SH, Rim HJ (2009) Foodborne intestinal flukes in Southeast Asia. Korean J Parasitol 47(suppl):S69–S102

Cheng YZ, Xu LS, Chen BJ et al (2005) Survey on the current status of important human parasitic infections in Fujian Province. Chin J Parasitol Parasit Dis 23:283–287 (in Chinese)

Fujino T, Takahashi Y, Fried B (1995) A comparison of *Echinostoma trivolvis* and *E. caproni* using random amplified polymorphic DNA analysis. J Helminthol 69:263–264

Kostadinova A (1999) Cercarial chaetotaxy of *Echonostoma miyagawai* Ishii, 1932 (Digenea: Echinostomatidae), with a review of the sensory patterns in the 'revolutum' group. Syst Parasitol 44:201–209

Kostadinova A (2005) Family Echinostomatidae Looss, 1899. In: Jones A, Bray RA, Gibson DI (eds) Keys to the Trematoda, vol 2. Natural History Museum, London, pp 9–64

Kostadinova A, Gibson DI (2000) The systematic of the echinostomes. In: Fried B, Graczyk TK (eds) Echinostomes as experimental models for biological research. Kluwer Academic Publishers, Dordrecht/Boston/London/Amsterdam, pp 31–57

Kostadinova A, Gibson DI (2002) *Isthmiophora* Lühe, 1909 and *Euparyphium* Dietz, 1909 (Digenea: Echinostomatidae) re-defined, with comments on their nominal species. Syst Parasitol 52:205–217

Kostadinova A, Herniou EA, Barrett J et al (2003) Phylogenetic relationships of *Echinostoma* Rudolphi, 1809 (Digenea: Echinostomatidae) and related genera re-assessed via DNA and morphological analyses. Syst Parasitol 54:159–176

Looss A (1899) Weitere Beitrage zur Kentniss der Trematoden-Fauna Aegyptens, zugleich Versuch einer naturalischen Gliedrung des Genus *Distomum* Retzius. Zool Yb 12:521–784

Maldonado AJ, Vieira GO, Lanfredi RM (2003) *Echinostoma luiseryi* n. sp. (Platyhelminthes: Digenea) by light and scanning electron microscopy. J Parasitol 89:800–808

Marcilla A (2009) Chapter 9. Echinostomes: genomics and proteomics. In: Fried B, Toledo R (eds) The biology of echinostomes. Springer, New York, pp 207–228

Morgan JA, Blair D (1995) Nuclear rDNA ITS sequence variation in the trematode genus *Echinostoma*: An aid to establishing relationships within the 37-collar-spine group. Parasitology 111:609–615

Morgan JA, Blair D (1998a) Relative merits of nuclear ribosomal internal transcribed spacers and mitochondrial CO1 and ND1 genes for distinguishing among *Echinostoma* species (Trematoda). Parasitology 116:289–297

Morgan JA, Blair D (1998b) Mitochondrial ND1 gene sequences used to identify echinostome isolates from Australia and New Zealand. Int J Parasitol 28:493–502

Rim HJ (1982) Echinostomiasis. CRC Handbook Series in Zoonoses, Section C: Parasitic Zoonoses, Vol. III. Trematode Zoonoses. CRC Press Inc., Boca Raton, pp 53–69

Sorensen RE, Curtis J, Minchella DJ (1998) Intraspecific variation in the rDNA ITS loci of 37-collar-spined echinostomes from North America: implications for sequence-based diagnoses and phylogenetics. J Parasitol 84:992–997
Tkach VV, Kudlai O, Kostadinova A (2016) Molecular phylogeny and systematics of the Echinostomatoidea Looss, 1899 (Platyhelminthes: Digenea). Int J Parasitol 46:171–185
Toledo R, Muñoz-Antoli C, Esteban JG (2000) The life-cycle of *Echinostoma friedi* n. sp. (Trematoda: Echinostomatidae) in Spain and a discussion on the relationships within the '*revolutum*' group based on cercarial chaetotaxy. Syst Parasitol 45:199–217
Toledo R, Esteban JG, Fried B (2006) Immunology and pathology of intestinal trematodes in their definitive hosts. Adv Parasitol 63:285–365
Xiao X, Wang T, Zheng X et al (2005) In vivo and in vitro encystment of *Echinochasmus liliputanus* cercariae and biological activity of the metacercariae. J Parasitol 91:492–498
Yamaguti S (1958) Systema Helminthum. Vol. I. The digenetic trematodes of vertebrates (Part I). Interscience Publishers Inc, New York, pp 1–979

References for Section 2.2

Agger MK, Simonsen PE, Vennervald BJ (1993) The antibody response in serum, intestinal wall and intestinal lumen of NMRI mice infected with *Echinostoma caproni*. J Helminthol 67:169–178
Ahn YK, Ryang YS, Chai JY et al (1989) Cercarial shedding of *Echinostoma cinetorchis* and experimental infection of the cercariae to several kinds of snails. Korean J Parasitol 27:203–211 (in Korean)
Alekseev VM (1968) The life cycles of *Echinostoma revolutum* (Froelish, 1802) and *E. robustum* Yamaguti, 1935 in the Primorsk Region. Soobshch dal'nevost. Fil. V.L. Komarova sib. Otdel. Akad. Nauk SSSR 26:3–7
Anazawa K (1929) On a human case of *Echinostoma revolutum* and its infection route. Taiwan Igahkai Zasshi 288:221–241 (in Japanese)
Ando R, Ozaki Y (1923) On four new species of trematodes of the family Echinostomatidae. Dobutsugaku Zasshi 35:108–119 (in Japanese)
Ando R, Tsuyuki H (1923) Studies on intestinal parasites taking rats as their final host (II). On the trematode *Echinostoma* and its 2nd intermediate host in Nagoya City. Tokyo Iji Shinshi 2340:1487–1499 (in Japanese)
Andressen K, Simonsen PE, Andressen BJ et al (1989) *Echinostoma caproni* in mice: shedding of antigens from the surface of an intestinal trematode. Int J Parasitol 19:111–118
Anh NTL, Madsen H, Dalsgaard A et al (2010) Poultry as reservoir hosts for fishborne zoonotic trematodes in Vietnamese fish farms. Vet Parasitol 169:391–394
Anthony RM, Rutitzky LI, Urban JF Jr et al (2007) Protective immune mechanisms in helminth infection. Nat Rev Immunol 7:975–987
Ashford RW, Crewe W (2003) The parasites of *Homo sapiens*. Taylor & Francis Inc, London
Bang NP, Cuong TP (2015) A potential risk from dog helminths for human health and some update information. J Sci (An Giang University, Vietnam) 3:76–90
Bashikirova EI (1947) Echinostomatidae. In: Skrjabin KI (ed) Trematodes and animals and man, vol 1. Akademiya Nauk Publishers, Moscow-Leningrad, pp 246–305
Beaver PC (1937) Experimental studies on *Echinostoma revolutum* (Froelich) a fluke from birds and mammals. Illinois Biol Monogr 15:1–96
Beaver PC, Jung RC, Cupp EW (1984) Clinical parasitology, 9th edn. Lea and Febiger, Philadelphia
Bernal D, Carpena I, Espert AM et al (2006) Identification of proteins in excretory/secretory extracts of *Echinostoma friedi* (Trematoda) from chronic and acute infections. Proteomics 6:2835–2843

Bhaibulaya M, Harinasuta C, Trirachantra S (1966) The finding of *Echinostoma revolutum* infection in man in Thailand. J Med Assoc Thailand 49:83

Bindseil E, Christensen NØ (1984) Thymus-independent crypt hyperplasia and villous atrophy in the small intestine of mice infected with the trematode *Echinostoma revolutum*. Parasitology 88:431–438

Bisseru B (1967) Stages in the development of larval echinostomes recovered from schistosome transmitting molluscs in Central Africa. J Helminthol 2:89–108

Bonne C, Bras G, Lie KJ (1953) Five echinostomes in man in the Malayan Archipelago. Am J Dig Dis 20:12–16

Borgsteede FHM, Okulewicz A, Okulewicz I (2000) A study of the helminth fauna of birds belonging to the Passeriformes in the Netherlands. Acta Parasitol 45:14–21

Brasil MD, Amato SB (1992) Faunistic analysis of the helminths of sparrows (*Passer domesticus* L, 1758) captured in Campo Grande, Rio de Janeiro, R. J. Mem Inst Oswaldo Cruz 87:43–48

Brunet IR, Joseph S, Dunne DW et al (2000) Immune responses during the acute stage of infection with the intestinal trematode *Echinostoma caproni*. Parasitology 120:565–571

Carney WP (1991) Echinostomiasis-a snail-borne intestinal trematode zoonosis. Southeast Asian J Trop Med Public Health 22:206–211

Carney WP, Sudomo M, Purnomo (1980) Echinostomiasis: a disease that disappeared. Trop Geogr Med 32:101–105

Carpena I, Espert A, Muñoz-Antoli C et al (2007) Antigenic characterization of *Echinostoma friedi* (Trematoda) in hamsters and rats experimentally infected. Rev Ibérica Parasitol 67:127–134

Chai JY (2007) Intestinal flukes. In: Murrell KD, Fried B (eds) food-borne parasitic zoonoses. Fish and plant-borne parasites. Springer, New York, pp 53–115

Chai JY (2009) Echinostomes in humans. In: Fried B, Toledo R (eds) The biology of echinostomes. Springer, New York, pp 147–183

Chai JY (2015) Chapter 19. Echinostomes. In: Xiao L, Ryan U, Feng Y (eds) Biology of foodborne parasites. CRC Press, Taylor & Francis Group, Boca Raton, pp 427–443

Chai JY, Lee SH (2002) Food-borne intestinal trematode infections in the Republic of Korea. Parasitol Int 51:129–154

Chai JY, Park JH, Han ET et al (2005) Mixed infections with *Opisthorchis viverrini* and intestinal flukes in residents of Vientiane Municipality and Saravane Province in Laos. J Helminthol 79:283–289

Chai JY, Han ET, Guk SM et al (2007) High prevalence of liver and intestinal fluke infections among residents of Savannakhet Province, Laos. Korean J Parasitol 45:213–218

Chai JY, Park JH, Jung BK et al (2009a) Echinostome infections in the striped-field mouse, *Apodemus agrarius*, and the Ussuri white-toothed shrew, *Crocidura lassiura*, caught near the demilitarized zone, Gyeonggi-do (province), Republic of Korea. Korean J Parasitol 47:311–314

Chai JY, Shin EH, Lee SH et al (2009b) Foodborne intestinal flukes in Southeast Asia. Korean J Parasitol 47(suppl):S69–S102

Chai JY, Han ET, Shin EH et al (2009c) High prevalence of *Haplorchis taichui, Prosthodendrium molenkampi*, and other helminth infections among people in Khammouane province, Lao PDR. Korean J Parasitol 47:243–247

Chai JY, Sohn WM, Ka BK et al (2011) *Echinostoma revolutum*: metacercariae in *Filopaludina* snails from Nam Dinh Province, Vietnam, and adults from experimental hamsters. Korean J Parasitol 49:449–455

Chai JY, Sohn WM, Yong TS et al (2012) Echinostome flukes recovered from humans in Khammouane Province, Lao PDR. Korean J Parasitol 50:269–272

Chai JY, Sohn WM, Cho J et al (2018) *Echinostoma ilocanum* infection in two residents of Savannakhet Province, Lao PDR. Korean J Parasitol 56 (in press)

Chantima K, Chai JY, Wongsawad C (2013) *Echinostoma revolutum*: freshwater snails as the second intermediate hosts in Chiang Mai Province, Thailand. Korean J Parasitol 51:183–189

Chen HT (1934) Helminths of dogs in Canton, with a list of those occurring in China. Lingnan Sci J 13:75–87
Chen HT, Chen S, Chu H et al (1985) Chapter 5. Echinostomatidae Dietz, 1909. Platyhelminthes, Trematoda, Digenea (1). Fauna Sinica. Science Press, Beijing, pp 333–403
Chen B, Li L, Xie H et al (2013) Morphology and characteristics of five types of Echinostomatidae in Fujian. J Pathogen Biol:2013–2003
Cheng YZ, Lin JX, Fang YY et al (1992) Discovery of human infection with *Echinostoma angustitestis*. Chin J Zoon 8:7–8 (in Chinese)
Cheng YZ, Xu LS, Chen BJ et al (2005) Survey on the current status of important human parasitic infections in Fujian Province. Chin J Parasitol Parasit Dis 23:283–287 (in Chinese)
Cho J (2016) Molecular differentiation of echinostomes occurring in Asia with description of *Echinostoma mekongi* n. sp. from humans in Cambodia. M.S. thesis to Seoul National University Graduate School, Department of Medicine, Seoul, Korea, February 2016
Cho SY, Kang SY, Ryang YS (1981) Helminthes infections in the small intestine of stray dogs in Ejungbu City, Kyunggi Do, Korea. Korean J Parasitol 19:55–59 (in Korean)
Christensen NØ, Knudsen J, Fagbemi B et al (1985) Impairment of primary expulsion of *Echinostoma revolutum* in mice concurrently infected with *Schistosoma mansoni*. J Helminthol 59:333–335
Christensen NØ, Odaibo AB, Simonsen PE (1988) *Echinostoma* population regulation in experimental rodent definitive hosts. Parasitol Res 75:83–87
Christensen NØ, Fried B, Kanev I (1990) Taxonomy of 37-collar spines *Echinostoma* (Trematoda: Echinostomatiade) in studies on the population regulation in experimental rodent hosts. Angewandte Parasitol 31:127–130
Chu JK, Cho YJ, Chung SB et al (1973) Study on the trematode parasites of the birds in Korea. Korean J Parasitol 11:70–75 (in Korean)
Chung PR, Jung Y (1999) *Cipangopaludina chinensis malleata* (Gastropoda: Viviparidae): a new second molluscan intermediate host of a human intestinal fluke *Echinostoma cinetorchis* (Trematoda: Echinostomatidae) in Korea. J Parasitol 85:963–964
Chung PR, Jung Y, Park YK (2001a) *Segmentina hemisphaerula*: a new molluscan intermediate host for *Echinostoma cinetorchis* in Korea. J Parasitol 87:1169–1171
Chung PR, Jung Y, Park YK et al (2001b) *Austropeplea ollula* (Pulmonata: Lymnaeidae): a new molluscan intermediate host of a human intestinal fluke, *Echinostoma cinetorchis* (Trematoda: Echinostomatidae) in Korea. Korean J Parasitol 39:247–253
Chung PR, Jung Y, Park YK et al (2001c) *Corbicula fluminea* (Bivalvia: Corbiculidae): a possible molluscan intermediate host of *Echinostoma cinetorchis* (Trematoda: Echinostomatidae) in Korea. Korean J Parasitol 39:329–332
Chung PR, Jung Y, Joo CY (2001d) *Biomphalaria glabrata* (Pulmonata: Planorbidae): a potential second molluscan intermediate host of a human intestinal fluke, *Echinostoma cinetorchis* (Trematoda: Echinostomatidae). Korean J Malacol 17:57–61
Cortés A, Sotillo J, Muñoz-Antoli C et al (2016) Definitive host influences the proteomic profile of excretory/secretory products of the trematode *Echinostoma caproni*. Parasit Vectors 9:185
Cortés A, Sotillo J, Muñoz-Antoli C et al (2017) Antibody trapping: a novel mechanism of parasite immune evasion by the trematode *Echinostoma caproni*. PLoS Negl Trop Dis 11:e0005773
Cross JH (1984) Changing patterns of some trematode infections in Asia. Arzneim-Forsch/Drug Res 34 (II), Nr, 9b:1224–1226
Cross JH, Basca-Sevilla V (1986) Studies on *Echinostoma ilocanum* in the Philippines. Southeast Asian J Trop Med Public Health 17:23–27
Davis NE (2005) Storage and incubation of *Echinostoma revolutum* eggs recovered from wild *Branta canadensis*, and their infectivity to *Lymnaea tomentosa* snails. J Helminthol 79:321–326
DeGirolami PC, Kimber J (1983) Intestinal parasites among Southeast Asian refugees in Massachusetts. Am J Clin Pathol 79:502–504
Detwiler JT, Bos DH, Minchella DJ (2010) Revealing the secret lives of cryptic species: Examining the phylogenetic relationships of echinostome parasites in North America. Mol Phylogen Evol 55:611–620

Detwiler JT, Zajac AM, Minchella DJ, Belden LK (2012) Revealing cryptic parasite diversity in a definitive host: echinostomes in muskrats. J Parasitol 98:1148–1155

Dietz E (1909) Die Echinostomatiden der Vogel. Zool Anz 34:180–192

Dietz E (1910) Die Echinostomatiden der Vogel. Zool Jarb Suppl 12:265–512

Dollfus PR (1925a) Distomens Parasites de Muridae du Genre Mus. Ann Parasitol (France) 3:85–102

Dollfus PR (1925b) Distomens Parasites de Muridae du Genre Mus (I). Ann Parasitol (France) 3:185–205

Eduardo SL (1991) Food-borne parasitic zoonoses in the Philippines. Southeast Asian J Trop Med Public Health 22:16–22

Eduardo SL, Lee GQ (2006) Some zoonotic trematodes from the Philippine field rat, *Rattus mindanensis mindanensis* (Mearns, 1905) (Mammalia: Rodentia) in Bay, Laguna, Philippines with redescription and new records of species. Phil J Vet Med 43:33–45

Eom KS, Rim HJ, Jang DH (1984) A study on the parasitic helminths of domestic duck (*Anas platyrhynchos* var. *domestica* Linnaeus) in Korea. Korean J Parasitol 22:215–221

Fagasinski A (1962) Helminth parasites of domestic galliform birds in Poland. Acta Parasitol Pol 10:347–368

Farahnak A, Shiekhian R, Mobedi I (2004) A faunistic survey on the bird helminth parasites and their medical importance. Iranian J Public Health 33:40–46

Faltýnková A, Georgieva S, Soldánová et al (2015) A reassessment of species diversity within the '*revolutum*' group of *Echinostoma* Rudolphi, 1809 (Digenea: Echinostomatidae) in Europe. Syst Parasitol 90:1–25

Ferraz J, Souza J, Costa-Silva M et al (2012) Effect of praziquantel on adult *Echinostoma paraensei* worms in experimentally infected mice. Parasitol Res 111:143–148

Fischthal JH, Kuntz RE (1975) Some digenetic trematodes of mammals from Taiwan. Proc Helminthol Soc Wash 42:149–157

Fischthal JH, Kuntz RE (1981) addicitonal records of digenetic trematodes of mammals from Taiwan. Proc Helminthol Soc Wash 48:71–79

Frazer BA, Fried B, Fujino T et al (1999) Host-parasite relationships between *Echinostoma caproni* and RAG-2-deficient mice. Parasitol Res 85:337–342

Fried B, Fujino T (1984) Scanning electron microscopy of *Echinostoma revolutum* (Trematoda) during development in the chick embryo and domestic chick. Int J Parasitol 14:75–81

Fried B, Graczyk TK (2004) Recent advances in the biology of *Echinostoma* species in the 'revolutum' group. Adv Parasitol 58:139–195

Fried B, Huffman JE (1996) The biology of the intestinal trematode *Echinostoma caproni*. Adv Parasitol 38:311–368

Fried B, Reddy A (1997) Comparative studies on excystation and morphological features of the metacercariae of *Echinostoma paraensei* and *E. caproni*. Int J Parasitol 27:899–901

Fried B, Huffman JE, Franco J (1988) Single- and five-worm infections of *Echinostoma revolutum* (Trematoda) in the golden hamster. Int J Parasitol 18:179–181

Fried B, Huffman JE, Weiss PM (1990) Single and multiple infections of *Echinostoma caproni* (Trematoda) in the golden hamster. J Helminthol 64:75–78

Fried B, Schmidt KA, Sorensen RE (1997) In vivo and ectopic encystment of *Echinostoma revolutum* and chemical excystation of the metacercariae. J Parasitol 83:251–254

Fujino T, Fried B (1993a) Expulsion of *Echinostoma trivolvis* (Cort, 1914) Kanev, 1985 and retention of *E. caproni* Richard, 1964 (Trematoda: Echinostomatidae) in C3H mice: pathological, ultrastructural, and cytochemical effects on the host intestine. Parasitol Res 79:286–292

Fujino T, Fried B (1993b) *Echinostoma caproni* and *E. trivolvis* alter the binging of glycoconjugates in the intestinal mucosa of C3H mice as determined by lectin histochemistry. J Helminthol 67:179–188

Fujino T, Fried B, Tada I (1993) The expulsion of *Echinostoma trivolvis*: worm kinetics and intestinal cytopathology in conventional and congenitally athymic BALB/c mice. Parasitology 106:297–304

Fujino T, Fried B, Hosier DW (1994) The expulsion of *Echinostoma trivolvis* (Trematoda) from mice: extension/retraction mechanisms and ultrastructure of the collar spines. Parasitol Res 80:581–587

Fujino T, Takahashi Y, Fried B (1995) A comparison of *Echinostoma trivolvis* and *E. caproni* using random amplified polymorphic DNA analysis. J Helminthol 69:263–264

Fujino T, Ichikawa H, Fried B et al (1996a) The expulsion of *Echinostoma trivolvis*: suppressive effects of dexamethasone on goblet cell hyperplasia and worm rejection in C3H/HeN mice. Parasite 3:283–289

Fujino T, Fried B, Hidetaka et al (1996b) Rapid expulsion of the intestinal trematodes *Echinostoma trivolvis* and *E. caproni* from C3H mice by trapping with increased goblet cell mucins. Int J Parasitol 26:319–324

Fujino T, Wu Z, Nagano I et al (1997) Specific primers for the detection of genomic DNA of *Echinostoma trivolvis* and *E. caproni* (Trematoda: Echinostomatidae). Mol Cell Probes 11:77–80

Fujino T, Ichikawa H, Fukuda K et al (1998a) The expulsion of *Echinostoma trivolvis* cause by goblet cell hyperplasia in severe combined immunodeficiency (SCID) mice. Parasite 5:219–222

Fujino T, Ichikawa H, Fried B (1998b) The immunosuppressive compound FK506 does not affect expulsion of *Echinostoma trivolvis* in C3H mice. Parasitol Res 84:519–521

Fujino T, Shinohara T, Fukuda K (2000) The expulsion of *Echinostoma trivolvis*: worm kinetics and intestinal cytopathology in jirds, *Meriones unguicalatus*. Comp Parasitol 67:236–240

Garcia JS, Hooper CS, Simões RO et al (2011) Biochemical and histological responses of *Rattus novergicus* (Wistar) infected by *Echinostoma paraensei* (Trematoda: Echinostomatidae). Vet Parasitol 178:86–92

Garcia JS, Pinheiro J, Hooper CS et al (2012) Haematological alterations in *Rattus norvegicus* (Wistar) experimentally infected with *Echinostoma paraensei* (Trematoda: Echinostomatidae). Exp Parasitol 2012:300–303

Garrison PE (1908) A new intestinal trematode of man. Phil J Sci B3:385–393

Georgieva S, Selbach C, Faltýnková A et al (2013) New cryptic species of the '*revolutum*' group of *Echinostoma* (Digenea: Echinostomatidae) revealed by molecular and morphological data. Parasit Vectors 6:64

Georgieva S, Faltýnková A, Brown R et al (2014) *Echinostoma* '*revolutum*' (Digenea: Echinostomatidae) species complex revisited: species delimitation based on novel molecular and morphological data gathered in Europe. Parasit Vectors 7:520

Georgieva S, Blasco-Costa I, Kostadinova A (2017) Molecular characterization of four echinostomes (Digenea: Echinostomatidae) from birds in New Zealand, with description of *Echinostoma novaezealandense* n. sp. and *Echinoparyphium poulini* n. sp. Syst Parasitol. https://doi.org/10.1007/s11239-017-9712-x

Gonçalves JP, Oliveira-Menezes A, Maldonado A Jr et al (2013) Evaluation of praziquantel effects on *Echinostoma paraensei* ultrastructure. Vet Parasitol 194:16–25

Graczyk TK, Fried B (1994) ELISA method for detecting anti-*Echinostoma caproni* (Trematoda: Echinostomatidae) immunoglobulins in experimentally infected ICR mice. J Parasitol 80:544–549

Graczyk TK, Fried B (1995) An enzyme-linked immunosorbent assay for detecting anti-*Echinostoma trivolvis* (Trematoda) IgG in experimentally infected ICR mice. Parasitol Res 81:710–712

Graczyk TK, Fried B (1998) Echinostomiasis: a common but forgotten food-borne disease. Am J Trop Med Hyg 58:501–504

Grover M, Dutta R, Kumar R et al (1998) *Echinostoma ilocanum* infection. Indian Pediatr 35:549–552

Guillou F, Roger E, Moné et al (2007) Excretory-secretory proteome of larval *Schistosoma mansoni* and *Echinostoma caproni,* two parasites of *Biomphalaria glabrata*. Mol Biochem Parasitol 155:45–56

Gürler AT, Bakan N (2017) Helminths of laboratory animals in Turkey: review. J Lab Anim 1:41–48

Haas W, Körner M, Hutterer E et al (1995) Finding and recognition of the snail intermediate hosts by 3 species of echinostome cercariae. Parasitology 110:133–142

Hansen K, Nielsen JW, Hindsbo O et al (1991) *Echinostoma caproni* in rats: worm population dynamics and host blood eosinophilia during primary infection with 6, 25 and 50 metacercariae and resistance to secondary and superimposed infections. Parasitol Res 77:686–690

Haque M, Siddiqi AH (1982) Histochemical and electrophoretic studies on phosphatases of some Indian trematodes. J Helminthol 56:111–116

Harinasuta T, Bunnag D, Radomyos P (1987) Intestinal fluke infections. Bailliere's Clin Trop Med Commun Dis 2(3):695–721

Haseeb MA, Eveland LK (2000) Human echinostomiasis: mechanisms of pathogenesis and host resistance. In: Fried B, Graczyk TK (eds) Echinostomes as experimental models for biological research. Kluwer Academic Publishers, Dordrecht, pp 83–98

Heyneman D, Faulk WP, Fudenberg HH (1971) *Echinostoma lindoense*: larval antigens from the snail intermediate host, *Biomphalaria glabrata*. Exp Parasitol 29:480–492

Higón M, Monteagudo C, Fried B et al (2008) Molecular cloning and characterization of *Echinostoma caproni* heat shock protein-70 and differential expression in the parasite derived from low- and high-compatible hosts. Parasitology 135:1469–1477

Hilario JS, Wharton LD (1917) *Echinostoma ilocanum* (Garrison): a report of five cases and a contribution to the anatomy of the fluke. Phil J Sci (Sec B Trop Med) 12:203–211

Hirazawa I (1929) An experimental study on trematodes which take tadpoles of *Rana catesbiana* Show (bullfrog) as their intermediate host. Kumamoto Igakkai Zasshi 5:599–612 (in Japanese)

Holland MP, Skelly DK, Kashgarian M et al (2007) *Echinostoma* infection in green frogs (*Rana clamitans*) is stage and age dependent. J Zool 271:455–462

Hosier DW, Fried B (1986) Infectivity, growth, and distribution of *Echinostoma revolutum* in Swiss Webster and ICR mouse. Proc Helminthol Soc Wash 53:173–176

Huffman JE, Fried B (1990) *Echinostoma* and echinostomiasis. Adv Parasitol 29:215–269

Huffman JE, Michos C, Fried B (1986) Clinical and pathological effects of *Echinostoma revolutum* (Digenea: Echinostomatidae) in the golden hamster, *Mesocricetus auratus*. Parasitology 93:505–515

Huffman JE, Iglesias D, Fried B (1988) *Echinostoma revolutum*: pathology of extraintestinal infection in the golden hamster. Int J Parasitol 18:873–874

Humphries JE, Reddy A, Fried B (1997) Infectivity and growth of *Echinostoma revolutum* (Froelich, 1802) in the domestic chick. Int J Parasitol 27:129–130

Hung NM, Madsen H, Fried B (2013) Global status of fish-borne zoonotic trematodiasis in humans. Acta Parasitol 58:231–258

Hyodo M, Matsuyama S (1958) A human case of *Echinostoma revolutum*. 11th Nippon Kiseichu Gakkai Minami Nippon Shibu Taikai (in Kagoshima) (in Japanese)

Isaacson AC, Huffman JH, Fried B (1989) Infection, growth, development and pathology of *Echinostoma caproni* (Trematoda) in the golden hamster. Int J Parasitol 19:943–955

Ishii N (1935) Studies on rat trematodes. Jikken Igaku Zasshi 19:1122–1128 (in Japanese)

Islam MR, Shaikh H, Baki MA (1988) Prevalence and pathology of helminth parasites in domestic ducks of Bangladesh. Vet Parasitol 29:73–77

Isshiki O (1934) On a trematode parasite *Echinostoma revolutum* (Froelich, 1802) from a Korean wild duck. Chuo Juigaku Zasshi 47:639–647 (in Japanese)

Ito J (1964) A monograph of cercariae in Japan and adjacent territories. In: Progress of medical parasitology in Japan, vol 1. Meguro Parasitological Museum, Tokyo, pp 395–550

Ito M, Itagaki T (2003) Survey on wild rodents for endoparasites in Iwate Prefecture, Japan. J Vet Med Sci 65:1151–1153

Ivanov VM, Semenova NN (2000) Parasitological consequences of animal introduction. Russ J Ecol 31:281–283

Jang DH (1958) Studies on intestinal parasites of chickens. Vet Med World (Korea) 2(2):149–155, 2(3):222–226, 2(4):330–334 (in Korean)

Jeyarasasingam U, Heyneman D, Lim HK et al (1972) Life cycle of a new echinostome from Egypt, *Echinostome liei* sp. nov. (Trematoda: Echinostomatidae). Parasitology 65:203–222

Johnson PTJ, McKenzie VJ (2009) Effects of environmental change on helminth infections in amphibians exploring the emergence of *Ribeiroia* and *Echinostoma* infections in North America. In: Fried B, Toledo R (eds) The biology of echinostomes. Springer, New York, pp 249–280

Jourdane J, Kulo SD (1981) Etude expérimentale du cycle biologique de *Echinostoma togoensis* n. sp., parasite a l-état larvaire de *Biomphalaria pfeifferi* au Togo. Ann Parasitol (Paris) 56:477–488

Jung WT, Lee KJ, Kim HJ et al (2014) A case of *Echinostoma cinetorchis* (Trematoda: Echinostomatidae) infection diagnosed by colonoscopy. Korean J Parasitol 52:287–290

Kanev I (1985) On the morphology, biology, ecology and taxonomy of *E. revolutum* group (Trematoda: Echinostomatidae: *Echinostoma*). Ph.D. thesis, University of Sofia, Bulgaria

Kanev I (1994) Life-cycle, delimitation and redescription of *Echinostoma revolutum* (Froelich, 1802) (Trematoda: Echinostomatidae). Syst Parasitol 28:125–144

Kanev I, Odening K (1983) Further studies on *Cercaria spinifera* La Valette, 1855 in Central Europe. Helminthology (Bulgaria) 15:24–34

Kanev I, Vassilev I, Bayssade-Dufour C et al (1987) Cercarial chaetotaxy of *Echinostoma revolutum* (Froelich, 1802) and *E. echinatum* (Zeder, 1803) (Trematoda, Echinostomatidae). Ann Parasitol Hum Comp 62:222–234

Kanev I, Dimitrov V, Radev V et al (1995a) Redescription of *Echinostoma jurini* (Skvortzov, 1924) with a discussion of its identity and characteristics. Ann Naturhist Mus Wien 97B:37–53

Kanev I, Fried B, Dimitrov V et al (1995b) Redescription of *Echinostoma trivolvis* (Cort, 1914) (Trematoda: Echinostomatidae) with a discussion on its identity. Syst Parasitol 32:61–70

Kanev I, Dezfuli BS, Nestorov M et al (1999) Scanning electron microscopy of the collar region of *Deropristis inflate* and *Echinostoma revolutum*. J Helminthol 73:51–57

Kawahara S, Yamamoto E (1933) Human cases of *Echinostoma cinetorchis*. Tokyo Iji Shinshi 2840:1794–1796 (in Japanese)

Kechemir N, Jourdane J, Mas-Coma S (2002) Life cycle of a new African echinostome species reproducing by parthenogenesis. J Nat Hist 36:1777–1784

Keiser J, Brun R, Fried B et al (2006) Trematodicial activity of praziquantel and artemisinin derivatives: in vitro and in vivo investigations with adult *Echinostoma caproni*. Antimicrob Agents Chemonther 50:803–805

Khalil M, Abaza MS (1924) A new trematode parasite of the rat, *Echinostoma aegyptiaca* nov. sp. Rep Notes Public Health Lab, Cairo, Egypt 6:187–189

Kim S, Fried B (1989) Pathological effects of *Echinostoma caproni* (Trematoda) in the domestic chick. J Helminthol 63:227–230

Kishore N, Sinha DP (1982) Observations on *Echinostoma revolutum* infection in the rectum of domestic ducks (*Anas platyrhynchos domesticus*). Agric Sci Dig. http://aims.fao.org/serials/c_dce294e2

Komiya Y (1965) Metacercariae in Japan and adjacent territories. In: Progress of medical parasitology in Japan, vol 2. Meguro Parasitological Museum, Tokyo, pp 1–328

Kostadinova A (2005) Family Echinostomatidae Looss, 1899. In: Jones A, Bray RA, Gibson DI (eds) Keys to the Trematoda, vol 2. Natural History Museum, London, pp 9–64

Kostadinova A, Gibson DI (2000) The systematic of the echinostomes. In: Fried B, Graczyk TK (eds) Echinostomes as experimental models for biological research. Kluwer Academic Publishers, Dordrecht/Boston/London/Amsterdam, pp 31–57

Kostadinova A, Gibson DI (2002) *Isthmiophora* Lühe, 1909 and *Euparyphium* Dietz, 1909 (Digenea: Echinostomatidae) re-defined, with comments on their nominal species. Syst Parasitol 52:205–217

Kostadinova A, Gibson DI, Biserkow V, Chipev N (2000a) A quantitative approach to the evaluation of the morphological variability of two echinostomes, *Echinostoma miyagawai* Ishii, 1932 and *E. revolutum* (Froelich, 1802), from Europe. Syst Parasitol 45:1–15

Kostadinova A, Gibson DI, Biserkow V, Chipev N (2000b) Re-validation of *Echinostoma miyagawai* Ishii, 1932 (Digenea: Echinostomatidae) on the basis of the experimental completion of its life-cycle. Syst Parasitol 45:81–108

Kostadinova A, Herniou EA, Barrett J et al (2003) Phylogenetic relationships of *Echinostoma* Rudolphi, 1809 (Digenea: Echinostomatidae) and related genera re-assessed via DNA and morphological analyses. Syst Parasitol 54:159–176

Kotelnikof GA (1961) The biology of *Echinostoma robustum* Yamaguti, 1935 causing diseases in ducks. Sbornik Nauchno-Tekhnicheskoi Informatsii Vsesoyuznogo Instituta Gelminthologii im No. 7/8: p 29

Kurisu Y (1932) Studies on trematodes which take Japanese house hen as the definitive host. Kumamoto Igakkai Zasshi 8:283–298 (in Japanese)

Kusharyono C, Sukartinah S (1991) The current status of food-borne parasitic zoonoses in Indonesia. Southeast Asian J Trop Med Public Health 22(suppl):8–10

Latham ADM, Poulin R (2002) New records of gastrointestinal helminths from the southern black-backed gull (*Larus dominicanus*) in New Zealand. N Z J Zool 29:253–257

Lee SH, Lee JK, Sohn WM et al (1988a) Metacercariae of *Echinostoma cinetorchis* encysted in the freshwater snail, *Hippeutis* (*Helicorbis*) *cantori*, and their development in rats and mice. Korean J Parasitol 26:189–197

Lee SK, Chung NS, Ko IH et al (1988b) A case of natural human infection by *Echinostoma cinetorchis*. Korean J Parasitol 26:61–64 (in Korean)

Lee SH, Sohn WM, Chai JY (1990a) *Echinostoma revolutum* and *Echinoparyphium recurvatum* recovered from house rats in Yangyang-gun, Kangwon-do. Korean J Parasitol 28:235–240

Lee SH, Chai JY, Hong ST et al (1990b) Experimental life history of *Echinostoma cinetorchis*. Korean J Parasitol 28:39–44

Lee SH, Jun HS, Sohn WM, Chai JY (1992) Tegumental ultrastructure of juvenile and adult *Echinostoma cinetorchis*. Korean J Parasitol 30:65–74 (in Korean)

Leles D, Cascardo P, Freire A dos S et al (2014) Insights about echinostomiasis by paleomolecular diagnosis. Parasitol Int 63:646–649

Li T, He S, Zhao H et al (2010) Major trends in human parasitic diseases in China. Trends Parasitol 26:264–270

Lie KJ (1964) Studies on Echinostomatidae (Trematoda) in Malaya. VII. The life history of *Echinostoma lindoense* Sandground and Bonne, 1940. Trop Geogr Med 16:72–81

Lie KJ (1966) Studies on Echinostomatidae (Trematoda) in Malaya. XIV. Body gland cells in cercariae of *Echinostoma audyi* Lie and Umathevy, and *E. lindoense* Sandground and Bonne. J Parasitol 52:1049–1051

Lie KJ (1968) Further studies on the life history of *Echinostoma lindoense* Sandground and Bonne, 1940 (Trematoda: Echinostomatidae) with a report on its occurrence in Brazil. Proc Helminthol Soc Wash 35:74–77

Lie KJ, Basch PF (1966) Life history of *Echinostoma barbosai* sp. n (Trematoda: Echinostomatidae). J Parasitol 52:1052–1057

Lie KJ, Basch PF (1967) The life history of *Echinostoma paraensei* sp. n (Trematoda: Echinostomatidae). J Parasitol 53:1192–1199

Lie KJ, Heyneman D (1975) Studies on resistance in snails: a specific tissue reaction to *Echinostoma lindoense* in *Biomphalaria glabrata* snails. Int J Parasitol 5:621–625

Lie KJ, Kanev I (1983) Identification and distribution of *Echinostoma lindoense, E. audyi* and *E. revolutum* (Trematoda: Echinostomatidae). Z Parasikenkd 69:223–227

Lie KJ, Nasemary S (1973) Studies on Echinostomatidae (Trematoda) in Malaya. XVI. The life history of *Echinostoma ilocanum* (Garrison, 1940). Proc Helminthol Soc Wash 40:59–65

Lie KJ, Umathevy T (1965) Studies on Echinostomatidae (Trematoda) in Malaya. VIII. The life history of *Echinostoma audyi* sp. n. J Parasitol 51:781–788
Lie KJ, Nasemary S, Impand P (1973) Five echinostome species from Thailand. Southeast Asian J Trop Med Public Health 4:96–101
Lo CT (1995) *Echinostoma macrorchis*: life history, population dynamics of intramolluscan stages, and the first and second intermediate hosts. J Parasitol 81:569–576
Lu SC (1982) Echinostomiasis in Taiwan. Int J Zoon 9:33038
Lutz A (1924) Untersuchung über die Entwicklungsgeschichte brazilianischer Trematoden. Spezieller Teil. I. Echinostomatidae. Mem Inst Oswaldo Cruz 17:75–93
Mabus J, Huffman JE, Fried B (1988) Humoral and cellular response to infection with *Echinostoma revolutum* in the golden hamsters, *Mesocricetus auratus*. J Helminthol 62:127–132
Majima M (1927) On *Echinostoma macrorchis* found in man. Kumamoto Igakkai Zasshi 2252:2260–2263 (in Japanese)
Makino Y, Nakagawa A, Yamane Y et al (1982) A human case of echinostomiasis in Shimane Prefecture and experimental infection in rats. Jpn J Parasitol 31:385–390 (in Japanese)
Maldonado A Jr, Lanfredi RM (2009) Echinostomes in the wild. In: Fried B, Toledo R (eds) The biology of echinostomes. Springer Science + Business Media, LLC, New York, pp 129–145
Maldonado A Jr, Loker ES, Morgan JAT et al (2001a) Description of the adult worms of a new Brazilian isolate of *Echinostoma paraensei* (Platyhelminthes: Digenea) from its natural vertebrate host Nectomys squamipes by light and scanning electron microscopy and molecular analysis. Parasitol Res 87:840–848
Maldonado A Jr, Vieira GO, Garcia JS et al (2001b) Biological aspects of a new isolate of *Echinostoma paraensei* (Trematoda: Echinostomatidae): susceptibility of sympatric snails and the natural vertebrate host. Parasitol Res 87:853–859
Maldonado A Jr, Coura R, Garcia JS et al (2001c) Changes on *Schistosoma mansoni* (Digenea: Schistosomatidae) worm load in *Nectomys squamipes* (Rodentia: Sigmodontinae) concurrently infected with *Echinostoma paraensei* (Digenea: Echinostomatidae). Mem Inst Oswaldo Cruz 96:193–198
Maldonado AJ, Vieira GO, Lanfredi RM (2003) *Echinostoma luisreyi* n. sp. (Platyhelminthes: Digenea) by light and scanning electron microscopy. J Parasitol 89:800–808
Marcilla A (2009) Chapter 9. Echinostomes: genomics and proteomics. In: Fried B, Toledo R (eds) The biology of echinostomes. Springer, New York, pp 207–228
Marcilla A, Pérez-García A, Espert A et al (2007) *Echinostoma caproni*: identification of enolase in excretory/secretory products, molecular cloning, and functional expression. Exp Parasitol 117:57–64
Matos FA, Sant'Anna V, Maldonado A Jr et al (2018) Morphology of *Echinostoma paraensei* Lie & Basch, 1967 (Trematoda) cercariae. Braz J Biol. https://doi.org/10.1590/1519-6984.169855
Matskási I (1971) The trematode fauna of rodents and insectivora (Mammalia) in Hungary I. Parasit Hung 4:125–136
McMaster RP, Huffman JE, Fried B (1995) The effect of dexamethasone on the course of *Echinostoma caproni* and *E. trivolvis* infections in golden hamster (*Mesocricetus auratus*). Parasitol Res 81:518–521
Meece JK, Nollen PM (1996) A comparison of the adult and miracidial stages of *Echinostoma paraensei* and *E. caproni*. Int J Parasitol 26:37–43
Mohandas A (1973) Studies on the life history of *Echinostoma ivaniosi* n. sp. J Helminthol 47:421–438
Mohanta UK, Watanabe T, Anisuzzaman et al (2019) Characterization of *Echinostoma revolutum* and *Echinostoma robustum* from ducks in Bangladesh based on morphology, nuclear ribosomal ITS2 and mitochondrial *nad1* sequences. Parasitol Int 69:1–7
Monte TC, Garcia J, Gentile R et al (2016) In vivo and in vitro effects of the herbicide Roundup® on developmental stages of the trematode *Echinostoma paraensei*. Exp Parasitol 169:43–50

Morgan JA, Blair D (1995) Nuclear rDNA ITS sequence variation in the trematode genus *Echinostoma*: An aid to establishing relationships within the 37-collar-spine group. Parasitology 111:609–615

Morgan JA, Blair D (1998a) Relative merits of nuclear ribosomal internal transcribed spacers and mitochondrial CO1 and ND1 genes for distinguishing among *Echinostoma* species (Trematoda). Parasitology 116:289–297

Morgan JA, Blair D (1998b) Mitochondrial ND1 gene sequences used to identify echinostome isolates from Australia and New Zealand. Int J Parasitol 28:493–502

Moriyama S (1952) A human case of *Echinostoma cinetorchis* Ando et Ozaki, 1923. Nippon Kiseichu Gakkai Kiji 21:132 (in Japanese)

Muñoz-Antoli C, Sotillo J, Monteagudo C et al (2007) Development and pathology of *Echinostoma caproni* in experimentally infected mice. J Parasitol 93:854–859

Mustafa T (1994) Karyological studies on some species of the families Echinostomatidae and Plagiorchiidae and aspects of chromosome evolution in trematodes. Syst Parasitol 28:229–238

Nagatani M, Tantrawatpan C, Agatsuma T et al (2015) Mitochondrial DNA sequences of 37 collar-spined echinostomes (Digenea: Echinostomatidae) in Thailand and Loa PDR reveals presence of two species: *Echinostoma revolutum* and *E. miyagawai*. Infect Genet Evol 35:56–62

Nassi H, Dupouy J (1988) Experimental study of the life history of *Echinostoma parvocirrus* n. sp. (Trematoda: Echinostomatidae), a larval parasite of *Biomphalaria glabrata* in Guadeloupe. Ann Parasitol Hum Comp 63:103–108 (in French)

Noikong W, Wongsawad C, Chai JY et al (2014) Molecular analysis of echinostome metacercariae from their second intermediate host found in a localized geographic region reveals genetic heterogeneity and possible cryptic speciation. PLoS Negl Trop Dis 8:e2778

Nowak TS, Loker ES (2005) *Echinostoma paraensei*: differential gene transcription in the sporocyst stage. Exp Parasitol 109:94–105

Ochi S (1931) Studies on the life cycle of *Echinostoma macrorchis*. Tokyo Joigaku Zasshi 1:12–32 (in Japanese)

Odaibo AB, Christensen NØ, Ukoli FMA (1988) Establishment, survival, and fecundity in *Echinostoma caproni* (Trematoda) infections in NMRI mice. Proc Helminthol Soc Wash 55:265–269

Odhner T (1911) *Echinostoma ilocanum* (Garrison), ein neuer menschenparasit aus ostasien. Zool Anz 38:65 (in German)

Okabe N, Okabe K (1972) On a human case infected by three species of trematodes. Nippon Iji Shimpo 2531:46–48 (in Japanese)

Okahashi K (1966) Researches on *Heterophyes*. (2) *Metagonimus yokogawai* parasitic on the loach: its infection test on birds and its adult form. Okayama Igakkai Zasshi 78:15–24 (in Japanese)

Papazahariadou M, Diakou A, Papadopoulos E et al (2008) Parasites of the digestive tract in free-ranging birds in Greece. J Nat Hist 42:381–398

Park SK, Kim DH, Deung YK et al (2004) Status of intestinal parasite infections among children in Bat Dambang, Cambodia. Korean J Parasitol 42:201–203

Park YK, Soh CT, Park GM et al (2006a) Host specificity of *Pisidium coreanum* (Bivalvia: Sphaeriidae) to larval infection with a human intestinal fluke *Echinostoma cinetorchis* (Trematoda: Echinostomatidae) in Korea. J Parasitol 92:1118–1120

Park YK, Hwang MK, Chung PR (2006b) Encystment and metacercariae development of *Echinostoma cinetorchis* cercariae in an in vitro culture system. J Parasitol 92:1010–1013

Patnaik MM, Ray SK (1966) On the life history and distribution of Echinostoma revolutum (Froelich, 1802) in Orisa. Indian Vet J 43:591–600

Pethleart A, Nateeworanart S, Kaewsook P (2005) Infection rate of the echinostome fluke in domestic ducks from Yaowarach Market, Bangkok. Thammasat Med J 6:22–27 (in Thai)

Petrie JL, Burg EF III, Cain G (1996) Molecular characterization of *Echinostoma caproni* and *E. paraensei* by random amplification of polymorphic DNA (RAPD) analysis. J Parasitol 82:360–362

Pinheiro J, Maldonado A, Lanfredi RM (2004a) Light and scanning electron microscopy of the miracidium of *Echinostoma paraensei* (Trematoda: Echinostomatidae). Vet Parasitol 121:265–275
Pinheiro J, Maldonado A Jr, Attias M et al (2004b) Morphology of the rediae of *Echinostoma paraensei* (Trematoda: Echinostomatidae) from its intermediate host *Lymnaea columella* (Mullusca, Gastropoda). Parasitol Res 93:171–177
Pisciotta JH, Ponder EL, Fried B et al (2005) Hemozoin formation in *Echinostoma trivolvis* rediae. Int J Parasitol 35:1037–1042
Poland GA, Navin TR, Sarosi GA (1985) Outbreak of parasitic gastroenteritis among travelers returning from Africa. Arch Intern Med 145:2220–2221
Radomyos P, Bunnag D, Harinasuta T (1982) *Echinostoma ilocanum* (Garrison, 1908) Odhner, 1911, infection in man in Thailand. Southeast Asian J Trop Med Public Health 13:265–269
Radomyos P, Radomyos B, Tungtrongchitr A (1994) Multi-infection with helminths in adults from northeast Thailand as determined by post-treatment fecal examination of adult worms. Trop Med Parasitol 45:133–135
Radomyos B, Wongsaroj T, Wilairatana P et al (1998) Opisthorchiasis and intestinal fluke infections in northern Thailand. Southeast Asian J Trop Med Public Health 29:123–127
Rankin JS Jr (1946) Helminth parasites of birds and mammals in western Massachusetts. Am Midl Naturalist 35:756–768
Rayski C, Fahmy MAM (1962) Investigation on some trematodes of birds from the East Scotland. Z Parazitenkd 22:186–195
Richard J (1964) Trématodes d-oiseax de Madagascar (Notes III). Espèces de la familie des Echinostomatidae. Ann Parasitol Hum Comp 34:607–620
Richard J, Brygoo ER (1978) Life cycle of the trematode *Echinostoma caproni* Richard, 1964 (Echinostomatidae). Ann Parasitol Hum Comp 53:265–275
Rim HJ (1982) Echinostomiasis. CRC Handbook Series in Zoonoses, Section C: Parasitic Zoonoses, Vol. III. Trematode Zoonoses. CRC Press Inc., Boca Raton, pp 53–69
Rondelaud D, Vignoles P, Dreyfuss G (2015) Larval trematode infections in *Lymnaea glabra* populations living in the Brenne Regional Natural Park, central France. Parasite 22:38
Rondelaud D, Vignoles P, Dreyfuss G (2016) Larval trematode infections in *Galba truncatula* (Gastropoda, Lymnaeidae) from the Brenne Regional Natural Park, central France. J Helminthol 90:256–261
Ryang YS, Ahn YK, Kim WT et al (1986) Two cases of human infection by *Echinostoma cinetorchis*. Korean J Parasitol 24:71–76 (in Korean)
Saijuntha W, Sithithaworn P, Andrews RH (2010a) Genetic differentiation of *Echinostoma revolutum* and *Hypoderaeum conoideum* from domestic ducks in Thailand by multilocus enzyme electrophoresis. J Helmnthol 84:143–148
Saijuntha W, Tapdara S, Tantrawatpan C (2010b) Multilocus enzyme electrophoresis analysis of *Echinostoma revolutum* and *Echinostoma malayanum* (Trematoda: Echinostomatidae) isolated from Khon Kaen Province, Thailand. Asian Pac J Trop Med 3:633–636
Saijuntha W, Tantrawatpan C, Sithithaworn P et al (2011a) Genetic characterization of *Echinostoma revolutum* and *Echinoparyphium recurvatum* (Trematoda: Echinostomatidae) in Thailand and phylogenetic relationships with other isolates inferred by ITS1 sequence. Parasitol Res 108:751–755
Saijuntha W, Tantrawatpan C, Sithithaworn P et al (2011b) Spatial and temporal genetic variation of *Echinostoma revolutum* (Trematoda: Echinostomatidae) from Thailand and the Lao PDR. Acta Trop 118:105–109
Saijuntha W, Sithithaworn P, Duenngai K et al (2011c) Genetic variation and relationships of four species of medically important echinostomes (Trematoda: Echinostomatidae) in South-East Asia. Infect Gen Evol 118:105–109
Saijuntha W, Duenngai K, Tantrawatpan C et al (2013) Zoonotic echinostome infections in free-grazing ducks in Thailand. Korean J Parasitol 51:663–667

Saito S, Tani S (1982) Comparision of meracercariae of *Echinostoma hortense* Asada, 1926 and *Echinostoma cinetorchis* Ando et Ozaki, 1923 in loach, *Misgurnus anguillicaudatus*. Jpn J Parasitol 31:281–287 (in Japanese)

Sanchaisuriya P, Pongpaew P, Saowakontha S et al (1993) Nutritional health and parasitic infection of rural Thai women of the child bearing age. J Med Assoc Thailand 76:138–145

Sandground JH (1938) On the occurrence of human echinostomiasis in Java. II. The discovery of an endemic focus of infection with *Echinostoma ilocanum* and the elucidation of the parasite's life cycle. Cteneesk Tijdschr v Nederl-Indie 79:1722–1734

Sandground JH (1939) On the occurrence of human echinostomiasis in Java. Preliminary report. Geneesk Tijdschr v Nederl-Indie 79:1497–1503

Sandground JH, Bonne C (1940) *Echinostoma lindoensis* n. sp., a new parasite of man in the Celebes with an account of its life history and epidemiology. Am J Trop Med 20:511–536

Sapp KK, Meyer KA, Loker ES (1998) Intramolluscan development of the digenean *Echinostoma paraensei*: rapid production of a unique mother redia that adversely affects development of conspecific parasites. Invertebr Biol 117:20–28

Sato H, Inaba T, Ihama Y et al (1999) Parasitological survey on wild carnivora in north-western Tohoku, Japan. J Vet Med Sci 61:1023–1026

Schell SC (1970) How to Know the Trematodes. Wm. C. Brown Company Publishers. Dubuque, pp 1–355

Schuster R, Schaffer T, Shimalov V (2002) The helminth fauna of indigenous white storks (*Ciconia ciconia*). Berliner und Munchener Tierarztliche Wochenschrift 115:435–439 (in Germany)

Seo BS, Rim HJ, Lee CW (1964) Studies on the parasitic helminths of Korea. I. Trematodes of rodents. Korean J Parasitol 2:20–26

Seo BS, Cho SY, Chai JY (1980) Studies on intestinal trematodes in Korea I. A human case of *Echinostoma cinetorchis* infection with an epidemiological investigation. Seoul J Med 21:21–29

Seo BS, Cho SY, Hong ST, Hong SJ, Lee SH (1981) Studies on parasitic helminths of Korea. V. Survey on intestinal trematodes of house rats. Korean J Parasitol 19:131–136

Seo BS, Park YH, Chai JY et al (1984) Studies on intestinal trematodes in Korea. XIV. Infection status of loaches with metacercariae of *Echinostoma cinetorchis* and their development in albino rats. Korean J Parasitol 22:181–189

Seo BS, Chun KS, Chai JY et al (1985) Studies on intestinal trematodes in Korea XVII. Development and egg laying capacity of *Echinostoma hortense* in albino rats and human experimental infection. Korean J Parasitol 23:24–32

Shimalov VV, Shimalov VT (2002) Human parasitic echinostomatata (Trematoda, Fasciolidae) in mammals in Belorussian forest zone. Med Parazitol (Mosk) (1):47–50 (in Russian)

Shin EH, Lee SH, Kim JL et al (2007) T-helper-1 and T-helper-2 immune responses in mice infected with the intestinal fluke *Neodiplostomum seoulense*: their possible roles in worm expulsion and host fatality. J Parasitol 93:1036–1045

Sianto L, Duarte AN, Borba VH et al (2016) Echinostomes in felid coprolites from Brazil. J Parasitol 102:385–387

Simonsen PE, Andersen BJ (1986) *Echinostoma revolutum* in mice: Dynamics of the antibody attack to the surface of an intestinal trematode. Int J Parasitol 16:475–482

Simonsen PE, Bindseil E, Køie M (1989) *Echinostoma caproni* in mice: studies on the attachment site of an intestinal trematode. Int J Parasitol 19:561–566

Skrjabin KI, Bashikirova EI (1956) Family Echinostomatidae Dietz, 1909. In: Skrjabin KI (ed) Trematodes and animals and man. Moscow-Leningrad Akademiya Nauk Publishers XII: 51-930 (in Russian)

Sloss B, Meece J, Tomano M, Nollen P (1995) The genetic relationships between *Echinostoma caproni, E. paraensei,* and *E. trivolvis* as determined by electrophoresis. J Helminthol 69:243–246

So K (1955) Studies on the pathogenicity of *Echinostoma cinetorchis*. Okayama Iggaku Zasshi 67:1023–1047 (in Japanese)

Sohn WM, Chai JY (2005) Infection status with helminthes in feral cats purchased from a market in Busan, Republic of Korea. Korean J Parasitol 43:93–100
Sohn WM, Na BK (2017) *Echinostoma macrorchis* (Digenea: Echinostomatidae): metacercariae in *Cipangopaludina chinensis malleata* snails and adults from experimental rats in Korea. Korean J Parasitol 55:541–548
Sohn WM, Chai JY, Yong TS et al (2011a) *Echinostoma revolutum* infection in children, Pursat Province, Cambodia. Emerg Infect Dis 17:117–119
Sohn WM, Kim HJ, Yong TS et al (2011b) *Echinostoma ilocanum* infection in Oddar Meanchey Province, Cambodia. Korean J Parasitol 49:187–190
Sohn WM, Yong TS, Eom KS et al (2012) Prevalence of *Opisthorchis viverrini* infection in humans and fish in Kratie Province, Cambodia. Acta Trop 124:215–220
Sohn WM, Chai JY, Na BK et al (2013) *Echinostoma macrorchis* in Lao PDR: metacercariae in *Cipangopaludina* snails and adults from experimentally infected animals. Korean J Parasitol 51:191–196
Sohn WM, Na BK, Song HJ et al (2014) Intestinal helminthic infections in striped field mice, *Apodemus agrarius*, from two southern regions of Korea. Korean J Parasitol 52:419–423
Son WY, Huh S, Lee SU, Woo HC, Hong SJ (1994) Intestinal trematode infections in the villagers in Koje-myon, Kochang-gun, Kyongsangnam-do, Korea. Korean J Parasitol 32:149–155
Sorensen RE, Minchella DJ (1998) Parasite influences on host life history: *Echinostoma revolutum* parasitism of *Lymnea elodes* snails. Oecologia 115:188–195
Sorensen RE, Kanev I, Fried B, Minchella DJ (1997) The occurrence and identification of *Echinostoma revolutum* from North American *Lymnaea elodes* snails. J Parasitol 83:169–170
Sorensen RE, Curtis J, Minchella DJ (1998) Intraspecific variation in the rDNA ITS loci of 37-collar-spined echinostomes from North America: implications for sequence-based diagnoses and phylogenetics. J Parasitol 84:992–997
Sotillo J, Muñoz-Antoli C, Marcilla A et al (2007) *Echinostoma caproni*: Kinetics of IgM, IgA and IgG subclasses in the serum and intestine of experimentally infected rats and mice. Exp Parasitol 116:390–398
Sotillo J, Valero ML, Del Pino S et al (2010) Excretory/secretory proteome of the adult stage of *Echinostoma caproni*. Parasitol res 107:691–697
Stein PC, Basch PF (1977) Metacercarial cyst formation in vitro of *Echinostoma paraensei*. J Parasitol 63:1031–1040
Sugimoto M (1933) On a trematode parasite (*Echinostoma cinetorchis* Ando and Ozaki, 1923) from a Formosan dog. Nippon Juigakkai Zasshi 12:231–236 (in Japanese)
Taft JL, Fried (1968) Oxygen consumption in adult *Echinostoma revolutum*. Exp Parasitol 23:183–186
Takahashi S (1927) The life cycle of *Echinostoma cinetorchis* and *Echinostoma macrorchis*, particularly their first and second intermediate hosts. Fukuoka Ika Daigaku Zasshi 20:712–723 (in Japanese)
Takahashi S, Ishii T, Ueno N (1930a) A human case of *Echinostoma cinetorchis*. Tokyo Iji Shinshi 2757:141–144 (in Japanese)
Takahashi S, Ishii T, Ueno N (1930b) The second human case of *Echinostoma cinetorchis* and a case of tapeworm in a man. Tokyo Iji Shinshi 2678:1326–1327 (in Japanese)
Tantrawatpan C, Saijuntha W, Sithithaworn P et al (2013) Genetic differentiation of *Artyfechinostomum malayanum* and *A. surfrartyfex* (Trematoda: Echinostomatidae) based on internal transcribed spacer sequences. Parasitol Res 112:437–441
Tesana S, Thabsripair P, Suwannatrai A et al (2014) Parasite surveys and environmental management for prevention of parasitic infection in cultivated *Barbonymus gonionotus* (Cyprinidae) in fishponds, in an opisthorchiasis endemic area of northeast Thailand. Aquaculture 428–429:54–60
Tkach VV, Kudlai O, Kostadinova A (2016) Molecular phylogeny and systematics of the Echinostomatoidea Looss, 1899 (Platyhelminthes: Digenea). Int J Parasitol 46:171–185

Toan PQ, Luc PV, Ha PV (2008) Some supplementary data on parasitic trematode of house rat (*R. flavipectus*) Nghe An, Ha Tinh Provinces and describe to *Centrocestus formosanus* (Heterophyidae) which species the first time found from the rat in Vietnam. Tap chi SINH HOC 31:9–13 (in Vietnamese)

Toledo R, Esteban JG (2016) An update on human echinostomiasis. Trans R Soc Trop Med Hyg 110:37–45

Toledo R, Fried B (2005) Echinostomes as experimental models for interactions between adult parasites and vertebrate hosts. Trends Parasitol 21:251–254

Toledo R, Fried B (2013) Echinostomes. In: Liu D (ed) Molecular detection of human parasitic pathogens. CRC Press-Taylor & Francis Group, Boca Raton, pp 333–342

Toledo R, Muñoz-Antoli C, Esteban JG (2000) The life-cycle of *Echinostoma friedi* n. sp. (Trematoda: Echinostomatidae) in Spain and a discussion on the relationships within the '*revolutum*' group based on cercarial chaetotaxy. Syst Parasitol 45:199–217

Toledo R, Espert A, Carpena et al (2003) An experimental study of the reproductive success of *Echinostoma friedi* (Trematoda: Echinostomatiae) in the golden hamster. Parasitology 126:433–441

Toledo R, Espert A, Carpena et al (2004a) The comparative development of *Echinostoma caproni* (Trematoda: Echinostomatiae) adults in experimentally infected hamsters and rats. Parasitol Res 93:439–444

Toledo R, Espert A, Muñoz-Antoli C et al (2004b) Kinetics of *Echinostoma caproni* (Trematoda: Echinostomatidae) antigens in feces and serum of experimentally infected hamsters and rats. J Parasitol 90:752–758

Toledo R, Espert A, Muñoz-Antoli C et al (2005) Kinetics of antibodies and antigens in serum of mice experimentally infected with *Echinostoma caproni* (Trematoda: Echinostomatidae). J Parasitol 91:978–980

Toledo R, Esteban JG, Fried B (2006a) Immunology and pathology of intestinal trematodes in their definitive hosts. Adv Parasitol 63:285–365

Toledo R, Monteagudo C, Espert A et al (2006b) *Echinostoma caproni*: intestinal pathology in the golden hamster, a highly compatible host, and the Wistar rat, a less compatible host. Exp Parasitol 112:164–171

Toledo R, Esteban JG, Fried B (2009) Recent advances in the biology of echinostomes. Adv Parasitol 69:147–204

Toledo R, Bernal MD, Marcilla A (2011) Proteomics of foodborne trematodes. J Proteomics 74:1485–1503

Toledo R, Radev V, Kanev I et al (2014a) History of echinostomes (Trematoda). Acta Parasitol 59:555–567

Toledo R, Muñoz-Antoli C, Esteban JG (2014b) Intestinal trematode infections. Digenetic Trematodes. Adv Exp Med Biol 766:201–240

Tsuchimochi K (1924) On the life cycle of two species of echinostomatid trematodes. I. Studies on trematodes of domestic fowls in Formosa. Dobutsugaku Zasshi 36:245–259 (in Japanese)

Tubangui MA (1931) Worm parasites of the brown rat (*Mus norvegicus*) in the Philippine Islands, with special reference to those forms that may be transmitted to human beings. Phil J Sci 46:537–589

Vasilev I, Kanev I, Shvetlikovski M et al (1982) Establishment of an echinostome with the features of *Echinostoma lindoense* Sanground et Bonne (1940) (Echinostomatidae: Trematoda) in Poland and Czechoslovakia. Khelmintologiya. http://aims.fao.org/serials/c_1b4a8a25

Voltz A, Richard J, Pesson B (1987) A genetic comparison between natural and laboratory strains of *Echinostoma* (Trematoda) by isoenzymatic analysis. Parasitology 95:471–477

Wang PQ (1977) Description of a new species of Echinostomatidae and Paramphistomata. Bull Fujian Normal Univ 2:62 (in Chinese)

Weinstein MS, Fried B (1991) Expulsion of *Echinostoma trivolvis* and retention of *Echinostoma caproni* in the ICR mouse: pathological effects. Int J Parasitol 21:255–257

Wu G (2013) Human parasitology, 4th edn. Rin Min Hu Sheng Publ Co, Beijing
Yamaguti S (1933) Studies on the helminth founa of Japan. Part 1. Trematodes of birds, reptiles and mammals. Jpn J Zool 5:1–134
Yamaguti S (1934) Studies on the helminth founa of Japan. Part 3. Avian trematodes, II. Jpn J Zool 5:542–583
Yamaguti S (1939a) Studies on the helminth founa of Japan. Part 25. Trematodes of birds, IV. Jpn J Zool 8:129–210
Yamaguti S (1939b) Studies on the helminth founa of Japan. Part 27. Trematodes of mammals, II. Jpn. J Med Sci (VI. Bacteriol Parasitol) 1:131–153
Yamaguti S (1958) Systema Helminthum. Vol. I. The digenetic trematodes of vertebrates (Part I). Interscience Publishers Inc, New York, pp 1–979
Yamaguti S (1971) Synopsis of digenetic trematodes of vertebrates, vol I. Keigaku Publishing Co., Tokyo, pp 1–1074
Yamashita J (1964) Echinostome. In: Progress of medical parasitology in Japan, vol 1. Meguro Parasitological Museum, Tokyo, pp 287–313
Yokohata Y, Abe H, Jiang YP (1989) Gastrointestinal helminth fauna of Japanese moles, *Mogera* spp. Jpn J Vet Res 37:1–13
Yong TS, Shin EH, Chai JY et al (2012) High prevalence of *Opisthorchis viverrini* infection in a riparian population in Takeo Province, Cambodia. Korean J Parasitol 50:173–176
Yousuf MA, Das PM, Anisuzzaman et al (2009) Gastro-intestinal helminths of ducks: some epidemiologic and pathologic aspects. J Bangladesh Agric Univ 7:91–97
Yu SH, Mott KE (1994) Epidemiology and morbidity of food-borne intestinal trematode infections. Trop Dis Bull 91:R125–R152
Żbikowski J, Żbikowska E (2009) Invaders of an invader-trematodes in *Potamopyrgus antipodarum* in Poland. J Inverteb Pathol 101:67–70
Zhan XD, Li CP, Yang BH et al (2017) Investigation on the zoonotic trematode species and their natural infection status in Huainan areas of China. Nutr Hosp 34:175–179

References for Section 2.3

Ahn YK, Ryang YS (1986) Experimental and epidemiological studies on the life cycle of *Echinostoma hortense* Asada, 1926 (trematode: Echinostomatidae). Korean J Parasitol 24:121–136 (in Korean)
Ahn YK, Kang HS (1988) Development and cercarial shedding of *Echinostoma hortense* in the snail host, *Radix auricularia coreana*. J Wonju Med Coll 1:137–152 (in Korean)
Ahn YK, Ryang YS, Chung PR et al (1985) *Echinostoma hortense* metacercariae naturally encysted in *Odontobutis obscura interrupta* (a freshwater fish) and experimental infection to rats. Korean J Parasitol 23:230–235 (in Korean)
Arizono N, Uemoto K, Kondo K et al (1976) Studies on *Echinostoma hortense* Asada, 1926 with special reference to its human infection. Jpn J Parasitol 25:36–45 (in Japanese)
Asada J (1926) A new echinostomatid trematode and its life history. Trans Jpn Soc Pathol 16:293–294 (in Japanese)
Asada J (1939) A new species of a trematode belonging to the family Echinostomatidae and its life cycle. Eiseidobutsu (A Jubilee Number of Prof. Dr. Yoshida):39–69 (in Japanese)
Barsiene J, Kiseliene V (1991) Karyological studies of trematodes within the genus *Echinostoma*. Acta Parasitol Pol 36:23–29
Bashikirova EI (1947) Echinostomatidae. In: Skrjabin KI (ed) Trematodes and animals and man, vol 1. Akademiya Nauk Publishers, Moscow-Leningrad, pp 246–305
Beaver PC (1941) Studies on the life history of *Euparyphium melis* (Trematoda: Echinostomatidae). J Parasitol 27:35–44
Beaver PC, Jung RC, Cupp EW (1984) Clinical parasitology, 9th edn. Lea and Febiger, Philadelphia

Besprozvannykh VV (2001) The structure and life cycle of trematodes *Euparyphium melis* and *Euparyphium amurensis* sp. n. (Echinostomatidae) from Primorye. Zoolologicheskii Zhurnal 80:5–11 (in Russian)

Brunet IR, Joseph S, Dunne DW et al (2000) Immune responses during the acute stage of infection with the intestinal trematode *Echinostoma caproni*. Parasitology 120:565–571

Chai JY (2007) Intestinal flukes. In: Murrell KD, Fried B (eds) Food-borne parasitic zoonoses. Fish and plant-borne parasites. Springer, New York, pp 53–115

Chai JY (2009) Echinostomes in humans. In: Fried B, Toledo R (eds) The biology of echinostomes. Springer, New York, pp 147–183

Chai JY (2015) Chapter 19. Echinostomes. In: Xiao L, Ryan U, Feng Y (eds) Biology of foodborne parasites. CRC Press, Taylor & Francis Group, Boca Raton, pp 427–443

Chai JY, Lee SH (2002) Food-borne intestinal trematode infections in the Republic of Korea. Parasitol Int 51:129–154

Chai JY, Hong SJ, Sohn WM et al (1985a) Studies on intestinal trematode in Korea XVI. Infection status of loaches with the metacercariae of *Echinostoma hortense*. Korean J Parasitol 23:18–23

Chai JY, Hong SJ, Son DW et al (1985b) Metacercariae of the *Echinochasmus japonicus* encysted in a freshwater fish, *Pseudorasbora parva*, and their development in experimental mice. Korean J Parasitol 23:221–229

Chai JY, Hong ST, Lee SH et al (1994) A case of echinostomiasis with ulcerative lesions in the duodenum. Korean J Parasitol 32:201–204

Chai JY, Han ET, Park YK et al (2001) *Acanthoparyphium tyosenense*: the discovery of human infection and identification of its source. J Parasitol 87:794–800

Chai JY, Shin EH, Lee SH et al (2009) Foodborne intestinal flukes in Southeast Asia. Korean J Parasitol 47(suppl):S69–S102

Chang YD, Sohn WM, Ryu JH et al (2005) A human infection of *Echinostoma hortense* in duodenal bulb diagnosed by endoscopy. Korean J Parasitol 43:57–60

Chen HT, Chen S, Chu H et al (1985) Chapter 5. Echinostomatidae Dietz, 1909. Platyhelminthes, Trematoda, Digenea (1). Fauna Sinica. Science Press, Beijing, pp 333–403

Chen YZ, Feng GX, Qian ZF et al (1993) A preliminary survey on infection with *Echinostoma hortense* in Liaoning province. Chin J Parasitol Parasit Dis 11:226 (in Chinese)

Cho CM, Tak WY, Kweon YO et al (2003) A human case of *Echinostoma hortense* (Trematoda: Echinostomatidae) infection diagnosed by gastroduodenal endoscopy in Korea. Korean J Parasitol 41:117–120

Cho SY, Kang SY, Ryang YS (1981) Helminthes infections in the small intestine of stray dogs in Ejungbu City, Kyunggi Do, Korea. Korean J Parasitol 19:55–59 (in Korean)

Cho YK, Ryang YS, Kim IS et al (2007) Differential immune profiles following experimental *Echinostoma hortense* infection in BALB/c and C3H/HeN mice. Parasitol Res 100:1053–1061

Cross JH (1974) Diagnostic methods in intestinal fluke infections: a review. SEAMEO-TROPMED technical meeting: diagnostic methods for important helminthiasis and amoebiasis in Southeast Asia and the Far East, Tokyo, 5–8 February 1974. pp 87–108

Churchill HM (1950) Germ cell cycle of *Echinostoma revolutum* (Froelich, 1802). J Parasitol 36(6 suppl):15

Dietz E (1909) Die Echinostomiden der Vögel. Zoologischer Anzeiger 34:180–192

Dönges J (1967) The modifying effect of the final host on the development of the intestinal fluke *Isthmiophora melis* (Schrank, 1788). A rehabitation of the genus *Isthmiophora* Luhe, 1909 (Trematoda: Echinostomatidae). Z Parasitenkd 35:169–172 (in Germany)

Dönges J (1970) The modifying effect of the final host on the development of the intestinal fluke *Isthmiophora melis* (Schrank, 1788). III. The development in the brown rat (*Rattus norvegicus*), a natural final host. Z Parasitenkd 35:169–172 (in Germany)

Dönges J (1971) The potential number of redial generations in echinostomatids (Trematoda). Int J Parasitol 1:51–59

Dönges J, Götzelmann M (1975) *Isthmiophora melis* (Trematoda: Echinostomatidae): normal adults after 41 snail passages in 7 years of redial transplantation. Int J Parasitol 5:421–422

Dönges J, Götzelmann M (1977) *Isthmiophora melis*; experimental reinfection of *Lymnaea stagnalis* by implantation of miracidia after implantation of rediae. Exp Parasitol 42:318–321
Fan SQ, Sun MF (1989) A case of *Echinostoma hortense* first found in the human body in China and morphological observation of the worm. J Harbin Med Univ 23:161–163 (in Chinese)
Fried B (2001) Biology of echinostomes except *Echinostoma*. Adv Parasitol 49:163–210
Fried B, Fujino T (1984) Scanning electron microscopy of *Echinostoma revolutum* (Trematoda) during development in the chick embryo and domestic chick. Int J Parasitol 14:75–81
Fried B, Graczyk TK, Tamang L (2004) Food-borne intestinal trematodiases in humans. Parasitol Res 93:159–170
Fujino T, Fried B (1993) Expulsion of *Echinostoma trivolvis* (Cort, 1914) Kanev, 1985 and retention of *E. caproni* Richard, 1964 (Trematoda: Echinostomatidae) in C3H mice: pathological, ultrastructural, and cytochemical effects on the host intestine. Parasitol Res 79:286–292
Fujino T, Fried B, Tada I (1993) The expulsion of *Echinostoma trivolvis*: worm kinetics and intestinal cytopathology in conventional and congenitally athymic BALB/c mice. Parasitology 106:297–304
Grabda-Kazubska B, Lakowski Z (1996) On the morphology and chaetotaxy of rediae and cercariae of *Isthmiophora melis* (Schrank, 1788) (Trematoda, Echinostomatidae). Acta Parasitol 4:7–12
Gupta SP (1962) A redescription of *Euparyphium melis* (Schrank, 1788) Dietz, 1909 and *Echinostoma revolutum* (Froelich, 1802) Looss, 1899 parasitic in the intestine of mink (*Mustela visoni*) and muskrat (*Ondatra zibethica*) from Canada. Indian J Helminthol 14:77–85
Hamamoto T, Kawasaki H, Maejima J et al (1997) A case of *Echinostoma hortense* infection diagnosed by the upper gastrointestinal endoscopy. Nippon Shokkibyo Gakkai Zasshi 94:487–491 (in Japanese)
Harada H, Yamaguchi K, Yoshida Y et al (1983) *Echinostoma hortense* infection diagnosed by the endoscopical examination. Gastroenterol Endosc 25:622–627 (in Japanese)
Harinasuta T, Bunnag D, Radomyos P (1987) Intestinal fluke infections. Bailliere's Clin Trop Med Commun Dis 2(3):695–721
Hildebrand J, Adamczyk M, Laskowski Z et al (2015) Host-dependent morphology of *Isthmiophora melis* (Schrank, 1788) Luhe, 1909 (Digenea, Echinostomatidae)-morphological variation vs. molecular stability. Parasit Vectors 8:481
Hsü HF (1940) *Euparyphium jassyense* Leon and Ciurea (= *E. melis* (Schrank)) found at the auropsy of a Chinese. Chin Med J 58:552–555
Huffman JE, Michos C, Fried B (1986) Clinical and pathological effects of *Echinostoma revolutum* (Digenea: Echinostomatidae) in the golden hamster, *Mesocricetus auratus*. Parasitology 93:505–515
Isaacson AC, Huffman JH, Fried B (1989) Infection, growth, development and pathology of *Echinostoma caproni* (Trematoda) in the golden hamster. Int J Parasitol 19:943–955
Ivanov VM, Semenova NN (2000) Parasitological consequences of animal introduction. Russ J Ecol 31:281–283
Kamiya H, Ishigaki K (1972) Helminths of Mustelidae in Hokkaido. Jpn J Vet Res 20:117–128
Kifune T, Takao Y (1973) Description of *Psilorchis hominis* sp. nov. from man (Trematoda: Echinostomatidae: Psilostomidae). Jpn J Parasitol 22:111–115
Kim DC, Cho SS (1996) A case report of *Echinostoma hortense* infection. Korean J Clin Pathol Med Exam 28:222–225 (in Korean)
Kim I, Im JA, Lee KJ et al (2000) Mucosal mast cell reponses in the small intestine of rats infected with *Echinostoma hortense*. Korean J Parasitol 38:139–143
Komiya Y (1965) Metacercariae in Japan and adjacent territories. In: Progress of medical parasitology in Japan, vol 2. Meguro Parasitological Museum, Tokyo, pp 1–328
Korol EN, Varodi EI, Kornyushin VV et al (2016) Helminths of wild predatory mammals (Mammalia, Carnivora) of Ukraine. Trematodes. Vestnik Zoologii 50:301–308
Kostadinova A (2005a) Family Echinostomatidae Looss, 1899. In: Jones A, Bray RA, Gibson DI (eds) Keys to the trematoda, vol 2. Natural History Museum, London, pp 9–64

Kostadinova A (2005b) Family Psilostomidae Looss, 1900. In: Jones A, Bray RA, Gibson DI (eds) Keys to the trematoda, vol 2. Natural History Museum, London, pp 99–118

Kostadinova A, Gibson DI (2002) *Isthmiophora* Lühe, 1909 and *Euparyphium* Dietz, 1909 (Digenea: Echinostomatidae) re-defined, with comments on their nominal species. Syst Parasitol 52:205–217

Kostadinova A, Herniou EA, Barrett J et al (2003) Phylogenetic relationships of *Echinostoma* Rudolphi, 1809 (Digenea: Echinostomatidae) and related genera re-assessed via DNA and morphological analyses. Syst Parasitol 54:159–176

Kudlai O, Tkach VV, Pulis EE et al (2015) Redescription and phylogenetic relationships of *Euparyphium cpitaneum* Dietz, 1909, the type-species of *Euparyphium* Dietz, 1909 (Digenea: Echinostomatidae). Syst Parasitol 90:53–65

Law RG, Kennedy AH (1932) Parasites of fur-bearing animals. Bull Department of Game Fisher (Ontario, Canada) No. 4:30

Lee OJ, Hong SJ (2002) Gastric echinostomiasis diagnosed by endoscopy. Gastroint Endosc 55:440–442

Lee SH, Hong SJ, Chai JY et al (1986a) Tegumental ultrastructures of *Echinostoma hortense* observed by scanning electron microscopy. Korean J Parasitol 24:63–70 (in Korean)

Lee SK, Chung NS, Ko IH et al (1986b) Two cases of natural human infection by *Echinostoma hortense*. Korean J Parasitol 24:77–81 (in Korean)

Lee SK, Chung NS, Ko IH et al (1988) An epidemiological survey of *Echinostoma hortense* infection in Chongsong-gun, Kyongbuk Province. Korean J Parasitol 26:199–206

Lee SH, Noh TY, Sohn WM et al (1990) Chronological observation of intestinal lesions of rats experimentally infected with *Echinostoma hortense*. Korean J Parasitol 28:45–52 (in Korean)

Lee SH, Hwang SW, Sohn WM et al (1991) Experimental life history of *Echinostoma hortense*. Korean J Parasitol 29:161–172 (in Korean)

Lee KJ, Park SK, Im JA et al (2004) Susceptibility of several strains of mice to *Echinostoma hortense* infection. Korean J Parasitol 42:51–56

Lee KJ, Jin D, Chang BS et al (2009) The immunological effects of electrolyzed reduced water on the *Echinostoma hortense* infection in C57BL/6 mice. Biol Pharm Bull 32:456–462

Lee D, Choe S, Park H et al (2013) Complete mitochondrial genome of *Haplorchis taichui* and comparative analysis with other trematodes. Korean J Parasitol 51:719–726

Liu XQ, Shi HH (2011) Two cases infected by *Echinostoma hortense* in Guangxi. Chin J Parasitol Parasit Dis 29:77 (in Chinese)

Liu ZX, Zhang Y, Liu YT et al (2016) Complete mitochondrial genome of *Echinostoma hortense* (Digenea: Echinostomatidae). Korean J Parasitol 54:173–179

Loy C, Motzel W, Haas W (2001) Photo- and geo-orientation by echinostome cercariae results in habitat selection. J Parasitol 87:505–509

Lühe M (1909) Parasitische Plattwurmer. I. Trematodes. In: Brauer A (ed) Die Süsswasserfauna Deuschlands. Eine exkursionfauna. Part 17. Jena, Gustav Fischer, 217 pp

Makino Y, Nakagawa A, Yamane Y et al (1982) A human case of echinostomiasis in Shimane Prefecture and experimental infection in rats. Jpn J Parasitol 31:385–390 (in Japanese)

Matskási I (1971) The trematode fauna of rodents and insectivora (Mammalia) in Hungary I. Parasit Hung 4:125–136

Mendheim H (1943) Beiträge zur Systematic und Biologie der Familie Echinostomatidae (Trematoda). Archiv für Naturgeschichte 12:175–302

Miyamoto K, Nakao M, Inaoka T (1983) Studies on the zoonoses in Hokkaido, Japan. 5. On the epidemiological survey of *Echinostoma hortense* Asada, 1926. Jpn J Parasitol 32:261–269 (in Japanese)

Morgan JA, Blair D (1998a) Relative merits of nuclear ribosomal internal transcribed spacers and mitochondrial CO1 and ND1 genes for distinguishing among *Echinostoma* species (Trematoda). Parasitology 116:289–297

Morgan JA, Blair D (1998b) Mitochondrial ND1 gene sequences used to identify echinostome isolates from Australia and New Zealand. Int J Parasitol 28:493–502

Motzel W, Haas W (1985) Studies on the attachment response of *Isthmiophora melis* cercariae (Trematoda: Echinostomatidae). Z Parasitenkd 71:519–526

Mustafova T, Kanev I, Eizenhut U (1991) Karyological studies of *Isthmiophora melis* (Schrank, 1788) from its type locality. J Helminthol 65:255–258

Nicoll W (1923) A reference list of the trematode parasites of British mammals. Parasitology 15:236–252

Nugaraitė D, Mažeika V, Paulauskas A (2017) Molecular and morphological characterization of *Isthmiophora melis* (Schrank, 1788) Luhe, 1909 (Digenea: Echinostomatidae) from American mink (*Neovison vison*) and European polecat (*Mustela putorius*) in Lithuania. Helminthologia 54:97–104

Okahashi K (1966) Researches on *Heterophyes* (2) *Metagonimus yokogawai* parasitic on the loach: its infection test on birds and its adult form. Okayama Igakkai Zasshi 78:15–24 (in Japanese)

Okamoto F (1954) Distinguishing characteristics between *Echinostoma hortense* Asada, 1926 and *Echinostoma campi* Ono, 1930. Jpn J Parasitol 3:117–118 (in Japanese)

Okanishi H, Matsumoto J, Nogami S et al (2013) *Echinostoma hortense* infection with enteritis diagnosed by upper gastrointestinal endoscopy in a dog. J Vet Med Sci 75:991–994

Ono S (1930) The life history of *Echinostoma campi* n. sp. found in the vicinity of Mukden, with special reference to the second intermediate host. Dobutsugakku Zasshi 42:7–16 (in Japanese)

Park JT (1938) A rat trematode, *Echinostoma hortense* Asada, from Korea. Keijo J Med 9:283–286

Park CJ, Kim J (2006) A human case of *Echinostoma hortense* infection diagnosed by endoscopy in area of southwestern Korea. Korean J Med 71:229–234 (in Korean)

Park KY, Lee KJ, Kim IS et al (2005) Reaction of mast cells and goblet cells in the small intestine of C57BL/6 and C3H/HeN mice infected with *Echinostoma hortense*. J Exp Biomed Sci 11:259–266

Qiu JH, Zhang Y, Zhang XX et al (2017) Metacercaria infection status of fishborne zoonotic trematode, except for *Clonorchis sinensis* in fish from the Heilongjiang Province, China. Foodborne Pathog Dis 14. https://doi.org/10.1089/fpd.2016.2249

Radev V, Kanev I, Khrusanov D et al (2009) Reexaminaion of the life cycle of *Isthmiophora melis* (Trematoda: Echinostomatidae) on material from a southeast Europe. Parazitologiia 43:445–453

Rhee JK, Rim BM (1970) Observation on the infection rate of helminths in Korean autochthonal dogs with special reference to the viewpoint of public health. Chon-Puk Nat Univ Theses Coll 12:27–38 (in Korean)

Rim HJ (1982) Echinostomiasis. CRC Handbook Series in Zoonoses, Section C: Parasitic Zoonoses, Vol. III. Trematode Zoonoses. CRC Press Inc., Boca Raton, pp 53–69

Ryang YS (1990) Studies on *Echinostoma* spp. in the Chungju Reservoir and upper streams of the Namhan River. Korean J Parasitol 28:221–233 (in Korean)

Ryang YS, Ahn YK, Lee KW et al (1985) Two cases of natural human infection by *Echinostoma hortense* and its second intermediate host in Wonju area. Korean J Parasitol 23:33–40 (in Korean)

Ryang YS, Yang EJ, Kim JL et al (2007) Immune response and inhibitory effect of ketotifen on the BALB/c and C3H/HeN mice infected with *Echinostoma hortense*. Parasitol Res 101:1103–1110

Saito S (1984) Development of *Echinostoma hortense* in rats, with special reference to the genital organs. Jpn J Parasitol 33:191–201

Saito S, Tani S (1982) Comparison of metacercariae of *Echinostoma hortense* Asada, 1926 and *Echinostoma cinetorchis* Ando et Ozaki, 1923 in loach, *Misgurnus anguillicaudatus*. Jpn J Parasitol 31:281–287 (in Japanese)

Sato H, Suzuki K (2006) Gastrointestinal helminths of feral raccoons (*Procyon lotor*) in Wakayama Prefecture, Japan. J Vet Med Sci 68:311–318

Sato H, Inaba T, Ihama Y et al (1999) Parasitological survey on wild carnivora in north-western Tohoku, Japan. J Vet Med Sci 61:1023–1026

Sato H, Suzuki K, Osanai A et al (2006) Identification and characterization of the threadworm, *Strongyloides procyonis*, from feral raccoons (*Procyon lotor*) in Japan. J Parasitol 92:63–68

Seo BS, Rim HJ, Lee CW (1964) Studies on the parasitic helminths of Korea. I. Trematodes of rodents. Korean J Parasitol 2:20–26

Seo BS, Cho SY, Chai JY (1980) Studies on intestinal trematodes in Korea I. A human case of *Echinostoma cinetorchis* infection with an epidemiological investigation. Seoul J Med 21:21–29

Seo BS, Cho SY, Hong ST et al (1981) Studies on parasitic helminths of Korea. V. Survey on intestinal trematodes of house rats. Korean J Parasitol 19:131–136

Seo BS, Hong ST, Chai JY et al (1983) Studies on intestinal trematodes in Korea. VII. A human case of *Echinostoma hortense* infection. Korean J Parasitol 21:219–223

Seo BS, Park YH, Chai JY et al (1984) Studies on intestinal trematodes in Korea. XIV. Infection status of loaches with metacercariae of *Echinostoma cinetorchis* and their development in albino rats. Korean J Parasitol 22:181–189

Seo BS, Chun KS, Chai JY et al (1985) Studies on intestinal trematodes in Korea. XVII. Development and egg laying capacity of *Echinostoma hortense* in albino rats and human experimental infection. Korean J Parasitol 23:24–32

Shimalov VV, Shimalov VT (2001) Helminth fauna of the American mink (*Mustela vison* Schreber, 1777) in Belorussian Polesie. Parasitol Res 87:886–887

Shimalov VV, Shimalov VT (2002a) Human parasitic echinostomatata (Trematoda, Fasciolidae) in mammals in Belorussian forest zone. Med Parazitol (Mosk) 1:47–50 (in Russian)

Shimalov VV, Shimalov VT (2002b) Helminth fauna of the European polecat (*Mustela putorius* Linnaeus, 1758) in Belorussian Polesie. Parasitol Res 88:259–260

Shin SS, Oh DS, Ahn KS et al (2015) Zoonotic intestinal trematodes in stray cats (*Felis catus*) from riverside areas of the Republic of Korea. Korean J Parasitol 53:29–213

Skrjabin KI, Bashikirova EI (1956) Family Echinostomatidae Dietz, 1909. In: Skrjabin KI (ed) Trematodes and animals and man, vol XII. Akademiya Nauk Publishers, Moscow-Leningrad, pp 51–930 (in Russian)

Smales LR, Blankespoor HD (1984) *Echinostoma revolutum* (Froelich, 1802) Looss, 1899 and *Isthmiophora melis* (Schrank, 1788) Luhe, 1909 (Echinostomatinae, Digenea): scanning electron microscopy of the tegumental surfaces. J Helminthol 58:187–195

Sohn WM, Chai JY (2005) Infection status with helminthes in feral cats purchased from a market in Busan, Republic of Korea. Korean J Parasitol 43:93–100

Sohn WM, Na BK, Cho SH (2009) *Echinostoma hortense* and heterophyid metacercariae in yellowfin goby, *Acanthogobius flavimanus*, from Shinan-gun and Muan-gun (Jeollanam-do, Korea). Korean J Parasitol 47:307–310

Sohn WM, Na BK, Song HJ et al (2014) Intestinal helminthic infections in striped field mice, *Apodemus agrarius*, from two southern regions of Korea. Korean J Parasitol 52:419–423

Sohn WM, Na BK, Shin SS (2017) New definitive hosts and differential body indices of *Isthmiophora hortensis* (Digenea: Echinostomatidae). Korean J Parasitol 55:287–294

Sohn WM, Na BK, Cho SH et al (2018) Infections with zoonotic trematode metacercariae in yellow goby, *Acanthogobius flavimanus*, from coastal areas of Republic of Korea. Korean J Parasitol 56:259–265

Soltys A (1962) Helminth parasites of Mustelidae of the Lublin Palatinate. Acta Parasitol Pol 10:73–76

Son WY, Huh S, Lee SU et al (1994) Intestinal trematode infections in the villagers in Koje-myon, Kochang-gun, Kyongsangnam-do, Korea. Korean J Parasitol 32:149–155

Sugár L, Matskási I (1962) Occurrence of *Isthmiophora melis* (Schrank, 1788) and *Alaria alata* (Goeze, 1782) in wild carnivora in Hungary. Parasit Hung 11:142 (in Hungarian)

Tanaka T, Kamada T, Koga H et al (2008) *Echinostoma hortense* Asada infection in the duodenum: incidental findings during routine gastrointestinal endoscopy. Digest Endosc 20:87–89

Tani S (1976a) Studies on *Echinostoma hortense* Asada, 1926 (1) Species identification of human echinostomiasis and its infection source. Jpn J Parasitol 25:262–273 (in Japanese)

Tani S (1976b) Studies on *Echinostoma hortense* Asada, 1926 (2) The intermediate and final hosts in Akita Prefecture. Jpn J Parasitol 25:461–467 (in Japanese)

Tani S (1976c) Studies on *Echinostoma hortense* Asada, 1926 (3) Experimental infection in man and laboratory animals. Jpn J Parasitol 25:495–501 (in Japanese)

Tani S (1979) Studies on *Echinostoma hortense* Asada, 1926 (4) Variation of egg count, peripheral eosinophils and antibodies in human volunteers experimentally infected with *E. hortense*. Jpn J Parasitol 28:57–62 (in Japanese)

Tani S, Yoshimura K (1988) Spontaneous expulsion of *Echinostoma hortense* Asada, 1926 (Trematoda: Echinostomatidae). Parasitol Res 74:495–497

Tani S, Yoshimura H, Ohmori Y et al (1974) A case of human echinostomiasis found in Akita Prefecture, Japan. Jpn J Parasitol 23:404–408 (in Japanese)

Terasaki K, Moriyama N, Tani S et al (1982) Comparative studies on the karyotypes of *Echinostoma cinetorchis* and *E. hortense* (Echinostomatidae: Trematoda). Jpn J Parasitol 31:569–574

Tkach V, Pawlowski J, Mariaux J (2000) Phylogenetic analysis of the suborder Plagiorchiata (Platyhelminthes, Digenea) based on partical lsrDNA sequences. Int J Parasitol 30:83–93

Toledo R, Fried B (2005) Echinostomes as experimental models for interactions between adult parasites and vertebrate hosts. Trends Parasitol 21:251–254

Toledo R, Muñoz-Antoli C, Sánchez et al (1998) Cercarial chaetotaxy of *Euparyphium albuferensis* Esteban et al., 1997 (Trematoda: Echinostomatidae), with a review of some genera of the Echinostomatinae. Syst Parasitol 39:35–44

Toledo R, Esteban JG, Fried B (2006a) Immunology and pathology of intestinal trematodes in their definitive hosts. Adv Parasitol 63:285–365

Toledo R, Monteagudo C, Espert A et al (2006b) *Echinostoma caproni*: intestinal pathology in the golden hamster, a highly compatible host, and the Wistar rat, a less compatible host. Exp Parasitol 112:164–171

Torres J, Miquel J, Fournier P et al (2008) Helminth communities of the autochthonous mustelids *Mustela lutreola* and *M. putorius* and the introduced *Mustela vision* in south-western France. J Helminthol 82:349–355

Yamaguti S (1933) Studies on the helminth founa of Japan. Part 1. Trematodes of birds, reptiles and mammals. Jpn J Zool 5:1–134

Yamaguti S (1939) Studies on the helminth founa of Japan. Part 27. Trematodes of mammals, II. Jpn J Med Sci (VI. Bacteriol Parasitol) 1:131–153

Yamaguti S (1941) Zur Entwicklungsgeschichte von *Echinostoma hortense* Asada, 1926, mit besonderer Berücksichtigung der Structur der Caercarie. Z Parasitenkd 12:273–276 (in Germany)

Yamaguti S (1958) Systema Helminthum. Vol. I. The digenetic trematodes of vertebrates (Part I). Interscience Publishers Inc, New York, pp 1–979

Yamaguti S (1971) Synopsis of digenetic trematodes of vertebrates, vol I. Keigaku Publishing Co., Tokyo, pp 1–1074

Yu SH, Mott KE (1994) Epidemiology and morbidity of food-borne intestinal trematode infections. Trop Dis Bull 91:R125–R152

Zhan XD, Li CP, Yang BH et al (2017) Investigation on the zoonotic trematode species and their natural infection status in Huainan areas of China. Nutr Hosp 34:175–179

Zschille J, Heidecke D, Stubbe M (2004) Distribution and ecology of feral American mink *Mustela vision* Schreber, 1777 (Carnivora, Mustelidae) in Saxony-Anhalt. Hercynia 37:103–126 (in Germany)

References for Section 2.4

Abdel Azim M (1938) On the intestinal helminths of dogs in Egypt. J Egypt Med Assoc 21:118–122

Abdel Azim M (1939) Helminthes Parasites des Chiens et des Chats en Egypte. Ann Parasitol 17:32–36

Abe T (1941) Studies on metacercariae of trematodes parasitic in *Rhodeus lanceolata* (2nd report). Kinds of metacercariae and location of infections in *R. lanceolata*. Okayama Igakkai Zasshi 53:1206–1219 (in Japanese)

Abou-Eisha AM, Saleh RE, Fadel HM et al (2008) Role of freshwater fishes in the epidemiology of some zoonotic trematodes in Ismailia Province. SCVMJ 13:653–673

Acharijyo LN (2004) Helminthiasis in captive wild carnivores and its control in India. Zoos' Print J 19:1540–1543

Al-Sabi MNS, Halasa T, Kapel CMO (2014) Infections with cardiopulmonary and intestinal helminths and sarcoptic mange in red foxes from two different localities in Denmark. Acta Parasitol 59:98–107

Anh NTL, Phuong NT, Johansen MV et al (2009a) Prevalence and risks for fishborne zoonotic trematode infections in domestic animals in a highly endemic area of North Vietnam. Acta Trop 112:198–203

Anh NTL, Phuong NT, Murrell KD et al (2009b) Animal reservoir hosts and fish-borne zoonotic trematode infections on fish farms, Vietnam. Emerg Infect Dis 15:540–546

Bang NP, Cuong TP (2015) A potential risk from dog helminths for human health and some update information. J Sci An Giang Univ (Part C. Agricult Sci Fisher Biotechnol) 3:76–90

Barsiene J, Kiseliene V (1990) Karyological studies of trematodes within the families Psilostomidae and Echinochasmidae. Helminthologia 27:99–108

Bashikirova EI (1947) Family Echinostomatidae Dietz, 1909. In: Skrjabin KI (ed) Trematodes and animals and man, vol 1. Akademiya Nauk Publishers, Moscow, pp 310–391

Beaver PC, Jung RC, Cupp EW (1984) Clinical parasitology, 9th edn. Lea and Febiger, Philadelphia

Besprozvannykh VV (2009) Life cycle of trematodes *Echinochasmus japonicus* Tanabe, 1926 and *E. beleocephalus* (Linstow, 1873) (Echinostomatidae) in Prymorye Region. Parazitologia 43:248–258 (in Russian)

Besprozvannykh VV, Ngo HD, Ha NV et al (2013) Descriptions of digenean parasites from three snail species, *Bithynia fuchsiana* (Morelet), *Parafossarulus striatulus* Benson and *Melanoides tuberculata* Muller, in North Vietnam. Helminthologia 50:190–204

Bhalerao GD (1935) Helminth parasites of the domesticated animals in India. ICAR Sci Monogr no. 6, p 365

Bhalerao GD (1936) Studies on the helminths of India. Trematoda III. J Helminthol 14:207–228

Chai JY (2007) Intestinal flukes. In: Murrell KD, Fried B (eds) Food-borne parasitic zoonoses. Fish and plant-borne parasites. Springer, New York, pp 53–115

Chai JY (2009) Echinostomes in humans. In: Fried B, Toledo R (eds) The biology of echinostomes. Springer, New York, pp 147–183

Chai JY (2015) Chapter 19. Echinostomes. In: Xiao L, Ryan U, Feng Y (eds) Biology of foodborne parasites. CRC Press, Taylor & Francis Group, Boca Raton, pp 427–443

Chai JY, Lee SH (2002) Food-borne intestinal trematode infections in the Republic of Korea. Parasitol Int 51:129–154

Chai JY, Hong SJ, Son DW et al (1985) Metacercariae of the *Echinochasmus japonicus* encysted in a freshwater fish, *Pseudorasbora parva*, and their development in experimental mice. Korean J Parasitol 23:221–229 (in Korean)

Chai JY, Shin EH, Lee SH et al (2009a) Foodborne intestinal flukes in Southeast Asia. Korean J Parasitol 47(suppl):S69–S102

Chai JY, Park JH, Jung BK et al (2009b) Echinostome infections in the striped-field mouse, *Apodemus agrarius*, and the Ussuri white-toothed shrew, *Crocidura lassiura*, caught near the demilitarized zone, Gyeonggi-do (province), Republic of Korea. Korean J Parasitol 47:311–314

Chai JY, Sohn WM, Yong TS et al (2012) Echinostome flukes recovered from humans in Khammouane Province, Lao PDR. Korean J Parasitol 50:269–272

Chai JY, Bahk YY, Sohn WM (2013) Trematodes recovered in the small intestine of stray cats in the Republic of Korea. Korean J Parasitol 51:99–106

Chandler AC (1925) The helminth parasites of cats in Calcutta and the relation of cats to human helminthic infection. Indian J Med Res 13:213–227

Chebotarev RS, Zaskind LN, Kubenko AL (1960) *Echinochasmus* infection of pigs. Trudy Nauchno-Issledovatelskogo Vet Inst 1:21–203 (in Russian)

Chen HT (1934) Helminths of dogs in Canton, with a list of those occurring in China. Lingnan Sci J 13:75–87

Chen SL, Yang QR (1988) Investigations on species and distribution of human parasites in Hubei Province, Peoples' Republic of China. J Central China Normal Univ 32:470–475 (in Chinese)

Chen HT, Chen S, Chu H et al (1985) Chapter 5. Echinostomatidae Dietz, 1909. Platyhelminthes, Trematoda, Digenea (1). Fauna Sinica. Science Press, Beijing, pp 333–403

Chen BJ, Li LS, Xie HG et al (2013) Morphology and characteristics of five types of Echinostomatidae in Fujian. J Pathog Biol 8:204–202 (in Chinese)

Cheng YZ, Fang YY (1989) The discovery of *Melanoides tuberculuta* as the first intermediate host of *Echinochasmus japonicus*. Chin J Parasitol Parasit Dis 7:47–48 (in Chinese)

Cheng YD, Ye LY (1988) A survey of parasitic helminths in wild *Nyctereutes procyonoides*. Chin J vet Sci Technol 8:25–27 (in Chinese)

Cheng YZ, Lin JX, Wang XP et al (1986) A survey of the freshwater fishes harbouring metacercariae of *Echinochasmus japonicus* and animal experimentation. Chin J Zoon 2:13–16 (in Chinese)

Cheng YZ, Lin JX, Fang YY (1990) Ecological studies on the cercariae of *Echinochasmus japonicus*. Chin J Parasitol Parasit Dis 8:26–28 (in Chinese)

Cheng YZ, Lin JX, Chen BJ et al (1992) A new species of *Echinochasmus* parasitic in human and observation of its experimental infection. Wuyi Sci J 9:135–140 (in Chinese)

Cheng YZ, Lin JX, Fang YY et al (1994) Epidemiological surveys and experimental infection of *Echinochasmus fujianensis*. Acta Parasitol Med Entomol Sin 1:10–15 (in Chinese)

Cheng YZ, Xu GF, Feng ZH et al (1997) Studies on efficacy of praziquantel and mebendazole-medicated salt in treatment of *Echinochasmus fujianensis* infection. Southeast Asian J Trop Med Public Health 28:344–346

Cheng YZ, Zhang YJ, Lin CX et al (1999) Taxonomic studies on *Echinochasmus fujianensis* and its related species by random amplified polymorphic DNA analysis and experimental infection. Chin J Parasitol Parasit Dis 17:135–139 (in Chinese)

Cheng YZ, Li YS, Lin JX et al (2000a) Survey of mixed infections of fish-borne trematodes in Pinyuan County and DNA (RAPD) analysis. Chin J Zoon 16:52–55 (in Chinese)

Cheng YZ, Xu YD, Yang WC et al (2000b) Analyses on LDH isoenzyme and protein from both Guangdong strain and Fujian strain of Echinochasmus fujianensis. Chin J Zoon 16:80–83 (in Chinese)

Chi TTK, Dalsgaard A, Turnbull JF et al (2008) Prevalence of zoonotic trematodes in fish from a Vietnamese fish-farming community. J Parasitol 94:423–428

Choi DW, Chung DI, Kee SK (1990a) Infestation of larval trematodes from fresh-water fish collected in the River Chongdo. Kyungpook Nat Univ Med J 31:32–38 (in Korean)

Choi DW, Chung DI, Kim JS (1990b) Infestation status of digenetic larval trematodes from freshwater fish collected in the River Yang, Kyungpook Province, Korea. Kyungpook Nat Univ Med J 31:17–25

Choi MH, Kim SH, Chung JH et al (2006) Morphological observations of *Echinochasmus japonicus* cercariae and in vitro maintenance of its life cycle from cercariae to adults. J Parasitol 92:236–241

Chun SK (1962) Studies on some trematodes whose intermediate hosts are fishes in the Naktong River. Bull Fisher Coll Pusan Nat Univ (Korea) 4:21–38 (in Korean)

Chun SK (1964) Studies on the experiment of mode of infection of *Clonorchis sinensis*. I. Studies on the metacercariae of some trematodes parasitic in fresh water fishes and experimental infection of the cercaria of *Clonorchis sinensis* to fresh water fishes. Bull Pusan Fisher Coll 6:1–14 (in Korean)

Ciurea J (1915) Un Echinostome dans l'intestin du porc. Centrabl Bacteriol (Org 1) 74:392–394

Ciurea J (1920) Sur La Source d'Infection du Chien et du Chat avec l'*Echinochasmus perfoliatus* (v. Ratz) et la Question d'Infection de l'Homme avec les Distomes de la Familie des Echinostomidés: Note Préliminaire. J Parasitol 6:173–177

Dietz E (1909) Die Echinostomatiden der Vogel. Zool Anz 34:180–192

Dietz E (1910) Die Echinostomatiden der Vogel. Zool Jarb Suppl 12:265–512

Dimitrov V, Kanev I, Bezprozvannykh V et al (1998) Argentophilic structures of the miracidium of *Echinochasmus perfoliatus* (Trematoda: Echinostomatidae). Parasite 5:185–188

El-Azazy OME, Abdou NMI, Khalil AI et al (2015) Potential zoonotic trematodes recovered in stray cats from Kuwait Municipality, Kuwait. Korean J Parasitol 53:279–287

El-Dakhly KM, Aboshinaf ASM, El-Nahass ES et al (2017) A preliminary study on the helminth fauna in necropsied stray cats (*Felis catus*) in beni-Suef, Egypt. J Adv Vet Res 7:87–92

El-Gayar AK (2007) Studies on some trematode parasites of stray dogs in Egypt with a key to the identification of intestinal trematodes of dogs. Vet Parasitol 144:360–365

Eom KS, Rim HJ, Jang DH (1984) A study on the parasitic helminths of domestic duck (*Anas platyrhynchos* var. *domestica* Linnaeus) in Korea. Korean J Parasitol 22:215–221

Fahmy MAM, Selim MK (1959) Studies on some trematode parasites of dogs in Egypt with special reference to the role played by fish in their transmission. Z Parasitenkd 19:3–13

Fang F, Huang T, Guillot J et al (2015) Zoonotic helminths parasites in the digestive tract of feral dogs and cats in Guangxi, China. BMC Vet Res 11:211

Filmonova LV (1973–1974) On the biology of *Echinochasmus* (*Ech.*) *japonicus*. Tanabe, 1926 (Trematoda: Echinostomatidae). Helminthologia 14–15:653–660 (in Russian)

Filmonova LV (1979) The phenomenon of "amphixeny" in the trematode *Echinochasmus japonicus*. Zool Z 58:1103–1109 (in Russian)

Fischthal JH, Kuntz RE (1981) addicitonal records of digenetic trematodes of mammals from Taiwan. Proc Helminthol Soc Wash 48:71–79

Fried B (2001) Biology of echinostomes except *Echinostoma*. Adv Parasitol 49:163–210

Gedoelst L (1911) Synopsis de parasitologie de l'homme et des animax domestiques. Bruxelles, pp 1–332

Gupta VP, Pande BP (1963) On a trematode of the genus *Echinochasmus* Dietz, 1909, with remarks on the species occurring in Indian carnivores. Parasitology 53:169–175

Harada H, Yamaguchi K, Yoshida Y et al (1983) *Echinostoma hortense* infection diagnosed by the endoscopical examination. Gastroenterol Endosc 25:622–627 (in Japanese)

Harinasuta T, Bunnag D, Radomyos P (1987) Intestinal fluke infections. Bailliere's Clin Trop Med Commun Dis 2(3):695–721

Hasegawa I (1926) Studies on trematodes having mud-snails as intermediate host. I & II. Tokyo Iji Shinshi (2493):555 & (2502):7–12 (in Japanese)

Hirazawa I (1928) *Echinochasmus perfoliatus* (Ratz) found in man. Tokyo Iji Shinshi (2577):1328–1334 (in Japanese)

Hung NM, Madsen H, Fried B (2013) Global status of fish-borne zoonotic trematodiasis in humans. Acta Prasitol 58:231–258

Hwang JT, Choi DW (1980) Changing pattens of infestation with larval trematodes from fresh-water fish in River Kumho, Kyungpook Province. Korea. Kyungpook Nat Univ Med J 21:460–475

Ito J (1962) Studies on cercariae from fresh water snails in Thailand. Jpn J Med Sci Biol 15:249–270

Ito J (1964) A monograph of cercariae in Japan and adjacent territories. In: Progress of medical parasitology in Japan, vol 1. Meguro Parasitological Museum, Tokyo, pp 395–550

Ito J, Papasarathorn T, Tongkoom B (1962) An investigation on parasitic helminths of stray dogs in Bangkok. Jpn J Med Sci Biol 15:53–60

Ivanov VM, Semenova NN (2000) Parasitological consequences of animal introduction. Russ J Ecol 31:307–309

Jiang ZX, Xu LQ, Tang JS et al (1988) Human natural infection of *Echinochasmus perfoliatus* in Anhui Province. Acta Acad Med Sin 10:68–71 (in Chinese)

Joo CY (1984) Infestation of larval trematodes from fresh-water fish and brackish-water fish in River Hyungsan, Kyungpook Province, Korea. Korean J Parasitol 22:78–84 (in Korean)

Kamiya Y, Ohbayashi M (1975) Some helminths of the red fox, *Vulpes vulpes schlencki,* Kishida, in Hokkaido, Japan, with a description of a new trematode, *Massaliatrema yamashitai* n. sp. Jpn J Vet Res 23:60–68

Kannangara DWW (1971) On some hitherto unreported digenetic trematodes of vertebrates in Ceylon, with a description of *Bilorchis dissanaikei* n. sp., and a revision of the genus *Bilorchis*. Ceylon J Sci Biol Sci 9:131–165

Kobayasi H (1942) Studies on the flukes in Hainan Island. III. On the flukes belonging to the Family Echinostomatidae Odhner, 1910, *Episthochasmus caninum* Verma, 1935. Acta Nipponica Medicinae Tropicalis 4:97–105

Kogame Y (1941) Study on the trematode whose intermediate host is the freshwater fish in the Mitsu River, Kamo Gun, Hiroshima Prefecture. Nippon Ikadaigaku Zasshi 12:345–351 (in Japanese)

Komiya Y (1949) The cercariae of *Echinochasmus perfoliatus* (Ratz) and its excretory system. Tokyo Iji Shinshi 66:8–10 (in Japanese)

Komiya Y (1951) The cercariae of *Echinochasmus perfoliatus* Ratz and its excretory system. Japan Med J 4:239–244

Komiya Y (1965) Metacercariae in Japan and adjacent territories. In: Progress of medical parasitology in Japan, vol 2. Meguro Parasitological Museum, Tokyo, pp 1–328

Komiya Y, Murase K (1952) On the distribution of various metacercariae of trematodes within the fish body. Jpn J Med Sci Biol 5:277–282

Korol EN, Varodi EI, Kornyushin VV et al (2016) Helminths of wild predatory mammals (Mammalia, Carnivora) of Ukraine. Trematodes. Vestnik Zool 50:301–308

Kostadinova A (2005) Family Echinostomatidae Looss, 1899. In: Jones A, Bray RA, Gibson DI (eds) Keys to the trematoda, vol 2. Natural History Museum, London, pp 9–64

Kostadinova A, Gibson DI (2001) A redescription of *Uroproctepisthmium bursicola* (Creplin, 1837) n. comb. (Digenea: Echinostomatidae), and re-evaluation of the genera *Episthmium* Lühe, 1909 and *Uroproctepisthmium* Fischthal & Kuntz, 1976. Syst Parasitol 50:63–67

Kumar GM, Sahai BN (1972) A note on the incidence of helminthic infections in dogs at Patna, Bihar. Indian Vet J 49:737

Kuntz RE, Chandler AC (1956) Studies on Egyptian trematodes with special reference to the heterophyid of mammals. I. Adult flukes, with descriptions of *Phagicola longicollis* n. sp., *Cynodiplostomum namrui* n. sp., and a *Stephanoprora* from cats. J Parasitol 42:445–459

Kuo SC, Kiang LM (1943) The animal parasites of dogs in Chengtu. Chin Med J 1:15–18

Kurisu Y (1932) Studies on trematodes which take Japanese house hen as the definitive host. Kumamoto Igakkai Zasshi 8:283–298 (in Japanese)

Le NT (2000) The trematodes parasitic in man and animals (Fauna of Vietnam), vol 8. Science and Technology Publishing House, Hanoi, p 385 (in Vietnamese)

Le TH, Nguyen NTB, Nguyen KT et al (2016) A complete mitochondrial genome from *Echinochasmus japonicus* supports the elevation of Echinochasminae Odhner, 1910 to family rank (Trematoda: Platyhelminthes). Infect Gen Evol 45:369–377

Lee JT (1968) Studies on the metacercariae from fresh water fishes in the Kum Ho River. Korean J Parasitol 6:77–99 (in Korean)

Lee HS (1979) A survey on helminth parasites of cats in Gyeongbug Area. Korean J Vet Res 19:57–61 (in Korean)

Lee YC, Liu CC, Huang RI (1976) Investigation of the cause of death of growing ducks in rice fields after harvesting. J Chin Soc Vet Sci 2:56–58 (in Chinese)
Lee DM, Ahn DH, Choi DW (1979) Larval trematodes from fresh water fish in River Oseep. Kyungpook Nat Univ Med J 20:219–233 (in Korean)
Lee SH, Sohn WM, Hong ST (1987) Scanning electron microscopical findings of *Echinochasmus japonicus* tegument. Korean J Parasitol 25:51–58
Liang C, Ke XL (1988) *Echinochasmus jiufoensis* sp. nov., a human parasite from Guangzhou. Acta Zootax Sinica 13:4–8 (in Chinese)
Lin JX, Cheng YZ (1981) *Echinochasmus perfoliatus* infection in a man: a case report. Nat Med J China 61:249–250 (in Chinese)
Lin JX, Gao YG, Cheng YZ et al (1982) Discovery of natural human infections with *Echinochasmus japonicus*. Fujian Med J 2:30–33 (in Chinese)
Lin JX, Cheng YZ, Liang CZ et al (1985) Epidemiological investigation and experimental infection of *Echinochasmus japonicus*. Chin J Parasitol Parasit Dis 3:89–91 (in Chinese)
Lin JX, Cheng YZ, Zhuang HI (1990) Experimental observation on the life cycle of *Echinochasmus japonicus*. Chin J Parasit Dis Control 3:294–297 (in Chinese)
Liu DG, Yao QF, Yao TJ et al (1982) A case report on human infection of *Echinochasmus japonicus*. Nat Med J China 62:736 (in Chinese)
Looss A (1896) Recherches sur la faune parasitaire de l'Egypte. Premiere Partie. Memoires de l'Institut Egyptien. 3:1–252
Machnicka B, Dziemian E, Rocki B et al (2003) Detection of *Echinococcus multilocularis* antigens in faeces by ELISA. Parasitol Res 91:491–496
Mori J (1935) Study on trematodes who take *Salangichthys microdon* Bleeker as the intermediate host. Tokyo Iji Shinshi (2952):2679–2686 (in Japanese)
Muto M (1918) On a trematode taking the fish as its intermediate host in Ogura Pond in Kyoto Prefecture. Chuo Igaku Zasshi 25:1–7 (in Japanese)
Nagasawa K, Nitta M (2012) A checklist of the parasites of freshwater and brackish-water fishes of Hiroshima Prefecture, Japan (192502012). Bull Hiroshima Univ Mus 4:53–71 (in Japanese)
Nicoll W (1923) A reference list of the trematode parasites of British mammals. Parasitology 15:236–252
Odhner T (1910) Nordafrikanische Trematoden, grösstenteils vom Weissen Nil. I. Fascioliden. Results of the Swedish Zoological Expedition to Egypt and the White Nile 1901, under the direction of L. A. Jägerskiöld. No. 23A, 170 pp
Okabe K (1940) A synopsis of trematode cysts in fresh water fishes from Fukuoka Prefecture. Fukuoka Ika Daigaku Zasshi 33:309–335 (in Japanese)
Okahashi K (1966) Researches on *Heterophyes*. (2) *Metagonimus yokogawai* parasitic on the loach: its infection test on birds and its adult form. Okayama Igakkai Zasshi 78:15–24 (in Japanese)
Ondračkova N, Slováčkova I, Trichkova T et al (2012) Shoreline distribution and parasite infection of black-striped pipefish *Syngnathus abaster* Risso, 1827 in the lower River Danube. J Appl Ichthyol 2012:1–7
Otagaki H, Kanemitsu T (1953) Study on the encysted metacercariae of the brackish water fishes sold in the market in Binan area in Hiroshima Prefecture. Tokyo Iji Shinshi 70:575–578 (in Japanese)
Otranto D, Dantas-Torres F, Mihalca AD et al (2017) Zoonotic parasites of sheltered and stray dogs in the era of the global economic and political crisis. Trends Parasitol 33:813–825
Patnaik B (1959) The trematode parasites of dogs in Orissa. Indian Vet J 36:595–600
Patton S, Rabinowitz AR (1994) Parasites of wild Felidae in Thailand: a coprological survey. J Wildl Dis 30:472–475
Pavlović I, Kulišić Z, Trifković A et al (2011) Trematode of foxes (*Vulpes vulpes* L.) hunting at Belgrade area [Serbia] during 1993–2000. In: Међународни симпозијум о ловству и одрживом коришћењу биодиверзитета, 6, Жагубица (Serbia), 2011. Ловачки савез Србије, 2011

Price EW (1931) Four new species of trematode worms from the muskrat, *Ondatra zibethica*, with a key to the trematode parasites of the muskrat. Proc US Natl Mus 79:1–13
Proshin YG (1962) Anthelmintics against *Echinochasmus* infection in pigs. Veterinariya 39:37–38 (in Russian)
Radomyos P, Bunnag D, Harinasuta T (1985) Report of *Episthmium caninum* (Verma, 1935) Yamagui, 1958 (Digenea: Echinostomatidae) in man. Southeast Asian J Trop Med Public Health 16:508–511
Radomyos P, Charoenlarp P, Radomyos B (1991) Human *Episthmium caninum* (Digenea: Echinostomatidae) infection: report of two more cases. J Trop Med Parasitol 14:48–50
Radomyos P, Radomyos B, Tungtrongchitr A (1994) Multi-infection with helminths in adults from northeast Thailand as determined by post-treatment fecal examination of adult worms. Trop Med Parasitol 45:133–135
Radomyos B, Wongsaroj T, Wilairatana P et al (1998) Opisthorchiasis and intestinal fluke infections in northern Thailand. Southeast Asian J Trop Med Public Health 29:123–127
Railliet A, Henry ACL (1909) Sur un èchinostome de l'intestin du chien. C R Soc Biol 66:447–449
Rajković-Janje R, Zagreb SB, Rimac D et al (2002) Prevalence of helminths in wild boar from hunting grounds in eastern Croatia. Z Jagdwiss 48:261–270
Rhee JK, Baek BK, Lee SB et al (1983a) Epidemiological studies of *Clonorchis sinensis* in Mangyeong Riverside Areas in Korea. Korean J Parasitol 21:157–166 (in Korean)
Rhee JK, Lee HI, Baek BK et al (1983b) Survey on encysted cercariae of trematodes from freshwater fishes in Mangyeong Riverside Area. Korean J Parasitol 21:187–192 (in Korean)
Rhee JK, Rim MH, Baek BK et al (1984) Survey on encysted cercaria of trematodes from freshwater fishes in Tongjin Riverside Area in Korea. Korean J Parasitol 22:190–202 (in Korean)
Rim HJ (1982) Echinostomiasis. CRC Handbook Series in Zoonoses, Section C: Parasitic Zoonoses, Vol. III. Trematode Zoonoses. CRC Press Inc., Boca Raton, pp 53–69
Rim HJ, Kim KH, Joo KH et al (1996) The infestation states and changing patterns of human infecting metacercariae in freshwater fish in Kyongsang-do and Kyonggi-do, Korea. Korean J Parasitol 34:95–105
Ritchie LS, Hunter GW III, Pan C et al (1952) Parasitological studies in the Far East. VI. An epidemiological survey on Kyushu Island, Japan. Jpn J Med Sci Biol 5:299–310
Ritchie LS, Hunter GW III, Pan C et al (1953) Parasitological studies in the Far East. VIII. An epidemiological survey of the Tone River area, Japan. Jpn J Med Sci Biol 6:33–43
Ryang YS, Ahn YK, Yoon MB (1991) Trematode infections in the small intestine of *Egretta alba medesta* in Kanhwon-do. Korean J Parasitol 29:227–233 (in Korean)
Saeed I, Maddox-Hyttel C, Monrad J et al (2006) Helminths of red foxes (*Vulpes vulpes*) in Denmark. Vet Parasitol 139:168–179
Sahai BN, Srivastava HD (1970) Studies on *Echinochasmus perfoliatus* (Ratz, 1908) Dietz, 1909: incidence in dogs and development of the miracidium. J Helminthol 44:315–320
Saleh RS, Abou-Eisha AM, Fadel HM et al (2009) Occurrence of encysted metacercariae of some zoonotic trematodes in freshwater fishes and their public health significance in port Said Province. Abbassa Int J Aquacult (Special Issue for Global Fisher Aquacult Res Conferene, 24–26 October 2009):341–351
Sayasone S, Tesana S, Utzinger J et al (2009a) Rare human infection with the trematode *Echinochasmus japonicus* in Lao PDR. Parasitol Int 58:106–109
Sayasone S, Vonghajack Y, Vanmany M et al (2009b) Diversity of human intestinal helminthiasis in Lao PDR. Trans R Soc Trop Med Hyg 103:247–254
Seo BS, Lee SH, Chai JY et al (1985) Studies on intestinal trematodes in Korea. XX. Four cases of natural human infection by *Echinochasmus japonicus*. Korean J Parasitol 23:214–220
Shimalov VV, Shimalov VT (2002) Human parasitic echinostomatata (Trematoda, Fasciolidae) in mammals in Belorussian forest zone. Med Parazitol Parazitamye Bolezni (1):47–50 (in Russian)

Skrjabin KI, Bashikirova EI (1956) Family Echinostomatidae Dietz, 1909. In: Skrjabin KI (ed) Trematodes and animals and man, vol XII. Akademiya Nauk Publishers, Moscow-Leningrad, pp 51–930 (in Russian)
Sohn WM, Choi YS (1997) Infection status with trematode metacercariae in the fresh-water fish from Chunamchosuchi (pond), Uichang-gun, Kyongsangnam-do, Korea. Korean J Parasitol 35:165–170 (in Korean)
Sohn WM, Chai JY (2005) Infection status with helminthes in feral cats purchased from a market in Busan, Republic of Korea. Korean J Parasitol 43:93–100
Sohn WM, Eom KS, Min DY et al (2009) Fishborne trematode metacercariae in freshwater fish from Guangxi Zhuang Autonomous Region, China. Korean J Parasitol 47:249–257
Sosipatrov GV (1961a) Diagnosis of a new disease of pigs – *Echinochasmus* infection. Veterinariya 38:36–39 (in Russian)
Sosipatrov GV (1961b) Pathological changes in pigs infected with *Echinochasmus perfoliatus*. Sbornik Nauchno-Technicheskol Informatsii Vsesoyuznogo Inst Gelminthol im K. I. Skrjabina (7/8):60–62 (in Russian)
Sosipatrov GV (1962) *Echinochasmus* infection of pigs. Veterinariya 39:30–32 (in Russian)
Sosipatrov GV (1964) Life cycle of *Echinochasmus perfoliatus* (Ratz, 1908). Trudy vsesoyuznogo Inst Gel'minthol 11:151–155 (in Russian)
Stanevičiūte G, Stunžėnas V, Petkevičiūte R (2015) Phylogenetic relationships of some species of the family Echinostomatidae Odhner, 1910 (Trematoda), inferred from nuclear rDNA sequences and karyological analysis. Comp Cytogen 9:257–270
Tanabe H (1915) On a new trematode with freshwater fishes as its intermediate hosts. Okayama Iggakai Zasshi (305):7–18 (in Japanese)
Tanabe H (1922) Studies on trematodes with freshwater fishes as their intermediate hosts. II. On *Echinochasmus perfoliatus* (Ratz) found in Japan. Okayama Iggakai Zasshi (387):1–20 (in Japanese)
Tanabe H (1926) Studies on trematodes with freshwater fishes as their intermediate hosts. III. On a new species, *Echinochasmus japonicus* (n. sp.). Nippon Byori Gakkai Kaishi 16:295–296 (in Japanese)
Tawfik MAA, Elnawawi FA, Shaapan RM (2000) Studies on some fish-borne trematodes in Egypt. Egypt J Vet Sci 34:39–48
Tkach VV, Kudlai O, Kostadinova A (2016) Molecular phylogeny and systematics of the Echinostomatoidea Looss, 1899 (Platyhelminthes: Digenea). Int J Parasitol 46:171–185
Tubangui MA (1922) Two new intestinal trematodes from the dog in China. Proc US Natl Mus 60:1–16
Tungtrongchitr A, Radomyos P (1989) Human intestinal fluke infections in Thailand. Bull Chulalongkorn Med Tech 3:417–427 (in Thai)
Ujiie N (1936a) On the development, the structure of *Echinochasmus japonicus* and its parasitism in man. Taiwan Igakkai Zasshi 35:535–546 (in Japanese)
Ujiie N (1936b) On the structure and function of Mehlis' gland on the formation of the egg shell of *Echinochasmus japonicus*. Taiwan Igakkai Zasshi 35:1000–1010 (in Japanese)
Verma SC (1935) Studies on the Indian species of the genus *Echinochasmus*, Part I. and on an allied new genus *Episthochasmus*. Proc Indian Acad Sci 1:837–856
Wang TP, Gao JF, Xiao Q et al (1993) Efficacy of pyquiton in the treatment of *Echinochasmus liliputanus* infection. Chin J Parasitol Parasit Dis 11:165–167 (in Chinese)
Wang TP, Zhu CG, Fang GR et al (1998) Studies on seasonal distribution and influence factors of *Echinochasmus liliputanus* infection. Chin J Parasit Dis Contr 11:295–297 (in Chinese)
Wang TP, Xiao X, Lu D et al (1999) Case-control study on risk factors of *Echinochasmus liliputanus* infection. Practic Prev Med 6:420–421 (in Chinese)
Wang CR, Qiu JH, Zhou JP et al (2006) Prevalence of helminthes in adult dogs in Heilongjiang Province, the Peoples' Republic of China. Parasitol Res 99:627–630

Witenberg G (1932) Über Zwei in Palästina in Hunden und Katzen Parasitierende *Echinochasmus*-Arten (Trematoda). Z Parasitenkd 5:213–216 (in Germany)
Wu K (1937) Susceptibility of various mammals to experimental infection with *Fasciolopsis buski* (Trematoda: Fasciolidae). Ann Trop Med Parasitol 31:361–372
Wu WD, Xiao X, Xu FL et al (1997) Observation on the fine structures of *Echinochasmus liliputanus* tegument by scanning electron microscopy. Chin J Parasitol Parasit Dis 15:205–207 (in Chinese)
Wu G (2013) Human parasitology, 4th edn. Rin Min Hu Sheng Publ Co, Beijing
Wuhan Medical College (1979) Case report on *Echinochasmus perfoliatus*. Bull Wuhan Med Coll 8:24 (in Chinese)
Xiao X, Wong TP, Lu DB et al (1992) The first record of human natural infection of *Echinochasmus liliputanus*. Chin J Parasitol Parasit Dis 10:132–135 (in Chinese)
Xiao X, Lu DB, Wang TP et al (1994) Epidemiological studies on *Echinochasmus liliputanus* infection. I. Parasite infection and distribution in final hosts. Chin J Parasit Dis Contr 7:285–298 (in Chinese)
Xiao X, Lu DB, Wang TP et al (1995a) Epidemiological studies on *Echinochasmus liliputanus* infection. II. Infection and seasonal variations in intermediate hosts. Chin J Parasit Dis Contr 8:24–27 (in Chinese)
Xiao X, Lu DB, Wang TP et al (1995b) Experiment on direct infection of definitive hosts with *Echinochasmus liliputanus* cercariae. Chin J Parasit Dis Contr 8:28–30 (in Chinese)
Xiao X, Lu DB, Wang TP et al (1995c) Studies on mode of human infection with *Echinochasmus liliputanus*. Chin J Parasitol Parasit Dis 13:197–199 (in Chinese)
Xiao X, Li CT, Fang GR et al (2000) Studies on biology of *Echinochasmus liliputanus* cercariae. Chin J Parasit Dis Contr 13:199–204 (in Chinese)
Xiao X, Wang TP, Zheng X et al (2005) In vivo and in vitro encystment of *Echinochasmus liliputanus* cercariae and biological activity of the metacercariae. J Parasitol 91:492–498
Xu LQ, Jiang ZX, Cheng ZS (1988) Preliminary study on praziquantel in the treatment of *Echinochasmus perfoliatus* and *Metagonimus yokogawai* infections. Zhonghua nei ke za shi. Chin J Intern Med 27:399–401 (in Chinese)
Xu YD, Lin RH, Sun S et al (2002) Analysis of protein and genomic DNA of Echinochasmus fujianensis. J Xiamen Univ, Natur Sci 41:117–120 (in Chinese)
Yamaguchi T (1967) *Clonorchis sinensis* (The first subject parasite). Proc Southeast Asia Research 4:766–771 (in Japanese)
Yamaguti S (1939) Studies on the helminth founa of Japan. Part 25. Trematodes of birds, IV. Jpn J Zool 8:129–210
Yamaguti S (1951) Zur Entwicklungsgeschichte von *Echinochasmus japonicus* Tanabe, 1926, mit besonderer Berucksichtigung der Struktur der Cercarie. Mit 4 Textabbildungen. Acta Med Okayama 7:338–342 (in Germany)
Yamaguti S (1958) Systema Helminthum. Vol. I. The digenetic trematodes of vertebrates (Part I). Interscience Publishers Inc, New York, pp 1–979
Yamaguti S (1971) Synopsis of digenetic trematodes of vertebrates, vol I. Keigaku Publishing Co., Tokyo, pp 1–1074
Yamashita J (1937) Studies on the Echinostomatidae. II. A list of the family Echinostomatidae, trematode parasites of reptiles, birds and mammals arranged systematically. Trans Sapporo Nat Hist Soc 15:82–95. in Japanese
Yamashita J (1964) Echinostome. In: Progress of medical parasitology in Japan, vol 1. Meguro Parasitological Museum, Tokyo, pp 287–313
Yong TS, Chung KH, Ree HI (1991) Infection status of intestinal parasites of field rodents in Korea. Yonsei Rep Trop Med 22:55–59
Yu SH, Mott KE (1994) Epidemiology and morbidity of food-borne intestinal trematode infections. Trop Dis Bull 91:R125–R152

Zhao HQ, Li CE, Xie SH et al (2001) Investigation of intestinal parasites in shar-pei in Nanhai. J Animal Sci Vet Med 20:23–25 (in Chinese)
Zhou J, Wang X (1987) Studies on the trematode family Echinostomatidae Dietz, 1909 from Jiangxi I. Jiangxi Sci 5:13–20
Zhou Y, Wang Y, Xu S et al (1987) A survey of helminth fauna of dogs along Tangwang River valley in Heilongjiang Province China. J Northeast Agric Coll 18:24–30 (in Chinese)
Zhu D, Lin J, Cheng Y et al (1986) Pyquiton treatment of *Echinochasmus japonicus* infection. Chin J Parasitol Parasit Dis 4:1–4 (in Chinese)

References for Section 2.5

Chai JY (2009) Echinostomes in humans. In: Fried B, Toledo R (eds) The biology of echinostomes. Springer, New York, pp 147–183
Chai JY, Han ET, Park YK et al (2001) *Acanthoparyphium tyosenense*: the discovery of human infection and identification of its source. J Parasitol 87:794–800
Chai JY, Shin EH, Lee SH et al (2009) Foodborne intestinal flukes in Southeast Asia. Korean J Parasitol 47(suppl):S69–S102
Chen HT, Chen S, Chu H et al (1985) Chapter 5. Echinostomatidae Dietz, 1909. Platyhelminthes, Trematoda, Digenea (1). Fauna Sinica. Science Press, Beijing, pp 333–403
Chung OS, Joo KH, Lee WS (2007) *Acanthoparyphium tyosenense* infection in great knots and turnstone on the Western Coast of Korea. J Ecol Field Biol 30:97–99
Han ET, Chai JY (2008) *Mactra veneriformis*, an intertidal clam, as a new second intermediate host for *Acanthoparyphium marilae* (Digenea: Echinostomatidae). Korean J Parasitol 46:101–104
Han ET, Kim JL, Chai JY (2003) Recovery, growth and development of *Acanthoparyphium tyosenense* (Digenea: Echinostomatidae) in experimental chicks. J Parasitol 89:176–179
Han ET, Choi MS, Choi SY et al (2011) Surface ultrastructure of juvenile and adult *Acanthoparyphium tyosenense* (Digenea: Echinostomatidae). J Parasitol 97:1049–1054
Ito J (1957) Studies on the brackish water cercariae in Japan. III. Three new echinostome cercariae in Tokyo Bay, with a list of Japanese echinostome cercariae (Trematoda). Jpn J Med Sci Biol 10:439–453
Kim YG (1988) Studies on a trematode parasitized on bivalves. V. On metacercaria of Echinostomatidae detected from *Mactra veneriformis, Cyclina sinensis* and *Solen strictus*. Bull Korean Soc Fish Pathol 1:31–37 (in Korean)
Kim YG, Chun SK (1969) Studies on a trematode parasite of pelecypoda. I. Trematode of the genus *Echinostoma* found in the clam, *Mactra sulcataria* Reeve. Bull Pusan Fish Coll 9:21–24 (in Korean)
Kim YG, Yu JE (2001) Studies on the life history of *Acanthoparyphium tyosenense* Yamaguti, 1939. J Korean Fish Soc 34:720–728
Kim YK, Yu JE, Chung EY et al (2004) *Acanthoparyphium tyosenense* (Digenea: Echinostomatidae): experimental confirmation of the cercaria and its complete life history in Korea. J Parasitol 90:97–102
Skrjabin KI, Bashikirova EI (1956) Family Echinostomatidae Dietz, 1909. In: Skrjabin KI (ed) Trematodes and animals and man, vol XII. Akademiya Nauk Publishers, Moscow-Leningrad, pp 51–930 (in Russian)
Sohn WM, Na BK, Cho SH et al (2017) Prevalence and density of digenetic trematode metacercariae in clams and oysters from western coastal regions of the Republic of Korea. Korean J Parasitol 55:399–408
Yamaguti S (1939) Studies on the helminth founa of Japan. Part 25. Trematodes of birds, IV. Jpn J Zool 8:129–210
Yamaguti S (1958) Systema Helminthum. Vol. I. The digenetic trematodes of vertebrates (Part I). Interscience Publishers Inc, New York, pp 1–979

References for Section 2.6

Acharjyo LN (2004) Helminthiasis in captive wild carnivores and its control in India. Zoos' Print J 19:1540–1543

Ahluwalia SS (1962) Studies on some helminths of the domestic pigs (*Sus scrofa domestica*) in western Uttar Pradesh. J Helminthol 36:347–364

Bandyopadhyay AK, Nandy A (1986) A preliminary observation on the prevalence of echinostomes in a tribal community near Calcutta. Ann Trop Med Parasitol 80:373–375

Bandyopadhyay AK, Manna B, Nandy A (1989) Human infection of *Artyfechinostomum oraoni* n. sp. (Paryphostominae: Echinostomatidae) in a tribal community, Oraons in West Bengal, India. Indian J Parasitol 13:191–196

Bandyopadhyay AK, Maji AK, Manna B et al (1995) Pathogenicity of *Artyfechinostomum oraoni* in naturally infected pigs. Trop Med Parasitol 46:138–139

Beaver PC, Jung RC, Cupp EW (1984) Clinical parasitology, 9th edn. Lea and Febiger, Philadelphia

Belizario VY, Geronilla GG, Anastacio MBM et al (2007) *Echinostoma malayanum* infection, the Philippines. Emerg Infect Dis 13:1130–1131

Bhalerao GD (1931) *Artyfechinostomum sufrartyfex* (Lane), assigned to genus *Paryphostomum*, occurrence in the pig. Bengal. Rec Indian Mus 33:475–479

Bisseru B (1957) On three known trematodes from African birds, with notes on the genera *Typhlocoelum, Paryphostomum* and *Petasiger*. J Helminthol 31:173–186

Bonne C, Bras G, Lie KJ (1953) Five echinostomes in man in the Malayan Archipelago. Am J Dig Dis 20:12–16

Brier JW (1992) Emerging problems in seafood-borne parasitic zoonoses. Food Contr:2–7

Chai JY (2009) Echinostomes in humans. In: Fried B, Toledo R (eds) The biology of echinostomes. Springer, New York, pp 147–183

Chai JY (2015) Chapter 19. Echinostomes. In: Xiao L, Ryan U, Feng Y (eds) Biology of foodborne parasites. CRC Press, Taylor & Francis Group, Boca Raton, pp 427–443

Chai JY, Shin EH, Lee SH et al (2009) Foodborne intestinal flukes in Southeast Asia. Korean J Parasitol 47(suppl):S69–S102

Chai JY, Sohn WM, Yong TS et al (2012) Echinostome flukes recovered from humans in Khammouane Province, Lao PDR. Korean J Parasitol 50:269–272

Chen HT, Chen S, Chu H et al (1985) Chapter 5. Echinostomatidae Dietz, 1909. Platyhelminthes, Trematoda, Digenea (1). Fauna Sinica. Science Press, Beijing, pp 333–403

Divina BP, Pulmano JA (1996) Occurrence of *Artyfechinostomum malayanum* (Leiper, 1911) Mendheim, 1943 in a Philippine monkey (*Macaca fascicularis*). Phil J Vet Med (abstract from AGRIS. http://agris.fao.org/agris-search/search.do?recordID=PH1999100072

Dubey JP, Srivastava HOP, Sahasrabudhe VK (1969) *Artyfechinostomum sufrartyfex* infection in cat and dog in India. Trop Geogr Med 21:210–213

Eduardo SL (1989) *Artyfechinostomum malayanum* (Leiper, 1911) Mendheim 1943 (Trematoda: Echinostomatidae) from pigs in the Philippines. Phil J Vet Med 26:25–27

Eduardo SL (1991) Food-borne parasitic zoonoses in the Philippines. Southeast Asian J Trop Med Public Health 22:16–22

Faruqui AJ (1930) On a new species of cercariae indicae found in *Indoplanorbis exustus* (Deshayes). Indian J Med Res 17:1205–1214

Jain GP (1958) On *Cercaria mehrai* Faruqui, 1930 with notes on its life-history. Parasitology 48:413–418

Jain GP (1960a) On the genus *Artyfechinostomum* (Lane, 1915) (Echinostomatidae: Trematoda). Parasitology 50:1–5

Jain GP (1960b) Further observations on *Artyfechinostomum mehrai* (Faruqui) (Echinostomatidae: Trematoda). Parasitology 50:7–11

Jaw CY, Lo CT (1974) In vitro cultivation of *Echinostoma malayanum* Leiper, 1911. Chin J Microbiol 7:157–164

Kaul BK, Singhal CD, Pillai PN (1974) *Artyfechinostomum mehrai* infestation with bowel perforation. J Indian Med Assoc 63:263–265

Khanna V, Tilak K, Mukim Y et al (2016) An unusual case of echinostomiasis in a retropositive patient: a case report. Human Parasit Dis 8:43–45

Kostadinova A (2005) Family Echinostomatidae Looss, 1899. In: Jones A, Bray RA, Gibson DI (eds) Keys to the Trematoda, vol 2. Natural History Museum, London, pp 9–64

Kostadinova A, Gibson DI (2002) *Isthmiophora* Lühe, 1909 and *Euparyphium* Dietz, 1909 (Digenea: Echinostomatidae) re-defined, with comments on their nominal species. Syst Parasitol 52:205–217

Kostadinova A, Vaucher C, Gibson DI (2002) Redescription of two echinostomes from birds in Paraguay, with comments on *Drepanocephalus* Dietz, 1909 and *Paryphostomum* Dietz, 1909 (Digenea: Echinostomatidae). Syst Parasitol 53:147–158

Lane C (1915) *Artyfechinostomum sufrartyfex*. Indian J Med Res 2:977–983

Leiper RT (1915) Notes on the occurrence of parasites presumably rare in man. J Royal Army Med Corps 24:569–575

Lie KJ (1963a) Studies on Echinostomatidae in Malaya. III. The adult *Echinostoma malayanum* Leiper, 1911 (Trematoda) and the probable synonymy of *Artyfechinostomum sufrartyfex* Lane, 1915. Z Parasitenkd 23:124–135

Lie KJ (1963b) The life history of *Echinostoma malayanum* Leiper, 1911 (Trematoda, Echinostomatidae). Acta Leidencia 32:180–190

Lie KJ, Virik HK (1963) Human infection with *Echinostoma malayanum*. J Trop Med Hyg 66:77–82

Maji AK, Bera DK, Manna B et al (1993) First record of human infection with *Echinostoma malayanum* in India. Trans R Soc Trop Med Hyg 87:673

Maji AK, Manna B, Bandyopadhyay AK et al (1995) Studies on the life cycle of *Artyfechinostomum oraoni* Bandyopadhyay, Manna & Nandy, 1989: embryogenesis and development in the intermediate host. Indian J Med Res 102:124–128

Maleewong W, Intapan PM, Wongkham C et al (2003) Detection of *Opisthorchis viverrini* in experimentally infected bithynid snails and cyprinoid fishes by a PCR-based method. Parasitology 126:63–67

Mendheim H (1943) Beiträge zur Systematic und Biologie der Familie Echinostomatidae (Trematoda). Archiv für Naturgeschichte 12:175–302

Mohandas A (1971) *Artyfechinostomum sufrartyfex* Lane, 1915 a synonym of *Echinostoma malayanum* Leiper, 1911 (Trematoda: Echinostomatidae). Acta Parasitol Pol 19:361–368

Mohandas A, Nadakal AM (1978) In vivo development of *Echinostoma malayanum* Leiper, 1911 with notes on effects of population density, chemical composition and pathogenicity and in vitro excystment of the metacercariae (Trematoda: Echinostomatidae). Z Parasitenkd 55:139–151

Monzon RB, Kitikoon V (1989) *Lymnaea* (*Bullastra*) *cummingiana* Pfeiffer (Pulmonata: Lymnaeidae): second intermediate host of *Echinostoma malayanum* in the Philippines. Southeast Asian J Trop Med Public Health 20:453–460

Monzon RB, Kitikoon V, Thammapalerd N et al (1993) Ecological observations on *Lymnaea* (*Bullastra*) *cummingiana*. Southeast Asian J Trop Med Public Health 24:563–569

Mukherjee RP, Ghosh RK (1968) On the synonymy of the genus *Artyfechinostomum* Lane, 1915 (Trematoda: Echinostomatidae). Proc Indian Acad Sci 67:52–58

Namue C, Wongsawad C (1997) A survey of helminth infection in rats (*Rattus* spp.) from Chiang Mai Moat. Southeast Asian J Trop Med Public Health 28(suppl 1):179–183

Nath D (1969) *Rana cyanophlyctis* as the second intermediary of *Artyfechinostomum sufrartyfex*. Curr Sci 14:342–343

Nath D (1974) Pathology of *Artyfechinostomum sufrartyfex* Lane, 1915 infection in experimental animals. Indian J Med Res 28:381–383

Ngo HD, Emolenko AV, Gerasev PI (2011) *Artyfechinostomum sufrartyfex* Lane, 1915 (Trematoda: Echinostomatidae), a parasite of mammals in southern Vietnam. Parazitologiia 45:54–59 (in Russian)

Noikong W, Wongsawad C (2014) Epidemiology and molecular genotyping of echinostome metacecariae in *Filopaludina* snails in Lamphun Province, Thailand. Asian Pac J Trop Med 2014:26–29

Odhner T (1913) Ein zweites *Echinostomum* aus dem Menschen in Ostasian (*Ech. malayanum* Leiper). Zool Anz 41:577–582 (in Germany)

Premvati G, Pande V (1974) On *Artyfechinostomum malayanum* (Leiper, 1911) Mendheim, 1943 (Trematoda: Echinostomatidae) with synonymy of allied species and genera. Proc Helminthol Soc Wash 41:151–160

Radomyos B, Wongsaroj T, Wilairatana P et al (1998) Opisthorchiasis and intestinal fluke infections in northern Thailand. Southeast Asian J Trop Med Public Health 29:123–127

Raghunathan VS, Srinivasan T (1962) *Artyfechinostomum mehrai* infestation. J Indian Med Assoc 38:485–487

Ramanujachari G, Alwar VS (1954) *Paryphostomum sufrartyex* (Lane, 1915) Bhalerao, 1931 in pigs (*Sus scrofa domestica*) in madras. Indian vet J 30:498–500

Reddy G, Varmah K (1950) *Paryphostomum sufrartyfex* (intestinal fluke) infection in man. Indian Med Gazette 85:546–547

Reddy DB, Ranganaykamma I, Venkataratnam D (1964) *Artyfechinostomum mehrai* infestation in man. J Trop Med Hyg 67:58–59

Roy B, Tandon V (1992) Seasonal prevalence of some zoonotic trematode infections in cattle and pigs in the north-east montane zone in India. Vet Parasitol 41:69–76

Roy B, Tandon V (1996) Effect of root-tuber extract of *Flemingia vestita*, a leguminous plant, on *Artyfechinostomum sufrartyfex* and *Fasciolopsis buski*: a scanning electron microscopy study. Parasitol Res 82:248–252

Saijuntha W, Tapdara S, Tantrawatpan C (2010) Multilocus enzyme electrophoresis analysis of *Echinostoma revolutum* and *Echinostoma malayanum* (Trematoda: Echinostomatidae) isolated from Khon Kaen Province, Thailand. Asian Pac J Trop Med 3:633–636

Singh S (1991) Trematode infections in India: a review. Trop Gastroenterol 12:119–132

Skrjabin KI, Bashikirova EI (1956) Family Echinostomatidae Dietz, 1909. In: Skrjabin KI (ed) Trematodes and animals and man, vol XII. Akademiya Nauk Publishers, Moscow-Leningrad, pp 51–930 (in Russian)

Sohn WM, Na BK, Cho SH et al (2017) Prevalence and density of digenetic trematode metacercariae in clams and oysters from western coastal regions of the Republic of Korea. Korean J Parasitol 55:399–408

Songsri J, Aukkanimart R, Boonmars T et al (2016) Animal models for *Echinostoma malayanum* infection: worm recovery and some pathology. Korean J Parasitol 54:47–53

Srisawangwong T, Sithithaworn P, Sukkasaem P et al (2011) Concomitant and protective immunity in mice exposed to repeated infections with *Echinostoma malayanum*. Exp Parasitol 127:740–744

Tandon V, Goswami LM, Prasad PK et al (2008) Molecular characterization of intestinal fluke, *Artyfechinostomum sufrartyfex* (Trematoda: Echinostomatidae) using PCR amplification of rDNA ITS regions. In: Tandon V, Yadav AK, Roy B (eds) Current Trends in Parasitology. Proceedings of the 20th National Congress Parasitol, India, November 3–5, 2008. Panima Publication Corption, New Delhi, India, pp 153–161

Tandon V, Shylla JA, Ghatami et al (2015) Neglected tropical diseases: trematodiases-the Indian scenario. Proc Natl Acad Sci India (Sect B Biol Sci) 85:901–907

Tangrtrongchitr A, Monzon RB (1991) Eating habits associated with *Echinostoma malayanum* infection in the Philippines. Southeast Asian J Trop Med Public Health 22(suppl):212–216

Tantrawatpan C, Saijuntha W, Sithithaworn P et al (2013) Genetic differentiation of *Artyfechinostomum malayanum* and *A. surfrartyfex* (Trematoda: Echinostomatidae) based on internal transcribed spacer sequences. Parasitol Res 112:437–441

Tesana S, Kania P, Maleewong W et al (1987) Scanning electron microscopy of adult *Echinostoma malayanum*. Southeast Asian J Trop Med Public Health 18:233–240

Toledo R, Esteban JG (2016) An update on human echinostomiasis. Trans R Soc Trop Med Hyg 110:37–45

Tran BT, Nguyen ST, Nguyen TT et al (2016) Endoparasites of Vietnamese lizards recorded in the last 50 years (1966–2015). Jpn J Vet Parasitol 15:34–58

Veciana M, Chaisiri K, Morand S et al (2012) Helminths of the Asian house shrew *Suncus murinus* from Cambodia. Cambodian J Nat Hist 2012:115–122

Wu G (2013) Human parasitology, 4th edn. Rin Min Hu Sheng Publ Co, Beijing

Yadav DC (1959) Further observations on *Artyfechinostomum sufrartyfex* (Lane) Bhalerao, 1931 (Trematoda: Echinostomatidae) with a note on its systematic position. Proc Natl Acad Sci B 29:157–167

Yamaguti S (1958) Systema Helminthum. Vol. I. The digenetic trematodes of vertebrates (Part I). Interscience Publishers Inc, New York, pp 1–979

Yamaguti S (1971) Synopsis of digenetic trematodes of vertebrates, vol I. Keigaku Publishing Co, Tokyo, pp 1–1074

Yu SH, Mott KE (1994) Epidemiology and morbidity of food-borne intestinal trematode infections. Trop Dis Bull 91:R125–R152

References for Section 2.7

Abdel Azim M (1939) Helminthes Parasites des Chiens et des Chats en Egypte. Ann Parasitol 17:32–36

Adam ME, Lewis JW (1992) Sites of encystment by the metacercariae of *Echinoparyphium recurvatum* in *Lymnaea peregra*. J Helminthol 66:96–99

Akagi K (1916) Demonstration of the echinostome parasitic in man. Taiwan Igakkai Zasshi 165:681

Anazawa K (1929) On a human case of *Echinostoma revolutum* and its infection route. Taiwan Igahkai Zasshi 288:221–241 (in Japanese)

Annereaux RF (1940) A not on *Echinoparyphium recurvatum* (von Linstow) parasitic in California turkeys. J Am Vet Med Assoc 96:62–64

Bashikirova EI (1947) Echinostomatidae. In: Skrjabin KI (ed) Trematodes and animals and man, vol 1. Akademiya Nauk Publishers, Moscow-Leningrad, pp 246–305

Beaver PC, Jung RC, Cupp EW (1984) Clinical parasitology, 9th edn. Lea and Febiger, Philadelphia

Beckett JV, Gallicchio V (1967) A survey of helminths of the muskrat, *Ondatra z. zibethica* Miller, 1912 in Portage County, Ohio. J Parasitol 53:1169–1172

Bonne C, Bras G, Lie KJ (1953) Five echinostomes in man in the Malayan Archipelago. Am J Dig Dis 20:12–16

Buscher HN (1978) *Echinoparyphium speotyto* sp. n. (Trematoda: Echinostomatidae) from the burrowing owl in Oklahoma, with a discussion on the genus *Echinoparyphium*. J Parasitol 64:52–58

Bush AO, Holmes JC (1986) Intestinal helminths of lesser scaup ducks: an interactive community. Can J Zool 64:142–152

Chai JY (2009) Echinostomes in humans. In: Fried B, Toledo R (eds) The biology of echinostomes. Springer, New York, pp 147–183

Chai JY, Shin EH, Lee SH et al (2009) Foodborne intestinal flukes in Southeast Asia. Korean J Parasitol 47(suppl):S69–S102

Chen HT, Chen S, Chu H et al (1985) Chapter 5. Echinostomatidae Dietz, 1909. Platyhelminthes, Trematoda, Digenea (1). Fauna Sinica. Science Press, Beijing, pp 333–403

Dietz E (1909) Die Echinostomiden der Vögel. Zoologischer Anzeiger 34:180–192

Dietz E (1910) Die Echinostomiden der Vögel. Zool Jahrb (suppl 12):18–512

Dimitrov V (1990) The chaetotaxy of *Echinoparyphium recurvatum* (Linstow, 1873) Lühe, 1909 cercariae from Bulgaria. Khelmintologiya 28:21–27

Evans NA (1983) The establishment and survival of *Echinoparyphium recurvatum* in the definitive host. Z Parasitenkd 69:401–402
Evans NA, Gordon DM (1983) Experimental studies on the transmission dynamics of the cercariae of *Echinoparyphium recurvatum* (Digenea: Echinostomatidae). Parasitology 87:167–174
Evans NA, Whitfield PJ, Dobson AP (1981) Parasite utilization of a host community: the distribution and occurrence of metacercarial cysts of *Echinoparyphium recurvatum* (Digenea: Echinostomatidae) in 7 species of mollusk at Harting Pond, Sussex. Parasitology 83:1–12
Fain A, Galal A (1977) Presence du Trematode *Echinoparyphium recurvatum* (von Linstow, 1873) chez l'Homme et chez un Rongeur en Egypte. Ann Soc Belge Med Trop 57:583–587 (in French)
Faltýnková A (2005) Larval trematodes (Digenea) in molluscs from small water bodies near České Budějovice, Czech Republic. Acta Parasitol 50:49–55
Fredensborg BL, Latham AD, Poulin R (2004) New records of gastrointestinal helminths from the red-billed gull (*Larus novaehollandiae scopulinus*). New Z J Zool 31:75–80
Fried B (2001) Biology of echinostomes except *Echinostoma*. Adv Parasitol 49:163–210
Grabda-Kazubska B, Borsuk P, Laskowski Z et al (1998) A phylogenetic analysis of trematodes of the genus *Echinoparyphium* and related genera based on sequencing of internal transcribed spacer region of rDNA. Acta Parasditol 43:116–121
Hon LT, Forrester DJ, Williams LE Jr (1975) Helminths of wild turkeys in Florida. Proc Helminthol Soc Wash 42:119–127
Huffman JE, Fried B (2012) The biology of *Echinoparyphium* (Trematoda, Echinostomatidae). Acta Parasitol 57:199–210
Ishii N (1932) Studies on bird trematodes (I & II). Jikken Igaku Zasshi 16:1205–1231 (in Japanese)
Kanev I (1990) A checklist of the helminth parasites of *Echinis, Echinostoma*, Echinostomatidae (Trematoda) with references for their renaming, replacement and reclassify. Publishing House of the Bulgarian Academy of Sciences, Sofia
Keymer IH, Rose JH, Beesley WN et al (1962) A survey and review of parasitic diseases of wild and game birds in Great Britain. Vet Rec 74:887–894
Kiseliene V, Grabda-Kazubska B (1990) *Echinoparyphium pseudorecurvatum* sp. n. (Trematoda: Echinostomatidae) and its life cycle. Acta Parasitol Pol 35:285–295
Kiseliene V, Grabda-Kazubska B (1993) The structure and life cycle of sibling species of trematodes of the genus *Echinoparyphium* Dietz. Biologiya, Vilnius 1:40–41
Kostadinova A, Herniou EA, Barrett J et al (2003) Phylogenetic relationships of *Echinostoma* Rudolphi, 1809 (Digenea: Echinostomatidae) and related genera re-assessed via DNA and morphological analyses. Syst Parasitol 54:159–176
Lajtner J (2012) Presence of *Bucephalus polymorphus, Echinoparyphium recurvatum* and *Aspidogaster limacoides* (Platodes, Trematoda) in the visceral mass of *Dreissena polymorpha* (Mollusc, Bivalvia). Helminthologia 49:147–153
Lee SH, Sohn WM, Chai JY (1990) *Echinostoma revolutum* and *Echinoparyphium recurvatum* recovered from house rats in Yangyang-gun, Kangwon-do. Korean J Parasitol 28:235–240
Lie KJ (1951) Some human flukes from Indonesia. Doc Neerland et Indonesia Morb Trop 3:105–116
Lühe M (1909) Parasitische Plattwürmer. I. Trematodes. Die Süsswasserfauna Deutschlands 17:1–217 (in Germany)
McCarthy AM (1990) Speciation of echinostomes: evidence for the existence of two sympatric species in the complex *Echinoparyphium recurvatum* (von Linstow 1873) (Digenea: Echinostomatidae). Parasitology 101:35–42
McCarthy AM (2011) Scanning electron microscopy of adult *Echinoparyphium recurvatum* (von Linstow 1873) (Digenea: Echinostomatidae) from Britain. J Helminthol 85:453–457
Meyer MC, Reilly JR (1950) Parasites of muskrats in Maine. Am Midl Natur 44:467–477
Penner LR (1940) Morphological and biological studies on certain helminths of the muskrat. Ph.D. dissertation, University of Minnesota, USA, 275 pp

Probert AJ (1966) Histochemical studies on the rediae and cercariae of *Echinoparyphium recurvatum* Linstow. Nature 210:550–551

Rim HJ (1982) Echinostomiasis. CRC Handbook Series in Zoonoses, Section C: Parasitic Zoonoses, Vol. III. Trematode Zoonoses. CRC Press Inc., Boca Raton, pp 53–69

Saijuntha W, Tantrawatpan C, Sithithaworn P et al (2011a) Genetic characterization of *Echinostoma revolutum* and *Echinoparyphium recurvatum* (Trematoda: Echinostomatidae) in Thailand and phylogenetic relationships with other isolates inferred by ITS1 sequence. Parasitol Res 108:751–755

Saijuntha W, Sithithaworn P, Duenngai K et al (2011b) Genetic variation and relationships of four species of medically important echinostomes (Trematoda: Echinostomatidae) in South-East Asia. Infect Gen Evol 118:105–109

Saijuntha W, Duenngai K, Tantrawatpan C et al (2013) Zoonotic echinostome infections in free-grazing ducks in Thailand. Korean J Parasitol 51:663–667

Senger CM (1954) Notes on the growth, development, and survival of two echinostome trematodes. Exp Parasitol 3:491–496

Sereno-Uribe AL, Pinacho-Pinacho CD, Cordero VS et al (2015) Morphological and molecular analyses of larval and adult stages of *Echinoparyphium recurvatum* von Linstow 1873 (Digenea: Echinostomatidae) from central Mexico. J Helminthol 89:458–464

Skrjabin KI (1915) Trématodes des oiseaux de l'Oural. Petrograd Ann Zool Mus Imp Akad Nauk 20:395–417 (in Russian)

Sohn WM (1998) Life history of *Echinoparyphium recurvatum* (Trematoda: Echinostomatidae) in Korea. Korean J Parasitol 36:91–98

Sohn WM, Woo HC, Hong SJ (2002) Tegumental ultrastructures of *Echinoparyphium recurvatum* according to developmental stages. Korean J Parasitol 40:67–73

Soulsby EJL (1955) Deaths in swans associated with trematode infection. Br Vet J 111:498–500

Toledo R, Muňoz-Antolí C, Pérez M et al (1998) Larval trematode infections in freshwater gastropods from the Albufera Natural Park in Spain. J Helminthol 72:79–82

Tsuchimochi K (1924) On the life cycle of two species of echinostomatid trematodes. I. Studies on trematodes of domestic fowls in Formosa. Dobutsugaku Zasshi 36:245–258 (in Japanese)

Tubangui MA (1932) Trematode parasites of Philippine vertebrates. V. Flukes from birds. Phil J Sci 47:369–402

Verma SC (1936) Notes on trematode parasites of Indian birds (Part I). Allahabad Univ Stud 12:147–188

Weeks PJ (1982) Checklist of helminth parasites of birds in New Zealand. New Z J Zool 9:451–460

Yamaguti S (1933) Studies on the helminth founa of Japan. Part 1. Trematodes of birds, reptiles and mammals. Jpn J Zool 5:1–134

Yamaguti S (1934) Studies on the helminth founa of Japan. Part 3. Avian trematodes, II. Jpn J Zool 5:542–583

Yamaguti S (1939) Studies on the helminth founa of Japan. Part 25. Trematodes of birds, IV. Jpn J Zool 8:129–210

Yamaguti S (1958) Systema Helminthum. Vol. I. The digenetic trematodes of vertebrates (Part I). Interscience Publishers Inc, New York, pp 1–979

Yamaguti S (1971) Synopsis of digenetic trematodes of vertebrates, vol I. Keigaku Publishing Co, Tokyo, pp 1–1074

Yamashita J (1964) Echinostome. In: Progress of medical parasitology in Japan, vol 1. Meguro Parasitological Museum, Tokyo, pp 287–313

Yu SH, Mott KE (1994) Epidemiology and morbidity of food-borne intestinal trematode infections. Trop Dis Bull 91:R125–R152

Yurlova NI, Vodyanitskaya SN, Serbina EA et al (2006) Temporal variation in prevalence and abundance of metacercariae in the pulmonate snail *Lymnaea stagnalis* in Chany Lake, West Siberia, Russia: long-term patterns and environmental covariates. J Parasitol 92:249–259

References for Section 2.8

Beaver PC, Jung RC, Cupp EW (1984) Clinical parasitology, 9th edn. Lea and Febiger, Philadelphia
Diaz JI, Cremonte F (2004) *Himasthla escamosa* n. sp. (Digenea: Echinostomatidae) from the kelp gull, *Larus dominicanus* (Charadriformes: Laridae), on the Patagonian Coast, Argentina. J Parasitol 90:308–314
Dietz E (1910) Die Echinostomiden der Vögel. Zool Jahrb (suppl 12):18–512
Fried B (2001) Biology of echinostomes except *Echinostoma*. Adv Parasitol 49:163–210
Han ET, Whang JD, Chai JY (2009) *Himasthla alincia* (Echinostomatidae): metacercariae in brackish water bivalves and their growth and development in experimental animals. J Parasitol 95:1415–1420
Stunkard HW (1938) The morphology and life cycle of the trematode *Himasthla quissetensis* (Miller and Northup, 1926). Biol Bull 75:145–164
Stunkard HW (1939) Determination of species in the trematode genus *Himasthla*. Z Parasitenkd 10:719–721
Stunkard HW (1960) Further studies on the trematode genus *Himasthla* with descriptions of *H. mcintosh* n. sp., *H. piscicola* n. sp., and stages in the life-history of *H. compacta* n. sp. Biol Bull 119:529–549
Vogel H (1933) *Himasthla muehlensi* n. sp., ein neuer menschlicher Trematode der Familie Echinostomidae. Z Bakteriol Paratitenkd Infektionskrankh 127:387–391
Yamaguti S (1971) Synopsis of digenetic trematodes of vertebrates, vol I. Keigaku Publishing Co, Tokyo, pp 1–1074

References for Section 2.9

Dietz E (1909) Die Echinostomiden der Vögel. Zoologischer Anzeiger 34:180–192
Dietz E (1910) Die Echinostomiden der Vögel. Zool Jahrb. (suppl (12):18–512
Haas W, Körner M, Hutterer E et al (1995) Finding and recognition of the snail intermediate hosts by 3 species of echinostome cercariae. Parasitology 110:133–142
Harinasuta T, Bunnag D, Radomyos P (1987) Intestinal fluke infections. Bailliere's Clinical Tropical Medicine and Communicable Diseases 2(3):695–721
Jakovleva GA, Lebedeva DI, Ieshko EP (2012) Trematode fauna of waterfowl birds in Karelia. Parazitologiia 46:98–110 (in Russian)
Morishita K, Tsuchimochi K (1925) Notes on four avian trematodes from Formosa, with remarks on the life history of *Hypoderaeum conoideum* (Bloch, 1782). Taiwan Igakkai Zasshi 243:544–562 (in Japanese)
Muñoz-Antolí C, Toledo R, Esteben JG (2000) The life cycle and transmission dynamics of the larval stages of *Hypoderaeum conoideum*. J Helminthol 74:165–172
Rim HJ (1982) Echinostomiasis. CRC Handbook Series in Zoonoses, Section C: Parasitic Zoonoses, Vol. III. Trematode Zoonoses. CRC Press Inc., Boca Raton, pp 53–69
Skrjabin KI, Bashikirova EI (1956) Family Echinostomatidae Dietz, 1909. In: Skrjabin KI (ed) Trematodes and animals and man, vol XII. Akademiya Nauk Publishers, Moscow-Leningrad, pp 51–930 (in Russian)
Toledo R, Muñoz-Antolí C, Esteben JG (1996) Redescription of the adult stage of *Hypoderaeum conoideum* (Bloch, 1782) (Trematoda: Echinostomatidae) and new record in Spain. Res Rev Parasitol 56:195–201
Toledo R, Muñoz-Antolí C, Pérez M et al (1998) Larval trematode infections in freshwater gastropods from the Albufera Natural Park in Spain. J Helminthol 72:79–82

Toledo R, Muñoz-Antolí C, Pérez M et al (1999) Survival and infectivity of *Hypoderaeum conoideum* and *Euparyphium albuferensis* cercariae under laboratory conditions. J Helminthol 73:177–182

Yamaguti S (1958) Systema Helminthum. Vol. I. The digenetic trematodes of vertebrates (Part I). Interscience Publishers Inc, New York, pp 1–979

Yamaguti S (1971) Synopsis of digenetic trematodes of vertebrates, vol I. Keigaku Publishing Co, Tokyo, pp 1–1074

Yokogawa M, Harinasuta C, Charoenlarp P (1965) *Hypoderaeum conoideum* (Block, 1782) Dietz, 1909, a common intestinal fluke of man in the north-east Thailand. Jpn J Parasitol 14:148–153 (in Japanese)

Yurlova NI (1987) Morphology and biology of trematodes of *Hypoderaeum cubanicum* comb. n. and *H. conoideum* (Echinostomatidae). Parazitologiia 21:35–42 (in Russian)

Chapter 3
Amphistomes

3.1 Families Gastrothylacidae and Gastrodiscidae

Amphistomes (= superfamily Paramphistomoidea Fischoeder, 1901) are those flukes lacking a true oral sucker (the pharynx is well-developed) and having a ventral sucker at or close to the posterior extremity of the body in both adults and cercariae (Jones 2005a). They lack body spines and armature of any kind but frequently have tegumental papillae; in most taxa, they (in adults and cercariae) have postero-lateral pharyngeal sacs or diverticula usually paired but rarely single or absent (Jones 2005a). At first these parasites were considered to belong to a family, Paramphistomidae, by Fischoeder in 1901, but later this group was raised to a superfamily level, Paramphistomoidea, by Stiles and Goldberger in 1910; they recognized 3 families in this group; the Paramphistomidae Fischoeder, 1901, Gastrothylacidae Stiles and Goldberger, 1910, and Gastrodiscidae Monticelli, 1892 (Jones 2005a; Tandon et al. 2014). Maplestone (1923) treated this group as a suborder Amphistomata acknowledging the 3 families. Skrjabin (1949) recognized 2 superfamilies Paramphistomoidea and Cladorchioidea Fischoeder, 1901 within the order Paramphistomatata Szidat, 1936. However, Yamaguti (1971) recognized only one superfamily, the Paramphistomoidea, but reduced the Cladorchioidea to a family level (Cladorchiidae Fischoeder, 1901) which is followed by Jones (2005b).

Now in the superfamily Paramphistomoidea, 12 families are recognized, including the family Paramphistomidae (lacking a ventral pouch), Cladorchiidae (pharyngeal sac and cirrus sac present), Gastrothylacidae (having a ventral pouch), and Gastrodiscidae (lacking a ventral pouch and having a divided body into cephalic and caudal portions) (Jones 2005a, b, c, d; Tandon et al. 2014). Human infections are known in 3 amphistome species, namely, *Fischoederius elongatus, Gastrodiscoides hominis,* and *Watsonius watsoni* (Table 3.1) (Tandon et al. 2014). *F. elongatus* belongs to the Gastrothylacidae, and *G. hominis* and *W. watsoni* belong to the Gastrodiscidae.

J.-Y. Chai, *Human Intestinal Flukes*,
https://doi.org/10.1007/978-94-024-1704-3_3

Table 3.1 Dimensions of adults, eggs, cercariae, and metacercariae of zoonotic intestinal flukes other than heterophyids and echinostomes

Species	Adults (mm)	Eggs (μm)	Cercariae (μm) body (tail length)	Metacercariae (μm)
Amphistomes				
Fischoederius elongatus	10.0–15.0 × 3.0–4.0	120–150 × 66–75	320–360 × 208–260 (460–760)	240–280
Gastrodiscoides hominis	8.0–14.0 × 8.0	127–160 × 62–75	403–865 × 192–310 (468–923)	201–227
Watsonius watsoni	8.0–10.0 × 4.0–5.0	122–130 × 75–80	Not found	Not found
Diplostomes				
Neodiplostomum seoulense	0.76–1.28 × 0.37–0.50	81–102 × 51–63	81–121 × 37–57 (138–175)	232–385
Fibricola cratera	0.65–0.84 × 0.24–0.33	115–135 × 65–75	105–146 × 30–61 (153–228)	450–525 × 240–300
Fasciolids				
Fasciolopsis buski	20.0–100.0 × 8.0–30.0	130–140 × 80–85	207 × 126 (392)	140 × 130
Gymnophallids				
Gymnophalloides seoi	0.33–0.50 × 0.23–0.33	20–25 × 11–15	Not found	310–390 × 210–260
Lecithodendriid-like flukes				
Caprimolgorchis molenkampi	0.55–0.92 × 0.41–0.77	20–28 × 9–14	Not described	Not described
Phaneropsolus bonnei	0.45–0.85 × 0.30–0.50	23–33 × 13–18	Not described	Not described
Phaneropsolus spinicirrus	0.55–0.76 × 0.43–0.63	27–33 × 13–16	Not found	Not found
Plagiorchiids				
Plagiorchis muris	2.85–2.99 × 0.82–0.95	38 × 19	248–275 × 90–105 (135–143)	117–140 × 165–185
Plagiorchis javensis	1.82 × 0.68	36 × 22–24	Not found	Not found
Plagiorchis philippinensis	1.5–2.0 × 0.39	28–30 × 19–21	Not found	Not found
Plagiorchis harinasutai	1.87 × 0.61	33–34 × 17–18	Not found	Not found
Plagiorchis vespertilionis	2.6 × 0.7	33 × 18	220 × 92 (150)	170 × 126

(continued)

Table 3.1 (continued)

Species	Adults (mm)	Eggs (μm)	Cercariae (μm) body (tail length)	Metacercariae (μm)
Miscellaneous zoonotic species				
Brachylaima cribbi	3.8–6.0 × 0.52–0.79	26–32 × 16–18	240–330 × 60–110 (12–35)	630–1910 × 180–610
Cotylurus japonicus	0.65–0.54 × 0.83–0.36	106–115 × 74–78	Not found	Not found
Gynaecotyla squatarolae	0.83 × 0.31	21–27 × 15–18	Not described	300–350
Isoparorchis hypselobagri	12.0–23.0 × 6.0–16.0	38–51 × 21–25	Not described	1900–1950 × 850–900
Microphallus brevicaeca	0.5–0.7 × 0.3–0.4	15–16 × 9–10	Not described	416–560 × 360–520
Nanophyetus salmincola	0.8–2.5 × 0.3–0.5	64–97 × 34–55	310–470 × 30–150	170–250
Nanophyetus schikhobalowi	0.58 × 0.47	52–82 × 32–56	220–430 × 30–120	160–220
Prohemistomum vivax	0.74–1.55 × 0.45–0.78	90–108 × 45–77	986–1300	320

The family Gastrothylacidae are parasites in the stomach of ruminants (rarely humans) morphologically characterized by the presence of a sucker-like attachment organ and a ventral pouch and without pharyngeal sacs and a cirrus sac (Jones 2005a, c). Four genera are enlisted; *Velasquezotrema* Eduardo & Javellana, 1987, *Gastrothylax* Poirier, 1883, *Carmyerius* Stiles and Goldberger, 1910, and *Fischoederius* Stiles and Goldberger, 1910 (Jones 2005c).

The family Gastrodiscidae are parasites in the intestine of mammals (rarely humans) morphologically characterized by a dorsoventrally flattened body and the presence of a pharyngeal bulb and pharyngeal sacs (paired; primary and secondary sacs) but without a hermaphroditic sac (Jones 2005a, d). Eight genera are acknowledged; *Gastrodiscus* Leuckart in Cobbold, 1877, *Homalogaster* Poirier, 1883, *Macropotrema* Blair, Beveridge, and Speare, 1979, *Pseudodiscus* Sonsino, 1895, *Hawkesius* Stiles and Goldberger, 1910, *Choerocotyle* Baer, 1959, *Gastrodiscoides* Leiper, 1913, and *Watsonius* Stiles and Goldberger, 1910 (Jones 2005d).

3.2 *Fischoederius, Gastrodiscoides,* and *Watsonius*

3.2.1 Fischoederius elongatus

3.2.1.1 *Fischoederius elongatus* (Poirier, 1883) Stiles and Goldberger, 1910

[syn. *Gastrothylax elongatus* Poirier, 1883; *Fischoederius fischoederi* Stiles and Goldberger, 1910; *Fischoederius ceylonensis* Stiles and Goldberger, 1910; *Fiscoederius siamensis* Stiles and Goldberger, 1910; *Fischoederius compressus* Wang, 1979]

Taxonomy and Morphology

The genus *Fischoederius* (Gastrothylacidae) was erected by Stiles and Goldberger in 1910 based on worms collected from the cattle stomach by Poirier in 1883 (*Gastrothylax elongatus* Poirier, 1883) as the type species, *F. elongatus* Stiles and Goldberger, 1910 (Mukherjee and Chauhan 1972). Thereafter, at least 21 species have been reported to occur in mammals; *F. elongatus*, *F. fischoederi* Stiles and Goldberger, 1910, *F. ceylonensis* Stiles and Goldberger, 1910, *F. cobboldi* (Poirier, 1883) Stiles and Goldberger, 1910, *F. japonicus* (Fukui, 1922) Yamaguti, 1939, *F. siamensis* Stiles and Goldberger, 1910, *F. skrjabini* Kadenatsii, 1963, *F. ovatus* Wang, 1977, *F. compressus* Wang, 1979, *F. poyangensis* Wang, 1979, *F. yunnanensis* Hoang, 1979, *F. brevisaccus* Eduardo, 1981, *F. sichuanensis* Wang and Jiang, 1982, *F. explanatus* Wang and Jiang, 1982, *F. philippinensis* Eduardo and Javellana, 1988, *F. baliensis* Kurniasih, 1995, *F. foliacae* Kurniasih, 1995, *F. brotoi* Kurniasih, 1995, *F. donsoni* Kurniasih, 1995, *F. tatoi* Kurniasih, 1995, *F. emiljavieri* Eduardo, 2009, and *F. upiensis* Eduardo and Javellana, 2009 (Yamaguti 1958, 1971; Eduardo 1981; Chen et al. 1985; Eduardo and Javellana 1988; Morgan and Blair 1998; Eduardo 2009; Eduardo and Javellana 2009). However, *F. fischoederi, F. ceylonensis, F. siamensis,* and *F. compressus* were suggested to be synonyms of *F. elongatus* (Eduardo and Javellana 1988).

Fischoederius elongatus is a parasite in the stomach (first, second, third, and fourth) of ruminants originally reported by Poirier in 1883 in Java, Indonesia (Chai 2007). This fluke has a narrow and elongated body, short intestinal caecae, and large and oval excretory bladder placed just in front of the acetabulum (Yamaguti 1939; Tandon 1961). *F. elongatus* morphologically resembles *Fischoederius cobboldi* but differs from it in having short caecae never extending beyond the middle portion of the body, whereas *F. cobboldi* has caecae extending at least to the testes (Maplestone 1923). Yamaguti (1935) compared the morphology of *F. elongatus* and *F. siamensis* and concluded that the 2 species are taxonomically distinct from each other. However, Edurado and Javellana (1988) did not agree to this and suggested that *F. siamensis* is a synonym of *F. elongatus*. Human infections with *F. elongatus* have been described in 2 reports in China (Li 1991; Huang 1992); however, it seems that the 2 dealt with an identical patient. The patient was a 35-year-old woman from Guangdong Province, China who complained of epigastric pain for months and vomited a worm (20 mm long and 4 mm wide) one morning while brushing her teeth, after which the symptoms disappeared (Li 1991; Huang 1992; Yu and Mott 1994).

Adult flukes of *F. elongatus* recovered from cattle (*Bos taurus*) in Kyoto, Japan were 10.0–15.0 mm long and 3.0–4.0 mm wide (Yamaguti 1939). Eggs are elliptical and 120–150 μm long and 66–75 μm wide (Yamaguti 1939). The cercarial body is 320–360 μm long and 208–260 μm wide, and the tail is 460–760 μm long and 64–86 μm wide; the metacecariae are round, surrounded by 2 thick walls, and 240–280 μm in diameter (Chen et al. 1985).

The surface ultrastructure of adult flukes of *F. cobboldi*, a species morphologically related to *F. elongatus*, has been reported (Anuracpreeda et al. 2012). The tegumental surface exhibited high corrugations and transverse folds alternating with grooves and without spines, and the surface of each fold was further increased with a meshwork of ridges separated by irregular-sized pits; the anterior sucker (mouth) and the ventral sucker have thick edges covered with transverse folds and appear to be spineless (Anuracpreeda et al. 2012). Two types of sensory papillae, type I (round swellings without a cilium) and type 2 (round swellings with a short cilium), were seen to be abundant on the ventral surface and around the anterior suckers; however, the dorsal side of the body had less numerous papillae and smaller in size (Anuracpreeda et al. 2012). The surface ultrastructure of *F. elongatus* was studied by Fan et al. (1990) in China but the content of the paper is unavailable to the author.

Life Cycle

When the eggs of *F. elongatus* were collected from the feces of infected cattle and incubated in vitro, miracidia developed in 7 days (Mukherjee 1966). The first intermediate host was found to be the freshwater snail *Lymnaea luteola* in Madras, India, and this snail host produced *Cercariae indicae* XXIX Sewell, 1922 (Rao and Ayyar 1932; Vaidyanathan 1941). *Lymnaea luteola* var. *succinea* collected near Bareilly, India were also found to shed the cercariae of *F. elongatus* (Mukherjee 1966). *Lymnaea acuminata, Lymnaea leuteola* var. *australis*, *Gyraulus euphraticus*, and *Galba pervia* have been added as the snail host (Mukherjee 1966; Chen et al. 1985). These cercariae encysted on blades of grass or on vegetables, and the encysted cercariae (= metacercariae) developed into adult flukes when fed to a calf (Vaidyanathan 1941). The natural definitive hosts are ruminants, including cattle (*Bos taurus*), buffaloes, caribous (*Rangifer tarandus*), goats, and sheep (Kobayashi 1921; Yamaguti 1939, 1954; Zhaltsanova 1972; Mukherjee and Chauhan 1972; Tandon 1973a; Fischthal and Kuntz 1975; Roy and Tandon 1992a). Experimental definitive hosts included cows (Mukherjee 1966).

Epidemiology and Geographical Distribution

Human infection with this amphistome is very rare, with only one patient from China (Li 1991; Huang 1992). It is presumed that the human case may have consumed aquatic plants having the metacercariae. The geographical distribution is known to extend from Indonesia to India, Sri Lanka, England, China, Japan, Thailand, Vietnam, Taiwan, and Russia (Fig. 3.1; Table 3.2) (Nicoll 1923; Yamaguti

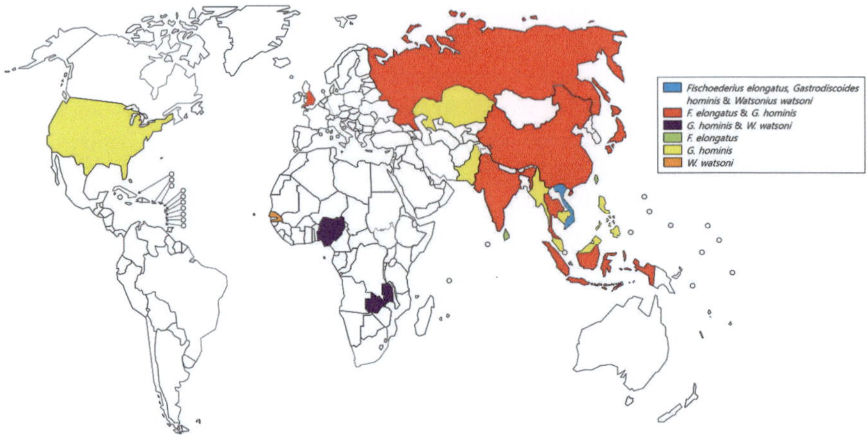

Fig. 3.1 Global distribution of amphistome species (*Fischoederius elongatus, Gastrodiscoides hominis,* and *Watsonius watsoni*) based on the presence of their life cycles

1939, 1954; Zhaltsanova 1972; Fischthal and Kuntz 1975; Chen et al. 1985; Sey 1985; Wongsawad et al. 2006; Tandon et al. 2014).

China Maplestone (1923) obtained 25 adult specimens of *F. elongatus* from a bullock in Hong Kong. Chen (1937) described the morphology of *F. elongatus* collected from buffaloes in Canton (Guangdong). Chen et al. (1985) listed various species of freshwater snails as the first intermediate host and also listed various localities, including Guangdong, Fujian, Jiangxi, Zhejiang, Guangxi, Yunnan, Jiangsu, Sichuan, Guizhou, and Hebei Provinces as the areas of this fluke distrbution. Fan et al. (1990) studied on the tegumental ultrastructure of *F. elongatus* in comparison with that of *Cotylophoron fuelleborni*. Li (1991) and Huang (1992) reported a human case infected with *F. elongatus* in a 35-year-old woman from Guangdong Province, China who complained of epigastric pain for several months and vomited an adult worm. Yang et al. (2015) analyzed the complete *F. elongatus* mitochondrial genome using worms collected from cattle in Hubei Province.

England Nicoll (1923) listed this fluke among the helminth species found from cattle.

India Rao and Ayyar (1932) discovered the cercariae of *F. elongatus* (*Cercaria indicae* XXVI by Sewell) from the freshwater snail *Lymnaea leuteola* near Madras. Vaidyanathan (1941) reconfirmed that *Lymnaea leuteola* snails shed the cercariae of *F. elongatus* in Madras, and further observed that the cercariae encyst on blades of grass; 250 metacercariae were fed to a calf and after 9 weeks 90 adult flukes were collected from the wall of the rumen. Tandon (1961) observed the excretory system of *F. elongatus* adults which showed a H-shaped pattern together with 2 other amphistome species *F. cobboldi* and *Gastrothylax crumenifer*. Tandon (1973a) further studied on the crowding effect of *F. elongatus* and *G. crumenifer* amphistomes

Table 3.2 Geographical distribution of zoonotic intestinal flukes other than heterophyids and echinostomes

Species & Nominator	Country/Region
Amphistomes	
Fischoederius elongatus (Poirier, 1883) Stiles and Goldberger, 1910	China, England, India, Indonesia, Japan, Russia, Sri Lanka, Taiwan, Thailand, Vietnam
Gastrodiscoides hominis (Lewis and McConnell, 1876) Leiper, 1913	Cambodia, China, England, India, Indonesia, Japan, Kazakhstan, Malaysia, Myanmar, Nigeria, Pakistan, The Philippines, Russia, Thailand, USA, Vietnam, Zambia
Watsonius watsoni (Conyngham, 1904) Stiles and Goldberger, 1910	Nigeria, Senegal, Vietnam, Zambia
Diplostomes	
Neodiplostomum seoulense (Seo et al. 1964) Hong and Shoop 1995	China, South Korea
Fibricola cratera (Barker and Noll, 1915) Dubois, 1932	Canada, USA
Fasciolids	
Fasciolopsis buski (Lankester, 1857) Odhner, 1902	Bangladesh, Cambodia, China, India, Indonesia, Japan, South Korea, Lao PDR, Malaysia, Myanmar, Nepal, Pakistan, The Philippines, Singapore, Taiwan, Thailand, Vietnam
Gymnophallids	
Gymnophalloides seoi Lee, Chai and Hong, 1993	South Korea
Lecithodendriid-like flukes	
Caprimolgorchis molenkampi (Lie, 1951) Baugh, 1957	Cambodia, Indonesia, Lao PDR, Thailand
Phaneropsolus bonnei Lie, 1951	Cambodia, India, Indonesia, Lao PDR, Malaysia, Thailand
Phaneropsolus spinicirrus Kaewkes et al, 1991	Thailand
Plagiorchiids	
Plagiorchis muris (Tanabe, 1922) Schulz and Skworzow, 1931	Cambodia, England, Europe (Central), Iran, Ireland, Japan, South Korea, Lao PDR, Mexico, The Netherlands, The Philippines, Spain, Taiwan, Thailand, USA, Vietnam
Plagiorchis javensis Sandground, 1940	Indonesia
Plagiorchis philippinensis Sandground, 1940	The Philippines
Plagiorchis harinasutai Radomyos, Bunnag and Harinasuta, 1989	Thailand
Plagiorchis vespertilionis (Müller, 1780) Braun, 1900	Afghanistan, Belarus, Canada, China, Denmark, Egypt, France, Hungary, India, Iraq, Italy, Japan, South Korea, Madagascar, Mexico, Mongolia, Poland, Romania, Russia, Spain, Taiwan, Turkey, Ukraine, USA

(continued)

Table 3.2 (continued)

Species & Nominator	Country/Region
Miscellaneous zoonotic species	
Brachylaima cribbi Butcher and Grove, 2001	Australia
Cotylurus japonicus Ishii, 1932	China, India, Japan, South Korea, Russia
Gynaecotyla squatarolae (Yamaguti, 1934) Yamaguti, 1939	Japan, South Korea, Taiwan
Isoparorchis hypselobagri (Billet, 1898) Odhner, 1927	Australia, Bangladesh, China, India, Indonesia, Japan, Pakistan, Russia, Thailand, Vietnam
Microphallus brevicaeca (Africa & Garcia, 1935)	Papua New Guinea, The Philippines
Nanophyetus salmincola (Chapin, 1926) Chapin in Hall, 1927	Canada, USA
Nanophyetus schikhobalowi Skrjabin and Podjapolskaya, 1931	Russia
Prohemistomum vivax (Sonsino, 1892) Azim, 1933	Egypt, Israel, Europe

in buffaloes. Balachandran et al. (2010) reported an outbreak of amphistomiasis in a sheep farm; amphistome eggs of presumably *F. elongatus* or *F. cobboldi* were detected from the feces. Ghatani et al. (2012) performed molecular characterization of amphistome parasites, including *F. elongatus*, collected from north-east India. Sarmah et al. (2014) reported human consumption of rumen flukes of cattle in Meghalaya for their nutrition and dietary benefits. Arunkumar and Krupakaran (2016) analyzed polypeptide profile of excretory-secretory antigens of *F. elongatus* from cattle origin.

Indonesia *F. elongatus* was first found in the stomach of ruminants (*Palonia frontalis*) in Java by Poirier in 1883 (Maplestone 1923; Chai 2007).

Japan *F. elongatus* was found frequently and numerously in the stomach (first and second) of Japanese cattle (*Bos taurus*) (Kobayashi 1921). Fukui in 1929 regarded *F. elongatus* and a related species *F. siamensis* Stiles and Goldberger, 1910 to be identical (Yamaguti 1935). However, Yamaguti (1935) morphologically compared *F. elongatus* and *F. siamensis*, and concluded that the 2 species are taxonomically distinct (Later, these 2 species were again synonymized by Eduardo and Javellana in 1988).

Russia Zhaltsanova (1972) reported the occurrence of *F. elongatus* in a caribou (*Rangifer tarandus*) in the Buryat ASSR.

Sri Lanka Yamaguti (1954) found *F. elongatus* adults in the abomasum of a buffalo at Macassar, Ceylon.

Taiwan Fischthal and Kuntz (1975) obtained adult specimens of *F. elongatus* from the stomach of domestic cattle at Taipei.

Thailand Wongsawad et al. (2006) successfully isolated DNA from a single specimen of trematodes, including *F. elongatus, Paramphistomum epiclitum*, and several other species. Sripalwit et al. (2007) used PCR-RAPD method to detect the genomic DNA of 3 paramphistome flukes, including *F. elongatus*. Wongsawad (2011) developed a HAT-RAPD (high annealing temperature-random amplified polymorphic DNA) PCR technique to detect the genes of trematode species, including *Stellantchasmus falcatus* and *F. elongatus*.

Vietnam Sey (1985) reported infection of ruminants, including cattle and buffaloes, with *F. elongatus* and various other amphistome species.

3.2.2 Gastrodiscoides hominis

3.2.2.1 *Gastrodiscoides hominis* (Lewis and McConnell, 1876) Leiper, 1913

[syn. *Amphistomum hominis* Lewis and McConnell, 1876; *Amphistomum* (*Gastrodiscus*) *hominis* Sonsino, 1895; *Gastrodiscus hominis* Fischoeder, 1902]

Taxonomy and Morphology

The genus *Gastrodiscoides* (Gastrodiscidae) was created by Leiper (1913) using *G. hominis* (syn. *Amphistomum hominis* Lewis and McConnell, 1876) originally collected from the cecum of an Indian patient as the type species (Khalil 1923; Beaver et al. 1984). In human infections, worms attach to the cecum and ascending colon and may cause mucous diarrhea (Beaver et al. 1984). This species (Fig. 3.2) was tentatively placed in the genus *Gastrodiscus* by Fischoeder in 1902 under the name *Gastrodiscus hominis* which was agreed by Stephens in 1906 who also found this parasite from a human in Assam, India and redescribed its internal morphology (Khalil 1923). However, Leiper (1913) erected a new genus for this fluke, *Gastrodiscoides*, considering that the nearness of the genital pore to the edge of the ventral disc-like expansion is a characteristic feature differentiated from other related species of *Gastrodiscus*, including *Gastrodiscus aegyptiacus, Gastrodiscus secundus,* and *Gastrodiscus minor*. Other characteristics of this new genus included the presence of a large genital cone, smooth ventral disk, and 2 tandem testes (Leiper 1913). Mathis and Leger in 1911 found pigs in Annam (Vietnam) infected with this fluke (Leiper 1913). It was stated that a large number of worms were collected from a person by Wise in British Guiana (an imported case), and Mackie saw these flukes

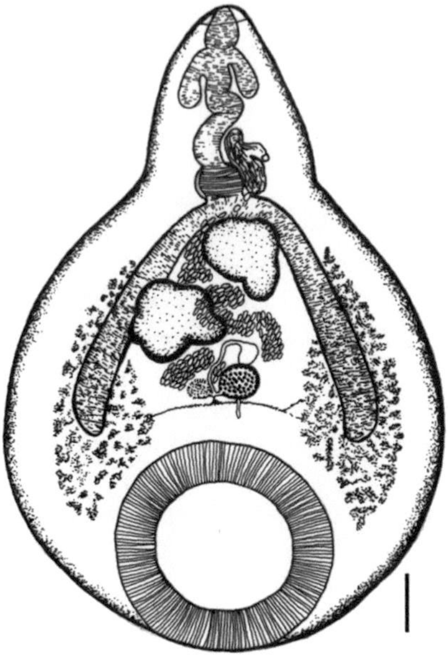

Fig. 3.2 Line drawing of an adult fluke of *Gastrodiscoides hominis*. Scale bar = 1 mm. Redrawn from the figure in Yamaguti (1971) Synopsis of Digenetic Trematodes of Vertebrates. Keigaku Publishing Co., Tokyo, Japan

in 7 human cases in Assam; in one, as many as 200 worms were passed after treatment with thymol (Leiper 1913). Lane (1922) did not agree to this genus and retained this parasite in the genus *Gastrodiscus*. However, Khalil (1923) discovered this fluke from the Napu mouse deer (*Tragulus napu*) that died in Zoological gardens in London which originated from Malay States, Indonesia and named it as *G. hominis* acknowledging the genus *Gastrodiscoides*. Nevertheless, Lane (1924) kept on assigning this species in the genus *Gastrodiscus*. However, Stunkard (1925), Nicoll (1927), Chatterji (1938), Buckley (1939), Varma (1954), and Yamaguti (1958, 1971) unanimously agreed to accept *Gastrodiscoides* as the generic name of this parasite. Besides *G. hominis*, Varma (1954) proposed a variant on specimens collected from pigs in India naming it as *G. hominis* var. *suis*. However, Shrivastav and Shah (1970) reviewed a number of *G. hominis* var. *suis* specimens and notified that those variations were not constantly recognizable. Consequently, Jones (2005d) acknowledges only one species in the genus *Gastrodiscoides, G. hominis*.

Adult flukes of *G. hominis* are thick, fleshy, and pink in color when fresh, with an anterior conical portion and a discoidal posterior portion, and 8.0–14.0 mm long and up to 8.0 mm wide (Kumar 1980; Mas-Coma et al. 2005, 2006). Eggs are ovoid and 127–160 µm long and 62–75 µm wide (Mas-Coma et al. 2006). The cercarial body is 403–865 µm long and 192–310 µm wide, and the tail is 468–923 µm long and 56–94 µm wide; the metacecariae are hemispherical and brown, surrounded by 6 thick walls, and 201–227 (mean 216) µm in diameter (Dutt and Srivastava 1966, 1972; Chen et al. 1985; Mas-Coma et al. 2005, 2006).

The surface ultrastructure of *G. hominis* adult flukes has been studied by Tandon and Maitra (1983). The tegumental surface of the huge ventral disc has a prominent pattern of convolutions and folds, including tubercle-like protuberances; such tegumental characteristics extend to the surface of the subterminal acetabulum (Tandon and Maitra 1983; Mas-Coma et al. 2006). Along the acetabular rim, there are conspicuous globular or cup-shaped mini sucker-like protuberances (= suckerlets), which probably aid the strong anchorage of the acetabulum to the host surface (Tandon and Maitra 1983; Mas-Coma et al. 2006). Numerous bosses and small button-like circular patches (look like sensory papillae) are present on the circumoral surface near the anterior end arranged in 2 or 3 concentric rings (Tandon and Maitra 1983).

Life Cycle

Buckley (1939) and Ahluwalia (1960) reported that the minimum time required for the development of the miracidium in vitro was 15–17 days at a temperature of 80–90 °F. The planorbid aquatic snail *Helicorbis coenosus* has been experimentally shown to shed the cercariae of *G. hominis* (Dutt and Srivastava 1966). Live adult specimens were collected from the intestines of domestic pigs slaughtered at the abattoir at Nekpur, a suburb of Bareilly, India; eggs recovered from the worms were cultured in vitro, and miracidia obtained were exposed to laboratory-reared snails *Helicorbis coenosus* (Dutt and Srivastava 1966). The cercariae were shed at 51–74 days after the miracidial infection at 20–30 C; from the dead snails rediae (mother and daughter) were found to contain cercarial germinal balls (Dutt and Srivastava 1966, 1972). In the laboratory, encystation of the cercariae took place on the flat bottom of various subjects that included glass containers, shell of the snail host (live or dead), stalk of an aquatic plant *Nymphoea*, cellophane sheet, or castoff skin of crustaceans (Dutt and Srivastava 1972). The pig is the most common reservoir host, and the Napu mouse deers (*Tragulus napu*), field rats (*Rattus brevicaudatus*), rhesus monkeys, and cynomolgus monkeys have been reported as natural definitive hosts (Honjo et al. 1963; Beaver et al. 1984; Yu and Mott 1994). Experimental definitive hosts included pigs (Dutt and Srivastava 1972).

Epidemiology and Geographical Distribution

Human infection with *G. hominis* is known to be acquired by ingestion of the metacercariae encysted on the surface of aquatic plants, live or dead crustaceans (crayfish), amphibians (tadpoles and frogs), squid, or molluscs (Yu and Mott 1994; Mas-Coma et al. 2006). It is a common parasite of pigs in India, Pakistan, Myanmar, Vietnam, the Philippines, Indonesia, Malaysia, Thailand, Cambodia, China, Japan, England, Kazakhstan, the Volga Delta in Russia, USA (?), and Indian immigrants in Guyana (West Indies; imported case), Zambia, and Nigeria (Table 3.2) (Nicoll 1923; Graham 1960; Honjo et al. 1963; Beaver et al. 1984; Harinasuta et al. 1987; Mas-Coma et al. 2005, 2006). Human infections have been reported in India, Vietnam, the Philippines, Thailand, Myanmar, China, Kazakhstan, Russia, Indian migrants in Guyana, and Nigeria (Surinthrangkul et al. 1965; Beaver et al. 1984; Yu and Mott 1994; Dada-Adegbola et al. 2004; Mas-Coma et al. 2005, 2006; Sergiev et al. 2008; Tandon et al. 2014).

Cambodia A high percentage (22.3%) of cynomolgous monkeys (n = 1108) imported from Cambodia, Malaya, and the Philippines were found to be infected with *G. hominis* adult flukes (Honjo et al. 1963).

China Chen et al. (1985) described that Jiangsu Province is an area of this fluke distribution; humans, pigs, boars, deers, mice, and rats are the definitive hosts.

England Nicoll (1923) listed this fluke among the helminth species found from pigs.

India Lewis and McConnell in 1876 first discovered *G. hominis* infection in a human patient in Assam, and Giles in 1890 also found human infection with *G. hominis* (Buckley 1939). Stephens in 1906 examined sectioned material of *G. hominis* collected from humans by Ross in Assam (Lane 1924). Leiper (1913) described that Mackie around 1910 also found *G. hominis* flukes in 7 human cases in Assam, and in one case, as many as 200 worms were passed after treatment with thymol. Ramsay (1923) discovered *G. hominis* (?) adults in the intestine of pigs from Assam. Sharma in 1933 recorded *G. hominis* infection in 3.2% of soldiers and civilians in Shillong, and Bose in 1934 reported that over 200 specimens were recovered from 2 human cases from Bihar and Orissa (Buckley 1939). This parasite is very common in Bengal and Assam pigs, and in Kamrup district of Assam, 41.2% of 221 people examined were positive for the eggs of *G. hominis* in stool (Buckley 1939). Varma (1954) proposed a variant of *G. hominis* on specimens collected from pigs in India naming it as *G. hominis* var. *suis*; later, however, Shrivastav and Shah (1970) reviewed a number of *G. hominis* var. *suis* specimens from pigs in Madhya Pradesh and did not agree to its taxonomic validity. Ahluwalia (1960) studied on the pathology of *G. hominis* infection in pigs; the cecal mucosa was dragged up into a plug by the acetabulum of the fluke and showed desquamation and infiltration with eosinophils, lymphocytes, and plasma cells. Dutt and Srivastava (1966) studied on the life cycle of this parasite and discovered the snail host (*Helicorbis coenosus*) shedding the cercariae. Dutt and Srivastava (1972) further studied on the life cycle and described the larval morphology (miracidium, redia, cercaria, and metacercaria); encystation of the cercaria occurred on the flat surface of various objects, including the glass containers, cellophane sheet, shell of the snail host (live or dead), stalk of aquatic plants, or castoff skin of crustaceans. The rhesus monkeys were reported to be a natural definitive host (Dutt and Srivastava 1966; Harinasuta et al. 1987). The presence of *G. hominis* infections in pigs of Uttar Pradesh and Madras presidency has also been reported (Buckley 1939; Dutt and Srivastava 1966; Mas-Coma et al. 2006). The excretory system of *G. hominis* was studied by Tandon (1973b). A case of *G. hominis* infection was reported from a central state of India (Murty and Reddy 1980). Tandon and Maitra (1983) and Brennan et al. (1991, 1992) studied on the surface ultrastructure and histochemical characteristics of the tegument and lymph system of *G. hominis* adults. Pigs from Assam, Meghalaya, Mizoram, and Tripura were infected with *G. hominis* (Roy and Tandon 1992a). This parasite showed a seasonal occurrence similar to that of *Fasciolopsis buski* (Roy and Tandon 1992b).

Goswami et al. (2009) performed molecular studies on ITS rDNA of *G. hominis* collected from India. Pigs from Jammu district were shown to be infected with *G. hominis* by recovery of fecal eggs (Khajuria et al. 2010). A 15-year-old girl from North India suffered from dull aching, periumbilical abdominal pain for 7 months, and a parasite identified as *G. hominis* was removed from the mucosa of the large intestine under colonoscopy (Gupte et al. 2014). A human case (young adult) infected with *G. hominis* suffered from irritable bowel syndrome with excessive mucoid stools for 3 months; a moving worm was seen under colonoscopy with was removed and morphologically identified (Shukla et al. 2016).

Indonesia Sandground (1940) reported that field rats from Java were confirmed as a natural definitive host for *G. hominis*.

Japan Hashimoto and Honjo (1966) reported 21.4% infection of cynomolgous monkeys (*Macaca irus*) imported from tropical countries with *G. hominis*. Field rats in Japan were reported to be the natural definitive hosts for *G. hominis* (Harinasuta et al. 1987).

Kazakhstan Human infections are known in Kazakhstan (Beaver et al. 1984).

Malaysia The Napu mouse deers originated from Malay States and died in Zoological gardens in London were found infected with a large number of *G. hominis* specimens (Khalil 1923). A high percentage (22.3%) of cynomolgous monkeys (n = 1108) imported from Malaya, Cambodia, and the Philippines were found to be infected with *G. hominis* adult flukes (Honjo et al. 1963). The presence of *G. hominis* has been reported in Malaysia but the prevalence in the community has never been investigated (Shekhar 1997).

Myanmar The presence of *G. hominis* in pigs was first described by Chatterji (1938). Human infections are known in Myanmar (Mas-Coma et al. 2006).

Nigeria Dada-Adegbola et al. (2004) reported a 7-year-old girl who presented with malnutrition and anemia and was diagnosed by finding eggs in stools. Uzairue et al. (2013) detected eggs of *G. hominis* contaminated on vegetables (cabbages) sold in Ekpoma Markets, Edo State.

Pakistan *G. hominis* is distributed in Pakistan as a parasite of humans (Buckley 1964; Mas-Coma et al. 2006).

The Philippines Tuttle in 1910 reported a human case (Buckley 1964). A high percentage (22.3%) of cynomolgous monkeys (n = 1108) imported from the Philippines, Cambodia, and Malaya were found to be infected with *G. hominis* adult flukes (Honjo et al. 1963).

Russia The Volga Delta area was reported to have *G. hominis* infection (Mas-Coma et al. 2006). Gastrodiscoidosis has been highlighted as an important and dangerous zoonosis in humans and animals in Russia (Sergiev et al. 2008).

Thailand A 17-year-old Thai female from Pichit Province suffered from fecal urine, general edema with a palpable mass in the suprapubic area, and passing many intestinal worms; the worms were identified as *G. hominis* (Surinthrangkul et al. 1965). Field rats were found to be the natural definitive hosts for *G. hominis* (Harinasuta et al. 1987). *G. hominis* is listed as a human-infecting parasite in Thailand (Waikagul 1991).

USA Graham (1960) reported recovery of *G. hominis* adult specimens from the intestine and cecum of rhesus monkeys in Philadelphia, although the origin of the monkeys was not clearly described. A 2-year-old rhesus monkey (*Macaca mulatta*) was heavily infected with *G. hominis* in the ileum, cecum, and colon which led to protracted diarrhea, emaciation, marked dehydration, and death (Fox and Hall 1970); the origin of the monkey was not clearly stated.

Vietnam The presence of this fluke in pigs from Cochinchina (a southern part of Vietnam) was confirmed by Brau and Bruyant in 1911 (Buckley 1964). Mathis and Leger in 1911 found that no less than 5% of the pigs in Annam were infected with this fluke (Leiper 1913). Humans and pigs are listed as the definitive hosts of *G. hominis* (Sey 1985).

Zambia Hira (1983) found eggs of a paramphistome species (possibly *G. hominis*) in human stools, although the positive cases were considered a spurious infection.

3.2.3 Watsonius watsoni

3.2.3.1 *Watsonius watsoni* (Conyngham, 1904) Stiles and Goldberger, 1910

[syn. *Amphistomum watsoni* Conyngham, 1904; *Cladorchis watsoni* Shipley, 1905; *Watsonius macaci* Kobayashi, 1915; *Pseudodiscus watsoni* Maplestone, 1923]

Taxonomy and Morphology

The genus *Watsonius* (Gastrodiscidae) was proposed by Stiles and Goldberger in 1910 for the flukes found from a naturally infected West African Negro (a Nigerian) by Watson in 1904 and named as *Amphistoma watsoni* Conyngham, 1904 (Maplestone 1923; Goldsmid 1975). Kobayashi (1915, 1921) used this name. This fluke was once assigned to another genus *Pseudodiscus* Sonsino, 1895 by Maplestone (1923) naming as *Pseudodiscus watsoni*, and Bhalerao (1933) followed this name. However, Stunkard (1925) was of opinion to restore the genus *Watsonius*. Later, Yamaguti (1958, 1971) assigned this species to the genus *Watsonius*, and the name

Watsonius watsoni (Conyngham, 1904) Stiles and Goldberger, 1910 has been settled. The genus *Skrjabinocladorchis* was created by Chertkova in 1959 and the genus *Prochiorchis* was proposed by Dollfus in 1963; however, these 2 genera were synonymized with *Watsonius* by Jones (2005d). In the genus *Watsonius*, 5 additional species have been recorded; *W. noci* (Barrois, 1908), *W. ornatus* Railliet and Henry, 1912, *W. macaci* Kobayashi, 1915, *W. deschiensi* Pick, 1951, and *W. papillatus* Sey, 1984 (Kobayashi 1915, 1921; Yamaguti 1971; Sey 1984; Jones 1986). The name *W. noci* (reported from a monkey *Macaca mulatta*) appeared one more time in Sey (1985) but Yamaguti (1958, 1971) did not list this species. *W. ornatus* was synonymized with *Hawkesius hawkesi* by Bhalerao in 1933 and not listed by Yamaguti (1958, 1971). The morphology of *W. macaci* was redescribed by Kobayashi (1921); however, Maplestone (1923) treated this species as a synonym of *W. watsoni* (under the name *Pseudodiscus watsoni*). Jones (1986) reported the comparative morphology of the subfamily Gastrodiscinae members including *W. watsoni* and *W. deschiensi* adults. However, there has been little further evaluation of the validity of *W. papillatus*. Thus, only 3 species, including *W. watsoni, W. deschiensi,* and *W. papillatus*, can be listed in *Watsonius*.

Human *W. watsoni* infection was confirmed only one time in a Nigerian who died of severe diarrhea in 1904; many worms were recovered from the intestine, some attached to the duodenal and jejunal wall, and others free in the lumen of the colon (Goldsmid 1975; Beaver et al. 1984). However, 2 more suspected cases have been reported. Manson in 1908 detected a patient presumed to be *W. watsoni* infection who had violent diarrhea and revealed many flukes in the feces (Pick and Deschiens 1947). Another case (adult female) suspected as *W. watsoni* infection was found by recovery of eggs in feces in Northern Rhodesia (currently Nigeria) (Buckley 1946).

A green monkey (*Cercopithecus callitrichus*) from Africa was also found to have *W. watsoni* infection by Joyeux in 1912 (Maplestone 1923). Natural infection of baboons (*Papio cynocephalus*), each with 200–1000 worms, was reported (Pick and Deschiens 1947). The grey monkey (*Cercopithecus aethiops*) from Northern Rhodesia (currently Zambia) was also found to be infected wth *W. watsoni* (Buckley 1946). Crab-eating monkeys imported from Vietnam to Japan were found to have *W. watsonius* infection (Hayama and Nigi 1963). Various species of primates were added to be natural definitive hosts in East Asia and Africa (Beaver et al. 1984).

Adult flukes of *W. watsoni* are pear-shaped, somewhat flattened dorsoventrally, and reddish yellow when alive, have a translucent glistening appearance; their size is 8.0–10.0 mm in length and 4.0–5.0 mm in width (Maplestone 1923; Kuntz 1972; Beaver et al. 1984). The eggs are ovoid, operculate, light yellow, and immature when laid; they measure 122–130 m long and 75–80 m wide (Beaver et al. 1984). The morphology and dimension of larval stages have not been described.

Life Cycle

The life cycle has not been completely determined. The snail host was reported to be a species of *Physa* by Neveu-Lemaire in 1921 (Yamaguti 1971). Human or animal infection is probably acquired by ingesting vegetation on which the metacercariae have encysted (Beaver et al. 1984). The natural definitive hosts are monkeys (Beaver et al. 1984); the green monkey (*Cercopithecus callitrichus*), grey monkey (*Cercopithecus aethiops*), crab-eating monkeys (*Macaca irus*), and baboons (*Papio cynocephalus, Papio papio,* and *Papio sphinx*) are the major species involved (Maplestone 1923; Buckley 1946; Pick and Deschiens 1947; Hayama and Nigi 1963; Kuntz 1972; Ebbert et al. 2013, 2015).

Epidemiology and Geographical Distribution
There have been only 1 (confirmed) to 3 (including 2 suspected cases by Manson in 1908 and Buckley in 1946) human case reports infected with this fluke (Buckley 1946; Pick and Deschiens 1947; Beaver et al. 1984). The mode of human infection is unknown but ingesting metacercaria-containing vegetation is strongly suggested (Beaver et al. 1984). The geographical distribution of this fluke is limited in Africa and Asia (Table 3.2) (Nigeria, Zambia, Senegal, Vietnam) (Leiper 1913; Buckley 1946; Hayama and Nigi 1963; Goldsmid 1975; Ebbert et al. 2013).

Nigeria The first and only confirmed human case was found in Nigeria who died of severe diarrhea by Conyngham in 1904 (Goldsmid 1975; Beaver et al. 1984).

Senegal Ebbert et al. (2013) reported the prevalence (44.0%; n = 100) of *W. watsoni* eggs in deposited feces of baboons (*Papio papio*) at Mt. Assirik.

Vietnam Hayama and Nigi (1963) working in Japan Monkey Center investigated helminth parasites of monkeys imported from different countries in Asia, Africa, and South America; *W. watsoni* was found in the cecum and colon of 20 out of 81 crab-eating monkeys imported from Vietnam.

Zambia Buckley (1946) performed a helminthological survey of humans in North Rhodesia (currently Zambia) and found amphistome eggs in an adult female (presumed to be *W. watsoni* eggs). It was aslo mentioned that *W. watsoni* specimens were recovered post-mortem from a gray monkey at Mwamfuli (Buckley 1946).

3.2.4 Potentially Zoonotic amphistome spp.

Potentially zoonotic amphistome species include *F. cobboldi* (Poirier, 1883) Stiles and Goldberger, 1910, *W. deschiensi* Pick, 1951, and *W. papillatus* Sey, 1984.

3.2.5 Genomics and Proteomics

The karyotypes of several amphistome species were investigated. One example was the karyotype study of *F. cobboldi* performed in South Korea (Rhee et al. 1988). The chromosome numbers in the haploid and diploid cells of *F. cobboldi* were n = 9 and

2n = 18, respectively; the meiotic divisions were observed frequently, and 1904 haploid and 49 diploid cells were recognized (Rhee et al. 1988).

Genomic studies on amphistomes began from the study of Morgan and Blair (1998) who analyzed rRNA ITS2 gene sequences of various trematode species, including *Fischoederius* spp. (*F. baliensis, F. folicae, F. brotoi, F. dobsoni,* and *F. tatoi*); the results revealed that the 5 species clustered together and showed high phylogenetic relationships with each other. Wongsawad et al. (2006) investigated the minimum DNA quantities of various trematodes, *F. elongatus*, to be detected by optical (by electrophotometer) and HAT-RAPD methods; only a single specimen of eggs, metacercariae, and adults could be amplified with distinct bands. Sripalwit et al. (2007) used PCR-RAPD method to detect the genomic DNA of 3 paramphistome flukes, including *F. elongatus*, from Thailand; 50 polymorphic markers were detected. Wongsawad (2011) developed a HAT-RAPD PCR technique to detect the genes of trematode species, including *F. elongatus* and *Stellantchasmus falcatus*. Ghatani et al. (2012) analyzed the ribosomal ITS sequence and secondary structure of 5 species of pouched amphistomes (Gastrothylacidae) from cattle in north-east India, including *F. elongatus* and *F. cobboldi*; the results revealed that the 5 species studied were clustered and separated from the other species of amphistomes, including *G. hominis* and *Homalogaster paloniae*. Mitochondrial cytochrome *c* oxidase 1 (CO1) was used to differentiate the species of the family Gastrothylacidae from India, including *F. elongatus* and *F. cobboldi* (Ghatani et al. 2014). The complete mitochondrial genome of *F. elongatus* was finally analyzed in China using specimens collected from cattle in Hubei Province (Yang et al. 2015).

Genomic studies on *G. hominis* are very few and began by Goswami et al. (2009). The phylogeny of *G. hominis* was studied using ITS rDNA sequence of worms obtained from pigs of Assam and Meghalaya origin; the maximum similarity was observed with *Homalogaster paloniae*, a bovine amphistome species belonging to the Gastrodiscidae (Goswami et al. 2009). Shylla et al. (2013) analyzed 28S rRNA D2 domain of several paramphistome species from India and observed close relationships between *G. hominis* and *H. paloniae*. Molecular studies on *W. watsoni* are unavailable.

3.2.6 Pathology and Immunology

Most of the studies on the pathology of amphistome infections have been performed on *G. hominis*, and those on *F. elongatus* and *W. watsoni* are hardly available. In *G. hominis* infection in pigs, Ahluwalia (1960) reported subacute inflammation of the cecum where the parasites caused desquamation of the mucosa, cellular infiltrations with eosinophils, lymphocytes, and plasma cells, and edematous and thickened submucosa; these lesions were thought to be ascribed to the continual impact of the discoidal region of the parasite body on the mucosa of the cecum. The acetabulum was seen to drag the mucosa as a plug which stood like a papilla and occupied an eccentric position in the sharply defined circular area (Ahluwalia 1960). Worms can be seen in the cecum, especially near the ileocecal valve, and at the site of attachment a deep imprint of the fluke is seen (Ahluwalia 1960). Marked desquamation of the epithelial lining, hypersecretion of the mucus, and necrosis of the mucous glands were observed in a histopathological examination; the lamina propria showed massive infiltration of eosinophils in the crypt of Lieberkühn along with lymphocytes, macrophages, and plama cells (Shrivastav and Shah 1970; Mas-Coma et al. 2006). Sometimes, the infected ceca are so severely destroyed that any healthy tissue can hardly be seen (Shrivastav and Shah 1970). Death occurred in a 2-year-old rhesus monkey reared in US Army after developing anorexia, emaciation, protracted diarrhea, and marked dehydration; post-mortem examination revealed intussusception of the colon and multifocal necrosis of the intestinal mucosa, and more than 200 adult specimens of *G. hominis* were recovered in the ileum, cecum, and colon (Fox and Hall 1970).

In humans, *G. hominis* infection may cause severe mucosal inflammation in the cecum and ascending colon and severe diarrhea, and in untreated patients, especially children, death may occur (Kumar 1980). For example, in a 17-year-old Thai girl, the main clinical complaint was passing urine containing feces for 15 days and passing many worms on the day before admission to the hospital; she also had general edema with a palpable mass in the suprapubic area (Surinthrangkul et al. 1965). A jejuno-vesical fistula was confirmed by means of X-ray barium enema; she finally died, and the autopsy revealed a jejuno-ileo-vesico-vaginal fistula and additional lymphosarcoma of the large intestine and mesenteric lymph nodes (Surinthrangkul et al. 1965). In Russia, Sergiev et al. (2008) defined *G. hominis* infection as a dangerous zoonosis causing severe infections in animals and humans. In India, inflammation of the cecum and ascending colon was found in a 15-year-old girl, and in colonoscopy multiple parasites diagnosed as *G. hominis* were found attached to the mucosa which bled on removal of the parasite (Gupte et al. 2014). Another patient from India (a young adult male) presented with irritable bowel syndrome, and colonoscopy revealed *G. hominis* worms; however, it was suggested that *G. hominis* infection may not be the cause of the symptoms (Shukla et al. 2016).

Immunological studies on human-infecting amphistomes are scarce. The so-called crowding effect was observed in *F. elongatus* infection in buffaloes; when the intensity of infection, either by its own species or other parasites also, is low they attain a very large size but remain immature, on the other hand, in a heavily crowded state very small worms become fully mature and gravid (Tandon 1973a). ELISA, dot-ELISA, and plate-ELISA have been introduced for serodiagnosis of amphistomiasis of ruminants but its practical use is only at its rudimentary stage (Tandon et al. 2014). Three prominent bands (66 kDa, 20 kDa, and 14 kDa) and 3 minor bands (95 kDa, 40 kDa, and 35 kDa) were observed in SDS-PAGE of the excretory-secretory antigen of *F. elongatus* from India (Arunkumar and Krupakaran 2016).

3.2.7 Clinical Manifestations, Diagnosis and Treatment

Human amphistome infections have been reported occasionally in *G. hominis* but extremely rare in *F. elongatus* (one confirmed case) and *W. watsoni* (3 suspected cases). Therefore, clinical details are known only in *G. hominis* infection. Severe mucosal inflammation in the cecum and colon with diarrhea may occur, and in untreated patients, especially children, death may occur (Kumar 1980). In a 17-year-old Thai girl, the clinical complaints included passing urine containing feces for 15 days; she also had a long history of weakness, anemia, and weight loss for 8 months before passing fecal urine and having general edema with a palpable mass in the suprapubic area (Surinthrangkul et al. 1965). A jejuno-vesical fistula was confirmed by means of X-ray barium enema; she finally died, and the autopsy revealed a jejuno-ileo-vesico-vaginal fistula (Surinthrangkul et al. 1965). A 7-year-old Nigerian child presented with malnutrition and anemia and found to have *G. hominis* infection; after deworming with 500 mg single dose of mebendazole there was tremendous improvement of the health status of the child (Dada-Adegbola et al. 2004). In colonoscopy of a 15-year-old girl in India who suffered from inflammation of the cecum and ascending colon, multiple parasites diagnosed as *G. hominis* were found attached to the mucosa which bled on removal of the parasite (Gupte et al. 2014). She was prescribed with mebendazole 100 mg twice a day for 3 days, the follow-up colonoscopy showed a reduced number of parasites; mebendazole for 3 days was given again resulting in normal colon and marked improvement in weight gaining (Gupte et al. 2014). Another patient from India presented with irritable bowel syndrome, and colonoscopy revealed *G. hominis* worms with moving proboscis in the cecum; he was treated with praziquantel (Shukla et al. 2016).

Human *G. hominis* infection can be easily diagnosed by finding the characteristic eggs in feces (Mas-Coma et al. 2006). Care should be taken to differentiate *G. hominis* eggs from those of *Fasciolopsis buski* which is commonly mixed distributed in endemic areas of Asia; however, the eggs of *G. hominis* are ovoid and pale greenish grey, whereas those of *F. buski* are oval and yellowish-brown in color (Mas-Coma et al. 2006). In order to distinguish the eggs of different species more clearly, it is advisable to use contrast stains such as methylene blue or methyl green, instead of Lugol (Tandon et al. 2014). Immunological and molecular diagnosis are not yet practicable and feasible.

Treatment can be done using conventional drugs, such as thymol, carbon tetrachloride, and tetrachlorethylene; however, praziquantel can be used as a promising drug (Mas-Coma et al. 2006). A patient was treated with praziquantel (Shukla et al. 2016). Alternatively, mebendazole (Dada-Adegbola et al. 2004) and albendazole can also be used for treatment of human *G. hominis* infection.

3.2.8 Prevention and Control

For prevention and control of amphistome infections in ruminant animals, several methods can be employed as follows: control of grazing water and water resources, chemotherapeutic control, immunization (using homologous or heterologous antigens), and control of intermediate hosts (snail control) (Tandon et al. 2014). The control strategy for human *G. hominis* infection is similar and can include prevention of the human contamination, actions at human level to cut disease dissemination by humans, control of the disease at the animal reservoir level, and actions at the level of the intermediate molluscan host (Mas-Coma et al. 2006; Tandon et al. 2014).

References

Ahluwalia SS (1960) *Gastrodiscoides hominis* (Lewis and McConnell) Laiper, 1913 (the amphistome parasite of man and pig). Ind J Med Res 48:315–325

Anuracpreeda P, Panyarachun B, Ngamniyom A et al (2012) *Fischoederius cobboldi*: a scanning electron microscopy investigation of surface morphology of adult rumen fluke. Exp Parasitol 130:400–407

Arunkumar S, Krupakaran RP (2016) Analysis of polypeptide profile of excretory/secretory antigens of *Fischoederius elongatus* from cattle origin using silver staining. Life Sci Int Res J 3:111–113

Balachandran C, Raman A, Pazhanivel N (2010) An outbreak of amphistomiasis in an organized sheep farm. Tamilnadu J Vet Anim Sci 6:286–288

Beaver PC, Jung RC, Cupp EW (1984) Clinical parasitology, 9th edn. Lea and Febiger, Philadelphia

Bhalerao GD (1933) The trematode parasites of the Indian elephant, *Elaphas indicia*. Ind J Vet Sci Anim Husb 3:103–115

Brennan GP, Hanna REB, Nizami WA (1991) Ultrastructural and histochemical observations on the tegument of *Gastrodiscoides hominis* (Paramphistoma: Digenea). Int J Parasitol 21:897–905

Brennan GP, Hanna REB, Nizami WA (1992) Studies on the ultrastructure and histochemistry of the lymph system of *Gastrodiscoides hominis* (Paramphistoma: Digenea). Int J Parasitol 22:479–489

Buckley JJC (1939) Observation on *Gastrodiscoides hominis* and *Fasciolopsis buski* in Assam. J Helminthol 17:1–12

Buckley JJC (1946) A helminthological survey in Northern Rhodesia. J Helminthol 21:111–174

Buckley JJC (1964) The problem of *Gastrodiscoides hominis* (Lewis and McConnell, 1876) Leiper, 1913. J Helminthol 38:1–6

Chai JY (2007) Intestinal flukes. In: Murrell KD, Fried B (eds) Food-borne parasitic zoonoses. Fish and plant-borne parasites. Springer, New York, pp 53–115

Chatterji RC (1938) Annotated list of the helminths recorded from domesticated animals of Burma. Part I. Trematoda. Proc Nat Acad Sci India 8:93–104

Chen HT (1937) Parasites in slaughter houses in Canton. Part III. Trematodes and cestodes parasitic in the alimentary tract of buffaloes. Lingnan Sci J 16:585–590

Chen HT, Chen S, Chu H et al (1985) Chapter 5. Echinostomatidae dietz, 1909. Platyhelminthes, Trematoda, Digenea (1). Fauna Sinica. Science Press, Beijing, pp 333–403

Dada-Adegbola HO, Falade CO, Oluwatoba OA et al (2004) *Gastrodiscoides hominis* infection in a Nigerian-case report. West Afr J Med 23:185–186

Dutt SC, Srivastata HD (1966) The intermediate host and the cercaria of *Gastrodiscoides hominis* (Trematoda: Gastrodiscidae). Prelim Rep J Helminthol 40:45–52

Dutt SC, Srivastata HD (1972) The life history of *Gastrodiscoides hominis* (Lewis and McConnell, 1876) Leiper, 1913-the amphistome parasite of man and pig. J Helminthol 46:35–46

Ebbert MA, McGrew WC, Marchant LF (2013) Community composition, correlations among taxa, prevalence, and richness in gastrointestinal parasites of baboons in Senegal, West Africa. Primates 54:183–189

Ebbert MA, McGrew WC, Marchant LF (2015) Differences between chimpanzee and baboon gastrointestinal parasite communities. Parasitology. https://doi.org/10.1017/S0031182015000104

Eduardo SL (1981) *Fischoederius brecaudatus*, a new species of pouched amphistome (Gastrothylacidae) from ruminants in the Philippines. Syst Parasitol 3:1–6

Eduardo SL (2009) *Fischoederius emiljavieri,* a new species of pouched amphistome from ruminants in the Philippines and Indonesia and redescription of *Fischoederius cobboldi* (Poirier, 1883) Stiles & Goldberger, 1910 (Trematoda: Gastrothylacidae). Phil J Vet Med 46:44–52

Eduardo SL, Javellana CRH (1988) *Fischoederius philippinensis,* a new species of gastrothylacid parasites from ruminants in the Philippines. Trans Nat Acad Sci Technol (Phil) 10:177–186

Eduardo SL, Javellana CRH (2009) *Fischoederius upiensis* new species from ruminants in the Philippines with remarks on other species of the genus *Fischoederius* Stiles & Goldberger, 1910 (Trematoda: Paramphistomoidea: Gastrothylacidae). Phil J Vet Med 45:22–29

Fan PF, Chen KO, Liu YI et al (1990) Ultrastructure of tegumental surface of *Cotylophoron fuelleborni* and *Fischoederius elongatus*. J Shanghai Agric Coll 8:35–40

Fischthal JH, Kuntz RE (1975) Some digenetic trematodes of mammals from Taiwan. Proc Helminthol Soc Wash 42:149–157

Fox JG, Hall WC (1970) Fluke (*Gastrodiscoides hominis*) infection in a rhesus monkey with related intussusception of the colon. J Am Vet Med Assoc 157:714–716

Ghatani S, Shylla JA, Tandon V et al (2012) Molecular characterization of pouched amphistome parasites (Trematoda: Gastrothylacidae) using ribosomal ITS2 sequence and secondary structures. J Helminthol 86:117–124

Ghatani S, Shylla JA, Roy B et al (2014) Multilocus sequence evaluation for differentiating species of the trematode family Gastrothylacidae, with a note on the utility of mitochondrial COI motifs in species identification. Gene 548:277–284

Goldsmid JM (1975) Ecological and cultural aspects of human trematodiasis (excluding schistosomiasis) in Africa. Cent Afr J Med 21:49–53

Goswami LM, Prasad PK, Tandon V et al (2009) Molecular characterization of *Gastrodiscoides hominis* (Platyhelminthes: Trematoda: Digenea) inferred from ITS rDNA sequence analysis. Parasitol Res 104:1485–1490

Graham GL (1960) Parasitism in monkeys. Ann N Y Acad Sci 85:842–860

Gupte A, Shah C, Koticha A et al (2014) *Gastrodiscoides hominis* infestation of colon: endoscopic appearance. Gastrointest Endosc 79:549–550

Harinasuta T, Bunnag D, Radomyos P (1987) Intestinal fluke infections. Bailliere's Clin Trop Med Commun Dis 2(3):695–721

Hashimoto I, Honjo S (1966) Survey of helminth parasites in cynomolgous monkeys (*Macaca irus*). Jpn J Med Sci Biol 19:215–227

Hayama S, Nigi H (1963) Investigation on the helminth parasites in the Japan Monkey Centre during 1959–1961. Primates 4:97–112

Hira PR (1983) Further spurious parasitic infestations of man in Zambia. Cent Afr J Med 29:33–40

Honjo S, Muto K, Fujiwara T et al (1963) Statistical survey of intestinal parasites in cynomolgous monkeys (*Macaca irus*). Jpn J Med Sci Biol 16:217–224

Huang ZQ (1992) First case report of *Fischoederius elongatus*. Proc Third Symp Parasitol (Chin Soc Parasitol), pp 116 (in Chinese)

Jones A (1986) A comparative morphological study of the subfamily Gastrodiscinae Monticelli, 1892 (Paramphistomidae) with comments on some members of related subfamilies. J Nat Hist 20:863–880

Jones A (2005a) Superfamily Paramphistomoidea Fischoeder, 1901. In: Jones A, Bray RA, Gibson DI (eds) Keys to the Trematoda, Natural history museum, vol 2. CABI, London, pp 221–227
Jones A (2005b) Family Cladorchiidae Fischoeder, 1901. In: Jones A, Bray RA, Gibson DI (eds) Keys to the trematoda, Natural history museum, vol 2. CABI, London, pp 257–317
Jones A (2005c) Family Gastrothylacidae Stiles and Goldberger, 1910. In: Jones A, Bray RA, Gibson DI (eds) Keys to the Trematoda, Natural History Museum, vol 2. CABI, London, pp 337–341
Jones A (2005d) Family Gastrodiscidae Monticelli, 1892. In: Jones A, Bray RA, Gibson DI (eds) Keys to the trematoda, Natural history museum, vol 2. CABI, London, pp 325–336
Khajuria JK, Katoch R, Yadav A et al (2010) Prevalence of gastrointestinal parasites affecting pigs in Jammu district of Jammu and Kashmir. Vet Pract 11:167–168
Khalil M (1923) A description of *Gastrodiscoides hominis* from the Napu Mouse deer. Proc R Soc Med 16 (Sect Trop Dis Parasitol):8–14
Kobayashi H (1915) Studies on digenetic trematodes in Japan. Part 8. A new species of *Watsonius* infecting monkeys. Dobutsugaku Zasshi (322):421–427 (in Japanese)
Kobayashi H (1921) On some digenetic trematodes in Japan. Parasitology 12:380–410
Kumar V (1980) The digenetic trematodes, *Fasciolopsis buski, Gastrodiscoides hominis* and *Artyfechinostomum malayanum*, as zoonotic infections in South Asian countries. Ann Soc Belge Med Trop 60:331–339
Kuntz RE (1972) Trematodes of the intestinal tract and biliary passages. In: Pathology of Simian Primates, Part II. Karger, Basel, pp 104–123
Lane C (1922) A demonstration. Trans R Soc Trop Med Hyg 16:22
Lane C (1924) Gastrodiscus hominis. Ann Trop Med Parasitol 18:27–32
Leiper RT (1913) Observations on certain helminths of man. Trans Soc Trop Med Hyg London (1912–1913) 6:265–297
Li D (1991) A case of human *Fischoederius elongatus* infection in China. Ann Bull Soc Parasitol Guangdong Province 12:155–156 (in Chinese)
Maplestone PA (1923) A revision of the Amphistomata of mammals. Ann Trop Med Parasitol 17:113–213
Mas-Coma S, Bargues MD, Valero MA (2005) Fascioliasis and other plant-borne trematode zoonoses. Int J Parasitol 35:1255–1278
Mas-Coma S, Bargues MD, Valero MA (2006) Gastrodiscoidiasis, a plant-borne zoonotic disease caused by the intestinal amphistome fluke *Gastrodiscoides hominis* (Trematoda: Gastrodiscidae). Rev Iberica Parasitol 66:75–81
Morgan JAT, Blair D (1998) Trematode and monogenean rRNA ITS2 secondary structures support a four-domain model. J Mol Evol 47:406–419
Mukherjee RP (1966) Studies on the life history of *Fischoederius elongatus* (Poirier, 1833) Stiles and Goldberger, 1910, an amphistome parasite of cow and buffalo in India. Ind J Helminthol 18:5–14
Mukherjee RP, Chauhan BS (1972) On Indian amphistomes. Rec Zool Sur India 67:65–80
Murty CV, Reddy CR (1980) A case report of *Gastrodiscoides hominis* infestation. Ind J Pathol Microbiol 23:303–304
Nicoll W (1923) A reference list of the trematode parasites of British mammals. Parasitology 15:236–252
Nicoll W (1927) A reference list of the trematode parasites of man and the primates. Parasitology 19:338–351
Pick F, Deschiens R (1947) Infection of baboons with *Watsonius watsoni*. Bull Soc Pathol Exot 40:202–211. (in French)
Ramsay GC (1923) The dissemination of human helminthic infections by animals. Ind Med Gaz 1923:422–424
Rao MAN, Ayyar LSP (1932) A preliminary report on two amphistome cercariae and their adults. Ind J Vet Sci Anim Husb 2:402–405

Rhee JK, Youn RH, Lee HI (1988) The karyotype of *Fischoederius cobboldi* (Poirrier, 1883) from Korean cattle. Korean J Parasitol 26:107–111 (in Korean)

Roy B, Tandon V (1992a) Trematodes in North-East India: a study on the spectrum of digenetic trematodes among pigs, buffaloes, cattle, goats and sheep. Ind J Anim Health 13:5–14

Roy B, Tandon V (1992b) Seasonal prevalence of some zoonotic trematode infections in cattle and pigs in the northeast mountain zone in India. Vet Parasitol 41:69–76

Sandground JH (1940) *Gastrodiscus hominis* a parasite of rats in Java. J Parasitol 26(Suppl):34: abstract no. 33

Sarmah PC, Laha R, Bhattacharjee K et al (2014) Human consumption of rumen flukes of cattle in India. Southeast Asian J Trop Med Public Health 45:26–30

Sergiev VP, Uspenskiĭ AV, Gorokhov et al (2008) Gastrodiscoidosis is a dangerous zoonosis. Med Parazitol Parazit Bolezni 3:47–51 (in Russian)

Sey O (1984) Description of *Watsonius papillatus* sp. n. and the revision of the subfamily Watsoniinae Näsmark, 1937 (Trematoda: Paramphistomata). Acta Zool Hung 30:493–510

Sey O (1985) Amphistomes of Vietnamese vertebrates (Trematoda: Amphistomida). Parasit Hung 18:17–24

Shekhar KC (1997) Epidemiological aspects of aquaculture in relation to fish borne trematodiasis in Malaysia. Southeast Asian J Trop Med Public Health 28:54–57

Shrivastav HO, Shah HL (1970) On *Gastrodiscoides hominis* (Lewis and McConnell, 1876) Leiper, 1913 from pigs (*Sus scrofa domesticus*) in Madhya Pradesh, its pathology and pulic health importance. Ind J Pathol Bacteriol 13:68–72

Shukla SK, Asati PK, Banerjee T et al (2016) Rare trematode infestation in irritable bowel syndrome: pathogen or commensal? J Digest Endosc 7:123–124

Shylla JA, Ghatani S, Tandon V (2013) Utility of divergent domains of 28S ribosomal RNA in species discrimination of paramphistomes (Trematoda: Digenea: Paramphistomoidea). Parasitol Res 112:4239–4253

Skrjabin KI (1949) Suborder Paramphistomata (Szidat, 1936) Skrjabin & Schulz, 1937. In: Skrjabin KI (ed) Trematodes of animals and man, vol 3. Academy of Sciences of the Union of Soviet Socialist Republics, Moscow, pp 1–623. (translated from Russian)

Sripalwit P, Wongsawad C, Wongsawad P et al (2007) High annealing temperature-random amplified polymorphic DNA (HAT-RAPD) analysis of three paramphistome flukes from Thailand. Exp Parasitol 115:98–102

Stunkard HW (1925) The present status of the amphistome problem. Parasitology 17:137–148

Surinthrangkul B, Gonthian S, Pradatsundarasar A (1965) *Gastrodiscoides hominis* from man in Thailand. J Med Assoc Thailand 48:96–103

Tandon RS (1961) Studies on the excretory system of amphistome parasites of ruminants. Parasitology 51:127–132

Tandon RS (1973a) Studies on "crowding effect" on *Gastrothylax crumenifer* and *Fischoederius elongatus*, the common amphistome parasites of ruminants, observed under natural conditions. Res Bull Meguro Parasitol Mus 7:12–14

Tandon RS (1973b) Excretory system of *Gastrodiscoides hominis* (Lewis and McConnell, 1876) Leiper, 1913, a common amphistome parasite of man and pigs in India. Zool Anz 1973:317–320

Tandon V, Maitra SC (1983) Surface morphology of *Gastrodiscoides hominis* (Lewis & McConnell, 1876) Leiper, 1913 (Trematoda: Digenea) as revealed by scanning electron microscopy. J Helminthol 57:339–342

Tandon V, Roy B, Shylla JA et al (2014) Chapter 11. Amphistomes. In Toledo R, Fried B (eds) Digenetic trematodes. Springer. Adv Exp Med Biol 766:365–392

Uzairue LI, Ugbor CI, Ezeah GA et al (2013) *Gastrodiscoides hominis* infestation on vegetables (cabbages) sold in Ekpoma Markets, Edo State, Southern Nigeria – a case report. Int J Basic Appl Innov Res 2:37–39

Vaidyanathan SN (1941) Experimental infestation with *Fischoederius elongatus* in a calf at Madras. Ind J Vet Sci 11:243

Varma AK (1954) Human and swine *Gastrodiscoides*. Ind J Med Res 42:475–479

Waikagul J (1991) Intestinal fluke infections in Southeast Asia. Southeast Asian J Trop Med Public Health 22(suppl):158–162
Wongsawad C (2011) Development of HAT-RAPD marker for detection of *Stellantchasmus falcatus* infection. Southeast Asian J Trop Med Public Health 42:46–52
Wongsawad C, Wongsawad P, Chai JY et al (2006) DNA quatities and qualities from various stages of some trematodes using optical and HAT-RAPD methods. Southeast Asian J Trop Med Public Health 37(suppl 3):62–68
Yamaguti S (1935) *Fischoederius elongatus* (Poirier, 1883) and *F. siamensis* Stiles et Goldberger, 1910. J Parasitol 21:416
Yamaguti S (1939) Studies on helminth fauna of Japan. Part 27. Trematodes of mammals, II. Jpn J Med Sci VI. Bact Parasitol 1:131–153
Yamaguti S (1954) Parasitic worms mainly from Celebes. Part 5. Trematodes of mammals. Acta Med Okayama 8:341–353
Yamaguti S (1958) Systema Helminthum. Vol. I. The digenetic trematodes of vertebrates (Part I). Interscience Publishers Inc, New York, pp 1–979
Yamaguti S (1971) Synopsis of digenetic trematodes of vertebrates. Keigaku Publishing Co., Tokyo
Yang X, Zhao Y, Wang L et al (2015) Analysis of the complete *Fichoederius elongatus* (Paramphistomidae, Trematode) mitochondrial genome. Parasit Vectors 8:279
Yu SH, Mott KE (1994) Epidemiology and morbidity of food-borne intestinal trematode infections. Trop Dis Bull 91:R125–R152
Zhaltsanova DSD (1972) Occurrence of *Fischoederius elongatus* in the Buryat ASSR. Materialy Nauchnykh Issledovanii Chlenov Vsesoyuznogo Obshchestva Gel'mintologov 1970–1971 24:49–50 (in Russian)

Chapter 4
Diplostomes

4.1 Family Diplostomidae

The family Diplostomidae Poirier, 1886, which belongs to the superfamily Diplostomoidea Poirier, 1886 of which name has been used after Gibson (1996), is a group of trematodes infecting the intestines of birds and mammals (Niewiadomska 2002a, b). This family has a foliate, spatulate, or calyciform forebody, and 'neascus' or 'diplostomulum' type metacercariae (Shoop 1989a; Niewiadomska 2002b). Two genera, *Neodiplostomum* (*Neodiplostomum seoulense*) and *Fibricola* (*Fibricola cratera*), have been known to be zoonotic (with natural human infections) (Table 3.1) or potentially zoonotic (having a successful human experimental infection), respectively (Seo et al. 1982; Shoop 1989b; Chai 2007, Chai et al. 2009). The Strigeidae Railliet, 1919, another family, which is closely related to the Diplostomidae, infects the intestines of birds and rarely mammals and has a tubular, cup-shaped, or bulbiform forebody, and 'tetracotyle' type metacercariae (Niewiadomska 2002c). A species of this family, *Cotylurus japonicus*, is known to infect humans (Chai 2007) which has been described in Chap. 9 (Miscellaneous zoonotic species reported from humans) in this book.

The family Diplostomidae has 4 subfamilies, including Alariinae Hall and Wigdor, 1918, Codonocephalinae Sudarikov, 1959, Crassiphialinae Sudarikov, 1960, and Diplostominae Poirier, 1886 (Niewiadomska 2002b). The subfamily Alariinae infects mammals and has 'diplostomulum' type metacercariae; it includes 11 genera (*Podospathalium, Bursotrema, Pharyngostomum, Pharyngostomoides, Procyotrema, Fibricola, Prudhoella, Cynodiplostomum, Didelphiodiplostomum, Paralaria,* and *Alaria*) (Niewiadomska 2002b). The subfamily Conodocephalinae infects birds, lacks pseudosuckers, and has only one genus *Conodocephalus* Diesing, 1850 (Niewiadomska 2002b). The subfamily Crassiphialinae infects birds, may have pseudosuckers, and has metacercariae of 'neascus' type; it includes 15 genera (*Pulvinifer, Posthodiplostomoides, Bolbophorus, Pseudoscolopacitrema, Allodiplostomum, Subuvulifer, Cercocotyla, Crassiphiala, Pseudodiplostomum,*

J.-Y. Chai, *Human Intestinal Flukes*,
https://doi.org/10.1007/978-94-024-1704-3_4

Uvulifer, Mesoophorodiplostomum, Scolopacitrema, Conodiplostomum, Ornithodiplostomum, and *Posthodiplostomum*) (Niewiadomska 2002b). The subfamily Diplostominae infects birds (can also infect mammals, such as in *Neodiplostomum seoulense*; Chai et al. 2009), may have pseudosuckers, having 'diplostomulum' type metacercariae, and consists of 14 genera (*Harvardia, Sphincterodiplostomum, Hysteromorpha, Neoharvardia, Adenodiplostomum, Austrodiplostomum, Bursatintinnabulus, Bursacetabulus, Diplostomum, Dolichorchis, Glossodiplostomoides, Tylodelphys, Lophasicyadiplostomum,* and *Neodiplostomum*) (Niewiadomska 2002b).

Shoop (1989a) studied the significance of the metacercarial type for the systematics of the superfamily Diplostomoidea, using 27 species of adults and 7 species of metacercariae representing 2 families, the Diplostomidae and Strigeidae. He obtained several sister groups that showed a remarkable concordance of phylogenetic trees based on morphological types of adults and metacercariae (Shoop 1989a). He accepted the classification of the family Strigeidae with a cup-shaped forebody and bilobed holdfast organ, the monophyly of which is supported by having 'tetracotyle' type of metacercariae (Shoop 1989a). However, in the case of the Diplostomidae (sensu Dubois, 1970), he did not find characters to support its monophyly but considered this as paraphyletic, composed of 3 monophyletic groups of family rank, the Neodiplostomidae (a new family with 2 new subfamilies Crassiphialinae and Neodiplostominae), Bolbophoridae (a new family), and Diplostomidae (with subfamilies Diplostominae and Alariinae) (Shoop 1989a). Crassiphialinae has 'neascus' type metacercariae, Neodiplostomidae has 'neodiplostomulum' type, Bolbophoridae has 'prodiplostomulum' type, Diplostominae and Alariinae have 'diplostomulum' type, and Strigeidae has 'tetracotyle' type metacercariae (Shoop 1989a). This classification seems to be useful, and the genera grouped together have a common metacercarial type; however, this systematics will be more readily discernible if more abundant data can be accumulated (Niewiadomska 2002a). In this context, Niewiadomska (2002a, b) acknowledged the family Diplostomidae Poirier, 1886 (and the subfamily Diplostominae Poirier, 1886) to which the genus *Neodiplostomum* belongs but did not accept the new family name, the Neodiplostomidae, proposed by Shoop (1989a).

Molecular phylogeny of the families Diplostomidae and Strigeidae was also studied by Lapierre (2011). Analyses of 4 molecular markers of varying evolutionary rates (SSU, LSU, ITS, and COI) revealed that genera currently included in the Diplostomidae and Strigeidae cluster into a single monophyletic clade having a single common ancestor, and it was justifiable to consider the clade as a single family, the Diplostomidae Poirier, 1866 (Lapierre 2011). The division of the Diplostomidae into 3 families (including 2 new families) by Shoop (1989a) which was supported by Brooks and McLennen (1993), i.e., the Neodiplostomidae, Bolbophoridae, and Diplostomidae, with the Strigeidae remaining monophyletic was not supported by this molecular study (Lapierre 2011). However, the significant systemic value of the metacercarial types, an important conclusion of Shoop (1989a), was agreed (Lapierre 2011).

4.2 *Neodiplostomum* and *Fibricola*

Two genera (species) of the Diplostomidae are known to be able to infect the human host; one is *Neodiplostomum* (*Neodiplostomum seoulense*), and the other is *Fibricola* (*Fibricola cratera*) (Chai 2007; Chai et al. 2009). *Neodiplostomum* was assigned to the subfamily Diplostomidae as it has vitellaria in both fore- and hindbody and is parasite of birds (primarily); it has the metacercariae of 'diplostomulum' type which consists of only the forebody (Niewiadomska 2002b) or 'neodiplostomulum' type which consists of the forebody and a small primordial stage of the hindbody. *Fibricola* was assigned to the subfamily Alariinae as it has vitellaria mostly in forebody and may penetrate the anterior part of the hindbody and is parasite of mammals; it also has the metacercariae of 'diplostomulum' type (Niewiadomska 2002b). However, the status of the genera *Neodiplostomum* Railliet, 1819 and *Fibricola* Dubois, 1932 still represents a special problem (Niewiadomska 2002b).

Dubois (1970) distinguished *Neodiplostomum* and *Fibricola* on the basis of host specificity and distribution of vitellaria. However, both criteria did not warrant generic distinction (Pearson 1959; Cribb and Pearson 1993; Niewiadomska 2002b). Pearson (1959, 1961) reported a diplostomid species from allied rats from Australia and assigned it as *Neodiplostomum intermedium* despite that the worms were recovered from a mammalian host and revealed limited distribution of vitellaria in the hindbody. In addition, Cribb and Pearson (1993) compared their material of diplostomids (assigned as *Neodiplostomum*) from Australian mammals with representatives from birds and showed that the distribution of vitellaria represented from extensive distribution as in specimens from avian hosts to that confined to the forebody as in those from mammalian hosts. In this context, Pearson (1959) proposed that the genus *Fibricola* be made a subgenus of the genus *Neodiplostomum*, and 3 subgenera were listed in this genus; *Neodiplostomum* (*Neodiplostomum*) not having a genital cone, having a symmetrical anterior testis, and parasitic in birds, *Neodiplostomum* (*Fibricola*) not having a genital cone, having an asymmetrical anterior testis, and parasitic in mammals, and *Neodiplostomum* (*Conodiplostomum*) having a genital cone and a symmetrical anterior testis. Later, however, Cribb and Pearson (1993) did not use the subgenera names and placed Australian species from mammals into a single genus *Neodiplostomum* without any subgenera. Nevertheless, resolution of the real phylogenetic relationships between these genera needed to be supported by both morphological and molecular evidences (Niewiadomska 2002b). Due to these difficulties, Niewiadomska (2002b) retained the classical generic and subfamily status of *Neodiplostomum* (Diplostominae) and *Fibricola* (Alariinae) to which this book followed.

4.2.1 Neodiplostomum seoulense

4.2.1.1 *Neodiplostomum seoulense* (Seo, Rim and Lee, 1964) Hong and Shoop, 1995

[syn. *Fibricola seoulensis* Seo, Rim and Lee, 1964; *Neodiplostomum seoulensis* Hong and Shoop 1994]

Taxonomy and Morphology

Neodiplostomum seoulense (Fig. 4.1a, b) was originally described from naturally infected house rats in the South Korea under the name *Fibricola seoulensis* (Seo et al. 1964). It was morphologically unique having a bisegmented body, a prominent tribocytic organ, 2 butterfly-shaped testes, and wide vitellaria distribution in the forebody and also to some extent in the hindbody (Seo 1990). Using the generic name *Fibricola* was because it was recovered from rats, a mammalian species (Seo

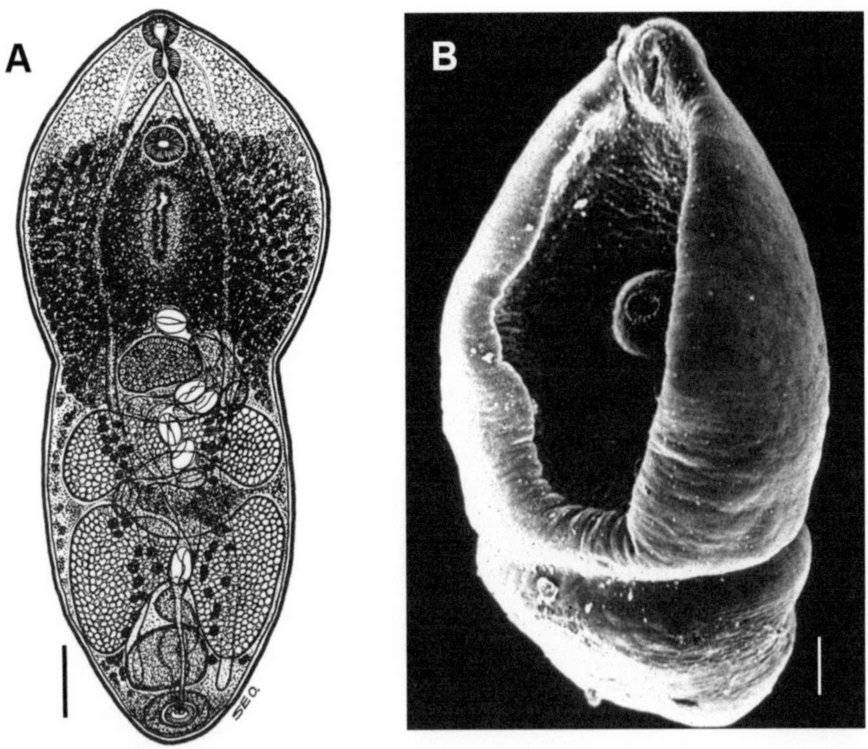

Fig. 4.1 *Neodiplostomum seoulense*. (**a**) Line drawing of an adult fluke. Scale bar = 0.1 mm. Reproduced from Seo (1990) Seoul J Med 31:61–96 with permission and courtesy of the late Prof. B.-S. Seo (**b**) Scanning electron microscopic view of a 5-day-old adult fluke recovered from an experimental mouse. Scale bar = 0.05 mm. Reproduced from Seo et al. (1984) Korean J Parasitol 22:21–29 with permission

et al. 1964). Later, however, Hong and Shoop (1994) recombined the name as *Neodiplostomum seoulensis* considering several significant points enough to transfer this species to *Neodiplostomum*. First of all, the number of transverse commissures in the excretory system (paranephridial plexus) of the metacercariae was 4 in living specimens (Hong and Shoop 1994), as recognizable in *Neodiplostomum*, while it was 3 or less in *Fibricola* (Shoop 1989a). Second, its anterior testis was almost symmetrical being compatible with *Neodiplostomum*, whereas it is usually asymmetrical in *Fibricola* (Shoop 1989a). Third, the vitellaria distribution is largely confined to the anterior body in *Fibricola*, whereas this fluke had extensive vitellaria distribution both in the fore- and hindbody which was compatible to *Neodiplostomum* (Shoop 1989a). A year later, the name was further amended as *Neodiplostomum seoulense* (Hong and Shoop 1995). Human *N. seoulense* infection was first diagnosed by the recovery of adult specimens in a young male patient suffering from acute abdominal discomfort after consumption of undercooked grass snakes (Seo et al. 1982). Thereafter, 26 additional human cases were reported from soldiers who had eaten raw snakes during their survival training in the military (Hong et al. 1984, 1986; Huh et al. 1994). Subsequently, the presence of *N. seoulense* was also reported in a northeastern part of China (Quan et al. 1995). Until now, the presence of *N. seoulense* is known only in South Korea and China (Chai 2007; Chai et al. 2009).

Adult flukes are 0.76–1.28 mm long and 0.37–0.50 mm wide (in humans; Seo et al. 1982) or 1.10–1.92 mm long and 0.51–0.70 mm wide (in experimental rats; Hong et al. 1982); they have a conspicuously bisegmented body separated into the fore- and hindbody and are spoon-shaped, with a well-developed ventral concavity (i.e., tribocytic organ) in the forebody (Fig. 4.1a, b) (Seo 1990). The elongate, ellipsoid hindbody is slightly shorter than the forebody or almost equal in length, tapering conically to a rounded end; the anterior end of the forebody is not bearing pseudosuckers (Seo 1990). The tribocytic organ is approximately circular or elliptical, about 1/3 length of the forebody, lying just behind the posterior border of the ventral sucker (Seo 1990). Ceca extend to near the posterior end of the body (Seo 1990). The vitelline follicles densely distribute in the concave part of the forebody, from the anterior border of the ventral sucker to the junctional portion of the 2 segments, and the density of vitelline follicles abruptly decreases in the hindbody; however, a few scattered follicles are reaching to the level of the posterior testis or even beyond, and the vitelline reservoir is seen in an area between the 2 testes (Seo 1990). The ovary is located median or submedian at the junction between the fore- and hindbody, in front of the anterior testis; 2 testes are tandem, symmetrical, and transversely elongated with a marked median constriction resembling butterfly-shaped cufflinks, occupying almost entire width of the hindbody (Seo 1990). The uterine tubule is descending ventrally from the anterior border of the ovary or anterior testis to the genital atrium which displays subterminal aperture (Seo 1990). The number of eggs in the uterus is 1–10 or slightly more, and the eggs are ovoidal, slightly attenuated at the opercular side, golden yellow or brown, thin-shelled, bilaterally asymmetrical, and slightly flattened on one side (Hong et al. 1984; Seo 1990). The operculum is well-demarcated and obliquely located to the equatorial plane of the egg, which is 81–102 (av. 92) × 51–63 (av. 56) μm in size (Hong et al. 1984; Seo

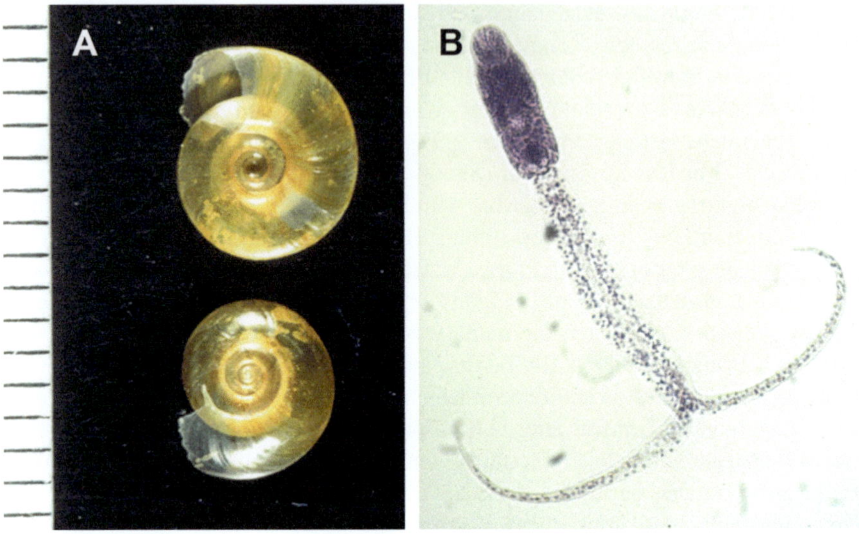

Fig. 4.2 *Neodiplostomum seoulense*. (**a**) Freshwater snails, *Hippeutis cantori*, the snail intermediate host (**b**) Bifurcated cercaria shed from the snail. The cercarial body is 93 μm long, and the tail is 157 μm long

1990). In experimentally infected mice, the EPDPW (number of eggs produced per day per worm) was estimated to be >100 during the first 2 weeks of infection, and in experimental rats, the EPDPW was over 300 even at 6 months after the infection; the patent period lasted longer than 12 months in both of these animal hosts (Hong et al. 1988).

The cercaria shed from the freshwater snail, *Hippeutis cantori* (Fig. 4.2a), is elongated and folk-tailed, a furcocercus type (Fig. 4.2b); the cercarial body is 81–121 (av. 93) μm long and 34–57 (av. 45) μm wide, and the tail is 138–175 (av. 157) μm long and 25–42 (av. 33) μm wide (Seo 1990). In tadpoles and frogs (second intermediate hosts) (Fig. 4.3a), the cercariae develop into metacercariae, and remain unchanged when these hosts are eaten by grass snakes (paratenic host) (Fig. 4.3b) (Seo 1990). The metacercariae are slightly elliptical (Fig. 4.4a, b), without cysts, 232–385 (av. 302) μm long and 213–338 (av. 240) μm wide in frog muscles, and 279–385 (av. 326) μm long and 232–298 (av. 258) μm wide in snake viscera (Hong et al. 1982). They are 'neodiplostomulum' type which possesses the forebody and a tiny primordial stage of the hindbody protruded from the dorsal subterminal end of the forebody (Hong et al. 1982).

In sectional morphologies, the internal structures of the genital atrium were clearly shown; the genital atrium is almost wholly occupied by the outward directed genital papilla or genital cone which is found protruded in the cavity (Seo 1990). The presence or absence of the genital cone is an important taxonomic key for the diplostomid flukes (Shoop 1989a; Niewiadomska 2002b).

The tegumental surface of *N. seoulense* adults is covered with cobblestone-like cytoplasmic processes in the forebody and finger-like processes in the hindbody in

Fig. 4.3 *Neodiplostomum seoulense*. (**a**) Tadpoles and frogs of *Rana* spp., the second intermediate host (**b**) Grass snake, *Rhabdophis tigrina*, a paratenic host

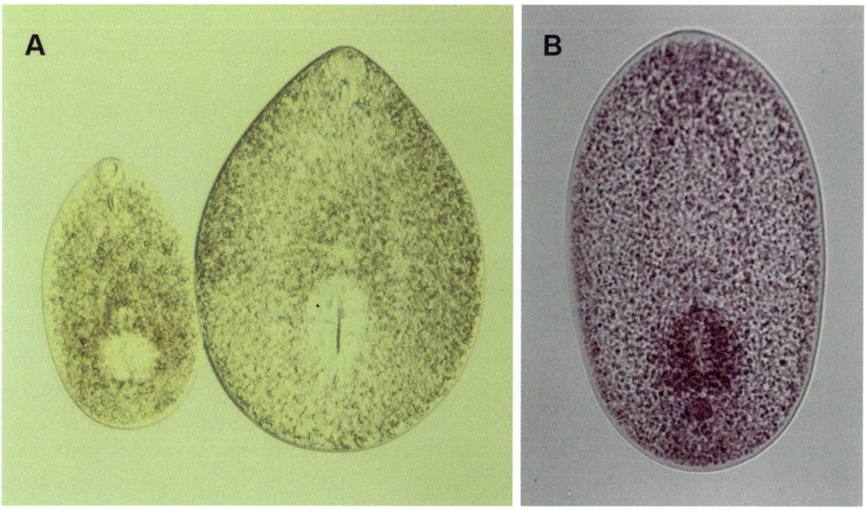

Fig. 4.4 *Neodiplostomum seoulense*. (**a**) Metacercariae of *N. seoulense* (left; smaller) in comparison with that of *Pharyngostomum cordatum* (right; bigger) isolated from the grass snake in South Korea. The metacercaria of *N. seoulense* is 326 μm long and 258 μm wide (**b**) Metacercaria of *N. seoulense*, acetocarmine-stained. Same size as the left one in (**a**)

which 4–5 large transverse wrinklings form many discontinued ridges (Seo et al. 1984; Lee et al. 1985a). The entire surface of the forebody is regularly covered with tegumental spines with 3–4 tips; in particular, densely packed spines are seen in anterior mid-median portion of the dorsal surface where a few spines with up to 5 tips are also visible (Seo et al. 1984; Lee et al. 1985a). The pointed spines of the forebody become sparse posterolaterally and single-tipped, of which style extends to the anterior one-third of the hindbody; the tribocytic organ is armed with many stout recurved pile-like spines arranged radially (Seo 1990). The anteriormost dorsal surface is armed with 60–70 spade-shaped spines (Seo et al. 1984; Lee et al.

1985a). There are 4 types of sensory papillae, which include ciliated knob-like papillae (Type I), non-ciliated round swellings (Type II), plate-like elevated papillae without a cilium (Type III), or with a cilium (Type IV) (Seo 1990). Type I papillae are almost bilaterally seen in ventral and dorsal surfaces of the forebody and abundant especially around the bases of the oral and ventral suckers, tribocytic organ, and lateral margins of the forebody; Type II papillae, about 24 in number, are present around each lip of the oral and ventral suckers; Type III and IV papillae are found only in the hindbody (Seo 1990). They seem to be tangoreceptive and/or rheoreceptive in function when their morphology and distributions are considered (Seo 1990). The surface ultrastructure of the cercariae of *N. seoulense* was also studied, and it has been shown that short tegumental spines, with a broad base and single pointed tip, were densely distributed at the anterior body surface which became sparse at the posterior part of the body; the acetabulum had stout spike-like spines, centropetally oriented on the inner surface, and sensory papillae, each with a short cilium, were concentrated around the oral sucker and those, each with a long cilium, were observed on the tail (Hong et al. 1996). On the surface of the tribocytic organ, microvilli were observed, and below the muscle layer 3 types of cells, Type I, Type II, and Type III cells, were recognized (Huh and Song 1993). Among them, Type III cells had many granules and thought as glandular cells having secretory function and specific to the tribocytic organ (Huh and Song 1993).

Life Cycle

N. seoulense has the life cycle stages of eggs, miracidia, sporocysts, rediae, cercariae, metacercariae (no mesocercarial stage), and adults (Seo 1990). The development of eggs into miracidia was studied by Seo et al. (1988); adult flukes were collected from the small intestine of experimentally infected rats 10 days after the infection which were incubated in Tyrode's solution for 12 days at 36.5 °C, and the eggs laid were collected. The eggs were thoroughly rinsed with distilled water were transferred to petri dishes containing distilled water; the dish was stored at 26 °C in a dark incubator with aeration, and developing miracidia were observed under a phase contrast microscope with vital staining with neutral red or after fixation with hot 0.5% silver nitrate (Seo et al. 1988). The intraoval cell divided into a 4-cell stage, on the second day to morular stage, and morular or blastular stage on the third day; all eggs were developed into embryos on the fourth day, and at this stage the presence of black or dark brown eyespots in the anterior portion of the miracidia and short cilia on the body surface was conspicuous (Seo et al. 1988). On the fifth day, all embryos had eyespots of conical shape, and on the sixth day miracidia moved actively, their eyespots became darker and larger, and the terebratorium appeared at the anterior end (Seo et al. 1988). On the seventh and eighth day the miracidia were nearly ready to hatch, and almost all miracidia were hatched out on the ninth day when the petri dishes containing the miracidia were placed under light (Seo et al. 1988). Lee et al. (1986a) performed a study on the effect of temperature, salinity, and aeration on maturation and hatching of *N. seoulense* eggs. At 28 °C, the egg hatching rate 2 weeks after incubation was 90%, whereas it was below 5% at 11–26 °C, and 0% at 5–15 °C and at 4 °C (Lee et al. 1986a). They also reported that the rate of eyespot appearance on the 7th day was over 90% at <0.6% salinity but it was 55% in 0.9% salinity at the 20th day and 0.2% in 1.2% salinity; aeration influenced neither the eyespot appearance nor hatching of the miracidia (Lee et al. 1986a). It was also noted that only 12.5% of the eggs incubated in the dark hatched until the tenth day, whereas 85.7% of them hatched after exposure to light within 2 hours (Lee et al. 1986a).

Three freshwater snail species, namely, *Hippeutis cantori* (Seo et al. 1988), *Segmentina* (*Polypylis*) *hemisphaerula* (Chung et al. 1996), and *Austropeplea ollula* (Chung et al. 2002) were confirmed to be the first intermediate host of *N. seoulense*. In *Hippeutis cantori*, both natural and experimental infections were confirmed (Seo et al. 1988). To detect natural infections, a total of 1410 *Hippeutis cantori* snails were collected from 5 small localities of Namyangju-gun, Gyeonggi-do (Province), South Korea, and examined for the cercariae of *N. seoulense*; 12 (0.85%) of them were found to shed furcocercus cercariae morphologically identical with those obtained from the experimentally infected snails (Seo et al. 1988). With regard to experimental infection, *Hippeutis cantori* snails, reared in the laboratory for over 1 year, were exposed to active miracidia, 10–20 per snail, in Petri dishes (55 mm in diameter) containing tap water; the dishes were placed at window side for 3–4 h to facilitate penetration of the miracidia, and then kept in an aquarium for 41 days at 26 °C (Seo 1990). The first appearance of cercariae was observed from the 13th to 33rd day after the miracidial challenge, and the infected snails shed the cercariae 4–5 days and then died; the dead snails revealed a large number of daughter sporocysts, tubular in shape, in and out of the liver, ovotestes, genital tract, digestive gland, and adjacent tissue of the snails (Seo 1990). The long tubular daughter sporocysts contained numerous developing furcocercus cercariae which slipped out here and there with their sluggish movements; the cercariae when undisturbed hung down quietly with their body either contracted or stretched with the tail stem straight and 2 furcae separated from each other by a right-angle (Seo 1990). The cercariae showed positive phototaxis and rested beneath the surface of water even in shallow containers; they sank slowly and from time to time swam upwards, and while they swam the cercarial body and tail stem extended with the tail stem bent first to one side then the other and furcae slipped back and forth (Seo 1990). The cercariae were shown to have propelling movement by the vibratory motion and pulled by the furcae of the tail foremost (Seo 1990). Another snail species, *Physa acuta*, was also tried for experimental infection with the miracidia; however, none of the 448 *Physa acuta* snails challenged with the miracidia revealed sporocysts or cercariae of *N. seoulense* (Seo 1990). In the field, a total of 3936 *Lymnaea* sp. snails were collected and examined for *N. seoulense* sporocysts or cercariae but none were found positive for these larval trematodes (Seo 1990). The tail of the cercariae of *N. seoulense* degraded when they were incubated with animal sera; it seemed that alternative complement pathway was related with this tail degradation (Park et al. 2006).

Tadpoles and frogs of *Rana nigromaculata* and possibly other species are the second intermediate host of *N. seoulense* (Seo et al. 1988), and the grass snake *Rhabdophis tigrina* (= *Natrix tigrina lateralis*) is regarded as a paratenic host (Seo 1990). Hong et al. (1985) detected natural infections of *N. seoulense* metacercariae in tadpoles of *Rana nigromaculata* caught from several localities of South Korea, including Seoul, Hoengseong-gun, Munkyong-gun, Seongju-gun, Miryang-gun, and Jinyang-gun; the prevalence ranged from 3.3% to 100% according to locality, with the mean prevalence of 48.6% (107/220), and the intensity of infection per tadpole of 1–584 (av. 47.3 per tadpole). Most of the metacercariae were detected in the abdominal cavity (476 metacercariae; 98.3%) of tadpoles, and only a small number was found in the proximal tail (6; 1.2%) and trunk (2; 0.4%) (Hong et al. 1985). Natural *N. seoulense* metacercarial infection was also detected in adult frogs of *Rana nigromaculata* caught from several localities of central parts of Korea (South Korea), including Namyangju-gun, Yongin-gun, Yeoju-gun, Hoeongseong-gun, and Jungwon-gun; the prevalence ranged from 97% to 100% according to locality, with the mean prevalence of 94.1% (80/85), and the intensity of infection per frog of 3–390 (av. 100.1 per frog). The metacercariae were detected most frequently in the hindleg (52.7%), followed by trunk (28.8%), foreleg (10.9%), head (6.6%), abdominal wall (0.9%), and abdominal cavity (0.04%) of the adult frogs (Hong et al. 1982). Similar results were obtained in adult frogs caught in different localities (Seoul and ten other localities of South Korea); the prevalence ranged from 0–100% by locality, and the mean prevalence was 62.4% (73/117) with the intensity of infection of 1–470 per frog (av. 53.8) (Hong et al. 1985). Histological sections of the frog skeletal muscles revealed the presence of the metacercariae, unencysted, within the endothelium-lined spaces with greatly dilated lymphatics and blood vessels; these spaces seldom contained red blood cells but some of the larvae were accompanied with inflammatory reactions and cell infiltrations (Hong et al. 1982).

Tadpoles were used for experimental infection with *N. seoulense* cercariae (Lee et al. 1986b). Eggs of the frogs (*Rana nigromaculata*) were collected from rice paddies in Yangju-gun, Gyeonggi-do (Province), South Korea, and reared for a month in the laboratory to develop into tadpoles; they were experimentally exposed to the cercariae of *N. seoulense,* and their development was observed until day 65 post-exposure (Lee et al. 1986b). The metacercarial stage, though small in size, was recognized from day 2 post-exposure in the abdominal cavity of the frogs, which grew progressively in size until day 14 and remained constant or slightly decreased in size but alive until day 65 of observation (Lee et al. 1986b). The metacercariae older than 14 days in tadpoles were infective to experimental mice when infected orally: the worm recovery rate was the highest (60–61%) when the metacercariae of 25–30 day of age in tadpoles were given (Lee et al. 1986b).

Terrestrial snakes are also carrying the metacercarial stage of *N. seoulense*; however, they are not an indispensable host in the life history of *N. seoulense* as only 3 hosts, namely, the snails *Hippeutis cantori*, amphibia *Rana nigromaculata* (tadpoles and frogs), and mammalia, rats and mice, are sufficient for completing the life history of this diplostomid species in the field, and the snake is considered to play the role of a prolonged, paratenic host (Seo 1990). In fact, the snakes played the role of a source of human infection with *N. seoulense* in South Korea (Seo 1990). Hong et al. (1982) reported that all (100%) of 79 *Rhabdophis tigrina* (= *Natrix tigrina lateralis*) non-venomous grass snakes caught from Yeoju-gun, Hoengseong-gun, and Jungwon-gun, South Korea were found positive for *N. seoulense* metacercariae. The intensity of infection (n = 10) per snake ranged from 3 to 34,813 (mean 9229) metacercariae; a great majority of the metacercariae were detected from the stomach (88.4%), followed by skeletal muscle in the trunk (7.1%), peritoneal fat (2.3%), liver (0.6%), intestine (0.6%), heart (0.2%), and others (Hong et al. 1982). Another survey by Cho et al. (1983) reported that 24 (64.9%) of 37 *Rhabdophis tigrina*, 3 (14.3%) of 21 *Agkistrodon blomhoffii brevicaudus*, one (14.3%) of 7 *Elaphe rufudorsata*, one (10.0%) of *Dinodon rufosanatum rufosonatum,* and one (5.9%) of 17 *Elaphe dione* were infected with the metacercariae of *N. seoulense*. The predilection sites of the metacercariae were the stomach and liver (86.7%), followed by the small intestine and gallbladder (8.4%), colon, genitalia, and kidney (1.9%), lung, esophagus, and liver (1.7%), cloaca (0.8%), and others (0.5%) (Cho et al. 1983). Histological sections of the snake stomach revealed massive metacercarial infections especially in the submucosal layer and sometimes the location of metacercariae extended to inner circular and outer longitudinal muscle layers; a few metacercariae were found even in the serosal layer of the stomach, and also in the peritoneal cavity (on fat tissues) and skeletal muscles, and rarely in other tissues (Hong et al. 1982). The metacercariae were surrounded by loose areolar tissue of the host; although some metacercariae were not accompanied with tissue reactions, many metacercariae were with tissue reactions and necrotized to form granulomas which consisted of histiocytes, plasma cells, and eosinophils (Hong et al. 1982).

Rats *Rattus norvegicus* (Seo et al. 1981, 1988) and mice *Apodemus agrarius* (Seo et al. 1964; Chai et al. 2007) have been identified to be natural definitive hosts. Rats, mice, and guinea pigs were found to be susceptible experimental hosts, whereas dogs, cats, and rabbits were less susceptible hosts (Hong 1982; Hong et al. 1983; Cho et al. 1983; Seo 1990). Chickens (>12-day old) were refractory to *N. seoulense* infection (Hong et al. 1983; Seo 1989). Fully mature adult flukes were recovered in new born chicks (≤2-day old) (Seo 1989). Later, however, those metacercariae from grass snakes attaining fully mature adult flukes in chicks were identified as *Neodiplostomum leei* (Chai and Shin 2002) or *Neodiplostomum boryongense* (Shin et al. 2008), both of which are intestinal flukes of avian hosts but not mammalian hosts; *N. leei* metacercariae migrate to the liver of mice and rats but never become adult flukes in the intestine, and they become adults only in the intestine of chicks (Chai and Shin 2002). Therefore, the adult flukes recovered from chicks and reported as *N. seoulense* (= *Fibricola seoulensis*) by Seo (1989) require further verification.

In experimentally infected rats and mice, the worm recovery rate was 21–64% at days 2–7 post-infection; the majority (>90%) of the adult worms were recovered in the duodenum, and only a few were found in the jejunum and ileum (Hong 1982). The body growth and sexual maturity of the worms was completed in as early as 6–7 days after the infection; the growth of the hindbody started quickly, and by day 4 post-infection the hindbody was well segmented from the forebody by a junctional constriction (Hong 1982). On the 5th day, the reproductive organs completed maturation and a few eggs appeared in the uterus; on the 6th day almost all worms had uterine eggs, and the average number of uterine eggs in 6~14-day-old worms was 11–19 (Hong 1982). The worm recovery rate was found to decrease as the infection progressed to 2–4 weeks in rats and mice; the optimum number of metacercariae to be given to these animals, with the highest worm recovery rate, was 1000 and 200 to rats and mice, respectively (Hong et al. 1983). In experimental rats, some worms (23.6% of infected) survived at least until week 7 post-infection (Kho et al. 1990); a few proportion of worms were found to survive in rats up to 36 weeks post-infection (unpublished observation). In dogs, a small number of worms survived from day 7 (38.4% in worm recovery rate) to day 56 post-infection (0.4%), whereas in cats a less number of worms survived for a shorter time from day 7 (30.1%) to day 14 (2.6%); the worm maturity index (no. of mature worms/no. of recovered worms) was 22.7% in dogs (only 2 of 27 worms had 10 or 15 uterine eggs) and 0% in cats (none of 40 worms recovered contained uterine eggs) (Hong et al. 1983). However, later, 6 adult flukes each having a few uterine eggs were recovered in the small intestine of stray cats caught from South Korea (Chai et al. 2013). In experimental rabbits, only one immature worm (0.05%) among 2000 metacercariae given to 4 rabbits was recovered in the duodenum at day 14 post-infection, and in 2 chickens no worms were recovered at days 3–56 post-infection (Hong et al. 1983).

Epidemiology and Geographical Distribution
Tadpoles and frogs of *Rana nigromaculata* and terrestrial snakes including *Rhabdophis tigrina* (grass snake) harbor the metacercariae (Seo 1990). However, the source of human infections was confirmed to be exclusively the grass snake but never the tadpoles or frogs (these animals are seldom eaten by the Korean people). The major reasons for consuming grass snakes are as a high calory diet or high protein diet and also as a man's tonic. Moreover, there is a local misbelief that the snakes under raw or incompletely cooked conditions exhibit a better effect to health than those cooked completely. Another important reason for consuming snakes in South Korea was the so-called 'survival training' among some military soldiers particularly during the period 1950s–1980s; the soldiers were trained to eat raw or undercooked snakes to survive in mountains or other hazardous areas where no other proper food could be found. Fortunately, however, eating snakes during the military survival training has been avoided since the 1990s, and after the report of Huh et al. (1994) no more human infections with *N. seoulense* have been documented. The geographical distribution is until now South Korea and China (Table 3.2).

China This fluke was reported to be present also in a northeastern part of China (Quan et al. 1995). The metacercariae were detected in several species of snakes sold in a market of Yanji, Yanbian, Jilin Province, namely, *Elaphe dione, Elaphe rufordorsata,* and *Agkistrodon halys brevicaudus*; 31 (70.5%) of 44 snakes examined harbored the metacercariae (Quan et al. 1995).

South Korea This fluke was first discovered in 2 field rats (*Rattus norvegicus*) captured from suburban Seoul and reported under the name *Fibricola seoulensis* (Seo et al. 1964). It was discovered again in field rats (*Rattus norvegicus*) captured from north central areas of South Korea, including Namyangju-gun, Yongin-gun,

Yongweol-gun, and Jungwon-gun (Seo et al. 1981). Later, its scientific name was revised as *Neodiplostomum seoulense* (Hong and Shoop 1995). The first human case infected with *N. seoulense* was found in a young man suffering from acute abdominal pain and fever, who had consumed viscera of 2 undercooked grass snakes 9 days prior to admission to a hospital (Seo et al. 1982). Large operculated trematode eggs were detected in the feces of this patient, and under the impression of an intestinal fluke infection bithionol (an anthelmintic drug) was given and magnesium purgation was tried; total 79 specimens of small adult trematodes were recovered from the diarrheal stool, and morphologically identified as *N. seoulense* (under the name *F. seoulensis*) (Seo et al. 1982). Subsequently, 15 human cases were detected among soldiers who had a history of survival training in the military and revealed *N. seoulense* eggs in their feces; they were all men, 21–28 years old, with no special clinical symptoms, and 6 of them expelled adult flukes, 1–78 in number, after treatment with praziquantel and purging with magnesium salts (Hong et al. 1984). Further, ten more human cases were detected among a group of soldiers serving around Seoul; all of them were positive for *N. seoulense* eggs, with no special clinical symptoms, and in one patient 59 adult specimens of *N. seoulense* were collected after praziquantel treatment and purging (Hong et al. 1986). Later, one more Korean soldier was found to reveal *N. seoulense* eggs in a follow-up fecal examination; thus, the total number of egg- and/or worm-confirmed cases of *N. seoulense* infection in South Korea was 27 (Huh et al. 1994).

Directly after the discovery of the first human case (Seo et al. 1982), various aspects of *N. seoulense* and its host-parasite relationships were studied, and until 2018, more than 30 research articles have been published from South Korea. Important progress has been achieved as follows. A part of its life cycle had been elucidated, and frogs (*Rana nigromaculata*) and snakes (*Rhabdophis tigrina*) were verified to be a second intermediate host and a paratenic host of this fluke, respectively (Hong et al. 1982). Cho et al. (1983) reported that, in addition to *Rhabdophis tigrina*, several other snake species, including *Agkistrodon blomhoffii brevicaudus*, *Elaphe rufudorsata*, *Dinodon rufosanatum rufosonatum,* and *Elaphe dione* were confirmed to be the paratenic host for *N. seoulense* harboring its metacercariae. Hong et al. (1985) first detected infection of tadpoles of *Rana nigromaculata* with the metacercariae of *N. seoulense*, and concluded that *N. seoulense* cercariae infect the tadpole stage of *Rana nigromaculata* first, and the cercariae become the metacercariae in the abdominal cavity of the tadpoles, and then the frogs harbor the metacercarial stage. Seo et al. (1988) first detected natural as well as experimental first intermediate host of *N. seoulense* which proved to be a freshwater snail species, *Hippeutis cantori*; they reconfirmed tadpoles of *Rana nigromaculata* as its second intermediate host, and experimentally obtained adult flukes infecting laboratory rats with the metacercariae in the tadpoles. A review article on *N. seoulense* morphology, life cycle, in vitro cultivation, classification, and human infections has been published (Seo 1990). In a field study, a new snail intermediate host, *Segmentina* (*Polypylis*) *hemisphaerula*, a planorbid species, has been found to shed the furcocercus cercariae of *N. seoulense* (Chung et al. 1996). In addition, another snail species, a lymnaeiid snail, *Austropeplea ollula*, has also been confirmed to be a first intermediate host of *N. seoulense* (Chung et al. 2002). Seven adult specimens were recovered in 2 feral cats purchased from Busan (Sohn and Chai 2005), and their morphologic details were described later (Chai et al. 2013). In the meantime, this fluke was discovered in field mice, *Apodemus agrarius*, collected from 3 localities (Yeoncheon, Paju, and Pocheon) of Gyeonggi-do (Province); the prevalence was the highest in autumn season, and the intensity was the highest in spring season (Chai et al. 2007).

An interesting study was performed with small diplostomid metacercariae (uniform in morphology) parasitic in the grass snakes, *Rhabdophis tigrina*, from South Korea (Chai and Shin 2002). When they were experimentally fed to mice and rats, only some of them developed into adults in their intestines (*N. seoulense*), and some others migrated to the liver of these rodents and did not develop into adult flukes in the intestine (Chai and Shin 2002). However, when the metacercariae isolated from the liver were fed to chicks they developed into adults in the intestine; they were morphologically unique and described as a new diplostomid species, *Neodiplostomum leei* (Chai and Shin 2002). Moreover, in the above experimental setting, some metacercariae neither developed into adults in rodent intestines nor they migrated into the liver of rodents; they developed into adult flukes only in the intestine of chicks, and their morphology was unique, and thus they were reported as a new species, *Neodiplostomum boryongense* (Shin et al. 2008).

4.2.2 Fibricola cratera

4.2.2.1 *Fibricola cratera* (Barker and Noll, 1915) Dubois, 1932

[syn. *Hemistomum craterum* Barker and Noll, 1915; *Fibricola laruei* Miller, 1940; *Fibricola nana* Chandler and Rausch, 1946]

Taxonomy and Morphology

Fibricola cratera was originally described from musk rats (*Ondatra zibethica*) under the name *Hemistomum craterum* in USA in 1915 by Barker and Noll (Sudarikov 1960). Dubois (1932) erected the genus *Fibricola* to include this species as the type and named it as *Fibricola cratera*. In 1936 Dubois assigned this species in the subfamily Alariinae, where parasites of mammals were placed (Dubois 1938, 1953; Sudarikov 1960). In 1944 Dubois created another genus *Theriodiplostomum* for *T. lucidum* but later concluded that *Theriodiplostomum* is identical with *Fibricola* (Dubois and Rausch 1950a, b). Pearson (1959) proposed to move *Fibricola* to a subgenus of *Neodiplostomum*, listing 3 subgenera in this genus; *Neodiplostomum* (*Neodiplostomum*) parasitic in birds, lacking a genital cone, but with a symmetrical anterior testis, *Neodiplostomum* (*Fibricola*) parasitic in mammals, lacking a genital cone, but with an asymmetrical anterior testis, and *Neodiplostomum* (*Conodiplostomum*) having a genital cone and a symmetrical anterior testis. Later,

Cribb and Pearson (1993) did not use the subgeneric names and placed Australian specimens from mammals in a single genus *Neodiplostomum* without any subgenera. Ching et al. (2000) followed this and reported their specimens from raccoons in British Columbia, Canada as *Neodiplostomum cratera*. However, Niewiadomska (2002b) retained the classical generic and subfamily status of *Neodiplostomum* (Diplostominae) and *Fibricola* (Alariinae). Thus, the name *Fibricola cratera* has been preferred by other workers (Richardson 2013). *F. cratera* has been popularly found from various mammalian species, including the rat, squirrel, chipmunk, skunk, American mink, raccoon, opossum, and shrew in USA and Canada (Sudarikov 1960). However, this species was also found in avian hosts (Ulmer 1955; Lumsden 1961). In addition, an experimental human infection was proved to be successful with recovery of eggs in the feces; the worms lived longer than 3 years in the human body (Shoop 1989b). However, no natural human infections have been discovered.

The adult flukes are bisegmented, 0.65–0.84 (av. 0.73) mm long and 0.24–0.33 (av. 0.29) mm wide, with the forebody 0.39–0.54 (av. 0.45) mm long and 0.27–0.42 (av. 0.33) mm wide and the hindbody 0.23–0.33 (av. 0.27) mm long and 0.24–0.33 (av. 0.29) mm wide (Turner 1958). In avian hosts, the length of adults may be slightly smaller, 0.60–0.67 mm in length (Lumsden 1961). The eggs are operculated, ovoid, yellowish brown, 115–135 (av. 125) μm long and 65–75 (av. 70) μm wide (Shoop 1989b). The cercariae are furcocercus type; the cercarial body is 105–146 (av. 126) μm long and 30–61 (av. 35) μm wide, and the tail is 153–228 (av. 195) μm long and 34–47 (av. 42) μm wide excluding the furcae; the furcae are each 146–173 (av. 156) μm long (Turner 1958). The metacercariae are diplostomulum type without cysts, and 450–525 (av. 490) μm long and 240–300 (av. 276) μm wide (Turner 1958).

The tegument of *F. cratera* adults is a syncytial layer connected via protoplasmic channels to underlying subtegumental cell bodies (Jansma 1971). Tegumental spines protrude from the ventral surface of the forebody, especially near the tribocytic organ; spines appear either as blunt, blade-like structures on the ventral forebody surface or as pointed tegumental projections on the tribocytic organ (Jansma 1971). The tribocytic organ is characterized by a highly-folded tegumental surface and many secretory gland cells peripheral to a central holdfast chamber (Jansma 1971). Tegumental sensory receptors are of at least 4 distinct types; ciliated and non-ciliated sensory bulbs are more numerous around the oral sucker, acetabulum, and genital aperture, but they are also located over the entire forebody surface (Jansma 1971).

Life Cycle

Freshwater snails, *Physa gyrina* and *Physa sayii,* were found naturally infected with the cercariae of *F. cratera* in Lake Macbride, Iowa City, Iowa and Carrol Lake, Woodruff, Wisconsin, respectively (Hoffman 1955). Experimental studies were also performed to complete the life cycle (Hoffman 1955). Eggs were obtained from the feces of raccoons (*Procyon lotor*) infected with *F. cratera*; 4 lots of eggs were incubated at room temperature, and miracidia first appeared at days 9, 10, 14, and

14 days, respectively, which survived about 7 h in water (Hoffman 1955). Laboratory reared *Physa gyrina* snails were exposed to miracidia, and cercariae were first seen at 30 days; the maximum longevity of the cercariae was 52 h, and they were infective for tadpoles at least 21 h, or probably longer, after emerging (Hoffman 1955). Tadpoles of *Rana pipiens* (leopard frog), *Pseudacris triceriata* (western chorus frog), and *Rana clamitans*, 1-day or older after hatching, exposed to the cercariae were successfully infected; the metacercariae were located free in the body cavity of the tadpoles from 12.5 h or less until shortly after metamorphosis of the tadpoles, when the metacercariae migrated to the hind legs and became encapsulated (Hoffman 1955; Cook 1978). Naturally infected tadpoles and frogs were collected in Dickinson County, Iowa (Cook 1978). Snakes, including garter snakes and Graham's water snakes, were found to have large numbers of diplostomula (Cuckler 1940); the snakes are regarded as paratenic hosts (Shoop 1989b). Muskrats, brown rats, meadow mice, and a short-tailed shrew have been found infected naturally (Cuckler 1940). In the laboratory, rats, mice, cats, and a Syrian hamster were successfully infected with this fluke maturing into adults in their small intestines (Cuckler 1940; Hoffman 1955); new born chicks were also infected with this fluke to become adults although the worms were expelled after 10 days (Lumsden 1961).

4.2.2.2 Epidemiology and Geographical Distribution

No natural human infections with *F. cratera* have been found. However, Shoop (1989b) demonstrated a successful human experimental infection with *F. cratera*. He obtained the metacercariae from the mesenteric fat deposits of cottonmouth snakes, *Agkistrodon piscivorus*, collected at Head-of-Island, Louisiana, USA, and orally fed the human volunteer with 100 metacercariae; at 42 days the eggs of *F. cratera* began to be detected in the feces and continued to be positive for about 3.5 years (41 months) (Shoop 1989b). Now this fluke is known to distribute in North America, including USA and Canada (Table 3.2) (Shoop 1989b; Seo 1990).

Canada *F. cratera* was first detected in fur-bearing animals (mink) in Ontario (Law and Kennedy 1932). Miller (1940) described *Fibricola laruei* from raccoons (*Procyon lotor*) in Quebec Province. However, it has been synonymized with *F. cratera* due to several reasons (Read 1948). In British Columbia, raccoons (14.5% of 82 examined) were found to have *F. cratera* infection in the intestine (described under the name *Neodiplostomum cratera*) (Ching et al. 2000).

USA This fluke was first discovered in the intestine of muskrats and described under the name *Hemistoma craterum* (Barker 1915). It was found again in a new host, raccoon (*Procyon lotor lotor*), in Iowa (Morgan and Waller 1940), in rodent animals including muskrats, brown rats, meadow mice, and a shrew in Nebraska (Cuckler 1940), in skunk (*Mephitis nigra*), opossum (*Didelphis virginiana*), and raccoon in Michigan (Chandler and Rausch 1946), in Texas mink (*Mustela vison*) in Houston, Texas (Read 1948). *Fibricola nana* was recorded as a new species from squirrels (Chandler and Rausch 1946) but it was considered a dwarfed form of *F. cratera* in an unusual host (Read 1948) and subsequently synonymized with *F. cratera* (Dubois 1953). Byrd et al. (1942) found *F. cratera* specimens from opossums (*Didelphis virginiana*) in Georgia and Tennessee. Rausch and Tiner (1949) reported infection of opossums with *F. cratera* in their small intestines in Wisconsin. Cuckler (1940) and Hoffman (1955) completed the complete life history of *F. cratera* in the laboratory and in the field. Ulmer (1955) studied on the host-parasite specificity of *F. cratera* and found that 1-day old chicks were successfully infected with this parasite (though not 10-day chicks), thus, questioned about Dubois (1953)'s hypothesis of host-specificity of *Fibricola* spp. exclusively for mammalian animals. Subsequently, Lumsden (1961) recovered 2 specimens of *F. cratera* from a naturally infected avian species, *Eudocimus albus* (white ibis), in Louisiana. Ulmer (1970) detected metacercariae of *F. cratera* in 2 tadpole species (*Pseudacris triseriata* and *Rana pipiens*) in Iowa. Jansma (1971) studied on the ultrastructure and histochemistry of *F. cratera* in Iowa. Cook (1978) collected naturally infected frogs and tadpoles with *F. cratera* in Iowa for a laboratory study of metacercarial migration in metamorphosing *Rana pipiens* tadpoles and frogs. Adult flukes were collected in opossums (*Didelphis virginiana*) from Florida (Premvati and Bair 1979) and Louisiana (Shoop and Corkum 1981, 1982; Alden 1995). Thousands of specimens were collected in some raccoons from Kentucky; the mean prevalence was 71% (n = 70) (Cole and Shoop 1987). One (3%) of 30 raccoons from Arkansas (Richardson et al. 1992) and one (11.1%) of 9 raccoons from Nebraska (Richardson 2013) were found infected with adult *F. cratera*.

4.2.3 Potentially Zoonotic **Neodiplostomum** *and* **Fibricola** *spp.*

Potentially zoonotic *Neodiplostomum* and *Fibricola* spp. include *Neodiplostomum oriolinum* Oschmarin, 1963, *Neodiplostomum spratti* Cribb and Pearson, 1993, *Neodiplostomum leei* Chai and Shin, 2002, *Neodiplostomum boryongense* Shin, Kim, and Chai, 2007, *Fibricola lucida* (La Rue and Bosma, 1927) Dubois and Rausch 1950a, b, *Fibricola minor* Dubois, 1936, *Fibricola texensis* Chandler, 1942, *Fibricola caballeroi* Cerecero, 1943, *Fibricola sudarikovi* Sadovskaya, 1952, *Fibricola sarcophila* Sanders, 1957, *Fibricola intermedia* (Pearson, 1959) Sudarikov, 1960, and *Fibricola ramachandrani* (Betterson, 1976) Palmieri et al., 1979.

4.2.4 Genomics and Proteomics

The genetic characteristics of *N. seoulense* and *F. cratera* have seldom been the subjects of intensive studies, although a few studies have been available on *N. seoulense*. Park et al. (1998) analyzed the karyotype of *N. seoulense* and reported that its chromosome number was n = 10 and 2n = 20, and each chromosome length ranged 1.3–4.0 μm; the chromosome pairs consisted of 2 pairs of metacentric, 5 pairs of submetacentric/subtelocentric, and 3 pairs of telocentric pieces.

Phylogenetic relationships of 3 *Neodiplostomum* species occurring in South Korea, *N. seoulense* (Seo et al. 1964), *N. leei* (Chai and Shin 2002), and *N. boryongense* (Shin et al. 2008), were analyzed using partical mitochondrial cytochrome *c* oxidase subunit 1 (CO1) gene (Pyo et al. 2014). The results demonstrated a closer phylogenetic relationship between *N. seoulense* and *N. boryongense* than between *N. seoulense* and *N. leei* and *N. leei* and *N. boryongense*; this high relationship between *N. seoulense* and *N. boryongense* may be related to their similar morphologies, in particular, a limited distribution of vitellaria in the forebody and the presence of a genital cone, in comparison to extensive distribution of vitellaria in the forebody and lacking a genital cone in *N. leei* (Pyo et al. 2014). Studies on genetic characteristics of the Diplostomidae have been reported targeting on *Diplostomum, Tylodelphis,* and *Austrodiplostomum* (Locke et al. 2015) and *Posthodiplostomum* (López-Hernández et al. 2018); however, their relationship with *Neodiplostomum* or *Fibricola* has not been analyzed.

A cysteine protease of *N. seoulense*, with the molecular weight of 54 kDa, was purified from the crude extract of adult flukes; its function was suggested to aid nutrient uptake, rather than host tissue lysis (Choi et al. 1999). Further, 2 cystatin-binding cysteine proteinases were successfully purified from *N. seoulense*; they were suggested to be useful for cystatin-capture ELISA of human *N. seoulense* infection (Kim et al. 2008). The distribution of acetylcholinesterases (nervous system) were histochemically demonstrated in metacercariae and adults of *N. seoulense*, and 2 bands (69 kDa and 132 kDa) were purified by enzyme electrophoresis (Cheon and Kim 1993). Other enzymes, proteases, and unique proteins should be purified and characterized for better understanding of the host-parasite relationships of *N. seoulense* and other diplostomid flukes.

4.2.5 Pathology and Immunology

In experimental rats and mice, *N. seoulense* was found to infect the mucosa of the duodenum (probably the same in human natural infections); however, in heavy infections, if infected with more than 1000 metacercariae in rats and more than 200 metacercariae in mice, some worms migrated to the jejunum and ileum (Hong 1982; Hong ST et al. 1982, 1983; Seo 1990). In the duodenal or jejunal mucosa, *N. seoulense* worms were found to entrap the host intestinal villi with their concave ventral curvature of the forebody, piercing into the villous stroma using the tribocytic organ (Fig. 4.5a,b), and the affected villi underwent severe destruction with hemorrhages and inflammation, and finally complete lost of mucosal integrity ensued (Lee et al. 1985b). In the lesions, the worms embraced the host villi, looking like 'eating' the villi using the tribocytic organ which penetrated into the mucosal tissues (Lee et al. 1985b). The major histopathological features of the affected mucosa are villous atrophy and crypt hyperplasia with decreased villus/crypt length ratio, mucosal inflammation with stromal edema, loss of villi, and bleeding (Lee et al. 1985b; Huh et al. 1988; Hong et al. 1993). The intestinal damage was not normalized until day 14 and day 28 post-infection in mice and rats, respectively (Lee et al. 1985b); it is unknown from when the mucosal damages become normalized in these animals. These histopathological changes due to *N. seoulense* were severer compared with those observed in other intestinal trematode infections including *Metagonimus*, *Pygidiopsis*, and *Isthmiophora hortensis* (formerly *E. hortense*) infections (Chai 2007; Chai et al. 2009). Death occurred in mice given 1000 metacercariae within day 16 post-infection, and malnutrition and severe fluid loss due to malabsorption, together with mucosal bleeding and intractable diarrhea, was suggested to be the major cause of death (Huh et al. 1988).

Hong et al. (1993) reported an interesting finding that a mixed infection with *N. seoulense* (inhabit mainly in the duodenum) and *Metagonimus yokogawai* (inhabit mainly in the jejunum), another species of intestinal fluke, in rats revealed more severe intestinal damages particularly in the duodenum with lower worm recovery of *N. seoulense* compared with single *N. seoulense* infection group. In addition, the survival of *M. yokogawai* worms in the jejunum was also markedly inhibited in mixed infection group compared with single *M. yokogawai* infection group (Hong

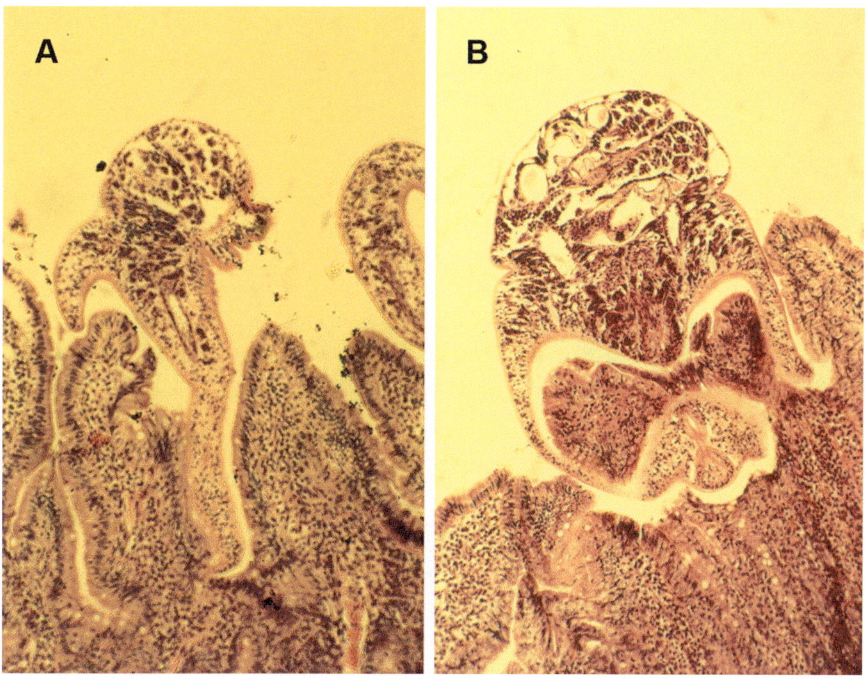

Fig. 4.5 Intestinal sections of rats (**a**, **b**) experimentally infected with the metacercariae of *Neodiplostomum seoulense*. Day 7 after infection. Intestinal mucosa is severely destroyed by the flukes, and severe inflammatory reactions are seen in the villous stroma. x 200

et al. 1993). Another interesting study was reported by Yu et al. (1995) that reinfection (after treatment of a primary infection with praziquantel) with *N. seoulense* revealed earlier onset of histopathological changes, from day 3 post-infection, as well as earlier resolution of the changes from day 7 post-infection.

The tribocytic organ of *N. seoulense* was shown to be an important somatic organ responsible for host mucosal damages (Huh et al. 1990; Seo 1990). It secretes alkaline phosphatases (Huh et al. 1990; Kim and Kim 1993), which could lyse the host villi and help mucosal invasion of worms; moreover, it was also shown to contain neutral mucopolysaccharides, and thus it is suggested to play a protective role against host digestive enzymes (Huh et al. 1990). Activities of acid phosphatase and other non-specific esterase which have adhesive and digestive functions were also present in the tribocytic organ of *N. seoulense* (Huh 1993; Kim and Kim 1993).

Regarding the pathogenesis of diarrhea in *N. seoulense* infection, it was shown in experimental mice and rats that the activities of sucrase, lactase, trehalase, alkaline phosphatase, and leucine aminopeptidase were decreased at the host intestinal mucosa after day 7 until day 32 post-infection (Lee et al. 1991; Yu et al. 1995). *N. seoulense* infection disturbed the final step of digestion and absorption of water and nutrients on the brush border membrane of the host which eventually caused osmotic diarrhea; this was recovered after treatment with praziquantel (Lee et al. 1991).

As to the pathogenicity of *N. seoulense* to definitive hosts, the most striking feature is its high pathogenicity and lethality to laboratory mice (Huh et al. 1988; Kook et al. 1998). When conventionally reared ICR mice were each given 1000 metacercariae of *N. seoulense*, all infected mice died by day 16 post-infection, whereas none of the uninfected control ICR mice were dead until day 28 of observation (Huh et al. 1988). The high lethality also occurred when only 200 metacercariae were given to C3H/HeJ (all mice died by day 29) and C57BL/6 mice (60% died by day 21) reared under specific pathogen-free conditions, whereas only a small proportion (13.3% by day 29) of BALB/c mice reared under the same conditions died (Kook et al. 1998). These results suggested that the lethality of mice was dependent upon the mouse genetic background; thus, Chai et al. (2000) studied on the genetic influence on susceptibility of the host to lethality due to *N. seoulense* infection. The results revealed that BALB/c [H-2*d*], C3H/He [H-2*k*], and C57BL/6 [H-2*b*] mice having different genetic background (H-2 gene products) exhibited different capacity to expel *N. seoulense*, with different worm recoveries, and to the fatality of the host themselves (Chai et al. 2000).

The pathogenetic mechanisms and pathogenesis of lethality in *N. seoulense*-infected mice have not been clearly understood. However, it has been shown that the infected mice revealed severely shortened and contracted intestines, strongly suggestive of an intestinal paralysis which may lead to the mortality of mice (Kook et al. 1998). In relation to this, neuronal growth associated protein (GAP)-43 expression in the myenteric plexus of the small intestinal wall has been shown to be depressed in *N. seoulense*-infected mice compared to uninfected controls from day 7 to day 28 post-infection and slightly normalized at day 35 post-infection; this strongly suggested that neuronal damage occurred in the intestinal mucosa of *N. seoulense*-infected mice (Pyo et al. 2012) which supports the intestinal paralysis theory (Kook et al. 1998). In addition, it has also been demonstrated that BALB/c mice, though many mice (>80%) of this strain survived from *N. seoulense* infection, undergo fecundity reduction after their survival (Shin et al. 2016). BALB/c mice were given 100 or 200 metacercariae of *N. seoulense,* and 1–3 weeks later their fertility rate, birth time, litter size, and size and weight of testes and ovary-oviduct-uterus of male and female mice, respectively, were measured; the number of apoptotic cells in the testicular tissue and serum testosterone levels of male mice were also determined (Shin et al. 2016). The results together revealed that BALB/c mice surviving *N. seoulense* infection underwent severe destruction and apoptosis of gonad tissues with significantly reduced fecundity; the next generation mice (F1-F4) were finally infertile, with no ability to produce their F5 next generation (Shin et al. 2016).

In *N. seoulense* infection, the protective immunity of the host and survival of worms in the host intestine are known to be variable depending on different host strains, for example, in BALB/c and C3H mice (Chai et al. 1998). Possible candidates of immune effectors in intestinal fluke infection include mast cells, goblet cells, macrophages, eosinophils, lymphocytes, and antibodies, including IgA (Chai 2007; Chai et al. 2009); however, the role of individual type of immune effectors in *N. seoulense* infection remains to be determined.

Throughout days 3, 7, 14, 21, and 28 post infection with 200 metacercarae of *N. seoulense*, BALB/c mice revealed significantly higher worm recoveries than C3H mice, and mastocytosis and goblet cell hyperplasia were more prominent in BALB/c mice than in C3H mice; thus, it was suggested that these cell reactions are rather local immune responses against *N. seoulense* worms but not important components in actual defense and worm expulsion (Chai et al. 1998). Mast cell proliferation (Fig. 4.6a,b) was also notified in experimental rats and suggested to be a local inflammatory response due to the presence of worms in the intestine (Kho et al. 1990). However, treatment of *N. seoulense*-infected rats with 3 kinds of anti-inflammatory drugs, namely, hydroxyzine (histamine receptor H_1 blocker), cimetidine (histamine receptor H_2 blocker), and cyclosporine-A (helper-T-cell suppressant), significantly enhanced worm recovery rates (>10%), particularly in the former 2 drugs (Shin et al. 2003). This indicated that inflammatory reactions, including mast cell responses, are at least in part positively involved in worm expulsion and host defense (Shin et al. 2003). It was also suggested that binding of histamines released from mast cells to its receptors on intestinal smooth muscles would be more important in mast cell actions than the level of histamine alone or mastocytosis (Shin et al. 2003). Prednisolone (both T- and B-cell suppressant) was also given to a group of *N. seoulense*-infected rats, but no recognizable changes were seen in the worm recovery rate compared to *N. seoulense*-infection only group (Shin et al. 2003); no effects of prednisolone and its underlying mechanisms should be further clarified.

The role of goblet cells and eosinophils in *N. seoulense* infection has yet to be determined; however, the role of macrophages was highlighted and shown to be an important effector for worm expulsion (Shin et al. 2007). In BALB/c mice infected with *N. seoulense*; the level of IFN-γ (a Th1 cytokine) was significantly increased in the spleen and small intestines of infected mice, and heavy infiltrations of

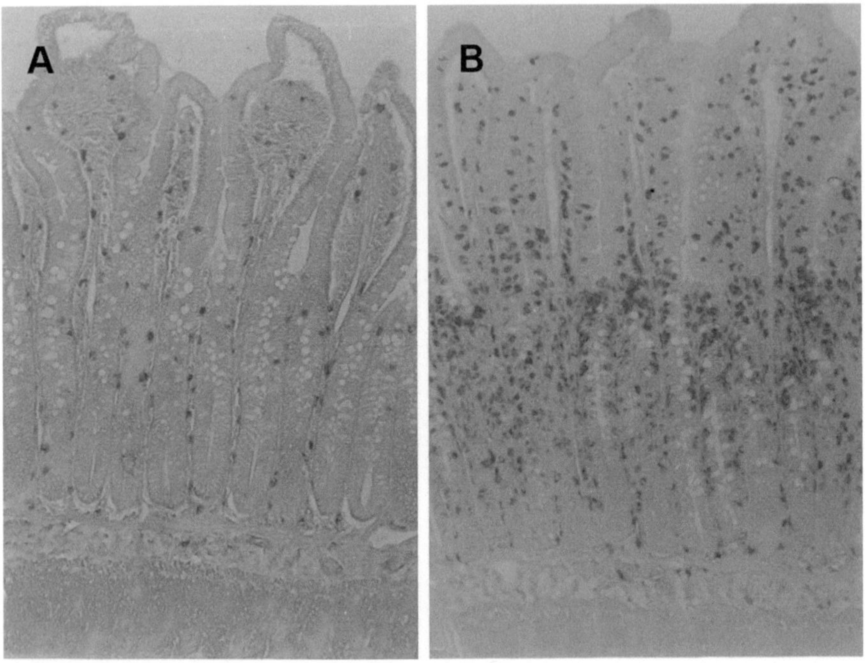

Fig. 4.6 Intestinal sections of rats (**a**, **b**) experimentally infected with the metacercariae of *Neodiplostomum seoulense* showing mastocytosis (blue spots; mucosal mast cells stained with alcian blue-safranin). Day 7 (**a**) and day 21 (**b**) after infection. × 100. Reproduced from the figure in Kho et al. (1990) Seoul J Med 31:191–199 with permission

macrophages were seen in intestinal tissues (Shin et al. 2007). The macrophages were found to kill *N. seoulense* worms in vitro, and thus it was strongly suggested that macrophages participate in worm expulsion and may also in damage to the host (Shin et al. 2007). Moreover, in these mice, IL-4 (a Th2 cytokine), IgG, IgA, and IgG2a were also increased in the spleen and small intestines of infected mice; therefore, it was suggested that mixed Th1 and Th2 immune responses occur in BALB/c mice infected with *N. seoulense* (Shin et al. 2007).

The locality of major parasite antigens was investigated using immunogold transmission electron microscopy; it has been shown that the tribocytic organ, seminal vesicle, ceca, and vitelline follicles are the major organs showing strong antigenicity (Lee et al. 1997). Seven somatic protein bands (26, 30, 35, 43, 54, 67, and 94 kDa) reacted strongly with serum IgG antibodies against *N. seoulense* from ICR, BALB/c, and C3H mice (Han et al. 2008). IgA levels were significantly increased in serum and intestinal mucosa-submucosa after an experimental infection in BALB/c mice, but the increase was not directly related to worm expulsion (Huh et al. 1995).

4.2.6 Clinical Manifestations, Diagnosis and Treatment

Clinical manifestations in *N. seoulense* infection are not well documented except in the first patient, who experienced severe abdominal discomfort with cramping pain and fever which led to admission to an emergency room of a university hospital (Seo et al. 1982; Seo 1990; Chai et al. 2009). The first patient was a 25-year old Korean male residing in a rural village of Gyeonggi-do (Province) and experienced epigastric discomfort, fullness and pain, and anorexia 5 days after consumption of 2 undercooked grass snakes; he tried to relieve the symptoms with medication at a drugstore, without effects (Seo et al. 1982). Two days later, he visited a local private clinic because of sudden onset of fever up to 40 °C which subsided by antipyretics but epigastric discomfort was not relieved; he began to pass diarrheal stools 2–3 times a day (Seo et al. 1982). Two days later, high fever reappeared and epigastric discomfort and pain continued; so he visited the Emergency Room of a university hospital in Seoul (Seo et al. 1982). The significant laboratory findings included high eosinophilia of 18% and 34% in 2 examinations during the hospital days (Seo et al. 1982).

However, in other 25 patients infected with *N. seoulense*, no recognizable clinical symptoms were complained (Hong et al. 1984, 1986). It is speculated that the patients were repeatedly infected cases and had milder symptoms than primarily infected patients; they were military soldiers and had consumed undercooked snakes more than one time (Hong et al. 1984, 1986). Another reason may include low intensity of infection in these patients except 2 cases from whom 78 (Hong et al. 1984) and 59 specimens were recovered (Hong et al. 1986), respectively, after anthelmintic treatment and purging; from other 12 cases (in the remaining 11 cases worm collection was not tried) 0–17 specimens were collected (Hong et al. 1984, 1986).

However, *N. seoulense* has been reported to be highly pathogenic and even lethal to laboratory mice (Kook et al. 1998). Therefore, infected humans may also experience a severe clinical course as seen in the first patient (Seo et al. 1982). The severity of symptoms due to *N. seoulense* may be dependent not only upon the individual worm burdens and frequency of infections, but also upon miscellaneous factors related to the acquired and innate immunity of each individual (Chai 2007; Chai et al. 2009). Potential symptoms that may occur in patients infected with *N. seoulense* include acute epigastric/abdominal discomfort and pain, diarrhea, lethargy, fever, and weight loss (Chai 2007; Chai et al. 2009).

Clinical manifestations due to *F. cratera* infection were described only in one occasion of human experimental infection; epigastric discomfort, loose stools, and flatulence occurred from 4 weeks after the infection and those symptoms continued over the first year of infection and ameliorated thereafter until 40 months of patent infection, positive for eggs in the feces (Shoop 1989b).

The diagnosis of *N. seoulense* or *F. cratera* infection can be done by recovery of typical eggs in the feces (Seo et al. 1982; Shoop 1989b; Seo 1990). The eggs are ellipsoid to elliptical, thin-shelled, with an inconspicuous operculum, which are frequently asymmetrical in *N. seoulense* (Seo 1990) or symmetrical in *F. cratera* (Shoop 1989b). These eggs differ from echinostome eggs, for example, the eggs of *Isthmiophora hortensis* or *Echinostoma cinetorchis*; the eggs of *N. seoulense* have a clean shell surface and, unlike the echinostome eggs, they do not have abopercular wrinkles at the posterior end (Chai 2007; Chai et al. 2009). Praziquantel in a single oral dose of 10–20 mg/kg is highly effective for treatment of human *N. seoulense* infection (Seo 1990; Chai 2007; Chai et al. 2009).

4.2.7 Prevention and Control

For prevention of *N. seoulense* or *F. cratera* infection, ingestion of raw or improperly cooked flesh of snakes (paratenic host) or frogs (second intermediate host) should be avoided (Chai 2007; Chai et al. 2009).

References

Alden KJ (1995) Helminths of the opossum, *Didelphis virginiana*, in Southern Illinois, with a compilation of all helminths reported from this host in North America. J Helminthol Soc Wash 62:197–208

Barker FD (1915) Parasites of the American muskrat (*Fiber zibethicus*). J Parasitol 1:184–197

Brooks DR, McLennen DA (1993) Parascript. Parasites and the language of evolution. Smithsonian Institution Press, Washington, DC/London, pp 1–429

Byrd EE, Reiber RJ, Parker MV (1942) Mammalian trematodes. I. Trematodes from the opossum, *Didelphis virginiana* Kerr. Rep Reelfoot Lake Biol Sta 6:130–142

Chai JY (2007) Intestinal flukes. In: Murrell KD, Fried B (eds) Food-borne parasitic zoonoses. Fish and plant-borne parasites. Springer, New York, pp 53–115

Chai JY, Shin EH (2002) *Neodiplstomum leei* n. sp. (Digenea: Neodiplostomidae) from chicks infected with metacercariae from the grass snake, *Rhabdophis tigrina*. J Parasitol 88:1181–1186

Chai JY, Kim TK, Cho WH et al (1998) Intestinal mastocytosis and goblet cell hyperplasia in BALB/c and C3H mice infected with *Neodiplostomum seoulense*. Korean J Parasitol 36:109–119

Chai JY, Shin EH, Han ET et al (2000) Genetic difference in susceptibility and fatality of three strains of mice experimentally infected with *Neodiplostomum seoulense*. J Parasitol 86:1140–1144

Chai JY, Park JH, Guk SM et al (2007) *Apodemus agrarius* as a new definitive host for *Neodiplostomum seoulense*. Korean J Parasitol 45:157–161

Chai JY, Shin EH, Lee SH et al (2009) Foodborne intestinal flukes in Southeast Asia. Korean J Parasitol 47(Suppl):S69–S102

Chai JY, Bahk YY, Sohn WM (2013) Trematodes recovered in the small intestina of stray cats in the Republic of Korea. Korean J Parasitol 51:99–106

Chandler AC, Rausch R (1946) A study of strigeids from Michigan mammals, with comments on the classification of mammalian strigeids. Trans Am Microsc Soc 65:328–337

Cheon EW, Kim CH (1993) The nervous system of *Fibricola seoulensis* by acetylcholinesterase histochemistry. Korean J Parasitol 31:321–329

Ching HL, Leighton BJ, Stephen C (2000) Intestinal parasites of raccoons (*Procyon lotor*) from southwest British Columbia. Can J Vet Res 64:107–111

Cho SY, Cho BH, Kang SY (1983) Trematode parasites of Korean terrestrial snakes. Chung-Ang J Med 8:13–31 (in Korean)

Choi MH, Choe SC, Lee SH (1999) A 54 kDa cysteine protease purified from the crude extract of *Neodiplostomum seoulense* adult worms. Korean J Parasitol 37:39–46

Chung PR, Jung Y, Kim DS (1996) *Segmentina* (*Polypylis*) *hemisphaerula* (Gastropoda: Planorbidae): a new molluscan intermediate host of a human intestinal fluke *Neodiplostomum seoulense* (Trematoda: Diplostomatidae) in Korea. J Parasitol 82:336–338

Chung PR, Jung Y, Park YK et al (2002) Host specificity of *Austropeplea ollula* (Gastropoda: Lymnaeidae) to miracidial infection with a human intestinal fluke *Neodiplostomum seoulense* (Trematoda: Diplostomatidae) in Korea. J Parasitol 88:630–631

Cole RA, Shoop WL (1987) Helminths of the raccoon (*Procyon lotor*) in western Kentucky. J Parasitol 73:762–768

Cook TW (1978) The migration of *Fibricola cratera* (Trematoda: Diplostomatidae) in metamorphosing *Rana pipiens*. J Parasitol 64:938–939

Cribb TH, Pearson JC (1993) *Neodiplostomum spratti* n. sp. (Digenea: Diplostomidae) from *Antechinus* spp. (Marsupialia: Dasyuridae) in Australia, with notes on other diplostomids from Australian mammals. Syst Parasitol 25:25–35

Cuckler AC (1940) The life cycle of *Fibricola cratera* (Barker and Noll, 1915) Dubois, 1932 (Trematoda: Strigeata). J Parasitol 26(Suppl 1):32–33

Dubois G (1932) Révision des “Hémistomes” et étude de forms nouvelles. Bull Soc Neuch Sci Nat 56:375–412

Dubois G (1938) Monographie des Strigeida (Trematoda). Mem Soc Neuchateloise Sci Nat VI:1–535

Dubois G (1953) Systematique des Strigeida. Complement de la Monographie Mem Soc Neuchateloise Sci Nat VIII:1–141

Dubois G (1970) Synopsis des Strigeidae et des Diplostomatidae (Trematoda). Mémoires de la Société Neuchâteloise des Sciences Naturalles 10:259–727

Dubois G, Rausch R (1950a) Troisième contribution à Pétude des Strigeidés nord-americains. Inst Zool Univ Neuchât 73:19–50 (in Swedish)

Dubois G, Rausch R (1950b) A contribution to the study of North American Strigeids (Trematoda). Am Midl Nat 43:1–31

Gibson DI (1996) Trematoda. In: Margolis L, Kabata Z (eds) Guide to the parasites of fishes of Canada (Part IV), Canadian Special Publication of Fisheries and Aquatic Sciences, No. 124. NRC Press, Otawa, pp 1–373

Han ET, Chen JH, Chai JY (2008) Antibody responses in sera of different mouse strains experimentally infected with *Neodiplostomum seoulense*. Korean J Parasitol 46:279–283

Hoffman GL (1955) Notes on the life cycle of *Fibricola cratera* (Trematoda: Strigeida). J Parasitol 41:327

Hong ST (1982) Studies on intestinal trematodes in Korea. VII. Growth, development and recovery of *Fibricola seoulensis* from experimentally infected rats and mice. Korean J Parasitol 20:112–121

Hong ST, Shoop WL (1994) *Neodiplostomum seoulensis* n. comb. (Trematoda: Neodiplostomidae). J Parasitol 80:660–663

Hong ST, Shoop WL (1995) *Neodiplostomum seoulense*, the emended name for *Neodiplostomum seoulensis*. Korean J Parasitol 33:399

Hong ST, Hong SJ, Lee SH et al (1982) Studies on intestinal trematodes in Korea. VI. On the metacercariae and the second intermediate host of *Fibricola seoulensis*. Korean J Parasitol 20:101–111

Hong SJ, Lee SH, Seo BS et al (1983) Studies on intestinal trematodes in Korea. IX. Recovery rate and development of *Fibricola seoulensis* in experimental animals. Korean J Parasitol 21:224–233

Hong ST, Cho TK, Hong SJ et al (1984) Fifteen human cases of *Fibricola seoulensis* infection in Korea. Korean J Parasitol 22:61–65

Hong ST, Lee SH, Chai JY et al (1985) A study on the infection status of tadpoles and frogs by the metacercariae of *Fibricola seoulensis* in Korea. Korean J Parasitol 23:73–78 (in Korean)
Hong ST, Chai JY, Lee SH (1986) Ten human cases of *Fibricola seoulensis* infection and mixed one with *Stellantchasmus* and *Metagonimus*. Korean J Parasitol 24:94–96
Hong ST, Kim CH, Huh S et al (1988) Egg laying capacity of *Fibricola seoulensis* in mice and rats. Korean J Parasitol 26:117–119
Hong SJ, Woo HC, Lee SY et al (1993) Worm recovery rate and small intestinal lesions of albino rats coinfected with *Fibricola seoulensis* and metagonimus yokogawai. Korean J Parasitol 31:109–116
Hong SJ, Lee DH, Hong ST et al (1996) Surface ultrastructure of the cercaria of *Neodiplostomum seoulense* (Trematoda: Neodiplostomidae). J Parasitol 82:837–840
Huh S (1993) Activities of acid phosphatase and non-specific esterase are present in the tribocytic organ and the caecum of *Fibricola seoulensis*. Korean J Parasitol 31:165–167
Huh S, Song HB (1993) Transmission electron microscopic findings of the tribocytic organ of *Fibricola seoulensis*. Korean J Parasitol 31:315–320
Huh S, Chai JY, Hong ST et al (1988) Clinical and histopathological findings in mice heavily infected with *Fibricola seoulensis*. Korean J Parasitol 26:45–53
Huh S, Lee SH, Seo BS (1990) Histochemical findings of the tribocytic organ and tegument of *Fibricola seoulensis*. Korean J Parasitol 28:155–160
Huh S, Lee SU, Huh SC (1994) A follow-up examination of intestinal parasitic infections of the Army soldiers in Whachon-gun, Korea. Korean J Parasitol 32:61–63
Huh S, Lee SU, Won MH et al (1995) IgA response in mice infected with *Neodiplostomum seoulensis*. Korean J Parasitol 33:55–60
Jansma WB (1971) Ultrastructure and histochemistry of *Fibricola cratera* (Trematoda: Diplostomatidae). PhD thesis to Iowa State University, Iowa, USA
Kho WG, Chai JY, Chun CH et al (1990) Mucosal mast cell responses to experimental *Fibricola seoulensis* infection. Seoul J Med 31:191–199
Kim HJ, Kim CH (1993) Localization and isoenzyme patterns of phosphatase in *Fibricola seoulensis*. Korean J Parasitol 31:353–361
Kim TY, Han KY, Shin EH et al (2008) Antigenic properties of cystatin-binding cysteine proteinases from *Neodiplostomum seoulense*. J Parasitol 94:654–658
Kook J, Nawa Y, Lee SH et al (1998) Pathogenicity and lethality of a minute intestinal fluke, *Neodiplostomum seoulense*, to various strains of mice. J Parasitol 84:1178–1183
Lapierre AR (2011) Molecular phylogeny of the trematode families Diplostomidae and Strigeidae. Master of Science Thesis to Concordia University, Montreal, Quebec, Canada
Law RG, Kennedy AH (1932) Parasites of fur-bearing animals. Bull Dept Game Fisher Ontario Canada 4:1–30
Lee SH, Hong SJ, Chai JY et al (1985a) Studies on intestinal trematodes in Korea. XV. Tegumental ultrastructures of *Fibricola seoulensis* according to developmental stages. Seoul J Med 26:52–63
Lee SH, Yoo BH, Hong ST et al (1985b) A histopathological study on the intestine of mice and rats experimentally infected by *Fibricola seoulensis*. Korean J Parasitol 23:58–72
Lee SH, Lee HJ, Hong ST et al (1986a) The effect of temperature and salinity on maturation and hatching of *Fibricola seoulensis* eggs. Korean J Parasitol 24:115–120
Lee SH, Shin SM, Hong ST et al (1986b) Growth and development of *Fibricola seoulensis* metacercariae in tadpoles. Korean J Parasitol 24:109–114
Lee CK, Hong ST, Yu JR et al (1991) Activity of brush border membrane bound enzymes in the small intestine of mice infected with *Fibricola seoulensis*. Seoul J Med 32:139–148
Lee JC, Kong Y, Lee SU et al (1997) Localization of worm antigen in *Neodiplostomum seoulense* by immuno-electronmicroscopy. Korean J Parasitol 35:95–104
Locke SA, Al-Nasiri FS, Caffara M et al (2015) Diversity, specificity and speciation in larval Diplostomidae (Platyhelminthes: Digenea) in the eyes of freshwater fish, as revealed by DNA barcodes. Int J Parasitol. https://doi.org/10.1016/j.ipara.2015.07.001

López-Hernández D, Locke SA, de Melo AL et al (2018) Molecular, morphological and experimental assessment of the life cycle of *Posthodiplostomum nanum* (Trematoda: Diplostomidae) from Brazil, with phylogenetic evidence of the paraphyly of the genus *Posthodiplostomum* Dubois, 1936. Infect Genet Evol. https://doi.org/10.1016/j.meegid.2018.05.010

Lumsden RD (1961) The white ibis, *Eudocimus albus* (Linn.), host for the diplostomatid trematode *Fibricola cratera* (Barker and Noll, 1915) Dubois, 1932, in Louisiana. J Parasitol 47:897

Miller MJ (1940) A new trematode, *Fibricola laruei*, from the raccoon in Canada. Can J Res (D) 18:333–335

Morgan BB, Waller EF (1940) Severe parasitism in a raccoon (*Procyon lotor lotor*, Linnaeus). Trans Am Microbiol Soc 59:523–527

Niewiadomska K (2002a) Superfamily Diplostomoidea Poirier, 1886. In: Gibson DI, Jones, Bray RA (eds) Keys to the Trematoda, vol 1. Natural History Museum, London, pp 159–166

Niewiadomska K (2002b) Family Diplostomidae Poirier, 1886. In: Gibson DI, Jones A, Bray RA (eds) Keys to the Trematoda, vol 1. Natural History Museum, London, pp 167–196

Niewiadomska K (2002c) Family Strigeidae Railliet, 1919. In: Gibson DI, Jones A, Bray RA (eds) Keys to the Trematoda, vol 1. Natural History Museum, London, pp 231–241

Park GM, Lee SU, Park HY et al (1998) Karyotype analysis of *Neodiplostomum seoulense*. Korean J Parasitol 36:277–279

Park YK, Hwang MK, Jung YJ (2006) Complement-mediated tail degradation of *Neodiplostomum seoulense* cercariae. Korean J Parasitol 44:127–131

Pearson JC (1959) *Neodiplostomum intermedium* n. sp. from the allied rat, *Rattus assimilis*, with remarks on the genera *Neodiplostomum* and *Fibricola* (Trematoda: Diplostomatidae). Parasitology 49:111–120

Pearson JC (1961) Observations on the morphology and life cycle of *Neodiplostomum intermedium* (Trematoda: Diplostomatidae). Parasitology 51:133–172

Premvati G, Bair TD (1979) Trematode parasites of the opossum, *Didelphis virginiana*, from Florida. Proc Helminthol Soc Wash 46:207–212

Pyo KH, Kang EY, Jung BK et al (2012) Depressed neuronal growth associated protein (GAP)-43 expression in the small intestinaes of mice experimentally infected with *Neodiplostomum seoulense*. Korean J Parasitol 50:89–93

Pyo KH, Lee JWY, Lee JJ et al (2014) Phylogenetic relationships of 3 Korean *Neodiplostomum* species (Digenea: Neodiplostomidae) based on partial CO1 gene. Korean J Parasitol 52:325–329

Quan F, Jiang T, Ma H et al (1995) The first discovery of *Fibricola seoulensis* in China. J Yanbian Med Coll 18:17–20 (in Chinese)

Rausch R, Tiner JD (1949) Studies on the parasitic helminths of the north central states. II. Helminths of voles (*Microtus* spp.) preliminary report. Am Midl Naturalist 41:665–694

Read CP (1948) Strigeids from Texas mink with notes on the genus *Fibricola* Dubois. Trans Am Microsc Soc 67:165–168

Richardson DJ (2013) Helminth parasites of the raccoon (*Procyon lotor*), Virginia opossum (*Didelphis virginiana*), and striped skunk (*Mephitis mephitis*) from Keith County, Nebraska. Trans Nebraska Acad Sci 33:35–38

Richardson DJ, Owen WB, Snyder DE (1992) Helminth parasites of the raccoon (*Procyon lotor*) from north-central Arkansas. J Parasitol 78:163–166

Seo BS (1989) Comparative growth and development of the metacercariae of *Fibricola seoulensis* (Trematoda: Diplostomidae) in vitro, in vivo and on the chick chorioallantois. Korean J Parasitol 27:231–248

Seo BS (1990) *Fibricola seoulensis* Seo, Rim and Lee, 1964 (Trematoda) and fibricoliasis in man. Seoul J Med 31:61–96

Seo BS, Rim HJ, Lee CW (1964) Studies on the parasitic helminths of Korea. I. Trematodes of rodents. Korean J Parasitol 2:20–26

Seo BS, Cho SY, Hong ST et al (1981) Studies on parasitic helminths of Korea. V. Survey on intestinal trematodes of house rats. Korean J Parasitol 19:131–136

Seo BS, Lee SH, Hong ST et al (1982) Studies on intestinal trematodes in Korea. V. A human case infected by *Fibricola seoulensis* (Trematoda: Diplostomatidae). Korean J Parasitol 20:93–99

Seo BS, Lee SH, Chai JY et al (1984) Studies on intestinal trematodes in Korea. X.Scanning electron microscopic observation o n the tegument of *Fibricola seoulensis*. Korean J Parasitol 22:21–29 (in Korean)

Seo BS, Lee SH, Chai JY et al (1988) The life cycle and larval development of *Fibricola seoulensis* (Trematoda: Diplostomatidae). Korean J Parasitol 26:179–188

Shin EH, Kim TH, Hong SJ et al (2003) Effects of anti-allergic drugs on intestinal mastocytosis and worm expulsion of rats infected with *Neodiplostomum seoulense*. Korean J Parasitol 41:81–87

Shin EH, Lee SH, Kim JL et al (2007) T-helper-1 and T-helper-2 immune responses in mice infected with the intestinal fluke *Neodiplostomum seoulense*: their possible roles in worm expulsion and host fatality. J Parasitol 93:1036–1045

Shin EH, Kim JL, Chai JY (2008) A new neodiplostomid (Digenea) from the intestine of chicks infected with metacercariae from the grass snake *Rhabdophis tigrina*. J Parasitol 94:1379–1384

Shin EH, Kim TK, Park YK et al (2016) Fecundity reduction of BALB/c mice after survival from lethal *Neodiplostomum seoulense* infection. Parasitol Res 115:2051–2059

Shoop WL (1989a) Systematic analyses of the Diplostomidae and Strigeidae (Trematoda). J Parasitol 75:21–32

Shoop WL (1989b) Experimental human infection with *Fibricola cratera* (Trematoda: Neodiplostomidae). Korean J Parasitol 27:249–252

Shoop WL, Corkum KC (1981) Some trematodes of mammals in Louisiana. Tulane Stud Zool Bot 22:109–121

Shoop WL, Corkum KC (1982) Additional trematodes of mammals in Louisiana with a compilation of all trematodes reported from wild and domestic mammals in the state. Tulane Stud Zool Bot 23:109–122

Sohn WM, Chai JY (2005) Infection status with helminthes in feral cats purchased from a market in Busan, Republic of Korea. Korean J Parasitol 43:93–100

Sudarikov VE (1960) Suborder Strigeata La Rue, 1926. Part 3. Superfamily Diplostomatoidea Nicoll, 1937. In: Skrjabin KI (ed) Trematodes of animals and man, vol 18. Moscow, Russia, pp 323–531 (translated from Russian)

Turner HF (1958) The life history of *Fibricola cratera* (Barker and Noll, 1915) Dobois, 1932 (Trematoda: Diplostomatidae). PhD thesis to Iowa State University, Iowa, USA

Ulmer ML (1955) Notes on the morphology and host-parasite specificity of *Fibricola cratera* (Barker and Noll, 1915) Dubois, 1932 (Trematoda: Diplostomatidae). J Parasitol 41:460–466

Ulmer ML (1970) Studies on the helminth fauna of Iowa. I. Trematodes of amphibians. Am Midl Naturalist 83:38–64

Yu JR, Hong ST, Chai JY et al (1995) The effect of reinfection with *Neodiplostomum seoulensis* on the histopathology and activities of brush border membrane bound enzymes in the rat small intestine. Korean J Parasitol 33:37–43

Chapter 5
Fasciolids

5.1 Family Fasciolidae

The family Fasciolidae Railliet, 1895 are a group of trematodes infecting the liver and bile ducts, intestine or, rarely, lungs of herbivorous and omnivorous mammals (Jones 2005). They can be divided into 3 subfamilies; Fasciolinae Railliet, 1895 (having branched ceca), Fasciolopsinae Odhner, 1910 (having simple ceca and branched dendritic testes), and Protofasciolinae Skrjabin, 1948 (having simple ceca and entire testes) (Yamaguti 1971; Jones 2005). The subfamily Fasciolinae contain 3 genera; *Fasciola* Linnaeus, 1758, *Fascioloides* Ward, 1917, and *Tenuifasciola* Yamaguti 1971, and the subfamily Protofasciolinae has one genus, *Protofasciola* Odhner, 1926 (Jones 2005). The subfamily Fasciolopsinae has 2 genera, *Fasciolopsis* Looss 1899 (type genus) and *Parafasciolopsis* Ejesmont, 1932 (Yamaguti 1971; Jones 2005). Members of *Fasciola, Fascioloides, Tenuifasciola,* and *Parafasciolopsis* are parasites of the liver, bile ducts, or lungs of herbivorous mammals, whereas members of *Protofasciola* and *Fasciolopsis* are intestinal parasites (Yamaguti 1971).

5.2 *Fasciolopsis*

Flukes of the genus *Fasciolopsis* have a cirrus sac extending posteriorly far beyond the ventral sucker, dendritic ovary and testes, a long uterus, whereas flukes of *Parafasciolopsis* have a cirrus sac entirely pre-acetabular or almost so, an entire ovary, and a short uterus, and flukes of *Protofasciola* have simple testes (Jones 2005). Other morphological characters of *Fasciolopsis* include a very large and broad, lanceolate to linguiform body without a cephalic cone (Yamaguti 1971). Its acetabulum is strongly muscular, produced backward, much larger than the oral sucker, close to the cephalic end; its testes are with numerous digitiform branches, tandem, intercecal and postequatorial (Yamaguti 1971). In the genus *Fasciolopsis*,

J.-Y. Chai, *Human Intestinal Flukes*,
https://doi.org/10.1007/978-94-024-1704-3_5

only one species *Fasciolopsis buski* is now recognized to be taxonomically valid and infect humans (Table 3.1).

5.2.1 Fasciolopsis buski

5.2.1.1 *Fasciolopsis buski* (Lankester, 1857) Odhner, 1902

[syn. *Distoma crassum* Busk, 1859; *Distoma rathouisi* Porier, 1887; *Fasciolopsis rathouisi* (Porier, 1887) Ward, 1903; *Fasciolopsis fülleborni* Rodenwaldt, 1909; *Fasciolopsis godaardi* Ward, 1910; *Fasciolopsis spinifera* Brown, 1917]

Taxonomy and Morphology

Fasciolopsis buski (Fig. 5.1), the giant intestinal fluke, one of the largest digeneans infecting humans, was first discovered by G. Busk, an English surgeon, in 1843 from the duodenum of an Indian sailor who died in London (Beaver et al. 1984). It was named as *Distoma buski* by Lankester in 1857, but the name was given again as *Distoma crassum* by Busk in 1859 and Cobbold in 1960 (Yamaguti 1971; Beaver et al. 1984). However, it emerged later that this name was already occupied by another parasite described in 1836 (Tandon et al. 2013). In 1874, this parasite was observed again in a missionary couple residing in China; the adult flukes passed out in their stool were identified by Busk to be the same fluke as the ones he had first seen decades ago (Tandon et al. 2013). In the following years, more than once

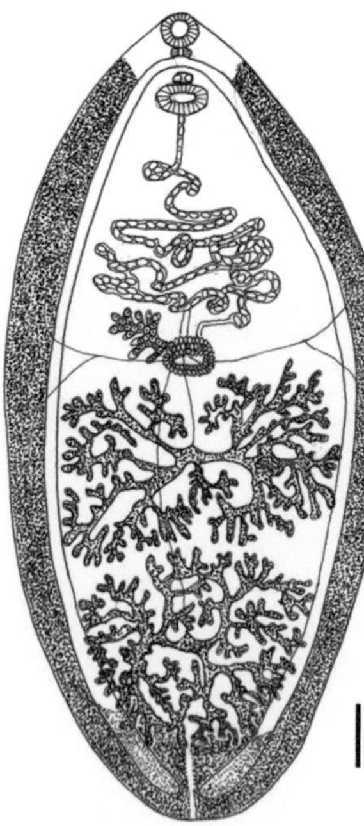

Fig. 5.1 Line drawing of an adult fluke of *Fasciolopsis buski* (original figure). Scale bar = 5 mm

similar-looking worms were reported from Chinese subjects (Tandon et al. 2013). Looss (1899) proposed the genus *Fasciolopsis*, and the name of this parasite was given as *Fasciolopsis crassa* (Cobbold, 1960) Looss, 1899 (Yamaguti 1971). However, this name was not accepted but further changed into *Fasciolopsis buski* (Lankester, 1857) by Odhner, 1902 (Beaver et al. 1984). In 1887, *Distoma rathouisi* was reported by Porier, and in 1903 Ward amended it into *Fasciolopsis rathouisi*; but it was synonymized with *F. buski* (Yamaguti 1971; Rim 1982a; Beaver et al. 1984). Other species reported later, *Fasciolopsis fülleborni* Rodenwaldt, 1909, *Fasciolopsis godaardi* Ward, 1910, and *Fasciolopsis spinifera* Brown, 1917, were all synonymized with *F. buski* (Yamaguti 1971; Rim 1982a; Beaver et al. 1984). It is now known to be a common intestinal parasite of man and pigs in South and Southeast Asia (Yu and Mott 1994; Mas-Coma et al. 2005; Rohela et al. 2005; Tandon et al. 2013; Chai 2014). Human infection occurs by ingestion of raw aquatic vegetation or food plants contaminated with the metacercariae (Tandon et al. 2013). The parasite chiefly inhabits the duodenum and jejunum but also can be found in the stomach in moderate and heavy infections (Graczyk et al. 2001). The prevalence of human infection varied according to countries, 10% in Thailand (Bunnag et al. 1983), 25% in Taiwan (Shyu et al. 1984), 57% in China (Lee 1972), and 60% in India (Muttalib and Islam 1975). The infection mainly prevails among the socioeconomically underdeveloped and impoverished areas of tropical and subtropical areas where high rainfalls and moderate water temperature offer suitable environmental conditions for the propagation of snail intermediate hosts that are essential for continuing the life cycle of the parasite (Tandon et al. 2013).

Adult flukes are, when live, thick, fleshy, pinkish, or dark brown in color, broadly leaf-shaped, ovate, elliptical with rounded posterior end, and 20–100 mm (mostly 20–70 mm) in length and 8–30 mm (mostly 20 mm) in width, and 0.5–3.0 mm in thickness, without cephalic cone (Rim 1982a; Mas-Coma et al. 2005; Tandon et al. 2013). The ventral sucker is large and muscular, and lies lose to the oral sucker; the prepharynx is very short and the esophagus is short (Tandon et al. 2013). The intestinal ceca are long, lateral, sinous but unbranched and extend to the subterminal region of the body; the testes are markedly branched and placed one behind the other in the posterior half of the body (Tandon et al. 2013). The ovary is also branched and lies to the right of the midline and the uterus is also highly branched which occupies the anterior half of the body containing an enormous number of eggs enabling each worm to deposit approximately 25,000 eggs daily (Stoll et al. 1927). The eggs are large and operculated, unembryonated when laid, and 130–140 μm long and 80–85 μm wide (Kumar 1980; Rim 1982a; Beaver et al. 1984; Mas-Coma et al. 2005). The cercarial body is 207 μm long and 126 μm wide, having 2 types of cytogenous glands (round-celled glands secrete the material for the outer cyst wall, and rhabdoidal-celled glands secrete the material for the inner cyst wall), and the tail 392 μm long and 54 μm (Nakagawa 1922; Ito 1964). The metacercariae are flat and almost round, 140 m long and 130 m wide, enveloped with inner thin and outer thick layers (Komiya 1965).

The surface ultrastructure of *F. buski* was studied by several workers; the ventral surface of the adult flukes was provided with densely packed and posteriorly directed broadly rounded scale-like spines, and this normal surface topography showed little variation according to specimens originating from different geographical regions (Taraschewski et al. 1986; Roy and Tandon 1993; Tandon et al. 2013).

Life Cycle

This fluke has the life cycle stages of the eggs, miracidium, sporocyst, rediae (mother and daughter rediae), cercaria, and metacercaria, and adult (Rim 1982a). When an immature egg is discharged in the feces of definitive hosts and reach fresh water; it requires 3–7 weeks at 27–32 °C for them to complete its incubation, where it develops into miracidia and hatch out from the eggs and swim in water (Rim 1982a; Beaver et al. 1984). On contact with an appropriate snail host, the miracidium penetrates the soft tissues of the snail, and within a few weeks (25–30 days) it develops into a sporocyst, and then rediae (mother and daughter rediae), and cercariae. After penetration of miracidia into the snail, the sporocyst develops quickly and then mother rediae develop rapidly inside the sporocyst within 9–10 days; mother rediae migrate to the ovotestis and form daughter rediae inside themselves (Mas-Coma et al. 2005). The mature daughter rediae harbor up to 45 cercariae (gymnocephalous type) (Mas-Coma et al. 2005). The first intermediate host is freshwater snails, including *Segmentina hemisphaerula* (syn. *Segmentina coenosus, Segmentina nitidella, Segmentina calathus*, and *Segmentina largeillierti*), *Segmentina trochoideus*, *Hippeutis cantori* (syn. *Hippeutis schmackeri*), *Hippeutis umbilicalis*, *Indoplanorbis exustus*, *Helicorbis coenosus*, *Gyraulus convexiusculus*, and *Gyraulus chinensis* (Yu and Mott 1994; Graczyk et al. 2000; Mas-Coma et al. 2005; Chai 2007a; Tandon et al. 2013). The cercariae stay a while in the liver of the snail before escaping from the snail (Barlow 1925). The emergence of cercariae is dependent on light, with great variation in daily emergence patterns (Preet and Prakash 2001). The freely swimming cercariae are morphologically almost identical with those of *Fasciola hepatica* (Rim 1982a). The cercarial survival period in water varies from 64 to 72 days (Mas-Coma et al. 2005; Tandon et al. 2013). They usually encyst on the seed pods of the water caltrop (*Trapa natans, Trapa bispinosa,* or *Trapa bicornis*) or on the bulb of the water chestnut (*Eliocharis tuberose*) (Rim 1982a). Other second intermediate hosts include various aquatic vegetations, including the water hyacinth (*Eichhornia speciosa*), roots of the water lotus or water lily (*Nymphaea lotus*), water cress (*Neptunia oleracea*), water bamboo (*Zizania* sp.), or morning glory (*Ipomoea aquatica*) (Manning and Ratanarat 1970; Beaver et al. 1984; Yu and Mott 1994; Fried et al. 2004). The metacercariae are located on their body surface, and they may float encysted on the water surface (Beaver et al. 1984; Yu and Mott 1994; Fried et al. 2004).

Infection of the definitive host takes place through the ingestion of encysted metacercariae along with infested vegetations or water (Tandon et al. 2013). Pigs are the only important natural reservoir host, although they harbor a relatively small number of flukes (usually 3–12 flukes per pig) (Rim 1982a). Pigs, rabbits, dogs, and squirrel monkeys can also be successful experimental hosts (Wu 1937; Malviya 1985; Mas-Coma et al. 2005). On entering the duodenum, the metacercariae excyst and liberate a juvenile worm, which develops into the adult fluke in the course of

3-months time; the adult flukes soon begin egg production and their life span is about 6 months (Tandon et al. 2013).

Epidemiology and Geographical Distribution

Pigs are the main source of eggs and drainage of pig excreta in farms is an important factor for maintaining high endemicity (Yu and Mott 1994). The major mode of human infection is consumption of raw or improperly cooked aquatic plants, or peeling off the hull or skin of the plants by mouth before eating the raw nut (Yu and Mott 1994). For example, up to 200 metacercariae may be present in one water caltrop, although the usual number per water caltrop is about 15–20 (Tandon et al. 2013). Cercariae may also encyst on the water surface; reportedly 10–13% of the patients and 35–40% of the infected pigs had possibly contracted infection by drinking metacercariae-contaminated water (Weng et al. 1989). Therefore, fasciolopsiasis is a type of plant- or water-borne parasitic infection.

F. buski is now known to be a common intestinal parasite of man and pigs in South and Southeast Asia, including China, Taiwan, Thailand, Vietnam, Lao PDR, Cambodia, Bangladesh, India, Indonesia, Myanmar, Malaysia, and the Philippines (Fig. 5.2; Table 3.2) (Yu and Mott 1994; Mas-Coma et al. 2005; Rohela et al. 2005; Tandon et al. 2013; Chai 2014). In 1947, it was estimated that over 10 million people in the Far East were infected with this fluke; most of these infections were reported from mainland China (Cross 1969; Tandon et al. 2013). Small endemic foci or a small number of cases have been reported from Taiwan, Thailand, Vietnam, Lao PDR, East Pakistan, India, Nepal, Singapore, and Japan (Ryukyu Islands); however, the distribution of infections in these countries is limited, and the overall prevalence rates are considerably lower than those of mainland China (Cross 1969). Case reports from South Korea (Brooke et al. 1956; Kuntz et al. 1958) may have been due to misidentification of fecal eggs. Reports from USA, Venezuela, Australia,

Fig. 5.2 Global distribution of *Fasciolopsis buski* based on the presence of their life cycles

Guatemala, Israel (Palestine), and Cuba may be due to immigrant from the Far East (Greenberg et al. 1994) or misidentification of fecal eggs (Schubert and Grantz 1981). Sex- and age-tendency of infection has been reported; in coprological surveys in Thailand, a higher prevalence was noted among females (16%) than in males (11%); the prevalence varied from 8% among adults (>15 years) to 15% in children (5–14 years old), with an average of 13% for all age groups (Sadun and Maiphoom 1953). The severity of infection increased up to 10–14 years of age and decreased in older groups, and the differences in prevalence and intensity were related to activities of individual (Mas-Coma et al. 2005).

Bangladesh The first *F. buski* case was reported in 1958 in a refugee family from Bihar, India, a known endemic area; it was thus considered that this parasite may have been introduced by immigrants recently; however, it is now clearly occurring in the native population (Gilman et al. 1982). Subsequently, 4 (16%) of 24 teenagers examined were found infected with this fluke (Muazzam and Ali 1961). Thereafter, a parasitic survey of a village (Maradia) in Dacca District revealed 39.2% prevalence of *F. buski,* while the corresponding figure in another village (Manda) was 8.6% (Muttalib and Islam 1975). In addition, a larger survey in 27 villages within Dacca District revealed that 10 villages located in the south and eastern parts were areas with positive prevalences ranging from 2.2% to 73.7% (Gilman et al. 1982).

Cambodia No information had been available before 1965 regarding the prevalence of *F. buski*; however, it was reported that in the region of Phnom Penh this parasite was positive in 0.04% of the humans and 5% of the pig population (Brumpt and Kong-Kim-Chuon 1965). In a recent survey in Kandal Province, one of 221 stool samples (large trematode egg-positive) tested positive by PCR for *Fasciola* spp., whereas none of them was positive for *F. buski* by PCR (Bless et al. 2015).

China Human and pig infections have been reported from 17 or 18 provinces with the prevalence ranging from 4.6% to 57.7% (Li 1991; Wu 2013). In some areas, like Chekiang and Kiangsi Province, the prevalence was up to 85%; however, recent nationwide surveys suggested a decrease in the prevalence (national prevalence; 0.169%) (Yu et al. 1994; Mas-Coma et al. 2005; Tandon et al. 2013). A clinical case report dealing with 2 patients which caused appendicitis has been published in Anhui Province (Cao et al. 2015).

India Morbidity due to fasciolopsiasis has been recorded since 1843 when the first human infection with *F. buski* was discovered from an Indian sailor who died in England (Tandon et al. 2013, 2015). Subsequently, this parasite was reported from different provinces of India, namely, Assam, Bengal, Bihar, Orissa, Maharashtra, Madhya Pradesh, and Uttar Pradesh where poverty and hygienic socio-cultural practices and food habits are associated with the existence of open types of large-scale piggeries (Buckley 1939; Chandra 1984; Tandon et al. 2013). In Kamrup district, Assam, up to 60% of human population (with 1–57 worms per person) and 40% pigs were infected with *F. buski* (Buckley 1939; Singh 1991). In Uttar Pradesh,

Chandra (1984) reported 22.4% egg prevalence among the people; the pigs of this locality were also found to be highly (29.4%) infected. Infection in pigs (29% prevalence) was also reported in Mumbai (Tandon et al. 2013). A new endemic focus of human *F. buski* infection was found in Maharashtra (Manjarumkar and Shah 1972). In Uttar Pradesh, there were no cases detected in the 1990s, but there were reports of a reemerging infection thereafter (Bhatti et al. 2000; Muralidhar et al. 2000). Consequently, a severe clinical case of a 10-year old body presenting with intestinal perforation was reported from Uttar Predesh; this child had 25 adult flukes detected in surgery and treated orally with praziquantel 25 mg/kg divided into 3 doses (Bhattacharjee et al. 2009). Khurana (2016) made a commentary that *F. buski* infection in Bihar area is an important but neglected parasitic disease. A human case presenting with an intestinal mass was reported in Kolkata (Roy et al. 2017).

Indonesia Borneo and Sumatra have been recorded where *F. buski* is distributed (Rim 1982a; Beaver et al. 1984). However, there have been very few actual reports on this parasite in Indonesia (Cross 1969; Hadidjaja et al. 1982). In 1923, Hegner first mentioned the presence of this parasite in Indonesia (Cross 1969), which was followed by Hsü and Li (1953) and Ressang et al. (1959). Hadidjaja et al. (1982) was the first who reported the first autochthonous human case that occurred in South Kalimantan, Indonesia. Handoyo et al. (1986) reported 27.0% prevalence among residents of Kalimantan and 20.3% outside that area, including high prevalence in the 5–14-year group but decreasing with age.

Japan It was mentioned in a textbook written by Simmons et al. in 1944 that *F. buski* occurs in some of the inhabitants of the Ryukyu Islands (Cross 1969). A few egg positive cases were reported in other areas of Japan; however, they were considered as imported cases from endemic countries (Morishita 1964).

South Korea Brooke et al. (1956) reported eggs of either *F. buski* or *Fasciola hepatica* in 6 North Korean prisoners of war. In the same year, Maschke reported *F. buski* in a child who had recently immigrated from South Korea to Germany (Cross 1969). Moreover, Kuntz et al. (1958) found *F. buski* eggs in the feces of a retired Turkish soldier who had served with the United Nations Forces in South Korea during the Korean War. Under these circumstances, it was speculated that *F. buski* might be present in South Korea (Cross 1969). However, it may be possible that the eggs found in the feces of above cases were of *F. hepatica* rather than *F. buski* since it is very difficult to differentiate between the eggs of these 2 species of trematodes (Cross 1969). Thereafter, 20–30 cases of *F. hepatica* have been continuously occurring, whereas no cases of *F. buski* have been diagnosed in South Korea (Chai 2007b). Thus, it is strongly suggested that South Korea is not an endemic area of *F. buski* infection.

Lao PDR No information had been available before 1968 regarding the prevalence of *F. buski*; however, it has been mentioned that human infection with this parasite is present in Lao PDR, without proper literature backgrounds (Segal et al. 1968). In 1989, fecal surveys were performed on people around Nam Ngum Dam, Vientiane

Province, which revealed 2.4–3.8% egg positive rate of *F. buski* out of 757 subjects (Giboda et al. 1991). Later, *F. buski* infection, together with *Fasciola gigantica*, was diagnosed by recovery of eggs (both *F. buski* and *F. gigantica*) or by serology (*F. gigantica*) among residents in Savannakhet Province; the egg prevalence of *F. buski* was 33.7% (Quang et al. 2008).

Malaysia Lie (1964) detected 2 human cases (an adult and a 13-year old girl) in Kuala Lumpur after treatment with carbon tetrachloride; it was presumed that one case (adult; Chinese) acquired the infection in China and the other (young girl) was infected through eating chest nuts imported from China. However, it seemed unlikely in the second case since this would have required the water chest nuts to be maintained in a wet or moist condition for an extended period of time in order to enable the metacercariae to remain viable (Cross 1969). Shekhar (1991) mentioned that domestic food animals in Malaysia had been found to harbor less common zoonotic parasites, including *F. buski*. Rohela et al. (2005) detected a patient (a native of Sabah, East Malaysia) positive for the eggs of *F. buski*, although the adult worm was not recovered from this case.

Myanmar Infections with *F. buski* were found in pigs (Bhalerao 1924; Bhattacharjee 1937; Chatterjee 1938); however, human infections were never discovered (Cross 1969).

Nepal It has been recently mentioned that the eggs of *F. buski* were detected from a Nepalese patient at Tribhuvan University Hospital, Kathmandu (Sah et al. 2018).

Pakistan Kuntz (1960) first detected an egg positive case among 295 schoolchildren in the vicinity of Dacca, East Pakistan. Subsequently, 5 (0.2%) of 2412 individuals of East Pakistan were found to be positive for *F. buski* eggs (Muazzam and Ali 1961). Later, in 12 localities (6 urban and 6 rural), 27 *F. buski* egg positive individuals were detected among 3600 examinees; 10 were from urban areas and 17 were from rural areas (Maqbool et al. 2007).

The Philippines Garrison and Lago (1910) mentioned on *F. buski* infection in the Philippines. In 1924, Schwartz found eggs in the stool of several Chinese; however, it was unknown whether these infections were acquired locally or in China (Cross 1969). Nearly 4000 residents in Northern Luzon were examined by NAMRU-2 but no infections of *F. buski* were found; thus, the Philippines should be considered a non-endemic area of *F. buski* (Cross 1969).

Singapore Singapore is included among the list of countries where *F. buski* is existing (Waikagul 1991; Mas-Coma et al. 2005).

Taiwan The most severely affected endemic area is located in southern parts; the prevalence reached 48% and the intensity of infection per person was 10 worms (Hsieh 1960), and the prevalence was even 61% in a village of Pa-Weng (Lee 1972).

From Tainan, South Taiwan, 2 of 3 primary schools examined revealed infected children (13.0% and 3.5%) with *F. buski*; they had a recent experience of eating raw water caltrop (Shyu et al. 1984).

Thailand The presence of human fasciolopsiasis was first recognized by Daengsvang and Mangalasmaya (1941) in 5 people from Dhonburi Province. Viranuvatti et al. (1953) reported a fatal case of fascioplopsiasis in a 15-year-old female who was infected with 466 worms. Sadun and Maiphoom (1953) also mentioned about this fatal case and reported 13.3% egg prevalence (208 people) among 1563 examined in 3 provinces (Ayuthia, Dhonburi, and Nakorn Phatom), areas of water caltrop cultivation, in central Thailand. Endemic areas were also found by Soavakontha et al. (1966), and clinical illness due to *F. buski* infection was defined in detail (Plaut et al. 1969). In 3 provinces (Ayuthaya, Angthong, and Suphaburi) of central Thailand, the egg positive rate of people was 39.3%, 5.2%, and 12.1%, respectively, and the estimated number of infected people was 100,000 in these areas (Manning and Ratanarat 1970). Two species of snails, *Segmentina hemisphaerula* and *Segmentina trochoideus*, were found to be infected with the cercariae, and 5 species of plants, morning glory (*Ipomoea aquatica*), water caltrop (*Trapa bicornis*), lotus (*Nymphaea lotus*), water cress (*Neptunia oleracea*), and water hyacinth (*Eichhornia speciosa*) were important source of infection (Manning and Ratanarat 1970). Catalytic models were applied to analyze the age-specific prevalence of *F. buski* infection in 2 endemic areas; the peak prevalence was found in 10–15 year children and the prevalence became zero in old age, suggesting an involvement of acquired immunity in old people (Manning et al. 1971). Bunnag et al. (1983) evaluated the therapeutic efficacy of praziquantel for treatment of human *F. buski* infection; the number of enrolled patients was 85 schoolchildren (10.4% prevalence among 816 examined) in Ayuthaya Province (Bunnag et al. 1983). Adult specimens of *F. buski* were recovered in a male patient from northeastern parts of Thailand (Radomyos et al. 1994, 1998). In addition, a high prevalence (7.1%) of *F. buski* was notified in Udonthani Province, located in a northeastern part, in stool examination of 183 villagers who were also positive for *Opisthorchis viverrini* eggs (8.7%); many of these population were immigrants from other parts of Thailand (Wiwanitkit et al. 2002). However, a survey in 3 (Ayuthaya, Suphanburi, and Angthong) provinces in central Thailand revealed no egg positive cases of *F. buski* (Saksirisampant et al. 2006).

Vietnam The earliest report on *F. buski* infection in pigs in Vietnam was made by Brau and Bruyant (1913). Later, in Tonkin (northern area), 5 human cases were detected by Galliard and Ngu in 1942, and 2 more cases were diagnosed by Galliard (1948). In 1953, Bauge found 15% prevalence among Asians living in Vietnam and 3% prevalence among Europeans (Cross 1969). Founier (1954) also reported this parasite in Asians as well as Europeans in Saigon (Ho Chi Min city). However, in studies by NAMRU-2 in Da Nang, only one of several hundred people examined were found to be passing eggs in the feces (Cross 1969). Buffle and canines have also been listed as possible definitive hosts in Vietnam (Segal et al. 1968). Pigs were confirmed to be reservoir host of this parasite (Yoshihara et al. 1999). An interesting case of a boy who vomited 8 live *F. buski* adult flukes has been described (Le et al. 2004). An immigrant from Vietnam to Taiwan was diagnosed as *F. buski* infection through gastrointestinal endoscopy in a hospital in Taipei (Lee et al. 2011). Another case of *F. buski* was reported in a pregnant woman who was accompanied by systemic lupus erythematosus (Fiamma et al. 2015). De and Minh (2016) reported 130 (1.23%) egg positive cases among 10,540 people examined from 14 provinces in Vietnam; adult worms were collected in several provinces and also molecular studies were done for species identification.

5.2.2 *Potentially Zoonotic* Fasciolopsis *spp*

Only one species, *F. buski*, is available in the genus *Fasciolopsis*. Therefore, there is no other potentially zoonotic species.

5.2.3 *Genomics and Proteomics*

In 1985 and 1990, the chromosome number of *F. buski* was reported to be 2n = 14 (Gao 1985; Dai 1990). However, few molecular studies had been performed on *F. buski* until the early 2000s; only 2 sequences corresponding to the 18S rDNA gene were available in GenBank (Mas-Coma et al. 2005). Comparing with this DNA sequence, fluke specimens vomited by a child in Vietnam, whose 18S rDNA was analyzed, was confirmed to be *F. buski*; the molecular identity between their samples and that deposited in GenBank was 99.9% (Le et al. 2004). However, it was notified that ITS2 sequences of isolates of *F. buski* from India and Vietnam differ by 6.7%, a divergence that is much larger than that between *F. hepatica* and *F. gigantica* (Ma et al. 2017). The stage (egg and adult)-specific ITS (ITS1 and ITS2) sequences of rDNA were determined, and those sequences from eggs and adults were identical in length and composition; phylogenetically, *F. buski* resembled closely the other members of the family Fasciolidae, including *Fasciola hepatica* and *Fasciola gigantica* (Prasad et al. 2007). However, using ITS2 rDNA analysis of *F. buski,* in comparison with *F. gigantica,* and *Paragonimus westermani*, it was possible to generate species-specific primers that can unequivocally discriminate one species from another (Prasad et al. 2011). Complete mtDNA sequences of *F. buski* from India were decoded using the next-generation sequencing (NGS) technologies (Biswal et al. 2013). The complete mtDNA sequence of *F. buski* from China was14,833 bp, with 36 genes, including 12 protein-coding genes (PCGs), 22 tRNA genes, and 2 rRNA genes (Ma et al. 2017). It was notified that the sequence difference in the nicotinamide dehydrogenase subunit 1 (*nad1*) gene between the *F. buski* isolates from India and Vietnam was 17.7%, which was higher than that (15%) between *Fascioloides magna* and *F. hepatica* (Ma et al. 2017). Moreover, by analyzing the mitochondrial and nuclear rDNA sequences, it was suggested that *F. buski* from China and India may represent distinct taxa, while *F. buski* in Vietnam and China represent the same species (Ma et al. 2017). Further studies with decoding mtDNA and rDNA sequences of *F. buski* from various geographical isolates may bring about better understanding of the species complex in *F. buski* (Ma et al. 2017).

In different developmental stages, parasites may express RNA differentially, which have been of increasing interests in studying the RNAs of parasites, especially microRNAs (miRNAs), which exercise important functions in gene expression regulation and protein translation in parasite development (Chen et al. 2016). Studies on miRNAs of *F. buski* were initiated by Chen et al. (2016) using Solexa deep sequencing and bioinformatics analysis; approximately 12 million high-quality reads were obtained from adult *F. buski* and a total of 286 miRNA candidates were found and among them 24 miRNA candidates were conserved miRNAs in the miRBase database. Three novel miRNAs were identified and confirmed by stem-loop reverse transcriptase polymerase chain reaction (RT-PCR); they belonged to 13 families whose members showed high bias, and guanine (G) was the dominant nucleotide (Chen et al. 2016).

5.2.4 Pathology and Immunology

The pathogenic effects of *F. buski* infection in humans are not clearly understood; however, this fluke is reputed to cause a rather severe clinical illness in humans, characterized by toxicity and constitutional symptoms, diarrhea, abdominal pain, edema, and passage of undigested food in the feces (Plaut et al. 1969). The severity of fasciolopsiasis is markedly variable depending on parasite load (Graczyk et al. 2001; Mas-Coma et al. 2005; Sripa et al. 2010). The damage that the worms produce can be categorized into traumatic, obstructive, and toxic (Beaver et al. 1984). At the site of attachment, the worms can cause inflammation and ulceration of the mucosa, and large numbers of worms may provoke increased secretion of mucus, hemorrhage, abscess, partial obstruction of the bowel, and sometimes acute ileus; in massive infections these changes may be less important than the profound intoxication and sensitization that result from absorption of the worm metabolites into the system (Beaver et al. 1984; Mas-Coma et al. 2005). Absorption of toxic and allergic worm metabolites can cause ascites, and facial, orbital, and generalized edema (Mas-Coma et al. 2005). In severe cases, this infection can be fatal (Sadun and Maiphoom 1953).

With regard to susceptibility of different animal species to *F. buski* infection, pigs were shown to be a highly susceptible host, whereas guinea pigs and rabbits were only partially susceptible to infection (Malviya 1985). Mice, rats, monkeys, and dogs were completely refractory to the experimental infection with this fluke (Malviya 1985). However, little information is available on the host immunity and immune responses agasint *F. buski* infection. Excretory-secretory (ES) antigens were prepared by in vitro culture of adult flukes, and their immunological properties were analyzed in comparison with crude soluble adult and egg antigens; there were many common antigenic components between ES and soluble adult antigens but only a few between ES and soluble egg antigens (So 1993). Adult antigens of *F. buski* and 3 other trematode species (*F. hepatica, Clonorchis sinensis,* and *Schistosoma japonicum*) analyzed in terms of their sensitivities and specificities for use in enzyme-linked immunoblotting (ELIB) studies in rabbits revealed many cross-reacting bands (Yang 1989). Similar cross-reactivities were also found in sera of human patients infected with *C. sinensis* (3 bands) and *F. buski* (5 bands) (Luo et al. 1994). Also, in pigs, antisera against *F. buski* cross-reacted with crude antigens of larval *Taenia solium* (Cheng and Ko 1991). Serum antibodies were detected in human patients using enzyme-linked immunosorbent assay (ELISA) technique (Chen et al. 2004).

5.2.5 Clinical Manifestations, Diagnosis and Treatment

Clinical manifestations can vary remarkably from subclinical to fatal infections (Beaver et al. 1984; Mas-Coma et al. 2005). Light infections may be subclinical but in some cases diarrhea, constipation, abdominal pain, anemia, eosinophilia, headache, dizziness, gastric pain, and loose stools can occur, with signs of asthenia, pallor, malnutrition, protuberant abdomen, and abdominal distention (Mas-Coma et al. 2005). In moderate and heavy infections, severe epigastric pain, abdominal pain, diarrhea, bowel obstruction, nausea (occurring especially in the morning and resolving after the first meal), acute ileus, anasarca, marked eosinophilia, and leucocytosis may occur (Gilman et al. 1982; Graczyk et al. 2001). In particular, due to allergic reactions to toxic worm metabolites, patients infected with *F. buski* may suffer from facial and orbital edema, and anasarca (Mas-Coma et al. 2005).

Clinical complications and accompanying diseases in fasciolopsiasis are diverse, including intestinal perforation (Bhattacharjee et al. 2009), small bowel stricture and perforation (Singh et al. 2011), acute kidney injury (Karthikeyan et al. 2013), acute gastrointestinal bleeding (Sarma et al. 2015), appendicitis (Cao et al. 2015), systemic lupus erythematosus (Fiamma et al. 2015), and intestinal mass (Roy et al. 2017). In patients having polyparasitism with other parasites in India such as *Giardia lamblia, Entamoeba histolytica, Ascaris lumbricoides, hookworms, Trichuris trichiura, Strongyloides stercoralis,* and *Hymenolepis nana*, acute diarrhea with dehydration, nausea, vomiting, abdominal pain, abdominal distention, and anemia were the major clinical symptoms (Ranjan et al. 2017).

The diagnosis is carried out by coprological examinations to detect eggs or occasionally by examination of expelled adult worms vomited or passed in the stool (Rim 1982a; Le et al. 2004; Mas-Coma et al. 2005). However, the eggs of *F. buski* are highly similar in size and shape to the eggs of *F. hepatica, F. gigantica*, and various species of echinostomes (Rim 1982a, 1982b; Mas-Coma et al. 2005). Thus, the coprological diagnosis of *F. buski* is frequently problematic, especially in previously unknown endemic areas. However, a useful key to differentiate eggs of *F. buski* from those of *F. hepatica* or *F. gigantica* is that the size of the former is slightly smaller in length, 130–140 µm (Kumar 1980; Rim 1982a; Beaver et al. 1984; Mas-Coma et al. 2005) or 120–130 µm (Miyazaki 1991), whereas that of the latter is slightly or considerably larger in length, 130–145 µm (Andrews 1999), 130–150 µm (Beaver et al. 1984) or 152–198 µm in Japanese deer (Miyazaki 1991). In addition, the eggs of *F. buski* are, compared to those of *F. hepatica* (or *F. gigantica*), slightly lighter in color, with a very small operculum, and the vitelline cells inside the eggs are not easily seen (Miyazaki 1991). The eggs of echinostomes can be as large as 130–149 µm in some zoonotic species, including *Artyfechinostomum malayanum, Artyfechinostomum oraoni, Echinochasmus perfoliatus, Isthmiophora hortensis* (= *Echinostoma hortense*), *Isthmiophora melis,* and *Himasthla muehlensi* (Chai 2009), and thus difficult to discriminate from those of *F. buski*. A few hints to differentiate them may include smaller and inconspicuous operculum, less prominent vitelline cells, and almost no recognizable abopercular wrinkles in *F. buski*, whereas in echinostome eggs the operculum and the vitelline cells within the egg shell may be clearly seen, and the prominent abopercular wrinkles are distinctively seen. The clinical pictures may be highly suggestive of *F. buski* infection in endemic areas; however, they usually are not distinctive (Mas-Coma et al. 2005). Serodiagnosis detecting serum antibodies may help the diagnosis (Quang et al. 2008). For example, ELISA using soaked adult antigens of *F. buski* was useful to detect serum antibodies in human patients (Chen et al. 2004).

Hexylresorcinol (McCoy and Chu 1937), stilbazium iodide (Hsieh et al. 1963), and tetrachlorethylene (Shah et al. 1966) were former drugs used for treatment of human fasciolopsiasis. Thereafter, niclosamide was introduced but its therapeutic efficacy against *F. buski* was less than that of tetrachlorethylene (Suntharasamai et al. 1974). Thiabendazole, mebendazole, levamisole, and pyrantel pamoate were ineffective, whereas hexylresorcinol and tetrachlorethylene showed some effects (Rabbani et al. 1985). Praziquantel was first tried in Thailand, and 100% cure rate was obtained using a single oral dose of 15–40 mg/kg (Bunnag et al. 1983). Thereafter, a 15 mg/kg single dose has been prescribed even in severe fasciolopsiasis patients, although this dose could not save the life of a heavily infected 20-year-old woman in India (Mas-Coma et al. 2005). A new drug, triclabendazole, has been introduced showing a promising efficacy without side effects in pigs (Datta et al. 2004; Mas-Coma et al. 2005). Two other new drugs, oxyclozanide and rafozanide, were nearly equally effective as triclabendazole in pigs (Datta et al. 2004). In addition, various kinds of natural plants have been tried for treatment of *F. buski* infection, particularly by Indian researchers. Root-tuber extract of a leguminous plant, *Flemingia vestita*, was shown to induce severe tegumental alterations and deformities on *F. buski* worms exposed to this drug (Roy and Tandon 1996). Its active compound, genistein, was shown to cause flaccid paralysis and deformity of tegumental architectures of worms, and alterations in the activity of several worm enzymes, free amino acid pool, and ammonia levels (Kar et al. 2002, 2004). Another traditional medicinal plant, *Alpinia nigra*, and its bioactive compound, astragalin, were also tested for its efficacy on *F. buski* in vitro with ultrastructural observations (Roy and

Tandon 1999; Roy et al. 2009; Swargiary and Roy 2015). The alcoholic extract of *Lysimachia ramosa*, another medicinal plant in India, also showed killing effects of 3 helminth species, including *F. buski* (Challam et al. 2010). Several kinds of medicinal plants, including *Alpinia nigra, Potentilla fulgens,* and *Carex baccans*, were examined on their helminthotoxic effects through inhibition of glycolytic enzymes (Swargiary et al. 2013).

5.2.6 Prevention and Control

Several ways of prevention and control of fasciolopsiasis have been reported, which included (1) reduction of the infection source (mostly humans and pigs) by anthelmintic treatment, (2) destruction of eggs and larvae (miracidia) in night soil, water, and soil, (3) reduction of snail hosts, and (4) thorough cooking of edible plants by health education of people in endemic localities (Rim 1982a). Mass deworming using anthelmintic treatment of people and livestock (pigs, in particular) is highly important for prevention and control of fasciolopsiasis. Human population can be mass-treated using praziquantel; however, for mass deworming of pigs cheaper anthelmintics should be developed and used. Pollution of ponds or reservoirs with human or pig excreta should be avoided where water plants are cultivated (Mas-Coma et al. 2005). Killing the eggs, miracidia, and cercariae in water can be tried by treatment of night soil by storage with unslaked lime (100 ppm) or copper sulfate (20 ppm); the eggs can also be killed by prolonged storage of night soil in vats or by treatment with unslaked lime (Rim 1982a). Control of snail hosts is a kind of active preventive measure, but this unfortunately is not an easy task (Rim 1982a).

Avoiding raw eating of water-derived food (water caltrop, water chestnut, water hyacinth, water cress, water bamboo, morning glory, and others) is one of the simplest and most effective preventive measures; however, it is extremely difficult to achieve this in the field because of the people's long-standing traditional food habit (Rim 1982a; Mas-Coma et al. 2005). In addition, water plants are a common food source because they are cheap and readily available from the environment (Mas-Coma et al. 2005). Infections follow a familial trait, as food preparation and eating habits are passed from one generation to the next generation (Mas-Coma et al. 2005).

Studies on resistance of larval stages were reported. Direct solar radiation for 20–30 min can kill the metacercariae contaminated on water plants (Rim 1982a). Drying of suspected water plants for an appropriate duration or, if eaten fresh, dipping them into boiling water for a few seconds can kill the metacercariae (Rim 1982a). All metacercariae are killed in 1% HCl in 18 days, 2% acetic acid in 9 days, 5% salt solution in 3 hours, in Japanese soybean sauce in 30 min, and 10% cane sugar in 3 days (Komiya 1964). Consistent educational programmes to the people in endemic areas, stressing the importance of thorough cooking of aquatic plants, immersing plants and fruits in boiling water for a few minutes, and boiling water before drinking, are essential for prevention of fasciolopsiasis (Mas-Coma et al.

2005). In Uttar Pradesh, India, *F. buski* infection was once considered to be almost controlled, but unfortunately it was pointed out that cases reemerged (Bhatti et al. 2000; Muralidhar et al. 2000).

References

Andrews SJ (1999) The life cycle of *Fasciola hepatica*. In: Dalton JP (ed) Fasciolosis. CABI Publishing, Wallingford, pp 1–29

Barlow CH (1925) Life cycle of *Fasciolopsis buski* (Human) in China. China Med J 37:453–472

Beaver PC, Jung RC, Cupp EW (1984) Clinical parasitology, 9th edn. Lea and Febiger, Philadelphia

Bhalerao G (1924) A contribution to the knowledge of the trematode parasites of the food mammals of Rangoon. Ann Trop Med Parasitol 18:139

Bhattachajee J (1937) A checklist of the trematode and cestode parasites of the domesticated animals of Burma. Indian Vet J 14:1

Bhattachajee HK, Yadav D, Bagga D (2009) Fasciolopsiasis presenting as intestinal perforation: a case report. Trop Gastroenterol 30:40–41

Bhatti HS, Malla N, Mahajan RC et al (2000) Fasciolopsiasis, a re-emerging infection in Azamgarh (Uttar Pradesh). Indian J Pathol Microbiol 43:73–76

Biswal DK, Ghatani S, Shylla JA et al (2013) An integrated pipeline for next generation sequencing and annotation of the complete mitochondrial genome of the giant intestinal fluke, *Fasciolopsis buski* (Lankester, 1857) Looss, 1899. PeerJ 1:e207. https://doi.org/10.7717/peerJ.207

Bless PJ, Schar F, Khieu V et al (2015) High prevalence of large trematode eggs in schoolchildren in Cambodia. Acta Trop 141:295–302

Brau P, Bruyant L (1913) Quelques notes sur les helminthes du porc en Cochinchine. Bull Soc Pathol Exot 15:41–43 (in French)

Brooke MM, Schwartzwelder C, Payne FJ et al (1956) Intestinal parasite survey of Korean prisoner-of-war camp. US Armed Forces Med J 7:708–714

Brumpt V, Kong-Kim-Chuon (1965) Les Helminthes Intestinaux chez l'Homme au Cambodge. Bull Soc Pathol Exot 58:501–510 (in French)

Buckley JJC (1939) Observations on *Gastrodiscoides hominis* and *Fasciolopsis buski* in Assam. J Helminthol 17:1–12

Bunnag D, Prayong R, Harinasuta T (1983) Field trial on the treatment of fasciolopsiasis with praziquantel. Southeast Asian J Trop Med Public Health 14:216–218

Cao YH, Ma YM, Qiu F et al (2015) Rare cause of appendicitis: mechanical obstruction due to *Fasciolopsis buski* infestation. World J Gastroenterol 21:3146–3149

Chai JY (2007a) Intestinal flukes. In: Murrell KD, Fried B (eds) Food-borne parasitic zoonoses. Fish and plant-borne parasites. Springer, New York, pp 53–115

Chai JY (2007b) Trends of parasitic diseases in the Republic of Korea. Infect Chemother 39(Suppl 2):S156–S172 (in Korean)

Chai JY (2009) Echinostomes in humans. In: Fried B, Toledo R (eds) The biology of echinostomes. Springer, New York, pp 147–183

Chai JY (2014) Epidemiology of trematode infections. In: Toledo R, Fried B (eds) Digenetic trematodes. Springer, New York. Adv Exp Med Biol 766:241–292

Challam M, Roy B, Tandon V (2010) Effect of *Lysimachia ramose* (Primulaceae) on helminth parasites: motility, mortality and scanning electron microscopic observations on surface topography. Vet Parasitol 169:214–218

Chandra SS (1984) Epidemiology of *Fasciolopsis buski* in Uttar Pradesh. Indian J Med Res 78:55–59

Chatterjee RC (1938) Annotated list of the helminths recorded from domesticated animals of Burma. Part I. Trematoda. Proc Nat Acad Sci India 8:93

Chen SL, Chen Q, Yuan Y et al (2004) Studies on detecting antibodies in human sera of *Fasciolopsis buski* by ELISA. Hubei Agric Sci 4:123–125 (in Chinese)
Chen MX, Hu W, Li J et al (2016) Identification and characterization of microRNAs in the zoonotic fluke *Fasciolopsis buski*. Parasitol Res 115:2433–2438
Cheng RW, Ko RC (1991) Cross-reactions between crude antigens of larval *Taenia solium* (Cysticercus cellulosae) and other helminths of pigs. Vet Parasitol 39:161–170
Cross JH (1969) Fasciolopsiasis in Southeast Asia and the far east: a review. In: Harinasuta C (ed) Proceedings of the 4th SEA seminar on parasitology and tropical medicine, schistosomiasis and other snail-transmitted helminthiases. Bangkok, Thailand, pp 177–196
Daengsvang S, Mangalasmaya M (1941) A record of some cases of human infestation with *Fasciolopsis buski* occurring in Thailand. Ann Trop Med Parasitol 35:43–44
Dai X (1990) Karyotype analysis of *Fasciolopsis buski*. J Chongquin Med Univ 4:11 (in Chinese)
Datta S, Mukerjee GS, Ghosh JD (2004) Comparative efficacy of triclabendazole, oxyclozamide and rafoxanide against *Fasciolopsis buski* in naturally infected pigs. Ind J Anim Health 43:53–56
De NV, Minh PN (2016) Prevalence and species of *Fasciolopsis buski* in Vietnam. Ind J Med Res Pharm Sci 3:8–12
Fiamma M, Longoni SS, Ngo TMC et al (2015) *Fasciolopsis buski* infection in a Vietnamese pregnant woman with systemic lupus erythematosus. J Infect Dev Ctries 9:670–673
Founier J (1954) Services pratiques. Rapp Inst Pasteur Saigon 1954:1–109
Fried B, Graczyk TK, Tamang L (2004) Food-borne intestinal trematodiases in humans. Parasitol Res 93:159–170
Galliard H (1948) La Distomatose Intestinale Humaine a *Fasciolopsis buski* au Tonkin. Bull Soc Pathol Exot 41:214–217 (in French)
Gao L (1985) Observation of meiosis of *Fasciolopsis buski*. Hereditas (Beijing) 7:22–23 (in Chinese)
Garrison OE, Lago FP (1910) Specimens added to the helminthological collection. US Naval Medical School, June and August. US Naval Med Bull 4:511
Giboda M, Ditrich O, Scholz T et al (1991) Current status of food-borne parasitic zoonoses in Laos. Southeast Asian J Trop Med Public Health 22(suppl):56–61
Gilman RH, Mondal G, Maksud M et al (1982) Endemic focus of *Fasciolopsis buski* infection in Bangladesh. Am J Trop Med Hyg 31:796–802
Graczyk TK, Alam K, Gilman RH et al (2000) Development of *Fasciolopsis buski* (Trematoda: Fasciolidae) in *Hippeutis umbilicalis* and *Segmentina trochoideus* (Gastropoda: Pulmonata). Parasitol Res 86:324–326
Graczyk TK, Gilman RH, Fried B (2001) Fasciolopsiasis: is it a controllable food-borne disease? Parasitol Res 87:80–83
Greenberg Z, Giladi L, Bashary A et al (1994) Prevalence of intestinal parasites among Thais in Israel. Harefuah 126:507–509
Hadidjaja P, Dahri HM, Roesin R et al (1982) First autochthonous case of *Fasciolopsis buski* infection in Indonesia. Am J Trop Med Hyg 31:1065
Handoyo I, Ismuljowono B, Darwis F et al (1986) A survey of fasciolopsiasis in Sei Papuyu village of Babirik subdistrict, Hulu Sungei Ultara Regency, South Kalimantan Province. Trop Biomed 3:113–118
Hsieh HC (1960) Studies on the epidemiology of *Fasciolopsis buski* in South Taiwan. Formosan Sci 14:95–120
Hsieh HC, Brown HW, Chen ER et al (1963) Treatment of *Fasciolopsis buski, Ancylostoma duodenale, Ascaris lumbricoides, Trichuris trichiura,* and *Enterobius vermicularis* infections with stilbazium iodide. J Parasitol 49:425–427
Hsü HF, Li SY (1953) Notes on *Fasciolopsis buski* in China. Thapar commemoration volume, 1953. Department of Zoology, National Taiwan University, Taipei, Taiwan, China
Ito J (1964) A monograph of cercariae in Japan and adjacent territories. Progr Med Parasitol Japan 1:395–550

Jones A (2005) Family Fasciolidae Railliet, 1895. In: Jones A, Bray RA, Gibson DI (eds) Keys to the Trematoda, vol 2. Natural history museum, London, pp 79–85

Kar PK, Tandon V, Saha N (2002) Anhelmintic efficacy of *Flemingia vestita*: genistein-induced effect on the activity of nitric oxide synthase and nitric oxide in the trematode parasite, *Fasciolopsis buski*. Parasitol Int 51:249–257

Kar PK, Tandon V, Saha N (2004) Anhelmintic efficacy of genistein, the active principle of *Flemingia vestita* (Fabaceae): alterations in the free amino acid pool and ammonia levels in the fluke, *Fasciolopsis buski*. Parasitol Int 53:287–291

Kathikeyan G, Ramkumar V, Kumar SP et al (2013) Intestinal infestation with *Fasciolopsis buski* leading to acute kidney injury. J Assoc Physicians India 61:936–938

Khurana S (2016) Fasciolopsiasis: endemic focus of a neglected parasitic disease in Bihar. Indian J Med Microbiol 34:247

Komiya Y (1964) Fasciolopsis buski. Prog Med Parasitol Japan 1:277–285

Komiya Y (1965) Metacercariae in Japan and adjacent territories. Prog Med Parasitol Japan 2:1–328

Kumar V (1980) The digenetic trematodes, *Fasciolopsis buski, Gastrodiscoides hominis* and *Artyfechinostomum malayanum*, as zoonotic infections in South Asian countries. Ann Soc Belge Med Trop 60:331–339

Kuntz RE (1960) Intestinal protozoa and helminths in school children of Dacca, East Pakistan (East Bengal). Am J Trop Med Hyg 9:168–172

Kuntz RE, Lawless DK, Langbehn HR (1958) Intestinal protozoa and helminths in people of Western (Anatolia) Turkey. Am J Trop Med Hyg 7:298–302

Le TH, Nguyen VD, Phan BU et al (2004) Case report: unsual presentation of *Fasciolopsis buski* in a Viet Namese child. Trans R Soc Trop Med Hyg 98:193–194

Lee HH (1972) *Fasciolopsis buski* infection among children of Liu-ying primary school in Tainan Hsien. South Taiwan Chin J Microbiol 5:114

Lee TH, Huang CT, Chung CS et al (2011) Gastrointestinal: *Fasciolopsis buski* infestation diagnosed by upper gastrointestinal endoscopy. J Gastroenterol Hepatol 26:1464

Li D (1991) A case of *Fischoederius elongatus* infections in China. Annual Bull Soc Parasitol (Guangdong Province) 12:155–156 (in Chinese)

Lie KJ (1964) Prevalence of intestinal helminths among patients of the General Hospital in Kuala Lumpur, Malaya. Trop Geogr Med 16:229–237

Looss A (1899) Weitere Beitrage zur Kentniss der Trematoden-Fauna Aegyptens, zugleich Versuch einer naturalischen Gliedrung des Genus *Distomum* Retzius. Zool Yb 12:521–784

Luo W, Xie K, Hu Y et al (1994) Studies on the cross antigens and their serological reactivities among *Schistosoma japonicum, Clonorchis sinensis* and *Fasciolopsis buski*. J Pract Parasit Dis 2:4–7 (in Chinese)

Ma J, Sun MM, He JJ et al (2017) Fasciolopsis buski (Digenea: Fasciolidae) from China and India may represent distinct taxa based on mitochondrial and nuclear ribosomal DNA sequences. Parasit Vectors 10:101

Malviya HC (1985) The susceptibility of mammals to *Fasciolopsis buski*. J Helminthol 59:19–22

Manjarumkar PV, Shah PM (1972) Epidemiological study of *Fasciolopsis buski* in Palghar Taluk. Indian J Public Health 16:3–6

Manning GS, Ratanarat C (1970) *Fasciolopsis buski* (Lankester, 1857) in Thailand. Am J Trop Med Hyg 19:613–619

Manning GS, Brockelman WY, Viyanant V (1971) An analysis of the prevalence of *Fasciolopsis buski* in central Thailand using catalytic models. Am J Epidemiol 93:354–361

Maqbool A, Ali SA, Tanveer A et al (2007) Prevalence and control of food borne parasitic zoonosis in Pakistan. Malays Appl Biol 36:15–21

Mas-Coma S, Bargues MD, Valero MA (2005) Fascioliasis and other plant-borne trematode zoonoses. Int J Parasitol 35:1255–1278

McCoy OR, Chu TC (1937) *Fasciolopsis buski* infection among school children in Shaohsing and treatment with hexylresorcinol. Chin Med J 51:937–944

Miyazaki I (1991) An illustrated book of helminthic zoonoses. International Medical Foundation of Japan, Tokyo, pp 60–65
Morishita K (1964) Outline of human parasites in Japan. Prog Med Parasitol Japan 1:35–60
Muazzam MG, Ali MT (1961) Intestinal parasites in East Pakistan. J Pakistan Med Assoc 11:185–191
Muralidhar S, Srivastava I, Aggarwal P et al (2000) Fasciolopsiasis: a persisting problem in eastern U. P.: a case report. Indian J Pathol Microbiol 43:69–71
Muttalib MA, Islam N (1975) *Fasciolopsis buski* in Bangladesh-a pilot study. J Trop Med Hyg 78:135–137
Nakagawa K (1922) The development of *Fasciolopsis buski* Lankester. J Parasitol 8:161–166
Plaut AG, Kampanart-Sanyakorn C, Manning GS (1969) A clinical study of *Fasciolopsis buski* infection in Thailand. Trans Roy Soc Trop Med Hyg 63:470–478
Prasad PK, Tandon V, Chatterjee A et al (2007) PCR-based determination of internal transcribed spacer (ITS) regions of ribosomal DNA of giant intestinal fluke, *Fasciolopsis buski* (Lankester, 1857) Looss, 1899. Parasito Res 101:1581–1587
Prasad PK, Goswani LM, Tandon V (2011) PCR-based molecular characterization and in-silico analysis of food-borne trematode parasites *Paragonimus westermani*, *Fasciolopsis buski* and *Fasciola gigantica* from northeast India using ITS2 rDNA. Bioinformatics 6:64–68
Preet S, Prakash S (2001) Cercarial emergence in *Fasciolopsis buski* (Lankester). J Parasit Dis 25:108–110
Quang TD, Duong TH, Richard-Lenoble D et al (2008) Emergence in humans of fascioliasis (from *Fasciola gigantica*) and intestinal distomatosis (from *Fasciolopsis buski*) in Laos. Cashiers Sante 18:119–124 (in French)
Rabbani GH, Gilman RH, Kabir I et al (1985) The treatment of *Fasciolopsis buski* infection in children: a comparison of thiabendazole, mebendazole, levamisole, pyrantel pamoate, hexylresorcinol and tetrachlorethylene. Trans R Soc Trop Med Hyg 79:513–515
Radomyos P, Radomyos B, Tungtrongchitr A (1994) Multi-infection with helminths in adults from northeast Thailand as determined by post-treatment fecal examination of adult worms. Trop Med Parasitol 45:133–135
Radomyos B, Wongsaroj T, Wilairatana P et al (1998) Opisthorchiasis and intestinal fluke infections in northern Thailand. Southeast Asian J Trop Med Public Health 29:123–127
Ranjan S, Saurabh K, Prasad RR (2017) Gastrointestinal manifestations of *Fasciolopsis buski* associated polyparasitism in patients of an endemic area: a hospital based study. Int J Commun Med Public Health 4:1898–1900
Ressang AA, Fischer H, Muchlis A (1959) The Indonesian veterinarian: his education, activities and problems. Comman Fac Vet Sci (Bogor, Indonesia) 3:55
Rim HJ (1982a) Fasciolopsiasis. CRC handbook series in zoonoses, section C: Parasitic zoonoses, Vol. III. Trematode zoonoses. CRC Press Inc, Boca Raton, pp 89–97
Rim HJ (1982b) Echinostomiasis. CRC handbook series in zoonoses, section C: Parasitic zoonoses, Vol. III. trematode zoonoses. CRC Press Inc, Boca Raton, pp 53–69
Rohela M, Jamaiah I, Menon J et al (2005) Fasciolopsiasis: a first case report from Malaysia. Southeast Asian J Trop Med Public Health 36:456–458
Roy B, Tandon V (1993) Morphological and microtopograhical strain variations among *Fasciolopsis buski* originating from different geographical areas. Acta Parasitol Pol 38:72–77
Roy B, Tandon V (1996) Effect of root-tuber extract of *Flemingia vestita*, a leguminous plant, on *Artyfechinostomum sufrartyfex* and *Fasciolopsis buski*: a scanning electron microscopy study. Parasitol Res 82:248–252
Roy B, Tandon V (1999) Flukicidal activity of *Alpinia nigra* (Zingiberaceae) against the trematode, *Fasciolopsis buski,* in humans. Biomed Lett 60:23–29
Roy B, Dasgupta S, Tandon V (2009) Ultrastructural observations on *Fasciolopsis buski* and its alterations caused by shoot extract of Alpinia nigra. Microsc Res Tech 72:61–66
Roy S, Dalal BS, Mitra S et al (2017) Intestinal mass caused by Fasciolopsis buski. J Evol Res Med Microbiol 3:15–16

Sadun EH, Maiphoom C (1953) Studies on the epidemiology of the human intestinal fluke, *Fasciolopsis buski* (Lankester) in Central Thailand. Am J Trop Med Hyg 2:1070–1084

Sah R, Khadka S, Hamal R et al (2018) Human echinostomiasis: a case report. BMC Res Notes 11:17

Saksirisampant W, Prownebon J, Kulkumthorn M et al (2006) The prevalence of intestinal parasitic infections among school children in the central region of Thailand. J Med Assoc Thail 89:1928–1933

Sarma MS, Yachha SK, Srivastava A et al (2015) Endoscopic extraction of *Fasciolopsis buski* presenting as acute upper gastrointestinal bleeding in a child. Gastrointest Endosc 82:743

Schubert S, Granz W (1981) Problems in the differential diagnosis of intestinal diseases in patients who have traveled in the tropics. Z Gesamte Med 36:230–233 (in German)

Segal DB, Humphrey JM, Edwards SJ et al (1968) Parasites of man and domestic animals in Vietnam, Thailand, Laos and Cambodia. Exp Parasitol 23:412–464

Shah A, Gadgil RK, Manohar KD (1966) Fasciolopsiasis in Bombay. A preliminary communication. Indian J Med Sci 20:805–811

Shekhar KC (1991) Epidemiological assessment of parasitic zoonoses in Malaysia. Southeast Asian J Trop Med Public Health 22:337–339

Shyu LY, Lee HH, Chen ER (1984) A preliminary study on epidemiology of fasciolopsiasis in Tainan Hsien, south Taiwan. Chin J Microbiol Immunol 17:118–120 (in Chinese)

Singh S (1991) Trematode infections in India: a review. Trop Gastroenterol 12:119–132

Singh UC, Kumar A, Srivastava A et al (2011) Small bowel stricture and perforation: an unusual presentation of *Fasciolopsis buski*. Trop Gastroenterol 32:320–322

So QML (1993) Immunological studies on the extraction and immunological properties of excretory-secretory antigens of *Fasciolopsis buski*. Chin J Vet Parasitol 1:23–26 (in Chinese)

Soavakontha S, Charoenlarp P, Radomyos P et al (1966) A new endemic area of *Fasciolopsis* in Thailand. In: Proceedings of 1st international congress of parasitology, Rome, Italy, 21–26 September 1964. Vol. II, p 809

Sripa B, Kaewkes S, Intapan PM et al (2010) Food-borne trematodiases in Southeast Asia: epidemiology, pathology, clinical manifestation and control. Adv Parasitol 72:305–350

Stoll NR, Cort WW, Kwei WS (1927) Egg-worm correlations in cases of *Fasciolopsis buski*: with additional data on the distribution of this parasite in China. J Parasitol 13:166–172

Suntharasamai P, Bunnag D, Tejavanij S et al (1974) Comparative clinical trials of niclosamide and tetrachlorethylene in the treatment of *Fasciolopsis buski* infection. Southeast Asian J Trop Med Public Health 5:556–559

Swargiary A, Roy B (2015) In vitro anthelmintic efficacy of *Alpinia nigra* and its bioactive compound, astragalin against *Fasciolopsis buski*. Int J Pharm Pharm Sci 7:30–35

Swargiary A, Roy B, Giri BR et al (2013) A comparative study on the anthelmintic efficacy of some medicinal plants of North-East India: alteration in the glycolytic enzymes of *Fasciolopsis buski*, a giant intestinal fluke. Asian Pac J Trop Med 6:412–420

Tandon V, Roy B, Prasad PK (2013) Fasciolopsis. In: Liu D (ed) Molecular detection of human parasitic pathogens. CRC Press/Taylor & Francis Group, Boca Raton, pp 353–364

Tandon V, Shylla JA, Ghatami et al (2015) Neglected tropical diseases: trematodiases-the Indian scenario. Proc Nat Acad Sci, India (Sect B Biol Sci) 85:901–907

Taraschewski H, Mehlhorn H, Bunnag D et al (1986) Effects of praziquantel on human intestinal flukes (*Fasciolopsis buski* and *Heterophyes heterophyes*). Zentralbl Bakteriol Mikrobiol Hyg 262:542–550

Viranuvatti V, Stitnimankarn T, Tansurat P (1953) A fatal case of infection with *Fasciolopsis buski* in Thailand. Ann Trop Med Parasitol 47:132–133

Waikagul J (1991) Intestinal fluke infections in Southeast Asia. Southeast Asian J Trop Med Public Health 22(suppl):158–162

Weng YL, Zhuang ZL, Jiang HP et al (1989) Studies on ecology of Fasciolopsis buski and control strategy of fasciolopsiasis. Chin J Parasitol Parasit Dis 7:108–111 (in Chinese)

Wiwanitkit V, Suwansaksri J, Chaiyakhun Y (2002) High prevalence of *Fasciolopsis buski* in an endemic area of liver fluke infection in Thailand. MedGenMed 4:6

Wu K (1937) Susceptibility of various mammals to experimental infection with *Fasciolopsis buski* (Trematoda: Fasciolidae). Ann Trop Med Parasitol 31:361–372

Wu G (2013) Human Parasitology, 4th edn. Rin Min Hu Sheng Publ Co, Beijing

Yamaguti S (1971) Synopsis of digenetic trematodes of vertebrates, vol I. Keigaku Publishing Co, Tokyo, pp 1–1074

Yang W (1989) Analysis of antigens of four adult trematodes by ELIB. Chin J Zoon 5:11–13 (in Chinese)

Yoshihara S, Hung NP, Hung NH et al (1999) Helminths and helminthosis of pigs in the Mekong Delta, Vietnam with special reference to ascariosis and *Fasciolopsis buski* infection. Jpn Agric Res Q 33:193–199

Yu SH, Mott KE (1994) Epidemiology and morbidity of food-borne intestinal trematode infections. Trop Dis Bull 91:R125–R152

Yu SH, Xu L, Jiang Z et al (1994) Report on the first nationwide survey of the distribution of human parasites in China. I. Regional distribution of parasite species. Chin J Parasitol Parasit Dis 12:241–247 (in Chinese)

Chapter 6
Gymnophallids

6.1 Family Gymnophallidae

The family Gymnophallidae Odhner, 1905 which belongs to the superfamily Gymnophalloidea Odhner, 1905 is a group of intestinal flukes (can also parasitize the gallbladder and Bursa Fabricii) of mainly birds of the orders Charadriiformes (shore birds, including gulls) and Anseriformes (diving ducks), and rarely mammals (Scholz 2002). Two taxa were reported from mammals; *Gymnophalloides seoi* Lee, Chai and Hong, 1993 which infects humans, rodents, and birds (Lee and Chai 2001; Chai et al. 2003), and *Gymnophalloides heardi* Ching, 1995 which infects rats (Ching 1995a). Other families of the superfamily Gymnophalloidea include Botulisaccidae Yamaguti, 1971, Callodistomidae Odhner, 1910, Tandanicolidae Johnston, 1927, and Fellodistomidae Nicoll, 1909, although the Callodistomidae and the Botulisaccidae are enigmatic families in this superfamily (Bray 2002).

The morphologic characters of the Gymnophallidae adults include small to minute worms with oval to pyriform body, and the oral sucker is usually larger than the ventral sucker with or without muscular lateral projections (Scholz 2002). Intestinal ceca are short, terminate blindly, not reaching midbody, and widely divergent, often wide, with or without dorsal diverticula; the genital pore is medial, postbifurcal, frequently inconspicuous at anterior margin of the ventral sucker, or wide, pit-like at some distance anterior to the ventral sucker, and the pore may be surrounded by muscle fibers (Scholz 2002).

In the subfamily Gymnophallinae, Yamaguti (1958) included 10 species of *Gymnophallus* and 10 larval forms of *Gymnophallus* or *Gymnophalloides* (including *Gymnophalloides tokiensis*), and in the subfamily Parvatrematinae he included only one species of one genus *Parvatrema*. He included these 2 subfamilies in the family Microphallidae. Later, however, Yamaguti (1971) adopted the family name Gymnophallidae to accept the subfamilies Gymnophallinae (*Gymnophallus* Odhner, 1900, *Gymnophalloides* Fujita, 1925, and *Meiogymnophallus* Ching, 1965) and Parvatrematinae (*Parvatrema* Cable, 1953). He synonymized *Lacunovermis* Ching,

J.-Y. Chai, *Human Intestinal Flukes*,
https://doi.org/10.1007/978-94-024-1704-3_6

1965 with *Gymnophalloides*. After then, the genus *Paragymnophallus* was erected by Ching (1973), and *Pseudogymnophallus* was created by Hoberg (1981). Later, Ching (1995b) was of opinion that the family Gymnophallidae consist of 7 genera that included *Gymnophallus, Gymnophalloides, Parvatrema, Meiogymnophallus, Lacunovermis, Paragymnophallus,* and *Pseudogymnophallus* and compared the descriptive morphologies of adult worms of these genera. However, Scholz (2002) acknowledged only 4 of these genera, which included *Gymnophalloides* Fujita, 1925 (syn. *Lacunovermis* Ching, 1965), *Parvatrema* Cable, 1953 (syn. *Meiogymnophallus* Ching, 1965), *Gymnophallus* Odhner, 1900 (syn. *Paragymnophallus* Ching, 1973), and *Pseudogymnophallus* Hoberg, 1981, synonymizing the remaining 3 with the others and acknowledged a new genus (*Bartolius*) raised by Cremonte (2001), finally making the family to be composed of 5 genera.

The most recent study on the taxonomy of the family Gymnophallidae was performed by Cremonte et al. (2015) through morphological and molecular analyses. They used the presence or absence of the pars prostatica as the essential key to differentiate the subfamilies Gymnophallinae and Parvatrematinae, respectively, and the sequencing results of ITS1-5.8S-ITS2-28S rDNA strands were used for differentiation of each genus (Cremonte et al. 2015). The results showed that 4 genera were accepted in the subfamily Gymnophallinae, including *Gymnophallus* Odhner, 1900 (syn. *Meiogymnophallus* Ching, 1965), *Paragymnophallus* Ching, 1973, *Pseudogymnophallus* Hoberg, 1981, and *Bartolius* Cremonte, 2001, and 3 genera were listed in the subfamily Parvatrematinae, including *Gymnophalloides* Fujita, 1925, *Parvatrema* Cable, 1953, and *Lacunovermis* Ching, 1965 (Cremonte et al. 2015). The important morphologic characters used to differentiate the 7 genera included the location of the ovary, size and location of the genital pore, presence of cecal pockets, and presence of a ventral pit (Cremonte et al. 2015).

Among the subfamily Gymnophallinae (having a pars prostatica), *Gymnophallus* (syn. *Meiogymnophallus*) has an inconspicuous genital pore located at the anterior margin of the ventral sucker, but *Paragymnophallus* has a conspicuous genital pore located at some distance anterior to the ventral sucker (Cremonte et al. 2015). *Gymnophallus* has an ovary located anterior to the testes and intestinal ceca without dorsal diverticula, but *Pseudogymnophallus* has an ovary located between the 2 testes and intestinal ceca with dorsal diverticula (Scholz 2002; Cremonte et al. 2015). Both *Gymnophallus* and *Pseudogymnophallus* lack lateral projections on the oral sucker and have Y-shaped excretory vesicle (Scholz 2002). Adult flukes of the genus *Bartolius* lack a ventral pit, have no lateral projections on the oral sucker, but have an ovary located at a post-testicular position, and inconspicuous genital pore (Scholz 2002; Cremonte et al. 2015).

Among the subfamily Parvatrematinae (not having a pars prostatica), *Gymnophalloides* and *Lacunovermis* differ from *Parvatrema* in having a ventral pit on the ventral surface (Ching 1995b; Scholz 2002). *Parvatrema* are equipped with 2 lateral projections on the oral sucker and V-shaped excretory vesicle (Scholz 2002). The ventral pit of *Gymnophalloides* is well developed (similar in size with the ventral sucker), whereas that of *Lacunovermis* is poorly developed (smaller in size than the ventral sucker) (Cremonte et al. 2015). The genital pore of

Gymnophalloides is inconspicuous and located at the anterior margin of the ventral sucker, but that of *Lacunovermis* is conspicuous and located at some distance from the anterior margin of the ventral sucker (Cremonte et al. 2015).

6.2 *Gymnophalloides*

The genus *Gymnophalloides* was erected by Fujita in 1925 based on metacercariae in oysters (*Ostrea gigas*) collected from Tokyo Bay, Japan, under the species name *Gymnophalloides tokiensis*; the specimen was reviewed by Dollfus RP with some revisions (Fujita 1925). However, there were many errors among the morphologic descriptions; one of the main errors is misinterpretation of the ventral pit as the genital pore (the real genital pore is much smaller being only a half size of the ventral pit) and several other errors included the misinterpretation of a part of the bipartite seminal vesicle as a seminal receptacle (Ching 1972). In the meantime, James (1964) reviewed gymnophallid species and emended the generic diagnosis of *Gymnophalloides* Fujita, 1925 to include *G. somateriae* (Levinsen, 1881), *G. macroporus* (Jameson and Nicoll, 1913), *G. oedemiae* (Jameson and Nicoll, 1913), and *G. macrostomus* (Yamaguti, 1939) in this genus. However, James (1964) considered *Gymnophallus macrostoma* (Yamaguti, 1939) and *Gymnophalloides tokiensis* synonymous and used the descriptions of *G. macrostoma* as the basis for the emended genus *Gymnophalloides*. Ching (1965, 1972) disagreed to this because the presence of a ventral pit was not considered as a characteristic feature for *Gymnophalloides* by James (1964). Ching (1965) thus erected a new genus for *Gymnophalloides* of James (1964) as *Meiogymnophallus*, and included 5 species, namely, *M. multigemmulus* Ching, 1965, *M. somateriae* (Levinsen, 1881), *M. macroporus* (Jameson and Nicoll, 1913), *M. oedemiae* (Jameson and Nicoll, 1913), and *M. macrostomus* (Yamaguti 1939). Later, the new generic and specific descriptions of *Gymnophalloides* and *G. tokiensis* (metacercariae) were provided by Ching (1972).

In 1988, adult gymnophallid flukes apparently belonging to this genus were recovered in a woman patient who habitually consumed raw oysters in a southwestern part of South Korea (Lee et al. 1993). The flukes were assigned as a new species, *Gymnophalloides seoi* Lee, Chai and Hong, 1993, because they were distinct from the pre-existing *G. tokiensis* in several aspects (Lee et al. 1993). *G. seoi* was based on adult flukes whereas *G. tokiensis* was based only on metacercariae (Lee et al. 1993). In addition, the position and orientation of the bipartite seminal vesicle were different; it is located between the ventral pit and ventral sucker in *G. tokiensis,* and its posterior portion is curved dorsally, whereas it is located more anteriorly between the ceca and ventral pit, and it is not curved dorsally in *G. seoi* (Lee et al. 1993). The comparison of other reproductive organs including the terminal genitalia and size and shape of eggs was not possible because the adult stage of *G. tokiensis* is unknown until present (Lee et al. 1993).

Ching (1995a) reported a new species of this genus, *Gymnophalloides heardi*, recovered from a mammalian host (rodent; marsh rice rat, *Oryzomys palustris*) in

Florida, USA. It is the first gymnophallid digenean found to parasitize a rodent host and differs morphologically from *G. tokiensis* and *G. seoi* in that *G. heardi* is smaller in body size and has a less muscular ventral pit than the other 2, and *G. heardi* has a single lobed vitellaria whereas *G. seoi* has 2 compact masses of vitellaria (Ching 1995a). Also, the seminal vesicle of *G. heardi* is undivided, whereas the seminal vesicle of *G. seoi* and *G. tokiensis* is bipartite (Lee et al. 1993; Ching 1972, 1995a). Ching (1995a) synonymized *Parvatrema* sp. II of Heard (1970) from the clapper rail (*Rallus longirostris*) and *Parvatrema* sp. of Kinsella (1988) from rice rats (*Oryzomys palustris*) with *G. heardi*.

Another species, *Gymnophalloides nacellae*, Cremonte, Pina, Gilardoni, Rodrigues, Chai and Ituarte, 2013 (metacercariae) was reported as a new species recovered in clams, *Nacella* (*Patinigera*) *magellanica* and *Nacella* (*Patinigera*) *deaurata*, from Argentina (Cremonte et al. 2013). This new species differs from *G. tokiensis, G. seoi,* and *G. heardi*, in having a group of papillae located between the ventral pit and ventral sucker (Cremonte et al. 2013). In addition, the new species is distinguished from *G. heardi* by the shape of vitellaria, i.e., single lobe in *G. heardi* (Ching 1995a) and paired follicular structures in *G. nacellae* (Cremonte et al. 2013). Moreover, *G. tokiensis* (metacercaria) and *G. seoi* (adult) have bipartite seminal vesicles (Ching 1972; Lee et al. 1993), whereas the seminal vesicle of *G. nacellae* is unipartite (Cremonte et al. 2013).

Therefore, 4 species are now acknowledged as taxonomically valid in the genus *Gymnophalloides*; *G. tokiensis* (type species), *G. seoi, G. heardi,* and *G. nacellae* (Cremonte et al. 2013). Among them, *G. seoi* is the only species ever known to infect humans (Table 3.1) (Lee and Chai 2001; Chai et al. 2003).

6.2.1 Gymnophalloides seoi

6.2.1.1 *Gymnophalloides seoi* Lee, Chai and Hong, 1993

Taxonomy and Morphology

Gymnophalloides seoi (Fig. 6.1a, b) was first discovered from the diarrheic stool of a Korean woman suffering from acute pancreatitis and gastrointestinal discomfort after anthelmintic treatment and purging (Lee et al. 1993; Chai et al. 2003). She had habitually consumed raw naturally produced oysters every time when she visited her home village on a southwestern coastal island named Aphaedo Island, Shinan-gun, the South Korea (= South Korea) (Lee et al. 1993). By fecal examinations performed in a university hospital, small trematode eggs (19–21 μm long and 14–16 μm in width) with a thin shell and peculiar morphology were detected, and to obtain adult flukes the patient was treated with praziquantel 10 mg/kg in a single dose and purged; 910 adult specimens of *G. seoi* together with 40 *Heterophyes nocens* and 2 *Stictodora fuscata* specimens were recovered from the diarrheic stools of this patient (Lee et al. 1993).

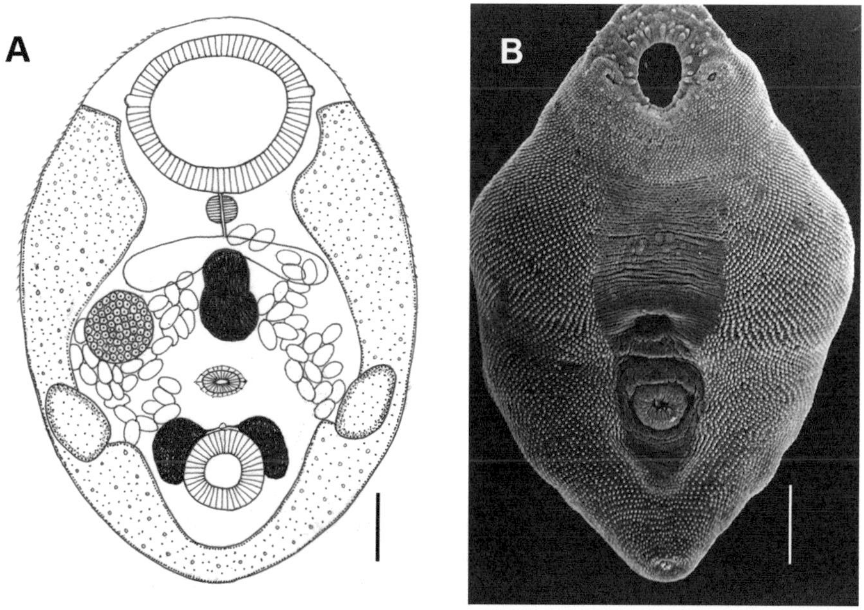

Fig. 6.1 *Gymnophalloides seoi*. (**a**) Line drawing of an adult fluke (original figure). Scale bar = 0.05 mm. (**b**) Scanning electron microscopic view of a 3-day-old juvenile fluke recovered from an experimental mouse. Scale bar = 0.05 mm. Reproduced from the figure in Choi et al. (1995) Korean J Parasitol 33:289–296 with permission

The adult specimens of *G. seoi* recovered from this patient morphologically resembled the previously known adult flukes of *Gymnophallus macrostoma* Yamaguti, 1939 and the metacercariae of *Gymnophalloides tokiensis* Fujita, 1925 (Lee et al. 1993). However, *G. seoi* showed the presence of a ventral pit separately from the genital pore and 2 ventrolateral projections on the oral sucker, whereas *G. macrostoma* had no ventral pit and no lateral projections on the oral sucker (Lee et al. 1993). Because *G. seoi* was based on adult flukes whereas *G. tokiensis* was on metacercariae, comparison of their reproductive organs, in particular, the terminal genitalia and eggs, was not possible (Lee et al. 1993). The seminal vesicle of *G. seoi* is frequently bipartite in adults (Lee et al. 1993) but in a great majority of metacercariae it is monopartite (Lee et al. 1995a), whereas in *G. tokiensis* (metacercariae) the seminal vesicle is bipartite (Ching 1972). In addition, the seminal vesicle of *G. seoi* (adults) is located anteriorly between the ceca and ventral pit, whereas the seminal vesicle of *G. tokiensis* (metacercariae) is located between the ventral pit and ventral sucker (Ching 1972; Lee et al. 1993).

Subsequently, the home village of this patient was found to be a highly endemic area of human *G. seoi* infection (Lee et al. 1994). Thereafter, numerous small endemic foci have been discovered, and to date, more than 28 villages, including 25 on western and southern coastal islands and 3 non-island coastal villages, have been recorded as the endemic areas (Chai et al. 1997, 1998, 2003; Lee et al. 1996; Chai et al. 2001a;

Guk et al. 2006; Park et al. 2007). A subsequent interesting finding to notify was the discovery of this fluke in a seventeenth century femal mummy in Hadong, a southern coastal area of South Korea; thus, this species is thought to have been prevalent in South Korea for a longer period than at least several hundred years (Seo et al. 2008). Until present, this parasite has been known to be existing only in South Korea. A closely related species, *G. tokiensis* was reported from Tokyo Bay, Japan, but it is uncertain whether the life cycle of this species is still present or not in Japan.

Adult flukes of *G. seoi* are 0.33–0.50 (av. 0.42) mm long and 0.23–0.33 (0.28) mm wide in specimens from humans (Lee et al. 1993) and 0.39–0.53 mm long and 0.23–0.29 mm wide in specimens from experimentally infected mice (Lee et al. 1997). They are broadly oval, rounded anteriorly, and slightly pointed posteriorly, with anterior 2/3 of the body covered with fine tegumental spines (Lee et al. 1993). They have a large, muscular, and subterminal oral sucker, with small but prominent lateral projections on both sides, and short, saccate, and inflated ceca, usually ending before midbody (Lee et al. 1993). The ventral pit is located median, transversely elongated, and surrounded by strong muscle fibers, and does not have any connection with other parenchymal organs; the ventral sucker is small, round, and located at a posterior part of the posterior half of the body (Lee et al. 1993). Two testes are ovoid, symmetrical, and located laterally at the level between the ventral pit and ventral sucker, and the seminal vesicle is frequently bipartite and located between the ceca and ventral pit; the genital atrium shallow with a small, inconspicuous genital pore opened at the level of the anterior margin of the ventral sucker, not surrounded by muscle fibers (Lee et al. 1993). Vitellaria are 2 compact follicular masses, symmetrical, and anterolateral to the ventral sucker; the uterus with anterior loops reaches to the level of the pharynx but is distributed mostly in middle 1/3 of the body; the excretoary bladder is V-shaped, with arms reaching to the oral sucker (Lee et al. 1993). The uterine eggs are ovoid to elliptical in shape, operculate (operculum conspicuous), with a thin transparent shell, and 20–25 (av. 21) μm long and 11–15 (av. 13) μm in width (Lee et al. 1993).

Mature miracidia with cilia were experimentally obtained 3 days after incubation of the eggs at 37 °C in Dulbecco's Modified Eagle Medium (DMEM), and their size after hatch-out in water was slightly larger than that of the eggs; no exact measurements were given (Park 2005). Sporocysts, rediae, and cercariae have never been detected in nature as well as in laboratory settings; the first intermediate host has not yet been determined (Park 2005; Lee and Chai 2001; Chai et al. 2003). However, the oysters *Crassostrea gigas* have been proved to be the second intermediate host harbouring the metacercariae (Lee et al. 1995a; Sohn et al. 1998). The metacercariae (Fig. 6.2a, b) are attached on the mantle of the oysters or free in the mantle cavity, small and pyriform in shape, without a cyst, 310–390 (av. 350) μm long and 210–260 (av. 230) μm wide, and covered entirely with fine tegumental spines; its anterior end is rounded, and its posterior end is slightly pointed (Lee et al. 1995a; Lee and Chai 2001).

The surface ultrastructure of the metacercariae (Fig. 6.2a) and adults (Fig. 6.1b) of *G. seoi* was reported by Choi et al. (1995). In metacercariae, uniciliated sensory papillae (type I) were arranged bilaterally in a row throughout the entire body length

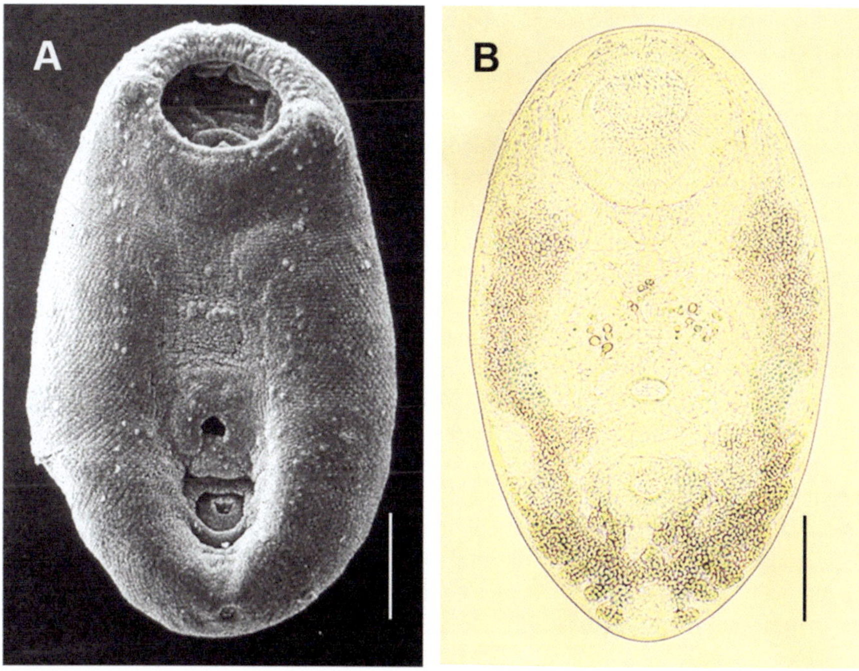

Fig. 6.2 *Gymnophalloides seoi*. (**a**) Scanning electron microscopic view of a metacercaria (unencysted) isolated from an oyster, *Crassostrea gigas*, collected in an endemic area in South Korea. Scale bar = 0.05 mm. Reproduced from the figure in Choi et al. (1995) Korean J Parasitol 33:289–296 with permission (**b**) Metacercaria (unstained) isolated from an oyster. Scale bar = 0.05 mm

(Choi et al. 1995). The tegument of the lip of the oral sucker was radially wrinkled and devoid of tegumental spines; the lip has 2 kinds of type I papillae (small and large ones), with the small ones distributed mainly along the dorsal side of the lip and the large ones forming a circle along the lip of the oral sucker (Choi et al. 1995). On each side of the oral sucker, there is a small lateral projection (= ventrolateral lip) of elevated dome-shape, covered with 3–5 digitated tegumental spines, and many type I papillae are distributed around and on these lateral projections; the lumen of the ventral pit is circular or transverse slit shaped, and its surface is not covered with tegumental spines (Choi et al. 1995). The ventral sucker is covered with cobblestone-like cytoplasmic processes, having 6 type I papillae on its lip (Choi et al. 1995).

In adult flukes, with the exception of the ventromedian area between the 2 suckers, the almost whole body surface is covered with tegumental spines (Fig. 6.1b) (Choi et al. 1995). The oral sucker has 2 kinds (small and large) of type I sensory papillae encircling its lip (same as in metacercariae), and the lateral projections are sometimes retracted slightly and have many type I papillae on its base; the tegumental spines around the oral sucker have tegumental spines with 5–6 digitations (Choi et al. 1995). The ventral pit is well developed, and covered with cobblestone-like cytoplasmic processes and 12–15 type I papillae around its border; the surface lateral to the ventral pit is covered with 6–7 digitated spines, larger than those around the oral sucker (Choi et al. 1995). The genital pore is a transverse slit, just anterior to the ventral sucker, and the surface around the ventral sucker is devoid of spines; the lip of the ventral sucker is wrinkled radially and its lumen is very small compared to the oral sucker, and type I papillae are distributed along its margins (Choi et al. 1995). Tegumental spines digitated into 5–7 points are distributed in the middle and posterior one-third of the ventral body (Choi et al. 1995). On the dorsal body surface, many type I papillae are scattered through the entire body, and the tegumental spines digitated into 8–10 (anterior body) or 6–7 (middle and posterior body) points are distributed densely in the anterior part of the body and become sparse toward the posterior part of the body (Choi et al. 1995).

The tegumental ultrastructure of *G. seoi* was studied using a transmission electron microscope (TEM) on metacercariae and adults; there was little difference on the tegumental ultrastructure between metacercariae and adults (Seo et al. 1995). The tegumental layer generally revealed a small number of foldings, and numerous small vacuoles, spines, and muscle bundles, and beneath the muscle layer, nuclei of tegumental cells were located; the oral and ventral suckers were well developed having well-developed muscle layers, except the presence of numerous foldings in the ventral sucker (Seo et al. 1995). The ventral pit was surrounded by a thin syncytial layer, where a number of microtubules and mitochondria were seen, and around the ventral pit located well-developed circular and longitudinal muscles; it seemed that the function of the ventral pit is a sphincter or an accessory adhesive organ (Seo et al. 1995). The basement membrane is relatively thick, and along the basement membrane circular and longitudinal muscle bundles are well-developed, and several mitochondria are observed at the margin of the longitudinal muscles (Seo et al. 1995). The results revealed that *G. seoi* metacercariae and adults have similar tegumental ultrastructures, shown by TEM, to other trematode species in general.

Life Cycle

This fluke has the life cycle stages of eggs, miracidia, sporocysts and daughter sporocysts (or germinal sacs), cercariae, metacercariae, and adults, although sporocysts and cercarial stages have not yet been discovered either in nature or in the laboratory (Lee and Chai 2001). It is generally accepted that rediae are not existing in the life cycle of the Gymnophallidae (Ching 1995b). The term "primary (cercarial) germinal sac" was used for a miracidium-mother sporocyst or the daughter sporocyst generation of *Parvatrema homoeotecnum* James, 1964 (James 1964), and "metacercarial germinal sac" was found in *Gymnophallus australis* Szidat, 1962 (Ching 1995b). However, the stage of germinal sacs was not found in species of *Gymnophalloides* (Ching 1995b).

The first intermediate host of *G. seoi* has not yet been determined; therefore, the larval development from the sporocyst to cercariae is unknown (Lee and Chai 2001; Lee et al. 2005). However, the first intermediate host can also be the oysters, considering the general life cycle of other gymnophallid flukes, and this should be determined (Lee and Chai 2001). Loos-Frank (1969) categorized 3 types of gymnophallid life cycles. One is that free swimming cercariae and metacercariae occur in one host (*Lacunovermis mocamae*) or 2 different hosts (*Parvatrema borinquenae*); the second is that free swimming cercariae and metacercariae occur in 2 intermediate hosts in phase of the life cycle alternating seasonally with a cercaria that loses its tail and remain in sporocysts within the same host (*Gymnophallus choledochus*); the third is that cercaria loses its tail and remains within the same host (*Meiogymnophallus affinis*) or remains in germinal sac in the same host (*Parvatrema homoeoecnum*) (Loos-Frank 1969). Park (2005) tried to establish the life cycle of *G. seoi* in the laboratory; however, he only succeeded in culture of eggs into miracidia and recovery of adult flukes from laboratory mice after experimental infection with metacercariae obtained from naturally infected oysters. The metacercariae could be successfully cultured in vitro into adults using NCTC 109 medium or minimum essential medium (Kook et al. 1997; Lee et al. 2009).

The adult flukes were recovered in the small intestines of immunosuppressed Sprague-Dawley rats at day 7 post-infection (Park 2005). They were washed with phosphate-buffered saline 5 times and incubated in DMEM containing 1% antibiotics and 5% CO_2 at 37 °C for 24 h, and eggs were separated from adult flukes using a 56-μm diameter mesh (Park 2005). More than 20,000 eggs were collected from numerous (>1000) adult flukes after 24 h of incubation in DMEM medium; some eggs were already matured containing miracidia when collected from adults and some others matured a few days after incubation but still others did not mature even at 15 days after incubation (Park 2005). Higher temperature (37 °C than 25 °C) facilitated maturation of the eggs (Park 2005). Several miracidia hatched out 3 days after incubation in DMEM at 37 °C; however, light and dark stimuli, enzyme treatment with trypsin or chitinase, and mechanical stimuli with 1000–7000 rpm centrifugation for 2 min did not affect the miracidial hatching (Park 2005). Slight mechanical pressure such as weak spout out with a pipette or a cover slip pressure helped hatch-out of the miracidia; however, the miracidia looked alive only 10–20 min under a cover slip on a glass slide (Park 2005).

Natural oysters (*Crassostrea gigas*) (Fig. 6.3a, b) collected in the sea village (Shin-Jang-3-Ri, Aphaedo Island, Jeollanam-do Province, South Korea) where the first human patient resided and consumed oysters have been proved to be the second intermediate host of *G. seoi* harbouring the metacercariae (Lee et al. 1995a; Lee and Chai 2001). The metacercariae were mainly located on the mantle surface near the hinge of the shell (Fig. 6.3a), sucking the extrapallial epithelia of the mantle, frequently in groups (Fig. 6.3b), and as the infection density increased they were spread toward the mouth of the oyster; heavily infected regions appeared as whitish spots and easily seen with the naked eyes, and some shell side of the infected oysters revealed brownish pigmentation (Lee and Chai 2001). The metacercariae were isolated and experimentally fed to ICR mice, each with 100 metacercariae, and 7 days later adult flukes were recovered in their small intestines; the adult flukes were morphologically confirmed to be *G. seoi* (Lee et al. 1995a). The metacercarial density per oyster in this village was 610 on average (n = 50), and the worm recovery rate from experimentally infected mice at day 7 post-infection averaged 19.0% (n = 5) (Lee et al. 1995a).

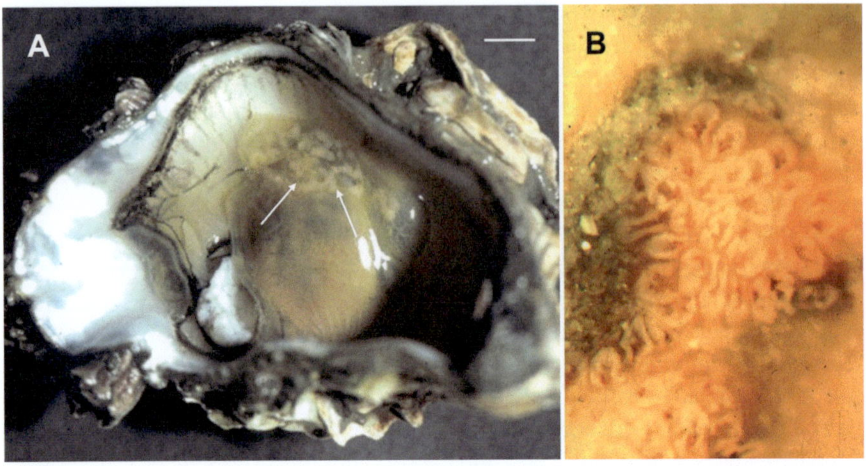

Fig. 6.3 *Gymnophalloides seoi*. (**a**) Grouped metacercariae (arrows) on the mantle surface of an oyster, *Crassostrea gigas*, collected in an endemic area in South Korea. Scale bar = 1 cm. Reproduced from the figure in Lee et al. (1995) Korean J Parasitol 33:1–7 with permission (**b**) Close-up view of the grouped metacercariae on the mantle of the oyster

An experimental study was performed to induce metacercarial infections of oysters transferred from a non-endemic locality (Taean-gun) and then put in sea water around the endemic sea village; oysters previously negative for *G. seoi* metacercariae became positive for *G. seoi* metacercariae 5–7 months (July-August-September) after the transfer of oysters (Park 2005). This undoubtedly means the existence of its life cycle in this sea village. However, it still remains to be determined whether *G. seoi* uses a snail first intermediate host separately from the oysters, or whether the oysters play a dual role of the first and second intermediate hosts. The present author and group repeatedly examined the oysters from endemic areas whether they had the sporocyst and cercarial stages but could not find these larval stages; we also examined several species of brackish water snails which were popularly scattered in the endemic areas but sporocysts and cercariae of *G. seoi* were never found (unpublished observations).

Seven species of mammals (gerbils, hamsters, cats, dogs, guinea pigs, rats, and 7 strains of mice) and 2 species of birds (ducks and chicks) were subjected to an experimental infection with *G. seoi* metacercariae (Lee et al. 1997). The worm recovery rate at day 7 post infection was the highest in hamsters (14.2%) followed by cats (10.9%), rats (4.0%), dogs (1.3%), and ducks (1.3%); guinea pigs and chicks revealed no worms (Lee et al. 1997). In different strains of mice, the highest worm recovery was obtained in KK mice (12.4%) followed by C3H/HeN (11.8%), ICR (9.6%), BALB/c (6.4%), ddY (6.3%), A (1.8%), and C57BL/6 mice (0%) (Lee et al. 1997). Immunosuppression of C3H/HeN mice with prednisolone injection for 7, 14, or 21 days remarkably enhanced the worm recovery rate up to 27.8% (7 days), 33.8% (14 days), and 67.5% (21 days) (Lee et al. 1997). Thus, C3H/HeN mice were used to observe the worm development and maturation (Fig. 6.4); the worms

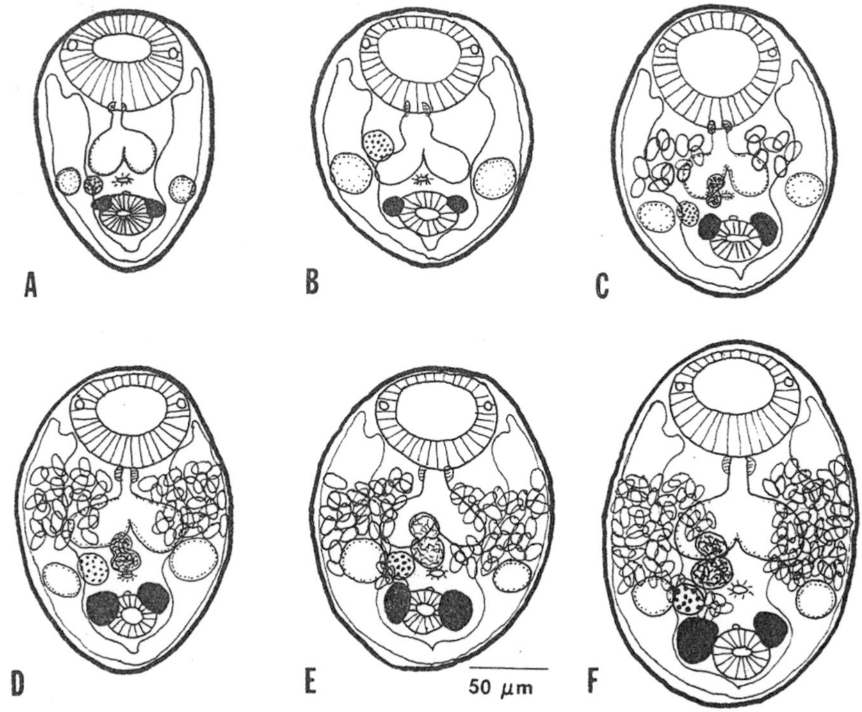

Fig. 6.4 Growth and development of *Gymnophalloides seoi* in experimental mice. (**a**) Excysted metacercaria (**b**) 1-day-old worm (**c**) 3-day-old worm (**d**) 5-day-old worm (**e**) 6-day-old worm (**f**) 14-day-old worm. Reproduced from the figure in Chai et al. (1999) Korean J Parasitol 37:21–26 with permission

attained sexual maturity by day 3 post-infection with eggs in the uterus, and the worm dimensions and number of uterine eggs increased continuously until day 14 post-infection both in immunocompetent and immunosuppressed mice (Chai et al. 1999). Immunosuppression also enhanced the fecundity of *G. seoi* worms; worms recovered from immunosuppressed C3H/HeN mice at day 7 post infection were fully matured, containing more than 120 uterine eggs per worm, whereas those from immunocompetent C3H/HeN mice were less matured with much less number of uterine eggs (Lee et al. 1997; Chai et al. 1999).

Natural definitive hosts for *G. seoi* so far reported include humans, cats, and birds (oystercatchers) (Lee and Chai 2001; Shin et al. 2009). In addition to human population infected with *G. seoi*, 2 of 4 feral cats caught at the endemic area on Aphaedo Island were found to harbor the adult flukes, 3 and 307 specimens each of *G. seoi* (Shin et al. 2009). The Palearctic oystercatchers *Haematopus ostralegus* were also verified to be a natural definitive host; 5 of 7 oystercatchers caught and examined in total (1 of 1 oystercatcher from Namyang Bay, 3 of 4 oystercatchers from Yubudo Island, 1 of 1 oystercatcher from Aphaedo Island, and none of 1 oystercatcher from Gangwhado Island) were found to harbor the adult flukes of *G. seoi*

(Ryang et al. 2000). In addition, wading birds, such as, the Kentish plover *Charadrius alexandrinus*, Mongolian plover *Charadrius mongolus*, and grey plover *Pluvialis squatarola*, were experimentally proved to be susceptible to infection with this fluke (Ryang et al. 2001). These results suggest strongly that various species of migrating birds visiting South Korea, other than the oystercatcher, may also be the definitive host for *G. seoi*, and the geographical distribution of this fluke may be wider than which has been imagined.

6.2.1.2 Epidemiology and Geographical Distribution

The source of human infection with *G. seoi* is raw consumption of oysters naturally produced at endemic areas (Lee and Chai 2001; Chai et al. 2003). Oyster dishes pickled slightly (within 1–2 days) and oysters mixed with 'kimchi' may also cause *G. seoi* infection in endemic areas. However, experimental proof on this has never been provided.

So far, this fluke has been found only in South Korea (Table 3.2) (Lee and Chai 2001; Chai et al. 2003). In Japan, the metacercariae of *G. tokiensis* were reported from oysters caught at Tokyo Bay (Fujita 1925), and if its life cycle exists until now, the adult flukes should be obtained and compared with those of *G. seoi*.

South Korea The presence of *G. seoi* was first documented in a woman patient who suffered from severe epigastric discomfort, indigestion, and diarrhea; laboratory findings suggested acute pancreatitis with elevated serum and urine amylase levels (Lee et al. 1993). Subsequently, a high prevalence (49.0%) with heavy worm loads (106–26,373 specimens per person) was discovered in a sea village (Shinjang-3-ri) on a southwestern island, Aphaedo Island, Jeollanam-do (Province), South Korea where the first patient resided and frequently consumed bivalves, including the oysters (Lee et al. 1994). Natural oysters (*Crassostrea gigas*) were then collected from this village which were found positive for the metacercariae of a gymnophallid; they were experimentally fed to ICR mice, and adult flukes recovered at day 7 post-infection were morphologically confirmed to be *G. seoi* (Lee et al. 1995a). The metacercarial density per infected oyster ranged from 2 to 4792 (av. 610, n = 50); they were unencysted, attached on the mantle surface near the hinge of the shell or free in the extrapallial cavity of the oyster (Lee et al. 1995a). The metacercarial density in oysters from this village was checked again 22 years later, and it was found that the density remained to be still high, ranging from 27 to 4704 per oyster (av. 646, n = 30) (Sohn et al. 2017). However, cultivated oysters have never been found to be infected with *G. seoi* metacercariae (unpublished observation).

Thereafter, sporadic human infections as well as endemic foci (based on human or oyster infections) were continually discovered in different localities. Two diabetic patients who visited hospitals in Seoul were found to have *G. seoi* infection (Lee et al. 1995b). A 62-year-old man in Mokpo City (near the high endemic area, Aphaedo Island) was found to be infected with this fluke; 500 adult specimens were recovered after praziquantel treatment and purging (Kim et al. 1995). The effect of gamma-irradiation to kill the metacercariae of *G. seoi* was reported to be great; irradiation of oysters with 200–1000 Gy was effective to control infectivity of the metacercariae to C3H mice and could be applied as a control measure for gymnophalloidiasis (Chai et al. 1996). After then, oysters were collected nationwide from 37 coastal areas of South Korea (nearby the western, southern, and eastern seas), including 13 areas in Shinan-gun (the already known endemic county), and examined for *G. seoi* metacercariae; the results revealed that one of the 2 areas of Buan-gun (Jeollabuk-do) and 10 of 13 areas of Shinan-gun (Jeollanam-do) were positive for the metacercariae (Lee et al. 1996). A low-grade endemic focus of *G. seoi* (3.7% in egg prevalence), together with heavy *Heterophyes nocens* and *Pygidiopsis summa* infections, was found in Muan-gun, Jeollanam-do, slightly north to the known endemic area of Shinan-gun, Jeollanam-do (Chai et al. 1997). Another low-grade endemic focus, with 2 villagers from whom 8 adult specimens were recovered, was subsequently detected in Buan-gun, more north to Muan-gun and Shinan-gun (Chai et al. 1998). Natural oysters collected from Yubudo (Chungcheongnam-do), Sonyudo and Munyodo (Jeollabuk-do), and Chumoondo Islands (Gangwha-gun) were positive for *G. seoi* metacercariae, although the metacercarial density was comparatively lower than that in Shinan-gun (Sohn et al. 1998). A few people (5.1% in 1997 and 3.8% in 1998) on these islands (Sonyudo and Munyodo, Jeollabuk-do Province) turned out to be positive for eggs of *G. seoi* (Lee et al. 1999). Despite repeated mass deworming using praziquantel on villagers of Aphaedo Island, *G. seoi* infection persisted during 6 years of 2 follow-up examinations; the prevalence of villagers was initially 49.0% in 1994 (Lee et al. 1994), but it was elevated markedly to 71.3% in 1997 and again to 72.0% in 2000 (Chai et al. 2000). In the same study, the egg laying capacity of *G. seoi* in humans was estimated to vary individually 0.01–0.42 in EPG/worm and 2.0–84.3 in EPD/worm (Chai et al. 2000). To estimate the prevalence of *G. seoi* infection in humans, a total of 4178 fecal specimens were collected from residents of 45 western or southern coastal islands, excluding Aphaedo Island (a formerly well-known endemic area); *G. seoi* eggs were detected from 160 (3.8%) specimens from 22 islands, and Amtaedo Island revealed the highest prevalence (25.3%) followed by Cheungdo Island (25.0%) and Anchwado Island (20.9%), Shinan-gun (Chai et al. 2001a). On Aphaedo Island, another village named Bokyong-ri, different from the first confirmed endemic village, was later confirmed to be an endemic area of *G. seoi* infection, with 57.9% egg prevalence of villagers; from 13 infected villagers a total of 86,558 adult specimens were recovered after praziquantel treatment and purging (Park et al. 2007).

It is of note that *G. seoi* infection (one of 67 HIV patients) was included among the list of parasitic infections in HIV-infected patients who visited Seoul National University Hospital, South Korea during the period 1995–2003 (Guk et al. 2005). Two coastal villages where natural oysters are unavailable but they consumed raw oysters were also confirmed to have *G. seoi* infection; the prevalence of *G. seoi* infection was 24.1% (Haenam-gun) and 9.3% (Youngam-gun), respectively, and the total number of worms recovered from the villagers were 34,044 (n = 10; av. 3404 per infected person) and 3445 (n = 5; av. 345 per infected person) specimens, respectively (Guk et al. 2006). The villagers stated that natural oysters are not available around their villages, and they purchased the oysters from a local market in southern Youngam-gun (Guk et al. 2006). It is also of note that 4 (0.1%) of 4137 people from Provinces nationwide and Metropolitan Cities, who did not reside in seaside villages, were positive for the eggs of *G. seoi* (Chai et al. 2006).

Later, epidemiological information has been added regarding the infection status of Korean people. An example included a survey of villagers in Muan-gun, Jeollanam-do, and 75 adult specimens of *G. seoi* were recovered from 9 villagers (8.4 specimens per person, low-grade infections) after treatment with praziquantel and purging (Cho et al. 2010). By contrast, in another village of Muan-gun, 3070 and 845 specimens (heavy infections) of *G. seoi* were recovered from 2 gymnophallid or heterophyid egg positive patients after treatment and purging (Chung et al. 2011). In fecal examinations of patients (including those for health check-up) who visited Samsung Medical Center (located in Seoul), a few egg positive cases were detected; 6 (0.01%) among 56,301 examined in 2010, 26 (0.05%) among 57,272 examined in 2011, and 21 (0.04%) among 46,681 examined in 2012 (Kim et al. 2013).

An interesting finding reported by Seo et al. (2008) was that a great number of *G. seoi* eggs (21,417 in eggs per gram of feces; EPG) were detected in the feces of a female mummy (seventeenth century; Joseon Dynasty) found in Hadong, Gyeongsangnam-do (Province), an area located in the eastern part of the contemporary high endemic area, Aphaedo Island. It was speculated that *G. seoi* may have occurred more widely around that time and that the endemic areas reduced more or less to restricted regions thereafter (Seo et al. 2008, 2014). In addition, *G. seoi* infection was detected again from a sixteenth century male mummy unearthed from Sapgyo of Yesan, a Yellow Sea coastal country; the EPG was 150.8 for *G. seoi* eggs (Shin et al. 2012).

The definitive host of *G. seoi*, other than humans, has not been studied extensively. A few researches on this aspect included the discovery of a natural definitive host (also a reservoir host), the Palearctic oystercatcher (*Haematopus ostralegus*), in 3 localities of the western coast of the Korean peninsula (Namyang Bay, Yubudo Island, and Aphaedo Island); 5 oystercatchers were captured by shooting and examined for their intestinal parasites, and 302–1660 (av. 892) adult specimens of *G. seoi* were recovered (Ryang et al. 2000). Seven species of birds were experimentally infected with the metacercariae, and 3 of them, namely, the Kentish plover (*Charadrius alexandrinus*), Mongolian plover (*Charadrius mongolus*), and grey plover (*Pluvialis squatarola*), were susceptible hosts harboring mature adult flukes, whereas 3 other bird species, including the great knot (*Calidris tenuirostris*), dunlin (*Calidris alpine*), and mallard (*Anas platyrhnychos*), were less susceptible hosts harboring only a small number of juvenile flukes, and one species, the black-tailed gull (*Larus crassirostris*), was refractory to the infection with no worms recovered (Ryang et al. 2001). Other than humans and oystercatchers, cats were the only confirmed natural definitive host so far; 2 of 4 feral cats caught in Aphaedo Island harboured adult specimens (3 and 307 from each cat) of *G. seoi* (Shin et al. 2009).

6.2.2 Potentially Zoonotic Gymnophallid spp.

Potentially zoonotic gymnophallid species include *Gymnophalloides heardi* Ching, 1995, *Parvatrema duboisi* (Dollfus, 1923) Bartoli, 1974, and others.

6.2.3 Genomics and Proteomics

Marked genetic heterozygosities are known among the metacercariae of gymnophallid species (Leung et al. 2007). In metacercariae of a species of *Gymnophallus* (*Gymnophallus* sp.) isolated from a bivalve host (*Austrovenus stutchburyi*) in New Zealand, 10 polymorphic microsatellite gene loci, namely, G1C10, G3A4, GYM6b, GYM8, GYM9, GYM11, GYM12, GYM14, GYM15, and GYM16, were found, and in each locus, 3–23 alleles were detected (Leung et al. 2007). In addition, 406 metacercariae of the same species isolated from 15 cockles from New Zealand were genotyped using 6 of the 10 microsatellite loci, and as many as 400 unique genotypes were identified; the results supported the role of the second intermediate host as an accumulator of genetic diversity in the trematode life cycle (Leung et al. 2009).

Cremonte et al. (2015) used molecular data (ITS1-5.8S-ITS2-28S rDNA) for revision of the trematode family Gymnophallidae, including *G. seoi*; the nucleotide sequences obtained were 2199 bp for *G. seoi*, 2141 bp for *G. nacellae*, 2157 bp for *L. macomae*, 2137 bp for *Parvatrema* sp., 2171 for *G. choledochus*, and 2210 bp for *G. australis* and *G. minutus* (syn. *Meiogymnophallus minutus*). The 28S region of *Parvatrema duboisi* could not be sequenced, so the nucleotide sequence of ITS1-5.8S-ITS2 in this species was 1394 (Cremonte et al. 2015). Maximum-likelihood (ML) and Bayesian Inference (BI) analyses resulted in trees with the same topology each other; they revealed the presence of 2 clades corresposponding with the 2 subfamilies suggested by morphology; Gymnophallinae and Parvatrematinae (Cremonte et al. 2015). Moreover, Gymnophallinae included *G. australis, G. minutus*, and *G. choledochus*, and Parvatrematinae included *G. seoi, G. nacellae, P. duboisi, Parvatrema* sp., and *L. macomae* (Cremonte et al. 2015). Furthermore, phylogenetic trees supported the synonymy between the genera *Gymnophallus* and *Meiogymnophallus* forming a highly supported clade, and also showed strong clustering of *L. macomae* and *P. duboisi/Parvatrema* sp. to be in the same subfamily (Cremonte et al. 2015).

A polymerase chain reaction-based restriction fragment length polymorphism (PCR-RFLP) analysis was used to detect 18S rRNA genes of foodborne trematodes in South Korea, including *G. seoi* (733 bp), *Clonorchis sinensis* (739 bp), *Metagonimus yokogawai* (739 bp), *Pygidiopsis summa* (739 bp), and *Heterophyopsis continua* (738 bp) (Pyo et al. 2013). The restriction enzymes Acc1 and Ava2 successfully digested the 18S rRNA of *G. seoi* but not the other 4 species of trematodes; *Msp1* successfully digested the 18S rRNA of the other 4 trematode species but could not differentiate *M. yokogawai* and *H. continua* (Hinf digested *M. yokogawai* but not *H. continua*) and could not digest *G. seoi* gene (Pyo et al. 2013). A multiplex quantitative real-time PCR assay was developed to detect parasites customized to the Korean population, including *G. seoi*; this assay offered a potential use for detecting various intestinal parasites infecting Korean people (Won et al. 2016).

Little study has been performed on molecular biology and proteomics of *G. seoi*. Crude extracts of *G. seoi* containing antigenic proteins were found to enhance mRNA expressions of Toll-like receptors 2 (TLR2) and 4 (TLR4) on a human intestinal epithelial cell line (HT29 cells) cultured in vitro (Lee et al. 2010). However, monoclonal antibodies against *G. seoi* 46 kDa antigen revealed no significant effects on the TLR2 and TLR4 mRNA expression on HT29 cells; therefore, the responsible antigenic proteins should be further clarified (Lee et al. 2010). In 2 papers, cysteine proteinases were isolated from the metacercariae and adults, and functionally characterized (Choi et al. 1998a, b).

6.2.4 Pathology and Immunology

The susceptibility of animals to *G. seoi* infection is variable among different species of animals and even strains, and there has been few highly susceptible experimental animals (Lee et al. 1997). Fairly susceptible animal species so far known include gerbils, hamsters, cats, mice (C3H/HeN, KK, ICR, ddY, BALB/c, and A strains), and some avian species including the Kentish plover, Mongolian plover, and gray plover (Lee et al. 1997; Ryang et al. 2001). Among mouse strains, C3H/HeN mice were the highest susceptible and the best for growth and development of worms, although the worm recovery rate at days 7–21 post-infection was not sufficiently high (Lee et al. 1997; Chai et al. 1999). However, when C3H/HeN mice were immunosuppressed by prednisolone injection, the survival and the recovery of the worms were greatly enhanced, and the enhancement was strongly related with the duration of immunosuppression of mice; immunosuppression also enhanced the fecundity of worms (Lee et al. 1997; Chai et al. 1999). On the other hand, ICR and BALB/c mice were quite resistant against *G. seoi* infection; they retained a fair number of worms by day 3 post-infection but most worms were expelled by day 7 post-infection (Lee et al. 1997; Chai et al. 1999; Chai 2007). Dogs, guinea pigs, ducks, and chicks revealed low susceptibility to *G. seoi* infection (Lee et al. 1997). With regard to avian species other than ducks and chicks, compared to the 3 species of plovers mentioned above, the great knot (*Calidris tenuirostris*), dunlin (*Calidris alpine*), and mallard (*Anas platyrhnychos*) were less susceptible hosts harboring only a small number of juvenile flukes by day 4 post-infection (no worms remained at day 6), and one species, the black-tailed gull (*Larus crassirostris*) was completely refractory to *G. seoi* infection (Ryang et al. 2000).

The pathogenicity of *G. seoi* as well as histopathology in the definitive host have not been extensively studied, mainly because there have been few highly susceptible experimental animals. Mechanical irritation and antigenic stimulation by the flukes as well as the immune status of the host are considered to be important factors in eliciting pathogenicity to the host (Chai et al. 2001b; Chai 2007). However, possible antigens such as enzymes produced by the worms, including cysteine proteases, were shown to be involved in immune evasion mechanisms but not eliciting pathogenicity to the host (Choi et al. 1998a, b). A 100-kDa somatic antigen from *Metagonimus yokogawai* adults was found to cross-react with *G. seoi*; it reacted also with *Clonorchis sinensis, Paragonimus westermani,* and *Fasciola hepatica*, and it seemed that this 100-kDa protein is a common antigen of various species of trematodes (Han et al. 2014).

In C3H/HeN mice, though they were not an excellent host, *G. seoi* grew to be adults (Chai et al. 1999). The worms were shown to parasitize the small intestine, chiefly the duodenum and jejunum, pinching and sucking the intestinal villi with their oral suckers; the infected intestinal mucosa showed villous atrophy and crypt hyperplasia, with inflammatory reactions in the villous stroma and the crypt (Fig. 6.5a, b) (Chai et al. 1999, 2001b, 2009). However, in immunocompetent mice, the histopathological changes were not so severe in general and in these mice the deteriorated mucosal integrity restored around day 14–21 post-infection (Chai et al. 2001b). It was also shown that in immunocompetent mice the worms did not invade the submucosal layer, whereas in immunosuppressed mice by prednisolone injection, worms were shown to have invaded into deeper levels beyond the submucosa

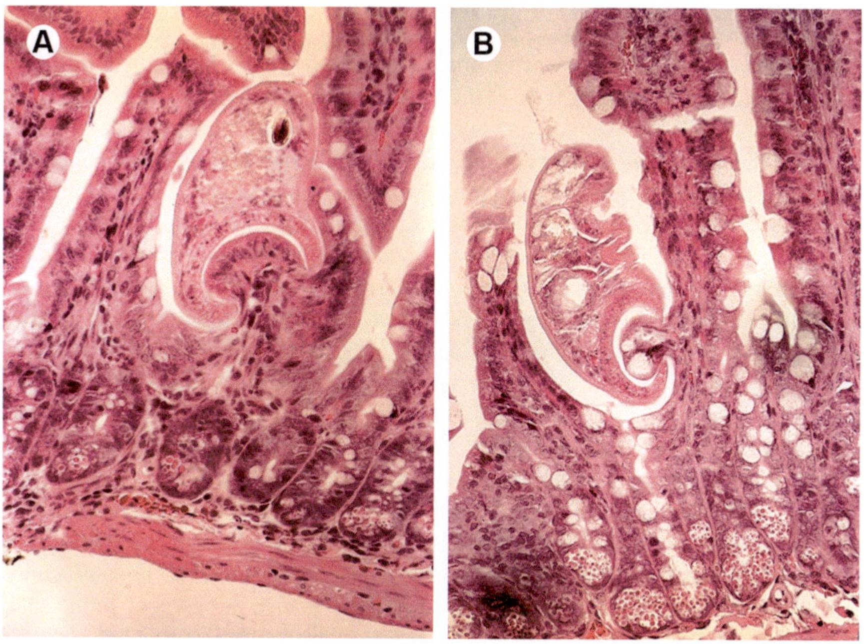

Fig. 6.5 Intestinal sections of mice (**a**, **b**) experimentally infected with the metacercariae of *Gymnophalloides seoi.* Day 5 after infection. Intestinal mucosa is sucked by the oral sucker of the fluke, becoming atrophic, and crypts show hyperplasia. Goblet cell hyperplasia is also seen. × 200

almost facing the serosa, and mucosal damages were severe with frequent displacement as well as complete loss of villi in areas adjacent to the flukes (Chai et al. 2001b). Nevertheless, the histopathology was generally mild with minimal goblet cell hyperplasia even in immunosuppressed C3H/HeN mice (Chai et al. 2001b).

In the human host, the normal habitat of *G. seoi* is presumed to be the small intestine as was demonstrated in experimental mice (Lee et al. 1997; Chai et al. 2001b; Chai 2007). However, in the first human patient, acute pancreatitis was the clinical diagnosis as evidenced by the elevated serum and urine amylases (Lee et al. 1993). In addition, it was reported that diabetes mellitus was accompanied in 2 patients (Lee et al. 1995b). Thus, *G. seoi* is suspected to invade the pancreatic duct and other organs/tissues of the human body (Chai et al. 2003, 2009; Chai 2007). In this connection, it is referable that other gymnophallid species, such as *Gymnophallus choledochus* and *Gymnophallus dapsilis*, were found in the gallbladder and bursa Fabricii of shorebirds as well as in the intestines (Yamaguti 1958). In addition, it is also of interest that a colon cancer patient who received anti-cancer chemotherapy, a *G. seoi* worm was found to have penetrated the colonic lymphoid tissue (Seo et al. 2006). Therefore, it is presumed that *G. seoi* can invade various organs/tissues other than the small intestines. In order to understand better the pathogenesis, pathology, and pathogenicity of *G. seoi* infection in the definitive host, experiments using larger animals, such as monkeys, seem to be necessary (Chai 2007). It is also worth to note that there is a possibility for *G. seoi* eggs to be transferred to remote organs to cause erratic parasitisms in immunocompromised hosts, as was reported in heterophyid trematode infections (Africa et al. 1940).

Spontaneous expulsion of worms from the intestine of mice has been observed in *G. seoi* infection (Fig. 6.6a) (Lee et al. 1997; Chai et al. 1999, 2001b; Song et al. 2018). ICR and BALB/c mice retained quite a number of worms by day 3 post-infection but most of worms were expelled by day 7 post-infection (Lee et al. 1997; Chai et al. 1999, 2001b). Goblet cell proliferation was marked in the small intestines of infected mice, in particular, in the villous epithelia of the jejunum during days 3–7 post-infection (Fig. 6.6b); thus it was suggested that goblet cells play an important role in expulsion of worms (Chai et al. 2001b, 2003; Song et al. 2018). The role of goblet cells in worm expulsion was further suggested by that only a small number of worms were retained in the intestines of C57BL/6 mice at days 7–14 post-infection, whereas goblet cell hyperplasia was marked in these mice during days 3–7 post-infection (Seo et al. 2003). However, in mmunocompromised C57BL/6 mice, worm recovery became higher at day 7 post-infection, while goblet cell hyperplasia was suppressed significantly at day 7 post-infection (Seo et al. 2003).

The goblet cell proliferation was shown to be highly dependent on $CD4^+$ T-helper cells (Guk et al. 2009). C57BL/6 mice expelled all *G. seoi* worms by day 4 post-infection, while ICR mice did not completely expel worms until day 7 post-infection; this difference in worm expulsion was associated with high numbers of goblet cells in C57BL/6 mice along with alteration of the mucin quality, with changes in the terminal sugar chain and high levels of IL-4 and IL-5 mRNA expression in mesenteric lymph nodes (Guk et al. 2009). Adoptive transfer of mucosal CD4+ T-cells from *G. seoi*-infected C57BL/6 mice to syngeneic mice elicited strong goblet cell

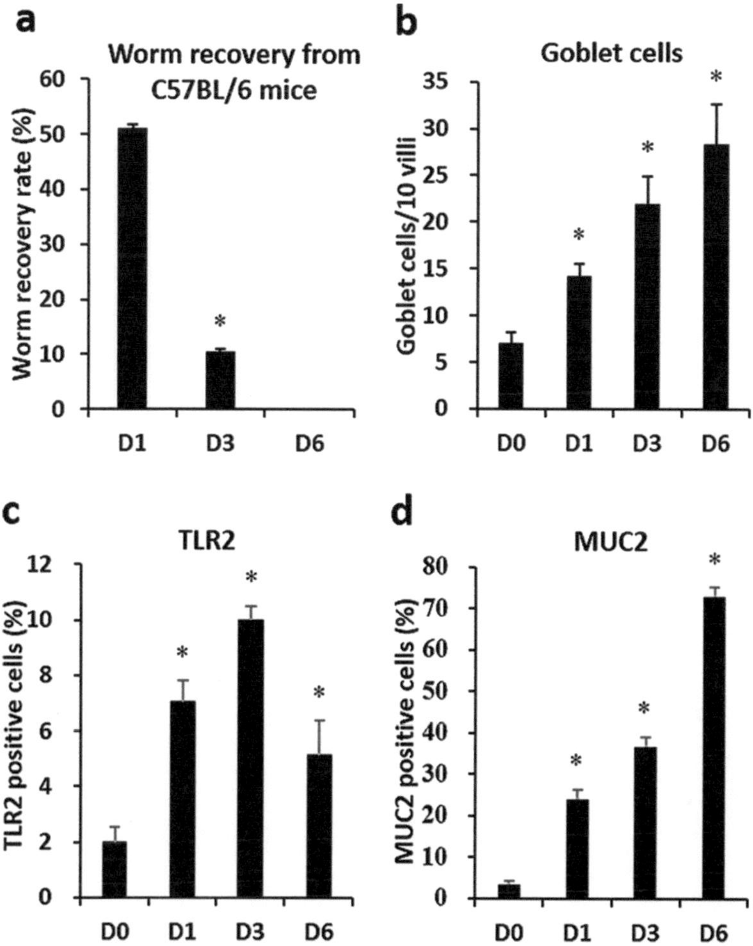

Fig. 6.6 Worm recovery of *Gymnophalloides seoi* from experimentally infected mice (**a**), goblet cell hyperplasia in their small intestines (**b**), and TLR2 and MUC2 expressions (**c**, **d**) in intestinal tissues of mice at different time points. Day 0 (D0); day 1 (D1); day 3 (D3); day 6 (D6) after infection. Reproduced from the figure in Song et al. (2018) Parasitol Res 117:3309–3314 with permission

hyperplasia and a notably accelerated worm expulsion; however, this T-helper cell transfer had no relationship with the alteration of mucin quality, which suggested involvement of both T-cell dependent and independent mechanisms in expulsion of *G. seoi* worms from C57BL/6 mice (Guk et al. 2009).

In order to understand better the innate immunity of the host against *G. seoi* infection, the effects of *G. seoi* antigens on the host's intestinal epithelial cells were studied using a human intestinal epithelial cell line (HT29 cells), on Toll-like receptor (*TLR*) and mucin-related (*MUC*) gene expressions (Lee et al. 2010). *G. seoi* antigen was shown to upregulate *TLR2, TLR4,* and *MUC2* expressions on human intestinal epithelial cells (Fig. 6.6c, d) (Lee et al. 2010; Song et al. 2018). IFN-γ was found to be an accelerator of *TLR* and *MUC* gene expressions on the surface of these cells (Lee et al. 2010). These results were considered to be a helminth-induced, mucosal innate immune mechanism to expel intestinal worms (Lee et al. 2010). Recently, exosomes were highlighted as an important component inducing mRNA and protein expressions of TLRs (*TLR2*) and MUC (*MUC2*) genes from host cells (Song et al. 2018). When exosomes (Fig. 6.7a) isolated from *G. seoi* metacercariae were co-cultured with HT29 cells, cellular internalization of the exosomes (Fig. 6.7b) were visualized using a confocal microscope, and upon stimulation with the exosomes *TLR2* and *MUC2* expressions were significantly up-regulated in HT29 cells (Fig. 6.7c) (Song et al. 2018). It was suggested that *G. seoi* secreted exosomes offered a new point of view in the mechanisms of worm expulsion from the host through enhancement of *TLR2* and *MUC2* expression (Song et al. 2018).

To understand better the mucosal defense mechanisms against *G. seoi* infection, the role of signal transducer and activator of transcription 6 (STAT6) and IL-13 (a Th2 cytokine related with intestinal mucus production via STAT6 signaling) was studied (Lee et al. 2013). In C57BL/6 mice (resistant to *G. seoi* infection), *G. seoi* induced a remarkable expression of STAT6 gene from day 2 post-infection and

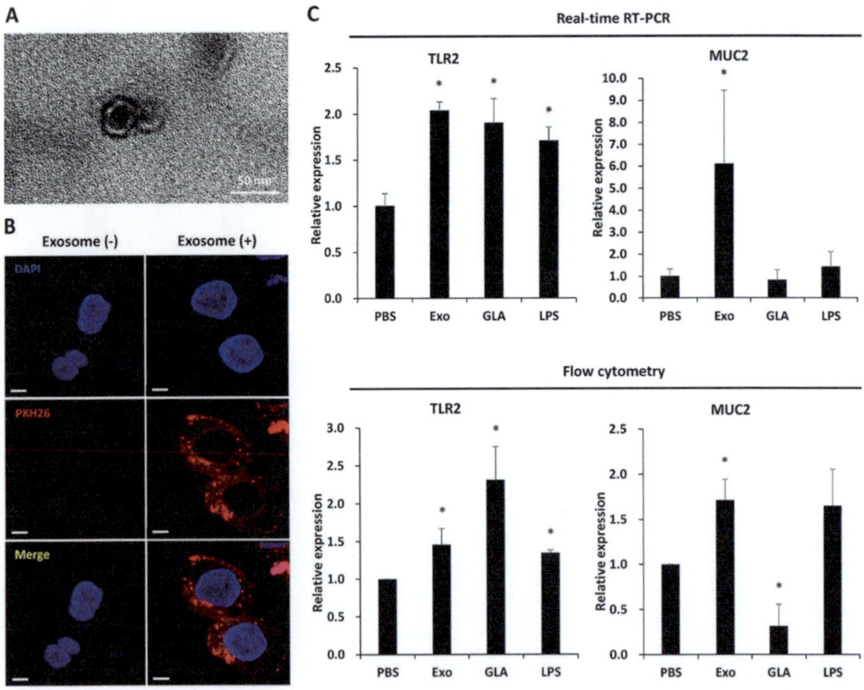

Fig. 6.7 *Gymnophalloides seoi* metacercarial exosomes (**a**), uptake by HT-29 human intestinal epithelial cells shown in pinkish color (**b**), and expression of TLR2 and MUC2 in human intestinal epithelial cells (**c**). Reproduced from the figure in Song et al. (2018) Parasitol Res 117:3309–3314 with permission

significant increase of IL-13 from day 4 post-infection in the spleen of infected mice; worm expulsion actively occurred during days 1–2 post-infection and at this time goblet cells began to proliferate in the small intestine (Lee et al. 2013). The results indicated that goblet cell hyperplasia followed by worm expulsion of *G. seoi* from C57BL/6 mice are induced by STAT6 signaling in which IL-13 may be involved as a dominant triggering cytokine (Lee et al. 2013).

In C57BL/6 (resistant strain) and ICR mice (susceptible strain) infected with *G. seoi*, the role of intestinal epithelial cell turnover and intestinal motility, in connection with goblet cell hyperplasia, was investigated (Lee et al. 2014). Whereas ICR mice retained *G. seoi* worms until day 7 post-infection, C57BL/6 mice showed a rapid worm expulsion within day 3 post-infection; however, immunosuppression significantly delayed the worm expulsion in C57BL/6 mice (Lee et al. 2014). Goblet cell counts were increased to become a peak at day 1 post-infection in C57BL/6 mice but increased slowly until day 7 post-infection in ICR mice; in the crypt newly proliferating intestinal epithelial cells were remarkably increased in number at day 1 post-infection but increased slowly until day 7 post-infection in ICR mice (Lee et al. 2014). Intestinal motility was increased positively correlated with the worm load in the 2 mouse strains (Lee et al. 2014). However, immunosuppression abrogated the goblet cell proliferation, reduced the intestinal epithelial cell proliferation, and suppressed the intestinal motility; these results showed that goblet cell hyperplasia, increased intestinal epithelial cell turnover, and increased intestinal motility are all important components of mucosal defense mechanisms in *G. seoi*-infected C57BL/6 mice (Lee et al. 2014).

6.2.5 Clinical Manifestations, Diagnosis and Treatment

Human *G. seoi* infection was first confirmed in a Korean woman by recovery of adult flukes after anthelmintic treatment and purging (Lee et al. 1993). She habitually consumed naturally produced oysters under raw or improperly cooked conditions when she visited her home village, and experienced repeated episodes of epigastric discomfort, indigestion, and diarrhea (Lee et al. 1993). She was admitted to a university hospital, and laboratory tests revealed elevated serum and urine amylase levels, increased serum alkaline phosphatase activity, and slight to moderate (3–12%) eosinophilia; the tentative diagnosis was acute pancreatitis or acute cholecystitis (Lee et al. 1993). In fecal examinations performed by Kato-Katz thick smear technique and formalin-ether sedimentation technique, small trematode eggs of peculiar morphology were detected, and the patient was treated with praziquantel 10 mg/kg in a single dose and purged with magnesium salts (Lee et al. 1993). From the diarrheic stool, total 910 adult specimens of *G. seoi,* together with 40 *Heterophyes nocens* and 2 *Stictodora fuscata* specimens, were recovered; the *G. seoi* specimens (adults) were reported as a new gymnophallid species (Lee et al. 1993), distinct from *G. tokiensis* (metacercaria) described from oysters in Tokyo Bay (Fujita 1925). Five days after the treatment, epigastric pain and diarrhea of this patient completely disappeared, and serum and urine amylase levels returned to their normal levels (Lee et al. 1993).

In other *G. seoi*-infected patients, occurrence of variable degrees of gastrointestinal troubles together with indigestion, fever, anorexia, weight loss, easy fatigue, and weakness has been reported (Lee et al. 1994; Chai et al. 2000, 2003). But, in most of the infected patients, there occurred only mild gastrointestinal troubles with indigestion (Lee et al. 1994; Chai et al. 2000, Chai 2007). However, it is noteworthy that, in 2 patients infected with *G. seoi,* diabetes mellitus with high blood glucose levels was accompanied, and thus some relations were suspected between *G. seoi* infection and diabetes mellitus (Lee et al. 1995; Lee and Chai 2001; Chai 2007). Moreover, some of the infected villagers living in a highly endemic area (Aphaedo Island) had symptoms, such as thirst, polydipsia, and polyuria that may occur among diabetic patients (Chai et al. 2000). A HIV-infected patient was found to have *G. seoi* infection based on recovery of eggs in the feces; however, clinical details of this patient were not pursued (Guk et al. 2005).

G. seoi infection can be diagnosed by detection of eggs in the feces; however, an expert is needed to identify the eggs (Lee and Chai 2001; Chai 2007). They may be overlooked as an air bubble or other artifacts in routine fecal examinations performed by Kato-Katz thick smear or formalin-ether sedimentation techniques (Chai et al. 2003). The eggs of *G. seoi* are very small (20–25 μm in length and 11–15 μm in width), immature without a developed miracidium when laid, and operculated having a prominent operculum and a thin- and transparent shell (Lee et al. 1993, 1994; Lee and Chai 2001). They are similar in size with those of *Pygidiopsis summa* but smaller than those of *Clonorchis sinensis*, *Metagonimus yokogawai*, or other heterophyids (Lee et al. 1993, 1994; Chai and Lee 2002; Chai et al. 2003). Another diagnostic problem is a very low egg laying capacity of *G. seoi*, for example, only 2–84 eggs per adult fluke in the human host (Chai et al. 2000) in comparison to other intestinal parasites (Chai and Lee 2002). It is assumed that unless a patient is infected with more than 100 worms, lower than 8400 eggs would be discharged in a whole-day stool, and the eggs per gram of feces (EPG) would be only 42 if the daily stool weight is assumed to be 200 g (Chai 2007). This represents the appearance of only 1–2 eggs on the whole field of a fecal smear made by the Kato-Katz technique (41.7 mg of feces/smear) (Chai and Lee 2002; Chai 2007).

Praziquantel in a single oral dose of 10 mg/kg is satisfactory for the treatment of human *G. seoi* infection (Lee et al. 1993; Chai et al. 2003; Chai 2007). A half dose, 5 mg/kg, may also be effective against *G. seoi* infection. Albendazole may also be effective, but this needs confirmation (Chai 2007).

6.2.6 Prevention and Control

The best way to prevent *G. seoi* infection is the avoidance of raw eating of natural oysters particularly produced in endemic areas (Chai 2007). As control measures, irradiation of oysters was tried to kill the metacercariae (Chai et al. 1996). Repeated mass chemotherapy of the people in endemic areas were tried with some successes but reinfection continued in endemic areas (Chai et al. 2000).

References

Africa CM, de Leon W, Garcia EY (1940) Visceral complications in intestinal heterophyidiasis of man. Acta Med Philip Monogr Ser 1:1–132

Bray RA (2002) Superfamily Gymnophalloides Odhner, 1905. In: Gibson DI, Jones, Bray RA (eds) Keys to the Trematoda, vol 1. Natural History Museum, London, pp 243–244

Chai JY (2007) Intestinal flukes. In: Murrell KD, Fried B (eds) Food-borne parasitic zoonoses. Fish and plant-borne parasites. Springer, New York, pp 53–115

Chai JY, Lee SH (2002) Food-borne intestinal trematode infections in the Republic of Korea. Parasitol Int 51:129–154

Chai JY, Han MS, Seo M et al (1996) Effects of gamma-irradiation on the survival and development of *Gymnophalloides seoi* in C3H mice. Korean J Parasitol 34:21–25

Chai JY, Kim IM, Seo M et al (1997) A new endemic focus of *Heterophyes nocens, Pygidiopsis summa,* and other intestinal flukes in a coastal area of Muan-gun, Chollanam-do. Korean J Parasitol 35:233–238

Chai JY, Song TE, Han ET et al (1998) Two endemic foci of heterophyids and other intestinal fluke infection in southern and western coastal areas in Korea. Korean J Parasitol 36:155–161

Chai JY, Chung WJ, Kook J et al (1999) Growth and development of *Gymnophalloides seoi* in immunocompetent and immunosuppressed C3H/HeN mice. Korean J Parasitol 37:21–26

Chai JY, Lee GC, Park YK et al (2000) Persistant endemicity of *Gymnophalloides seoi* infection in a southwestern coastal village of Korea with special reference to its egg laying capacity in the human host. Korean J Parasitol 38:51–57

Chai JY, Park JH, Han ET et al (2001a) A nationwide survey of the prevalence of human *Gymnophalloides seoi* infection on western and southern coastal islands in the Republic of Korea. Korean J Parasitol 39:23–30

Chai JY, Lee HS, Hong SJ et al (2001b) Intestinal histopathology and in situ postures of *Gymnophalloides seoi* in experimentally infected mice. Korean J Parasitol 39:31–41

Chai JY, Choi MH, Yu JR et al (2003) *Gymnophalloides seoi*: a new human intestinal trematode. Trends Parasitol 19:109–112

Chai JY, Park JH, Guk SM et al (2006) Status of intestinal parasite infections among 4,137 residents from Provinces nationwide and Metropolitan areas in the Republic of Korea. Infect Chemother (Korea) 38:198–203

Chai JY, Shin EH, Lee SH et al (2009) Foodborne intestinal flukes in Southeast Asia. Korean J Parasitol 47(suppl):S69–S102

Ching HL (1965) Life cycles of *Lacunovermis conspicuus* n. gen., n. sp. and *Meiogymnophallus multigemmulus* n. gen., n. sp. (Gymnophallidae: Trematoda) from *Macoma inconspicua* and diving ducks from Vancouver, Canada. Proc Helminthol Soc Wash 32:53–63

Ching HL (1972) A redescripition of *Gymnophalloides tokiensis* Fujita, 1925 (Trematoda: Gymnophallidae). Can J Zool 50:1299–1302

Ching HL (1973) *Paragymnophallus odhneri* gen. n., sp. n. (Trematoda: Gymnophallidae) for *Gymnophallus somateriae sensu* Odhner (1900, 1905). Can J Zool 51:807–810

Ching HL (1995a) Four new species of gymnophallid digeneans from rice rats, willets, and molluscs in Florida. J Parasitol 81:924–928

Ching HL (1995b) Evaluation of characters of the digenean family Gymnophallidae Morozov. 1955. Can J Fish Aquat Sci 52(suppl 1):78–83

Cho SH, Cho PY, Lee DM et al (2010) Epidemiological survey on the infection of intestinal flukes in residents of Muan-gun, Jeollanam-do, the Republic of Korea. Korean J Parasitol 48:133–138

Choi MH, Park WJ, Chai JY et al (1995) Surface ultrastructure of metacercaria and adult of *Gymnophalloides seoi* (Digenea: Gymnophallidae). Korean J Parasitol 33:289–296

Choi MH, Chai JY, Lee SH (1998a) Purification and characterization of a 16-kDa cysteine proteinase of *Gymnophalloides seoi* (Gymnophallidae) metacercariae. J Parasitol 84:350–355

Choi MH, Park WJ, Park YK et al (1998b) Isolation and characterization of a 40 kDa cysteine protease from *Gymnophalloides seoi* adult worms. Korean J Parasitol 36:133–141

Chung OS, Lee HJ, Kim YM et al (2011) First report of human infection with *Gynaecotyla squatarolae* and first Korean record of *Haplorchis pumilio* in a patient. Parasitol Int 60:227–229

Cremonte F (2001) *Bartolius pierrei* n. g., n. sp. (Digenea: Gymnophallidae) from the Peninsula Valdés, Argentina. Syst Parasitol 49:139–147

Cremonte F, Pina S, Gilardoni C et al (2013) A new species of gymnophallid (Digenea) and an amended diagnosis of the genus *Gymnophalloides* Fujita, 1925. J Parasitol 99:85–92

Cremonte F, Gilardoni C, Pina S et al (2015) Revision of the family Gymnophallidae Odhner, 1905 (Digenea) based on morphological and molecular data. Parasitol Int 64:202–210

Fujita T (1925) Etudes sur les parasites de L'huitre comestible du Japon *Ostrea gigas* Thunberg. Traduction accompagnée de notes, de diagnoses et d'une bibliographie, par Robert-Ph. Dollfus. Ann Parasitol 3:37–59

Guk SM, Seo M, Park YK et al (2005) Parasitic infections in HIV-infected patients who visited Seoul National University Hospital during the period 1995–2003. Korean J Parasitol 43:1–5

Guk SM, Park JH, Shin EH et al (2006) Prevalence of *Gymnophalloides seoi* infection in coastal villages of Haenam-gun and Yeongam-gun, Republic of Korea. Korean J Parasitol 44:1–5

Guk SM, Lee JH, Kim HJ et al (2009) CD4+ T-cell-dependent goblet cell proliferation and expulsion of *Gymnophalloides seoi* from the intestine of C57BL/6 mice. J Parasitol 95:581–590

Han ET, Yang HJ, Park YJ et al (2014) *Metagonimus yokogawai*: a 100-kDa somatic antigen commonly reacting with other trematodes. Korean J Parasitol 52:201–204

Heard RW III (1970) Parasites of the clapper rail, *Rallus longirostris* Boddaert. II. Some trematodes and cestodes from *Spartina* Marshes of the Eastern United States. Proc Helminthol Soc Wash 37:147–153

Hoberg EP (1981) *Pseudogymnophallus alcae* gen. n. et sp. n. (Treatoda: Gymnophallidae) from Alcids (Charadriiformes) in Subarctic Seas. Proc Helminthol Soc Wash 48:190–194

James BL (1964) The life cycle of *Parvatrema homoeotecnum* sp. nov. (Trematoda: Digenea) and a review of the family Gymnophallidae Morozov, 1955. Parasitology 54:1–41

Kim DC, Kim JW, Cho SS et al (1995) A case report of *Gymnophalloides seoi* infection. J Korean Soc Clin Pathol 27:228–229

Kim YE, Huh HJ, Hwang YY et al (2013) A survey of intestinal parasite infection during a 10-year period (2003–2012). Ann Clin Microbiol 16:134–139

Kinsella JM (1988) Comparison of helminths of rice rats, *Oryzomys palustris*, from freshwater and saltwater marshes in Florida. Proc Helminthol Soc Wash 55:275–280

Kook J, Lee SH, Chai JY (1997) In vitro cultivation of *Gymnophalloides seoi* metacercariae (Digenea: Gymnophallidae). Korean J Parasitol 35:25–29

Lee SH, Chai JY (2001) A review of *Gymnophalloides seoi* (Digenea: Gymnophallidae) and human infections in the Republic of Korea. Korean J Parasitol 39:85–118

Lee SH, Chai JY, Hong ST (1993) *Gymnophalloides seoi* n. sp. (Digenea: Gymnophallidae), the first report of human infection by a gymnophallid. J Parasitol 79:677–680

Lee SH, Chai JY, Lee HJ et al (1994) High prevalence of *Gymnophalloides seoi* infection in a village on a southwestern island of the Republic of Korea. Am J Trop Med Hyg 51:281–285

Lee SH, Choi MH, Seo M, Chai JY (1995a) Oysters, *Crassostrea gigas,* as the second intermediate host of *Gymnophalloides seoi* (Gymnophallidae). Korean J Parasitol 33:1–7

Lee SH, Chai JY, Seo M et al (1995b) Two cases of *Gymnophalloides seoi* infection accompanied by diabetes mellitus. Korean J Parasitol 33:61–64

Lee SH, Sohn WM, Hong SJ et al (1996) A nationwide survey of naturally produced oysters for infection with *Gymnophalloides seoi* metacercariae. Korean J Parasitol 34:107–112

Lee SH, Park SK, Seo M et al (1997) Susceptibility of various species of animals and strains of mice to *Gymnophalloides seoi* infection and the effects of immunosuppression in C3H/HeN mice. J Parasitol 83:883–886

Lee KJ, Park GM, Yk A (1999) Surveys on *Gymnophalloides seoi* infection in the Gogunsan Gundo (Islands) of Korea. Korean J Malacol 15:121–125

Lee SH, Chai JY, Park JH (2005) Studies on *Gymnophalloides seoi* (Digenea: Gymnophallidae). (2) Search for intermediate hosts. J Nat Acad Sci (Natural Science Series, Korea) 44:113–122

Lee SH, Kim HJ, Pyo KH et al (2009) Effects of several culture conditions on in vitro growth and development of *Gymnophalloides seoi*. J Nat Acad Sci (Natural Science Series, Korea) 48:199–212

Lee KD, Guk SM, Chai JY (2010) Toll-like receptor 2 and MUC2 expression on human intestinal epithelial cells by *Gymnophalloides seoi* adult antigen. J Parasitol 96:58–66

Lee JJ, Kim D, Pyo KH et al (2013) STAT6 expression and IL-13 production in association with goblet cell hyperplasia and worm expulsion of *Gymnophalloides seoi* from C57BL/6 mice. Korean J Parasitol 51:589–594

Lee SH, Jung BK, Park JH et al (2014) Increased intestinal epithelial cell turnover and intestinal motility in *Gymnophalloides seoi*-infected C57BL/6 mice. Korean J Parasitol 52:273–280

Leung TLF, Poulin R, Keeney DB (2007) Ten polymorphic microsatellite loci for the trematode *Gymnophallus* sp. Mol Ecol Notes 7:1039–1041

Leung TLF, Poulin R, Keeney DB (2009) Accumulation of diverse parasite genotypes within the bivalve second intermediate host of the digenean *Gymnophallus* sp. Int J Parasitol 39:327–331

Loos-Frank B (1969) Zur Kentniss der gymnophalliden Trematoden des Nordseeraumes. I. Die Alternativ-Zyklen von *Gymnophallus choledochus* Odhner, 1900. Z Parasitenkd 32:135–156

Park JH (2005) Studies on biological and epidemiological characteristics of Gymnophalloides seoi. Ph.D. thesis to Seoul National University College of Medicine, Seoul, Korea

Park JH, Guk SM, Shin EH et al (2007) A new endemic focus of *Gymnophalloides seoi* infection on Aphae Island, Shian-gun, Jeollanam-do. Korean J Parasitol 45:39–44

Pyo KH, Kang EY, Hwang YS et al (2013) Species identification of medically important trematodes in aquatic food samples using PCR-RFLP targeting 18S rRNA. Foodborne Pathog Dis 10(3):1–3

Ryang YS, Yoo JC, Lee SH et al (2000) The palearctic oystercatcher *Haematopus ostralegus,* a natural definitive host for *Gymnophalloides seoi*. J Parasitol 86:419–419

Ryang YS, Yoo JC, Lee SH et al (2001) Susceptibility of avian hosts to experimental *Gymnophalloides seoi* infection. J Parasitol 87:454–456

Scholz T (2002) Family Gymnophallidae Odhner, 1905. In: Gibson DI, Jones A, Bray RA (eds) Keys to the Trematoda, vol 1. Natural History Museum, London, pp 245–251

Seo M, Chai JY, Lee SH (1995) TEM ultrastructure of the tegumental layer of *Gymnophalloides seoi* (Digenea: Gymnophallidae). Korean J Parasitol 33:165–172

Seo M, Guk SM, Han ET et al (2003) Role of intestinal goblet cells in the expulsion of *Gymnophalloides seoi* from mice. J Parasitol 89:1080–1082

Seo M, Chun H, Ahn G et al (2006) A case of colonic lymphoid tissue invasion by *Gymnophalloides seoi* in a Korea man. Korean J Parasitol 44:87–89

Seo M, Shin DH, Guk SM et al (2008) *Gymnophalloides seoi* eggs from the stool of a 17th century female mummy found in Hadong, Republic of Korea. J Parasitol 94:467–472

Seo M, Araujo A, Reinhard K et al (2014) Paleoparasitological studies on mummies of the Joseon Dynasty, Korea. Korean J Parasitol 52:235–242

Shin EH, Park JH, Guk SM et al (2009) Intestinal helminth infections in feral cats and a raccoon dog on Aphae Island, Shian-gun, with a special note on *Gymnophalloides seoi* infection in cats. Korean J Parasitol 47:189–191

Shin DH, Oh CS, Min JJ et al (2012) Sixteenth century *Gymnophalloides seoi* infection on the coast of the Korean peninsula. J Parasitol 98:1283–1286

Sohn WM, Ryang YS, Chai JY et al (1998) Discovery of *Gymnophalloides seoi* metacercariae in oysters from islands of the West Sea known as the habitats of palearctic oystercatchers. Korean J Parasitol 36:164–169

Sohn WM, Na BK, Cho SY et al (2017) Prevalence and density of digenetic trematode metacercariae in clams and oysters from western coastal regions of the Republic of Korea. Korean J Parasitol 55:399–408

Song H, Jung BK, Cho J et al (2018) Worm expulsion of *Gymnophalloides seoi* from C57BL/6 mice: role of metacercarial exosomes in upregulating TLR2 and MUC2 expression in intestinal tissues. Parasitol Res 117:3309–3314

Won EJ, Kim SH, Kee SJ et al (2016) Multiplex real-time PCR assay targeting eight parasites customized to the Korean population: potential use for detection in diarrheal stool samples from gastroenteritis patients. PLoS One 11(11):e0166957

Yamaguti S (1939) Studies on the helminth fauna of Japan. Part 25. Trematodes of birds IV. Jpn J Zool 8:129–210

Yamaguti S (1958) Systema Helminthum. Vol. I. The digenetic trematodes of vertebrates (Part I). Interscience Publishers Inc, New York, pp 1–979

Yamaguti S (1971) Synopsis of digenetic trematodes of vertebrates. Keigaku Publishing Co., Tokyo, Japan

Chapter 7
Lecithodendriid-Like Flukes

7.1 Families Lecithodendriidae and Phaneropsolidae

Lecithodendriid-like flukes (= virgulate digeneans) are parasites of amphibians and mammals, including bats and humans, and occasionally birds, characterized by having virgulate xiphidocercariae (Lotz and Font 2008a). These include 5 families Pleurogenidae Looss, 1899, Lecithodendriidae Lühe, 1901, Leyogonimidae Lühe, 1901, Phaneropsolidae Mehra, 1935, and Gyrabascidae Macy, 1935 (Lotz and Font 2008a). Among them, Phaneropsolidae (*Phaneropsolus bonnei* and *Phaneropsolus spinicirrus*) and Lecithodendriidae (*Caprimolgorchis molenkampi*) are the 2 families infecting humans (Table 3.1) (Yu and Mott 1994; Chai 2007; Chai et al. 2009a). In an abstract of an international meeting, 2 more lecithodendriids (*Paralecithodendrium obtusum* and *Paralecithodendrium glandulosum*) were stated to have been found from humans in northeastern Thailand (Kaewkes et al. 1992); however, no detailed description of the cases nor the morphology of the worms has been available. Thus, these 2 lecithodendriid species were excluded from this review book.

Lühe (1901) erected the subfamily Lecithodendriinae, and Odhner (1911) elevated it to a family status (Lecithodendriidae), considering it to include "brachycoelid" (having short ceca) digeneans (Lotz and Font 2008a). Odhner (1911) divided this family into 2 subfamilies, Lecithodendriinae (parasites of mammals with a median or submedian genital pore) and Pleurogeninae Looss, 1899 (parasites of amphibians with a lateral or sublateral genital pore). Thereafter, a number of genera and species were added in the Lecithodendriidae. Mehra (1935) divided it into 6 subfamilies, which included Lecithodendriinae Lühe, 1901, Pleurogeninae Looss, 1899, Phaneropsolinae Mehra, 1935, Eumegacetinae Travassos, 1922, Anchitreminae Mehra, 1935, and Exotidendriinae Mehra, 1935. Later, however, Skarbilovich (1948) recognized only 4 subfamilies, the Lecithodendriinae (containing 2 tribes Lecithodendriea and Phaneropsolea) for species with the median genital pore anterior to the ventral sucker, the Pleurogeninae for those with a lateral genital pore

J.-Y. Chai, *Human Intestinal Flukes*,
https://doi.org/10.1007/978-94-024-1704-3_7

anterior to the ventral sucker, the Gyrabascinae Macy, 1935 for those with the genital pore median but posterior to the ventral sucker, and the Allassogonoporinae Skarbilovich, 1948 for those with a lateral pore anterior to the ventral sucker. Odening (1959) elevated the subfamily Lecithodendriinae to a family level Lecithodendriidae Lühe, 1901, the subfamily Pleurogeninae to the family Pleurogenidae Looss, 1899, and the Allassogonoporinae to the family Allassogonoporidae Skarbilovich, 1948. However, Lotz and Font (2008a, b) accepted the concept of Mehra (1935) who divided the subfamilies Lecithodendriinae and Phaneropsolinae and of Skarbilovich (1948) who divided the tribes Lecithodendriea and Phaneropsolea within the Lecithodendriinae; they accepted the 2 as distinct families Lecithodendriidae and Phaneropsolidae. Within the Lecithodendriidae, 12 genera, including *Caprimolgorchis* Jha, 1943 (written as *Caprimulgorchis*), *Acanthatrium* Faust, 1919, *Lecithodendrium* Looss, 1896, and *Paralecithodendrium* (Odhner, 1911) Travassos, 1921 (syn. *Prosthodendrium* Dollfus, 1931) are enlisted (Lotz and Font 2008a).

The family Phaneropsolidae Mehra, 1935 (syn. The subfamily Phaneropsolinae Mehra, 1935) are morphologically characterized by the presence of a well-developed cirrus sac and median position of the genital pore (Lotz and Font 2008b). Skarbilovich (1948) included this group as a tribe of the subfamily Lecithodendriinae naming it as the Tribe Phaneropsolea Skabilovich, 1943. Yamaguti (1958) assigned the subfamily Phaneropsolinae Mehra, 1935 in the family Lecithodendriidae. However, Khotenovskii (1970) assigned this taxon in the family Pleurogenidae under the name Parabascinae Yamaguti, 1958, a synonym of Phaneropsolinae Mehra, 1935 (Lotz and Font 2008b). The subfamily Parabascinae (= Phaneropsolinae) were to accept mammalian parasites possessing a cirrus and cirrus sac with the genital pore opening medially or submedially, and the subfamily Pleurogeninae were amphibian parasites possessing a well-developed cirrus and cirrus sac with the genital pore opening laterally or sublaterally (Khotenovskii 1970). Lotz and Font (2008b, c) accepted both subfamilies as distinct families, the Phaneropsolidae Mehra, 1935 and the Pleurogenidae Looss, 1899. Molecular studies using 28S rRNA gene from *Phaneropsolus praomydis* Baer, 1971, in comparison with *Microtrema barusi* (reported to belong to the Phaneropsolidae by Sitko, 2013 but it seems to be a member of the Microphallidae) and *Cortrema magnicaudata* (Pleurogenidae) supported the validity of the family status of the Phaneropsolidae (Kanarek et al. 2014). Within the Phaneropsolidae, 26 genera (20 from mammals, 9 from birds, and 2 from reptiles) were enlisted by Lotz and Font (2008b). A new genus, *Microtrema*, was created by Sitko (2013) with *Microtrema barusi* as a new species and included in the Phaneropsolidae; however, this genus appeared to be more close to the family Microphallidae based upon the sequences of its 28S rRNA gene (Kanarek et al. 2014). Thus, total 26 genera are available in the Phaneropsolidae, including *Phaneropsolus* Looss, 1899, *Ornithodendrium* Oshmarin and Dotsenko, 1950, and *Combesia* Mas-Coma, Roset and Mantoliu, 1985 (Lotz and Font 2008b).

7.2 *Caprimolgorchis* and *Phaneropsolus*

7.2.1 Caprimolgorchis molenkampi

7.2.1.1 *Caprimolgorchis molenkampi* (Lie, 1951) Baugh, 1957

[syn. *Paralecithodendrium molenkampi* Lie, 1951; *Prosthodendrium molenkampi* (Lie, 1951) Yamaguti, 1958; *Fontius molenkampi* (Lie, 1951) Lotz and Palmieri, 1985].

Taxonomy and Morphology

The history of the genus *Caprimolgorchis* Jha, 1943 (syn. *Fontius* Lotz and Palmieri, 1985) is closely related with that of the genus *Paralecithodendrium* Travassos, 1921 (syn. *Prosthodendrium* Dollfus, 1931 (Lotz and Font 2008a). Odhner (1911) proposed a subgenus *Paralecithodendrium* for the lecithodendriid-like flukes that have a lobed or branched ovary anterior to the ventral sucker, without type designation. Travassos (1921) elevated *Paralecithodendrium* to the rank of genus adding the characteristic of pretesticular vitellaria, designating *Paralecithodendrium anticum* (Stafford, 1905) as the type species. Later, the genus *Prosthodendrium* was erected by Dollfus (1931) based on specimens reported by Bhalerao (1926), originally named as *Lecithodendrium dinanatum,* collected from bats *Nycticejus pallidus* in Rangoon (currently Yangon), Myanmar. This species became the type species, *Prosthodendrium dinanatum* (Bhalerao, 1926) Dollfus, 1931. Macy (1936) acknowledged the genus *Prosthodendrium* Dollfus, 1931 and assigned 13 species retaining *Paralecithodendrium* Odhner, 1911 as a subgeneric status including 6 other species in this subgenus; *P. anticum* (Stafford, 1905) Travassos, 1921, *P. glandulosum* (Looss, 1896) Bhalerao, 1936, *P. obtusum* (Looss, 1896) (synonymized with *P. glandulosum* by Yamaguti, 1971), *P. ovimagnosum* (Bhalerao, 1926) Yamaguti, 1958, *P. nokomis* Macy, 1936, and *P. lucifugi* Macy, 1936. Dollfus (1937) revised the genus *Prosthodendrium* (having pretesticular vitellaria) and listed 2 subgenera *Paralecithodendrium* (with a lobed ovary) and *Prosthodendrium* (with an entire ovary). However, Skarbilovich (1948) elevated the status of *Paralecithodendrium* Odhner, 1911 to a generic level together with the genus *Prosthodendrium* Dollfus, 1931. Soon after this, Lie (1951) described a new species of *Paralecithodendrium, P. molenkampi,* recovered from humans in Indonesia. However, Yamaguti (1958) synonymized the genus *Paralecithodendrium* with *Prosthodendrium,* subdividing the genus *Prosthodendrium* into 2 subgenera, *Acanthatrium* and *Prosthodendrium,* and assigned *Paralecithodendrium molenkampi* Lie, 1951 as *Prosthodendrium molenkampi.*

Nevertheless, the subgeneric status of *Paralecithodendrium* was continuously used by several other authors, including Macy et al. (1961), Heyneman and Macy (1962), and Agrawal (1966). Yamaguti (1971) himself began to admit the subgeneric status of *Paralecithodendrium* within the genus *Prosthodendrium.* Meanwhile, Cain (1966) treated *Paralecithodendrium* and *Prosthodendrium* as 2 distinct genera accepting that the former had a lobed ovary anterior to right testis and a round cirrus sac, whereas the latter had a round or oval ovary between testes and an oval cirrus sac in forebody. However, Lotz and Font (1983) was of opinion that *Paralecithodendrium* Odhner, 1911 and *Prosthodendrium* Dollfus, 1931 should be incorporated in a single genus, and the name of the genus should be the preceding *Paralecithodendrium* Odhner, 1911 according to the rule of priority. They (Lotz and Font 1983) added 6 new combinations in the genus *Paralecithodendrium*, including *P. chilostomum, P. macnabi, P. naviculum, P. nokomis, P. swansoni*, and *P. transversum* recovered from bats in Wisconsin and Minnesota, USA. In the genus *Paralecithodendrium*, more than 100 species have been accumulated according to the available literature (Yamaguti 1971; Matskasi 1973, 1980; Lotz and Font 1983; Lotz and Palmieri 1985; Kifune et al. 1983, 1997; Nahhas et al. 2005; McAllister and Bursey 2009; Morozova and Zhokhov 2016).

The genus *Caprimolgorchis* was newly proposed by Jha in 1943 in the family Lecithodendriidae using the type species, *Caprimolgorchis karchanii* recovered from birds, *Caprimulgus asiaticus,* in India (Jha 1943). According to Yamaguti (1971), Baugh in 1957 added 2 additional species from mammalian hosts in this genus, *Caprimolgorchis narendrai* Baugh, 1957 from horseshoe bats and another, *Caprimolgorchis molenkampi* (Lie, 1951) from humans, after transferring from *Prosthodendrium molenkampi* (Lie, 1951) Yamaguti 1958. Later, Lotz and Palmieri (1985) proposed a new combination for this species under a new genus *Fontius* proposed by themselves, *Fontius molenkampi* n. comb. (Lie, 1951) Lotz and Palmieri, 1985. However, Lotz and Font (2008a) themselves synonymized the genus *Fontius* with *Caprimolgorchis* (written as *Caprimulgorchis*). Thus, it seems to be appropriate here to use the name of this zoonotic lecithodendriid returning to *Caprimolgorchis molenkampi* (Lie, 1951) Baugh, 1957. Another species infecting birds, *Caprimolgorchis jhai*, was reported from Egyptian house sparrows (Ramadan et al. 1988). So far, only *C. molenkampi* is known to infect humans.

Caprimolgorchis molenkampi (syn. *Paralecithodendrium molenkampi, Prosthodendrium molenkampi,* and *Fontius molenkampi*) (Fig. 7.1) was first

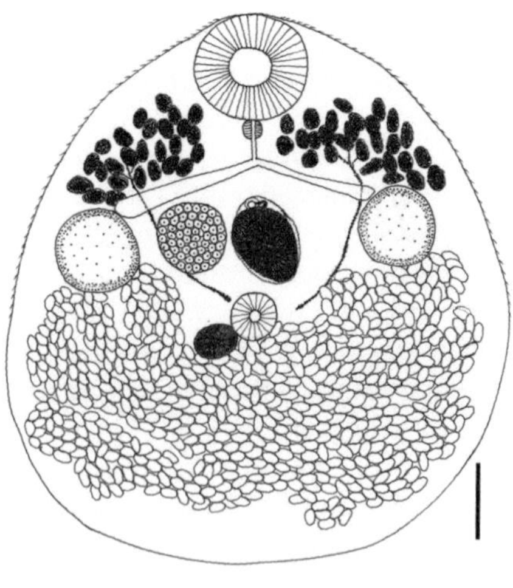

Fig. 7.1 Line drawing of an adult fluke of *Caprimolgorchis molenkampi* (original figure). Scale bar = 0.1 mm

reported from humans in Indonesia by Lie Kian Joe (1951) together with several other species of intestinal flukes, *Phaneropsolus bonnei, Haplorchis yokogawai, Plagiorchis javensis,* and *Plagiorchis* sp. The specimens of *C. molenkampi* were morphologically characterized by possessing a structure resembling the genital sucker (= hermaphroditic organ by Lotz and Palmieri, 1985), the projection of the ventral and genital suckers from the body surface, and the presence of small cuticular spines (Lie 1951). Baugh in 1957 moved *Paralecithodendrium molenkampi* to *Caprimolgorchis* genus proposed by Jha in 1943 and named it as *Caprimolgorchis molenkampi* (Lie, 1951) Baugh, 1957 to which Yamaguti (1971) agreed. On the other hand, Yamaguti (1958) and Dubois (1962) transferred this species to *Prosthodendrium* Dollfus, 1931 naming it as *Prosthodendrium molenkampi.* Thai authors, when they described human infections with this fluke, used this name for a long time (Manning et al. 1970a, b, 1971; Manning 1971; Manning and Lertprasert 1971, 1973; Manning and Viyanant 1972; Radymoys et al. 1984, 1994, 1998; Tesana et al. 1991; Kaewkes et al. 1991a; Sukontason et al. 1999; Sayasone et al. 2009), and Korean workers, including the present author, who worked on its human infections in Lao PDR also used the name *Prosthodendrium molenkampi* (Chai et al. 2005, 2007, 2009b). Lotz and Palmieri (1985) assigned this species under a new genus *Fontius* proposed by them, *Fontius molenkampi*; however, Lots and Font (2008a) synonymized the genus *Fontius* with *Caprimolgorchis* (written as *Caprimulgorchis*). Thus, it seems reasonable here to use the former name, *Caprimolgorchis molenkampi,* for this species.

Human infections with *C. molenkampi* were first reported in Indonesia (Lie 1951) followed by Thailand (Manning 1971; Manning et al. 1971; Manning and Lertprasert 1971; Radomyos et al. 1984, 1994, 1998), Lao PDR (Manning 1971; Chai et al. 2005, 2007, 2009b; Sayasone et al. 2009), and Cambodia (Chai et al. 2019).

Adult flukes of *C. molenkampi* recovered from natural human (n = 21) and animal (tomb bats and common rats) infections (n = 5 specimens each) are oval to pyriform and 0.55–0.92 mm long and 0.41–0.77 mm wide; the tegumental surface is beset with minute cuticular spines (Manning et al. 1971). The oval or reniform cirrus pouch is located between the testes and acetabulum mostly in anterior half of the body; the cirrus pouch and genital pore may be at right or left side of the midline (amphitypic) (Manning et al. 1971). The eggs are 20–28 (av. 23) μm long and 9–14 (av. 12) μm wide (Manning et al. 1971). Cercariae were found in *Bithynia goniomphalus* snails but the dimension is unknown; metacercariae were found in naiads and adults of various species of insects, including the dragonflies and damselflies, but the dimension of the metacercariae has not been given (Manning and Lertprasert 1973). The surface ultrastructure has not been studied in detail.

Life Cycle

C. molenkampi is a zoonotic parasite infecting both animals and humans. However, life cycle of this parasite have seldom been the subject of studies except for a report from Thailand (Manning and Lertprasert 1973). It seems that *C. molenkampi* has the life cycle stages of eggs, sporocysts, cercariae, metacercariae, and adults. The snail

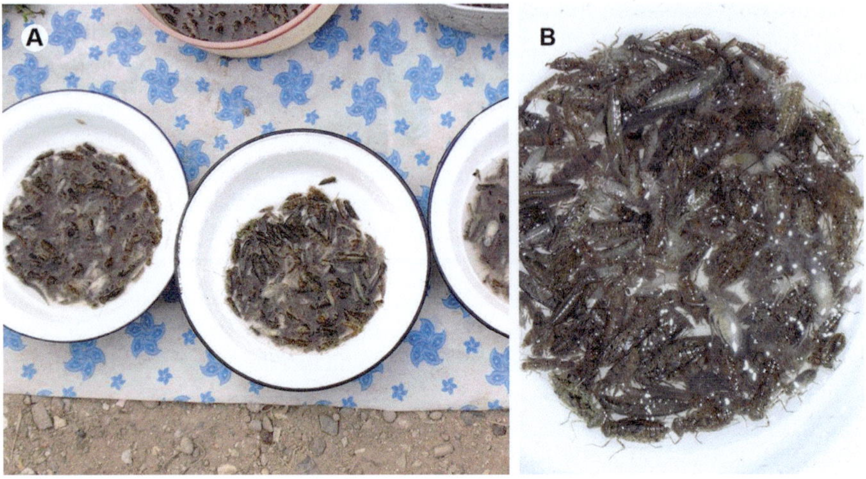

Fig. 7.2 *Caprimolgorchis molenkampi*. (**a**) Naiads of dragonflies, a second intermediate host, sold in a local market in Lao PDR (**b**) Close-up view of the naiads of dragonflies

host was suggested to be a freshwater species *Bithynia goniomphalus* (Manning and Lertprasert 1973). The second intermediate hosts include naiads (Fig. 7.2a, b) and adults of dragon- and damselflies (*Crocothemis servilia, Orthetrum sabina, Trithemis pallidinervis*, and *Brachythemis contaminata*) (Manning and Lertprasert 1973). However, the larval development from sporocysts to cercariae and from cercariae to metacercariae are unknown. Natural definitive hosts include humans, rats (*Rattus rattus*), and bats (*Scotophilus kuhlii* and *Taphozous melanopogon*) (Lie 1951; Manning et al. 1971; Manning and Lertprasert 1971, 1973). Experimental definitive hosts included house rats (*Rattus rattus*) and white rats (Fischer) (Manning and Lertprasert 1973).

Epidemiology and Geographical Distribution
The principal mode of human infection with *C. molenkampi* is presumed to be eating naiads of dragon- or damselflies in water, whereas the infection of other definitive hosts is acquired from ingesting the adult insects (Manning and Lertprasert 1973). The geographical distribution of *C. molenkampi* so far reported extends from Indonesia, Thailand, Lao PDR, and Cambodia (Table 3.2) (Lie 1951; Manning 1971; Manning et al. 1971; Chai et al. 2005, 2007, 2009a,b, 2019). Human cases were reported in Indonesia, Thailand, Lao PDR, and Cambodia (Lie 1951; Manning et al. 1971; Chai et al. 2005, 2007, 2009a,b, 2019).

Cambodia Chai et al. (2019) detected a low-grade infection of a few residents in Prey Vihear Province with *C. molenkampi* after treatment with praziquantel and purging with magnesium salts.

Indonesia Adult specimens of *C. molenkampi* were recovered from a human autopsy case in a mental hospital in Jakarta which were described as a new species (Lie 1951).

Lao PDR Manning (1971) first mentioned on the occurrence of human infections with *C. molenkampi* in Lao PDR, in areas adjacent to northeastern Thailand. Later, Chai et al. (2005) recovered total 441 adult specimens from 14 of 18 residents examined (small trematode egg positive and treated with praziquantel and purged) in Vientiane and Saravane Province. Chai et al. (2007) also detected adult fluke (total 887 specimens) infections in 12 of 29 residents examined (small trematode egg positive and treated with praziquantel and purged) in Savannakhet Province. Chai et al. (2009b) further detected a high prevalence and worm burdens of *C. molenkampi* in Khammouane Province where 26 (78.8%) of 33 residents (positive for small trematode eggs) expelled a total of 7510 adult specimens after praziquantel treatment and purging. Sayasone et al. (2009) performed a similar survey in Vientiane, Savannakhet, and Saravane Province and detected total 562 *C. molenkampi* adult specimens in 14 (14.4%) of 97 community people or hospital patients treated with praziquantel and purged with monosodium solution. In a mountainous area of Phongsaly Province, one adult specimen of *C. molenkampi* was recovered from one of the ten volunteer residents for intestinal fluke surveys who were treated with praziquantel and purged with magnesium salts (Chai et al. 2010).

Thailand Manning (1971) and Manning et al. (1971) reported natural human infections with *C. molenkampi* in northeastern areas. Fourteen (58%) of 24 human autopsies performed at the Udornthani Provincial Hospital were positive for *C. molenkampi* (Manning et al. 1971; Manning and Lertprasert 1973). A life cycle study revealed that the first intermediate host is freshwater snails *Bithynia goniomphalus*, and the second intermediate host is naiads and adults of dragon- and damselflies (Manning and Lertprasert 1973). The natural definitive hosts included humans, house rats (*Rattus rattus*), and bats (*Scotophilus kuhlii* and *Taphozous melanopogon*), and experimental infection was successful to house rats and white rats (Fischer) (Manning and Lertprasert 1973). During 1970–1980, a total of 411 patients were undergone intestinal helminth collection after treatment with praziquantel and purging with magnesium salts at Hospital for Tropical Diseases, Bangkok; 60 patients were positive for *C. molenkampi* from whom a total of 5363 specimens were recovered (max. Per person; 1339) (Radomyos et al. 1984).

The eggs of *C. molenkampi* were studied using light and scanning electron microscopies in comparison with eggs of other trematode species, including *Opisthorchis viverrini, Haplorchis taichui, Haplorchis pumilio,* and *Phaneropsolus bonnei*; the eggs of *C. molenkampi* and *P. bonnei* were found to be similar in shape but differed from the other 3 in that they have clean and smooth shell surface, indistinct shoulders, and small knobs (Tesana et al. 1991). Further, the eggs of *C. molenkampi* were smaller in length and width than those of *P. bonnei*, and the latter had a curved miracidium but not the former (Kaewkes et al. 1991a). In addition, the embryonated eggs of *C. molenkampi* and *P. bonnei* commonly had small iodophilic bodies inside the egg, whereas those of *Opisthorchis viverrini* very rarely had such bodies (Kaewkes et al. 1991a). In 16 northeastern provinces, total 681 small trematode egg positive residents were treated with praziquantel, and adult flukes were collected from 3 days' whole stool; 132 (19.4%) were positive for *C. molenkampi* adult specimens (Radomyos et al. 1994). However, in 16 northern provinces, only 4 (0.93%) of the 431 residents who revealed small trematode eggs and treated with praziquantel and purged with magnesium sulfate, were positive for adult flukes of *C. molenkampi* (Radomyos et al. 1998). A methylene blue staining method was developed to differentiate the eggs of *C. molenkampi* from those of *Opisthorchis viverrini* and *Haplorchis taichui* (Pasuralertsakul et al. 2005). By this staining, the eggs of *O. viverrini* showed prominent musk-melon like ridges on the shell surface, whereas the eggs of *H. taichui* had flat, thread-like curly ridges, and those of *C. molenkampi* had smooth shell surfaces (Pasuralertsakul et al. 2005).

7.2.2 Phaneropsolus bonnei

7.2.2.1 *Phaneropsolus bonnei* Lie, 1951

Taxonomy and Morphology

The genus *Phaneropsolus* was erected by Looss, 1899 using specimens (*P. sigmoideus*) collected from the intestine of house sparrows (*Passer domesticus*) and European nightjars (*Caprimulgus europaeus*) in Egypt (Yamaguti 1958; Khotenovskii 1970). At the same time, Looss included 2 more species in this genus, *P. longipenis* collected from apes in Egypt and *P. oviformis* (syn. *Distomum oviforme* Poirier, 1886) reported from a Javanian ape species (Saoud 1964; Khotenovskii 1970). Braun (1901) placed 3 species in this genus, *P. micrococcus* (syn. *Distomum micrococcum* Rudolphi, 1819), *P. orbicularis* (syn. *Distomum orbiculare* Diesing, 1850), and *P. oviformis*, and synonymized *P. sigmoideus* with *P. micrococcus*. Thus, the type species of this genus became *P. micrococcus* (Rudolphi, 1819) Looss, 1899 (Khotenovskii 1970; Lotz and Font 2008b). Seven new species of *Phaneropsolus* were reported thereafter until 1961; *P. lakdivensis* Fernando, 1933, *P. bonnei* Lie, 1951; *P. philanderi* Caballero and Grocott, 1952, *P. simiae* Yamaguti, 1954, *Phaneropsolus* sp. Zajiçek and Valenta, 1958, *P. magnitesticulatus* Rysavý and Dudek, 1960, and *P. alternans* Capron et al. 1961 (Khotenovskii 1970). Reporting a new species, *Phaneropsolus philanderi*, Caballero and Grocott (1952) synonymized *P. lakdivensis* with *P. oviformis* and *P. bonnei* with *P. longipenis*; however, Yamaguti (1971) denied these synonymies.

Premvati (1958) proposed a new genus *Primatotrema* for a species found in the Rhesus monkey, *Primatotrema macacae*. This genus differed from *Phaneropsolus* in that *Primatotrema* had an ovary on the right side of the ventral sucker, a genital pore located anterior to the pharynx, and no esophagus (Premvati 1958). However, Saoud (1964) demoted *Primatotrema* to a synonym of *Phaneropsolus*, and synonymized *P. magnitesticulatus* with *Phaneropsolus macacae* (Premvati, 1958) and admitted the taxonomic validity of *P. lakdivensis*. Khotenovskii (1970) agreed to the synonymy of *Primatotrema* with *Phaneropsolus* and regarded *P. macacae, P. bonnei, P. magnitesticulatus, P. simiae,* and *Phaneropsolus* sp. of Zajiçek and Valenta, 1958 to be synonymous with *P. oviformis*. Thus, Khotenovskii (1970) listed 7 species in *Phaneropsolus*, which included *P. philanderi, P. lakdivensis, P. alternans, P. micrococcus, P. longipenis, P. orbicularis,* and *P. oviformis*. On the other hand, Yamaguti (1971) accepted *Phaneropsolus* and *Primatotrema* as 2 subgenera of the genus *Phaneropsolus* and listed 10 species, including 6 species in the subgenus *Phaneropsolus* (*P. sigmoideus, P. bonnei, P. lakdivensis, P. orbicularis, P. oviformis,* and *P. philanderi*) parasitic in birds and mammals and 4 species in the subgenus *Primatotrema* (*P. longipenis, P. macacae, P. magnitesticulatus,* and *P. simiae*) parasitic exclusively in monkeys. Baer (1971) reported *Phaneropsolus praomidis* as a new species from West African forest mice in Cote d'Ivore, and Palmieri and Krishnasamy (1978) added a new species, *Phaneropsolus aspinosus*, from the leaf monkey in Malaysia and compared it with *P. bonnei* and *P. oviformis* which are deposited at the Institute of Medical Research, Malaysia. Goodman and Panesar (1986) described *Phaneropsolus perodictici* as a new species from the primate (*Perodicticus potto*) in Uganda. Another new species, *Phaneropsolus spinicirrus*, was described from a human infection in Thailand (Kaewkes et al. 1991b). Thus, total 14 species have been described in the genus *Phaneropsolus*. Among them, 2 species, namely, *Phaneropsolus bonnei* and *Phaneropsolus spinicirrus* have been reported to cause human infections (Lie 1951; Kaewkes et al. 1991b; Chai et al. 2009a). Presumed to be a new species of *Phaneropsolus* was found from the bird (Indian paradise flycatcher) in China; molecular analysis using 28S rRNA gene revealed a 100% homology with *P. praomydis* Baer, 1971 (Kanarek et al. 2017).

Phaneropsolus bonnei (Fig. 7.3) was first reported from humans in Indonesia by Lie Kian Joe (1951) together with several other species of intestinal flukes, *Paralecithodendrium molenkampi, Haplorchis yokogawai, Plagiorchis javensis,* and *Plagiorchis* sp. Lie (1962) also found *P. bonnei* specimens in the intestine of several species of monkeys in Malaysia (*Macaca irus* and *Nycticebus coucang*) and India (*Macaca mulatta*). Saoud (1964) noted morphological similarity of *P. bonnei* Lie, 1951 with *P. macacae* (Premvati, 1958) but retained the validity of both species because of the differences in the position of the ovary in relation to the acetabulum and the position of the seminal receptacle in relation to the ovary. Later, Khotenovskii (1970) synonymized these 2 (*P. bonnei* and *P. macacae*) with *P. oviformis* (Poirier, 1886). However, Manning et al. (1970a, b) described human infections with *P. bonnei* in northeastern Thailand pointing out that their specimens revealed previously unrecognized features or variation from the previous descriptions of *P. bonnei* (Lie 1951) such as (1) longer posterior cuticular spines, (2) position of the oral sucker subterminal, (3) presence of a small prepharynx or esophagus, (4) shape of the excretory bladder (either V or Y-shaped), (5) number of vitelline follicles (n = 8), (6) presence of a Laurer's canal, (7) size of the seminal receptacle determined, (8) location of the metraterm just lateral to the cirrus, and (9) description of eggs done. Yamaguti (1971) acknowledged the validity of both *P. bonnei* and *P. oviformis*.

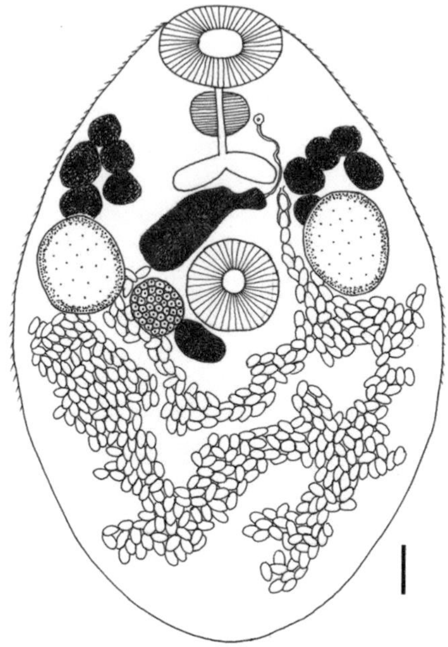

Fig. 7.3 Line drawing of an adult fluke of *Phaneropsolus bonnei* (original figure). Scale bar = 0.05 mm

Manning and Lertprasert (1971), Manning et al. (1971), and Manning and Viyanant (1972) further reported human *P. bonnei* infections from northeastern Thailanders. Further, Manning and Lertprasert (1973) studied on the life cycle of *P. bonnei* and *Caprimolgorchis molenkampi* (syn. *Prosthodendrium molenkampi*) in northeastern Thailand.

Human infections with *P. bonnei* were first reported in Indonesia (Lie 1951) followed by Thailand (Manning et al. 1970a, b, 1971; Manning 1971; Manning and Lertprasert 1971; Manning and Viyanant 1972; Wijit et al. 2013), Lao PDR (Manning 1971; Chai et al. 2005, 2007, 2009b, 2010; Sayasone et al. 2009), and Cambodia (Chai et al. 2019, manuscript to be published).

Adult flukes of *P. bonnei* recovered from natural human infections are pyriform to oval and 0.45–0.85 mm long and 0.30–0.50 mm wide; the tegumental surface is beset with numerous conical spines (Manning et al. 1970b). Characteristically, the cirrus pouch is located in anterior half of the body consisting of a long, rather straight cirrus and a curved portion which includes the pars prostatica and seminal vesicle; the positions of the pars prostatica and seminal vesicle may be reversed (amphitypic) (Manning et al. 1970b). The eggs are 23–33 (av. 27) μm long and 13–18 (av. 15) μm wide (Manning et al. 1970b). Cercariae were found in *Bithynia goniomphalus* snails but the dimension is unknown; metacercariae were found in naiads and adult of various species of insects, including the dragonflies and damselflies, but the dimension of the metacercariae has not been given (Manning and Lertprasert 1973). The surface ultrastructure has not been studied in detail.

Life Cycle
Despite that *P. bonnei* is a zoonotic parasite infecting both animals and humans, the life cycle of this parasite has seldom been the subject of extensive studies except for a single research paper from Thailand (Manning and Lertprasert 1973). It is evident that *P. bonnei* has the life cycle stages of eggs, sporocysts, cercariae, metacercariae, and adults. The snail host was presumed to be a freshwater species *Bithynia goniomphalus* (Manning and Lertprasert 1973). However, the larval development from sporocysts to cercariae has not yet been clearly demonstrated. The second intermediate hosts include naiads and adults of dragon- and damselflies (*Crocothemis servilia, Orthetrum sabina, Trithemis pallidinervis*, and *Brachythemis contaminata*) (Manning and Lertprasert 1973). However, the biological characteristics of the metacercarial development are yet to be determined. Natural definitive hosts include humans and monkeys (*Macaca fascicularis, Macaca irus, Macaca mulatta,* and *Nycticebus coucang*) (Lie 1951, 1962; Manning et al. 1970a; Manning and Lertprasert 1971, 1973). Experimental definitive hosts included monkeys (*Macaca fascicularis* and *Hylobates lar*) and white rats (Fischer) (Manning and Lertprasert 1973).

Epidemiology and Geographical Distribution
The principal mode of human infection with *P. bonnei* was presumed to be eating naiads of dragon- or damselflies in water, whereas the infection of other definitive hosts is acquired from ingesting the adult insects (Manning and Lertprasert 1973). The geographical distribution of *P. bonnei* so far reported extends from Indonesia, Malaysia, India, Thailand, Lao PDR, and Cambodia (Table 3.2) (Lie 1951, 1962; Manning et al. 1970a, b; Chai et al. 2005, 2007, 2009b, 2019). Human cases were reported in Indonesia, Thailand, Lao PDR, and Cambodia (Lie 1951; Manning et al. 1970a, b; Chai et al. 2005, 2007, 2009b, 2019).

Cambodia Chai et al. (2019) detected a low-grade infection of a few residents in Prey Vihear Province with *P. bonnei* after treatment with praziquantel and purging with magnesium salts.

India Lie (1962) found *P. bonnei* specimens in the intestine of a monkey species (*Macaca mulatta*).

Indonesia Adult specimens of *Phaneropsolus* were recovered from a single human autopsy case in a mental hospital in Jakarta which were described as a new species, *P. bonnei* (Lie 1951).

Lao PDR Manning (1971) first mentioned on the occurrence of human infections with *P. bonnei* in Lao PDR, in addition to northeastern Thailand. Later, Chai et al. (2005) recovered total 336 adult specimens from 4 of 18 residents examined (small trematode egg positive and treated with praziquantel and purged) in Saravane Province. Chai et al. (2007) also detected adult fluke (total 27 specimens) infections in 3 of 29 residents examined (small trematode egg positive and treated with praziquantel and purged) in Savannakhet Province. Chai et al. (2009b) further detected a high prevalence and worm burdens of *P. bonnei* in Khammouane Province where 20 (60.6%) of 33 residents (positive for small trematode eggs) expelled a total of 910 adult specimens after praziquantel treatment and purging. Sayasone et al. (2009) performed a similar survey in Vientiane, Savannakhet, and Saravane Province and detected *P. bonnei* adult specimens in 22 (22.7%) of 97 community people or hospital patients treated with praziquantel and purged with monosodium solution.

Malaysia Lie (1962) found *P. bonnei* specimens in the intestine of 2 species of monkeys (*Macaca irus* and *Nycticebus coucang*).

Thailand Manning et al. (1970a, b) reported natural human infections with *P. bonnei* in northeastern parts. First, they (Manning et al. 1970a) detected small trematode eggs of undetermined species, including those of *Opisthorchis viverrini*, in 156 of 413 stool specimens from a village of Udornthani Province, northeastern Thailand. Fifteen of such egg positive cases were given hexylresorcinol and adult flukes were recovered from 3 days' stools but the internal morphology of the worms was unsatisfactory (Manning et al. 1970a). An autopsy was performed at Udornthani Provincial Hospital on a 43-year-old woman, and more than 100 small pyriform trematodes (< 1 mm) were recovered from the duodenum and upper jejunum, together with several other helminth species, including *Opisthorchis viverrini* from the liver, and hookworms, pinworms, and a *Taenia saginata* tapeworm from the intestine (Manning et al. 1970a). The morphology of *P. bonnei* was redescribed using forty specimens from this autopsy case and ten specimens from another patient from northeastern Thailand (Manning et al. 1970b). *P. bonnei* was also found in 7 of 48 cynomolgus monkeys (*Macaca fascicularis*) in Thailand (Manning and Lertprasert 1971). Until 1971, 15 of 24 human autopsies performed at the Udornthani Provincial Hospital were positive for *P. bonnei* (Manning et al. 1971). In fecal surveys performed on villagers in Udornthani Province, the overall prevalence of *P. bonnei* eggs ranged 10–40% (Manning and Viyanant 1972). A life cycle study revealed that the first intermediate host of *P. bonnei* is freshwater snails *Bithynia goniomphalus*, and the second intermediate host is naiads and adults of dragon- and damselflies; the natural definitive hosts included humans and monkeys (*Macaca fascicularis*) and experimental infection was successful to monkeys (*Macaca fascicularis* and *Hylobates lar*) and white rats (Fischer) (Manning and Lertprasert 1973). During 1970–1980, a total of 411 patients were undergone intestinal helminth collection after treatment with praziquantel and purging with magnesium salts at Hospital for Tropical Diseases, Bangkok; 34 patients were positive for *P. bonnei* from whom a total of 5647 specimens were recovered (max. Per person; 4356) (Radomyos et al. 1984).

The eggs of *P. bonnei* were studied using light and scanning electron microscopies in comparison with eggs of other trematode species, including *Opisthorchis viverrini, Haplorchis taichui, Haplorchis pumilio,* and *C. molenkampi* (under the name *Prosthodendrium molenkampi*); the eggs of *P. bonnei* and *C. molenkampi* were found to be similar in shape but differed from the other 3 in that they have clean and smooth shell surface, indistinct shoulders, and small knobs (Tesana et al. 1991). Further, the eggs of *P. bonnei* were larger in length and width than those of *C. molenkampi*, and the former had a curved miracidium; in addition, the embryonated eggs of *P. bonnei* and *C. molenkampi* commonly had small iodophilic bodies inside the egg, whereas those of *Opisthorchis viverrini* very rarely had such bodies (Kaewkes et al. 1991a). In 16 northeastern provinces, total 681 small trematode egg positive residents were treated with praziquantel, and adult flukes were collected from 3 days' whole stool; 102 (15.0%) were positive for *P. bonnei* adult specimens (Radomyos et al. 1994). However, in 16 northern provinces, only 2 (0.46%) of the 431 residents who revealed small trematode eggs and treated with praziquantel and purged with magnesium sulfate, were positive for adult flukes of *P. bonnei* (Radomyos et al. 1998). A temporary potassium permanganate staining method was developed for differentiation of *P. bonnei* eggs from those of *Opisthorchis viverrini* and *Haplorchis taichui*; the eggs of *P. bonnei* differed from the eggs of the other 2 in different size ranges and having no musk-melon patterns on the egg shell surface (*O. viverrini* has such patterns), a small abopercular protrusion or knob, and not prominent shoulders (Sukontason et al. 1999). Adult specimens were recovered from 4 (4.0%) of 100 residents examined in Lampang Province, northern Thailand (Wijit et al. 2013).

7.2.3 Phaneropsolus spinicirrus

7.2.3.1 *Phaneropsolus spinicirrus* Kaewkes et al., 1991

Taxonomy and Morphology

This species was reported as a new species from a human in northeastern Thailand (Kaewkes et al. 1991b). Lecithodendriid-like flukes resembling *P. bonnei* were recovered from a 44-year-old woman in Kalasin Province, northeastern Thailand (Kaewkes et al. 1991b). The worm was morphologically characterized by the presence of a spiny cirrus which was reported only in another species, *P. perodictici* Goodman and Panesar, 1986, and never in the other 12 previously reported species of *Phaneropsolus* (Kaewkes et al. 1991b). *P. spinicirrus* is differed from *P. perodictici* in having larger spines on the cirrus, a longer cirus sac, and the more anterior position of the genital pore, and in different forms of the tegumental spines, ovary, and excretory bladder (Kaewkes et al. 1991b). It differs from *P. bonnei* Lie, 1951 in having a spined cirrus, a larger V-shaped excretory bladder, and uniform and regular distribution of conical spines on the tegument, whereas *P. bonnei* does not have a spined cirrus, has a small V- or Y-shaped excretory bladder, and long fine hair-like projections (tegumental spines) near the posterior end (Manning et al. 1970b; Kaewkes et al. 1991b). *P. spinicirrus* is morphologically similar to *P. philanderi* Caballero and Grocott, 1952 in having abundant tubercles on the surface of the cirrus but the latter species has a larger cirrus sac and transverse position of the cirrus sac, the genital pore located at the posterior border of the pharynx, and different suck ratio (Kaewkes et al. 1991b).

Adult flukes are small, oval, and 0.550–0.758 mm long and 0.430–0.629 mm wide; the tegumental surface is covered regularly with conical spines (Kaewkes et al. 1991b). The cirrus sac is elongate and coiled, extending from the level of the ventral sucker to the posterior border of the oral sucker, containing bipartite seminal vesicle, elongate pars prostatica, and short bulbous cirrus with numerous conical spines on its surface (Kaewkes et al. 1991b). The eggs are 27–33 (av. 29) μm long and 13–16 (av. 14) μm wide (Kaewkes et al. 1991b). The cercariae and metacercariae have not yet been found. The surface ultrastructure has not been studied in detail.

Life Cycle
The life cycle of *P. spinicirrus* has not yet been determined. The only finding is that this species can infect the human host (Kaewkes et al. 1991b).

Epidemiology and Geographical Distribution
The mode of human infection with *P. spinicirrus* remained to be determined; however, it is presumed that eating naiads of dragon- or damselflies may contract the infection. The geographical distribution of *P. spinicirrus* is yet confined to northeastern Thailand (Table 3.2) (Kaewkes et al. 1991b).

Thailand From Kalasine Province, northeastern Thailand, a 44-year-old woman patient expelled numerous specimens of *P. spinicirrus* after treatment with praziquantel and purging with magnesium sulfate, together with other trematode species, including *P. bonnei, Paralecithodendrium* sp., *Opisthorchis viverrini, Echinostoma malayanum,* and *Echinostoma ilocanum* (Kaewkes et al. 1991b).

7.2.4 Potentially Zoonotic Caprimolgorchis *and* Phaneropsolus *spp.*

The potentially zoonotic *Caprimolgorchis* and *Phaneropsolus* spp. include *Caprimolgorchis karchanii* Jha, 1943, *C. narendrai* Baugh, 1957, *C. jhai* Ramadan et al., 1988, *Phaneropsolus sigmoideus* Looss, 1899, *P. oviformis* (Poirier, 1886) Looss, 1899, *P. longipenis* Looss, 1899, *P. orbicularis* (Diesing, 1850) Braun, 1901, *P. lakdivensis* Fernando, 1933, *P. philanderi* Caballero and Grocott, 1952, *P. simiae* Yamaguti, 1954, *P. magnitesticulatus* Ryšavý and Dudek, 1960, *P. alternans* Capron et al., 1961, *P. macacae* (Premvati, 1959) Saoud, 1964, *P. praomidis* Baer, 1971, *P. aspinosus* Palmieri and Krishnasamy, 1978, and *P. perodictici* Goodman and Panesar, 1986 (see Yamaguti 1971; Baer 1971; Palmieri and Krishnasamy, 1978; Goodman and Panesar, 1986).

7.2.5 Genomics and Proteomics

Genomic and proteomic studies regarding *Caprimolgorchis* and *Phaneropsolus* spp. have seldom been performed with the exception of a few works. Kanarek et al. (2014) performed a systematic and phylogenetic study on the families Phaneropsolidae and Cortrematidae using 28S rRNA sequenes of *Phaneropsolus praomydis* (Phaneropsolidae), *Microtrema barusi* (reported to belong to the Phaneropsolidae by Sitko, 2013 but it seemed to be a member of the Microphallidae by Kanarek et al., 2014), and *Cortrema magnicaudata* (Cortrematidae). The results revealed that the family status of the Phaneropsolidae as an independent family should be maintained because *P. praomydis* appeared in the phylogenetic tree as an independent family-level branch not showing close relationships with other families of the Microphalloidea (Kanarek et al. 2014). Another study of Kanarek et al. (2017) confirmed again the family status of the Phaneropsolidae adding a possible new species of *Phaneropsolus* which was collected from birds (Indian Paradise Flycatchers) in Guangxi Province, China.

7.2.6 Pathology and Immunology

The pathogenicity, pathology, and immunology of human *Caprimolgorchis* and *Phaneropsolus* spp. infection are known. Most of the reported human cases were mixed infections with the liver fluke *Opisthorchis viverrini* and other minute intestinal flukes (heterophyids or echinostomes) (Manning et al. 1971; Radomyos et al. 1984, 1994, 1998; Chai et al. 2005, 2007, 2009a, b). Therefore, specific clinical symptoms solely due to *C. molenkampi* or *P. bonnei* (or *P. spinicirrus*) infection could not be properly determined. Another factor is relatively low worm loads of *C. molenkampi* or *P. bonnei* in reported human cases (Chai et al. 2005, 2007, 2009b); thus, the pathogenic effects and clinical symptoms due to lecithodendriid infections in such patients may be largely negligible. Innate as well as acquired immunity in human or animal infections have never been investigated.

7.2.7 Clinical Manifestations, Diagnosis and Treatment

The reported human cases had relatively low worm burdens; thus no significant clinical symptoms have been complained by the patients (Manning et al. 1971; Radomyos et al. 1984, 1994, 1998; Chai et al. 2005, 2007, 2009a). A tentative diagnosis can be made if small trematode eggs resembling the eggs of *Opisthorchis viverrini* or *Haplorchis taichui* but having clean shell surface are recovered in stool examinations. Potassium permanganate staining was reported to be useful for discrimination of *P. bonnei* eggs from those of *Opisthorchis viverrini* and *Haplorchis taichui* (Sukontason et al. 1999), and methylene blue staining was useful for discrimination of *C. molenkampi* eggs from those of *Opisthorchis viverrini* and *Haplorchis taichui* (Pasuralertsakul et al. 2005). However, worm recovery is needed to confirm a true infection and for specific diagnosis of the worms (to determine the worm species). Treatment can be done by praziquantel in a single dose of 10 mg/kg or 40 mg/kg (this high dose is required for treatment of the concomitant liver fluke *Opisthorchis viverrini* infection) (Radomyos et al. 1989).

7.2.8 Prevention and Control

To prevent lecithodendriid-like trematode infections, eating naiads or adults of dragon- or damselflies should be avoided. Killing naiads of such insects in water using insecticides or natural enemy may not be feasible and may be difficult to adopt in the field.

References

Agrawal V (1966) Two new trematodes from the intestine of a yellow bat, *Nycticeius kuhlii* from Lucknow, India. Trans Am Microscop Soc 85:559–563

Baer JG (1971) Trématodes de Rongeurs récoltés en Côte d'Ivore. Z Parasitenkd 37:226–254

Bhalerao GD (1926) XXXVI.-A new species of trematode from *Nycticejus pallidus*, with a key to the species of *Lecithodendrium*. Ann Mag Nat Hist 18:299–304

Braun M (1901) Zur Revision der Trematoden der Vögel. Zentralbl Bakteriol Parasitenkd Infekt (Abt 1) 29:560–568. in Germany

Caballero E, Grocott R (1952) Helminths from the Republic of Panama. II. A new trematode from the intestine of *Philander laniger pallidus* Thomas and key to the species of the genus *Phaneropsolus* Looss, 1899 (Trematoda: Lecithodendriidae). J Wash Acad Sci 42:388–391

Cain GD (1966) Helminth parasites of bats from Carlsbad Caverns, New Mexico. J Parasitol 52:351–357

Chai JY (2007) Intestinal flukes. In: Murrell KD, Fried B (eds) Food-borne parasitic Zoonoses, fish and plant-borne parasites. Springer, New York, pp 53–115

Chai JY, Park JH, Han ET et al (2005) Mixed infections with *Opisthorchis viverrini* and intestinal flukes in residents of Vientiane Municipality and Saravane Province in Laos. J Helminthol 79:283–289

Chai JY, Han ET, Guk SM et al (2007) High prevalence of liver and intestinal fluke infections among residents of Savannakhet Province, Laos. Korean J Parasitol 45:213–218

Chai JY, Shin EH, Lee SH et al (2009a) Foodborne intestinal flukes in Southeast Asia. Korean J Parasitol 47(suppl):S69–S102

Chai JY, Han ET, Shin EH et al (2009b) High prevalence of *Haplorchis taichui, Prosthodendrium molenkampi*, and other helminth infections among people in Khammouane province, Lao PDR. Korean J Parasitol 47:243–247

Chai JY, Yong TS, Eom KS et al (2010) Prevalence of the intestinal flukes *Haplorchis taichui* and *H. yokogawai* in a mountainous area of Phongsaly Province, Lao PDR. Korean J Parasitol 48:339–342

Chai JY, Sohn WM, Jung BK et al (2019) Trematode parasites recovered from residents after praziquantel treatment in Prey Vihear Province, Cambodia (manuscript in preparation)

Dollfus RP (1931) Amoenitates helminthologicae. I A propos de la création de *Lecithodendrium laguncula* Ch W Stiles et M O Nolan 1931. Ann Parasitol Hum Comp 9:483–484

Dollfus RP (1937) Sur *Distoma ascidia* P. J. Van Beneden 1873 (nec Linstow, nec Looss) et le genre *Prosthodendrium* R. Ph. Dullfus 1931 (Trematoda: Lecihodendriidae). Bull Mus Roy Hist Nat Belg 13:1–21

Dubois G (1962) Contribution à l'étude des trématodes de chiroptères. Revision du sous-genre *Paralecithodendrium* Odhner 1911. Rev Suisse Zool 69:385–407

Goodman JD, Panesar TS (1986) *Phaneropsolus* (*Phaneropsolus*) *perodictici* n. sp. (Trematoda: Lecithodendriidae) from the potto *Perodicticus potto* in Uganda. Trans Am Microscop Soc 105:76–78

Heyneman D, Macy RW (1962) Helminths reported from bats (Chiroptera) in Egypt with an illustrated key to the common flukes. J Egypt Public Health Assoc 37:109–142

Jha VR (1943) Three new distomes of the family Lecithodendriidae Odhner. Proc Nat Acad Sci India (Sect B Biol Sci) 13:9–19

Kaewkes S, Elkins DB, Sithithawarn P et al (1991a) Comparative studies on the morphology of the eggs of Opisthorchis viverrini and lecithodendriid trematodes. Southeast Asian J Trop Med Public Health 22:623–630

Kaewkes S, Elkins DB, Haswell-Elkinds MR et al (1991b) *Phaneropsolus spinicirrus* n. sp. (Digenea: Lecithodendriidae), a human parasite in Thailand. J Parasitol 77:514–516

Kaewkes S, Elkins DB, Pearson JC et al (1992) The taxonomy and epidemiology of minute intestinal flukes in northeast Thailand. The XIII International Congress for Tropical Medicine and Malaria, Pattaya, Thailand. Abstract Vol. 2:207

Kanarek G, Zalesny G, Sitko J et al (2014) Phylogenetic relationships and systematic position of the families Cortrematidae and Phaneropsolidae (Platyhelminthes: Digenea). Folia Parasitol 61:523–528

Kanarek G, Zalesny G, Sitko J et al (2017) The systematic position and structure of the genus *Leyogonimus* Ginetsinskaya, 1948 (Platyhelminthes: Digenea) with comments on the taxonomy of the superfamily Microphalloidea Ward, 1901. Acta Parasitol 62:617–624

Khotenovskii IA (1970) Family Pleurogenidae Looss, 1899. In Skrjabin KI (ed) Trematodes of Animals and Man. Academy of Sciences of the USSR. Vol. 23:126–316 (English translation from Russian by US Department of Agriculture and National Science Foundation, Amerind Publishing Co., New Delhi, India, 1982)

Kifune T, Sawada I, Lee WC (1983) Trematode parasites of two Korean bats. Med Bull Fukuoka Univ 10:3–8

Kifune T, Harada M, Sawada I et al (1997) Trematode parasites of five Korean bats. Med Bull Fukuoka Univ 24:225–232

Lie KJ (1951) Some human flukes from Indonesia. Doc Neerl Indon Morb Trop 3:105–116

Lie KJ (1962) *Phaneropsolus bonnei*. A trematode found in man in Indonesia, occurring in monkeys. Med J Malaya 17:83

Lotz JM, Font WF (1983) Review of the Lecithodendriidae (Trematoda) from *Eptesicus fuscus* in Wisconsin and Minnesota. Proc Helminthol Soc Wash 50:83–102

Lotz JM, Font WF (2008a) Family Lecithodendriidae Lühe, 1901. In: Bray RA, Gibson DI, Jones A (eds) Keys to the Trematoda, vol 3. CAB Publishing, Natural History Museum, London, pp 527–536

Lotz JM, Font WF (2008b) Family Phaneropsolidae Mehra, 1935. In: Bray RA, Gibson DI, Jones A (eds) Keys to the Trematoda, vol 3. CAB Publishing, Natural History Museum, London, pp 545–562

Lotz JM, Font WF (2008c) Family Pleurogenidae Looss, 1899. In: Bray RA, Gibson DI, Jones A (eds) Keys to the Trematoda, vol 3. CAB Publishing, Natural History Museum, London, pp 563–575

Lotz JM, Palmieri JR (1985) Lecithodendriidae (Trematoda) from *Taphozous melanopogon* (Chiroptera) in Perlis, Malaysia. Proc Helminthol Soc Wash 52:21–29
Lühe M (1901) Zwei neue Distomen aus indischen Anuren. Centralbl Bacteriol Parasitenkd Infektionskrankh I Abteilung 30:166–177
Macy RW (1936) Three new trematodes of Minnesota bats with a key to the genus *Prosthodendrium*. Trans Am Microscop Soc 55:352–359
Macy RW, Heyneman D, Kuntz RE (1961) Records of trematodes of the families Lecithodendriidae, Dicrocoeliidae, and Heterophyidae from Chiroptera collected in Egypt and Yemen, S. W. Arabia. Proc Helminthol Soc Wash 28:13–17
Manning GS (1971) The study of novel intestinal parasites in Thailand. Rep First Int Sem Southeast Asia Treaty Organ Med Res Lab 1:43–46
Manning GS, Lert prasert P (1973) Studies on the life cycle of *Phaneropsolus bonnei* and *Prosthodendrium molenkampi* in Thailand. Ann Trop Med Parasitol 67:361–365
Manning GS, Lertprasert P (1971) Four new trematodes of man from Thailand. Trans R Soc Trop Med Hyg 65:101–102
Manning GS, Viyanant V (1972) *Phaneropsolus bonnei* Lie Kian Joe, 1951, established as a naturally occurring parasite of humans. J Parasitol 58:652
Manning GS, Diggs CL, Viyanant V et al (1970a) Preliminary report on *Phaneropsolus bonnei* Lie Kian Joe, 1951 a newly discovered human intestinal fluke from northeastern Thailand. J Med Assoc Thailand 53:173–177
Manning GS, Anluchai T, Nganpanya B et al (1970b) Redescription of the intestinal fluke *Phaneropsolus bonnei* Lie Kian Joe, 1951 (Trematoda: Lecithodendriidae). Southeast Asian J Trop Med Public Health 1:492–495
Manning GS, Lertprasert P, Watanasirmkit K et al (1971) A description of newly discovered intestinal parasite endemic to northeastern Thailand. J Med Assoc Thailand 54:466–474
Matskási I (1973) Trematodes of bats in India. Parasit Hung 6:77–97
Matskási I (1980) Trematodes of bats in Iraq. Parasit Hung 13:7–12
McAllister CT, Bursey CR (2009) New host and geographic distribution records for helminths (Trematoda, Nematoda) in three species of vespertilionid bats (Chiroptera) from the pine ridge of Dawes County, Nebraska, U.S.A. Comp Parasitol 76:117–121
Mehra HR (1935) New trematodes of the family Lecithodendriidae Odhner, 1911, with a discussion on the classification of the family. Proc Acad Sci (UP, India) 5:99–121
Morozova DA, Zhokhov AE (2016) Finding of *Paralecithodendrium chilostomum* (Trematoda: Lecithodendriidae) in a roundleaf bat and in the African sharptooth catfish from Ethiopia. Parazitologiia 50:156–160 (in Russian)
Nahhas FM, Yang P, Uch S (2005) Digenetic trematodes of *Tadarida brasiliensis mexicana* (Chiroptera: Molossidae) and *Myotis californicus* (Chiroptera: Vespertilionidae) from Northern California, U.S.A. Comp Parasitol 73:196–199
Odening K (1959) Das Exkretionssystem von *Omphalometra* und *Brachycoelium* (Trematoda, Digenea) und die Taxonomie der Unterordnung Plagiorchiata. Z Parazitenkd 19:442–457
Odhner T (1911) Nordostafrikanische Trematoden, grösstentiels vom Weissen Nil. I. Fascioliden. Results of Swedish Zool Exped to Egypt and the White Nile 1901 under the Direction of L.A. Jägerskiöld 23A:1–170
Palmieri JR, Krishmasamy M (1978) *Phaneropsolus aspinosus* sp. n. (Lecithodendriidae: Phaneropsolinae) from the leaf monkey *Macaca fascicularis* (Raffles). J Helminthol 52:155–158
Pasuralertsakul S, Ngrenngarmlert W, Sripochang S et al (2005) Methylene blue staining method for identification of *Opisthorchis viverrini* egg. Southeast Asian J Trop Med Public Health 36.(suppl(4):107–109
Premvati (1958) *Primatotrema macacae* gen. nov., sp. nov. from Macaque Rhesus monkeys, and a redescription of *Phaneropsolus oviforme* Poirier (1886) Looss, 1899 (Lecithodendriidae). J Parasitol 44:639–642

Radomyos P, Bunnag D, Harinasuta T (1984) Worms recovered in stool following praziquantel treatment. Arzneim/Forch (Drug Res) 34:1186–1188

Radomyos P, Tadomyos B, Tungtrongchitr A (1994) Multi-infection with helminths in adults from northeast Thailand as determined by post-treatment fecal examination of adult worms. Trop Med Parasitol 45:133–135

Radomyos P, Wongsaroj T, Wilairatana P et al (1998) Opisthorchiasis and intestinal fluke infections in northern Thailand. Southeast Asian J Trop Med Public Health 29:123–127

Ramadan MM, Saoud MFA, Aly AH (1988) *Caprimolgorchis jhai* sp. nov. (Trematoda: Lecithodendriidae), an intestinal parasite of the Egyptian house spprow. Parasitol Res 75:28–30

Saoud MFA (1964) On a new trematode, *Tremajoannes buckleyi* gen. et sp. nov. (Lecithodendriidae) from Central American bats with some notes on *Phaneropsolus orbicularis* (Diesing, 1850) Braun, 1901. J Helminthol 38:97–108

Sayasone S, Vonghajack Y, Vanmany M et al (2009) Diversity of human intestinal helminthiasis in Lao PDR. Trans R Soc Trop Med Hyg 103:247–254

Sitko J (2013) *Microtrema barusi* gen. n. and sp. n. (Digenea: Phaneropsidae) from *Prunella modularis* (Aves, Passeriformes) in the Czech Republic. Helminthologia 50:43–45

Skarbilovich TS (1948) Family Lecithodendriidae Odhner, 1911. In: Skrjabin KI (ed) Trematodes of Animals and Man. Academy of Sciences of the USSR. Vol. 2:268–457 (English translation by Amerind Publishing Co., New Delhi, India, 1981)

Sukontason K, Piangjai S, Sukontason K et al (1999) Potassium permanganate staining for differentiation of the surface morphology of *Opisthorchis viverrini, Haplorchis taichui,* and *Phaneropsolus bonnei* eggs. Southeast Asian J Trop Med Public Health 30:371–374

Tesana S, Srisawangwonk T, Kaewkes S et al (1991) Eggshell morphology of the small eggs of human trematodes in Thailand. Southeast Asian J Trop Med Public Health 22:631–636

Travassos L (1921) Contribuições para o conhecimento da funa helmintolojica Brasileira. XV. Sobre as especies Brasileiras da familia Lecithodendriidae Odhner, 1911. Arch Esc Sup Agric Med Vet Nictheroy 5:73–79

Wijit A, Morakote N, Klinchid J (2013) High prevalence of haplorchiasis in Nan and Lampang Provinces, Thailand, proven by adult worm recovery from suspected opisthorchiasis cases. Korean J Parasitol 51:767–769

Yamaguti S (1958) Systema Helminthum. Vol. I. The digenetic trematodes of vertebrates (Part I). Interscience Publishers Inc, New York, pp 1–979

Yamaguti S (1971) Synopsis of digenetic trematodes of vertebrates, vol I. Keigaku Publishing Co., Tokyo, pp 1–1074

Yu SH, Mott KE (1994) Epidemiology and morbidity of food-borne intestinal trematode infections. Trop Dis Bull 91:R125–R152

Chapter 8
Plagiorchiids

8.1 Family Plagiorchiidae

The family Plagiorchiidae Lühe, 1901 are large digeneans parasitic in the intestine of tetrapod hosts (birds and mammals) and accidentally amphibians and reptiles; they can also be found in all parts of the digestive tract, including the mouth, cloaca, and also the bile-ducts, gall-bladder, liver, lungs, ureters, and kidneys (Tkach 2008). This is the family with most complex taxonomic history and most controversial content of all digeneans; about 150 genera have been included in this family but many of them werc either synonymized or transferred to other families (Tkach 2008). In addition, the family Plagiorchiidae have been over-inflated and may potentially contain at least 5 or 6 different families, and revisionary works are ongoing; however, 39 genera are listed in this family with *Plagiorchis* Lühe, 1899 the type genus (Tkach 2008). Regarding the content of subfamilies, there is disagreement between different authors; the use of subfamilies was mainly counterproductive, brought even more instability into the systematics of the family, and made identification of genera more difficult (Tkach 2008).

Morphologically, flukes of the family Plagiorchiidae are characterized by a slender or plump, elongated, elliptical, cylindrical, fusiform, lanceolate, or pyriform body, a well-defined cirrus sac containing a bipartite seminal vesicle, a uterus that passes between the testes or partly overlaps them, a Y-shaped excretory vesicle with short arms, a protonephridial formula of 2 [(3 + 3 + 3) + (3 + 3 + 3)] = 36, and arthropods as intermediate hosts (Tkach 2008). Flukes of the genus *Plagiorchis* are morphologically characterized by oval to fusiform, elliptical or somewhat elongate body, 2 obliquely located testes, an ovary at some distance from the ventral sucker, a cirrus sac barely extending posterior to the ventral sucker, and some uterine folds between 2 testes (Schell 1985; Tkach 2008). Morphologically close genera to *Plagiorchis* include *Microderma* Mehra, 1931, *Bilorchis* Mehra, 1937, *Skrjabinoplagiorchis* Petrov and Merkusheva, 1963, and *Choledocystus* Pereira and Cuocolo, 1941 (Tkach 2008). *Microderma* and *Bilorchis* are parasites of intestine or

J.-Y. Chai, *Human Intestinal Flukes*,
https://doi.org/10.1007/978-94-024-1704-3_8

gall-bladder of turtles and have a very elongate body (*Microderma*) and an ovary closely adjacent to the ventral sucker (*Bilorchis*) (Tkach 2008). *Skrjabinoplagiorchis* is parasitic in the gall-bladder, liver, and small intestine of Palaearctic mammals, and *Choledocystus* is parasitic in the gall-bladder, bile-ducts, and liver of Neotropical anuran amphibians; they are morphologically differed from *Plagiorchis* in that the body of *Skrjabinoplagiorchis* is almost round or oval, and that of *Choledocystus* is rounded-oval to fusiform (Tkach 2008).

8.2 *Plagiorchis*

Plagiorchis is the only known genus of the Plagiorchiidae infecting the human host. Yamaguti (1958, 1971) listed 55 species from mammals and 49 species from birds, with *P. vespertilionis* (Müller, 1780) Braun, 1900 [syn. *P. lima* (Rudolphi, 1809) Lühe, 1899] as the type species. Thereafter, at least more than ten species have been added, which included *Plagiorchis neomidis* Brendow, 1970, *Plagiorchis kyushuensis* Kifune and Sawada, 1979, *Plagiorchis corpulentus* Kifune and Sawada, 1979, and *Plagiorchis harinasutai* Radomyos et al., 1979 (Radomyos et al. 1979; Kifune et al. 1983; Faltýnkova and Haas 2006). Among them, 5 species, namely, *Plagiorchis muris, Plagiorchis javensis, Plagiorchis philippinensis, Plagiorchis harinasutai,* and *Plagiorchis vespertilionis*, have been reported to cause human infections (Table 3.1) (Chai et al. 2009; Chai 2014). Studies on *Plagiorchis* have been mainly focused on *P. muris* and *P. vespertilionis* because of their wide geographical distributions, high prevalences in the definitive hosts (McMullen 1937a; Tkach et al. 2000), and high possibility of zoonotic potential raised through an experimental human infection (*P. muris*) at an earlier time (McMullen 1937a).

For species identification of *Plagiorchis* spp., the location and morphology of the cirrus sac, cirrus, testes, ovary, and Mehlis' gland, the position and extents of vitellaria and uterus, and the sucker ratio are important (Sandground 1940; Sogandares-Bernal 1956; Kifune et al. 1983, 1997; Radomyos et al. 1989; Tkach et al. 2000). *P. muris* is morphologically differed from *P. vespertilionis* in several points. The adult worm has more extensive distribution of vitellaria, from the posterior extremity to the pharynx or prepharynx level in *P. muris* (Tanabe 1922; Hong et al. 1996), whereas only to the ventral sucker level in *P. vespertilionis* (Sogandares-Bernal 1956; Guk et al. 2007). The location of the ovary is also different, i.e., submedian, dextral, or nearly lateral in *P. muris* (Tanabe 1922; Hong et al. 1996) but median, or near the left side of the cirrus sac in *P. vespertilionis* (Tkach et al. 2000). The location of the 2 testes is also comparable, post-equatorial in *P. muris* (Asada et al. 1962; Hong et al. 1996) but pre-equatorial, equatorial, or slightly post-equatorial in *P. vespertilionis* (Sogandares-Bernal 1956; Tkach et al. 2000; Guk et al. 2007). *P. philippinensis* is differed from *P. muris* by its smaller body size, bigger ventral sucker size, and smaller egg size (Velasquez 1964). *P. javensis* differs from *P. muris* in its smaller body size, bigger ventral sucker, almost same size of the oral and ventral suckers (oral sucker is bigger than ventral sucker in *P. muris*), and bigger testes

(Velasquez 1964). The location of the ovary is just posterior to the rim of the ventral sucker in *P. javensis*, but the ovary is separated from the ventral sucker in *P. muris* (Sandground 1940; Radomyos et al. 1989). *P. harinasutai* is smaller in body size and egg size than *P. muris*, has the same size of the oral and ventral suckers unlike *P. muris*, and larger size of the ovary compared to testes (ovary is smaller in size than testes in *P. muris*) (Radomyos et al. 1989).

8.2.1 Plagiorchis muris

8.2.1.1 *Plagiorchis muris* (Tanabe, 1922) Schulz and Skworzow, 1931

[syn. *Lepoderma muris* Tanabe, 1922].

Taxonomy and Morphology

This species (Fig. 8.1a) was originally described from the intestine of experimental mice and rats fed the metacercariae encysted in *Lymnaea* sp. snails and aquatic insect *Chironomus pulmosus prasinus* larvae, nymphs, and adults under the name *Lepoderma muris* (Tanabe 1922; Komiya 1965). The name was later changed into *Plagiorchis muris* by Schulz and Skworzow (1931). Cercariae (xiphidiocercariae) and metacercariae (in the sporocysts) of a *Plagiorchis* species found large numbers in *Stagnicola emarginata angulata* snails at Douglas Lake, Michigan, USA were determined experimentally to be the larval stages of *P. muris* (McMullen 1937a, b). The metacercariae were also experimentally fed to a human volunteer, and eggs were detected in the feces from day 9 post-infection until day 37 post-infection (McMullen 1937a). Precocious metacercarial development of this species in the *Stagnicola* snails (in sporocysts) was reported in detail (McMullen 1938; Cort and Olivier 1943). However, Yamaguti (1975) was of opinion that the *P. muris* of McMullen may not be identical with *P. muris* reported from Japan. The reasons included that such precocious development of metacercariae in sporocysts had never been seen in *P. muris* in Japan, and natural emergence of cercariae occurred in Japanese *P. muris,* whereas it was not observed in *P. muris* of McMullen (Yamaguti 1971, 1975). He (Yamaguti 1975) further indicated that the natural definitive hosts of *P. muris* of the U.S. were mostly birds, including the robin, herring gull, nighthawk, and spotted sandpiper, whereas those in Japan were chiefly mammals, especially rodents, though experimentally sparrows and chicks were also susceptible for the Japanese type. This issue of *P. muris* in Japan and the U.S. needs further elucidation by ecological and molecular studies. In the meantime, the presence of *P. muris* has been reported from different parts of the world, including Asia (Japan, South Korea, and Vietnam) (Okabe and Shibue 1952; Seo et al. 1964, 1981; Anh et al. 2009), Middle East (Iran) (Mowlavi et al. 2013; Yousefi et al. 2014), Europe, including England, Ireland, Spain, and central Europe (Langlet and Fairley 1982; de Bellocq et al. 2003; Rogan et al. 2007), and Central America, particularly Mexico (Barragán-Sáenz et al. 2009).

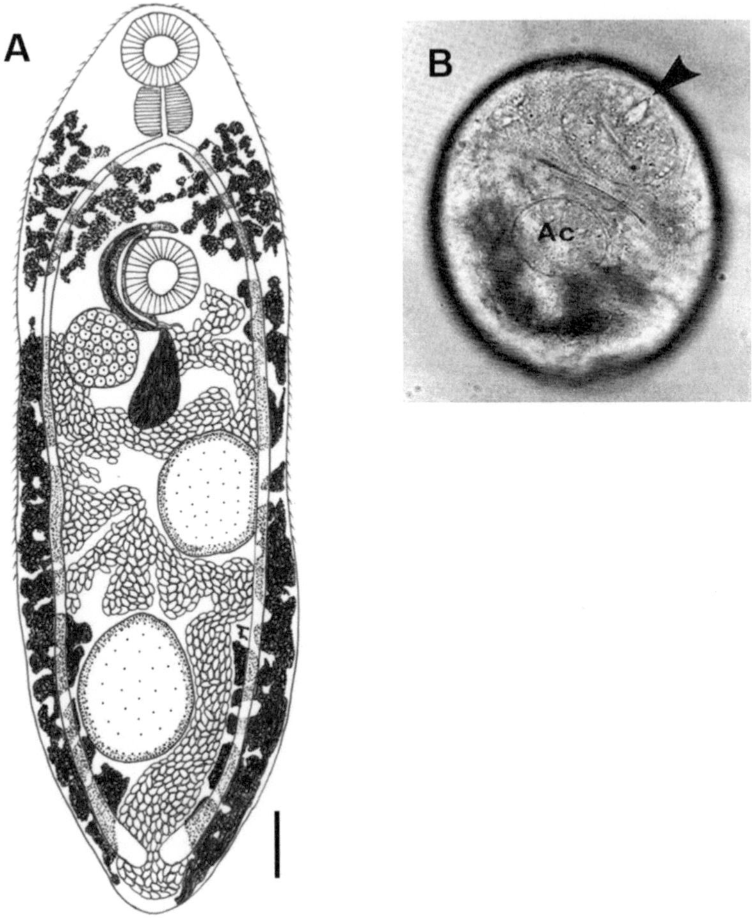

Fig. 8.1 *Plagiorchis muris*. (**a**) Line drawing of an adult fluke (original figure). Scale bar = 0.2 mm (**b**) Metacercaria (150 μm in diameter) collected from a dragonfly, *Sympetrum darwinianum*, in South Korea. (Courtesy of Prof. S.-J. Hong, Chung-Ang University, Seoul, South Korea)

A successful human experimental infection was reported for *P. muris* of the U.S. using the metacercariae precociously developed in sporocysts (McMullen 1937a). Natural human infection was first reported for *P. muris* of Japan in a 54-year-old man in Hiroshima Prefecture, Japan; the possible mode of infection was drinking a large amount of water containing aquatic insect larvae, a second intermediate host, during his swimming at the Lake Shin-no (Asada et al. 1962). Another natural human infection was reported from a 40-year-old Korean man who frequently consumed raw freshwater fish from a small stream near his village; these were presumed to be the source of infection, and metacercariae were detected in 3 species of fish collected there (Hong et al. 1996).

Adult flukes of *P. muris* are plump, but not oval, with almost parallel sides or somewhat spindle-shaped; they are broadest a little behind the equator (Yamaguti 1933). They are characterized by having a submedially or laterally located ovary, 2 obliquely tandem testes, and extensive distribution of vitellaria from the posterior end of the body to the level of the pharynx (Tanabe 1922; Chai et al. 2009). They are 2.1 mm long and 0.84 mm wide (Asada et al. 1962) or 2.85-2.99 mm long and 0.82-0.95 mm wide (Hong et al. 1996) in human infections and 0.8-2.2 mm long and 0.24-0.8 mm wide in rodents or 2.09 ± 0.18 mm long and 0.65 ± 0.03 mm wide in experimentally infected rats at day 28 post-infection (Hong et al. 1998). The size of uterine eggs in human infections was 32-38 (av. 34) μm long and 20-24 (av. 22) μm wide (Asada et al. 1962; Hong et al. 1996). The eggs in the feces of an experimentally infected human with *P. muris* of the U.S. were 38 μm long and 19 μm wide (McMullen 1937a). The sporocyst is 1150-1500 μm long and 200-280 μm wide (Tanabe 1922). The cercarial body is 248-275 μm long and 90-105 μm wide, and the tail is 135-143 μm long and 22-26 μm wide for Japanese *P. muris* (Yamashita 1952); the body is 240 μm long and 92 μm wide, and the tail is 190 μm long and 27 μm wide for *P. muris* of the U.S. (McMullen 1937b). The metacercarial cyst is 117-140 μm in diameter (Tanabe 1922; Komiya 1965) or 165-185 (av. 173) μm in a long radius for Japanese/Korean *P. muris* (Hong et al. 1998), whereas it measured about 200 in diameter for *P. muris* of the U.S. (McMullen 1937b). The metacercaria is equipped with a stylet on the oral sucker and U-shaped excretory bladder; the ventral sucker is smaller than the oral sucker (Hong et al. 1998).

Ultrastructural studies on *P. muris* have seldom been performed with the exception of 2 papers from South Korea (Hong 2009; Chae et al. 2012). Hong (2009) reported the ultrastructure of metacercariae, juvenile, and adult flukes of *P. muris*. In excysted metacercariae, the whole tegumental surface was covered with peg-like tegumental spines, ciliated sensory papillae (type I) were concentrated around the oral sucker, and non-ciliated sensory papillae (type II) were aligned on the lip of the oral and ventral suckers (Hong 2009). In juvenile flukes, cytoplasmic processes were band-shaped on the anterior body surface and velvety on the posterior body surface, and in adult flukes, the surface ultrastructure was generally similar to that of the metacercariae and juvenile flukes; distribution and types of the processes were differentiated into velvety forms, and the density of tegumental spines were reduced on the posterior half of the body (Hong 2009). In adult flukes, the cirrus was seen protruded from the genital pore which is located just anterior to the ventral sucker (Chae et al. 2012).

Life Cycle

This fluke has the life cycle stages of the eggs, miracidium, sporocyst (mother and daughter), cercaria, and metacercaria, and adult (Tanabe 1922; Yamaguti 1975). Freshwater snails, including *Lymnaea pervia* and *Lymnaea japonica* in Japan (Tanabe 1922; Yamaguti 1943; Yamashita 1952) and *Stagnicola emarginata angulata* in the U.S. (McMullen 1937a, b, 1938; Cort et al. 1937; Pratt and Barton 1941; Cort and Olivier 1943) were found to be the first intermediate host of *P. muris*. Two types of the life cycle were suggested for *P. muris* of Japan; one is the infection of the definitive host through the first intermediate host, *Lymnaea* snails, which not only contain the cercariae but also the metacercariae at the same time, and the second is the infection of the definitive host through the second intermediate host, including the larvae of insects (*Chironomous* sp.), shrimps, and small fishes (Tanabe 1922). Cercarial shedding occurred from *Lymnaea* snails in Japanese *P. muris*; the cercariae enter into other snails of the same species and insect larvae, shrimps, and fish (Yamaguti 1975), whereas cercarial shedding was not observed from *Stagnicola* sp. snails in the U.S. form of *P. muris,* and formation of metacercariae within the sporocysts (= precocious development of metacercariae) was a characteristic feature (McMullen 1937b, 1938).

The second intermediate host of *P. muris* ever recorded included snails (*Lymnaea* spp.), insects (non-biting midges *Chironomous pulmosus prasinus* and *Chironomous dorsalis*, mosquitoes *Culex pipiens pallens,* beach-fleas *Anisogammarus annandalei,* and dragonflies *Sympetrum eroticum, Sympetrum darwinianum, Sympetrum pedomontanum, Sympetrum infuscatum, Pantala flavoscens,* and *Calopteryx atrata*), shrimp (*Neocaridina denticulata*), and fish (*Misgurnus anguillicaudatus, Puntungia herzi, Liobagrus andersonii,* and *Odontobutis platycephala*) (Tanabe 1922; Hirasawa and Asada 1927; Yamashita 1952; Okabe and Shibue 1952; Komiya 1965; Hong et al. 1996, 1998, 1999). The metacercariae (Fig. 8.1b) encyst in the body cavity, muscles, and occasionally liver of these hosts (Komiya 1965). Metacercariae that are 1 week old or more are infective to the definitive hosts (McMullen 1937b).

The natural definitive hosts included rats (*Rattus rattus, Rattus rattus rufescens, Rattus alexandrinus,* and *Rattus norvegicus*), mice (*Apodemus agrarius* and *Apodemus speciosus*) (Tanabe 1922; Seo et al. 1964, 1981; Kasai 1978; Ito and Itagaki 2003; Chai et al. 2007), bats, sparrows (Hirasawa and Asada 1929), dogs (Miyata 1940, Kamiya et al. 1973), raccoons (Yamada 2000; Sato and Suzuki 2006; Matoba et al. 2006), and cats (Sohn and Chai 2005) for *P. muris* of Japan and South Korea. For *P. muris* of the U.S., birds, including the robin, herring gull, night-hawk, and spotted sandpiper were naturally infected (McMullen 1937b). Experimental hosts included mice, rats, sparrows, and chicks for *P. muris* of Japan and South Korea (Tanabe 1922; Yamaguti 1943, 1975; Yamashita 1952; Hong et al. 1996) and humans, mice, rats, and pigeons for *P. muris* of the U.S. (McMullen 1937a, b). In experimental albino rats, most of the flukes stay in the host small intestine until day 14 post-infection; however, thereafter (day 28 post-infection), the worm recovery became remarkably decreased (Hong et al. 1998).

Epidemiology and Geographical Distribution

The source of human infection included accidental drinking of a large amount of water contaminated with insect larvae (chironomid) infected with larvae of *P. muris* (Asada et al. 1962) or consumption of freshwater fish under raw or inadequately cooked conditions (Hong et al. 1996). Ingestion of raw or inadequately cooked *Lymnaea* sp. snails or drinking water contaminated with larvae of aquatic insects (including dragonfly larvae) may also cause infection in humans. The geographical distribution of this fluke is very wide, including Asia (Japan, South Korea, Taiwan, and Vietnam) to the Middle East (Iran) and western countries, including Mediterranean areas, central and northern Europe, and North and Central America (Fig. 8.2; Table 3.2).

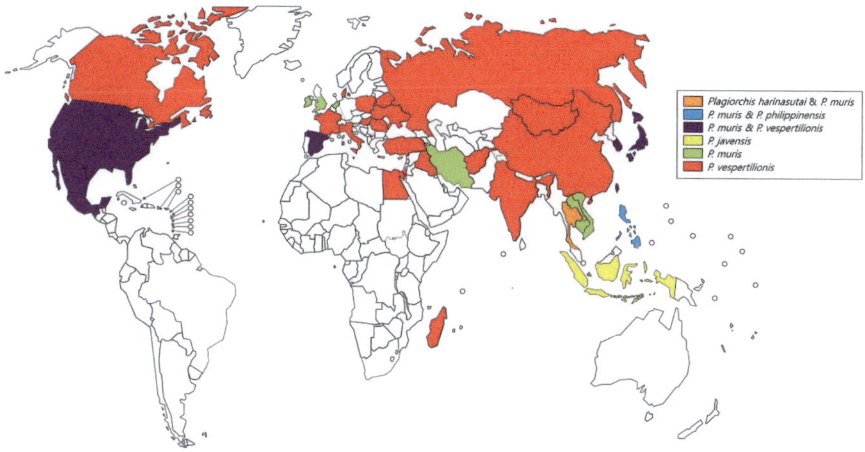

Fig. 8.2 Global distribution of *Plagiorchis* spp. (*P. muris, P. harinasutai, P. javensis, P. philippinensis,* and *P. vespertilionis*) based on the presence of their life cycles

Cambodia Mice *Mus caroli* and *Mus cookii* and rats *Rattus tanezumi* caught from Cambodia were found infected with *P. muris* (Chaisiri et al. 2015).

England Wood mice *Apodemus sylvaticus* caught from a wooded area of North Yorkshire were found to be infected with *P. muris*, which was the dominant intestinal trematode species occurring every year of sampling, with an average prevalence of 16.9% (42 of 248 mice examined) and mean worm burden of 2.03 (Rogan et al. 2007; Behnke et al. 2009).

Europe *P. muris* infection was found in wood mice *Apodemus sylvatus* in central Europe; detailed locality not described (de Bellocq et al. 2003).

Iran One (0.2%) of 500 rats *Rattus norvegicus* caught from an area of northern Teheran was found infected with 64 specimens of *P. muris* (Mowlavi et al. 2013). In addition, one (1.67%) of 60 wood mice *Apodemus sylvaticus* caught from suburban areas of Hamadan City, Western Iran were infected with 12 specimens of *P. muris* (Yousefi et al. 2014).

Ireland Wood mice *Apodemus sylvaticus* caught at Merlin Park which borders the eastern suburbs of Galway were found to be infected with *P. muris* in the small intestine; the infection rate was 1.2% (4 mice) out of 323 examined (Langley and Fairley 1982).

Japan *P. muris* was first described as a new species based on experimentally obtained adult flukes from mice and rats fed the metacercariae in *Lymnaea* snails or larvae and adults of non-biting midges *Chironomus pulmosus prasinus* (Tanabe 1922). Hirazawa and Asada (1929) reported various species of flying insects, including mosquitoes, as the second intermediate hosts and bats and sparrows as the natural definitive hosts. Miyata (1940) added dogs from Kobe Prefecture among the natural definitive hosts of *P. muris*; 16 adult specimens were recovered from 14 dogs examined. Yamaguti (1933) redescribed *P. muris* based on his own specimens obtained experimentally from albino rats. He (Yamaguti 1943) also redescribed the cercariae from *Lymnaea pervia* snails, and metacercarial cysts in *Chironomus* larvae were fed to obtain adult flukes at day 10 post-infection. Yamashita (1952) performed experimental studies on the morphology, behavior, infectivity, and artificial encystation of cercariae in vitro. Okabe and Shibue (1952) found a new second intermediate host, *Neocaridina denticulata* (shrimp); 15-day-old cysts were given to an albino rat, and 9 days later, 34 adult flukes were harvested from the small intestine. In 1962, the first report of a human infection with this fluke was made in Hiroshima Prefecture; the patient (54-year-old man) was infected with one specimen of *P. muris* together with 127 specimens of *Metagonimus yokogawai*, and drinking of a large amount of water containing the aquatic insect larvae during swimming at Lake Shin-no (Asada et al. 1962). Stray dogs in Sapporo, Hokkaido were found to be infected with *P. muris*, the prevalence being 19.7% (12/61) (Kamiya et al. 1973). Rats *Rattus norvegicus* and *Rattus rattus* in Sapporo, Hokkaido (Kasai 1978) and raccoons *Procyon lotor* in Sapporo and Nopporo, Hokkaido (Yamada 2000; Matoba et al. 2006) and Wakayama Prefecture (Sato and Suzuki 2006) were found to have intestinal infection with *P. muris*. Infection of a wild mouse *Apodemus speciosus* was also reported in Iwate Prefecture (Ito and Itagaki 2003).

South Korea The presence of *P. muris* in South Korea was first documented from 5 field mice (*Apodemus agrarius*) and one rat (*Rattus alexandrinus*) caught in central parts; total 33 adult specimens were harvested (Seo et al. 1964). Subsequently, one rat each from Yongin-gun and Hadong-gun were found infected with one specimens each of *P. muris* (Seo et al. 1981). Later, Hong et al. (1996) detected a naturally infected human (40-year-old man) from Hamyang-gun, Gyeongsangnam-do (Province); 3 mature specimens were recovered after treatment with praziquantel and purging. Three species of freshwater fish (*Puntungia herzi, Liobagrus andersonii*, and *Odontobutis platycephala*) caught near his village were confirmed to have the metacercariae of this fluke, and he stated that he used to consume freshwater fish raw (Hong et al. 1996). Hong et al. (1998) studied on recovery, growth, and development of worms in albino rats fed metacercariae isolated from dragonflies (*Sympetrum eroticum*); mature flukes were established in the lower part of the small intestine from day 5 post-infection, with a peak egg production at day 14 post-infection, until day 28 post-infection. Hong et al. (1999) added 5 more species of dragonflies (*Sympetrum darwinianum, Sympetrum pedomontanum, Sympetrum infuscatum, Pantala flavoscens,* and *Calopteryx atrata*) caught from different part of South Korea as new second intermediate hosts of *P. muris*. Lee et al. (2004) studied on the molecular phylogeny of *P. muris* based on sequences of partial 28S D1 rDNA and mitochondrial cytochrome *c* oxidase subunit I (mtCOI). The 28S D1 tree of *P. muris* showed the closest relation with that of *Plagiorchis elegans* (this was suggested to be a synonym of *P. muris* by Krasnolobova, 1977), followed by *Plagiorchis koreanus, Plagiorchis muelleri*, and *P. vespertilionis* (Tkach et al. 2000; Lee et al. 2004). Hong (2009) studied on the surface ultrastructure of developmental stages of *P. muris*, and Chae et al. (2012) reported light and scanning electron microscopic morphologies of *P. muris* obtained from experimental mice fed metacercariae from the dragonfly *Sympetrum darwinianum*. Feral cats (Sohn and Chai 2005; Chai et al. 2013) and wild mice (Chai et al. 2007; Lee et al. 2013; Sohn et al. 2014) caught from various localities were found to be infected with *P. muris*.

Lao PDR Mice *Mus caroli* and *Mus cookii* and rats *Rattus tanezumi* caught from Lao PDR were found infected with *P. muris* (Chaisiri et al. 2015).

Mexico Cercariae of *P. muris* were detected in hepatopancreas of *Lymnaea stagnalis* snails (2/572; 0.35%) collected in Lake Chicnahuapan (Barragán-Sáenz et al. 2009).

Netherlands Brown rats *Rattus norvegicus* caught from a rural environment (Friesland) were found infected with *P. muris*, with the prevalence of 4.1% (Franssen et al. 2016).

The Philippines Rats *Rattus norvegicus* and *Rattus mindanensis* caught from Manila and 10 provinces were infected with *P. muris* (Jueco and Zabala 1990).

Spain *P. muris* infection was found in wood mice *Apodemus sylvatus* (de Bellocq et al. 2003).

Taiwan Adult specimens of *P. muris* were recovered from the small intestine of rats *Rattus rattus* collected from different areas (Fischthal and Kuntz 1975).

Thailand Mice *Mus caroli* and *Mus cookii* and rats *Rattus tanezumi* caught from Thailand were found infected with *P. muris* (Chaisiri et al. 2015).

USA *Stagnicola emarginata angulata* snails collected at the University of Michigan Biological Station at Douglas Lake were found infected with a common xiphidiocercaria (*P. muris*) together with numerous metacercariae of the same species in the sporocysts (McMullen 1937a). The metacercarial cysts were experimentally fed to rats, mice, and pigions, and adult flukes were recovered and identified as *P. muris*; experimental infection of a human was also successful, and eggs were detected in feces until day 37 post-infection (McMullen 1937a). Natural definitive hosts in this area were avian species, including the robin, herring gull, night-hawk, and spotted sandpiper (McMullen 1937b). Precocious development of the metacercariae inside the sporocyst was recognized, but cercarial emergence from the snail was not observed (McMullen 1937b, 1938). The development of larval stages of *P. muris* in the snail host was studied in detail; the morphology of mother and daughter (immature and mature) sporocysts was described (Cort and Olivier 1943). Ash (1962) detected *P. muris* infection in a rat from the Island of Oahu, Hawaii. Kinsella (1974) reported infection of cotton rats (*Sigmodon hispidus*) from saltwater marshes in Florida with *P. muris*. One migrant yellowleg (*Tringa melanoleuca*) shot in Texas harboured specimens of *P. muris* (Secord and Canaris 1993). Yamaguti (1975) mentioned that *P. muris* reported from the U.S. may be a different species from the original *P. muris* reported from Japan; this issue needs verification in the near future.

Vietnam Rats *Rattus sladeni* caught from southern parts of Vietnam were found infected with *P. muris* (Nguyen 1991). One of 25 dogs necropsied in Nam Dinh Province, a northern area, was found infected with 4 adult specimens of *P. muris* (Anh et al. 2009).

8.2.2 Plagiorchis javensis

8.2.2.1 *Plagiorchis javensis* Sandground, 1940

Taxonomy and Morphology

This plagiorchiid species (Fig. 8.3) was originally described from the small intestine of a post-mortem human case (a Javanese native) in Indonesia based on a single worm who was also heavily infected with *Echinostoma ilocanum* (Sandground 1940). Later 2 more cases, each with a single specimen, were found in Indonesia, at autopsy of an Indonesian and a Chinese in a hospital in Java (Lie and Bras 1950; Yu and Mott 1994). Lie (1951) added another human case (man) in Indonesia with 158 specimens of *P. javensis* and a specimen of *Plagiorchis* sp. (species undetermined). Adult flukes of *P. javensis* are smaller in body size (1.82 mm long and 0.68 mm wide) than *P. muris*, but has a bigger ventral sucker and almost the same size of the oral and ventral sucker (oral sucker is bigger than ventral sucker in *P. muris*), and bigger testes (Sandground 1940; Velasquez 1964). In *P. javensis,* the ovary is located just posterior to the rim of the ventral sucker (Sandground 1940); however, in *P. muris* and the other zoonotic *Plagiorchis* spp., the ovary is separately located from the ventral sucker (Radomyos et al. 1989; Hong et al. 1996; Guk et al. 2007). The egg size of *P. javensis* is 36 μm long and 22-24 μm wide (Sandground 1940). The cercariae and metacercariae have never been described.

Life Cycle

Freshwater snails are presumed to be the first intermediate host, and snails, larval insects, or fish may be the second intermediate host (studies not done). Birds and bats seem to be natural definitive hosts (Yu and Mott 1994).

Epidemiology and Geographical Distribution

The mode of human infection with *P. javensis* is unknown but insect larvae may be a source of infection (Yu and Mott 1994). This fluke is so far known to be distributed only in Indonesia (Fig. 8.2; Table 3.2) (Sandground 1940; Lie and Bras 1950).

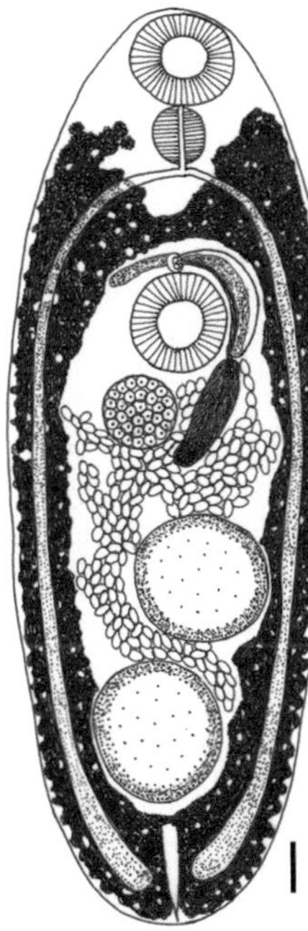

Fig. 8.3 Line drawing of an adult worm of *Plagiorchis javensis*. Modified from the figure in Sandground (1940) Rev Med Trop Parasitol 6:207–211. Scale bar = 0.1 mm

Indonesia A case of natural human infection with *P. javensis* was first reported at post-mortem necropsy of a man who was an inmate of a rural psychopathic asylum; he also had a heavy *Echinostoma ilocanum* infection (Sandground 1940). Subsequently, 2 additional human infections were found at autopsy in Java (Lie and Bras 1950), and 1 more human case was reported by Lie (1951).

8.2.3 Plagiorchis philippinensis

8.2.3.1 *Plagiorchis philippinensis* Sandground, 1940

[syn. *Plagiorchis* sp. of Africa and Garcia, 1937].

Taxonomy and Morphology
Five specimens of a plagiorchiid fluke which was named as *Plagiorchis* sp. were recovered by Africa and Garcia (1937) in Manila, the Philippines from the small intestine of a native Ilocanoan man at autopsy, together with specimens of *Echinostoma ilocanum* and *Microphallus brevicaeca* (syn. *Spelotrema brevicaeca*) (Beaver et al. 1984). The inhabitants of the local areas eat the grubs of certain insects which is believed to be the second intermediate host (Beaver et al. 1984). This fluke (Fig. 8.4) was subsequently named as *Plagiorchis philippinensis* by Sandground (1940) because of the characteristic location of the ovary just under (or dorsal to) the acetabular rim, whereas in most other species, including *P. muris* and *P.*

Fig. 8.4 Line drawing of an adult worm of *Plagiorchis philippinensis*. Redrawn from the figure in Skrjabin and Antipin (1958) Trematodes and Animals and Man (ed. Skrjabin KI). Moscow-Leningrad, Russia, Vol XIV: 73–620. Scale bar = 0.1 mm

javensis, the ovary is quite distantly separated from the cirrus which is less lunate in form that the other species (Sandground 1940; Skrjabin and Antipin 1958). No other reports have appeared since then until Eduardo and Lee (2006) detected 1.27% prevalence among rats in Bay, Laguna (Eduardo et al. 2008). Adult flukes are 1.5-2.0 mm long and 0.385 mm wide, and their eggs are 28-30 μm long and 19-21 μm wide (Africa and Garcia 1937). The cercariae and metacercariae have never been discovered.

Life Cycle

Insect larvae may be a second intermediate host, and reservoir hosts are rats and possibly birds (Yu and Mott 1994).

Epidemiology and Geographical Distribution

Only one human case was reported in the Philippines, and the mode of human infection seems to be raw eating of insect larvae (Beaver et al. 1984). The geographical distribution of this fluke is confined to the Philippines (Fig. 8.2; Table 3.2).

The Philippines Africa and Garcia (1937) detected this fluke (5 specimens) for the first time in Manila from a native Ilocanoan man at autopsy which was named as *Plagiorchis* sp. Sandground (1940) named this fluke as *P. philippinensis* based on its characteristic morphological features. Eduardo and Lee (2006) detected 1.27% prevalence among rats in Bay, Laguna.

8.2.4 Plagiorchis harinasutai

8.2.4.1 *Plagiorchis harinasutai* Radomyos, Bunnag and Harinasuta, 1989

Taxonomy and Morphology

This plagiorchiid species (Fig. 8.5) was reported as a new species based on 6 adult flukes recovered from 4 human cases in Thailand; the worms were recovered during a clinical trial of praziquantel treatment for opisthorchiasis patients (Radomyos et al. 1989). The patients were 3 men and a woman aged 28-37 years of age residing in northeastern parts of Thailand (Radomyos et al. 1989). One more human case (man) was detected by recovery of adult worms in northeastern Thailand (Radomyos et al. 1994). Two more human cases were detected from Mae Hong Son area by worm recovery but the worms were described just as plagiorchid fluke (Radomyos et al. 1998), which are considered to be *P. harinasutai.*

Adult flukes (1.87 mm long and 0.61 mm wide) of *P. harinasutai* differ from those of *P. muris* and *P. philippinensis* in that its oral and ventral suckers are the same size, whereas in the latter 2 species the oral sucker is bigger than the ventral sucker (Radomyos et al. 1989). In *P. harinasutai*, the ovary is larger than its testes but in *P. muris, P. javensis,* and *P. philippinensis* the ovary is smaller than their testes; the vitelline follicles of *P. harinasutai* do not unite in front of the ventral sucker but those of *P. muris* and *P. javensis* unite in front of the ventral sucker (Radomyos et al. 1989). The eggs of *P. harinasutai* are 33-34 μm long and 17-18 μm wide (Africa and Garcia 1937). The cercariae and metacercariae have not been discovered.

Life Cycle

The life cycle of this species has never been studied; however, freshwater snails such as *Lymnaea* spp. are presumed to be the first intermediate host, and the same snails, insect larvae, and fish are suspected as the second intermediate hosts. Rodents, bats, and birds may be the natural definitive hosts.

Epidemiology and Geographical Distribution

Eating raw snails, insect larvae, or fish may be the mode of human infection. This species is so far known to be distributed only in Thailand (Fig. 8.2; Table 3.2) (Radomyos et al. 1989, 1994, 1998).

Thailand *P. harinasutai* was first detected from 4 patients infected with *Opisthorchis viverrini* in northeastern parts of Thailand; during praziquantel treatment 1-2 specimens each of *P. harinasutai* were incidentally collected from their diarrheic stools (Radomyos et al. 1989). One (Radomyos et al. 1994) and 2 (Radomyos et al. 1998) additional human infections were detected in northeastern parts of Thailand.

Fig. 8.5 Line drawing of an adult worm of *Plagiorchis harinasutai*. Redrawn from the figure in Radomyos et al. (1989) Southeast Asian J Trop Med Public Health 20:101-107. Scale bar = 2 mm

8.2.5 Plagiorchis vespertilionis

8.2.5.1 *Plagiorchis vespertilionis* (Müller, 1780) Braun, 1900

[syn. *Fasciola vespertilionis* Müller, 1780; *Distoma lima* Rudolphi, 1809; *Plagiorchis lima* (Rudolphi, 1809) Lühe, 1899; *Plagiorchis obensis* Schulz, 1932; *Plagiorchis magnacotylus* Park, 1939; *Plagiorchis eptesici* Ogata, 1940; *Plagiorchis vespertilionis parorchis* Macy, 1960; *Plagiorchis amplehaustoria* Mituch, 1964].

Taxonomy and Morphology

This plagiorchiid species (Fig. 8.6) was originally described from the brown long-eared bat *Plecotus auritus* (syn. *Vespertilio auritus*) in Denmark by Müller in 1780 and 1784 under the name *Fasciola vespertilionis* (Sogandares-Bernal 1956; Tkach et al. 2000). Braun (1900) found this fluke again in Europe and renamed it as *Plagiorchis vespertilionis*. Before this, Rudolphi described *Distoma lima* in 1809, which was later renamed as *Plagiorchis lima* by Lühe in 1899 (Yamaguti 1958). However, Dubois (1955) regarded this as a synonym of *P. vespertilionis*. Many other species described under the names *Plagiorchis obensis* Schulz, 1932, *Plagiorchis magnacotylus* Park, 1939, *Plagiorchis eptesici* Ogata, 1940, and *Plagiorchis amplehaustoria* Mituch, 1964 were regarded as synonyms of *P. vespertilionis* (Sogandares-Bernal 1956; Tkach et al. 2000). On the other hand, almost all *Plagiorchis* worms found by different authors in bats throughout Europe and other parts of the Holarctic region were simply assigned as *P. vespertilionis*, and some of

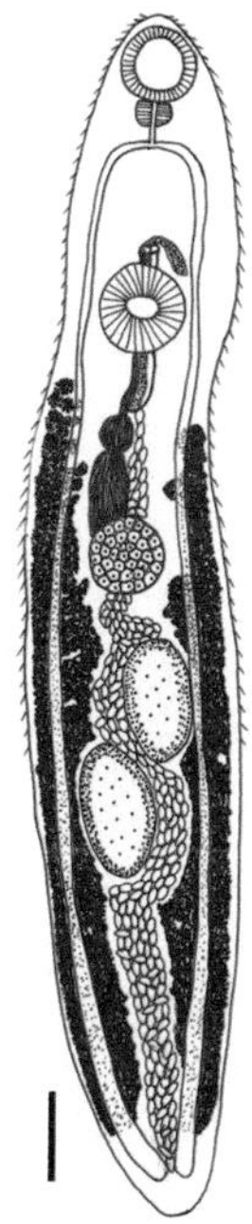

Fig. 8.6 Line drawing of an adult worm of *Plagiorchis vespertilionis*. Redrawn from the figure in Tkach et al. (2000) Syst Parasitol 47:9–22. Scale bar = 0.2 mm

them may be different species (Tkach et al. 2000). Using morphological and molecular data, Tkach et al. (2000) have clearly differentiated *Plagiorchis* spp. in European bats into several species, including *P. vespertilionis, P. elegans* (Rudolphi, 1802), *P. koreanus* Ogata, 1938, and *P. muelleri* Tkach and Sharpilo, 1990.

Stafford (1905) reported *P. vespertilionis* from Canadian vertebrates, and Caballero (1940) described this species in Mexico. A subspecies named *P. vespertilionis parorchis* (later synonymized with *P. vespertilionis* by Nahhas et al. 2005) was reported from bats (natural infection) and mice (experimental infection) in Oregon, U.S. (Macy 1960). Tkach et al. (2000) questioned about the presence of *P. vespertilionis* in the Nearctic and American Continent, considering only European forms to be true representatives of *P. vespertilionis*. However, reports of this species from areas other than Europe should be reconsidered until firm evidences are drawn out. Here, the author tentatively designated the *P. vespertilionis* reported from European bats as "European type", and the *P. vespertilionis* reported from the U.S. and Canada as "American type".

There has been only one case report of human infection with *P. vespertilionis*; the patient was a 34-year-old male who lived in a coastal village of a southwestern part of South Korea (Guk et al. 2007). Only one worm was recovered after treatment with praziquantel and purging with magnesium salt for treatment of *Gymnophalloides seoi* infection which is prevalent in this village (Guk et al. 2007). The patient had habitually eaten raw flesh of snakehead mullet and gobies caught nearby his village (Guk et al. 2007); however, it is uncertain whether these fish were truly the source of infection with *P. vespertilionis*.

Adult flukes of *P. vespertilionis* are 2.6 mm long and 0.7 mm wide (human case) (Guk et al. 2007) or 2.28-4.14 (mean 3.27) mm wide and 0.24-0.54 (mean 0.45) mm wide in specimens from European bats (Tkach et al. 2000) and 2.68-4.80 mm long and 0.80-1.58 mm wide in specimens from Korean bats (Sogandares-Bernal 1956). Eggs are 32.5 ± 1.3 μm long and 17.5 ± 0.5 μm wide (uterine eggs in human case) (Guk et al. 2007), 29-34 (mean 32) μm long and 16-21 (mean 18) μm wide in specimens from European bats (Tkach et al. 2000), or 37 μm long and 18 μm wide in specimens from Korean bats (Sogandares-Bernal 1956). The cercaria of *P. vespertilionis parorchis* (a synonym of *P. vespertilionis*) is a xiphidiocercarial type; its body is 220 μm long and 92 μm wide, and the tail is 150 μm long and 28 μm wide (Macy 1960). Its sporocyst is elongated, yellowish orange, and 700 μm long and 110 μm wide (Macy 1960). The metacercarial cyst are 170 μm long and 126 μm wide, and the metacercaria is equipped with a stylet on its oral sucker but sometimes disappear soon after encystment in the insect larvae (Macy 1960).

Life Cycle

In the European type of *P. vespertilionis*, the life cycle has been poorly known; only natural definitive hosts (various species of bats) have been reported (Tkach et al. 2000). In the American type, the life cycle studies were performed by Macy (1960), and numerous reports are available regarding the natural definitive hosts and geographical localities of the parasites in North America (Ching et al. 2000; Nahhas et al. 2005; McAllister and Bursey 2009; Eckerlin 2011).

The snail host of the American type is an aquatic snail *Lymnaea stagnalis*, and the second hosts included mosquito larvae, caddis-fly larvae, mayfly larvae, and dragonfly nymphs (Macy 1960). In the snail host, cercariae are produced in sporocysts; however, no precocious development of metacercariae inside the sporocyst, which occurs in a related species *P. muris* (McMullen 1937b, 1938), was found. The cercariae showed very little photosensitivity, and they often swam near the bottom of the container and frequently crept for brief periods; at room temperature they may live as long as 36 h and be able to penetrate mosquito larvae (Macy 1960). The cercariae can emerge almost entirely at night; even more than during the daytime (Macy 1960). Insect larvae were readily penetrated by the cercariae, and encystment ensued shortly thereafter, within 30–45 min with the formation of a thin cyst wall; cysts formed in mosquito larvae (*Culex* sp.) remained viable in the pupae even when the pupae were kept for an extended period at 4 °C (Macy 1960). Seven-day-old metacercariae in caddis-fly larvae, mayfly larvae, and dragonfly nymphs were infective when fed to experimental mice; after 7 days in mice the worms were fully developed but egg production occurred from day 10 post-infection (Macy 1960).

The natural definitive hosts of *P. vespertilionis* are bats and rodents, in both European and American types as well as in those occurring in other continents including Asia (Sogandares-Bernal 1956; Macy 1960; Tkach et al. 2000). Important species of bats involved included *Asellia tridens, Barbastella barbastella, Coelops frithii, Eptesicus fuscus, Eptesicus serotinus, Lasionycteris noctivagans, Lasiurus borealis, Lasiurus cinereus, Miniopterus schreibersi, Myotis aurescense, Myotis adversus, Myotis leibii Myotis capaccinii, Myotis californicus, Myotis ciliolarum,*

Myotis daubentoni, Myotis emarginatus, Myotis keenii, Myotis longipes, Myotis lucifugus, Myotis macrodactylus, Myotis mystacinus, Myotis sodalis, Myotis volans, Nyctalus noctyla, Pipistrellus abramus, Pipistrellus pipistrellus, Pipistrellus kuhli, Pipistellus subflavus, Plecotus auritus (syn. *Vespertilio auritus*), *Plecotus murinus* (syn. *Vespertilio murinus*), *Plecotus superans* (syn. *Vespertilio superans*), *Rhinolophus blasii, Rhinolophus euryale, Rhinolophus ferrum-equinum, Rhinolophus hipposideros, Rhinolophus mehelyi, Tadarida brasiliensis,* and *Taphozous nudiventris* (Sogandares-Bernal 1956; Soltys 1959; Macy 1960; Dancáu and Capuse 1966; Nickel and Hansen 1967; Combes and Clerc 1970; Matskási 1973, 1980; Webster and Casey 1973; Pistole 1988; Kifune et al. 1997; Tkach et al. 2000; Nahhas et al. 2005; McAllister and Bursey 2009; Sümer and Yildirimhan 2018). A rodent host, gerbil *Meriones persicus* was also found to be a natural definitive host (Groschaft and Tenora 1971). Racoon dogs (Ching et al. 2000), and hares, rodents, and cats (Shimalov et al. 2002) were also recorded as the natural definitive hosts for *P. vespertilionis*. Experimental definitive hosts included mice *Mus musculus* (Macy 1960).

Epidemiology and Geographical Distribution

The source of human infection with *P. vespertilionis* reported from South Korea is unknown (Guk et al. 2007). The patient used to eat raw mullet and goby; however, the fish seems to be a less possible source of infection (Guk et al. 2007). It is presumed that the patient may have accidentally drunk water containing insect larvae infected with the metacercariae. Currently, the geographical distribution of this fluke is almost cosmopolitan (Fig. 8.2; Table 3.2) according to available literature, which includes Denmark (Tkach et al. 2000), Spain (Mészáros and Mas-Coma 1980; Alvarez et al. 1991; Feliu et al. 2006), France (Combes and Clerc 1970), Poland (Soltys 1959), Turkey (Sümer and Yildirimhan 2017, 2018), Italy (Ricci 1995), Hungary (Matskási 1967), Romania (Dancáu and Capuse 1966), Russia (Lagocheva 1974; Krasnolobova 1977; Kirilov et al. 2012), Belarus (Shimalov et al. 2002), Ukraine (Tkach et al. 2000), Egypt (Yamaguti 1971), Madagascar (Yamaguti 1971), Afghanistan (Groschaft and Tenora 1971), Iraq (Mahmoud and Jawdat 1982; Matskási 1980), India (Matskási 1973), South Korea (Sogandares-Bernal 1956; Kifune et al. 1997; Guk et al. 2007), Japan (Kagei and Sawada 1983), Taiwan (Fischthal and Kuntz 1981), China (Ono 1934; Ma et al. 2008; Li and Wu 2011), Mongolia (Tinnin et al. 2008), Canada (Stafford 1905; Webster and Casey 1973; Ching et al. 2000), Mexico (Caballero 1940), and U.S. (Macy 1960; Nickel and Hansen 1967; Blankespoor and Ulmer 1970; Lotz and Font 1985, 1991; Pistole 1988; Nahhas et al. 2005; McAllister and Bursey 2009; Eckerlin 2011).

Afghanistan A gerbil *Meriones persiscus*, a rodent species, was found to be infected with *P. vespertilionis* (Groschaft and Tenora 1971).

Belarus *P. vespertilionis* was found in *Myotis daubentoni* and *Plecotus auritus* bats in the south-west part of Belarus; this species was also found in hares, rodents, and cats (Shimalov et al. 2002).

Canada Trematode fauna in Canadian bats *Myotis leibii* included *P. vespertilionis* (Stafford 1905). Six of 9 species of bats from British Columbia examined for their intestinal parasites were found infected with *P. vespertilionis* (Webster and Casey 1973). Two (2.4%) of 82 racoon dogs captured from British Columbia were also found to be infected with *P. vespertilionis* (Ching et al. 2000).

China Adult worms of *P. vespertilionis* were detected from bats in Manchuria (Ono 1934). In Henan Province, 2 (3.4%) of 59 bats belonging to 4 genera were found infected with *P. vespertilionis* (Ma et al. 2008). In 3 localities of Guangdong Province, *P. vespertilionis* infection was found in 10% of 6 bat species examined (Li and Wu 2011).

Denmark In 1780 and 1784, *P. vespertilionis* (under the name *Fasciola vespertilionis*) was first described based on specimens obtained from the intestine of bats (*Plecotus auritus*) (Tkach et al. 2000).

Egypt Egypt is included among the list of countries where *P. vespertilionis* has been recorded (Yamaguti 1958, 1971).

France Helminth fauna of ten bat species caught from Pyrénées was studied; 8 of the 10 species were found infected with *P. vespertilionis* (Combes and Clerc 1970).

Hungary A systematico-faunistical survey was performed on trematodes infecting Hungarian bats; 15 digenean species, including *P. vespertilionis*, were recorded from 22 localities (Matskási 1967).

India *P. vespertilionis* specimens were collected from the rectum of 4 species of Indian bats (Matskási 1973).

Iraq Alcohol-fixed intestines of bats from Iraq were brought to Hungary and intestinal parasites were recovered; *P. vespertilionis* was collected from 5 species of bats, *Miniopterus schreibersi, Pipistrellus kuhli, Asellia tridens, Rhinolophus mehelyi,* and *Taphozous nudiventris* (Matskási 1980). *P. vespertilionis* was found again in *Taphozous nudiventris* bats from southern Iraq (Mahmoud and Jawdat 1982).

Italy A total of 289 bats belonging to 13 species were examined for their intestinal helminths; special attention was given to *P. verspertilionis* (Ricci 1995).

Japan *P. vespertilionis* is recorded among the helminth fauna of bats in Japan (Kagei and Sawada 1983).

South Korea Adult specimens of *P. vespertilionis* were recovered from the small intestine of the Korean bats *Plecotus superans* and *Pipistrellus* sp. (Sogandares-Bernal 1956). This fluke was found again in the intestine of another species of bat *Myotis macrodactylus* from Geochang-gun, Gyeongsangnam-do Province (Kifune et al. 1997). Subsequently, the only human case known so far was found in a 34-year-old man from Haenam-gun, Jeollanam-do Province; only one adult specimen was recovered together with numerous specimens of gymnophallid and heterophyid flukes (Guk et al. 2007).

Madagascar Madagascar is included among the list of countries where *P. vespertilionis* has been recorded (Yamaguti 1971).

Mexico *P. vespertilionis* was first reported in bats *Tadarida brasiliensis* from Chapultepec, Mexico City (Caballero 1940, 1942); however, subsequently this fluke has been never collected again from any bat species in Mexico despite significant survey effort (Guzmán-Carnejo et al. 2003).

Mongolia Two species of bats *Plecotus murinus* (syn. *Vespertilio murinus*) and *Eptesicus gobiensis* caught from Ulaan Tsutgaalan were found infected with *P. vespertilionis* (Tinnin et al. 2008).

Poland *P. vespertilionis* was detected in 11 bat species caught from Lublin Palatinate. (Soltys 1959).

Romania *P. vespertilionis* specimens were recovered from various bat species, including the new hosts *Rhinolophus blasii* and *Myotis capaccinii* (Dancáu and Capuse 1966).

Russia Seven species of bats from Kirgizia were found infected with *P. vespertilionis* (Lagocheva 1974). In the Middle Volga Region, *P. vespertilionis* was found in bats and also in other animal species (Kirilov et al. 2012).

Spain The presence of *P. vespertilionis* in Spanish bats was first documented by López-Neyra (1947) which was followed by several other papers. Mészáros and Mas-Coma (1980) also found *P. vespertilionis* in bats *Miniopterus schreibersi* from Catalonia. Alvarez et al. (1991) detected *P. vespertilionis* infection in 2 bat species captured from northwest Spain. This fluke species is distributed across the entire Iberian Peninsula (Feliu et al. 2006).

Taiwan *P. vespertilionis* adult specimens were recovered from the small intestine and liver of Taiwan bats, including the long-winged bat *Miniopterus schreibersi* (Fischthal and Kuntz 1981).

Turkey Helminth parasites of the whiskered brown bats *Myotis aurescens* were studied in a forested area of Bursa Province; 2 (13.3%) of 15 bats examined were found infected with *P. vespertilionis* (Sümer and Yildirimhan 2018). DNA sequencing of partial (613 bp) nuclear ribosomal gene (28S rDNA) was obtained and compared with other *Plagiorchis* spp., and *Lecithodendrium* spp., and *Prosthodendrium* spp. (Sümer and Yildirimhan 2017).

Ukraine Specimens of *P. vespertilionis* collected from bats *Barbastella barbastella* and *Plecotus auritus* in Ukraine were used to describe the neotype of *P. vespertilionis*; the morphological details of *P. vespertilionis* were re-described (Tkach et al. 2000).

USA A subspecies *P. vespertilionis parorchis* was newly reported from Portland, Oregon (Macy 1960). This new subspecies was later synonymized with *P. vespertilionis* (Nahhas et al. 2005), although Tkach et al. (2000) suggested this American form to be a separate species. Its first intermediate host was freshwater snail *Lymnaea stagnalis*, which was confirmed in nature and in the laboratory, and the second host was laboratory-confirmed to be mosquito larvae, caddis-fly larvae, and dragonfly nymphs (Macy 1960). Mice were found to be an experimental definitive host, and bats *Myotis lucifugus* were confirmed to be a natural definitive host (Macy 1960). One bat each from Kansas (*Eptesicus fuscus*) and Nebraska (*Myotis lucifugus*) were found to harbor one specimen each of *P. vespertilionis* in their intestines (Nickel and Hansen 1967). In Iowa, 8 (28.6%) of 28 bats *Eptesicus fuscus*, one (50.0%) of 2 *Lasiurus cinereus*, and 7 (25.0%) of 28 *Myotis lucifugus* were found infected with *P. vespertilionis* (Blankespoor and Ulmer 1970). *P. vespertilionis* specimens were recovered from *Eptesiscus fuscus* bats from Wisconsin (Lotz and Font 1985). In Indiana, 8 bat species, including *Eptesicus fuscus, Lasionycteris noctivagans, Lasiurus borealis, Lasiurus cinereus, Myotis keenii, Myotis lucifugus, Myotis sodalis,* and *Pistrellus subflatus,* were found infected with *P. vespertilionis* with variable prevalences of 3.3-35.3% (Pistole 1988). In Northern California, 2 bat species *Tadarida brasiliensis mexicana* and *Myotis californicus* were reported to be infected with *P. vespertilionis* (Nahhas et al. 2005). In Nebraska, 2 more bat species *Eptesicus fuscus* and *Myotis ciliolarum*, in addition to an ever known one *Myotis lucifugus* (Nickel and Hansen 1967), were added among the natural definitive hosts of *P. vespertilionis* (McAllister and Bursey 2009). *P. vespertilionis* was recovered from the digestive tract of 2-6 bats *Lasionycteris noctivagans* caught from Virginia (Eckerlin 2011).

8.2.6 Potentially Zoonotic **Plagiorchis** *spp.*

Potentially zoonotic *Plagiorchis* spp. include numerous species, including *P. koreanus* Ogata, 1938, *P. dilamanensis* Velasquez, 1964, *P. siamensis* Yamashita, 1967, and *P. muelleri* Tkach and Sharpilo, 1990 (see Yamaguti 1971; Tkach et al. 2000).

8.2.7 Genomics and Proteomics

Phylogenetic studies were performed on *P. muris, P. vespertilionis*, and several other non-zoonotic *Plagiorchis* spp. (Tkach et al. 2000; Platt and Tkach 2003; Lee et al. 2004; Zikmundová et al. 2014; Sümer and Yildirimhan 2017). The sequences from the nuclear rDNA ITS region (ITS1, 5.8S, ITS2) of *P. vespertilionis, P. muelleri* Tkach and Sharpilo, 1990, and *P. koreanus* Ogata, 1938 were used to test the validity of these species (Tkach et al. 2000). The results revealed that all 3 species were clearly distinguishable using these ITS sequences; *P. koreanus* occupied a basal position, while *P. vespertilionis* and *P. muelleri* appeared as a cluster of 2 closely related, derived species (Tkach et al. 2000). The sequences from 28S D1 rDNA and mitochondrial cytochrome *c* oxidase subunit I (mtCOI) of *P. muris* were obtained and compared with other *Plagiorchis* spp., including *P. elegans, P. koreanus, P. muelleri,* and *P. vespertilionis*, and other trematode genera (Lee et al. 2004). According to the sequences of 28S D1 rDNA, *P. muris* was more closely related with *P. elegans* than with *P. koreanus, P. muelleri*, or *P. vespertilionis*; the sequences of mtCOI showed a distinct position of *P. muris* among the trematode family Plagiorchiidae (Lee et al. 2004). Cercariae of *Plagiorchis* spp., including *P. elegans, Plagiorchis maculosus, P. koreanus,* and *Plagiorchis neomidis*, emerged from lymnaeid snails (*Lymnaea stagnalis* and *Radix auricularia*) in central Europe were morphologically and molecularly analyzed (using the sequences of partial 28S rRNA, complete ITS1-5.8S-ITS2, and mtCOI) to see their phylogenetic relationships (Zikmundová et al. 2014). In Turkey, partial nuclear 28S rDNA of *Plagiorchis* spp., including *P. vespertilionis, P. koreanus,* and *P. muelleri*, was sequenced for a phylogenetic study of bat trematodes (Sümer and Yildirimhan 2017).

8.2.8 Pathology and Immunology

The pathogenicity of *Plagiorchis* spp. and pathology in human or animal infections are unknown. The number of worms in human infections has been usually lower than 5 specimens per case (Africa and Garcia 1937; Sandground 1940; Asada et al. 1962; Harinasuta et al. 1989; Hong et al. 1996; Guk et al. 2007); thus the pathogenic effects of *Plagiorchis* spp. infection in these human cases seem to be negligible. Innate as well as acquired immunity in human or animal infections have never been investigated.

8.2.9 Clinical Manifestations, Diagnosis and Treatment

Human cases have been very few in number, each case with low worm burdens, and thus no significant clinical symptoms have been complained by the patients (Sandground 1940; Asada et al. 1962; Hong et al. 1996; Guk et al. 2007). A tentative diagnosis can be made if plagiorchiid eggs are recovered in stool examinations; however, worm recovery is needed to confirm a true infection and for specific diagnosis of the worms (to determine the worm species). Treatment can be done by praziquantel in a single dose of 10 mg/kg (Hong et al. 1996) or 40-50 mg/kg (this high dose was for treatment of the concomitantly infected liver fluke *Opisthorchis viverrini*) (Radomyos et al. 1989). Kamala (4 g) was also used for treatment of the human case from Japan (Asada et al. 1962).

8.2.10 Prevention and Control

The second intermediate hosts of *Plagiorchis* spp. include freshwater snails, larvae or nymphs of insects (such as mosquitoes and dragonflies), and freshwater fish, eating these hosts under raw or inadequately cooked conditions should be avoided. Drinking untreated water should also be avoided, because, in a case from Japan, drinking a large amount of water which had been contaminated with insect larvae infected with *Plagiorchis* spp. was suspected as the source of infection (Asada et al. 1962).

References

Africa CM, Garcia EY (1937) *Plagiorchis* sp. a new trematode parasite of the human intestine. Papers on Helminthology: 30th Jubileum of the Activities of K.J. Skrjabin. Moscow, Russia. pp 9–10

Alvarez F, Rey J, Quinteiro P et al (1991) Helminth parasites in some Spanish bats. Wiadom Parazytol 37:321–329

Anh NTL, Phuong NT, Johansen MV et al (2009) Prevalence and risks for fishborne zoonotic trematode infections in domestic animals in a highly endemic area of North Vietnam. Acta Trop 112:198–203

Asada J, Otagaki H, Morita D et al (1962) A case report on the human infection with *Plagiorchis muris* (Tanabe, 1922) in Japan. Jpn J Parasitol 11:512–516. in Japanese

Ash LR (1962) The helminth parasites of rats in Hawaii and the description of *Capillaria traverae* sp. n. J Parasitol 48:66–68

Barragán-Sáenz FA, Sánchez-Nava P, Hernández-Gallegos O et al (2009) Larval stages of trematodes in gastropods from Lake Chicnahuaphan, State of Mexico, Mexico. Parasitol Res 105:1163–1167

Beaver PC, Jung RC, Cupp EW (1984) Clinical parasitology, 9th edn. Lea and Febiger, Philadelphia

Behnke JM, Eira C, Rogan M et al (2009) Helminth species richness in wild wood mice, *Apodemus sylvaticus*, is enhanced by the presence of the intestinal nematode *Heligmosomoides polygyrus*. Parasitology 136:793–804

Blankespoor HD, Ulmer MJ (1970) Helminths of six species of Iowa bats. Proc Iowa Acad Sci 77:200–206

Braun M (1900) Trematoden der Chiroptera. Annal K K Natur Hofmus (Wien) 15:217–236

Caballero CE (1940) Algunos trematodos intestinales de los murciélagos de México. Annal Inst Biol (México) 11:215–223

Caballero CE (1942) Trematodos de los murcielagos de Mexico. IV. Description de un nuevo de la subfamilia Lecithodendriinae Looss, 1902 y una nuevo especia de *Prosthodendrium*

Chae JS, Park MK, Kim HC et al (2012) Ultrastructural study of the three trematodes *Plagirochis muris, Pleurogenoides japonicus* and *Loxogenes librum* collected from dragonflies. Int J Vet Sci 1:59–63

Chai JY (2014) Chapter 8: Epidemiology of trematode infections. In: Toledo R, Fried B (eds) Digenetic trematodes. Springer. Adv Exp Med Biol 766:241–292

Chai JY, Park JH, Guk SM et al (2007) *Plagiorchis muris* infection in *Apodemus agrarius* from northern Gyeonggi-do (Province) near the demilitarized zone. Korean J Parasitol 45:153–156

Chai JY, Shin EH, Lee SH et al (2009) Foodborne intestinal flukes in Southeast Asia. Korean J Parasitol 47(suppl):S69–S102

Chai JY, Na BK, Sohn WM (2013) Trematodes recovered in the small intestine of stray cats in the Republic of Korea. Korean J Parasitol 51:99–106

Chaisiri K, Siribat P, Ribas A et al (2015) Potentially zoonotic helminthiases of murid rodents from the Indo-Chinese Peninsula: impact of habitat and the risk of human infection. Vector-Borne Zoon Dis 15:73–85

Ching HL, Leighton BJ, Stephen C (2000) Intestinal parasites of raccoons (*Procyon lotor*) from southwest British Columbia. Can J Vet Res 64:107–111

Combes C, Clerc B (1970) Recherches éco-parasitologiques sur l'helminthofaune des Chiroptères dans l'est des Pyrénés. Ann Parasitol (Paris) 45:537–561

Cort WW, Olivier L (1943) The development of the larval stages of *Plagiorchis muris* Tanabe, 1922, in the first intermediate host. J Parasitol 29:81–99

Cort WW, McMullen DB, Brackett S (1937) Ecological studies on the cercariae in *Stagnicola emarginata angulata* (Sowerby) in the Douglas Lake region, Michigan. J Parasitol 23:504–599

Dancáu D, Capuse I (1966) A contribution to the study of the helminth fauna of Ciroptera in Rumania. Lucrdrile Inst Speol 5:81–89. in Romanian

de Bellocq JG, Sarà M, Casanova JC et al (2003) A comparison of the structure of helminth communities in the woodmouse, *Apodemus sylvaticus*, on islands of the western Mediterranean and continental Europe. Parasitol Res 90:64–70

Dubois G (1955) Les Trématodes de chiroptères de la collection Villy Aellen. Rev Suiss Zool 62:469–506. in French

Eckerlin RP (2011) The rare fluke *Urotrematulum attenuatum* (Trematoda: Digenea) in Virginia. Comp Parasitol 78:395–396

Eduardo SL, Lee GQ (2006) Some zoonotic trematodes from the Philippine field rat, *Rattus mindanensis mindanensis* (Mearns, 1905) (Mammalia: Rodentia) in Bay, Laguna, Philippines with description and new records of species. Phil J Vet Med 43:33–45

Eduardo SL, Domingo CYJ, Divina BP (2008) Zoonotic parasites of rats in the Philippines. In: Singleton GR, Joshi RC, Sebastian LS (eds) Phil Rats Ecol Managem. Philippine Rice Research Institiute, Manila, pp 157–190

Faltýnkova A, Haas W (2006) Larval trematodes in freshwater molluscs from the Elbe to Danube rivers (Southeast Germany): before and today. Parasitol Res 99:572–582

Feliu C, Torres J, Miquel J et al (2006) Digenean trematodes. In: Morand S, Krasnov BR, Poulin R (eds) Micromammals and macroparasites. Springer, Tokyo, pp 13–28

Fischthal JH, Kuntz RE (1975) Some digenetic trematodes of mammals from Taiwan. Proc Helminthol Soc Wash 42:149–157

Fischthal JH, Kuntz RE (1981) Addicitonal records of digenetic trematodes of mammals from Taiwan. Proc Helminthol Soc Wash 48:71–79

Franssen F, Swart A, van Knapen F et al (2016) Helminth parasites in black rats (*Rattus rattus*) and brown rats (*Rattus norvegicus*) from different environments in the Netherlands. Infect Ecol Epidemiol 6:31413

Groschaft J, Tenora J (1971) *Plagiorchis vespertilionis* (Muller, 1780) (Trematoda)-a parasite of *Meriones persicus* (Rodentia) in Afghanistan. Folia Parasitol 18:40

Guk SM, Kim JL, Park JH et al (2007) A human case of *Plagiorchis vespertilionis* (Digenea: Plagiorchiidae) infection in the Republic of Korea. J Parasitol 93:1225–1227

Guzmán-Carnejo C, García-Prieto L, Pérez-Ponce de León G et al (2003) Parasites of *Tadaria brasiliensis mexicana* (Chiroptera: Molossidae) from arid regions of Mexico. Comp Parasitol 70:11–25

Hirazawa I, Asada J (1929) Studies on the life history of *Lepoderma muris*. Tokyo Iji Shinshi (no. 2614):507-516. (in Japanese)

Hong SJ (2009) Surface ultrastructure of *Plagiorchis muris* growth and developmental stages in rats, the final host. Parasitol Res 105:1077–1083

Hong SJ, Woo HC, Chai JY (1996) A human case of *Plagiorchis muris* (Tanabe, 1922: Digenea) infection in the Republic of Korea: Freshwater fish as a possible source of infection. J Parasitol 82:647–649

Hong SJ, Ahn JH, Woo HC (1998) *Plagiorchis muris*: recovery, growth and development in albino rats. J Helminthol 72:251–256

Hong SJ, Woo HC, Lee SU et al (1999) Infection status of dragonflies with *Plagiorchis muris* metacercariae in Korea. Korean J Parasitol 37:65–70

Ito M, Itagaki T (2003) Survey of wild rodents for endoparasites in Iwate Prefecture, Japan. J Vet Med Sci 65:1151–1153

Jueco NL, Zabala ZR (1990) The cestode and trematodes of *Rattus norvegicus* and *Rattus rattus mindanensis*. Phil J Vet Med 27:47–51

Kagei N, Sawada I (1983) Helminth fauna of bats in Japan. XXVIII Annot Zool Japon 56:19–26

Kamiya H, Ishimoto T, Araki J et al (1973) Helminths of stray dogs in Sapporo, Hokkaido, Japan. Jpn J Vet Sci 21:51–56

Kasai Y (1978) Studies on helminth and protozoan parasites of rats in Sapporo. Jpn J Vet Res 26:31

Kifune T, Sawada I, Lee WC (1983) Trematode parasites of two Korean bats. Med Bull Fukuoka Univ 10:3–8

Kifune T, Harada M, Sawada I et al (1997) Trematode parasites of five Korean bats. Med Bull Fukuoka Univ 24:225–232

Kinsella JM (1974) Comparison of helminth parasites of the cotton rat, *Sigmodon hispidus*, from several habitats in Florida. Am Mus Novitates (no. 2540):1-12

Kirilov AA, Kirilova N, Vekhnik VP (2012) Trematodes (Trematoda) of bats (Chiroptera) from the Middle Volga Region. Parazitologiia 46:384–413

Komiya Y (1965) Metacercariae in Japan and adjacent territories. Progress Med Parasitol Japan 2:1–328

Krasnolobova TA (1977) The principles of systematics in trematodes of the genus *Plagiorchis* Lühe, 1899. Trudy gel'mint. Lab 27:65–100. in Russian

Lagocheva LS (1974) Helminths of Chiroptera in Kirgizia. Fauna gel'mintov zhivotnykh rastenii Kirgizii pp 49-51

Langley R, Fairley JS (1982) Seasonal variations in infestations of parasites in a wood mouse *Apodemus sylvaticus* population in the West of Ireland. J Zool Lond 198:249–261

Lee SU, Huh S, Sohn WM (2004) Molecular phylogenic location of the *Plagiorchis muris* (Digenea: Plagiorchiidae) based on sequences of partial 28S D1 rDNA and mitochondrial cytochrome *c* oxidase subunit I. Korea J Parasitol 42:71–75

Lee YI, Pyeon HJ, Seo M (2013) Intestinal parasites among wild rodents in northern Gangwon-do, Korea. Korean J Parasitol 51:603–606

Li HY, Wu Y (2011) Study on two species of trematodes in Plagiorchiidae in six bat species from Guangdong Province. J Guangzhou Univ (Nat Sci Ed):2011–2006

Lie KJ (1951) Some human flukes from Indonesia. Docum Neerland Indon Morbis Trop 3:105–116
Lie KJ, Bras G (1950) *Plagiorchis javensis* in Indonesia. Docum Neerland Indon Morbis Trop 2:182–184
López-Neyra CR (1947) Helmintos de los Vertebrados Ibéricos. T. I, II et III. C.S.I.C., Granada
Lotz JM, Font WF (1985) Structure of enteric helminth communities in two populations of *Eptesicus fuscus* (Chiroptera). Can J Zool 63:2969–2978
Lotz JM, Font WF (1991) The role of positive and negative interspecific associations in the organization of communities of intestinal helminths of bats. Parasitology 103:127–138
Ma JY, Feng WF, Chen ZT (2008) Studies on trematodes of Plagiorchiidae from Henan Province. Sichuan J Zool:2008–2002
Macy RW (1960) The life cycle of *Plagiorchis vespertilionis parorchis* n. spp. (Trematoda: Plagiorchiidae) and observation on the effects of light on the emergence of the cercaria. J Parasitol 46:337–345
Mahmoud SN, Jawdat SZ (1982) First record of two digenetic trematodes (*Plagiorchis vespertilionis* and *Prosthodendrium ovimagnosum*) from the naked bellied tomb bat *Taphozous nudiventris* in Iraq. J Biol Sci 13:59–70
Matoba Y, Yamada D, Asano M et al (2006) Parasitic helminths from feral raccoons (*Procyon lotor*) in Japan. Helminthologia 43:139–146
Matskási I (1967) The systematico-faunistical survey of the trematode fauna of Hungarian bats. I. Ann Hist Nat Mus Natn Hung 59:217–238
Matskási I (1973) Trematodes of bats in India. Parasit Hung 6:77–97
Matskási I (1980) Trematodes of bats in Iraq. Parasit Hung 13:7–12
McAllister CT, Bursey CR (2009) New host and geographical distribution records for helminths (Trematoda, Nematoda) in three species of vespertilionid bats (Chiroptera) from the Pine Ridge of Daws County, Nebraska, U.S.A. Comp Parasitol 76:117–121
McMullen DB (1937a) An experimental infection of *Plagiorchis muris* in man. J Parasitol 23:113–115
McMullen DB (1937b) The life histories of three trematodes, parasitic in birds and mammals, belonging to the genus *Plagiorchis*. J Parasitol 23:235–243
McMullen DB (1938) Observations on precocious metacercarial development in the trematode superfamily Plagiorchioidea. J Parasitol 24:273–280
Mészáros F, Mas-Coma S (1980) On some parasitic helminths from Spanish bats. Parasit Hung 13:59–64
Miyata I (1940) On a new trematode, *Opisthoglyphe canis*, parasitic to the small intestine of dogs. Dobutsugaku Zasshi 52:367–371
Mowlavi G, Mobedi I, Abedkhojasteh H et al (2013) *Plagiorchis muris* (Tanabe, 1922) in *Rattus norvegicus* in Iran. Iran J Parasitol 8:486–490
Nahhas FM, Yang P, Uch S (2005) Digenetic trematodes of *Tadarida brasiliensis mexicana* (Chiroptera: Molossidae) and *Myotis californicus* (Chiroptera: Vespertilionidae) from Northern California, U.S.A. Comp Parasitol 72:196–199
Nguyen TL (1991) The trematodes of birds and mammals in South Vietnam. Tap Chi Sinh Hoe (Vietnam). pp 23–26
Nickel PA, Hansen MF (1967) Helminths of bats collected in Kansa, Nebraska and Oklahoma. Am Midl Natur 78:481–486
Okabe K, Shibue H (1952) A new second intermediate host, *Neocaridina denticulata*, for *Plagiorchis muris* (Tanabe): Plagiorchiidae. Jpn J Med Sci Biol 5:257–258
Ono S (1934) On the life-history of *Plagiorchis* (*Lepoderma*) and *Prosthogonimus* of dragonflies found in the vicinity of Mukden. J Jpn Soc Vet Sci 13:267–280. in Japanese
Pistole DH (1988) A survey of helminth parasites of Chiropterans from Indiana. Proc Helminthol Soc Wash 55:270–274
Platt TR, Tkach VV (2003) Two new species of *Choanocotyle* Jue Sue and Platt, 1998 (Digenea: Choanocotylidae) from an Australian freshwater turtle (Testudines: Pleurodira: Chelidae). J Parasitol 89:145–150

Pratt I, Barton GD (1941) The effects of four species of larval trematodes upon the liver and ovotestis of the snail, *Stagnicola emarginata angulata* (Sowerby). J Parasitol 27:283–288
Radomyos P, Bunnag D, Harinasuta T (1989) A new intestinal fluke, *Plagiorchis harinasutai* n. sp. Southeast Asian. J Trop Med Public Health 20:101–107
Radomyos P, Radomyos B, Tungtrongchitr A (1994) Multi-infection with helminths in adults from northeast Thailand as determined by post-treatment fecal examination of adult worms. Trop Med Parasitol 45:133–135
Radomyos P, Wongsaroj T, Wilairatana P et al (1998) Opisthorchiasis and intestinal fluke infections in northern Thailand. Southeast Asian J Trop Med Public Health 29:123–127
Ricci M (1995) Trematode parasites of Italian bats. Parassitologia 37:199–214
Rogan MT, Craig PS, Hide G et al (2007) The occurrence of the trematode *Plagiorchis muris* in the wood mouse *Apodemus sylvaticus* in North Yorkshire, UK. J Helminthol 81:57–62
Sandground JH (1940) *Plagiorchis javensis* n. sp. a new trematode parasitic in man. Rev Med Trop Parasitol 6:207–211
Sato H, Suzuki K (2006) Gastrointestinal helminths of feral raccoons (*Procyon lotor*) in Wakayama Prefecture, Japan. J Vet Med Sci 68:311–318
Schell SC (1985) Handbook of Trematodes of North America North of Mexico. University Press of Idaho, Moscow, pp 1–263
Schulz RE, Skworzow AA (1931) *Plagiorchis arvicolae* n. sp. aus der Wasserratte. Z Parasitenkd 3:765–774. in Germany
Secord ML, Canaris AG (1993) The metazoan parasite community of migrating greater yellowlegs, *Tringa melanoleuca*, from the Rio Grande Valley, Texas and New Mexico. J Parasitol 79:690–694
Seo BS, Rim HJ, Lee CW (1964) Studies on the parasitic helminths of Korea. I. Trematodes of rodents. Korean J Parasitol 2:20–26
Seo BS, Cho SY, Hong ST et al (1981) Studies on parasitic helminths of Korea. V. Survey on intestinal trematodes of house rats. Korean J Parasitol 19:131–136
Shimalov VV, Demyanchik MG, Demyanchik VT (2002) A study on the helminth fauna of the bats (Mammalia. Chiroptera: Vespertilionidae) in Belarus. Parasitol Res 88:1011
Skrjabin KI, Antipin DN (1958) Superfamily Plagiorchioidea Dollfus, 1930. In: Skrjabin KI (ed) Trematodes and Animals and Man. Moscow-Leningrad, Russia, Vol XIV: 73–620 (in Russian)
Sogandares-Bernal F (1956) Four trematodes from Korean bats with description of three new species. J Parasitol 42:200–206
Sohn WM, Na BK, Sonh HJ et al (2014) Intestinal helminthic infections in striped field mice, Apodemus agrarius, from two southern regions of Korea. Korean J Parasitol 52:419–423
Sohn WM, Chai JY (2005) Infection status with helminthes in feral cats purchased from a market in Busan, Republic of Korea. Korean J Parasitol 43:93–100
Soltys A (1959) The helminth fauna of bats (Chiroptera) of Lublin Palatinate. Acta Parasitol Pol 7:599–613. Polish
Stafford J (1905) Trematdes from Canadian vertebrates. Zool Anz (Leipzig) 28:681–694
Sümer N, Yildirimhan HS (2017) DNA sequencing of Digenea nuclear lsrDNA of the whiskered brown bat, *Myotis aurescens* (Vespertilionidae: Chiroptera). Turk J Zool 41:64–66
Sümer N, Yildirimhan HS (2018) Helminth parasites of the whiskered brown bat, *Myotis aurescens* (Kuzyakin, 1935) (Chiroptera: Vespertilionidae) from Turkey. Acta Zool Bulg 70:113–116
Tanabe H (1922) A contribution to the study of the life cycle of hermaphroditic distomes. A study of the new species *Lepoderma muris* n. sp. Okayama Igakkai zasshi:47–68. in Japanese
Tinnin DS, Gardner SL, Ganzorig S (2008) Helminths of small mammals (Chiroptera, Insectivora, Lagomorpha) from Mongolia with a description of a new species of *Schizorchis* (Cestoda: Anoplocephalidae). Comp Parasitol 75:107–114
Tkach VV (2008) Family Plagiorchiidae Lühe, 1901. In: Bray RA, Gibson DI, Jones A (eds) Keys to the Trematoda, vol 3. CAB Publishing, Natural History Museum, London, pp 295–325

Tkach VV, Pawlowski J, Sharpilo VP (2000) Molecular and morphological differentiation between species of the *Plagiorchis vespertilionis* group (Digenea, Plagiorchiidae) occurring in European bats, with a re-description of *P. vespertilionis*. Syst Parasitol 47:9–22

Velasquez CC (1964) Observations on the life history of *Plagiorchis dilimanensis* sp. n. (Trematoda: Digenea). J Parasitol 50:557–563

Webster WA, Casey GA (1973) Studies on the parasites of Chiroptera. III. Helminths from various bat species collected in British Columbia. Can J Zool 51:633–636

Yamada D (2000) Studies on the parasite fauna of raccoons (*Procyon lotor*) naturalized in Hokkaido, Japan. Jpn J Vet Res 48:70–71

Yamaguti S (1933) Studies on the helminth founa of Japan. Part 1. Trematodes of birds, reptiles and mammals. Jpn J Zool 5:1–134

Yamaguti S (1943) Cercaria of *Plagiorchis muris*. Annot Zool Jap 22:1–3

Yamaguti S (1958) Systema Helminthum. Vol. I. The digenetic trematodes of vertebrates (Part I). Interscience Publishers Inc, New York, pp 1–979

Yamaguti S (1971) Synopsis of digenetic trematodes of vertebrates, vol I. Keigaku Publishing Co., Tokyo, pp 1–1074

Yamaguti S (1975) Synoptical review of life histories of digenetic trematodes of vertebrates. Keigaku Publishing Co, Tokyo, pp 1–590. with 219 figure plates

Yamashita J (1952) Studies on the cercaria of the rat trematode *Plagiorchis muris* (Tanabe). J Faculty Agric (Hokkaido Imper Univ) 48:305–358

Yousefi A, Eslami A, Mobedi I et al (2014) Helminth infections of house mouse (*Mus musculus*) and wood mouse (*Apodemus sylvaticus*) from the suburban areas of Hamadan City, Western Iran. Iran J Parasitol 9:511–518

Yu SH, Mott KE (1994) Epidemiology and morbidity of food-borne intestinal trematode infections. Trop Dis Bull 91:R125–R152

Zikmundová J, Georgieva S, Faltýnková A et al (2014) Species diversity of *Plagiorchis* Luhe, 1899 (Digenea: Plagiorchiidae) in lymnaeid snails from freshwater ecosystems in central Europe revealed by molecules and morphology. Syst Parasitol 88:37–54

Chapter 9
Miscellaneous Zoonotic Species

In addition to heterophyids (Heterophyidae), echinostomes (Echinostomatidae), diplostomes (Diplostomidae), fasciolids (Fasciolidae), gymnophallids (Gymnophallidae), lecithodendriid-like flukes (Lecithodendriidae and Phaneropsolidae), plagiorchiids (Plagiorchiidae), and amphistomes (Gastrothylacidae and Gastrodiscoides), there have been at least 6 digenetic families (8 species) ever reported to cause human infections. They include Brachylaimidae (*Brachylaima cribbi*), Strigeidae (*Cotylurus japonicus*), Microphallidae (*Gynaecotyla squatarolae* and *Microphallus brevicaeca*), Isoparorchiidae (*Isoparorchis hypselobagri*), Troglotrematidae (*Nanophyetus salmincola* and *N. schikhobalowi*), and Cyathocotylidae (*Prohemistomum vivax*) (Table 3.1). Each species has been briefly reviewed in this part.

9.1 Species Involved

9.1.1 Brachylaima cribbi *(Brachylaimidae)*

9.1.1.1 *Brachylaima cribbi* Butcher and Grove, 2001

Brachylaima cribbi (Fig. 9.1) belongs to the family Brachylaimidae Joyeux and Foley, 1930 (Pojmańska 2002). In this family, 2 subfamilies (Brachylaiminae and Ityogoniminae) and 7 genera (*Glaphirostomum, Parabrachylaima, Postharmostomum, Brachylaima, Ectosiphonus, Ityogonimus,* and *Scaphiostomum*) were listed by Pojmańska (2002). Later, a new genus (*Renylaima*) was described by Sirgel and Mas-Coma (2010). The subfamily Panopistinae which was included in the Brachylaimidae family by Yamaguti (1958) was proposed to be raised as a family level by Pojmańska (2002). However, Sirgel and Mas-Coma (2010) did not accept this taxonomic move because of absence of important morphological differences between the subfamilies Brachylaiminae, Ityogoniminae, and Panopistinae.

J.-Y. Chai, *Human Intestinal Flukes*,
https://doi.org/10.1007/978-94-024-1704-3_9

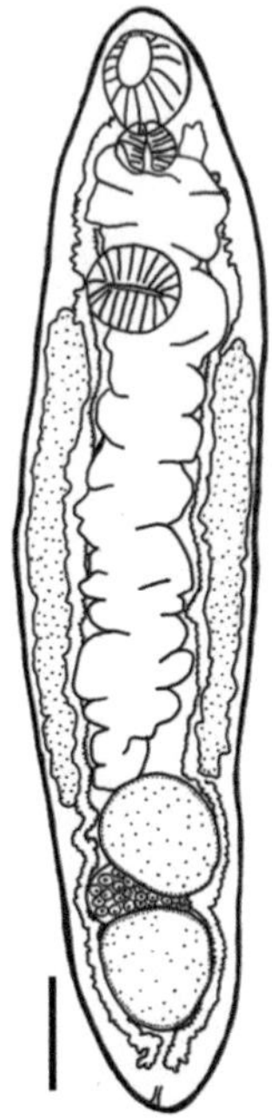

Fig. 9.1 Line drawing of an adult worm of *Brachylaima cribbi*. Redrawn from the figure in Cribb and O'Callaghan (1992) Aust Vet J 69:69–70. Scale bar = 0.5 mm

The life cycle of the species in the Brachylaimidae has 2 intermediate hosts, both terrestrial molluscs (land snails), and their adult flukes usually live in the alimentary tract of birds and mammals, rarely amphibians (Pojmańska 2002), and a few of them parasitize the urinary system (Sirgel and Mas-Coma 2010).

Brachylaima Dujardin, 1843 is the type genus of the Brachylaimidae (Yamaguti 1958, 1971; Pojmańska 2002), and *Brachylaima migrans* Dujardin, 1843 is the type species of this genus. Yamaguti (1975) listed 30 *Brachylaima* species from mammals and 30 *Brachylaima* species from birds, 60 species in total. New species have been added since then, for example, *Brachylaima mascomai* by Gracenea and González-Moreno (2002) and *Brachylaima llobregatensis* by González-Moreno and Gracenea (2006) in Spain and *Brachylaima ezohelicis* by Nakao et al. (2017) in Japan. Currently, about 70 species are known in this family (Butcher 2016).

B. cribbi was described as a new species in South Australia by Butcher and Grove (2001) based on adult flukes from experimentally infected mice with the metacercariae obtained from the laboratory completed life cycle originating from eggs obtained in a human patient reported by Butcher et al. (1998). This fluke was actually first detected from the house mouse (*Mus domesticus*) in South Australia with no species name, *Brachylaima* sp., by Angel and Mutze (1987) and Cribb (1990). This fluke was later considered to be identical with *B. cribbi* (Butcher and Grove 2001). It was hypothesized that *B. cribbi* was introduced from Europe, because it used the introduced European snails *Cernuella virgata* and *Cochlicella barbara* as the first intermediate host and the same 2 snail species and *Theba pisana* as the second intermediate host (Cribb 1990). Probably the same species, *B. cribbi,* was recovered also from avian hosts (domestic chickens) in South Australia (Cribb and O'Callaghan 1992).

Human infections with this fluke were first found in two 21-month-old children from a rural district of South Australia who presented with mild abdominal pain and diarrhea showing helminth eggs in their feces (Butcher et al. 1996). By morphology, the eggs were suggestive of a *Brachylaima* species, and treatment with praziquantel resulted in egg clearance and resolution of gastrointestinal symptoms (Butcher et al. 1996). Adult flukes were not recovered; however, both infants had been seen eating raw land snails, and snails from their environment were found to be infected with metacercariae of a brachylaimid trematode (Butcher et al. 1996). Later, these infections were regarded as *B. cribbi* infections (Butcher et al. 2003). The second report of human *B. cribbi* infection was documented by Butcher et al. (1998). The patient was a 78-year-old woman presenting with an 18-month history of intermittent diarrhea; examination of her stools revealed brachylaimid eggs in 3 separate specimens over a week (Butcher et al. 1998). After treatment with praziquantel, a degenerate adult *Brachylaima* sp. worm was recovered from her feces (Butcher et al. 1998) which was later confirmed to be an adult specimen of *B. cribbi* (Butcher and Grove 2001; Butcher et al. 2003). The patient lived in a rural area of South Australia and ate vegetables grown in her own garden which had been contaminated with helicid snails, that are considered to be the source of infection (Butcher et al. 1998). Eggs from this patient were laboratory-passaged through first intermediate snail hosts and resulting cercariae were used to infect second intermediate snail hosts, and then Swiss outbread mice were infected with the metacercariae; adult flukes recovered from these mice were identified as *B. cribbi* (Butcher et al. 1998; Butcher and Grove 2001). Subsequently, further 12 egg positive human infections, with the majority of them (80%) in children under 2 years of age, were detected in South Australia (Butcher et al. 2003; Butcher 2016).

Adult flukes of *B. cribbi* from experimental mice are elongate, with dense covering of fine tegumental spines on the forebody but diminishing towards the posterior body, and 3.8–6.0 mm long and 0.52–0.79 mm wide (Butcher and Grove 2001). The eggs are ovoid, asymmetrical with one side slightly flattened, with a smooth shell, inconspicuous operculum, and an abopercular knob or thickening, and measure 26.0–32.0 μm long and 16.0–17.5 μm wide (Butcher 2016). The sporocyst (3–12 mm in length) is seen in the digestive gland of infected snails, and highly branched sporocysts are containing developing and mature cercariae within the branches and having a terminal birth pore (Butcher and Grove 2001). The cercariae have an elongate spinose body, 240–330 μm long and 60–110 μm wide, and a short simple tail (length 12–35 μm) (Butcher and Grove 2001). The metacercariae are unencysted, and 630–1910 μm long and 180–610 μm wide, and found only in kidneys of the snails (Butcher and Grove 2001).

The life history of *B. cribbi* has been completely elucidated (Butcher and Grove 2001, 2003). The first intermediate host is helicid land snails, including *Theba pisana, Cernuella virgata, Cochlicella barbara*, and *Cochlicella acuta* (Cribb 1990; Butcher and Grove 2001, 2003, 2005a). In these snail hosts, cercariae begin to emerge 8 weeks after exposure to the eggs (Butcher and Grove 2001). The second intermediate host is also helicid and hygromiid land snails, including the same species listed as the first intermediate host; *Theba pisana, Cernuella virgata, Cochlicella barbara, Cochlicella acuta, Helix aspersa, Microxeromagna armillata, Succinea australis,* and *Strangesta gawleri* (Butcher and Grove 2005a, b). Birds (Australian little ravens, black birds, and starlings), reptiles (lizards), and mammals (field mice and other rodents, cats, sheep, and red foxes) were found to be naturally infected with this fluke (Butcher et al. 1998; Butcher and Grove 2001, 2005b; Dybing et al. 2013). Experimental definitive hosts included various strains of mice and rats (Cribb 1990; Butcher et al. 2002a, b; Butcher and Grove 2001, 2005b).

The principal mode of human infections is consuming raw snails serving as the second intermediate host (Butcher and Grove 2005b; Chai 2007). In children, mouthing of objects including land snails seems to be an accidental mode of infection, and in adults, the patients had eaten home-grown garden vegetables contaminated with land snails (Butcher 2016). The geographical distribution of *B. cribbi* is known so far to be confined to Australia (southern and western parts) (Table 3.2) (Butcher and Grove 2005a, b; Dybing et al. 2013; Butcher 2016).

Studies on host-parasite relationships and immunology of *B. cribbi* infection have been performed by Butcher et al. (2002a, b, 2003). The susceptibility of different sex and age of C57BL/6 J mice appeared to be variable; mature female mice were significantly more resistant to *B. cribbi* infection than older mature females and adolescent females (Butcher et al. 2002a). It was suggested to be due to physiological factors, such as hormones, which provided a significant level of protection of the host (Butcher et al. 2002a). In addition, non-obese diabetic severe combined immunodeficient (NOD SCID) mice were highly susceptible to *B. cribbi* infection with the infection persisting with a relatively unchanged worm burden for the life of the mouse with the longest surviving mice being 31 weeks post infection, whereas the life span of the worms in normal C57BL/6 J mice was 9–12 weeks with a peak excretion of eggs at 4 weeks post infection (Butcher et al. 2002a). Eight strains of inbred mice (AKR, C3H/HeJ, CBA/CaH, BALB/c, DBA/2 J, SJL/J, A/J, and C57BL/6 J) and Swiss albino white mice were also tested for their susceptibility to *B. cribbi* infection; C57BL/6 J mice were the most highly susceptible having the highest egg excretion and the longest duration of infection, and all other strains, inbred or outbred, showed low susceptibility to infection with low egg excretion and short worm survival (Butcher et al. 2002b). C57BL/6 J and immunodeficient non-obese diabetic severe combined immunodeficient (NOD SCID) mice were used for infection and reinfection with *B. cribbi*, and the course of infection was observed (Butcher et al. 2003). In the case of C57BL/6 J mice, there were significant differences between primary and challenge infections in the mean fecal egg counts and worm fecundity, having lower egg counts and reduced fecundity in challenge infections; in contrast, no significant differences were observed in NOD SCID mice between primary and challenge infections (Butcher et al. 2003).

Infections in humans usually become chronic and can persist as long as 18 months (Butcher et al. 1996, 1998). Symptoms in human infections due to this fluke infection vary depending on the worm burden; heavy infections are associated with diarrhea with offensive stools several times a day, abdominal pain, low-grade fever, and fatigue (Butcher et al. 2003; Toledo et al. 2014). Among these, the main presenting symptoms were mucoid, watery diarrhea, abdominal pain, anorexia, and weight loss or poor weight gain in children (Butcher 2016). However, there have been no studies on experimental pathology of infections with brachylaimids. The diagnosis can be done by recovery of typical eggs in fecal examinations; they are 26–32 μm long and 16.0–17.5 μm wide, the eggs are fully mature containing a miracidium and morphologically characterized by ovoid shape with one side flattened, smooth and relatively thick shell, inconspicuous operculum, an abopercular knob or thickening, and typically asymmetrical (Butcher 2016). Treatment can be done using praziquantel 20 mg/kg once a day for 3 days (Butcher 2016); however, using a single dose of 10–20 mg/kg for only 1 day may also show the same efficacy.

9.1.2 Cotylurus japonicus *(Strigeidae)*

9.1.2.1 *Cotylurus japonicus* Ishii, 1932

Cotylurus japonicus belongs to the family Strigeidae Railliet, 1919 (Niewiadomska 2002). Dubois (1938) defined this family to include genera with a cup-shaped forebody separated from hindbody and a bilobed holdfast organ. In this family, 2 subfamilies are included, Strigeinae Railliet, 1919 (parasites of birds, occasionally reptiles) and Duboisiellinae Baer, 1938 (parasites of mammals) (Niewiadomska 2002). In the Duboisiellinae, only one genus *Duboisiella* Baer, 1938 is known and in the Strigeinae 12 genera are included; *Strigea* Abildgarrd, 1790, *Cotylurus* Szidat, 1928, *Apatemon* Szidat, 1928, and *Australapatemon* Sudarikov, 1959 (Niewiadomska 2002).

The genus *Cotylurus* Szidat, 1928 (syn. *Choanodiplostomum* Vigueras, 1944; *Cotylurostrigea* Sudarikov, 1961) is morphologically characterized by the presence of a genital bulb (no genital cone), spherical forebody, proteolytic gland dispersed, and trilobed testes with smooth lobes (Niewiadomska 2002). The type species is *C. cornutus* (Rudolphi, 1808) Szidat, 1928 (Yamaguti 1958, 1971; Niewiadomska 2002). Its metacercariae are found in snails and leeches as 'tetracotyle' type (Niewiadomska 2002). Yamaguti (1971) listed 22 species in this genus, including *C. japonicus* Ishii, 1932. Thereafter, Birmani et al. (2009) and Das and Ghazi (2012) added 2 new species *Cotylurus sindhense* and *Cotylurus fuscicollisi* from birds in Pakistan, and Zazornova described a new species *Cotylurus szidati* from birds in Russia in 1991 (Terenina and Movsesyan 2018).

C. japonicus was originally described by Ishii (1932) from the intestine of aquatic birds in Tokyo, Japan. This fluke was also found in wild and domestic ducks in several places of South Korea (Chu et al. 1973), Madras, India (Lalitha and Alwar 1960), and Amur and Kamchatka, Russia (Yamaguti 1971). Human infection with this fluke was reported only one time from a 13-year-old girl in Hunan Province, China (Chen and Cai 1985).

Adult flukes of *C. japonicus* from ducks are 1.3–2.0 mm long and 0.50–0.86 mm wide, and morphologically characterized by a bisegmented body, a well-developed and bilobed tribocytic organ, and large testes with smooth surface (Ishii 1932). The adult from the human infection was 1.48 mm long with its forebody 0.65 x 0.54 mm and hindbody 0.83 x 0.36 mm in size (Chen and Cai 1985). The eggs are 106–115 μm long and 74–78 μm wide in worms from ducks (Ishii 1932), and those from the human infection were markedly smaller (Chen and Cai 1985). The cercariae and metacercariae of *C. japonicus* have not yet been discovered.

The first intermediate hosts of *Cotylurus* spp. are in general freshwater snails belonging to the genera *Stagnicola, Lymnaea, Physa*, and *Heligsoma*, and cercariae encyst in the same snail hosts to become specialized metacercariae known as tetracotyles (Fried et al. 2004). The genus and species of the snail host for *C. japonicus* remain to be confirmed. Wild and domestic ducks can be the natural definitive host for *C. japonicus* (Ishii 1932; Yu and Mott 1994).

Infection may occur when birds or mammals (including humans) ingest tetracotyles in infected snails (Fried et al. 2004). The geographical distribution of *C. japonicus* extends from Japan to South Korea, China, India, and Russia (Table 3.2) (Ishii 1932, Lalitha and Alwar 1960; Chu et al. 1973; Chen and Cai 1985; Yamaguti 1971).

The pathogenicity of *C. japonicus* in humans can be significant and notifiable (Chen and Cai 1985; Yu and Mott 1994). In the child case reported from Hunan Province, China, eggs resembling strigeoid species were initially observed in the necrotic tissue of the liver cysts and pericardium and diagnosed as hepatic cysts and chronic constrictive pericarditis of unknown etiology (Chen and Cai 1985; Yu and Mott 1994). It was thus consented to perform exploratory surgery on this patient, and an adult fluke was eventually found in the feces of the patient (Chen and Cai 1985; Yu and Mott 1994). Local ducks were examined for the enteric parasites, and the same parasites, eggs and adults, with those seen in the patient were collected; the parasite was identified as *C. japonicus* (Chen and Cai 1985; Yu and Mott 1994). The mode of infection in this patient is unknown (Yu and Mott 1994).

The diagnosis may be done by fecal examination to detect strigeoid eggs. However, the specific diagnosis is possible after collection of the adult flukes. Treatment may be successfully done using praziquantel.

9.1.3 Gynaecotyla squatarolae *(Microphallidae)*

9.1.3.1 *Gynaecotyla squatarolae* (Yamaguti, 1934) Yamaguti, 1939

[syn. *Levinseniella squatarolae* Yamaguti, 1934].

The fluke family Microphallidae Ward, 1901 is a group of small worms found in the intestine of most vertebrate classes, but mainly birds, acquired by consumption of crustaceans (Deblock 2008). Initially, this family was considered a subfamily of the Heterophyidae Odhner, 1914 but it was raised to full family rank by Travassos (1921) and 3 genera were included; *Microphallus* Ward, 1901, *Maritrema* Nicoll,

1907, and *Levinseniella* Stiles and Hassall, 1901. Yamaguti (1971) included 6 subfamilies within the Microphallidae; Ornithotrematinae (cirrus pouch unusually long), Gynaecotylinae (acetabulum double), Austromicrophallinae (no digestive tract), Maritrematinae (having digestive tract and vitellaria in hindbody), Microphallinae (cirrus pouch absent), and Basantisiinae (cirrus pouch encircling acetabulum). However, Deblock (2008) adopted a supersubfamily concept and revised the classification of the Microphallidae, including 4 supersubfamilies Maritrematidi Nocoll, 1907 (Pseudolevinseniellinae and Maritrematinae), Promicrophallidi Fischthal and Kuntz, 1981 (containing only one genus *Promicrophallus*), Gynaecotylidi Guschanskaya, 1952 (Androcotylinae, Sphairiotrematinae, Gynaecotylinae, and Basantisiinae), and Microphallidi Ward, 1901 (Levinseniellinae, Microphallinae, and Endocotylinae). Two species, namely, *Gynaecotyla squatarolae* (Gynaecotylinae) and *Microphallus brevicaeca* (Microphallinae), are known to infect the human host.

Flukes of the genus *Gynaecotyla* Yamaguti, 1939 (syn. *Cornucopula* Rankin, 1939) are intestinal parasites of birds (Charadriiformes) and morphologically characterized by having double acetabulum, separate male and female genital pores, a well-developed genital atrium, and a large transverse cirrus pouch anterior to the ventral sucker (Dery 1958). The differential points from 3 other genera in the Gynaecotylinae, *Diacetabulum* Belopolskaia, 1952, *Derytrema* (Rebecq, 1962) Yamaguti, 1971, and *Sonkulitrema* Ablasov and Chibichonko, 1960 included vitellaria massed together behind testes, ceca comparatively short, not incurved, and uterus extending to lateral margins of hindbody (Yamaguti 1971). In the genus *Gynaecotyla*, 8 species were listed by Yamaguti (1971); *G. squatarolae* (type species), *G. adunca* (Linton, 1905) Yamaguti, 1939, *G. gallica* (Rebecq, 1962), *G. jägerskiöldi* (Travassos, 1921) Yamaguti, 1939, *G. longiintestinata* Leonov, 1958, *G. nassicola* (Cable and Hunninen, 1938) Yamaguti, 1939, *G. simillima* (Travassos, 1921) Yamaguti, 1939, and *G. sippiwissettensis* (Rankin, 1939) Baer, 1944. *Gynaecotyla riggini* was reported as a new species from the ruddy turnstone by Dery (1958); however, Rebecq in 1962 created a new genus for this species, *Derytrema*, naming it as *Derytrema riggini* (Yamaguti 1971). Thereafter, Deblock and Pearson (1968) added a new species *Gynaecotyla brisbanensis* from Australia, and Deblock (1974) reported another new species *Gynaecotyla bridgmani* from Japan. In China, Ke (1980) reported 2 new species *Gynaecotyla beihaiensis* and *Gynaecotyla zhanjiangensis* from Guangxi and Guangdong Province. Now, total 12 species can be listed among the genus *Gynaecotyla*.

G. squatarolae (Fig. 9.2) was originally reported from the intestine of birds (*Squatarola squatarola hypomelaena*) in Kanagawa Prefecture, Japan, under the name *Levinseniella squatarolae* (Yamaguti 1934). Soon after this, a new genus *Gynaecotyla* was proposed by Yamaguti (1939) for *L. squatarolae* and 3 other species *Levinseniella adunca, Levinseniella jägerskiöldi*, and *Levinseniella simillima* because the genital sinus has neither finger-cap-like structures nor female pouch, which occur sometimes in *Levinseniella*. Yamaguti (1939) transferred these species to the new genus, and named as *G. squatarolae, G. adunca, G. jägerskiöldi*, and *G.*

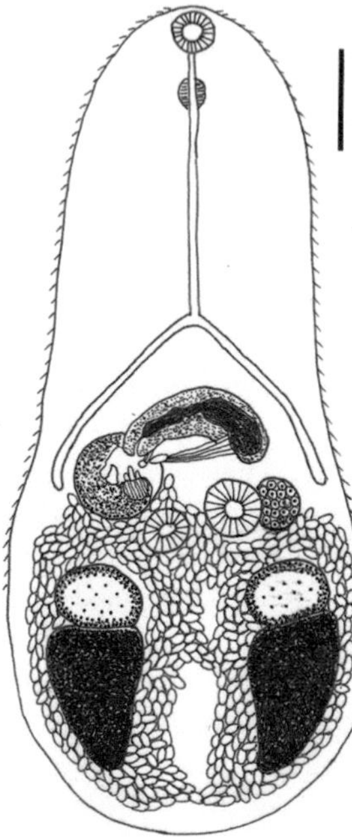

Fig. 9.2 Line drawing of an adult worm of *Gynaecotyla squatarolae*. Redrawn from the figure in Deblock (2008) Keys to the Trematoda. Vol. 3. CAB Publishing, Natural History Museum, London, UK. Scale bar = 0.1 mm

simillima. Human infection was reported only one time in a Korean female who habitually consumed brackish water crabs in soy sauce (Chung et al. 2011a).

Adult flukes of *G. squatarolae* are elongated pear-shaped, flattened dorsoventrally, covered with exceedingly small spines all over, and 0.83 mm long and 0.31 mm wide (Yamaguti 1934). The eggs are oval, brownish yellow, thick-shelled, and 21–27 μm long and 15–18 μm wide in specimens from the bird (Yamaguti 1934). The morphology of the cercariae seems never been described in detail, although a brackish water snail *Batillaria cumingi* has been strongly suggested to be the first intermediate host (Koga 2002; Yamanishi 2014). The metacercariae encysted in the crab host *Macrophthalmus dilatatus* are round with a thin transparent inner and a thicker outer membrane, and 300–350 μm in diameter (Yamaguti 1934).

The tegumental ultrastructure of *G. squatarolae* adult flukes was studied by Lim et al. (2008). They were pyriform, and their anterior half was concave ventrally; the whole body surface was covered with tegumental spines, and between oral and ventral suckers the spines were wide and 16–17 digitated (Lim et al. 2008). On the dorsal surface, the tegumental spines were sparsely distributed; type I and type II sensory papillae were seen densely around the oral sucker and also 2 ventral suckers (Lim et al. 2008).

The life cycle of *G. squatarolae* has been almost completely elucidated. A potamidid brackish water snail *Batillaria cumingi* has been shown to be a presumed first intermediate host (Koga 2002; Yamanishi 2014). Brackish water crabs, including *Macrophthalmus dilatatus* (the shore crab), *Macrophthalmus japonicas* (the mud crab), *Scopimera globosa* (the sand-bubbler crab), *Hemigrapsus sanguineus* (the

Asian shore crab), and *Helice depressa* have been found to carry the metacercariae (Yamaguti 1934, 1971; Otagaki 1958; Kifune and Koga 1996, 2001; Seo et al. 2007; Lee et al. 2010; Chung et al. 2010). Natural definitive hosts include various species of shore birds, including *Squatarola squatarola hypomelaena, Erolia alpine sakhalina, Arenaria interpres interpres* (the ruddy turnstone), *Trigna cinereus* (the Terek sandpiper), *Xenus cinereus* (the Terek sandpiper), *Charadrius alexandrinus* (the Kentish plover), *Charadrius mongolus* (the Mongolian plover), *Calidris ruficollis* (the red necked stint), *Numenius phaeopus* (the whimbrel) (Yamaguti 1934, 1939; Seo et al. 2008; Chung et al. 2011b; Yoo et al. 2012; Lee et al. 2016). Experimental definitive hosts were albino rats, rabbits, chicks, chickens, and quails (Otagaki 1958; Seo et al. 2007; Lim et al. 2008).

Human or animal infection can be achieved through eating shore crabs containing the metacercariae. In the seashore village where the human case (50-year-old female) was found, the brackish water crabs were commonly consumed raw as a food (Chung et al. 2011a). This fluke has been reported only from the Far East (Japan, Taiwan, and South Korea) (Table 3.2) (Yamaguti 1971; Seo et al. 2007, 2008). In Japan, this fluke was discovered from Kanagawa (Yamaguti 1934), Mie (Yamaguti 1939), Fukuoka, Chiba, Wakayama (Kifune and Koga 1996, 2001), and Kyushu Prefecture (Koga 2002, 2008). In Taiwan, the crab *Helice depressa* was reported as a second intermediate host (Yamaguti 1971). In South Korea, the metacercariae of this fluke was discovered in shore crabs from a seashore village of Tae-An, Chungcheongnam-do (Seo et al. 2007), and then also from 6 other localities of the western coast, from Jebudo Island to Aphaedo Island (Lee et al. 2010; Chung et al. 2010). Several avian species were added as a natural definitive hosts in South Korea, which included *Arenaria interpres interpres*, *Trigna cinereus*, *Charadrius alexandrinus*, *Charadrius mongolus*, *Calidris ruficollis*, and *Numenius phaeopus* (Seo et al. 2008; Chung et al. 2011b; Yoo et al. 2012; Lee et al. 2016). A human case infected with 3 adult specimens of *G. squatarolae* was discovered in South Korea (Chung et al. 2011a).

The pathogenicity, pathology, and immunology have not been studied. A tentative diagnosis could be made by detection of eggs in feces; however, the definite diagnosis can be done after recovery of the adult flukes. Treatment is successful using praziquantel 10 mg/kg in a single doe (Chung et al. 2011a).

9.1.4 Isoparorchis hypselobagri *(Isoparorchiidae)*

9.1.4.1 *Isoparorchis hypselobagri* (Billet, 1898) Odhner, 1927

[syn. *Distomum hypselobagri* Billet, 1898].

Isoparorchis hypselobagri belongs to the family Isoparorchiidae Travassos, 1922, a group of piscivorous freshwater fishes, teleosts (Gibson 2002). This family was erected by Travassos in 1922 for a single genus, *Isoparorchis* Southwell, 1913 (syn. *Leptolecithium* Kobayashi, 1915), from the swim bladder of freshwater fishes, and raised to full family level by Poche in 1926 (Gibson 2002). Yamaguti (1971) broadened the concenpt to include 2 more genera *Elongoparorchis* Rao, 1960 and *Cladolecithotrema* Ichihara, 1970. However, Gibson and Bray (1979) and Gibson (2002) considered them to be 3 unrelated hemiuroid genera and accepted only one genus *Isoparorchis* in the Isoparorchiidae. Gibson and Bray (1979) considered that *Isoparorchis* differs from the other swim bladder forms in that it occurs in freshwater fishes rather than marine fishes and possesses several different and more primitive features, including a Laurer's canal, a tubular vitellarium, a tubular ovary, and a well-developed muscular sinus-organ.

I. hypselobagri was originally reported from the swim bladder of siluroid fishes in 1898 under the name *Distomum hypselobagri* by Billet in Vietnam (Cribb 1988; Shimazu et al. 2014). The genus *Isoparorchis* was established by Southwell in 1913 using a new species *I. trisimilitubis* Southwell, 1913 collected from the air bladder of *Wallago attu*, a siluroid fish in India (Shimazu et al. 2014). Soon after this, another new species *I. eurytremum* (Kobayashi, 1915) was reported under the name *Leptolecithum eurytremum* from *Silurus asotus* fish in Japan (Kobayashi 1921). Travassos in 1922 recognized this species to belong to *Isoparorchis*, and thus the name became *I. eurytremum* (Kobayashi, 1915) Travassos, 1922 (Ejsmont 1923). Odhner in 1927 suggested to move *Distoma hypselobagri* to *Isoparorchis* and Ejsmont (1923) agreed to do it; thus, the name became *I. hypselobagri* (Billet, 1989) Odhner, 1927. Thereafter, 3 more species have been added in *Isoparorchis*. *I. tandani* Johnston, 1927 was reported from *Tandanus tandanus* fish from Australia (Ejsmont 1923), and *I. pakistani* Bilqees and Khatoon, 1972 was collected from *Wallago attu* fish in Pakistan (Shimazu et al. 2014). Finally, *Isoparorchis* sp. 3 (species name undetermined) was described as a potentially valid species by Shimazu et al. (2014) in Japan.

There had been debates on the synonymy among the species of *Isoparorchis*. Ejsmont (1923) treated *I. trisimilitubis, I. eurytremum,* and *I. tandani* as synonyms of *I. hypselobagri* because of their morphological similarity. Yamaguti (1958, 1971) accepted the synonymy. *I. pakistani* was also synonymized with *I. hypselobagri* by Bhutta and Khan in 1975 and Zaidi and Khan in 1977 (Cribb 1988). By this, only one species remained to be valid within the genus *Isoparorchis* (Cribb 1988). However, Cribb (1998) suggested that the Australian isolates may not be conspecific with the Asian (original description from Vietnam) *I. hypselobagri* considering some evidence regarding the life cycle of this parasite. In this regard, Shimazu et al. (2014) studied on the molecular (ITS2 rDNA gene anaylsis) as well as morphological characteristics of all 5 ever reported *Isoparorchis* species collected from Russia, Japan, Vietnam, Cambodia, Bangladesh, India, and Australia, and concluded that the 4 of the 5 species, including *I. hypselobagri, I. trisimilitubis, I. eurytremum,* and *I. tandani*, were taxonomically valid, whereas *I. pakistani* remained to be a *species inquirenda*. They also detected another potential new species *Isoparorchis* sp. 3 Shimazu et al., 2014 from India and Bangladesh (Shimazu et al. 2014). Human infections with *I. hypselobagri* were reported among the literature (Seo 1978; Ashford and Crewe 2003); one in India by Chandler in 1926 and another in China by Faust in 1929 through recovery of eggs in feces (Seo 1978; Cribb 1988). It was also stated that adult worms were expelled from the alimentary tract of a human following treatment but the literature background is unavailable (Ashford and Crewe 2003).

Adult flukes of *I. hypselobagri* are large, robust, fleshy, oval or oblong with a translucent tegument (Tamuli et al. 2017). They are 12.0–23.0 mm long and 6.0–16.0 mm wide, with forebody having squaring shoulders in large specimens and hindbody with broad-elliptical in shape (Shimazu et al. 2014). The eggs are large and 38–51 μm long and 21–25 μm wide in specimens from the fish host (Shimazu et al. 2014). The cercariae have never been described. The metacercariae are very large, non-encysted, thick, and elongated, 1900–1950 μm long and 850–900 μm wide (Sen 2014).

In large gravid specimens of *I. hypselobagri* (or *I. tandani* for Australian species; Shimazu et al. 2014) the uterine eggs were numerous in number (total uterine eggs: up to 200,000), and those in the terminal parts of the uterus were fully embryonated; miracidia had cilia in bunches and a crown of apical spines (Cribb 1988). However, the eggs did not hatch spontaneously when maintained in water at room temperature for several weeks; it seemed that the eggs must be eaten by a gastropod (Cribb 1988). It is strongly suggested that the gastropod host is prosobranch snails, such as *Posticobia brazieri* and *Melanoides tuberculatus* (Cribb 1988; Ashford and Crewe 2003). The cercariae are released from the gastropod and are consumed by a small invertebrate second intermediate host, probably a small crustacean, in which the cercariae develop into metacercariae up to 1 mm long (Cribb 1988). Metacercariae are also found in the body cavity of fishes, for example, *Mystus vittatus* (catfish), *Oxygaster bacaila,* and *Gagata cenia* (Pandey 1969; Cribb 1988; Sen 2014). Some fish take the role of both second intermediate and definitive host successively (Cribb 1988). The natural definitive hosts are siluroid or non-siluroid fishes, including *Hemibargus* sp. (most likely the same as *Hypselobagrus* sp.), *Wallago attu*, *Silurus asotus*, *Parasilurus asotus, Pelteobagrus fulvidraco, Odontobutis obscura, Ophicephalus argus, Pseudogobio esocinus, Hemibarbus barbus*, *Channa punctatus*, and *Channa maculata* (Bhalerao 1932; Wu 1938; Suzuki et al. 1967; Pandey 1969; Mahajan et al. 1979; Shimazu et al. 2014). Gravid flukes were also recovered from the bile duct of a domestic pig in India; it was assumed that the pig had eaten infected fish and is not a normal host (Varma and Ahluwalia 1980). This fluke was also recovered from various body sites of various host species, including the body cavity of a turtle, the stomach of a crocodile, the intestine of a snake, the liver of frogs, and the feces of humans (Cribb 1988).

Humans may be an accidental host; they may be infected through eating raw or undercooked freshwater fish or crustaceans. The geographical distribution of this parasite has been reported in India, Pakistan, Bangladesh, Thailand, Vietnam, Indonesia, China, Australia, Japan, and Russia (Table 3.2) (Cribb 1988). The flukes from Vietnam was molecularly (and morphologically) defined as *I. hypselobagri sensu stricto*, whereas those from India were defined as *I. trisimilitubis*, those from Japan and Russia were *I. eurytremum*, and those from Australia were *I. tandani* (Shimazu et al. 2014).

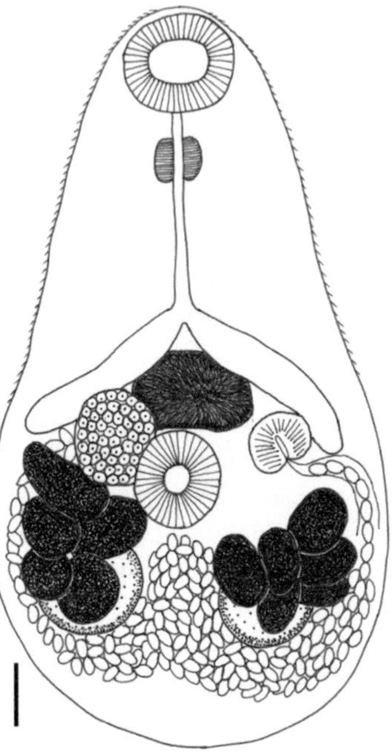

Fig. 9.3 Line drawing of an adult worm of *Microphallus brevicaeca*. Redrawn from the figure in Africa and Garcia (1935) Phil J Sci 57:253–267. Scale bar = 0.05 mm

9.1.5 Microphallus brevicaeca *(Microphallidae)*

9.1.5.1 *Microphallus brevicaeca* (Africa & Garcia, 1935)

[syn. *Heterophyes brevicaeca* Africa and garcia, 1935; *Spelotrema brevicaeca* Tubangui and Africa, 1938; *Carneophallus brevicaeca* Velasquez, 1975].

Microphallus brevicaeca (Fig. 9.3) belongs to the subfamily Microphallinae and family Microphallidae (Velasquez 1975; Deblock 2008). It was originally reported from a human autopsy case (50-year-old man) in Manila, the Philippines under the name *Heterophyes brevicaeca* (Heterophyidae) by Africa and Garcia (1935). Soon after this, Tubangui and Africa (1938) transferred it to the family Microphallidae because of its absence of a seminal receptacle (Heterophyidae usually has a seminal receptacle; Yamaguti 1971) and assigned it in the genus *Spelotrema* Jägerskiöld, 1901 under the name *Spelotrema brevicaeca*.

After then, there have been long debates on the nomenclature of this fluke. Baer (1943) suppressed *Spelotrema* to a synonym of *Microphallus* because the only difference was differet type of hosts and transferred all known species of *Spelotrema* to the genus *Microphallus* Ward, 1901, naming it as *Microphallus brevicaeca*. However, Belopol'skaia (1952) and Yamaguti (1958, 1971) acknowledged the genus *Spelotrema* and returned the name of this species back to *Spelotrema brevicaeca*. Meanwhile, Rausch and Loker (1951), Cable and Kuns (1951), and Stunkard (1951) agreed to the Baer (1943)'s synonymy of *Spelotrema* with *Microphallus*. Capron et al. (1957) also followed Baer (1943)'s opinion and assigned this species as

Microphallus brevicaeca. Separately from this, Cable and Kuns (1951) erected a new genus *Carneophallus* to include 2 species *Carneophallus trilobatus* (new species) and *Carneophallus pseudogonotylus* (Chen, 1944) which have characteristic features of divided lobes of the genital papilla, one of which is penetrated by the ejaculatory duct, and an unmodified metraterm. Thus, Velasquez (1975) proposed a new combination *Carneophallus brevicaeca* for this fluke and discovered the crustacean intermediate host in the Philippines. However, Deblock and Pearson (1969) synonymized *Spelotrema* Jägerskiöld, 1901 and *Carneophallus* Cable and Kuns, 1951 with *Microphallus* Ward, 1901 and gave diagnostic characters of each species of *Microphallus,* including *M. brevicaeca*. This taxonomic move has been adopted by Deblock (2008) who extensively reviewed the flukes belonging to the family Microphallidae. Nevertheless, the 3 names, *Microphallus brevicaeca* (Heard and Overstreet 1983), *Carneophallus brevicaeca* (Waikagul 1991; Eduardo 1991; Kumar 1999), and *Spelotrema brevicaeca* (Fried et al. 2004; Goldberg et al. 2008; Bursey and Goldberg 2016) have been chaotically used by various workers. The present author used the name *M. brevicaeca* following Deblock (2008).

M. brevicaeca was originally reported from one human autopsy in the Philippines (Africa and Garcia 1935) but thereafter recovered from 11 additional human autopsies and also from the intestine of birds named turns (*Sterna albifrons sinensis*) (Africa et al. 1940). Later, this fluke (a single specimen) was recovered in a lizard species *Emoia atrocostata* from Papua New Guinea; whether this fluke is a common parasite of skinks (tropical lizards) or an accidental infection is to be determined (Goldberg et al. 2008). In humans, eggs of this fluke caused acute cardiac dilatation and egg granuloma in the heart, brain, and spinal cord (Africa et al. 1940). The presence of this fluke has been known in the Philippines (Africa et al. 1940) and Papua New Guinea (Goldberg et al. 2008) (Table 3.2).

Adult flukes of *M. brevicaeca* are pyriform to triangular, dorsally convex and ventrally concave, and 0.5–0.7 mm long and 0.3–0.4 mm wide (Velasquez 1975; Beaver et al. 1984). Eggs are small, yellow, operculate, and 15.0–16.0 μm long and 9.4–10.0 μm wide (Beaver et al. 1984). The cercariae have never been described. The metacercariae were ovoid covered with 2 walls, consisting of a thin hyaline inner wall and an outer fibrous, circularly and radially striated layer, and 416–560 μm long and 360–520 μm wide (Velasquez 1975).

The life cycle is not completely known. The snail host is yet undetermined. The second intermediate host has been confirmed to be a freshwater shrimp species *Macrobrachium* sp. (Velasquez 1975). Excysted metacercariae and ovigerous flukes were found in the intestine of freshwater fish *Glossogobius giurus*, and the stomach content of which showed the fish to feed predominantly on the shrimp *Macrobrachium* sp. having the metacercariae (Velasquez 1975). However, whether freshwater fish is a natural definitive host of this species remains to be determined. Natural definitive hosts include fish (?), lizards, birds, and mammals, including humans and monkeys (*Macaca* sp.) (Yamaguti 1971; Velasquez 1975; Ashford and Crewe 2003; Goldberg et al. 2008). Experimental infection of rats was successful to obtain adult flukes (Velasquez 1975).

The eggs of *M. brevicaeca* were found, together with the eggs of other minute intestinal flukes such as *Haplorchis taichui, H. pumilio, H. yokogawai,* and *Stellantchasmus falcatus*, in lesions in the heart, brain, and spinal cord or persons dying of acute cardiac dilatation (Africa et al. 1940). At least 12 fatal patients in the Philippines were diagnosed with *M. brevicaeca* infection mixed-infected with those minute intestinal fluke species (Africa et al. 1940). However, intestinal histopathology and immunology in *M. brevicaeca* infection have not been studied in detail. Diagnosis can be made by recovery of eggs in feces; however, specific diagnosis needs adult worm recovery. Treatment may be successful with praziquantel.

9.1.6 Nanophyetus salmincola *and* Nanophyetus schikhobalowi *(Troglotrematidae)*

9.1.6.1 *Nanophyetus salmincola* (Chapin, 1926) Chapin in Hall, 1927

[syn. *Nanophyes salmincola* Chapin, 1926; *Troglotrema salmincola* Witenberg, 1932].

Nanophyetus salmincola was first described from the intestine of dogs dead (due to so-called salmon poisoning disease) after ingestion of uncooked salmon in North America (Chapin 1926; Witenberg 1932). This fluke was at first assigned to the family Heterophyidae Leiper, 1909 (Chapin 1926). Witenberg (1932) restudied the original specimens and found that they do not have a genital sucker or seminal receptacle but had a large cirrus pouch, and thus, transferred them to the Troglotrematidae Odhner, 1914. Wallace (1935) also restudied this fluke and agreed to assign it in the Troglotrematidae; however, he erected a subfamily Nanophyetinae to include this fluke and another (*Sellacotyle mustelae*). Dollfus (1939) considered the Troglotrematidae to be an unnatural group and proposed to divide it into 6 families, including 4 new families, Nanophyetidae (Wallace, 1935) Dollfus, 1939, Paragonimidae Dollfus, 1939, Pholeteridae Dollfus, 1939, and Renicolidae Dollfus, 1939, and 2 pre-existing ones, Troglotrematidae Odhner, 1914 and Collyriclidae Ward, 1917. Yamaguti (1958, 1971) accepted the family Nanophyetidae (with subfamilies Nanophyetinae, Sellacotylidae, and Macroorchiinae) including *N. salmincola* in this family and also accepted the family Troglotrematidae which included the genera *Troglotrema, Nephrostoma,* and *Xiphidiotrema*. However, molecular evidence favoring synonymy of the Troglotrematidae and Nanophyetidae has been obtained by analysis of the nuclear 28S rRNA gene (Olson et al. 2003). This and other evidence together showed that troglotrematids and nanophyetids were scarcely diverged enough to merit separate family status; thus, they were all assigned in the family Troglotrematidae (Blair et al. 2008). Members of the Troglotrematidae are characterized by small to medium-sized gorgoderoids found in the lumen of the intestine, cavities of the upper respiratory tract, or kidneys or liver of mammals and seabirds (Blair et al. 2008).

The generic name of this fluke had been changed several times. When this fluke was originally described, the generic name was given as *Nanophyes* (*Nanophyes salmincola*) by Chapin (1926). However, the name *Nanophyes* was found to be preoccupied by another taxon, and so it was amended to *Nanophyetus* (Chapin 1927). Witenberg (1932) was of opinion that *Nanophyetus* is a synonym of *Troglotrema* Odhner, 1914 and renamed this parasite as *Troglotrema salmincola*. However, Wallace (1935) acknowledged the validity of the genus *Nanophyetus* and retained the name *N. salmincola*. Yamaguti (1958, 1971) agreed to the validity of this genus. Thereafter, most authors use *Nanophyetus salmincola* (Philip et al. 1954; Yamaguti 1958, 1971; Bennington and Pratt 1960; Farrell et al. 1964; Gebhardt et al. 1966; Porter 1970; Brassard et al. 1982; Eastburn et al. 1987; Jacobson et al. 2008; Sandell et al. 2015) as the name of this fluke. However, some others also use *Troglotrema salmincola* (Shaw 1947; Baker 1950; Mongeau 1961; Beaver et al. 1984; Garcia 2007; Nwoha and Ekwuruike 2010; Mirzaei and Fooladi 2013; Amissah-Reynolds et al. 2016). The present author preferred to use the name *N. salmincola* rather than *T. salmincola* in a review article on fish-borne trematodes (Chai et al. 2005) and also in this book.

Within the genus *Nanophyetus*, 4 species, *N. salmincola* (Chapin, 1926) and *N. schikhobalowi* Skrjabin and Podjapolskaya, 1931, *N. japonensis* Saito, Saito, Yamashita, Watanabe and Sekikawa, 1982, and *N. asadai* (Yamaguti, 1971) Voronova and Chelomina, 2018 (syn. *Pseudotroglotrema asadai* Yamaguti, 1971) have been recorded. *N. schikhobalowi* was described as a new species based on worms from natives in far eastern Siberia (Skrjabin and Podjapolskaja 1931). Witenberg (1932) synonymized *N. schikhobalowi* with *N. salmincola*. Later, Gebhardt (1966) and Filimonova (1966) proposed a subspecific status of this fluke, as *N. salmincola schikhobalowi*. However, a recent molecular study using the nuclear ribosomal gene family (18S, ITS1-5.8S-ITS2, and 28S) provided strong support for *N. salmincola* and *N. schikhobalowi* as independent species (Voronova et al. 2016; Voronova and Chelomina 2018).

N. japonensis was first described from the small intestine of Japanese martens, weasels, raccoon dogs, Japanese badgers, and Japanese water shrews (Saito et al. 1982). The metacercariae were detected from salamanders and freshwater fishes (Saito et al. 1982), and the cercariae were found in the freshwater snail *Semisulcospira libertina* (Saito 1985). *N. japonensis* has been genetically (analyzing the nuclear ribosomal gene family and mitochondrial *nd1* gene) confirmed to be distinct from the pre-existing *N. salmincola* and *N. schikhobolawi* (Voronova and Chelomina 2018). Salmon poisoning disease has not been known in *N. japonensis* (Saito et al. 1982). *N. asadai* was first described from the intestine of stray dogs in Tokyo, Japan under the name (new genus and new species) *Pseudotroglotrema asadai* (Yamaguti 1971). Blair et al. (2008) synonymized *Pseudotroglotrema* with *Nanophyetus*, but they did not make a new combination. Thus, Voronova and Chelomina (2018) proposed a new combination for this species; the new combined name is *N. asadai* (Yamaguti, 1971) Voronova and Chelomina, 2018.

N. salmincola (Fig. 9.4) was first found by Donham (1925) in the intestine of dogs dead after eating "sore-back" salmon in the Pacific Coast of North America.

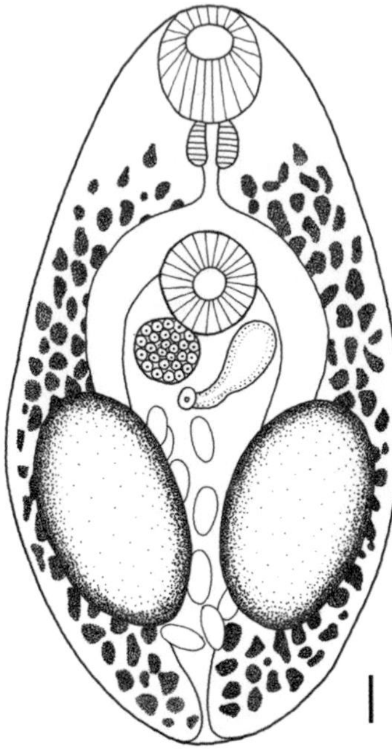

Fig. 9.4 Line drawing of an adult worm of *Nanophyetus salmincola*. Redrawn from the figure in Witenberg (1932) J Parasitol 18:258–293. Scale bar = 0.1 mm

The worm was identified by Chapin (1926) who named it as *Nanophyes salmincola*. The generic name was soon changed into *Nanophyetus* by Chapin (1927). Cram (1926) found this parasite in various mammalian animals in North America, including the coyote (*Canis lestes*), raccoon (*Procyon psora pacifica*), and lynx (*Lynx fasciatus fasciatus*). This parasite has been found to be the vector of a pathogenic microbe named *Neorickettsia helmintheca*, a rickettsia-like organism that is the causative agent of the salmon poisoning disease in canid hosts, in particular, dogs (Millemann and Knapp 1970). The possibility of human infection was first proved by Philip (1958) who successfully infected himself experimentally.

Adult flukes of *N. salmincola* are minute, ovoid to pyriform, characterized by the presence of 2 large testes in the posterior half of the body, and 0.8–2.5 mm long and 0.3–0.5 mm wide (Millemann and Knapp 1970). The uterus contains 5–16 eggs, and the cirrus sac contains a large bipartite seminal vesicle but there is no cirrus (Millemann and Knapp 1970). The eggs are light brown in color with an indistinct operculum at one end and a small blunt point at the other, 64–97 μm long and 34–55 μm wide, and unembryonated when passed in the feces (Millemann and Knapp 1970). The rediae are 450–3000 μm long, and the cercariae are microcercus type and 310–470 μm long (including the short tail) and 30–150 μm wide (Millemann and Knapp 1970). The metacercariae are round, enclosed by a thin, transparent wall of parasite origin, and older ones also by a fibrous wall of host origin, and 170–250 μm in diameter (Simms et al. 1931).

The life cycle of *N. salmincola* was studied extensively (Bennington and Pratt 1960; Millemann and Knapp 1970). The time required for eggs to hatch when held in standing water at room temperature was 90 days (Millemann and Knapp 1970). The first intermediate host, *Oxytrema silicula*, the pleurocerid stream snail, was confirmed in Oregon west of the Cascade Mountains, north to the Olympic Peninsula in Washington, and in northern California (Millemann and Knapp 1970). The metacercariae were found in salmonid (*Oncorhynchus* sp., *Brachymystax* sp., and *Coregonus* sp.) and non-salmonid fishes and the Pacific giant salamander (Millemann and Knapp 1970; Yu and Mott 1994). The natural definitive hosts are fish-eating birds (3 species) and mammals, including humans, dogs, cats, raccoons, rats, foxes, minks, and bears (Millemann and Knapp 1970; Rogers and Rogers 1976; Eastburn et al. 1987). Experimental definitive hosts included dogs, raccoons, and golden hamsters (Bennington and Pratt 1960; Millemann and Knapp 1970).

The number of human *N. salmincola* infection documented so far is at least 21 cases in North America (Eastburn et al. 1987; Fritsche et al. 1989; Harrell and Deardorff 1990). In a clinic located in a northwestern part of the U.S., 10 natural human cases were diagnosed with *N. salmincola* between 1974 and 1985 (Eastburn et al. 1987). Subsequently, 10 additional human patients (9 in 1986 and 1987, and 1 in 1982) were reported also from the same area of the U.S. (Fritsche et al. 1989). Another human case was reported to be infected through handling naturally infected coho salmon in the U.S. (Harrell and Deardorff 1990).

The principal mode of human infection with *N. salmincola* is consumption of raw or undercooked salmonid or non-salmonid fishes (Eastburn et al. 1987; Fritsche et al. 1989). However, handling infected fish can also be a mode of human infection (Harrell and Deardorff 1990). The geographical distribution of this fluke is confined to North America, including the U.S. and Canada (Table 3.2) (Millemann and Knapp 1970; Booth et al. 1984). The distribution of *N. schikhobalowi*, another species found in Russia and proved to be a distinct species molecularly (Voronova et al. 2016), is described below.

Infected people with *N. salmincola* may experience diarrhea, abdominal discomfort, and eosinophilia, but the symptoms are generally mild (Eastburn et al. 1987; Fritsche et al. 1989). Salmon poisoning has not been reported in humans. However, this fluke has been proven to be the vector of a rickettsia *Neorickettsia helminthoeca* which causes a serious and often fatal systemic infection known as salmon poisoning in animals such as dogs, foxes, and coyotes (Millemann and Knapp 1970). *N. salmincola* was also found to harbor a second species of *Neorickettsia* which can cause Elokomin fluke fever in bears (a febrile disease similar to salmon poisoning in dogs) but cause only low grade illness in dogs (Greiman et al. 2016).

Human nanophyetiasis can be diagnosed by recovery of eggs in fecal examinations if the infection is endemic in that area. However, recovery of adult flukes may be necessary to draw a specific diagnosis. Treatment can be done using praziquantel in both human and animal infections (Eastburn et al. 1987; Foreyt and Gorham 1988; Fritsche et al. 1989). Niclosamide and bithionol were also used with favorable effects (Eastburn et al. 1987).

9.1.6.2 *Nanophyetus schikhobalowi* Skrjabin and Podjapolskaya, 1931

[syn. *Nanophyetus salmincola schikhobalowi* Gebhardt, 1966].

Nanophyetus schikhobalowi was discovered from natives in far eastern Siberia and described as a new species mainly because of smaller egg size compared to *N. salmincola* (Skrjabin and Podjapolskaya 1931). However, Witenberg (1932) considered the description to be incomplete and concluded that *N. schikhobalowi* is a synonym of *N. salmincola*. However, Gebhardt (1966) and Filimonova (1966) relegated *N. schikhobalowi* to a subspecific status, *N. salmincola schikhobalowi*. At that time, the major differences between the 2 subspecies were that the Siberian form does not carry a rickettsia and that natural human infections with the U.S. form had not been reported until the 1960s (Millemann and Knapp 1970). Later, however, human infections were also reported for the U.S. form (Eastburn et al. 1987). A recent molecular study using the nuclear ribosomal gene family (18S, ITS1-5.8S-ITS2, and 28S) provided strong support for *N. salmincola* and *N. schikhobalowi* to be independent species (Voronova et al. 2016; Voronova and Chelomina 2018).

Adult flukes of *N. schikhobalowi* are morphologically similar to *N. salmincola*; they are minute, pyriform, characterized by the presence of 2 large testes in the posterior half of the body, and 0.58 mm long and 0.47 mm wide in specimens from Amur aborigines in Russia (Millemann and Knapp 1970; Yamaguti 1971). The eggs are light brown in color with an indistinct operculum at one end and a small blunt point at the other, and slightly smaller than those of *N. salmincola*, 52–82 μm long and 32–56 μm wide (Filimonova 1965; Millemann and Knapp 1970). The rediae of *N. schikhobalowi* are very similar to those of *N. salmincola* (Millemann and Knapp 1970). The cercariae are microcercus, xiphidiocercarial type, and 220–430 μm long (including the short tail) and 30–120 μm wide (Bennington and Pratt 1960; Filimonova 1964). The metacercariae are round, enclosed by a thin, transparent wall of parasite origin, and older ones also by a fibrous wall of host origin, and 160–220 μm in diameter (22-day-old ones in experimentally infected fish) (Filimonova 1965).

The life cycle of *N. schikhobalowi* was studied extensively by Russian researchers (Filimonova 1964, 1965, 1966; Millemann and Knapp 1970). The eggs first appear in the feces of experimental animals 5–8 days after they have eaten infected fish (Filimonova 1965). The first intermediate host is *Semisulcospira laevigaeta* and *Semisulcospira cancellata* (Filimonova 1965). The metacercariae occur in salmonid (*Oncorhynchus keta*, the chum salmon, and others) and non-salmonid fishes (Cottidae and Cyprinidae) and the Pacific giant salamander (Millemann and Knapp 1970). The natural definitive hosts are fish-eating mammals, including humans, dogs, wolves, sea otters, cats, martens, badgers, minks, raccoon dogs, rats, foxes, and bears (Millemann and Knapp 1970). Experimental definitive hosts included dogs, cats, and white rats (Millemann and Knapp 1970).

People acquire the infection by ingestion of improperly cooked salmon or trout (Yu and Mott 1994). The infection is endemic in the far eastern part of Russia including Amur and Ussuri valleys of Khabarovsk territory and north Sakhalin (Table 3.2), where the average prevalence among human population was 5.0% (Yu and Mott 1994). In local ethnic minorities, the prevalence was higher, 20%, and may reach up to 60% in some localities (Yu and Mott 1994). Some 18,500 human infections were estimated in 1993 in the far eastern part of Russia (Kumar 1999). Infection incidences in snails on the Aneu and Khor Rivers were 9.3% and 16.7%, respectively (Filimonova 1965).

People harbouring more than 500 flukes may manifest clinical symptoms primarily of abdominal discomfort; however, rickettsial transmission by this fluke to humans has not been known (Kumar 1999; Voronova et al. 2016). The diagnosis can be done by recovery of eggs in fecal examinations if the infection is endemic in that area. However, recovery of adult flukes may be necessary to draw a specific diagnosis. Treatment was successfully done using either fern extract or quinacrine in endemic areas in Russia (Fritsche et al. 1989). However, praziquantel seems to be the best drug for treatment of both human and animal infections.

9.1.7 Prohemistomum vivax *(Cyathocotylidae)*

9.1.7.1 *Prohemistomum vivax* (Sonsino, 1892) Azim, 1933

[syn. *Prohemistomum spinulosum* Odhner, 1913].

Prohemistomum vivax (Fig. 9.5) was previously considered a member of strigeids and to belong to the family Strigeidae (Azim 1933; Olivier 1940; Chandler and Rausch 1946; Dubois and Pearson 1963). However, Yamaguti (1958, 1971) and

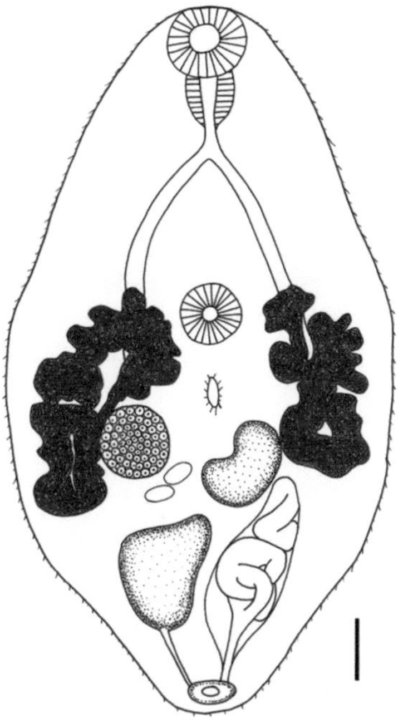

Fig. 9.5 Line drawing of an adult worm of *Prohemistomum vivax*. Redrawn from the figure in Fahmy and Selim (1959) Z Parasitenkd 19:3–13. Scale bar = 0.1 mm

Niewiadomska (2002) assigned *Prohemistomum* in the family Cyathocotylidae Mühling, 1898. The family Cyathocotylidae is morphologically characterized by the presence of a cirrus-sac that encloses the seminal vesicle, pars prostatica, and an eversible ejaculatory duct that forms a cirrus, a sucker-like holdfast organ extending over all or part of the ventral surface of the body, and round or oval testes and ovary variable in position (Niewiadomska 2002). Another characteristic feature of the Cyathocotylidae is broad host spectrum ranging from reptiles to birds and mammals (Niewiadonska 2002). Yamaguti (1958, 1971) divided this family into 4 subfamilies, Cyathocotylinae Mühling, 1898, Pseudhemistominae Szidat, 1936, Prohemistominae Lutz, 1935, and Szidatiinae Dubois, 1938. Niewiadomska (2002) acknowledged 3 of these subfamilies (Cyathocotylinae, Prohemistominae, and Szidatiinae) and added 2 more subfamilies, Muhlinginae Mehra, 1950 and Prosostephaninae Szidat, 1936. *P. vivax* belongs to the subfamily Prohemistominae, in which 5 genera are included, *Mesostephanoides* Dubois, 1951, *Mesostephanus* Lutz, 1935, *Prohemistomum* Odhner, 1913, *Linstowiella* Szidat, 1933, and *Paracoenogonimus* Katsurada, 1914 (Niewiadomska 2002).

The generic characteristics of *Prohemistomum* include elongate body without caudal appendage, ventral concavity in form of shallow pocket which may overlie holdfast organ, round, oval or transversely oval holdfast organ situated in posterior part of body, well-developed vitallarium and cirrus sac, and absence of vaginal sphincter (Niewiadomska 2002). Within the genus *Prohemistomum*, more than ten species have been described, including *P. fregatae* (Tubangui and Masiluñgan, 1941) Dubois, 1951, *P. indicum* (Mehra, 1947) Dubois, 1951, *P. lutzi* (Vidyarthi, 1948) Dubois, 1951, *P. secundum* Vidyarthi, 1948, *P. vidyarthii* Yamaguti, 1959, *P. chandleri* Vernberg, 1952, and *P. azimi* Saoud and Ramadan, 1977 (Yamaguti 1971; Saoud and Ramadan 1977). In 1916, Ciurea described *Prohemistomum appendiculatum* but Lutz in 1935 transferred this to another genus under the name *Mesostephanus appendiculatus* (Dubois 1982). In 1934, Price reported *Prohemistomum fajardensis* but Lutz in 1935 also transferred this to *Mesostephanus* genus under the name *M. fajardensis* (Dubois 1982). Travassos in 1924 described *Prohemistomum odhneri* from an Indian hawk, but later it was synonymized with *P. indicum* (Yamaguti 1971). *P. vivax* is the type species of this genus (Yamaguti 1958, 1971; Niewiadomska 2002), and the only species causing zoonotic infection to humans (Nasr 1941).

P. vivax was originally reported as a cercaria (*Cercaria vivax*) shed from the snail *Cleopatra bulimoides* in Egypt by Sonsino in 1892 (Azim 1933). The genus *Prohemistomum* was erected in 1913 by Odhner using *Prohemistomum spinulosum* collected from the common Egyptian kite (*Milvus migrans aegyptius*) (Azim 1933). Later, the cercariae (*Cercaria vivix*) were experimentally exposed to brackish and freshwater fish *Gambusia affinis* and *Tilapia nilotica,* and metacercariae were obtained from these fish; adults were also recovered from cats and dogs experimentally fed the fish and were named as *P. vivax* (Azim 1933). Then, *P. spinulosum* was synonymized with *P. vivax* because of the rule of priority (Azim 1933; Gohar 1934). A human infection was found in Cairo, Egypt (Nasr 1941). The geographical distribution of this parasite includes Egypt, Israel (Palestine), and Europe (Table 3.2) (Bowman 2014; Faltýnková et al. 2016).

Adult flukes of *P. vivax* are elongate ovoid or broadly pyriform, with more attenuated posterior end than anterior end, and 0.74–1.55 mm long and 0.45–0.78 mm wide (Fahmy and Selim 1959). The eggs are large, operculate, and 90–108 μm long and 45–77 μm wide (Fahmy and Selim 1959). In the snail host, young sporocysts contained germinal cells, and adult sporocysts had cercariae in different stages of development; the cercaria is a furcocercus type, called as vivax cercaria, with the total length of 986–1300 μm (Azim 1933). The metacercarial cyst is round having a thin membranous wall and a thick external one with the maximum diameter of 320 μm; black pigments are deposited in the tissues of the metacercariae (Azim 1933).

The eggs of *P. vivax* obtained from the adult flukes were kept at 28 ± 2 °C with light; they developed to maturity and hatched to free-swimming miracidia which were pyriform and covered with cilia (El-Kewaisny 2011). The first intermediate host is known to be *Cleopatra bulimoides* snails (Azim 1933; Saad 1998). The second intermediate hosts are freshwater fishes, including *Tilapia zilli, Tilapia nilotica, Gambusia affinis, Clarias lazera, Clarias gariepinus, Oreochromis niloticus, Bagrus bayad, Shilbe mystus, Atherina* sp., *Hydrocyon* sp., *Alestes* sp., *Schibe* sp., and *Eutropius* sp. (Azim 1933; Tawfik et al. 2000; El-Seify et al. 2003; Saad 2007; Amin et al. 2010; Shalaby et al. 2011; Bowman 2014; Kirrella et al. 2018) and frogs (Walton 1949). Natural definitive hosts include kites (*Milvus migrans aegyptius*) and other fish-eating birds, and mammals including dogs, cats, and humans (Gohar 1934, 1935; Nasr 1941; Abo-Shady 1980; El-Dakhly et al. 2017). Experimental definitive hosts included dogs, cats, rats, mice, chickens (chicks), and hamsters (Azim 1933; Fahmy and Selim 1959; Fahmy et al. 1976; Tawfik et al. 2000; Mahdy et al. 2000; El-Seify et al. 2003; Saleh et al. 2009; El-Kewaisny 2012). In rats, first eggs were detected in the feces at day 3 after metacercarial infection (Alghabban 2014).

In experimentally infected BALB/c mice, histopathological findings in the small intestine included compression and sometimes erosion of intestinal epithelial lining especially at the site of worm attachment (Mahfouz et al. 2005). The intestinal villi underwent deformation in the form of shortening, blunting, and fusion, which progressed with time; some villi were totally destroyed at the parasite localization, and hypertrophy of crypts with inflammatory cell infiltration in the stroma were observed in parallel (Mahfouz et al. 2005). In these mice, the level of TGF-β was progressively increased along with the infection time compared with uninfected controls (Mahfouz et al. 2005). Immunostimulating effects were observed in mice infected with *P. vivax* using a medicinal plant, *Pelagonium reinforme/sidoides* (Amer et al. 2006). In hamsters experimentally infected with *P. vivax*, the serum level of iron but not vitamin B_{12} was significantly decreased compared to uninfected controls (El-Kewaisny 2012).

Nasr (1941) reported a human case infected with *P. vivax* who was 30-year-old resident of Cairo, a fez seller, admitted to a hospital for bilateral pulmonary tuberculosis; he died and 5 adult specimens of *P. vivax* were recovered from his small intestine. The death of this case seems not directly due to *P. vivax* infection. For serological diagnosis of *P. vivax* infection, ELISA technique was developed in experimentally infected rats (Mahdy et al. 2000). The herb drug, named *Moringa oleifera*, was proved to be effective in treatment of experimental *P. vivax* infection in rats (Alghabban 2014). Aqueous extract of dried papaya seed (*Carica papaya*) showed anthelmintic activity against metacercariae as well as adult flukes of *P. vivax* (Ibrahim and Mahdy 2017).

References

References for Section 9.1.1

Angel LM, Mutze GJ (1987) On the occurrence of *Brachylaima* sp. (Trematoda) in the feral house mouse, *Mus musculus*, in South Australia. Trans R Soc South Australia 111:121–122

Butcher AR (2016) Children, snails and worms: the *Brachylaima cribbi* story. Microbiol Australia 37:30–33

Butcher AR, Grove DI (2001) Description of the life-cycle stages of *Brachylaima cribbi* n. sp. (Digenea: Brachylaimidae) derived from eggs recovered from human faeces in Australia. Syst Parasitol 49:211–221

Butcher AR, Grove DI (2003) Field prevalence and laboratory susceptibility of southern Australian land snails to *Brachylaima cribbi* sporocyst infection. Parasite 10:119–125

Butcher AR, Grove DI (2005a) Seasonal variation in rates of sporocyst and metacercarial infection by *Brachylaima cribbi* in helicid and hygromiid land snails on the Yorke Peninsula, South Australia. Austral J Zool 53:375–382

Butcher AR, Grove DI (2005b) Second intermediate host land snails and definitive host animals of *Brachylaima cribbi* in South Australia. Parasite 12:31–37

Butcher AR, Talbot GA, Norton RE et al (1996) Locally acquired *Brachylaima* sp. (Digenea: Brachylaimidae) intestinal fluke infection in two South Australian infants. Med J Aust 164:475–478

Butcher AR, Parasuramar P, Thompson CS et al (1998) First report of the isolation of an adult worm of the genus *Brachylaima* (Digenea: Brachylaimidae), from the gastrointestinal tract of a human. Int J Parasitol 28:607–610

Butcher AR, Palethorpe HM, Grove DI (2002a) Effects of sex and age on the susceptibility of C57BL/6J mice to infection with *Brachylaima cribbi* and the course of infection in NOD SCID mice. Parasitol Res 88:668–674

Butcher AR, Palethorpe HM, Grove DI (2002b) The susceptibility of inbred mice to infection with *Brachylaima cribbi* (Digenea: Brachylaimidae). Parasitol Int 51:109–115

Butcher AR, Palethorpe HM, Grove DI (2003) Response to a re-infection with *Brachylaima cribbi* in immunocompetent and immunodeficient mice. Parasitol Int 52:219–228

Chai JY (2007) Intestinal flukes. In: Murrell KD, Fried B (eds) Food-borne parasitic zoonoses. Fish and plant-borne parasites. Springer, New York, pp 53–115

Cribb TH (1990) Introduction of a *Brachylaima* species (Digenea: Brachylaimidae) to Australia. Int J Parasitol 20:789–796

Cribb TH, O'Callaghan M (1992) An unusual trematode infecting domestic chickens. Aust Vet J 69:69–70

Dybing NA, Fleming PA, Adams PJ (2013) Environmental conditions predict helminth prevalence in red foxes in Western Australia. Int J Parasitol: Parasit Wildl 2:165–172

González-Moreno O, Gracenea M (2006) Life cycle and description of a new species of brachylaimid (Trematoda: Digenea) in Spain. J Parasitol 92:1305–1312
Gracenea M, González-Moreno O (2002) Life cycle of *Brachylaima mascomai* n. sp. (Trematoda: Brachylaimidae), a parasite of rats in the Llobregat Delta (Spain). J Parasitol 88:124–133
Nakao M, Waki T, Sasaki M et al (2017) *Brachylaima ezohelicis* sp. nov. (Trematoda: Brachylaimidae) found from the land snail *Ezohelix gainesi*, with a note of an unidentified *Brachylaima* species in Hokkaido, Japan. Parasitol Int 66:240–249
Pojmańska T (2002) Family Brachylaimidae Joyeux and Foley, 1930. In: Gibson DI, Jones A, Bray RA (eds) Keys to the Trematoda, vol 1. CAB Publishing, Natural History Museum, London, pp 37–43
Sirgel WF, Mas-Coma S (2010) *Renylaina capensis* n. gen., n. sp. (Trematoda: Brachylaimidae) from the urinary system of the shrew *Myosorex varius* Smuts, 1832 (Insectivora: Soricidae). Parasitol Res 106:1443–1453
Toledo R, Muñoz-Antoli C, Esteban JG (2014) Intestinal trematode infections. Digenetic trematodes. Adv Exp Med Biol 766:201–240
Yamaguti S (1958) Systema Helminthum. Vol. I. The digenetic trematodes of vertebrates (Part I). Interscience Publishers Inc, New York, pp 1–979
Yamaguti S (1971) Synopsis of digenetic trematodes of vertebrates, vol I. Keigaku Publishing Co, Tokyo, Japan, pp 1–1074
Yamaguti S (1975) Synoptical review of life histories of digenetic trematodes of vertebrates. Keigaku Publishing Co, Tokyo, Japan, pp 1–590 with 219 figure plates

References for Section 9.1.2

Birmani NA, Dharejo AM, Khan MM (2009) *Cotylurus sindhense*, new species (Digenea: Strigeidae) in black coot *Fulica atra* (Rallidae) of Manchhar Lake, Sindh, Pakistan. Proc Parasitol (Pakistan) 48:133–138
Chen C, Cai G (1985) Morphological testimony, demonstration of a case of human infested with *Cotylurus japonicus* Ishii, 1932 (Trematoda: Strigeidae). Bull Hunan Med Coll 10:31–34 (in Chinese)
Chu JK, Cho YJ, Chung SB et al (1973) Study on the trematode parasites of the birds in Korea. Korean J Parasitol 11:70–75 in Korean
Das SN, Ghazi RR (2012) *Cotylurus fuscicollisi* (Trematoda: Strigeidae) from *Phalacrocorax fuscicollis* (Stephens) in Thatta District, Sindh, Pakistan. Proc Parasitol (Pakistan) 53:37–42
Dubois G (1938) Monographie des Strigeida (Trematoda). Mem Soc Neuchateloise Sci Natur VI:1–535
Fried B, Graczyk TK, Tamang L (2004) Food-borne intestinal trematodiases in humans. Parasitol Res 93:159–170
Ishii N (1932) Studies on bird trematodes. I. Taxonomic study of trematodes. II. Description of new and known species. Jikken Igaku Zasshi 16:1205–1231 (in Japanese)
Lalitha CM, Alwar VS (1960) Parasites of domestic ducks (*Anas boschas domesticus*) in Madras (a preliminary note). Ind Vet J 37:179–181
Niewiadomska K (2002) Family Strigeidae Railliet, 1919. In: Gibson DI, Jones, Bray RA (eds) Keys to the Trematoda, vol 1. Natural History Museum, London, pp 231–241
Terenina NB, Movsesyan SO (2018) Distribution pattern of serotoninergic neurons in trematode cercariae. J Evol Biochem Physiol 54:1–7
Yamaguti S (1958) Systema Helminthum. Vol. I. The digenetic trematodes of vertebrates (Part I). Interscience Publishers Inc, New York, pp 1–979
Yamaguti S (1971) Synopsis of digenetic trematodes of vertebrates. In: Vol, vol I. Keigaku Publishing Co, Tokyo, pp 1–1074
Yu SH, Mott KE (1994) Epidemiology and morbidity of food-borne intestinal trematode infections. Trop Dis Bull 91:R125–R152

References for Section 9.1.3

Chung OS, Lee HJ, Sohn WM et al (2010) Discovery of *Maritrema jebunensis* n. sp. (Digenea: Microphallidae) from the Asian shore crab, *Hemigrapsus sanguineus*, in Korea. Korean J Parasitol 48:335–338

Chung OS, Lee HJ, Kim YM et al (2011a) First report of human infection with *Gynaecotyla squatarolae* and first Korean record of *Haplorchis pumilio* in a patient. Parasitol Int 60:227–229

Chung OS, Sohn WM, Chai JY et al (2011b) Discovery of *Maritrema obstipum* (Digenea: Microphallidae) from migratory birds in Korea. Korean J Parasitol 49:457–460

Deblock S (1974) Contribution à l'étude des Microphallidae Travassos, 1920 (Trematoda). XXIX. A propos d'espèces décrites au Japon par S. Yamaguti. B. Le genre *Gynaecotyla* Yamaguti, 1939. Ann Parasitol 49:319–335

Deblock S (2008) Family Microphallidae Ward, 1901. In: Bray RA, Gibson DI, Jones A (eds) Keys to the Trematoda, vol 3. CAB Publishing, Natural History Museum, London, pp 451–492

Deblock S, Pearson JC (1968) Contribution à l'étude des Microphallidae Travassos, 1920 (Trematoda). XIV. Trois Gynaecotylinae nouveaux d'Australie. Considérations systématiques. Ann Parasit Hum Comp 43:131–148 (in French)

Dery DW (1958) A revision of the genus *Gynaecotyla* (Microphallidae: Trematoda) with a description of *Gynaecotyla riggini* n. sp. J Parasitol 44:110–112

Ke XL (1980) Studies on microphallid trematodes from China. V. Genus *Gynaecotyla*, with descriptions of 2 new species. Acta Zootaxon Sin 5:235–239 (in Chinese)

Kifune T, Koga T (1996) Metacercaria of *Gynaecotyla squatarolae* (Digenea: Microphallidae) found in *Scopimera globosa* (Decapoda: Ocypodidae) on the seashore of the eastern part of Fukuoka City, Kyushu. Trans Nagasaki Biol Soc 47:51–54 (in Japanese)

Kifune T, Koga T (2001) On the microphallid metacercaria (Trematoda: Microphallidae) found in *Scopimera globosa* inhabiting the tidal flats in Tokyo Bay (Chiba Prefecture) and in an estuary of the Waka River (Wakayama Prefecture). Trans Nagasaki Biol Soc 53:50–53 (in Japanese)

Koga T (2002) Parasite and species richness: association of *Scopimera globose* (Crustacea: Decapoda: Ocypodidae), *Batillaria cumingi* (Mollusa: Gastropoda: Potamididae) and *Gynaecotyla squatarolae* (Trematoda: Digenea: Microphallidae). Jpn J Benthol 57:67–70 (in Japanese)

Koga T (2008) A trematode infection with no effect on reproductive success of a sand-bubbler crab. Ecol Res 23:557–563

Lee HJ, Chai JY, Lee JW et al (2010) Surveys of *Gynaecotyla squatarolae* and *Microphallus koreana* (Digenea: Microphallidae) metacercariae in two species of estuarine crabs in western coastal areas, Korea. Korean J Parasitol 48:81–83

Lee YI, Chung OS, Seo M (2016) Recovery of *Oswaldotrema nacinovici* from whimbrels (Aves) in Korea. Korean J Parasitol 54:809–812

Lim DS, Cho KJ, Guk SM et al (2008) Tegumental ultrastructure of adult *Gynaecotyla squatarolae* (Digenea: Microphallidae). Korean J Parasitol 46:87–90

Otagaki H (1958) A study on some trematodes whose intermediate hosts are crabs inhabiting mouth of rivers flowing into Inland Sea of Japan. Jpn J Parasitol 7:167–182 (in Japanese)

Seo M, Guk SM, Lee SH et al (2007) *Gynaecotyla squatarolae* (Digenea: Microphallidae) from rats experimentally infected with metacercariae from the shore crab, *Macrophthalmus dilatatus*. Korean J Parasitol 45:199–204

Seo M, Guk SM, Chai JY (2008) The ruddy turnstone, *Arenaria interpres interpres*, a new definitive host for *Gynaecotyla squatarolae* (Digenea: Microphallidae). Korean J Parasitol 46:41–43

Travassos L (1921) Contribuçâo para o conhecimento da fauna helmintologica brasileira. IX. Sobre as espéces da subfamilia Microfalinae Ward, 1901. Arch Escola Sup Agric Med Vet. Nictheroy 4(1920):85–91

Yamaguti S (1934) Studies on the helminth fauna of Japan. Part 3. Avian trematodes, II. Jpn J Zool V:543–583

Yamaguti S (1939) Studies on the helminth fauna of Japan. Part 25. Trematodes of birds, IV. Jpn J Zool 8:129–210
Yamaguti S (1971) Synopsis of digenetic trematodes of vertebrates, vol I. Keigaku Publishing Co, Tokyo, pp 1–1074
Yamanishi H (2014) Infection rates of larval lung flukes, *Paragonimus ohirai*, in the brackish water crabs, *Sesarma dehaani*, from Kikuyajima Sandbank in the Maruyama River in Hyogo prefecture from 2010 to 2013. Med Entomol Zool 65:157–162 (in Japanese)
Yoo HJ, Chung OS, Seo M (2012) Discovery of *Endocotyle incana* and *Spelotrema psudogonotyla* (Digenea: Microphallidae) from scolopacid migratory birds in Korea. Korean J Parasitol 50:273–276

References for Section 9.1.4

Ashford RW, Crewe W (2003) The parasites of *Homo sapiens*. Liverpool School of Tropical Medicine, London
Bhalerao GD (1932) A note on the probability of infection of man and domestic carnivores by *Isoparorchis hypselobagri* (Billet, 1898). Ind J Vet Sci Anim Husb 11:406–407
Cribb TH (1988) Two new digenetic trematodes from Australian freshwater fishes with notes on previously described species. J Nat Hist 22:27–43
Cribb TH (1998) The diversity of the Digenea of Australian animals. Int J Parasitol 28:899–911
Ejsmont L (1923) Note sur le genre *Isoparchis*. Ann Parasitol 10:453–457 in French
Gibson DI (2002) Family Isoparorchiidae Travassos, 1922. In: Gibson DI, Jones A, Bray RA (eds) Keys to the Trematoda, vol 1. CAB Publishing, Natural History Museum, London, pp 379–380
Gibson DI, Bray RA (1979) The Hemiuroidea: terminology, systematics and evolution. Bull Brit Mus (Nat Hist) (Zool) 36:35–146
Kobayashi H (1921) On some digenetic trematodes in Japan. Parasitology 12:380–410
Mahajan CL, Agrawal NK, John MJ et al (1979) Effect of the digenean *Isoparorchis hypselobagri* (Bilet, 1898) on airbreathing fish *Channa punctatus* (Bloch) with particular reference to biochemical and haematological changes. J Fish Dis 2:519–528
Pandey KC (1969) Studies on the metacercaria of freshwater fishes of India. VI. On the morphology of metacercaria of *Isoparorchis hypselobagri* (Billet, 1898) with a note on its development. Proc Nat Acad Sci India (Sect B) 39:185–190
Sen JM (2014) Occurrence of *Isoparorchis hypselobagri* (Billet, 1898) Odhner, 1927 (Family: Isoparorchiidae Poche, 1926) as parasite of *Oxygaster bacaila* (Ham.) and *Gagata cenia* (Ham.) in Baruasagar Reservoir, Jhansi. J Entomol Zool Stud 2:32–34
Seo BS (1978) Clinical Parasitology. Revised ed. Il-Cho-Kak, Seoul, Korea (a textbook in Korean)
Shimazu T, Cribb TH, Miller TL et al (2014) Revision of *Isoparorchis* Southwell, 1913 (Digenea: Hemiuroidea, Isoparchiidae), parasites of the air bladder of freshwater catfishes: a molecular and morphological study. Bull Natl Mus Nat Sci Ser A 40:15–51
Suzuki K, Kamegai S, Kamegai S et al (1967) The occurrence of *Isoparorchis hypselobagri* Billet, 1898 (Trematoda) in Eastern Japan. Res Bull Meguro Parasitol Mus (1):15–19 (in Japanese)
Tamuli S, Kalita B, Islam S et al (2017) Prevalence of *Isoparorchis hypselobagri* Southwell, 1913 (Digenea: Hemiuroidea, Isoparorchiidae), in some bottom dwelling fishes of Kolong River. Assam Env Ecol 35:2032–2037
Varma TK, Ahluwalia SS (1980) An unusual record of *Isoparorchis hypselobagri* (Billet, 1898), a trematode parasite of fishes from the bile duct of a pig. Ind Vet J 57:688–689
Wu K (1938) On the occurrence of *Isoparorchis* among fishes in China (Trematoda: Isoparorchiidae). Peking Nat Hist Bull 12:273–277
Yamaguti S (1958) Systema Helminthum. Vol. I. The digenetic trematodes of vertebrates (Part I). Interscience Publishers Inc, New York, pp 1–979
Yamaguti S (1971) Synopsis of digenetic trematodes of vertebrates, vol I. Keigaku Publishing Co, Tokyo, pp 1–1074

References for Section 9.1.5

Africa CM, Garcia EY (1935) Heterophyid trematodes of man and dog in the Philippines with descriptions of three new species. Phil J Sci 57:253–267

Africa CM, de Leon W, Garcia EY (1940) Visceral complications in intestinal heterophyidiasis of man. Acta Med Philippina, Monogr Series No. 1, pp 1–132

Ashford RW, Crewe W (2003) The parasites of *Homo sapiens*. Taylor & Francis Inc, London

Baer JG (1943) Les trématodes parasites de la musraigne d'eau Neomys fodiens (Schreb.). Bull Soc Neuchatel Sci Nat 68:33–84

Beaver PC, Jung RC, Cupp EW (1984) Clinical parasitology, 9th edn. Lea and Febiger, Philadelphia

Belopol'skaia MM (1952) Trematode family Microphallidae Travassos, 1920. In Trematodes of Animals and Man. Moscow. Vol. 6, pp. 619–756 (in Russian)

Bursey CR, Goldberg SR (2016) A new species of *Physalopteroides* (Nematode: Physalopteridae) in *Emoia atrocostata* (Squamata: Scincidae) from Peninsular Malaysia. Comp Parasitol 83:221–226

Cable RM, Kuns ML (1951) The trematode family Microphallidae with the description of *Carneophallus trilobatus* gen. et sp. nov. from Mexico. J Parasitol 37:507–514

Capron M, Deblock S, Biguet J (1957) Premièr contribution à la connaissance des Microphallidae Travassos, 1920 (Trematoda). I. Description de deux nouveaux microphallides de Charadriformes: *Microphallus chabaudi* et *M. tringae*. Non-validité du genre *Carneophallus* Cable et Kuns, 1951. Bull Soc Zool France 82:378–392 (in French)

Deblock S (2008) Family Microphallidae Ward, 1901. In: Bray RA, Gibson DI, Jones A (eds) Keys to the Trematoda, vol 3. CAB Publishing, Natural History Museum, London, pp 451–492

Deblock S, Pearson JC (1969) Contribution à l'étude des Microphallidae Travassos, 1920 (Trematoda). XVIII. De cinq Microphallus d'Australie done deux mouveaux. Ann Parasit (Paris) 44:391–414 (in French)

Eduardo SL (1991) Food-borne parasitic zoonoses in the Philippines. Southeast Asian J Trop Med Public Health 22(suppl):16–22

Fried B, Graczyk TK, Tamang L (2004) Food-borne intestinal trematodiases in humans. Parasitol Res 93:159–170

Goldberg SR, Bursey CR, Kraus F (2008) Gastrointestinal helminths of eleven species of *Emoia* (Squamata: Scincidae) from Papua New Guinea. J Nat Hist 42:1923–1935

Heard RW, Overstreet RM (1983) Taxonomy and life histories of two north American species of "*Carneophallus*" (= *Microphallus*) (Digenea: Microphallidae). Proc Helminthol Soc Wash 50:170–174

Kumar V (1999) Echinostomiasis, heterophyiasis, metagonimiasis and other intestinal trematode infections. In: Trematode infections and diseases of man and animals. Springer, Dordrecht, pp 322–353

Rausch R, Locker B (1951) Studies on the helminth fauna of Alaska. II. On some helminths parasitic in the sea otter, *Enhydra lutris* (L.). Proc Helminthol Soc Wash 18:77–81

Stunkard HW (1951) Observations on the morphology and life-history of *Microphallus limuli* n. sp. Biol Bull 101:307–318

Tubangui MA, Africa CM (1938) The systematic position of some trematodes reported from the Philippines. Phil J Sci 67:117–125

Velasquez CC (1975) Observation on the life cycle of *Carneophallus brevicaeca* (Africa et Garcia 1935) comb. n. (Digenea: Microphallidae). J Parasitol 61:910–915

Waikagul J (1991) Intestinal fluke infections in Southeast Asia. Southeast Asian J Trop Med Public Health 22(suppl):158–162

Yamaguti S (1958) Systema Helminthum. Vol. I. The digenetic trematodes of vertebrates (Part I). Interscience Publishers Inc., New York, pp 1–979

Yamaguti S (1971) Synopsis of digenetic trematodes of vertebrates, vol I. Keigaku Publishing Co., Tokyo, pp 1–1074

References for Section 9.1.6

Amissah-Reynolds PK, Monney I, Adowash LM et al (2016) Prevalence of helminths in dogs and owners' awareness of zoonotic diseases in Mampong, Ashanti, Ghana. J Parasitol Res 1715924:1–6

Baker GA (1950) *Troglotrema salmincola* in mink. J Parasitol 36:503

Beaver PC, Jung RC, Cupp EW (1984) Clinical Parasitology, 9th edn. Lea and Febiger, Philadelphia

Bennington E, Pratt I (1960) The life history of the salmon poisoning fluke, *Nanophyetus salmincola* (Chapin). J Parasitol 46:91–100

Blair D, Tkach VV, Barton DP (2008) Family Troglotrematidae Odhner, 1914. In: Bray RA, Gibson DI, Jones A (eds) Keys to the Trematoda, vol 3. Natural History Museum, London, pp 277–289

Booth AJ, Stogdale L, Grigor JA (1984) Salmon poisoning disease in dogs on southern Vancouver Island. Can Vet J 25:2–6

Brassard P, Rau ME, Curtis MA (1982) Parasite-induced susceptibility to predation in diplostomiasis. Parasitology 85:495–501

Chai JY, Murrell KD, Lymbery AJ (2005) Fish-borne parasitic zoonoses: status and issues. Int J Parasitol 35:1233–1254

Chapin EA (1926) A new genus and species of trematode, the probable cause of salmon poisoning in dogs. North Am Vet 7:36–37

Chapin EA (1927) New name *Nanophyetus* to replace *Nanophyes* Chapin 1926, nec *Nanophyes* Chaudoir, 1845. J Parasitol 14:60 (society proceeding of Helminthological Society of Washington, written by Dr. Hall)

Cram EB (1926) Wild carnivores as hosts of trematode previously found in dogs as the result of salmon poisoning. North Am Vet 7:42–43

Dollfus RP (1939) Distome d'un abcès palpébro-orbitaire chez une panthère. Possibilité d'affinités lointaines entre ce distome et les Paragonimidae. Ann Parasitol 17:209–235

Donham CR (1925) So-called salmon poisoning of dogs. J Am Vet Med Assoc 66:637–639

Eastburn RL, Tritsche TR, Terhune CA Jr (1987) Human intestinal infection with *Nanophyetus salmincola* from salmonid fishes. Am J Trop Med Hyg 36:586–591

Farrell RK, Lloyd MA, Earp B (1964) Persistence of *Neorickettsia helminthoeca* in an endoparasite of the Pacific Salmon. Science 145:162–163

Filimonova LV (1964) New first and second intermediate hosts of the trematode *Nanophyetus schikhobalowi*. Trudy Gel'mintologicheskoĭ laboratorii 14:246–251

Filimonova LV (1965) An experimental study of the biology of *Nanophyetus schikhobalowi*. Trudy Gel'mintologicheskoĭ laboratorii 15:172–184

Filimonova LV (1966) Distribution of *Nanophyetus schikhobalowi* in the Soviet territory of the Far East. Trudy Gel'mintologicheskoĭ laboratorii 17:240–244

Foreyt WJ, Gorham JR (1988) Evaluation of praziquantel against induced *Nanophyetus salmincola* infections in coyotes and dogs. Am J Vet Res 49:563–565

Fritsche TR, Eastburn RL, Wiggins LH et al (1989) Praziquantel for treatment of human *Nanophyetus salmincola* (*Troglotrema salmincola*) infection. J Infect Dis 160:896–899

Garcia LS (2007) Diagnostic medical parasitology, 5th edn. ASM Press, Washington, DC

Gebhardt GA (1966) Studies on the molluscan and fish hosts of the "salmon poisoning" fluke, *Nanophyetus salmincola* (Chapin). M.S. Thesis to Oregon State Univ., June 1966

Gebhardt GA, Millemann RE, Knapp SE et al (1966) "Salmo poisoning" disease. II. Second intermediate host susceptibility studies. J Parasitol 52:54–59

Greiman SE, Kent ML, Betts J et al (2016) *Nanophyetus salmincola*, vector of the salmon poisoning disease agent *Neorickettsia helminthoeca*, harbors a second pathogenic *Neorickettsia* species. Vet Parasitol 229:107–109

Harrell LW, Deardorff TL (1990) Human nanophyetiasis: transmission by handling naturally infected coho salmon (*Oncorhynchus kisutch*). J Infect Dis 161:146–148

Jacobson KC, Teel D, Van Doornik DM et al (2008) Parasite-associated mortality of juvenile Pacific salmon caused by the trematode *Nanophyetus salmincola* during early marine residence. Mar Ecol Prog Ser 354:235–244
Kumar V (1999) Echinostomiasis, heterophyiasis, metagonimiasis and other intestinal trematode infections. In: Trematode infections and diseases of man and animals. Springer, Dordrecht, pp 322–353
Millemann RE, Knapp SE (1970) Biology of *Nanophyetus salmincola* and "salmon poisoning" disease. Adv Parasitol 8:1–41
Mirzaei M, Foodladi M (2013) Coproscopy survey of gastrointestinal parasites in owned dogs of Kerman City, Iran. Vet Ital 49:309–313
Mongeau N (1961) Hepatic distomatosis and infectious canine hepatitis in Northern Manitoba. Can Vet J 2:33–38
Nwoha RIO, Ekwuruike JO (2010) Prevalence of gastrointestinal parasites in dogs from Umuahia City of Abia State. Glob J Med Sci 9:35–42
Olson PD, Cribb TH, Tkach VV et al (2003) Phylogeny and classification of the Digenea (Platyhelminthes: Trematoda). Int J Parasitol 33:733–755
Philip CB (1958) A helminth replaces the usual arthropod as vector of a rickettsia-like disease. Proc 10th Int Congr Entomol, Montreal, Canada, 1956, 3:651–653
Philip CB, Hadlow WJ, Hughes LE (1954) Studies on salmon poisoning disese of canines. I. The rickettsial relationships and pathogenicity of Neorickettsia helmintheca. Exp Parasitol 3:336–350
Porter CA (1970) A histochemical study of the cyst wall of the metacercaria of *Nanophyetus salmincola* (Chapin). Proc Helminthol Soc Wash 37:13–17
Rogers LL, Rogers SM (1976) Parasites of bears: a review. In: Bears: Their Biology and Management, Vol. 3, A selection of papers from the Third International Conference on Bear Research and Management. New York, USA. no. 40:411–430
Saito S (1985) Cercaria of *Nanophyetus japonensis* from the freshwater snail, *Semisulcospira libertina*, in Japan and its experimental infection. Jpn J Parasitol 34:41–53
Saito Y, Saito S, Yamashita T et al (1982) On *Nanophyetus japonensis* n. sp. from Northern District, Honshu, Japan (Trematoda: Nanophyetidae). Acta Med Biol 30:1–15
Sandell TA, Teel DJ, Fischer J et al (2015) Infections by *Renibacterium salmoninarum* and *Nanophyetus salmincola* Chapin are associated with reduced growth of juvenile Chinook salmon, *Oncorhynchus tsawytscha* (Walbaum), in the Northeast Pacific Ocean. J Fish Dis 38:365–378
Shaw JN (1947) Some parasites of Oregon wild life. Station Tech Bull 11:1–16
Simms BT, Donham CR, Shaw JN et al (1931) Salmon poisoning. J Am Vet Med Assoc 78:181–195
Skrjabin KJ, Podjapolskaja WP (1931) *Nanophyetus schikhobalowi* n. sp., ein neuer Trematode aus dem Darm des Menschen. Centralbull Bakteriol Orig 119:294–297
Voronova AN, Chelomina GN (2018) Genetic diversity and phylogenetic relations of salmon trematode *Nanophyetus japonensis*. Parasitol Int 67:267–276
Voronova AN, Chelomina GN, Besprozvannykh et al (2016) Genetic divergence of human pathogens *Nanophyetus* spp. (Trematoda: Troglotrematidae) on the opposite side of the Pacific Rim. Parasitology https://doi.org/10.1017/S0031182016002171
Wallace FG (1935) A morphological and biological study of the trematode, *Sellacotyle mustelae* n. g., n. sp. J Parasitol 21:143–164
Witenberg G (1932) On the anatomy and systematic position of the causative agent of so-called salmon poisoning. J Parasitol 18:258–263
Yamaguti S (1958) Systema Helminthum. Vol. I. The digenetic trematodes of vertebrates (Part I). Interscience Publishers Inc., New York, pp 1–979
Yamaguti S (1971) Synopsis of digenetic trematodes of vertebrates, vol I. Keigaku Publishing Co., Tokyo, pp 1–1074
Yu SH, Mott KE (1994) Epidemiology and morbidity of food-borne intestinal trematode infections. Trop Dis Bull 91:R125–R152

References for Section 9.1.7

Abo-Shady AF (1980) Intestinal helminths among stray dogs in Mansoura City, Egypt. J Egypt Soc Parasitol 10:289–294

Alghabban AJM (2014) Fish farms as a source for parasites transport: parasitological and developmental studies of *Prohemistomum vivax* with the ameliorating role of *Moringa oleifera* in the treatment. J Am Sci 10:6–14

Amer SE, El-Shazly KA, El-Shazly SA (2006) Immunostimulating effects of *Pelargonium reinforme/sidoides* extract (Kalobin®) on mice infected with *Prohemistomum vivax*. Egypt J Exp Biol 2:117–121

Amin MA, Hassam AO, Awadallah AI et al (2010) Role of *Atherina* fish in transmitting some trematodes of public health importance. Proc 3rd Global Fisher Aquacult Res Conf. Foreign Agricult Relat (FAR), Egypt. pp 120–133

Azim MA (1933) On *Prohemistomum vivax* (Sonsino, 1892) and its development from *Cercaria vivax* Sonsino, 1892. Z Parasitenkd 5:432–436

Bowman A (2014) *Prohemistomum vivax* (Sonsino, 1892) Azim, 1933. Am Assoc Vet Parasitol. www.aavp.org/wiki/trematodes-2/trematodes-small-intestine/cyathocotylidae

Chandler AC, Rausch R (1946) A study of strigeids from Michigan mammals, with comments on the classification of mammalian strigeids. Trans Am Microscop Soc 65:328–337

Dubois G (1982) Les trématodes des genre *Mesostephanus* Lutz, 1935 et *Mesostephanoides* Dubois, 1951 (Strigeata: Cyathocotyloidea). Ann Parasitol 57:329–343 (in French)

Dubois G, Pearson JC (1963) Les Strigeida (Trematoda) d'Egypte (collection William H. Wells). Ann Parasitol 38:77–91 (in French)

El-Dakhly MM, Aboshinaf ASM, El-Nahass E et al (2017) A preliminary study on the helminth fauna in necropsied stray cats (*Felis catus*) in Beni-Suef, Egypt. J Adv Vet Res 7:87–92

El-Kewaisny NM (2011) Effect of borax and niclosamid (Bayluscide or Bayer 73) on egg development and hatching of *Prohemistomum vivax*. Egypt J Zool 57:69–82

El-Kewaisny NM (2012) Vitamin B_{12} and iron in the plasma of hamster infected with the intestinal parasite *Prohemistomum vivax*. J Basic Appl Zool 65:106–108

El-Seify MA, Desouky ARY, Bazh EK (2003) Epidemiological studies on some fish-borne parasites. Egypt Vet Med Soc Parasitol J 2:570–590

Fahmy MA, Selim MK (1959) Studies on some trematode parasites of dogs in Egypt with special reference to the role played by fish in their transmission. Z Parasitenkd 19:3–13

Fahmy MA, Mandour AM, El-Naffar MK (1976) Successful infection of dogs and cats by *Prohemistomum vivax* Sonsino, 1892 and *Haplorchis yokogawai* Katsuta, 1922. J Egypt Soc Parasitol 6:77–82

Faltýnková A, Sures B, Kostadinova A (2016) Biodiversity of trematodes in their intermediate mollusc and fish hosts in the freshwater ecosystems of Europe. Syst Parasitol 93:283–293

Gohar N (1934) Les trématodes parasites du milan Egyptien *Milvus migrans* avec description d'une nouvelle espèce et remarques sur les genres *Haplorchis* Looss 1899 et *Monorchotrema* Nishigori 1924. Ann Parasitol 12:218–227 (in French)

Gohar N (1935) Liste des trématodes parasites et de leurs hôtes vertébrés signalés dans la vallée du nil (1). Ann Parasitol 13:80–90 (in French)

Ibrahim TB, Mahdy OA (2017) *In vitro* and *in vivo* effects of *Carica papaya* seed extract on the ultrastructure of the tegument of *Prohemistomum vivax* (Sonsino, 1892) (Trematoda: Prohemistomatidae). Int J Zool Res 13:45–53

Kirrella GAK, Elhawary NM, Bazh EK et al (2018) *Oreochromis niloticus* and *Clarias gariepinus* fish infected with digenean metacercariae: experimental infection of puppies and some chemical alterations in fish. Asian J Anim Vet Adv 13:352–359

Mahdy OA, Mousa WM, Kandil OM (2000) Some serological and biological control studies on *Heterophyes heterophyes* and *Prohemistomum vivax* in experimentally infected rats. Assiut Vet Med J 43:186–198

Mahfouz ME, Mira NM, Amer SRE (2005) Histopathological and molecular studies on the intestine of experimentally infected mice by *Prohemistomum vivax* (Trematoda: Cyathocotylidae). Egypt J Exp Biol 1:77–86

Nasr M (1941) The occurrence of *Prohemistomum vivax* (Sonsino, 1892) Azim, 1933 infection in man, with a redescription of the parasite. Lab Med Progr 2:135–149

Niewiadomska K (2002) Family Cyathocotylidae Mühling, 1898. In: Gibson DI, Jones A, Bray RA (eds) Keys to the Trematoda, vol 1. Natural History Museum, London, pp 201–214

Olivier L (1940) Life history studies on two strigeid trematodes of the Douglas Lake Region, Michigan. J Parasitol 26:447–477

Saad AI (1998) Studies on some cercaria from two fresh water snails at Aswan. Part III. Furcocercous cercariae. J Egypt Ger Soc Zool 27D:1–11

Saad AI (2007) A comparative study of different metacercarial infections in two freshwater fishes from Lake Nasser, Nile River and hatcheries at Aswan-Egypt. J Egypt Ger Soc Zool 51D:107–125

Saleh RS, Abou-Eisha AM, Fadel HM et al (2009) Occurrence of encysted metacercariae of some zoonotic trematodes in freshwater fishes and their public health significance in Port Said Province. Abbassa Int J Aquacult (special issue for Global Fisher Aquacult Res Conf, Cairo, Egypt). pp 341–351

Saoud MFA, Ramadan MM (1977) On a new trematode, *Prohemistomum azimi* n. sp. (Trematoda: Cyathocotylidae) from the Egyptian slit-faced bat. Z Parasitenkd 53:281–285

Shalaby SI, Shalaby SI, Awad MA et al (2011) Experimental clinicopathological studies on enteric parasitic diseases of the final host (man) that are transmitted from fish. Proc Zool Soc India (special issue-Parasitol) 1:25–31

Tawfik MAA, Elnawawi FA, Shaapan RM (2000) Studies on some fish-borne trematodes in Egypt. Egypt J Vet Sci 34:39–48

Walton AC (1949) Parasites of the Ranidae (Amphibia). VII. Trans Am Microscop Soc 68:49–54

Yamaguti S (1958) Systema Helminthum. Vol. I. The digenetic trematodes of vertebrates (Part I). Interscience Publishers Inc., New York, pp 1–979

Yamaguti S (1971) Synopsis of digenetic trematodes of vertebrates, vol I. Keigaku Publishing Co., Tokyo, pp 1–1074

Index

J.-Y. Chai, *Human Intestinal Flukes*,
https://doi.org/10.1007/978-94-024-1704-3

D

H

I

J

K

O

Q

R

S

CONSTITUCIÓN DE 1949

Claves para una interpretación latinoamericana y popular
del constitucionalismo argentino

Javier Azzali

CONSTITUCIÓN DE 1949

Claves para una interpretación latinoamericana y popular del constitucionalismo argentino

70 Años

1949 - 2019

Azzali, Javier
Constitución de 1949: claves para una interpretación latinoamericana y popular del constitucionalismo argentino / Javier Azzali. - 2a ed ampliada. - Ciudad Autónoma de Buenos Aires : Punto de Encuentro, 2019.
320 p. ; 22 x 16 cm.

ISBN 978-987-4465-15-3

1. Constitucionalismo. 2. Peronismo. 3. Historia Constitucional. I. Título.
CDD 342.8202

Av. de Mayo 1110
Ciudad Autónoma de Buenos Aires, República Argentina.
(54-11) 4382-1630

Diseño interiores y cubierta: Cristina Angelini
Para el collage de cubierta se utilizó un fragmento de obra plástica del **Colectivo Político Ricardo Carpani** cedida al autor.

Este libro se compuso con las tipografías:
Unna de De Buen & Omnibus-Type Team (SIL Open Font License, 1.1)
Saira y **Saira Condensed** de Gatti & Omnibus-Type Team (SIL Open Font License, 1.1).
www.omnibus-type.com

Se terminó de imprimir durante el mes de marzo de 2019 en Punto de Encuentro, Ceballos 885, Avellaneda.

www.puntoed.com.ar

Queda hecho el depósito que establece la ley 11.723.
Libro de edición argentina.

Índice

Prólogo

Han transcurrido casi 20 años desde la sanción de la Constitución que nos rige. Sin embargo, tantas transformaciones se han producido desde entonces, tan rotunda ha sido la crisis del neoliberalismo que hundió al país en todos los órdenes hasta el abismo del 2001/2002 y tan enorme el cambio producido entre esa fecha y el día de hoy, que cualquier hombre de derecho, sin ataduras con el pasado, admite que estamos viviendo otra época y que resultaría necesario actualizarla. Por supuesto, ello no es fácil porque las exigencias que la misma Constitución impone para su reforma son difíciles de cumplimentar y los mezquinos intereses de muchos dirigentes políticos se opondrían seguramente a un proyecto de esta clase.

Pero lo más curioso que ocurre en este campo del derecho constitucional no solo consiste en este envejecimiento veinteañero, sino que si nos abocáramos seriamente a la tarea de una reforma modernizadora resultaría imprescindible retrotraernos medio siglo atrás y recurrir a la Constitución del 49, cuyos contenidos resultan, a todas luces, mucho más adecuados a las nuevas situaciones que la sancionada en 1994. Tan enorme ha sido el retroceso sufrido por la Argentina que aquella Constitución, cuestionada por aspectos puramente formales, aborda las cuestiones actuales con mayor sentido de futuro.

Por eso, procede muy bien Javier Azzali cuando aborda el análisis de la Constitución desde el principio, pues después de reflexionar en profundidad acerca de la cuestión nacional y aspectos relevantes como lo son el liberalismo y el proteccionismo, analiza el rol de la Constitución e inclusive se remite hasta la de 1853, para adoptar frente a ella una posición muy equilibrada, ajena totalmente a los vituperios lanzados por el

nacionalismo rosista, como expresión del centralismo porteño –al cual le dolió demasiado que hubieran sido los federales del interior los que la dictaron y echaron la base de la República, sancionando la federalización de Buenos Aires que significaba la nacionalización de la Aduana–. Un análisis profundo de los enfrentamientos de clase en 1853 evidencia que no fue la oligarquía en formación –los Anchorena (estancias) y los Mitre (comercio probritánico)– quien la sancionó, sino los federales del interior. Por eso la Constitución fue federal y estuvo adecuada al marco político general en el que se aprobó, por más que el nacionalismo oligárquico la denigrara y que José María Rosa se hubiera burlado injustamente de los convencionales constituyentes en su libro *Nos los representantes del pueblo.*

Azzali avanza luego un siglo y aborda la reforma constitucional de 1949, valorando la modernización que significó en las más diversas áreas, como reflejo de los cambios operados por el peronismo en el gobierno desde 1946. Se detiene, entonces, en el estudio pormenorizado de distintos aspectos de la Constitución, entre otros, la elección directa de presidente, vice y senadores, los derechos de la familia del trabajador y de la ancianidad, la función social de la propiedad, el artículo 40 que resguarda las riquezas naturales, y otros derechos que hoy deben ser plenamente reivindicados.

El libro no va dirigido por supuesto a los académicos, aferrados con uñas y dientes a las cátedras, ni a los nonagenarios que se resisten a abandonar la judicatura, sino especialmente a los jóvenes, y proporciona los fundamentos acerca de que toda reforma constitucional futura deberá tomar como base, en mayor medida, las reformas del 49 que las de 1994.

La experiencia de estos años le ha servido a Azzali para sacar conclusiones sobre la efectividad de unas y otras en la aplicación e interpretación de las leyes, así como en las polémicas producidas últimamente con respecto al voto popular en la elección de los integrantes del Consejo de la Magistratura o en el desastre jurídico que significan las cautelares capaces de paralizar la aplicación de leyes que han obtenido la sanción del Poder Ejecutivo y del Poder Legislativo. Surge entonces el análisis de la

libertad y habrá que recordar al Alberdi viejo, no al de *Las Bases* sino al de los *Escritos Póstumos*, cuando sostenía que el liberalismo oligárquico apuntaba a la libertad para los liberales y a la dictadura de los liberales sobre los otros. Alberdi, después de años de destierro por culpa del mitrismo, había aprendido que "nadie está contra la libertad, a lo sumo, está contra la libertad del otro" y que "los amantes de la libertad son los tiranos, pero que quieren la libertad ellos solos". De ahí la necesidad de un debate profundo en el seno del pueblo acerca del país que queremos y, por tanto, qué Constitución ha de presidir las transformaciones necesarias.

Por todas estas razones, el libro de Azzali resulta sumamente oportuno y valioso en estos momentos en que la crisis de la justicia es muy honda. El lector que se acerque a el sin viejos prejuicios, se abrirá a un amplio campo de elaboración jurídica y comprenderá que las leyes dependen de la realidad social, que no solo basta que "la idea clame por expresarse, sino que es necesario que la realidad clame por la idea" y que entonces sí la Constitución y los Códigos operarán en el futuro progreso de los argentinos, dando respuestas a los nuevos problemas, y abriendo camino a las transformaciones, en vez de paralizarlas u obstaculizarlas.

Sumérjase el lector en este excelente ensayo de Javier Azzali y estoy seguro de que nos dará la razón.

Norberto Galasso

Introducción a la segunda edición

Cuando se publicó la primera edición de este libro, los argentinos nos encontrábamos en la encrucijada de definir el modelo de crecimiento para el país, en el camino hacia la autodeterminación nacional y la integración sudamericana. La reivindicación de la reforma constitucional de 1949 buscaba aportar a ese debate sobre el proyecto de nación, mediante el conocimiento del antecedente fundamental que fue el programa de país promovido por el movimiento político liderado por Juan Perón.

Ahora, el presente nos muestra la cara opuesta. De un país donde las decisiones en materia económica se adoptaban en la Casa Rosada, con un rol activo del Estado que impulsaba políticas de inclusión social, derechos de los trabajadores, desarrollo productivo, desendeudamiento externo y unidad sudamericana en las relaciones exteriores, pasamos a uno que promueve exactamente todo lo contrario. La saga del oprobio actual es desmesurada: predominio de la especulación financiera por sobre la producción, caída en picada de la industria y del empleo, deterioro de la situación social, pérdida generalizada de los derechos y en particular en las relaciones del trabajo, presos políticos, persecución a opositores y sindicalistas, manipulación de la justicia, violencia institucional, una insólita toma de deuda externa combinada con la fuga de capitales, y ni qué decir sobre el abandono de la senda sudamericana, cuando el Grupo de Lima y la OEA son la contracara geopolítica de la UNASUR y la CELAC.

Como en el tradicional juego de la oca, la historia nos depara una sucesión de avances y retrocesos, de ciclos de progreso y atraso, de transformaciones y de reacciones conservadoras; pero el curso de la acción no es determinado por el azar inocente de un lanzamiento de dados, sino por la cruel

y fría puja de las relaciones de fuerza entre las clases sociales, dentro del país, y por la presión de las potencias imperialistas, a quienes los sectores reaccionarios responden. La magnitud social, económica y política de estas reacciones tienen el carácter de auténticas rupturas del orden establecido, lo cual rebasa los límites de simples alternancias entre opciones de centro, izquierda y derecha dentro del sistema democrático. No son cambios sino quiebres del proyecto de nación, dando paso al cauce de la dependencia, en cuyas aguas turbias intentamos no hundirnos. El asunto se revela con claridad apenas se advierte que detrás del cambio no hay nada parecido a un programa de país o al menos de política pública, tan solo se trata de cumplir con el objetivo de retornar a la dependencia. Y para renunciar a la soberanía y a la justicia social no hace falta mucho plan de gobierno...

La presión imperialista debilita los espacios nacionales mediante la destrucción de la capacidad de conducir de los Estados, la fragmentación de los territorios, el quiebre de cualquier alianza entre los trabajadores y el capital productivo, y empuja a nuestros países a que sean simples productores de materias primas, desde el agro, los minerales, hasta los recursos como los hidrocarburos y el agua. Se impone la idea de que nuestros pueblos no tienen la capacidad de producir y crear; que estamos inmersos en la corrupción, en la incapacidad y en la ignorancia; y por ende, que solo la tutela extranjera nos puede orientar hacia el progreso. Las mayorías populares se ven en la encerrona del fracaso de la política como alternativa única, que solo conduce a la resignación y desesperanza. El dominio oligárquico e imperialista se sustenta, justamente, en una visión de la realidad, en la que el pueblo aparece sin historia, el país sin clases sociales y las mayorías populares sin lucha nacional. En fin, nuevos formatos para actualizar las viejas relaciones de dependencia, justo cuando el escenario mundial destierra el unilateralismo estadounidense y gira hacia la multilateralidad, con el protagonismo de potencias como China y Rusia, en las que, además, el Estado cumple un rol central.

Pero la esperanza de nuestros pueblos muestra una vigencia admirable en el ideario de la igualdad, la justicia y la solidaridad como la única

posibilidad para el progreso y la paz. Para esto, la creación de proyectos nacionales aparecen como la vía para la autodeterminación, con base en el rol activo y planificador del Estado, la democracia económica y la organización popular. Las funciones esenciales del Estado en la dirección de las áreas estratégicas de la economía tienen base especialmente en el dominio de los recursos naturales y su capacidad de ahorro interno para promover y planificar políticas desde las inversiones social, popular y pública. El destino del conjunto de los pueblos latinoamericanos se juega, por partes, en cada uno de los países –especialmente lo hace en el núcleo formado por Brasil y Argentina–, por eso, la reconstrucción de los movimientos nacionales es un capítulo en ese largo y fluctuante desarrollo histórico. Los sindicatos, las organizaciones sociales de base, las diversas formas de asociación en los barrios y las comunidades, y de los trabajadores de la agricultura familiar, así como los partidos políticos, son parte fundamental de esta tarea de resistencia y construcción de una alternativa.

Adquiere valor, una vez más, la tesis de que solo los pueblos que saben de dónde vienen y conocen el camino recorrido, están en condiciones de poder sacar conclusiones razonadas y fundadas sobre hacia dónde quieren y pueden ir, acerca de sus facultades reales, posibilidades y límites. El deber de cada persona a comprometerse con su tiempo y lugar tiene fundamento en el derecho a opinar y participar en la cosa pública. Se trata, como dice el maestro E. Raúl Zaffaroni, del derecho constitucional a ejercer los atributos de la ciudadanía en un país que se pretende democrático. Este mandato fortalece las reservas culturales e ideológicas necesarias para la resistencia cultural, en la que abreva una larga lista de pensadores, en distintos tiempos y geografía de nuestro continente, como Darcy Ribeiro, Leopoldo Zea, Juan Brom, y, entre nosotros, Arturo Jauretche, Juan José Hernández Arregui y Norberto Galasso. El estudio de la reforma constitucional de 1949 se entiende con la intención de mantener el ideario de la igualdad social y la necesidad de la autodeterminación nacional como la condición para el adecuado ejercicio de la totalidad de los otros derechos, como los civiles, políticos, sociales, económicos y culturales.

Mi agradecimiento y reconocimiento al compromiso de todos aquellos que desde los más diversos espacios y diferentes rincones del país, reivindican ese derecho a una patria libre, justa y soberana. A los sindicatos que luchan por los derechos de los trabajadores, en la huella del sindicalismo de liberación y al movimiento estudiantil. A los compañeros y compañeras del Centro Cultural Enrique Santos Discépolo y del periódico *Señales Populares*, quienes, como decía Homero Manzi en un poema, "sueñan con la paz y hacen la simbiosis –pampeanamente rara– de Yrigoyen y Marx". A Norberto Galasso, quien no solo ha aportado una obra extraordinaria a la memoria colectiva de nuestro pueblo, sino que también con su trayectoria es una referencia esencial para el camino a seguir. Al Colectivo Político Ricardo Carpani, a los Vagos y Vagas Peronistas, a los compañeros docentes de la Universidad de Buenos Aires, de la Universidad Nacional de José C. Paz y de la Diplomatura de Pueblos Indígenas e Interculturalidad de la Facultad de Humanidades de la Universidad Nacional del Nordeste –Resistencia, Chaco–; a mis compañeros y compañeras de la Defensa Pública por su aliento diario para la defensa de los derechos humanos, y de los derechos económicos, sociales y culturales; al Instituto para la Producción Popular. A Gabriel Fernández, Jorge Thierbach y los compañeros que hacen la fundamental Radio Gráfica, por una comunicación desde el pueblo y el sur del mundo. A Mara Espasande, Carlos Cháves, Carlos Elorza, Claudio Castelli, Juan Carlos Jara, Luís Roa e Iván Garbarino. Al historiador León Pomer. A los queridos Tito Ateiro y Antonio el Negro Coria. A Gimol, a mis padres y hermana, y especialmente a Lautaro, Facundo, Malena, Julián, Niky, Elías y Abi, quienes atentamente miran la patria para realizar su futuro.

Y por supuesto, a la editorial Punto de Encuentro, ese equipo dirigido por Carlos Benítez, a quienes les agradezco de corazón la confianza brindada, así como va mi reconocimiento a su trabajo para forjar la conciencia histórica y la cultura nacional. Como decía Raúl Scalabrini Ortiz, se lucha también con la pluma, porque "luchar es, en cierta manera, sinónimo de vivir y el que no lucha, se estanca como el agua."

Esta segunda edición respeta a la primera y solo contiene modificaciones mínimas; pero incluye, al final, el texto constitucional que a setenta años de su aparición presenta una importante vigencia ideológica.

El autor
Buenos Aires, enero de 2019

Palabras preliminares

Las crisis que en forma recurrente han venido desgraciando a nuestro país en los últimos decenios tienen una causa esencial que predomina por sobre todas las demás: la dependencia económica, política y cultural de nuestra nación respecto de las potencias mundiales. Solo en una lectura aparente de la realidad podrían adjudicarse los problemas sociales y las crisis últimas de representación política y de carácter institucional que estallaron en 2001 a errores de coyuntura o al desliz de algún gobernante de turno. Por el contrario, estos obedecen a nuestra condición de país que aún no ha logrado el ejercicio pleno de su autodeterminación nacional. Al desatarse el nudo de la dependencia económica, el resto de la vida social estará en condiciones de recrearse libremente a partir del desarrollo pleno de las fuerzas productivas y del uso consiente de la totalidad de nuestras posibilidades. La etapa de los gobiernos peronistas entre 1945 y 1955 es un ejemplo de esa búsqueda, mientras que los períodos de la última dictadura cívico-militar: 1976-1983 y la etapa de democracia abierta en los 80 y 90, lo son, con matices, de lo contrario.

Desde 2003 se ha abierto una etapa política de reivindicaciones sociales, civiles y culturales de gran importancia, en la que el país reconstruye de a poco su autodeterminación, lo que ha hecho que los argentinos, después de mucho tiempo, nos encontremos debatiendo qué modelo de nación queremos. También se ha dado, de modo consecuente, un reverdecimiento del pensamiento nacional y popular y un renovado interés por la historia reciente del país y el continente, en clave revisionista, ratificando eso de que "yerba mala nunca muere". La denominada historia oficial –de raigambre antiperonista– es el relato del poder acerca de los hechos del

pasado que tiende a justificar la dominación del presente, es decir, el orden injusto impuesto por los poderes oligárquicos a las mayorías, a través de la economía, la política y la cultura. El conocimiento de la historia, que solo puede ser útil para la desmitificación de aquel relato dominante y, por ende, posibilita la crítica de la interpretación liberal conservadora, es la clave para la comprensión de la cuestión nacional y de sus causas, porque sin memoria histórica no hay sujeto y sin sujeto que cuestione la dominación no hay cambio posible[1].

El ejercicio del poder con óptica neoliberal, desde la época de la dictadura cívico-militar de 1976, ha dejado un conjunto de normas propio de una economía de especulación financiera, de disciplinamiento social y un modelo de país europeísta, dependiente del capital extranjero y de las corporaciones financieras multinacionales. En otras palabras, una patria enajenada y un pueblo subyugado. Ante ello, entiendo que se justifica el estudio de la reforma constitucional de 1949, como modo de aportar a la recuperación de los antecedentes normativos principales que nos permitan a los argentinos encontrar, en nuestra historia, los fundamentos del camino de la liberación nacional. Es este, entonces, un trabajo intelectual y más que nada de divulgación, aunque no por eso una actividad solitaria y estéril. Al contrario, lo impulsa la certeza de que con el estudio de la Constitución de 1949 acompañamos al esfuerzo de los argentinos por encontrarnos como nacionales y latinoamericanos, en la perspectiva de unidad continental que alumbra la nueva era abierta y con la esperanza de que las transformaciones más profundas son posibles. Nuestro destino de realización social solo puede darse con el "país en movimiento"[2], auténtico

1 "Lo que se nos ha presentado como historia es una política de la historia en que esta es solo un instrumento para impedir que la historia verdadera contribuya a la formación de una conciencia histórica nacional que es la base de toda política de la nación" de Arturo Jauretche, lo que impide todo progreso histórico, desarrollo cultural y el paso de las transformaciones sociales más profundas y justas (Galasso, Norberto, *Imperialismo y pensamiento colonial en la Argentina*, Buenos Aires, Roberto Vera Editor, 1985).

2 "El proletariado lleva en sí mismo la liberación de la sociedad y los intelectuales de clase media deben aprender de su accionar, alejarse de la atractiva

sujeto de la historia con capacidad de cuestionar el orden oligárquico y sus injusticias y desigualdades inherentes.

Después de diferentes versiones desde 2003, al vaivén de los debates y la militancia que tuvieron lugar en el Centro Cultural Enrique Santos Discépolo (en sus sucesivas casas de Av. La Plata, del barrio de Once y finalmente en la calle Rivarola), de charlas, cursos, seminarios y debates en diferentes lugares y espacios en la ciudad de Buenos Aires y barrios bonaerenses, arribé finalmente a esta versión algo más formada pero que decido dar a la editorial. En cuanto al contenido, en primer lugar haremos reflexiones básicas respecto de la cuestión nacional y del significado del fenómeno constitucional en general. En segundo lugar, seguiremos con una aproximación breve a la historia política argentina y el constitucionalismo, desde una óptica revisionista popular y latinoamericana, así como del fenómeno jurídico-político en tanto expresión discursiva del ejercicio del poder, con su significación concreta en nuestros países semicoloniales. Todo proyecto de nación implica la creación de una base jurídica sobre la cual se sustenta y legitima, de ahí que la explicación del fenómeno jurídico adquiere cierta importancia, tarea que es propia de la teoría general de las normas y que en este trabajo asumimos desde la perspectiva de la crítica jurídica latinoamericana. En tercer lugar, incursionaremos en el estudio concreto de la reforma constitucional de 1949, tanto en su significado como parte de un proceso histórico –el peronismo y su proyecto de nación– así como en su contenido normativo e ideológico específico. Finalmente, haremos un repaso general de las reformas de 1957 y 1994.

maquinaria del prestigio hacia el país en movimiento", en *Primera Plana*, 27/06/1972, citado en el mensuario *Señales Populares* nro. 22, diciembre de 2010, de la Corriente E. S. Discépolo.

I. ¿Qué es la cuestión nacional?

"Hay que diferenciar el nacionalismo de un país oprimido del de un país opresor, lo que suponía la interpretación y reinterpretación del imperialismo, no solo como factor frenador del desarrollo de las fuerzas productivas en el mundo colonial y semicolonial sino como causa de la conformación del movimiento nacional."[3]

En uno, el nacionalismo tiene carácter conservador por representar los intereses de la burguesía contra los de la clase trabajadora (en este caso ocultos bajo la forma abstracta de "patriotismo" o "igualdad jurídica"), mientras que en los países semicoloniales, tiene significado progresivo en tanto tiende a superar al orden oligárquico –ligado al esquema internacional imperialista–, como condición para realizar la cuestión social. Por eso, el auténtico nacionalismo es aquel que expresa los anhelos de las mayorías populares, en contraposición a un pseudonacionalismo que se propone, bajo la apariencia de defender lo autóctono, la defensa de objetivos elitistas, como en el caso del nacionalismo aristocrático o de derecha, aun recurriendo a interpretaciones revisionistas de la historia liberal conservadora. Una de las claves que nos aproxima a la condición semicolonial la brinda Raúl Scalabrini Ortiz, cuando, como conclusión de sus investigaciones económicas sobre el funcionamiento del país[4], decía a propósito de la situación histórica antes de la irrupción del peronismo:

3 Alberti, Blas, *El revisionismo histórico socialista*, Buenos Aires, octubre de 1974.

4 La tarea de Raúl Scalabrini Ortiz guarda similitud con lo que Carlos Marx hizo a mediados del siglo XIX con su obra *El Capital* en la Inglaterra industrial: explicar el funcionamiento del capital en la sociedad, solo que a diferencia de este, lo hizo con Argentina, un país semicolonial y primario, mientras que Inglaterra era la sociedad más industrializada del planeta. La tesis central es la misma: la política no puede explicarse sin su vinculación efectiva con la economía.

> La Argentina es una nación ficticia porque gozamos de apariencia de nación hasta donde esa apariencia no perjudica los intereses de Inglaterra. Tenemos un escudo, una bandera y hasta una constitución, pero nuestra voluntad política, nuestra conducta financiera, nuestra organización social, nuestra ruta económica y hasta la interpretación de nuestra historia, nos es dictada solapadamente desde Londres.[5]

La dependencia constituye así el hecho principal de la historia política argentina y, de este modo, la cuestión nacional es la clave de su interpretación. Desde la formación definitiva de la hegemonía oligárquica a mediados del siglo XIX hasta los actuales inicios del siglo XXI, aquella tiene el efecto de distorsionar toda la vida social y se experimenta subjetivamente en las más variadas formas de desprecio de lo nacional, lo autóctono y lo latinoamericano. Una inversión del lenguaje ha deformado nuestra percepción de la realidad, ya que en nombre de la libertad y la civilización han sido cometidos los peores crímenes colectivos y defendidos los intereses de los propietarios de los medios de producción y de los grupos económicos extranjeros. Una consigna resume la problemática: no hay igualdad social sin liberación nacional, y esta solo puede ser entendida en su mayor expresión como unidad latinoamericana. De la fragmentación de nuestra América (como hecho histórico-político), a la dependencia y desarrollo insuficiente (como hecho económico), y a la negación de nuestra condición de latinoamericanos (como hecho cultural), se ha construido y perdura la principal causa de nuestros problemas.

La cuestión nacional es en verdad la tarea de construir la unidad nacional de nuestra América, esa Patria Grande cuyo lineamiento encuentra fundamento histórico en el proyecto frustrado de Bolívar y San Martín hace casi doscientos años[6]. De ello depende también la vida de millones de compatriotas latinoamericanos, en especial de los sectores populares.

5 Periódico *Señales*, 23/10/1935.

6 Ramos, J. A., *Historia de la Nación Latinoamericana*, Buenos Aires, Continente, 2011, p. 23.

Al mismo tiempo, la unidad nacional latinoamericana exige la búsqueda de formas superadoras de producción social con respecto a las impuestas por el capitalismo imperialista y depredador, por lo que su norte de igualdad social y soberanía solo podrá ser logrado y consolidado en la originalidad de un socialismo latinoamericano. Se reivindica, así, al nacionalismo democrático y a los movimientos nacionales como portadores de la posibilidad de realización nacional y del camino hacia el socialismo latinoamericano[7].

> En América Latina el nacionalismo no es separable del socialismo ni de la democracia. Tales aspiraciones indisociables reflejan de modo combinado las claves de su necesario salto histórico hacia la revolución unificadora y la liberación social de toda explotación. (*Historia de la Nación Latinoamericana* de J. A. Ramos).

El ideario nacional democrático en el siglo XX tuvo su expresión con el yrigoyenismo primero y el peronismo después, dando continuidad a las posiciones proteccionistas y latinoamericanistas del federalismo del siglo anterior y levantando la consigna de la revolución nacional. Su programa antiimperialista –aunque no socialista– puede resumirse en la posición de FORJA[8]: "Somos una Argentina colonial, queremos ser una Argentina libre", que va encontrar en la etapa peronista su concreción.

En esta línea, el peronismo histórico fue expresión del nacionalismo democrático en la medida en que representó la apertura política y social de un país elitista, que se encontraba clausurado para las mayorías populares que, como podían, intentaban dar cauce a sus pulsiones de liberación. Ese carácter democrático se complementó con la ampliación en todos sus ámbitos de la base de representación política, tanto en el ámbito electoral (aumento considerable del padrón electoral) para la ciudadanía, en el gremial para los trabajadores como hasta en el empresarial para las

7 Ramos, J. A., *Historia de la Nación Latinoamericana, op. cit*, p. 29. Ver también Galasso, Norberto, *América Latina, unidos o dominados*, Buenos Aires, Instituto Arturo Jauretche, 2008.

8 Fuerza de Orientación Radical de la Joven Argentina.

pequeñas y medianas industrias. Esta época constituyó sin duda la segunda experiencia democrática del país, después de la del yrigoyenismo, que se vio frustrada con el inicio de la larga proscripción electoral y la sucesión de golpes de Estado y dictaduras que culminaron en 1983, año de la nueva experiencia democrática abierta en la que, con fuertes vaivenes y retrocesos, aún nos encontramos.

El peronismo es reivindicado por la corriente revisionista socialista en su aspecto más progresivo por su vocación de movimiento de liberación nacional. Desde esta óptica, que es la concepción marxista aplicada al caso concreto de América Latina, a países semicoloniales y del Tercer Mundo como el nuestro, se sostiene la necesidad de resolver la cuestión nacional, que significa romper con la dependencia extranjera a partir de la reivindicación de los movimientos nacionales como frentes de liberación y la lucha por lograr la unidad latinoamericana.

Esta corriente de interpretación histórica y política nace a la par que irrumpe el peronismo como movimiento nacional, en 1945, con las tesis elaboradas por el Frente Obrero, una pequeña agrupación de militantes populares cuya formación intelectual se inspiraba en las ideas de Trotsky sobre América Latina. Para mejor, se sugieren las lecturas de Enrique Rivera *José Hernández y la guerra del Paraguay*; *La larga lucha de los argentinos y Aportes críticos a la historia de la izquierda argentina* de Norberto Galasso; *El revisionismo histórico socialista*, de Ediciones Octubre; o *Nacionalismo oligárquico y nacionalismo revolucionario* y *La cuestión nacional en Marx* de Jorge Enea Spilimbergo, entre muchas otras obras valiosas. La intersección entre el marxismo (máximo nivel de conciencia crítica del pensamiento de la modernidad) y el revisionismo histórico (como crítica a la pedagogía colonial del liberalismo oligárquico) ha dado origen a fórmulas originales como el "marxismo bolivariano", cuya expresión política hoy se advierte en el socialismo del siglo XXI de Hugo Chávez, Rafael Correa y Evo Morales. Sus objetivos políticos expresan el ala izquierda del campo nacional y popular: a las tres banderas del peronismo –independencia económica, soberanía

política y justicia social– se le suma el gobierno obrero y popular como garantía del cumplimiento de las anteriores[9].

Para esta interpretación solo se puede avanzar en la cuestión social con firmeza, al mismo tiempo que se supera la cuestión nacional, cuya tarea requiere el protagonismo principal de la clase trabajadora organizada. Los sectores populares son quienes hacen la historia a través de una actividad política consciente en su contradicción dialéctica con las oligarquías locales y extranjerizantes, o, dicho de otro modo, la lucha de clases es la que explica la historia de acuerdo a las particularidades propias de nuestro continente y de cada país. Desde esta posición –latinoamericana, federal y popular– intentamos este ensayo de interpretación que intenta incursionar en lo histórico, jurídico y político.

¿Librecambio o proteccionismo?

La cuestión nacional ha encontrado expresión histórica en el debate acerca del rol del Estado. La disyuntiva "proteccionismo o librecambio" ha sido clave en la historia económica argentina y está presente desde el origen mismo de las luchas emancipadoras a principios del siglo XIX, e incluso es posible rastrearla en la época virreinal, como lo demuestran las reformas borbónicas y la actuación de Manuel Lavardén, o en el programa emancipador de la Primera Junta de Mariano Moreno y Manuel Belgrano.

Desde temprano también surgía otro programa que priorizaba la libertad de comercio y la vinculación con el capital europeo en general e inglés en particular, un liberalismo que olvidaba su costado político para resaltar su visión librecambista, como forma ideológica de justificar la dependencia. Bernardino Rivadavia, Manuel García y Martín Rodríguez fueron sus principales referentes políticos como expresión de la creciente burguesía comercial del puerto de Buenos Aires. La libre importación de manufacturas en perjuicio del desarrollo regional y una concepción

9 "¿Qué es la izquierda nacional? Introducción al socialismo nacional", de José Luís Madariaga, Buenos Aires, Ediciones del Sur, con comentarios de Norberto Galasso y Néstor Gorojovsky, 2010.

aristocrática y elitista de la política (el voto calificado) daban forma a un modelo de desarrollo económico al servicio del mercado externo (de dependencia del interés británico), al inicio del endeudamiento externo (con la Baring Brothers) y a los Bancos de Descuentos y Nacional (1822 y 1826) bajo el dominio del comercio inglés. Un antecedente de relevancia es el "Tratado de Amistad, Comercio y Navegación con el Reino de Gran Bretaña", del 2 de febrero de 1825 firmado por Rivadavia, en el que se proclamaba una "reciprocidad" para el libre comercio de los habitantes de uno y los súbditos del otro, que en los hechos solo legitimaba la penetración financiera y de manufacturas del capital inglés. El siglo XIX pronto se colmaría de tratados similares entre los británicos y los países latinoamericanos.

Para esta visión el progreso solo era posible mediante el predominio del capital extranjero, como se observa cuando Bartolomé Mitre en su carácter de presidente de la nación justificaba la Guerra de la Triple Alianza contra el Paraguay en nombre del libre cambio y comercio "para mayor gloria y felicidad de los hombres". Lo mismo durante el siglo XX, cuando el 2 de abril de 1976 Martínez de Hoz, ministro de economía de la dictadura cívico-militar, anunciaba que se había terminado "el intervencionismo estatizante y agobiante de la actividad económica para dar paso a la liberación de las fuerzas productivas", en premisas que decían "achicar el Estado es agrandar la nación". En la década del noventa, el Consenso de Washington y el ALCA también se justificaron en nombre de la libertad en el mismo sentido elitista. Estamos entonces ante la imposición de un concepto de "Estado", una suerte de naturalización acerca de su aparente posición pasiva y abstencionista en la economía. Estas ideas son tan fuertes que nociones como libre comercio exterior e interior, libre cambio, propiedad privada o capital extranjero son presentadas algo así como atributos naturales de la sociedad que el Estado debe respetar para no interferir en el progreso y desarrollo de las fuerzas económicas. Por eso se utiliza habitualmente el término "intervención" del Estado o "intervencionismo estatal" para describir políticas públicas activas que regulan a través de límites al empresariado o al sector financiero, con una evidente carga de valor negativo.

El mito de la intervención del Estado en el mercado deviene de los países semicoloniales, de la separación entre economía y política que opera en los países centrales por el predominio del liberalismo economicista en el siglo XX. Varios fueron sus refutadores, entre ellos Hans Kelsen cuando sostenía: "mediante esta diferenciación entre una esfera jurídica pública, o sea, política, y una esfera privada, es decir, no política, se trata de evitar la evidencia de que el derecho 'privado' producido a través de un contrato (negocio jurídico) no es menos escenario del poder político que el derecho público"[10]

Pero el crecimiento industrial de los países más desarrollados del planeta muestra un curso histórico diferente, con dos etapas bien marcadas: la primera –con el fin del desarrollo interno– de fuerte proteccionismo, y la segunda –con el fin de expandirse hacia afuera– de promoción del librecambio. Dice Mario Rapoport:

> Gran Bretaña se hizo librecambista a mediados del siglo XIX (más precisamente en 1846, con la abolición de las leyes de granos), cuando ya era la principal potencia industrial del mundo y podía colocar ventajosamente sus manufacturas y bienes de capital.[11]

10 Ver Kelsen, Hans, *Teoría Pura del Derecho*, México, UNAM, 1993. Aunque su reconocimiento le viene por los aportes en el campo de la teoría del derecho, su figura es la de uno de los grandes pensadores del siglo XX de la filosofía política. Su pensamiento ha sido reducido, por parte de la interpretación liberal conservadora, a una supuesta mirada neutra del derecho, en la que el fenómeno jurídico se analiza al margen de consideraciones políticas. Pero, como muy bien señala el pensador Oscar Correas, su objeto de estudio, al contrario, ha sido el del ejercicio del poder a través del derecho. No obstante, esta manera particular de leer a Kelsen se convirtió en hegemónica en las escuelas de derecho, con implicancias devastadoras para entender la condición semicolonial y dependiente de nuestro país. Por eso resultan de gran importancia las originales y fecundas interpretaciones de Correas sobre Kelsen en libros fundamentales como *El otro Kelsen* o *Kelsen y los marxistas*. Hans Kelsen nació en Praga, en 1881, y con la consolidación del nazismo en el poder tuvo que irse a Estados Unidos, donde residió en California hasta su fallecimiento en 1973.

11 "Verdades y mitos del libre comercio", *Página/12*, suplemento *Cash* del 11/01/09.

En el caso de los Estados Unidos, la otra gran potencia industrial heredera, en el siglo XX, de la posición hegemónica en el mundo, su desarrollo económico pasó por etapas similares, y la disputa entre proteccionistas y librecambistas se dirimió en principio con una guerra de independencia contra Inglaterra, y finalmente por la guerra civil entre el Norte de base industrial y el Sur de condición pastoril cuya base de sustentación era el esclavismo. El triunfo del proyecto burgués industrial fue determinante para el destino de la incipiente potencia imperialista.

En estos casos ejemplares de desarrollo productivo se advierte sin dificultad la denominada intervención fundamental del Estado. Lo mismo en nuestro caso, aunque en sentido inverso. Detrás de las relaciones privadas, la extranjerización de la economía y la concentración de las riquezas se encuentra la organización nacional diseñada por las leyes que son expresión del poder político y económico creado. La cuestión queda reducida entonces a determinar a favor de qué intereses y clases sociales se dictan las normas y las políticas que las sustentan, y en nuestro país, aquellas tesis antiestatales y antipopulares han servido desde hace doscientos años al predominio de las élites y del capital privado y extranjero.

El proclamado rol ausente del Estado es una mistificación que oculta el origen histórico de la formación de las grandes propiedades de tierras, cuya explicación está en las diferentes decisiones políticas adoptadas por los poderes públicos y promovidos por el poder real a lo largo del tiempo. Desde el apoderamiento de tierras "de nadie" en la época colonial, la enfiteusis de Rivadavia, la distribución realizada por Rosas, la Ley de Tierras de Mitre en la Buenos Aires de la secesión, e incluso después de la persecución contra los pueblos indígenas en las distintas campañas de expansión y la avanzada militar en la región del Chaco.

Pero en nuestro continente se impuso, de a poco, como ideología hegemónica del orden oligárquico, un liberalismo que olvidaba su origen igualitario para resaltar únicamente su visión librecambista. En la otra vía, una tradición del liberalismo político pero de contenido nacional va

a encontrar expresión en las políticas morenistas y su continuidad en la parte final del siglo XIX en el autonomismo y el roquismo, para luego en el inicio del siglo XX, reaparecer en las consignas de voto libre y secreto del yrigoyenismo, y mayor participación política del peronismo, con sus propuestas de desarrollo productivo interno y de soberanía nacional[12].

La relación entre el librecambio, la inversión de capital privado y el progreso de la "civilización" ha sido objeto de estudio por grandes pensadores de nuestro tiempo, como por ejemplo Carlos Marx. En julio de 1853, el mismo año en que la Confederación Argentina sancionaba la Constitución Nacional, Marx esbozaba su tesis inicial favorable al rol progresivo del libre cambio en los países periféricos, al sostener que en la India el capital inglés y el libre comercio echarían las bases de la modernidad y del desarrollo productivo capitalista industrial, superando el atraso del antiguo orden de castas. Pero con el tiempo Marx modificó este criterio sustancialmente, ante la evidencia de la historia signada por la división internacional entre países dominadores y dominados y el reconocimiento de la gravitación de la cuestión nacional. Marx ya no habló de progreso sino de vandalismo inglés en la India, cuando en el devenir de los hechos comprobaba el carácter esencialmente opresivo y hasta destructor de la influencia capitalista extranjera[13].

En marzo de 1857 Carlos Pellegrini, que integraba el autonomismo, resumía el problema: "No hay en el mundo hoy día, un solo Estado serio que sea librecambista. Todas las naciones son proteccionistas y diré algo más, siempre lo han sido y tienen fatalmente que serlo para mantener su importancia económica y política". Y agregaba: "Nosotros somos y seremos

12 Sobre su origen puede resumirse en las siguientes palabras de Alberdi: "La revolución de Mayo es un capítulo de la revolución hispanoamericana, así como esta lo es de la española y esta, a su vez, de la revolución europea que tenía por fecha liminar el 14 de julio de 1789 en Francia" en *Grandes y Pequeños hombre del Plata.*

13 Marx afirmó, en relación a la cuestión de la liberación de Irlanda respecto de Inglaterra, que "el problema no es solo de orden económico sino que se plantea al mismo tiempo la cuestión nacional", es decir la liberación del país opresor (Carta a Luís Kugelman, del 29 de noviembre de 1869, en Marx, Engels, *Acerca del colonialismo*, Moscú: Editorial Progreso, 1981.

por mucho tiempo, si no ponemos remedio al mal, la granja de las grandes naciones manufactureras".

En el siglo XX, tanto el yrigoyenismo como el peronismo fueron momentos políticos de desmitificación de las alegadas bondades librecambistas. Durante el primer gobierno de Perón, la oposición de Argentina a la firma del convenio final hizo naufragar el primer intento por realizar una Organización Mundial del Comercio –institución que tiempo después sería clave para el entramado de la globalización neoliberal–, propuesta por los Estados Unidos para crear un mercado mundial "libre y abierto", en la Conferencia de las Naciones Unidas sobre Comercio y Empleo de La Habana en 1947[14].

Especialmente los fundamentos de los constituyentes de 1949 dieron sustento teórico al proceso político destruyendo con argumentos el mito del "intervencionismo estatal", como intentaremos dar cuenta en este trabajo. Arturo Sampay, en la Asamblea Constituyente decía al respecto que "La no intervención es una forma de intervención a favor del más poderoso". Y John William Cooke, en ocasión de presentar la Ley de Precios Máximos, explicaba que

> Los hasta ayer valores eternos del librecambio revisten hoy carácter de mito [...] El libre juego de la demanda no es libre ni es juego [...] Queremos dejar constancia que intervención ha habido siempre en este país, y sobre todo en los gobiernos anteriores a la revolución. El intervencionismo no es nuevo. Lo que es nuevo es el intervencionismo en favor de la clase necesitada y el intervencionismo por medio de la planificación.

Aún hoy, la falsa disyuntiva proteccionismo o libre comercio, con base en el mito de la "intervención del Estado", continúa vigente y su superación es una de las tareas político-culturales fundamentales a realizar[15].

14 Rapoport, *op. cit.*

15 La intervención del Estado a favor de la clase dominante como una constante en la historia argentina tuvo un capítulo especial en la dictadura cívico-militar en los años ochenta, cuando se nacionalizó la deuda externa contraída por sec-

¿Qué es la Constitución?

Un primer aspecto a considerar cuando se analiza el fenómeno jurídico es la relación inherente de la dimensión normativa con la política, la economía, la historia o la sociología. El derecho debe ser analizado desde la óptica de la lucha de clases, ya que sus categorías son las creadas en el seno de la sociedad moderna, pero aquellos análisis que son válidos para explicar las relaciones del capitalismo desarrollado y plenamente industrializado, requieren de una readaptación en ocasión de ser utilizados para el estudio de los países semicoloniales y oprimidos en el concierto de las naciones, como el nuestro[16].

Con esta aclaración previa, corresponde definir al derecho como un conjunto de normas –denominado sistema normativo– que dota de sentido a las relaciones sociales y pertenece al orden de los usos prescriptivos del lenguaje al establecer deberes. Con más claridad, el sistema normativo tiene el atributo de ser un orden coercitivo que, en líneas generales, es respetado y obedecido por la población, que tiene la función de otorgar "el sentido de lo bueno y lo malo, de lo aceptable y lo repudiable, de lo plausible y lo reprimible, solo que, a diferencia de otros usos prescriptivos del lenguaje, el derecho: a) regula su propia producción y b) amenaza con una sanción"[17]. La obediencia a las normas –su eficacia– es indicio de legitimidad por parte del ejercicio de poder, o en palabras de Norberto Bobbio "la legitimidad hace del poder de mandar un derecho y de la obediencia un deber, es decir, transforma una relación de mera fuerza en una relación

---

tores privados y, a la vez, se establecieron tipos de cambio diferenciales con el fin de dar financiamiento público a las importaciones de la burguesía local, con grave perjuicio de la economía nacional.

16 Este fenómeno de la dualidad es observado también por Peter Fitzpatrick, cuando dice que el "derecho occidental avanzado, dedicado en su apoteosis a la libertad, a su igualdad, se vuelve totalmente despótico cuando es enviado al resto del mundo en los procesos de colonización que se realizaron desde fines del siglo XV hasta comienzos del siglo XX" en *La mitología del derecho moderno*, México, Siglo XXI, 1998, p. 113.

17 Correas, Oscar, *Kelsen y los marxistas*, México, Coyoacán, 1994.

jurídica"[18]. En ese paso de la "fuerza" al "derecho" justamente consiste el oficio de hacer política. El ejercicio del poder es siempre crear derecho, por eso detrás de los derechos viven las luchas sociales, políticas y económicas, y en las sociedades capitalistas expresan fundamentalmente la contradicción principal que las atraviesa, es decir el estado de las relaciones de producción a partir del conflicto capital-trabajo. En los países latinoamericanos, que tienen órdenes oligárquicos, esta última fórmula contradictoria adopta, al mismo tiempo, los términos de la contradicción principal entre el pueblo y el bloque oligárquico imperialista.

Desde esta óptica –que, a rasgos generales, es la perspectiva de la crítica jurídica latinoamericana– la ley es el discurso del poder, y lo es en un doble sentido: normativo, al establecer derechos y deberes, e ideológico, al transmitir al mismo tiempo ideas, creencias, escala de valores, intenciones políticas[19]. El derecho "es la ideología que, como ninguna otra puede indicar posesión, crisis o falta de hegemonía" (Correas), y, para nuestros países latinoamericanos en los que la injerencia extranjera económica y política es la marca del sometimiento, sirve para indicar la existencia o no de soberanía nacional. Esta puede ser definida como el derecho de un Estado de no tener superior sobre la tierra a quien deba rendir cuenta de sus actos[20] o, dicho de otro modo, la hegemonía realizada a través del dictado de un sistema normativo de parte de un grupo social determinado en un espacio territorial cuya delimitación y condición de autoridad de aquellos es reconocida por el resto de los países.

18 Bobbio, Norberto, "El poder y el derecho" en *El origen y fundamentos del poder político*, México, Grijalbo, 1986.

19 Decía Carlos Marx: "El derecho no puede ser nunca superior a la estructura económica y al desarrollo cultural de la sociedad por ella condicionado". Algún día "podrá escribir en sus banderas: de cada uno, según sus capacidades; a cada uno, según sus necesidades", en la *Crítica del programa de Gotha*. Esto último lo diferencia del derecho romano –base del derecho universalizado bajo el capitalismo– de carácter privatista, que regla a una sociedad de economía mercantil –e incluso esclavista–, y cuyo principio de justicia, al contrario del postulado por Marx, consiste en mantener la circulación de bienes en el mercado de la propiedad privada.

20 Así define la soberanía Isidoro Ruiz Moreno, en *El derecho internacional público ante la Corte Suprema*, Buenos Aires, Eudeba, 1970.

Volviendo al sistema normativo, en su cúspide encontramos a la Constitución Nacional. En ella se establece, entre otras cosas, el modo de organización y las autoridades del país –que son los sujetos autorizados a crear y hacer cumplir las normas–, y cuáles son las reglas más importantes para regular la producción de derecho bajo amenaza de sanción. En el origen de un sistema normativo, o si se prefiere de la nación entendida como comunidad jurídica, se encuentra un hecho de poder que tiene la fuerza de ser fundador, como por ejemplo la Asamblea Constituyente que dictó la primera Constitución, o fenómenos jurídico-políticos similares como la Revolución de Mayo de 1810, o los acuerdos políticos plasmados en los denominados "pactos preexistentes", para los habitantes de un territorio determinado que han resuelto obedecer las normas que, a raíz de ese primer texto legal –la Constitución Nacional o los pactos–, se legislen. Dice Correas, "este primer constituyente es el grupo de individuos que, consiguiendo hacerse con el poder, ganando por tanto la hegemonía, consigue producir una Constitución que, luego a su vez, consigue hacer efectiva y por tanto eficaz"[21].

La eficacia de esa Constitución y, por lo tanto, de todo el sistema normativo consiste en que quien tiene el poder consigue hacerse obedecer con continuidad en el tiempo: "Rebeldes fueron los que dictaron la Constitución de los Estados Unidos, fuerzas irregulares hicieron lo mismo con la Constitución mexicana de 1917, guerrilleros triunfantes fueron quienes produjeron la Constitución cubana y la nicaragüense actualmente vigentes" (Correas). En todos estos casos estamos ante sistemas jurídicos que han logrado obediencia[22].

21 Correas, Oscar, *Introducción a la sociología jurídica*, México, Fontamara, 1994.
22 Dice Correas: "Si no lo son, constituyen un *intento* de alguien de ejercer el poder sobre ciertos individuos, en un territorio y en un tiempo preciso. Si, en cambio, las normas son efectivas, al menos en cierto grado, debe decirse que existe 'alguien' que consigue ejercer su poder sobre ciertos individuos, en cierto territorio, y en cierto tramo de la historia. Esto quiere decir que los sistemas normativos son *reales*. Existen porque *en la realidad* alguien consigue que otros produzcan ciertas conductas y no otras [...]", en *Derecho indígena mexicano I*, México, UNAM/Coyoacán, 2007, p.30.

Esta hegemonía lograda se va a autodenominar Poder Constituyente, que es el modo en que se nombra a la facultad soberana del pueblo para darse su propia Constitución, establecer el orden jurídico y político elegido, y a revisarlo cada vez que lo crea necesario. Al realizarlo por primera vez, es decir al fundarlo, el poder se autodenomina de carácter originario, mientras que en el último caso, ese ejercicio de poder es denominado constituido o derivado[23].

En el caso del ejercicio del poder constituyente originario estamos ante un hecho revolucionario en la medida en que el dictado de sus normas sea "eficaz"[24]. Si no lo es, si no tiene eficacia, si no logra la hegemonía necesaria para que la acción política sea revolucionaria, será una revolución frustrada y la formación política que le había dado origen será despreciada y descalificada con términos como autoritaria, dictadora o tirana. Su líder, el presidente de la nación, será nombrado como "el tirano depuesto", y si se puede, prohibido su nombre, como ocurrió con Juan Perón a partir de 1955. Se trata, en definitiva, de un capítulo esencial en la lucha por sustituir un bloque histórico por otro, o bien por consolidarlo[25].

23 Linares Quintana, Segundo, "Introducción al estudio de la teoría del poder constituyente", en *La Ley*, T. 65, pp. 787 y ss., 1955.

24 Julio Oyhanarte escribió que: "Poder constituyente originario es el que se ejerce sin sujeción a ninguna norma constitucional anterior y vigente. Poder constituyente derivado, en cambio, es aquel que tiende a revisar un ordenamiento constitucional en vigor y se somete a las normas procesales que este ordenamiento establece en previsión de su propia reforma", en "Derecho Constitucional: Doctrinas Esenciales" en *La Ley*, T. 1, pp. 84-779, 2008.

25 Para Gramsci la hegemonía consiste en lograr la dirección de la sociedad por medio de un dominio abarcador tanto de las relaciones de producción como del ámbito de la cultura en general. En cuanto al derecho, Gramsci decía que "si todo Estado tiende a crear y a mantener un cierto tipo de civilización y ciudadano (y, por consiguiente, de convivencia y de relaciones individuales), si tiende a hacer desaparecer ciertas costumbres y actitudes y a difundir otras, el derecho será el instrumento para este fin (junto a la escuela y a otras instituciones y actividades) y debe elaborarse de modo que resulte conforme al fin, y sea máximamente eficaz y productor de resultados positivos". (En *La política y el Estado moderno*, Barcelona, Planeta Agostini, 1993, p. 159).

En los países semicoloniales la soberanía adopta la doble forma de nacional y popular. La primera expresa la vocación de la comunidad de defenderse del dominio extranjero –que puede ser militar en el caso de una invasión, o económico en el caso de la mayoría de nuestros países–, mientras que la segunda se trata del ejercicio de los derechos políticos y civiles por parte la totalidad de la población, el interior de esa comunidad, en especial por parte de los más débiles y oprimidos. El poder constituyente es entonces la expresión jurídica de la soberanía en ambos sentidos. Más allá de los debates histórico-políticos, tanto en 1853 como en 1949 se ejerció el poder constituyente, obviamente de diferentes modos, pero en 1957 aquel se vio frustrado por la proscripción de la opción política de las mayorías populares (el peronismo).

Ahora bien, llegando a la Asamblea Constituyente Argentina de 1949, estimo que debe atribuírsele el carácter de poder constituyente derivado, sin importar los alcances y la importancia de la reforma encarada. Cooke sostenía que las transformaciones se realizaron dentro del texto constitucional que regía –el de 1853– porque "no se hizo una revolución contra la Constitución sino dentro de ella, buscando interpretarla lealmente en lo mucho que tiene de democrático, de popular, de justiciero". La concepción liberal de base fue respetada pero resignificada al interior del ciclo nacional popular, por lo que perdía su carácter conservador. Por ejemplo, la reforma respetó la declaración de igualdad entre todos los habitantes consagrada en el anterior artículo 16, y luego en el nuevo artículo 28 con el agregado que la nación "no admite diferencias raciales", por lo que no solo se respetaba un principio clave del liberalismo político sino que se lo completaba con el principio de no discriminación. En fin, la reforma de 1949 pertenece a la tradición del liberalismo político de contenido nacional con sus primeras raíces en el morenismo de 1810.

También los momentos constituyentes han sido en nuestro continente hitos en la acción de los movimientos nacionales[26]. Ahí están como ejemplos, la Constitución mexicana dictada como consecuencia de la etapa

26 En este sentido también la Profesora Mara Espasande, "Las Constituciones de la Patria Grande" en *El Cronista del Bicentenario*, nro. 6, junio 2012.

revolucionaria en 1917[27] –que entre otras medidas dispuso la nacionalización de las minas, la prohibición de los latifundios, limitaciones para tener propiedades o concesiones de servicios para los extranjeros, medidas de originalidad histórica cuando aún no había tenido lugar la Revolución rusa–, la brasilera de 1946 del varguismo –los artículos 147 y 148 disponían la función social de la propiedad, la intervención estatal en el mercado y cláusulas antimonopolistas–, la de Colombia de 1936 con Alfonso López Pumarejo –su artículo 30 disponía que la función social de la propiedad y el método indemnizatorio–, y la guatemalteca –disponía la función social de la propiedad, prohibía los latifundios y autorizaba la expropiación forzosa por utilidad pública– adoptada después de la revolución de 1944 y que mantuvo su vigencia durante las presidencias de Arévalo y Árbenz, hasta el golpe de Estado de 1954[28]. Del mismo modo puede citarse la reforma constitucional de Chile de 1967 –que incorpora al artículo 10 una cláusula que favorece a la reforma agraria– y de 1971 –que incorpora un texto similar al del artículo 40 de la argentina de 1949, de nacionalización de bienes, impulsada por el frente popular de Salvador Allende–.

En los últimos años, acompañando al momento político económico de unidad continental, ha habido reformas constitucionales que se corresponden a respuestas originales de nuestra América, como en el caso de Ecuador y Bolivia en las que, entre muchos otros temas, crean nuevos límites a la propiedad privada a favor de los sectores sociales más oprimidos (los indígenas y los campesinos) al consagrar a la naturaleza como sujeto de derechos (la Pachamama y el "buen vivir")[29]. Incluso no está de

27 Dijo José Nicolás Matienzo: "Se ve que los autores de la Constitución Mexicana de 1917 no la han adquirido hecha en Europa o en los Estados Unidos, sino que han tratado de hacerla a medida de las necesidades del país [...] de afirmar su soberanía nacional contra toda intervención exterior", en "El derecho y la soberanía argentina" Buenos Aires, Juárez Editor, 1970.

28 Con influencia de la Constitución española de 1931 declara que Guatemala es "Una república de trabajadores de todas las clases", en García Laguarda, Jorge M., *Constituciones Iberoamericanas*, México, UNAM, 2006.

29 "La naturaleza o Pacha Mama, donde se reproduce y realiza la vida, tiene derecho a que se respete integralmente su existencia [...] Toda persona, comuni-

más citar el caso del socialismo de la URSS en el que Vyshinski, el jurista con rol institucional más destacado del Estado soviético, justificaba tanto la propiedad colectiva de los bienes de producción como la propiedad particular de los de uso y consumo.

En todos los casos nos encontramos con el avance de programas de movimientos nacionales latinoamericanos, en donde la principal contradicción social se reactualiza bajo nuevas formas, recordándonos a Hernández Arregui cuando decía que "el desarrollo de la conciencia histórica sigue un curso paralelo a las épocas de las grandes transformaciones de la realidad nacional".

Se trata de la necesaria dimensión normativa del desarrollo de esa conciencia histórica con que los pueblos avanzan en las grandes realizaciones sociales.

¿Cuál es el significado general de la reforma constitucional de 1949?

La Constitución de 1949 expresó en el más alto plano jurídico la resolución de la cuestión nacional en aquel momento y el modelo de país con soberanía y justicia social que pregonaba el peronismo. La reforma constitucional fue la máxima expresión jurídica de su voluntad política por consolidar el cambio y la orientación dada al país, desde una perspectiva nacional y democrática.

Así como no es posible caracterizar en forma ligera al peronismo como la versión criolla del Estado de Bienestar, tampoco la Constitución del 49 fue un simple reflejo de la corriente del constitucionalismo social a nivel mundial –aunque comparta elementos– sino la sustitución de las obsoletas relaciones jurídicas de producción del país oligárquico por las del nuevo modelo productivo y soberano.

---

dad, pueblo o nacionalidad podrá exigir a la autoridad pública el cumplimiento de los derechos de la naturaleza [...]", dice el artículo 71 de la Constitución de Ecuador. Sin dejar de señalar la justa advertencia de lo que Pablo Stefanoni ha llamado el "pachamamismo ingenuo", para designar a aquellas interpretaciones del mundo indígena por fuera de su articulación al interior del movimiento nacional.

Su principal logro no fue únicamente dar rango constitucional a los derechos de los trabajadores, sociales y económicos –lo que de por sí no es poca cosa–, sino especialmente el de crear los instrumentos para que el Estado pudiera viabilizar esos derechos por medio del ejercicio de la soberanía nacional. De este modo, la reforma sentaba las bases para un proyecto de nación a largo plazo y duradero, a través del diseño jurídico de un modelo de sociedad que trascendiera la coyuntura[30]. No fue, en este sentido, una reforma de partido, pese a que en la Asamblea Constituyente quedaron finalmente solo los legisladores del peronismo. La inclusión en el texto constitucional de las políticas implementadas hasta 1949 tuvo la consecuencia de mutar la categoría jurídica de los avances logrados: de programas gubernamentales de coyuntura pasaron a ser derechos cuyos titulares corresponden a toda la población y tienen la facultad de exigir su cumplimiento.

En cuanto a la naturaleza del poder constituyente de la Convención formada, en la primera sesión del 24 de enero se expusieron las posiciones encontradas. Para Domingo Mercante –peronista–, la potestad de la Convención estaba en la búsqueda del orden social justo que hacía efectiva la libertad y la igual dignidad de las personas. Mientras que Moisés Lebensohn –radical– se opuso a legitimar la Convención por no haber sido producto de la participación y "decisión esclarecida del pueblo" y ser "inconstitucional la declaración legislativa que promovió la reforma por no existir en el país el clima de libertad indispensable para el libre debate de las ideas"[31]. Fue parte del error histórico que se le puede atribuir al radicalismo, que se concretó con el retiro de sus legisladores de la Asamblea

30 Carlos Vilas, en *Página/12*, 10/03/2009: "Una Constitución es la expresión jurídica de la estructura de poder en la sociedad. Por eso, cuando tienen lugar cambios significativos en esa estructura, la Constitución experimenta modificaciones. La reforma de 1949, de cuya sanción se cumplen sesenta años este 11 de marzo, fue la arquitectura jurídica de los cambios en las relaciones de poder que tenían lugar desde la reforma electoral de 1912, completada con la sanción del voto femenino en 1947".

31 *Diario de sesiones de la Convención Nacional Constituyente*. Buenos Aires, Imprenta del Congreso, pp. 13 a 17.

Constituyente, alejándose de las viejas consignas yrigoyenistas –por otro lado ya abandonadas por el alvearismo–, el hecho de no aportar a un consenso social que hubiera permitido la consolidación política del bloque de poder emergente para sostener el proyecto de nación con soberanía.

El eje ideológico que recorre el nuevo texto constitucional está atravesado por la contradicción nación-antinación –cuestión nacional– y la de pueblo-oligarquía –cuestión social–. Por la primera cuestión, la Constitución puede ser caracterizada como antiimperialista. En relación al segundo aspecto, debe advertirse que bajo el rótulo pueblo subyace una alianza de clases sociales, aglutinadas en el poder político del Estado, con el objetivo de alcanzar un desarrollo superador de las fuerzas productivas del país elitista y primario propio del esquema oligárquico. Este carácter policlasista del frente nacional es la clave para entender el proceso histórico de liberación, tanto en sus posibilidades como en sus límites, al mismo tiempo que se vio expresado en los nuevos mandatos constitucionales.

El Estado cumplía un rol central en la producción de riqueza –especialmente las empresas estatales– y distribución de la renta –intervención en el comercio exterior, el mercado financiero y la política social–, a través de instrumentos que adquirieron categoría constitucional. A diferencia de lo que ocurrió en las décadas siguientes, en las que se verificó una creciente concentración y extranjerización del aparato productivo y repliegue del Estado de las áreas estratégicas. Una síntesis de la finalidad del Estado comprende a la protección del trabajo, como fuente de producción de riqueza; de los recursos naturales, como patrimonio público; y la autodeterminación nacional como sentido general e integrador de la propuesta constitucional. En definitiva, el Estado como constructor de la nación, al asumir las realizaciones propias de una comunidad nacional: la justicia social, la soberanía política y la independencia económica.

Es cierto que no puede decirse que la reforma haya sido específicamente latinoamericanista, al no incluir normas de expresa connotación continental, pero hay que tener en cuenta que el mismo peronismo no

pudo concretar formas más profundas de una confluencia sudamericana que ya se anunciaba en políticas de integración como las practicadas con Brasil y Chile, interrumpidas por el golpismo conservador.

Arturo Sampay expresó que la reforma constitucional se

> [...] proponía hacer efectivo el gobierno de los sectores populares, liberar el país del imperialismo, estatizando el manejo de los recursos financieros, de los recursos naturales y de los principales bienes de producción, con la finalidad de ordenarlos planificadamente para conseguir un desarrollo autónomo y armónico de la economía, que conceda el bienestar moderno a todos y a cada uno de los miembros de la comunidad. Apuntaba a consumar en la Argentina la revolución social requerida por el mundo contemporáneo[32].

Aunque también el mismo Sampay expuso lo que entendía como el talón de Aquiles de la reforma: la falta de organización adecuada del "ejercicio del poder político de los sectores populares", por lo que el peronismo "iba a mantenerse hasta que la oligarquía cautivara a los oficiales de las Fuerzas Armadas"[33]. Identifica, así, Sampay en el plano constitucional una de las claves del desarrollo histórico-político del movimiento nacional en nuestro país: la ilusión de crear una comunidad organizada de imposible equilibrio –como se revelaría crudamente en 1955– en lugar de asumir con todas sus consecuencias la tarea de construir un frente de liberación nacional. Aquellas realizaciones nacionales incluidas en el señalado tríptico constitucional expuesto en el preámbulo de la nueva constitución encontraron su límite dentro del marco del capitalismo autónomo de difícil sustento.

Aun así, el momento constituyente de 1949 debe analizarse como expresión de la conciencia nacional que correspondió al nivel de desarrollo de las fuerzas productivas de la época y del estado de organización de los

32 Sampay, Arturo, *Constitución y Pueblo*, Buenos Aires, Instituto Superior Arturo Jauretche, 2011 p. 101.
33 *Ídem.*

trabajadores[34]. Y como el modo de dar respuesta propia a las cuestiones que planteaban las condiciones reales de nuestro país con vocación por la igualdad social. Si como decía Fermín Chávez, "cada pueblo da en su momento su propia contestación original al llamado de la historia, sin reglas absolutas prefijadas ni medidas dictadas desde ese mundo que Sarmiento llamaba Civilización", la Constitución de 1949 expresó, en el plano jurídico, el modo concreto en que se asumió "el llamado de la historia"[35]. O, lo que sería en términos de Marx, la acción real y no meramente imaginaria, que correspondió a la transformación de las condiciones reales de la vida social de aquel momento, más concretamente la superación de la semicolonia pastoril. Como las condiciones reales de la vida de un pueblo tienen un desarrollo continuo a lo largo del tiempo, el conocimiento de la historia representa la conciencia de esa continuidad, de sus avances y retrocesos, y la posibilidad de asumir la conducción de su propio destino colectivo.

34 El jurista venezolano Carlos Escarrá Malave, acerca del significado de una Constitución decía que, en ocasión del llamado a consulta popular por una posible reforma constitucional en su país, creía "que ahorita constitucionalistas somos todos los venezolanos. Aquí hay algo que me interesa precisar: el problema de la Constitución no es cosa de abogados y ahí radica el error fundamental de un sector del país. La Constitución es un pacto político, un pacto afectivo, un pacto de piel entre todos los ciudadanos. Por lo tanto, si se lo dejas a los abogados y al método racional positivista echaste a perder esa broma. Yo creo que es más un problema de gente, de pueblo, de ciudad, de expectativas de cada uno de nosotros" (Entrevista realizada por Hugo Prieto).

35 Chávez, Fermín, *Historicismo e iluminismo en la cultura argentina*, Buenos Aires, Trafac, 1957. Esta característica historicista, de algún modo va a ser denominada también como de "carácter sociológico" por Juan Fernando Segovia en *El peronismo y la Constitución de 1949 en la crisis de legitimidad argentina* al incorporarse como miembro correspondiente a la Academia Nacional de Ciencias Morales y Políticas, en sesión del 24 de agosto de 2005, disponible en la web.

II.
Breve reseña histórica constitucional argentina: de 1853 al país oligárquico

Antecedentes

"¡Soldados federales! Nuestro programa es la práctica estricta de la Constitución jurada, el orden común, la paz, la amistad con el Paraguay y la unión con las demás Repúblicas Americanas". Con esta consigna, la proclama de Felipe Varela del 6 de diciembre de 1866 realiza su llamado a la lucha federal contra el mitrismo y por la unidad de los pueblos americanos, reivindicando la Constitución de 1853. No obstante, era la misma Constitución que la Buenos Aires mitrista había jurado en 1860 y que finalmente formaría parte de la superestructura normativa del país oligárquico hasta su lejana reforma en 1949. Se trata, pues, del devenir de la historia y el desarrollo de las luchas sociales y de clase, ante lo cual la Constitución se rinde como letra muerta al servicio de los combates de la política práctica. Si ante la historia su texto parece estático, su significado ha variado según quien la levantara como consigna.

Las distintas corrientes historiográficas han sido parte de este proceso interpretativo. Para la historia mitrista y liberal conservadora, la Constitución de 1853 es reivindicada como fuente de derechos y garantías individuales contra el abuso del Estado, y valora una supuesta inspiración en la Carta Magna estadounidense. Resalta su aspecto liberal y de reivindicación de los derechos del hombre, aunque olvida el proteccionismo económico y la capacidad del Estado para intervenir en la economía (Germán Bidart Campos). En general, se le atribuye la condición de símbolo de la paz y de la unión nacional a la que por fin arriban los bandos encontrados en 1860, sin profundizar en el significado de clase de ese conflicto para el desarrollo nacional y el carácter regresivo impuesto después de Pavón. Para esta corriente no tienen ningún significado las luchas de los caudillos

federales, ni las miserias de los pueblos de las provincias, ni la política de represión desatada desde Buenos Aires.

La posición del nacionalismo oligárquico o conservador ha sido, por el contrario, la de denigrar la Constitución justamente por considerarla también simple calco de la del imperio del gran garrote, y por lo tanto ajena a la realidad nacional. En este sentido, la impugna por "antirosista" y probritánica, y suele destacar que Rosas aportó el orden social necesario como antecedente de la organización nacional (Carlos Ibarguren). Una posición similar proviene de quienes atribuyen a la Constitución el estar al servicio del capital extranjero y promover la dependencia.

En el fondo, estos últimos, muestran una coincidencia fundamental con la historia oficial, al omitir valorar las luchas de los caudillos (Peñaloza, Varela, Guayama, Saá, etc.) y el apoyo de los federales de las provincias a la Constitución, así como también el olvido del hecho fundamental que trataba de resolver: la nacionalización de los recursos aduaneros y la federalización de Buenos Aires. Tampoco ninguna de las interpretaciones suele avanzar en la perspectiva continental del constitucionalismo y el estado de retroceso de la cuestión nacional latinoamericana.

Desde una posición revisionista popular y latinoamericana, el constitucionalismo argentino del siglo XIX es interpretado como expresión de las tensiones existentes entre los dos proyectos de nación opuestos[36]. La recurrentemente invocada organización nacional no fue más que parte de la disputa entre sectores sociales históricamente encontrados (Buenos Aires, el litoral y los pueblos del resto de las provincias del país) y no un acuerdo pacífico a la espera de su tiempo idílicamente oportuno. Así, en un inicio, la sanción constitucional estuvo en el escenario de la lucha entre el proyecto federal y democrático de la Confederación del Paraná y el centralismo porteño separatista y aristocrático –correspondiente al proyecto federal–, pero con el tiempo quedó reducida a formar parte de la hegemonía triunfante. Se trata, por un lado, pues, de una variación en el contenido de las interpretaciones otorgadas por parte de diferentes

36 Galasso, Norberto, "La Constitución de 1853, proyectos e intereses contrapuestos", en *El Cronista del Bicentenario*, junio 2012.

fuerzas políticas. Variación que, por otro lado, es característica del fenómeno de la interpretación de la ley y la lucha por alcanzar la hegemonía, como vimos antes.

Si la Confederación del 53 fue una oportunidad nacional, la Constitución expresó la voluntad constituyente de ese poder político que buscó, sin éxito, consolidarse. Esta posición se encuentra en la huella de la corriente democrática con eje en la soberanía popular y el desarrollo económico autocentrado, con origen en las luchas contra los realistas[37]. En cambio, las Constituciones de 1819 y 1826 fueron impugnadas en su eficacia normativa y aceptación, como parte de la lucha federal de los pueblos de las provincias contra el centralismo porteño que, al arrebatarles las rentas aduaneras del puerto a las que todos contribuían, les privaba de la única posibilidad de un desarrollo productivo integrado y más justo.

La reivindicación de una Constitución para todo el país fue expresión de la lucha por la organización nacional que llevaron adelante los caudillos federales (desde Dorrego a Facundo Quiroga, pasando por el "Chacho" Peñaloza y Felipe Varela, e incluso el mismo Urquiza). El federalismo no nació en nuestras tierras de la doctrina de Hamilton o Jefferson sino de la lucha contra el centralismo despótico del porteñismo, así como las autonomías provinciales fueron el intento de los pueblos del interior por sustraerse de su influjo regresivo (Enrique Rivera). Y el retraso constitucional hasta 1853 no tuvo causas telúricas, sino más bien concretas e históricas: mantener la hegemonía bonaerense o, como decía Terzaga, "los intereses de siempre de la vieja metrópoli –por Buenos Aires–: nada de organización si es que la organización tenía que ser federal; nada de capitalización de la ciudad; nada de libertad de los ríos; nada de nacionalización aduanera".

En cambio, "cada vez que en Buenos Aires apareció un movimiento o una actitud de carácter ´federal´ (Tratado del Cuadrilátero, Santa Federación,

37 Sobre los cambios que trajo la Revolución de Mayo y sus limitaciones, dice León Pomer: "Todo lo nuevo que traerá Mayo no alcanzará para imponer una cultura democrática e igualitaria. Los portadores de la modernidad no navegarán en un mar de rosas". En *Continuidades y rupturas. De la Colonia a Mayo*, Buenos Aires, Ed. Colihue, 2012, p. 9.

entre otros), lo fue para aferrarse al puerto, bajo el manto federal, a los mismos privilegios y exclusivismos que defendiera bajo la cubierta del unitarismo"[38].

En la misma línea David Peña –ese abogado protorevisionista–, en 1903 desde su cátedra en la Facultad de Derecho, reivindicó a Facundo Quiroga desmitificando la ideología de "civilización o barbarie", y lo consideró como uno de los que más habían hecho para lograr la organización nacional dictando el "cuadernito", como le llamaba a la Constitución, causa por la cual fue asesinado en Barranca Yaco. Como dice Norberto Galasso:

> [...] en su última conferencia, Peña sostuvo, ante una concurrencia perpleja: "Por 16 años enmudece la palabra Constitución en los labios argentinos. Quiroga se la ha llevado a la tumba [...] si no muere Quiroga el año 35, él habría llegado a fundar la organización de la República (como dijo Vicente Fidel López). ¡Sombra ensangrentada! No has sido entonces el mito aterrador que el nombre de Facundo evoca. Representas en germen un ideal que unido al del vasto laboreo, da origen después a la organización de que hoy gozamos"[39].

Si al principio la vocación separatista portuaria, y el desinterés por un proyecto de desarrollo interno integrador, dio lugar a políticas como la de Rivadavia con apoyo de la burguesía comercial, con Rosas se instaló una posición defensiva que negociaba con las provincias pero no modificaba la esencia de la estructura monopólica de las rentas. Rosas fue expresión de un nacionalismo ganadero en la medida en que fue el mejor y más lúcido representante de la clase terrateniente bonaerense que, todavía distanciada de los importadores de manufactura británica, anheló hacia 1835 poner fin al desorden de las luchas civiles, promover sin sobresaltos el saladero (producción de tasajo y carne salada para

38 En *Historia de Roca*, Buenos Aires, Peña Lillo, p. 218 y ss.
39 Galasso, Norberto, "A 83 años del fallecimiento de David Peña, un rosarino 'maldito'", en *Tiempo Argentino*, 8 de abril de 2014.

alimentar a los esclavos de los imperios) y la ganadería exportadora, negociar con las provincias y hacerles concesiones pero sin socializar la aduana porteña –expresada en la carta de la hacienda de Figueroa de 1834–[40]. Las dos posiciones históricas se resumen en la expresión de Olegario Andrade, de "las dos políticas" o, desde el bando opuesto, en Carlos Tejedor cuando decía: "No hemos de consentir en ser gobernados por un chino o un japonés, ni en el Estado actual por un provinciano" (en los debates de la legislatura porteña en 1854, en referencia al líder entrerriano Urquiza)[41]. Y por eso era el programa federal y popular de Felipe Varela.

> El nacionalismo territorial expresado por Rosas y los estancieros bonaerenses –en su enfrentamiento con las potencias extranjeras– significaba asimismo la defensa del orden. Podía ser anticolonialista y al mismo tiempo ideológicamente conservador. Años después, cuando el imperialismo británico se instala con sus ferrocarriles, bancos, puertos, etc., ya los estancieros de la pampa húmeda abandonan toda posición nacional pues la defensa del orden, es decir de sus privilegios, solo es compatible con la subordinación al imperio. (Galasso)
> El tiempo posterior sería el de la fase superior del capitalismo.[42]

40 Una interpretación similar es asumida por Arturo Sampay en *Las ideas políticas de Juan Manuel de Rosas*, Buenos Aires, CEAL, 1975, p. 42. Decía: "Rosas [...] por fidelidad a su posición adversa a las implicancias sociales de la sociedad moderna, oponíase tanto a las instituciones democráticas como al de un mercado interno nacional que permitiera la incorporación de todas las regiones del país a la órbita de desarrollo del capitalismo europeo, entonces concurrencial". Le atribuía su pensamiento conservador.

41 Ruiz Moreno, Isidoro, *Campañas militares aregntinas,* T3 (2012), Ed. Claridad, Buenos Aires.

42 De Lenin hacemos referencia, quien ponía a Argentina como ejemplo de los países dependientes que gozan de independencia formal pero se hallan envueltos en las redes de la dependencia financiera y diplomática, en nuestro caso de Inglaterra, que pasan a ser eslabones en la cadena del capital financiero mundial. En *El imperialismo, fase superior del capitalismo* (1917), en el capítulo VI titulado "El reparto del mundo entre las grandes potencias".

Fue entonces, el de 1853, un programa urgente para crear un país con desarrollo capitalista autónomo de carácter integrador de todas las regiones. Como decía Rodolfo Puiggrós:

> [...] en tanto carta magna tenía más de programa que de estatuto constitucional, si entendemos que este último, por lo general, consagra un orden social preexistente y expresa el grado de desarrollo alcanzado por un país[43].

Al igual que Alberdi cuando sostenía que "hay constituciones de transición y creación, y constituciones definitivas y de conservación. Las que hoy pide la América del Sud son de la primera especie, son de tiempos excepcionales"[44].

Pero al mismo tiempo las intenciones de los constituyentes encontraron las dificultades que la época les ofrecía, en factores estructurales como: 1) la insuficiencia del desarrollo económico nacional sin resolver desde la caída del virreinato (ausencia de una burguesía autóctona e industrialista que, como en la Europa moderna, sostuviera la unificación de los territorios); 2) la presión que fue ejerciendo el imperio británico para incorporar a la cuenca del Plata dentro de su área de influencia económica; 3) la fragmentación continental en "patrias chicas"[45]. No eran otras que las dificultades para resolver la cuestión nacional en el contexto de consolidación del poderoso y voraz capitalismo industrial a nivel mundial.

43 Puiggrós, Rodolfo, *Historia crítica de los partidos políticos argentinos*, T. 1, Buenos Aires, Hyspamérica, p.69.
44 Alberdi, Juan B., *Bases y puntos de partida para la organización política de la República Argentina,* Cap. X (2017), Buenos Aires, Biblioteca del Congreso.
45 Cito la opinión en igual sentido de Arístides Horacio Corti en relación al modelo utilizado por los legisladores constituyentes para su obra: "Y si es cierto que, más allá de sus diferencias, nuestra Carta se basó, esencialmente, en el modelo de la Constitución de Estados Unidos, también lo es que si en dicho país sirvió de marco jurídico para un proyecto de desarrollo capitalista autónomo, no sucedió así en la Argentina cuyas oligarquías gobernantes promovieron un desarrollo parcial (solo agropecuario), deformado y dependiente", en *Algunas reflexiones sobre leyes de facto y derechos adquiridos*, Buenos Aires, La Ley 1984-B, 970.

El capitalismo en la segunda mitad del siglo XIX –modelo civilizatorio a escala mundial impulsado por Gran Bretaña, a quien Vivian Trías denominó "el imperio del mar"– ingresó en su etapa financiera, monopolista, con hegemonía de bancos, sociedades anónimas, la industria de las armas, los ferrocarriles y el sistema de transporte con la navegación a vapor[46]. También hacia 1885, en Berlín, las potencias europeas se repartieron el continente africano. El imperialismo era entonces un hecho consumado difícil de enfrentar, y lejos quedaban los proyectos emancipatorios de Bolívar, San Martín y Artigas. La separación de los pueblos americanos, en tanto ausencia de un proyecto unificador triunfante, ahondó aun más las divisiones, y el riesgo de una disolución nacional más profunda fue potenciado por la miseria, los años de luchas y el predominio creciente de las oligarquías portuarias en todo el continente.

1853: Constitución y después

Entre las principales disposiciones constitucionales, como ya señalamos, estuvieron la nacionalización de las rentas de la aduana con sede en el puerto de Buenos Aires, la libre navegabilidad de los ríos del interior –reclamo concreto de los estancieros del litoral para su participación en el mercado exterior y el desarrollo de su renta–; la igualdad entre todas las provincias, incluida Buenos Aires; la supresión de las aduanas interiores y la futura federalización de Buenos Aires, pensada como capital del país, así como la creación de un poder central que dictara la ley con validez de alcance nacional y uniforme en materia civil, comercial, penal y de minería[47].

46 Trías sostiene que el "secreto de tal hazaña" imperialista a nivel mundial, consistió en "la existencia, en cada sociedad sometida, de una clase nativa dominante constituida por terratenientes o mineros, grandes comerciantes, abogados de empresas inglesas [...] cuyos intereses, carreras, cuyo status, están íntimamente ligados a la política del imperio británico [...] y que asegura la articulación de la economía dependiente local con la economía mundial dirigida desde la City", en "El imperio británico", *Cuadernos de Crisis*, Buenos Aires, 1976 p. 59.

47 Decía Juan Álvarez en *Las guerras civiles argentinas*: "La aduana, además de constituir el principal recurso del gobierno central, pareció ser la mejor solución

Y, por un lado, también el artículo 16 que establecía la igualdad entre todos los habitantes[48], en cuya norma encontramos la influencia progresiva de aquel liberalismo político igualitario con origen en las revoluciones europeas (la francesa de 1789, la española de 1808) y las luchas de emancipación americana. Aunque por otro lado, esa igualdad encontraba algún límite en la relación diferenciada con los pueblos originarios, cuando en el artículo 67 inciso 15 establecía que correspondía "proveer a la seguridad de las fronteras; conservar el trato pacífico con los indios, y promover su conversión de ellos al Catolicismo". Esta última norma evidentemente regulaba la relación con los indígenas que se mantenían en conflicto con el Estado y no la de aquellos que habían pasado a formar parte de la sociedad mestiza, a quienes les correspondía el derecho a la igualdad del artículo 16.

La constitución establecía un instrumento macroeconómico fundamental para el ejercicio de la soberanía económica, como la atribución estatal de ejercer los derechos de exportación e importación, lo que prestaba respaldo normativo al plan económico de Mariano Fragueiro, sancionado el 9 de diciembre de 1853 por el mismo Congreso Constituyente al aprobar el Estatuto para la Organización de la Hacienda y Crédito Público[49].

Por su parte, Alberdi sostenía la necesidad de industrializar a partir de la colonización agrícola, pero también con el protagonismo de la inmigración

económica hallada durante el siglo XIX, para transar el viejo pleito entre la región del Litoral productora de materias exportables, y las del Interior fabricantes de artículos industriales susceptibles de ser consumidos en el país".

48 El artículo 16 decía: "La Confederación Argentina no admite prerrogativas de sangre, ni de nacimiento: No hay en ella fueros personales ni títulos de nobleza. Todos sus habitantes son iguales ante la ley, y admisibles en los empleos sin otra consideración que la idoneidad. La igualdad es la base del impuesto y de las cargas públicas".

49 El importante programa de Mariano Fragueiro, expresado en el Estatuto para la Organización de la Hacienda y Crédito Público de la Confederación Argentina, consagró la intervención del Estado en la economía mediante el monopolio del crédito público, convirtiéndolo no solo en receptor de los tributos, monopolizador de funciones bancarias y acuñación de moneda, sino también en hacedor de obras públicas esenciales para impulsar la actividad económica nacional, por la inversión de sus recursos. También promovía la protección de las industrias locales estableciendo controles a la importación de manufacturas.

europea ("poblador anglosajón y alemán de raza") para poblar el territorio y la libertad de ingreso de capitales europeos. *Las Bases* (1852) y *Sistema Económico y Rentístico de la Confederación Argentina según su Constitución de 1853* (1854) tributan en el liberalismo económico y librecambista de Adam Smith (como explica Bernardo Canal Feijóo[50]): "la riqueza es hija del trabajo, del capital y de la tierra", debiéndose limitar el Estado a garantizar la seguridad necesaria para el desarrollo de esos factores de producción. "Los capitales son la civilización argentina" los que merecen una "amplia y entera libertad de acción y aplicación" y "la libertad ilimitada en la tasa del interés" (¡aunque se trate de la usura!). Esto último y su desvalorización por lo criollo e indígena –como la expresada en *Las Bases*– constituyen el aspecto reaccionario de su pensamiento, mientras que la fundamentación de la nacionalización de las rentas aduaneras y una posición política a favor del federalismo lo es del progresivo[51]. Aunque es justo precisar que el tucumano no podía imaginar los alcances que la concentración monopólica adquiriría, ni la expansión capitalista en su rol de fase superior del imperialismo. Como tampoco lo hicieron los constituyentes (interpretación abonada por Sampay, como ya señalamos), e incluso no terminaba de hacerlo Marx desde la propia Inglaterra industrial.

Ha sido objeto de crítica el reconocimiento a los extranjeros de los mismos derechos civiles (art. 20)[52]. Pero, siguiendo a José Matienzo, ello razonablemente lo era solo respecto de los habitantes incorporados personalmente al país, lo que excluía a los monopolios extranjeros[53]. Más aun, según la interpretación propiciada por Sampay, con la incorporación de capitales extranjeros "se refiere a los que se incorporan al país dejando

50 En *Constitución y Revolución*, dos tomos, Buenos Aires, Hyspamérica.

51 Es justo también señalar que, tiempo después, varió hacia posturas reivindicatorias de lo nativo, fue crítico de la guerra contra el Paraguay, manteniendo un antimitrismo militante. Este Alberdi contradictorio ha llevado a decir a León Pomer, "el de las Bases y el otro".

52 Así, entre varios, José Pablo Feinmann en su obra *Filosofía y Nación*, Buenos Aires, Sudamericana, 1996.

53 *La doctrina de Monroe y la Constitución Argentina*, Buenos Aires, Valerio Abeledo, 1929.

de ser tales y que, por lo mismo, no generan beneficios remesables al exterior, porque si no se propugnaría que la economía nacional estuviese manejada desde afuera"[54]. También debe precisarse que el texto constitucional no disponía que el rol del Estado en materia cambiaria se redujese a una caja de conversión del peso a la moneda metálica –como ocurrió especialmente desde la presidencia de Mitre y permaneció, salvo por los períodos de crisis, hasta los años 30–, dispositivo que sería clave para someter la economía a las exigencias del capital inglés para los empréstitos, la remisión de utilidades o la compra de bienes públicos.

Otras disposiciones establecían que las contribuciones directas correspondían en principio a las provincias y excepcionalmente a la nación (art. 64, inc. 2°, conjugado con el art. 101), mientras que las provincias cuyas rentas no alcanzaran según sus presupuestos, tenían derecho a requerir subsidios del Tesoro nacional (inc. 8°, art. 64), renunciando todas a sus aduanas locales y a imponer derechos de tránsito (arts. 9, 10 y 11).

La composición del Senado de la Nación garantizaba a las provincias su peso político en la toma de decisiones de gobierno, como por ejemplo la facultad de regular la política de protección arancelaria (art. 42). "Esta Cámara era la verdadera llave maestra del sistema: se le atribuía virtualmente la custodia del texto fundamental sancionado, por la primacía que importaba otorgarle la iniciativa de la reforma constitucional (art. 51)"[55].

Como buena síntesis, encontramos que para Arturo Sampay el polo axiológico constitucional de 1853 se encuentra en el preámbulo cuando enuncia al pueblo como fuente originaria del poder constituyente, declara el fin supremo de "promover el bienestar general", y en el plano de las relaciones exteriores sostiene en forma incipiente la igualdad jurídica entre las naciones. Esta tradición encontró una expresión contundente con la Doctrina Drago (1898 y 1902) como posición asumida por

54 *Constitución y Pueblo*, Buenos Aires, Instituto Superior Arturo Jauretche, 2011, p. 201.
55 Explica Luís Iriarte en "Programa económico del federalismo argentino, reflexiones sobre modelos de inserción nacional en distintas etapas de la globalización" (*La Ley*, Suplemento Actualidad, Buenos Aires, 16 de diciembre de 2004).

la nación argentina en defensa de la soberanía de los países contra la opresión de las potencias imperialistas, opuesta en la época al Corolario Roosevelt de la doctrina Monroe (EUA)[56]. También marcó distancia con el Pacto de la Liga de las Naciones (1919) en el que se establecía el derecho a tutela de los países más poderosos contra los más débiles, justo cuando las dos terceras partes del planeta se encontraban bajo el poder de hecho de EUA, Inglaterra, Francia y Japón.

En definitiva, entre Fragueiro y Alberdi se debatía la posibilidad de una Confederación que vio frustrado su destino nacional. Ni uno ni otro prosperó, sino el centralismo porteñista, aristocrático y librecambista, promotor y aliado de la penetración imperialista al que le otorgaba la correspondiente cobertura de la legislación civil, comercial y minera. En esa *intelligentsia* se comprende cómo, según los artículos 34 y 41 del Código Civil, los Estados extranjeros, las grandes corporaciones y sus magnates particulares, tienen los mismos derechos que cualquier habitante de nuestro país para adquirir bienes y constituir derechos reales, lo que favorece la opresión económica de las potencias mundiales. Reproducen así la misma lógica mistificadora de la desigualdad real entre las naciones que en los acuerdos de libre comercio con Inglaterra, cuya flagrancia debe haber inspirado a alguien como José Nicolás Matienzo –uno de los juristas más reconocidos del primer cuarto del siglo XX que combinó la tarea de Procurador General de la Nación de Yrigoyen con la de político conservador de peso hasta su deceso en 1936– a opinar que estas normas no respetaban el sentido de la Constitución de 1853[57].

56 En uno de los hechos más relevantes en la historia de la política exterior argentina, Luís María Drago, ministro de Relaciones Exteriores en la segunda presidencia de Julio A. Roca, en 1902 exigió el respeto al principio de no intervención, especialmente por motivos de deudas externas, y condenó el bloqueo y bombardeo de los puertos de Venezuela, por parte de Inglaterra, Alemania e Italia, para lograr el cobro de empréstitos. Drago la llamaba "la nota argentina" (Russo, Carlos, en *Revista Panorama*, junio 1972, nro. 22).

57 "El imperialismo y las leyes argentinas" (1929) en *El derecho y la soberanía argentina*, Buenos Aires, Juárez Editor, 1969, p.102 y ss.

Volviendo a la Confederación de Paraná, su sola existencia provocó la reacción de Buenos Aires que, al ver peligrar su política porteñista y los privilegios rentísticos, rechazó la Constitución sancionada y dividió al país[58]. El partido centralista encontró su prolongación histórica en el acuerdo entre los antiguos unitarios y los cuadros del rápidamente diluido rosismo, cimentado en la intención de enfrentarse a Urquiza y su organización constitucional. Ahí desfilaron, en mezcla de facciones porteñas, Alsina, Lorenzo Torres, Mitre, Vélez Sarsfield (alias el "Dr. Mandinga"), Flores, Anchorena (los primos de Rosas), entre otros[59].

Con una Constitución propia desde 1854, el Estado de Buenos Aires se separó de la Confederación, ejerció una pretendida soberanía externa frente a las potencias europeas, con fundamento económico en la apropiación de la aduana y el banco emisor de moneda. De un lado, la arrogante "República del Río de la Plata", del otro, "los treces ranchos" que, hundidos en la miseria y sin fuente de recursos disponible al haber perdido toda posibilidad de comercio exterior, solo pudieron unirse contra el separatismo portuario y respaldar a Urquiza como única esperanza posible de sostener objetivos nacionales.

La derrota militar definitiva de la Confederación, con el abandono de Urquiza en Pavón (1861) y el triunfo de la oligarquía bonaerense representada

58 En las sesiones de junio de la legislatura porteña, al estudiar el acuerdo de San Nicolás, Mitre fundamentó su rechazo y la secesión: "¿De dónde pues todos ellos reunidos han obtenido esa plenitud de autoridad y soberanía para legislar como han legislado el acuerdo de San Nicolás, como no legislaría el Poder Ejecutivo Nacional? ¿Quién los invistió con un poder constituyente de la nación, poder que no tenían como gobernantes de provincia?" (cit. en López Rosas, Rafael, *Historia Constitucional Argentina*, Buenos Aires, Astrea, 3ª ed., p. 521). Como citamos antes, esta argumentación jurídica "es la ideología que, como ninguna otra puede indicar posesión, crisis o falta de hegemonía" (O. Correas).

59 El 11 de septiembre de 1852 había tenido lugar en Buenos Aires el "Abrazo del Coliseo", representado en Lorenzo Torres y Valentín Alsina, en el que los dos sectores dominantes de la economía, que hasta el momento habían permanecido separados, se unen: los terratenientes ganaderos de la pampa húmeda y los comerciantes porteños vinculados al negocio de la importación de manufacturas. Esta puede ser tenida como la fecha de nacimiento del bloque dominante argentino.

en el liderazgo político de Bartolomé Mitre, se tradujeron en la resolución infausta del largo conflicto[60], con la posición de dominio para dictar las líneas del nuevo país oligárquico que se proyectaba, pese a que la Constitución imponía la forma de gobierno "representativa, republicana y federal" (como señala en su artículo 1).[61] Su triunfo, más económico que militar significó "la organización nacional con dependencia económica" (Puiggrós) porque, de algún modo la unidad nacional era necesaria para el desarrollo de la república aristocrática al someter a todo el territorio a las leyes del modelo agroexportador de carácter semicolonial[62]. Como dice Alfredo Terzaga:

> El triunfo militar enfrentó a Buenos Aires con una realidad: había que contar con el país, aunque el país fuera esa odiosa porción formada por las trece provincias restantes [...] Relegando al olvido su antiguo proyecto de segregar del todo a Buenos Aires para formar la famosa República del Río de la Plata, Mitre desoyó a los extremistas de su partido, que eran legión, y se dedicó a "contar con el país", según su propia expresión.[63]

60 Lo infausto no fue el conflicto en sí, que en todo caso expresaba el estado de la lucha de clases en el país, sino su resolución a favor del partido del atraso, la dependencia y la represión.

61 Como dice Norberto Galasso mediante nota dirigida al autor: "para el orden oligárquico 'fue mucho más Pavón que Caseros', porque si bien en Caseros los liberales oligárquicos habían concurrido al frente antirrosista, fue en Pavón donde lograron el allanamiento completo del camino para la realización de sus objetivos elitistas de organización nacional.".

62 Es posible adjudicarle a Mitre el rol de intelectual orgánico del bloque dominante en la etapa de formación de nuestra nación. Dice Duhalde: "Sorprende la modernidad de Mitre en el diseño de la estructura ideológica de la clase dirigente, es decir, en términos gramscianos, de la organización material destinada a mantener, defender y desarrollar el frente teórico e ideológico [...] Alternó la dirección del Estado –provincial y nacional– y su presencia en los campos de batalla con las tareas de esforzado traductor, poeta, ensayista, historiador y periodista, advirtiendo que el principio de autoridad exigía revestirse de componente culturales [...] Comprendió como ninguno el papel de la prensa, fundando diarios y clausurando los de sus opositores, y nadie como él advirtió en su tiempo el papel de la historia como elaboradora de los paradigmas constitutivos de la Argentina liberal". En *Contra Mitre. Los intelectuales y el poder: de Caseros al 80.* Bs. As: Punto Crítico, p. 30 y ss.

63 Terzaga, Alfredo, *Historia de Roca*, Buenos Aires, Peña Lillo Editor, 1976, p. 118.

Y contar con el país significó la inmediata implementación de una feroz guerra de policía, a cargo de lugartenientes mitristas como Paunero, Sandes, Rivas, y que incluso contó con el apoyo fervoroso de Sarmiento.

Según Fermín Chávez, entre 1852 y1868 estallaron en las provincias argentinas 117 revoluciones y se libraron 91 combates, con un total de 4.728 muertos[64]. Las rebeliones popular y federal del "Chacho" Peñaloza, Felipe Varela y luego de López Jordán fueron, aunque justas y dignas, a destiempo, y "quienes no aceptaron la nueva situación terminaron en la cuchilla del enemigo"[65]. La guerra contra el Paraguay (1865) definió el escenario en la cuenca del Plata –impulsada por Mitre, los colorados uruguayos y el Imperio del Brasil, bajo la influencia británica–, al dejar como saldo el primer gran genocidio latinoamericano y el fin de la experiencia de desarrollo autónomo cuyo ejemplo de crecimiento amenazaba a los intereses oligárquicos.

El americanismo asomó con fuerza en las proclamas jordanistas y varelistas que convocaban a la lucha federal y repudiaban la Guerra de la Triple Alianza contra el Paraguay por ser "guerra ambiciosa de dominio", porque como también señala Fermín Chávez, tal convicción "republicana, anticentralista y americanista" era común a "una generación nacional y a un partido: el de la Confederación Argentina después de Pavón"[66]. Felipe Varela, como expresión avanzada del caudillismo popular del Noroeste instó vanamente por una acción decididamente federal y americanista que tampoco triunfó[67].

64 Chávez, *op. cit.*

65 "Primero, con la deserción de Urquiza como jefe del partido federal, y después, la resistencia al poder armado de Buenos Aires que invadió, ocupó el interior con sus batallones de línea, e impuso gobernadores de facto" en Chávez, Fermín, *Vida de López Jordán*, Buenos Aires, Hyspamérica, 1986.

66 Chávez, Fermín, "El revisionismo y las montoneras", Buenos Aires, Theoría, 1984, p.27.

67 Sobre este extraordinario caudillo citemos lo siguiente: "Felipe Varela nace en Huaycama, departamento de Valle Viejo, Catamarca, en 1821. Desde muy joven vive y sufre la pobreza de su provincia arruinada por la política librecambista de Buenos Aires que destruye la economía doméstica y artesanal. No es casualidad, entonces, su lucha como lugarteniente del Chacho Peñaloza. Inte-

El régimen político imperante después de Pavón dio baños de racionalismo absoluto y mesiánico a su política de guerra e intolerancia, lo que también caracterizó a las campañas contra los pueblos indígenas, realizadas con la legítima excusa de consolidar fronteras nacionales y extender la presencia del Estado, pero al costo inaceptable de someter comunidades por métodos criminales contrarios a la propia Constitución y de promover el etnocidio, lo que finalmente contribuyó a la formación terrateniente[68]. La vieja Constitución de 1853 pasó a tener el mismo valor que una pieza de museo, en donde se podría exhibir junto con la Confederación del Paraná y los restos de las luchas federales. Su lugar fue ocupado por el reinado de la legalidad infraconstitucional,

grará bajo su mando la Coalición del Norte contra Rosas. Entiende la política del Restaurador de puerto único y monopolio de las rentas aduaneras como una continuidad de la practicada por los unitarios rivadavianos. No le temblará el pulso para denunciar la sangrienta represión de los ejércitos mitristas, y denunciar el carácter de "guerra de policía" que le da Mitre a su lucha contra los montoneros para que sus esbirros (Paunero, Rivas, Sandes y otros) puedan asesinarlos impunemente sindicándolos como meros "ladrones". Viaja a Chile y Bolivia a expandir los comités de la "Unión Americana". Este será el punto medular de su política ya que impugna las fronteras artificiales, las políticas portuarias de las burguesías mercantiles pro británicas y llama a la unidad hispanoamericana", en Molocznik, Maximiliano, *Señales Populares*, Buenos Aires, Centro Cultural E. S. Discépolo, 2012.

68 No es tema de estudio en este trabajo la vida de los pueblos indígenas, solo acoto que ellos integran la identidad nacional y latinoamericana. Carlos Montemayor solía decir que tal vez los mexicanos todavía no estén preparados para saber qué tanto de la cultura indígena hay en ellos, lo mismo se podría decir de los argentinos. Según el estudio genético de Daniel Corach (UBA) más del cincuenta por ciento de la población argentina podría ser descendiente de pueblos indígenas, lo que sería "una sustancial contribución genética de las poblaciones originarias de América a la constitución actual de la población argentina [...] Todos tendemos hacia el amerindio" (*Página/12*, 10/08/2005). Ello concurre a ratificar una vez más la certeza de que la condición del hecho americano es el mestizaje, lo que incluye por supuesto a los pueblos indígenas con el aporte de la riqueza cultural y política de su diversidad. En relación a la conquista del desierto de 1879, ver Jara, Juan Carlos, "Julio A. Roca y la conquista del desierto", en *Cronista del Bicentenario*, Buenos Aires, Dirección General de Cultura y Educación de la Provincia de Buenos Aires, donde se pondera certeramente y con justeza histórica.

en especial el Código Civil legislado en 1869. La de 1853 fue, de algún modo, la Constitución "ausente" –como uno de sus inspiradores– y su lugar ocupado por el texto de Vélez Sarsfield[69], proyectado entre 1865 y 1869 y en vigencia desde 1871, por lo que fue expresión normativa de la voluntad política del mitrismo. Hasta ese momento regía el Código de Comercio legislado por la provincia de Buenos Aires en 1858 –que luego, con la integración de Buenos Aires en la Confederación, se volvió ley nacional– cuyo fin era la protección del interés de la burguesía mercantil portuaria. El andamiaje jurídico de carácter federal inicial también fue producto de la necesidad de organizar al país, por medio de las Leyes 27, 48, 49 y 50, y la novel e importante institución: la Corte Suprema de Justicia de la Nación. Leyes de organización pero de contenido antinacional en el sentido de integrar para consolidar la dependencia y el orden elitista. Más que una Constitución para el país semicolonial, lo que hubo fue una interpretación normativa que adecuó las leyes a la realidad histórica fraguada. Por ejemplo, la Ley 49 de 1863, el antecedente legislativo en materia penal más importante, sirvió como marco legal para la política represiva mitrista contra los pueblos del Noroeste, al establecer la competencia de tribunales federales (es decir, al servicio del centralismo) y la pena de muerte[70].

El principal de los derechos lo constituía, como en toda sociedad capitalista, el de la propiedad privada, con especial protección del poder de los grandes propietarios sobre las llanuras fértiles y tierras ricas en posibilidades de cultivo o ganadería. La propiedad de las tierras estaba

69 En esta construcción de la hegemonía jurídica corresponde incluir al dictado de la Ley N° 48 (de tanta importancia que aún hoy está vigente), bajo la presidencia de Mitre, en 1863. Esta norma, inspirada en la *Judiciary Act* de los Estados Unidos (1789), dispone el alcance federal del recurso extraordinario, el que en ese momento histórico funcionó como un elemento político para mantener la unión del país bajo el poder político de la Buenos Aires mitrista, al establecer la supremacía de las normas federales sobre las normas locales. Ese sería el sentido también de las cláusulas incorporadas a la Constitución en 1860.

70 Ver Mercado Luna, Ricardo, *Los coroneles de Mitre*, Córdoba, Alcion Editora, 2006. Obra prohibida por la última dictadura militar y reeditada por Alcion Editora.

definida por la concesión, donación y venta de tierras públicas: es decir, un incesante proceso de privatización de las tierras estatales. La derrota del cacique indígena Calfucurá en 1858 aseguraría una posesión tranquila de la pampa húmeda para los terratenientes bonaerenses, aunque aún quedaría para más adelante la ofensiva hacia el denominado "desierto", dejando atrás la política más contemplativa de asegurar posiciones llevada a cabo por Nicolás Avellaneda y Adolfo Alsina.

El Código Civil establecía un principio que con el tiempo fue clave para consolidar el poder de una clase social ausente del territorio y de paso terminar de expulsar definitivamente al gauchaje: el título constituye el derecho de propiedad sin necesidad de acreditar la posesión efectiva. Esta norma los protegía frente a los reclamos de nativos, indígenas y criollos pobres sobre la base de una ocupación de hecho tradicional, y les permitía consagrarse propietarios con solo ordenarlo desde los escritorios de las ciudades.

Esta protección se completó con la omisión de Vélez en el Código Civil de la regulación del requisito de la publicidad y la anotación registral para constituir el tan protegido derecho a la propiedad. Como la implantación de los registros de propiedad locales se daría recién al iniciarse los años ochenta,

> Vélez organiza de tal modo esta materia porque no entraba en los cálculos de política fomentar la negociación sobre tierras. Menos aun podía arriesgar el "congelamiento" de la extensión de las propiedades mediante su inmatriculación registral.[71]

Es que los "dueños de la tierra" en rigor eran en su mayoría simples poseedores, muchos carentes de títulos y en vías de ser "propietarios" una vez que la expansión encontrara su límite "natural" (es decir, hasta que los alambrados se chocaran). Pero por entonces aún no se había terminado de repartir la tierra disponible, por lo que la exclusión inicial en la legislación de la "publicidad registral" del título de propiedad era un modo de proteger el interés terrateniente y no entorpecer su expansión con requisitos formales.

71 Siperman, Arnoldo, "Código Civil y Propiedad", en *Rev. Polémica*, Buenos Aires, CEAL, 1970,

La intención del nuevo sistema normativo no era el de fomento de la inmigración rural para el crecimiento del país, como a su modo querían los constituyentes de Paraná en 1853, sino la de proteger a los terratenientes bonaerenses, triunfantes con el mitrismo y en curso de constante expansión.

En síntesis, como en el resto de los países latinoamericanos, la oligarquía terminó siendo la clase social hegemónica, auténtica causa del atraso económico, las desigualdades sociales y la dependencia con los poderes extranjeros. En nuestro país, el liberalismo conservador resguardó al Estado librecambista, cuyo principal derecho consagrado era el de la propiedad privada y la autonomía de la voluntad del individuo en abstracto, que en concreto era la de los sectores dominantes. Fue el garante jurídico del ingreso del capitalismo financiero extranjero y de vocación imperialista, con los ferrocarriles, los talleres, el sistema de bancos y el financiamiento externo, y el reparto de tierras. Ya por entonces hasta el mismo Marx había cambiado de opinión acerca del rol regresivo del ferrocarril en manos imperialistas en los países sometidos. Lejos quedaría aquel liberalismo constitucional de contenido nacional y democrático que inspirara a la Carta Magna, por el contrario, fue sustituido por un liberalismo de carácter economicista y aristocrático[72]. "La posesión del gobierno: he ahí toda su libertad. El monopolio del gobierno: he ahí todo su liberalismo", diría con meridiana claridad el exembajador de Paraná, de inspiración liberal pero antiporteño con claro sentido nacional.

En todo lo que no era útil para la hegemonía porteña la Constitución fue descartada, como demuestra la persecución a muerte de los caudillos y sus huestes (Vicente "Chacho" Peñaloza y Santos Guayama, entre otros).

72 Vilas, Carlos, en *Derecho y Estado en una economía dependiente*, Buenos Aires, Guadalupe, 1974, señala que los extranjeros a los que la Constitución Nacional acordó los derechos civiles de los ciudadanos no eran las corporaciones multinacionales, sino como lo destacó Matienzo "los habitantes de la República incorporados personalmente a nuestra población" o sea los inmigrantes, que volcaron su sangre y sus esfuerzos a la nueva patria; y "la importación de capitales extranjeros" se refiere "a los que se incorporan al país dejando de ser tales, y que por lo mismo, no generan beneficios remesables al exterior". Citado por Arístides H. Corti, en *op. cit.*

El historiador León Pomer, al referirse al mundo de los sectores populares, dice que:

> [...] muchos se jactaban de que la Argentina tenía la constitución más liberal del mundo. Al amparo de ese liberalismo se torturaba al gauchisoldado con increíble ferocidad. "No era nada del otro mundo" sin duda no lo era. Era del mundo que aquí estaban construyendo los que se pretendían iluminados. El lomo de los hombres del pueblo aguantaba.[73]

La cuestión federal tendría sus últimos ecos hacia 1880. El dominio de Buenos Aires sobre el resto del país no había cambiado en lo sustancial y mantuvo siempre a la aduana bajo su poder de hecho[74]. La reforma constitucional de 1860 que integró a Buenos Aires, favoreció a esta en las nuevas disposiciones y solo recién en 1866 fueron nacionalizados los derechos de exportación, es decir, la aduana y su renta, cuando ya los ganaderos bonaerenses y la burguesía porteña importadora se habían consolidado a sangre y fuego. Pero igualmente 1880 fue un año crucial. Buenos Aires tuvo su último intento por profundizar su hegemonía y lugar de privilegio, y se insurreccionó para evitar la llegada al poder del tucumano Roca, que era representante de la Liga de Gobernadores del interior y al que consideraba un adversario. El levantamiento armado dio lugar a terribles batallas en la zona sur de la ciudad, como Los Corrales, Parque Patricios, Puente Alsina, Barracas, con el fin de que "la provincia (de Buenos Aires) reasuma temporalmente su soberanía de Estado independiente". La derrota militar del mitrismo, con Carlos Tejedor como su conspicua expresión, evitó la posibilidad de una nueva segregación y selló definitivamente la unidad nacional con la federalización

73 Pomer, León, *Historia de gauchos y gauchisoldados*, Buenos Aires, Colihue, 2007.

74 Alberdi opinaba críticamente de la forma en que se dio la integración de Buenos Aires a la nación argentina, con la reforma constitucional y el convenio de noviembre de 1860, porque "no hay tal unión, hay dos países unidos como la colonia puede estar unida a la metrópoli, la una para obedecer, la otra para gobernar". Ver Alberdi, J. B., *Proceso a Mitre*, Buenos Aires, Punto de Encuentro, 2013, p. 162 y ss.

de la ciudad y el reparto –ahora sí efectivo– de la renta de la aduana, impuesto por Roca.

El autonomismo, de este modo, recogió las banderas del viejo federalismo de naturaleza política antimitrista y no se resignó a un país exclusivamente pastoril sino que promovió cierta protección al desarrollo nacional[75]. Pero entre la declinación final del PAN –Partido Autonomista Nacional– (su *mitrificación*, en palabras de Eduardo Wilde) y las circunstancias socioeconómicas derivadas de la división internacional del trabajo impuesta por el capitalismo industrial expansionista de los países imperialistas, el orden oligárquico se impuso. En 1904, el año clave en el que la oligarquía se hizo cargo del gobierno nacional por su propia cuenta cuando Roca cedió el poder a Quintana –exabogado de la banca inglesa–, ya se había consolidado una legalidad y doctrina librecambista que aseguraba el orden en el país semicolonial. La seguridad jurídica tenía como contenido histórico la protección de la renta agraria diferencial como propiedad privada de la "oligarquía"[76]. Los dueños de la tierra de la pampa húmeda constituyeron el núcleo de la clase dominante, en tanto que usufructuaban vastas extensiones de gran fertilidad y clima excepcional, aptas para la invernada y cercanas al puerto. Estas condiciones fueron causa de una rentabilidad extraordinaria por sus bajos costos en comparación con el promedio mundial, en especial con el cereal, el ganado y las carnes. Es "el poder secreto de la oligarquía", según Hernández Arregui, "el centro de su filosofía política es el carácter inalienable de la propiedad de la tierra", en la que el único progreso aceptable es el de servir a la tierra[77]. Pero la

75 Del autonomismo surgió el Informe sobre el estado de las Clases Obreras Argentinas de 1904, para la comisión organizada por el presidente Roca. Juan Bialet Massé, su autor, expresó, además de un alegato a favor de los derechos de los trabajadores, una posición nacional, industrialista y de denuncia de la influencia perniciosa y antipopular del capital extranjero.

76 La clase dominante se formaba con las familias propietarias de grandes extensiones de tierra en la pampa húmeda, productores privilegiados de las provincias (como los bodegueros de Cuyo o los azucareros de Tucumán) y los financistas y comerciantes vinculados al comercio exterior.

77 Hernández Arregui, J. J., *La formación de la conciencia nacional*, Buenos

clave está en su alianza con el capital británico que ejerce su predominio en los bancos, en la infraestructura de transporte ferroviario, puerto, flota mercante, compañías de seguro y el comercio de importación de manufacturas.

Al país oligárquico y agroexportador con dependencia económica le correspondió una superestructura jurídica que consagraba, formalmente, un Estado neutro (con la aclaración explicada en el capítulo anterior sobre la falsa dualidad librecambio o intervencionismo), pero que en el campo social y político era altamente represivo, en el que los sectores populares –orilleros, peones, artesanos y obreros– fueron objeto de explotación laboral y represión ante cualquier manifestación de protesta. En este aspecto, los postulados liberales propios de la escuela penal clásica, que regían según el texto constitucional, fueron postergados por un sistema de control social, a través de una legislación infraconstitucional integrada por bandos de Policía y normas que reprimían la vagancia como sinónimo de "desocupado" y "sin patrón o estancia", con sanciones como azotes, leva o destierro a la frontera, impuestas por jueces de paz o la Policía[78]. Este sistema punitivo de ideología positivista fue el que rigió, aun contrariando los postulados de igualdad jurídica y otras garantías penales que en la letra consagraba la Constitución Nacional: esa fue la Argentina del centenario y de inicios del siglo XX[79].

El autonomismo se esfumó con el siglo anterior y hubo que esperar la continuidad de sus posiciones en el primer movimiento de masas del siglo veinte: el yrigoyenismo. Un hito inicial de importancia fue la reforma electoral de 1912 –de voto secreto, obligatorio y universal, aunque en ese entonces solo para los varones–, producto del pacto entre Yrigoyen y

Aires, Peña Lillo/Continente, 2004, pp. 54 y ss..

78 Puebla, María Daniela, *El modelo criminológico argentino*, San Juan, Fundación Universidad Nacional de San Juan, 1997.

79 Zaffaroni explica que en definitiva, "el Estado gendarme desemboca en el Estado autoritario" porque se "limita a conceder una libertad abstracta, ficticia, que solo puede gozar el poderoso. El grupo económicamente poderoso resiste todos los embates y cuando ese mismo ámbito abstracto de libertad pone en peligro su estabilidad, lo cancela [...]". Por esta vía su derecho penal pasa a ser un derecho penal autoritario, en *Manual de Derecho Penal*, Buenos Aires, Ediar, 1994, p. 275.

Roque Sáenz Peña, que respondía al alza de masas populares y abrió el camino a la presidencia del primero en 1916.

La política de Yrigoyen fue de naturaleza democrática y de posición nacional, y marcó un período de ascenso de los sectores populares dentro del régimen agroexportador[80]. Se caracterizó, al contrario de la doctrina liberal conservadora y contra los intereses dominantes, de promover un rol activo del Estado en la economía y en las relaciones sociales. Dio impulso a una incipiente legislación laboral –la jornada de ocho horas es de su segundo período– y a una serie de leyes de defensa del pequeño y mediano productor agropecuario, a la creación de YPF, a la defensa de la soberanía en política exterior –un acentuado latinoamericanismo y el difícil sostenimiento de la neutralidad en la guerra–, y tuvo un intento fallido de crear un Banco de la República –antecedente que se concretó en 1935–. Acerca de los gobiernos yrigoyenistas es relevante la observación de Galasso, que pone de relieve la vinculación entre el ejercicio del poder político y el fenómeno jurídico, al señalar que

"de esta experiencia puede obtenerse la conclusión que el respeto a la "institucionalidad" cuando ella viene impuesta por el enemigo, deviene en obstáculo para un gobierno popular y la experiencia latinoamericana muestra de qué modo los movimientos populares, no bien se consolidan, proceden a crear su propia legitimidad, sancionando una nueva constitución o estableciendo nuevas formas de representación política"[81].

Yrigoyen no hizo lo que Perón sí haría años después, tal vez un poco por la conciencia agraria que lo inspiraba, y otro por aquel respeto casi sagrado a la legalidad instituida.

La crisis social: del liberalismo conservador al peronismo

Los años treinta marcaron la reformulación del orden oligárquico construido desde el siglo anterior, a partir de la crisis del orden capitalista internacional y la reacción conservadora en Europa como salida ante

80 Galasso, Norberto, *Historia de la Argentina*, Buenos Aires, Colihue, 2011.
81 Galasso, *op. cit.*, p. 134.

la crisis (tanto la nazifascista, la anglobritánica como la consolidación del stalinismo en la URSS, todas de vocación imperialista)[82]. La inmersión de los países imperiales en las luchas fratricidas por el poder mundial afectó con gravedad a nuestra América. Las dificultades para seguir adquiriendo productos manufacturados ante la caída del desarrollo industrial y la falta de mercados donde colocar los granos, cereales y carnes, provocaron la ruina del país oligárquico y agrario. La crisis mundial había tenido efectos concretos sobre la vida económica de la Argentina pastoril a partir de la abrupta caída de los términos del intercambio comercial exterior[83]. A esto hay que agregarle el colapso de la bolsa de comercio en los EUA, la fuerte inestabilidad cambiaria a nivel internacional que derivó en el abandono del patrón oro por Gran Bretaña, el desequilibrio generalizado de las balanzas de pago y el proceso inflacionario en alza imparable, los movimientos anormales de los capitales especulativos y el retroceso inevitable del sector productivo, y el aumento sideral de las deudas por las guerras. Este cuadro de crisis extraordinaria no encontró solución sino hasta la reconfiguración definitiva del mapa mundial en

82 Mientras, la teoría liberal clásica fue criticada por John Maynard Keynes, en especial con su obra publicada en 1936 *Teoría general sobre la ocupación, el interés y el dinero*, en la que afirmaba como principio que el capitalismo debía ser regulado por la acción estatal. Las filosofías que criticaban a la razón como centro del universo social empezaban a resurgir, mientras, la razón dejaba de iluminar para oscurecer medio planeta, con sus campos de concentración y la ciencia y tecnología puestas al servicio de las máquinas de matar. Los imperialismos estaban en juego; el entonces vigente (Inglaterra), el que pretendía vencer (Alemania), y el finalmente ganador (los EUA y la URSS). El resultado de su lucha marcó la nueva era de la Guerra Fría tras las bombas genocidas contra Hiroshima y Nagasaki.

83 Algunos datos son reveladores: por un lado, la producción nacional cayó el 44% entre 1928 y 1933, y las exportaciones se redujeron a menos del 50%, mientras que el área sembrada sufrió una notable reducción en hectáreas (Rapoport, Mario, "Historia de la economía argentina del siglo XX", en La Página, 2007). Y por otro lado "[...] el intercambio total que alcanzaba a 1.815 millones de pesos oro en 1929 cayó a 1.157 millones en 1931 y a 934 millones en 1932, mientras que las exportaciones que superaban los mil millones de pesos en 1929 bajaron bruscamente hasta 566 millones en 1932" en Rouquié, Alain, *Poder militar y sociedad política en la Argentina*, Buenos Aires, Emecé, 1982.

la era abierta después de 1945. Argentina definió su rol en función del cambio abrupto de escenario.

Pero en 1930 con la caída de Yrigoyen se terminaban en el país las políticas nacionales. La toma del poder por parte del gobierno de Agustín Justo, de tendencia probritánica –y tras el breve ciclo de Uriburu–, dio origen a una nueva etapa en el país y al "giro intervencionista". Las políticas estatales de esa época signada por el Pacto Roca-Runciman, en defensa de los intereses del orden oligárquico amenazado por la crisis internacional, tuvieron lugar a través de una serie de leyes que, por su contenido antinacional, fueron definidas por el forjismo como "el estatuto legal del coloniaje". También se ha denominado a ese período "intervencionismo estatal a la defensiva", por su predisposición a favor del capital extranjero y los sectores concentrados de la economía, pero en este caso bajo formas intervencionistas, socavando la tradicional tesis de la neutralidad liberal que, como señalamos, venía del siglo anterior[84]. La necesidad de la regulación estatal en la economía para proteger los intereses de la clase dominante llevó a adoptar medidas inéditas hasta el momento: el control de cambios (1931), la creación del Banco Central (1935), el Instituto Movilizador de Inversiones Bancarias (1935), que favoreció a los dueños de grandes extensiones de tierras endeudados, la creación de la Dirección Nacional de Elevadores de Granos, la Junta Reguladora de Granos, la Junta Nacional de Carnes (1933), etcétera.

La crisis del principio del patrón oro, principal mecanismo de dependencia y fundamento de la libre convertibilidad de nuestra moneda y la desregulación cambiaria y financiera dependiente del centro financiero de Londres, derivó en la necesidad de diseñar un esquema de intervención que garantizara una estabilidad mínima del sistema económico. La creación del Banco Central fue parte de la respuesta.

84 La intervención del Estado a favor de la clase dominante es una constante en la historia argentina, como lo fue en los últimos años de la dictadura cívico-militar en los años ochenta, cuando se nacionalizó la deuda externa contraída por sectores privados y a la vez se establecieron tipos de cambio diferenciales con el fin de dar financiamiento público a las importaciones de la burguesía local, con grave perjuicio de la economía nacional.

Con miras a mantener la estructura oligárquica y la dependencia de Gran Bretaña, el intervencionismo estatal de la década infame y la crisis general implicaron, al mismo tiempo, la puesta en tensión de los postulados del liberalismo en su versión conservadora, dando origen a una reconfiguración tanto económica como cultural del país que incluía también el aspecto normativo. El modo en que el orden oligárquico pretendió reconducir el rumbo del país al finalizar el régimen de los años treinta, después de junio de 1943, fue explicado por Federico Pinedo:

> La vida económica del país gira alrededor de una gran rueda maestra que es el comercio exportador. Nosotros no estamos en condiciones de reemplazar esa rueda maestra por otra, pero estamos en condiciones de crear al lado de ese mecanismo algunas ruedas menores que permitan cierta circulación de la riqueza, cierta actividad económica, la suma de lo cual mantenga el nivel de vida de este pueblo a cierta altura.
> (Ministerio de Hacienda de la Nación, Discurso del Sr. Ministro de Hacienda en ocasión de la presentación del Plan de Reactivación Económica)

Es decir, la propuesta de Pinedo consistía en mantener en lo esencial la matriz productiva agroexportadora del país en forma planificada desde el Estado, pero permitiendo una industrialización de menor peso –"una rueda menor"– que no pusiera en riesgo la hegemonía de la clase terrateniente y que, a la vez, fuera una respuesta posible a la crisis.

Frente a esto, el peronismo, en el 45, planteó la necesidad de que el país dispusiera de esa "gran rueda maestra" para el beneficio de toda la sociedad, por lo cual debía ser reemplazada, mediante la planificación económica estatal y el crecimiento de las industrias argentinas. Con la creación del Consejo Nacional de Posguerra se pasará definitivamente a la planificación estatal con el objeto de reorganizar social y económicamente al país bajo la dirección general del Estado. En agosto de 1944 Perón creó el Consejo Nacional de Posguerra como órgano consultivo de la

Vicepresidencia de la Nación –primer intento orgánico de planificación económica en la Argentina– con fines de crear una política nacional[85].

El plan de ordenamiento económico y social definió que

> [...] todo el proceso de la economía nacional requiere un plan estable y sistemático [...] [que] contribuyan al incremento y próspero desarrollo de las empresas comerciales e industriales, permitan a estas, poner ese mismo progreso estimulado, reconocer el derecho que tienen las clases trabajadoras de disfrutar de un bienestar moral y material concorde con su propia condición humana.

Se creó el Consejo Económico Social como órgano consultivo del mismo, en el que el acuerdo programático entre el Estado, los trabajadores organizados y la clase empresarial "constituye un modo nuevo de tratar los problemas socioeconómicos". En ese sentido, el Ordenamiento atribuyó al Estado un rol nuevo: el de "ser el fiel de la balanza Capital- Trabajo". Los estudios y propuestas de ese Consejo fueron la base para el Primer Plan Quinquenal del peronismo a partir de 1947.

Al mismo tiempo, durante los años treinta y a la par de la sustitución de importaciones, se fue desarrollando una línea industrialista en la Fuerzas Armadas como búsqueda de respuestas ante la situación internacional. Ella proponía que el Estado adoptara una política proteccionista y

85 Perón contó con la colaboración especial de José Miguel Francisco Luís Figuerola y Tresols. Nació en Barcelona, España, en 1897, donde estudió derecho y filosofía. En los años 20 fue funcionario de la dictadura de Miguel Primo de Rivera, que a su caída emigró a Buenos Aires y en 1944 Perón lo designó secretario general del Consejo Nacional de Posguerra, donde tuvo un rol importante por su conocimiento de estadísticas, planificación de la economía y de legislación social en general. En 1943 Figuerola había publicado *La colaboración social en Hispanoamérica*, en que explica su concepto sobre la intervención del Estado en las relaciones sociales para colaborar con los trabajadores y los sectores corporativos. En 1948 presentó un anteproyecto de reforma constitucional que no tuvo apoyo, ya que se optó por el propuesto por Sampay, en el que postulaba una política débil, de nacionalización de servicios públicos en la medida en que así fuera determinado por ley. Luego de ello, se alejó del gobierno peronista. Falleció en Buenos Aires en 1970.

una función empresarial, así como incentivar la creación de industrias necesarias para la fabricación de armamentos. El concepto de defensa nacional volvió a integrarse a la necesidad de consolidar una actividad industrial propia, lo que se reflejó en la creación de diferentes fábricas militares en el país, en el impulso a la primera Flota Mercante del Estado y la Dirección General de Fabricaciones Militares. En síntesis, la industrialización del país se tornó un reclamo de sectores militares de avanzada que ya contaban con los importantes antecedentes del Gral. Mosconi (en el petróleo) y el Gral. Savio (en la siderurgia).

Al comenzar los años cuarenta, en el orden social ya se había consolidado la presencia del proletariado urbano, a partir de la migración interna a las ciudades más importantes, el crecimiento de una industria nacional y del mercado interno. Esta transformación de la estructura socioeconómica puso en crisis los postulados liberales. Si por un lado se hacía evidente que no eran las relaciones privadas de los individuos lo que movilizaba a la sociedad sino la regulación estatal, por el otro había nuevas fuerzas sociales que motorizaban y transformaban las relaciones sociales: el proletariado urbano y la pequeña burguesía industrial incipiente. El surgimiento de nuevas clases sociales rompieron el débil y limitado esquema de la representación política del país semicolonial, por derecha y por izquierda.

En ese contexto, del 43 al 45 se jugó el destino del país: se avanzaba hacia adelante transformándolo, o se regresaba al viejo y caduco orden oligárquico al costo social que fuera. La bifurcación histórica alcanzó su brillante síntesis en la consigna Braden o Perón. El peronismo representó esa ruptura con el pasado semicolonial y el liberalismo conservador, y la larga jornada del 17 de octubre de 1945 decidió el partido a favor del proyecto nacional y popular. Pese a la propuesta de represión de Vernengo Lima, jefe de la Armada, y la perplejidad de sectores medios capitalinos que vieron avanzar las columnas de obreros, nada pudo detener la definitiva irrupción del movimiento obrero como sujeto político. El movimiento nacional se creó en la acción histórica y encontró su expresión política en la forma de adhesión a Perón: en esas coordenadas nació el peronismo

como un frente político policlasista que forjaba un nuevo liderazgo[86]. El peronismo significó el momento histórico en el que se forjó la dignidad de los trabajadores frente a la prepotencia patronal y el desprecio racista de las élites. "Hoy es San Perón, que trabaje el patrón" fue la consigna del paro general celebrado el 18 de octubre de 1945[87]. Como dice Roberto Ferrero,

> [...] todo el aparato político de la vieja Argentina; todos los prejuicios de sus clases medias; antimilitarismo, formalismo legal, moralismo, etcétera, toda la artillería de la prensa comercial, todo el peso de una gran potencia continental, todo el prestigio de los centros universitarios, se movilizaban contra la candidatura de Perón; pero sus resultados fueron opuestos a lo que esperaban[88].

Unos años bastaron para dejar en claro que la obra del gobierno peronista significó el mayor avance social de la clase trabajadora en la historia del país.

86 John W. Cooke fue quien interpretó el fenómeno con justeza: "No es que la izquierda hiciera crisis: es que era una parte de la superestructura política del imperialismo y saltó junto con los demás pedazos de esa superestructura [...] El movimiento popular que atacó a la oligarquía y al imperialismo pasó a ser la izquierda, por cuanto representaba las fuerzas del progreso nacional y de la independencia del extranjero. Fue una situación revolucionaria.", citado por Norberto Galasso en *Perón, tomo I*. Buenos Aires, Colihue, p. 531. Sin embargo, también digamos que el peronismo ocupó ese sitio sin asumir las consignas socialistas más propias de una posición de izquierda nacional.

87 Baschetti, Roberto, *La clase obrera peronista. T. 1*, La Plata, De la Campana, 2010, p. 10.

88 Ferrero, Roberto, *Del fraude a la soberanía popular: 1938-1946*, Buenos Aires, Memorial de la Patria, 1976.

III.
La reforma constitucional de 1949 y su contexto

Si la Revolución Francesa terminó con el gobierno de las aristocracias,
la Revolución Rusa termina con el gobierno de las burguesías.
Empieza el gobierno de las masas populares.

La constitución que nos rige no debe ser artículo de museo
que cuanto mayor es su antigüedad mayor es su mérito.
No podemos aceptar sin desmedro de la lógica,
que en la época de la navegación estratosférica
que permite trasladarnos a Europa en un día,
usemos la constitución creada en los tiempos de la carreta,
cuando para ir a Mendoza debíamos soportar un mes de viaje.
Juan Perón

Entre esas dos frases de Perón se encuentra el sentido de la reforma constitucional. La necesidad de expresar jurídicamente las transformaciones sociales para consolidarlas, y la de adaptar y reactualizar el sistema normativo nacional a la etapa de la historia contemporánea de la posguerra de mediados del siglo XX.

Hacia 1949 el nuevo escenario mundial adoptó perfiles más definidos que fueron los que caracterizaron al resto del siglo XX: del reparto mundial en manos de las dos potencias (Estados Unidos y la Unión de Repúblicas Socialistas Soviéticas) y el sistema de Naciones Unidas, al largo proceso de descolonización de los países del tercer mundo respecto de las potencias europeas. En 1947 la India de Ghandi se había liberado de Gran Bretaña, aunque sufrió la separación de Pakistán, y en 1949 se inició la República-

Popular de China de Mao Tse Tung[89] reconocida en 1951 por Gran Bretaña, e Indonesia lograba su liberación de Holanda. Francia dio inicio a la guerra colonialista contra Vietnam, cuyo pueblo empezaba una larga lucha por su liberación que culminó con la derrota estadounidense en 1975. En Egipto en 1953 se consagró la república tras ser derrotada la monarquía el año anterior. En Colombia, el 9 abril de 1948 fuerzas reaccionarias asesinaron a Jorge Eliécer Gaitán, quien anunciaba la profundización del camino iniciado por Alfonso Portillo, y abrieron una larga era de conflictos y luchas internas. En Paraguay concluía abruptamente la experiencia nacionalista de Juan Natalicio González, mientras que poco antes ocurría el golpe de Estado contra Rómulo Gallegos en Venezuela, lo que dio inicio a la larga dictadura militar de Marcos Pérez Jiménez. Todos truncados por la violencia proimperialista y oligárquica. En 1949 EE.UU., en plena implementación del Plan Marshall (1947-1951), consolidaba su hegemonía militar en la parte occidental del planeta al ser creada la OTAN. Pero, simultáneamente, la URSS hacía público su primer ensayo nuclear y dejaba entrever que aquel país ya no tenía el monopolio de las armas nucleares.

En el terreno de la cultura, 1949 es el año en que, en México, Octavio Paz publicó *El laberinto de la soledad* y Leopoldo Zea su ensayo *Dos etapas del pensamiento en Hispanoamérica*; el guatemalteco Miguel Ángel Asturias, *Hombres de maíz*, y Simone de Beauvoir, en Francia, *El segundo sexo*. En Argentina, Jorge Abelardo Ramos hizo lo propio ese año con *América Latina, un país* y la CEPAL publicó *El desarrollo económico de América Latina y sus principales problemas* de Raúl Prebisch, donde se mencionaba la relación centro-periferia. Eduardo Astesano hizo lo mismo con su *Historia de la independencia económica*, y en San Miguel de Tucumán, bajo el sello editorial La Raza salió a la luz *Shunko* de Jorge Washington Ábalos.

89 En 1949, Mao Tse Tung, en su conocido artículo "Sobre la dictadura democrática popular", señalaba que "la combinación de la democracia en el seno del pueblo y la dictadura sobre la reacción configura la dictadura democrática popular", la que constituía el camino al socialismo y el modo de resolver –o superar dialécticamente– las pujas del Estado con los sectores sociales aliados y con los oligárquicos proimperialistas. A los aliados les reservaba la democracia, mientras que a los enemigos, la dictadura.

En 1949 visitó el país Hans Kelsen, y su debate con Carlos Cossio en esa ocasión fue uno de los puntos más altos de la filosofía del derecho argentina[90].

Desde el punto de vista normativo fue una época de cambios fundamentales a nivel internacional, como consecuencia del nuevo ordenamiento de las relaciones de poder entre las naciones. Los doctrinarios del derecho internacional suelen afirmar que después de 1945 tuvo origen un cambio de paradigma jurídico, cuyo eje fue un nuevo constitucionalismo en Occidente con fundamento en el sistema normativo de Naciones Unidas. En este encontramos la Declaración Universal de los Derechos Humanos, adoptada por la Asamblea de las Naciones Unidas el 10 de diciembre de 1948 sobre la base de la Carta de San Francisco (del 24 de octubre de 1945). Para darnos una idea del vínculo entre los cambios políticos y la nueva juridicidad, basta notar el carácter fundacional de las Naciones Unidas de este último documento, tras los acuerdos de la Conferencia de Yalta en febrero de ese mismo año, que impulsaba la creación de un sistema de cargos, y el Consejo de Seguridad integrado por los Estados

90 Carlos Cossio nació en San Miguel de Tucumán en 1903 y falleció en Buenos Aires en 1987. En una encuesta realizada entre profesores de la Facultad de Derecho y Ciencias Sociales de la Universidad de Buenos Aires, él opinó favorablemente sobre la reforma constitucional, "para acomodar al Estado argentino a la situación histórica" mundial de posguerra. Para ello, "el contenido de la nueva Constitución debe significar lo siguiente: economía planeada pero con subsistencia de los derechos individuales" (en Sampay, de González Arzac, A., *Sampay y la constitución del futuro*, Buenos Aires, Peña Lillo editor, 1982, p.43). Como ya hemos mencionado, la etapa de mayor desarrollo de la teoría egológica del derecho de Carlos Cossio fue durante el peronismo. En 1956 Cossio se vio obligado a abandonar la universidad por resolución del interventor José Luís Romero, quien alegó el motivo de la participación de aquel en la señalada encuesta sobre la reforma constitucional. Manuel Atienza, filósofo español, en alguna oportunidad puso atención en el hecho de que "la actitud de los iusfilósofos argentinos frente a la egología guarda ciertos paralelismos con la de los intelectuales políticos argentinos frente al peronismo". (Cossio, Carlos, *Los Malditos, T. III*, Buenos Aires, Madres de Plaza de Mayo, 2008, p. 437). Cossio pretendía pensar la filosofía del derecho desde nuestra posición nacional. Para ello criticaba el pensamiento jurídico liberal conservador y esbozaba su teoría egológica para superar los diferentes modelos eurocéntricos positivista e iusnaturalista.

Unidos, la URSS, China, Francia y el Reino Unido. El fundamento escrito y declamado de la Carta era asegurar la paz mundial y un mínimo de derechos para todos los habitantes. Su preámbulo dice:

> Nosotros, los pueblos de las Naciones Unidas resueltos a preservar a las generaciones venideras del flagelo de la guerra que dos veces durante nuestra vida ha infligido a la Humanidad sufrimientos indecibles, a reafirmar la fe en los derechos fundamentales del hombre, en la dignidad y el valor de la persona humana, en la igualdad de derechos de hombres y mujeres y de las naciones grandes y pequeñas, a crear condiciones bajo las cuales puedan mantenerse la justicia y el respeto a las obligaciones emanadas de los tratados y de otras fuentes del Derecho Internacional, a promover el progreso social y a elevar el nivel de vida dentro de un concepto más amplio de la libertad, y con tales finalidades a practicar la tolerancia y a convivir en paz como buenos vecinos, a unir nuestras fuerzas para el mantenimiento de la paz y la seguridad internacionales, a asegurar, mediante la aceptación de principios y la adopción de métodos, que no se usará la fuerza armada sino en servicio del interés común, y a emplear un mecanismo internacional para promover el progreso económico y social de todas los pueblos, hemos decidido aunar nuestros esfuerzos para realizar estos designios. Por lo tanto, nuestros respectivos Gobiernos, por medio de representantes reunidos en la ciudad de San Francisco que han exhibido sus plenos poderes, encontrados en buena y debida forma, han convenido en la presente Carta de las Naciones Unidas, y por este acto establecen una organización internacional que se denominará las Naciones Unidas.[91]

El sistema normativo de las Naciones Unidas tuvo sus pilares en la Declaración Universal y en los Pactos Internacionales de Derechos Humanos y sus Protocolos. Es fundamental señalar que a la par de la expansión y

91 Ver http://www.un.org/es/documents/udhr/law.shtml.

mantenimiento de la opresión colonial por parte de las potencias mundiales, la nueva organización normativa del orden internacional afirmaba tener una inédita preocupación por consagrar derechos. Este doble discurso encontró expresión en la política exterior de los Estados Unidos y sus reiteradas invasiones militares de carácter imperialista realizadas en nombre de la paz mundial, o en la actitud sistemática de no suscribir o ratificar tratados de derechos humanos[92]. Así como el ascenso de la modernidad capitalista en Europa derivó en el liberalismo igualitario y las revoluciones y la consolidación de la burguesía, en un liberalismo conservador, de contenido de clase y librecambista, y su crisis en el nazifascismo; la etapa de la posguerra trajo una suerte de inversión del lenguaje, al extenderse al resto de los países oprimidos en Occidente en competencia interimperialista con el bloque del este[93].

En 1948 tuvo lugar en nuestro continente la Conferencia de Bogotá, en la que se constituyó la Organización de Estados Americanos, curiosamente en medio del "bogotazo" que siguió al crimen político de Gaitán. El impulso de este organismo tuvo su antecedente en encuentros de países

92 El Pacto de San José de Costa Rica fue suscripto por Estados Unidos pero no ratificado. En 2002, Estados Unidos comunicó que dejaba de considerarse obligado por el Estatuto de Roma de la Corte Penal Internacional.

93 Franz Hinkelammert le llama a esto la "inversión de los derechos humanos" a partir de describir cómo "se violan y destruyen los derechos fundamentales de pueblos enteros –vidas de mujeres, hombres, niñas y niños concretos– en nombre de los "derechos humanos de la humanidad". El autor encuentra el fundamento de esta operación ideológica (tal vez Jauretche la hubiera llamado "zoncera") en John Locke con su *Segundo ensayo sobre el gobierno civil de 1690*, quien en nombre de los derechos del hombre justificaba la invasión inglesa de Norteamérica y el tráfico de esclavos. La conquista de África por la denuncia de canibalismo, la de la India por la de la quema de las viudas, y la destrucción de China por las Guerras del Opio se basaron igualmente en la denuncia de la violación de derechos humanos en China. El Occidente conquistó el mundo, destruyó culturas y civilizaciones, cometió genocidios nunca vistos, sin embargo todo eso lo hizo para salvar los derechos humanos. En Hinkelammert, Franz, "La inversión de los derechos humanos: el caso de John Locke" en Herrera Flores, Joaquín, *El vuelo de Anteo. Derechos humanos y crítica de la razón liberal*, Bilbao, Desclée de Brouwer, 2000, p. 79 y ss.).

americanos realizados desde mediados del siglo XIX, en el contexto del impulso expansionista de los Estados Unidos hacia el continente, bajo el rótulo de panamericanismo. Su creación encontró su complemento ideal en la hegemonía política, económica y militar del nuevo orden mundial, en el cual Latinoamérica y el Caribe quedaban bajo la órbita de dominio de los Estados Unidos. El sistema interamericano creado se constituyó normativamente con la Carta de la Organización de los Estados Americanos, el Tratado Americano de Soluciones Pacíficas (Pacto de Bogotá) y la Declaración Americana de los Derechos y Deberes del Hombre. En 1950 se creó el Banco Interamericano de Desarrollo y en 1962 se expulsó a Cuba con la acusación de ser marxista-leninista (decisión revocada 47 años después, en 2009). En 1969 una conferencia interamericana de la OEA redactó la Convención Americana sobre Derechos Humanos (en Costa Rica), que entró en vigencia recién en 1978 con la última ratificación de países necesaria para ello.

La OEA durante todo el siglo XX y principios del XXI fue el principal organismo regional del continente dentro de las Naciones Unidas, con el objetivo declarado, entre otros, de afianzar la paz y la seguridad continental, promover la democracia representativa con respeto al principio de no intervención, y asegurar la solución pacífica de controversias que surgieran entre los Estados miembro. Fue durante mucho tiempo el lenguaje político normativo expresión de la hegemonía de los Estados Unidos en nuestro continente.

Su enunciado principal, aún vigente, es que existe un mínimo de derechos destinados a garantizar la división de poderes institucionales y los derechos fundamentales de las personas que no pueden ser afectados por los Estados, lo que se encuentra normativamente en la Carta de la ONU (1945), en la Declaración Universal de los Derechos Humanos (1948), en el ámbito europeo en la Constitución de Italia (1947)[94] y en la Ley Fundamental de la República Federal de Alemania (1948), todo en una nueva

94 Esta norma fundamental tuvo inspiración demócrata cristiana, y al menos en su filosofía guarda relación con la reforma de 1949 que aquí analizamos.

lectura de la Declaración de los Derechos del Hombre de 1789[95]. Se afirma, entonces, la existencia de principios generales no disponibles por los órdenes estatales para que sean considerados en la comunidad internacional como legales, con criterios de validez condicionada por vínculos formales (de procedimiento acerca de los modos de su creación) y sustanciales (de contenido). Este enunciado general puede servir de referencia en la cuestión cívico-política y social de los países, pero omite la cuestión nacional y, más aun, la realización de la nación latinoamericana.

En síntesis, el orden político internacional imperante, diseñado por las potencias mundiales, dio lugar a este sistema normativo con base en la juridicidad creada por las Naciones Unidas, en un contexto histórico de reinicio de la cuestión nacional a partir de la desigualdad real entre los países, con la división entre naciones opresoras y oprimidas. En esta contradicción cabalga el liberalismo político revivido en el igualitarismo social de los derechos humanos, pero sometido a los vaivenes de esa inversión del lenguaje que lo hunde en una abstracción sin correspondencia real ni histórica. Su destino es superarlo o declinar.

Bajo esta perspectiva, en nuestro país, la derogación de la Constitución de 1949 y el regreso a la Constitución de 1853, implicó, además del regreso a la dependencia económica y al conservadurismo político, un retroceso jurídico internacional en términos del paradigma de posguerra de los derechos humanos. En esta línea conceptual hay que interpretar la reforma constitucional de 1949 –además Argentina integra la ONU y la OEA desde sus orígenes–, como expresión de una corriente similar a nivel latinoamericano (que incluye a México, Bolivia y Brasil), que pugna por el establecimiento de un mínimo necesario de derechos sociales y garantías normativas, así como de condiciones de funcionamiento del Estado cuyo cumplimento posibilite la existencia nacional en los programas de gobierno de los movimientos populares de la época. Es decir, los procesos constituyentes latinoamericanos han significado un avance progresivo real en

95 Ver entre varios, Ferrajoli, Luigi, "La Democracia Constitucional" en *Desde otra mirada, textos de teoría crítica del Derecho*, Buenos Aires, Eudeba, 2009. Así como también su obra *Derecho y Razón*, Madrid, Trotta, 1995.

tanto impliquen avances en la resolución de la cuestión social y nacional al mismo tiempo como expresión de nacionalismo popular.

El movimiento nacional de liberación en marcha

Caracterización del peronismo

El peronismo histórico puede ser caracterizado como expresión de nacionalismo popular y democrático en la medida en que representó, al mismo tiempo, la defensa de la soberanía nacional y una apertura política y social clausurada hasta entonces para las mayorías que, como podían, dieron cauce a sus pulsiones de liberación. Su búsqueda dio lugar al hecho político de masas en nuestro país de mayor trascendencia del siglo XX: la marcha de los trabajadores hacia la Plaza de Mayo el 17 de octubre de 1945. Hacia 1943 el país mantenía, pese al proceso de sustitución de importaciones en ascenso, una estructura semicolonial cuya función era proveer alimentos baratos a Gran Bretaña a cambio del consumo de productos manufacturados. Es decir, el nuevo mundo que venía creciendo en los últimos años no encajaba en el viejo orden semicolonial (modelo agroexportador con dependencia económica y una superestructura cultural que lo legitimaba) y clamaba, huérfano, por quien lo expresara políticamente. Hombres y mujeres del interior, de cultura criolla y mestiza, emigraban en forma masiva a las ciudades del país, y poblaban especialmente el Gran Buenos Aires y otros centros urbanos para transformarse en obreros y trabajadores industriales. También emergía pujante una pequeña burguesía industrial, mientras los sectores nacionalistas del ejército se sentían disconformes por el nivel de subordinación a los intereses extranjeros. Todos ellos empujaban por concluir el ciclo liberal oligárquico de la década infame.

Por eso, dice Galasso:

> Más allá del afecto que perdura en las mayorías populares argentinas, nadie supone que Perón gestó la industria, inventó la clase trabajadora y convirtió en nacional a un sector del ejército sino que, por el contrario, esa industria en crecimiento, esos trabajadores

> concentrados en el Gran Buenos Aires y esos soldados enemigos de los ingleses y yanquis, generaron un líder[96].

El principal legado de la etapa abierta en 1945 fue haber alcanzado la condición de nación soberana con el protagonismo de organizaciones de los trabajadores. El peronismo significó el despliegue de un proyecto de desarrollo productivo, político, económico y cultural que, en sus rasgos más sustanciales, encarnó la ruptura de la dependencia con el imperialismo británico a través de diversas medidas que avanzaban en resolver la cuestión nacional. De este modo se recuperaron

> [...] los resortes de la economía que estaban en manos del capital inglés: la nacionalización del Banco Central que pone en manos del Estado el control de los cambios, la tasa de interés y la circulación monetaria; la nacionalización de los depósitos de la banca privada que entrega al Banco Central el control del crédito, la creación del Instituto Argentino de Promoción del Intercambio (IAPI) que significa el control estatal del comercio exterior (antes en manos de un puñado de consorcios internacionales); la nacionalización de los ferrocarriles y de empresas de transporte automotor que permite reglar las comunicaciones terrestres [...] el impulso a la flota mercante [...] la implantación de un régimen estatal de reaseguros [...] el recupero de la soberanía sobre nuestros puertos[97].

Así como también la aparición de ENTEL, ELMA, la CNEA, SOMISA, la televisión pública, las aerolíneas de bandera argentina, las Industrias Aeronáuticas y Mecánicas del Estado (IAME) para la producción de tractores, automóviles y motocicletas, Gas del Estado, la red de Agua y Energía, entre numerosas empresas públicas[98]. Para la época nuestro país era

96 Galasso, Norberto, "Peronismo y Liberación nacional", en *Cuadernos para la otra historia*, nro. 23, 2003.

97 Galasso, Norberto, *op. cit.*

98 En octubre de 1949 se sancionó la Ley13.653 de organización del funcionamiento de las empresas del Estado, las que eran definidas como "entidades

el único de América Latina que se había negado a pertenecer al novel Fondo Monetario Internacional, cuyas acciones no ocultaban la intencionalidad de implantar un nuevo orden financiero mundial al servicio de los intereses de las potencias, al mismo tiempo que el país registraba el fundamental dato de haber reducido a cero la deuda externa.

El control estatal del comercio exterior es una herramienta fundamental para avanzar en un sentido transformador en países que, como el nuestro, tienen su eje en la producción primaria, por los fuertes condicionamientos de dependencia de la demanda externa y el desequilibrio en su estructura productiva por la desigual relación entre el sector agropecuario y el industrial[99]. El primero goza de ventajas comparativas debido a la alta rentabilidad de la pampa húmeda por sus características naturales –que actualmente se expresa, por ejemplo, mayormente en la soja–, mientras que el sector industrial, debido a la alta e imposible competencia existente en el mercado mundial, tiene una productividad dificultosa y mucho menor, por lo que necesita de las divisas que solamente se pueden obtener de la exportación de productos primarios[100]. Uno se aprovecha del librecambio, mientras que el otro requiere de la protección y activa promoción del Estado, sin las cuales fracasa irremediablemente. El establecimiento de tipos de cambio diferenciados, implementados en los gobiernos peronistas, ha sido el mecanismo más apto para ello[101].

---

descentralizadas de la administración nacional, que cumplen funciones de índole comercial, industrial o de prestación de servicios públicos de carácter similar", bajo control del Poder Ejecutivo.

99 La modalidad de generación, apropiación y uso del excedente económico es clave para el desarrollo productivo. El destino de esos recursos puede ser la expansión del producto social y la inversión productiva, o el consumo suntuoso y los privilegios de la clase dominante. Ver Sbatella, José y otros, "Excedente económico y distribución del ingreso en la Argentina de la posconvertibilidad", en *Revista de Ciencias Sociales, segunda época*, año 4, nro. 23, Buenos Aires, UNQUI, pp. 123-143, 2013.

100 Esta situación es expuesta con claridad en "La estructura productiva desequilibrada. Argentina y el tipo de cambio", de Marcelo Diamand. Desarrollo Económico, Vol. 12, 1972.

101 En ocasión de informar sobre la Ley 13.571 de reforma financiera, el Min-

En esta línea, el IAPI –creado en 1946 mediante el Decreto-Ley 15.350/1946[102]– fue un instrumento fundamental para la estrategia de desarrollo productivo, y sus funciones estuvieron previstas en el Primer Plan Quinquenal (1947-1952), que permitió captar los recursos del comercio exterior para financiar la planificación del proyecto nacional, en una política de uso directo del excedente extraordinario. Así, se lo utilizaba para impulsar al sector industrial, para el fortalecimiento estatal con las nacionalizaciones de los servicios públicos, compra de materias primas esenciales, bienes de capital y buques para la flota mercante. El IAPI cumplió el rol de regular las relaciones de comercio, financieras y el mercado interno, de colocar el capital al servicio de la producción nacional alejándolo de la influencia recesiva –y por ende regresiva– del sistema financiero internacional[103].

Las políticas monetaria, de crédito, cambiaria y financiera formaban parte de un plan integral de desarrollo productivo estratégico, para promover el mercado interno, la industria manufacturera local, el trabajo y la redistribución del ingreso nacional, para lo cual fue clave la nacionalización de los depósitos bancarios y del Banco Central. De este modo el Estado echaba bases firmes para la autonomía nacional para conducir el destino social del país.

Para el peronismo ni la soberanía nacional ni la justicia social se podían alcanzar sin lograr al mismo tiempo la independencia económica.

istro de Finanzas explicaba que *"la preocupación principal en materia monetaria de los más importantes países se manifiesta con el propósito de asegurar el mantenimiento de adecuados niveles de ocupación, de precios, de réditos y de vida en el orden interno, aun a costa de la inestabilidad de los tipos de cambio...la necesidad de resguardar la estabilidad económica interna impuso la necesidad de desarrollar políticas flexibles de crédito al margen de la rigidez imperante bajo el patrón oro; a aplicar diversos procedimientos monetarios compensatorios y al establecimiento del control de cambios"*. De este modo, destacaba la importancia de una política de administración y control del tipo de cambio.

102 El decreto, firmado por Farrell, le daba carácter de entidad autárquica, y fue derogado por el Decreto-Ley 2.539 del 4 de noviembre de 1955.

103 Al respecto, ver la obra de Novick, Susana, *IAPI: auge y decadencia*, Buenos Aires, CEAL, 1986.

El capitalismo autóctono es nacional al alcanzar un grado de desarrollo que le permita autodeterminarse frente al capital extranjero. En este sentido, una forma de autonomía nacional adquirida al interior del mundo capitalista en su etapa imperialista y global. Tal desarrollo autónomo encuentra su base en la producción de bienes de capital, es decir, en la medida de la capacidad de crear fábricas de fábricas. No solo se trata de producir bienes de consumo, sino especialmente de tener la capacidad de producir los bienes (de capital) con los cuales se producen esos bienes de consumo masivo por la población local. Esta base de producción industrial será más nacional en tanto mayor sea la capacidad de autonomizarse frente al capital extranjero, es decir, menos sea la necesidad de adquirir por importación bienes de capital para su sustentabilidad y, por lo tanto, el desarrollo productivo se pueda independizar de los mandatos del sistema financiero mundial y del rol sumiso que se le adjudica a los países semicoloniales. Por eso, los problemas de restricción externa, primarización de la economía y aumento de precios internos, son parte del mismo problema: la dependencia del país y la primacía del núcleo oligárquico.

Frente a esto surge la necesidad de planificar la dirección del crédito, la moneda, el tipo de cambio y toda la política en materia de aranceles de comercio exterior y fomento de inversión local, regulación de precios y captación de la renta al interior de la cadena de valor y comercio interno, de acuerdo con fines y modos establecidos por el Estado a partir de un sistema financiero público con capacidad suficiente para hacerlo. Y por supuesto este es el sentido de la existencia de empresas públicas en sectores estratégicos de la economía. Esa autonomía económica solo puede ser consecuencia de la capacidad de autodeterminarse políticamente pero, al mismo tiempo, esta soberanía política (y popular) solo puede sustentarse en el tiempo en la medida en que se construya el proyecto de nación sobre la firmeza de esa base económica. Este será el grado de desarrollo autónomo de una nación. Por el contrario, la dependencia del capital extranjero (industrial y financiero) es en definitiva dependencia de todo el país. No hay posibilidad de sostener en el tiempo una política nacional sin

alcanzar ese grado de desarrollo económico autocentrado y autónomo. Con razón, Raúl Scalabrini Ortiz decía "tenemos industria, luego nuestra nación existe" (casi parafraseando a Descartes), vinculando la necesidad de la industrialización como clave para la autonomía política y económica del país o, dicho con mayor precisión, su liberación nacional.

En síntesis, la etapa del peronismo abierta en 1945 significó un desarrollo extraordinario de las fuerzas productivas y una transformación en la vida cotidiana, fenómeno que recuerda a esa referencia en el Manifiesto Comunista (1848) cuando señalaban que la burguesía industrial europea, en el siglo XIX, hacía que "todo lo sólido se desvaneciera en el aire". Aunque en nuestro caso, esta tarea de desarrollo productivo fue cumplida principal y mayormente por el Estado, ante la ausencia de una burguesía nacional fuerte con capacidad suficiente para conducirlo. Un capitalismo nacional que no fue socialismo, pero sí fue autónomo y antiimperialista, y dio lugar a la etapa de mayor acumulación de capital autóctona y desarrollo de fuerzas productivas conocidas hasta ese momento en el país, con dos características específicas:

> [...] por un lado, el crecimiento de las fuerzas productivas se caracterizó por una poderosísima franja de empresas estatales [...] [y]por otro, la acumulación del capital no se basó fundamentalmente en la explotación de los asalariados, sino en la translación de ingresos desde el sector agrario al sector industrial [...] [todo ello con] un alto grado de "socialización" y el apoyo fervoroso y consecuente de los trabajadores, convertidos en columna importantísima del sistema[104].

La estatización de una importante franja de la economía y su correspondiente planificación nos autoriza a catalogar a la economía como mixta y no meramente privada o de mercado, en la que una de sus notas salientes fue la participación central del movimiento obrero organizado como base de sustentación en el poder, lo que no hubiera sido posible sin

104 Galasso, Norberto, *op. cit*, p.12.

esa redistribución de la riqueza y la ampliación del consumo interno[105]. Esta última característica explica en buena medida las reiteradas alusiones al bienestar y a la felicidad del pueblo que están presente tanto en los discursos de Perón como en el texto de la Constitución del 49. Es cierto que es posible remitirse al lenguaje cristiano de las encíclicas, pero en este contexto de modo específico y original de acumulación de capital, la mención adquiere un significado histórico concreto, en especial si tenemos en cuenta que al mismo tiempo la URSS desarrollaba un intenso y acelerado desarrollo productivo e industrializador de su economía agraria. Por todo ello, nuestro país transitó un camino propio de desarrollo nacional sobre la base del bienestar de las clases populares, inédito a esa altura en muchas de sus políticas si tenemos en cuenta que Cuba recién tuvo su revolución en 1959.

La reforma constitucional de 1949 fue el cauce jurídico abierto por este creciente modelo de país, cuyo despliegue precisaba de una institucionalidad adecuada en sus formas a la nueva realidad histórica. Alcira Argumedo explica con razón que en la Constitución de 1949 se definió una forma de Estado que la vinculaba con otros movimientos populares latinoamericanos, como el caso del México de Lázaro Cárdenas y el Brasil de Getulio Vargas. Un Estado que buscaba responder a los conflictos del escenario de posguerra, afirmando la soberanía nacional y la integración de nuevos sujetos sociales, al mismo tiempo que era expresión de los anhelos de las aspiraciones mayoritarias, continuadoras de las tradiciones federales y populares del país del siglo anterior[106].

Pero más allá de las interpretaciones más explicativas, la reforma constitucional también se justifica por el mismo paso del tiempo, ya que la misma evolución de la historia torna fuera de tiempo a cualquier ley por más justa y adecuada a su época que haya sido. Como se desprende de la siguiente opinión de Perón, quien con la fuerza de las verdades simples decía:

105 1949 fue también el año en que la CGT, ya como única central sindical de los trabajadores, se proclamó como "fiel depositario de la ideología peronista".
106 En Argumedo, Alcira, *Los silencios y las voces en América Latina. Notas sobre el pensamiento nacional y popular*, Buenos Aires, Colihue, 2004.

> La constitución que nos rige no debe ser artículo de museo que cuanto mayor es su antigüedad mayor es su mérito. No podemos aceptar, sin desmedro de la lógica, que en la época de la navegación estratosférica que permite trasladarnos a Europa en un día, usemos la constitución creada en los tiempos de la carreta, cuando para ir a Mendoza debíamos soportar un mes de viaje". (1949)

La convocatoria para reformar la Constitución

Durante la primera presidencia de Juan Domingo Perón el Congreso declaró la necesidad de reformar la Constitución Nacional a través de la Ley 13.233, proyecto inicialmente presentado por el diputado Eduardo Colom –exradical y director de *La Época*– y sancionado en sesión especial extraordinaria los días 13 y 14 de agosto de 1948[107]. Esa era una legislatura en la que, poco antes, el diputado radical Ernesto Sammartino había lanzado en el recinto su voz de alerta contra el "aluvión zoológico", expresión despectiva contra legisladores representantes de los hombres y mujeres del interior que llegaban a Buenos Aires para ocuparse como trabajadores de la nueva y creciente industria, los "cabecita negra".

La sesión fue conformada por 129 diputados: 96 votaron a favor de la ley de la reforma y 33 en contra. Ha sido recurrente la impugnación de la convocatoria constituyente, a partir del modo en que se interpretó el artículo 30 de la Constitución del 53, en el que se establecía el procedimiento para realizar las reformas de la Carta Magna a partir de una mayoría especial y la procedencia de una declaración: la necesidad de reforma debía ser declarada por el Congreso "con el voto de dos terceras partes, al menos, de sus miembros". La mencionada ley fue votada por los dos

107 Hay que señalar que Colom había presentado uno similar el año anterior (1947). Tras una serie de iniciativas legislativas para reformar la Constitución, según cuenta Segovia "once proyectos se presentaron: dos de ellos de declaración, procuraban la formación de comisiones especiales para que estudiasen la reforma; solo uno, el de Cámpora y otros, avanzó en una reforma total o general; los ocho restantes propusieron cambios parciales" (*op. cit.*). El de John W. Cooke fue el de mayor importancia por el desarrollo de sus fundamentos, pero no prosperó.

tercios de los miembros presentes, mientras que la bancada opositora había interpretado que los "dos tercios" eran sobre la totalidad de los miembros y no solo de los presentes[108].

En el debate entre los legisladores constituyentes en la propia asamblea se expusieron los términos de las posiciones. Por el oficialismo lo hicieron especialmente Sampay, el jurista sanjuanino Pablo Ramella y Berraz Montyn. Este último señaló:

> [...] cuando se sancionó la ley declarando la necesidad de la reforma, el peronismo contaba, efectivamente, con los dos tercios de mayoría, y esto es cosa que nadie puede negar. El peronismo no quiso hacer una trampa porque no estaba en sus designios y porque no tenía necesidad, pues contaba con el número exigido por la ley. La minoría, en cambio, no tenía ese número que la ley requiere para poder oponerse eficazmente. ¿Cómo nos viene entonces la minoría con estas argumentaciones? ¿Cree la minoría que por la sola existencia de un voto en contra dentro del recinto es necesaria la existencia de 106 votos para contrarrestarlo? ¿A quién puede ocurrírsele semejante criterio? [...] el peronismo tenía el número necesario para sancionar lo que sancionó válidamente.

Por parte del bloque opositor, el legislador Parry opinó a favor de la nulidad de la convocatoria inicial por entender que la norma en debate era lo suficientemente clara en su simple interpretación literal.

> El presidente Perón, al redactar el anteproyecto de reformas a la Constitución, ha creído necesario agregar a ese artículo la palabra "presentes" para que la disposición analizada coincida con la interpretación peronista. El agregado evidencia el concepto de que

108 Según una crónica periodística, el diputado Colom intentó sin éxito suspender la votación por 24 horas "hasta que regresen a la Capital los dos diputados que nos faltan para completar los dos tercios", pero en la madrugada se votó en la Cámara de Diputados la declaración de necesidad de la reforma constitucional. *Revista Primera Plana nro. 233* del 13 de junio de 1967.

> era necesaria su inclusión para que la Constitución dijera lo que el peronismo quiere que diga.

Y sobre el fondo de la cuestión, expuso:

> Las mayorías gobiernan, pero con el control de las minorías bien intencionadas. La Constitución, en la sabia disposición del artículo 30, establece que no es la simple mayoría la que puede reformar la Constitución y que se requiere para ello los dos tercios de votos, a fin de que exista el concurso de la minoría al declarar la necesidad de la reforma.

Agregó el mismo constituyente que "en presencia de esta gravísima irregularidad y del estado de subversión existente durante el proceso electoral [...] no existe un Estado de derecho".

Sobre esto corresponde realizar algunas precisiones. Se trata, por sobre todo, de una cuestión de hermenéutica de la norma que, como toda cuestión de esa índole, se resuelve por la vía de la argumentación. Es decir, no hay una única interpretación posible sino que estamos frente a la disyuntiva de tener que escoger entre varias diferentes, de acuerdo con el interés al que se pretende dar protección. Nada extraordinario ni irregular hay en ello, al contrario, debe reconocerse que tal condición conflictiva forma parte de la naturaleza del fenómeno jurídico, donde no es posible arribar a una certeza absoluta en la que una de las partes prevalezca sobre la otra. Tal pretensión sería ilusoria. Tanto es así que incluso Juan Perón habría manifestado su disgusto por el modo de su aprobación legislativa.

> ¿A quién se le puede ocurrir que basta con alcanzar a los dos tercios de los diputados presentes y no respecto del total de los integrantes del cuerpo? Dicen que yo soy desaprensivo, que no le doy importancia a las formas pero esos ´se pasaron´ [...] con el criterio de ellos, en cualquier sesión con poca gente, los dos tercios podrían convocar una reforma constitucional [...] En fin, ahora no

> habrá más remedio que seguir adelante y defender la situación con los argumentos que se puedan[109].

Parece lo más atinado sostener que para reformar la Constitución se requiera de una mayoría especial, pero desde el punto de vista jurídico la cuestión se reduce a una disputa interpretativa entre argumentos, mientras que, desde lo político, Perón tenía razón ya que la cuestión podría haber sido resuelta por medio de la obtención de una concurrencia perfecta, lo que le hubiera significado clausurar apenas un flanco de la crítica fácil[110].

En cambio, la afirmación de la ausencia de "Estado de derecho" parece en retrospectiva un anuncio de la posición extrema que adoptó, de ahí en adelante, el partido radical, la cual lo llevó a la virulencia golpista de figuras como Roque Carranza y Zavala Ortiz, y marcó el punto de inicio de su declinación como fuerza nacional, al menos hasta su próxima oportunidad con la presidencia de Frondizi. Ello colocó al radicalismo en el campo antidemocrático y oligárquico, más allá de la fraseología republicana que defendió la mayoría especial de la letra de la ley. Para el partido radical, la asamblea constituyente de 1949 pudo haber representado la oportunidad histórica para participar, aunque sea desde la oposición, de las transformaciones sociales, y cumplir así un rol progresivo en línea ideológica con el programa de Avellaneda. Pero las relaciones de fuerza internas derivaron hacia otro camino, en el que predominó el cálculo político de evitar de cualquier modo la continuidad de Perón en el poder. En términos de Jauretche se podría decir que en el radicalismo primó una posición de partido por sobre la posibilidad de una política nacional.

Las elecciones para legisladores constituyentes se realizaron en diciembre: el peronismo sacó 1.730.000 votos (61,38%), mientras el radicalismo contó con 757.000 votos (26%). A la luz del resultado y la alta

109 Galasso, Norberto, *Perón*, Tomo I, Buenos Aires, Colihue, 2005, p. 539.

110 En este sentido, lo afirma Terroba, *op. cit.*: "Se debe hacer notar que, aun para la postura más exigente, los dos tercios sumaban 106 representantes y la bancada parlamentaria peronista reunía 108 miembros". En *La Constitución Nacional de 1949, una causa nacional*, Buenos Aires, Fundación Ross, 2010, p. 65.

participación, la convocatoria a la reforma debe ser considerada legitimada desde los parámetros de la representación democrática, y el argumento de impugnación de todo el proceso constituyente por no coincidir acerca del modo en que se realizó el primer acto de convocatoria, se convierte en una manera oblicua de criticar el fondo de la reforma. Más allá de que el argumento de la concurrencia de la mayoría especial sea el más atinado, la discusión sobre el modo de la convocatoria nada agrega al contenido de la reforma constitucional: no la hace ni mejor ni peor.

A mi juicio, lo más importante es dar cuenta de que, más allá de las interpretaciones posibles sobre el significado de una norma, la reforma constitucional era necesaria para el avance social. La dimensión de las transformaciones económicas y políticas así lo ameritaba, bajo el riesgo de que la norma fundamental del sistema jurídico se convirtiera en un obstáculo para el desarrollo del país: el viejo problema del progreso social entorpecido por relaciones de producción y jurídicas propias de una etapa anterior, cuya resolución era la transformación progresiva de estas.

Finalmente, la doctrina liberal conservadora impugnó la reforma constitucional fundamentando su crítica en la cláusula que permitía la reelección presidencial, la no inclusión del derecho a huelga y la legislación de ciertas normas que legalizaban una ampliación del poder de las fuerzas de seguridad en determinados casos. En opinión del que escribe, si bien todo ello es materia de debate histórico –en el que con este trabajo pretendo modestamente tomar parte– y más allá del grado de veracidad que puedan tener algunas de las posiciones, estimo que no configuran los aspectos principales de la reforma constitucional. En una observación que busque integrar la totalidad de los aspectos en juego con la reforma, hay otros elementos que adquieren una relevancia muy superior para caracterizarla en sus rasgos fundamentales, que serán enumerados más adelante. De lo contrario, estaríamos cometiendo el error de observar la parte ocultando al todo –metodología recurrente en la doctrina liberal conservadora– bajo una interpretación fetichista de la Constitución de 1949 y, por ende, inválida.

La sanción definitiva de la Ley 13.233 fue el 27 de agosto de 1948 en la Cámara de Senadores, con el despacho del sanjuanino Pablo Ramella y con el fin de una "mejor defensa de los derechos del pueblo y del bienestar de la nación". En ocasión de su promulgación el 3 de septiembre, Perón criticó a "las declaraciones de sociedad y clubes que nada tienen que hacer con la marcha del gobierno", por referencia a círculos de abogados ligados a intereses corporativos, porque "no constituyen sino meras opiniones de grupos de personas. Podrían formarse artificiosamente millones de ellos en la República, pero el pueblo no delibera ni gobierna sino por medio de sus representantes"[111]. La convocatoria a elecciones de convencionales constituyentes incluyó la de diputados nacionales y electores para senadores (cfr. Ley 13.262 del 20 de septiembre).

En el radicalismo la posición a asumir frente al llamado a elecciones estuvo dividida. El sector unionista proponía directamente la abstención electoral, pero se impuso la idea de los intransigentes de concurrir con la condición de no presentar proyectos de reforma. Los socialistas también tuvieron posiciones encontradas entre quienes proponían concurrir "para evitar que las reformas fueran contrarias a la clase obrera", y los que optaban por la oposición a "colaboracionismos estériles". Se impuso esta última actitud promovida por la conducción del Partido Socialista con su llamado a "votar en blanco contra la reforma fascista de la Constitución". Los peronistas por entonces les recordaron a los socialistas el pedido a Uriburu en 1931 de reformar la Constitución para darle "algunos retoques". Por su parte, los demócratas progresistas adoptaron la misma actitud; los comunistas, al igual que los conservadores, se presentaron a las elecciones pero sin obtener ninguna banca en la asamblea.

En las elecciones del 5 de diciembre triunfó el peronismo ampliamente, por lo que el resto de la oposición, a excepción de los radicales, decidió reunirse en forma paralela a la asamblea en un denominado "Congreso de la Defensa de la Constitución Nacional".

111 *Revista Primera Plana, op. cit.*

La reforma de la Constitución fue finalmente concretada y el proyecto nacional en ese momento contó con un sistema normativo adecuado para su realización histórica. El peronismo tenía su autoría exclusiva, mientras en el camino quedaba el radicalismo con sus aguas divididas entre intransigentes y unionistas, y el resto de una oposición políticamente débil.

La Convención Constituyente

La Convención Constituyente tuvo lugar en el Congreso de la Nación e inició su funcionamiento con 110 constituyentes peronistas y 48 radicales, el 24 de enero de 1949 –primera reunión preparatoria–, ocasión en la que se designó a las autoridades y a la Comisión de Reglamento. Las sesiones ordinarias de debate, seis en total, finalizaron el día 11 de marzo, y una última posterior, a modo de clausura, celebrada el 16 de marzo[112]. En la segunda reunión preparatoria, ocurrida el 27 de enero, el presidente Perón visitó la asamblea y dio un discurso. En la sesión ordinaria del 1º de febrero ingresaron a despacho los proyectos de reforma y aquellos relativos a los planteos de nulidad de la convocatoria, y las elecciones realizadas a partir del mandato de reforma de la Ley 13.233. El 15 de febrero, durante la tarde, se rechazó la nulidad presentada por los constituyentes de la oposición y se declaró cumplido el artículo 30 por la convocatoria.

La presidencia de la Convención estuvo a cargo de Domingo Mercante, que fue el candidato con mayor cantidad de votos, electo como convencional de la provincia de Buenos Aires de donde era gobernador. En la vicepresidencia primera fue designado Héctor Cámpora y en la segunda, José Espejo. Parecía una suerte de eco del policlasismo de la coalición de gobierno, a través de las figuras del líder sindical, el legislador partidario leal y el gobernador bonaerense. Después de la reforma constitucional,

112 El 6 de enero de 1949 se conoció la propuesta de reforma constitucional del Consejo Superior del Partido Peronista, la que dio lugar a la formación de una Comisión de estudio de ese proyecto, encabezada por Arturo Sampay, con duración hasta el 24 del mismo mes.

comenzó una nueva etapa dentro del peronismo, en la cual las figuras de Mercante y Espejo, ambas con cierta autonomía del liderazgo de Perón, se opacaron y perdieron posiciones dentro del proyecto político.

Los convencionales radicales, como ya dijimos, bajo la conducción de Moisés Lebensohn, abandonaron la Asamblea el 8 de marzo –la tercera sesión ordinaria– antes de la lectura del informe de Sampay[113].

El fundamento esgrimido fue el planteo de ilegitimidad de la convocatoria –rechazado en la primera sesión– y el incumplimiento por parte de Perón con la promesa inicial de no incluir la cláusula de la reelección en la reforma. El mismo Perón en una reunión en la residencia de Olivos con los constituyentes electos de su partido en ese momento, en un cambio de opinión, sostenía: "el partido, aun contra mi voluntad ha colocado la reelección en el proyecto [...] a mí me han convencido a ese respecto". No obstante, Perón manifestó en esa misma ocasión sus reservas de pretender una reelección suya, por razones personales y por existir en el movimiento hombres con capacidad para reemplazarlo.

A esa altura, la retirada no impidió la continuidad constituyente, ya que la bancada peronista contaba con *quorum* propio[114].

113 Según Osvaldo Álvarez Guerrero, "al retirarse con su bloque de la Convención Constituyente reunida en tan irregulares condiciones, y en respuesta a los gritos de la mayoría '¡Que se vayan!' exclamó: 'Volveremos, para dictar la Constitución de los argentinos'. Poco más tarde, Lebensohn sufrió la cárcel por razones políticas durante más de un año y allí se quebrantó su salud física definitivamente" (http: //www.historia.radicales.org.ar/lebensohn.htm. consultada el 15/04/2009). Lo cierto es que el ideario de Lebensohn –quien tuvo una relación de amistad personal con Evita–, expresado en el programa de Avellaneda de los radicales intransigentes de 1945, coincidía con las líneas esenciales de la reforma constitucional.

114 En Sánchez Zinny, E. F., *El Culto de la Infamia*, Buenos Aires, Artes Gráficas de Bartolomé Chiesino S.A., 1958 citado por Jorge Vanossi: "Sr. Lebensohn: —El propio miembro informante de la mayoría ha confesado ante la conciencia argentina que la Constitución se modifica en el artículo 77 para Perón, con el espíritu de posibilitar la reelección de Perón."(Hablan varios señores convencionales a la vez y suena la campana.) Sr. Lebensohn: —La representación radical desiste de seguir permaneciendo en este debate, que constituye una farsa. (¡Muy bien! ¡Muy bien! Aplausos) (Hablan varios señores convencionales a la vez y suena la

Los días 9 y 10 de marzo tuvieron lugar la cuarta y quinta sesiones ordinarias, y el 11 de marzo la sexta, cuando se sancionó la nueva Constitución Nacional y la juraron los convencionales.

En las elecciones presidenciales de 1951 el resultado fue el siguiente: sobre un total de 7.500.000 electores, el peronismo fue votado por 4.745.000 (62,5%), el radicalismo por 2.415.000 (32%), mientras que el resto (comunismo, socialismo, conservador y demócrata progresista) por 300.000 (4%), y hubo 122.600 votos en blanco y anulados (1,5%). Estos datos, en relación con el acto electoral de 1948, denotan un sensible aumento del padrón electoral y de la participación popular, lo que a mi juicio concurre a respaldar la legitimidad democrática de la reforma constitucional.

En sus disposiciones transitorias finales, la Convención Nacional Constituyente estableció que, en un plazo de noventa días se autorizaba a las "legislaturas provinciales para reformar totalmente sus constituciones, con el fin de adaptarlas a los principios, declaraciones, derechos y garantías consagrados" en la nueva Constitución, lo que así hicieron al poco tiempo[115]. La nueva Constitución fue jurada por Juan Perón, a las 14:20 horas del 16 de marzo de 1949, en el Congreso Nacional, sin la presencia de los radicales.

Con posterioridad, los legisladores radicales juraron la nueva Constitución, previo debate interno en el que el sector unionista proponía la medida extrema del directo abandono de las bancas.

---

campana.) En tanto la representación radical se retira del recinto, el presidente Mercante, anuncia, entre vivas y aplausos, que continúa la sesión. En medio de la batahola, los convencionales peronistas, puestos de pie, entonan el Himno Nacional. En esos instantes, la palabra 'Libertad' consignada en la canción patria, adquiere un extraño sentido; el de algo que no existe".

115 Entre ellas sobresale la Constitución de Chaco (1951) que integraba a una única Cámara de representantes por mitades iguales de políticos y sindicalistas, dando lugar a lo más parecido a un Estado sindical o corporativo en el que el sujeto de la representación está constituido por las fuerzas sociales.

Fundamentos políticos e ideológicos de la reforma constitucional

En el peronismo, el liberalismo político de posición nacional, cuya expresión más consecuente era el forjismo, concurría en el mismo cauce con otras corrientes de pensamiento como el social cristianismo (expresado en Arturo Sampay) y el nacionalismo revisionista (en el caso de José María Rosa, Ernesto Palacio, Fermín Chávez y John W. Cooke). Lo mismo puede decirse por su importancia ideológica, aunque sin un correlato proporcional en lo político, del latinoamericanismo de Manuel Ugarte y el trotskismo nacional del Frente Obrero (Enrique Rivera, Aurelio Narvaja, Adolfo Perelman, entre varios) o, desde otra perspectiva, filósofos como Carlos Astrada o Nimio de Anquín. A los fines de difusión propia de la tarea política cultural, la revista *Hechos e Ideas* fue un bastión[116]. Esta diversidad ideológica –de convivencia no necesariamente pacífica ni exenta de contradicciones– expresa a su modo el hecho político del carácter policlasista del movimiento nacional popular. Por eso, en el sentido ideológico de las nuevas normas constitucionales puede advertirse la existencia de varias fuentes de distinto origen, que le otorgan complejidad a la trama jurídica y semántica del texto, sin que ninguna adquiera el carácter de exclusiva o de primacía por sobre las otras.

En lo esencial, la Constitución de 1949 expresó en su letra un proyecto de patria caracterizada como "socialmente justa, económicamente libre y políticamente soberana". Fue la expresión jurídica de la etapa de consolidación de las transformaciones sociales de la revolución nacional y un punto alto en el proceso histórico –y nunca acabado– de la formación de la conciencia nacional, al adoptar formas institucionales concretas en superación de las interpretaciones propias del liberalismo conservador.

116 Ver al respecto de Alejandro Cataruzza, "Una empresa cultural del primer peronismo: la revista *Hechos e Ideas* (1947-1955)", en *Revista Complutense de Historia de América, nro. 19*, Madrid, 1993. Para Roberto Baschetti la revista de origen radical fue un intento "por dotar a su discurso de una serie de apoyos técnicos, de citas prestigiosas, de una impronta 'académica' que lo legitime ante el público" (consultado en http://www.robertobaschetti.com). Se registraron números especiales sobre la reforma constitucional de 1949, discursos de Perón, de varios ministros, y acerca del Segundo Plan Quinquenal.

Es cierto que tiempo antes habían tenido lugar reformas constitucionales en algunas provincias con predominio de una innovadora legislación social, como los casos de Tucumán, Mendoza, Entre Ríos (1933) y San Juan (la más antigua, de 1927), pero más allá del indudable valor de estos importantes antecedentes del constitucionalismo provincial no puede concluirse sin más que la reforma de 1949 haya sido consecuencia de un proceso de nacionalización de estos[117]. El texto constitucional expresó principalmente el modo de organización política y económica del programa nacional del peronismo, como una forma particular de capitalismo nacional o autónomo. En el vocabulario del peronismo "capitalismo nacional" significa independencia económica y justicia social.

A esta revolución nacional le debe su impronta ideológica el texto normativo, en el cual subyace la certeza de que los individuos solo pueden realizar sus derechos en la medida en que la nación se autodetermine, lo que en el plano jurídico se denomina el derecho a la autodeterminación de los pueblos –derecho de carácter colectivo que se encuentra consagrado en el derecho internacional público–, y que para la filosofía política puede ser traducido como la búsqueda de la liberación nacional. Es lo que tanto Manuel Ugarte como Arturo Jauretche denominaron la libertad nacional. Algo así como el derecho de los derechos para los pueblos de nuestra América Latina y del tercer mundo[118]. Es la facultad que posibilita el ejercicio real del resto de los derechos, incluidos los individuales, que legitima la existencia de instituciones propias del Estado en las distintas áreas de la economía con miras a lograr la realización social. El Estado asumía el rol de constructor de la nación, para lo cual resultaba fundamental considerar a la protección del trabajo como fuente de producción de riqueza, de los recursos naturales como patrimonio público y a la autodeterminación

117 Ver AA.VV. "Las reformas sociales en la Constitución de San Juan de 1927", en *Revista de Historia del Derecho*, Buenos Aires, Instituto de Investigaciones de Historia del Derecho, 1977.

118 "El tercer mundo está compuesto por los países que no están bajo el dominio del imperialismo americano o del imperialismo ruso", dijo Juan Perón, citado en *América Latina, ahora o nunca*, Buenos Aires, Punto de Encuentro, 2009.

nacional como sentido general e integrador de la propuesta constitucional.

En la Asamblea Constituyente el discurso de Sampay ocupó un lugar central como expresión del pensamiento social cristiano, con eje en la comunidad organizada, el bien común y la función social del individuo y de la propiedad. Este perfil ideológico difería del presentado por Cooke en ocasión de fundamentar en la Cámara de Diputados la necesidad de la reforma. No obstante, ambos deben considerarse referentes de la interpretación del texto constitucional.

Desde esta posición, la reforma constitucional debe ser vista como integrada por aquellos actos legislativos que a modo de antecedentes le dan sustento como, a la vez, por los posteriores, que obran a modo de reglamentación de sus artículos.

Así, si bien la figura de Sampay sobresalió en su rol central en la Asamblea Constituyente, debe destacarse la actuación de Cooke en forma previa especialmente en su actuación parlamentaria, en la cual presentó fundamentos políticos, económicos, históricos e ideológicos, respecto de los debates de aquella normativa, y reveló una estatura de jurista con conciencia nacional, pese a no haber sido convocado por Perón para la asamblea, ni a participar de la redacción del anteproyecto. En sus discursos parlamentarios desfilaron conceptos que dieron contenido concreto a una nueva visión del derecho y la sociedad: economía nacional, imperialismo, países semicoloniales, liberación social, proletariado[119]. Al tiempo que encaró una crítica desmitificadora de la falsa sacralización de la propiedad privada, el libre cambio y el libre comercio, el concepto liberal de la libertad en nuestros países oprimidos, la dualidad librecambio o proteccionismo. Utilizó un vocabulario acorde con una perspectiva nacional popular para fundamentar una nueva legalidad, en la cual la Constitución del 49 fue su corolario. Por eso en cada tema desarrollado de la reforma haremos referencia a sus aportes como legislador.

119 Ver Cooke, John William, Duhalde, Eduardo Luís (comp.) y Baschetti, R., *Acción Parlamentaria, Tomo I*, Buenos Aires, Colihue, 2007. En adelante, las citas textuales de Cooke se corresponden a esta fuente de consulta.

Algunas de las principales fuentes: Cooke, Scalabrini Ortiz, Sampay y el movimiento obrero

En los fundamentos vertidos por Cooke para justificar la reforma constitucional encontramos una de las fuentes de interpretación jurídica e ideológica. En ocasión de proponer la reforma, dijo:

> Los mitos del librecambio están abandonando sus sitiales para dar lugar a imágenes todavía imprecisas, cuyas formas se insinúan pero cuyas líneas definitivas aún no conocemos. La Constitución actual es en parte síntesis de la realidad argentina, solo el sistemático y malicioso falseamiento de la historia argentina ha llevado a muchos espíritus al convencimiento que los errores cometidos por la clase dirigente tienen por causa la Constitución, ello no es así.

Este señalamiento lo hace Cooke contra los principios del librecambio

> [...] al que se apegan fervientemente las grandes potencias, una vez que por medio del proteccionismo han dominado el comercio internacional [...] pero el espíritu nacional ha logrado también sus triunfos, y el texto de 1853 con todos sus errores, pudo haber sido la base de un ordenamiento jurídico político compatible con la realidad argentina.

Aunque,

> [...] en realidad el país se organizó tomando como modelo una sociedad anónima con directorio en el extranjero. Rieles, muelles, barcos, empresas, bolsas, se entremezclan en un desparramo de teorías y concepciones que nos iban a llevar a un progreso y civilización jamás alcanzados. [...] No nos dimos cuenta de que, una vez más, nos daban collares de vidrio por nuestro auténtico oro. Ni los rieles sirvieron a nuestra producción, ni los muelles fueron ocupados por nuestros barcos. El progreso, la fuerza económica, los kilómetros de rieles, las

> toneladas de productos extraídos del suelo, los balances, los presupuestos, las memorias de las sociedades anónimas, tal o cual avenida, tal o cual camino, según esos clamores expresaban la pujanza y la dinámica de la patria, manejadas con las fórmulas cuyo secreto solo poseían los directores con asiento en remotos países y el mítico capital extranjero.
> Así la Constitución llegó a ser un instrumento que respondía a la interpretación única de la clase dirigente [...] lo que tenía de democrático y social no llegó a concretarse nunca. Y lo que tenía en su aspecto económico, al estar condicionado por las doctrinas de la época –que sostenían la inmutabilidad de una escuela económica determinada– ha quedado superado por una realidad completamente distinta a los moldes y fórmulas del pasado.

En estas palabras de Cooke están los fundamentos que justificaron el emprendimiento de una reforma constitucional que, sin haber constituido el poder constituyente originario, por sus innovaciones tuvo el carácter de integral. Cooke se encargó también de destacar que las transformaciones peronistas fueron realizadas dentro del texto constitucional que regía –el de 1853– porque

> [...] no se hizo una revolución contra la Constitución sino dentro de ella, buscando interpretarla lealmente en lo mucho que tiene de democrático, de popular, de justiciero. Con las modificaciones que proponemos, a las que indudablemente habrán de agregarse otras, podrá adaptarse nuestro supremo texto a la realidad de la República Argentina, que va reencauzándose por la trayectoria auténtica de su destino como Nación.

En ocasión de presentarse en el Congreso de la Nación[120] el proyecto de la mencionada Ley 13.233, Cooke expresó:

120 Nos explayaremos sobre esto más adelante. Entre sus compañeros se contaban Ernesto Palacio, Antonio Benítez, Alejandro Leloir, entre varios.

> [...] esta revolución es típicamente americana [...] que sigue la reconquista económica, la liberación nacional, el afianzamiento de sus propios valores espirituales y morales, y el tiempo está trabajando a nuestro favor, estamos construyendo para el futuro. Hay que reglamentar constitucionalmente el derecho de *habeas corpus* y de amparo a los derechos y a las personas porque nosotros –lo podemos decir– somos partidarios de la intervención estatal en todos los órdenes de la vida argentina, menos en lo que atañe a la personalidad íntima del individuo. Creemos que el Estado debe intervenir en las cuestiones económicas y que debe regular todo tipo de relación entre capital y trabajo, que debe ejercer el control de todo lo económico; pero, al mismo tiempo, necesitamos reglamentar en forma más completa lo que establece el actual texto, el amparo de los derechos individuales.
> Hay que incorporar los derechos del trabajador, que posiblemente sean una simple declaración de anhelos, que por sí solos no significan nada, pero que tienen mucho valor porque cristalizan en el texto constitucional la voluntad de los argentinos de distribuir equitativamente la riqueza de la Nación.

Cooke interpretaba a la Constitución que regía (la de 1853) como una "buena Constitución" debido al sentido democrático e igualitario que le inspiraba, pero de la que también podía decirse que era una

> constitución fracasada [...] a causa del apoderamiento de la oligarquía de los comandos de la maquinaría del país, desde los que vició continuada y permanentemente todos los principios que afirmaba defender en su vocinglería declamatoria.

Y en otra parte dijo:

> El hecho es que la Constitución, bien o mal interpretada, sirvió siempre para justificar las grandes entregas de la soberanía, porque lo mismo se la invocaba para malvender un ferrocarril construido

> por el esfuerzo de los argentinos que para regalar a un ferrocarril extranjero una legua a ambos costados de la vía.

Esa era la cuestión que determinaba la necesidad política de la reforma: la alternativa nación o factoría, como Arregui definió la disyuntiva de nuestros pueblos latinoamericanos; y por eso Cooke alertó, con ironía, que "al pensar en la reforma de la Constitución del 53, hará que algunos se desgarren sus túnicas, se cubran sus rostros horrorizados y llenen sus cabezas de ceniza".

Otra de las fuentes que aporta sentido ideológico e interpretativo viene de Raúl Scalabrini Ortiz quien realizó, además de sus investigaciones económicas, un aporte singular desde el intento de dar sustento filosófico a la etapa que se abría con el peronismo. En noviembre de 1948, reivindicaba la idea de Perón de "humanizar el capital", lo que parecía un absurdo, decía Scalabrini. Sin embargo se trata de "una fecunda fuente de reflexión analítica" porque el capital era la invención social de un ente "eterno". El capital, según Scalabrini Ortiz,

> [...] pasa sobre las cosas perecederas sin perecer, pasa sobre los hombres mortales sin fenecer. Si el rédito o parte de él se incorpora al capital, el capital crece hasta el infinito [...] Humanizar el capital significa a mi entender emplazarlo, transformarlo en mortal y perecedero como las cosas a las cuales está aplicado.

El mandato de Perón ("hay que humanizar el capital") abría la puerta a nuevas relaciones sociales progresistas e intervencionistas porque "afirmar que la propiedad es violable con fines de utilidad pública es proyectar de inmediato nuevas perspectivas para la convivencia". En otra parte el mismo autor había sostenido que encontraba acreditada la "inexistencia de verdaderas inversiones extranjeras en el país" y que "el llamado capital ferroviario extranjero no fue sino la capitalización a favor del extranjero del trabajo y la riqueza natural argentina". Es que "los argentinos tuvieron bienes, inmuebles, mercaderías, valores, dinero

a veces, pero jamás tuvieron capitales; el capital fue un mito para uso exclusivo de los extranjeros".

En esta concepción el capital aparece como una relación social ajena a los intereses nacionales, en la que quedan subordinadas a su proceso de formación, tanto la fuerza de trabajo de las mayorías populares como los recursos naturales del país. La declaración de utilidad pública o de interés público, la cláusula antimonopolio y la función social de la propiedad –fórmulas jurídicas que expresan un rol activo del Estado en las relaciones de producción– son instrumentos que habilitan la nacionalización de la economía y del capital, y su puesta al servicio de un proyecto nacional que promueva los intereses de las clases populares o, en palabras de Scalabrini, que procure "la humanización del capital". En fin, se trata de afirmar la naturaleza social del capital, es decir, de enunciar las relaciones sociales ocultas detrás. "Humanizar el capital" no es otra cosa que mostrar las relaciones de dominio entre los sujetos y las clases sociales a las que pertenecen, con el fin de ponerlo al servicio del bien común.

"Henchido de reconfortante esperanza en el porvenir de la patria", Scalabrini les sugirió a los constituyentes los "cinco principios de cooperación interna", ya formulados durante la primera campaña presidencial de Perón. Estos eran: 1) el principio del hombre colectivo: en el que el conjunto debe primar por sobre lo individual; 2) el de la comprensión del hombre: para que no se sacrifique jamás la realidad humana en su totalidad compleja, en pos de una abstracción normativa; 3) el de protección al más débil: para que se elimine la "ley de la selva" porque la igualdad teórica es una desigualdad práctica a favor del poderoso; 4) el de la comunidad de la riqueza natural: en el que la propiedad es una delegación de la fuerza de la organización colectiva que la hizo posible y mantiene; 5) el de la utilidad colectiva del provecho: para que nadie tenga derecho a obtener beneficios de actividades perjudiciales o inútiles para la sociedad[121].

121 En "El capital, el hombre y la propiedad en la vieja y en la nueva Constitución", en *Hechos e Ideas*, IX (56/57), Buenos Aires, noviembre-diciembre de 1948 y "Análisis de las prerrogativas constitucionales para los extranjeros y el

Estos principios filosóficos encuentran coherencia con las nuevas disposiciones constitucionales. En ellos, no hay lugar para la concentración de la riqueza en pocas manos, ya sea de parte de las oligarquías locales –burguesías comercial, financiera y agropecuaria– como de los conglomerados multinacionales.

Perón expuso en el discurso del 1º de mayo de 1948, en línea con Scalabrini Ortiz, que

> [necesitamos] capitales que se humanicen en su función específica, que extraigan la riqueza del seno de la tierra en el trabajo fecundo y que sepan anteponer su función social a la meramente utilitaria. Repudio al dios Oro, improductivo y estático, al supercapitalismo frío y calculador.

También Perón diría que era

> [...] un convencido de que el peor azote de nuestros pueblos es precisamente la intervención económica, política y social de los Estados Unidos en nuestros países [...] Las dificultades entre nuestro gobierno y el de Washington comenzaron cuando me di cuenta que pretendían hacernos pagar parte de sus deudas de guerra [...][122].

Otra fuente conceptual de importancia que aporta sentido a las normas de la reforma constitucional proviene directamente de Arturo Sampay. Aunque Perón le había encargado a José Figuerola en su carácter de Secretario Técnico de la Presidencia de la Nación –aunque no era convencional constituyente–, la elaboración del anteproyecto de reforma constitucional, que contaba con antecedentes como el Plan Quinquenal de 1946 y el IV Censo nacional de 1947, en los que aquel había tenido participación fundamental, finalmente optó por delegar la tarea de la redacción final a la Comisión de Estudio del Anteproyecto de Reformas a la Constitución

desamparo de los argentinos. La reforma constitucional", en *Cuatro verdades sobre nuestras crisis*, F.R.S.O., Buenos Aires, Ediciones Theoría, 1948.

122 Galasso, *op. cit.* p. 538

Nacional, del bloque del partido peronista, cuya presidencia estaba a cargo de Arturo Sampay, de línea política e ideología diferente a Figuerola.

Arturo Sampay expresó la política de nacionalismo económico antiimperialista y antioligárquico a través del pensamiento social cristiano de donde proviene la noción de comunidad organizada, de bien común y función social de la propiedad[123]. Su obra ha tenido la dimensión suficiente como para dar lugar a un derecho político iusnaturalista de notable profundidad, merecedor de un mayor reconocimiento del que actualmente tiene y un estudio más dedicado que el presente ensayo. Su pensamiento, de contenido católico y de orientación social[124], coincide con la formación de un "imaginario cristiano peronista", aunque no desde la recepción pasiva y acrítica del mensaje de la jerarquía eclesiástica como factor de poder real, sino desde el espacio católico más popular –social cristianismo– inspirado en la crítica a la dominación liberal conservadora, que surgió en esos años cuyos voceros, entre otros, fueron el padre Hernán Benítez o monseñor Miguel De Andrea[125]. También se cuenta, además de Sampay, a Pablo Ramella –senador de San Juan y juez de la Corte Suprema en 1975/76–[126]. Hay en líneas generales en estos planteos –en los cuales la

123 No era el único, también estaba la figura de Pablo Ramella, o la de Oscar Salvador Martini quien afirmaba "la concepción aristotélica tomista como base de la revolución nacional" y el "principio del bien común de la tercera posición".

124 La interpretación cristiana de Arturo Sampay del sistema normativo se desprende también de su texto "La filosofía jurídica del art. 19 de la Constitución Nacional", en el que señala que "el art. 19 viene a reconocer implícitamente la vigencia de las leyes naturales de la moral que reglan los actos libres de los hombres, porque cuando reserva a Dios el juicio sobre la bondad o malicia de actos humanos, acepta, evidentemente, que tal juzgamiento se hace sobre la base de normas instituidas por Dios, porque la entidad que dicta un orden es también quien pena y premia la conducta de los sujetos a ese orden".

125 Acerca de la influencia del social cristianismo en Perón, ver Chávez, Fermín, *El peronismo visto por Víctor Frankl*, Buenos Aires, Theoría, 1999.

126 Ver Cucchetti, Humberto, "Religión y Política en Argentina y en Mendoza (1943-1955): lo religioso en el primer peronismo", con cita de Fortunato Mallimacci, en www.clacso.org.ar/biblioteca. El Dr. Pablo Ramella fue perseguido por la dictadura de 1955 y preso. Al ser liberado, el partido demócrata cristiano le ofreció integrarse a sus filas, lo que rechazó por no haber defendido a católicos

prédica católica crítica adquiere un contenido nacional popular– un antecedente de la teología de la liberación de los años 60, donde el cristianismo llega por momentos a converger con el marxismo.

Para esta filosofía católica, preconciliar y con base en las ideas de Tomás de Aquino y Aristóteles, la *polis* es la finalidad a la cual tiende el derecho, que solo puede darse en el interior de la sociedad política[127]. Pero no se da de cualquier forma, ni tampoco cualquier formación social alcanza la condición de *polis*, sino solo aquella en la que el orden establecido guarda correlación con lo justo y el bien común. De tal forma que una ley contraria al orden social justo no es considerada derecho, así como solo la sociedad puede ser considerada *polis* cuando está orientada al bien común[128].

La doctrina social católica sirvió para relativizar la propiedad privada como derecho absoluto –tesis jurisprudencial que rigió en el país hasta bien entrado el siglo XX–, impugnando su sacralidad y justificando un rol activo del Estado en la economía, como bien ensayó Sampay en una frase recortada de la asamblea de 1949:

> Sobre la base de la libre actividad económica de los particulares [...] está el Estado, como promotor del bien de la colectividad, interviene para orientar la economía conforme a un plan general de beneficios comunes.

"Lo que no es justo no es legal" es la consigna de tono insurrecto capaz de alcanzar la prédica iusnaturalista cuando es adoptada como horizonte de sentido por los oprimidos. El movimiento nacional peronista mayormente se presentó como la expresión política de la comunidad organizada, cuya forma histórica adoptada en aquel momento fue el nacionalismo

peronistas encarcelados, en "Carta dirigida a Lozano Gil", San Juan, 3 de junio de 1958, en "Archivo de Pablo Ramella, Carpeta 212", citado por Susana Ramella en Ramella, Susana, "La concepción antropológica del derecho del trabajo en el constitucionalismo social del siglo XX", en *Revista de Historia del Derecho, nro. 42*, Buenos Aires, INHIDE, junio-diciembre de 2011.

127 La función social de la propiedad estaba mencionado en las Encíclicas de la Iglesia Católica, "Rerum Novarum", "Quadragessimo Anno" y "Populorum Progressio", así como la condición de derecho natural de los derechos de los trabajadores.

128 Del Vecchio, G., *Sobre la politicidad del derecho*, T. 75, Buenos Aires, La Ley.

económico. "El justicialismo es una nueva filosofía de vida, simple, práctica, popular, profundamente humana y cristiana", definía Perón en *Las veinte Verdades del justicialismo* (1950). Según esta interpretación, la comunidad se constituye en la afirmación de lo nacional y en el equilibrio de los diferentes factores sociales de producción que, sin postergar la búsqueda de sus intereses particulares, se subordinan al bien común.

Cabe señalar que en esta noción de bien común coincide tanto la voluntad general del liberalismo igualitario de la Revolución francesa como la tradición social cristiana, pero en el caso concreto del programa de nación propuesto por el peronismo, el bien común era una manifestación de la defensa de la soberanía nacional y popular. La "comunidad organizada"[129] es una interpretación de la sociedad donde los factores de la producción –el capital y el trabajo– conciliaban sus intereses a través del rol del Estado en procura de ese bien común, mediante un modelo social de capitalismo nacional, de independencia económica y justicia social.

Este planteo filosófico está presente en la ideología expresada por la letra constitucional, con la particularidad señalada de realizarse en formas concretas de nacionalismo económico, pero es una visión de mundo correspondiente a un orden social antiguo y precapitalista y, sobre todo, demasiado lejano en tiempo y lugar. La comunidad organizada expresaba la utopía de un nacionalismo burgués con justicia social solo viable en un capitalismo concurrencial. Pero nuestro país era de condición dependiente y semicolonial, en un capitalismo mundial que hacía décadas había dejado atrás su etapa concurrencial para ingresar definitivamente en su fase expansionista y dominante, sin espacio para nuevas naciones capitalistas y competitivas. Por eso la opción principal, para los países como los nuestros, era la liberación o la dependencia.

129 Aunque presente en momentos anteriores, como en la asamblea de 1949, la noción de comunidad organizada tuvo su expresión más fuerte en el Congreso de Filosofía de Mendoza de 1949, a través del discurso brindado por Perón. Según testimonios, su importancia habría sido relativizada por el mismo Perón (ver Galasso, Norberto, *Perón, T. 1, op. cit.*, testimonio de Hernán Benítez).

Esta concepción hizo crisis ante su insuficiente respuesta en la crisis final del peronismo y el comportamiento antisocial, destructivo e impregnado de odio de clase de la oligarquía. En 1955, cuando el conflicto social no tenía contención posible, la comunidad organizada (ese pacto social donde la lucha de clases parece suspenderse) se tornó imposible. Es que, en rigor, el peronismo, más allá de cómo se presente, no instauró una "comunidad organizada" con eje en la conciliación social y el consenso, sino un frente de liberación nacional en disputa dramática contra el bloque oligárquico conservador.

La clave es que aunque la alianza social sostenedora del proyecto nacional no era clerical, al carecer de una ideología propia por la cual expresarse de modo más consecuente, el socialcristianismo se presentaba como una opción. Recién después de 1955, tras la caída de Perón y el protagonismo exclusivo adquirido por la clase trabajadora en el movimiento nacional, el pensamiento nacional popular encontró una expresión más profunda en la obra posterior elaborada por Jauretche, Hernández Arregui, Ramos y el mismo John William Cooke, con un ejercicio de crítica intelectual nacional de profundidad y entroncando el movimiento peronista con el socialismo nacional.

El pensamiento social cristiano como explicación de la realidad social ha sido objeto de la crítica, a mi juicio con acierto, por Spilimbergo –en *Hombre, Estado, Comunidad*–, quien señalaba su insuficiente explicación de las contradicciones entre las clases sociales, que serían permanentes si no se superara dialécticamente el modelo de desarrollo capitalista por uno de emancipación social. Con mayor detalle –y ojo crítico– explicaba que

> [...] la ideología clerical medievalista y nacionalista-oligárquica pretendió suministrar para un problema moderno de un país moderno de relativo desarrollo burgués y con fuerte incidencia del movimiento obrero, una teoría paternalista y estamentaria del "equilibrio de clases", reaseguro estático ante desbordes socializantes de la base obrera del movimiento. Esta asfixia ideológica no solo debilitó programáticamente al movimiento sino que, además, contribuyó a aislar a la clase trabajadora de otros sectores

> populares como la pequeña burguesía estudiantil, al privarla de un discurso articulador del frente nacional.

Spilimbergo calificaba a esta concepción como antihistórica y estática.

> De allí que los principales aportes favorecedores del desarrollo de una conciencia nacional haya que buscarlos en "intelectuales periféricos" como Jauretche, Scalabrini Ortiz, Hernández Arregui, Jorge Abelardo Ramos, Rodolfo Puiggrós, John William Cooke sin acceso (salvo, circunstancialmente, Cooke y Arregui) a la cátedra universitaria[130].

Es que principalmente la interpretación social cristiana no se planteaba teóricamente el dilema de la superación de las relaciones de producción, ni tampoco avanzar en una de las cuestiones más problemáticas para el peronismo: el rol de las clases sociales (la oligarquía, la burguesía industrial y los trabajadores) y la posibilidad de su superación en el curso progresivo de la revolución nacional. Por eso Sampay –quien pese a su pensamiento católico no pertenecía a las filas del nacionalismo oligárquico– justamente avanzó hacia tesis más radicales o jacobinas en *Constitución y Pueblo*, en donde explicaba que la función social de la propiedad privada y la "humanización del capital" habían sido expresión jurídica y filosófica de una conciencia antiimperialista hacia el socialismo[131].

130 Es lo que sostiene, con razón, el sociólogo Alberto Franzoia. "Este planteo es medular, ya que un frente nacional siempre es policlasista en su constitución pero no puede serlo en su ideología. Las ideologías, independientemente de cómo se presenten a la consideración pública, no pueden tener un contenido policlasista real, pues son por definición las visiones de mundo que desarrollan cada una de las clases fundamentales de una sociedad. Por lo que si el nacionalismo popular del frente no logra expresarse a través de la visión de una burguesía fuerte, necesariamente debe hacerlo mediante la clase obrera, o en su defecto sucumbir ante el bloque oligárquico-imperialista. La historia posterior es muy conocida." en Franzoia, A., "¿Quién es Jorge Enea Spilimbergo?", versión disponible en www.elortiba.org.

131 Sobre la concepción de la función social de la propiedad, nos explayaremos un poco más adelante.

La Declaración de los Derechos del Trabajador de 1947

Otra fuente la constituyen las demandas del movimiento obrero organizado, cuya expresión se dio en la Declaración de los Derechos del Trabajador de 1947. Las luchas sindicales por reivindicar los derechos de los trabajadores había sido el eje de la acumulación política de Juan Perón, a partir de las inéditas conquistas en materia laboral alcanzadas especialmente en el período 1943-1945. En 1947 tuvieron su síntesis en un documento, de inspiración socialcristiana, que proclamaba los derechos básicos: derecho al trabajo, a una justa distribución, a la capacitación, a condiciones dignas de trabajo y de vida, a la salud, al bienestar, a la seguridad social, a la protección de la familia, al mejoramiento económico y a la defensa de los intereses profesionales. Perón los promulgó mediante el Decreto 4.865 del 7 de marzo del mismo año, y en 1949 fueron incorporados al artículo 37 del texto constitucional.

En un acto realizado el 24 de febrero de 1947 –al conmemorar en la Plaza Lavalle de la ciudad de Buenos Aires, un año del triunfo electoral–, el presidente Perón entregó la proclama en custodia al secretario general de la Confederación General del Trabajo. En su Preámbulo señalaba:

> El presidente de la Nación Argentina, haciéndose interprete de los anhelos de Justicia Social que alientan los pueblos y teniendo en cuenta que los derechos derivados del trabajo, al igual que las libertades individuales, constituyen atributos naturales inalienables e imprescriptibles de la personalidad humana, cuyo desconocimiento o agravio es causa de antagonismos, luchas y malestares sociales, considera necesario y oportuno enunciarlos mediante una declaración expresa, a fin de que en el presente y en el futuro sirva de norma para orientar la acción de los individuos y los poderes públicos, dirigida a elevar la cultura social, dignificar el trabajo y humanizar el capital como la mejor forma de establecer el equilibrio entre las fuerzas concurrentes de la economía y afianzar en un nuevo ordenamiento jurídico los principios que inspiran la legislación social. Por ello y de acuerdo

> con estos propósitos y fines, formula solemnemente la siguiente
> DECLARACIÓN DE LOS DERECHOS DEL TRABAJADOR.

Todo ello expresó un proceso de transformación social profundo, en una sociedad donde hasta hacía poco tiempo atrás, en junio de 1945, los sectores patronales confiaban en su capacidad de influencia y acción restauradora, como en el caso de los patrones de la industria y el comercio cuando se organizaron para presionar al presidente Farell ante el proyecto de salario mínimo, vital y móvil, aumentos a los trabajadores y su participación en las ganancias. En esa oportunidad dieron su alerta por

> [...] la intranquilidad creciente de un ambiente de agitación social, que venía a malograr la disciplina y pujante eficiencia del esfuerzo productor y cuya gravedad hallaba origen en el constante impulso que se deparaba desde dependencias oficiales.

Fue el preludio de la ofensiva contra Perón, su renuncia y detención en la isla Martín García, contrarrestada por la gesta popular del 17 de octubre.

La Declaración de los Derechos del Trabajador dibujaba en el mundo de las leyes lo que el pueblo había forjado en la práctica política. Luego, las leyes de Asociaciones Profesionales de 1945 y de Negociaciones Colectivas de 1953 completaron el escenario de reivindicaciones.

Para Perón, con su inclusión constitucional "el trabajador podía afirmar con fundamento que la era de la explotación del hombre por el hombre ha sido barrida para siempre de la tierra argentina".[132] Lo que guarda coherencia con esa comunidad organizada donde la lucha de clases parecía suspenderse y sustituida por un sistema de una economía social en que se pone "al capital al servicio de la economía" (Discurso de Perón del 1º de mayo de 1950: "Las luchas entre el capital y el trabajo son siempre destructivas y no hay ganancia ni para una parte ni para la otra. Y como queremos una Argentina constructiva y no destructiva, sumamos un

132 Baschetti, Roberto *La clase obrera peronista*, Buenos Aires, De la campana, 2010, p.29.

tercer factor que es el Estado. El Estado al servicio de esas dos fuerzas)."[133]

En verdad, como ya dijimos, el peronismo tensionó la cuerda del conflicto de clase contra el bloque oligárquico-imperialista. En esa dirección, hay réditos productivos para las dos partes del conflicto capital-trabajo y derrota política para la oligarquía. Aunque, pese a ello, la naturaleza de la política peronista, más que conciliadora, fue proletaria. Perón ponía el eje en los trabajadores porque

> [...] todas las conquistas sociales están dirigidas a dignificar el trabajo y a dignificar a quien lo ejecuta, el trabajador [...] lo que hemos establecido en la Constitución Justicialista de 1949 [es] que la explotación del hombre por el hombre es un delito penado por la ley.[134]

Si en un principio la ideología peronista había sido antioligárquica, en determinados momentos de la historia –en especial después de 1955– fue, al mismo tiempo, decididamente antipatronal. Lo que fue tenido en cuenta en todo momento por una burguesía que, aunque manufacturera y mercadointernista, fue siempre antipática y reaccionaria ante el peronismo, aunque desde una equívoca conciencia de clase y suicida posición antinacional.

Después de 1955 el movimiento nacional acentuó su rasgo popular y obrero, y dio origen a dos hitos en la historia de los trabajadores: los documentos de La Falda (1957) y de Huerta Grande (1962). Sus contenidos representan un auténtico programa de país porque profundizan la línea de la reforma de 1949, con la nacionalización del comercio exterior, los recursos naturales, los frigoríficos y los bancos; salarios altos, protección del mercado interno y de la industria nacional; expropiación del latifundio y control obrero de la producción. El programa de la CGT de los Argentinos del 1º de mayo de 1968 también retomó estos puntos y cuestionó el fundamento de la sociedad capitalista: la compraventa del trabajo y la propiedad privada de los medios de producción.

133 *Ídem* Baschetti, p. 29.
134 *Ídem* Baschetti, p. 31.

Contenido y fundamentos normativos de la reforma constitucional

Ya ingresando en la normativa constitucional de la reforma, lo primero a señalar es que el preámbulo fue respetado, por lo que es lícito afirmar la continuidad de ese "polo axiológico" como decía Sampay respecto del texto constitucional de 1853. Sin embargo, se le agregó la conocida síntesis de la filosofía política del proyecto nacional: "la irrevocable decisión de constituir una Nación socialmente justa, económicamente libre y políticamente soberana" y de "promover la cultura nacional". Ahí están los principios básicos guía del proyecto de nación: justicia social, liberación nacional y soberanía popular.

La primera parte de los Principios Fundamentales mantuvo sus enunciados generales, pero con importantes agregados y modificaciones. El Capítulo I tomó el título de "Forma de gobierno y declaraciones políticas", y se reformaron los artículos 15 (sobre la libertad de emitir opinión o de expresión), 16 (promoción de reformas constitucionales en las provincias), 17 (era el anterior artículo 25 que "fomentaba la inmigración europea", del cual quedó solo el fomento de la inmigración sin distinción), 18 (era el anterior artículo 26 que legislaba sobre la libre navegación de los ríos), 21 (que establecía los requisitos para la convocatoria y reforma constitucional). El Capítulo II llevó el título de "Derechos, deberes y garantías de la libertad personal" y comenzaba con el artículo 26, que era el anterior artículo 14, de considerable importancia en el anterior armado jurídico según la pacífica y tradicional interpretación de los tribunales federales. Los principios de reserva y de legalidad pasaron al artículo 30. También contenía varios artículos nuevos, como el 29 que incluía nuevas garantías procesales penales. Se destaca la derogación del anterior artículo 17 que disponía la inviolabilidad de la propiedad, entre otras normativas. El artículo 34 refería a los casos de conmoción interior o ataque exterior, mientras que el 35 incluía la fórmula de la reglamentación de derechos prevista en el anterior 28, con el agregado de la prohibición del abuso de derecho.

El Capítulo III llevaba el título de "Derechos del trabajador, de la familia, de la ancianidad y de la educación y la cultura", en el que el artículo 37 establecía lo que denominaba derechos especiales: ahí estaban las conquistas laborales y sociales. El Capítulo IV con el título "La función social de la propiedad, el capital y la actividad económica", incluía desde los artículos 38 a 40 con la normativa clave promotora del rol activo y fundamental del Estado en las relaciones sociales. A continuación venía la Segunda Parte que legislaba sobre las autoridades de la nación con los distintos títulos y capítulos.

Es posible caracterizar a las nuevas concepciones constitucionales a partir de los siguientes enunciados, con la sola intención de sistematizar, y sin ánimo de que sean los únicos, o establecer algún orden de prioridad: 1) la función social de la propiedad, el capital y la actividad económica; 2) el sistema político de protagonismo popular sobre la base de la democracia social; 3) la soberanía nacional y antiimperialista; 4) los derechos de la clase trabajadora y los nuevos sujetos de derecho; 5) la distribución y el trabajo de la tierra; 6) el federalismo; 7) la cultura nacional y la educación; 8) las garantías penales y 9) la libertad de prensa. A continuación, les daremos desarrollo.

1) La función social de la propiedad, el capital y la actividad económica

Así se titulaba el Capítulo IV, integrado por los nuevos artículos 38, 39 y 40, una de las claves de la reforma al diseñar las funciones del Estado y sus modos de actuación. La trascripción completa del artículo 40 de la Constitución es la siguiente:

> La organización de la riqueza y su explotación tienen por fin el bienestar del pueblo, dentro de un orden económico conforme a los principios de la justicia social. El Estado, mediante una ley, podrá intervenir en la economía y monopolizar determinada actividad, en salvaguardia de los intereses generales y dentro de los límites fijados por los derechos fundamentales asegurados en esta Constitución. Salvo la importación y exportación, que estarán a

> cargo del Estado, de acuerdo con las limitaciones y el régimen que se determine por ley, toda actividad económica se organizará conforme a la libre iniciativa privada, siempre que no tenga por fin ostensible o encubierto dominar los mercados nacionales, eliminar la competencia o aumentar usurariamente los beneficios.
> Los minerales, las caídas de agua, los yacimientos de petróleo, de carbón y de gas, y las demás fuentes naturales de energía, con excepción de los vegetales, son propiedad imprescriptible e inalienable de la Nación, con la correspondiente participación en su producto que se convendrá con las provincias.
> Los servicios públicos pertenecen originariamente al Estado, y bajo ningún concepto podrán ser enajenados o concedidos para su explotación. Los que se hallaran en poder de particulares serán transferidos al Estado, mediante compra o expropiación con indemnización previa, cuando una ley nacional lo determine.
> El precio por la expropiación de empresas concesionarias de servicios públicos será el del costo de origen de los bienes afectados a la explotación, menos las sumas que se hubieren amortizado durante el lapso cumplido desde el otorgamiento de la concesión y los excedentes sobre una ganancia razonable que serán considerados también como reintegración del capital invertido.

Se ha señalado la intervención en su redacción de Arturo Sampay, Jorge Del Río y Juan Sábato, en consulta con Raúl Scalabrini Ortiz y José Luís Torres[135]. Scalabrini y Del Río colaboraron con Sampay en su gestión como fiscal de Estado en la provincia de Buenos Aires, en especial en los juicios contra el Grupo Bemberg y la CADE[136]. Según González

135 Según otra versión, se le adjudica su autoría a Juan E. Maggi, titular de Agua y Energía Eléctrica en aquel momento. *Revista Primera Plana, nro. 233*, del 13 de junio de 1967.

136 Las citas del jurista Alberto González Arzac son de las revistas *Línea* (febrero 1999) y *Todo es historia* (noviembre de 1969), y Galasso, Norberto, *Perón, T. 1*, Buenos Aires, Colihue, 2005, p. 542.

Arzac, Sampay fue quien en forma directa había incorporado los dos incisos finales del artículo 40, y cuenta las presiones sufridas por Perón, días previos a su aprobación definitiva.

El 9 de marzo de 1949 Perón llamó a Mercante diciéndole que diplomáticos italianos, suizos, estadounidenses e ingleses sugerían modificar el artículo 40 [...] Una vez con Perón, Sampay le expresó que bajo ningún concepto consideraba posible modificar el artículo 40 porque ya había tomado publicidad el proyecto de la comisión. Por otra parte, sostuvo que los radicales, antes de retirarse, habían dejado sentada su expresa conformidad con las reformas sobre servicios públicos.

En esas circunstancias, Perón contestó: "Está bien. Prefiero pelear contra los gringos y no soportar a los lenguaraces de adentro". La anécdota finaliza en

> la noche del 11, en casa de José Luís Torres, hubo empanadas tucumanas, caldo y vino. Estaban el dueño de casa, su mujer y su hijo, junto a Scalabrini Ortiz y Jorge Del Río. Esperaban a Sampay. El héroe de la noche contó con lujo de detalles las alternativas que permitieron sancionar el artículo 40. La vocación nacionalista y antiimperialista que yacía en el espíritu del peronismo lo había salvado.

Es importante destacar que las presiones llevaron incluso a que el Departamento de Estado y la Embajada de EUA manifestaran su disgusto por la sanción de la norma[137].

137 Sampay había proyectado incluir como causal de nulidad insanable y asimilado a la traición a la patria (art. 20 de la reforma), la enajenación de la propiedad o concesión a empresas extranjeras de "los transportes ferroviarios, de los puertos, de las redes de comunicación telefónicas, de las fuentes de energía, del banco oficial encargado de emitir monedas o de cualquier otra riqueza nacional que originariamente perteneciera al patrimonio público o fuera recuperado para él, ni adoptar medida alguna que directamente o indirectamente entregue al extranjero el manejo de la economía de país [...]". Pero la propuesta se habría frustrado por iniciativa de Perón, conforme sostiene Alberto González Arzac, en "Vida, pasión y muerte del artículo 40", en *Todo es historia*, Buenos Aires, noviembre de 1969.

Con posterioridad a 1955, Raúl Scalabrini Ortiz, ya desde la semiclandestinidad, denominó a esta norma el "bastión de la República", el lugar donde "están los huevos del tero", porque "la alharaca que se alza en torno a la reelección es una coartada de disimulo [...] es el artículo 40 el que se quiere eliminar". "El artículo 40 sí es un obstáculo, una verdadera muralla que nos defiende de los avances extranjeros y está entorpeciendo y retardando el planeado avasallamiento y enfeudamiento de la economía argentina". Scalabrini tenía en mente un asunto concreto:

> Mientras esté vigente el artículo 40, no podrán constituirse las sociedades mixtas, porque todo lo que se urde estará incurablemente afectado de inconstitucionalidad. Ni los transportes, ni la electricidad, ni el petróleo podrán enajenarse ni subordinarse al interés privado, con que se enmascara el interés extranjero.
> Cada párrafo del artículo 40 tiene la recia estructura de un bastión, y sus nítidas aristas no se prestan a torcidas interpretaciones [...] Son párrafos perfectos, concluyentes y sonoros, como una cachetada.

Perón llegó a opinar que en el contrato petrolero con la Standard Oil de California –que no llegó a concretarse por falta de aprobación del Congreso–, debido a su carácter de sociedad mixta constituida con mitad de capital nacional, solo hubiera sido constitucionalmente aceptable la extracción de petróleo al servicio de YPF

> [...] porque, de acuerdo con el artículo 40 de la Constitución Nacional, tanto el mineral como las caídas de agua eran de propiedad imprescriptible e inalienable de la Nación Argentina[138].

La nacionalización de los recursos naturales ha sido por lo general un capítulo fundamental de las políticas del nacionalismo popular latinoamericano, porque como se ha dicho con razón "en los países semicoloniales, la defensa de los recursos naturales es el contenido concreto de su liberación nacional"[139]. El objetivo de nacionalización de la energía y

138 Testimonio de Perón del 7 de noviembre de 1967 a Norberto Galasso, citado en *Perón, T. I*, p.705, *op. cit.*
139 Chávez, Guido, "Bolivia, las luchas por el gas y el petróleo", en *Desafíos*,

el petróleo de Hipólito Yrigoyen había sido atacado desde los sectores oligárquicos y fue una de las principales causas del golpe de Estado que lo derrocó en 1930. La nacionalización del petróleo ha sido la base de lanzamiento del proyecto de liberación en Bolivia en 1937, 1969 y 2006 con los gobiernos de David Toro, Alfredo Ovando y Evo Morales. Al contrario, en nuestro país ha sido una estrategia contraproducente el fraccionamiento de la propiedad del subsuelo nacional en la reforma constitucional de 1994, un falso federalismo que debilita la posición nacional[140].

En la discusión sobre la actividad económica es donde aparecen las definiciones clave. Dijo Arturo Sampay en la asamblea:

> La reforma constitucional asigna al Estado la directiva de una política social, de una política familiar, y también de una política económica, que podríamos bifurcar en dos campos: la actividad económica privada y la actividad económica del Estado, con su condigno plan de nacionalización del Banco Central, de los servicios públicos y de las fuentes naturales de energía, y con la autorización para desarrollar actividades industriales cuando comporten monopolios de hecho, y estatizar sectores del comercio externo del país en la medida en que lo dispongan las leyes.
>
> Frente al capitalismo moderno ya no se plantea la disyuntiva entre economía libre o economía dirigida, sino que el interrogante versa sobre quién dirigirá la economía y hacia qué fin. Porque economía libre, en lo interno y en lo exterior, significa fundamentalmente una economía dirigida por los 'cartels' capitalistas, vale decir, encubre la dominación de una plutocracia que, por eso mismo, coloca en gran parte el poder político al servicio de la economía.

El fin de la economía política consiste en

> [...] alcanzar el bien de todos, para lograr la libertad democrática que es la que asegura el máximo de libertad al conjunto del

nro. 15, 2005. El enunciado textual corresponde a Adolfo Perelman.
140 Herrero, Félix, "¿Se puede en Argentina? Comentario a la nota de Guido Chávez", en *Desafíos*, *nro.5*, 2006.

> pueblo, y para derogar la libertad de explotación, la libertad de los poderosos que siempre traba la libertad de los débiles.

La idea de libertad, tal como la presentaba el liberalismo conservador, era contextualizada en el juego de las asimétricas relaciones sociales y adquiría, de ese modo, un contenido de clase y nacional (contra los "cartels capitalistas"). Por lo que la libertad solo podía ser la del pueblo y para que sea posible había que crear las condiciones materiales para su real ejercicio:

> La economía programática tiene dos fines: uno concreto e inmediato, la ocupación total de los trabajadores, esto es, la supresión definitiva de la desocupación cíclica, de la desocupación en masas que se verificaba en las sucesivas depresiones económicas: y otro último, al que este se subordina: brindar a todos los habitantes de la Nación las condiciones materiales necesarias para el completo desarrollo de la personalidad humana [...].

Queda claro que Sampay incluía tanto el derecho a la libertad como los derechos de los trabajadores y los económicos, sociales y culturales.

Para Sampay había terminado

> [...] la época en que la política –según el esquema liberal– era considerada como un factor de "perturbación" para la economía libre, y hoy es verdad lo contrario, o sea que la economía libre es un factor de "perturbación" para la política.

Es decir, no hay economía sin política, ni tampoco política sin economía, sino economía política. Entender a la política sin la economía es desmembrar la realidad social; la economía sin la política es en la práctica entregarse a la voluntad de las potencias hegemónicas. Por eso, se imponía ensayar una mirada completa que integrara a ambas esferas bajo el riesgo de "que la economía libre se convierta en un factor de "perturbación" para la política". Las libertades del mercado, del comercio o de empresa, las

políticas de libre cambio ya no integraban las formas naturales en que las sociedades se relacionaban de acuerdo a las formas superiores de la civilización moderna. En ese entonces, las formas eran determinaciones propias de un desarrollo productivo impuesto por las potencias extranjeras que atrofiaba las posibilidades nacionales.

Algo parecido, desde otro lugar, dijo el convencional Valenzuela –uno de los miembros de la Corte Suprema que integraba la asamblea–:

> El Estado no puede limitarse a reconocer la independencia jurídica del individuo sino que debe establecer un mínimo de condiciones necesarias para asegurar la independencia social.

En igual sentido opinaba el convencional Maturo:

> La falta de una estructuración orgánica del capitalismo industrial privado del país, la carencia de altos valores de especialización técnica y económica, las condiciones de la explotación y la pugna de los diversos intereses en juego, impone la intervención del Estado como único capaz de movilizar los recursos del país en defensa de la economía nacional.

Luego del golpe de 1955, Raúl Scalabrini Ortiz explicaba que

> [...] la industria es una integral creación del hombre [...] es la actividad humana que solo puede nacer, crecer y desarrollarse con la actividad combinada y la cooperación de otros hombres. En el mundo moderno, esa cooperación se llama crédito. El crédito es el vientre fecundo de la industria. Sin él nada pueden la inventiva, la iniciativa ni el espíritu de empresa [...] Cegar las fuentes del crédito industrial es herir mortalmente el destino industrial del país, y eso es justamente lo que está previsto en el ignominioso plan de aniquilamiento que lleva el nombre del doctor Raúl Prebisch y que las autoridades del Banco Industrial aplican tan sigilosa como implacablemente.[141]

141 En *Bases para la Reconstrucción Nacional. Aquí se aprende a defender a la patria*, Buenos Aires, Plus Ultra, 1985.

En este punto es importante citar al jurista Julio Oyhanarte, para quien el artículo 40 instauraba un trato diferencial para la propiedad, entre los bienes de uso o consumo y los de los medios de producción: los primeros solo implicaban poder sobre la cosa propia, mientras que los segundos "atribuye poder sobre los hombres y las cosas de los demás". En esta última situación se justificaba la subordinación de la propiedad de los medios de producción al interés público determinado por el Estado.

Para dar cuenta de lo valioso de la afirmación de Oyhanarte hay que señalar, como bien lo hace Correas, el error frecuente entre los juristas quienes

> [...] confunden las relaciones entre los individuos con relaciones entre estos y los objetos inertes. Si hay algo que pueda ser una "relación de propiedad" tiene que ser una relación entre seres humanos, aun cuando sea con motivos de las cosas. Pero tratándose de normas, y el derecho es eso, no cabe hablar de relaciones entre seres humanos y cosas, solamente cabe hablar de relaciones entre seres humanos. Y esto es de la mayor importancia, pues una teoría de la propiedad requiere aprehender correctamente esto: la propiedad es una relación social.[142]

El "interés público" se nos aparece como un modo específico de desenvolvimiento de las relaciones sociales, con objetivos democráticos y nacionales para definir el vínculo con los medios de producción, sostenidos por la política del Estado.

El poder expropiatorio, que es una pieza del derecho público económico, tuvo recepción especial en el artículo 38 del texto de la reforma de 1949, en relación con el principio de igualdad ante las cargas públicas con el que debía regularse el costo monetario de esa función estatal. Esto explicaba que el régimen de expropiación de los servicios públicos que estaban en manos privadas se basara en una fórmula de indemnización que correspondía exclusivamente al derecho público constitucional, sustancialmente diferente a la protección brindada a la propiedad privada

142 Correas, Oscar, "La propiedad y las comunidades indígenas en México", en *Rev. Pueblos y Fronteras*, México, UNAM, 2008.

por el derecho patrimonial clásico. En el derecho privado, al otorgarle a la propiedad particular la condición de preexistente al Estado y por ende inviolable, la indemnización se medía tanto por el valor real del bien como por el lucro cesante que le causaba al propietario[143].

Oyhanarte también llegaba al punto de comparar el poder de expropiar por parte del Estado con el mandato constitucional de la liberación de esclavos (anterior artículo 15 de la Constitución de 1853) que, a su modo y en otro tiempo histórico, había sido también el ejercicio de un poder estatal de naturaleza similar.

En ocasión de brindar fundamento para la Ley 12.906 de represión de los monopolios (sancionada y publicada en el Boletín Oficial en febrero de 1947), Cooke vertió conceptos trascendentes para la función activa del Estado frente a los monopolios. Este caracterizaba al capital concentrado y extranjero como un rasgo propio del actual estadio del capitalismo mundial y a la vez como un grave riesgo para la soberanía nacional, lo que exigía un rol activo y planificado del Estado para la defensa de la economía nacional, con citas de Marx, Engels, Lenin, Roosevelt y Mannheim.

> Existe también un problema que afecta ya a la soberanía del Estado, porque al lado de las autoridades constituidas de acuerdo con las cartas constitucionales se forma el gobierno de los consorcios financieros, de los hombres de la banca, del comercio y la industria [...] que llegan a posesionarse del gobierno en defensa de sus intereses. (AP, p. 87)

143 Dice Oyhanarte: "La Constitución Nacional adopta el sistema de la Suprema Corte de Estados Unidos en orden a servicios públicos [...] Las empresas de servicios públicos cuentan con un capital que puede reducirse a una cifra monetaria determinada. Ese capital, conforme el artículo 40, es establecido según la fórmula del costo histórico o la inversión prudente y traduce lo que la empresa vale [...] por regla constitucional existe un concepto unitario de "valor" destinado a actuar como denominador común en la operación expropiatoria y en la regulación de las tarifas" ("La expropiación de las empresas y el artículo 40 de la Constitución Nacional", en *La Ley, T. II*, Buenos Aires, La Ley, 1951, pp. 60 y ss.). Esto coincide con lo que prescribía la Ley Mitre (L. 5.315/1907) que otorgaba privilegios aduaneros a los ferrocarriles ingleses y la "Federal Power Act" de 1935 en los EUA; aunque, es preciso señalarlo, en ambos casos en un sentido político conservador.

Pero esa defensa del interés nacional alcanza también a comprender los intereses sociales en juego en el interior de las relaciones sociales de nuestro país y su disputa por el destino nacional, ante lo cual el Estado no puede ser prescindente y utilizar las diferentes formas de acción. Por eso,

> Es necesario vigilar ese proceso de industrialización porque, por un lado, hay interesados en que este siga siendo un país agrícola ganadero exclusivamente y, por otro lado, hay interesados en que ese proceso industrial redunde en beneficio de pequeños grupos económicos. (AP, p. 90)
>
> Debe asegurarse la defensa de la industria contra las maniobras internas y externas. Deben adoptarse medidas diversas: regulación aduanera, reordenación del régimen impositivo, nacionalización de empresas de servicios públicos, confección de estadísticas que nos den una noción exacta y al día de nuestra economía, y al mismo tiempo nos informen del grado de desarrollo que tiene la tendencia hacia la concentración monopolista en cada industria [...] Hay que hacer una planificación para la libertad.

El tratamiento completo de normas antimonopolistas exige el debate sobre la viabilidad del desarrollo capitalista en nuestros países dependientes. De ahí que Cooke reivindicara la posibilidad de la libre concurrencia capitalista, pero con la aclaración de que no lo hacía desde "el viejo concepto de liberalismo sin restricciones" sino del "bien social como fin de la economía del Estado" (AP, p. 92). Esto solo puede ser interpretado como la imposibilidad para una economía de dependencia de alcanzar un desarrollo capitalista de mercado, debiendo hacerlo bajo la forma de un capitalismo de Estado. Por eso aseguraba con firmeza que "el libre juego de la oferta y la demanda no es libre ni es juego". En otras palabras, la burguesía nacional en un país semicolonial, al verse imposibilitada ante la expansión de la fuerza poderosa del capital financiero de la banca internacional, no es nacional ni es burguesía. En su lugar solo puede estar el Estado en representación de los intereses

populares. Con el tiempo, Cooke radicalizaría su posición en búsqueda de formas directamente socialistas.

El rol transformador del Banco Central y el sistema financiero nacionalizado

Desde el preámbulo se declara el valor constituyente que significa la "independencia económica y la soberanía política", mientras que en el artículo 68 inciso 5, entre las atribuciones del Congreso, se establecía la de legislar sobre el régimen bancario, el crédito y la emisión de moneda, y que "en ningún caso los organismos correspondientes podrán ser entidades mixtas o particulares", con lo que se buscaba evitar la injerencia extranjera en este área vital de la economía. Se buscó dar sustento a la política oficial de nacionalización del sistema financiero. Recordemos que en el artículo 40 se establecía la autorización constitucional para estatizar el comercio externo. Arturo Sampay lo definía como "el único dispositivo que se posee para defender la economía del país" porque se trata de evitar caer "en el comercio internacional explotador, en el de la libertad de los países imperialistas para esquilmar a los países coloniales [...]". Sampay recurrió, para justificar, a un acontecimiento de la historia cercano a la época:

> Hipólito Yrigoyen, pocos meses antes de su derrocamiento, decía que "el subsuelo mineral de la República no puede ni debe ser objeto de otras explotaciones que las de la Nación misma", y cuya deposición, que impidió sancionar la ley que nacionalizaba el petróleo, –según anota Waldo Frank, testigo del 6 de septiembre–, fue festejada "por los ricos terratenientes sacando de sus bodegas el champaña de las mejores vendimias para acompañar el menú de los petroleros americanos".

En 1946, el presidente Farrell había sancionado, a instancias de Perón quien ya era presidente electo, el Decreto-Ley 8.503[144] de nacionalización del Banco Central. Se enunciaban como objetivos "promover el desarrollo de la

144 El decreto fue ratificado por la Ley 12.962 sancionada por el Congreso Nacional en marzo de 1947, en una de las medidas iniciales del gobierno de Perón.

industria", "el mejoramiento de la producción agrícola", "alcanzar los más altos niveles de consumo", "orientar y planificar la economía, garantizando la estabilidad, el nivel de vida y el pleno empleo", "la intensificación racional de la capacidad productiva de la Nación", "expandir la economía" y "la elevación de la riqueza nacional". Y la conversión de una entidad mixta a una completamente estatal se fundamentó en que "el interés privado no constituye una garantía de coincidencia con las necesidades del interés general".

Al mismo tiempo se disponía que los establecimientos bancarios procedieran a registrar los depósitos y redescuentos a nombre del Banco Central de la República Argentina –por medio del Decreto-Ley 11.554/1946–. De este modo, se confería "a los bancos mandato legal para actuar como agentes directos del Banco Central de la República Argentina, con las responsabilidades y deberes propios de ese carácter" porque las funciones desempeñadas por el Banco Central "son fines propios del Estado". También se señalaba "que los depósitos bancarios son trabajo y ahorro del pueblo argentino" por lo que "deben cumplir los fines que les establezca el Banco Central", en ese momento bajo la órbita del poder público. Porque, como la misma norma decía, es claro que recibir fondos que la población depositaba en los bancos era en verdad un privilegio a conceder bajo severas condiciones de vigilancia y contralor ejercida por el Estado, "como intérprete del interés general de la colectividad".

En septiembre de 1949 se promulgó la Ley 13.571 de reforma de la organización bancaria del país, del Banco Central y los bancos particulares, la que en buena medida fue reglamentación del nuevo artículo 40. Allí se estableció que el Banco Central tendría por objeto

> [...] concentrar y movilizar reservas y ejercer el control de los cambios, para moderar los efectos que sobre el valor de la moneda y la actividad económica puedan tener las fluctuaciones del comercio exterior y los movimientos internacionales de capitales y su inversión, y efectuar la regulación del crédito y de los medios de pago a fin de crear condiciones que permitan mantener un alto grado de ocupación y el poder adquisitivo de la moneda [...].

Luego de la reforma constitucional se consolidó la política activa del Estado en la economía, por medio de la culminación del proceso de regulación y control público sobre el Banco Central y el sistema financiero, en otras palabras, su nacionalización. En oportunidad de presentarse el proyecto de ley en el Congreso Nacional, el ministro de hacienda Ramón Cereijo expuso los motivos principales de la normativa que venía a dar formas jurídicas definitivas al programa de gobierno hasta entonces realizado:

> [...] que el programa se realizara mediante un amplio proceso crediticio y la utilización de las reservas metálicas para capitalizar el país. El Estado cuenta hoy con el control de los ferrocarriles y de los buques que lo colocan en favorables condiciones, con líneas abundantes de aviones comerciales y otras tantas inversiones o participaciones que le permiten intervenir en la dirección y promoción económica nacional [...] Abarca un programa amplísimo que puede encuadrarse en estos mojones fundamentales: empleo, planificación, estabilidad económica y elevación del nivel de vida. Es que el gobierno del General Perón, en su propósito profundamente ético de transformar una economía capitalista en una economía social informada de un contenido hondamente humano, consideró que la moneda y el crédito constituyen, en realidad, el medio más eficaz de realizar los objetivos de la política económica [...].

La reforma legal previó la creación de un departamento de Estado encargado primordialmente del control monetario y cambiario, lo que fue consecuencia de las facultades que la nueva Constitución Nacional en su artículo 83 inciso 13 le otorgaba al Poder Ejecutivo en ese sentido. Junto con la consagración normativa de vincular la política monetaria, cambiaria y crediticia a la planificación económica del Estado, se regulaba acerca del uso de las reservas del Banco Central, porque la política económica

> [...] tiende a buscar un respaldo muy superior que el de un montón de oro apilado en los sótanos de un banco o en las entrañas de la tierra. El respaldo económico de nuestra estructura económica lo

> hemos buscado en la potencialidad de nuestro pueblo y de nuestra propia riqueza; en la ocupación total de nuestros brazos y en el incremento positivo y consolidado de nuestra renta nacional.

Esa formación de enormes saldos no era otra cosa que el proceso de fuerte acumulación de capital promovida por el peronismo, base para financiar la política de nacionalización de la economía con aumento del patrimonio público (estatización de empresas de capital extranjero, compra de barcos mercantes, etc.) y la repatriación de deuda. Hasta entonces la regla vigente seguía siendo una relación rígida entre el nivel de las reservas y el volumen de moneda en circulación y obligaciones a la vista del Banco Central. Ahora era necesario que

> [...] esa norma rígida sea substituida por una política de utilización de las reservas de oro y divisas de que disponga el país, formulada en atención a las necesidades presentes y futuras de la Argentina con respecto a sus adquisiciones en el exterior.

En definitiva se trataba de alejar definitivamente al Banco Central de la fórmula adoptada en 1935, en la que primaba el criterio de la protección del capital extranjero y especulativo, porque,

> [...] la permanente preocupación del Banco Central por mantener la liquidez bancaria, lo desvió del que debió constituir su objetivo fundamental: promover el desarrollo industrial del país mediante el recurso del crédito a largo plazo, dejando sin resolver este importante problema. Desde luego no podía esperarse que los hombres que entonces actuaban y sobre los que privaba la opinión de los asesores foráneos, tomaran decisiones que pudieran afectar los intereses de una de las principales potencias industriales de entonces.

Lo significativo de esta fundamentación consiste en la formación de una conciencia nacional sobre la base de la producción industrial y

agropecuaria, por un lado, y las funciones financieras (de crédito, cambio y moneda) por otro, con la finalidad de alcanzar una ocupación laboral plena y una justa redistribución de la riqueza social. Esta unidad de acción es el sentido nacional de la política del Estado. Resurgía, un siglo después, la senda abierta por Manuel Belgrano y Mariano Fragueiro.

Por su cuenta, John William Cooke sostenía la defensa del interés nacional como fundamento del rol activo del Estado porque:

> Somos un país de economía semicolonial, dirigida desde el extranjero y campo propicio para el juego de todos los monopolios. Frente a ello, ¿qué puede hacer el Estado? ¿Cruzarse de brazos y esperar que empiecen a actuar los famosos automatismos reguladores, último bastión de los defensores del libre cambio? (AP, p.101)

La función de emitir moneda y la política crediticia fueron atributos esenciales de la soberanía nacional, la que no podía estar

> librada al beneplácito de quienes están investidos de la facultad de conceder los créditos. Es necesario que exista una doble fiscalización y que el Estado esté en condiciones de realizar una verdadera política, es decir, dar orientaciones, señalar derroteros, evitando que el capital disponible vaya a incidir en el aumento de la inflación, en vez de crear riqueza. (AP, p. 108)

Se trataba de crear formas jurídicas hábiles para la protección de la capacidad de hacer daño del capital financiero extranjero, a través del traslado de las crisis de los países centrales a los periféricos, por eso decía Cooke:

> La única manera de realizar política anticíclica es por medio de la nacionalización de los depósitos, que permite al Estado revertir sobre el mercado los fondos en momentos de depresión y restringir los créditos cuando el proceso inflacionista se acentúa. (AP, p. 109)

La búsqueda de la soberanía económica era el sentido de la defensa de la repatriación de la deuda externa, por la ventaja de que "los servicios

no serán pagados en el extranjero" (AP, p. 111). Se había disminuido la tasa de interés y aumentado el plazo. Era una medida antiinflacionaria porque al "emitirse el empréstito para rescatar la deuda externa se han absorbido del mercado una serie de fondos que estaban gravitando en la inflación". (AP, p. 112)

> La deuda externa ha sido fomentada por los países de penetración imperialista en nuestro continente, porque muchos gobiernos endeudados han sido arcilla en manos de los fuertes consorcios internacionales". (AP, p. 112)

El artículo 40 y el antecedente de la Constitución de México

Para confirmar una vez más la concepción nacional latinoamericana que debe inspirar al constitucionalismo, no podemos dejar de mencionar que el artículo 40 encontró un antecedente importante en el artículo 27 de la Constitución de México. En 1917, como consecuencia de la larga revolución desatada en ese país, una coalición de diferentes sectores sociales y grupos se dieron cita en la ciudad de Querétaro durante la presidencia de Venustiano Carranza, para dar forma a una nueva organización nacional y atender las exigencias sociales de las rebeliones populares. Algunas de las normas fundamentales están en aquel artículo, en el que se declaraba que la tierra pertenecía a la nación y que existían diferentes formas de propiedad que limitaban sustancialmente a la privada. También se estableció el dominio imprescriptible de la nación sobre el subsuelo, los minerales y el petróleo.

Una trascripción apretada de algunas partes relevantes es la siguiente:

> La propiedad de las tierras y aguas comprendidas dentro de los límites del territorio nacional corresponde originariamente a la Nación, la cual ha tenido y tiene el derecho de transmitir el dominio de ellas a los particulares constituyendo la propiedad privada. Las expropiaciones solo podrán hacerse por causa de utilidad pública y mediante indemnización [...] Corresponde a la Nación

el dominio directo de todos los minerales [...] los combustibles minerales sólidos; el petróleo y todos los carburos de hidrógeno sólidos, líquidos o gaseosos [...] [que] La Nación tendrá en todo tiempo el derecho de imponer a la propiedad privada las modalidades que dicte el interés público, así como el de regular el aprovechamiento de los elementos naturales susceptibles de apropiación, para hacer una distribución equitativa de la riqueza pública y para cuidar de su conservación. Con este objeto se dictarán las medidas necesarias para el fraccionamiento de los latifundios; para el desarrollo de la pequeña propiedad [...] [que] los pueblos, rancherías y comunidades que carezcan de tierras y aguas o no las tengan en cantidad suficiente para las necesidades de su población tendrán derecho a que se les dote de ellas, tomándolas de las propiedades inmediatas, respetando siempre la pequeña propiedad [...] [que] solo los mexicanos por nacimiento o por naturalización y las sociedades mexicanas tienen derecho para adquirir el dominio de las tierras, aguas y sus accesiones, o para obtener concesiones de explotación de minas, aguas o combustibles minerales [...] [que] las asociaciones religiosas denominadas Iglesias, cualquiera que sea su credo, no podrán en ningún caso tener capacidad para adquirir, poseer o administrar bienes raíces, ni capitales impuestos sobre ellos; los que tuvieren actualmente, por sí o por interpósita persona, entrarán al dominio de la Nación, concediéndose acción popular para denunciar los bienes que se hallaren en tal caso [...] [que] se declaran revisables todos los contratos y concesiones hechos por los gobiernos anteriores desde el año de 1876, que hayan traído por consecuencia el acaparamiento de tierras, aguas y riquezas naturales de la Nación por una sola persona o sociedad, y se faculta al Ejecutivo de la Unión para declararlos nulos, cuando impliquen perjuicios graves para el interés público.

Esta normativa puede ser considerada aún hoy, de carácter emancipatorio. También en el artículo 123 se consignaban los derechos sociales y de los trabajadores, como la jornada de ocho horas, el salario mínimo, el derecho a la asociación sindical, a la huelga, a la indemnización en caso de despido injustificado, entre otros. En su letra se puede leer:

"Las huelgas serán lícitas cuando tengan por objeto conseguir el equilibrio entre los diversos factores de la producción, armonizando los derechos del trabajo con los del capital."

Unos años después, con la presidencia de Lázaro Cárdenas (1934-1940), los mexicanos vieron cumplido, en gran medida, el mandato constitucional, tanto en cuanto a la reforma agraria prometida como a la nacionalización de las empresas petroleras en 1938. Su base legal era el señalado artículo 27 constitucional, sustentado en las luchas sindicales y populares.

En México aún el artículo 27 está vigente, pero con importantes reformas introducidas en 1992 por el entonces presidente Carlos Salinas de Gortari[145]. Con ellas se autorizó a dividir los ejidos en parcelas individuales con derecho a venderlas, y así se promovió el negocio inmobiliario y la concentración de tierras, con las consecuentes pérdidas de los derechos de campesinos e indígenas. Ello facilitó el ingreso del país al Tratado de Libre Comercio de América del Norte el 1º de enero de 1994, fecha en la que también, levantando las banderas de la revolución mexicana y, entre ellas, las del artículo 27 constitucional, se sublevó el Ejército Zapatista de Liberación Nacional[146].

Finalmente, con la misma mirada latinoamericana, hay que destacar que el artículo 40 de la reforma constitucional argentina de 1949 ha servido de inspiración para reformas realizadas en Uruguay (1967) y Chile (1971)[147]. La ley de reforma de la Constitución en Chile decía:

145 Las reformas introducidas por el neoliberalismo de Salinas de Gortari fueron denominadas por un académico mexicano, como "el regreso enmascarado de Pedro Páramo" (Berumen, Arturo Campos, en *Crítica Jurídica, nro. 16*, México, 1995.

146 Brom, Juan, *Esbozo de Historia de México*, México, Grijalbo, 1998.

147 Centro de Estudios Políticos Simón Bolívar y Fundación Presidente Allende (España), disponible en http://www.salvador-allende.cl/Documentos/1970-73/proyecto_constitucion.pdf.

> El Estado tiene el dominio absoluto, exclusivo, inalienable e imprescriptible de todas las minas, las covaderas, las arenas metalíferas, los salares, los depósitos de carbón e hidrocarburos y demás sustancias fósiles, con excepción de las arcillas superficiales [...].

También se destaca *Un Estado democrático y soberano: Mi propuesta a los chilenos* (texto póstumo) de Salvador Allende, base de la reforma de la Constitución política que propuso y sometió a plebiscito en 1973, interrumpida por el golpe de Estado proimperialista.

El derecho de la propiedad y su función social

El artículo 38 establecía:

> La propiedad privada tiene una función social y, en consecuencia, estará sometida a las obligaciones que establezca la ley con fines de bien común. Incumbe al Estado fiscalizar la distribución y la utilización del campo o intervenir con el objeto de desarrollar e incrementar su rendimiento en interés de la comunidad, y procurar a cada labriego o familia labriega la posibilidad de convertirse en propietario de la tierra que cultiva. La expropiación por causa de utilidad pública o interés general debe ser calificada por ley y previamente indemnizada. Solo el Congreso impone las contribuciones que se expresan en el artículo 4°. Todo autor o inventor es propietario exclusivo de su obra, invención o descubrimiento por el término que le acuerda la ley. La confiscación de bienes queda abolida para siempre de la legislación argentina. Ningún cuerpo armado puede hacer requisiciones ni exigir auxilios de ninguna especie en tiempo de paz.

Mientras el artículo 39 establecía lo siguiente:

> El capital debe estar al servicio de la economía nacional y tener como principal objeto el bienestar social. Sus diversas formas de explotación no pueden contrariar los fines de beneficio común del pueblo argentino.

Esta norma se vincula con el artículo 26 cuya letra respeta el anterior artículo 17 en cuanto al derecho de usar y disponer de la propiedad pero, a diferencia de este, agrega como causa de expropiación por utilidad pública el concepto de "interés general"[148].

La concepción de la función social de la propiedad, y en especial los límites a un ejercicio absoluto del poder privado, encontró antecedente en la tradición hispánica de raíz medieval, trasladada a los territorios de ultramar[149]. En ella, los límites del poder central a la propiedad privada operaban como valla contra el desafío de un capitalismo en ascenso. Luego, en las luchas emancipadoras de principio del siglo XIX, el mismo concepto adquirió un sentido plebeyo al ser puesto al servicio de la búsqueda de la igualdad social, en especial en la política ensayada por Artigas con el Reglamento de 1815[150]. También estuvo presente en el Plan de Operaciones de la Primera Junta de 1810, de Mariano Moreno, y en la actuación política

148 En el anteproyecto aprobado por el Consejo Superior del Partido Peronista y presentado al Congreso de la Nación, establecía una descripción levemente diferente, en el artículo 20 que decía: "La Nación garantiza la propiedad como función social y, en consecuencia, la misma estará sometida a las contribuciones, restricciones y obligaciones que establezca la ley con fines de utilidad general. Asimismo, se adoptarán las medidas necesarias para el fraccionamiento de los latifundios; para el desarrollo de la pequeña propiedad agrícola en explotación; para la creación de nuevos centros de población con las tierras y aguas que les sean indispensables y para el fomento agrícola ganadero". Presidencia de la Nación, La reforma de la Constitución Nacional sancionada por la Convención Nacional Constituyente el 11 de marzo de 1949, Buenos Aires, p. 147.

149 Un ejemplo del traslado a tierras americanas, lo explica María Victoria Daract (en http://bdigital.uncu.edu.ar/objetos_digitales/1509/ramellainforme07.pdf) cuando señaló que para Ricardo Levene la repoblación de Buenos Aires por Garay en 1580 con la creación de lugares de uso común (huertas) indicó una forma de propiedad con función social: "[...] estos requisitos y otros como la confirmación real de las mercedes de tierras hechas por las autoridades de Indias, revelan el fundamento de la teoría jurídica que está en las leyes de Indias, inspiradas en el principio de que la propiedad privada de la tierra era considerada en los orígenes como una función social" (en *Manual de Historia del Derecho Argentino*, 4°edición, Buenos Aires, Depalma, 1969, p. 95).

150 Pomer, León, *Continuidades y rupturas. De la colonia a Mayo*, Buenos Aires, Colihue, 2012, p. 266

de San Martín en Cuyo (1814-1817). En el proceso de codificación de la segunda mitad del siglo XIX, los límites a la propiedad privada formaban parte de las atribuciones de los poderes públicos para diseñar las relaciones de producción en la organización definitiva de los países. En la nota al artículo 2508 del Código Civil, Vélez Sárfield señalaba limitaciones al derecho real de dominio por consideraciones del "interés general y colectivo, por sobre el interés individual". Lo mismo en los artículos 14 y 17 de la Constitución de 1853[151]. Ya en el siglo XX, el nacionalismo popular latinoamericano le dio a la función social de la propiedad un sentido antiimperialista[152].

Arturo Sampay, con tono iusnaturalista, la fundamentaba en la misma Asamblea Constituyente de este modo:

> El hombre no está solo en la tierra, sino que, por su propia naturaleza, está vinculado y depende de sus semejantes, por lo que no se le es dado cumplir su destino sin el concurso de la comunidad que lo circunda y que le ayuda a alcanzar su fin personal; además, cada uno de sus semejantes tiene derecho a sustentarse con los bienes exteriores, de donde resulta que, en el orden natural de las cosas, tiene prioridad el derecho de todos al uso de los bienes materiales sobre el derecho a la apropiación privada, instituida solamente en razón de la utilidad que presta en la vida social.
>
> Se deriva así que la propiedad privada –no obstante conservar su carácter individual– asume una doble función: personal y social; personal, en cuanto tiene como fundamento la exigencia de que se garantice la libertad y afirmación de la persona; social, en cuanto esa afirmación no es posible fuera de la sociedad, sin el concurso de la comunidad que la sobrelleva, y en cuanto es previa la destinación de los bienes exteriores en provecho de todos los hombres [...] A ello se debe que la reforma constitucional consagre, junto a la

151 Ver De Franchini, María Florencia, *Función social de la propiedad en la legislación argentina*, La Plata: UNLP, 2005, pp. 36, 214.

152 En la época adquiría una perspectiva latinoamericana, con las Constituciones de Bolivia, art. 17 (1947), Ecuador, art. 183 (1946), Panamá, art. 45 (1946), o Perú, arts. 207 a 212, (1947).

> garantía de la función personal de la propiedad, la obligatoriedad de la función social que le incumbe –ya legalmente consagrada en el país por la ley de transformación agraria–, y que haga de esta institución la piedra sillar del nuevo orden económico argentino.

Para el convencional Valenzuela, en representación del bloque de la mayoría, se trataba de una modificación conceptual de la propiedad privada en línea con la economía social:

> El pueblo ha hecho ya el proceso del liberalismo y de los males económicos, que son su consecuencia. Al analizar el nuevo concepto que se propone para la propiedad privada [...] queremos suprimir la economía capitalista de explotación, reemplazándola por una economía social en la que no haya ni explotadores ni explotados y donde cada uno reciba la retribución justa de su capacidad y de su esfuerzo.

Nótese que el objetivo declarado no era abolir la propiedad privada, sino crear un nuevo concepto, de acuerdo con un principio al que, ella, debía subordinarse: la justicia social[153]. Es sugerente también el enunciado de la utopía de avanzar hacia una sociedad sin "explotadores ni explotados". El mismo legislador Valenzuela continuó con lo siguiente:

> El capital debe estar al servicio de la economía y no como hasta ahora ha sucedido, que nuestra economía ha estado al servicio del

153 De modo distinto el constitucionalista Rafael Bielsa opinaba que "Hay garantías fundamentales que implican la atribución directa de derechos subjetivos, como la relativa al derecho de propiedad establecido en la Constitución de 1853, que es oponible a los demás y al propio Estado. En la reciente reforma se ha intercalado una cláusula según la cual "la propiedad privada tiene una función social y estará sometida las obligaciones que establezca la ley con fines de bien común (art. 38)".. Esta disposición nada agrega, pues bajo la égida de la Constitución anterior, tanto la legislación como la jurisprudencia han concebido la propiedad como un derecho compatible con las limitaciones en el interés público, como lo hemos demostrado en una monografía escrita hace más de treinta años (por referencia a "Limitaciones impuestas a la propiedad en interés público" de 1923), en *La Ley, T. 75*, "La cuestión de las jurisdicciones especiales", Buenos Aires, septiembre de 1954, pp. 797 y ss..

> capitalismo internacional [...] el individualismo así practicado forja una sociedad de egoístas y desalmados que solo piensan en enriquecerse, aunque para ello sea necesario hacerlo sobre el hambre, la miseria y la desesperanza de millones de hermanos de la clase menos favorecida por la fortuna.

Luego, con cita de Harold Laski, dijo:

> El dominio de los ricos, bien sea de los terratenientes o de los que poseen capital industrial, se ha consagrado primero a la acumulación de riquezas y después a impedir su difusión. El carácter de la vida social y por consiguiente el carácter del Estado, se determina, sobre todo, por su división en un número reducido de personas ricas y un vasto número de individuos que viven al margen de la subsistencia [...] [así las cosas] el orden es la salvaguardia de los menos frente a la demanda de los demás por una vida más digna y halagüeña.[154]

Una buena síntesis podría ser:

> El artículo 39 fija claramente cuál ha de ser en adelante el papel del capital. No puede ser ya factor de explotación inhumana e injusta, sino tener por principal objeto el bienestar social. Lo que se busca es la humanización del capital: se lo convierte, de instrumento de dominación económica, en factor de colaboración con el trabajo, para alcanzar la felicidad de los más" (palabras de Valenzuela).

Scalabrini Ortiz explicaba que:

> [...] el capital es un ente de por sí incorpóreo, una entelequia, una voluntad de poder que necesita un cuerpo, un punto de aplicación para actuar y operar y esa es la propiedad. Y por eso la propiedad fue protegida con los mayores recaudos que pudieron argüirse.

154 Nacido en Manchester, Inglaterra, en 1893. Laski fue un influyente intelectual que llegó a liderar el Partido Laborista en 1945. Fundó el Left Book Club, dedicado a la difusión de ideas socialistas y a resistir el fascismo en su país. Falleció en 1950.

La Corte Suprema avaló la función social de la propiedad en los términos establecidos, como en el caso "Comercial Staudt" de 1954[155], que limitó la autonomía de la voluntad establecida en el artículo 1.197 del Código Civil sobre la base de aquel y en el principio de abuso del derecho.

La función social de la propiedad, una vez consagrada en la Constitución, fue fundamento de legislación posterior. Una de ellas fue la Ley 13.581 de locación de inmuebles de propiedad privada de octubre de 1949, por la que se declaraba a esta actividad subordinada a la función social de la propiedad. Según las sesiones de debate, se trataba de un criterio de interpretación general derivado del artículo 38 de la Constitución en relación al acceso a la vivienda. En sus disposiciones principales se establecía la obligatoriedad de denunciar por parte de los propietarios las viviendas deshabitadas, para que en un término determinado la arrendaran. También se autorizaba a hacerlo por cuenta del propietario, al Poder Ejecutivo Nacional o Provincial, quien tomaba posesión del inmueble a tal fin. En esta cuestión se revelaba discursivamente la filosofía que inspiraba al peronismo cuando se invocaba el artículo 37 punto 3 de la Constitución Nacional reformada, que obligaba a garantizar el "bien de familia".

> Nuestro fin ulterior es la consecución de una casa habitación en propiedad para cada familia argentina. Entendemos este principio como fundamental para la estructuración definitiva de la sociedad argentina ya que la consecución de este fin será la valla insalvable contra las doctrinas colectivistas que postulan la destrucción de la unidad familiar como basamento del Estado [...] Ni el nomadismo primitivo ni la colectivización de la colmena. La casa familiar, centro de todos los afectos nobles que da el sello definitivo de toda personalidad.

En 1950 se dictó la Ley 13.995, en donde se establecía el deber del Poder Ejecutivo Nacional de promover "el cumplimiento de la función social de la tierra fiscal, mediante su arrendamiento y enajenación en forma progresiva

155 Fallos de la Corte Suprema de Justicia Nacional (CSJN) 229: 368 (1954).

y orgánica, a favor de los auténticos trabajadores del campo", complementada por la Ley 14.392, cuyo objeto era la facilitación de tierras a trabajadores agrarios para su colonización a cargo del Banco de la Nación Argentina. Ambas fueron derogadas por decretos leyes de dictaduras: la primera en 1956, y la segunda en 1980 con la firma de Videla y Martínez de Hoz.

Con anterioridad a la reforma constitucional, en agosto de 1946, el Congreso Nacional había dictado una importante norma contra la suba de precios (Ley12.591, modificada por la Ley 12.830), por la cual se le otorgaban al Poder Ejecutivo Nacional las atribuciones necesarias para la regulación principalmente de los precios máximos de las materias primas, manufacturas, locaciones de obra y productos de consumo de diferente naturaleza. La norma le daba amplias facultades para ejercer el poder de policía en todo el país, aunque especialmente en Capital Federal y el Gran Buenos Aires, a incautar y secuestrar bienes, suspender patentes y permisos, congelar precios, fijar remuneraciones, obligar a fabricar determinados productos dentro del sistema de cuota mínima, a declarar de utilidad pública y sujetos a expropiación las mercaderías, productos y materias primas necesarias para su elaboración. También facultaba al presidente de la nación y a los gobernadores de provincia y territorio a tomar posesión de las mercaderías expropiadas previa consignación judicial del precio de costo y una indemnización del 10% para las materias primas y hasta el precio máximo fijado por la ley. Incluso lo facultaba a organizar comisiones populares a fin de cooperar con las autoridades administrativas. A partir de 1949, se delegó la facultad de intervención en la Dirección Nacional de Vigilancia de Precios y Abastecimiento.

Esta normativa constituyó un instrumento de actuación estatal de importante valor para el control de precios y para mantener el nivel del poder adquisitivo de los ingresos y la estabilidad económica general. Su sustento constitucional lo encontraba en la atribución del Congreso Nacional de "proveer lo conducente a la prosperidad, al adelanto y bienestar de todas las provincias", lo que autorizaba a delegar las facultades

del poder de policía en la nación[156]. Pero también es evidente su apoyatura legal en el principio de la función social de la propiedad, dado que, como decía el artículo 39 de la reforma constitucional, las "diversas formas de explotación (del capital) no pueden contrariar los fines de beneficio común del pueblo argentino".

Esta norma fue antecedente de la Ley 16.454 de Abastecimiento bajo la presidencia de Arturo Illia, y de la Ley 20.680 del 24 de junio de 1974 –actualmente vigente– que otorga amplias atribuciones al Estado para proteger el orden público económico nacional contra el agio y la especulación. Toda esa normativa establecía diferentes instrumentos y facultades cuyo ejercicio por parte del Estado posibilitaba el despliegue de una política autónoma de los monopolios y poderes económicos concentrados, en protección de la producción local, el empleo, el ingreso y el mercado interno.

Como se señaló anteriormente, el capital y el derecho a la propiedad son modos específicos de una relación social, concreta e histórica, que justamente se mantiene oculta en el enunciado jurídico. Por lo que no existe a ciencia cierta un único significado de la "función social de la propiedad" –aunque sí es clara la definición utilizada por los constituyentes en 1949–, sino que ella adquiere diversos contenidos en la medida de la naturaleza del proyecto histórico del cual es expresión; o, en otras palabras, de las relaciones sociales de las que es portadora. Puede ser, entonces, motor de las relaciones capitalistas industriales y de servicio, y por ende de un empresariado mercadointernista, en la medida en que es fundamento de normas antimonopolio que procuran la competencia –aspecto nacional burgués o desarrollista–, o bien de una posición antiimperialista, y por ende producto de la alianza policlasista antioligárquica en el Estado, si se trata de nacionalizar la economía frente a los capitales extranjeros –aspecto nacional popular y antiimperialista–. La reforma constitucional de 1949 habilitaba ambos sentidos, la legislación que la sustituyó no.

156 La CSJN en el caso Lares, Gabino Alberto del 10/04/1959, en ocasión de juzgar en un caso ocurrido en 1953, afirmó la constitucionalidad de las leyes contra el agio con base en esos argumentos. *Revista Jurisprudencia Argentina, III*, 1959, pp. 527 y ss..

En oportunidad de darse el debate sobre el plan quinquenal (47-51) de las sesiones del 27 y 28 de marzo de 1947, Cooke tomaba posición acerca del librecambismo porque "el libre juego de la demanda no es libre ni es juego":

> El siglo XIX marca la muerte del liberalismo y lo marca en lo conceptual con las ideas de List, pero sobre todo en la realidad de los hechos económicos, con el proceso de concentración de capitales que viene a dar plena ratificación a las teorías que combaten el sistema de libre cambio.
>
> Voy a establecer la necesidad de la intervención estatal provocada por el fracaso del libre cambio, cuyos factores actúan en contra, por medio del crecimiento de las organizaciones monopolísticas que engendrara la revolución industrial.

Tras aclarar –a mi juicio en forma innecesaria– que "aunque no se acepten sus conclusiones es evidente que el análisis es certero", afirma: "Marx no alcanza a contemplar el pleno florecimiento del monopolio, pero lo intuye, lo ve en su nacimiento y acierta en sus predicciones". (AP, p.146)

Y con cita de Lenin, dice:

> El capitalismo ha de encontrar en última instancia su forma de actuación, por medio del imperialismo. El imperialismo, consecuencia del capitalismo, encierra en sí sus contradicciones, como las llama él, que son el germen de su propia muerte y constituye su última etapa. (AP, p. 147)

Y de este análisis extrae la siguiente conclusión:

> [...] es preciso que nuestros sistemas económicos, sin llegar a la socialización, encuentren en sí mismos las formas que les permitan cumplir los fines sociales del Estado, sin que ello constituya un desmedro para los fueros de la personalidad humana.

Con esto, Cooke hacía un aporte fundamental para la realización de la soberanía nacional, con un análisis marxista para la construcción de la comunidad organizada. Vamos a creerle a Cooke, por ahora, cuando decía

que no era marxista, aunque compartiera la interpretación de la realidad de Marx, y aunque bien visto, ya de jovencito se pareciera bastante al viejo Bebe, al que desde Cuba anhelaba la llegada del socialismo.

De todas maneras, lo importante es, como decíamos al principio, el fundamento del rol activo del Estado para conducir la economía, en crítica al liberalismo conservador propio de orden oligárquico y dependiente. Por eso en ese entonces Cooke insistía:

> La función del Estado moderno es de carácter dinámico como elemento de coordinación de los factores económicos y redistribuidor de la riqueza, debiendo estimular las inversiones tendientes al cumplimiento de los fines sociales del Estado, incrementar la producción y fomentar la elevación de los niveles de vida de la población. Ya no puede discutirse la necesidad de una planificación [...] la única perspectiva que le queda a la democracia, de salvarse. (AP, p. 150)

Ese rol era "la función social del Estado", como le llamó Cooke.

La naturaleza de la propiedad empresarial

Sampay alguna vez describió a la naturaleza de la propiedad de las grandes empresas monopólicas como "comunidades públicas de inversión, trabajo, producción y distribución"[157], cuya fuente de financiamiento es, principalmente, el ahorro del pueblo a través de bancos y bolsas, mediante la utilización de la fuerza de trabajo de masas de obreros, técnicos y profesionales, y la capacidad de consumo de la población. En virtud de ello, tienen una naturaleza de bien colectivo a partir de la cual merecen una nueva regulación distinta a la establecida en los artículos 14 y 17 de la Constitución, cuya protección alcanza a la propiedad individual y a la indemnización del valor absoluto del bien sin considerar ese aspecto colectivo y social.

157 En *Constitución y Pueblo*, Buenos Aires, Instituto Superior Arturo Jauretche, 2011, p. 201 y ss..

Ante esta cuestión jurídica, Sampay daba una respuesta audaz y contundente: la nacionalización de los grandes monopolios con el fin del desarrollo económico y un procedimiento de indemnización a largo plazo. El cálculo monetario compensatorio, según Sampay, se practicaría utilizando como base el precio de origen del bien de la empresa, menos todo aquello de pertenencia a la comunidad a saber: la amortización del capital fijo, las ganancias usurarias y la falta de reinversión productiva.

Sampay incluso fundamentaba su propuesta en el preámbulo del texto constitucional de 1853, por el cual el ejercicio de los derechos individuales se subordinaba al fin supremo de promover el bienestar general (el polo axiológico de la Constitución). En definitiva, Sampay afirmaba que la protección constitucional dispensada a la propiedad privada prevista en los artículos 14 y 17 de la Constitución de 1853, no tenía como destino a la de las empresas concentradas y monopólicas[158]. Lo cual, además, es razonable, a poco que se medite en que los convencionales de entonces no pudieron nunca haber tenido en mente la protección de fenómenos sociales que todavía no habían ocurrido, como lo fue, justamente, la concentración de capital en los grandes monopolios y las empresas multinacionales.

2) El sistema político de protagonismo popular sobre la base de la democracia social

El fin del fraude con las elecciones libres de 1945 y la aparición del liderazgo de Juan Perón, como representante de los anhelos y reclamos de mayorías, constituyó un aspecto vital para el surgimiento de la democracia después del largo período de la década infame. Con la inclusión del electorado femenino tuvo lugar un sustancial aumento en la cantidad y calidad de la representación política, y la reforma de 1949 incluyó la

158 Como reverso, la Comisión de juristas convocada para el estudio de la reforma constitucional, por la Junta de Comandantes presidida por Lanusse en 1971, dictaminó que el alcance de la protección del texto de 1853 incluía a la propiedad de los grandes monopolios. He aquí, una vez más y como si a esta altura hiciera falta insistir, un ejemplo de diferentes interpretaciones al servicio de la protección de intereses sociales opuestos.

representación profesional como forma de organización que autorizaba y mejoraba la participación popular de los trabajadores. También en este aspecto hay que considerar la elección directa del presidente de la nación y la de los senadores, dado que esto último era el modo de eludir la posibilidad de retornar a los contubernios locales –reaseguro político del poder oligárquico– que, en su época, habían jaqueado a Yrigoyen.

La reelección presidencial

La autorización para la reelección del presidente de la nación y la del vice era clave desde el punto de vista político, en tanto significaba la posibilidad de darle continuidad al proceso de liberación nacional en marcha a través del voto libre de los electores, al mismo tiempo que receptaba la eventual voluntad de los electores de confirmar su opción[159].

Este punto merece un párrafo aparte. La experiencia histórica en nuestro continente indica que el avance de los movimientos nacionales populares, así como la posibilidad de realizaciones progresivas y reformas sociales de importancia, dependen en buena medida de la consolidación de un liderazgo político fuerte. Aun a riesgo de personalismos y construcciones verticales, las figuras fuertes no aparecen como una opción sino como una necesidad para aglutinar a su alrededor a una heterogeneidad de sectores sociales como base de sustento para la política nacional. Eso han significado en nuestro país Yrigoyen y Perón en el siglo XX, quienes han sufrido por igual la impugnación a sus liderazgos, bajo la equívoca etiqueta de autoritarismo en países como el nuestro, azotados por violentas y crueles dictaduras. La disputa en el terreno estrictamente constitucional se traslada a la posibilidad de la reelección presidencial, por eso el análisis de la cláusula de la reelección debe ser abordada desde la óptica del significado de la alternancia en el poder político.

159 Sampay opinaba que el fin era "la democratización de los modos de elegir los sujetos del poder político, pues ya no queda la elección indirecta ni para los senadores nacionales ni para el Presidente de la República [ya que es] indudable que un Presidente de la República con basamento democrático se constituya en el mejor defensor del orden constitucional".

La respuesta ensayada por Sampay fue su justificación por razones democráticas porque, señalaba, "si el pueblo elige a los sujetos del poder político es contradictorio que la constitución le impida hacerlo con determinada persona que llena las capacidades morales, ciudadanas e intelectuales exigidas como regla general"[160].

En nuestra opinión, la exigencia de la alternancia en el poder político como recaudo para garantizar una mayor participación y democracia podrá tener cierta validez y utilidad social en aquellas naciones en donde la totalidad de las instituciones responden a la defensa del interés nacional. Esto ocurre en los países poderosos cuyos proyectos nacionales están en expansión y el sistema de representación política muestra diferencias de matices en un consenso de postulados básicos. Entonces la alternancia no se da entre proyectos de nación –como sí ocurre en los países semicoloniales o dependientes–, sino más bien entre distintas formas partidarias de una misma política.

Pero en aquellos países de condición semicolonial donde la disputa política se tiñe de una reacción poderosa por parte de los intereses conservadores, como lo demuestran las reiteradas y prolongadas dictaduras militares, o la influencia del capital extranjero como causa de la atrofia económica, la alternancia es causa de debilidad del sistema político porque interrumpe la continuidad del liderazgo en el poder. Los motivos institucionales (la crítica al cesarismo) se convierten así en coartada para impedir la consolidación de la política nacional a través de la figura central en quien se proyectan los intereses del movimiento nacional.

El problema de la sucesión presidencial no radica entonces en la posibilidad de la alternancia –exigencia innecesaria y contraproducente–, sino en el riesgo de la representación de intereses económicos ajenos a la soberanía popular. Esto no lo resuelve la letra de la Constitución sino la realidad política. La emergencia de liderazgos fuertes que conduzcan los movimientos nacionales como vía de representación de los sectores populares es una característica de la vida política latinoamericana insoslayable al momento del análisis de constitucionalidad.

160 Sampay, Arturo Enrique, *Las Constituciones de la Argentina (1810-1972)*. Buenos Aires, EUDEBA, 1972, p. 514.

Pero esta cuestión no solo se presenta en Latinoamérica, también ha sido el caso de los Estados Unidos en alguna etapa de su historia reciente. Franklin Delano Roosevelt, una de las figuras políticas de mayor trascendencia en el siglo XX de ese país, fue elegido presidente de la nación cuatro veces consecutivas (1932, 1936, 1940 y 1944). En 1951 se aprobó la Enmienda XXII a la Constitución de los Estados Unidos para limitar a dos mandatos sucesivos el ejercicio de la presidencia.

El problema de la institucionalidad en nuestro país se revela con cierta claridad al comparar las convenciones constituyentes de 1949 y 1957. La primera fue hegemonizada por un solo partido (el peronista), al menos tras el retiro de la bancada radical, pero contó con indudable apoyo electoral previo. La segunda, en cambio, tuvo la participación de once partidos políticos pero el proceso electoral que le dio sustento fue realizado bajo la proscripción de la fuerza política mayoritaria. Como se ve, la institucionalidad solo puede ser entendida en términos de garantía de la participación popular de las mayorías nacionales.

El viejo orden conservador se había reformado con la importante Ley Sáenz Peña de 1912, y luego del golpe de Uriburu (1930) y los años de la década infame se encontraba definitivamente caduco e impotente ante el surgimiento del movimiento nacional. Este es el sentido político del artículo 77 de la reforma. En ocasión de expresar los fundamentos del proyecto de declaración de la necesidad de la reforma constitucional por él presentado, Cooke sentó su posición sobre la políticamente espinosa cuestión de la reelección presidencial. Antes citó la opinión contraria del propio interesado, es decir la de Perón, quien aducía razones de prudencia para evitar una "incitación a la violencia", al fraude o a "la tentación a la acción política por el gobierno". Y luego discrepó sobre la base de que la cláusula de no reelección no había servido en la práctica para evitar nada, ni el fraude, siendo además que "nuestro país ha sufrido una larga experiencia en materia de violación de los derechos de la soberanía popular". (AP, p. 234)

Los derechos de las mujeres

El voto femenino no integra el texto constitucional pero sin lugar a dudas merece ser mencionado por su importancia dentro de la estrategia de ampliación del derecho electoral y la participación popular. Una vez al frente de la Secretaría de Trabajo, Perón creó la División y Asistencia a la Mujer –receptora de esa larga lucha de las argentinas– desde donde se empezó a bregar por reformas legales. Desde 1871, por disposición del Código Civil (como ya mencionamos en otra parte, la norma fundamental que rigió las relaciones sociales y económicas durante el país oligárquico), las mujeres eran consideradas "incapaces" y recién en 1926, mediante la Ley 11.357, se dispuso formalmente la igualdad jurídica, aunque no incluía el derecho al voto ni la patria potestad compartida. El 23 de septiembre de 1947 se aprobó finalmente la Ley 13.010, y en noviembre de 1951 3.800.000 mujeres emitieron su sufragio: el 63% de ellas lo hizo por la fórmula peronista y el 30% por la de la UCR.

Pese a esto, las militantes feministas que tradicionalmente habían levantado sus reclamos se opusieron a la ley con el argumento de que "ahora no queremos votar". Evita vinculó expresamente el derecho al voto de las mujeres con el "despertar nacional", es decir la formación de la conciencia nacional que encontraba cauce político concreto en un reclamo democrático de género:

> En cuanto a la hostilidad oligárquica, no puedo menos que sonreírme. Y me pregunto: ¿por qué hubiese podido rechazarme la oligarquía? ¿Por mi origen humilde? ¿Por mi actividad artística? ¿Pero acaso alguna vez esa clase de gente tuvo en cuenta aquí o en cualquier parte del mundo, estas cosas, tratándose de la mujer de un presidente? Nunca la oligarquía fue hostil con nadie que pudiera serle útil. El poder y el dinero no tuvieron nunca malos antecedentes para un oligarca genuino [...] Pero además, yo no era solamente la esposa del Presidente de la República, era también la mujer del conductor de los argentinos.

La versión actualizada de hoy sería la vinculación de las reivindicaciones de género con los avances del proyecto nacional. El voto femenino era la dimensión política de la igualdad en el derecho de familia que consagraba la nueva Constitución con el ejercicio de la patria potestad y la igualación entre los cónyuges, así como también expresaba el reconocimiento profundo de las mujeres del interior del país que unos años atrás había irrumpido definitivamente en el escenario político de la nación[161]:

> Este siglo no pasará a la historia con el nombre de "Siglo de las Guerras Mundiales" ni acaso con el nombre de "Siglo de la Desintegración Atómica", sino con otro nombre mucho más significativo: "Siglo del feminismo victorioso". (Del mensaje a la mujer española de Eva Duarte de Perón, el 15 de junio de 1947)

La política de provincialización de territorios nacionales

El proyecto de nación encontró un punto de importancia en la creación de nuevas provincias. La provincialización de territorios nacionales fue el modo de integrar en una igualdad ciudadana a las poblaciones que, según la opinión de Pablo Ramella, se encontraban bajo un sistema de verdadero coloniaje.

161 Kogan, Hilda, "El Bicentenario: el rol de la mujer", en *La Ley*, Buenos Aires, 21 de mayo de 2010. Kogan señala que "los siglos XVIII y XIX encuentran a la mujer en una situación de total subordinación, que se trasluce en el temprano y desigual matrimonio y la Iglesia como único lugar permitido para interrelacionarse y apartarse de la reclusión hogareña. En esta etapa el trabajo femenino es prácticamente nulo, su ocupación radicaba en lo que los documentos de la época han denominado "trabajos mujeriles", los cuales consistían en costuras y granjerías [...] [y que] ese triunfo es tal vez el más decisivo en la historia de la mujer argentina. Significó comenzar a andar con pasos femeninos en el mundo democrático y adquirir influencia en su desarrollo. De todas formas, y no obstante haber obtenido una merecida conquista, también en el recorrido por ese camino fueron encontrados obstáculos que impedían un verdadero ingreso al parlamento, ya que eran excepcionales los casos en los que las mujeres lograban integrar las listas en lugares de orden que les permitieran ser electas para acceder a una banca. Por lo tanto, en la realidad de los hechos, y más allá del supuesto amparo dado a sus derechos cívicos, estaban apenas representadas".

Perón reformó la ley vigente desde 1884 y autorizó el derecho a voto de los habitantes de los territorios nacionales en 1951 y 1954 para, en 1955, haber dado rango de provincias a Chaco, La Pampa, Misiones, Río Negro, Neuquén, Formosa, Santa Cruz y Chubut. Mientras que Tierra del Fuego, Antártida e Islas del Atlántico Sur –el último territorio nacional del país– fueron provincializadas recién en 1990[162]. Según el censo nacional de 1947, los territorios nacionales tenían una población de más de un millón trescientos mil habitantes, lo que provocó un aumento en el padrón electoral de 1951. El padrón electoral de 1948 tenía 3.794.000 inscriptos, mientras el de 1951, tanto masculino como femenino, ya incluía a 8.634.000 inscriptos[163].

3) La soberanía nacional y antiimperialista

Ya mencionamos la concepción básica de la reforma constitucional: el individuo como parte integrante del pueblo al que pertenece, por lo que sus derechos y garantías individuales solo pueden tener vigencia en la medida de la fortaleza del proyecto nacional, entendido como la autodeterminación del pueblo, o "la tercera posición" en términos de la filosofía política del peronismo:

> La tercera posición arranca de un doble rechazo del demoliberalismo capitalista y del Estado totalitario. En consecuencia tiene también un objeto último diferenciado. En el liberalismo el objetivo es el ascenso de la sociedad mediante el éxito de los individuos más aptos. En el socialismo marxista, el desarrollo económico

162 En relación a la provincialización de Misiones, ver Pedranzini, Maximiliano, "La provincialización de Misiones Aportes críticos para una interpretación histórica (1919-1953)", en revista *Historia y Frontera, nro. 1*, 2013, www.historiayfrontera.org.

163 Según Pablo Ramella, su retraso "debilitó el cuerpo político de la Nación e hipertrofió el poder central", mientras que Arturo Frondizi, en 1951, dijo que "mantener esa diferencia hoy entre argentinos y argentinos, impedirles elegir sus gobernantes, votar sus impuestos, darse sus leyes y, negarles el derecho a enviar diputados es posición antirrepublicana, antidemocrática y antiargentina", en Freaza, Julián Francisco, "Misiones debe ser provincia por imperio de la constitución", en *Jurisprudencia Argentina 1953, T. II.*, 1953.

> integral. En la tercera posición el objetivo es la felicidad del hombre, como individuo, como familia, como comunidad.[164]

El 20 de mayo de 1947, la Oficina de Asuntos de las Repúblicas Americanas expresó su preocupación por "el peligro de que la Argentina aspire a organizar un bloque del Cono Sur, bajo la dominación política y económica argentina [...]"[165]. Juan Perón, el 6 de julio de 1947, había dado su mensaje para los pueblos del mundo. Allí reiteró su concepto de "elevar la cultura social, dignificar el trabajo y humanizar el capital, y, especialmente, reemplazar los sistemas de lucha por el de colaboración". Galasso concluye sobre el significado de la tercera posición:

> Con este planteo, en momentos en que la "guerra fría" divide a la humanidad en países capitalistas y países comunistas, la Argentina se coloca en una posición centrada en la paz y el mejoramiento económico de los países expoliados, como si fuera posible un ordenamiento social superador del egoísmo que impera en Estados Unidos y del colectivismo que impera en la URSS.

En una explicación más profunda, Galasso entiende que, en definitiva,

> [...] esa Tercera Posición es el traslado al campo internacional de la confluencia policlasista del campo nacional en que se sustenta el Gobierno y que, poco más tarde, será teorizada como comunidad organizada.[166]

Esto parece ser cierto a poco que se piensa que ninguno de los sectores concurrentes al frente nacional mostró adhesión absoluta a esos sistemas sociales, por lo que era un corolario de una fórmula superadora.

En similar sentido se ha destacado la aparición en el escenario internacional de la época de un "tercer Estado mixto", que era una forma de Estado

164 Salvador Ferla, *Revista Redacción*, febrero 1974, en http://www.elortiba.org/pdf/Salvador_Ferla_Tercera_Posicion.pdf.
165 Galasso, Norberto, *Perón, tomo I*, Buenos Aires, Colihue, 2005, p. 474.
166 *Ídem*, p. 473.

que, aun estando bajo la órbita del bloque capitalista o del comunista, mantenía formas de organización propias en las que participaban características de ambos sistemas socioeconómicos. En este contexto se computaba la "tesis argentina de la tercera posición" que se caracterizaba por la adopción de un sistema intermedio cuyo instrumento básico era la justicia social (Juan Perón en la apertura de sesiones del Congreso Nacional en 1950)[167].

Es relevante destacar que la Tercera Posición –que incluso volvió a ser sostenida con políticas concretas por Perón en su tercera presidencia– configura un momento de altura del pensamiento nacional y latinoamericano, porque afirma la necesidad de que nuestra América construya un camino propio, fuera del dominio de las grandes potencias mundiales. En la construcción de una posición semejante necesariamente concurrieron tanto el pensamiento de la modernidad occidental, en su más avanzada y solidaria versión, como el marxismo –en miradas nuestras como las de Manuel Ugarte[168], José Mariátegui, Natalicio González y Hernández Arregui–, el pensamiento antiimperialista y bolivariano, las voces de los pueblos indígenas y la filosofía cristiana en su opción por los pobres y oprimidos.

4) Los derechos de la clase trabajadora y los nuevos sujetos de derecho

El protagonismo de los trabajadores en el período peronista tuvo lugar a través de la participación concreta de las organizaciones sindicales. La expresión jurídica de este proceso histórico de contenido popular y emancipador fue la consagración de los derechos de los trabajadores

167 Según José Julio Santa Pinter, "este intento idealista ha encontrado cálido eco en el mundo: es muy sugestiva la situación político económico social de la liga árabe; la ideología particularísima del mundo hispánico; la posición del laborismo inglés, etcétera.", en "¿Un nuevo derecho internacional?", *Rev. Jurisprudencia Argentina*, Buenos Aires, *II-1953*.

168 "El socialismo debe ser nacional" dijo este pensador argentino, nacional y latinoamericanista. Haya de la Torre y Mariátegui lo consideraban una de las más prestigiosas figuras del continente; Sandino le escribió para agradecerle su apoyo a la causa del pueblo nicaragüense. Fue uno de los grandes "malditos" del siglo XX. Falleció en 1951. Ver Galasso, Norberto, *Manuel Ugarte y la lucha por la unidad latinoamericana*, Buenos Aires, Colihue, 2012 y Ramos, Jorge Abelardo, *Manuel Ugarte y la revolución latinoamericana*, Buenos Aires, Coyoacán, 1951.

–cuyo punto más alto fue la reforma constitucional–, la ley de asociaciones profesionales y la fijación de numerosos convenios colectivos.

El artículo 37 inciso 10 establecía como atribuciones esenciales de los trabajadores "el derecho de agremiarse libremente y de participar en otras actividades lícitas tendientes a la defensa de los intereses profesionales". Esta norma tenía un valor fundamental al darle respaldo constitucional a lo que la importante ley de asociaciones profesionales había consagrado un tiempo antes: la protección del sindicalismo como forma de organización propia de los trabajadores para reclamar contra el empresariado, y su fortalecimiento mediante el reconocimiento de una única organización nacional de la rama de la industria. Esta disposición le otorgaba a la comunidad organizada o pacto social un contenido de defensa de los intereses de los trabajadores.

En 1947 el presidente Perón había proclamado los derechos del trabajador en un documento cuyo contenido sirvió de base para los nuevos derechos que fueron incluidos en el texto constitucional, y donde se destacaba el reconocimiento a la centralidad social del trabajo como actividad creadora.

La nueva Constitución nacional fue producto de una reforma realizada en respeto de las normas constitucionales preexistentes, pero incorporó en forma expresa a nuevos sujetos de derecho como el trabajador, la familia y el anciano. Los derechos de los trabajadores tuvieron una especial y primordial referencia, plasmando en el más alto plano jurídico lo que ya se había establecido en la realidad y, en general, también ya se había obtenido mediante leyes, en especial en el período de la política desarrollada por Perón desde la Secretaría de Trabajo de 1943 hasta 1945. Su mediación en la puja entre patrones y trabajadores tuvo como resultado conquistas muy profundas en materia social que mejoraron las condiciones de vida de los más desprotegidos y quedaron grabadas en la memoria histórica: vacaciones pagas, aguinaldo, horario de ocho horas, sábado medio turno, domingo libre, jubilaciones, asignaciones familiares, indemnización por despido, estatuto del peón, y distintos tipos de beneficios sociales fueron algunas de las conquistas de los trabajadores que hasta entonces no existían[169].

169 Jornadas de Formación Política en el Gran Buenos Aires "En el Bicentenario, hacia la unidad latinoamericana" a cargo del equipo de formación del C. C. E. S.

Como bien señala Héctor Recalde, el fuerte aumento del salario industrial entre 1947 y 1949 negó el falso augurio empresarial de que el aumento del "costo laboral" afectaría la productividad industrial[170]. La coexistencia de intervención estatal, aumento de derechos de los trabajadores y desarrollo industrial lo desmiente. Otro mito "antiobrero" del país semicolonial se derrumbaba.

En este punto es fundamental la derogación del principio de autonomía contractual de los individuos, que en la década del 90 fue la esencia de la flexibilización laboral y el retroceso en los derechos de los trabajadores. El artículo 37 (I) decía que "el derecho de trabajar debe ser protegido por la sociedad, considerándolo con la dignidad que merece y proveyendo ocupación a quien la necesite".

Esto es posible advertirlo en la reformulación de una norma clave en el sistema liberal:

> Los derechos y garantías reconocidos por esta Constitución no podrán ser alterados por las leyes que reglamenten su ejercicio [...] pero tampoco amparan a ningún habitante de la Nación en perjuicio, detrimento o menoscabo de otro. Los abusos de esos derechos que perjudiquen a la comunidad o que lleven a cualquier forma de explotación del hombre por el hombre, configuran delitos que serán castigados por las leyes.

Es este un principio general del constitucionalismo liberal reformulado con la concepción solidaria que capta tanto la dimensión individual del sujeto como la colectiva. Durante el año 1951 se registró la firma de, al menos, 133 convenios colectivos de trabajo para las más variadas categorías de trabajadores (por ejemplo, pintores, gastronómicos, empleados de comercios minoristas, obreros de la industria maderera, de las fábricas

Discépolo con la coordinación de Mara Espasande y Norberto Galasso, 2009.

170 "Las cargas sociales pasaron de representar el 13% del salario bruto al 20% en 1943 y el 25% en 1952", en Recalde, Héctor, *Una historia laboral jamás contada... El relato empresario ante conquistas y nuevos derechos de los trabajadores en Argentina (1869-2012)*, Buenos Aires, Corregidor, 2012, p. 90.

de cigarros, de confecciones y medidas, de la industria del aceite, de luz y fuerza, de las metalúrgicas, de las empresas petroleras, de la industria de plásticos, de la industria del sombrero, de las importadoras de tejido, etc.), mientras que entre enero y febrero de 1952 fueron 57 los convenios acordados. Los convenios colectivos de trabajo, así como el Pacto Social, son políticas de avances y logros de los trabajadores organizados, y constituyen el modo propio y específico que adquiere la lucha de clases en nuestros países americanos.

En el convenio de los trabajadores de Luz y Fuerza puede leerse la firma conjunta de la declaración de los derechos del trabajador de 1947, y que

> [...] el trabajo es la causa de todas las conquistas de la civilización y el fundamento de la prosperidad general, de ahí que el derecho de trabajar debe ser protegido por la sociedad, considerándolo con la dignidad que merece y proveyendo ocupación a quien la necesite.

En el artículo 37 (I) 2 se expresa en buena medida la filosofía peronista cuanto se justifica el derecho del trabajador a una retribución justa:

> Siendo la riqueza, la renta y el interés del capital frutos exclusivos del trabajo humano, la comunidad debe organizar y reactivar las fuentes de producción en forma de posibilitar y garantizar al trabajador una retribución moral y material que satisfaga sus necesidades vitales y sea compensatoria del rendimiento obtenido y del esfuerzo realizado.

Es decir, aparecen los distintos factores constituyentes del mercado interno: el Estado debe organizar a la sociedad de tal modo que asegure al trabajador, que solo cuenta con su fuerza de trabajo, una "retribución moral y material" que sea justa, frente al propietario de los medios de producción. Aquí vuelve a aparecer la tesis de una conciliación posible entre ambas partes, en donde el conflicto capital-trabajo se difiere en tiempo y espacio. Se trata evidentemente, de una disposición normativa de fuerte sentido ideológico que expresa la utopía de la comunidad organizada.

Finalmente cabe citar a Susana Ramella, cuando precisa sobre la distinción entre el derecho a trabajar y el derecho al trabajo. El primero, previsto en el artículo 14 de la Constitución del 53, consiste en la facultad individual de elegir libremente la actividad laboral a realizar. Mientras que el segundo, además de incluir la citada facultad, comprende la garantía de obtener empleo, lo que compromete la prosperidad general de la nación, entendida como una economía de pleno empleo. Este último es el caso del artículo 37 de la reforma de 1949, el derecho "al" y no la preposición "de".[171]

Esta fue la perspectiva de José Espejo, el convencional obrero, uno de los más interesados en la incorporación del derecho al trabajo, quien acusaba a "la prepotencia patronal, la indiferencia estatal y la injusticia descarada de los jueces" del país oligárquico que se dejaba atrás,

> [...] cuando la patria fue gobernada por hombres surgidos de la clase de los estancieros y los universitarios aristócratas, que constituyó la oligarquía que vendió al país al extranjero y mantuvo sojuzgada a la mayoría de los argentinos.

En esta línea, el derecho al trabajo aparece como una fórmula jurídica superadora, cuya amplitud de alcance y concepto configura un piso mínimo para el derecho constitucional.

El derecho de huelga

Finalmente, cabe referirse a la interpretación que correspondía dar del ejercicio del derecho de huelga a partir de la reforma. Su no inclusión ha dado lugar a cierto debate. Según Sampay, el derecho de huelga es un derecho natural derivado del derecho del pueblo a la resistencia al tirano, cuyo carácter natural torna innecesaria su positivización. Pero además porque si el nuevo orden social tenía la pretensión de ser un orden justo

171 Ramella, Susana, "La concepción antropológica del derecho del trabajo en el constitucionalismo social del siglo XX", en *Revista de Historia del Derecho, nro. 42*, Buenos Aires, INHIDE, junio-diciembre 2011.

(en los términos de la filosofía de Tomás de Aquino), su inclusión legal implicaría aceptar la posibilidad de su ruptura. Este argumento, más allá de lo acertado o no, respeta las reglas de la lógica iusnaturalista. Pero más importante aun, indica qué lejos estaba en el ánimo de Sampay la instauración de un sistema totalitario que oprimiera a los trabajadores, como sugiere la doctrina liberal conservadora[172].

En todo caso, agregamos nosotros, el derecho de huelga es siempre un recurso legítimo de los trabajadores que se utiliza con el fin de recuperar o defender el ejercicio de los derechos, por lo que si bien su inclusión en el texto constitucional es una herramienta de utilidad para las luchas gremiales, no es una condición ineludible para ello. Además la existencia de numerosas huelgas en la época indica que su ejercicio no estaba prohibido. Véase si no que el mismo fue normado en la reforma constitucional de 1957, en el contexto de una persecución sistematizada de la dictadura contra el sindicalismo, por lo que su regulación fue tan inútil como hipócrita.

Solo cabe agregar que en las ocasiones en las que se lo ha prohibido en otros lugares, se lo hizo con la intención de superar la crisis de capital, para disminuir el ingreso de los trabajadores y limitar su capacidad de resistencia. Como surge del debate y demuestra la realidad político-económica del período 45-55, no fue ese el sentido de la omisión constitucional[173].

172 Dijo Sampay en la Asamblea Constituyente: "El derecho de huelga es un derecho natural del hombre en el campo del trabajo, como lo es el de la resistencia a la opresión en el campo político, pero si bien existe un derecho natural de huelga no puede haber un derecho positivo de huelga, porque –aunque esto haya sonado como un galimatías– es evidente que la huelga implica un rompimiento con el orden jurídico establecido, que, como tal, tiene la pretensión de ser un orden justo, y no olvidemos que la exclusión del recurso a la fuerza es el fin de toda organización social. El derecho absoluto de huelga, por tanto, no puede ser consagrado en una Constitución, a pesar de lo cual, dentro del derecho positivo argentino, se reglamenta esa zona de guerra extrajurídica que era la huelga –como se hizo en Francia después de la ley de arbitraje y contratos colectivos de 1936, en Suiza después de la ley de 1937, y en la de Italia posfascista– para que pueda cumplirse en los casos en que los patronos no se avienen a satisfacer reclamaciones legítimas de los sindicatos obreros".

173 Sin embargo cabe citar el caso de la FOTIA. En 1949 tuvo lugar la huel-

Acerca del debate, el constituyente Salvo, de origen gremial, expuso su crítica a las razones de la bancada radical:

> Rechazo terminantemente el atrevimiento que se tomó el miembro informante de la minoría [...] Los hombres que tenemos origen obrero y que nos sentamos con gran honor en esta Asamblea, no podemos aceptar el calificativo de amigos de parte de hombres que, con toda responsabilidad, han asumido una actitud que los señala como hombres sin honor y sin patria.

Salvo marcaba en sus palabras un desencuentro que se reiteró a lo largo de la historia entre el radicalismo y la clase obrera, especialmente mediante sus representaciones gremiales, y que llevó a esa fuerza política de origen nacional y popular a su declinación.

En relación con el derecho de huelga, el convencional peronista sostuvo:

> La huelga era un hecho más que un derecho y que, por lo tanto, los obreros que tenemos conciencia de dirigentes, que sabemos cuánto sufren nuestros hogares durante las huelgas, a veces interminables, no necesitamos el derecho cuando nos disponemos a ese sacrificio: vamos a los hechos y triunfamos.

De este modo, con toda la validez que puedan tener las diferentes posiciones asumidas sobre la conveniencia o no de incluir el derecho de huelga en la Constitución, lo cierto es que la posición en la asamblea del movimiento obrero organizado era contraria a su regulación.

---

ga de 50 días de los obreros azucareros conducido por la FOTIA, con sede en Tucumán, por reclamo salarial. La medida fue declarada ilegal por el Ministerio de Trabajo y varios dirigentes fueron desplazados y perseguidos. El gremio se había originado en 1944 con el apoyo de Perón, había tenido una participación importante en las jornadas que desembocaron en el 17 de octubre, y su nivel de movilización de bases, con delegados y comisiones en cada ingenio, le dio independencia de acción. Con el tiempo, el carácter combativo de los obreros del azúcar los llevó a protagonizar la resistencia peronista, e incluso algunos de ellos se vincularon a los Uturuncos, primera experiencia guerrillera del país.

Los derechos especiales

Se adjudicaba categoría de "derechos especiales" a los derechos del trabajador, de la familia, de la ancianidad y de la educación y la cultura. Respecto del trabajador se protegía su derecho a trabajar, a una retribución justa, a la capacitación, a condiciones dignas de trabajo, a la preservación de la salud, al bienestar (dentro del cual se incluye el derecho "de disponer de vivienda, indumentaria y alimentación adecuadas, de satisfacer sin angustias sus necesidades y las de su familia en forma que les permita trabajar con satisfacción"), a la seguridad social, a la protección de su familia ("la protección de la familia responde a un natural designio de individuo"), al mejoramiento económico, a la defensa de los intereses profesionales ("el derecho de agremiarse libremente y de participar en otras actividades lícitas tendientes a la defensa de los intereses profesionales, constituyen atribuciones esenciales de los trabajadores").

Se constituía a la familia como sujeto de derecho, en la medida en que la declaraba como "de preferente protección por parte del Estado, el que reconoce sus derechos en lo que respecta a su constitución, defensa y cumplimento de sus fines". Al mismo tiempo que se le otorgaba categoría constitucional al matrimonio, a la igualdad jurídica de los cónyuges y de la patria potestad, a la unidad económica familiar, al bien de la familia, y a la atención y asistencia de la madre y del niño con privilegiada consideración estatal[174].

El anciano era consagrado como sujeto de derecho constitucional con derecho a la asistencia, a su protección integral, por cuenta y cargo de su familia; y en caso de desamparo, le correspondía al Estado proveerla; con derecho a la vivienda, a la alimentación, al vestido, al cuidado de la salud física y de la salud moral ("el libre ejercicio de las expansiones espirituales, concordes con la moral y el culto"), al esparcimiento, al trabajo ("la laborterapia productiva"), a la tranquilidad y al respeto.

174 Sobre los criterios actuales de interpretación normativa de los derechos de las niñas, niños y adolescentes ver Pinto, Gimol, *El sistema penal juvenil argentino*, Buenos Aires, UNICEF, 2009.

En síntesis, los derechos de los trabajadores y los derechos sociales, como el de la vivienda, adquirían jerarquía constitucional y por lo tanto su protección era normativa de orden público y formaba parte del diseño de nación que la nueva Constitución proyectaba. Tanto es así, que Cooke sostenía el paralelismo entre el poder del amo sobre su esclavo y el del acreedor sobre su deudor, que exigía "una valoración del trabajo frente al capital hasta llegar al equilibrio, fórmula de coexistencia de la justicia social". Por eso, proponía que la declaración inicial del anterior artículo 15 ("en la Nación Argentina no hay esclavos") debía ser mantenida, para extender su alcance tuitivo a la formas de explotación laboral y romper "las cadenas del miedo al hambre, a la indignidad, al sufrimiento". (AP, p. 316)

Los pueblos indígenas

Hasta 1949 rigió el artículo 67 inciso 15 de la Constitución de 1853 que le imponía al Congreso el deber de proveer la seguridad de las fronteras y de "conservar el trato pacífico con los indios y promover la conversión de ellos al catolicismo"[175]. La reforma de aquel año suprimió esta leyenda –quedó el deber de "proveer a la seguridad de las fronteras"–, por lo que, al mismo tiempo, superó la idea segregacionista que la norma suponía[176].

La justificación de la reforma fue que:

> [...] la modificación de este artículo consiste en eliminar la alusión al trato pacífico con los indios y su conversión al catolicismo, aspecto que hoy resulta anacrónico, por cuanto no se pueden establecer distinciones raciales, ni de ninguna clase, entre los habitantes del país.

175 La norma expresaba una posible vocación de diálogo para la integración por parte de quienes conformaban la Confederación del`Paraná, como continuación de la tradición que, en líneas generales, habían sostenido tanto Rosas como Urquiza, y que unos años después de su sanción apoyó Adolfo Alsina. Sin embargo, con la instauración del orden oligárquico del proyecto mitrista, ese mandato quedó postergado para dar lugar a una política de guerra interior bajo el mando de Roca.

176 Según Pablo Ramella, la supresión se debió a que "los reducidos núcleos de indios que todavía existen en el país no exigían una norma expresa", en *Derecho Constitucional*, Buenos Aires, De Palma, 1986, p. 312.

Martínez Sarasola ha sostenido que el reconocimiento de la persona indígena como ciudadana fue un importante avance y destacó que, en general, el período peronista se caracterizó por una revalorización de los pueblos indígenas[177]. Se subraya la ratificación interna por la Ley 13.560 (1949) del convenio número 50 de la Conferencia Internacional del Trabajo –sobre derechos en el "reclutamiento" de trabajadores indígenas–, y las colonias granjas creadas para pueblos indígenas en Salta, Jujuy, Presidente Perón y en los territorios nacionales de Formosa y Neuquén. También la inclusión en el Primer Plan Quinquenal (1947-1952) de un programa de entrega de tierras fiscales sobre medio millón de hectáreas, en etapas sucesivas (reserva, reducción y colonia), mientras que en el Segundo Plan Quinquenal (1953-1957) se incluía a los pueblos indígenas en el capítulo de las organizaciones del pueblo, para establecer su protección con el fin de ser integrados en forma progresiva al nivel de vida ordinario de la nación. El objetivo particular se explica por el general: poblar el campo de pequeños productores, lugar social propio e histórico para los indígenas. Es importante tener en cuenta que el derecho al territorio es la clave de las luchas y el destino de los pueblos originarios[178].

En 1946 se creó la Dirección de Protección al Aborigen en el ámbito de la Secretaría de Trabajo para reemplazar a la Comisión Honoraria de Reducciones de Indios. Hubo casos de expropiación de tierras a favor de comunidades, como el del Decreto 18.341 (1949) en la provincia de Jujuy, cuyo texto sostenía "la prohibición de enajenar o ceder las tierras que se entreguen a los aborígenes".

Es importante señalar un hecho de relevancia histórica para los reclamos de los derechos colectivos indígenas ocurridos en la época. En agosto de 1946 tuvo lugar el mítico Malón de la Paz o la Caravana de la Paz, que

177 Por su parte, el Dr. Manuel Moreira sostiene en *El derecho de los pueblos originarios. Reflexión y hermenéutica*, Universidad Nacional del Litoral: Santiago Álvarez Editor, de importante consulta en la materia de derechos colectivos de los pueblos indígenas, que "aun la Constitución de 1949 lo ignoró, ya que suprimió del texto la palabra "indígena" y evitó considerarlo de cualquier otra manera" (p. 97).
178 La obra citada es el clásico e indispensable Sarasola, Carlos Martínez, *Nuestros paisanos los indios*, Buenos Aires, Del nuevo extremo, 2011.

consistió en una larga travesía de pueblos collas hasta Buenos Aires, para reclamar por sus tierras usurpadas por latifundistas. Pero, tras ser alojados en el Hotel de los Inmigrantes, fueron obligados a regresar en forma abrupta sin respuestas a sus legítimas demandas. En 1947 ocurrió la "Matanza de Rincón Bomba", en las cercanías de Las Lomitas, en el entonces Territorio Nacional de Formosa, en la cual miles de braceros pilagás, tobas y wichís fueron despedidos sin indemnización alguna del Ingenio San Martín de El Tabacal. Según los abogados Carlos Alberto Díaz y Julio García, fueron asesinados en la "campaña" entre 400 y 500 argentinos de etnia pilagá, aproximadamente, por el accionar de las ametralladoras de la Gendarmería Nacional, además de los heridos y los más de 200 "desaparecidos". Ello, sumado a más de 50 muertos por intoxicación, hambre y falta de atención médica y la desaparición de un número indeterminado de niños, eleva las bajas a más de 750, entre niños, ancianos, mujeres y hombres[179]. Esta masacre se sumó a muchas realizadas contra pueblos indígenas en nuestro país, como producto de la discriminación, la violencia, la injusticia social y el racismo que, ya desde la persecución a las montoneras y los caudillos federales en el siglo XIX, fueron las notas características de la ideología dominante que aún perdura en la actualidad.

Finalmente, hay que señalar también que en 1956 se quitó la Dirección de Protección al Aborigen de la órbita nacional, y se provincializó el organismo así como también los bienes fiscales, por lo que se sustrajeron las relaciones jurídicas del ámbito federal, lo que a la larga debilitó la protección de los derechos. También en este punto hay que tener en cuenta la regresión que significó la vuelta al anterior artículo 67 inciso 15 de la Constitución, tras la derogación de la reforma de 1949.

En líneas generales, la política peronista podría ser caracterizada como integracionista y con rasgos propios del indigenismo con origen en México, en el Primer Congreso Indigenista Interamericano de Patzcuaro, Michoacán, en 1940. Hay que precisar que recién con la reforma constitucional de 1994 se estableció la propiedad comunitaria indígena con sus caracteres

179 Ver en *Los Malditos, tomo IV*, Buenos Aires, Madres de Plaza de Mayo.

propios, como la inenajenabilidad, y que en 2001 se ratificó a nivel nacional el Convenio 169 de la Organización General del Trabajo de 1989, por lo que aquella política, para la época resultaba, aun con sus limitaciones, lo más progresiva posible. Pero también le corresponden al peronismo las críticas que pueden adjudicarse a otros movimientos nacionales latinoamericanos, en tanto que el nacionalismo popular ha mantenido, en las diferentes expresiones en nuestro continente, una relación con los pueblos indígenas de marcadas tensiones y no exenta de conflictos. Su dialéctica de contradicción entre mayorías populares y minorías oligárquicas, en principio y pese a su proyecto emancipatorio, pareció no darle cabida a los originarios en su especificidad étnica, en tanto minorías discriminadas y como pueblos integrantes de la gran nación latinoamericana. A partir de la creciente reivindicación de la identidad indígena, los movimientos nacionales populares tendrán como tarea histórica en el siglo XXI reconfigurar la categoría "pueblo" y la de igualdad desde una dimensión de mayor pluralidad cultural y política, para mantener con suerte su vocación transformadora, como lo es la senda iniciada por el pueblo boliviano con Evo Morales[180].

5) La distribución y el trabajo de la tierra

El artículo 38, antes citado, también establecía:

> Incumbe al Estado fiscalizar la distribución y la utilización del campo e intervenir con el objeto de desarrollar e incrementar su rendimiento en interés de la comunidad, y procurar a cada labriego o familia labriega la posibilidad de convertirse en propietario de la tierra que cultiva.

De esto último, se deriva lo que Sampay denominó como

> [...] un derecho del Estado a controlar la distribución y la utilización del suelo, interviniendo con el fin de desarrollar su

180 Como dice, en un criterio que compartimos, Manuel Moreira: "La cuestión indígena llega muy tarde pero paradójicamente muy temprano en la idea de pluralidad jurídica, modelo que avanza con gran dificultad sobre la matriz disciplinaria más conservadora del derecho, generando polémica y hostilidad" *op. cit.*, p. 239.

> rendimiento en interés de todo el pueblo y de garantizar a cada labriego o familia labriega que demuestre aptitudes para ello, la posibilidad de convertirse en dueño de la tierra que trabaja.

La cláusula del progreso, prevista en el inciso 16 del artículo 68 (anterior 67), agregaba el mandato de la colonización rural. Se enunciaba así uno de los principios fundamentales para el desarrollo colectivo de cualquier nación en nuestra América: la tierra debe ser de quien la trabaja. El fin buscado era "introducir una profunda transformación agraria sobre la base del concepto de que el campo –según expresaba el general Perón– no debe ser bien de renta, sino instrumento de trabajo". El latifundio –característica de la injusticia social en toda América Latina y el Caribe– encuentra aquí sus grandes obstáculos: 1) la tierra no es para beneficio de unos pocos (la renta), sino para el bien común (para los que la trabajan, es decir, los trabajadores campesinos y pequeños productores), y, por ello, 2) debe cumplir una función social determinada por una política de Estado, a partir, en especial, del control de la exportación e importación (recordemos el artículo 40 que establecía que "la importación y exportación estarán a cargo del Estado").

La función social de la propiedad de la tierra implica la negación de la usura como ejercicio concreto de la libertad de contratación en el mundo capitalista. La Ley 13.246, de arrendamiento y aparcería sobre la propiedad de la tierra, corría el riesgo de ser declarada inconstitucional por algún juez defensor de los intereses de los grandes estancieros con la redacción de la Carta Magna de 1853. Aquella ley, del 18 de septiembre de 1948, establecía que sus normas se aplicaban a todo contrato de finalidad agroeconómica, en calidad de orden público y con sanción de nulidad por pactos en contrario, cualquiera que sea la denominación que las partes le hayan asignado por un tiempo mínimo determinado. Su objetivo fue dar estabilidad a la familia labriega, la redistribución de las tierras por medio del arrendamiento rural.

Tuvo su origen primero en la Ley 11.170 de 1921, sancionada a raíz del Grito de Alcorta de 1912 en el sur de Santa Fe, donde sobresalió la

actuación de los hermanos Netri. La ley era similar y disponía un plazo mínimo de cuatro años de alquiler respecto de predios de hasta 300 hectáreas y la prohibición de obligar al arrendatario a comercializar su producción con persona o empresa determinada. En fin, superaba la situación anterior que era regida directamente por el Código Civil que, entre otros, en su artículo 1.197 consagraba la autonomía de la voluntad de las partes. Por su reiterado incumplimiento se sancionó en 1932 la Ley 11.627, vigente hasta 1948.

Se discutió sobre el valor de la denominada "renta nacional". En nombre de la subcomisión, habló el convencional Marini:

> La organización de la riqueza implica la solución del problema de la renta individual, es decir, la justa distribución de la renta entre los tres factores principales de la producción: tierra, trabajo y capital [...] el concepto de renta nacional [...] y el de mayor rendimiento del trabajo, es lo que ha de liberar a las masas en su futuro, porque es con lo que se podrá enfrentar el problema de la seguridad social.

De la renta individual a la renta social, de los beneficios personales a la solidaridad colectiva. De ahí se derivó un nuevo enfoque de lo que es el valor, en tanto relación social: "Ya la riqueza no será valorada en función de lo subjetivo, como se hacía en el mundo liberal; la riqueza será valorada en función de lo subjetivo y exteriorizada hacia lo social."

Por eso, como estábamos frente a una nueva idea del valor, había que cambiar el modo en que se veían las cosas, en especial aquella mirada que la ideología liberal había logrado imponer en el sentido común.

> Necesitamos abolir de la mentalidad de muchos argentinos aquello de que nuestro país carece de riquezas ubérrimas fuera del mundo agrícola y ganadero. No, señor presidente; hay extensas regiones del país donde productos como el carbón, el hierro y otros minerales esperan la mano del hombre para poder reivindicarlos a favor de la sociedad, como bienes de consumo de factible adquisición". (Marini)

Es decir, somos mucho más que un país con un destino natural a ser el "granero del mundo" o a estar condenado a vivir en dependencia de acuerdo a la suerte del modelo agroexportador.

En aquella época, el valor utilidad estaba fijado por el patrón oro –aunque ya en su etapa final–, por eso el mismo convencional advirtió que el patrón oro valía como medida de la moneda pero, a la vez, aclaró que no iba a

> [...] darle un valor superior a aquel que podría tener el valor adquisitivo respaldado por el trabajo productor de bienes [...] Es el respaldo del factor mercancía el que está impulsando a los pueblos a la liberación, y no el oro acumulado en manos de los poderosos que es la opresión y la miseria de la clase proletaria.

Solo a partir de esta conciencia del valor trabajo en la vida social los pueblos adquieren las mejores condiciones para su desarrollo productivo. Tal vez la misma vara podría utilizarse para juzgar en la actualidad a la sobrevalorización de la economía especulativa y financiera por sobre la productiva e industrial. El rol del Estado en esta relación es fundamental:

> "La organización de la riqueza implica la dirección del crédito en lo nacional [...] El crédito argentino estaba en manos del poder extranjero" (convencional Marini).

Al decir del convencional Simini, la reforma constitucional implicaba en sí misma, "una verdadera declaración de los derechos del trabajador rural". Entonces proclamaba:

> Tierra en propiedad para el que la trabaja, impuestos progresivos al latifundio, está constituyendo ya la hermosa realidad de la República. Con la reforma constitucional podrán crearse legalmente las condiciones favorables para radicar al labriego y al productor rural de la tierra. Ya no ocurrirá que el capital tome la tierra para que después venga el hombre. Con la revolución vendrá primero el hombre a la tierra para poner en ella su capital, que es su trabajo.

6) La cuestión del federalismo

La Constitución de 1853 había establecido una relación entre la nación y las provincias en la que estas se reservaban todo el poder no delegado expresamente a aquella. Pero, la verdad histórica es que el federalismo constitucional fue siempre letra muerta en el país agroexportador. La relación desigual signada por el fuerte centralismo porteño, la disímil posición de privilegios económicos y de posibilidades de crecimiento de las regiones, de acuerdo a su cercanía con el puerto de Buenos Aires o la posibilidad de acceso a los ríos de navegación (en la cuenca del Plata) tornó difícil el vínculo.

Con la reforma de 1949, sin variar el concepto general de soberanía residual, se modificó el concepto de federalismo a partir de que se estableció la propiedad nacional en forma inalienable e imprescriptible de los recursos naturales en el artículo 40. Había allí nuevas atribuciones y facultades para la nación que modificaban las relaciones con las provincias, al darle al poder nacional facultades absolutas y exclusivas sobre un bien estratégico para el desarrollo socioeconómico, abriendo la posibilidad de una actuación coordinada. La existencia de un poder federal orientado a la promoción del interés nacional e integrador de todo el país, constituye la condición para neutralizar la vocación fragmentadora del centralismo porteñista.

Al respecto, Pablo Ramella destacaba la dificultad de constituir una nación sin "un plan de gobierno de sostenido fortalecimiento de las necesidades culturales, sociales, políticas y económicas de las diversas regiones del país"[181]. En nuestro país, señalaba, por el proceso histórico, la entidad política por excelencia era la provincia, a diferencia de otros países como España o Italia. Así, la región debía ser considerada como una relación entre provincias o parte de ellas para atender las necesidades diversas que se presentaran, por lo que la determinación de las regiones "nunca deben ser impuestas por el gobierno federal sino por la libre concertación de las provincias". La soberanía nacional y la justicia social se constituyen a partir de la indispensable integración regional, de su tejido productivo y la igualdad de oportunidades y derechos entre los habitantes de todo el país.

181 González Arzac, Alberto, *Federalismo y justicialismo*, Buenos Aires, Peña Lillo, 1984.

Otra cuestión importante es la de la atención de las realidades regionales. El concepto de lo regional y de instituciones de carácter corporativo o intermedio es un aporte de la reforma constitucional. Dice González Arzac que

> [...] tradicionalmente los políticos y economistas liberales omitieron considerar la presencia de realidades regionales, dado que ideológicamente evitaban todo tipo de institución intermedia entre el Estado y el individuo, así como también negaron los sindicatos [...].[182]

De algún modo, ello fue antecedente del federalismo de concertación o de competencia concurrente que en forma doctrinaria se fue estableciendo para describir situaciones de políticas conjuntas, y que luego se consagró constitucionalmente con la reforma de 1994 en el ámbito del derecho ambiental (artículo 43). En esta última reforma se introdujo nuevamente el concepto de regiones (artículos 75 inciso 19 y 124), vinculado con la necesidad de promover políticas tendientes a equilibrar el desigual desarrollo económico y social.

En este punto corresponde remitirnos a la opinión de Cooke sobre la cuestión de la libre navegación de los ríos. Cooke le daba suma importancia a esta cuestión, a la que comparaba con los ferrocarriles:

> La libertad de los ríos es, paralelamente, la libertad de los ferrocarriles, en resumen, la entrega de la libertad del tráfico a las fuerzas foráneas, al margen del Estado, de nuestra soberanía y de la iniciativa nacional.

Es que, como decía Cooke, "los grandes lineamientos han sido siempre conformados y condicionados por la propia geografía", por eso existe un factor determinante de nuestra política nacional: la cuenca del Río de la Plata.

> El dominio del estuario implica, en principio, el dominio del país. Dividir el estuario, internacionalizar sus afluentes, imponer la

182 *Ídem.*

> libre navegación, desintegrar sus regiones, fueron medidas diplomáticas y económicas tendientes a conseguir por otros medios lo que nunca pudo conseguirse por las armas. (AP, p. 263)

La cuestión del federalismo solo se comprende en el estudio del desarrollo histórico del país, por lo que cabe remitirse a lo explicado en el capítulo II de este libro.

Como expresión de la conciencia histórica de nuestro pueblo, Cooke citaba a Pedro Ferré, el gobernador de Corrientes, "el campeón de la tendencia proteccionista" que exigía "que se prohíban o impongan altos derechos a aquellos efectos extranjeros que se produzcan por la industria rural del país". (AP, p. 264)

La asamblea de 1853 suprimió las trabas impuestas al tráfico fluvial y decretó la libertad de navegar y comerciar, así como la apertura de los ríos interiores (artículos 11 y 12, 14 y 20, 26 y 67 inciso 9 de la Constitución del 53), en la creencia de que esa era la vía para neutralizar el centralismo porteñista. Pero el resultado fue el inverso. Desde entonces, esa disposición ha mantenido su vigencia por lo que Cooke afirmaba que el artículo 26 debía ser abolido, "así como la prohibición de crear zonas francas o de conceder preferencias a un puerto respecto de otro". Con esta propuesta, Cooke tenía la intención de impulsar el desarrollo económico integral de todo el país, el intercambio comercial entre las regiones, racionalizar la producción y consolidar el mercado interno y la creación de trabajo.

En relación al sistema impositivo y de rentas, Cooke sostenía la necesidad de adaptar el sistema rentístico a las cambiantes condiciones económicas y a la creciente extensión de las funciones del Estado, lo que hacía más conveniente la inclusión de los recursos provenientes de la explotación o venta de esos bienes como parte del Tesoro Nacional.

Cooke explicaba que, desde 1890 y tras la crisis financiera producto de la caída de la Baring Brothers, se habían creado impuestos internos que hasta entonces subsistían. La múltiple imposición fue un efecto no resuelto

sino hasta 1934 al sancionarse la Ley 12.139, cuya normativa unificaba los impuestos internos. En este contexto, Cooke afirmaba el principio realista de que "el sistema tributario de la Nación pueda seguir el ritmo de su desarrollo económico". Por eso en aquel momento eran

> [...] cuantiosos los recursos que obtiene el Tesoro Nacional de la explotación de los bienes que constituyen el dominio privado del Estado. Este es propietario de los principales bancos, de la red telefónica y ferroviaria, yacimientos petrolíferos y destilerías, de ingenios y de importantes establecimientos industriales, se encarga de la venta al exterior de la mayor parte de la producción nacional, y por último se asocia al capital privado para constituir sociedades de economía mixta que realizan toda clase de actividades. (AP, p. 272 y ss.)

En otro orden, en ocasión de fundamentar sobre la necesidad de legislar una instancia de casación a nivel de jurisdicción nacional, Cooke expresó que "entre nosotros no existe una soberanía que se hayan reservado los Estados, paralela a la soberanía de la Nación", por lo que solo existe una única soberanía –de la nación– y múltiples autonomías –de las provincias–. "Menos aun si se quiere entrar en el distingo entre la soberanía política y soberanía jurídica, toda vez que esta última aparece delegada expresamente a la Nación con respecto a los códigos de fondo" (AP, p. 294)

7) La cultura nacional y la educación

La importancia de la promoción de una cultura de raíz nacional se comprende con el agregado al preámbulo en cuanto a la obligación de "[...] promover la cultura nacional", más el artículo 37 (IV, 7) que decía que

> [...]las riquezas artísticas e históricas, así como el paisaje natural, cualquiera sea su propietario, forman parte del patrimonio cultural de la Nación y estarán bajo la tutela del Estado, que puede decretar las expropiaciones necesarias para su defensa y prohibir la exportación o enajenación de los tesoros artísticos [...].

Hay también una nueva concepción de la educación que se expresa en términos de que "la elección profesional redunde en beneficios suyo –del individuo– y de la sociedad", y "el ejercicio de las profesiones y de las artes técnicas, en función del bien de la colectividad". Estas fórmulas lingüísticas expresan la concepción colectiva del sujeto en la que la auténtica realización individual consiste en el aporte concreto a la vida de los demás, a los más débiles, al bienestar general.[183]

Sampay ante la asamblea, dijo:

> La cultura nacional, se refiere a la naturaleza, condiciones, historia y exigencias de la Nación en que se vive y a la que se pertenece, porque teniendo cada nación su genio y destino, el ciudadano que solo por serlo tiene la obligación de responder a ellos, necesita naturalmente, conocerlos [...] para comprender y vivir íntegramente la vida nacional.

La conciencia de los individuos, ya no considerados en forma aislada sin el sentido de pertenencia al pueblo, sino como parte integrante de la cultura nacional y, por lo tanto, en su verdadera dimensión política, como afirmación de lo nacional. Consecuencia de esta concepción integradora entre lo nacional y lo popular (donde la nación es el pueblo) y no aristocrática (donde la nación son las élites dominantes), es la ampliación del acceso al sistema universitario.[184]

En el artículo 37 se establecía el régimen de autonomía universitaria, recuperando el legado de la reforma universitaria de 1918, hasta

183 Ya lo escribió Jauretche: "La sociedad entera es puesta a contribución para capacitar sus mejores elementos en beneficio de la misma; el estudiante se sabe a su vez un producto de la colectividad a la que debe servir, y el egresado no se cree, como entre nosotros, el propietario de una patente de corso, costeada por el bolsillo de papá, aunque el máximo aporte haya sido del Estado" (en *Los profetas del odio y la yapa*).

184 En palabras de Juan Perón: "Deseo anunciar que desde hoy quedan suprimidos los actuales aranceles universitarios en forma tal que la enseñanza sea absolutamente gratuita y al alcance de todos los jóvenes argentinos que anhelan instruirse para el bien del país".

ese momento no realizado[185]. También disponía que la enseñanza primaria fuera obligatoria y gratuita, mientras que la universitaria tenía como fin "que los jóvenes capaces y meritorios encausaran sus actividades siguiendo los impulsos de sus naturales aptitudes en su propio beneficio y en el de la Nación misma", así como que les encomendaba a las universidades el dictado de cursos de formación política con el objeto de que

> [...] cada alumno conozca lo esencial de lo argentino, la realidad espiritual, económica, social y política de su país, la evolución y misión histórica de la República Argentina, y para que adquiera conciencia de la responsabilidad que debe asumir en la empresa de lograr y afianzar los fines reconocidos y fijados en esta Constitución.

Luego, con un decreto firmado y promulgado el 22 de noviembre de 1949 (Decreto 29.337/49) el presidente Perón suspendió el cobro de los aranceles universitarios que regían. Es más, con posterioridad mediante el Decreto 9.695/1951, se creó el Consejo Nacional de Investigaciones Técnicas y Científicas, que luego sería el CONICET actual[186].

En 1953 se estableció la Doctrina Nacional Justicialista –después del golpe de 1955 fue prohibida–, conforme lo dispuesto por el artículo 3 de la Ley 14.184. Esto último ha merecido críticas como las de Jauretche, quien la veía como una doctrina de partido en "una versión exclusivamente personalista". Esta "doctrina nacional" ha sido flanco de críticas, aunque, en

185 Señalemos en este punto, que la reforma del 18 "puede resumirse en cuatro puntos fundamentales: revolución democrática, unificación de América Latina, democratización universitaria y formación de intelectuales y de técnicos para una nueva Nación" (Oporto, Mario, *De Moreno a Perón, pensamiento argentino de la unidad latinoamericana*, Buenos Aires, Planeta, 2011, p. 60.

186 "La matrícula universitaria pasó de 40.284 alumnos en 1945 a 138.871 en 1955 (cabe aclarar que este crecimiento sostenido continuó en la próxima década, ya que en 1965 concurrían 206.032 alumnos a las universidades, según la misma fuente). Similares índices de crecimiento se observan tanto en lo que hace al presupuesto de las Universidades Nacionales como en la cantidad de profesores", de acuerdo a Ángel Márquez en *Educación y Peronismo (1946 – 1955)*, Buenos Aires, CEAL, 1984.

nuestra opinión, para emitir un juicio completo y más justo es necesario observar la totalidad de la política nacional educativa, lo que incluye como elemento más importante lo antes señalado en orden a la ampliación de la base social con acceso a la educación.

Por eso, en líneas generales, parece haber habido predominio de un concepto de socialización de la cultura, como parte del derecho de todos y no como un atributo de distinción "civilizada" de las elites[187].

La reforma constitucional y la Iglesia

La Iglesia fue inicialmente parte de la alianza gobernante. Cabe recordar la Carta Pastoral del 15 de noviembre de 1945, por la cual la jerarquía eclesiástica consignó: que ningún católico podía votar a candidatos que propiciaran la separación de la Iglesia del Estado, la supresión de los derechos de la religión, el laicismo escolar y el divorcio, lo que, en la práctica, implicaba una adhesión a la fórmula Perón-Quijano. Véase que la reforma constitucional respeta estos principios, y en el artículo 2 se mantenía la obligación por parte del gobierno federal de sostener el culto católico apostólico romano. También se respetaba la pertenencia a la religión católica apostólica romana como requisito para ser elegido presidente o vicepresidente de la nación. Pero, como señala Loris Zanatta, la reforma constitucional, al continuar con el Patronato fue un "quiebre de confianza" en el vínculo con la Santa Sede, y un punto de inflexión en la relación entre la Iglesia y el peronismo, cuyo distanciamiento se fue profundizando aun más con el tiempo[188]. En efecto, la Iglesia tenía la pretensión de suprimir el Patronato, pero la reforma constitucional mantuvo la facultad

187 El citado decreto de suspensión de los aranceles universitarios decía: "[...] que atendiendo al espíritu y la letra de la nueva constitución es función social del Estado ampliar la enseñanza universitaria a fin de que los jóvenes capaces y meritorios encaucen sus actividades siguiendo los impulsos de sus naturales aptitudes, en su propio beneficio y en el de la Nación misma".

188 Zanatta, Loris, "Perón, la Iglesia y la reforma que no fue. Patronato nacional y conflicto con la Santa Sede en la reforma constitucional de 1949", ponencia en el 49 Congreso Americanista, Quito, Ecuador, julio de 1997, disponible en http://www.naya.org.ar/congresos/contenido/49CAI/Zanatta.htm.

del Estado para designar obispos prevista en los anteriores artículos 65 y 86 de la Constitución. Aquellos méritos del gobierno nacional frente a la Iglesia, como la ley de enseñanza religiosa, quedaban opacados ante esta negativa. Según el padre Hernán Benítez, en definitiva, se trataba de que las masas populares antes que nada fueran peronistas, es decir, la opción política tenía predominio por sobre la religiosa[189]. De hecho, las bases movilizadas en el 55 por la jerarquía eclesiástica no fueron de origen popular, sino más bien de sectores medios y acomodados impulsados por una convicción antiperonista.

8) Las garantías penales

El positivismo fue la ideología que había utilizado el país oligárquico para legitimar el control social (las leyes de residencia, de defensa social y la Agote, son ejemplos de ello)[190]. Son los movimientos nacionales quienes cuestionan, de diversos modos e intensidad, los discursos hegemónicos; por eso su carácter humanista es una nota saliente a lo largo de nuestra historia política. De la época del yrigoyenismo, es en el Código Penal de 1921 en el que se introduce la condenación condicional y la abolición de la pena de muerte, así como la conmutación presidencial de las condenas a muerte existentes. Durante el peronismo el proceso de industrialización aparejó el fenómeno social de la concentración poblacional urbana a partir de las migraciones internas, lo que explicaría un mayor control policial en las ciudades (el origen de la policía en Europa nos remonta a la época de la Revolución Industrial en los puertos de Londres, Liverpool y Manchester, como fuerza de seguridad para proteger los *dockes*[191]).

189 Galasso, Norberto, *Yo fui el confesor de Eva Perón. Conversaciones con el Padre Hernán Benítez*, Rosario, Homo Sapiens Ediciones, 1999.

190 Zaffaroni dice para el siglo XIX en Europa central: “El industrialismo necesitaba previsibilidad, orden disciplina, domesticación para el trabajo fabril [...] no buscaba eliminar enemigos sino disciplinar a las masas [...] su humanismo fue el abandono de las penas aterradoras”. Mientras que en el siglo XX se inició bajo el signo de una ideología médico policial en donde cundieron “las leyes de Estado peligroso sin delito”.

191 Ver Foucault, Michel, *La verdad y las formas jurídicas*, Barcelona, Gedisa, 1996.

Sin embargo, hay que destacar dos características del peronismo: la casi nula persecución policial a las clases trabajadoras y las reformas de las instituciones carcelarias. Se organizó el Servicio Penitenciario Federal, se creó la Escuela Penitenciaria de la Nación, se suprimió el traje cebrado para los presos, los grilletes en los pies y se cerró el penal de Ushuaia donde iban los "relegados", reformas que fueron encaradas por Roberto Pettinato[192].

Esta política criminal –con características que hoy son similares a las posiciones garantistas– encuentra correlato en las reformas introducidas en la Constitución Nacional en su artículo 29. Además de las garantías ya establecidas, se incorporó el *habeas corpus*, la prohibición de la analogía, el principio *in dubio pro reo*, la aplicación de la ley penal más benigna, así como la función casatoria de la Corte Suprema para establecer y unificar una interpretación de los códigos de fondo, entre ellos el penal.

En el caso "San Miguel, José", de mayo de 1950, se realizaron interesantes interpretaciones sobre el *habeas corpus* constitucional introducido por la reforma. El voto de la mayoría de la Corte Suprema –Luís Longhi, Atilio Pessagno, Felipe Pérez y Rodolfo Valenzuela–, en ocasión de no hacer lugar a la presentación realizada (según se relata en el fallo, el presidente de la Comisión Parlamentaria Nacional dispuso la clausura del diario *La República*, de la ciudad de Rosario, porque en una edición no incluyó la leyenda "Año del Libertador General San Martín" impuesta en la Ley 13.661), opinó que la Constitución del 49 no había innovado respecto de la naturaleza del *habeas corpus*, que

> [...] lo que en verdad hizo fue reafirmar su fundamento institucional con el expreso propósito de no confiar ese recurso a la simple ley y menos aun a la forma, cuya sanción ha sido atribuida a las legislaturas locales. Por cierto, si alguien fuera detenido en virtud de una orden escrita de autoridad incompetente, o lo fuera sin orden alguna, o simplemente amenazado en el ejercicio de su

192 Dice Zaffaroni: "El fortalecimiento del control policial urbano es explicable por la necesidad de controlar el proceso de concentración poblacional que sufre la Argentina sin mayores sobresaltos ni costos de vidas humanas", en *Manuel de Derecho Penal*, Buenos Aires, Ediar, 1994, p.173.

> libertad, ¿qué recurso legal le quedaría para hacer cesar inmediatamente su detención o la amenaza? (Dr. Lascano citando al miembro informante de la mayoría en la Asamblea Constituyente)

Sin embargo, adviértase que la vigencia de tal disposición constitucional en los años siguientes hubiera obligado a los jueces de la nación a intervenir en los casos de desaparición forzada de personas, tanto durante el Plan Conintes como en los hechos posteriores alumbrados bajo la inspiración de la Doctrina de Seguridad Nacional. En el voto en disidencia en el mismo caso, el juez Tomás Casares sostuvo una interpretación extensiva del artículo 29 tendiente a la protección de derechos distintos al de la libertad personal, porque

> [...] el recurso tiene en el nuevo precepto constitucional una mayor amplitud a la que corresponde un nuevo espíritu, congruente, por lo demás, con la predominancia del sentido social sobre el sentido político en la nueva Ley Suprema.

Es que, dice, el ejercicio de la libertad depende de la posibilidad de ejercer otros derechos.

> Es así, por ejemplo, como una libertad, sin que el ejercicio del derecho de trabajar esté eficazmente amparado y sin posibilidad efectiva de acceso al derecho de propiedad, no sería un atributo real sino un espectro [...] Con ello no se atribuye a los derechos individuales una primacía absoluta que no tienen. La verdadera primacía es siempre la del bien común, fruto natural de un orden público justo y condición de todo bien individual.[193]

193 También cabe citar el caso "Codovilla, Victorio", de abril de 1950, en donde con el voto de la totalidad de los jueces de la Corte –Casares incluido–, se rechazó el *habeas corpus* porque el art. 29 de la Constitución requiere la demostración de la existencia del riesgo a la libertad individual porque la diligencia de notificación "lejos de configurar una amenaza a la libertad, importaría haber hecho conocer al interesado la existencia de actuaciones en las cuales le correspondería invocar, si fuere el caso, los derechos que creyere le asisten, aún antes de la adopción de cualquier disposición que pudiera afectar esa libertad, que así no aparece amenazada ni restringida".

Es en estas disposiciones penales, propias del liberalismo jurídico tradicional, en las que se advierte como este es adoptado para formar parte de un nuevo modelo de Estado de derecho, incluso alcanzando formas jurídicas –luego de su derogación en 1956– que recién volvieron a adquirir jerarquía constitucional en 1994[194]. Lo explica Zaffaroni:

> [...] hasta 1955 podemos señalar la tendencia a un severo control social con ideología racista por parte de los gobiernos elitistas y una distensión punitiva y cierta humanización por parte de los gobiernos populares[195].

John W. Cooke fundamentaba la inclusión constitucional de estas garantías penales en la Constitución de los Estados Unidos Mexicanos en sus artículos 16, 19, 20 y 107, porque decía: "una de las finalidades primordiales del Estado democrático es la protección de los derechos individuales" (AP, p. 274). El fundamento era su carácter imprescindible en "todas las revoluciones progresistas de la humanidad". Y citaba a Perón cuando alguna vez dijo:

> Queremos una nación con doctrina y cultura profundamente humanista, en todo cuanto no se oponga o debilite al Estado, y con sentido y sentimiento estatal en cuanto no anule o tiranice al hombre. (AP, p. 276 y ss.)

En estas palabras de Perón se resume la razón por la cual ese liberalismo cívico podía tener cabida en la política nacional.

194 Una posición contraria postuló por entonces el constitucionalista Rafael Bielsa, *op. cit.*, quien fue crítico de la reforma constitucional porque en su opinión "en diversas partes es represiva y por tanto destinada a no perdurar", por especial referencia al art. 29 y el denominado Código de Justicia Policial de octubre de 1952 (Ley 14.165), el cual impugnaba porque "decimos que no es constitucional esa jurisdicción y ese régimen, pero lo sería si fuese exclusivamente disciplinario, porque todo organismo debe tener su régimen disciplinario [...] con las garantías elementales de la defensa en juicio".

195 En *Manual de Derecho Penal*, Buenos Aires, Ediar, 1994.

Luego del 55 se impusieron los criterios propios del positivismo criminológico con miras a reprimir y perseguir a los sectores populares y sus reclamos políticos y sociales. Ello tuvo su versión más refinada y cruel en el derecho penal de la "seguridad nacional" de la dictadura cívico-militar de 1976, la política criminal propia del terrorismo de Estado originada en la masacre de junio del 55 en Plaza de Mayo, y que continuó con los fusilamientos del año 1956, el Plan Conintes[196], la política de Onganía y la aparición de comandos de ultraderecha como la Triple A.

La reforma introducía, entre los derechos de los habitantes, "el de reunirse" conforme las leyes que reglamentaran su ejercicio (artículo 26). El derecho de reunión hasta entonces no se encontraba normado expresamente y solo era reconocido en el sistema normativo nacional como uno de los derechos implícitos del artículo 33. La Corte Suprema de Justicia de la Nación había sostenido que su origen estaba "en la libertad individual, de palabra y de asociación, y que nace de la soberanía del pueblo y de la forma republicana de gobierno" (Armando Arjones y otros del 17/11/1941, entre otros). En 1947, la Corte declaró la inconstitucionalidad de un edicto policial emitido en 1945 que autorizaba únicamente reuniones públicas con fines de conmemoración patriótica[197], aunque esta defensa del derecho de reunión fue restringida en el caso "Sofía" de 1959[198].

196 Lo que vino después del peronismo fue, además de antidemocrático, terrorista. Sin embargo no mereció la objeción constitucional de la Corte Suprema. En 1962, ese tribunal convalidó la denominada Ley marcial, por la cual se juzgaba a civiles bajo la jurisdicción militar, en ocasión de tener que fallar en un caso en el marco del Plan Conintes ("Rodríguez, Juan C. Ruggero, Conrado Tambascio, Juan C. s/sumario por actividades terroristas, subversivas, intimidación pública, y otras" de 1962). Para ello, los jueces dijeron que las normas que integraban el Plan Conintes tenían validez porque habían sido dictadas por "los poderes constitucionales", es decir, el presidente y el Congreso de la nación.
197 Fallos de la Corte Suprema de Justicia Nacional (CSJN) 207:251 (1947).
198 La importancia del derecho de reunión está en que constituye la base para el ejercicio del respeto de la autonomía de la persona y la participación en el proceso colectivo de toma de decisiones, exigencias básicas de la democracia liberal.

El estado de prevención y alarma
Las críticas de autoritarismo

El artículo 34 de la nueva Constitución creaba el estado de prevención y alarma. Sobre su fundamento Sampay dijo en la asamblea

> [...] que apuntaba a poner en manos del Poder Ejecutivo un instrumento rápido de acción, muy limitado en cuanto a sus facultades y perentorio en cuanto a la duración de sus atribuciones, para los casos de turbación que no alcancen a requerir el estado de sitio [...].

El constituyente Julio Lafitte explicó que se diferenciaba del estado de sitio en que este era "una medida de defensa del Estado, y el estado de prevención y alarma, como una medida destinada a garantizar la seguridad de la vida civil y de la actividad social". Lo fundamentó en que se había desnaturalizado conceptualmente al estado de sitio en diferentes momentos de la vida institucional del país, por habérselo mantenido "en vigencia durante largo tiempo hasta casi convertirse en un estado de normalidad enfermiza, con verdadero agravio para la libertad y la cultura cívica y jurídica del país". Citó también como antecedente la legislación española de 1870, vigente entonces, y mencionó la importancia de la determinación de sus alcances por una ley posterior. Finalmente expuso que no se pretendía

> [...] permitir una dictadura, ni darle instrumentos legales. Por el contrario, queremos dar a los gobiernos legalistas y respetuosos de las leyes y del cumplimiento de su deber el medio exacto y adecuado para salvar la salud del pueblo, su bienestar y su tranquilidad, sin distinción de clases ni banderas.

Este punto ha sido de crítica recurrente por parte de la doctrina liberal conservadora. Debe mencionarse entre varios al constitucionalista Jorge Vanossi[199] quien fundamenta su crítica en aquellos rasgos que consideraba

199 Comunicación del académico Dr. Jorge Reinaldo Vanossi, en sesión privada de la Academia Nacional de Ciencias Morales y Políticas, 9 de noviembre de 2005, disponible en la web http://www.ancmyp.org.ar/user/files/La_constitucion.pdf.

autoritarios[200]. La reforma constitucional, según esta interpretación habría consagrado

> [...] un régimen de "cesarismo" [...]. [con] cláusulas tales como las que permitían un acentuado control cualitativo de los partidos políticos (artículo 15), extendían el ámbito de la represión penal (artículo 21), establecían el "estado de prevención y alarma" con restricciones para la libertad personal (artículo 34), ampliaban considerablemente los alcances de la jurisdicción militar sobre las personas (artículo 29)[201].

Esto último permitía el sometimiento de civiles a consejos de guerra bajo circunstancias excepcionales, pero en 1951 se sancionó el Código de Justicia Militar (Ley 14.029), que recién fue derogado con la Ley 26.394 del 29/8/2008[202].

200 Escribe Zaffaroni: "En el segundo gobierno del Gral. Perón las damas de beneficencia pertenecientes a los sectores más elitistas de la ciudad, en conflicto con el Ejecutivo y con la Fundación Eva Perón se reunieron para cantar el Himno Nacional en la calle Florida y fueron sancionadas con arresto por el edicto de escándalo público." En *Manual de Derecho Penal*, Buenos Aires, Ediar, 1994. En 1948, el joven abogado Ismael Viñas denunció "la detención canallesca de ocho damas que distribuían volantes en la calle Florida" recluidas en un asilo treinta días por repartir volantes con la leyenda "Salve la Constitución".

201 La Corte en el caso "Attias, Alberto" (1951) sostuvo la constitucionalidad de la Ley 14.062 que declaró el estado de guerra interno, porque "como lo consagra unánimemente la doctrina y la jurisprudencia, la declaración del estado de guerra –aun en el orden interno del país, en casos de insurrección u otros análogos– es, por su naturaleza, un acto indiscutiblemente político, que a semejanza del estado de sitio o de las intervenciones del artículo 6 en todos los casos en que el mismo las autoriza, es función privativa de los poderes políticos del Gobierno, a los que exclusivamente corresponde su verificación". Entonces, "la detención de los ciudadanos cuando media el estado de guerra interno, constitucionalmente autorizado por la ley que aprobara la declaración ejecutiva, constituye el ejercicio regular de uno de los poderes legítimos inherentes a ese estado". Casares, por su voto, opinó que esa declaración de estado de sitio (art. 34 de la Constitución) es "insusceptible de revisión judicial porque es de carácter político".

202 *Ídem* Zaffaroni, p. 141.

En efecto, tales normas parecen haber estado inspiradas en criterios de matriz positivista, que a la luz del derecho penal liberal y los criterios garantistas, hoy son criticables. Si bien se crearon garantías penales, como las señaladas en el punto anterior, lo cierto es que en la actualidad las normas criticadas no superarían el análisis de constitucionalidad (si fueran normas inferiores) o el de adecuación al Derecho internacional (si fueran normas constitucionales), porque el estado actual al que ha arribado la evolución de nuestro derecho –jurisprudencia, doctrina y legislación vigente– no lo permitiría. Pero también es necesario realizar algunas precisiones.

En primer lugar, aún no había tenido lugar la importante evolución que con posterioridad registró el derecho internacional de los derechos humanos y no existía el conjunto de tratados, pactos y reglas que condiciona al derecho penal interno. Tampoco el país había asumido la obligación de adecuar su legislación interna a tales principios y reglas propias del garantismo, bajo el riesgo de generar responsabilidad internacional, como ocurre en la actualidad (por ejemplo, con la Convención Americana de Derechos Humanos). No se había desarrollado una teoría crítica penal latinoamericana como ocurrió varias décadas después (Lola Aniyar de Castro, Roberto Bergalli, Rosa del Olmo, Eugenio Raúl Zaffaroni, entre muchos otros), ya sea en su variante abolicionista al estilo de Louk Hulsman, o de las tesis de la intervención mínima (Luigi Ferrajoli, entre otros)[203].

En segundo lugar, en un análisis histórico, debe concluirse que no es una normativa ni práctica que corresponda a un Estado autoritario al estilo "fascista", ya que el fascismo es una forma política de expresión de las posiciones imperialistas y expansionistas de las naciones más poderosas del mundo, y de avance del capital financiero.

203 Una política de seguridad ciudadana democrática ha sido una materia pendiente aún no resuelta, como se desprende del "Acuerdo para la seguridad democrática" en el 2010, que señala que "las respuestas estatales autoritarias e ineficientes frente al delito y la fuerte dosis de exclusión y violencia que domina el debate público y que orienta muchas de las acciones del Estado, exigen una discusión abierta y pluralista, capaz de alcanzar acuerdos básicos sobre políticas democráticas de seguridad que atiendan las legítimas demandas de la sociedad".

También debe mencionarse la existencia de un sistema judicial, que con los criterios propios de la época intervino en diferentes casos de relevancia social, y de la Corte Suprema de Justicia de la Nación, cuya presidencia estaba a cargo de Tomás Casares, distinguido jurista de ideología cristiana. Pero los cuerpos de seguridad del país estaban influenciados por una fuerte doctrina "anticomunista y antianarquista" con sesgo racista, clasista y antidemocrático –cuya matriz tenía origen en los EUA y los países europeos–, que mantenía su vigencia desde casi los orígenes de su formación a finales del siglo XIX[204]. Adviértase que pasaron décadas para que en nuestro país hubiera políticas de reformas democráticas, ya que recién a partir de 1983, con grandes dificultades y matices, formaron parte de la agenda pública, y se puede contar como antecedente la corta gestión de Esteban Righi como ministro de Interior en 1973 durante la "primavera camporista"[205].

Se conjugan varios factores que concurren a explicar las normas de prevención y alarma incluidas en la reforma –aunque no necesariamente a justificar–, entre los cuales se pueden mencionar: la previsión de una

204 En este punto debe considerarse a la Comisión Bicameral presidida por el diputado oficialista José Emilio Visca, que se dedicaba a investigar las "actividades antiargentinas", en el año 1950 y mediante la cual, según Félix Luna, se habría perseguido a unos sesenta periódicos de distintos pueblos y ciudades entre enero y febrero de 1950.

205 A modo de ejemplo, puede citarse lo ocurrido durante un gobierno democrático. Con motivo de la huelga ferroviaria y la paralización del servicio público que implicaba, el presidente Arturo Frondizi apeló a la Ley 13.234 dictada por el gobierno justicialista en 1948, que había creado el Servicio de Defensa Nacional, por el cual el Poder Ejecutivo podía movilizar a población civil cuando fuera necesario para la defensa, o en casos de catástrofe o emergencias graves que afectaran parte del territorio nacional, y en consecuencia dictó el Decreto 10.394/58 (*La Ley*, Anales de la Legislación Argentina, T. XVII-B, p. 1241) por el cual declaró "movilizado" a todo el personal ferroviario, y sometido al Código de Justicia Militar y su reglamentación. El obrero Vicente Pucci faltó a trabajar con motivo de la huelga y fue condenado por un consejo de guerra en un proceso sumarísimo de un día a la pena de dos años de prisión. Todo fue avalado por distintas instancias judiciales y la Corte misma (salvo la disidencia de Orgaz). Pucci fue indultado al año siguiente.

reacción opositora de conspiración que, con fines de derrocamiento, utilizó medios violentos, como ocurrió en los hechos de los años 51, 52 y 55; la ausencia de un sistema de partidos con vocación democrática e inserción popular y que padecía una crisis terminal de representación –adviértase que la crisis política alcanzó a todo el abanico partidario sin que quedara ningún espacio al amparo–; la falta de una cultura política democrática como resultado de la década infame, cuya principal característica había sido justamente una combinación de la corrupción institucional, el descrédito hacia la clase dirigente y el fraude electoral como mecanismo de elección de autoridades; las características del peronismo como un frente al que concurrían diferentes sectores, entre ellos, parte de las Fuerzas Armadas y la jerarquía eclesiástica, cuyas visiones verticales exigían un orden de iguales características.

Entonces, mal puede derivarse de la crítica a las normas de prevención y alarma, que por justa no deja de ser parcial, la conclusión de que el régimen político imperante era autoritario, y se extiende su impugnación a todo el sistema político y económico, cuando en verdad son aspectos claramente diferenciables. Mientras en lo social, en el diseño del modelo de nación la Constitución del 49 tiene, como señalamos, una inspiración esencial que se corresponde con el nacionalismo democrático –con variada influencia, como el liberalismo político y jurídico–, en lo relativo a la política de seguridad nacional aquella varía en algunos aspectos, que parecen ser continuación de los criterios del positivismo hasta entonces vigentes. Siguiendo aquella crítica, estaríamos transformando lo accesorio en lo principal, repitiendo la impugnación que usualmente ocurre con los movimientos nacionales en nuestro continente cuando intentan organizarse y acceder al poder[206]. Algunos han encontrado como caracterizadora del período la relación "amigo-enemigo" pero, aun con la razón que pueda entrañar ello, esa contradicción social debe ser explicada como consecuencia de la realización de las tareas nacionales por parte de

206 Raanan Rein, historiador israelí especialista en populismos latinoamericanos, critica la existencia del mito de un "peronismo antisemita" (*Tiempo Argentino*, 19/09/2011).

un país que intentaba desarrollarse en su plenitud, aun en perjuicio de aquellos sectores sociales cuyo interés estaba en mantener el antiguo orden. En este punto cobra cierta relevancia la raíz cristiana del peronismo que, de algún modo también es extensible a los movimientos nacionales populares de América Latina. Methol Ferré, con acierto, señalaba que "la dialéctica amigo-enemigo en términos cristianos no se resuelve con el aniquilamiento del enemigo, sino con la recuperación del enemigo como amigo"[207], enunciado con eco en la dialéctica del amo y el esclavo hegeliana, en la que la función liberadora está solo en manos del esclavo quien, al liberarse, libera también al amo de la relación de dominio; por lo que debe descartarse cualquier connotación fundamentalista que pretenda atribuírsele.

En tercer lugar, en este punto corresponde también señalar que la reforma constitucional no implicó cambios en cuanto a la facultad de los jueces para ejercer el control de constitucionalidad, con la función casatoria de la Corte Suprema y la obligatoriedad de sus fallos (art. 96).

> Es decir que si bien los jueces no pueden juzgar sobre la política jurídica de las leyes por errada que ella sea, sí están facultados para rever la que llega a lo absurdo, irrazonable o confiscatorio (de acuerdo al anterior art. 23 de la CN y el ahora vigente art. 35)[208].

En definitiva, como en toda política de Estado, existen causas históricas que deben ser analizadas. Las condiciones políticas en que asumió el poder el peronismo, y la magnitud y características de las tareas a realizar, le exigió la concreción de un frente fuertemente centralizado, en donde la ausencia de una clase política y dirigente con representatividad a la altura que tales circunstancias requerían propició un ejercicio del poder

207 Methol Ferré, Alberto y Metalli, Alver, *La América Latina del siglo XXI*, Buenos Aires, Edhasa, 2006, p. 31.

208 Según la opinión de Alejandro Ghigliani en "Del control jurisdiccional de constitucionalidad" y el comentario de Juan Francisco Linares en la *Revista Jurisprudencia Argentina, 1953-III*. En el mismo sentido se expresó en reiteradas oportunidades la Corte Suprema de Justicia de la Nación. Este criterio concurre a relativizar las críticas de falta de control y abuso de poder.

fuertemente personalizado, en cuyo análisis poco aportan las recurrentes críticas al "hiperpresidencialismo"[209].

9) La libertad de prensa

El artículo 15 de la reforma constitucional decía:

> El Estado no reconoce libertad para atentar contra la libertad. Esta norma se entiende sin perjuicio del derecho individual de emisión del pensamiento dentro del terreno doctrinal, sometido únicamente a las prescripciones de la ley [...].

Lo dispuesto hacía referencia a los medios de comunicación, a la libertad de prensa, o bien ya para intentar limitar la "libertad de empresa". Scalabrini Ortiz aportó una reflexión de notable actualidad y profundidad conceptual:

> En un país empobrecido, los grandes diarios son órganos de dominio colonialista. El periodismo es quizás la más eficaz de las armas modernas que las naciones eventualmente poderosas han utilizado para dominar pacíficamente hasta la intimidad del cuerpo nacional y sofocar casi en germen los balbuceos de todo conato de oposición. Su acción es casi indenunciable porque fundamentalmente opera, no a través de sus opiniones sino mediante el diestro empleo de la información que por su misma índole no puede proporcionar una visión integral y solo transfiere aquella parte de la realidad que conviene a los intereses que representa." (Bases para la reconstrucción nacional).

Los dos grandes matutinos de la época eran *La Nación* y *La Prensa*, fundados por Bartolomé Mitre y José C. Paz respectivamente, hombres de la

209 Dice J. A. Ramos: "Estas contradicciones eran habituales y sirven para que dibujemos a la distancia un retrato más o menos aproximado de un régimen que no puede ser simplificado con un simple aforismo, ya que expresa en último análisis la inmadurez histórica del país, sus debilidades, su osadía, su esperanza y su frustración". En *El marxismo de indias*, Barcelona, Planeta, 1973, p. 29. También ver: Zaffaroni E. R., "Estudio sobre la Constitución de la Nación Argentina de 1949", *Revista de Derecho Público INFOJUS*, Buenos Aires, 2014.

oligarquía nativa y dueños de la máquina de dar prestigio cultural en el país semicolonial como oportunamente denunciaron Manuel Ugarte y Ramón Doll. Su influencia sobre las clases medias los orientaba hacia un antiperonismo, lo que motivó el debate acerca de la validez de su pretendida neutralidad política y el rol de los medios de comunicación. El Poder Legislativo intervino en uso de sus facultades constitucionales, y el 18 de abril de 1951 se promulgó la ley de expropiación de *La Prensa*. En noviembre del mismo año, el periódico reapareció como órgano de la CGT[210]. Puede ser objeto de debate histórico la táctica elegida por Perón, pero sin duda debe ser reconocido el problema en su verdadera dimensión y la cuestión del rol de esos medios a lo largo de la historia en relación al derecho a la información de toda la población, incluido el derecho a expresar opiniones, lo que adquirió con el tiempo, y en especial a partir de los años noventa, una relevancia aun mayor con el surgimiento de los multimedios.

El estado del debate jurídico acerca del alcance del concepto de libertad de expresión aún esperó varios años para tener una evolución de mayor profundidad, tanto en lo nacional como en lo internacional. Incluso así, en nuestro país, en los años posteriores a 1955, aquel se vio gravemente afectado por la seguidilla de dictaduras[211].

210 El presidente Juan Perón decía: "Hay algunos diarios que sistemáticamente combaten todas nuestras medidas. Son los que dicen que los teléfonos andan mal porque ahora son argentinos y que antes andaban bien porque los manejan los extranjeros. Pero ya se sabe por qué dicen eso, porque frente a ese artículo leemos el aviso que los paga." Y Cooke: "Creemos en la libertad de prensa independiente [...] pero no en el derecho de estas empresas mercantiles y capitalistas para procurar que los resortes del Estado se pongan al servicio de sus intereses [...]". Cuando en 1957 Cooke se escapa con otros compañeros del penal de Ushuaia, monta una radio clandestina desde donde comunicaba: "Aquí radio justicialista, desde algún lugar de la patria".

211 Todavía faltaba para el fallo que fue utilizado como fuente por la doctrina internacional, pronunciado por el Supremo Tribunal de los EUA el 9/3/1964 en el caso "The New York Times C. Sullivan", por el cual se revocó una sentencia que condenaba al pago de medio millón de dólares por indemnización a un funcionario policial, que se había visto supuestamente agraviado por una solicitada publicada en un periódico en defensa de Martin Luther King Jr. y en la que se denunciaba el terror provocado por las fuerzas de seguridad. La Corte allí es-

La cuestión se vincula con la lucha ideológica, y en este punto el peronismo demostró una falencia importante por ausencia de una política cultural adecuada al proceso revolucionario. Eso mismo señala Terroba como uno de los elementos que concurren a explicar la reacción conservadora y la caída del partido en 1955: "Su única debilidad había sido ideológica" ya que "continuaba la ideología del colonialismo al rendir homenajes de desagravio a Rivadavia, Sarmiento y Alberdi, definiendo a Rivadavia como el visionario de la grandeza argentina"[212]. Scalabrini Ortiz llegó a decir que "durante la época de Perón me tuvieron la boca tapada, ni un diario me abrió sus columnas ni una revista ni una tribuna, solo alcancé a dar tres conferencias en un centro obrero y Borlenghi lo hizo clausurar"[213]. Jauretche hizo una crítica similar.

Habla Perón a los constituyentes

El 27 de enero de 1949 Perón habló ante la Asamblea Constituyente y sostuvo que el fundamento de la reforma estaba en la evolución de los pueblos.

> Al pueblo no puede impedírsele que exteriorice su modo de pensar y de sentir [...] No podía el pueblo argentino [...] tolerar que la persona humana, que el caballero que cada pecho criollo lleva dentro, permaneciera a merced de los explotadores de su trabajo y de los conculcadores de su conciencia.

El camino de la explotación conduce al pueblo "al escepticismo y a la postración moral, desvinculándolo de la cosa pública".

> Afirmada la personalidad humana del ciudadano anónimo, aventada la dominación que fuerzas ajenas a las de la soberanía de

tableció la protección más amplia de la libertad de expresión conocida hasta el momento con el único límite de no actuar con "malicia real". Esta doctrina fue adoptada recién en 1986 por nuestra Corte Suprema en el caso "Campillay".

212 Terroba, Luís Alberto, *La Constitución Nacional de 1949, una causa nacional*, Buenos Aires, Fundación Ross, 2010, p. 367.

213 En Galasso, Norberto, *La búsqueda de la identidad nacional en J. L. Borges y R. Scalabrini Ortiz*, Rosario, Ediciones Homo Sapiens, 1998, p. 150.

nuestra Patria ejercían sobre la primera de nuestras fuentes de riqueza, es decir, sobre nuestros trabajadores y sobre nuestra economía; revelada de nuevo el ansia popular de vivir una vida libre y propia, se patentizó en las urnas el deseo de terminar para siempre y el afán de evitar el retorno de las malas prácticas y malos ejemplos que impedían el normal desarrollo de la vida argentina, por cauces de legalidad y de concordia. El clamor popular que acompañó serenamente a las Fuerzas Armadas el 4 de junio y estalló pujante el 17 de octubre, se impuso, solemne, el 24 de febrero. [La senda] para interpretar el sentimiento argentino y conducirlo con paso firme hacia sus grandes destinos [...] no es otra que la libertad individual, base de la soberanía; pero ha de cuidarse que el abuso de la libertad individual no lesione la libertad de otros y que la soberanía no se limite a lo político, sino que se extienda a lo económico o, más claramente dicho, que para ser libres y soberanos no debemos respetar la libertad de quienes la usen para hacernos esclavos o siervos.

¿Podían imaginarse los Convencionales del 53 que la igualdad garantizada por la Constitución llevaría a la creación de entes poderosos, con medios superiores a los propios del Estado? ¿Creyeron que estas organizaciones internacionales del oro se enfrentarían con el Estado y se negarían a sojuzgarle y a extraer las riquezas del país? ¿Pensaron siquiera que los habitantes del suelo argentino serían reducidos a la condición de parias obligándoles a formar una clase social pobre, miserable y privada de todos los derechos, de todos los bienes, de todas las ilusiones y de todas las esperanzas? ¿Pensaron que la máquina electoral montada por los que se apropiaron de los resortes del poder llegaría a poner la libertad de los ciudadanos a merced del caudillo político, del "patrón" o del "amo", que contaba su "poderío electoral" por el número de conciencias impedidas de manifestarse libremente?

> Con las reformas propiciadas pretendemos correr definitivamente un tupido velo sobre las ficciones que los argentinos de nuestra generación hemos tenido que vivir. Deseamos que se desvanezca el reino de las tinieblas y de los engaños. Aspiramos a que la Argentina pueda vivir una vida real y verdadera. Pero esto solo puede alcanzarse si la Constitución garantiza la existencia perdurable de una democracia verdadera y real.
>
> Mientras se fundaban los grandes capitalismos, el pueblo permaneció aislado y expectante. Después, frente la explotación, fortaleció su propio descontento. Hoy no es posible pensar organizarse sin el pueblo, ni organizar un Estado de minorías para entregar a unos pocos privilegiados la administración de la libertad. Esto quiere decir que de la democracia liberal hemos pasado a la democracia social.
>
> Nuestra preocupación no es tan solo crear un ambiente favorable para que los más capaces o los mejor preparados labren su prosperidad, sino procurar el bienestar de todos. Junto al arado, sobre la tierra, en los talleres y en las fábricas, en el templo del trabajo, donde quiera que veamos al individuo que forma esas masas, al descamisado, que identifica entre nosotros nuestra orgullosa comprensión del acontecimiento de nuestro siglo, se halla hoy también el Estado.

Al final de su discurso, Perón decía que "queden con su conciencia [...] los que quieren convertir la Nación en un rencoroso régimen de trabajos forzados sin compensaciones y sin alegrías".

La exposición de Sampay en la Convención

Arturo Sampay actuó como el miembro informante en la Convención Nacional Constituyente de 1949. Fue su figura intelectual, y no solo por su función política sino también por la profundidad y el contenido de sus discursos. En su informe general ante la Asamblea Constituyente, como miembro informante y presidente de la comisión de reformas, Arturo Sampay comenzó su exposición refiriéndose a la cuestión social en nuestro país.

> La Constitución de 1853, como todo el liberalismo, se propone afianzar la libertad personal –en lo cual reside lo vivo del liberalismo, aunque no es criatura suya, sino del cristianismo–, pero en esa concepción la libertad comportaba, simplemente, la supresión de las constricciones jurídicas. En consecuencia, la visión del Estado que anima a la Constitución de 1853 tiende a contenerlo en un mínimo de acción, neutralizándolo en el mayor grado posible con respecto a las tensiones de intereses existentes en el seno de la sociedad.

Sampay, para ilustrar, citó a Juan Bautista Alberdi:

> He aquí –concluye Alberdi– todo el ministerio de la ley, todo el círculo de su intervención en la producción, distribución y consumo de la riqueza pública y privada: se reduce pura y sencillamente a garantizar su más completa independencia y libertad, en el ejercicio de esas tres grandes funciones del organismo económico argentino.

Sobre esto, contundente, Sampay opinó:

> No me ocuparé en poner de relieve los errores de esta concepción política, que tuvo efectos que produjeron una penosa realidad sociológica –la concentración de la riqueza en pocas manos y su conversión en un instrumento de dominio y de explotación del hombre por el hombre– y que, mientras algunas potencias extranjeras proclamaban al exterior la libertad económica para servirse de ella en su política de imperialismo y de monopolios mercantiles, nos llevaron a nosotros, en aras de ese esquema utópico, con toda buena fe –pues la generación liberal del 53 estaba constituida por doctores de una ideología, y no por servidores de una plutocracia– a poner en manos ajenas el usufructo de nuestras riquezas y hasta el contralor internacional de nuestros ríos interiores.

Respecto de la interpretación del significado histórico de la Asamblea Constituyente de 1853, nos remitimos a lo ya sostenido en el capítulo

anterior, en tanto que no es posible caracterizarla como un producto exclusivo del orden oligárquico sino como expresión de las relaciones sociales de la época. Entonces, Sampay definía el contenido real de la libertad jurídica en el juego de dos planos: el de la explotación del hombre por el hombre y el de la explotación de naciones por potencias extranjeras. En otras palabras, se trata de la cuestión nacional y la cuestión social, como parte de un mismo hecho.

Sampay, con el advenimiento de la democracia de masas, como contracara y superación del Estado neutro y abstencionista del liberalismo conservador hegemónico, considera a "toda actividad humana como potencialmente política, en la medida en que un acto humano privado puede significar una perturbación del bien común"[214]. De ahí que se necesitó de "una eficaz administración reglamentaria y controladora, que es atributo del poder ejecutivo". Hasta aquí tenemos una clara definición política del rol del Estado, ya no en la abstracción de las características concretas de la sociedad propuesta por el liberalismo europeísta, sino en el contexto de la lucha de clases y las cuestiones nacional y continental contra las estrategias geopolíticas de las potencias extranjeras, en una visión de conjunto que significa un análisis de la totalidad concreta, en cuyo interior la legalidad debe jugar un papel consciente y clarificador, es decir tomar partido y denunciar la falsedad de la declarada neutralidad del Estado y su pretendido abstencionismo normativo.

Haciendo un poco de historia para entender ese presente de profundos cambios sociales que clamaba por ser acompañado por una nueva Constitución, Sampay decía:

> Después de la Primera Guerra Mundial advino la democracia de masas, resultante de una convergencia de circunstancias históricas que no es del caso analizar aquí, y el Estado neutro y

214 Para Sampay "el fin natural de la autoridad es efectuar la justicia o el bien común, lo que equivale a decir obtener la plena participación de todos y cada uno de los miembros de la colectividad en los bienes materiales y culturales de la civilización". En *Constitución y Pueblo*, Buenos Aires, Instituto Superior Arturo Jauretche, 2011, p. 103.

> abstencionista del liberalismo se convirtió en el Estado que considera toda actividad humana como potencialmente política, en la medida en que un acto humano privado puede significar una perturbación del bien común.

La causa de ese cambio trascendental tiene nombre: “la democracia de masas”. Y aquí viene un párrafo trascendental para entender su interpretación de la historia inmediata:

> Aquí anoto que, justamente en ese momento histórico comienza la crisis de la parte dogmática de nuestra Constitución y la documentación de violaciones flagrantes de la Carta Fundamental por parte de los intereses afectados por los principios de la política social y económica de Yrigoyen, quienes propiciaban la petrificación de la letra y espíritu de la Constitución de 1853 como un medio de impedir que el poder político enfrentara al poder económico, y de permitir que este último siguiera teniendo, en la realidad, el poder político a su servicio.

Es que efectivamente el país oligárquico utilizó la carta constitucional a su favor, lo que consistía justamente en esa “petrificación” que advertía Sampay como recurso para volverla “neutral” ante el conflicto social, y que las posibilidades que su interpretación pudiera abrir, se clausuraran mediante la tradicional y conservadora interpretación de la Corte Suprema en su función de “guardián del orden”. Su conclusión fue contundente a la hora de impugnar la ideología dominante: “La no intervención (del Estado en materia económica) implica la intervención a favor del más fuerte”.

En este contexto, la democracia de masas, expresada en un “poder ejecutivo de vigorosos atributos”, intervenía activamente en la vida política para modificar la realidad, con una opción que señalaba una continuidad entre dos liderazgos populares de los movimientos nacionales: Yrigoyen y Perón. La activa participación política de los sectores populares (en palabras de Sampay: “el magnífico movimiento ascensional de

la clases obreras") era el proyecto de una nueva nación más justa; por lo tanto, era la realidad nacional la que exigía una nueva Constitución que la legitimara y le diera impulso. Para Sampay, el texto de la Constitución del 53, ante ese nuevo desafío de la época, era un escollo en el camino de la participación popular,

> [...] por lo que su dogmática ya no rige la vida argentina, malogrando una de las funciones primordiales de la Constitución, a saber: la docencia que cumple sobre los gobernados, su acatamiento e inviolabilidad.

Sampay, como muchos otros, preveía que la democracia liberal no iba a quedarse sentada observando pasivamente como el país cambiaba o, mejor dicho, como un país avanzaba sobre el otro transformándolo. Por eso, no ocultaba su preocupación:

> Cuando una constitución ha perdido vigencia histórica porque la realidad se ha desapareado de ella, debe abandonarse la ficción de una positividad que no existe, y adecuarla a la nueva situación [...] Además, si se acogen en la ley fundamental la realidad surgida por la exigencia de justicia, el nuevo orden socioeconómico y la garantía de una efectiva vigencia de los derechos sociales del hombre, se atajan las posibilidades de que un vaivén reaccionario, jurisprudencia o legislativo, eche por tierra el edificio alzado sobre la base de la justicia social, so pretexto de cumplir las normas de la Constitución.

Para afirmar esto, Sampay citaba, como ejemplo, al *New Deal* de Roosevelt, al que caracterizaba como

> [...] el conjunto de disposiciones concebidas para limitar la libertad absoluta de las poderosas organizaciones capitalistas americanas y el desenfreno de los productores, orientando socialmente la economía y protegiendo las clases obreras, cuyo espíritu, sin duda, estaba en oposición con el individualismo que alienta en la Constitución americana, modelo de la nuestra de 1853.

Temía que en nuestro país pasara lo que ocurrió en Estados Unidos, cuando en 1935 la Suprema Corte declaró la "inconstitucionalidad de las dos columnas que sustentaban el *New Deal*: el organismo de contralor para la industria, y el organismo de contralor para la producción agrícola."

En efecto, la política intervencionista del *New Deal* recibió fuertes embates y resistencia por parte de la clase dominante con el fin de impedir las transformaciones propuestas que afectaban sus intereses, reacción que contó con el apoyo activo de la Suprema Corte de los EUA.

A la luz de la Constitución del 53 y de una interpretación conservadora de la misma,

> [...] las leyes protectoras de la economía nacional que la libran de la expoliación de los consorcios capitalistas y la hacen servir al hombre, serían inconstitucionales porque contrarían la libertad de industria y comercio asegurada por la Constitución vigente [...].

Sampay tenía razón en alertarse. Lo que no se imaginaba era que en nuestro país, los pilares de la democracia de masas no serían destruidos por fallos judiciales que declararan la inconstitucionalidad del bien común y la revolución nacional, sino por bombardeos aéreos, fusilamientos y persecuciones en masa. Su concepción política tributaba a una antropología definida:

> Como Perón tantas veces lo proclamara diciendo: "El Estado es para el hombre y no el hombre para el Estado" [...] los hombres están subordinados al Estado, para de esta manera resultar coordinados a un mismo fin: el bien común [...] [pero]obsérvese que este sometimiento del interés individual al bien de todos no es, rigurosamente hablando, la renuncia que una persona hace de un "bien suyo" a favor de un "bien ajeno", sino que es la renuncia de un bien propio menor a favor de uno mayor, exigido por su esencia social, esto es por una de las dimensiones ontológicas del ser humano.

Si la voluntad política era construir una nación, era necesario crear un horizonte de sentido en el que se reflejaran las formas de un futuro mejor.

> Toda la legislación intervencionista que la reforma autoriza tiende a compensar la inferioridad contractual, la situación de sometimiento en que se haya el sector de los pobres dentro del sistema del capitalismo moderno, falto de moral y caridad, que aprovecha su prepotencia económica para la explotación del prójimo, sea obrero o consumidor; por eso, tal intervención irá perdiendo su razón de ser en la medida en que los elementos desquiciadores del mutuo acuerdo sean substancialmente dominados, haciendo que emerja per se la legitimidad de los negocios privados respectos de los principios de justicia.
>
> Lo típico del sesgo constitucional del siglo XX, confrontado con las declaraciones liberales de la centuria decimonónica, es el alargamiento de los derechos personales acompañado de una limitación de los derechos individuales que se consideraban absolutos e intocables, o sea, el derecho de propiedad y la libertad económica, y como consecuencia, una nueva concepción de las relaciones entre los individuos y de estos con la sociedad, al punto de que el abuso de la libertad, que equivale a una falta de solidaridad humana, es punido como un delito. Así lo proyecta la reforma.

Para terminar, Sampay, en perspectiva emancipadora, señaló alguna vez que "el progreso de la justicia es el sentido de la historia" porque el avance de las ciencias "posibilita, por primera vez en la historia, extender los beneficios de la civilización al género humano entero". Para ello, será necesario que los pueblos se den a sí mismos el mejor modo de organización política y económica que permita la más justa distribución y acceso a esos beneficios de la civilización: la eficacia del principio normativo de igualdad entre las personas y los pueblos. La superación del orden global elitista, así como la de los órdenes oligárquicos que someten y frustran nuestro destino colectivo, es el auténtico significado de ese sentido de la

historia que mencionaba Sampay. Ese es el mundo que se viene que, en nuestra América, es el de la unidad y la igualdad.

El fin del ciclo nacional popular peronista

El desarrollo productivo y la industrialización fueron rasgos salientes del período pero, no obstante los esfuerzos realizados, el país no había alcanzado a echar las bases suficientes para una industria pesada proveedora de insumos locales. La fuente más importante de ingresos de divisas seguía siendo la exportación de materias primas del campo por lo que, pese a los niveles de crecimiento y soberanía alcanzados, aún persistía un esquema económico con riesgos de estrangulamiento y restricción externa cuyos efectos nocivos dificultaban la evolución del proyecto nacional. Fue el mismo año de la reforma (1949), el que marcó el inicio de un declive en los términos de intercambio del comercio exterior y achicamiento de la renta agraria diferencial, que afectó al modelo de desarrollo productivo mercadointernista que impulsó el peronismo, con la aparición de los primeros indicios de la crisis económica que fue preponderante en los últimos años. El desplazamiento de Miguel Miranda por Alfredo Gómez Morales fue el anuncio del plan de estabilización que se impuso a partir de 1952 para hacer frente al déficit comercial y la crisis provocada por la suba constante de precios y, en especial, por la exclusión del país del Plan Marshall[215].

Pero también hubo motivos de carácter político. En 1952, como indicio de los límites de construcción política del modelo nacional revolucionario, Arturo Sampay se exilió, objeto de una persecución política. Su marcha coincidió con el destino de otras figuras que compartían con él una mirada similar. Según Galasso

215 El ministro de Finanzas, cuando presentó el proyecto de ley de reforma financiera en septiembre de 1949, reconoció los síntomas de la crisis provocada por "signos inequívocos de un importante cambio en la situación económica mundial [...] Por primera vez desde 1945 se producen bajas de precios, se detiene el aumento de la producción mundial y aparece la desocupación [...] baja de cotización internacional de los granos [porque] la producción ha crecido más rápidamente que la demanda efectiva".

> [...] se percibe de qué manera se produce el alejamiento de los hombres más valiosos [...] aquellos que se encontraban en condiciones de dar batalla ideológica a la oposición, llevando a cabo la pedagogía nacional que pudiese "desazonzar" a los sectores medios tomados por el discurso oligárquico[216].

Los que, de un modo u otro, dentro o fuera del país, se alejaron del poder político, fueron hombres de gran importancia: Manuel Ugarte (falleció en 1951), Raúl Scalabrini Ortiz, Ramón Carrillo, Domingo Mercante, Juan José Hernández Arregui, Arturo Jauretche y John William Cooke.

La debilidad del frente político se correspondió también con las limitaciones encontradas para profundizar aun más la ampliación de las fuerzas productivas y los horizontes de la estructura económica del país, por medio del desarrollo de la industria pesada –aunque ya se habían empezado a sentar sus bases–, y con el achicamiento del ingreso nacional que potenció las contradicciones al interior del movimiento nacional, en especial entre la burguesía y los trabajadores[217]. Por un lado, la rentabilidad nacional disminuyó –en relación a los años anteriores de la "época de oro"–; por otro, los nuevos industriales, beneficiarios del modelo productivo, se mostraron políticamente inconsecuentes al pasarse al frente opositor, confrontar con los sindicatos y el gobierno nacional. La disputa creciente con la Iglesia aportó una base social de importancia a la oposición, y llevó al gobierno a una escalada que derivó, incluso, en un intento de reforma constitucional que no se concretó[218]. Pero el terreno de la

216 En *Perón, T. I, op cit.*, p. 613.

217 Eduardo Basualdo destaca que el escollo insalvable para el desarrollo estuvo del lado de los sectores industriales y no de los trabajadores, es decir, del capital y no del trabajo. Agrega que "el peronismo consigue disciplinar a varios de los sectores centrales de la agotada economía agroexportadora pero será doblegado por las fracciones del capital que conducen la actividad dinámica que promueve enfáticamente, entre los que se encuentra, además del capital extranjero, la fracción dominante de la oligarquía argentina", en *Los primeros gobiernos peronistas y la consolidación del país industrial: éxitos y fracasos*, Buenos Aires, FLACSO, 2004.

218 El 23 de mayo de 1955 Perón promulgó la Ley 14.404 por la cual declaró

conspiración y el golpismo ya estaba abonado para que los sectores oligárquicos nativos en el mes de junio, impulsados por el odio de clase, bombardearan el centro de Buenos Aires y mataran a cientos de compatriotas.

> [El] poderoso frente nacional del 45 ya no existe. Solo la clase trabajadora permanece sosteniendo al gobierno. La oligarquía comprende el peligro que la acecha y la oportunidad que se le presenta. En ese escenario político, se produce el golpe militar del 16 de septiembre de 1955[219].

El 15 de julio de 1955, después de la masacre de Plaza de Mayo, Juan Perón habló a los legisladores nacionales, en el medio del luto, mediante un llamado a la pacificación nacional.

> Con una absoluta licencia para que todo el mundo hiciera lo que quisiese, nosotros no habríamos podido cumplir nuestro objetivo y nuestros objetivos eran irrenunciables [...] No hemos jamás instaurado el terror para cumplirlos [...] Muertos violentamente por la acción revolucionaria no tenemos. A nosotros nos han matado a mucha gente, pero nosotros no hemos muerto a nadie [...] Este objetivo (la restauración del país) ha sido cumplido al realizarse la independencia económica [...] También hemos realizado el objetivo político con la reforma básica de la Constitución [...] Por eso días pasados, he dado por terminada la revolución [...] Comienza ahora una nueva etapa que es de carácter institucional, sin revoluciones, porque el estado permanente de un país no puede ser la revolución[220].

El 27 de julio siguiente, Perón dijo ante dirigentes gremiales:

"necesaria la reforma parcial de la Constitución Nacional en todo cuanto se vincula a la Iglesia y sus relaciones con el Estado, a fin de asegurar la efectiva libertad e igualdad de culto frente a la ley".

219 Galasso, Norberto, *Cuadernos para otra historia, nro.* 3, Buenos Aires, Centro Cultural Enrique Santos Discépolo, 2003.

220 Galasso, Norberto, *Perón, T.1, op cit.*, p. 700.

> Hemos promovido una conciencia económica en el país [...] En el aspecto político, hemos desterrado el fraude y hemos reformado la Constitución [...] Nuestras conquistas no tienen aspecto reversible, no pueden volver atrás.

Perón parecía creer en eso de que "los hombres reales y actuantes se hallan condicionados por un determinado desarrollo de las fuerzas productivas" –como decía Marx–, al punto de que la imposibilidad de retornar al país oligárquico, dato real que se desprendía de la objetividad del estadio de las relaciones sociales, lo llevaba a confiar en la continuidad de los rasgos más fuertes de la revolución nacional aun después de su derrocamiento. Pero si bien fue cierto, por un lado, que no se pudo volver a las relaciones de producción vigentes antes de 1943, tampoco lo fue menos que el país se reconvirtió en un modelo dependiente a partir de la desnacionalización de la economía y crecimiento del capital extranjero, con la larga proscripción del peronismo y la sucesión de dictaduras o democracias débiles. Se inició, así, un largo y doble exilio: el de Perón de su patria y el del pueblo de su conductor.

IV.
El ciclo liberal y antidemocrático: de 1955 a 1957

Se vuelve cruda mentira
lo que fue tierna verdad
y hasta la tierra fecunda
se convierte en arenal.
Atahualpa Yupanqui

El proceso de liberación nacional se interrumpe y la película deja de proyectarse hacia adelante "mientras los más fervorosos gorilas del 55 pretenden incluso dar vuelta los carretes para regresar al 3 de junio de 1943" en su intento de volver al país semicolonial. El ciclo 55-58 se caracterizó principalmente por el giro sustancial del proyecto socioeconómico caracterizado por la desnacionalización de la economía, la pérdida de soberanía, la implementación de una política económica liberal y de ajuste, y la de un orden político elitista y duramente represivo con violaciones masivas a los derechos de los trabajadores y los derechos humanos. Rodolfo Puiggrós decía, sobre la oscura etapa iniciada, que

> [...] los consultores y asesores del gobierno militar nacido del golpe de fuerza hicieron del pueblo una entelequia y de la democracia una abstracción, por lo que se creyeron con derecho a violar las libertades del auténtico pueblo en nombre de un pueblo fantasma y a burlarse de las exigencias de las masas invocando una democracia sofisticada y vacía [...] con una soberbia respaldada por el poder del dinero y los recursos de la propaganda imperialista pretendieron que la sociedad argentina no fuera lo que era, sino lo que ellos deseaban que fuera, para cumplir las órdenes de sus mandantes[221].

221 En *Historia crítica de los partidos políticos argentinos*, Buenos Aires, Hyspamérica, 1986.

Hernández Arregui directamente hablaba de la barbarie de la oligarquía al señalar que en 1955 había bombardeado "a su propio pueblo y festejado su crimen como otro fasto triunfal de la civilización contra la barbarie". La dicotomía peronismo-antiperonismo expresó durante décadas la lucha de clases en nuestro país, reactualizando a su modo la histórica falsa dualidad civilización o barbarie del siglo XIX.

La Revolución Libertadora se autoproclamó defensora de la más "auténtica y absoluta libertad" y de "los principios democráticos y republicanos". El lenguaje del liberalismo oligárquico volvió a nuestro país para ahogar, en un mar sordo de abstracciones enunciativas, cualquier reclamo nacional y popular. En este contexto jurídico e ideológico se produjo la suspensión en sus cargos de 92.000 dirigentes sindicales y la sanción del Decreto 9.270/56 –que derogó la importante ley con la que el peronismo consagró el derecho sindical– por el que se procuró fragmentar la estructura gremial heredada pero que, en los hechos, no funcionó por el rechazo de los propios trabajadores[222]. Se buscaba imponer "la libertad sindical", como dice Héctor Recalde, "un eufemismo más del liberalismo ideológico detrás del cual está el riesgo de la debilidad sindical". También se dictó el Decreto-Ley 4.161/56 por el cual se instauraba un virtual delito de opinión al prohibir la propaganda peronista, o el uso de expresiones como

> [...] peronismo, peronista, justicialismo, justicialista, tercera posición, la abreviatura P.P., las fechas exaltadas por el régimen depuesto, las composiciones musicales denominadas *Marcha de los muchachos peronistas* y *Evita capitana* o fragmentos de las mismas, la obra *La razón de mi vida* o fragmentos, y los discursos del presidente depuesto y de su esposa o fragmentos.

La pena establecida era de treinta días –mínimo– a seis años –máximo– de prisión y multa, y no procedía la excarcelación ni la ejecución condicional[223].

222 Basualdo, Victoria, *Los delegados y las comisiones internas en la historia argentina: 1943-2007*, Buenos Aires, Cara o Ceca, 2011, p. 100.

223 Jauretche se refirió a la actuación ilegal de la Junta Nacional de

Todo un ejemplo de cómo un lenguaje cargado de formas sirvió para ocultar los verdaderos fines, de cómo un mar de palabras arremolinó para ocultar la ideología y las intenciones que acechaban desde el fondo. Si las clases populares querían vivir, ser reconocidas en su subjetividad y formar parte del nuevo país, debían hablar como correspondía al modo civilizado, abandonar su propio lenguaje y las normas de ese otro mundo indecible del que venían, el de las reivindicaciones sociales del país profundo. Lo innombrable era la barbarie, como el grito de "viva Perón" en la medianoche de una calle vacía o esa rebeldía colectiva desafiante de un grupo de hinchas cantando la marchita peronista. Pronto, ese nombre propio se tornaría el nombre de la resistencia y la revolución social, y el peronismo, en el hecho maldito del país burgués, como decía Cooke, por eso se proclamó el olvido –de cualquier modo, aunque sea por decreto, cesanteo o cárcel–, porque la memoria colectiva actualizaba nuevamente el recuerdo del 45.

En aquellos días emergió, como pudo, la resistencia peronista, con la espontaneidad como método de acción y la convicción como fuerza impulsora. Dice con acierto un documento de las Cátedras Nacionales: "Sería inútil buscar programas, planes de estudio. Una frase englobaba toda la ideología política del resistente: "el retorno incondicional de Perón"[224]. Eso pedían las frases escritas con tiza y carbón en las paredes de pueblos y ciudades. "Lo "democrático", lo antiobrero, lo bien (en el idioma de Landrú), lo proimperialista era lo antiperonista".

Recuperación Patrimonial creada después del golpe de 1955: "Era obligación de los interdictos presentarse ante la Comisión Especial constituida bajo el nombre de la Junta Nacional de Recuperación Patrimonial y aceptar las disposiciones absolutamente inconstitucionales y jurídicamente inmorales que contenía el decreto ley respectivo, disposiciones tales como la inversión del cargo de la prueba, la retroactividad de la ley penal, el juzgamiento por comisiones especiales, la indagación por funcionarios no hábiles jurídicamente y al margen de toda norma procesal. La sanción que penaba el no presentarse ante esa Junta era la "confiscación de bienes" también prohibida expresamente por la Constitución Nacional". (*Revista Mayoría*, 15/11/1959, citado en Galasso, Norberto e Ibáñez, Germán (eds.), *Arturo Jauretche. Textos Selectos*, Buenos Aires, Corregidor, 2004, p. 175.

224 En *Antropología del Tercer Mundo, nro. 10*, junio de 1972.

El 21 de septiembre de 1955, con la firma de Lonardi y Rial, por un lado, se dispuso una liberación de presos, mediante un decreto que, en sus fundamentos, ilustra sobre el contenido ideológico del nuevo poder de ese momento.

> Atento a que en muchas cárceles del país se encuentran presos políticos de las más variada condición, miembros de las Fuerzas Armadas y civiles, entre los cuales puede señalarse de modo muy especial a los oficiales de la Marina de Guerra y de Aeronáutica Militar que el 16 de junio pasado realizaron los actos preliminares de la Revolución que la Providencia ha permitido completar más tarde; que esos presos políticos, en su mayor parte, no han realizado otro delito que el de armar su brazo en defensa de la Constitución y las leyes o propagar principios de amor a la libertad y al decoro ciudadano.

Por otro lado, los jueces de la Corte Suprema y el procurador general fueron exonerados. En noviembre de ese año inició su desempeño la Junta Consultiva Nacional, creada por el Decreto 2.011 para sustituir al Congreso de la Nación –incluso tuvo sede en el mismo edificio–, con el objeto de asesorar al presidente de facto, e integrada por representantes de diferentes partidos políticos, con exclusión del peronismo –proscripto– y del Partido Comunista. Ahí desfilaron figuras como las del vicepresidente Isaac Rojas, Julio Noble, Reinaldo Pastor, Américo Ghioldi, Alicia Moreau de Justo, Juan Gauna, Miguel Zavala Ortiz (dirigente radical que protagonizó desde un avión los criminales bombardeos de junio de 1955), Oscar Alende y Nicolás Repetto, entre otros[225].

Las directivas básicas del 7 de diciembre de 1955 establecían los objetivos de la dictadura.

225 En ocasión de los levantamientos de junio de 1956, Américo Ghioldi justificó los fusilamientos porque, según él, "parece que es materia política, los argentinos necesitan aprender que la letra con sangre entra", y lanzó su tenebrosa frase: "se acabó la leche de la clemencia".

> La finalidad primera y esencial de la revolución ha sido derrocar al régimen de la dictadura [...] Debemos ahora [...] restablecer el imperio de la moral, de la justicia, del derecho, de la libertad y de la democracia. Cumplido ese objetivo y alcanzadas aquellas condiciones que permitan a la ciudadanía expresar su auténtica voluntad, ella decidirá sobre sus destinos. [...] Crear, con pleno resguardo de la soberanía nacional y sobre la base del respeto y garantía a la propiedad privada, las condiciones propicias a la inversión de capitales extranjeros que complementen y estimulen el esfuerzo de la producción argentina [...].

Si bien durante el breve tiempo de Lonardi no se adoptó ninguna medida respecto de la Constitución vigente –por lo cual continuó rigiendo la reforma de 1949–, la tesitura cambió luego del "golpe dentro del golpe" y su sustitución por el general Aramburu. Para González Arzac fue "la vuelta al liberalismo económico de los constituyentes de 1853, por lo que ahora sí la derogación de la Constitución de 1949 era imprescindible"[226]. Más allá de que no acuerde con el criterio de este importante jurista en el carácter exclusivamente regresivo que parece atribuirle a la Asamblea Constituyente de 1853, lo cierto es que la implementación del plan ideado por Raúl Prebisch, que provocó la advertencia de Scalabrini Ortiz acerca de que "el gato era mal guardián de las sardinas, por más ágil y de buena raza que sea el gato" (*El Líder*, 23/10/1955), significó efectivamente el regreso al libre cambio y la apertura al capital financiero extranjero, frente al cual el diseño constitucional de 1949 resultaba insuficiente[227].

226 *Revista Polémica, nro. 94*, año 1972, CEAL.
227 En mi opinión, cito a Sampay, quien resaltaba "la elasticidad" de la Constitución de 1853, ya que permitía, al no prohibirlo, que el comercio exterior estuviese bajo control exclusivo del Estado, o que se estableciera el monopolio público de la actividad bancaria. Igual, señalaba que "empero, todo lo que permite la Constitución escrita de 1853 por falta de preceptos prohibitivos, la de 1949 lo dispone de manera expresa y concede a los órganos del Estado las atribuciones precisas para tomar las decisiones conducentes al cambio de las estructuras económicas" (*Constitución y Pueblo*, Buenos Aires, Instituto Superior Arturo

En abril de 1956, mediante un decreto firmado por Aramburu, Rojas y Alsogaray, entre otros, se dispuso iniciar las "gestiones para el ingreso de la Argentina al Fondo Monetario Internacional y al Banco Internacional de Reconstrucción y Fomento [...] [y]la adhesión a las convenciones de Bretton Woods", porque era "perjudicial para la economía argentina continuar en el estado de aislamiento en que se la mantenía", lo que, finalmente, se aprobó con otro decreto del 31 de agosto. Si en la etapa anterior, Argentina era el único país del continente que no aceptaba las directivas del Fondo Monetario Internacional, en ese momento se dio inicio a un largo período, con algunas breves interrupciones, de sometimiento a sus dictados que abarcó hasta 2003.

Al mismo tiempo, la proclama del 27 de abril de 1956 expresaba lo siguiente:

> Que en la vida institucional de los Estados, el acto de mayor trascendencia es el de adoptar su Constitución o el de introducir en ella reformas sustanciales [...] Que el gobierno depuesto se ha caracterizado [...] por la presión oficial [...] por la violencia material con que los ha impuesto [...] Que la finalidad esencial de la reforma de 1949 fue obtener la reelección indefinida del entonces presidente de la República, finalidad probada fehacientemente por la representación opositora en la Convención constituyente [...]Que la revolución libertadora ha tenido su origen en la necesidad de poner término al caos imperante y a las causas que lo originaron [...] que a tal efecto [...] corresponde, en primer término, con carácter de deber impostergable, restablecer la Carta Fundamental que fue resultante de una libre autodeterminación [por lo que]corresponde restablecer, en su anterior vigencia, la Constitución de 1853 con las reformas anteriores al 11 de marzo de 1949, completando de este modo en el orden jurídico fundamental el acto revolucionario que tuvo por objeto abatir al régimen de la dictadura [...] Por ello, el Gobierno provisional de la Nación Argentina, en ejercicio de sus

---

Jauretche, 2011, pp. 204 y 205). Lo mismo puede decirse respecto de la reforma constitucional de 1994.

> poderes revolucionarios, proclama con fuerza obligatoria: Art. 1. Declarar vigente la Constitución nacional sancionada en 1853 [...] con exclusión de la de 1949 [...] Art. 2. El gobierno provisional de la Nación ajustará su acción a la Constitución que se declara vigente por el art. 1 en tanto y en cuanto no se oponga a los fines de la Revolución, enunciados en las directivas básicas del 7 de diciembre de 1955 y a las necesidades de la organización y conservación del gobierno provisional.

Este procedimiento de subordinar la estructura jurídica de la nación a un conjunto de "directivas" tuvo continuidad en el Acta de la Revolución Argentina de junio de 1966 y en el Estatuto Fundamental de agosto de 1972, ambos también autoproclamados superiores a la Constitución, y en especial, años después, cuando una junta militar usurpó el poder institucional el 24 de marzo de 1976 y colocó a la Constitución Nacional en un plano inferior al Estatuto para el Proceso de Reorganización Nacional. Frente a ello, las críticas dirigidas por la doctrina liberal conservadora contra la reforma constitucional de 1949 empalidecieron. Finalmente hay que agregar que la Corte Suprema de Justicia de la Nación legitimó con su jurisprudencia aquella inusual derogación de la reforma constitucional de 1949. Bernardo Velar de Irigoyen publicó una opinión de doctrina (*La Ley, T. 81*) en la que se consigna lo siguiente:

> El doctor Clodomiro Zavalía [...] llega a la conclusión de que "la Convención de 1949 se reunió bajo el signo de un movimiento social y económico que impuso por la fuerza sus enunciados [...] se trata de una creación espuria, susceptible de ser atacada en su esencia más que desde el punto de vista de las deficiencias formales que rodearon la sanción de la ley que dispuso la reforma".
> Por mi parte declaro, incurriendo en saludable indiscreción, que conocía la opinión del doctor Zavalía pues a su consejo y colaboración recurrí para confeccionar algunos proyectos –entre otros uno sobre derogación del Estatuto de 1949– para el llamado

> comando civil de un movimiento que se gestaba en 1952; estas actividades se interrumpieron cuando recibí alojamiento forzoso en la Penitenciaría Nacional.
> La Revolución de setiembre tuvo por declarada y esencial finalidad la restauración de las libertades escamoteadas y la vuelta al orden jurídico, y no escapa a la reflexión común que ese propósito no se lograría frente a disposiciones y enunciados introducidos en 1949 que no solo desfiguran la organización institucional de la República conforme con el régimen federal elegido para su gobierno sino que revisten acentuada concepción totalitaria, deslustrando la honrosa tradición democrática que llenó de orgullo a los argentinos. En condiciones tales no quedaría otro camino que el acto revolucionario francamente declarado como tal que implantara nuevamente la plena vigencia de la Carta política de 1853.

Como justificativo y para sustento cita

> [...] el fallo de la Corte Suprema que reconoció por primera vez el Gobierno "de facto de Mitre", con el derecho de la revolución triunfante y asentida por los pueblos y en virtud de los graves deberes que la victoria impone[228].

Es interesante este opúsculo jurídico porque el argumento de la nulidad de origen por vicios de forma cede y deja lugar a que emerja con nitidez la naturaleza golpista y antidemocrática del régimen. Pero aun así, el argumento de la "nulidad" de origen de la reforma constitucional de 1949 ha sido recurrente a la hora de buscar algún fundamento a la derogación de la Constitución. Al estilo de Vittorio Codovilla (Partido Comunista), Carlos Sánchez Viamonte (Partido Socialista), Luciano Molinas (Partido Demócrata Progresista), aparece una notable inversión en el lenguaje que supone a su vez la de los valores sociales, en donde se califica de "dictadura" a un gobierno constitucional y legítimo, y de "revolución libertadora"

228 Fallos de la CSJN 2:217 (1865).

a un golpe de Estado[229]. Pero no es menos cierto que el idioma al revés solo confundió a los sectores medios, acostumbrados a la influencia del aparato cultural oligárquico, y no a la clase trabajadora que reafirmó al peronismo como su identidad política.

Hernández Arregui decía que ante la desnacionalización de las clases altas y medias de nuestro país

> [...] es necesario encontrar el país desdibujado por ellas en otro lado, en su cantera real. Ese país está en las masas trabajadoras. Solo ellas, que no tienen que perder con la erradicación del colonialismo en tanto lo sufren directamente, pueden devolverle al país su silueta perdida[230].

De ahí la lealtad incondicional de los trabajadores hacia Perón, en tanto él era el líder popular que, en su regreso, podía reiniciar el proceso de liberación interrumpido.

El 9 de junio de 1956 se produjo el levantamiento del general Juan José Valle y otros militares y civiles, sin el apoyo activo del viejo líder, mediante una proclama propia en la que se señalaba:

> Las horas dolorosas que vive la República, y el clamor angustioso de su pueblo, sometido a la más cruda y despiadada tiranía, nos han decidido a tomar las armas para restablecer en nuestra patria el imperio de la libertad y la justicia al amparo de la Constitución y las leyes [...] no nos guía otro propósito que el de restablecer la soberanía popular, esencia de nuestras instituciones democráticas, y arrancar a la Nación del caos y la anarquía a que ha sido llevada por una minoría despótica encaramada y sostenida por el terror y la violencia en el poder [...] Este desborde de la arbitrariedad ha culminado con la abolición de la Constitución Nacional

229 El Partido Socialista, a través del periódico *La vanguardia*, calificó a la reforma de 1949 como la "constitución bastarda", por haber sido hecha a espaldas del pueblo.
230 Hernández Arregui, J. J., *Nacionalismo y liberación*, Buenos Aires, Peña Lillo/Ediciones Continente, 2004.

> vigente, sancionada por una Convención Reformadora libremente elegida por el pueblo, con la participación de los mismos sectores políticos que apoyan a la tiranía, Constitución que juraron acatar y defender los mismos que hoy la vulneran y suprimen a espaldas del pueblo y al margen de su libre voluntad soberana, con el evidente propósito inconfesable de abolir disposiciones como las del artículo 40, que impiden la entrega al capitalismo internacional de los servicios públicos y las riquezas naturales del país, juntamente con otras también fundamentales como las que sancionan los derechos del trabajador y las que estatuyen la función social de la economía y la riqueza [...] la felicidad del pueblo y la grandeza de la patria, en una nación socialmente justa, económicamente libre y políticamente soberana[231].

La nueva Asamblea Constituyente de 1957 llegó después de los fusilamientos y el país se transformó en un escenario en donde, citando a Yupanqui, hasta la tierra fecunda se había convertido en arenal, mientras los trabajadores pasaban largas noches buscando un rayo de luz de esperanza.

La cuestión constitucional

La Asamblea Constituyente fue convocada en el intento de reordenamiento "institucional" del país. Por eso también se convocó a un frustrado Congreso normalizador de la CGT en julio de 1957, que solo sirvió para

231 El levantamiento cívico-militar, de carácter peronista, tuvo como reacción del gobierno de Aramburu el asesinato masivo. En total hubo 31 fusilados (18 militares y 13 civiles), entre ellos los generales Juan José Valle y Raúl Tanco. Es posible pensarlo como uno de los puntos de partida del terrorismo de Estado que tuvo su mayor y nefasta expresión en la dictadura de 1976. Para Norberto Galasso "se trató, en ambos casos, de la instalación del terror como condición para impedir toda resistencia ante la reconversión económica decidida por los grandes poderes nativos y extranjeros. La coincidencia es aun mayor si se observan los métodos represivos y el grado de crueldad empleado", en *Clarín* del 4/06/06. Se recomienda la obra de Leónidas Chaves, Gonzalo, *La masacre de Plaza de Mayo*, Buenos Aires, Campana de Palo, 2003.

reorganizar la lucha del movimiento obrero a través, principalmente, del nacimiento de las 62 Organizaciones. El 12 de abril de 1957, mediante el Decreto 3.838, el gobierno declaró "necesario considerar la reforma parcial de la Constitución de 1853, con las reformas de 1860, 1866 y 1898". Entre otros temas, el Poder Ejecutivo expresó su preocupación para el debate por

> [...] si deben modificarse las bases del sistema electoral [...] afianzar la libertad individual y de expresión y los derechos individuales y sociales [...] e imponer un régimen adecuado de dominio y explotación de las fuentes naturales de energía.

Los temas a reformar fueron sugeridos por una comisión de juristas formada por Juan González Calderón, Sebastián Soler y Carlos Sánchez Viamonte. La convocatoria a elecciones de los constituyentes para el 28 de julio de 1957 fue mediante el sistema de representación proporcional, por el cual se garantizaba que todos los partidos políticos participantes, en especial los más pequeños, tuvieran representantes, como un intento sobreactuado de legitimar una elección en la que se proscribía –paradójicamente– a la fuerza mayoritaria. Juan Perón, desde el exilio, opinaba

> [...] La tiranía mediante el fraude piensa suprimir la Constitución justicialista, anulando los derechos del trabajador y la independencia económica, para retornar a la explotación y el colonialismo. Los peronistas, en cualquier caso, deben abstenerse de votar, no concurriendo a los comicios. Si, por cualquier causa, debieran hacerlo, votarán en blanco o anularán su voto con la palabra "asesinos"[232].

Pero no todo el campo nacional opinaba igual que Perón. Scalabrini Ortiz pensaba que con un triunfo de la lista opositora se podría haber declarado la nulidad de la Convención y entorpecido el plan político de la dictadura. Para él el voto en blanco aparecía como "un lírico gesto de protesta que no tendrá más consecuencia que el gesto mismo", aunque reconocía que era "un esfuerzo sorprendente que traduce una madurez

232 González Arzac, Alberto, en Revista *Qué*, año 1 nro. 4 (Director: Eric Calcagno), Buenos Aires, noviembre de 2005.

de conciencia y una disciplina colectiva, tanto más admirable cuando no tuvo vehículo alguno de comunicación"[233]. Jauretche mantuvo la misma posición que Scalabrini. En un artículo de la revista *Qué* del 26 de julio de 1957, explicaba:

> ¿Vamos a ser tan giles? Si la oligarquía gana el 28, arreglará las cosas para perpetuarse en el gobierno. Ya lo hizo otra vez. Y serán otros diez años de entrega, de persecuciones, de cárcel, de leyes antiobreras, de bajos salarios, de desocupación y de miseria popular [...] Tenemos un cañón de seis millones de votos. Utilicémoslo para impedir que la oligarquía haga su Constitución para afianzarse en el poder o aproveche la Convención para proclamar presidente a Rojas. Apoyemos a quien pueda derrotarla y disolver la Convención.

Mientras, Arturo Frondizi –a quien Jauretche hacía referencia– prometía la nulidad de la Convención y un nuevo llamado a elecciones libres donde el pueblo elegiría "qué Constitución es la que rige". En esta coincidencia encontró su origen la relación del peronismo con el futuro candidato presidencial, que mediante el pacto con Perón, en 1958, lo condujo al poder.

González Arzac recuerda que en las elecciones constituyentes

> [...] hubo muchos votos anulados con la palabra "asesinos" u otras palabrotas irreproducibles. Fue una derrota del gobierno militar y su constituyente. Perón felicitó al pueblo por el triunfo de los votos "en blanco" [...] ya que ganaron con 2.115.861 sufragios. La UCR del Pueblo (favorable al gobierno) sacó 2.106.524 votos; la UCR Intransigente (crítica al gobierno y contraria a la convocatoria) 1.847.603.

233 Galasso, Norberto, *Vida de Scalabrini Ortiz*, Buenos Aires, Colihue, 2008, y Scalabrini Ortiz, Raúl, "Abstenerse o votar en blanco es tirar su voto a la basura", en *Qué*, Bs. As., 23 de julio de 1957.

También muchos salieron a la calle bajo el grito de "¡Viva el General Blanco!"[234]. El Partido Comunista, por su parte, participó de las elecciones con la equívoca consigna "no vote en blanco, vote en rojo".

La Convención Constituyente de 1957

La Convención Nacional sesionó en la ciudad de Santa Fe desde el 30 de agosto hasta el 23 de septiembre de 1957. En la reunión del 2 de septiembre se tomaron los juramentos, aunque antes el bloque de la Unión Cívica Radical Intransigente (de 67 miembros) se retiró de la Convención. En la primera reunión, cuando se pasó lista, se registró la presencia de 192 convencionales electos más 13 que estaban momentáneamente ausentes; pero ya en la segunda, con el retiro de los radicales intransigentes y de otros partidos, la Asamblea se vio constantemente con el problema de la obtención del *quorum* que exigía la presencia de 104 convencionales. Cuando Oscar Alende (Unión Cívica Radical Intransigente) impugnó la legitimidad para luego retirarse con la bancada, el socialista Alfredo Palacios pidió una moción para que se les pidiera que retornaran al cuerpo, y su camarada Américo Ghioldi dijo "que se haga privadamente alguna sugestión para que se restablezca la perdida cordialidad". Pero no les hicieron caso y no volvieron. También se fueron los tres convencionales laboristas, nueve radicales sabattinistas, y uno de la Unión Federal (que apoyaba a Lonardi) y del Partido de los Trabajadores. Oscar Alende había dicho en la sesión preparatoria que "no estamos sentados aquí en calidad de constituyentes sino como simples ciudadanos que niegan validez al mandato de los señores convencionales".

En relación a las razones del retiro de los ucristas, Cooke señaló las diferentes versiones existentes:

> Fue una cosa espontánea, dice Perina. [Ramón] Prieto fue un misterio. La versión de Gómez dice que había tres posiciones: una era

234 Testimonio brindado al autor por el militante sindical Eduardo Corbalán, en ocasiones de conferenciar en el Centro Cultural Enrique Santos Discépolo en 2004. Acerca de su vida y obra, ver *Los Malditos, Tomo IV*, Buenos Aires, Madres de Plaza de Mayo, 2005 en la reseña realizada por Facundo Cersósimo y Cecilia Ferroni.

> la del propio Frondizi, de trabajar, de colaborar en la Convención y desde allí tratar de influir; otra que propugnaba la no concurrencia a las reuniones; y una tercera posición que fue la que se impuso, que consistía en concurrir a la Constituyente solo para impugnarla y retirarse de la misma[235].

Según Cooke, Perina le insistió a Frondizi desde Chile que había que obtener el retiro si se quería negociar con el peronismo su apoyo a la futura candidatura presidencial. Ello sobre la base de la promesa preelectoral a la Constituyente y la declaración del propio Perón en ese sentido. Tras el triunfo del voto en blanco, Perón dirigió un mensaje mediante el cual señalaba que

> [...] nos queda por ver ahora si los que prometieron abandonar la Asamblea Constituyente, como lo hicieron en 1949 cuando se sancionó la Constitución Justicialista, lo hacen. Allí sabremos si sus declaraciones preelectorales eran sinceras o si se trataba de una traición más al pueblo. (Mensaje a los compañeros peronistas).

Así fue nomás que las sesiones continuaron con la UCR del Pueblo, los demócratas cristianos, los demócratas progresistas, los socialistas, los comunistas, los conservadores y otros partidos provinciales, con un *quorum* tan ajustado que había que hacer números al inicio de cada sesión. Los constituyentes recibieron un mensaje firmado por Aramburu y dirigido al presidente de la Convención Reformadora –de la Unión Cívica Radical del Pueblo (UCRP) Ignacio Palacios Hidalgo– leído el 3 de septiembre:

> La Revolución Libertadora no es la simple reacción de la nacionalidad ofendida por el despotismo, que colma su aspiración en la expulsión del déspota. Es tanto más cuanto que su espíritu es aquel de Mayo, el que se anticipó al cuerpo institucional y aun a la misma nacionalidad, el que en Caseros impuso la organización y

235 Cooke, John William, "Peronismo y petróleo. Declaraciones ante la Comisión Especial Investigadora sobre Petróleo de la Cámara de Diputados de la Nación", publicado en www.ruinasdigitales.com.

> la ley, y el que en setiembre ofrendó sangre para reconquistar el derecho a la justicia, a la moralidad, a la verdad y al futuro, avasallado por un poder desbordado [...] Puede llegar a su término una etapa de inquietudes, desconcierto y zozobra, quedando expedito el sendero luminoso de un país fuerte y progresista, que ama a la libertad en el orden, y aspira a la unión y tranquilidad como factores imprescindible para su grandeza.

No obstante el espíritu optimista de Aramburu, la Convención, desde el primer día hasta su lánguida finalización –porque a esto se sumó que los legisladores dejaron de concurrir a las sesiones de forma inorgánica y progresivamente–, tuvo que dar cuenta del embrollo legal en el que se encontraba. Cipriano Reyes –antes de retirarse– dijo que “nadie, ni la propia Convención, sabría decir qué Constitución rige en estos momentos”. Y el constituyente Ricardo Bassi que “la Honorable Convención no es un oráculo para contestar preguntas, es un organismo llamado a dictar resoluciones”. Más aun, a tal punto no tenía solución ese embrollo, que no falta hoy quien arguye que la Constitución de 1949 estaba vigente. Es que la solución no podía ser legal ni constitucional; todo era una cuestión de hecho, o de “resoluciones”.

Las posiciones dentro de la Convención se pueden resumir así, conforme los proyectos presentados: 1) declaración de nulidad de la proclama del 56, de la Convención y vigencia de la reforma del 49 (Partidos Laborista, Laborista Federal, Unión Federal, y Provincial Salteño); 2) abrogación de la reforma de 1949 (Demócratas Progresistas); 3) vigencia de la Constitución de 1853, nulidad de la reforma de 1949 pero validados sus actos hasta la fecha de la proclama de 1956 (UCRP, Partido Socialista Democrático, Partido Comunista). Ante esto, la Convención Nacional resolvió rechazar las impugnaciones formuladas y declarar la validez del mandato de cada uno de los convencionales y la legitimidad de la convocatoria. Declaró que la Constitución nacional que regía era la de 1853, con las reformas de 1860, 1866, 1898 y exclusión de la de 1949.

Se discutió si la Convención tenía el mandato limitado por la convocatoria, o si eso era incumbencia de ella misma. Si la Constitución de 1853 regía desde la fecha de la proclama de abril de 1956 o desde que así lo disponía la Convención. Si a la Constitución de 1949 había que considerarla nula desde su origen, o desde la citada proclama. El constituyente Hardoy expresó la angustia existencial que pareció arrebatarlos:

> Tenemos que evitar que pueda interpretarse que recién desde ahora entra a regir la Constitución de 1853, porque eso crearía una situación sin salida, a la cual se refería Ghioldi. Todos deseamos darle al país esa salida cuanto antes. Quiero evitar que la discusión gire sobre si la reforma de 1949 era nula o anulable, si se la debió derogar o declarar abrogada, si tuvo o no el gobierno facultades, por sí, para dictar la proclama revolucionaria del 27 de abril de 1956 con los efectos expresados; si debemos ratificarla, convalidarla o aceptarla.

Américo Ghioldi (del Partido Socialista) tomó la palabra enseguida para aclarar que debía tenerse en cuenta la doctrina judicial del gobierno de facto y por la cual se sostenía la validez de los actos jurídicos cometidos por quien había tenido la fuerza para hacerlos cumplir, durante el tiempo de subsistencia de ese gobierno. Y agregó para que quedara claro su mensaje:

> [...] reconozco en el gobierno atribución para derogar la Constitución mal habida de 1949, la bastarda de 1949, y aplicar la Constitución de 1853: porque en este caso el gobierno ha procedido como si pudiera encontrarse razón en la alegoría: si en un mural un buen día alguien echa una capa de barro y, más tarde, por un aparato de succión, revolucionario, se suprime el barro adherido, el fresco continúa. Así es, a mi modo de ver, la situación de la Constitución de 1853, puesta en movimiento por el decreto o proclama de abril de 1956.

El legislador Aguirre Cámara (del conservador bloque del Centro) dijo:

> [...] el problema que plantea que hayamos llegado como hemos llegado a esta Asamblea, sin haberse dictado antes la Ley del Congreso, declarando la necesidad de la reforma, no puede resolverse con un criterio institucional estrictísimo porque entonces no tiene solución posible. La severidad legal es para tiempo de completa normalidad, por lo menos aparente [...] la nulidad de la reforma del 49 no estuvo tanto en el incumplimiento del requisito del art. 30 [...] la ilegalidad está sobre todo en que se la hizo cuando el país era presa de un aparato de sojuzgamiento, de tipo totalitario que hacía monstruosamente falsos todos los pronunciamientos electorales [...] ¿cómo quiere entonces articularse sobre la base de preceptos jurídicos la nulidad de esa reforma [por la de 1949]?[...] La ilegalidad de aquella no pudo ser prevista por la ley. Es por tanto una ilegalidad inasible. El mal terrible estaba en el magnífico y perfecto aparato totalitario que nos había atrapado, y contra el cual no hay sino que tratar, cuando todavía es posible, de no dejarse atrapar y, cuando ya se está subyugado, el de romperlo a cañonazos como lo hemos roto los argentinos. Porque no hay otra manera de salir de eso. Salvo, por supuesto, mediante la derrota en la guerra exterior.

La palabra cañonazos sonaba a eco terrible de los acontecimientos de junio de 1956.

En otra parte también se dijo, en una opinión compartida por muchos convencionales, que no era necesario declarar la nulidad o abrogar la reforma de 1949 porque era inexistente a partir del bando de abril de 1956.

> Comprendo que el poder de fuerza que lleva una revolución solo vale mientras dure esa revolución. Esta revolución no puede dictar normas para el futuro gobierno regular y normal del país. Para eso es necesario que nosotros le demos a ese futuro gobierno normal el instrumento jurídico cierto [...]. (Marini)

En efecto, para no parecer un teatro político sin valor jurídico –ya que su origen era el golpe de Estado de 1955 y no tenía ningún respaldo fuera del hecho de fuerza de la que derivaba–, era necesario que la Convención no terminara sin dictar alguna norma constitucional. Anhelaban darse la trascendencia de que en verdad estaban en Paraná convocados para legislar en resguardo de la futura democracia que algún día vendría. Fue entonces que legislaron sobre los derechos de los trabajadores, como si fueran los primeros en hacerlo y la reforma constitucional de 1949 que derogaban no hubiera consagrado ninguno. Pero hubo tiempo para que los constituyentes se indignaran por la repercusión que tuvo en la prensa una reunión de oficiales de la Fuerzas Armadas, en la que el almirante Perren se quejó por el proyecto a estudio en la Comisión Revisora. Entonces, para agravar la situación, ya iniciada la Asamblea, un grupo de once constituyentes conservadores del bloque del Centro con el fin de aventar cualquier riesgo, se retiraron con la siguiente declaración:

> Los convencionales que suscriben [...] concurrimos a la Convención Reformadora con el propósito de asegurar la vigencia de la Constitución de 1853 y colaborar con reformas limitadas [...] [pero] si las disposiciones del despacho de la Comisión Redactora hubieran llegado a aprobarse, grandes males habrían nacido para el país [...] El sistema económico que se intentaba, copiado del tristemente famoso art. 40 de la reforma de 1949, hubiera implicado no solo reincidir en un ensayo totalitario que ya se hizo con funestas consecuencias, sino la rehabilitación histórica del gobierno depuesto. (firmado: Mariano Gómez, Emilio Hardoy, Justo Medina, Reynaldo Pastor, entre otros)

La actitud de estos convencionales que determinó la parálisis virtual de la Asamblea, tuvo como intención evitar la posibilidad de que pudieran prosperar proyectos de reforma con contenido parecido al derogado artículo 40[236].

236 Cholbis, Jorge, "La constitución de 1949 (a 60 años de su sanción)", en *Equipo Federal de Trabajo, año IV, nro. 48.*

Sobre esto último es interesante advertir que el bloque mayoritario, el de la UCRP, propuso como proyecto en la Comisión Redactora una reforma integral que dispusiera: la función social de la propiedad, una cláusula antimonopólica, el poder expropiatorio del Estado, la elección directa del presidente y vice, el monopolio de los servicios públicos, la nacionalización del petróleo, el gas y el carbón, y de los impuestos, la división de latifundios, etc.; todas disposiciones que, en esencia, estaban previstas en la Constitución que el bloque había concurrido a derogar. Por lo que tal acción apenas tuvo un carácter testimonial. Por demás, el resto de los partidos realizó disidencias parciales[237].

Aramburu describió a la Convención como una "lección de genuina y sincera democracia", y Rojas confesó su "honda satisfacción" por lo resuelto en torno a los derechos sociales en el denominado "Artículo nuevo". Para sintetizar lo ocurrido, Palacios Hidalgo dijo, en su último mensaje, que eran facultades "implícitas al poder constituyente declarar el orden jurídico vigente y establecer el nexo entre el Estado revolucionario y el restablecimiento de la norma legal institucional", y que "al pronunciar este mensaje me acompañan los constituyentes que han permanecido hasta ahora en sus bancas". Entre la falta de *quorum* y los sesudos debates acerca de las facultades y límites de la Convención, se sucedieron las sesiones y la Convención solo legisló la incorporación del artículo 14 bis, en donde se incluyó una enumeración de derechos de los trabajadores –hoy en día aún tiene vigencia–, y, como complemento, se agregó la facultad del Poder Legislativo de dictar el Código del Trabajo y Seguridad Social. Jaureguiberry (convencional radical del pueblo) había sostenido que se trataba de "dotar al país, en su Carta Fundamental, de los principios del constitucionalismo social, etapa no prevista por los hombres de 1853 que hoy nadie discute". Ello pese a que Alfredo Palacios se esforzara en argumentar el carácter de poder constituyente de la Convención, para sostener que no había que aceptar "que el gobierno provisional disponga lo que

237 Entre muchas, la del Partido Comunista que, entre sus varias reformas, proponía el reconocimiento jurídico de las comunidades indígenas. De este modo se verifica eso de que el campo antinacional tiene sus alas derecha e izquierda.

debemos resolver de acuerdo a un temario consignado en la convocatoria" realizada por la Revolución Libertadora a la que, en la misma intervención en el debate, consideró "de la misma categoría de la de Caseros". Ya otro convencional había dicho que "Esta revolución es como la de Mayo y como la de Caseros: Revolución Libertadora" (Vergara Ocampo, UCRP). Américo Ghioldi lo ayudó a argumentar contra la reforma de 1949 porque, entre varias objeciones, está la que no se le dio oportunidad de votar a la mujer cuando "ya tenían derechos ciudadanos para expedirse". Aunque, al mismo tiempo, aclaró, "se ignoraba todavía cómo reaccionaría la mujer. Había que prepararla y formarla para las futuras votaciones organizadas".

Solo resta citar a Domingo Mercante, para quien esos hechos implicaban "la negación de la libertad del pueblo y el escarnio de la forma republicana de gobierno" lo que tornaba insanablemente nula, no solo la abrogación de la reforma constitucional de 1949, cumplida por derecho del Poder Ejecutivo, sino también las que podría sancionar una Convención elegida sin la libre manifestación de la voluntad del pueblo, especialmente de su clase trabajadora[238].

Arturo Sampay dijo:

238 Con motivo de la convocatoria constituyente, Sampay y Mercante redactaron y dieron a conocer en julio de 1957 un Manifiesto de reivindicación de la Constitución de 1949. Entre otras cosas ahí dicen: "El holding SOFINA –la mayoría de cuyas acciones controla el Banco de Lazard Brothers, Banco de la Royal Dutch, del trust que nos abastece de petróleo a cambio de las carnes que malvendemos a nuestra metrópoli– el holding SOFINA, decía, va a hacerse renovar la concesión para el abastecimiento de la energía eléctrica de Buenos Aires y el Gran Buenos Aires. Mas antes quiere, claro está, que una Convención Constituyente ratifique el decreto del Poder Ejecutivo que derogó el artículo 40 de la Constitución Nacional. Vale decir que busca, con tal medida, que dicha derogación se encubra bajo apariencias jurídicas [...] En consecuencia, es menester que el pueblo argentino sepa que la reforma constitucional que pretende engendrarse a sus espaldas, tiene los objetivos que enseguida numero. Primero, de dar visos de legalidad –por medio de una ratificación explícita o implícita que cumpliría la Convención Constituyente al poner como base de su labor la reforma parcial de la Constitución de 1853– a la derogación de la reforma constitucional de 1949, para que principalmente quede sin efecto, con todas las apariencias de legalidad, la estatización del banco Central y el art. 40".

> Pienso que la derogación de la Constitución de 1949 es el nudo de la trama de nuestra realidad económica y social presente, realidad que el pueblo no necesita que la describa porque la soporta y sufre[239].

Diestros en el arte de combinar abstracciones, a los convencionales se les fueron las horas, los días y las semanas en un intento por desentrañar la naturaleza jurídica de esa Convención a la que habían decidido pertenecer, cuya validez derivaba de la "facticidad" del gobierno convocante, como señaló, con sinuosidad argumentativa, Américo Ghioldi.

En definitiva, la cuestión para los constituyentes era "la continuidad jurídica y evitar el caos jurídico" –a juicio del convencional Bassi–, o, como decía sobre otro momento de la historia José María Rosa, salvar "el fetiche constitucional", porque en verdad la ley última, o la ley de leyes que regía en el país era el mando militar del gobierno de facto. Para el régimen instalado en el país a partir de 1955 el ejercicio del poder no daba derechos sino a partir de la fuerza y la coerción, porque su legalidad constitucional tuvo origen en el golpe de Estado mismo. Crear derecho fue un acto basado en el ejercicio de la fuerza y la represión. La condición de "fuerza de ley" la adquirió por la fuerza del fusil y la ruptura del orden constitucional vigente hasta septiembre de 1955. Por eso es que, a diferencia de la reforma de 1949, no hubo poder constituyente derivado de la continuidad de la institucionalidad vigente, sino meramente originario, entendiendo por "origen" ese hecho de fuerza que fue la instauración de la dictadura. Por eso mismo también puede impugnarse la condición de "poder constituyente" y adjudicarle el rótulo de poder destituyente o bando usurpador.

La reforma de 1994 incluyó en su artículo 36, la cláusula que dispone que la Constitución

> [...] mantendrá su imperio aun cuando se interrumpiere su observación por actos de fuerza contra el orden institucional y el sistema democrático. Estos actos serán insanablemente nulos.

239 González Arzac, Alberto, *Sampay y la Constitución del futuro*, Buenos Aires, Peña Lillo editor, 1982.

Y establece que serán considerados infames traidores a la Patria, y que

> Todos los ciudadanos tienen el derecho de resistencia contra quienes ejecutaren los actos de fuerza enunciados [...].

Si subsumiéramos aquella situación histórica a esta norma, la "asamblea de 1957" hubiera sido inválida, así como toda la legalidad impuesta por la fuerza por la dictadura, lo que dejaría en pie la Constitución de 1949.

Pero la nueva Constitución de 1957 fue jurada ante la Junta Consultiva Nacional con un acto celebrado en la Plaza del Congreso y desde ese momento el país dejó de proclamar su vocación por ser socialmente justo, políticamente soberano y económicamente libre. De este modo, la Convención de 1957 apenas sirvió para contribuir al sostén del poder que había irrumpido, dándole algún tipo de cobertura legal mediante la argumentación del país al revés, y la conciencia jurídica inició un largo desencuentro con los problemas centrales del país: porque a partir de ese momento la Constitución fue más que nada un texto alejado de la realidad social y política. Mientras unos discutían nebulosas abstracciones, otros ataban con fuerza los nudos de la dependencia económica y la represión. Sus consideraciones constituyentes estaban muy lejos de la conciencia histórica de los trabajadores, cuyas preocupaciones se batían entre el hecho diario de sobrevivir frente a tanta cárcel, persecución y cesanteo, y el reclamo de elecciones libres con la esperanza del regreso de Perón[240].

En fin, la convocatoria a la constituyente de 1957 es pasible de ser caracterizada como un fraude legal, ya que su verdadero fin era diferente al enunciado. La convocatoria tuvo como principal intención la de legitimar la anulación de la Constitución de 1949 y la instauración del nuevo régimen conservador liberal autoritario en el país. El resto de lo proclamado en cuanto a la consagración de derecho fue una puesta en escena destinada a distraer y falsear la realidad política.

240 La conciencia histórica de los sectores trabajadores se puede resumir en lo siguiente: "Los yanquis, los rusos y las potencias reconocen a la libertadora, Villa Manuelita no", rezaba una leyenda escrita para la época en el barrio homónimo de Rosario.

El proceso político y económico abierto en 1955 no se clausuró ni con las experiencias semidemocráticas de 1958 y 1963. No se volvió a mencionar la posibilidad de restablecer la vigencia de la Constitución de 1949. En 1973 se lograron, por fin, las primeras elecciones libres que consagraron a los gobiernos de Cámpora primero y de Perón después. Aunque ya los tiempos históricos eran muy diferentes a 1945, el gobierno peronista dictó una serie de normas de defensa del patrimonio nacional y promoción del mercado interno en el marco del Plan Trienal para la Reconstrucción y la Liberación Nacional (21/12/1973). A fines de 1973 se sancionó la Ley 20.557 de inversiones extranjeras que, en una suerte de remedo del viejo artículo 40, prohibía la intromisión del capital extranjero en áreas definidas como estratégicas, tales como defensa, seguridad nacional, servicios públicos, banca, seguros, medios de comunicación, entre otras[241]. Esta norma se complementaba con la ley de protección al mercado interno. En su discurso ante el Congreso de la Nación del 1º de Mayo de 1974, Perón expuso: "Habremos también de proponer al país una reforma de la Constitución Nacional. Para ello estamos trabajando desde dos vertientes: por un lado, recogiendo las opiniones del país; y por el otro, identificando las solicitaciones del Modelo argentino". En febrero de 1976, mediante el Decreto 620 se declaró la necesidad de la reforma constitucional con especial referencia a la Constitución de 1949 y se dispuso la remisión al Congreso de la Nación para que convocara a las elecciones a constituyentes, como un intento de instalar en la agenda de discusión política el contenido de aquella, junto con el adelanto de las elecciones presidenciales. Sin embargo, ya no había tiempo para nada, el golpe de Estado ya estaba en marcha[242].

241 Fue derogada expresamente por el Decreto-Ley 21.382 (Su art. 1 resume el sentido político de la norma: "los inversores extranjeros que invierten capitales en el país tendrán los mismos derechos y obligaciones que la Constitución y las leyes acuerdan a los inversores nacionales"), clave jurídica del neoliberalismo.

242 El decreto decía: "que el orden constitucional de la Nación Argentina ha sido de este modo profundamente alterado, al margen de la voluntad del pueblo libremente expresada, lo cual configura una inadmisible lesión a los principios básicos del régimen representativo, republicano y federal [...] constituiría una aberración jurídica la elección de autoridades sin fijar la ley básica fundamen-

V.
La reforma constitucional de 1994

El neoliberalismo de los años noventa fue la reactualización histórica del viejo pensamiento liberal conservador de carácter elitista y economicista, para justificar el diseño socioeconómico que en sus trazos más gruesos se venía imponiendo desde 1976. Este modelo condujo al país a una condición de dependencia aun más profunda al integrarlo sumisamente a los dictados del capital transnacional hegemónico. La clase dominante se reconfiguró internamente, con la hegemonía del sector financiero, y compartió el lugar con los tradicionales terratenientes. Ya no se trataba únicamente del viejo modelo agroexportador de economía primarizada, sino de la instauración de una economía con eje en la valorización financiera y en la especulación, donde los sectores ligados al capital financiero extranjero ocupaban el rol hegemónico en el interior del bloque dominante.

Para someter al país industrial con su poderosa clase obrera hizo falta, además del terrorismo de Estado, la imposición de una política de desmantelamiento del aparato productivo y de inédito endeudamiento externo, con desocupación masiva y "miseria planificada", como dijo Rodolfo Walsh en su conocida Carta Abierta a la Junta Militar. Ante la imposibilidad de regresar a la dependencia agroexportadora, propia del país del centenario, los sectores dominantes sostuvieron una dictadura cívico-militar para implementar un genocidio contra la población, cuya principal víctima fue la clase obrera. Se pasó a una etapa de mayor sometimiento a los

tal [...]". Se declaró "programáticamente prioritaria respecto de toda elección de autoridades [...] la reunión de Convención Constituyente que decidirá sobre la Constitución [...] Concluida la Convención Constituyente se verificará por el procedimiento y el plazo que corresponda la elección de las autoridades que ejercerán el poder del Estado [...]". Fue publicado en el Boletín Oficial el 13/02/1976.

poderes extranjeros, de disciplinamiento laboral y destrucción de la producción industrial autóctona, fuerte endeudamiento externo y fuga de capitales. Este modelo encontró su apogeo en los años noventa con el predominio regional del Consenso de Washington y los planes de consecuencias recesivas del Fondo Monetario Internacional: toda Latinoamérica y el Caribe, a excepción de Cuba, fue subyugada por el poder financiero en una suerte de neopanamericanismo de integración para la dominación[243]. La etapa superior de este proceso de dependencia se expresó en el ALCA (Tratado de Libre Comercio de América del Norte) o el Plan Dornbush[244].

En este contexto, en 1994 se reformó la Constitución Nacional. En primer lugar debe señalarse la intención del bloque mayoritario (a partir del Pacto de Olivos y el Núcleo de Coincidencias Básicas) por diseñar un país al servicio del mercado financiero internacional[245]. Los mitos del librecambio y comercio, del Estado ausente y del progreso a través del capital extranjero, se reeditaron bajo formas jurídicas como las leyes de reforma del Estado (agosto de 1989), de emergencia económica (septiembre de 1989), y de convertibilidad (marzo de 1991), los cuales hubieran merecido de parte de los viejos forjistas, la calificación de "nuevo estatuto legal del coloniaje". Otra vez "achicar el Estado era agrandar la Nación".

La baja de la tasa de inflación fue consecuencia del enfriamiento de la economía real y productiva, y los bajos precios de los bienes de consumo

243 "La crisis del constitucionalismo neoliberal de los años 90, con su concepción neoabsolutista del derecho de propiedad privada y de la libertad de empresa, no ha sido un fenómeno exclusivamente argentino. Más bien, es un elemento común de buena parte de la historia constitucional latinoamericana reciente" (Pisarello, Gerardo y Tedeschi, Sebastián, "Propiedad y Constitución: del 'derecho terrible' a la democracia económica", en Gargarella, Roberto (comp.), *La Constitución en 2020*, Buenos Aires, Siglo XXI, 2011). Por eso el desafío es ahora "repensar los derechos de propiedad en un sentido democrático e igualitario".

244 Rudiger Dornbusch, asesor de los principales bancos de inversión, a comienzos de 2002 aconsejó intervenir la Argentina con equipos del primer mundo para manejarle la moneda, el gasto público y los impuestos, en una cesión de soberanía previa a la prestación de asistencia del FMI.

245 Con esta interpretación parece coincidir el R. Gallardo en *Teoría y praxis del Estado nacional en la era global*, Buenos Aires, Madres de Plaza de Mayo, 2006.

masivo, de la apertura irrestricta de la importación, financiados artificialmente por la libre convertibilidad. Sus efectos en el corto plazo fueron la desindustrialización, la descapitalización del Estado y su pérdida de autonomía frente a los poderes extranjeros y financieros, primacía de la economía de especulación, aumento en el mediano plazo del desempleo y la pérdida de poder adquisitivo de los trabajadores.

En segundo lugar, 1994 fue también el año, entre otras cosas, en que la Argentina adhirió al CIADI (Ley 24.353) en abandono definitivo de las históricas doctrinas Drago y Calvo impulsadas por el autonomismo a fin del siglo XIX. Por medio de estas últimas se había defendido la integridad nacional con la primacía de la jurisdicción nacional y la protección contra el cobro compulsivo de deuda externa. El Centro Internacional de Arreglos de las Diferencias Relativas a Inversiones (CIADI), organismo dependiente del Banco Mundial, con sede en Washington, fue fundado en 1965 como reacción de las potencias mundiales ante los avances de nacionalización económica en casos como el canal de Suez o las empresas petroleras de Irán, e incluso también ante el fallido intento de reforma agraria en Guatemala (abortado por el golpe a Jacobo Árbenz en 1954) que afectaba a la United Fruit estadounidense. Su función aún hoy es la de atender las demandas de las compañías extranjeras contra los Estados por supuestos incumplimientos de tratados de inversiones bilaterales, pasando por alto los sistemas normativos nacionales, las constituciones, y hasta el propio derecho internacional sobre los derechos humanos. De este modo, estamos ante una flagrante afectación a la soberanía nacional por vía de una resignación propia de la Argentina –conducta sumisa que la adecua a la definición clásica de país semicolonial–, que ocurrió al mismo tiempo en que se procedió a convocar a la Asamblea Constituyente. La mayoría de las demandas fueron de Repsol, la multinacional con sede en España beneficiaria de la privatización de YPF que se revirtió 18 años después.

Tal renuncia a la soberanía nacional y a la jurisdicción interna se complementó con la suscripción de nuestro país a 58 tratados bilaterales de inversión con sus correspondientes prórrogas de jurisdicción a favor del

CIADI, y su apoyo inicial a la iniciativa del ALCA, en donde también se preveía la misma prórroga[246]. Finalmente, en 2005 en la IV Cumbre de las Américas celebrada en la ciudad de Mar del Plata, el ALCA fue rechazado en jornadas calificadas como históricas, pero tanto el CIADI como aquellos tratados continuaron vigentes.

La reforma constitucional tuvo como principal objetivo político posibilitar la reelección presidencial de Carlos Menem y, de este modo, dar continuidad a la planificación neoliberal conservadora. La segunda vuelta para la elección del presidente y vice, junto con otras disposiciones, como la inclusión del tercer senador por la minoría, intentó ser garantía del bipartidismo ante la crisis de la Unión Cívica Radical –que a su vez condicionaba la gobernabilidad–. Fueron cláusulas incorporadas mediante el Pacto de Olivos y el Núcleo de Coincidencias Básicas que limitaba las facultades reformadoras de la asamblea constituyente a la aprobación de un paquete cerrado de normas, pero también se habilitó la posibilidad para el debate y resolución respecto de otros temas determinados.

Pero también hay que advertir la creación de una serie de mandatos normativos y de recursos políticos destinados a aumentar la participación democrática[247]. Claro está que en este sentido la reforma significó una débil ampliación de derechos, en tanto no creó los instrumentos del Estado

246 En los tratados bilaterales de inversión, la finalidad proclamada es favorecer la inversión protegiéndola de la discriminación entre capitales nacionales y extranjeros. En algún punto del absurdo se realizan en nombre del repudio a la discriminación contra los extranjeros. Esto nos remite al antecedente del tratado celebrado por las Provincias Unidas del Río de la Plata con Gran Bretaña en 1825, en donde ambas partes se comprometían a dispensarse mutuamente en sus territorios "una recíproca libertad de comercio", que en los hechos, por supuesto, era ilusoria y solo favorecía a la parte más poderosa.

247 Como bien señala Pisarello, en relación a las constituyentes del continente en la época: "sería una caricatura reducir estas reformas a un simple ejercicio de fortalecimiento de la figura presidencial o a la apertura de la constitución económica a políticas privatizadoras o monetaristas. Evidentes razones de legitimidad, así como la existencia de fuerzas opositoras más o menos articuladas, obligaron a incluir también algunos principios e instituciones garantistas" ("El nuevo constitucionalismo latinoamericano y la constitución venezolana de 1999: balance de una década", en *Sin Permiso*, nro. 6, Barcelona, Ediciones de Intervención Cultural, 2009).

necesarios para su realización y defensa de la soberanía nacional, condición previa para alcanzar la plenitud de su ejercicio.

Hubo otros puntos clave en la reforma (previstos en el artículo 75 de las atribuciones del Congreso de la Nación), por su importancia en la organización nacional con consecuencias que se extienden más allá de las circunstancias históricas coyunturales: el mandato –aún hoy no cumplido– dirigido al Congreso de la Nación para que dictara una ley-convenio sobre la base de acuerdos entre la nación y las provincias para instituir regímenes de coparticipación con la creación de un organismo fiscal federal de control y fiscalización de su ejecución[248]. Esto iba en línea con el mandato expreso de "proveer al crecimiento armónico de la Nación y al doblamiento de su territorio" y "promover políticas diferenciadas que tiendan a equilibrar el desigual desarrollo relativo de provincias y regiones", lo que se vincula directamente con el avance de un desarrollo productivo integrado y la relación entre los mercados externo e interno y, por ende, con la cuestión nacional.

También se destacan la cláusula que establece el deber de proveer al desarrollo humano, al progreso económico con justicia social, a la productividad de la economía nacional (en línea con el "plan de inversiones públicas", también constitucionalmente previsto), a la generación de empleo, a la formación profesional de los trabajadores y a la investigación y al desarrollo científico y tecnológico, o el mandato a legislar acciones positivas que garanticen la igualdad real de oportunidades y de trato. Ello pese a que es evidente la contradicción que surge entre esta normativa fundamental y el programa de gobierno vigente en esa época[249]. Más coherente fue la

248 La reforma del 94 también dispuso derogar el principio por el cual "gastaba quien recaudaba, sustituido por criterios de solidaridad y equidad para el desarrollo igualitario de las provincias, calidad de vida e igualdad de oportunidades en todo el territorio nacional", según María Angélica Gelli en "Retenciones, federalismo, república y derechos fundamentales, Suplemento Especial sobre Retenciones a las exportaciones de enero de 2008, en *La Ley*, Buenos Aires, 2008.

249 Barcesat, abogado de derechos humanos y legislador constituyente en 1994, opinó que "en el año de 1994 cuando se reunió la convención constituyente dijimos que había que lavar una doble mácula, la de un usurpante que había derogado una constitución vigente y la del hecho de que una constitución con larga legitimación

inclusión del objetivo de "la defensa del valor de la moneda" (artículo 75 inciso 19), enunciado con un sentido ideológico monetarista.

La incorporación al sistema normativo nacional del derecho internacional de los derechos humanos –y la habilitación de los mecanismos de protección del sistema interamericano– constituye uno de sus mejores legados. Es el caso, por ejemplo, del artículo 21 de la Convención Americana sobre Derechos Humanos que establece el concepto de "interés social" de la propiedad[250].

Sin embargo, la reforma constitucional también estableció disposiciones que, con el tiempo, dieron lugar a polémicas, como el artículo 124 que dispuso que las provincias pudieran crear regiones para el desarrollo económico, establecer órganos y celebrar convenios internacionales, en tanto no fueran incompatibles con la política nacional y con conocimiento del Congreso de la Nación, y "el dominio originario de los recursos naturales existentes en su territorio". Este dispositivo apunta en la dirección contraria a lograr un desarrollo productivo equilibrado e integrado de las regiones, y tiende a debilitar la política nacional en un área clave para la economía del país como lo es el uso de los recursos naturales (hidrocarburos, minería)[251]. Esta última cláusula –que no estaba incluida en el Núcleo de Coincidencias Básicas– legitimó el ingreso del capital financiero

histórica hubiera sido repuesta por un usurpante. Me parece que la oportunidad de 1994, más allá de los condicionamientos del Pacto de Olivos, era la de poder resarcir esa doble falla histórica". En *Crítica Jurídica*, nro. 30, 2010.

250 Por vía del SIDH se consagran mejores derechos y se amplían otros, como ocurre con la libertad de expresión. Según el criterio establecido en "Kimel" y "Fontevecchia y D'Amico", y OC nro. 5 de la Corte IDH, los monopolios u oligopolios de los medios de información son considerados causa de afectaciones a este derecho. Se traza así una línea de la historia argentina entre estos parámetros jurídicos y el artículo 15 de la reforma constitucional de 1949.

251 Sin embargo es necesario precisar también que el ejercicio del dominio originario (art. 124 en función del 121 de la Constitución) debe compatibilizarse con los poderes concurrentes del Congreso de la Nación en materia de legislación de protección mínima ambiental (arts. 43 y 75 inc. 17), por medio de los cuales se restringen las facultades provinciales por razones de prosperidad y bienestar general, desarrollo sustentable o uso racional de un recurso natural estratégico y escaso.

extranjero para la extracción de materia prima básica sin valor agregado y promovió la fuga de capitales en perjuicio del país[252].

También deben enumerarse como valiosas, entre otras disposiciones, las que establecen los derechos ambientales y de los usuarios y consumidores, la solidaridad, la igualdad real de oportunidades y de trato, la elección directa del presidente, vice y senadores, la creación del Consejo de la Magistratura para la designación de los jueces de la nación, las garantías en el proceso penal, el mecanismo de participación política, y la ratificación de la soberanía sobre las islas Malvinas, Georgias del Sur y Sándwich del Sur y los espacios marítimos e insulares correspondientes. Como se advierte, las reformas excedieron el estrecho margen del Pacto de Olivos que expresaba el acuerdo circunstancial entre los dos partidos tradicionales (el justicialista y el radical) y que había dado lugar al "paquete cerrado". En definitiva, si bien la reforma constitucional ocurrió en la época del neoliberalismo conservador, no es posible caracterizarla como un exclusivo producto suyo, sino que la concurrencia de diferentes fuerzas políticas y sociales en la asamblea dio lugar a una confluencia ideológica que se plasmó, con suerte dispar, en lo normativo, como parte de la crisis del bipartidismo.

La desregulación del mercado de cambio y el comercio exterior, la fuga de capitales, el endeudamiento externo, las privatizaciones de los servicios públicos, la flexibilización laboral o la prórroga de la jurisdicción nacional[253], de ser contrastadas con el texto vigente por los constituyentes de 1949, hubieran sido ilegales.

252 Es el caso de los Tratados de Promoción y Protección Recíproca de Inversiones, por ende de rango supralegal, suscriptos por la República Argentina con naciones extranjeras y ratificados por el Congreso de la Nación.

253 Sampay opinaba que: "Los países dominantes, inversores de escasos capitales pero apropiadores en grande de los recursos naturales y financieros nativos, imponen a los países dominados una administración de justicia *ad hoc* para lograr la inmunidad de sus manejos. Los conflictos de intereses de los que son parte deben ser dirimidos en los tribunales del exterior", en *El derecho y la soberanía argentina*, Buenos Aires, Juárez Ed., 1970. Es relevante tener en cuenta que la jurisdicción de los jueces argentinos es uno de los atributos de la soberanía nacional.

VI. Últimas reflexiones: ¿era la Constitución de 1949 anticapitalista o socialista?

Gritar, gritar para qué
si a nadie le importa mi atardecer
total mi huella es de nadie
todos la caminan pero no la ven.
Hedgar Di Fulvio.

El texto constitucional concurrió a expresar en el campo de lo jurídico las nuevas relaciones de producción propias de un momento histórico de gran acumulación de capital, crecimiento de las fuerzas productivas y participación de los trabajadores en el ingreso nacional. Tanto la función social de la propiedad como la nacionalización de la economía y el control público de los servicios financieros y recursos naturales parecieron crear un esquema anticapitalista. Arturo Sampay en ocasión de la Convención dijo:

> La libertad de usura [...] impuso su concepción burguesa del mundo a todos los distritos de la cultura moderna [...] pues bien, solo legitimando la actividad económica no usuraria, como se lo propone la reforma constitucional, podrá restablecerse el espíritu económico precapitalista o tradicionalista –así llaman Max Weber y Sombart a la ética cristiana– con lo que la riqueza quedará sometida a una función social [...] Con este sentido, señor presidente, es que la reforma constitucional instaura un orden económico esencialmente anticapitalista.

Como ya vimos, para Sampay la noción de anticapitalista no era regresiva –por antiburguesa y por pretender volver atrás el tiempo histórico– sino progresiva por emancipadora. Si definimos al capitalismo como la apropiación particular por parte de la burguesía de la riqueza generada

colectivamente por los trabajadores, la superación de la democracia liberal burguesa por la democracia social en 1945 significó una formación social progresiva en relación al capitalismo tradicional, aunque no su superación total. De este modo se conjugaron elementos propios de formas capitalistas promovidas por una hegemonía estatal. La finalidad de la defensa de la soberanía nacional le daba al modelo productivo del peronismo un contenido antiimperialista.

Desde la corriente histórico-revisionista popular se podría afirmar que la Constitución de 1949 fue la máxima expresión jurídico-política del nacionalismo democrático, en donde incluso era posible advertir la existencia de formas presocialistas (como sostenía Hernández Arregui en *Peronismo y Socialismo*), en tanto que el socialismo es la posibilidad que dibujan en el horizonte los movimientos nacionales, como respuesta original latinoamericana que ya señalaban precursores como Mariátegui y Manuel Ugarte[254]. Es que el peronismo se define por su policlasismo y la superación del viejo orden oligárquico, pero no por plantearse objetivos socialistas superadores del capitalismo[255].

Cuando a partir de 1955 se inició la etapa de desnacionalización del país y su sometimiento a los dictados económicos de las potencias industriales, la clase trabajadora construyó su identidad política alrededor de la figura de Perón y en la memoria histórica de su gobierno, de cuyo seno brotaron aquellas reivindicaciones de socialismo nacional, único camino posible para que esa modernización se profundizara y no tuviera marcha atrás ante las recurrentes reacciones conservadoras.

254 "El socialismo debe ser nacional" dijo este pensador argentino, nacional y latinoamericanista. Haya de la Torre y Mariátegui lo consideraban una de las más prestigiosas figuras del continente; Sandino le escribió para agradecerle su apoyo a la causa del pueblo nicaragüense. Es uno de los grandes "malditos" del siglo XX. Falleció en 1951. Ver Galasso, Norberto, *Manuel Ugarte y la lucha por la unidad latinoamericana*, Buenos Aires, Colihue, 2012 y Ramos, Jorge Abelardo, *Manuel Ugarte y la revolución latinoamericana*, Buenos Aires, Coyoacán, 1961.
255 Es el caso de la Constitución bolivariana de 1999 o de Ecuador de 2008 o de Bolivia de 2006, que consagran economías mixtas y nuevas y originales formas de propiedad social.

VII. Algunas conclusiones

Es preciso fundar nuevamente la nación y ello debe dar lugar a una nueva Constitución, cuyo contenido no podrá obviar los mandatos que integraron la reforma de 1949, ni tampoco toda la rica tradición jurídica de defensa del interés nacional, la soberanía económica y justicia social. Pero, a la vez, en virtud del actual momento histórico del desarrollo del capitalismo mundial y de la ferocidad del expansionismo financiero transnacional y militar imperialista, no resultaría suficiente afirmar únicamente el predominio del rol del Estado en la economía. Actualmente, la denominada globalización ha implicado la estrecha interconexión entre los sistemas monetarios y los mercados financieros nacionales, como resultado de la liberalización y desregulación que se pretende imponer desde las potencias económicas. Este espacio financiero mundial impregna de incertidumbre a las economías regionales y nacionales, las cuales aparecen débiles frente a la capacidad de acción, movimiento y potencia de aquella instancia dominante. Esta tendencia depredadora del capitalismo mundial crea formas sociales antidemocráticas en la medida en que los poderes económicos, de carácter trasnacional y con formas volátiles (ahora sí, todo lo sólido se desvanece en el aire pero en un sentido destructivo), en su proceso de acumulación, se vuelven más poderosos que los Estados mismos y tornan ineficaces sus sistemas normativos. Ante ello, las cláusulas antimonopolistas y de regulación estatal de los mercados propias de los movimientos nacionales del siglo XX no garantizan de igual manera los niveles de autodeterminación económica necesarios para alcanzar la soberanía. Será fundamental un texto jurídico como expresión del proyecto nacional de unidad latinoamericana en el que, a su vez, se avizoren formas de producción originales con apropiación, uso y distribución

democrática del conocimiento y la tecnología, y la consolidación de modos de producción y circuitos de economía popular tendientes a garantizar el trabajo y la supervivencia de comunidades de base, lo más protegidos posibles de la influencia nociva del mundo financiero capitalista. Frente a la utopía conservadora de la extinción del Estado y la hegemonía de la ideología del fin de la historia, aquellas cláusulas antimonopolio aparecen como instrumentos jurídicos políticos a revalorizar, pero la fuerza del neoliberalismo de los países poderosos solo puede ser contrarrestada por una que surja de la construcción de la gran nación latinoamericana con igualdad social y soberanía popular.

Marx decía que las ideas dominantes en una sociedad son las de la clase dominante, lo que lleva a fundamentar una crítica al universo normativo del orden oligárquico si se pretende avanzar en una dirección emancipadora. En nuestro país se trata de sostener una concepción jurídica cuyo objeto sea la protección del interés nacional con un sentido de igualdad y justicia social. En concreto, el contenido nacional atraviesa todas las concepciones de igualdad y libertad, dándoles un tinte particular y diferente respecto del liberalismo europeo, para lo cual se impone la recuperación de la tradición jurídica enlazada con los movimientos nacionales, con nociones antimonopolistas, de interés y orden público, de ampliación del rol activo del Estado y de sus áreas de acción, de función social de la propiedad, de creación de diferentes formas de propiedad, entre otras, cuya expresión en nuestro país fue la Constitución de 1949 aquí analizada.

Por eso, en una provincia de una nación inconclusa, ese interés nacional y público solo puede ser interpretado, en su más profundo significado, con alcance nacional latinoamericano. El protagonismo de los pueblos es la condición necesaria para concretar una nueva institucionalidad latinoamericana y del Caribe, con fuerza suficiente como para emanciparnos de la tutela del mundo financiero internacional. Esa institucionalidad abarca una concepción normativa comprensiva de la cuestión nacional latinoamericana y la asunción de la contradicción fundamental cuya tensión es constitutiva de nuestra historia: el conflicto pueblo-oligarquía, igualdad-

desigualdad y nación-imperialismo. La soberanía nacional es ahora, definitivamente, la de la Patria Grande y los pueblos de Latinoamérica y el Caribe están asumiendo la tarea histórica de crear y darle forma a la voluntad política capaz de construir una alternativa depredadora del capitalismo mundial.

En los tiempos actuales, el derrumbe de la experiencia del socialismo soviético –con la digna excepción de Cuba– dio lugar a la etapa del neoliberalismo y la política imperial unilateral de los Estados Unidos. Fue la "era del vacío", el imperio de lo *light*, del individualismo y el escepticismo generalizado, con sociedades más violentas y excluyentes. El fin de la historia fue el relato que acompañó al triunfo del capitalismo financiero y global. Ahora, en los inicios del siglo XXI, nos encontramos en una nueva etapa de reconstrucción de los proyectos nacionales, en la que como nunca antes, existe una conciencia latinoamericana y política de unidad continental, mientras que la emergencia de un mundo multipolar abre posibilidades para el desarrollo de alternativas sin vernos condicionados por fórmulas ajenas de países más desarrollados[256]. Junto con el reverdecimiento de los movimientos nacionales, populares y democráticos, Hugo Chávez hablaba de "socialismo del siglo XXI", Rafael Correa, de "revolución democrática" y Evo Morales, de "revolución pluriétnica", y más recientemente, de "socialismo comunitario del buen vivir". En nuestro país, a partir de mayo de 2003 se vive otra vez una etapa de transformación, el capítulo nacional de una revolución latinoamericana cuya utopía apenas ha comenzado a andar con la fuerza de los que no se resignan después de años de sometimiento neoliberal. La utopía latinoamericanista es como

256 En la carta enviada por Chávez en la última reunión de la CELAC del 28/01/2013, dijo: "Recordemos a Bolívar: una sola debe ser la patria de todos los americanos, ya que en todo hemos tenido una perfecta unidad. Pero las oligarquías le cerraron el paso al proyecto histórico unitario, y el costo todavía lo estamos pagando. Tiene razón el escritor argentino Norberto Galasso: Lo que pudo ser la victoria de la Patria Grande se convirtió en las veinte derrotas de las patrias chicas. Esta historia no debe repetirse. Pongo toda mi convicción al reiterar unas palabras que dije en Caracas el histórico 2 de diciembre de 2011 al nacer la CELAC: ¡O somos una Patria, o no seremos Patria!".

esa huella en el camino que siempre aparece aun cuando más oculta está. Hagamos nuestras entonces, las palabras de Manuel Ugarte y creamos "en el advenimiento de un porvenir que incendia los horizontes"[257].

257 "El dolor de escribir" (1933), en Galasso, Norberto, *Hacia la unidad latinoamericana* (antología), Buenos Aires, Punto de Encuentro, 2013, p. 447.

CONSTITUCION

DE LA

NACION ARGENTINA

BUENOS AIRES
1949

CONSTITUCION DE LA NACION ARGENTINA

SANCIONADA POR EL SOBERANO CONGRESO GENERAL CONSTITUYENTE EL 1º DE MAYO DE 1853. REFORMADA Y CONCORDADA POR LA CONVENCION NACIONAL DE 25 DE SEPTIEMBRE DE 1860. REFORMADA POR LAS CONVENCIONES NACIONALES DE 1866 Y 1898 Y REFORMADA, CONCORDADA Y ORDENADA POR LA CONVENCION NACIONAL DE 1949

Publicación de la Secretaría del H. Senado de la Nación

INDICE

Preámbulo

Nos, los representantes del pueblo de la Nación Argentina, reunidos en Congreso General Constituyente por voluntad y elección de las provincias que la componen, en cumplimiento de pactos preexistentes, con el objeto de constituir la unión nacional, afianzar la justicia, consolidar la paz interior, proveer a la defensa común, promover el bienestar general y la cultura nacional, y asegurar los beneficios de la libertad, para nosotros, para nuestra posteridad y para todos los hombres del mundo que quieran habitar el suelo argentino; ratificando la irrevocable decisión de constituir una nación socialmente justa, económicamente libre y políticamente soberana, e invocando la protección de Dios, fuente de toda razón y justicia, ordenamos, decretamos y establecemos esta Constitución para la Nación Argentina.

PRIMERA PARTE

PRINCIPIOS FUNDAMENTALES

Capítulo I

Forma de gobierno y declaraciones políticas

Artículo 1º — La Nación Argentina adopta para su gobierno la forma representativa republicana federal, según lo establece la presente Constitución.

Art. 2º — El Gobierno federal sostiene el culto católico apostólico romano.

Art. 3º — Las autoridades que ejercen el Gobierno federal residen en la ciudad que se declare Capital de la República por una ley especial del Congreso, previa cesión hecha por una o más Legislaturas provinciales, del territorio que haya de federalizarse.

Art. 4º — El Gobierno federal provee a los gastos de la Nación con los fondos del

Tesoro nacional, formado del producto de derechos de importación y exportación, de la propia actividad económica que realice, servicios que preste y enajenación o locación de bienes de dominio del Estado nacional; de las demás contribuciones que imponga el Congreso Nacional, y de los empréstitos y operaciones de crédito que sancione el mismo Congreso para urgencias de la Nación o para empresas de utilidad pública.

Art. 5º — Cada provincia dictará para sí una Constitución bajo el sistema representativo republicano, de acuerdo con los principios, declaraciones y garantías de la Constitución Nacional; y que asegure su administración de justicia, su régimen municipal, la educación primaria, y la cooperación requerida por el Gobierno federal a fin de hacer cumplir esta Constitución y las leyes de la Nación que en su consecuencia se dicten. Con estas condiciones el Gobierno federal garantiza a cada provincia el goce y ejercicio de sus instituciones.

Art. 6º — El Gobierno federal interviene en el territorio de las provincias para garantir la forma republicana de gobierno, o repeler invasiones exteriores, y a requisición de sus

autoridades constituídas para sostenerlas o restablecerlas, si hubiesen sido depuestas por la sedición, o por invasión de otra provincia.

Art. 7º — Los actos públicos y procedimientos judiciales de una provincia gozan de entera fe en las demás; y el Congreso puede por leyes generales determinar cuál será la forma probatoria de estos actos y procedimientos, y los efectos legales que producirán.

Art. 8º — Los ciudadanos de cada provincia gozan de todos los derechos, privilegios e inmunidades inherentes al título de ciudadano en las demás. La extradición de los criminales es de obligación recíproca entre todas las provincias.

Art. 9º — En todo el territorio de la Nación no habrá más aduanas que las nacionales, en las cuales regirán las tarifas que sancione el Congreso.

Art. 10. — En el interior de la República es libre de derechos la circulación de los efectos de producción o fabricación nacional, así como la de los géneros y mercancías de todas clases, despachadas en las aduanas exteriores.

Art. 11. — Los artículos de producción o fabricación nacional o extranjera, así como los ganados de toda especie que pasen por

territorio de una provincia a otra, estarán libres de los derechos llamados de tránsito, estándolo también los vehículos, ferrocarriles, aeronaves, buques o bestias en que se transporten, y ningún otro derecho podrá imponérseles en adelante, cualquiera que sea su denominación, por el hecho de transitar por el territorio.

Art. 12. — Los buques o aeronaves destinados de una provincia a otra no serán obligados a entrar, anclar, descender, amarrar ni pagar derechos por causa de tránsito.

Art. 13. — Podrán admitirse nuevas provincias en la Nación; pero no podrá erigirse una provincia en el territorio de otra u otras, ni de varias formarse una sola, sin el consentimiento de la Legislatura de las provincias interesadas y del Congreso.

Art. 14. — El pueblo no delibera ni gobierna, sino por medio de sus representantes y autoridades creadas por esta Constitución. Toda fuerza armada o reunión de personas que se atribuya los derechos del pueblo y peticione a nombre de éste, comete delito de sedición.

Art. 15. — El Estado no reconoce libertad para atentar contra la libertad. Esta norma

se entiende sin perjuicio del derecho individual de emisión del pensamiento dentro del terreno doctrinal, sometido únicamente a las prescripciones de la ley.

El Estado no reconoce organizaciones nacionales o internacionales cualesquiera que sean sus fines, que sustenten principios opuestos a las libertades individuales reconocidas en esta Constitución, o atentatorias al sistema democrático en que ésta se inspira. Quienes pertenezcan a cualquiera de las organizaciones aludidas no podrán desempeñar funciones públicas en ninguno de los poderes del Estado.

Quedan prohibidos la organización y el funcionamiento de milicias o agrupaciones similares que no sean las del Estado, así como el uso público de uniformes, símbolos o distintivos de organizaciones cuyos fines prohibe esta Constitución o las leyes de la Nación.

Art. 16. — El Congreso promoverá la reforma de la actual legislación en todos sus ramos, con el fin de adaptarla a esta Constitución.

Art. 17. — El Gobierno federal fomentará la inmigración europea; y no podrá restringir, limitar ni gravar con impuesto alguno la entrada en el territorio argentino de los extranjeros que traigan por objeto labrar la

tierra, mejorar las industrias, e introducir y enseñar las ciencias y las artes.

Art. 18. — La navegación de los ríos interiores de la Nación es libre para todas las banderas, en cuanto no contraríe las exigencias de la defensa, la seguridad común o el bien general del Estado y con sujeción a los reglamentos que dicte la autoridad nacional.

Art. 19. — El Gobierno federal está obligado a afianzar sus relaciones de paz y comercio con las potencias extranjeras por medio de tratados que estén en conformidad con los principios de derecho público establecidos en esta Constitución.

Art. 20. — El Congreso no puede conceder al Ejecutivo nacional, ni las Legislaturas provinciales a los gobernadores de provincia, facultades extraordinarias, ni la suma del poder público, ni otorgarles sumisiones o supremacías por las que la vida, el honor o las fortunas de los argentinos queden a merced de gobiernos o persona alguna. Actos de esta naturaleza llevan consigo una nulidad insanable, y sujetarán a los que los formulen, consientan o firmen, a la responsabilidad y pena de los infames traidores a la patria.

Art. 21. — La Constitución puede reformarse en el todo o en cualquiera de sus partes.

La necesidad de la reforma debe ser declarada por el Congreso con el voto de dos terceras partes de sus miembros presentes; pero no se efectuará sino por una convención convocada al efecto.

Una ley especial establecerá las sanciones para quienes, de cualquier manera, preconizaren o difundieren métodos o sistemas mediante los cuales, por el empleo de la violencia, se propongan suprimir o cambiar la Constitución o alguno de sus principios básicos, y a quienes organizaren, constituyeren, dirigieren o formaren parte de una asociación o entidad que tenga como objeto visible u oculto alcanzar alguna de dichas finalidades.

Art. 22. — Esta Constitución, las leyes de la Nación que en su consecuencia se dicten por el Congreso y los tratados con las potencias extranjeras son la ley suprema de la Nación; y las autoridades de cada provincia están obligadas a conformarse a ella, no obstante cualquiera disposición en contrario que contengan las leyes o constituciones provinciales, salvo para la provincia de Buenos Aires, los tratados ratificados después del Pacto de 11 de noviembre de 1859.

Art. 23. — El Congreso federal no dictará leyes que restrinjan la libertad de impren-

ta o establezcan sobre ella la jurisdicción federal.

Art. 24. — Los jueces de los tribunales federales no podrán serlo al mismo tiempo de los tribunales de provincia, ni el servicio federal, tanto en lo civil como en lo militar, da residencia en la provincia en que se ejerza, y que no sea la del domicilio habitual del empleado, entendiéndose esto para los efectos de optar a empleos en la provincia en que accidentalmente se encuentre.

Art. 25. — Las denominaciones adoptadas sucesivamente desde 1810 hasta el presente, a saber: Provincias Unidas del Río de la Plata, República Argentina, Confederación Argentina, serán en adelante nombres oficiales indistintamente para la designación del Gobierno y territorio de las provincias, empleándose las palabras «Nación Argentina» en la formación y sanción de las leyes.

Capítulo II

Derechos, deberes y garantías de la libertad personal

Art. 26. — Todos los habitantes de la Nación gozan de los siguientes derechos con-

forme a las leyes que reglamenten su ejercicio, a saber: de trabajar y ejercer toda industria útil y lícita; de navegar y comerciar; de peticionar a las autoridades; de reunirse; de entrar, permanecer, transitar y salir del territorio argentino; de publicar sus ideas por la prensa sin censura previa; de usar y disponer de su propiedad; de asociarse con fines útiles; de profesar libremente su culto; de enseñar y aprender.

Art. 27. — En la Nación Argentina no hay esclavos. Los que de cualquier modo se introduzcan, quedan libres por el solo hecho de pisar el territorio de la República.

Art. 28. — La Nación Argentina no admite diferencias raciales, prerrogativas de sangre ni de nacimiento; no hay en ella fueros personales ni títulos de nobleza. Todos sus habitantes son iguales ante la ley, y admisibles en los empleos sin otra condición que la idoneidad. La equidad y la proporcionalidad son las bases de los impuestos y de las cargas públicas.

Art. 29. — Ningún habitante de la Nación puede ser penado sin juicio previo fundado en ley anterior al hecho del proceso, ni juzgado por comisiones especiales o sacado de los jueces designados por la ley antes del hecho de la

causa. Siempre se aplicará, y aun con efecto retroactivo, la ley penal permanente más favorable al imputado. Los militares y las personas que les están asimiladas estarán sometidos a la jurisdicción militar en los casos que establezca la ley. El mismo fuero será aplicable a las personas que incurran en delitos penados por el Código de Justicia Militar y sometidos por la propia ley a los tribunales castrenses. Nadie puede ser obligado a declarar contra sí mismo; ni arrestado, sino en virtud de orden escrita de autoridad competente. Es inviolable la defensa en juicio de la persona y de los derechos. El domicilio es inviolable, como también la correspondencia epistolar y los papeles privados; y una ley determinará en qué casos y con qué justificativos podrá procederse a su allanamiento y ocupación. Los jueces no podrán ampliar por analogía las incriminaciones legales ni interpretar extensivamente la ley en contra del imputado. En caso de duda, deberá estarse siempre a lo más favorable al procesado. Quedan abolidos para siempre la pena de muerte por causas políticas, toda especie de tormento y los azotes. Las cárceles serán sanas y limpias, y adecuadas para la reeducación social de los detenidos en ellas; y toda medida que, a pretexto de precaución,

conduzca a mortificarlos más allá de lo que la seguridad exija, hará responsable al juez o funcionario que la autorice.

Todo habitante podrá interponer por sí o por intermedio de sus parientes o amigos, recurso de hábeas corpus ante la autoridad judicial competente, para que se investiguen la causa y el procedimiento de cualquier restricción o amenaza a la libertad de su persona. El tribunal hará comparecer al recurrente, y, comprobada en forma sumaria la violación, hará cesar inmediatamente la restricción o la amenaza.

Art. 30. — Las acciones privadas de los hombres que de ningún modo ofendan al orden y a la moral pública, ni perjudiquen a un tercero, están sólo reservadas a Dios y exentas de la autoridad de los magistrados. Ningún habitante de la Nación será obligado a hacer lo que no manda la ley, ni privado de lo que ella no prohibe. Ningún servicio personal es exigible, sino en virtud de ley o de sentencia fundada en ley.

Art. 31. — Los extranjeros que entren en el país sin violar las leyes, gozan de todos los derechos civiles de los argentinos, como también de los derechos políticos, después de

cinco años de haber obtenido la nacionalidad. A su pedido podrán naturalizarse si han residido dos años continuos en el territorio de la Nación, y adquirirán automáticamente la nacionalidad transcurridos cinco años continuados de residencia, salvo expresa manifestación en contrario.

La ley establecerá las causas, formalidades y condiciones para el otorgamiento de la nacionalidad y para su privación, así como para expulsar del país a los extranjeros.

Art. 32. — Todo ciudadano argentino está obligado a armarse en defensa de la Patria y de esta Constitución, conforme a las leyes que al efecto dicte el Congreso y a los decretos del Ejecutivo nacional.

Nadie puede ejercer empleos y funciones públicas, civiles o militares, si previamente no jura ser fiel a la Patria y acatar esta Constitución.

Art. 33. — La traición contra la Nación consistirá únicamente en tomar las armas contra ella, o en unirse a sus enemigos prestándoles ayuda y socorro. El Congreso fijará por una ley especial la pena de este delito; pero ella no pasará de la persona del delincuente, ni la infamia del reo se transmitirá a sus parientes de cualquier grado.

Art. 34. — En caso de conmoción interior o de ataque exterior, que ponga en peligro el ejercicio de esta Constitución y de las autoridades creadas por ella, se declarará en estado de sitio la provincia o territorio en donde exista la perturbación del orden, quedando suspensas allí las garantías constitucionales. Pero durante esta suspensión no podrá el presidente de la República condenar por sí ni aplicar penas. Su poder se limitará en tal caso, respecto de las personas, a arrestarlas o trasladarlas de un punto a otro de la Nación, si ellas no prefiriesen salir del territorio argentino. Podrá declararse asimismo el estado de prevención y alarma en caso de alteración del orden público que amenace perturbar el normal desenvolvimiento de la vida o las actividades primordiales de la población. Una ley determinará los efectos jurídicos de tal medida, pero ésta no suspenderá, sino que limitará transitoriamente las garantías constitucionales en la medida que sea indispensable. Con referencia a las personas, los poderes del presidente se reducirán a detenerlas o trasladarlas de un punto a otro del territorio, por un término no mayor de treinta días.

Art. 35. — Los derechos y garantías reconocidos por esta Constitución no podrán ser alterados por las leyes que reglamenten su ejercicio, pero tampoco amparan a ningún habitante de la Nación en perjuicio, detrimento o menoscabo de otro. Los abusos de esos derechos que perjudiquen a la comunidad o que lleven a cualquier forma de explotación del hombre por el hombre, configuran delitos que serán castigados por las leyes.

Art. 36. — Las declaraciones, derechos y garantías que enumera la Constitución, no serán entendidos como negación de otros derechos y garantías no enumerados, pero que nacen del principio de la soberanía del pueblo y de la forma republicana de gobierno.

Capítulo III

Derechos del trabajador, de la familia, de la ancianidad y de la educación y la cultura

Art. 37. — Decláranse los siguientes derechos especiales:

I. — Del trabajador

1. — *Derecho de trabajar.* — El trabajo es el medio indispensable para satisfacer las ne-

cesidades espirituales y materiales del individuo y de la comunidad, la causa de todas las conquistas de la civilización y el fundamento de la prosperidad general; de ahí que el derecho de trabajar debe ser protegido por la sociedad, considerándolo con la dignidad que merece y proveyendo ocupación a quien la necesite.

2. — *Derecho a una retribución justa.* — Siendo la riqueza, la renta y el interés del capital frutos exclusivos del trabajo humano, la comunidad debe organizar y reactivar las fuentes de producción en forma de posibilitar y garantizar al trabajador una retribución moral y material que satisfaga sus necesidades vitales y sea compensatoria del rendimiento obtenido y del esfuerzo realizado.

3. — *Derecho a la capacitación.* — El mejoramiento de la condición humana y la preeminencia de los valores del espíritu imponen la necesidad de propiciar la elevación de la cultura y de la aptitud profesional, procurando que todas las inteligencias puedan orientarse hacia todas las direcciones del conocimiento, e incumbe a la sociedad estimular el esfuerzo individual proporcionando los medios para que, en igualdad de oportunidades,

todo individuo pueda ejercitar el derecho a aprender y perfeccionarse.

4. — *Derecho a condiciones dignas de trabajo.* — La consideración debida al ser humano, la importancia que el trabajo reviste como función social y el respeto recíproco entre los factores concurrentes de la producción, consagran el derecho de los individuos a exigir condiciones dignas y justas para el desarrollo de su actividad y la obligación de la sociedad de velar por la estricta observancia de los preceptos que las instituyen y reglamentan.

5. — *Derecho a la preservación de la salud.* — El cuidado de la salud física y moral de los individuos debe ser una preocupación primordial y constante de la sociedad, a la que corresponde velar para que el régimen de trabajo reúna los requisitos adecuados de higiene y seguridad, no exceda las posibilidades normales del esfuerzo y posibilite la debida oportunidad de recuperación por el reposo.

6. — *Derecho al bienestar.* — El derecho de los trabajadores al bienestar, cuya expresión mínima se concreta en la posibilidad de disponer de vivienda, indumentaria y alimen-

tación adecuadas, de satisfacer sin angustias sus necesidades y las de su familia en forma que les permita trabajar con satisfacción, descansar libres de preocupaciones y gozar mesuradamente de expansiones espirituales y materiales, impone la necesidad social de elevar el nivel de vida y de trabajo con los recursos directos e indirectos que permita el desenvolvimiento económico.

7. — *Derecho a la seguridad social.* — El derecho de los individuos a ser amparados en los casos de disminución, suspensión o pérdida de su capacidad para el trabajo, promueve la obligación de la sociedad de tomar unilateralmente a su cargo las prestaciones correspondientes o de promover regímenes de ayuda mutua obligatoria destinados, unos y otros, a cubrir o complementar las insuficiencias o inaptitudes propias de ciertos períodos de la vida o las que resulten de infortunios provenientes de riesgos eventuales.

8. — *Derecho a la protección de su familia.* — La protección de la familia responde a un natural designio del individuo, desde que en ella generan sus más elevados sentimientos afectivos, y todo empeño tendiente a su bienestar debe ser estimulado y favorecido por la

comunidad, como el medio más indicado de propender al mejoramiento del género humano y a la consolidación de principios espirituales y morales que constituyen la esencia de la convivencia social.

9. — *Derecho al mejoramiento económico.* — La capacidad productora y el empeño de superación hallan un natural incentivo en las posibilidades de mejoramiento económico, por lo que la sociedad debe apoyar y favorecer las iniciativas de los individuos tendientes a ese fin, y estimular la formación y utilización de capitales, en cuanto constituyan elementos activos de la producción y contribuyan a la prosperidad general.

10. — *Derecho a la defensa de los intereses profesionales.* — El derecho de agremiarse libremente y de participar en otras actividades lícitas tendientes a la defensa de los intereses profesionales, constituyen atribuciones esenciales de los trabajadores, que la sociedad debe respetar y proteger, asegurando su libre ejercicio y reprimiendo todo acto que pueda dificultarlo o impedirlo.

II. — De la familia

La familia, como núcleo primario y fundamental de la sociedad, será objeto de prefe-

rente protección por parte del Estado, el que reconoce sus derechos en lo que respecta a su constitución, defensa y cumplimiento de sus fines.

1. — El Estado protege el matrimonio, garantiza la igualdad jurídica de los cónyuges y la patria potestad;

2. — El Estado formará la unidad económica familiar, de conformidad con lo que una ley especial establezca;

3. — El Estado garantiza el bien de familia conforme a lo que una ley especial determine;

4. — La atención y asistencia de la madre y del niño gozarán de la especial y privilegiada consideración del Estado.

III. — De la ancianidad

1. — *Derecho a la asistencia.* — Todo anciano tiene derecho a su protección integral, por cuenta y cargo de su familia. En caso de desamparo, corresponde al Estado proveer a dicha protección, ya sea en forma directa o por intermedio de los institutos y fundaciones creadas o que se crearen con ese fin, sin perjuicio de la subrogación del Estado o de dichos institutos, para demandar a los familiares

remisos y solventes los aportes correspondientes.

2. — *Derecho a la vivienda.* — El derecho a un albergue higiénico, con un mínimo de comodidades hogareñas es inherente a la condición humana.

3. — *Derecho a la alimentación.* — La alimentación sana, y adecuada a la edad y estado físico de cada uno, debe ser contemplada en forma particular.

4. — *Derecho al vestido.* — El vestido decoroso y apropiado al clima complementa el derecho anterior.

5. — *Derecho al cuidado de la salud física.* — El cuidado de la salud física de los ancianos ha de ser preocupación especialísima y permanente.

6. — *Derecho al cuidado de la salud moral.* — Debe asegurarse el libre ejercicio de las expansiones espirituales, concordes con la moral y el culto.

7. — *Derecho al esparcimiento.* — Ha de reconocerse a la ancianidad el derecho de gozar mesuradamente de un mínimo de entretenimientos para que pueda sobrellevar con satisfacción sus horas de espera.

8. — *Derecho al trabajo.* — Cuando el estado y condiciones lo permitan, la ocupación por medio de la laborterapia productiva ha de ser facilitada. Se evitará así la disminución de la personalidad.

9. — *Derecho a la tranquilidad.* — Gozar de tranquilidad, libre de angustias y preocupaciones, en los años últimos de existencia, es patrimonio del anciano.

10. — *Derecho al respeto.* — La ancianidad tiene derecho al respeto y consideración de sus semejantes.

IV. — De la educación y la cultura

La educación y la instrucción corresponden a la familia y a los establecimientos particulares y oficiales que colaboren con ella, conforme a lo que establezcan las leyes. Para ese fin, el Estado creará escuelas de primera enseñanza, secundarias, técnicoprofesionales, universidades y academias.

1. — La enseñanza tenderá al desarrollo del vigor físico de los jóvenes, al perfeccionamiento de sus facultades intelectuales y de sus potencias sociales, a su capacitación profesional, así como a la formación del carácter

y el cultivo integral de todas las virtudes personales, familiares y cívicas.

2. — La enseñanza primaria elemental es obligatoria y será gratuita en las escuelas del Estado. La enseñanza primaria en las escuelas rurales tenderá a inculcar en el niño el amor a la vida del campo, a orientarlo hacia la capacitación profesional en las faenas rurales y a formar la mujer para las tareas domésticas campesinas. El Estado creará, con ese fin, los institutos necesarios para preparar un magisterio especializado.

3. — La orientación profesional de los jóvenes, concebida como un complemento de la acción de instruir y educar, es una función social que el Estado ampara y fomenta mediante instituciones que guíen a los jóvenes hacia las actividades para las que posean naturales aptitudes y capacidad, con el fin de que la adecuada elección profesional redunde en beneficio suyo y de la sociedad.

4. — El Estado encomienda a las universidades la enseñanza en el grado superior, que prepare a la juventud para el cultivo de las ciencias al servicio de los fines espirituales y del engrandecimiento de la Nación y para el ejercicio de las profesiones y de las artes

técnicas en función del bien de la colectividad. Las universidades tienen el derecho de gobernarse con autonomía, dentro de los límites establecidos por una ley especial que reglamentará su organización y funcionamiento.

Una ley dividirá el territorio nacional en regiones universitarias, dentro de cada una de las cuales ejercerá sus funciones la respectiva universidad. Cada una de las universidades, además de organizar los conocimientos universales cuya enseñanza le incumbe, tenderá a profundizar el estudio de la literatura, historia y folklore de su zona de influencia cultural, así como a promover las artes técnicas y las ciencias aplicadas, con vistas a la explotación de las riquezas y al incremento de las actividades económicas regionales.

Las universidades establecerán cursos obligatorios y comunes destinados a los estudiantes de todas las facultades para su formación política, con el propósito de que cada alumno conozca la esencia de lo argentino, la realidad espiritual, económica, social y política de su país, la evolución y la misión histórica de la República Argentina, y para que adquiera conciencia de la responsabilidad que debe asumir en la empresa de lograr y

afianzar los fines reconocidos y fijados en esta Constitución.

5. — El Estado protege y fomenta el desarrollo de las ciencias y de las bellas artes, cuyo ejercicio es libre; aunque ello no excluye los deberes sociales de los artistas y hombres de ciencia. Corresponde a las academias la docencia de la cultura y de las investigaciones científicas posuniversitarias, para cuya función tienen el derecho de darse un ordenamiento autónomo dentro de los límites establecidos por una ley especial que las reglamente.

6. — Los alumnos capaces y meritorios tienen el derecho de alcanzar los más altos grados de instrucción. El Estado asegura el ejercicio de este derecho mediante becas, asignaciones a las familias y otras providencias que se conferirán por concurso entre los alumnos de todas las escuelas.

7. — Las riquezas artísticas e históricas, así como el paisaje natural, cualquiera que sea su propietario, forman parte del patrimonio cultural de la Nación y estarán bajo la tutela del Estado, que puede decretar las expropiaciones necesarias para su defensa y prohibir la exportación o enajenación de los

tesoros artísticos. El Estado organizará un registro de la riqueza artística e histórica que asegure su custodia y atienda a su conservación.

Capítulo IV

La función social de la propiedad, el capital y la actividad económica

Art. 38.—La propiedad privada tiene una función social y, en consecuencia, estará sometida a las obligaciones que establezca la ley con fines de bien común. Incumbe al Estado fiscalizar la distribución y la utilización del campo e intervenir con el objeto de desarrollar e incrementar su rendimiento en interés de la comunidad, y procurar a cada labriego o familia labriega la posibilidad de convertirse en propietario de la tierra que cultiva. La expropiación por causa de utilidad pública o interés general debe ser calificada por ley y previamente indemnizada. Sólo el Congreso impone las contribuciones que se expresan en el artículo 4º. Todo autor o inventor es propietario exclusivo de su obra, invención o descubrimiento por el término que le acuerda la ley. La confiscación de bienes que-

da abolida para siempre de la legislación argentina. Ningún cuerpo armado puede hacer requisiciones ni exigir auxilios de ninguna especie en tiempo de paz.

Art. 39. — El capital debe estar al servicio de la economía nacional y tener como principal objeto el bienestar social. Sus diversas formas de explotación no pueden contrariar los fines de beneficio común del pueblo argentino.

Art. 40. — La organización de la riqueza y su explotación tienen por fin el bienestar del pueblo, dentro de un orden económico conforme a los principios de la justicia social. El Estado, mediante una ley, podrá intervenir en la economía y monopolizar determinada actividad, en salvaguardia de los intereses generales y dentro de los límites fijados por los derechos fundamentales asegurados en esta Constitución. Salvo la importación y exportación, que estarán a cargo del Estado de acuerdo con las limitaciones y el régimen que se determine por ley, toda actividad económica se organizará conforme a la libre iniciativa privada, siempre que no tenga por fin ostensible o encubierto dominar los mercados nacionales, eliminar la competencia o aumentar usurariamente los beneficios.

Los minerales, las caídas de agua, los yacimientos de petróleo, de carbón y de gas, y las demás fuentes naturales de energía, con excepción de los vegetales, son propiedades imprescriptibles e inalienables de la Nación, con la correspondiente participación en su producto, que se convendrá con las provincias.

Los servicios públicos pertenecen originariamente al Estado, y bajo ningún concepto podrán ser enajenados o concedidos para su explotación. Los que se hallaren en poder de particulares serán transferidos al Estado, mediante compra o expropiación con indemnización previa, cuando una ley nacional lo determine.

El precio por la expropiación de empresas concesionarias de servicios públicos será el del costo de origen de los bienes afectados a la explotación, menos las sumas que se hubieren amortizado durante el lapso cumplido desde el otorgamiento de la concesión, y los excedentes sobre una ganancia razonable, que serán considerados también como reintegración del capital invertido.

SEGUNDA PARTE

AUTORIDADES DE LA NACION

TITULO PRIMERO

GOBIERNO FEDERAL

SECCION PRIMERA

Del Poder Legislativo

Art. 41. — Un Congreso compuesto de dos Cámaras, una de diputados de la Nación y otra de senadores de las provincias y de la Capital, será investido del Poder Legislativo de la Nación.

Capítulo I

De la Cámara de Diputados

Art. 42. — La Cámara de Diputados se compondrá de representantes elegidos directamente por el pueblo de las provincias y de

la Capital, que se consideran a este fin como distritos electorales de un solo Estado, y a simple pluralidad de sufragios. El número de representantes será de uno por cada cien mil habitantes, o fracción que no baje de cincuenta mil. Después de la realización del censo general, que se efectuará cada diez años, el Congreso fijará la representación con arreglo a aquél, pudiendo aumentar, pero no disminuir la base expresada para cada diputado. La representación por distrito no será inferior a dos.

Art. 43. — Para ser elegido diputado se requiere haber cumplido la edad de veinticinco años, tener cuatro años de ciudadanía en ejercicio los argentinos nativos y diez los naturalizados, y ser nativo de la provincia que lo elija o con dos años de residencia inmediata en ella.

Art. 44. — Los diputados durarán en su representación seis años, y son reelegibles; pero la sala se renovará por mitad cada tres años. Para ese efecto, los nombrados para la primera Legislatura, luego que se reúnan, sortearán los que deban cesar en el primer período.

Art. 45. — En caso de vacante, el Gobierno de provincia, o de la Capital, hace proceder a elección legal de un nuevo miembro.

Art. 46. — Sólo la Cámara de Diputados ejerce el derecho de acusar ante el Senado al presidente, vicepresidente, sus ministros y a los miembros de la Corte Suprema de Justicia de la Nación, en las causas de responsabilidad que se intenten contra ellos, por mal desempeño o por delito en el ejercicio de sus funciones; o por crímenes comunes, después de haber conocido en ellos y declarado haber lugar a la formación de causa por mayoría de dos terceras partes de sus miembros presentes.

Capítulo II

Del Senado

Art. 47. — El Senado se compondrá de dos senadores por cada provincia y dos por la Capital, elegidos directamente por el pueblo. Cada senador tendrá un voto.

Art. 48. — Son requisitos para ser elegido senador: ser argentino nativo, tener la edad de treinta años, y diez años de ciudadanía en ejercicio, y ser natural de la provin-

cia que lo elija o con dos años de residencia inmediata en ella.

Art. 49. — Los senadores duran seis años en el ejercicio de su mandato, y son reelegibles; pero el Senado se renovará por mitad cada tres años, decidiéndose por la suerte quiénes deben cesar en el primer trienio.

Art. 50. — El vicepresidente de la Nación será presidente del Senado; pero no tendrá voto sino en el caso que haya empate en la votación.

Art. 51. — El Senado nombrará un presidente provisorio que lo presida en caso de ausencia del vicepresidente, o cuando éste ejerce las funciones de presidente de la Nación.

Art. 52. — Al Senado corresponde juzgar en juicio público a los acusados por la Cámara de Diputados, debiendo sus miembros prestar juramento para este acto. Cuando el acusado sea el presidente de la Nación, el Senado será presidido por el presidente de la Corte Suprema. Ninguno será declarado culpable, sino a mayoría de los dos tercios de los miembros presentes.

Art. 53. — Su fallo no tendrá más efecto que destituir al acusado, y aun declararle incapaz de ocupar ningún empleo de honor,

de confianza o a sueldo en la Nación. Pero la parte condenada quedará, no obstante, sujeta a acusación, juicio y castigo conforme a las leyes ante los tribunales ordinarios.

Art. 54. — Corresponde también al Senado autorizar al presidente de la Nación para que declare en estado de sitio, uno o varios puntos de la República en caso de ataque exterior.

Art. 55. — Cuando vacase alguna plaza de senador por muerte, renuncia u otra causa, el Gobierno a que corresponda la vacante hace proceder inmediatamente a la elección de un nuevo miembro.

Capítulo III

Disposiciones comunes a ambas Cámaras

Art. 56. — Ambas Cámaras se reunirán en sesiones ordinarias todos los años desde el 1º de mayo hasta el 30 de septiembre. El presidente de la Nación puede prorrogar las sesiones ordinarias y convocar a extraordinarias. En las sesiones extraordinarias no se tratarán sino los asuntos determinados en la convocatoria.

Durante el receso de las Cámaras Legislativas, el presidente de la Nación podrá con-

vocar a la de Senadores, al solo objeto de los acuerdos necesarios para los nombramientos que requieren tal requisito con arreglo a esta Constitución.

Art. 57. — Cada Cámara es juez de las elecciones, derechos y títulos de sus miembros en cuanto a su validez. Ninguna de ellas entrará en sesión sin la mayoría absoluta de sus miembros; pero un número menor podrá compeler a los miembros ausentes a que concurran a las sesiones, en los términos y bajo las penas que cada Cámara establecerá.

Art. 58. — Ambas Cámaras empiezan y concluyen sus sesiones simultáneamente. Ninguna de ellas, mientras se hallen reunidas, podrá suspender sus sesiones más de tres días, sin el consentimiento de la otra.

Art. 59. — Cada Cámara hará su reglamento, y podrá, con dos tercios de votos de los presentes, corregir a cualquiera de sus miembros por desorden de conducta en el ejercicio de sus funciones, o removerlo por inhabilidad física o moral sobreviniente a su incorporación, y hasta excluirlo de su seno; pero bastará la mayoría de uno sobre la mitad de los presentes para decidir en las renuncias que voluntariamente hicieren de sus cargos.

Art. 60. — Los senadores y diputados prestarán, en el acto de su incorporación, juramento de desempeñar debidamente el cargo, y de obrar en todo en conformidad a lo que prescribe esta Constitución.

Art. 61. — Ninguno de los miembros del Congreso puede ser acusado, interrogado judicialmente, ni molestado por las opiniones o discursos que emita desempeñando su mandato de legislador.

Art. 62. — Ningún senador o diputado, desde el día de su elección hasta el de su cese, puede ser arrestado; excepto el caso de ser sorprendido in fraganti en la ejecución de algún crimen que merezca pena de muerte, infamante, u otra aflictiva; de lo que se dará cuenta a la Cámara respectiva con la información sumaria del hecho.

Art. 63. — Cuando se forme querella por escrito ante las justicias ordinarias contra cualquier senador o diputado, examinado el mérito del sumario en juicio público, podrá cada Cámara, con dos tercios de votos de los presentes, suspender en sus funciones al acusado y ponerlo a disposición del juez competente para su juzgamiento.

Art. 64. — Cada una de las Cámaras puede solicitar al Poder Ejecutivo los informes que estime conveniente respecto a las cuestiones de competencia de dichas Cámaras. El Poder Ejecutivo podrá optar entre contestar el informe por escrito, hacerlo personalmente su titular, o enviar a uno de sus ministros para que informe verbalmente.

Art. 65. — Ningún miembro del Congreso podrá recibir empleo o comisión del Poder Ejecutivo, sin previo consentimiento de la Cámara respectiva, excepto los empleos de escala.

Art. 66. — Los gobernadores de provincia no pueden ser miembros del Congreso.

Art. 67. — Los servicios de los senadores y diputados son remunerados por el Tesoro de la Nación, con una dotación que señalará la ley.

Capítulo IV

Atribuciones del Congreso

Art. 68. — Corresponde al Congreso:

1. Legislar sobre las aduanas exteriores y establecer los derechos de importación y exportación;

2. Imponer contribuciones directas por tiempo determinado en todo el territorio de la Nación, siempre que la defensa, seguridad común y bien general del Estado lo exijan;
3. Contraer empréstitos sobre el crédito de la Nación;
4. Disponer del uso y de la enajenación de las tierras de propiedad nacional;
5. Crear y suprimir bancos oficiales y legislar sobre el régimen bancario, crédito y emisión de billetes en todo el territorio de la Nación. En ningún caso los organismos correspondientes podrán ser entidades mixtas o particulares;
6. Arreglar el pago de la deuda interior y exterior de la Nación;
7. Fijar por un año, o por períodos superiores hasta un máximo de tres años, a propuesta del Poder Ejecutivo, el presupuesto de gastos de administración de la Na-

ción, y aprobar o desechar anualmente la cuenta de inversión;

8. Acordar subsidios del Tesoro nacional a las provincias, cuyas rentas no alcancen, según sus presupuestos, a cubrir sus gastos ordinarios;

9. Reglamentar la navegación de los ríos, habilitar los puertos que considere convenientes, y crear y suprimir aduanas;

10. Adoptar un sistema uniforme de pesas y medidas para toda la Nación;

11. Dictar los códigos Civil, de Comercio, Penal, de Minería, Aeronáutico, Sanitario y de Derecho Social, sin que tales códigos alteren las jurisdicciones locales, correspondiendo su aplicación a los tribunales federales o provinciales, según que las cosas o las personas cayeren bajo sus respectivas jurisdicciones; y especialmente leyes generales para toda la Nación sobre naturalización y ciudadanía, con arreglo al

principio de la nacionalidad natural; así como sobre bancarrotas, falsificación de la moneda corriente y documentos públicos del Estado;

12. Reglar el comercio con las naciones extranjeras y de las provincias entre sí;

13. Ejercer una legislación exclusiva sobre los servicios públicos de propiedad de la Nación, o explotados por los órganos industriales del Estado nacional, o que liguen la Capital Federal o un territorio federal con una provincia, o dos provincias entre sí, o un punto cualquiera del territorio de la Nación con un Estado extranjero;

14. Arreglar definitivamente los límites del territorio de la Nación, fijar los de los provincias, crear otras nuevas y determinar por una legislación especial la organización, administración y gobierno que deben tener los territorios nacionales que queden

fuera de los límites que se asignen a las provincias, y establecer el régimen de las aguas de los ríos interprovinciales y sus afluentes;

15. Proveer a la seguridad de las fronteras;

16. Proveer lo conducente a la prosperidad del país, a la higiene, moralidad, salud pública y asistencia social, al adelanto y bienestar de todas las provincias y al progreso de la ciencia, organizando la instrucción general y universitaria; promover la industria, la inmigración, la construcción de ferrocarriles y canales navegables y el establecimiento de otros medios de transporte aéreo y terrestre; la colonización de tierras de propiedad nacional y de las provenientes de la extinción de latifundios, procurando el desarrollo de la pequeña propiedad agrícola en explotación y la creación de nuevos centros poblados con las tierras, aguas y servicios públicos que

sean necesarios para asegurar la salud y el bienestar social de sus habitantes; la introducción y establecimiento de nuevas industrias, la importación de capitales extranjeros y la exploración de los ríos interiores, por leyes protectoras de estos fines y por concesiones temporales de franquicias y recompensas de estímulo;

17. Establecer tribunales inferiores a la Suprema Corte de Justicia; crear y suprimir empleos, fijar sus atribuciones, dar pensiones, decretar honores y conceder amnistías generales;

18. Admitir o desechar, reunidas ambas Cámaras en Asamblea, los motivos de dimisión del presidente o vicepresidente de la República; y declarar el caso de proceder a una nueva elección;

19. Aprobar o desechar los tratados concluídos con las demás naciones, y los concordatos con la Silla Apostólica; y arreglar el

ejercicio del patronato en toda la Nación;

20. Admitir en el territorio de la Nación otras órdenes religiosas a más de las existentes;

21. Autorizar al Poder Ejecutivo para declarar la guerra o hacer la paz;

22. Autorizar represalias y establecer reglamentos para las presas;

23. Fijar las fuerzas armadas en tiempo de paz y de guerra; establecer reglamentos y ordenanzas para el gobierno de dichas fuerzas; y dictar leyes especiales sobre expropiaciones y requisiciones en tiempo de guerra;

24. Permitir la introducción de fuerzas extranjeras en el territorio de la Nación y la salida de las fuerzas nacionales fuera de él, excepto cuando tengan como propósito razones de cortesía internacional. En este caso bastará la autorización del Poder Ejecutivo;

25. Declarar en estado de sitio uno o varios puntos de la Nación en caso de conmoción interior, y aprobar o suspender el estado de sitio declarado durante su receso, por el Poder Ejecutivo;

26. Ejercer una legislación exclusiva sobre todo el territorio de la Capital de la Nación y en los demás lugares adquiridos por compra o cesión, en cualquiera de las provincias, para establecer fortalezas, arsenales, aeródromos, almacenes u otros establecimientos de servicios públicos o de utilidad nacional;

27. Hacer todas las leyes y reglamentos que sean convenientes para poner en ejercicio los poderes antecedentes, y todos los otros concedidos por la presente Constitución al gobierno de la Nación Argentina;

28. Sancionar el régimen impositivo del distrito federal y fijar por un año o por períodos superiores, hasta un máximo de tres años, a

propuesta del presidente de la República, el presupuesto de gastos de su administración;

29. Dictar la ley para la elección de presidente, vicepresidente, senadores y diputados.

Capítulo V

De la formación y sanción de las leyes

Art. 69. — Las leyes pueden tener principio en cualquiera de las Cámaras del Congreso, por proyectos presentados por sus miembros o por el Poder Ejecutivo.

Art. 70. — Aprobado un proyecto de ley por la Cámara de su origen, pasa para su discusión a la otra Cámara. Aprobado por ambas, pasa al Poder Ejecutivo de la Nación para su examen; y si también obtiene su aprobación, lo promulga como ley.

Art. 71. — Se reputa aprobado por el Poder Ejecutivo todo proyecto no devuelto en el término de 20 días hábiles.

Art. 72. — Ningún proyecto de ley, desechado totalmente por una de las Cámaras, podrá repetirse en las sesiones de aquel año. Pero si sólo fuese adicionado o corregido por

la Cámara revisora, volverá a la de su origen; y si en ésta se aprobasen las adiciones o correcciones por mayoría absoluta de los miembros presentes, pasará al Poder Ejecutivo de la Nación. Si las adiciones o correcciones fueren rechazadas, volverá por segunda vez el proyecto a la Cámara revisora, y si aquí fueren nuevamente sancionadas por una mayoría de las dos terceras partes de sus miembros presentes, pasará el proyecto a la otra Cámara, y no se entenderá que ésta reprueba dichas adiciones o correcciones si no concurre para ello el voto de las dos terceras partes de sus miembros presentes.

Art. 73. — Desechado totalmente un proyecto por el Poder Ejecutivo, vuelve con sus objeciones a la Cámara de origen; ésta lo discute de nuevo, y si lo confirma por mayoría de dos tercios de votos de los presentes, pasa otra vez a la Cámara de revisión. Si ambas Cámaras lo sancionan por igual mayoría, el proyecto es ley y pasa al Poder Ejecutivo para su promulgación.

Si el proyecto es desechado sólo en parte por el Poder Ejecutivo, vuelve únicamente la parte desechada con sus objeciones, procediéndose en igual forma que cuando el veto es total.

Las votaciones de ambas Cámaras serán en uno y otro caso nominales, por sí o por no; y tanto los nombres y fundamentos de los sufragantes, cuanto las objeciones del Poder Ejecutivo, se publicarán inmediatamente por la prensa. Si las Cámaras difieren sobre las objeciones, el proyecto no podrá repetirse en las sesiones de aquel año.

Art. 74. — En la sanción de las leyes se usará de esta fórmula: El Senado y Cámara de Diputados de la Nación Argentina, reunidos en Congreso, sancionan con fuerza de ley.

SECCION SEGUNDA

Del Poder Ejecutivo

Capítulo I

De su naturaleza y duración

Art. 75. — El Poder Ejecutivo de la Nación será desempeñado por un ciudadano con el título de «Presidente de la Nación Argentina».

Art. 76. — En caso de enfermedad, ausencia del país, muerte, renuncia o destitución del presidente, el Poder Ejecutivo será ejercido por el vicepresidente de la Nación. En caso de

destitución, muerte, dimisión o inhabilidad del presidente y vicepresidente de la Nación, el Congreso determinará qué funcionario público ha de desempeñar la Presidencia hasta que haya cesado la causa de la inhabilidad o un nuevo presidente sea elegido.

Art. 77. — Para ser elegido presidente o vicepresidente de la Nación, se requiere haber nacido en el territorio argentino, pertenecer a la comunión Católica Apostólica Romana, y las demás calidades exigidas para ser senador.

Art. 78. — El presidente y el vicepresidente duran en sus cargos seis años; y pueden ser reelegidos.

Art. 79. — El presidente de la Nación cesa en el poder el día mismo en que expira su período de seis años; sin que evento alguno que lo haya interrumpido, pueda ser motivo de que se le complete más tarde.

Art. 80. — El presidente y el vicepresidente disfrutan de un sueldo pagado por el Tesoro de la Nación. Durante el mismo período no podrán ejercer otro empleo, ni percibir ningún otro emolumento de la Nación, ni de provincia alguna.

Art. 81. — Al tomar posesión de su cargo, el presidente y vicepresidente prestarán

juramento en manos del presidente del Senado, estando reunido el Congreso, en los términos siguientes:

«Yo, N. N., juro por Dios Nuestro Señor y estos Santos Evangelios desempeñar con lealtad y patriotismo el cargo de presidente (o vicepresidente) de la Nación, y observar y hacer observar fielmente la Constitución de la Nación Argentina. Si así no lo hiciere, Dios y la Nación me lo demanden.»

Capítulo II

De la forma y tiempo de la elección del presidente y vicepresidente de la Nación

Art. 82. — El presidente y el vicepresidente de la Nación serán elegidos directamente por el pueblo y a simple pluralidad de sufragios, formando con este fin las provincias, Capital Federal y territorios nacionales un distrito único. La elección deberá efectuarse tres meses antes de terminar el período del presidente en ejercicio. El escrutinio se realizará por el o los organismos que establezca la ley.

Capítulo III

Atribuciones del Poder Ejecutivo

Art. 83. — El presidente de la Nación tiene las siguientes atribuciones:

1. Es el jefe supremo de la Nación y tiene a su cargo la administración general del país;
2. Expide las instrucciones y reglamentos que sean necesarios para la ejecución de las leyes de la Nación, cuidando de no alterar su espíritu con excepciones reglamentarias, y ejerce la policía de los ríos interprovinciales para asegurar lo dispuesto en el artículo 68, inciso 14;
3. Es el jefe inmediato y local de la Capital de la Nación, pudiendo delegar estas funciones en la forma que determinen los reglamentos administrativos;
4. Participa en la formación de las leyes con arreglo a la Constitución y las promulga;
5. Nombra los jueces de la Corte Suprema de Justicia y de los de-

más tribunales inferiores de la Nación, con acuerdo del Senado;

6. Puede indultar o conmutar las penas por delitos sujetos a la jurisdicción federal, previo informe del tribunal correspondiente, excepto en los casos de acusación por la Cámara de Diputados;

7. Concede jubilaciones, retiros, licencias y goce de montepíos conforme a las leyes de la Nación;

8. Ejerce los derechos del patronato nacional en la presentación de obispos para las iglesias catedrales, a propuesta en terna del Senado;

9. Concede el pase o retiene los decretos de los concilios, las bulas, breves y rescriptos del Sumo Pontífice de Roma con acuerdo de la Suprema Corte; requiriéndose una ley cuando contienen disposiciones generales y permanentes;

10. Nombra y remueve los embajadores y ministros plenipotenciarios con acuerdo del Senado; y

por sí solo nombra y remueve los ministros del despacho, los oficiales de sus secretarías, los agentes consulares y demás empleados de la administración cuyo nombramiento no está reglado de otra manera por esta Constitución;

11. Convoca e inaugura las sesiones del Congreso, reunidas al efecto ambas Cámaras, para el 1º de mayo de cada año; da cuenta en esta ocasión al Congreso del estado de la Nación, de las reformas prometidas por la Constitución, y recomienda a su consideración las medidas que juzgue necesarias y convenientes;

12. Prorroga las sesiones ordinarias del Congreso, o lo convoca a sesiones extraordinarias cuando un grave interés de orden o de progreso lo requiera, y convoca al Senado en el caso del artículo 56;

13. Hace recaudar las rentas de la Nación y decreta su inversión con arreglo a la ley o presupuesto

de gastos nacionales; hace sellar moneda, fija su valor y el de las extranjeras;

14. Concluye y firma tratados de paz, de comercio, de navegación, de alianza, de límites y de neutralidad, concordatos y otras negociaciones requeridas para el mantenimiento de buenas relaciones con las potencias extranjeras, recibe sus representantes y admite sus cónsules;

15. Es comandante en jefe de todas las fuerzas armadas de la Nación;

16. Provee los empleos militares de la Nación: con acuerdo del Senado, en la concesión de los empleos o grados de oficiales superiores de las fuerzas armadas; y por sí solo, en el cāmpo de batalla;

17. Dispone de las fuerzas armadas y corre con su organización y distribución, según las necesidades de la Nación;

18. Declara la guerra y concede cartas de represalia, con autorización y aprobación del Congreso;

19. Declara en estado de sitio uno o varios puntos de la Nación en caso de ataque exterior y por un término limitado, con acuerdo del Senado. En caso de conmoción interior, sólo tiene esta facultad cuando el Congreso está en receso, porque es atribución que corresponde a este cuerpo. Declara también el estado de prevención y alarma en uno o varios puntos del país en caso de alteración del orden público que amenace perturbar el normal desenvolvimiento de la vida o las actividades primordiales de la población, por un término limitado y da cuenta al Congreso. El presidente ejerce estas atribuciones dentro de los límites prescritos por el artículo 34;

20. Puede pedir a los jefes de todos los ramos y departamentos de la administración, y por su conducto, a los demás empleados los informes que crea convenientes, y ellos son obligados a darlos;

21. No puede ausentarse del territorio de la Nación, sino con permiso del Congreso. En el receso de éste, sólo podrá hacerlo sin licencia por graves objetos de servicio público;

22. El presidente tendrá facultad para llenar las vacantes de los empleos que requieran el acuerdo del Senado, y que ocurran durante su receso, por medio de nombramientos en comisión, que deberán ser considerados en la legislatura inmediata;

23. Provee lo conducente al ordenamiento y régimen de los servicios públicos a que se refiere el inciso 13 del artículo 68.

Capítulo IV

De los ministros del Poder Ejecutivo

Art. 84. — El despacho de los negocios de la Nación estará a cargo de ministros secretarios de Estado, quienes refrendarán y legalizarán los actos del presidente de la Nación

por medio de su firma, sin la cual carecen de eficacia. Por una ley de la Nación, y a propuesta del Poder Ejecutivo, se determinará la denominación y los ramos de los ministerios, así como la coordinación de los respectivos despachos.

Para ser ministro se requieren las mismas condiciones que para ser diputado, y ser argentino nativo. Los ministros estarán amparados por las inmunidades que otorgan a los miembros del Congreso los artículos 61 y 62 de la Constitución.

Gozarán por sus servicios de un sueldo establecido por la ley.

Art. 85. — Cada ministro es responsable de los actos que legaliza; y solidariamente de los que acuerda con sus colegas.

Art. 86. — Los ministros no pueden por sí solos, en ningún caso, tomar resoluciones a excepción en lo concerniente al régimen económico y administrativo de sus respectivos departamentos.

Anualmente presentarán al presidente de la Nación la memoria detallada del estado de los negocios de sus respectivos departamentos.

Art. 87. — No pueden ser senadores ni diputados, sin hacer dimisión de sus empleos de ministros.

Art. 88. — El presidente de la Nación y sus ministros tienen la facultad de concurrir a las sesiones conjuntas o separadas de las Cámaras de Senadores y Diputados, informar ante ellas y tomar parte en los debates, sin voto.

SECCION TERCERA

Del Poder Judicial

Capítulo I

De su naturaleza y duración

Art. 89. — El Poder Judicial de la Nación será ejercido por una Corte Suprema de Justicia, y por los demás tribunales inferiores que el Congreso estableciese en el territorio de la Nación.

Art. 90. — En ningún caso el presidente de la Nación puede ejercer funciones judiciales, arrogarse el conocimiento de causas pendientes o restablecer las fenecidas.

Art. 91. — Los jueces de la Corte Suprema de Justicia y de los tribunales inferiores de la Nación son inamovibles, y conservarán

sus empleos mientras dure su buena conducta. Recibirán por sus servicios una compensación que determinará la ley y que no podrá ser disminuída, en manera alguna, mientras permanezcan en sus funciones. Los jueces de los tribunales inferiores serán juzgados y removidos en la forma que determine una ley especial, con sujeción a enjuiciamiento por los propios miembros del Poder Judicial.

Art. 92. — Para ser miembro de la Corte Suprema de Justicia se requiere ser argentino nativo, abogado graduado en universidad nacional, con diez años de ejercicio y treinta años de edad.

Art. 93. — Los jueces de la Corte Suprema de Justicia, al tomar posesión de sus cargos, prestarán juramento ante el presidente de ésta de desempeñar sus obligaciones, administrando justicia bien y legalmente, y de conformidad con lo que prescribe la Constitución.

Art. 94. — La Corte Suprema de Justicia dictará su reglamento interno y económico, y nombrará sus empleados. Ejercerá superintendencia sobre los jueces y tribunales que integran la justicia de la Nación.

En la Capital de la República todos los tribunales tienen el mismo carácter nacional.

Capítulo II

Atribuciones del Poder Judicial

Art. 95. — Corresponde a la Corte Suprema de Justicia y a los tribunales inferiores de la Nación, el conocimiento y decisión de todas las causas que versen sobre puntos regidos por la Constitución; por las leyes de la Nación, con la reserva hecha en el inciso 11 del artículo 68, y por los tratados con las naciones extranjeras; de las causas concernientes a embajadores, ministros plenipotenciarios y cónsules extranjeros; de las de almirantazgo y jurisdicción marítima y aeronáutica; de los asuntos en que la Nación sea parte; de las causas que se substancien en la Capital Federal y en los lugares regidos por la legislación del Congreso; de las que se susciten entre dos o más provincias; entre una provincia y los vecinos de otra; y entre la Nación o una provincia o sus vecinos con un Estado extranjero.

La Corte Suprema de Justicia conocerá, como Tribunal de Casación, en la interpretación e inteligencia de los códigos a que se refiere el inciso 11 del artículo 68.

La interpretación que la Corte Suprema de Justicia haga de los artículos de la Cons-

titución por recurso extraordinario, y de los códigos y leyes por recurso de casación, será aplicada obligatoriamente por los jueces y tribunales nacionales y provinciales.

Una ley reglamentará el procedimiento para los recursos extraordinario y de casación, y para obtener la revisión de la jurisprudencia.

Art. 96. — La Corte Suprema de Justicia conocerá originaria y exclusivamente en las causas que se susciten entre la Nación o una provincia o sus vecinos con un Estado extranjero; en las causas concernientes a embajadores, ministros plenipotenciarios o cónsules extranjeros y asimismo originaria y exclusivamente en las causas entre la Nación y una o más provincias, o de éstas entre sí.

TITULO SEGUNDO

GOBIERNOS DE PROVINCIAS

Art. 97. — Las provincias conservan todo el poder no delegado por esta Constitución al Gobierno federal, y el que expresamente se hayan reservado por pactos especiales al tiempo de su incorporación.

Art. 98. — Se dan sus propias instituciones locales y se rigen por ellas. Eligen sus gobernadores, sus legisladores y demás funcionario de provincia, sin intervención del Gobierno federal.

Art. 99. — Cada provincia dicta su propia Constitución, conforme a lo dispuesto en el artículo 5º.

Art. 100. — Las provincias pueden celebrar tratados parciales para fines de administración de justicia, de intereses económicos y trabajos de utilidad común, con conocimiento del Congreso Federal; y promover su industria, la inmigración, la construcción de ferrocarriles y canales navegables, la colonización de tierras de propiedad provincial, la introducción y establecimiento de nuevas industrias, la importación de capitales extranjeros y la exploración de sus ríos, por leyes protectoras de estos fines y con sus recursos propios.

Art. 101. — Las provincias no ejercen el poder delegado a la Nación. No pueden celebrar tratados parciales de carácter político ni expedir leyes sobre comercio o navegación interior o exterior; ni establecer aduanas pro-

vinciales; ni acuñar moneda; ni establecer bancos con facultad de emitir billetes sin autorización del Congreso federal; ni dictar los códigos a que se refiere el artículo 68, inciso 11, después que el Congreso los haya sancionado; ni dictar especialmente leyes sobre ciudadanía y naturalización, bancarrotas, falsificación de moneda o documentos del Estado; ni establecer derechos de tonelaje; ni armar buques de guerra o levantar ejércitos, salvo en el caso de invasión exterior o de un peligro tan inminente que no admita dilación, de lo que dará cuenta al Gobierno federal; ni nombrar o recibir agentes extranjeros; ni admitir nuevas órdenes religiosas.

Art. 102. — Ninguna provincia puede declarar ni hacer la guerra a otra provincia. Sus quejas deben ser sometidas a la Corte Suprema de Justicia y dirimidas por ella. Sus hostilidades de hecho son actos de guerra civil, calificados de sedición o asonada, que el Gobierno federal debe sofocar y reprimir conforme a la ley.

Art. 103. — Los gobernadores de provincia son agentes naturales del Gobierno federal para hacer cumplir la Constitución y las leyes de la Nación.

DISPOSICIONES TRANSITORIAS

1ª — Hasta tanto el Congreso sancione la ley orgánica de los ministerios, el despacho de los negocios de la Nación estará a cargo de los siguientes departamentos: Relaciones Exteriores; Defensa Nacional; Ejército; Marina; Aeronáutica; Economía; Hacienda; Finanzas; Obras Públicas; Agricultura; Industria y Comercio; Trabajo y Previsión; Transportes; Interior; Justicia; Educación; Salud Pública; Comunicaciones; Asuntos Políticos; Asuntos Técnicos.

2ª — Esta Constitución entrará en vigencia a partir de la fecha de su publicación en el Diario de Sesiones.

3ª — El presidente de la Nación jurará ante la Convención Nacional Constituyente cumplir y hacer cumplir esta Constitución.

Los presidentes de las cámaras legislativas jurarán esta Constitución ante los cuerpos respectivos en la primera sesión preparatoria del período legislativo siguiente a la sanción de aquélla; y los miembros de cada cuerpo, ante su presidente.

El juramento que prescribe el artículo 32 de la Constitución, deberá ser prestado por

todo ciudadano que se halle actualmente en el ejercicio de una función pública.

La falta de cumplimiento del juramento a que se refiere el presente artículo, hará cesar inmediatamente a aquel que se negare a hacerlo en el desempeño de su mandato, función o empleo.

4ª — Durante el primer período legislativo siguiente a la sanción de la presente disposición, deberá solicitarse nuevamente el acuerdo del Senado a que se refieren los incisos 5 y 10 del artículo 83, de la Constitución Nacional y las leyes especiales que exijan igual requisito.

5ª — Autorízase por esta única vez a las Legislaturas provinciales para reformar totalmente sus constituciones respectivas, con el fin de adaptarlas a los principios, declaraciones, derechos y garantías consagrados en esta Constitución.

A tal efecto, en las provincias con poder legislativo bicameral, ambas Cámaras reunidas constituirán la Asamblea Constituyente, la que procederá a elegir sus autoridades propias y a tomar sus decisiones por mayoría absoluta.

La reforma de las constituciones provinciales deberá efectuarse en el plazo de 90 días

a contar de la sanción presente, con la excepción de aquellas provincias cuyo poder legislativo no se halle constituído, caso en el cual el plazo se computará a partir de la fecha de su constitución.

6ª — A los efectos de unificar los mandatos legislativos cuya duración regla esta Constitución, dispónese que los mandatos de los senadores y diputados nacionales en ejercicio caducarán el 30 de abril de 1952.

El mandato de los senadores cuya elección se efectúe para llenar las vacantes de los que concluyen el 30 de abril de 1949, expirará asimismo el 30 de abril de 1952. La elección correspondiente deberá realizarse por el procedimiento de elección por las legislaturas, que establecía el artículo 46 de la Constitución.

Dada en la Sala de Sesiones de la Honorable Convención Nacional Constituyente, en Buenos Aires, a los once días del mes de marzo del año mil novecientos cuarenta y nueve.

DOMINGO A. MERCANTE.
Presidente.

Bernardino H. Garaguso.
Convencional secretario.

Mario M. Goizueta.
Convencional secretario.

Esta Constitución está en
vigencia desde el día
16 de marzo de 1949
en que se publicó
en el Diario de
Sesiones de la
Convención Na-
cional Cons-
tituyente

Notas Bibliográficas

AA.VV., "Las reformas sociales en la Constitución de San Juan de 1927", en Revista de Historia del Derecho, Buenos Aires, Instituto de Investigaciones de Historia del Derecho, 1977.

Alberdi, Juan Bautista, "Grandes y pequeños hombres del Plata", Buenos Aires, Punto de Encuentro, 2007.

Alberdi, Juan Bautista, *Proceso a Mitre*, Buenos Aires, Punto de Encuentro, 2013.

Alberti, Blas, *El revisionismo histórico socialista*, Buenos Aires, Octubre, 1974.

Alberto González Arzac, "Vida, pasión y muerte del artículo 40", en *Todo es historia*, Buenos Aires, noviembre de 1969.

Álvarez, Juan, Las guerras civiles argentinas, Buenos Aires, Eudeba, 1983.

Argumedo, Alcira, *Los silencios y las voces en América Latina. Notas sobre el pensamiento nacional y popular*, Buenos Aires, Colihue, 2004.

Azzali, Javier, "Cossio, Carlos", en *Los Malditos, T. III*, Buenos Aires, Madres de Plaza de Mayo, 2008.

Barcesat, Eduardo, *Crítica Jurídica, nro. 30*, 2010.

Baschetti, Roberto, *La clase obrera peronista*, Buenos Aires, De la campana, 2010.

Baschetti, Roberto, *La clase obrera peronista, T. 1*, La Plata, De la Campana, 2010.

Basualdo, Eduardo, *Los primeros gobiernos peronistas y la consolidación del país industrial: éxitos y fracasos*, Buenos Aires, FLACSO, 2004.

Basualdo, Victoria, *Los delegados y las comisiones internas en la historia argentina: 1943-2007*, Buenos Aires, Cara o Ceca, 2011.

Bielsa, Rafael, "La cuestión de las jurisdicciones especiales", en *La Ley, T. 75*, Buenos Aires, septiembre de 1954.

Bobbio, Norberto, *El origen y fundamentos del poder político*, México, Grijalbo, 1986.

Brom, Juan, *Esbozo de historia de México*, México, Grijalbo, 1998.

Canal Feijóo, Bernardo, *Constitución y revolución, T. I y II*, Buenos Aires, Hyspamérica.

Cataruzza, Alejandro, "Una empresa cultural del primer peronismo: la revista Hechos e ideas (1947-1955)", en *Revista Complutense de Historia de América, nro. 19*, Madrid, 1993.
Cersósimo, Facundo, Ferrón, Cecilia y Eduardo Corbalán en *Los Malditos, Tomo IV*, Buenos Aires, Madres de Plaza de Mayo, 2005.
Chávez, Gonzalo Leónidas, *La masacre de Plaza de Mayo*, Buenos Aires, Campana de Palo, 2003.
Chávez, Fermín, *Historicismo e iluminismo en la cultura argentina*, Buenos Aires, Trafac, 1957.
Chávez, Fermín, *El revisionismo y las montoneras*, Buenos Aires, Theoría, 1984.
Chávez, Fermín, *Vida de López Jordán*, Buenos Aires, Hyspamérica, 1986.
Chávez, Fermín, *El peronismo visto por Víctor Frankl*, Buenos Aires, Theoría, 1999.
Chávez, Guido, "Bolivia, las luchas por el gas y el petróleo", en *Desafíos, nro. 15*, 2005.
Cholbis, Jorge, "La constitución de 1949 (a 60 años de su sanción)", en *Equipo Federal de Trabajo, año IV, nro. 48*, 2009.
Cooke, John William, "Peronismo y petróleo. Declaraciones ante la Comisión Especial Investigadora sobre Petróleo de la Cámara de Diputados de la Nación", publicado en www.ruinasdigitales.com.
Cooke, John William, Duhalde, Eduardo Luís (comp.) y Baschetti, R., *Acción Parlamentaria, T.I*, Buenos Aires, Colihue, 2007.
Correas, Oscar, *Introducción a la sociología jurídica*, México, Fontamara, 1994.
Correas, Oscar, *Kelsen y los marxistas*, México, Coyoacán, 1994.
Correas, Oscar, *Derecho indígena mexicano I*, México, UNAM/Coyoacán, 2007.
Correas, Oscar, "La propiedad y las comunidades indígenas en México", en *Pueblos y Fronteras*, México, UNAM, 2008.
Corti, Arístides Horacio, *Algunas reflexiones sobre leyes de facto y derechos adquiridos, T. B*, Buenos Aires, La Ley, 1984, p. 970.
De Franchini, María Florencia, *Función social de la propiedad en la legislación argentina*, La Plata, UNLP, 2005.

Del Vecchio, Giorgio, *Sobre la politicidad del derecho, T. 75*, Buenos Aires, La Ley.

Diamand, Marcelo, "La estructura productiva desequilibrada. Argentina y el tipo de cambio", en *Desarrollo Económico, Vol. 12*, 1972.

Duhalde, Eduardo Luís, *Contra Mitre. Los intelectuales y el poder: de Caseros al 80*, Buenos Aires, Punto Crítico, 2005.

Espasande, Mara, "Las Constituciones de la Patria Grande" en *El Cronista del Bicentenario, nro. 6*, Provincia de Buenos Aires, junio de 2012.

Feinmann, José Pablo, *Filosofía y Nación*, Buenos Aires, Sudamericana, 1996.

Ferrajoli, Luigi, "La Democracia Constitucional" en *Desde otra mirada, textos de teoría crítica del Derecho*, Buenos Aires, Eudeba, 2009.

Ferrero, Roberto, *Del fraude a la soberanía popular: 1938-1946*, Buenos Aires, Memorial de la Patria, 1976.

Fitzpatrick, Peter, *La mitología del derecho moderno*, México, Siglo XXI, 1998.

Foucault, Michel, *La verdad y las formas jurídicas*, Barcelona, Gedisa, 1996.

Fragueiro, Mariano, *Estatuto para la Organización de la Hacienda y Crédito Público de la Confederación Argentina*, Buenos Aires, Solar/ Hachette, 1976.

Franzoia, Alberto, "¿Quién es Jorge Enea Spilimbergo?", versión disponible en www.elortiba.org.

Freaza, Julián Francisco, "Misiones debe ser provincia por imperio de la constitución", en *Jurisprudencia Argentina 1953, T. II.*, 1953.

Galasso, Norberto, *Imperialismo y pensamiento colonial en la Argentina*, Buenos Aires, Roberto Vera Editor, 1985.

Galasso, Norberto, *La búsqueda de la identidad nacional en J. L. Borges y R. Scalabrini Ortiz*, Rosario, Ediciones Homo Sapiens, 1998.

Galasso, Norberto, *Yo fui el confesor de Eva Perón. Conversaciones con el Padre Hernán Benítez*, Rosario, Homo Sapiens Ediciones, 1999.

Galasso, Norberto, "Peronismo y liberación nacional", en *Cuadernos para la otra historia, nro. 23*, 2003.

Galasso, Norberto, "La corriente historiográfica socialista, federal - provinciana o latinoamericana", en *Cuadernos para otra historia, nro. 3*, Buenos Aires, Centro Cultural Enrique Santos Discépolo, 2003.

Galasso, Norberto e Ibáñez, Germán (eds.), *Arturo Jauretche. Textos Selectos*, Buenos Aires, Corregidor, 2004.

Galasso, Norberto, *Perón, T. I*, Buenos Aires, Colihue, 2005.

Galasso, Norberto (coord.), *Los Malditos, T. IV*, Buenos Aires, Madres de Plaza de Mayo, 2005.

Galasso, Norberto (comp.), *América Latina, unidos o dominados*, Buenos Aires, Instituto Arturo Jauretche, 2008.

Galasso, Norberto, *América Latina, ahora o nunca*, Buenos Aires, Punto de Encuentro, 2009.

Galasso, Norberto, *Historia de la Argentina*, Buenos Aires, Colihue, 2011.

Galasso, Norberto, "La Constitución de 1853, proyectos e intereses contrapuestos", en *El Cronista del Bicentenario*, Provincia de Buenos Aires, junio 2012.

Galasso, Norberto, *Manuel Ugarte y la lucha por la unidad latinoamericana*, Buenos Aires, Colihue, 2012

Galasso, Norberto, *Hacia la unidad latinoamericana* (antología), Buenos Aires, Punto de Encuentro, 2013.

Galasso, Norberto, "A 83 años del fallecimiento de David Peña, un rosarino 'maldito'", en *Tiempo Argentino*, Buenos Aires, 8 de abril de 2014.

Gallardo, Roberto, *Teoría y praxis del estado nacional en la era global*, Buenos Aires, Madres de Plaza de Mayo, 2006.

García Laguarda, Jorge M., *Constituciones Iberoamericanas*, México, UNAM, 2006.

Gelli, María Angélica, "Retenciones, federalismo, república y derechos fundamentales, Suplemento Especial sobre Retenciones a las exportaciones de enero de 2008", en *La Ley*, Buenos Aires, 2008.

Ghigliani, Alejandro, "Del control jurisdiccional de constitucionalidad", en *Jurisprudencia Argentina, T. III*, 1953.

González Arzac, Alberto, *Sampay, y la Constitución del futuro*, Buenos Aires, Peña Lillo editor, 1982.

González Arzac, Alberto, *Federalismo y justicialismo*, Buenos Aires, Peña Lillo, 1984.

González Arzac, Alberto, "Historia de un golpe a la constitución" en Revista *Qué*, año 1 nro. 4 (Director: Eric Calcagno), Buenos Aires, noviembre de 2005.

Gramsci, Antonio, *La política y el Estado moderno*, Barcelona, Planeta Agostini, 1993.

Hernández Arregui, J. J., *La formación de la conciencia nacional*, Buenos Aires, Peña Lillo/Ediciones Continente, 2004.

Hernández Arregui, J. J., *Nacionalismo y liberación*, Buenos Aires, Peña Lillo/Ediciones Continente, 2004.

Herrero, Félix, "¿Se puede en Argentina? Comentario a la nota de Guido Chávez", en *Desafíos, nro.5*, 2006.

Hinkelammert, Franz, "La inversión de los derechos humanos: el caso de John Locke" en Herrera Flores, Joaquín, *El vuelo de Anteo. Derechos humanos y crítica de la razón liberal*, Bilbao, Desclée de Brouwer, 2000.

Iriarte, Luís, "Programa económico del federalismo argentino, reflexiones sobre modelos de inserción nacional en distintas etapas de la globalización", en *La Ley*, Suplemento Actualidad, Buenos Aires, 16 de diciembre de 2004.

Jara, Juan Carlos, "Julio A. Roca y la conquista del desierto", en *Cronista del Bicentenario*, Buenos Aires, Dirección General de Cultura y Educación de la Provincia de Buenos Aires, 2013.

Jauretche, Arturo, *Los profetas del odio y la yapa*, Buenos Aires, Corregidor, 2001.

Kelsen, Hans, *Teoría pura del Derecho*, México, UNAM, 1993.

Kogan, Hilda, "El Bicentenario: el rol de la mujer", en *La Ley*, Buenos Aires, 21 de mayo de 2010.

Lenin, Vladimir Ilich., *El imperialismo, fase superior del capitalismo*, Moscú, Progreso, 1973.

Linares Quintana, Segundo, "Introducción al estudio de la teoría del poder constituyente", en *La Ley, T. 65*, Buenos Aires, 1955.

López Rosas, Rafael, *Historia Constitucional Argentina* (3ª ed.), Buenos Aires, Astrea.

Madariaga, José Luís, ¿Qué es la izquierda nacional? Introducción al socialismo nacional, (con comentarios de Norberto Galasso y Néstor Gorojovsky), Buenos Aires, Ediciones del Sur, 2010.

Márquez, Ángel, *Educación y Peronismo (1946-1955)*, Buenos Aires, CEAL, 1984.

Marx, Carlos, *Acerca del colonialismo*, Moscú, Editorial Progreso, 1981.

Matienzo, José Nicolás, *El derecho y la soberanía argentina*, Buenos Aires, Juárez Editor, 1970.

Matienzo, José Nicolás, *La doctrina de Monroe y la Constitución Argentina*, Buenos Aires, Valerio Abeledo, 1929.

Mercado Luna, Ricardo, *Los coroneles de Mitre*, Córdoba, Alcion Editora, 2006.

Methol Ferré, Alberto y Metalli, Alver, *La América Latina del siglo XXI*, Buenos Aires, Edhasa, 2006.

Molocznik, Maximiliano, *Señales Populares*, Buenos Aires, Centro Cultural E. S. Discépolo, 2012.

Moreira, Manuel, *El derecho de los pueblos originarios. Reflexión y hermenéutica*, Misiones, Universidad Nacional del Litoral/Santiago Álvarez Editor, 2009.

Novick, Susana, *IAPI: auge y decadencia*, Buenos Aires, CEAL, 1986.

Oporto, Mario, *De Moreno a Perón, pensamiento argentino de la unidad latinoamericana*, Buenos Aires, Planeta, 2011.

Oyhanarte, Julio, "Derecho Constitucional: Doctrinas Esenciales" en *La Ley, T. 1*, pp. 84-779, Buenos Aires, 2008.

Oyhanarte, Julio, "La expropiación de las empresas y el artículo 40 de la Constitución Nacional", en *La Ley, T. II*, pp. 60 y ss., Buenos Aires, 1951.

Pedranzini, Maximiliano, "La provincialización de Misiones. Aportes críticos para una interpretación histórica (1919-1953)", en revista digital *Historia y Frontera, nro. 1*, 2013. Puede consultarse en: http//www.historiayfrontera.org.

Pinto, Gimol, *El sistema penal juvenil argentino*, Buenos Aires, UNICEF, 2009.

Pisarello, Gerardo y Tedeschi, Sebastián, "Propiedad y Constitución: del 'derecho terrible' a la democracia económica", en Gargarella, Roberto (comp.), *La Constitución en 2020*, Buenos Aires, Siglo XXI, 2011.

Pisarello, Gerardo, "El nuevo constitucionalismo latinoamericano y la constitución venezolana de 1999: balance de una década", en *Sin Permiso, nro. 6*, Barcelona, Ediciones de Intervención Cultural, 2009.

Pomer, León, *Historia de gauchos y gauchisoldados*, Buenos Aires, Colihue, 2007.

Pomer, León, *Continuidades y rupturas. De la colonia a Mayo*, Buenos Aires, Colihue, 2012.

Puebla, María Daniela, *El modelo criminológico argentino*, San Juan, Fundación Universidad Nacional de San Juan, 1997.

Puiggrós, Rodolfo, *Historia crítica de los partidos políticos argentinos*, Buenos Aires, Hyspamérica, 1986.

Raanan, Rein, "Entrevista en Tiempo Argentino", 19 de septiembre de 2011.

Ramella, Pablo, *Derecho Constitucional*, Buenos Aires, De Palma, 1986.

Ramella, Susana, "La concepción antropológica del derecho del trabajo en el constitucionalismo social del siglo XX", en *Revista de Historia del Derecho, nro. 42*, Buenos Aires, INHIDE, junio-diciembre de 2011.

Ramos, Jorge Abelardo, *Manuel Ugarte y la revolución latinoamericana*, Buenos Aires, Coyoacán, 1961.

Ramos, Jorge Abelardo, *El marxismo de indias*, Barcelona, Planeta, 1973.

Ramos, Jorge Abelardo, *Historia de la Nación Latinoamericana*, Buenos Aires, Continente, 2011.

Rapoport, Mario, "Historia de la economía argentina del siglo XX", en *La Página*, Buenos Aires, 2007.

Rapoport, Mario, "Verdades y mitos del libre comercio", en *Página/12*, suplemento Cash del 11 de enero de 2009.

Recalde, Héctor, *Una historia laboral jamás contada... El relato empresario ante conquistas y nuevos derechos de los trabajadores en Argentina (1869-2012)*, Buenos Aires, Corregidor, 2012.

Rouquié, Alain, *Poder militar y sociedad política en la Argentina*, Buenos Aires, Emecé, 1982.

Ruiz Moreno, Isidoro, *El derecho internacional público ante la Corte Suprema*, Buenos Aires, Eudeba, 1970.

Salvador Ferla, "La tercera posición ideológica, en *Revista Redacción*, febrero 1974, disponible en http://www.elortiba.org/pdf/Salvador_Ferla_Tercera_Posicion.pdf.

Sampay, Arturo y otros, *El derecho y la soberanía argentina*, Buenos Aires, Juárez Editor, 1970.

Sampay, Arturo Enrique, *Las Constituciones de la Argentina (1810-1972)*, Buenos Aires, EUDEBA, 1972.

Sampay, Arturo, *Las ideas políticas de Juan Manuel de Rosas*, Buenos Aires, CEAL, 1975.

Sampay, Arturo, *Constitución y Pueblo*, Buenos Aires, Instituto Superior Arturo Jauretche, 2011.

Sánchez Zinny, Fernando, *El Culto de la Infamia*, Buenos Aires, Artes Gráficas de Bartolomé Chiesino S.A, 1958.

Santa Pinter, José Julio, "¿Un nuevo derecho internacional?", en *Jurisprudencia Argentina, II*, Buenos Aires, 1953.

Sarasola, Carlos Martínez, *Nuestros paisanos los indios*, Buenos Aires, Del nuevo extremo, 2011.

Sbatella, José y otros, "Excedente económico y distribución del ingreso en la Argentina de la posconvertibilidad", en *Revista de Ciencias Sociales, segunda época, año 4, nro. 23*, Buenos Aires, UNQUI, 2013, pp. 123-143.

Scalabrini Ortiz, Raúl, *Cuatro verdades sobre nuestras crisis*, Buenos Aires, Ediciones Theoría, 1948.

Scalabrini Ortiz, Raúl, *Bases para la Reconstrucción Nacional. Aquí se aprende a defender a la patria*, Buenos Aires, Plus Ultra, 1985.

Segovia, Juan Fernando, *El peronismo y la Constitución de 1949 en la crisis de legitimidad argentina*, en sesión de la Academia Nacional de Ciencias Morales y Políticas del 24 de agosto de 2005.

Siperman, Arnoldo, "Código Civil y Propiedad", en *Polémica*, Buenos Aires, CEAL, 1970,

Terroba, Luís Alberto, *La Constitución Nacional de 1949, una causa nacional*, Buenos Aires, Fundación Ross, 2010.

Terzaga, Alfredo, *Historia de Roca*, Buenos Aires, Peña Lillo, 1976.

Trias, Vivian, "El imperio británico", en *Cuadernos de crisis*, Buenos Aires, 1976.

Vanossi, Jorge Reinaldo, *Comunicación del académico*, en sesión privada de la Academia Nacional de Ciencias Morales y Políticas del 9 de noviembre de 2005.

Vilas, Carlos, *Derecho y Estado en una economía dependiente*, Buenos Aires, Guadalupe, 1974.

Zaffaroni, Eugenio Raúl, *Manual de Derecho Penal*, Buenos Aires, Ediar, 1994.

Zanatta, Loris, "Perón, la Iglesia y la reforma que no fue. Patronato nacional y conflicto con la Santa Sede en la reforma constitucional de 1949", ponencia en el 49 Congreso Americanista, Quito, Ecuador, julio de 1997 disponible en http://www.naya.org.ar/congresos/contenido/49CAI/Zanatta.htm.

Fuentes

Revistas y diarios:

Primera Plana, Hechos e Ideas, Todo es Historia, Panorama, Polémica, Crisis, Desarrollo Económico, Línea, Redacción, Antropología del Tercer Mundo, Qué (Director. Eric Calcagno), Equipo Federal de Trabajo, Revista Complutense de Historia de América, Revista de Historia del Derecho (Instituto de Investigaciones de Historia del Derecho, UBA), El Cronista del Bicentenario, Señales Populares, Desafíos, Página/12 (diario), Clarín (diario), Tiempo Argentino (diario), La Ley, Jurisprudencia Argentina, Crítica Jurídica (Universidad Nacional Autónoma de México), Pueblos y fronteras (Universidad Nacional Autónoma de México), Revista de Ciencias Sociales, segunda época (Universidad Nacional de Quilmes).

Sitios WEB:

*http://*www.clacso.org.ar/biblioteca
http://www.naya.org.ar/congresos/contenido/49CAI/Zanatta.htm
*http://*www.elortiba.org
http://www.salvador-allende.cl/Documentos/1970-73/proyecto_constitucion.pdf
http://www.ancmyp.org.ar/user/files/La_constitucion.pdf
http://www.un.org/es/documents/udhr/law.shtml
http://www.historia.radicales.org.ar/lebensohn.htm
http://www.robertobaschetti.com
http://www.ruinasdigitales.com

Leyes, decretos y documentos:

Diario de sesiones de la Convención Nacional Constituyente de la imprenta del Congreso de la Nación.
Anales de la legislación argentina de 1949 y 1957, de la Revista La Ley.
Ley 13.653.
Ley 5.315.
Ley 11.357.
Ley 12.906.
Ley 12.591.
Ley 12.962.
Ley 13.010.
Ley 13.246.
Ley 13560.
Ley 13.571.
Ley 13.233.
Ley 13.234.
Ley 13.262.
Ley 13.571.
Ley 13.581.
Ley 13.995.
Ley 14.029.
Ley 14.184.
Ley 14.165 (Código de Justicia Policial de octubre de 1952).
Ley 14.392.
Ley 14.404.
Ley 20.680.
Decreto del P.E.N. 4.865/1947.
Decreto-Ley 2.539 del 4 de noviembre de 1955.
Decreto-Ley 15.350 (1946).
Decreto-Ley 8.503 (1946).
Decreto-Ley 11.554 (1946).
Decreto 18.341 (1949).
Decreto 29.337 (1949).
Decreto 4.865 (1947).
Decreto-Ley 2.539 del 4 de noviembre de 1955.

Decreto-Ley 2.011 (1955).
Decreto-Ley 9.270/1956.
Decreto-Ley 4.161/1956 .
Decreto-Ley 3.838/1957.
Decreto 10.394/1958.
Decreto-Ley 21.382 (1976).
Decreto 620 (1976).
Directivas Básicas del 7 de diciembre de 1955.
Proclama del 27 de abril de 1956.
Acta de la Revolución Argentina de junio de 1966 y el Estatuto Fundamental de agosto de 1972.
Constitución de San Juan (1927).
Constitución de Chaco (1951).
Constitución de México (1917 y reforma de 1992).
Constituciones de Uruguay (1967) y Chile (1971).
Declaración de los Derechos del Trabajador de 1947.
Manifiesto de reivindicación de la Constitución de 1949 de julio de 1957.
La "Federal Power Act" de 1935, EUA.
Plan Nacional contra la Discriminación aprobado por Decreto 1.086/2005.

Fallos de la Corte Suprema de Justicia de la Nación
"Armando Arjones y otros", del 17 de noviembre de 1941.
"Attias, Alberto" (1951)
"Codovilla, Victorio, sobre Hábeas Corpus", de abril de 1950.
"Lares, Gabino Alberto" del 10 de abril de 1959.
"Rodríguez, Juan C. Ruggero, Conrado Tambascio, Juan C. s/sumario por actividades terroristas, subversivas, intimidación pública, y otras" de 1962,
"San Miguel, José", de 1950.
"Sofía", de 1959.

Made in the USA
Monee, IL
18 October 2026

66035225R10177

MIX
Papier aus verantwortungsvollen Quellen
Paper from responsible sources
FSC® C105338

If you have any concerns about our products,
you can contact us on
ProductSafety@springernature.com

In case Publisher is established outside the EU,
the EU authorized representative is:
Springer Nature Customer Service Center GmbH
Europaplatz 3, 69115 Heidelberg, Germany

Printed by Libri Plureos GmbH
in Hamburg, Germany